D1410678

Nineteenth-Century Literature Criticism

Guide to Gale Literary Criticism Series

For criticism on	Consult these Gale series
Authors now living or who died after December 31, 1999	*CONTEMPORARY LITERARY CRITICISM (CLC)*
Authors who died between 1900 and 1999	*TWENTIETH-CENTURY LITERARY CRITICISM (TCLC)*
Authors who died between 1800 and 1899	*NINETEENTH-CENTURY LITERATURE CRITICISM (NCLC)*
Authors who died between 1400 and 1799	*LITERATURE CRITICISM FROM 1400 TO 1800 (LC)* *SHAKESPEAREAN CRITICISM (SC)*
Authors who died before 1400	*CLASSICAL AND MEDIEVAL LITERATURE CRITICISM (CMLC)*
Authors of books for children and young adults	*CHILDREN'S LITERATURE REVIEW (CLR)*
Dramatists	*DRAMA CRITICISM (DC)*
Poets	*POETRY CRITICISM (PC)*
Short story writers	*SHORT STORY CRITICISM (SSC)*
Literary topics and movements	*HARLEM RENAISSANCE: A GALE CRITICAL COMPANION (HR)* *THE BEAT GENERATION: A GALE CRITICAL COMPANION (BG)*
Asian American writers of the last two hundred years	*ASIAN AMERICAN LITERATURE (AAL)*
Black writers of the past two hundred years	*BLACK LITERATURE CRITICISM (BLC)* *BLACK LITERATURE CRITICISM SUPPLEMENT (BLCS)*
Hispanic writers of the late nineteenth and twentieth centuries	*HISPANIC LITERATURE CRITICISM (HLC)* *HISPANIC LITERATURE CRITICISM SUPPLEMENT (HLCS)*
Native North American writers and orators of the eighteenth, nineteenth, and twentieth centuries	*NATIVE NORTH AMERICAN LITERATURE (NNAL)*
Major authors from the Renaissance to the present	*WORLD LITERATURE CRITICISM, 1500 TO THE PRESENT (WLC)* *WORLD LITERATURE CRITICISM SUPPLEMENT (WLCS)*

ISSN 0732-1864

Volume 150

Nineteenth-Century Literature Criticism

Criticism of the
Works of Novelists, Philosophers, and Other
Creative Writers Who Died between 1800
and 1899, from the First Published Critical
Appraisals to Current Evaluations

Russel Whitaker
Project Editor

THOMSON

GALE

Detroit • New York • San Francisco • San Diego • New Haven, Conn. • Waterville, Maine • London • Munich

Nineteenth-Century Literature Criticism, Vol. 150

Project Editor
Russel Whitaker

Editorial
Jessica Bomarito, Kathy D. Darrow, Jeffrey W. Hunter, Jelena O. Krstović, Michelle Lee, Thomas J. Schoenberg, Lawrence J. Trudeau

Data Capture
Francis Monroe, Gwen Tucker

Indexing Services
Laurie Andriot

Rights and Acquisitions
Margie Abendroth, Denise Buckley, Emma Hull

Imaging and Multimedia
Dean Dauphinais, Robert Duncan, Leitha Etheridge-Sims, Lezlie Light, Michael Logusz, Dan Newell, Kelly A. Quin, Denay Wilding

Composition and Electronic Capture
Kathy Sauer

Manufacturing
Rhonda Williams

Associate Product Manager
Marc Cormier

LIBRARY OF CONGRESS CATALOG CARD NUMBER 84-643008

ISBN 0-7876-8634-4
ISSN 0732-1864

Printed in the United States of America
10 9 8 7 6 5 4 3 2 1

Contents

Preface vii

Acknowledgments xi

Literary Criticism Series Advisory Board xiii

Preface

S ince its inception in 1981, *Nineteeth-Century Literature Criticism* (*NCLC*) has been a valuable resource for students and librarians seeking critical commentary on writers of this transitional period in world history. Designated an "Outstanding Reference Source" by the American Library Association with the publication of is first volume, *NCLC* has since been purchased by over 6,000 school, public, and university libraries. The series has covered more than 450 authors representing 33 nationalities and over 17,000 titles. No other reference source has surveyed the critical reaction to nineteenth-century authors and literature as thoroughly as *NCLC*.

Scope of the Series

NCLC is designed to introduce students and advanced readers to the authors of the nineteenth century and to the most significant interpretations of these authors' works. The great poets, novelists, short story writers, playwrights, and philosophers of this period are frequently studied in high school and college literature courses. By organizing and reprinting commentary written on these authors, *NCLC* helps students develop valuable insight into literary history, promotes a better understanding of the texts, and sparks ideas for papers and assignments. Each entry in *NCLC* presents a comprehensive survey of an author's career or an individual work of literature and provides the user with a multiplicity of interpretations and assessments. Such variety allows students to pursue their own interests; furthermore, it fosters an awareness that literature is dynamic and responsive to many different opinions.

Every fourth volume of *NCLC* is devoted to literary topics that cannot be covered under the author approach used in the rest of the series. Such topics include literary movements, prominent themes in nineteenth-century literature, literary reaction to political and historical events, significant eras in literary history, prominent literary anniversaries, and the literatures of cultures that are often overlooked by English-speaking readers.

NCLC continues the survey of criticism of world literature begun by Thomson Gale's *Contemporary Literary Criticism* (*CLC*) and *Twentieth-Century Literary Criticism* (*TCLC*).

Organization of the Book

An *NCLC* entry consists of the following elements:

- The **Author Heading** cites the name under which the author most commonly wrote, followed by birth and death dates. Also located here are any name variations under which an author wrote, including transliterated forms for authors whose native languages use nonroman alphabets. If the author wrote consistently under a pseudonym, the pseudonym will be listed in the author heading and the author's actual name given in parenthesis on the first line of the biographical and critical information. Uncertain birth or death dates are indicated by question marks. Single-work entries are preceded by a heading that consists of the most common form of the title in English translation (if applicable) and the original date of composition.

- The **Introduction** contains background information that introduces the reader to the author, work, or topic that is the subject of the entry.

- A **Portrait of the Author** is included when available.

- The list of **Principal Works** is ordered chronologically by date of first publication and lists the most important works by the author. The genre and publication date of each work is given. In the case of foreign authors whose works have been translated into English, the list will focus primarily on twentieth-century translations, selecting those works most commonly considered the best by critics. Unless otherwise indicated, dramas are dated by first performance, not first publication. Lists of **Representative Works** by different authors appear with topic entries.

- Reprinted **Criticism** is arranged chronologically in each entry to provide a useful perspective on changes in critical evaluation over time. The critic's name and the date of composition or publication of the critical work are given at the beginning of each piece of criticism. Unsigned criticism is preceded by the title of the source in which it appeared. All titles by the author featured in the text are printed in boldface type. Footnotes are reprinted at the end of each essay or excerpt. In the case of excerpted criticism, only those footnotes that pertain to the excerpted texts are included. Criticism in topic entries is arranged chronologically under a variety of subheadings to facilitate the study of different aspects of the topic.

- A complete **Bibliographical Citation** of the original essay or book precedes each piece of criticism.

- Critical essays are prefaced by brief **Annotations** explicating each piece.

- An annotated bibliography of **Further Reading** appears at the end of each entry and suggests resources for additional study. In some cases, significant essays for which the editors could not obtain reprint rights are included here. Boxed material following the further reading list provides references to other biographical and critical sources on the author in series published by Thomson Gale.

Indexes

Each volume of *NCLC* contains a **Cumulative Author Index** listing all authors who have appeared in a wide variety of reference sources published by Thomson Gale, including *NCLC*. A complete list of these sources is found facing the first page of the Author Index. The index also includes birth and death dates and cross references between pseudonyms and actual names.

A **Cumulative Nationality Index** lists all authors featured in *NCLC* by nationality, followed by the number of the *NCLC* volume in which their entry appears.

A **Cumulative Topic Index** lists the literary themes and topics treated in the series as well as in *Classical and Medieval Literature Criticism, Literature Criticism from 1400 to 1800, Twentieth-Century Literary Criticism,* and the *Contemporary Literary Criticism* Yearbook, which was discontinued in 1998.

An alphabetical **Title Index** accompanies each volume of *NCLC*, with the exception of the Topics volumes. Listings of titles by authors covered in the given volume are followed by the author's name and the corresponding page numbers where the titles are discussed. English translations of foreign titles and variations of titles are cross-referenced to the title under which a work was originally published. Titles of novels, dramas, nonfiction books, and poetry, short story, or essay collections are printed in italics, while individual poems, short stories, and essays are printed in roman type within quotation marks.

In response to numerous suggestions from librarians, Thomson Gale also produces an annual paperbound edition of the *NCLC* cumulative title index. This annual cumulation, which alphabetically lists all titles reviewed in the series, is available to all customers. Additional copies of this index are available upon request. Librarians and patrons will welcome this separate index; it saves shelf space, is easy to use, and is recyclable upon receipt of the next edition.

Citing *Nineteenth-Century Literature Criticism*

When citing criticism reprinted in the Literary Criticism Series, students should provide complete bibliographic information so that the cited essay can be located in the original print or electronic source. Students who quote directly from reprinted criticism may use any accepted bibliographic format, such as University of Chicago Press style or Modern Language Association style.

The examples below follow recommendations for preparing a bibliography set forth in *The Chicago Manual of Style,* 14th ed. (Chicago: The University of Chicago Press, 1993); the first example pertains to material drawn from periodicals, the second to material reprinted from books:

Guerard, Albert J. "On the Composition of Dostoevsky's *The Idiot.*" *Mosaic: A Journal for the Interdisciplinary Study of Literature* 8, no. 1 (fall 1974): 201-15. Reprinted in *Nineteenth-Century Literature Criticism.* Vol. 119, edited by Lynn M. Zott, 81-104. Detroit: Gale, 2003.

Berstein, Carol L. "Subjectivity as Critique and the Critique of Subjectivity in Keats's *Hyperion.*" In *After the Future: Postmodern Times and Places,* edited by Gary Shapiro, 41-52. Albany, N. Y.: State University of New York Press, 1990. Reprinted in *Nineteenth-Century Literature Criticism.* Vol. 121, edited by Lynn M. Zott, 155-60. Detroit: Gale, 2003.

The examples below follow recommendations for preparing a works cited list set forth in the *MLA Handbook for Writers of Research Papers,* 5th ed. (New York: The Modern Language Association of America, 1999); the first example pertains to material drawn from periodicals, the second to material reprinted from books:

Guerard, Albert J. "On the Composition of Dostoevsky's *The Idiot.*" *Mosaic: A Journal for the Interdisciplinary Study of Literature* 8. 1 (fall 1974): 201-15. Reprinted in *Nineteenth-Century Literature Criticism.* Ed. Lynn M. Zott. Vol. 119. Detroit: Gale, 2003. 81-104.

Berstein, Carol L. "Subjectivity as Critique and the Critique of Subjectivity in Keats's *Hyperion.*" *After the Future: Postmodern Times and Places.* Ed. Gary Shapiro. Albany, N. Y.: State University of New York Press, 1990. 41-52. Reprinted in *Nineteeth-Century Literature Criticism.* Ed. Lynn M. Zott. Vol. 121. Detroit: Gale, 2003. 155-60.

Suggestions are Welcome

Readers who wish to suggest new features, topics, or authors to appear in future volumes, or who have other suggestions or comments are cordially invited to call, write, or fax the Associate Product Manager:

Associate Product Manager, Literary Criticism Series
Thomson Gale
27500 Drake Road
Farmington Hills, MI 48331-3535
1-800-347-4253 (GALE)
Fax: 248-699-8054

Acknowledgments

The editors wish to thank the copyright holders of the criticism included in this volume and the permissions managers of many book and magazine publishing companies for assisting us in securing reproduction rights. We are also grateful to the staffs of the Detroit Public Library, the Library of Congress, the University of Detroit Mercy Library, Wayne State University Purdy/Kresge Library Complex, and the University of Michigan Libraries for making their resources available to us. Following is a list of the copyright holders who have granted us permission to reproduce material in this volume of *NCLC*. Every effort has been made to trace copyright, but if omissions have been made, please let us know.

COPYRIGHTED MATERIAL IN *NCLC*, VOLUME 150, WAS REPRODUCED FROM THE FOLLOWING PERIODICALS:

Australian Journal of French Studies, v. 16, January-April, 1979. Copyright © 1979 *Australian Journal of French Studies*. Reproduced by permission.—*Cuadernos de Investigacion Filologica*, v. 23-24, 1997-1998. Reproduced by permission of the publisher.—*Dalhousie French Studies*, v. 12, spring-summer, 1987; v. 33, winter, 1995. Copyright © 1987, 1995 *Dalhousie French Studies*. Both reproduced by permission.—*Dalhousie Review*, v.73, spring, 1993 for "Card-Playing and the Marriage Gamble in *Pride and Prejudice*" by Matthew Schneider. Copyright © 1994. Reproduced by permission of the publisher and the author.—*English Studies in Canada*, v. 10, June, 1984 for "The Art of Reading in *Pride and Prejudice*" by Gary Kelly. Copyright © 1984 Association of Canadian University Teachers of English. Reproduced by permission of the publisher and the author.—*Explicator*, v. 48, fall, 1989; v. 57, summer, 1999. Copyright © 1989, 1999 by Helen Dwight Reid Educational Foundation. Both reproduced with permission of the Helen Dwight Reid Educational Foundation, published by Heldref Publications, 1319 18th Street, NW, Washington, D.C. 20036-1802.—*Feminist Studies*, v. 4, February, 1978. Reproduced by permission of Feminist Studies, Inc., Department of Women's Studies, University of Maryland, College Park, MD 20724.—*French Review*, v. 52, April, 1979; v. 53, December, 1979; v. 58, May, 1985. Copyright © 1979, 1979, 1985 by the American Association of Teachers of French. All reproduced by permission.—*International Fiction Review*, v. 14, winter, 1987. Copyright © 1987 International Fiction Association. Reproduced by permission.—*Journal of Evolutionary Psychology*, v. 22, March, 2002. Copyright © 2002 *Journal of Evolutionary Psychology*. Reproduced by permission.—*Kentucky Romance Quarterly*, v. 32, 1985. Copyright © 1985 by Helen Dwight Reid Educational Foundation. Reproduced with permission of the Helen Dwight Reid Educational Foundation, published by Heldref Publications, 1319 18th Street, NW, Washington, D.C. 20036-1802.—*Language and Style*, v. 4, fall, 1971 for "The Significance of Style in *Fantasio*" by Adele King. Copyright © 1971 by the Southern Illinois University Board of Trustees. Reproduced by permission of the author.—*Legacy*, v. 19, 2002. Copyright © 2003 The University of Nebraska Press. Reproduced by permission.—*Mosaic*, v. 25, winter, 1992. Copyright © Mosaic 1992. All rights reserved. Reproduced by permission.—*Neophilologus*, v. 58, April, 1974. From "Linguistic and Stylistic Clues to Characterization in Musset's *Fantasio*" by Russel S. King. Copyright © 1974 Neophilologus. Reproduced with kind permission from Kluwer Academic Publishers and the author.—*Nineteenth-Century Contexts*, v. 20, 1997. Copyright © 1997 OPA (Overseas Publishers Association). Reproduced by permission of Taylor & Francis, Ltd.—*Nineteenth-Century French Studies*, v. 7, spring-summer, 1979; v. 12, summer, 1984; v. 15, fall, 1986-87; v. 16, fall-winter, 1987-1988; v. 18, fall-winter, 1989-1990; v. 20, fall-winter, 1991-1992. Copyright © 1979, 1984, 1986, 1987, 1989, 1991 by *Nineteenth-Century French Studies*. All reproduced by permission; v. 31, spring-summer, 2003. Copyright © The University of Nebraska Press 2003. Reproduced by permission.—*Nottingham French Studies*, v. 8, May, 1969; v. 8, October, 1969; v. 11, May, 1972. Copyright © The University of Nottingham 1969, 1972. Reproduced by permission.—*Persuasions*, December 16, 1979. Reproduced by permission of *Persuasions*: Journal of the Jane Austen Society of North America.—*Philological Quarterly*, v. 65, winter, 1986 for "Breaking Up/Down/Apart: 'L'Eclatement' as a Unifying Principle in Musset's *Lorenzaccio*" by Barbara T. Cooper. Copyright © 1986 by The University of Iowa, founded in 1847 as The State University of Iowa. Reproduced by permission of the author.—*Qui Parle*, v. 6, fall/winter, 1992 for "Delicacy and Disgust, Mourning and Melancholia, Privilege and Perversity:*Pride and Prejudice*" by Joseph Litvak. Copyright © 1992 by Joseph Litvak. Reproduced by permission of the publisher and the author.—*Resources for American Literary Study*, v. 11, spring, 1981. Copyright © 1981 by The Pennsylvania State University. Reproduced by permission of The Pennsylvania State University Press.—*Romance Notes*, v. 15, spring, 1974; v. 17, spring, 1977; v. 38, fall, 1997. Copyright © 1974, 1977, 1997 *Romance Notes*. Reproduced by permission.—*Studies in the American Renaissance*, 1988, 1990, 1996. Copyright © 1988, 1990, 1996 *Studies in the American Renaissance*. Reproduced by permission.—*Studies in the Humanities*, v. 12, December, 1985. Copyright © 1985 by Indiana University Press of Pennsylvania. Reproduced by permission.—*Style*, v. 20, fall, 1986 for "Characterization and Comment in *Pride and Prejudice*: Free Indirect Discourse and 'Double-voiced' Verbs of Speaking, Thinking, and Feeling" by Anne Waldron Neumann. Copyright ©

COPYRIGHTED MATERIAL IN *NCLC*, VOLUME 150, WAS REPRODUCED FROM THE FOLLOWING BOOKS:

PHOTOGRAPHS AND ILLUSTRATIONS APPEARING IN *NCLC*, VOLUME 150, WERE RECEIVED FROM THE FOLLOWING SOURCES:

Thomson Gale Literature Product Advisory Board

The members of the Thomson Gale Literature Product Advisory Board—reference librarians from public and academic library systems—represent a cross-section of our customer base and offer a variety of informed perspectives on both the presentation and content of our literature products. Advisory board members assess and define such quality issues as the relevance, currency, and usefulness of the author coverage, critical content, and literary topics included in our series; evaluate the layout, presentation, and general quality of our printed volumes; provide feedback on the criteria used for selecting authors and topics covered in our series; provide suggestions for potential enhancements to our series; identify any gaps in our coverage of authors or literary topics, recommending authors or topics for inclusion; analyze the appropriateness of our content and presentation for various user audiences, such as high school students, undergraduates, graduate students, librarians, and educators; and offer feedback on any proposed changes/enhancements to our series. We wish to thank the following advisors for their advice throughout the year.

Pride and Prejudice

Jane Austen

The following entry presents criticism of Austen's novel *Pride and Prejudice* (1813); for further discussion of this novel, see *NCLC,* Volume 13. For discussion of Austen's complete career, see *NCLC,* Volumes 1, 119; for discussion of the novel *Emma,* see *NCLC,* Volume 19; for discussion of the novel *Persuasion,* see *NCLC,* Volume 33; for discussion of the novel *Northanger Abbey,* see *NCLC,* Volume 51; for discussion of the novel *Sense and Sensibility,* see *NCLC,* Volume 81; and for discussion of the novel *Mansfield Park,* see *NCLC,* Volume 95.

INTRODUCTION

One of the world's most popular novels, Jane Austen's *Pride and Prejudice* has delighted readers since its publication with the story of the witty Elizabeth Bennet and her relationship with the aristocrat Fitzwilliam Darcy. Similiar to Austen's other works, *Pride and Prejudice* is a humorous portrayal of the social atmosphere of late eighteenth- and early nineteenth-century England, and it is principally concerned with courtship rituals of the English gentry. The novel is much more than a comedic love story, however; through Austen's subtle and ironic style, it addresses economic, political, feminist, sociological, and philosophical themes, inspiring a great deal of diverse critical commentary on the meaning of the work.

PLOT AND MAJOR CHARACTERS

Pride and Prejudice focuses on Elizabeth Bennet, an intelligent young woman with romantic and individualistic ideals, and her relationship with Mr. Darcy, a wealthy gentleman of very high social status. At the outset of the novel, Elizabeth's loud and dim-witted mother, her foolish younger sisters, and her beautiful older sister Jane are very excited because a wealthy gentleman, Mr. Bingley, is moving to their neighborhood. The young women are concerned about finding husbands because if Elizabeth's father, a humorous and ironical man, were to die, the estate would be left to their pompous cousin Mr. Collins. Mr. Bingley soon becomes attached to Jane while Elizabeth grows to dislike his close friend Mr. Darcy, whom the village finds elit-

ist and ill-tempered. Under the influence of his sisters and Mr. Darcy, Mr. Bingley eventually moves away to London. Mr. Collins, an irritating clergyman, then proposes to his cousin Elizabeth, who refuses him. He marries her friend Charlotte instead, and Elizabeth visits the couple at their estate, where she and Mr. Darcy meet again at the house of his aunt, also Mr. Collin's patroness, Lady Catherine de Bourgh. Mr. Darcy proposes to Elizabeth but she refuses him, partly based on her belief that he dissuaded Mr. Bingley from pursuing a relationship with Jane. In a letter to Elizabeth, Mr. Darcy explains his actions regarding Jane and Mr. Bingley, as well as the way in which he has treated his estranged childhood companion, Mr. Wickham. The next time Elizabeth sees Mr. Darcy, at his estate, she is better disposed toward him, but they are interrupted by a scandal involving Elizabeth's sister Lydia, who has eloped with Mr. Wickham. Mr. Bennet and his brother-in-law Mr. Gardiner attempt to resolve the situation, but it is actually Mr. Darcy who resolves the situation by paying Mr. Wickham and convincing him to marry Lydia. Mr. Bingley then returns to his estate in the Bennets' neighborhood and soon becomes engaged to Jane. Afterward, despite Lady Catherine's attempt to prevent the engagement, Elizabeth marries Mr. Darcy.

MAJOR THEMES

Austen's novel is principally concerned with the social fabric of late eighteenth- and early nineteenth-century England, a patriarchal society in which men held the economic and social power. In an often satirical portrait of the men and women attempting to gain a livelihood, Austen subtly and ironically points out faults in the system, raising questions about the values of English society and the power structure of the country. *Pride and Prejudice* contains many elements of social realism, and it focuses on the merging of the bourgeoisie and the aristocracy during the era of the Napoleonic wars and at the beginning of the industrial revolution. The novel is also engaged in an ideological debate that drives its plot and defines the essence of its main character. Interested in the balance between pragmatism, or the necessity of securing a marriage, and idealism, particularly Elizabeth's romanticism and individualism, Austen dramatizes her heroine's struggle to find a place within the conservative social institution of marriage. The precise nature of this balance is not necessarily clear, and despite what seems to be a happy marriage, it may not be entirely possible to reconcile Elizabeth's independence and naturalness with Mr. Darcy's conservatism and conventionality. Nevertheless, the novel seems to work toward an ideological balance and an alteration in the fundamental aspects of these characters that will lead to a reconciliation of the themes that they represent.

CRITICAL RECEPTION

Probably Austen's most widely read novel, *Pride and Prejudice,* which has been continuously in print since its publication in 1813, has been the subject of volumes of diverse critical reactions. Evaluations of this work have included condemnatory dismissals such as that of Mark Twain, measured praises of Austen's sophistication and wit, and plaudits for the novel as the author's masterpiece. Many early critics focused on the social realism of the novel, commenting on the depth, or lack of depth, of Austen's characters. Criticism of the novel from the nineteenth century through the early twentieth century also tended to regard Austen as a moralist, discussing the value system that *Pride and Prejudice* establishes. Critics from the 1920s through the 1950s focused on Austen's characteristic themes and stylistic devices, as well as discussing her choice of subject matter and the moral and ideological journey that Elizabeth undertakes throughout the course of the novel. During the 1960s and 1970s, commentators offered contextual criticism that evaluated *Pride and Prejudice* within the literary and social world in which Austen wrote. It was also during this period that new directions in criticism of the novel began to be explored. Since the late 1960s, for example, critics have approached Austen's novel from a variety of linguistic standpoints, such as Mikhail Bakhtin's theory of dialogism, as well as analyzing the work in terms of postmodern theory and applying new developments in psychology to the text. There has also been increased attention given to the political subtext of the novel, suggesting new ways of interpreting its relationship to the historical context of the late eighteenth and early nineteenth centuries. In the later decades of the twentieth century and into the early years of the twenty-first century, the most prominent trends in criticism of *Pride and Prejudice* have derived from the perspectives of literary feminism, including analysis of the novel's view of female oppression, its portrayal of the patriarchal society of the time, and its treatment of the possibility, fantasy, and reality of female power. Feminist critics such as Judith Lowder Newton have envisioned the novel as a triumphant fantasy of female autonomy, while Jean Ferguson Carr warns that Austen's exclusion of Mrs. Bennet from the social world reveals a persistent subjugation of women throughout the novel. In addition to strictly feminist readings of *Pride and Prejudice,* many essays not associated with this school of social and literary thought either incorporate or challenge various feminist claims in relation to Austen's work.

PRINCIPAL WORKS

Sense and Sensibility. 3 vols. (novel) 1811
Pride and Prejudice. 3 vols. (novel) 1813
Mansfield Park. 3 vols. (novel) 1814
Emma. 3 vols. (novel) 1816
Northanger Abbey and Persuasion. 4 vols. (novels) 1818
Lady Susan (novel) 1871
The Watsons (unfinished novel) 1871
Love and Friendship and Other Early Works, Now First Printed from the Original MS (juvenilia) 1922
[Sanditon] Fragments of a Novel (unfinished novel) 1925
Volume the First (juvenilia) 1933
Volume the Third (juvenilia) 1951
Volume the Second (juvenilia) 1963

CRITICISM

Joseph Wiesenfarth (essay date 1967)

SOURCE: Wiesenfarth, Joseph. "The Plot of *Pride and Prejudice.*" In *The Errand of Form: An Assay of Jane Austen's Art,* pp. 60-85. New York: Fordham University Press, 1967.

[*In the following essay, Wiesenfarth defends the aesthetic greatness of* Pride and Prejudice, *arguing that its plot is a sophisticated method of erecting an ideal value system.*]

Pride and Prejudice has long been considered a classic by the general reader,[1] but it no longer enjoys that distinction with many professional critics. To the latter, in the post-James and anti-plot era,[2] it seems too elegantly dressed in a strait jacket of form. "Exactness of symmetry," writes Mary Lascelles, ". . . carries with it one danger. The novelist's subtlety of apprehension may be numbed by this other faculty of his for imposing order on what he apprehends."[3] The question, of course, is whether this is truly the case with ***Pride and Prejudice.*** Has the form of the novel been preserved at the expense of the life of the characters it presents? Miss Lascelles herself objects to Darcy's letter: "The manner is right, but not the matter: so much, and such, information would hardly be volunteered by a proud and re-served man—unless under pressure from his author, anxious to get on with the story."[4] But the same proud and reserved man, we remember, rather loudly refused to dance with Elizabeth at Meryton. Did he do that on his own volition or on the author's? The difficulty of answering this question suggests the impossibility of dealing satisfactorily with the problem concerning the letter. A Darcy who could say within earshot of a young lady, "She is tolerable; but not handsome enough to tempt *me*; and I am in no humour at present to give consequence to young ladies who are slighted by other men"[5]—that same Darcy could certainly write a letter to justify *himself* when falsely accused. But even if one were disposed to admit that Darcy is inconsistent, he could find a view of character in eighteenth-century conduct books that sees such inconsistency as natural. Lady Sarah Pennington writes that "the best men are sometimes inconsistent with themselves . . . they may have some oddities of behaviour, some peculiarities of temper . . . blemishes of this kind often shade the brightest character . . ."[6] The kind of question that Darcy's letter raises is open to endless debate. It is too much involved with too many critical presuppositions to be satisfactorily answered. Miss Lascelles is troubled by it; I am not.

A problem raised by Reuben Brower—and later elaborated by Robert Liddell and Marvin Mudrick—can be more advantageously dealt with. The question of esthetic fitness that he introduces into the evaluation of *Pride and Prejudice* deserves serious consideration. Brower writes that "as all ambiguities are resolved and all irony is dropped, the reader feels the closing in of a structure by its necessary end, the end implied in the crude judgment of Dracy in the first ballroom scene."[7] It is his opinion that after the moment at Lambton, when Elizabeth admits "a real interest" in Darcy's welfare, *Pride and Prejudice* is "not quite the same sort of book."[8] "Once we have reached the scenes in which the promise of the introduction is fulfilled, the literary design both ironic and dramatic is complete."[9] If one admits Brower's objection to the design of *Pride and Prejudice,* he has to decide what he can conveniently do with the last fifteen chapters of the novel. If the promise of the introduction is fulfilled at Lambton, these last hundred pages must be considered supererogatory; and with such an excrescence marring its form, *Pride and Prejudice* will have to be considered something less than a classic.

If we turn to the Meryton ball, however, it becomes evident that Brower's analysis of the situation is not exact. The "promise of the introduction" has to do with more than the crude judgment of Darcy at the ball, which Elizabeth rectifies by her sensitive judgment of him at Lambton. The first eligible bachelor introduced into the novel is Charles Bingley. Everything is "Mr.

Bingley" until the ball; during and after it, Bingley is as much in the conversation of Hertfordshire as Darcy. The Meryton ball shows Bingley finding Jane "the most beautiful creature I ever beheld" (11) and asking her "to dance a second time" (14). Attention after the ball is as much directed to the friendly relationship between Bingley and Jane as to the fractured one between Darcy and Elizabeth. Then, after Jane is taken ill, she becomes the center of attention. While she recuperates at Netherfield Park, she and Bingley cautiously reveal their affection for each other. And because Jane is there, Elizabeth comes to visit her; this gives Darcy a chance to reconsider his refusal to dance with her at the ball. Mrs. Bennet also appears on the scene, carrying all but the marriage contract to Bingley and Jane. Unless one is ready to do without much that inspires the first twelve chapters of *Pride and Prejudice,* one has to admit the importance of Jane and Bingley and see them and their relationship as integral to "the promise of the introduction." In fact, one of the main reasons that Elizabeth gives to Darcy for her refusal to marry him concerns Jane:

> ". . . Had not my own feelings decided against you, had they been indifferent, or had they even been favourable, do you think that any consideration would tempt me to accept the man, who has been the means of ruining, perhaps for ever, the happiness of a most beloved sister?"
>
> (190)

Darcy remembers this statement so well that even after Lambton, when he knows that Elizabeth's feelings are favorable toward him, he sees to it that Bingley returns to Netherfield and consequently to Jane. When Elizabeth leaves Darcy at Lambton to attend to Lydia's elopement, the strand of action concerning Bingley and Jane—which was introduced into the novel before that concerning Darcy and herself—remains to be untangled. The dramatic design of *Pride and Prejudice* under these circumstances can hardly be thought at that point to be complete.

Another fact brings out the incompleteness quite clearly too. Before Darcy can accept Elizabeth, he has to accept her family. He has never yet entered the Bennet house at Longbourn. Also, he has still to realize that indecorum is not the specifying characteristic of the Bennets alone. The wonderful interference of the egregious Lady Catherine de Bourgh in his affairs has yet to make Darcy realize that his aunt's title is nothing more than a cover that keeps the skeleton in the family closet from rattling as loudly as the bumbling Mrs. Bennet. Darcy has yet to see completely through the personal-social equation that has been the cause of much of his hauteur. Lady Catherine has yet to clear his vision once and for all. The dramatic design of *Pride and Prejudice* is not complete at Lambton.

PRIDE

AND

PREJUDICE:

A NOVEL.

IN TWO VOLUMES.

BY THE
AUTHOR OF "SENSE AND SENSIBILITY," &c.

VOL. I.

THIRD EDITION.

London:
PRINTED FOR T. EGERTON,
MILITARY LIBRARY, WHITEHALL.

1817.

Title page of Pride and Prejudice, *1817.*

Nor is the ironic either, simply because the ironic is so completely implicated in the dramatic. Irony in *Pride and Prejudice* is more totally verbal in the first half of the novel than in the second. But the verbal irony is necessary to the ambiguity that enables Darcy and Elizabeth so completely to misunderstand each other. It would be rather foolish for Jane Austen to preserve such ironic ambiguity when she is trying to solve the problems caused by it. Such verbal irony in no sense controls the design of the novel. What is normative is personal development through perception, understanding, and affection. Irony is the handmaid of such a norm, not its master.

The norm of personal development through perception, understanding, and affection is developed by a symmetry of plot that involves a series of actions which are dramatically ironic. The plot of *Pride and Prejudice* builds to a statement of problems that arise through verbal ambiguity. Darcy comes to think that Elizabeth loves him whereas she could not care less for him because of the way she feels about his treatment of Jane and of

Wickham. It is on these matters that she is brooding when Darcy comes to her at Hunsford. When he proposes to Elizabeth, she refuses him; and Darcy wants to know why he is not accepted. His request for an explanation is soon answered with three specific accusations, but Elizabeth first asks Darcy why he proposed to her at all since it was (as he said) "against your reason, and even against your character" (190). For Darcy to have proposed irrationally to Elizabeth and to have insinuated that marriage to her would injure his character was for him simply to have insulted her. But Elizabeth puts aside the proposal for a moment and taxes Darcy, first, with preventing Bingley from marrying Jane; second, with hindering Wickham from receiving the living which he claimed was his by right. Then she doubles back to include the nature of his proposal in a third charge that indicts his manners, which impress "me with the fullest belief of your arrogance, your conceit, and your selfish disdain of the feelings of others" (193). Then Darcy places an obstacle of his own in the way of their marrying. He reminds Elizabeth of the indecorous and reprehensible conduct of her family. Darcy had hesitated to propose to Elizabeth because of her family, and he now accuses her of being piqued because "your pride [had] been hurt by my honest confession of the scruples that had long prevented my forming any serious design" (192). There is no question but that at Hunsford parsonage Darcy and Elizabeth for the first time understand each other completely and unequivocally.

The first thirty-three chapters have inevitably led to this moment of passionate clarity. The conflicts and organization of these chapters make it necessary for Elizabeth to charge Darcy with bad faith and worse manners and for Darcy to indict the manners of Elizabeth's mother and father and younger sisters. The Meryton ball, which organizes much of the action and conversation until the sixth chapter, introduces two main actions into the novel. It is at the ball that the romance between Bingley and Jane begins and that Elizabeth's first unfortunate encounter with Darcy occurs: he finds her tolerable but not tempting. Chapters 7 through 12 are organized around Jane, ill but in love at Netherfield Park. There Darcy becomes attracted to Elizabeth, who does not like him at all. There Mrs. Bennet visits her daughter and shows herself a matchmaker and an enemy of Darcy. The courtship of Collins runs sporadically through Chapters 13 to 26 (I. 13 to II. 3),[10] which present Bingley's puzzling retreat to London and Wickham's reports of Darcy's injustice to him. Elizabeth becomes increasingly impatient with Darcy because she believes that he has been unfair to Wickham, whom she likes, and because she believes he has forced Bingley to leave Jane. At the same time, Darcy's attraction to Elizabeth grows stronger. Charlotte's invitation brings Elizabeth to Hunsford—Chapters 26 to 38 (II. 3 to 15)—where she sees Darcy once again, and it is at the Collinses' parsonage that they meet in the fashion described above. Quite clearly, ***Pride and Prejudice*** builds to that moment of conflict.

Only when the four problems that have been so carefully developed and then explicitly stated at Hunsford are solved can the novel come to an end. The problems are not all solved by the time Elizabeth leaves Lambton, and the dramatic irony implicit in them is not fully released until after that point in the novel. The dramatic and ironic design of the novel is not complete until Darcy comes to Longbourn and proposes to Elizabeth. By the time he does that, both he and she have matured intellectually and emotionally as individuals and are ready for the personal encounter of marriage. It is a great triumph of form that one finds in the second half of ***Pride and Prejudice,*** and it is one of the great delights of reading ***Pride and Prejudice*** to see how Jane Austen worked out the design of the novel after Chapter 34 (II. 11) in relation to the four problems presented at Hunsford. One might best begin to demonstrate this position by returning to that letter of Darcy's that Mary Lascelles so much objected to.

Darcy's letter to Elizabeth, which she receives the day following his extraordinary proposal, directs itself in detail to two of the accusations she made against him. Because Elizabeth has called into question Darcy's moral character, he does more than ask her attention to his letter: "I demand it," he writes, "of your justice" (196).

Darcy's letter explains his role in Bingley's leaving Jane, and it explains his obligations toward Wickham as well. Elizabeth learns that Darcy thought that Jane's "look and manners were open, cheerful and engaging as ever, but without any symptom of peculiar regard" for Bingley (197); she learns that he did not think he was doing Jane a personal injury by separating Bingley from her. Moreover, Bingley was courting the danger of connecting himself with a family that Darcy taxes with a "total want of propriety" (198); Elizabeth had thought that he objected to her family's lack of connections. Darcy next turns to Wickham's conduct toward himself and Georgiana, and he offers Colonel Fitzwilliam, whom Elizabeth has found likable and charming, as a corroborating witness. So she is faced with what might be a satisfactory answer to two of her objections to Darcy, namely, his treatment of Jane and of Wickham.

Elizabeth must now decide whether her opinions of Darcy's conduct or his assertions of what his conduct has been are true. Assembling the evidence and calling memory to witness, she judges that she has been in error. "Proud and repulsive as were his manners," Mr. Darcy could not be accused of being "unprincipled or unjust," "irreligious or immoral" (207).

> She grew absolutely ashamed of herself.—Of neither Darcy nor Wickham could she think, without feeling that she had been blind, partial, prejudiced, absurd.

> "How despicably have I acted!" she cried.—"I, who have prided myself on my discernment!—I, who have valued myself on my abilities! who have often disdained the generous candour of my sister, and gratified my vanity, in useless or blameable distrust.—How humiliating is this discovery!—Yet, how just a humiliation!—Had I been in love, I could not have been more wretchedly blind. But vanity, not love, has been my folly.—Pleased with the preference of one [Wickham], and offended by the neglect of the other [Darcy], on the very beginning of our acquaintance, I have courted prepossession and ignorance, and driven reason away, where either were concerned. Till this moment, I never knew myself."

> (208)

The psychomachy is over.[11] Elizabeth has done Darcy the justice he had demanded of her.[12]

Though Elizabeth exonerates Darcy's conduct in relation to Jane and Bingley and to Wickham, she cannot excuse the manner of his proposal to her. In justice, also, she is forced to recognize in that the performance of a man made ridiculous by vanity. He was vain enough to think that his social consequence made him personally desirable. Just as vanity drove reason away in Elizabeth's case, so too has it acted in Darcy's: he proposed to Elizabeth, one remembers, against his reason. So the problem of Darcy's manners remains, as does that of the Bennets' conduct. Elizabeth and Darcy can find no satisfactory personal relationship until these two problems are solved.

At Pemberley, Elizabeth's objection to Darcy's manners disappears. When the Gardiners ask their niece if she would like to see Pemberley, the narrator relates that Elizabeth "was obliged to assume a disinclination for seeing it" (240). The party nevertheless enters Darcy's park, and Elizabeth's expectation is delightfully thwarted: "She had never seen a place for which nature had done more, or where natural beauty had been so little counteracted by an awkward taste" (245). Elizabeth had expected to find Darcy's house and park pretentious, like its owner; all that she sees, however, bespeaks nature: at Pemberley the only art is a natural art, and it configures a natural beauty unmarred by artificiality. Withindoors Elizabeth finds "less of splendor, and more real elegance" than she had anticipated (246). She meets a housekeeper "much less fine, and more civil, than she had any notion of finding" at Pemberley (246), and from her Elizabeth hears a storybook description of Fitzwilliam Darcy, whom Mrs. Reynolds had seen grow into "the best landlord, and the best master . . . that ever lived" (249). Elizabeth also recognizes a portrait of Darcy

> with such a smile over the face, as she remembered to have sometimes seen, when he looked at her. . . . [Now] as she stood before the canvas, on which he was represented, and fixed his eyes upon herself, she

thought of his regard with a deeper sentiment of gratitude than it had ever raised before.

(250-251)

Almost surrealistically the words Elizabeth has heard
and the colors and lines she has seen take life in the
person of Darcy. He greets her with the warm regard
the portrait pictured and shows the Gardiners that attentiveness beyond civility his housekeeper had attributed
to him. The Darcy of art comes alive, asks an introduction to the Gardiners, invites Mr. Gardiner to fish in his
streams, and asks Elizabeth's permission to introduce
Georgiana to her on the following day. Darcy's manners, which were artificial and strained in Hertfordshire
and Hunsford, are all naturalness at Pemberley. Elizabeth is literally charmed out of her objections to Darcy's manners by his cordial reception of herself and her
aunt and uncle, and we see his acceptance of the Gardiners as proleptic of his final acceptance of the Bennet
family.

Indeed, the acceptance of the Bennet family is the only
obstacle of the four mentioned at Hunsford parsonage
that still stands between Darcy and Elizabeth. Before
Elizabeth and the Gardiners leave the Derbyshire region
that obstacle becomes more formidable because Lydia
elopes with Wickham, and Wickham is hardly Darcy's
friend. Now for Darcy to make Elizabeth his wife, he
will have to make Wickham his brother. Nevertheless,
Darcy goes to London and clandestinely arranges the
marriage of Lydia and Wickham, and after he learns
from Lady Catherine that Elizabeth refused to promise
not to marry him if she were asked, he goes to Longbourn, proposes, and is accepted. His going to Longbourn and his entering the Bennet house for the first
time show that he accepts the family in spite of its
faults; and sitting down to dinner with Mrs. Bennet at
his side, Darcy dramatically destroys the last obstacle
to his and Elizabeth's love.

This very brief analysis of the plot of *Pride and Prejudice* shows a structure that is at once dynamic and ordered. Darcy, who could not propose to Elizabeth in the
midst of her family, seeks her out when she is a free
agent. He and she meet at Hunsford, but his social consciousness and her annoyance mar the encounter. Happily, however, they are able to speak directly and unambiguously to each other. This significant change in their
relationship enables Elizabeth to state her three objections to Darcy (he has ruined Jane's relation to Bingley;
he has been unjust to Wickham; he is ill-mannered and
no true gentleman) and he to state his objection to her
(the members of the Bennet family, save Jane and herself, act indecorously and irresponsibly). The dynamics
of their confused and ironic relationship in Hertfordshire are given an orderly perspective at Hunsford. Once
the truth is clear, meaningful reflection and action become possible.

This meeting at Hunsford, therefore, is the watershed
chapter of *Pride and Prejudice.* At the parsonage Elizabeth gives Darcy a cataclysmic piece of information:

"You are mistaken, Mr. Darcy, if you suppose that the
mode of your declaration affected me in any other way,
than as it spared me the concern which I might have
felt in refusing you, had you behaved in a more
gentleman-like manner."

(192)

The man gently born and gently reared is told that he is
not a gentleman, and this changes his life. Elizabeth's
accusation hits so true that it tortures Darcy until he becomes "reasonable enough to allow" its justice (368).
In Chapter 35 (II. 12) Darcy offers causes for effects
when he explains Bingley's presence in London and the
reason for Wickham's lies. Then, in Chapter 36 (II. 13),
Elizabeth judges the causes and her attitude changes,
because she comes for the first time to know herself.
From Chapters 1 to 35 (I. 1 to II. 12) the action of
Pride and Prejudice is for the most part founded on appearances, and these appearances give the lie to reality:
Darcy's manners give the lie to his moral integrity;
Jane's composure, to her feelings of love; Bingley's
leaving, to his love and candor; the Bennets' ill manners, to the worth of Jane and Elizabeth. To Chapter 36
(II. 13) *Pride and Prejudice* is burdened with what
Elizabeth calls an "incumbrance of mystery" (227), but
from that point on the novel proceeds on truth. The
truth that is suddenly revealed at the end of the first
half of *Pride and Prejudice* brings personal realization
through self-discovery to Darcy and Elizabeth. The second half, largely unencumbered by mystery, allows them
to pursue personal realization through love and marriage. After each learns to know himself, they learn
about each other, and seek happiness in the context of
marriage and community.

But before there can be marriage in Jane Austen, there
must be friendship; and before there can be a fitting social context for a particular marriage, there must be a
general acceptance of it on a reasonable basis. Pemberley shows Darcy and Elizabeth developing a friendship
that has a clearly reasonable and deeply affective foundation. Wickham's eloping with Lydia tests this new relationship of Darcy and Elizabeth and deepens it
through empathy. So too does Lady Catherine de
Bourgh's huff-and-puff visit to Elizabeth at Longbourn.
Darcy's return with Bingley to the Hertfordshire region
confirms his and Elizabeth's love and gives it a new
impetus with Jane's acceptance of Bingley. And the recognition of the rightness of the Darcy-Elizabeth engagement by Mr. Bennett and Jane and Bingley is a token of its approval by all in society who are reasonable.
I want now to look at these incidents and to show how
each of them is an elaboration of one of the four problems stated at Hunsford and to suggest how nicely Jane

Austen can turn her variations on principal into dramatic harmonies.

Just as the novel proceeds by dramatization and careful modulation to moments of self-discovery, so too does it move with care and rhythm to Darcy's second proposal and Elizabeth's acceptance. Elizabeth does not simply come to Pemberley, realize what she has denied herself, and set about redressing the error by falling in love with Darcy.[13] Nor does Darcy simply decide to buy off Elizabeth's objection to him by saving the honor of her sister. By the time Elizabeth comes to Pemberley, both she and Darcy have learned something about each other, and at Pemberley they learn more. Elizabeth first sees a house and park that bespeak the taste of true gentility, then she hears about a true gentleman and sees the portrait of one. At the moment when nature and art have conspired to dispose her to see Darcy in a new way, he appears, and he is a new man. Pemberley turns into dramatic truth the rules for judging a gentleman's worth:

> It is only from the less conspicuous scenes of life, the more retired sphere of action, from the artless tenor of domestic conduct, that the real character can, with any certainty, be drawn—these, undisguised, proclaim the man; . . . the best method, therefore, to avoid the deception in this case is, to lay no stress on outward appearances, which are too often fallacious, but to take the rule of judging from the simple unpolished sentiments of those, whose dependent connexions give them an undeniable certainty—who not only see, but who hourly feel, the good or bad effects of that disposition, to which they are subjected. By this, I mean, that if a man is equally respected, esteemed, and beloved by his tenants, by his dependents and domestics . . . you may justly conclude, he has that true good nature, that real benevolence, which delights in communicating felicity, and enjoys the satisfaction it diffuses. . . .[14]

At Pemberley, Darcy's house and park provide the more retired sphere of action, Mrs. Reynolds provides the testimony of a domestic, and Elizabeth is on hand to judge from something other than first impressions. Therefore, after Darcy takes his leave of Elizabeth at Lambton, the narrator takes occasion to comment on the course of their relationship:

> If gratitude and esteem are good foundations of affection, Elizabeth's change of sentiment will be neither improbable nor faulty. But if otherwise, if the regard springing from such sources is unreasonable or unnatural, in comparison of what is so often described as arising on a first interview with its object, and even before two words have been exchanged, nothing can be said in her defence, except that she had given somewhat of a trial to the latter method, in her partiality for Wickham, and that its ill-success might perhaps authorise her to seek the other less interesting mode of attachment.
>
> (279)

Three months have elapsed since we saw Darcy at Hunsford; nevertheless, Elizabeth has been constantly in view. During this three-month period she has come to understand Darcy's conduct. But by showing such a change in one of her characters, Jane Austen suggests the possibility of the same kind of change in an equally intelligent counterpart. She shows Elizabeth changing, but brings Darcy forward when his change is complete. Elizabeth, whom we have seen doing Darcy the justice he demanded of her, finds that he has done her justice as well. Her visit to Pemberley shows her return to reason to be a reflection of his, for herself as well as for the reader. The reality of the change in both—which resulted from Elizabeth's dealing honestly with his letter and Darcy's dealing honestly with her refusal of him—is now dramatized by Elizabeth's admiration of Darcy's manners, which are impeccable, and by his acceptance of Elizabeth's relatives, who are equally without fault.

Moreover, Jane Austen has not forgotten either Darcy's role in separating Jane and Bingley or Elizabeth's former admiration for Wickham. That mutual love existed between Jane and Bingley we are certain, but Bingley himself was unsure of Jane's affection. Now Darcy can be seen in exactly the same position as Bingley was in then. The Gardiners put the case succinctly: "Of the lady's sensations they remained a little in doubt; but that the gentleman was overflowing with admiration was evident enough" (262). Darcy, who split apart doubting lovers, is now a lover and in doubt about being loved himself. There is more than poetic justice in Darcy's feeling along his pulses the meaning of Elizabeth's strong objection to his interference with Jane and Bingley. Darcy's position moves him from mere understanding to empathy. He feels with Elizabeth her objection to his actions, and those objections in light of his own case now mean a great deal more to him. Darcy's becomes an intelligent heart.

Before Elizabeth leaves the Pemberley region, she too comes to feel the justice of Darcy's strong objections to Wickham, whereas formerly she had understood only their reasonableness. When Lydia elopes with Wickham, Elizabeth and her family are made to experience the same disgrace that threatened Darcy's when Wickham planned to elope with Georgiana. The parallel misfortunes of their sisters suggest the creation of a community of feeling between Darcy and Elizabeth. Experiencing in her own family what Darcy had experienced with Wickham in his, Elizabeth understands Darcy better and soon expresses her affection for him:

> She began now to comprehend that he was exactly the man, who, in disposition and talents, would most suit her. His understanding and temper, though unlike her own, would have answered all her wishes. It was an union that must have been to the advantage of both; by her ease and liveliness, his mind might have been softened, his manners improved, and from his judgment, information, and knowledge of the world, she must have received benefit of greater importance.
>
> (312)

But Elizabeth sees quite clearly that, at this time when they are so drawn to each other through understanding and gratitude and empathy, she and Darcy seem more separated than before by Lydia and Wickham's coming together.

> Had Lydia's marriage been concluded on the most honourable terms, it was not to be supposed that Mr. Darcy would connect himself with a family, where to every other objection would now be added, an alliance and relationship of the nearest kind with the man whom he so justly scorned.
>
> (311)

Fortunately, however, Darcy likens Elizabeth's sister to his own. The parallel between Lydia and Georgiana becomes complete as Darcy settles with Wickham and saves Lydia from "irremediable infamy" (335). And Elizabeth learns of Darcy's second encounter with Wickham the same way she learned of his first—by letter, this time Mrs. Gardiner's, rather than Darcy's.[15]

Darcy's motivation for his acts of kindness is not inconsistent with his character as it is developed in the novel. His sense of justice is clearly presented to Elizabeth in Chapter 35 (II. 12), and the chapters that treat Elizabeth's visit at Pemberley and Lambton make Darcy's love for her unmistakable. His sense of justice and his love for Elizabeth lead him to rescue Lydia, as he afterwards confesses. His acts seem completely consistent. His return to Netherfield Park is consistent too. He took Bingley from Netherfield by mistake; now he returns him by design. Bingley's return and his subsequent visit to Longbourn are salts to the faint hopes of Mrs. Bennet, who, to secure Jane a husband, rouses herself to the good health of robust impoliteness. She succeeds in spite of herself because the eminent good sense and superlative dispositions of Jane and Bingley outrun her train of contrivance. Bingley proposes, Jane accepts, Mr. Bennet approves. Elizabeth celebrates the "happiest, wisest, most reasonable end" (347). She sees every expectation for Jane and Bingley's happiness

> to be rationally founded, because they had for basis the excellent understanding, and super-excellent disposition of Jane, and a general similarity of feeling and taste between her and himself.
>
> (347-348)

These reflections of Elizabeth on the natural and reasonable foundations for the happiness of the new couple are the anti-thesis of Mrs. Bennet's comment to Jane: "I was sure you could not be so beautiful for nothing!" (348). Jane's own reaction terminates in a wish that Elizabeth may enjoy equal happiness, to which the younger sister replies, "Till I have your disposition, your goodness, I never can have your happiness" (350). It is interesting to note that Jane's goodness stands here as Elizabeth's model just as her candor did when Eliza-

beth suffered through her revaluation of Darcy after she read his letter. Jane, who appears so early in the novel and in the important role of beloved sister, has to be attended to before Elizabeth herself can find her place at Darcy's side. Jane represents an ideal that Elizabeth respects and loves so much that her reaction to other people is frequently conditioned by their reaction to Jane. This has been a pattern in *Pride and Prejudice.* The most serious charge that Elizabeth brought against Darcy was his interference with Jane's happiness. Now that happiness is complete. Darcy not only brought Bingley back but encouraged his proposal as well. It remains for Darcy to marry Elizabeth to lay to rest the last ghost of prejudice that haunts their relationship. But not without the help of his aunt.

Lady Catherine de Bourgh travels to Longbourn to claim a hereditary right to stupidity. Mrs. Bennet's obvious maneuvers are but pallid challenges to the vulgarity of an aunt who arrives with "chaise and four" to secure the marriage of her daughter to her nephew. Lady Catherine comes to Elizabeth in the name of "honour, decorum, prudence, nay, interest" (355) to order her not to marry Darcy.

It is highly amusing not only to listen to Lady Catherine argue the reasonableness of her demands but also to hear in turn Elizabeth's logical analysis demonstrate that both the premise under which Lady Catherine made her trip—if Elizabeth refused to marry Darcy, he would marry her daughter—and the arguments used to support that premise are ludicrous. Lady Catherine offends Elizabeth's good sense with rhetorical nonsense:

> "I will not be interrupted. Hear me in silence. My daughter and my nephew are formed for each other. They are descended on the maternal side, from the same noble line; and, on the father's, from respectable, honourable, and ancient, though untitled families. Their fortune on both sides is splendid. They are destined for each other by the voice of every member of their respective houses; and what is to divide them? The upstart pretentions of a young woman without family, connections, or fortune. Is this to be endured! But it must not, shall not be. If you were sensible of your own good, you would not wish to quit the sphere, in which you have been brought up."
>
> (356)

There is no mention here of compatibility of mind and disposition, no word about attraction or affection. Lady Catherine, like Mrs. Bennet, does not look upon marriage as a proposition of nature, but as one of stereotyped convention. Both women have daughters to marry: whether there is reason or love in the marriage made is a matter of no importance so long as a marriage takes place. Each recalls to mind a sentence of Dr. Johnson's:

> The miseries, indeed, which many ladies suffer under conjugal vexations are to be considered with great pity, because their husbands are often not taken by them as

objects of affection, but forced upon them by authority and violence or by persuasion and importunity, equally resistless when urged by those whom they have been accustomed to reverence and obey; and it very seldom appears that those who are thus despotic in the disposal of their children pay any regard to their domestic and personal felicity, or think it so much to be inquired whether they will be happy, as whether they will be rich.[16]

Marriage is something other than the ludicrous and tragic yoking of unsuitable partners. Those who would marry, Johnson cautions, should be aware that

marriage is the strictest tie of perpetual friendship; that there can be no friendship without confidence, and no confidence without integrity; and that he must expect to be wretched who pays to beauty, riches, or politeness, that regard which only virtue and piety can claim.[17]

This natural and reasonable basis for marriage, which Johnson delineates to extol, has no place in the system of a Lady Catherine or a Mrs. Bennet, because to them marriage is simply part of a system utterly divorced from nature itself. Lady Catherine does no more than describe the mechanism of the system when she details family, fortune, cradle engagements, connections, and family expectations. She dresses out in the vulgarity of irresponsible obligation what Dr. Johnson described generically as "friendship" based on "virtue and piety." She is the victim of an error that Johnson elsewhere warned against: a man ought to endeavor "to distinguish nature from custom; or that which is established because it is right from that which is right because it is established."[18] To the reasonable person, to one who respects nature, Lady Catherine—who holds that a thing is right only because it is established—can only be unreasonable, and Elizabeth tells her as much:

"Neither duty, nor honour, nor gratitude," replied Elizabeth, "have any possible claim on me, in the present instance. No principle of either, would be violated by my marriage with Mr. Darcy. And with regard to the resentment of his family, or the indignation of the world, if the former *were* excited by his marrying me, it would not give me one moment's concern—and the world in general would have too much sense to join in the scorn."

(358)

Thus beaten on her own terms, Lady Catherine travels to London to report the insolence of Elizabeth to her nephew before she returns to Rosings. But Lady Catherine again fails because Darcy finds her to be the insolent one. His aunt, in fact, makes Mrs. Bennet a bit easier for Darcy to accept as a mother-in-law.

I have dwelt at some length on Lady Catherine's visit to Longbourn because it shows her utter vulgarity and the depersonalizing pattern of life it represents. Lady Catherine shows the danger of money and position sup-

porting a weak mind. Because Mrs. Bennet is fortunately less wealthy, she is also less a threat to the personal order of value. And Darcy realizes this. He also realizes that when he proposed to Elizabeth at Hunsford, there was something of the de Bourgh in him:

He spoke well, but there were feelings besides those of the heart to be detailed; and he was not more eloquent on the subject of tenderness than of pride. His sense of her inferiority—of its being a degradation—of the family obstacles which judgment had always opposed to inclination, were dwelt on with a warmth which seemed due to the consequence he was wounding, but was very unlikely to recommend his suit.

(189)

When Darcy proposes a second time he takes a different tack because he is a different Darcy:

"The recollection of what I then said, of my conduct, my manners, my expressions during the whole of it, is now, and has been many months, inexpressibly painful to me. Your reproof, so well applied, I shall never forget: 'had you behaved in a more gentleman-like manner.' Those were your words. You know not, you can scarcely conceive, how they have tortured me;—though it was some time, I confess, before I was reasonable enough to allow their justice."

(367-368)

Darcy is capable of sympathizing with Elizabeth's rejection of his proposal and of her rejection of Lady Catherine's interference in her personal affairs because he himself was once what his aunt still is. Jane Austen again establishes a relation of sympathetic feeling between Darcy and Elizabeth and ironically forces him to realize that the objection he brought against Elizabeth's family at Hunsford applies as forcefully to his own.

The events from Lydia's elopement to Darcy's proposal clearly show that Jane Austen is still working out her novel in relation to the four problems introduced by Darcy's first proposal. Elizabeth accused Darcy of separating Bingley and Jane, of being unjust to Wickham, of acting generally in an ungentlemanly way. Darcy, in turn, indicted her family's lack of sense and decorum. Once stated, the problems are gradually solved. Darcy's letter to Elizabeth exonerates him of his conduct to Jane and Bingley and toward Wickham. At Pemberley Elizabeth sees Darcy's change in manners by his cordial reception of herself and the Gardiners, and his acceptance of her family is hinted at. But Jane Austen does not let go of her problems with these solutions. Each of them must not only be solved by reason but also dissolved in love. Darcy does not merely right the wrongs he was more or less guilty of, but he rights them to fault. Darcy's love of Elizabeth is dramatically revealed by his settling a sum of money on Wickham. The problem of Darcy's doing justice to Wickham is thus reintroduced and irrevocably solved. So, too, his interference in the love of Bingley and Jane is exonerated when he returns Bingley to Longbourn, and Bingley proposes. Lady Catherine's visit to Elizabeth makes Darcy feel how relatively unimportant his objection to the Bennets is, just as Mrs. Bennet's treatment of Darcy, when he visits Longbourn with Bingley, reminds Elizabeth of what there was of justice in Darcy's former objection to her family. At any rate, Darcy's visit shows how resilient to change are the good manners—the gentlemanly conduct—Elizabeth met at Pemberley. Darcy clearly comes to an unimproved Bennet family, but he comes willingly. He comes to pluck a flower among the thorns quite conscious that he is going to be pricked. This is all to his credit and shows that he has come to understand that the slight consequence of Elizabeth's family in no way diminishes her desirability; therefore, he comes to Elizabeth as a man to a woman on the basis of reason and affection. Elizabeth's expression of gratitude for his goodness to Lydia allows Darcy to tell her that "the wish of giving happiness to you" added "force to other inducements which led me on" (366). This conversation almost immediately turns into Darcy's second proposal, which shows him accepting the Bennets and bringing to a happy solution the last of the problems raised at Hunsford. The second half of *Pride and Prejudice* clearly shows Darcy and Elizabeth, who have already achieved self-knowledge, moving toward marriage on the bases of reason and gratitude, empathy and love.

The rhythm and modulation of the human events that lead Darcy and Elizabeth to the altar suggest that their marriage is an ideal. They achieve that friendship based on confidence and integrity that Johnson extolled in *The Rambler,* no. 18, as the foundation of true love and happy marriage. It is important in this connection to note how little emphasis is put on the marriage and how much on the courtship. Getting married is not just an end, a standing at the altar; rather, it is a going to the altar. The movement toward marriage in *Pride and Prejudice* is a ritual of human development. In this novel those who just want to get to the altar, no matter what, are different from those who get there in a distinctly human way. Therefore, the marriage of Darcy and Elizabeth compares favorably with that of the Bingleys and of the Gardiners; but it contrasts sharply with the Collinses' marriage, the Wickhams' marriage, and the Bennets' marriage. Their carefully developed love shows Darcy and Elizabeth to be truly human and completely ready to make of their marriage the meaningful union it can be within the limits of the society Jane Austen creates in her novel.

Marriage itself has a social extension in Jane Austen's novels that one must always expect to appear. Marriage is never a matter of personal recognition of individual worth only, important and indispensable as that is. One can presume that the "promise of the introduction" of any Jane Austen novel takes in the assimilation of the couple into a larger context. Jane Austen sees man, "not as a solitary being completed in himself, but only as completed in society."[19] Elizabeth by having her marriage accepted by others sees to it that her personal judgment of Darcy effectively replaces the crude judgments of him that temporarily prevail. As soon as Jane and Mr. Bennet understand that Elizabeth loves Darcy and is marrying him because she loves him, not because he is rich, they rejoice in her engagement. Elizabeth's mother, however, knows nothing about love's relation to respect, reason, and affection. Mrs. Bennet is the poor man's Lady Catherine. Marriage is good because every girl needs a husband to support her; it is the custom. Marriage to a rich man, since it implies indescribable wile, shows the greatest respect for custom.

> "Good gracious! Lord bless me! only think! dear me! Mr. Darcy! Who would have thought it! And is it really true? Oh! my sweetest Lizzy! how rich and how great you will be! What pin-money, what jewels, what carriages you will have! Jane's is nothing to it—nothing at all. I am so pleased—so happy. Such a charming man!—so handsome! so tall!—Oh, my dear Lizzy! pray apologise for my having disliked him so much before. I hope he will overlook it. Dear, dear Lizzy. A house in town! Every thing that is charming! Three daughters married! Ten thousand a year! Oh, Lord! What will become of me. I shall go distracted."
>
> (378)

One is hard-put to find any one paragraph in all of Jane Austen where so many exclamation marks are used. To Mrs. Bennet, as her speech reveals, Elizabeth's performance of her duty to marry is superior to anything a mother's heart has known. To Mrs. Bennet's thinking, certainly, her daughter has snatched a grace beyond the reach of a mother's art.

At the end of *Pride and Prejudice* it is clear that Mrs. Bennet is as crass and as stupid as she was at the beginning of the novel. Elizabeth has changed considerably, however. The vain and prejudiced girl has grown into the reasonable and loving woman. It is significant that physical movements correlate with her development. Indeed, Mrs. Bennet's stasis and Elizabeth's dynamism give the novel a total esthetic fitness. It is notable that Mrs. Bennet never leaves Hertfordshire, and for the most part stays in Longbourn. All her world is there. Darcy and Elizabeth first meet in Hertfordshire, where Elizabeth's family alienates Darcy's feelings. At Hunsford, Elizabeth and Darcy meet on more neutral ground. Elizabeth is there as a person to be valued for herself and separated from her family. There Darcy and she come face to face with each others' faults and virtues. Elizabeth is next at Pemberley. At Darcy's Derbyshire estate, she sees him in a new perspective, that of his home. There he is a new man and she a new woman. Lastly, she sees Darcy come to Longbourn, her own home, face her family, and ask her hand. From Hertfordshire, to Hunsford, to Pemberley, to Longbourn: the journey has been for Darcy and Elizabeth as much a journey of the spirit as of the body. The roads of the English countryside have been the way of man between meeting and marriage. By having the principal episodes of *Pride and Prejudice* occur at significant places, Jane Austen carefully coordinates physical and social events with spiritual experiences. The art of travel in Jane Austen is the art of putting people in the right place at the right time. Fielding and Smollett give way to Jane Austen, who places her people in parks and parsonages and who creates excitement in her novels through the movement of the mind and the affections. Her *homo viator* is a man on a more spiritual path than the heroes who trod the road in the novels of her dusty and muddy predecessors. Characteristically, then, the total configuration of events in the plot of the novel shows that in *Pride and Prejudice* the journey from Hertfordshire back to Hertfordshire becomes for Darcy and Elizabeth a movement from pride and prejudice to love.

Now what does it mean to read *Pride and Prejudice* in this way? It means, I think, that one comes to recognize that the plot of the novel expresses the values of the novel. *Pride and Prejudice* dramatizes the possibility of an ordered world in which people are frustrated when they cannot see or when they refuse to recognize what is real in the world about them. Conversely, in this ordered world people who see reality and act reasonably in relation to it find fulfillment and happiness.

In *Pride and Prejudice* Elizabeth Bennet makes a mistake that she finally rectifies. She misjudges Darcy because her prejudice against him leads her to misunderstand a series of incidents in which they are both involved. But by refusing to marry Darcy the first time he proposes, she does not irrevocably create a destiny for herself. Rather her destiny is created for her by his letter, by their accidental meeting at Pemberley, by her sister Lydia's elopement, by Lady Catherine's visit, and by Darcy's generosity. The mistake of one day does not press upon Elizabeth for the rest of her life because the world Jane Austen creates is benign to the degree that one is reasonable and virtuous. Therefore, the mistake of one day brings Elizabeth directly in the middle of *Pride and Prejudice* to a realization of her personal faults, to an understanding of her life, and to an awareness of her character in relation to a reasonable norm according to which men are good or bad. By the time the plot of the novel has reached its midpoint, its heroine is realized as a total and integral human being. After this moment of realization Elizabeth has to be patient and suffer not because of herself, but because of others. The consequences of her first rejection of Darcy are temporary and beneficial. The rejection brings both of them to a realization of their true humanity. Just as the realization overpowers Elizabeth's prejudice, it over-

powers Darcy's pride. A series of incidents over which Elizabeth has no control reunites them on the bases of understanding, empathy, gratitude, and love. The novel, then, ends not only with the total individual development of each character but also with his total social development, because personal love is satisfied in marriage and harmonized with society. The most divergent elements come to recognize the reasonableness of the marriage and give it their blessing. Darcy and Elizabeth are assumed into their social order and become exemplars of it in their reasonable and loving marriage. Under these circumstances, therefore, if *Pride and Prejudice* develops four problems and solves them—as I submit it does—it could have ended no sooner than it did.

As a novel that presents a society that has reason for its ideal for action, and marriage as its symbol for personal and societal fulfillment, *Pride and Prejudice* has a plot that controls the presentation of these values. It is so constructed that the characters confront situations that force to our attention those human values that are held to be most important. Through a complex series of interwoven incidents Elizabeth and Darcy are shown acting irrationally, coming to an awareness of their defection from reasonable conduct, experiencing events that enable them to empathize with each other, strengthening their friendship, falling in love, and marrying.

> [The] marriage of Elizabeth and Darcy resolves not only their personal differences but the conflicts they have represented, with the result that the novel provides a final pleasure unique in Jane Austen's fiction, a sense of complete fulfillment analogous to that which marks the end of some musical compositions.[20]

If this reading of *Pride and Prejudice* is valid, a radical reassessment of the significance of plot is needed, for the plot emphasizes an ideal pattern of conduct that shows Jane Austen sounding the classic note:

> If the poet can portray something superior to contemporary practice, it is not in the way of anticipating some later, and quite different code of behaviour, but by an insight into what the conduct of his own people at his own time might be, at its best.[21]

Only in relation to such an ideal does irony—so much emphasized in recent criticism—make sense, because irony demands such an ideal: "Unless there is something about which the author is never ironical," writes C. S. Lewis, "there can be no true irony in the work. 'Total irony'—irony about everything—frustrates itself and becomes insipid."[22] Also, only in relation to such an ideal does money find its place in Jane Austen's created world. Therefore the notion that the form of the novel develops through a vocabulary of mercantile metaphor, which Mark Schorer and Dorothy Van Ghent[23] have proposed, needs rethinking. The plot clearly suggests the true value of money by subjugating it to personal dignity and love in the relationship of Darcy and Elizabeth, and its false value by dramatizing its first importance in the lives of Lady Catherine, Mrs. Bennet, and Charlotte Lucas, none of whom is admirable. In short, in *Pride and Prejudice* the incidents and design of the plot expose an ideal of human conduct and fulfillment that Jane Austen treats neither ironically nor cynically. Rather, she disposes the incidents of the plot in such a way that they shape meaning, direct irony, control diction, and present themselves as an esthetic fact. Consequently, Jane Austen makes plot more than an arrangement of incidents in *Pride and Prejudice*: she makes it a mold of values. And from that mold she strikes a novel of classical delicacy and strength.

Notes

1. "I have called Miss Austen's earliest work, *Pride and Prejudice,* her masterpiece; and though some of her votaries have preferred to it *Emma,* or, as did the Prince Regent, *Mansfield Park,* the suffrage of the general reader has always been strong for *Pride and Prejudice,*" H. W. Garrod, "Jane Austen: A Depreciation" in *Discussions of Jane Austen,* ed. William Heath (Boston, 1961), p. 35.

2. "Trying to recover here, for recognition, the germ of my idea, I see that it must have consisted not at all in any conceit of a 'plot,' nefarious name, in any flash, upon the fancy of a set of relations, or in any one of those situations that, by a logic of their own, immediately fall, for the fabulist, into movement, into a march or a rush, a patter of quick steps; but altogether in the sense of a single character, the character and aspect of a particular engaging young woman, to which all the usual elements of a 'subject,' certainly of a setting, were to need to be super-added," *The Art of the Novel: Critical Prefaces* (New York, 1953), p. 42. James substituted the word "action" for the more nefarious "plot." For the more than nominal difference between "plot" and "action" as the terms achieve concrete realization in novels, see Joseph Wiesenfarth, "Henry James: Action and the Art of Life," *Four Quarters,* XV (1966), 18-26, an article which compares *The Portrait of a Lady* with *Pride and Prejudice.*

3. *Jane Austen and Her Art,* p. 163.

4. Ibid., p. 162.

5. *The Novels of Jane Austen,* ed. R. W. Chapman (3rd ed.), Vol. II: *Pride and Prejudice* (London, 1959), p. 12. All subsequent page references to this text will appear in parentheses following quotations from it.

6. "An Unfortunate Mother's Advice to Her Absent Daughters," reprinted in part in Appendix II of Frank W. Bradbrook, *Jane Austen and her Successors* (Cambridge, 1966), p. 152.

7. Reuben Brower, *The Fields of Light* (New York, 1962), p. 179.

8. Ibid., p. 180.

9. Ibid.

10. For sake of convenience I have given the chapter numbers from editions of *Pride and Prejudice* that are numbered consecutively and in parentheses the volume and chapter numbers of the standard three-volume edition.

11. I use the word *psychomachy* to describe, in relation to Elizabeth, a condition of mind and emotions that was well explained by an anonymous critic for the *North British Review,* LXXII (April 1870), 129-152. "Again, she contemplates virtues, not as fixed quantities, or as definable qualities, but as continual struggles and conquests, as progressive states of mind, advancing by repulsing their contraries, or losing ground by being overcome. Hence again the individual mind can only be represented by her as a battle-field where contending hosts are marshalled, and where victory inclines now to one side and now to another," quoted in Lionel Trilling, "Introduction," *Emma* (Cambridge, Mass., 1957), p. xxii.

12. The presence here of a value like justice raises a problem. Dorothy Van Ghent has written that the "general directions of reference taken by Jane Austen's language . . . are clearly materialistic" (*The English Novel: Form and Function* [New York, 1961], p. 110). When a rich man sees a marriageable daughter, Mrs. Van Ghent writes, there is "no doubt he will buy, that is to say, 'fall in love'" (p. 102). "Categories" such as "'trade,' 'arithmetic,' 'money,' 'material possessions' . . . indicate that kind of language Jane Austen inherited from her culture and to which she was confined . . ." (p. 109). Elsewhere, Mrs. Van Ghent affirms that "the moral life . . . will be equated with delicacy and integrity of feeling" (p. 103). But it is a logical necessity that one either eat his cake or have it: either one or the other, but not both. If Jane Austen's society allowed her a materialistic vocabulary only, then she could not express nonmaterialistic values like "delicacy and integrity of feeling" because she had no words to do so. Indeed, if "to fall in love" is no more than "to buy," one wonders how delicacy of feeling and integrity of moral life can be spoken of at all. There is no such dilemma if one discards the theory of "dead metaphor." Important and characteristic words like "ashamed," "think," "feeling," "prejudiced," "despicably," "prided," "discernment," "detained,"

"generous," "vanity," blameable," "humiliating," "just," "humiliation," "love" (all words taken from the two paragraphs quoted from p. 208) abound in *Pride and Prejudice.* These words suggest, as C. S. Lewis has written, that the "great abstract nouns of the classical English moralists are unblushingly and uncompromisingly used" by Jane Austen ("A Note on Jane Austen" in *Jane Austen: A Collection,* p. 28). And with the nouns there are verbs, adjectives, and adverbs to carry serious moral judgments. To remain alive, a theory of dead metaphor has to discount not only the literal meaning of these words and those like them but also the structure of a plot wherein the human development of the characters depends on a literal reading of the diction.

13. It seems hardly necessary to make such a bland statement of facts; however, Geoffrey Gorer proves that it is. He writes, "Elizabeth, in *Pride and Prejudice,* does, it is true, marry young Mr. Darcy, but has anybody, even the author, been convinced that she loved him, or that she entertained any feelings warmer than respect or gratitude? Surely her own remark, that she must date her affection 'from my first seeing his beautiful grounds at Pemberley' (ch. 59), represents the psychological truth" ("The Myth in Jane Austen" in *Five Approaches to Literary Criticism,* ed. Wilbur Scott [New York, 1962], p. 94).

14. Lady Sarah Pennington in Bradbrook, 151ff.

15. This episode of Lydia's elopement with Wickham has not been to the liking of many critics. Brower, Mudrick, and Liddell, for instance, feel a drop in Jane Austen's imaginative power, a loss of irony, and a lack of dramatic coordination in it. There is, however, a structural coordination with the plot, as I have shown in my text. Besides, three other points may be made in reference to irony. First, the episode is ironic in its own way: Wickham, who has been angling throughout the novel, makes the poorest catch in Lydia. Also, Elizabeth now reacts to Wickham in a manner for which she once condemned Darcy for reacting to Wickham. Again, the money Darcy once refused Wickham is now given him. Perhaps the irony is more attenuated than, and functionally different from what, it was previously, but irony nevertheless does function in this episode.

Another point that I cannot admit is that irony is the norm in the novel. An episode does not really have to be ironic to justify its presence in *Pride and Prejudice.* But Mudrick seems to argue that it does (*Irony,* pp. 111-115). In this episode, for instance, he maintains that Elizabeth is inconsistent because she does not react ironically to Lydia's elopement. Lydia, he argues, as a simple character is incapable of free choice; therefore, she is not susceptible to Elizabeth's moral indignation. Besides, Elizabeth's conventional moral reaction is atypical of her. But one need accept neither of these premises when evaluating the elopement. Elizabeth reacts in a straightforward manner to the faults of her mother, her sisters, Lady Catherine, Bingley, and occasionally even of Collins (all simple characters in Mudrick's opinion), and this suggests responsibility on their part and consistency on Elizabeth's when she reacts to Lydia. The "fogbank of bourgeois morality" that Mudrick feels conceals Jane Austen seems rather to be an acceptance on her part of a principle that holds fornication to be wrong. The principle may be conventional, but that does not discredit it. Neither Jane Austen nor Elizabeth needs to invoke irony here to discriminate good from bad. "Critics have seen [irony]," writes Donald J. Greene, ". . . as the mechanism of a refusal to make moral judgments about the world or to become emotionally involved with it. . . . This seems to me a fundamentally mistaken line of approach to any supremely great artist like Jane Austen" ("Jane Austen and the Peerage" in *Jane Austen: A Collection* p. 164).

16. *The Rambler,* no. 39.

17. *The Rambler,* no. 18.

18. *The Rambler,* no. 156.

19. *North British Review,* LXXII (April 1870), quoted in Trilling, "Introduction," *Emma* (Cambridge, Mass., 1957), p. xxii.

20. A. Walton Litz, *Artistic Development.* New York: Oxford University Press, 1965, p. 102. In a similar vein, Joseph M. Duffy remarks, "Her vision might almost be reduced to the assertion that, in spite of all evidence to the contrary, the sublime, the miraculous, and the ever possible human achievement is the love of two people for each other and the proliferation of that love in the family" ("Moral Integrity in *Mansfield Park,*" *ELH,* XXIII [1956], 82).

21. T. S. Eliot, "What is a Classic?" reprinted in *On Poetry and Poets* (New York, 1961), p. 63.

22. "A Note on Jane Austen" in *Jane Austen: A Collection,* p. 3. One ought certainly to add to Lewis' remarks those of Alan D. McKillop: ". . . The social comedy can never be separated from a basic system of moral judgments; the release of free and humorous criticism or irony, as it is now fashionable to call it, is never irresponsible though it may well be lighthearted; as an aspect of the art of the novelist it stands in vital relationship to a plot structure which embodies a social structure." (*Early Masters,* p. 96).

23. For Dorothy Van Ghent, see note 12 above. Schorer first proposed the theory of dead metaphor in an essay "Fiction and the 'Analogical Matrix'" (*Kenyon Review,* XI [1949], 541-560), in which he discussed *Persuasion.* More recently, he affirmed the applicability of his theory to *Pride and Prejudice*: see "Introduction," *Pride and Prejudice* (Cambridge, Mass., 1956), pp. xv-xvi.

Works Cited

Litz, A. Walton. *Jane Austen: A Study of Her Artistic Development.* New York: Oxford University Press, 1965.

McKillop, Alan Dugald. *The Early Masters of English Fiction.* Lawrence: University of Kansas Press, 1956.

Mudrick, Marvin. *Jane Austen: Irony as Defense and Discovery.* Princeton, N.J.: Princeton University Press, 1952.

Kenneth L. Moler (essay date 1968)

SOURCE: Moler, Kenneth L. "*Pride and Prejudice* and the Patrician Hero." In *Jane Austen's Art of Allusion,* pp. 74-108. Lincoln: University of Nebraska Press, 1968.

[*In the following essay, Moler discusses the relationship between* Pride and Prejudice *and the novels of Fanny Burney and Samuel Richardson.*]

In *Pride and Prejudice,* it is generally agreed, one encounters a variant of the eighteenth-century "art-nature" contrast when Elizabeth Bennet's forceful and engaging individualism clashes with Darcy's by no means indefensible respect for the social order and his class pride. Most critics agree that *Pride and Prejudice* does not suffer from the appearance of one-sidedness that makes *Sense and Sensibility* unattractive. It is obvious that neither Elizabeth nor Darcy embodies the moral norm of the novel. Each is admirable in his way, and each must have his pride and prejudice corrected by self-knowledge and come to a fuller appreciation of the other's temperament and beliefs. Ultimately their conflicting points of view are adjusted, and each achieves a mean between "nature" and "art." Elizabeth gains some appreciation of Darcy's sound qualities and comes to see the validity of class relationships. Darcy, under Elizabeth's influence, gains in naturalness and learns to respect the innate dignity of the individual.[1]

This essay is concerned with the relationship between certain elements in *Pride and Prejudice* and the novels of Richardson, Fanny Burney, and some of their imitators. Jane Austen's Mr. Darcy bears a marked resemblance to what may be called the "patrician hero," a popular character type in the novels of her day, and it is rewarding to investigate the relationship between Darcy and his love affair with Elizabeth Bennet and the heroes of Richardson's and Burney's novels and their relations with their heroines. Jane Austen's treatment of her patrician hero has a marked relevance to the theme of the reconciliation of opposite values and qualities that plays such an important part in *Pride and Prejudice.* Moreover, it is possible that the study of Darcy's origins may help to account for some inconsistencies in his character that have troubled a number of Jane Austen's readers. I shall begin by outlining some of the characteristics of the patrician hero.

I

Authority figures of various sorts play prominent roles in many eighteenth- and nineteenth-century novels. There is the patriarch or matriarch—Fielding's benevolent Allworthy, Godwin's terrifying Falkland, Dickens' Miss Havisham—whose relationship with a young dependent acts as a sort of metaphor for the relationship between the social order and individual, "natural" man. In the novels of Richardson the relationship—prosperous, or, in the case of Lovelace and Clarissa, mutually destructive—between a young man of rank and fortune and a girl who is naturally good but socially inferior performs a similar function. The chief concern here is with the particular sort of figure that Richardson's Sir Charles Grandison represents.[2]

Richardson's Lovelace is a lost soul; his Mr. B———— has to be reformed by the virtuous Pamela. In Sir Charles Grandison, however, Richardson depicted a perfect Christian aristocrat. Sir Charles, Richardson would have his readers feel, combines the glamor of a Lovelace with the principles of a Clarissa. He is handsome and accomplished, dresses exquisitely (out of respect for his father's memory!) and has charming manners. He is immensely wealthy, an owner of splendid mansions and manors, and a powerful, important landholder. Yet he is a man of the strictest Christian virtue, a just, benevolent, and superefficient steward of his estates, a protector of the weak and a friend to the poor. In short, as Richardson describes him in the preface to *Grandison,* Sir Charles is "a man of religion and virtue; of liveliness and spirit; accomplished and agreeable; happy in himself, and a blessing to others."[3]

In the concluding note to *Grandison,* Richardson admits that "it has been observed by some, that, in general [Sir Charles] approaches too near the faultless character which some critics censure as above nature" (7: 327). The reaction Richardson describes is not uncommon among readers of his novel. "Pictures of perfection," Jane Austen once wrote, ". . . make me sick and wicked" (*Letters,* pp. 486-487, March 23, 1817[4]); and most readers are wicked enough to resent a character who demands so much admiration as Sir Charles does. In addition to being dismayed by Sir Charles' incredible glamor and goodness, one tends to be annoyed by the sycophantic deference with which he is treated by nearly every character in his history. Sir Charles' male friends attempt to emulate his virtues—and admit it on every possible occasion. His female acquaintance worship him as "the best of men," take his word for law, and all too frequently fall in love with him. His admirers—repeatedly, indeed *ad nauseam*—entrust their most important affairs to him when they are living, and leave their estates to his management when they die. Thus, Sir Charles, at his sister's request, frees her from an unfortunate engagement; later he arranges a suitable marriage for her. He extricates his uncle from the clutches of an unmanageable mistress and, on the uncle's insistence, provides him with a worthy wife. He assists in bringing about a reconciliation between his friend Mr. Beauchamp and Beauchamp's stepmother. He sees to it that the relatives of Mr. Danby—Mr. Danby having left his estate in Sir Charles' hands—are provided with fortunes, employment, and matrimonial partners, and arranges for the distribution of the remainder of Danby's estate in charity. He is entrusted with the negotiation of a "treaty" between the unfortunate Lady Clementina della Poretta and the tyrannical relatives from whom she flees to England. Indeed, it is a rare moment when Sir Charles is not dispensing advice and assistance to half a dozen of his family and friends simultaneously. "Such a man," the lovelorn Harriet Byron writes shortly after she has come to visit Sir Charles and Miss Grandison, "cannot, ought not to be engrossed by one family. . . . Let me enumerate some of his present engagements that we know of."

> The Danby family must have some further portion of his time.
>
> The executorship in the disposal of the 3000 £ in charity, in France as well as in England, will take up a good deal more.
>
> My Lord W—— may be said to be under his tutelage, as to the future happiness of his life.
>
> Miss Jervois's affairs, and the care he has for her person, engage much of his attention.
>
> He is his own steward. . . .
>
> His sister's match with Lord G—— is one of his cares.
>
> He has services to perform for his friend Beauchamp, with his father and mother-in-law, for the facilitating his coming over.
>
> And the Bologna family in its various branches, and more especially Signor Jeronymo's dangerous state of health, and Signora Clementina's disordered mind—O Lucy!—What leisure has this man to be in love!
>
> (vol. 4, letter 5, pp. 49-50)

Among the most fervent of Sir Charles' *aficionados* is the heroine of *Grandison,* Miss Byron. Sir Charles is her oracle; she treasures up his every word, and is embarrassingly grateful when he "condescends" to give her advice. She makes no pretensions to equality with her hero. She asks only that he: "'Teach me, sir, to be good, to be generous, to be forgiving—like you!—Bid me do what you think proper for me to do'" (vol. 6, letter 24, p. 206). Her relationship with him is like that of an adoring younger sister to an older brother, or that of an infatuated pupil with a favorite teacher: he is, to use her own word, her "monitor," as much as he is her lover. Harriet is in love with Sir Charles long before she knows that he cares for her; and when, after months of heartburning, she learns that he has decided to marry her, she is overwhelmed with joy and gratitude. "My single heart, methinks," she writes in her last letter to her grandmother,

> is not big enough to contain the gratitude which such a lot demands. Let the over-flowings of your pious joy, my dearest grandmamma, join with my thankfulness, in paying part of the immense debt for
>
> Your undeservedly happy HARRIET GRANDISON.
>
> (vol. 8, letter 62, p. 325)

As noted above, all of this deference, added to Richardson's insistence on Sir Charles' perfection, tends to make the reader react unfavorably toward both Sir Charles and his creator. One is inclined, in spite of Richardson's insistence on his humility, to think of Sir Charles as a stuffily superior, rather supercilious character, rather than as the noble and magnanimous hero that Richardson envisioned, and inclined, too, to tax Richardson as well as some of the characters in his novel with an unduly sycophantic attitude toward his highborn hero. That Jane Austen reacted to *Grandison* in a similar fashion will become apparent later.

All of the three novels that Fanny Burney published before 1813 deal, as *Sir Charles Grandison* does, with the relationships between exemplary young authority figures who are wealthy or wellborn or both and heroines who are in some respects their social inferiors. *Cecilia,* however, is the Burneyan novel most frequently cited as a source for **Pride and Prejudice,** some critics, indeed, feeling that Jane Austen's novel is simply a realistic rewriting of *Cecilia.* R. Brimley Johnson, for instance, has referred to the "title and plot, the leading characters and most dramatic scenes of **Pride and Prejudice**" as "frank appropriations" from *Cecilia.*[5]

Cecilia is certainly an important source for **Pride and Prejudice.** In plot and theme it resembles Jane Austen's novel more nearly than any other single work does. It is possible—though by no means certain—that the title of **Pride and Prejudice** was borrowed from *Cecilia.*[6] It is often suggested that the first proposal scene in **Pride** *and Prejudice* was influenced to a large extent by the scenes in *Cecilia* in which Mortimer Delvile states his objections to a marriage with Cecilia, and there are similarities between the scene in which Mrs. Delvile prevails on Cecilia to give Mortimer up and the scene in which Lady Catherine de Bourgh descends on Elizabeth Bennet. There are, however, a number of significant points of resemblance between *Pride and Prejudice* and novels other than *Cecilia*. In some respects the situation of Fanny Burney's Evelina is closer to that of Elizabeth Bennet than Cecilia's is. Both Elizabeth and Evelina are relatively poor in addition to being inferior in rank to their heroes, while Cecilia is rich, and both are surrounded by sets of vulgar relatives who embarrass them in the presence of their lovers. Moreover, some specific scenes in *Pride and Prejudice* are almost certainly based on similar scenes in *Evelina*. Some others, on the other hand, would seem to have their originals in *Sir Charles Grandison*. I believe that in her novel Jane Austen is not rewriting *Cecilia*, but manipulating a character type and a situation made familiar to her audience in various novels by Richardson and Fanny Burney—and in numerous works by their imitators as well. The relationship between *Evelina* and *Pride and Prejudice* has never been fully explored; and since it seems in some respects rewarding to compare Jane Austen's Mr. Darcy to Fanny Burney's Lord Orville, I shall rely primarily on *Evelina* to illustrate Fanny Burney's treatment of the patrician hero.

While all of Fanny Burney's heroes resemble Richardson's patrician hero somewhat, Lord Orville is Sir Charles Grandison writ small. He is "a picture of perfection," a paragon among men—at least in the eyes of his heroine and his author. Evelina describes him as "one who seemed formed as a pattern for his fellow creatures, as a model of perfection" (p. 280). He is handsome, wellborn, rich, wise. "His conversation," Evelina gushes after her first encounter with him, "was sensible and spirited; his air and address were open and noble; his manners gentle, attentive, and infinitely engaging; his person is all elegance, and his countenance, the most animated and expressive I have ever seen" (p. 33).

The relationship between Orville and Evelina is much the same as that between Sir Charles Grandison and Harriet Byron. Evelina adores Orville from their first meeting, and she is fully convinced of her own inferiority. "That he should be so much my superior in every way, quite disconcerted me," she writes after their first dance together (p. 33). She cringes when she learns that he has referred to her as "a poor weak girl" and is "grateful for his attention" even after she believes that he has insulted her with a dishonorable proposal. Orville, like Sir Charles, is regarded as an oracular "monitor" by his heroine, and Evelina seeks, and is delighted to receive, his counsel. "'There is no young creature,

my Lord, who so greatly wants, or so earnestly wishes for, the advice and assistance of her friends, as I do,'" she says to him on one occasion (p. 331), and Orville quickly becomes a substitute for her absent guardian. It is he who arranges an interview with Mr. Macartney for her at Bristol, who persuades the repentant Sir John Belmont to receive her—and who, later on, magnanimously disposes of half of her fortune to provide for Macartney and the onetime Miss Belmont. Like Harriet Byron, Evelina is overcome with gratitude when her hero finally proposes to her. "To be loved by Lord Orville," she writes, "to be the honoured choice of his noble heart,—my happiness seemed too infinite to be borne, and I wept, even bitterly I wept, from the excess of joy which overpowered me" (p. 383). And just before her marriage she writes to Mr. Villars: "Oh my dearest Sir, the thankfulness of my heart I must pour forth at our meeting . . . when my noble-minded, my beloved Lord Orville, presents to you the highly-honoured and thrice-happy Evelina" (p. 438).

The relationship between the heroes and heroines of *Cecilia* and *Camilla* is similar to that between Orville and Evelina. In both of the later novels a most exemplary hero stoops to marry, and there is doubt as to whether the heroine will be found worthy of his hand. Both Cecilia and Camilla are "in love and in some doubt of a return" during a considerable part of their histories; both are left in suspense to await the approval of their heroes—and that of their heroes' advisors as well. And the reader reacts to all of Fanny Burney's first three novels in much the same way that he reacts to Richardson's "picture of perfection" Sir Charles Grandison, and his sycophant-heroine, Harriet Byron. One is amused and irritated by the relationship between hero and heroine: he longs for an Evelina who will tell Orville that her conversations with Mr. Macartney are her own affair; a Camilla who will tell Edgar Mandlebert to send Dr. Marchmont packing; a Cecilia who will tell the Delvile family what they really are. Such longings were apparently not felt by many novelists of the day, however, for the Burney-Richardson character type and situation were often imitated in the minor literature of the period. In Thomas Hull's *The History of Sir William Harrington,* for example (1771), the exemplary Lord C———, nobly born, extremely wealthy, and "as perfect as a human being can be" in person, mind, and character, is obviously modeled on Sir Charles Grandison. And Mr. Charlemont, the hero of a novel by Anna Maria Porter entitled *The Lake of Killarney* (1804), is "a young Apollo," "the god of his sex," and the son of a lord. Rose, a dependent in a family of Charlemont's acquaintance, loves him desperately, but is by no means unaware of his vast superiority to her. At one point in the novel, in an episode that seems to have been inspired by the scene in *Cecilia* in which Mrs. Delvile warns Cecilia to beware of falling in love with Delvile, Rose is cross-examined by an older woman who is a friend of Charlemont's family. "'If nothing else were wanting to crush presumptuous hopes on my part,'" Rose replies, "'. . . the difference in our rank, our birth, our fortune, would place them beyond all doubt. Mr. Charlemont is . . . a prize, for which all his equals may contend.'"[7] Similar heroes, often similarly difficult of attainment to admiring heroines, are to be found in numerous other works of Jane Austen's day. The patrician hero, clearly, was a character type that Jane Austen's audience could readily identify.

Jane Austen must have been as much amused by the all-conquering heroes and too humble heroines of Richardson and Fanny Burney and their followers as many later readers have been, for in the juvenile sketch entitled "Jack and Alice" she reduces the patrician hero to absurdity with gusto. Charles Adams, in that sketch, is the most exaggerated "picture of perfection" conceivable. He is a young man "of so dazzling a Beauty that none but Eagles could look him in the Face" (*Minor Works,* p. 13[8]). On one occasion, indeed, when he attends a masquerade disguised as the sun, the reader is told that "the Beams that darted from his Eyes were like those of that glorious Luminary tho' infinitely superior. So strong were they that no one dared venture within half a mile of them" (*Minor Works,* p. 13).[9] (The continual references in "Jack and Alice" to the brilliance of Charles' countenance are probably specific allusions to *Sir Charles Grandison*: Richardson repeatedly describes Sir Charles in similar language.)[10] But the beauties of Charles Adams' person, striking as they are, are nothing to those of his mind. As he tells us himself:

> ". . . I imagine my Manners & Address to be of the most polished kind; there is a certain elegance, a peculiar sweetness in them that I never saw equalled, & cannot describe—Partiality aside, I am certainly more accomplished in every Language, every Science, every Art and every thing than any other person in Europe. My temper is even, my virtues innumerable, my self unparalelled."

> (*Minor Works,* p. 25)

The superciliousness and conceit that readers, in spite of Richardson's and Fanny Burney's insistence on their modesty, cannot help attributing to Sir Charles Grandison or Orville or Delvile, becomes the very essence of Charles Adams' being; the kind of praise that Richardson and Fanny Burney heap on their heroes is most liberally bestowed by Charles on himself. And just as Charles himself is a burlesque version of the too perfect Burney-Richardson hero, so he is provided with two heroines who are ten times more inferior, and twenty times more devoted to him, than Evelina and Cecilia and Harriet Byron are to their heroes. Charles is the owner of the "principal estate" in the neighborhood in which the lovely Lucy lives, and Lucy adores him. She is the daughter of a tailor and the niece of an alehouse-

keeper, and she is "'fearful that tho' possessed of Youth, Beauty, Wit & Merit, and tho' the probable Heiress of my Aunts House & business'" Charles may think her "'deficient in Rank, & in being so, unworthy of his hand'" (*Minor Works,* p. 21). Screwing up her courage, however, she writes him a "'very kind letter, offering him with great tenderness my hand & heart,'" but, to her sorrow, receives "'an angry & peremptory refusal'" from the unapproachable young man (*Minor Works,* p. 21). Alice Johnson, the titular heroine of the novel, is also infatuated with Charles. Although, like the rest of her family, Alice is "a little addicted to the Bottle & the Dice," she hopes, after she has inherited a considerable estate, to be found worthy of him. But when Alice's father proposes the match to him, Charles declares:

> ". . . what do you mean by wishing me to marry your Daughter? . . . Your Daughter Sir, is neither sufficiently beautifull sufficiently amiable, sufficiently witty, nor sufficiently rich for me—. I expect nothing more in my wife than my wife will find in me—Perfection."

> (*Minor Works,* pp. 25-26)

Fortunately, Alice is able to find consolation in her bottle, and fortunately there is a feminine "picture of perfection"—the outrageously exemplary Lady Williams—in the neighborhood of Pammydiddle for Charles to marry. "Jack and Alice," however, was not Jane Austen's only attack on the patrician hero. There is a good deal of Charles Adams in her Mr. Darcy.

II

Darcy's actual circumstances are not an exaggeration of those of the patrician hero, as Charles Adams' are. In fact Jane Austen seems at times to be uncritically borrowing the popular Burney-Richardson character type and situation in *Pride and Prejudice*—altering them, if at all, only by toning them down a bit. Mr. Darcy is not the "picture of perfection" that Sir Charles Grandison is, but he shares many of the advantages of Sir Charles and Lord Orville, including a "fine, tall person, handsome features, noble mien . . . and ten thousand a year" (p. 10). He has a mind that even Elizabeth Bennet, his severest critic, can respect. "His understanding and temper," she admits when there seems to be little likelihood of their ever marrying, "though unlike her own, would have answered all her wishes . . . and from his judgment, information, and knowledge of the world, she must have received benefit . . ." (p. 312). Darcy is not as powerful and important as Sir Charles Grandison, but he is the owner of a large estate and a giver, and withholder, of clerical livings. He marries a woman who, like Evelina, is embarrassed by the inferiority of some of her nearest connections, although even Mrs. Bennet can scarcely approach the supreme vulgarity of a Madame Duval.

But Darcy is a Charles Adams in spirit, if not in circumstances.[11] It is his exaggerated conception of the importance of his advantages, his supercilious determination "'to think well of myself, and meanly of others'" who are not so fortunate that causes him at times to sound very much like a caricature of the Burney-Richardson hero. He may not expect to have to address "an angry & peremptory refusal" to a fawning, lovelorn Elizabeth Bennet; but during Elizabeth's visit at Netherfield he is anxious lest, by devoting so much of his conversation to her, he may have been encouraging her to hope for the honor of his hand. On the eve of her departure from Netherfield, the reader is told:

> He wisely resolved to be particularly careful that no sign of admiration should *now* escape him, nothing that could elevate her with the hope of influencing his felicity; sensible that if such an idea had been suggested, his behavior during the last day must have material weight in confirming or crushing it. Steady to his purpose, he scarcely spoke ten words to her through the whole of Saturday, and though they were at one time left by themselves for half an hour, he adhered most conscientiously to his book, and would not even look at her.
>
> (p. 60)

The idea of a proposal which is humiliating to a heroine may come from *Cecilia.* But the language of Darcy's first proposal to Elizabeth sounds like something that might have come from Charles Adams' lips, rather than the gallant, ardent language of a Delvile.[12] During Darcy's proposal, the reader is told: "His sense of her inferiority—of its being a degradation—of the family obstacles which judgment had always opposed to inclination, were dwelt on with a warmth which seemed due to the consequence he was wounding, but was very unlikely to recommend his suit" (p. 189). And when Elizabeth rebukes him, he declares himself not to be "'ashamed of the feelings I related. They were natural and just. Could you expect me to rejoice in the inferiority of your connections? To congratulate myself on the hope of relations, whose condition in life is so decidedly beneath my own?'" (p. 192).

On two occasions, Darcy is specifically a caricature of Fanny Burney's Lord Orville. The scene at the Meryton assembly in which Darcy makes his rude remarks about Elizabeth Bennet is a parody of Lord Orville's unfavorable first impression of Evelina.[13] In *Evelina,* shortly after Orville and Evelina have had their first dance together, Miss Mirvan overhears a conversation between Orville and Sir Clement Willoughby. She repeats the conversation to Evelina, much to Evelina's mortification, and the scene is recorded in a letter to Mr. Villars:

> . . . a very gay-looking man [Sir Clement Willoughby, as the reader learns later] stepping hastily up to him, cried, "Why, my Lord, what have you done with your lovely partner?"
>
> "Nothing!" answered Lord Orville, with a smile and a shrug.

> "By Jove," cried the man, "she is the most beautiful creature I ever saw in my life!"
>
> Lord Orville, as well he might, laughed, but answered, "Yes; a pretty modest-looking girl."
>
> "O my Lord!" cried the madman, "she is an angel!"
>
> "A *silent* one," returned he.
>
> "Why ay, my Lord, how stands she as to that? She looks all intelligence and expression."
>
> "A poor weak girl!" answered Lord Orville, shaking his head.
>
> (p. 39)

In Darcy's remarks about Elizabeth at the Meryton assembly, Orville's gentle mockery becomes supercilious rudeness. Mr. Bingley enters into conversation with Darcy on the merits of the various ladies at the assembly, hoping to persuade his friend to dance. Like Sir Clement Willoughby, Bingley praises the heroine: Elizabeth, he declares, is "'very pretty, and I dare say, very agreeable'"; and he proposes that Darcy ask her to dance. Darcy replies: "'She is tolerable; but not handsome enough to tempt *me*; and I am in no humour at present to give consequence to young ladies who are slighted by other men'" (p. 12).

A second ballroom scene in *Evelina* is also parodied in **Pride and Prejudice.** At one point in *Evelina* Sir Clement Willoughby, who is determined to punish the heroine for pretending that Lord Orville is to be her partner in a dance for which Sir Clement wished to engage her, conducts her to Lord Orville and presents him with her hand. Evelina writes:

> . . .—he suddenly seized my hand, saying, "think, my Lord, what must be my reluctance to resign this fair hand to your Lordship!"
>
> In the same instant, Lord Orville took it of him; I coloured violently, and made an effort to recover it. "You do me too much honour, Sir," cried he, (with an air of gallantry, pressing it to his lips before he let it go) "however, I shall be happy to profit by it, if this lady," (turning to Mrs. Mirvan) "will permit me to seek for her party."
>
> To compel him thus to dance, I could not endure, and eagerly called out, "By no means,—not for the world!—I must beg—. . . .
>
> (pp. 51-52)

Orville, with true politeness, attempts to help Evelina recover from her confusion. Darcy, "all politeness," as Elizabeth ironically describes him, signifies his willingness to oblige Elizabeth Bennet with a dance when Elizabeth is placed in a similarly embarrassing situation at Sir William Lucas' ball.[14] Sir William and Darcy are conversing. Elizabeth approaches them and Sir William, "struck with the notion of doing a very gallant thing," calls out to her:

"My dear Miss Eliza, why are you not dancing?—Mr. Darcy, you must allow me to present this young lady to you as a very desirable partner.—You cannot refuse to dance, I am sure, when so much beauty is before you." And taking her hand, he would have given it to Mr. Darcy, who, though extremely surprised, was not unwilling to receive it, when she instantly drew back, and said with some discomposure to Sir William,

"Indeed, Sir, I have not the least intention of dancing.—I entreat you not to suppose that I moved this way in order to beg for a partner."

Mr. Darcy with grave propriety requested to be allowed the honour of her hand; but in vain. Elizabeth was determined; nor did Sir William at all shake her purpose by his attempt at persuasion.

"You excel so much in the dance, Miss Eliza, that it is cruel to deny me the happiness of seeing you; and though this gentleman dislikes the amusement in general, he can have no objection, I am sure, to oblige us for one half hour."

"Mr. Darcy is all politeness," said Elizabeth, smiling.

(p. 26)

Mr. Darcy is a complex human being rather than a mere vehicle for satire such as Charles Adams. Nevertheless, I think it is likely that Darcy has somewhere in his ancestry a parody-figure similar to the ones in which Jane Austen's juvenilia abound. Such a theory of Darcy's origins is consistent with generally accepted assumptions about the development of Jane Austen's first three novels from prototypes. It is not unreasonable to assume that *Pride and Prejudice,* as well as *Sense and Sensibility,* grew, through a process of revision, from an original containing large amounts of satire of literature to a differently oriented work. Moreover, the theory helps to account for a feature of *Pride and Prejudice* that has been noted by a number of readers: the inconsistency between the Darcy of the first ballroom scene and the man whom Elizabeth marries at the end of the novel. It is often said that the transition between the conceited and arrogant young man of the book's early chapters and the polite gentleman whom Elizabeth loves and admires is too great and too abrupt to be completely credible.[15] Several critics have defended Jane Austen, showing among other things that some of Darcy's conversation can be interpreted in various ways, and that the reader's reactions to him are often conditioned by the fact that he is seen largely through the eyes of the prejudiced Elizabeth.[16] But even these theories do not account for all the things in *Pride and Prejudice* that trouble readers. Darcy's remark about Elizabeth at the Meryton assembly, for instance, remains almost unbelievably boorish, and there is no reason to believe that Elizabeth has misunderstood it.[17] His fears lest he should be encouraging Elizabeth to fall in love with him during the visit at Netherfield, the extraordinarily haughty language of his first proposal, and other such things remain stumbling blocks to the reader's ac-

ceptance of the later Darcy. The three things just mentioned could have originated in pardoy of the patrician hero, as has been shown. If one postulates an origin in parody for Darcy and assumes that, like many characters in Jane Austen's novels, he was subjected to a refining process, these and perhaps others of the early, exaggerated displays of rudeness and conceit can be accounted for, if not excused, as traces of the original purely parodic figure that Jane Austen was not able to manage with complete success.

Regardless of its origins, *Pride and Prejudice,* even as it stands, is in many respects a subtly humorous reflection on Richardson and Fanny Burney and their patrician heroes. In addition to Darcy's role as a comically treated Orville or Sir Charles Grandison, Lady Catherine de Bourgh is a reminiscence of Mrs. Delvile in *Cecilia* or Dr. Marchmont in *Camilla,* a humorous version of the kindly but mistaken friend who frowns upon the patrician hero's intended bride. And the scene in which she attempts to persuade Elizabeth not to marry Darcy is an exaggeration of what is potentially ridiculous in similar situations in *Cecilia*—not, as R. Brimley Johnson and others have suggested, a refined imitation. Mrs. Delvile is Mortimer's mother and exercises, according to Cecilia, an almost maternal prerogative upon Cecilia herself. Cecilia is grateful—exaggeratedly, unnecessarily grateful, many readers feel—to Mrs. Delvile for that lady's interest in her and for her kindness in providing her with a home during part of her minority. Mrs. Delvile has as much right as anyone could have to interfere in the love affair between Mortimer and Cecilia. And when she persuades Cecilia not to marry Mortimer, although what she says is prideful and humiliating to Cecilia, her language, at least, is kind and respectful. "'Acquit me, I beg,'" she says to Cecilia at one point,

"of any intentional insolence, and imagine not that in speaking highly of my own family, I mean to depreciate yours: on the contrary, I know it to be respectable, I know, too, that were it the lowest in the kingdom, the first might envy it that it gave birth to such a daughter."

And a little later she declares:

"You were just, indeed, the woman he had least chance to resist, you were precisely the character to seize his very soul. To a softness the most fatally alluring, you join a dignity which rescues from their own contempt even the most humble of your admirers. You seem born to have all the world wish your exaltation, and no part of it murmur at your superiority. Were any obstacle but this insuperable one in the way, should nobles, nay should princes offer their daughters to my election, I would reject without murmuring the most magnificent proposals, and take in triumph to my heart my son's nobler choice!"[18]

Lady Catherine is Darcy's aunt, and she hardly knows Elizabeth. Her attempt to prevent Elizabeth's and Darcy's marriage, her arrogant language and the manner in which she taxes Elizabeth with ingratitude, on the strength of having invited her to Rosings several times in the past, are a parody of the situation in *Cecilia*. Again, several scholars have remarked that Mr. Collins, with his moralizing and his flattery of his patroness and her family, parodies the didactic and obsequious clergymen found in Richardson's and Fanny Burney's works.[19] Darcy's relationship with Mr. Bingley is humorously reminiscent of Sir Charles Grandison and the friends who continually depend on him for advice and assistance. Richardson's supercompetent hero was notable for his propensity to manage the lives and loves of his friends. Darcy, to the reader's and Elizabeth Bennet's amusement, domineers over the spineless Bingley, arranging and rearranging Bingley's love life, and at one point officiously separating him from the amiable and disinterested young woman whom Bingley truly loves. Darcy is provided with a mock Evelina or Harriet Byron in Miss Bingley, who is all too obviously willing to play the role of the patrician hero's female adorer in order to become the mistress of Pemberley. "'Now be sincere'"; Elizabeth says to Darcy toward the end of the novel, "'did you admire me for my impertinence? . . .'"

> "The fact is, that you were sick of civility, of deference, of officious attention. You were disgusted with the women who were always speaking and looking, and thinking for *your* approbation alone. I roused, and interested you, because I was so unlike *them* . . . and in your heart, you thoroughly despised the persons who so assiduously courted you."
>
> (p. 380)

And it is not difficult to see whom she has chiefly in mind. The flattery Evelina and Harriet Byron unconsciously heap upon their heroes, their willingness to take their young men's pronouncements as law, become Miss Bingley's determined and obvious toadeating: when she is not praising Darcy's library or his sister, she is defending his views on the subject of feminine accomplishments or inviting his comments on the company at Sir William Lucas' ball.

Most important, while Miss Bingley is an exaggeration and distortion of qualities in Evelina or Harriet Byron, Elizabeth Bennet plays the role of an anti-Evelina in the novel's satiric pattern.[20] Throughout most of the novel she acts in a manner directly contrary to the way in which one would expect a heroine of Richardson's or Fanny Burney's to behave.[21] While the would-be Harriet Byron, Miss Bingley, courts Darcy in the traditional manner, Elizabeth makes him the butt of her wit and the prime target of her attacks on snobbery and class consciousness. "'My behavior to *you*,'" she says to him toward the end of the novel, "'was at least always bordering on the uncivil, and I never spoke to you without

rather wishing to give you pain than not'" (p. 380). While he worries lest he should have encouraged her to hope for the honor of his hand, she is regarding him as "only the man who made himself agreeable no where, and who had not thought her handsome enough to dance with" (p. 23). Instead of being overwhelmed with gratitude when he proposes to her, she prefaces her refusal by saying: "'. . . if I could *feel* gratitude, I would now thank you. But I cannot—I have never desired your good opinion, and you have certainly bestowed it most unwillingly'" (p. 190). And she goes on to tax him with "arrogance," "conceit," and a "selfish disdain for the feelings of others" (p. 193), and to accuse him of being snobbish and overbearing in his interference with Jane and Bingley and of abusing the power he holds over Wickham. Even when she and Darcy are reconciled she laughs, though only to herself, at his casual assumption of the right to arrange and rearrange his friend Bingley's love affairs. When Darcy described the manner in which he sent Bingley back to Jane Bennet with his blessing, "Elizabeth could not help smiling at his easy manner of directing his friend. . . . [She] longed to observe that Mr. Bingley had been a most delightful friend; so easily guided that his worth was invaluable; but she checked herself" (p. 371). Again, Elizabeth answers Lady Catherine de Bourgh's demand that she renounce Darcy in a manner calculated to warm the hearts of readers irritated by Cecilia Beverly's deference to Mrs. Delvile's pride and prejudice:

> "Allow me to say, Lady Catherine, that the arguments with which you have supported this extraordinary application, have been as frivolous as the application was ill-judged. You have widely mistaken my character, if you think I can be worked on by such persuasions as these. How far your nephew might approve of your interference in *his* affairs, I cannot tell; but you have certainly no right to concern yourself in mine. I must beg, therefore, to be importuned no farther on the subject."
>
> (p. 357)

> "I am . . . resolved to act in that manner, which will, in my own opinion, constitute my happiness, without reference to *you,* or to any person so wholly unconnected with me. . . .
>
> "Neither duty, nor honour, nor gratitude . . . have any possible claim on me, in the present instance. No principle of either, would be violated by my marriage with Mr. Darcy. And with regard to the resentment of his family, or the indignation of the world, if the former *were* excited by his marrying me, it would not give me one moment's concern—and the world in general would have too much sense to join in the scorn."
>
> (p. 358)[22]

In earlier stages of the novel's growth, probably Lady Catherine, Mr. Bingley, and Miss Bingley were more exaggerated and distorted versions of their prototypes in eighteenth- and early nineteenth-century literature than they are at present. Elizabeth Bennet was merely

an antitype to the Burney-Richardson sycophantic heroine; Darcy, a caricature of the patrician hero. Later, although she retained an element of ironic imitation, Jane
Austen refined her characters, transforming them from
mere vehicles for satire into human beings interesting
in their own right as well as because of their relationship to their literary prototypes.[23] And, as the remainder
of this chapter implies, she also changed her attitude toward her patrician hero and her anti-Evelina, and accordingly altered her treatment of Darcy drastically and
made Elizabeth, as well as Darcy, a target for her irony.
Theories about the development of the novel aside,
however, the fact remains that *Pride and Prejudice* in
its final form is not simply, as critics have suggested, an
imitation of the work of Jane Austen's fellow novelists.
It is, in part at least, an attack on Richardson and Fanny
Burney and their patrician heroes.

III

Jane Austen thoroughly humbles her patrician hero.
Darcy is subjected to a series of what Mrs. Bennet
would call "set-downs" at the hands of the anti-Evelina,
Elizabeth Bennet; and through his love for Elizabeth,
and the shock he receives from her behavior, he comes
to see himself as he really is and to repent of his pomposity and pride. Toward the end of the novel Darcy is
forced to admit to Elizabeth:

> "I have been a selfish being all my life, in practice,
> though not in principle. As a child I was taught what
> was *right*, but I was not taught to correct my temper. I
> was given good principles, but left to follow them in
> pride and conceit . . . my parents . . . allowed, en-
> couraged, almost taught me to be selfish and overbear-
> ing, to care for none beyond my own family circle, to
> think meanly of all the rest of the world, to *wish* at
> least to think meanly of their sense and worth com-
> pared with my own. Such I was, from eight to eight
> and twenty; and such I might still have been but for
> you, dearest, loveliest Elizabeth! What do I not owe
> you! You taught me a lesson, hard indeed at first, but
> most advantageous. By you, I was properly humbled. I
> came to you without a doubt of my reception. You sh-
> ewed me how insufficient were all my pretensions to
> please a woman worthy of being pleased."
>
> (p. 369)

But Darcy's humiliation and attainment of self-
knowledge do not constitute the whole story of *Pride
and Prejudice*: Jane Austen does not allow her anti-
Evelina to rout her patrician hero completely.

In discussing *Sense and Sensibility* it was noted that an
ironic reversal of attitude toward the traditional deluded
"sensibility" heroine and her sensible counterpart takes
place in that novel. Something a bit similar happens in
Pride and Prejudice, in Jane Austen's treatment of
Darcy and his relationship to Elizabeth Bennet. Once
Darcy has been humbled, Jane Austen turns her irony

on Elizabeth. She shows that Elizabeth, in her resentment of Darcy's conscious superiority, has exaggerated
his faults and failed to see that there is much in him
that is good. Elizabeth proves to have been blind and
prejudiced in her views on the relationship between
Darcy and Wickham, too willing to accept Wickham's
stories because they so nicely confirmed her own feelings about Darcy. When she reads the letter that follows
Darcy's first proposal, she is forced to admit that her
resentment has led her to be foolish and unjust. After
reading the letter,

> She grew absolutely ashamed of herself.—Of neither
> Darcy nor Wickham could she think, without feeling
> that she had been blind, partial, prejudiced, absurd.
>
> "How despicably have I acted!" she cried. . . . "Had I
> been in love, I could not have been more wretchedly
> blind. But vanity, not love, has been my folly.—Pleased
> with the preference of one, and offended by the neglect
> of the other, on the very beginning of our acquaintance,
> I have courted prepossession and ignorance, and driven
> reason away, where either were concerned. Till this
> moment, I never knew myself."
>
> (p. 208)

Again, until Darcy's letter shocks her into self-
knowledge, Elizabeth has seen Darcy's interference in
the affair between Jane and Bingley only as an instance
of coldhearted snobbery on Darcy's part. Reading Darcy's letter, and considering Jane's disposition, Elizabeth
is forced to admit that Darcy's view of the affair, his
belief that Jane was little more than a complacent pawn
in her mother's matrimonial game, is not unjustified.
Darcy's interference, Elizabeth must admit, was motivated not merely by snobbery, but by concern for his
guileless friend's welfare as well. With her eyes thus
opened, Elizabeth comes to see later in the novel that
Darcy's position and fortune, and his pride in them, can
be forces for good as well as sources of snobbery and
authoritarianism. Seeing Pemberley, and hearing his
housekeeper's praise of Darcy's conduct as a brother
and a landlord, she learns that Darcy's position is a
trust and a responsibility, and that his not unjustifiable
self-respect leads to a code of conduct worthy of admiration. And in his action in the Lydia-Wickham affair
she is provided with an impressive and gratifying instance of his power to do good and his sense of responsibility. At the end of the novel Jane Austen's anti-
Evelina is defending her patrician hero. "'I love him,'"
Elizabeth says of Darcy to the astounded Mr. Bennet.
"'Indeed, he has no improper pride'" (p. 376).

As noted earlier, a pattern of "art-nature" symbolism in
Pride and Prejudice served to add depth of suggestion,
for Jane Austen's early nineteenth-century audience, to
the novel's love plot. At the beginning of the story
Darcy is the representative of a bias toward "art," and
an excessive class pride, and Elizabeth is the exponent

of "nature" and aggressive individualism. In the course of the novel their mental and temperamental propensities are modified somewhat, and their marriage at the conclusion of the story is a union between a reasonable degree of "art" and a desirable degree of "nature." Jane Austen's treatment of the figure here called the patrician hero serves a similar purpose and follows a similar pattern. One cannot, of course, assume that Jane Austen thought of her Mr. Darcy as an "authority figure," in today's sense of the term, any more than one can assume that she considered *Pride and Prejudice* a treatise on the eighteenth-century "art-nature" antithesis. But she did expect the novel-reading audience for which she wrote to respond to her work on the basis of their impressions of the insufferable Sir Charles Grandisons and Lord Orvilles, the sycophantic Evelinas and Harriet Byrons, of noveldom. At the beginning of *Pride and Prejudice* Darcy is a pompous Burney-Richardson aristocrat, with many of the most disagreeable attributes of his literary progenitors as well as a representative of "art" and excessive class pride; Elizabeth is a determined anti-Evelina as well as a symbol for "nature" and aggressive individualism. The marriage at the end of the story joins a properly humbled patrician hero and an anti-Evelina who has also undergone a partial reformation.

In view of what has just been said, it is interesting to note that, paralleling Elizabeth's attainment of self-knowledge, there is a marked tendency on Jane Austen's part to cease laughing at the works of Richardson and Fanny Burney and even to imitate them rather obviously in the later chapters of *Pride and Prejudice.* At Pemberley, for instance, Darcy is allowed to behave toward Elizabeth with a marked tact and gallantry that is nonhumorously reminiscent of Sir Charles Grandison or Lord Orville. In the manner of Richardson's and Fanny Burney's heroes he takes over his heroine's affairs, rescuing Elizabeth and her family from imminent disgrace and providing for the erring Lydia.[24] Moreover, Jane Austen's audience might well have recognized some decidedly nonsatiric echoes of *Sir Charles Grandison* in the scenes in which Elizabeth visits Pemberley. Sir Charles, as one might expect, has excellent taste in landscaping. He "pretends not to level hills, or to force and distort nature; but to help it, as he finds it, without letting art be seen in his works, where he can possibly avoid it" (vol. 3, letter 23, p. 246). On his country estate he has a

> large and convenient house, . . . situated in a spacious park; which has several fine avenues leading to it.
>
> On the north side of the park flows a winding stream, that may well be called a river, abounding with trout and other fish; the current quickened by a noble cascade, which tumbles down its foaming waters from a rock, which is continued to some extent, in a ledge of rock-work, rudely disposed.

> The park is remarkable for its prospects, lawns, and rich-appearing clumps of trees of large growth.
>
> (vol. 7, letter 6, p. 30)

The Pemberley grounds are kept up with a similar regard for nature and timber, and there is even a similarly managed, artificially swelled trout stream. Pemberley House, the reader is told, was

> situated on the opposite side of a valley, into which the road with some abruptness wound. It was a large, handsome, stone building, standing well on rising ground, and backed by a ridge of high woody hills;—and in front, a stream of some natural importance was swelled into greater, but without any artificial appearance. Its banks were neither formal, nor falsely adorned. Elizabeth was delighted. She had never seen a place for which nature had done more, or where natural beauty had been so little counteracted by an awkward taste.
>
> (p. 245)

Was Jane Austen thinking of Harriet Byron's tour of Sir Charles Grandison's property when she described Elizabeth Bennet's visit to Pemberley? Both Elizabeth and Harriet are conducted around magnificent but tastefully appointed houses and both talk to elderly, respectable housekeepers who praise their masters' kindness to servants and tenants. "'Don't your ladyship see,'" Sir Charles' housekeeper asks Harriet Byron, "'how all his servants love him as they attend him at table? . . . Indeed, madam, we all adore him; and have prayed morning, noon, and night, for his coming hither, and settling among us'" (vol. 7, letter 9, p. 52). Darcy's housekeeper laments the fact that he is not at Pemberley "so much as I could wish" (p. 248), and declares that "'he is the best landlord, and the best master . . . that ever lived. Not like the wild young men now-a-days, who think of nothing but themselves. There is not one of his tenants or servants but what will give him a good name'" (p. 249). Harriet and Elizabeth are both conducted around noble picture galleries, and both view pictures of their lovers with admiration during their tours.[25]

As Darcy becomes a modified but genuine Sir Charles Grandison, so does Elizabeth cease to resemble an aggressive anti-Evelina or Harriet Byron. She becomes more and more impressed with her patrician hero, more and more attracted to his many good qualities. Indeed, as she stands in the gallery at Pemberley, there is even a trace of Evelina-like gratitude in her thoughts, and she feels honored by the love of such a man as Darcy:

> As a brother, a landlord, a master, she considered how many people's happiness were in his guardianship!— How much of pleasure or pain it was in his power to bestow!—how much of good or evil must be done by him! Every idea that had been brought forward by the housekeeper was favourable to his character, and as she stood before the canvas, on which he was represented,

and fixed his eyes upon herself, she thought of his regard with a deeper sentiment of gratitude than it had
ever raised before; she remembered its warmth, and
softened its impropriety of expression.

(pp. 250-251)

Pride and Prejudice is a story about two complex, sensitive and often blindly wrongheaded "intricate characters" and their progress toward a better understanding
of one another, the world, and themselves. The drama
of Elizabeth's and Darcy's conflict and ultimate harmony is played out in the context of a symbolism based
on the antithesis between "art" and "nature," in the
comprehensive eighteenth-century sense of those terms.
It is also referred at many points to the fiction of Jane
Austen's day—particularly to her fellow novelists' handling of the figure called here the patrician hero. It may
be that Jane Austen's first response to the patrician hero
was purely satiric and that later she refined and complicated her treatment of him; this would help to account
for some of the flaws in Darcy's character to which
most of her readers object. At any rate, *Pride and Prejudice* is something more than a much-improved imitation
of the novels Jane Austen knew. It is a work in which
she tumbles an eighteenth-century authority figure from
the pedestal on which Richardson and Fanny Burney
had placed him—and, with a gesture typical of both her
vision of life and her artistic technique, then stoops to
retrieve him from the dust.[26]

Notes

1. The most detailed study of *Pride and Prejudice* in
terms of the "art-nature" dichotomy is Samuel
Kliger's "Jane Austen's *Pride and Prejudice* in
the Eighteenth-Century Mode," *University of Toronto Quarterly,* 16 (1947): 357-370. To note only
a few more instances of similar interpretations,
Dorothy Van Ghent, in *The English Novel,* (New
York: Reinhart, 1953) p. 100, states that the novel
deals with "the difficult and delicate reconciliation
of the sensitively developed individual with the
terms of his social existence"; and David Daiches,
in the introduction to the Modern Library edition
of *Pride and Prejudice* (New York: Random
House, 1950), calls the conflict between Elizabeth
and Darcy an "adjustment between the claims of
personal and social life."

2. Jane Austen's Mr. Darcy is sometimes compared
to Richardson's patrician "villain-hero," Mr.
B———. E. E. Duncan-Jones, in "Proposals of
Marriage in *Pamela* and *Pride and Prejudice,*"
Notes and Queries, 202 (1957): 76, has suggested
that the proposal scene in *Pride and Prejudice* is a
reminiscence of Mr. B———'s first honorable
proposal to Pamela. More general resemblances in
situation and character types between *Pamela* and
Jane Austen's novel are discussed in Henrietta

Ten Harmsel's "The Villain-Hero in *Pamela* and
Pride and Prejudice," in *College English,* 23
(1961): 104-108, and in the chapter on *Pride and
Prejudice* in Miss Ten Harmsel's *A Study in Fictional Conventions.* While it may be profitable to
compare *Pamela* and *Pride and Prejudice,* it
seems more rewarding to compare Darcy to heroes modeled on Sir Charles Grandison, for reasons to be made apparent later.

3. *Sir Charles Grandison,* in *The Novels of Samuel
Richardson* (London: Chapman & Hall, 1902), 14:
x. All references will be to this edition.

4. *Jane Austen's Letters* (London: Oxford University
Press, 1952), p. 300 (February 4, 1813). All references to Jane Austen's letters will be to this edition.

5. The quotation is from Johnson's introduction to
Sense and Sensibility in *The Works of Jane Austen*
(London: J. M. Dent & Sons, 1950), p. v. The re-
lationship between *Cecilia* and *Pride and Preju-
dice* is more fully discussed in Johnson's *Jane
Austen,* pp. 124-127, and in his *Jane Austen: Her
Life, Her Work, Her Family, and Her Critics,*
(New York: Haskell House, 1974), pp. 137-139.

6. *Cecilia* is not necessarily the source for the title of
Pride and Prejudice, since the terms "pride" and
"prejudice" were frequently used in conjunction in
Jane Austen's day. R. W. Chapman's notes to the
Oxford edition of *Pride and Prejudice* and numerous articles in the *Times Literary Supplement* and
Notes and Queries testify to the popularity of the
expression. I have myself located versions of the
phrase within the Austen family circle, in the sermons of Jane Austen's cousin Edward Cooper.
(See my "*Pride and Prejudice* and Edward Cooper's *Sermons,*" *Notes and Queries,* 211 [1966]:
182.) And W. H. Welpley, in "Pride and Prejudice," *Notes and Queries,* 196 (1951): 93, remarks
that the expression is used in *Sir Charles Grandison.* See also above note 11 to the introduction.

7. Anna Maria Porter, *The Lake of Killarney*
(London, 1804), vol. 1, chap. 4, p. 219. Jane Austen mentions this novel in a letter of October 24,
1808 (*Letters,* pp. 58-59).

8. *The Novels of Jane Austen* (London: Oxford University Press, 1933), vol. 3: *Mansfield Park,* p.
459. All subsequent references to Jane Austen's
fiction will be to the five volumes of this edition
and to the subsequent *The Works of Jane Austen*
(London: Oxford University Press, 1954), vol. 6:
Minor Works.

9. The masquerade at which Charles shines is probably a humorous reminiscence of a similar scene
in *Cecilia,* as I have pointed out in "Fanny Bur-

ney's *Cecilia* and Jane Austen's 'Jack and Alice,'" *English Language Notes,* 3 (1965): 40-42.

10. As E. E. Duncan-Jones points out in "Notes on Jane Austen," *Notes and Queries,* 196 (1951): 14-16. Numbers of heroes in the minor fiction of the period, however, among them Lord C——,—— in *The History of Sir William Harrington* and Mr. Charlemont in *The Lake of Killarney,* are similarly described.

11. Compare the opinion of F. W. Bradbrook (*Jane Austen and Her Predecessors,* Cambridge University Press, 1966, pp. 96-97) regarding Jane Austen's treatment of the Burney-Richardson hero. Bradbrook feels that Jane Austen "accepts Fanny Burney's conception of the hero" although he does suggest that she "deflates" Darcy somewhat.

12. Bradbrook (*Jane Austen and Her Predecessors,* pp. 127-132) compares the first proposal scene to one in Sir Egerton Brydges' *Mary de Clifford,* and suggests other parallels between Brydges' work and Jane Austen's.

13. In "A Critical Theory of Jane Austen's Writings," pt. 1, *Scrutiny,* 10 (1941): 61-87, Q. D. Leavis recognizes the similarity between the two scenes.

14. Of course, as Reuben Brower, in *The Fields of Light* (New York: Oxford University Press, 1951), pp. 168-169, points out, the reader sees this scene largely through the eyes of the prejudiced Elizabeth Bennet. Darcy is actually happy to dance with Elizabeth, although his manner of expressing himself is not as gallant as it might be.

15. See, for example, the comments on Darcy in Mary Lascelles' *Jane Austen and Her Art* (Clarendon Press, 1939), pp. 22 and 162, and Marvin Mudrick's complaints about the change in Darcy's character in his *Irony as Defense and Discovery* (Princeton University Press, 1952), pp. 117-119.

16. See the chapters on *Pride and Prejudice* in Brower's *The Fields of Light* (Oxford University Press, 1951), pp. 164-181, and in Howard S. Babb's *The Fabric of Dialogue* (Ohio State University Press, 1962), pp. 115-118, and Charles J. McCann's "Setting and Character in *Pride and Prejudice,*" *Nineteenth Century Fiction,* 19 (1964): 65-75.

17. Compare, however, Philip Drew's "A Significant Incident in *Pride and Prejudice,*" *Nineteenth Century Fiction,* 13 (1958): 356-368, in which Darcy's asperity toward the opposite sex at the assembly is explained as the result of temporary chagrin engendered by his sister's affair with Wickham.

18. Fanny Burney, *Cecilia* (London, 1893), vol. 3, bk. 8, chap. 3, p. 22, and chap. 4, p. 37.

19. For fuller discussion of this point see Alan D. McKillop, "Critical Realism in *Northanger Abbey,*" in *From Jane Austen to Joseph Conrad: Essays in Honor of James T. Hillhouse,* eds. Robert C. Rathburn and Martin Steinmann, Jr. (Minneapolis: University of Minnesota Press, 1958), p. 37; B. C. Southam's "Jane Austen and *Clarissa,*" *Notes and Queries,* 208 (1963): 191-192; and Henrietta Ten Harmsel's *A Study in Fictional Conventions* (Mouton, 1964), pp. 83-84. For another aspect of Collins' literary background, see J. M. S. Tompkins' *The Popular Novel in England, 1770-1800* (Lincoln, Neb.: University of Nebraska Press, 1961), p. 132.

20. Q. D. Leavis ("Critical Theory," pt. 1) adopts a view of Elizabeth's origins that is somewhat similar to my own, holding that much of *Pride and Prejudice* was originally a satire on *Cecilia* and that Elizabeth is an "anti-Cecilia." She feels, however, that Darcy is simply a refined imitation of Mortimer Delvile, "Delvile with the minimum of inside necessary to make plausible his conduct"—an opinion with which, of course, I disagree; I believe, too, Elizabeth is an antitype to Harriet Byron, Evelina, and a number of other heroines as well as to Cecilia, and not simply a vehicle for satire of one particular novel.

21. According to Henrietta Ten Harmsel, in the chapter on *Pride and Prejudice* in her *A Study in Fictional Conventions,* Elizabeth is an antitype to conventional heroines in some ways other than the ones I am about to mention. She is a forceful, vigorous character, where the conventional heroine is passive. Where the traditional heroine is outstandingly beautiful and accomplished, Elizabeth is only "tolerably" handsome, and far from proficient in the feminine "accomplishments" of the period. The typical heroine of the Burney-Richardson tradition is a moral paragon (it would seem that Fanny Burney's Camilla is a notable exception to this rule), whereas Elizabeth's fallibility is stressed. Miss Ten Harmsel also feels that Elizabeth's originality is emphasized by contrast with Jane Bennet, who is a heroine of the conventional stamp.

22. Compare Ten Harmsel, *A Study in Fictional Conventions,* pp. 90-91. Miss Ten Harmsel notes the similarity between Lady Catherine de Bourgh and Mrs. Delvile, but feels that there is a more marked similarity between Lady Catherine's encounter with Elizabeth Bennet and the scene in *Pamela* where Lady Davers abuses Pamela for having captivated Mr. B——.

23. Another view of the novel's origins and development is found in B. C. Southam's *Jane Austen's Literary Manuscripts* (Oxford University Press,

1964), pp. 59-62, where it is suggested that *Pride and Prejudice* was originally a satire, in epistolary form, on the theme of "first impressions" that was so prevalent in the literature of Jane Austen's day.

24. In the chapter on *Pride and Prejudice* in Marvin Mudrick's *Irony as Defense and Discovery,* Darcy's resemblance to conventional heroes in the latter part of the novel is interpreted as one of its failings.

25. The fact that the episodes in *Grandison* just mentioned had been imitated in the minor literature of the period strengthens my belief that Jane Austen's borrowings are purposeful. In Thomas Hull's *The History of Sir William Harrington,* for example, similar scenes occur when Lord C—'s bride reaches her new habitation. See *Harrington* (London, 1772), vol. 3, letter 52, pp. 1-7. Compare the suggestion of F. W. Bradbrook (*Jane Austen and Her Predecessors,* pp. 58-59) that the descriptions of Pemberley may have been influenced by passages in William Gilpin's *Observations on the Mountains and Lakes of Cumberland and Westmorland.*

26. Jane Austen, of course, uses the patrician hero elsewhere. Henry Tilney, wiser and wealthier than his heroine, and adored by her almost from the moment they meet, is a more nearly "straight" Burney-Richardson hero. In a later chapter it will be noted that Edmund Bertram, mentor and eventual lover of Fanny Price, receives a treatment somewhat similar to Darcy's.

Judith Lowder Newton (essay date February 1978)

SOURCE: Newton, Judith Lowder. "*Pride and Prejudice*: Power, Fantasy, and Subversion in Jane Austen." *Feminist Studies* 4, no. 1 (February 1978): 27-42.

[*In the following essay, Newton examines the power dynamic in* Pride and Prejudice, *arguing that although men dominated Austen's society in economic and social privilege, Elizabeth Bennet represents a fantasy of female autonomy.*]

To read Jane Austen's letters—with their steady consciousness of bargains, pence, and shillings—is to be aware of one small but nagging way in which she experienced the restrictions of being an unmarried middle-class woman: she had little money, and she had almost no access to more. In 1813, for example, the year *Pride and Prejudice* was published, Jane Austen, her mother, and her sister, Cassandra, were dependent for their living on three sources: a small income of Mrs. Austen's, a small legacy of Cassandra's, and the £ 250 provided

annually by four of the Austen brothers.[1] The sum was enhanced to some degree by the money Jane earned through writing, for in July of that year she reports that "I have now . . . written myself into £ 250—which only makes me long for more."[2] But the £140 brought by *Sense and Sensibility* and the £110 by *Pride and Prejudice* did not go far, and Austen's letters for that year, as for every year, are full of reference to small economies.

To read Jane Austen's letters is also to be aware—to be reminded—of the privilege that belonged to middle-class men. For Austen had five brothers, and they had what she did not: access to work that paid, access to inheritance and preference, and access to the independence, the personal power, that belonged to being prosperous and male. In 1813, for example, all but one brother was rising in a career. James was earning £1100 a year as curate. Henry was partner in a successful banking firm, Frank was captain of a ship in the Baltic, Charles the flag captain of another, and Edward, the only brother without a profession, was living as a country gentleman on one of the two estates he had inherited from the family who adopted him.

The economic difference in the lots of Austen women and Austen men was certainly striking, and yet there is little indication in the letters that this difference was a source of oppression or discomfort to Jane. Her letters, for the most part, make a casual patchwork of details about her own economies and her brothers' expenditures, about her desire for money and their attainment of it, about her dependence in traveling and their liberties with horseback, carriage, and barouche, about the pressure she felt to marry and the freedom they assumed to marry or not to marry as they chose. Here and there, of course, we find some humorous consciousness of inequity, and there is more than one joke about the economic recommendations of marriage. But, for the most part, Jane Austen's attitude toward the economic restrictions of being a woman, and toward the resulting dependence, confinement, and pressure to marry is, in the letters, amused, uncomplaining, without emphasis.

It is only in Austen's fiction that we begin to feel a certain edge, a certain critical emphasis being given to the difference between the economic privilege of middle-class women and that of middle-class men. The first two sentences of *Pride and Prejudice,* for example, make subtle and ironic point of that distinction and suggest the weight of it in shaping male and female life: "It is a truth universally acknowledged, that a single man in possession of a good fortune must be in want of a wife. However little known the feelings or views of such a man may be on his first entering a neighborhood, this truth is so well fixed in the minds of the surrounding families that he is considered as the rightful property of some one or other of their daughters."[3] Some single men, it would appear, have independent access to money, but all single women, or "daughters," must marry for it. Families with daughters, therefore, think a great deal about marriage, while single men with fortunes do not. Families with daughters may try to control men too, to seize them as "property," but it is really "daughters," the sentence implies, who are controlled, who are "fixed" by their economic situation. Single men, in contrast, appear at liberty—at liberty to enter a neighborhood, for example, and presumably to leave it. Single men have a distinct mobility and a personal power that daughters do not.

The opening of *Pride and Prejudice* thus introduces a familiar distinction between the economic restrictions of middle-class women and the economic privilege of middle-class men, but it does so with an emphasis not characteristic of the letters. It also insinuates a causal connection between economic privilege and personal power, a connection which the letters reflect but hardly articulate. Austen's fiction, as is often observed, obviously did provide outlet for critical energies she could not otherwise express. But the effect of those energies is not what one might expect. For while the rest of the novel sustains an awareness of the economic inequality of women and men, it does not sustain a felt awareness of the causal connection between money and power. Indeed, for all its reference to money and money matters, *Pride and Prejudice* is devoted not to establishing but to denying the force of economics in human life. In the reading of the novel the real *force* of economics simply melts away.[4]

Despite the first two sentences of *Pride and Prejudice,* despite the implication that access to money in some way determines personal power, the difference between men's economic privilege and that of women is not something we are invited to *experience* as a cause of power and powerlessness in the novel. Men, with all their money and privilege, are not permitted to seem powerful in *Pride and Prejudice,* but rather bungling and absurd; and women, for all their impotence, are not seen as victims of economic restriction. What the novel finally defines as power has little to do with money, and the most authentically powerful figure in the novel is an unmarried middle-class woman without a fortune—a woman, we may note, who bears striking resemblance to Jane Austen.

Now, readers of *Pride and Prejudice* have not generally posed questions about the powerlessness and power of women and men. They have not posed these questions, I suspect, for all the usual historical and cultural reasons, but they have also failed to pose them because the author of *Pride and Prejudice* does not invite us to see what she is doing, because she is, in fact, hiding out. Subverting the force of economic privilege and inverting traditional power relations are not activities many

women undertake without misgivings and a desire for cover. And indirection, deviousness, evasion, are traditionally feminine covers, means of disguising aggression against things as they are. Much of the multiple irony, the lack of commitment, the irresponsibility which readers of *Pride and Prejudice* have marked again and again in its style[5] may be attributed, I suggest, to the traditional uneasiness with which Austen, *as a woman,* expresses discomposure about, and subtly subverts, the traditional lots, the traditional powerlessness and power of women and men.

In *Pride and Prejudice,* as in Austen's letters, the major difference in the lots of women and men is that men—all men of the upper- and middle-class—have an independent access to money that women do not. It is the unremarked privilege of men in the novel to have work that pays, to rise through preference and education, and to inherit. Women, in contrast, have no access at all to work that pays and are educated for nothing but display. Although women and men both inherit, women inherit a lump sum, a kind of dowry, while men inherit livings. The entail, then, which so obviously benefits Mr. Collins and so obviously restricts the Bennet daughters, is really the epitome of an economic privilege that is granted men in general and of an economic restriction that is imposed on women: for most women, lacking men's access to work and inheritance, economic survival means marriage.

As in the letters, then, the economic difference in the lots of women and men is hard to ignore, but once again there is no overt indication that Austen protested this division of privilege. Indeed, where the economic inequity of women's lot seems most unfair, Austen deflects criticism. Mrs. Bennet and Lady Catherine, for example, are the only persons in the novel allowed to object to the entail and neither is permitted to engage our sympathies.

But if, by deflecting criticism, Austen appears to accept, indeed to apologize for, the unequal division of money and privilege, she also appears to limit, subtly, and from the outset, what that inequity can mean. Although the Austen of the letters seems well aware of the status and sense of power involved in earning or preserving money, she omits from the novel almost any reference to, and all observation of, activity which has an economic reward. We may hear that men work, but we never see them at their labors, and if the enforced idleness of upper- and middle-class women seems oppressive in this novel, it is not out of contrast with the more productive activities of males.

It is principally in their personal rather than in their working lives that men appear at first to have more autonomy than women, more power to make decisions, to go, and to do as they please. Throughout *Pride and*

Prejudice, for example, men in general have a mobility that women, even women with money, do not, and that mobility must suggest a greater general autonomy. From the first sentence on, men are linked with entering and leaving, women with being "fixed," and it is not surprising that it is women in the novel who are dull or bored, who feel that the country is "bare of news," who suffer when it rains, who repine at "the dullness of everything," who feel "forlorn" (pp. 25, 84, 223, 311).

The patterns of movement in the novel do suggest a dramatic difference in the autonomy of women and men but they are only background, like the fact that men work, and the patterns are neither emphasized nor overthrown. It is in relation to the marriage choice that men's potential autonomy is brought most into conscious focus, and it is in relation to the marriage choice that men's power is most emphatically subverted. Men, as the first two sentences suggest, do not need to marry. They may "want" or desire wives as it turns out, but they do not *need* to want them as women must want husbands. Men in *Pride and Prejudice,* therefore, are conscious of having power to choose and they are fond of dwelling on it, of impressing it upon women. Mr. Collins, for example, assumes that there is nothing so central to his proposal as a rehearsal of his "reasons" for marrying and for choosing a Bennet in particular, nothing quite so central as the information that there were "many amiable young women" from whom he might have made his selection (pp. 101, 102). Darcy is scarcely less agreeably aware of his power to choose, and from his first appearance in the novel acts the role of high-class connoisseur, finding Elizabeth "tolerable, but not handsome enough to tempt *me*" (p. 9). Like Mr. Collins, moreover, Darcy remains preoccupied with the privilege of choice in the very act of proposing, for his first words are not "I love you" but "in vain have I struggled" (p. 178). Fitzwilliam, Wickham, and Bingley, the other single men in the novel, betray a similar consciousness. Although Fitzwilliam maintains that "younger sons cannot marry where they like," Elizabeth protests that they often choose to like and to propose to, "women of fortune" (p. 173). And Wickham, ever confident in his power to choose, first chooses Georgiana Darcy, and then in succession, Elizabeth Bennet, Mary King, and Lydia Bennet. Even Bingley, who is persuaded not to choose Jane, is still a conscious chooser at first, alive to arguments against her family and ready to oppose them.

Male privilege, then, and access to money in particular, makes men feel autonomous. It also makes them feel empowered to control others, especially women to whom they make advances. For as givers of economic benefit to women, men expect their advances to be received and even sought for. Mr. Collins dwells warmly upon the "advantages that are in [his] power to offer" Elizabeth and tactfully reminds her that she is bound to accept him, for "It is by no means certain that another offer of marriage may ever be made you" (p. 104). Darcy is also pleasantly aware of his power to bestow value, whether it is his desirable attention or his desirable fortune and station. At the first ball, for example, he will not dance with Elizabeth because he is in "no humor at present to give consequence to young ladies who are slighted by other men" (p. 9). His proposal, moreover, like Mr. Collins' is "not more eloquent on the subject of tenderness than of pride" and betrays his confidence in having his own way.

With the exception of Bingley, who is seen as an anomaly, and of Mr. Gardener, who scarcely exists, virtually every man in the novel reacts in the same fashion to his economic privilege and social status as a male. All enjoy a mobility that women do not have. All relish an autonomy that women do not feel. All aspire to a mastery that women cannot grasp. And yet, in spite of their mobility, their sense of autonomy, their desire to master and to control, we do not feel that men are powerful in this novel. Their sense of power and their real pomposity are at base, a setup, a preparation for poetic justice, a license to enjoy the spectacle of men witlessly betraying their legacy of power, of men demonstrating impressive capacities for turning potential control into ineffective action and submission to the power of others.

It is significant, I think, that the only proposals of marriage recorded in the novel are unsuccessful, and that both suitors are so immersed in their sense of power that they blindly offend the woman whose affections they mean to attach and in the process provoke what must be two of the most vigorous rejections in all of literature. It is also significant that Sir Lucas and Mr. Collins, the only two men in the novel who have risen through preference—another benefit of male privilege—enjoy little more than an inflated *sense* of power and succeed mainly in annoying those whom they propose to influence.

Our sense of male control is also undercut by the comic readiness with which some men submit to the influence of others. Mr. Collins and Sir Lucas manifest such slavish admiration of those who have raised them or of those who stand above them in rank that their own imagined influence is constantly and ironically juxtaposed with images of self-abasement. Collins, moreover, qualifies his potential autonomy by submitting virtually every life decision to the "particular advice and recommendation" of Lady Catherine, and Bingley surrenders Jane because he depends on Darcy's opinion more strongly than on his own (p. 101).

Men are also prone to misusing their autonomy by making bad investments. It is Mr. Bennet's own "imprudence" that must account for his unhappy domestic life and Wickham's failure of resolution that yokes him to Lydia, a woman without fortune (p. 222). Thus access to money, and male privilege in general, do grant men the potential for control of their lives and for control over women, but the men in *Pride and Prejudice* are essentially set up—to surrender, to misuse, to fail to realize the power that is their cultural legacy.

In obvious contrast to men, women in their economic dependence have far less potential to do as they like. Most women in the novel *must* marry and since access to money both shapes and is shaped by traditional attitudes toward women and their proper destiny, even women with money feel pressured to get a man. (The rich Miss Bingley pursues Darcy as does Lady Catherine on behalf of the wealthy Anne.) Women, for the most part, do not dwell on their power to choose, do not debate about getting a husband, and seldom give thought to the value of one husband over another. Some young women, like Lydia and Kitty, are so engrossed with male regard in general, that they lose sight of their reason for securing it, which is to marry, and make the attention of men—any men—an end in itself. Indeed the action in almost the entire first volume of the novel consists of very little but women talking or thinking or scheming about men.

Women in *Pride and Prejudice,* then, do not generally act like choosers, and since they devote a good deal of energy to compulsive scheming and plotting, they obviously do not entertain illusions of easy control. What control women do aspire to is manipulative and indirect and is further diminished by the fact that obsession makes them ineffective and unreflecting. It is important, moreover, to note that all young women in the novel are swept to some degree in the same currents, enforcing our sense of a universal female condition. All the Bennet women spend a good part of one evening conjecturing about Bingley and "determining when they should ask him to dinner" (p. 6). All are pleased with their own or with each others' triumphs. All are bored by the "interval of waiting" for the gentlemen, and the prospect of the Netherfield ball is "extremely agreeable to every female in the family" (pp. 72, 82). Our first introduction to Elizabeth, in fact, finds her trimming a hat.

Women, like men, therefore, appear to be determined almost uniformly by a shared economic and social condition, but just as we are not permitted to feel that men's economic privilege *must* result in power we are not permitted to feel that women's lack of privilege *must* result in powerlessness. The first two sentences of the novel may emphasize the idea that women's compulsive husband hunting has an economic base, but we are never allowed to *feel* that base as a determining force in women's experience. As I have suggested, almost every reference in the novel to economic necessity is relegated

to Mrs. Bennet, a woman whose worries we are not allowed to take seriously because they are continually undermined by their link with the comic and the absurd: "Miss Lizzy, if you take it into your head to go on refusing every offer of marriage in this way, you will never get a husband at all—and I am sure I do not know who is to maintain you when your father is dead" (pp. 108-109). This is the kind of financial threat which would be taken seriously in a novel by Charlotte Brontë, but in *Pride and Prejudice,* the threat, the sting of potential poverty is undercut. There is consciousness of economics to be sure, but that consciousness is raised and then subverted. It is a distinctly odd maneuver on the part of an author sometimes praised for her awareness of social and economic forces, but it serves a purpose in preparing the reader for Elizabeth by defining the nature of Elizabeth's world.

The Charlotte Lucas' episode is especially significant in this light, for at a distance it might suggest that economic forces do indeed have tragic power over "sensible, intelligent" young women (p. 15). But once again this is not what we are actually invited to feel. We are not allowed to dwell on the economic realities of Charlotte's situation because the shifting ironies almost continually direct us elsewhere: we look with irony at Mr. Collins, for example, or at Charlotte's family, or at Charlotte herself. And though we may feel sympathy for Charlotte when she refers to marriage as the "only honorable provision for well-educated women of small fortune," our sense of her as economic and social victim is not sustained. The narrator, in fact, abandons us to ambivalence, and the Charlotte Lucas' episode on the whole is left to suggest, on the one hand, the perverting force of women's economic lot, and to prevent us, on the other, from feeling that force as a reality in the universe of Elizabeth Bennet.

One effect of undermining the force of economic realities is to make most women, in their helpless fixation on men and marriage, look perverse, or merely silly, and to lay the blame on women themselves, not on their economic and social lot. Another effect, however, is to suggest, rather wishfully, that there is some way out. Men may go about acting more powerful than women; indeed their lot in life may give them the potential for having power, but because a sense of power seems to befuddle critical vision, they are not really powerful at all. Conversely, women may seem powerless as men are not, but because we are finally not to *feel* that they are victims of social and economic forces, they do not have to be powerless after all. What we have here, it seems, is a novel that recognizes the shaping influence of economics but that denies its force. The novel, in fact, all but levels what in life we know to have been the material base of power and powerlessness and defines real power as something separate from the economic.

Real power in *Pride and Prejudice,* as is often observed, is to have the intelligence, the wit, and the critical attitudes of Jane Austen; and Elizabeth Bennet, as it is also sometimes observed, is essentially an Austen fantasy, a fantasy of power. But while some critics have noticed that Elizabeth expresses Austen's wit and intelligence in a particularly free and exuberant manner, they have not observed that Elizabeth does more than that. For Elizabeth's world affords her a freedom that Jane Austen's world evidently did not—it affords her scope not only to express critical attitudes, with energy, but to put them into action. Thus Elizabeth not only criticizes women's extreme eagerness to please men, but puts herself at some distance from that eagerness and, in the process, is rather direct in challenging Darcy's traditional assumptions of power as a male.

Elizabeth's world, moreover, allows her the power to change her lot through acting upon it, in that it allows her the power to alter Darcy's behavior. Elizabeth's world, that is, in contrast to the world of Jane Austen, permits her something more than spiritual victories, permits her more than that *sense* of autonomy that comes with wittily observing the confinements of one's situation, with standing apart from them in spirit and having to bend to them in daily behavior. Elizabeth's world, in short, permits her not only the energetic expression but the forceful use of those critical energies which Austen herself diverted into ironic novels.

That we enjoy those energies as we do, that we feel safe with them, that generations of conventional readers have found Elizabeth charming rather than reckless, owes much to the fact that Austen's version of Elizabeth's universe is one that mitigates the punishing potential of her critical views and challenging behavior. If money, for example, were really a force in the novel, we might find Elizabeth heedless, radical, or at best naïve, for insulting and rejecting a man with £10,000 a year or for condemning her best friend, a plain and portionless twenty-seven-year-old, because she married a man who could at least support her in comfort. In similar fashion, if wealthy young men were less given to bungling the personal power and influence that is their legacy, we might feel uncomfortable or incredulous when Elizabeth takes on Darcy. It is Austen's subversion of economic realities and of male power that permits us to enjoy the rebellious exuberance and energy of Elizabeth because it is principally this subversion which limits, from the outset, the extent to which we feel Elizabeth is in conflict with the forces of her society.

But to allow a nineteenth-century heroine to get away with being critical and challenging—especially about male power and feminine submission—is still to rebel, no matter how charmingly that heroine may be represented, no matter how safe her rebellion is made to appear. When Austen allows Elizabeth to express critical attitudes, to act upon them without penalty, when she endows Elizabeth with the power to alter her lot, Austen is moving against traditional notions of feminine behavior and feminine fate. For by any traditional standards Elizabeth's departures from convention ought to earn her a life of spinsterhood, not a man, a carriage, and £10,000 a year. Elizabeth's universe, moreover, is real enough, the economic and social forces kept close enough to the surface, that we believe in it, that we do not dismiss it as fantasy, and Elizabeth herself is so convincing that we can't dismiss her either. For all its charm and relative safety, Elizabeth's rebellion invites us to take it seriously, and it is for this reason, I assume, that the rebelliousness of *Pride and Prejudice,* like the rebelliousness of most women's writing, is further qualified.

One major qualification of Elizabeth's resistance to male power, to men's assumption of power, and to women's powerless behavior, is that, like Austen, she accepts the basic division in women and men's economic lots. Men, moreover, have a right to money that women do not. Thus Wickham is "prudent" for pursuing Mary King, but Charlotte is mercenary for marrying Collins. Men also have a right to greater autonomy, to greater power of choice, for Elizabeth never challenges Darcy's right to criticize women or to act the connoisseur. Nor is it entirely clear that she objects to men's general assumption of control over women. Her real aim is to resist intimidation, to deny Darcy the power of controlling *her* through the expression of critical judgments: "He has a very satirical eye, and if I do not begin by being impertinent myself, I shall soon grow afraid of him" (p. 21). Elizabeth's habitual tactic with Darcy is thus to anticipate and to deflate him in the role of critic and chooser but never to challenge the privilege by which he is either one.

Elizabeth, of course, in defending herself against the power of Darcy's negative judgments, suggests that she is also defending herself against a desire to please Darcy and to enjoy the benefit of his positive attentions. Elizabeth's defense, that is, continually implies an underlying vulnerability to Darcy's good opinion, and this is another qualification of her rebellion. Elizabeth never does challenge the privilege by which Darcy bestows benefit through his regard, never entirely denies the benefit he does bestow, and is never wholly immune to enjoying it. She merely tries to avoid responding to his attention with that show of gratefulness and pleasure that Darcy egotistically expects and that her own feelings indeed prompt in her. At Netherfield, for example, when Darcy asks Elizabeth to dance she is at first "amazed at the dignity to which she had arrived," but her overriding, defensive purpose is to deny both to herself and to Darcy that the occasion affords her any sense of status or pleasure (p. 86). It is evident, then, that Elizabeth's resistance to Darcy is undermined by a lingering susceptibility to his attentions and by a lingering desire to please. Indeed, the very energy with which Elizabeth defends herself against both pleasing and being pleased argues that she is not only vulnerable to Darcy's power over her feelings but ironically and defensively controlled by it.

Elizabeth's qualified resistance to being controlled by one attractive male is juxtaposed, moreover, with her complete vulnerability to the power of another, for Elizabeth succumbs to pleasing and being flattered by Wickham even before he reveals himself as ally. Indeed, Elizabeth's readiness to believe Wickham is partially explained by the fact that, like all the young women in the novel, she is ready to approve any attractive and charming man who pays her attention, to decide absurdly that his "very countenance may vouch for [his] being amiable" (p. 77). Elizabeth's head is full, not only of what Wickham "had told her" about Darcy, but of Wickham himself, and even after Wickham has thrown her over for Mary King, or Mary King's fortune, she continues to be flattered by "a solicitude, an interest which she felt must ever attach her to him with the most sincere regard" (p. 44).

As it turns out, of course, Elizabeth is not only not autonomous with Darcy and Wickham, she is mistaken and wrong. She is wrong about Darcy's intentions and she is wrong about Wickham's. She is wrong, moreover, for the same reason that she is not self-directing. Despite her intelligence, wit, and critical energies, she cares too much about male regard. As she herself is aware, after reading Darcy's letter, it is her "vanity," her vulnerability to the good opinion of men, that has blinded her both to Darcy's character and to Wickham's (p. 196).

If there is any force left in Elizabeth's resistance to Darcy's traditional assumptions of power, it is certainly mitigated by our continuing awareness that the rebellion itself works in the interest of tradition. That is, Elizabeth's assertion of autonomy attracts Darcy rather than putting him off. Elizabeth, we are assured, has a "mixture of sweetness and archness in her manner which made it difficult for her to affront anybody; and Darcy had never been so bewitched by any woman as he was by her" (p. 48). Heightened aggression on Elizabeth's part is met by heightened feeling on Darcy's, by greater fears of "the danger of paying Elizabeth too much attention" (p. 54). Thus we may enjoy Elizabeth's self-assertions, but we are never invited to value them in themselves, as we are invited to value Maggie Tulliver's or Jane Eyre's or Lucy Snowe's. Elizabeth's qualified resistance to Darcy, attractive as relief from the extreme male-centering of most women in the novel, is valued in great measure, nevertheless, because it attracts the attention of a desirable man.

Elizabeth's rebelliousness, then, is quiet, is not intended to alarm. It invites the conventional female reader to identify with unconventional energies, but it commits her to nothing more. It permits the conventional male reader to admire Elizabeth's spirit while finding comfort in the fact that she is wrong, not autonomous after all, and that her whole resistance to male power only secures and gives value to the love of a good man. It is as if Austen could not be indirect or qualified enough in presenting this self-assertive heroine, for we almost never see Elizabeth's rebel energies without feeling the undermining force of one irony or another. It is, in fact, Austen's qualification of Elizabeth's power that accounts for most of the complexities and ironies in the first two-thirds of the novel, and it is these ironies, I suspect, that have permitted the most conventional readers to find Elizabeth charming, and most charming of all when she asserts her independence of Darcy's traditional powers as a male.

Elizabeth, then, as a power fantasy, is in some ways astoundingly modest. The remarkable thing, perhaps, is that her rebelliousness, undercut and qualified as it is, still maintains a quality of force, still strikes us as power. It does so in part because of its juxtaposition with Miss Bingley's ineffective machinations and Jane's well-intentioned passivity, both reminders of what it means to be traditionally feminine. But most importantly, Elizabeth's rebel energies retain a quality of force because, as I have noted, they really act upon her world; they change Darcy, change the way he responds to his economic and social privilege, change something basic to the power relation between him and Elizabeth. Without intending to, Elizabeth renders Darcy more courtly, less liable to impress upon her the power he has to choose and to give her benefits, less liable to assume control of her feelings.

Still, it is not Elizabeth's much qualified self-assertion or even her unintended alteration of Darcy that establishes her as the powerful character she is. The most profound source of what we feel as Elizabeth's power is her ability in the last third of the novel to turn her critical vision upon herself, upon her own unthinking vulnerability to male approval. It is at this point in the novel that Elizabeth establishes what we could call real autonomy. It is at this point in the novel, moreover—the point at which Elizabeth redirects her critical energies from Darcy to herself—that the multiple ironies which have characterized the first two-thirds of the novel are suddenly dropped. It is a less anxiety-provoking business for a woman to assert power against an aspect of herself, against the enemy within, than against the traditional power relations of her culture. And though it is necessary and vital to assert oneself against one's own blindness, in a patriarchal society, it is also a much surer and more lasting form of power than pitting oneself against the traditional privileges of men.

Yet Elizabeth's recognition of her vulnerability to male attention does force her into painful, even humiliating recognitions. It is a hard thing for a woman to have felt herself powerful against the greater power of a man and to discover after all that she had been led astray by her extreme vulnerability to his good opinion. It is humiliating to feel apologetic toward an oppressor—for Darcy has greater potential power than Elizabeth and he has made her feel it. Why, one wants to know, has Austen put her through it? One answer, perhaps, is that Elizabeth's recognition of her "vanity" is a further undercutting of her rebellion against male power. But Elizabeth's confessions may also be seen as a hard lesson in the difficulties of confronting the enemy within, a hard lesson in the fact that the most apparently powerful women may be creatures of their culture too.

Elizabeth's honesty, of course, is also a tribute to her potential for true self-direction, for no other character in the novel achieves her measure of self-knowledge or potential self-rule. The self-knowledge which comes to Darcy comes to him offstage and at the instigation of Elizabeth. Elizabeth alone is her own analyst, and in a novel in which Austen brilliantly arranges for intelligence to mitigate the force of economics and of social position, Elizabeth emerges for the readers as the most powerful because she is the most intelligent and self-directing character in her world.

In reading Darcy's letter, then, Elizabeth gains a measure of real autonomy, in that she gains a measure of freedom from unthinking desire for male regard. But what Elizabeth's freedom finally purchases is an ability to consider, to weigh, to choose which male's regard she really values. Elizabeth's autonomy, that is, frees her to choose Darcy, and Elizabeth's untraditional power is rewarded, not with some different life, but with woman's traditional life, with love and marriage.

Austen's commitment to the economic inequities of women's and of men's lives permits her no other happy ending, but there is, of course, a major difficulty in Elizabeth's reward. For marriage in this novel, as in life, involves a power relation between unequals, and that is hardly a fitting end for a fantasy of power. What we find at the end of *Pride and Prejudice,* therefore, is a complicated and not entirely successful juggling act in which all the economic and social powers of the traditional husband/hero must be demonstrated at last but demonstrated without diminishing the powers of the heroine. It is not until late in the novel, for example, not until Elizabeth rejects Darcy's proposal, reads Dar-

cy's letter, and establishes herself as the most powerful character in the book, that we are permitted first-hand exposure to Darcy's economic and social significance. It is only at Pemberly, for example, that we are made to *feel* the reality of Darcy's power to act upon the world: "As a brother, landlord, a master, she considered . . . how much of pleasure or pain it was in his power to bestow" (p. 234). Darcy's social and economic power, moreover, is juxtaposed on this visit with the first signs that he has been altered by Elizabeth's self-assertion: "Never in her life had she seen his manners so little dignified, never had he spoken with such gentleness as in this unexpected meeting" (p. 235).

Darcy's rescue of Lydia is another demonstration of the hero's traditional powers, the powers belonging to money, class, and male privilege, but it is also to be construed as further demonstration that Elizabeth has altered Darcy, that he is not only more courtly to her but more courtly to her family, whom he is now not above serving. Darcy's proposal, moreover, is brought on by still another spirited assertion of Elizabeth's autonomy, her refusal to conciliate Lady Catherine, and even the timing of the proposal scene is set by Elizabeth. The proposal itself, finally, is followed by Darcy's lengthy reminder that it is Elizabeth who has changed him: "You taught me a lesson, hard indeed at first but most advantageous. By you I was properly humbled" (p. 349).

But it "will never do" for Elizabeth to seem more controlling than Darcy (p. 361). That is not what traditional marriages, what "good" marriages are all about. Darcy must protest, then, that he would have proposed whether Elizabeth had opened the way or not, and Elizabeth, for her part, must betray some consciousness of, and gratefulness for, the traditional economic and social benefits. She must appreciate Pemberly not just for the taste that it exhibits but for its economic grandeur, for the "very large" park and for the "lofty and handsome" rooms (pp. 228, 229). She must acknowledge that to be mistress of Pemberly might be "something" and she must experience "gratitude" to Darcy for loving her (p. 228). And yet, Elizabeth's own power must not be diminished. She is allowed, therefore, to see more than Darcy to the last: "she remembered that he had yet to learn to be laughed at, and it was rather too early to begin" (p. 351). We leave her, in fact, in the last paragraph of the novel, surrounded by Pemberly's splendor but seeming to hold her own, astonishing Georgiana with her "lively, sportive manner" and her "open pleasantry" and persuading Darcy against his will to make peace with Lady Catherine (p. 367).

Austen's difficulties with Elizabeth's reward, her attempt to give her marriage but to alter what marriage means, her tinkering with heroine and hero, must account for the fact that most readers of *Pride and Prejudice* find the end of the novel less satisfactory than the beginning. On the one hand, the charge that Elizabeth, as witty heroine, is now too inclined to moralize and be grateful owes much to the fact that marriage requires her to dwindle by degrees into a wife. On the other hand, the observation that Darcy as hero is less convincing than as villain owes much to the requirements of Austen's fantasy, which are that Elizabeth not dwindle too far, that she maintain her equality with, if not her ascendency over, her husband. Darcy, therefore, although he must demonstrate all the economic and social powers of the traditional hero—which are plenty— may not have everything; he may not have Pemberly, £10,000 a year, rank, looks, intelligence, flexibility, wit, and a convincing reality as well. There is point, though unconscious point, to his stiffness and unreality, for both function at some level to preserve the fantasy of Elizabeth's power.

The end of *Pride and Prejudice,* nevertheless, witnesses a decline in Elizabeth Bennet, for in *Pride and Prejudice* as in much of women's fiction, the end, the reward, of woman's apprenticeship to life is marriage, and marriage demands resignation even as it prompts rejoicing, initiates new life while it confirms a flickering suspicion that the best is already over. Given the ambivalent blessing of marriage as a happy ending, it is simply a tribute to Austen's genius that what we take from *Pride and Prejudice* is not a sense of Elizabeth's untimely decline but a tonic impression of her intelligence, her wit, and her power, and it is an even greater tribute that we believe in her power, that we do not perceive it as fantasy. For Austen's brilliant construction of her heroine's world, her recognition and subtle subversion of economic forces, the mobile intelligence of the heroine herself, the ironies directed at that intelligence, the complexities of Elizabeth's failure in vision and of her recovery, complicate what is at base a wish fulfillment, give it an air of credibility which lends force to the power of the fantasy upon us; as one of my students put it, we need more fantasies like Elizabeth.

It is not, of course, that the fantasy of Elizabeth's power leaves us with any real hope for the majority of women—how many Elizabeths, how many Jane Austens are there? But what *Pride and Prejudice* does do is to give us a heroine who is at once credible, charming, and the deepest fulfillment of a woman's intelligent desire for autonomy. And that is more than most women's fiction has been able to accomplish. Most women in women's fiction pay a price for autonomy—madness, for example, or death by drowning—but Elizabeth does not. The brilliance, perhaps, and certainly the joy of *Pride and Prejudice* is that it makes us believe in her.

Notes

1. F. B. Pinion, *A Jane Austen Companion* (London: The Macmillan Press, Ltd., 1973), p. 15.

2. Jane Austen to Frank Austen, July 3, 1813, in *Jane Austen's Letters to her Sister Cassandra and Others,* ed., R. W. Chapman (London: Oxford University Press, 1959), p. 317.

3. Jane Austen, *Pride and Prejudice* (New York: Holt, Rinehart and Winston, Inc., 1949), p. 1. Subsequent references appear in the text.

4. Critics like Daiches and Schorer, for example, emphasize Austen's consciousness of economic forces. See David Daiches, "Jane Austen, Karl Marx, and the Aristocratic Dance," *American Scholar* 17 (1947-1948): 289. See also Mark Schorer, "Pride Unprejudiced," *Kenyon Review* 18 (1956): 83, 85.

5. Critics like Mudrick and Harding, of course, have written admirably about Austen's general evasiveness as critic of her culture, about her general unwillingness to risk confrontation, but they have not dealt with the particular relation of this evasion to Austen's situation as a woman, nor have they noted the relation between Austen's indirection and the central focus of her critical energies in this novel: the traditional power relations between women and men. See Marvin Mudrick, *Jane Austen: Irony as Defense and Discovery* (Berkeley and Los Angeles: University of California Press, 1968). See also D. W. Harding, "Regulated Hatred: An Aspect of the Work of Jane Austen" in *Jane Austen: A Collection of Critical Essays,* ed., Ian Watt, *Twentieth Century Views* (Englewood Cliffs, N.J.: Prentice-Hall, Inc., 1963).

A. Walton Litz (essay date 16 December 1979)

SOURCE: Litz, A. Walton. "The Picturesque in *Pride and Prejudice.*" *Persuasion,* no. 1 (16 December 1979): 13, 15-24.

[*In the following essay, Litz discusses Austen's use of landscape in* Pride and Prejudice, *focusing on how she employs "picturesque moments" to establish meaning and form.*]

When I learned that Donald Greene would be talking this evening about possible models for Pemberley, it set me thinking again about the role of landscape—both natural and "improved"—in Jane Austen's fiction. Over the past few years, following the early lead of E. M. Forster, a number of critics have examined Jane Austen's uses of landscape, and have discovered that she was affected far more profoundly than one might have thought—given her essentially classical mind—by the great shifts in taste and feeling that we call Romanticism. In the later novels landscape is used to express "states of feeling," and in *Persuasion* especially the intensely physical nature of Anne's life—her loss and recovery of "bloom," as Jane Austen calls it—is movingly imaged in the rhythms and moods of the changing seasons, which finally bring Anne "a second spring of youth and beauty."

Tonight, however, I want to build on Donald Greene's remarks by focusing on landscape in *Pride and Prejudice.* You might call my little talk, in imitation of the title-pages affixed to accounts of late eighteenth-century sketching tours, "Some Observations Relative Chiefly to Picturesque Beauty in *Pride and Prejudice,* With Particular Attention Given to the Approach to Pemberley House."

In the Biographical Notice of the Author supplied for *Northanger Abbey* and *Persuasion* by Henry Austen, Jane's favorite brother, we learn that she "was a warm and judicious admirer of landscape, both in nature and on canvass. At a very early age she was enamoured of Gilpin on the Picturesque; and she seldom changed her opinions either on books or men." Among the works of William Gilpin that Jane Austen certainly knew was his *Observations, Relative Chiefly to Picturesque Beauty, Made in the Year 1772, On Several Parts of England; Particularly the Mountains and Lakes of Cumberland and Westmoreland.* It was published in 1786 with aquatint illustrations and was an immediate success, going through four editions by 1808. Vestiges of this book have been located in *Pride and Prejudice* by many readers; but I would go further and speculate that Gilpin's tour provided the ground-plan for *First Impressions,* the lost original of *Pride and Prejudice* written in 1796-97. At the end of Book Two of *Pride and Prejudice,* when Elizabeth and her aunt and uncle embark on their tour, Jane Austen comments: "It is not the object of this work to give a description of Derbyshire, nor of any of the remarkable places through which their route thither lay; Oxford, Blenheim, Warwick, Kenilworth, Birmingham, etc. are sufficiently known." They were sufficiently known to Jane Austen because of Gilpin's book, which describes the area around Haddon Hall and Chatsworth in a late chapter that opens with a "General description of the peak of Derbyshire." Moreover, the route followed by Elizabeth and the Gardiners, by no means the only approach to the Lake Country, is exactly that followed by Gilpin in his first four chapters. Gilpin's tour culminates in a detailed and ecstatic survey of the Lake country, and we remember that Elizabeth is delighted when a trip to the Lakes is first proposed, and "excessively disappointed" when it has to be curtailed because of Mr. Gardiner's business commitments: "she had set her heart on seeing the Lakes."

But more than a ground-plan is visible in the revised novel. Some of Elizabeth's more obscure remarks have their explanations in Gilpin. When she decides to risk a visit to Pemberley, Elizabeth muses: "But surely . . . I may enter his county with impunity, and rob it of a few petrified spars without his perceiving me." The "spars" have puzzled commentators, but Gilpin has a paragraph on "that curious, variegated mineral . . . supposed to be a petrifaction . . . known in London by the name of the *Derbyshire Drop.*" According to the OED this is one of the first literary references to "Derbyshire spar" (flourspar), which could be held before a candle to reveal picturesque patterns.

There are many other details from Gilpin embedded in the revised novel, but the real interest in Jane Austen's relationship to Gilpin lies, of course, in a different world from "petrified spars." The picturesque tells us something important about her development as an artist, and about Elizabeth's changing sensibility in the novel, which reflects the changes in Jane Austen's own sensibility between 1797 and 1811-12. I think Jane Austen was so strongly attracted to Gilpin in her youth because his work appealed to her warm, pre-Romantic feelings about nature *and* her love of the comic, which is founded on her unshakeable good sense. The "picturesque moment," as Martin Price has so aptly named it, was a brief phase in English taste when the new sense of landscape already apparent in poets such as Jane Austen's favorite, William Cowper, was systematized in the language of sketching and painting. Jane Austen's early attitude toward the picturesque is neatly embodied in a passage which I think we all feel must be a substantial survivor from *First Impressions.* Elizabeth has just heard that the tour with the Gardiners may reach "perhaps to the Lakes."

> 'My dear, dear aunt,' she rapturously cried, 'what delight! what felicity! You give me fresh life and vigour. Adieu to disappointment and spleen. What are men to rocks and mountains? Oh! what hours of transport we shall spend! And when we do return, it shall not be like other travellers, without being able to give one accurate idea of any thing. We *will* know where we have gone—we *will* recollect what we have seen. Lakes, mountains, and rivers, shall not be jumbled together in our imaginations; nor, when we attempt to describe any particular scene, will we begin quarrelling about its relative situation. Let *our* first effusions be less insupportable than those of the generality of travellers.'

The language here is that of the late Juvenilia, and the attitude toward the picturesque—enthusiastic participation tempered by a sense of the absurdities in the vocabulary of "transport"—is very much the attitude of the young Jane Austen.

Jane Austen's keen, almost professional grasp of the techniques and jargon of the picturesque is reflected also in that marvelous passage in *Northanger Abbey* where Henry Tilney, who views the country with an eye "accustomed to drawing," lectures so brilliantly on "foregrounds, distances, and second distances—side-screens and perspectives—lights and shades" that Catherine is ready to reject the whole city of Bath as "unworthy to make part of a landscape." Although the young Jane Austen was deeply attracted to the picturesque, which organized her emotional responses to Nature and gave her a language for seeing, she was endlessly delighted by its pedantic absurdities, especially those of William Gilpin. In the section on Henry the 8th in her juvenile "History of England," Jane Austen comments: "nothing can be said in his vindication, but that his abolishing Religious Houses and leaving them to the ruinous depredations of time has been of infinite use to the landscape of England in general, which probably was a principal motive for his doing it." Here she is spoofing a paragraph in the introduction to Gilpin's *Observations,* where he exults over the number of ruined and therefore picturesque abbeys in England, which naturally make England superior to the continent: "Where popery prevails, the abbey is still entire and inhabited; and of course less adapted to landscape." But we must not think of Gilpin as an easy target for Jane Austen's satire. He can on occasion sound like Mr. Collins, yet at other times he resembles the ironic Mr. Bennet—or Elizabeth herself. The following passage on Scaleby-castle must have delighted the youthful author of "The History of England" and *First Impressions.*

> What share of picturesque genius Cromwell might have, I know not. Certain however it is, that no man, since Henry the eighth, has contributed more to adorn this country with picturesque ruins. The difference between these two masters lay chiefly in the style of ruins, in which they composed. Henry adorned his landscapes with the ruins of abbeys; Cromwell, with those of castles. I have seen many pieces by this master, executed in a very grand style; but seldom a finer monument of his masterly hand than this.

The delicate balance between affection and humor in Jane Austen's early attitude toward the picturesque is revealed in another scene in *Pride and Prejudice* which I suspect was carried over intact from *First Impressions.* When Darcy asks Elizabeth to join him in a walk with Mrs. Hurst and Miss Bingley, who has just been abusing Elizabeth's family, Elizabeth replies with a laugh:

> "No, no; stay where you are. You are charmingly group'd, and appear to uncommon advantage. The picturesque would be spoilt by admitting a fourth. Good bye."

> She then ran gaily off . . .

As several critics have noted, the "subtext" here is Gilpin's appendix on his prints, where he explains in technical jargon that there are problems in "forming *two* into a group," while "*four* introduce a new diffi-

culty in grouping." But with *three* you "are almost sure of a good group." Elizabeth shows herself to be a good student of Gilpin, like her creator; but the cause for her gay laugh is the little joke she shares with those of us who have read Gilpin, since what Gilpin is actually talking about is "the doctrine of grouping *larger cattle.*"

I think we all feel that the peculiar charm of *Pride and Prejudice* lies in the easy blending of youthful energy and humor, so evident in this scene, with a mature moral vision. In the years between *First Impressions* and the radical revisions that produced *Pride and Prejudice,* Jane Austen had grown from adolescence to middle-age, from expectations of marriage to almost certain spinsterhood. She had witnessed death and family tragedy, and had come to understand the pressures that drive Charlotte Lucas into a humiliating marriage with the grotesque Mr. Collins. She had, in short, learned the lessons of *Mansfield Park,* the first complete product of her mature years. What gives *Pride and Prejudice* its special quality, and makes so many readers think of Mozart, is the innocence and playfulness of the original novel, which shine through and soften the harder outlines of adult experience.

But the picturesque in *Pride and Prejudice* is more than a vestige of *First Impressions*: the way Jane Austen accommodates it to her mature vision becomes part of the novel's meaning and form. By the time she "lop't and crop't" *Pride and Prejudice* around 1811-12, the picturesque of William Gilpin was going out of fashion, replaced by the more sublime intimations of high Romanticism. It had also received a heavy blow in William Combe's *Tour of Dr. Syntax in Search of the Picturesque* (1809-12), which Jane Austen may have read while reworking *Pride and Prejudice.* Combe's satire and the wonderful Rowlandson illustrations exposed all the absurdities that had so delighted the young Jane Austen. A way of seeing could not long survive that preferred ruins to sound buildings, bandits to solid citizens, blasted oaks to "great-rooted blossomers." A world of painterly effects and aesthetic surfaces leaves too many of our deepest needs unsatisfied. Soon a new term evolved, reflecting a more profound involvement in landscape: the "moral picturesque." Hawthorn used it to describe one of his stories in *Mosses from an Old Manse,* and Henry James picked up the phrase in his study of Hawthorne. Ruskin in *Modern Painters* carefully distinguished between the nobler (or moral) picturesque and the surface-picturesque, which he felt was a kind of irresponsible, witty play separated from the world of social responsibility.

I would contend that Elizabeth Bennet's education in *Pride and Prejudice* involves a movement from the "surface-picturesque" to the "moral picturesque." Her early prejudiced behavior is marked by a witty arrangement of people and ideas, a playing with emotional effects for aesthetic ends. She misunderstands Darcy's inner nature because she is so delighted with surfaces, and enjoys seeing the world in artistic terms. She journeys to Derbyshire and the peak expecting to find Gilpin's picturesque delights, but finds instead a house and grounds that embody what can only be called moral values. It has often been remarked that the description of Pemberley which opens Book Three is covertly a description of Darcy: the landscape foreshadows the startling discoveries of the next few pages. Like Donwell Abbey in *Emma,* which embodies Knightley's frank personality—"It was just what it ought to be, and it looked what it was"—Pemberley speaks of its owner's personality.

> Elizabeth's mind was too full for conversation, but she saw and admired every remarkable spot and point of view. They gradually ascended for half a mile, and then found themselves at the top of a considerable eminence, where the wood ceased, and the eye was instantly caught by Pemberley House, situated on the opposite side of a valley, into which the road with some abruptness wound. It was a large, handsome, stone building, standing well on rising ground, and backed by a ridge of high woody hills;—and in front, a stream of some natural importance was swelled into greater, but without any artificial appearance. Its banks were neither formal, nor falsely adorned. Elizabeth was delighted. She had never seen a place for which nature had done more, or where natural beauty had been so little counteracted by an awkward taste.

The difference between this landscape, filtered through the consciousness of Elizabeth Bennet, and the surface-picturesque of Gilpin tells us how far Elizabeth and her creator have come in their journeys toward maturity. The "picturesque moment" of Jane Austen's youth has not been discarded; rather, it has been absorbed into a more complex and responsible view of life and art. As I have said before, *Pride and Prejudice* is so seductive because it allows us to feel that Elizabeth and Darcy are "right" for each other both morally and aesthetically: their marriage satisfies our desire to believe that what is "right" socially and ethically can also be stylish and beautiful. That belief may be an illusion, and Jane Austen could not rest with it, moving in her later fictions toward the calm, slow beauty of disciplined suffering. But it is an illusion so powerfully sustained within the created world of *Pride and Prejudice* that the novel has remained uniquely satisfying for over one hundred and fifty years, and has brought us together tonight.

Gary Kelly (essay date June 1984)

SOURCE: Kelly, Gary. "The Art of Reading in *Pride and Prejudice.*" *English Studies in Canada* 10, no. 2 (June 1984): 156-71.

[*In the following essay, Kelly explores the role of reading in* Pride and Prejudice, *drawing a parallel between Elizabeth's inclination to read her world like a book and the reader's epistemological approach to the novel.*]

It is by now well established that *Pride and Prejudice* is about perception and judgement as acts of the whole mind, with important ethical consequences in domestic and social life.[1] The story deals with characters who are, in varying degrees, good or bad observers and judges of themselves and the world around them, and the plot shows how some of these characters, and especially the heroine, can learn to be better observers and judges by learning to avoid the enemies of good judgement, namely prejudice, ignorance, and habit or convention. Luckily (for this is a providential given in Austen's plot),[2] the heroine also has the courage, the curiosity, and the right combination of circumstances to be able to express her improved competence as an observer and judge to others; therefore, she wins the appropriate reward, a marriage of true minds. What has not been much commented on, I think, is the central place that reading has, in *Pride and Prejudice* as in all of Austen's novels, in the plot of improved observation and judgement, and as a paradigm for those activities. Before examining Austen's use of reading in *Pride and Prejudice,* however, it will be useful to consider in detail the epistemological model which is dramatized in her novels.

Essentially, this model involves the process of forming hypotheses, more or less shapely and more or less accurate, which give meaning and thus value for an individual mind to the facts of observation, indeed, which give to facts themselves their very status. Here are some of the words of perception and hypothesis to be found in *Pride and Prejudice,* many of which could be cited with reference *"passim"*: suppose, surmise, conjecture, believe, credit, impute, account for, fancy, hope, doubt, see, observe, read, determine, judge, reason, know, and their nominal and adjectival variants; sensible, attentive/inattentive, ignorant, partial, prepossessed, blind, deceived, persuaded, decided, convinced, struck (forcibly), surprised, amazed, shocked; apparent, possible, probable, likely, unaccountable, plain, evident, certain, known/unknown; impression, observation, opinion, explanation, attention/inattention, penetration, conviction, reflection, presumption, sensibility/insensibility, prejudice. The key terms, however, the ones which occur again and again in Austen's novels, are "observation" (which is best when it is "attentive"), "reflection," and "judgement." Inattentive and unreflecting observers—and the novel is full of them, although Mr. Collins, Mrs. Bennet, Lydia Bennet, and Lady Catherine de Bourgh spring most immediately to mind—cannot of course arrive at true judgements because, "blinded" by prejudice or conventional attitudes, they will simply not be able to see things "as they are." "Partial," ignorant, or merely idle, they will only see what their bad habits of mind allow them to see, and so they are disastrously or comically (usually the latter) cut off from "reality"; they are isolated in a private world which is in fact a fantasy, and lacking self-knowledge as well, they are not even aware of the delusion. The true mind, however, is precisely the one which is subject to chastening, which wants to see clearly and reflect carefully, so that it can judge correctly and thereby enter the community of civilized intercourse.[3]

These ideas, and this model of the mind's advance from ignorance and error to knowledge, are themselves conventional enough in eighteenth-century epistemology,[4] but before we see how they are developed and dramatized in *Pride and Prejudice* three additional points must be made. First, Austen and her characters assume that there is an objective natural and social reality, and that it can be known with certainty.[5] Of course, these were by no means universal assumptions in eighteenth-century epistemology. However, secondly, there are certain individual predispositions of nature, certain "tempers" of mind, which seem to distinguish one individual from another absolutely and unalterably. Clearly there is a conflict between this assumption and the first, a conflict which is masked by the comic form and ironic mode of Austen's novels, and—the third point—by the fact that Austen uses such a varied vocabulary to describe judgements made by characters in her novels; in fact she usually prefers to refer to such judgements in some of the terms mentioned above, as "surmises," "opinions," "suppositions," "beliefs," "conjectures," "constructions," or (at best) "convictions"—in other words, as hypotheses which "acount for" one's observations.[6] For to "account for" something is to pretend to understand it, and understanding is the necessary precondition for evaluation. One cannot judge what one does not understand, and so understanding must precede judgement, even though understanding is *for* judgement. Idle curiosity, manifested in such activities as gossip and being a busybody, is always a vice in Austen's novels, and the desire to know and understand should always serve the higher end of judgement, of discrimination, of the drawing of distinctions between one thing and another.

It is this relationship between meaning and value which is the basis of any kind of valid individual or social culture in Austen's fictional worlds. That is why reflection is such an important activity, such an important index of moral improveability, such a dominant element in the plot as well as the story material of an Austen novel. And so her novels show characters trying, frequently with a comic but serious lack of success, to understand the world around them, and understanding or sound judgement, like "taste" and like "manners," has to be cultivated. That is why one of the most important words—or rather values—in Austen's novels is "elegance," and why the word is applied to mind as well as manners. Indeed, her novels seem designed to show

that one can hardly have elegance of manners without elegance of mind. And elegance for Austen is clearly the product of cultivation; the ability to judge correctly, to discriminate, to exercise proper taste is an art that is learned through practice. It is in this sense that Austen's novels are "novels of education." One observes, reflects, judges; one repeats the process; one becomes civilized, that is, one becomes fit to live in and with society.

Thus, true to the culture of her class, the Anglican gentry,[7] Jane Austen shows that observation and judgement are not ends in themselves, but they are for conduct, for the leading of one's life in a civil community. One wants a cultivated mind because one wants to behave properly, not just with propriety, but appropriately. One wants to be able to understand the conventions of the community so that one can critically respond to them, that is, so that one can, as an authentic moral individual, choose how one is to inhabit the society (like the estate) which one has inherited.[8] One wants to observe and judge well so that one can act well. That, I think, is the importance of reading books in Austen's novels. Not only is the ability to discriminate among books correlated with a character's ability to discriminate among people, from *Northanger Abbey* through to *Sanditon,* but reading books is implicitly a kind of practice in reading the world, and is therefore a preparation for conduct in society. Cultivation of mind alone produces a pedant such as Mary Bennet, or perhaps a mere cynical spectator such as her father. Cultivation of manners alone, however, produces a rake such as Willoughby, Wickham, or Henry Crawford, or a coquette such as Lydia Bennet or Mary Crawford, or a busybody such as Mrs. Elton or Emma Woodhouse, or snobs such as Lady Catherine de Bourgh and her toady, Mr. Collins. On the other hand, to observe and judge well and still be prevented from acting on one's penetration and judgement (just as, in a lesser way, to read well and have to remain silent, like Fanny Price) is to experience a kind of anguish in the deliberately reduced scale of emotions Austen deals with, and this is in fact what happens to all of her heroines in all or parts of her novels. Consequently, the novels are about love and marriage. For what could be a clearer demonstration of and a more acute problem for one's ability to base conduct on judgement, than the choice of a partner in marriage: marriage which is at once the formalization in the eyes of God and the world of one's personal emotional and intellectual commitment to one's judgement, and a continuation of those formalities and conventions which constitute human society and human civilization—but which must be as it were re-invented by each individual in order for those conventions to continue to have moral meaning.

Observation, reflection, judgement, action: the Arminian (or rather Pelagian) and Anglican insistence on moral freedom of action, both faith and works, on both true belief and appropriate action in the world in the light of that belief. If only that were all; but the truth is that man is in a fallen condition, flawed. And there is the paradox of the human mind: desiring true judgement, yet constantly exposed to error, through prejudice, ignorance, and idleness; wishing to see, yet constantly suffering defects of vision. It is a painful process. That is why so many Austen characters give up, or never set out, settling for convention, for received ideas, habits of thought, expression, conduct. But, on the other hand, that is also why the Austen heroines, like Elizabeth Bennet, are armed with both "curiosity" and "courage." For only by divine grace operating through a comic universe can we hope, through time and chance and the exercise of our free will, to have our errors corrected happily.

Elizabeth Bennet is of course described (humorously but significantly) as a "philosopher" because she does reflect strenuously (though of course she is somewhat too proud of her reflectiveness); and in terms of what I have just been saying, all of Austen's heroines are philosophers because they are all serious, and at times comically earnest, in their commitment to the process of creating meaning and value out of observation by the construction of hypotheses, of "surmises," "suppositions," "conjectures," or "convictions." The seriousness of their involvement in this process is due to personal character or "temper" (Austen's word) no doubt; but it is also due to circumstances: the heroine's hypothesizing concerns nothing less than her personal happiness, which involves self-approbation, but also a form of social recognition or approbation of her mental and (therefore) moral superiority: marriage to the right person, a person who for Austen is always himself a good observer and judge of others (that is how he comes to choose the heroine). Elizabeth's "curiosity" is her desire to know the truth and thus to have true judgement; her "courage" is her readiness to accept pain and embarrassment in order to get at the truth, her willingness to admit her errors, to re-examine what she has misperceived, and then to act on her revised judgement. Her curiosity and her courage make Elizabeth educable and "improveable." In this willingness to create meaning and value, and thus the proper grounds of conduct for herself, not only by constructing but also by tearing down and reconstructing her hypotheses until she has arrived at true judgement, perhaps Elizabeth is, rather than a philosopher, a critic. One is reminded that one of Austen's favourite moralists defined the task of criticism in *The Rambler* (92) as "to improve opinion into knowledge," and that is precisely what Elizabeth Bennet attempts and, however painfully for herself, is willing to do throughout *Pride and Prejudice.* It is just that the consequences of Elizabeth Bennet's perceptions and judgements are, for her, of rather more practical consequence than they are for most professional critics. In-

deed, for Elizabeth Bennet, as for Marianne and Elinor Dashwood, for Fanny Price, Emma Woodhouse, and Anne Elliott, the real practical importance of criticism (including self-criticism) is precisely in the "practice" that follows criticism, the conduct in domestic and social life which is based on perception and judgement. They must go beyond criticism to action.

However, to describe Elizabeth Bennet as a critic according to Samuel Johnson's definition is to recall to mind that one of Austen's most important and most frequently used techniques for dramatizing the process of observation and judgement is the act of reading itself. Of course in *Northanger Abbey* and *Sense and Sensibility,* novels still bound to the aims of literary parody,[9] there are young women who persist in forming the wrong hypotheses about the world around them because they have read the wrong books too uncritically. In *Pride and Prejudice,* however, the importance of correct reading is presented more immediately and dramatically by showing the heroine reading, misreading, and rereading a particular written text, a letter.[10] These readings may be dramatized as a kind of filtered interior monologue, filtered, that is, through the omniscient narrator's voice, and in this case the monologue is actually an interior dialogue or debate; or the readings may be dramatized in actual dialogue between two different readers, with two different readings, and thus the improvement of opinion into knowledge may take a form closely resembling a debate between two critics. In *Pride and Prejudice,* for example, the problem of forming correct hypotheses is shown in the early part of the novel in a series of dialogues between Elizabeth and her sister Jane as they read together the letters of others. In the complex cognitive task of improving opinion into knowledge Austen is very much aware of the problem of point of view or perspective, the apparently unresolvable differences in the personal outlook of different individuals (even though, as noted earlier, Austen does suggest very strongly in her novels her belief that there is a true, "objective" point of view from which the world may be known correctly). In *Pride and Prejudice,* then, this additional problem of relativism is presented clearly in the dialogues on letters between Elizabeth and Jane, for what is immediately obvious is the way the "temper" of each colours her own reading.

The first instance of such critical reading by Jane and Elizabeth is in their discussion of Miss Bingley's letter to Jane, informing her of the sudden removal of the Netherfield party to London.[11] Jane reads the letter silently to herself, but Elizabeth reads its probable contents in the changes in Jane's countenance as she reads, and as soon as the sisters are alone they engage in an earnest debate over what the contents might mean. In this debate, the temperamentally optimistic Jane tends to take a pessimistic interpretation of Bingley's sudden removal, while Elizabeth the sceptic tries out of love and kindness to devise a hypothesis which will allow her sister to hope. Jane quotes certain key passages in the letter which seem to support her own hypothesis, and the discussion moves from the letter to the conduct of the Bingleys, as observed and as interpreted by Jane and Elizabeth. The process which Jane and Elizabeth go through in this chapter, from surprise at the letter's contents, through supposition as to its "real" or "hidden" meaning, to decision on the most likely or comfortable explanation, is repeated several times in *Pride and Prejudice*—in fact it is one of the novel's basic narrative figures. But more than the basic figure is developed here: for the reading of the letter is also an occasion for developing the different but sympathetic characters of Jane and Elizabeth so that the reader of the novel is instructed in how to predict their responses, in how to read them, and thus the novel, more accurately. What this does is to enable the reader to perceive more accurately the situation of dramatic irony which is the primary perspective Austen wishes us to adopt: reading with the characters, but, like the narrator herself, reading better—reading more fully, more justly, and more quickly. What the reader should notice here, then, is the essential irony of the passage: Elizabeth, the most thoughtful and rational of the Bennet girls, uses the procedures of weighing and interpreting evidence (almost in a legal sense: "The case is this . . ." she tells Jane)[12] in order to come up with a hypothesis which will "answer every wish" of her more realistic sister's heart, a hypothesis which will perform for Jane what Jane usually does for Elizabeth, and put the best construction on the actions and characters of others. Reason and argument are being used here, we perceive, to serve fancy and desire. But then we know that where Jane is concerned Elizabeth cannot be impartial; and this prejudice, which seems laudable in itself because the narrator prevents us from seeing Jane in any other way than Elizabeth does, creates others, more dangerous for Elizabeth.

The irony is made apparent three chapters later, at the beginning of Volume II (Chapter 24 in editions with continuously numbered chapters), when a second letter from Miss Bingley seems to show that, in the first instance, Jane was right, Elizabeth wrong. This time, Jane's feelings are more deeply touched, and so a day or two passes before the sisters can debate the matter. Jane's fortitude, and her concern for others before herself, rouse Elizabeth's love for her, and this in turn leads her into a somewhat superficial cynicism towards others. There follows a short debate in which Jane clearly reveals her willingness to believe the best of people, against Elizabeth's strong resistance. Elizabeth's reasons we agree with, Jane's benevolence we admire, but after this preliminary Jane turns the debate closer home, and the dialogue is thick with suppositions, until one is found which will hurt Jane the least. We end up sharing Elizabeth's point of view on the

Bingley situation, and on Jane, and therefore, ironically, we end up agreeing with Jane that it is sometimes better to be mistaken than to be right. The passage is studded with the vocabulary of hypothesizing mentioned earlier,[13] and nothing in the novel so far could more clearly demonstrate the essential difference of "temper" (the word Austen uses) between the two sisters, the difference of temper which leads them to form different hypotheses to explain the same facts. The reader of the novel, of course, is kept in the dark about Bingley until eleven chapters later when Elizabeth and the reader learn for certain and at the same time that, ironically, Jane's hypothesis was, if not correct, at least better. And, more ironical still, this revelation comes about at the same time as a revelation of much greater consequence to Elizabeth herself, one which is the novel's decisive test of her abilities as a reader and critic, of her ability to observe, reflect, reason and judge.[14]

The occasion is of course her reading and re-reading of the letter Darcy gives her following his disastrous proposal of marriage at Hunsford Parsonage, the home of Elizabeth's friend Charlotte Lucas and of Elizabeth's first suitor, Mr. Collins. And since Elizabeth's debate with Jane over the propriety and wisdom of this marriage of Charlotte's, she has also been prejudiced against Darcy by the revelations of her second would-be suitor, Wickham, as to Darcy's character for pride, and of Col. Fitzwilliam as to Darcy's hand in the Bingley affair. Darcy's letter contains explanations of his actions on precisely these two accounts, but Elizabeth has already made up her own mind, and so she opens the letter "with no expectation of pleasure, but with the strongest curiosity" (174), curiosity which will lead to self-correction. But first, it is important to note that not only Elizabeth's abilities as a reader are tested; ours are also brought into play: Elizabeth opens the letter, but we are allowed to read it first, before we are told how Elizabeth reads it. This allows us to form our own "first impressions" (the novel's original title) of Darcy's arguments and explanations; and in the case of both we are liable to be as influenced by the vigorous, one might say manly style, as by any new information the letter contains. Having read the letter, as novel readers anxious for "intelligence," feeling for the letter's reader in the novel, but not as she will feel, we are then curious to compare our reading to hers.

Darcy's letter takes up the last part of Volume II, Chapter 12, which is nothing less than the complete shattering of Elizabeth's previous hypotheses about Darcy, Wickham, and the Bingley affair. Elizabeth's mind has, typically, already been prepared for a revolution in her point of view by the shock of Darcy's proposal, which has left her mind in a "tumult," a kind of epistemological anarchy which results in the suspension of the mind's usual cognitive powers (i.e., in a kind of blindness), and which is the opposite of the "tranquillity" which accompanies certainty. Nevertheless, Elizabeth begins to read "with a strong prejudice against every thing he might say" (181), a prejudice based on her own hypothesis about the Bingley business and Darcy's motives therein, about Wickham's character and Darcy's treatment of that charming young man, about Darcy's character in general. Thus forearmed, she can only read the first half of the letter, concerning Bingley and Jane, one way:

> She read, with an eagerness which hardly left her power of comprehension, and from impatience of knowing what the next sentence might bring, was incapable of attending to the sense of the one before her eyes. His belief of her sister's insensibility, she instantly resolved to be false, and his account of the real, the worst objections to the match, made her too angry to have any wish of doing him justice. He expressed no regret for what he had done which satisfied her; his style was not penitent, but haughty. It was all pride and insolence.
>
> (181)

In whatever affects Jane, she cannot be disinterested, and she knows in advance how to feel.

> But when this subject was succeeded by his account of Mr. Wickham, when she read with somewhat clearer attention, a relation of events, which, if true, must overthrow every cherished opinion of his worth, and which bore so alarming an affinity to his history of himself, her feelings were yet more acutely painful and more difficult of definition. Astonishment, apprehension, and even horror, oppressed her. She wished to discredit it entirely, repeatedly exclaiming, "This must be false! This cannot be! This must be the grossest falsehood!"— and when she had gone through the whole letter, though scarcely knowing any thing of the last page or two, put it hastily away, protesting that she would not regard it, that she would never look in it again.
>
> In this perturbed state of mind, with thoughts that could rest on nothing, she walked on; but it would not do; in half a minute the letter was unfolded again, and collecting herself as well as she could, she again began the mortifying perusal of all that related to Wickham, and commanded herself so far as to examine the meaning of every sentence.
>
> (181-82)

And so she "read, and re-read with the closest attention" (182), but is faced only with two opposing hypotheses which can make sense of the whole business: either Darcy or Wickham is lying. She tries to draw memory to her aid, wishing to believe in Wickham, not Darcy, trying to remember some circumstance besides Wickham's "countenance, voice, and manner" to confirm her judgement of him. "But no such recollection befriended her" (183). Instead, her memory, that most important faculty in the reading process, seems to condemn Wickham. There is for example Wickham's original disclosure of his connection with Darcy:

> Many of his expressions were still fresh in her memory. She was *now* struck with the impropriety of such communications to a stranger, and wondered it had escaped

her before. She saw the indelicacy of putting himself forward as he had done, and the inconsistency of his professions with his conduct.

> (183-84)

She sees, that is, for the first time, what she could not see before, because her eyes were blinded by her prejudice against Darcy and by the visible, sensible charms of Wickham's countenance, voice, and manner, which she had simply misread as establishing "him at once in the possession of every virtue" (183).

What is interesting here is that what Elizabeth did not see, we probably did not either, and like her, we should have. We are at this moment at one with Elizabeth, and so prepared to exclaim with her, of Wickham, "How differently did every thing now appear in which he was concerned!" It is at moments such as this especially, and in this particular example, that Austen slips into "free indirect discourse,"[15] that peculiar fusion of author's and character's point of view which was to become such an important technique for novelists in F. R. Leavis's "great tradition." Then, from condemning Wickham, Elizabeth must, by sheer force of logic, turn to the "justification" (184) of Darcy, and the meaning of this part of Darcy's letter is now clear to her: she has read both Darcy and Wickham wrongly. The consequence is immediate: it is a self-revelation:

> She grew absolutely ashamed of herself.—Of neither Darcy nor Wickham could she think, without feeling that she had been blind, partial, prejudiced, absurd.
>
> "How despicably have I acted!" she cried.—"I, who have prided myself on my discernment!—I, who have valued myself on my abilities! who have often disdained the generous candour of my sister, and gratified my vanity, in useless or blameable distrust.—How humiliating is this discovery!—Yet, how just a humiliation!—Had I been in love, I could not have been more wretchedly blind. But vanity, not love, has been my folly.—Pleased with the preference of one, and offended by the neglect of the other, on the very beginning of our acquaintance, I have courted prepossession and ignorance, and driven reason away, where either were concerned. Till this moment, I never knew myself."
>
> (185)

The shock of re-cognition drives her back on her self, that is, on the suppositions on which she has grounded her reading, and on her own competence as a reader. Then, having changed her reading of one part of the letter, and the "reality" it refers to, can she ignore the other part? Courage (her other major attribute besides curiosity) must now come to her aid.[16] And so "she read [the other part of the letter] again. Widely different was the effect of a second perusal.—How could she deny that credit to his assertions, in one instance, which she had been obliged to give in the other?" One by one she accepts the justness of Darcy's readings—of the likelihood of Jane, whose "temper" Elizabeth knows to be mild, manifesting for certain in her conduct a truly deep attachment for Bingley; of her family's essential vulgarity and foolishness even in public. Here the logic of alliteration reinforces Elizabeth's acceptance of Darcy's use of "terms of such mortifying, yet merited reproach" against her family (and we notice later how the novel itself seems to accept Darcy's criticism of Elizabeth's family, for just two chapters further on Lydia, the embodiment of all the worst weaknesses of the Bennets, advances into the foreground of the story).

It is in every way an active reading and re-reading of Darcy's letter by Elizabeth, an activity neatly underlined by the fact that Elizabeth is physically active as she reads, walking up and down the lane outside Rosings. And so, too, the reading turns into a period of reflection, with Elizabeth "wandering along the lane for two hours, giving way to every variety of thought; reconsidering events, determining probabilities, and reconciling herself as well as she could, to a change so sudden and so important" in her understanding of her immediate world. The "fatigue" which eventually forces her "home" to Hunsford Parsonage is, we feel, as much due to her exercise of mind as to her exercise of body (though, once again, the correlation of physical and mental states was learned by Austen from the conventions of sentimental fiction). From anger and prejudice against Darcy, Elizabeth has passed through confusion, to acceptance, to shame, to reflection, to fatigue of mind and body. Such is the effect on the whole person of such a rite of passage.[17] But now, having arrived at a complete understanding and acceptance of Darcy's point of view, can she do any more but love him? The attentive reader, familiar with the conventions Jane Austen is here recreating, must now suppose so.[18]

Elizabeth's acknowledgement that, "Till this moment, I never knew myself," is a turning point in the novel because Elizabeth learns to re-read not just Darcy's letter, or all that the letter refers to, or the writer of the letter himself; Elizabeth also learns to re-read herself. But the setting up of this turning point also involves the reader in the process of revision. The persuasiveness and force of Darcy's epistolary style is experienced by the novel-reader before it is experienced by the reader in the novel,[19] and so we learn to re-read what has already passed in the novel before Elizabeth does, because we cannot simultaneously read what the heroine is reading and read her too. It is a question of the ordering of the material of the story, and this is a question of artistic choice, of narrative strategy. The result, in this case, is that we come to read of Elizabeth's revisions already somewhat chastened by our own reading of Darcy's letter, and so we are both sympathetic to Elizabeth and prepared to judge her as she judges herself. It is a peculiar combination of sympathy and detachment, and so

the narrative strategy is matched precisely by Austen's use of "free indirect discourse": we read as the heroine reads, but we also read the heroine. We find that we are like her in fallibility as a reader; we learn, as she learns, to revise our hypotheses about the other characters, as well as about the heroine herself. But the management of the narration, by first the use of narrative voice and second the distribution of the story material, guides our reading. And so the chapter is a turning point for us as well. Henceforth we embark on a new exercise in hypothesizing: how will Elizabeth and Darcy now get together?

I said just now that the attentive reader will suppose, from Elizabeth's acceptance of Darcy's point of view, that she has nothing left to do but love him, and of this we are given hints in the very next chapter. Elizabeth continues to re-read and reflect on Darcy's letter, "studying" it until she has got it "by heart" (189). If Darcy as she now knows him to be *is* his letter (the letter replaces the person),[20] he has already won her mind and therefore her heart, though of course it is ironical that his writing, not his face-to-face proposal, should gain Elizabeth for him. Elizabeth has to have a text so that she can reflect on it, and take it to heart. The rest, the novel makes plain, is up to time and chance, for this is after all a comic world. When Elizabeth next sees Darcy, it will be but another image, a portrait, but one she can by then read right, and soon after she is surprised by the man himself, almost magically transformed,[21] in his physical absence from the novel, into the image of the letter. For, after the turning point of Volume II, Chapter 13, character has been revealed, and so character gives way to plot.

The drama of perception becomes increasingly comic as Elizabeth persists in one aspect of her original hypothesis, that Darcy is proud; but as, in incident after incident, Darcy shows that he does still love Elizabeth, her persistent belief that he must be too proud to propose again becomes, to us readers, an increasingly obvious comic error. Even before Darcy's first proposal other characters—Jane, Miss Bingley, Charlotte Lucas—had correctly read love in his behaviour towards Elizabeth, and the reader of the novel is willing to follow their surmise. After Darcy's failed proposal, Elizabeth's persistent shying from the possibility of a second proposal makes *us* more likely to entertain the possibility *she* will not; and we are encouraged to do so by our knowledge that Elizabeth does love Darcy, by the serious obstacle thrown in their way by the Lydia-Wickham affair, and by the recognizable comic tone.

All these are evident signs to the attentive and, in terms of the language of fiction, cultured reader to conjecture with growing confidence that Elizabeth will marry Darcy. Thanks not only to the superior knowledge conferred on us by the narrator, but also to our skill and attentiveness as readers in identifying the plot-signs of romantic comedy, we know pretty well how to read the second half of *Pride and Prejudice.* Only in the first part, up to Volume II, Chapter 13, are our skill and attentiveness tested, as Elizabeth's are tested. After that point we readers have little more to learn about reading Elizabeth, though Elizabeth still does. This is why Darcy is made by Jane Austen to propose the first time at Hunsford Parsonage, the home of Elizabeth's erstwhile bosom friend Charlotte Lucas Collins. As she leaves Hunsford, and the first part of the novel closes, Elizabeth reflects, "Poor Charlotte!—it was melancholy to leave her to such society [as that of her husband and Lady Catherine de Bourgh]!—But she had chosen it with her eyes open" (192). Surely the reader recognizes the irony here: Charlotte choosing a fool with her eyes open; Elizabeth rejecting a prince of a man out of blind prejudice. The plot of the three suitors—Collins, Wickham, Darcy—has in one way for Elizabeth come full circle. Henceforth, the novel shifts into a different mode, a shift symbolized by a certain kind of removal: it is the last we see of Elizabeth and Darcy meeting, as they have always met before, as the visitors in the houses of others. From now on their game of reading one another will be a home and home series; and for the reader, too, from now on the game can be played with an increasing sense of being at home with the conventions of romantic comedy.[22]

The clearest sign that this is so is that the narrator becomes positively playful about the conventions of novel-writing in the second half of *Pride and Prejudice.* There are direct and indirect references to conventions which are being rejected: the refusal to describe the scenery on Elizabeth's tour (213); Mary's novelish moralizing on Lydia's elopement (255); Collins's ditto (261-62); and "public opinion's" preference for novelishly disastrous fates for Lydia (273). There are obvious signs of structural symmetry: Lydia gets married; Jane gets engaged; the third time completes the conventional folk and popular literary pattern of three, and it can only be Elizabeth, and there is no one for her to marry but Darcy. There is use of repetition to tip us off to the joke, as time after time Elizabeth expects Darcy to be proud and aloof. There is also the increasingly evident shift in use of free indirect discourse, as the narrator cools sympathy for Elizabeth into a more ironic and detached rendering of her thoughts and feelings; and we sense the increasingly imminent closure in the gradual withdrawal of the narrative voice from sympathetic commitment to philosophic, if amused, spectating (I mean narrating) of Elizabeth's progress towards matrimony. Finally, after Darcy and Elizabeth have become engaged, there is their own comment on their complicated love-plot as though it were the plot of a novel (339).

However, none of these signs will be evident—or even signs—unless the reader is competent and willing to read them: the novel does not force a reading on us—no novel does—and we will be in the same position as Elizabeth is *vis-à-vis* Darcy in both parts of the novel unless we are able to recognize the conventions as well as the resistance that must be made to them, unless, that is, we recognize both the necessity and the danger of conventions, the necessity of habits of perception and their ability to blind us to the world as it is.[23] And so Austen's novels are about courtship and marriage as both social conventions and exercises for the individual in "reading" and "re-reading" others. Similarly, the novels engage the reader in an exercise in both using and resisting the conventions of the language of fiction. Our satisfaction with the marriage of Elizabeth and Darcy, for example, is partly in recognizing its function as a closure of the form, and this is a highly conventional satisfaction in terms of the genre of fictional romantic comedy to which *Pride and Prejudice* belongs.

Part of the satisfaction is also in recognizing Austen's particular use of the convention in her own *oeuvre,* the way a true marriage concludes a series of three (sometimes fewer), in which the others in the series are less satisfactory and satisfying versions. But there is for us also the realization that this marriage is inspired in the sense that the mere form of the social convention has been recreated by being filled with meaning and value for the particular individuals involved. And parallel to this satisfaction is a recognition of the way the literary convention has been recreated, by being filled with meaning and value.[24] A knowledge of the convention must go with an ability to recognize the ways the convention has been re-invented. Without the former knowledge, we will not have the latter: we will be as uncivilized as Lydia Bennet and all of her party in the novel. Without the latter we will be mere formalists, like Mr. Collins, and all of his ilk in the novel, mistaking convention alone for meaning and value. And so the novel offers us, as it offers Elizabeth Bennet, occasions for mis-reading, and then occasions for re-reading. All we need is curiosity and courage, or confidence in the providential design of the world we are, temporarily, inhabiting.

To summarize, then, the points I have tried to establish are these: that "reading" people and oneself is a problem in *Pride and Prejudice* for both the heroine and the reader; that Austen uses the reading of actual written texts in order to dramatize Elizabeth's problems in "reading" her social world; that there is a particular crisis of reading for Elizabeth and for the reader in Volume II, Chapter 13; and that thereafter the problem of reading remains, though it is partially resolved for the heroine, whereas it becomes, for the reader of the novel, increasingly a game played with the novelist, in which the reader is called upon to recognize both the conventions of the genre and the author's play with those conventions, and the author's own particular use of conventions.[25]

The conclusion I draw is that Austen's heroine "reads" herself and her world in terms of her knowledge of the norms and conventions of the languages of feeling and of social conduct in her world, just as the reader reads the novel in terms of the norms and conventions of a particular *genre* and the author's own *oeuvre*. **Pride and Prejudice** is not a modernist novel in which fictional conventions themselves become the subject of fiction; but it is, nevertheless, a novel in which the cultivated art of mediating between convention and originality, habit and freshness of perception, is an issue in both subject and form; and if the process of cultivating this art is demonstrated within the novel by, among other things, the heroine's difficulties in interpreting written texts, the process is actually imposed on the reader by the ways the novel as a whole plays on and plays off the conventions of fiction itself. To read **Pride and Prejudice** well is to learn how read better; that is why we go on re-reading it.[26]

Notes

1. See, for example, Susan Morgan, *In the Meantime: Character and Perception in Jane Austen's Fiction* (1980), where Austen's interest in perception is seen as similar to that of the Romantic poets; I argue here that Austen inherits, and alters, eighteenth-century models of perception and eighteenth-century fictional techniques (especially in the literature of Sensibility) for dramatizing perception and judgement. Moreover, Morgan does not treat the act of reading itself as a paradigm for the process of perception and judgement. On the whole, I feel that Morgan neglects moral judgement in favour of the act of perception, in order to bring Austen closer to the Romantic poets, and thus farther from her late eighteenth-century predecessors and the eighteenth-century moralists. Alistair Duckworth has also noted "the relativistic (or better, perspectivistic) aspects involved in knowing another person" as an important theme in *Pride and Prejudice; The Improvement of the Estate* (1971), p. 121.

2. See Joel Weinsheimer's remarks on chance in "Chance and the Hierarchy of Marriages in *Pride and Prejudice,*" *ELH,* 39 (1972), 404-19.

3. Cf. again Morgan, who argues that Austen treats perception and judgement as provisional; I feel she overstates the case for this, and neglects the relationship of perception and judgement to action, which I discuss below.

4. Cf. again Morgan, who sees Austen rejecting eighteenth-century epistemology. See also Gilbert

Ryle's essay, "Jane Austen and the Moralists" (in *Critical Essays on Jane Austen,* ed. B. C. Sontham, 1968). No one has really followed up on the suggestions in Ryle's essay.

5. Cf. Stuart Tave's argument in "Jane Austen and one of her contemporaries" (*Jane Austen. Bicentenary Essays,* ed. John Halperin, 1975) that Austen presents a version of Wordsworth's theme of the marriage of mind and world in the act of perception.

6. As noted above, Morgan argues that Austen presents perception as irreducibly provisional, and the point I make here would seem to support her argument; but I argue that the "provisional" terms Austen tends to use are "directed" towards assumptions of some discoverable certainty. I would adduce those critics who point out the presence of the narrative voice as a model consciousness which does have direct access to certainty, and which thus "places" and orients the provisional certainties ("surmises," etc.) in the minds of her heroines. Referring to Tave's argument (see n. 5) and considering the differences between Wordsworth and Austen, I would again adduce the role of the narrator and call on M. Bakhtin's distinction between the "dialogical" nature of prose fiction and the "monological" nature of personal lyric poetry.

7. On Jane Austen and the gentry see Samuel Kliger's "Jane Austen's *Pride and Prejudice* in the Eighteenth-Century Mode" (*University of Toronto Quarterly,* 16, 1947), Marilyn Butler's *Romantics, Rebels, and Reactionaries* (1981) and the sensible remarks in the Introduction to David Monaghan's *Jane Austen: Structure and Social Vision* (1980).

8. See ch. 3 of Alistair Duckworth's *The Improvement of the Estate.*

9. See A. Walton Litz's (as usual) discriminating remarks on the differences between *Sense and Sensibility* and *Pride and Prejudice,* in *Jane Austen: A Study of Her Artistic Development* (1965), pp. 97ff.

10. Elizabeth is also, of course, a discriminating reader of books; my point is that it is her reading of letters which is a decisive paradigm, and decisive in the plot of perception and judgement.

11. Jane Austen, *Pride and Prejudice,* ed. Frank W. Bradbrook and James Kinsley (London: Oxford University Press, 1970), I, Ch. 21. Subsequent citations in parentheses.

12. Reuben Brower has noted the "odd, rather legalistic process" by which Elizabeth weighs the mean-

ing of letters; "Light and Bright and Sparkling: Irony and Fiction in *Pride and Prejudice*" from his *The Fields of Light* (1951).

13. Some of the words in this passage which have to do with hypothesizing are: credit, doubted, reflection, opinion, unaccountable, believe, persuade, convinced, thinking, fancy, deceives, have no idea of, imagine, attributing, take it in the best light; see pp. 119-23 in the edition by James Kinsley and Frank Bradbrook.

14. Howard Babb's fine discussion of the use of dialogue in Austen's novels (*Jane Austen's Novels: The Fabric of Dialogue,* 1972) could, I feel, be usefully supplemented by attention to the way that the dialogues are so often exercises in refining hypotheses down to irreducible differences of "temper," as I have suggested above. One could also consider the incident described below, Elizabeth's reading of Darcy's letter, as a significant kind of dialogue, in terms of Babb's sensitive analysis of the conversations between Elizabeth and Darcy in the rest of the novel.

15. See the discussion of this topic by Norman Page in *The Language of Jane Austen* (1972).

16. Elizabeth declares her courage to Darcy just before he proposes; see p. 155.

17. Cf. Morgan, who sees *Pride and Prejudice* as a novel of crisis rather than of rite of passage.

18. Several critics have written on Austen's use of convention, notably Frank Bradbrook and Kenneth Moler; Marilyn Butler (*Jane Austen and the War of Ideas,* 1975) has also written on this topic; I feel there is still much more to be said on the subject, and, as my argument here suggests, especially on Austen's use of convention to cultivate and educate the reader's competence as a reader of fiction, and thus of the world the reader inhabits.

19. Note the discussion of letter-writing earlier in the novel, in ch. 10. Letter-writing is a parallel and correspondent theme to reading, and the two themes join in vol. II, ch. 13.

20. In his essay on *Mansfield Park* Lionel Trilling notes that Darcy exhibits "a formal rhetoric, traditional and rigorous" (*The Opposing Self,* 1955, p. 222); while just in its intent, this remark seems to me to diminish the richness of significance of Darcy's style (in his letter, at least), and to oversimplify the effect of Darcy's style in the universe of styles which is the novel as a whole.

21. Thus reinforcing the fact that a transformation has occurred in Elizabeth's perceptions, and giving this transformation a power, almost "magical" (the fairy-tale elements do lurk in Austen's novels), to transform the world—at least to transform Darcy. Cf. Marvin Mudrick's view of Darcy's character as simply inconsistent in the two halves of the novel (*Jane Austen: Irony as Defense and Discovery,* 1952, pp. 117-19).

22. Kenneth Moler, for example, argues that *Pride and Prejudice* "is in many respects a subtly humorous reflection on Richardson and Fanny Burney and their patrician heroes" (*Jane Austen's Art of Allusion,* 1968, pp. 94-95). I find Moler neglects to answer the question, What is such "reflection" for? Is it merely to "correct" Richardson and Burney? Or is it to instruct the reader? I am arguing of course that it is the latter (though it may do so by means of the former). Also Moler neglects the issue of Austen's ability to rely on and play off her readers' knowledge of and habituation to the generic properties of romantic-comic fiction; thus his study is too narrow.

23. Reuben Brower, in one of the more widely read essays in New Criticism's celebration of irony as form ("Light and Bright and Sparkling: Irony and Fiction in *Pride and Prejudice*"), sees a diminution of irony and thus of density and originality, and an increase of conventionality, in the last third of the novel. I am arguing that this "conventionality" is purposeful, meant to be noticed, far from unironic, and part of Austen's larger strategy in the novel as a whole.

24. The process is described by Hans-Georg Gadamer: "Every age has to understand a transmitted text in its own way, for the text is part of the whole of the tradition in which the age takes an objective interest and in which it seeks to understand itself" (*Truth and Method,* transl., 1975, p. 263). If one takes "text" as "institution," and "age" as "individual," one has a statement of Austen's interest in marriage, speech, reading, property, fictional conventions, etc., etc. I am not, of course, citing Gadamer in order to claim Austen as a hermeneutist.

25. Cf. Litz's attributing unity in the novel as a whole to "the indirect presence of Jane Austen's sensibility" and "the direct presence of Elizabeth Bennet as a commanding center of our interest," while noting the shift from "scenic" construction in the first half of the novel into "the less dramatic narrative" of the second (op. cit., p. 111). I have argued for exercise in reading as an important if not the unifying principle. Cf. also Robert Garis's denial of unity in *Pride and Prejudice,* in "Learning Experience and Change," in *Critical Essays on Jane Austen,* ed. B. C. Southam (1968).

26. An earlier version of this paper was read to the 1979 meeting of the Association of Canadian University Teachers of English.

Dvora Zelicovici (essay date December 1985)

SOURCE: Zelicovici, Dvora. "Reversal in *Pride and Prejudice*." *Studies in the Humanities* 12, no. 2 (December 1985): 106-14.

[*In the following essay, Zelicovici concentrates on the third volume of* Pride and Prejudice, *contending that it is vital in developing Mr. Darcy's and Elizabeth's reversals of conviction.*]

The third volume of **Pride and Prejudice** has frequently been regarded as not merely different from but also inferior to the previous two volumes. Marvin Mudrick sees it "diminish suddenly in intensity and orginality,"[1] and Reuben A. Brower argues that the perfect harmony achieved between the ironic dialogue and the movement toward the climactic scenes ceases when Elizabeth arrives at a new view of Darcy. Brower writes, "once we have reached the scenes in which the promise of the introduction is fulfilled, the literary design both ironic and dramatic is complete. Thereafter **Pride and Prejudice** is not quite the same sort of book."[2] Such a view derives from a misconception of the book's literary design and its overall thematic and dramatic structure.[3] The misconception also leads to adverse aesthetic judgments of Volume III. If Austen had intended to compose a novel, in which, as Tony Tanner puts it, "the most important events are the fact that a man changes his manners and a lady changes her mind,"[4] then the literary design would have been complete by the middle of the Pemberley section. By then, these two events have occurred, and a happy reconciliation is clearly in the offing. Instead of a proposal, Chapter IV of the third volume brings Jane's letters informing Elizabeth of Lydia's elopement. The happy end is delayed for a third of the novel, not through a need on Austen's part to conform to the fashionable demand for a triple-decker novel, but because in Austen's literary design, a rapprochement between Elizabeth and Darcy would have been premature and facile. The novel has been so structured that by the end a reversal has taken place.

Such a reversal is an integral part of most of Austen's novels, but does not always take the same form. The kind discernible in **Pride and Prejudice,** and also in **Emma,** occurs when a crucial event (or series of events) in the first part of the novel is virtually repeated in the last part, with the significant difference that the reactions, emotions, or attitudes of the protagonists are the opposite of what they were previously. The reversal also entails punishment for serious error, involves suffering, and yet allows for a happy resolution.

In **Pride and Prejudice** the reversal is so systematic and pronounced that it can be regarded as the major shaping principle of the novel. The novel falls into two perfect halves.[5] The first traces the chain of errors and misunderstandings that drives Elizabeth and Darcy apart and extends up to Elizabeth's first reading of Darcy's letter of explanation (Vol.II.,chap.xiii). Elizabeth's second reading (of the same letter) is the turning point, and is followed by a reversal for the characters. It has two phases: first a period of "re-cognition"[6] and then a painful ordeal. In Austen's books error always results from wrong reasoning. Austen is not, however, a pessimistic Christian, as Marian Butler would have it,[7] for her protagonists are capable of learning: they are not incorrigible. They learn to employ reason rightly and gain a clear sight and unimpaired judgment. With the possible exception of **Mansfield Park**[8] Austen's works are definitely rationalistic. But she is a Christian rationalist.[9] That is why acknowledgement of error is insufficient without suitable penance, and why that penance characterizes the protagonist's ordeals. The ordeal is a suffering, a testing, a way of paying and earning happiness once the lovers have been properly chastened. This process is not normally viewed as comedy, and is certainly not the "pure" comedy of the first two volumes. Perhaps this explains why the third volume jars on certain readers who sense it is different. They feel let down and, as a consequence, disparage this volume and label it melodrama. It is not. But to get a better appreciation of this volume we must see it as an indispensable part of the novel's reversal structure.

The Darcy that Elizabeth meets at Pemberley, in the first chapter of the third volume, has already completed the re-cognition phase, and is, consequently, capable of making a fresh start with Elizabeth. For the first time in the novel our hero, no longer automatically assuming he enjoys Elizabeth's esteem, is anxiously bent on courting her and on winning her approval. The great courtesy, warm hospitality, and attentions showered on Elizabeth and the Gardiners are clear evidence that Darcy has taken to heart Elizabeth's strictures regarding his presumptuous, ungentleman-like behaviour. But what is not always sufficiently heeded is the nature and extent of the change Darcy must still undergo, the need for which has sharply manifested itself in his attitude to Elizabeth. Though he started to fall in love with her after their second or third encounter, all his efforts were directed to conquering that love, which, as Elizabeth trenchantly remarked, he regarded as an unworthy passion, "against . . . [his] will, against . . . [his] reasons, even against . . . [his] character."[10] Stronger proof, therefore, has to be given that Darcy is indeed a changed man with a very different apprehension of the world and a different set of values. In Austen's scheme, the Lydia-Wickham elopement provides the ideal opportunity for this proof and at the same time exacts a full retribution for all Darcy's former sins of pride. The

Pemberley section is thus not an end so much as a beginning, allowing Darcy to put right the errors of the past, a singular demonstration of the reversibility of error in the world of comedy.

The reversal in Elizabeth's case, though similar to Darcy's, possesses subtle differences. The first phase of recognition, for instance, is not over by the time Elizabeth comes to Pemberley, for even after Darcy's letter of explanation removes the substance of her ill-opinion, she is still not favourably disposed towards him.[11] She has not forgiven him the insolence of his address; moreover, chagrin at her own conduct and her family's as well prevents her from ever wishing to see him again. For a better appreciation of him, Elizabeth must see Pemberley, hear the housekeeper and discover a new Darcy.[12] Elizabeth is Austen's only heroine actually seen falling in love with a man she has long known and cared nothing for. Were such a radical emotional change to occur only in a brief coda, it would be as unconvincing as Marianna's change toward Colonel Brandon in *Sense and Sensibility*. Austen's finer artistic sense in this later novel dictated that an entire second phase be devoted to this interesting development. Love is to be quickened by suffering. Elizabeth must therefore be submitted to an ordeal, but unlike Darcy's active testing, hers is a passive trial. This is just since Darcy's actions drove them apart in the first half, while Elizabeth's emotional and mental responses and not her actions spoilt her relationship with Darcy. For the sin of a willed dislike she must be punished, and suffering instructs her into the true nature of her feelings.

This then is the rationale for a third volume and for the elopement which does double duty by serving as the device for both the hero and heroine's ordeals. Volume III, chapter iv begins the ordeals for both protagonists. Elizabeth's suffering begins when Darcy's is eased. His suffering began when he believed his intolerable pride had lost him Elizabeth and his hope is only kindled during the meetings at Pemberley and strengthened by his opportunity to serve her. She, on the other hand, can only suffer on his account when it is her turn to be placed in a situation where she believes he is lost to her. Her disclosure to him of the news of the elopement will, she fears, have this result. Yet her willingness to tell him of such a shameful family matter is a measure both of her confidence in him and of the new intimacy that has sprung up between them. The same proneness to mutual misunderstanding that characterized the entire relationship is manifested here too, but the causes have changed. Elizabeth observes Darcy standing, rapt in thought, meditating the best course to reclaim Lydia, and misinterprets his silence:

> Her power was sinking; everything must sink under such a proof of family weakness, such an assurance of deepest disgrace. She could neither wonder nor con-
> demn, but the belief of his self-conquest brought nothing consolatory to her bosom, afforded no paliation to her distress. It was on the contrary, exactly calculated to make her understand her own wishes; and never had she so honestly felt that she could love him, as now, when all love must be vain.

(pp.189-190)

It is a brilliantly graphic stroke in the ironic pattern that Darcy's silence should, as at Hunsford,[13] be a pregnant source of misunderstanding. He, as usual, says too little, but whereas before his silence sprang from insensitive complacency and concern with family consequence, now it springs solely from consideration for Elizabeth's distress. A delicacy of obtruding himself on her thoughts at this painful juncture, and too great a humility to imagine himself of sufficient importance to her, testify not only to self-forgetfulness but also to the distance he has come since he proposed to her.

An equally significant change is observable in Elizabeth. Instead of her former indifference[14] now she is concerned above all else about his feelings for her. An exchange of sensibilities has occurred: ironically, when Darcy ceases to be bothered about the degradation of such a family alliance, she is not only positive he must be entertaining such considerations, but admits the justice of such claims and thinks much less of her own as a person.

Chapter four contains echoes of previous encounters between Elizabeth and Darcy, and Elizabeth is even shown "throwing a retrospective glance over their whole relationship." She reflects on how "full of contradictions and varieties" it has been, as she sighs "at the perverseness of those feelings which would now have promoted its continuance, and would formerly have rejoiced in its termination" (p.190).

Her ordeal imposes penance for the past feelings, and it is only after the most recent set of contradictions and varieties has satisfactorily resolved itself, that the design of the novel is complete. And this can only happen after the Lydia-Wickham elopement has been taken care of. Once we perceive how neatly that elopement fulfils the various functions of reversal we may stop complaining about its being a threadbare, hand-me-down literary device[15] and laud instead the economy and resourcefulness of Austen's art. The elopement is more than a demonstration of the hero's impeccability. It subtly tests out and confirms Darcy's realization of the sovereignty of individual human worth. It is not, as Wiesenfarth argues, that the problem posed in the first part of the novel and resolved in the last third is Darcy's acceptance of the Bennet family.[16] The question is not one of acceptance but of Darcy's discovering that love of the right lady knows no impediments. He who prevented the marriage of one sister on the grounds of its imprudence for Bingley, now brings about the marriage of another sister which must add disgrace to an alliance with his own family. And if this were not enough, he who was successful in frustrating Wickham's marrying Georgina for her share of the Darcy fortune (as well as out of spite at Darcy's refusal of his outrageous suit for the living), now has to undergo the humiliation of seeking out, pleading with, and bribing Wickham to become his brother-in-law. This is indeed a nemesis of reversal!

The Lydia-Wickham elopement, moreover, closes the gap between the previously diverse outlooks of the protagonists, for as we have already seen it leads to an equally drastic shift in Elizabeth's views regarding the relative importance of family and the individual. Elizabeth's acute embarrassment at her family's exhibition of itself at the Netherfield ball had, as Mary Lascelles has observed, every appearance of its being the first time she had been so sensitive,[17] and the reason is clearly Elizabeth's perception of the scene through Darcy's eyes. Yet at Hunsford she had allowed herself to forget the Bennets' total want of propriety, and it was only after her second reading of Darcy's letter that she understood that Jane's disappointment had been "the work of her nearest relations" (p.144). Understanding then how materially Jane's credit and her own must suffer from their family's conduct, she had attempted to dissuade her father from permitting Lydia's trip to Brighton. But even at this stage she did not yet grasp the true nature of the dangers inherent in Lydia's impropriety. Elizabeth was still primarily concerned with ill-breeding, with breaches of decorum, with relatives for whom she had to blush, that is, with society's opinion. Thus at Pemberley, Elizabeth could revel in the good breeding of the Gardiners and "glory in every expression, every sentence of her uncle which marked his intelligence, his taste, or his good manners" (p.174).

But it takes Lydia's elopement to reveal to Elizabeth the full impropriety of her family's behaviour, and realize the causes which have made such an elopement, if not inevitable, at least a likely consequence of her family's life-style. Only then does she recognize all the implications of her family's irresponsible attitudes.[18] Her strictures regarding her father, coming from a daughter so attached to Mr. Bennet as Elizabeth, are harsh indeed. As she explains to the Gardiners, Wickham need not have feared her father's intervention: "[Wickham] might imagine from his indolence and the little attention he has ever seemed to give his family, that he would do as little, and think as little, about it, as any father could do in such a matter" (p.193). She now perceives that Lydia's never having been taught to "think on serious subjects, but allowed to dispose of her time in the most idle and frivolous manner and to adopt any opinions that came in her way" (p.193), is a failure in upbringing. For Elizabeth, as for her author, the elope-

ment is thus not merely a matter for conventional moral condemnation,[19] but is to be seen within a framework of cause and effect. Frivolity and idleness are conducive to lack of principle and to reprehensible behaviour.

Austen not only exploits the device of an elopement as a vehicle for the structural and thematic elements of reversal, but has also treated it in a far more imaginative and rich manner than has usually been appreciated. The focus is never on the external action—elopement, chase, hasty wedding—but always on Elizabeth: her first learning about the elopement, her fears, conjectures and conclusions, her reactions to the various letters containing information about the events transpiring, her anxieties and regrets, and her response to the newlyweds. The essential action takes place, as it does in all the mature Austen novels "in the intimate and subtle chambers of her heroine's mind."[20] And what censorious critics may have failed to notice is that Volume III, even more insistently than the previous volumes, is presented almost throughout from Elizabeth's point of view. Everything is filtered through her consciousness. The main narrative technique is not dialogue but free indirect speech, and what should be stressed is the marvelously convincing rendering of the heroine's consciousness as she lives through this most severe crisis of her life.

The sensitive reader has a vivid sense of the way in which Elizabeth's growing apprehension of the moral and social implications of her sister's conduct is made all the more painful by her belief that it must sever her forever from Darcy. She reflects that "had she known nothing of Darcy, she could have borne the dread of Lydia's infamy somewhat better. It would have spared her, she thought, one sleepless night out of two" (p.205). Elizabeth is not yielding here or in other passages temporarily to a kind of hopeless "moralizing on Lydia's disgrace," nor is the term "infamy" evidence of the author's "inability to assimilate extra-marital sex to her unifying irony" (p.119). Elizabeth's moral judgments are not irrelevant, but as an involved and suffering person, she responds to and reflects on her family's conduct in a new and more mature manner. Her awareness of the price she is paying colors almost every thought and feeling. Instead of a happy marriage which could "teach the admiring multitude what connubial felicity really was" (p.214), she has to live with the bleak prospect of life without Darcy, a prospect all the more dismal now that her own view of her family is so depressing. Furthermore, it is a time of regrets, of reflection on the might-have-beens and should-have-beens resulting from her own folly.

No sooner, for example, does Elizabeth learn that Lydia is to marry Wickham than she regrets having disclosed the truth to Darcy. Second thoughts tell her it can make little difference as Darcy must shrink from any such family connection, and the thoughts which follow these illuminate the nemesis which is now overtaking her.

She was humbled, she was grieved; she repented though she hardly knew of what. She became jealous of his esteem, when she could no longer hope to be benefited by it. She wanted to hear of him, when there seemed the least chance of gaining intelligence. She was convinced that she could have been happy with him; when it was no longer likely they should meet.

(p.181)

She is convinced Darcy must be feeling triumph not because she attributes to him less than noble thoughts, but because she now quarrels with herself. She has been living with the memory of "the petulance and acrimony in her manner of rejecting him and all the unjust accusations that accompanied her rejection" (p.181), and it continues to be a source of constant vexation, as we see from her later apology to Darcy for "having abused . . . [him] so abominably to . . . [his] face" (p.253). But this is not all. What Elizabeth is also repenting, even if she is not as yet fully conscious of it, is her previously fostered dislike and wilful misconstructions. Some such thoughts clearly plague her, for these are her laments when she receives her aunt's letter informing her of Darcy's role in bringing about Lydia's marriage: "Oh how heartily did she grieve over every ungracious sensation she had ever encouraged, every saucy speech she had directed towards him" (p.224). And as she puts it later to Darcy, she has realized that she never "spoke to . . . [him] without rather wishing to give . . . [him] pain than not" (p.262). The censorious Elizabeth, previously so unfair to Darcy, is now no kinder to herself, and regrets having been the playful, satirical girl enjoying herself at Darcy's expense.

The reversal in Elizabeth's situation, is re-inforced by the structual device of a second letter received, perused, and re-perused. The first letter (the one she received from Darcy at the end of the first half of the novel) was opened with the certainty that it could offer no excuse for Darcy's base conduct, but the second is torn open with the anticipation of an account of an "exertion of goodness too great to be probable" (p.242). As marked a contrast exists in her response after perusal of each letter. Even after several readings of the first Elizabeth could only begrudgingly allow him "capable of some amiable feeling" (p.141). Now on rereading, even her aunt's warm recommendations do not appear to her to do him sufficient justice for she credits him with the greatest disinterested goodness.

Insufficient attention to the narrative perspective gives rise to the notion that there is a deterioration in the quality of writing in these chapters. There has been no suspension of the "author's characteristic response of comic irony" (p.112), nor is there any sign that she "must truncate, flatten, falsify, and disapprove" (p.101). The visit of the newly-weds to Longbourn, singled out in particular for criticsm by Mudrick, is a perfect instance of the danger of confusing Austen with Elizabeth. The visit is a further turning of the screw for our heroine. The sight of the young couple and her mother conducting themselves without the slightest trace of embarrassment makes Elizabeth run out of the room. For those responsible for her unhappiness blandly to ignore the wrong they have done is unendurable. A reader should surely appreciate the naturalness of such feelings of indignation and resentment. It would hardly be credible for a person in Elizabeth's situation to have the equanimity and capacity for a distanced, objective, ironic stance. It is more psychologically convincing that she over-reacts. But it is not Austen who has suspended her irony. Austen is, for the most part silent as Mudrick himself remarks (p.112), and while the author holds virtually the same moral position towards Lydia's conduct as Elizabeth, it is Austen who remarks: "Lydia was Lydia still, untamed, unabashed, wild and fearless" (p.216). It is Austen who is making precisely the point that Mudrick labours—that Lydia is merely "behaving true to character, and that the irony lies in her powerlessness to change, in the incongruity between her conviction of vitality and lack of choice" (pp.111-12). Elizabeth's efforts to shame Lydia are, of course, fruitless, and they are ill-tempered. Mudrick is correct, she should have known better, but it is a perceptive and accurate depiction of Elizabeth that she does try. She is acting in character, for she has shown herself, when provoked, perfectly capable of resentment, acrimony, and sarcasm.

While every person acts in character, our perception of them has undergone a substantial change. Our response, for instance, to Mrs. Bennet's lamentations and subsequent raptures is very different form the ear we turned, so much earlier in the novel, to her complaints about the entail, her nerves, and Elizabeth's refusal of Mr. Collins. She is no longer an object of fun, of broad satire, as Brower would have it.[21] We are no longer amused. Every word she now utters grates as we understand the serious implications not of a mean intelligence but of a moral vacuity, a complete incomprehension of all questions of right and wrong. She is not, for example, the least troubled that her brother may have pledged himself to assist Mr. Wickham with money:

> Well . . . it is all very right; who should do it but her own uncle? If he had not a family of his own, I and my children must have had all his money you know . . . Well! I am so happy. In a short time, I shall have a daughter married. Mrs. Wickham! how well it sounds, and she was only sixteen last June.

We have been made painfully conscious of what it must be like for a sensitive individual to live at Longbourn, and to be "ambushed by an imbecility,"[22] but it is an awareness that we gain primarily in this last part of the novel.

On the other hand, while identifying with Elizabeth and sharing her changed apprehension, we are by no means limited to seeing, feeling, and reacting only as she does. We are in the privileged position of enjoying the author's perspective, which is not, as Brower asserts, that of a world which is suddenly simpler than the rest of the novel "where outright judgments of good and bad or happy and unhappy are in place."[23] It is a perspective which allows for a much more complex comprehension and discrimination than Brower notices or than Mudrick appears to require when he insists on the value of the aloof vision of the ironist. This perspective enables the reader to perceive that Elizabeth is not the playful, satirical, lively girl of the previous volumes, and it is perfectly right psychologically, thematically, and structurally that she should not be. Only after her ordeal comes to an end do her captivating wit and liveliness reemerge.

If the novel is the art of preparations, as Henry James affirmed, then **Pride and Prejudice** is an instance of such art. The holding off of the rapprochement of the two lovers till they have given every proof of being completely ready for each other is an integral part of Austen's design and a perennial source of satisfaction for the novel's constant readers.

The build-up to a second proposal scene, paralleling the climax of the first half of the novel but its ironic antithesis, completes the counter-movement of reversal in the second half. Elizabeth's reaction to the insolent and presumptuous interference, not of Mr. Darcy in her sister's affairs, but of his aunt in her own, paves the way to the opposite conclusion; Darcy's needing his aunt's report to summon up enough courage to speak to Elizabeth is a telling touch of irony that highlights not only his great diffidence but also his better understanding of Elizabeth. The scene of two hesitant lovers fearful that their dearest wishes may not be fulfilled replaces the earlier one where an unwarranted confidence in themselves and in their knowledge of the other had transformed a proposal into a direct and nasty collision. This summation of the chastening process has been subtly effected by a third volume without which, I submit, the novel would have been inestimably the poorer.

Notes

1. Marvin Mudrick, *Jane Austen: Irony as Defense and Discovery* (Berkeley: Univ. of California Press, 1968), p. 119.

2. Reuben A. Brower, "Light and Bright Sparkling: Irony and Fiction in *Pride and Prejudice*," reprinted in *The Fields of Light: An Experiment in Reading* (New York: Oxford Press, 1968), p. 180.

3. Cf. J. Wiesenfarth, F.S.C., *The Errand of Form* (New York: Fordham Univ. Press, 1967), p. 61 and A. Walton Litz, *Jane Austen: A Study of Her Artistic Development* (New York: Oxford Univ. Press, 1965), pp. 110-111.

4. Tony Tanner, Introd., *Pride and Prejudice* by Jane Austen (Harmondsworth, England: Penguin Books, 1972), p. 7.

5. Cf. E. Halliday, "Narrative Perspective in *Pride and Prejudice*," *Nineteenth Century Fiction*, 15 (1961), 68.

6. Tony Tanner, p. 26.

7. Marian Butler, *Jane Austen and the War of Ideas* (Oxford: Clarendon Press, 1975), p. 212.

8. *Mansfield Park* is perhaps the exception because three important, central characters, Henry and Mary Crawford and Maria Bertram, prove incorrigible. They show themselves to be incapable of learning even when given ample opportunity. Yet they are none of them unintelligent. Austen would thus appear to be entertaining very grave doubts in this novel as to the possibility of re-educating the vision when wrong reasoning springs from deeply ingrained false values. See my article "The Inefficacy of Lovers' Vows," *ELH*, 50 (1983), 531-540.

9. Butler is correct that Austen is no rationalist as Maria Edgeworth in *Belinda* for Austen is sceptical about intelligence in a way Edgeworth is not. See also Alistair M. Duckworth for the view that Austen's novels are informed by the traditions of Christian rationalism. In "Prospects and Retrospects," in *Jane Austen Today,* ed. Joel Weinsheimer (Athens: Univ. of Georgia Press, 1975), p. 21.

10. All quotations from the novel are from the Norton Critical Edition, ed. D. J. Gray (New York: Norton, 1966), p. 132.

11. See Vol.II., Chap. xiv.

12. The significance of Pemberley for Elizabeth's understanding of Darcy has been variously discussed. See Dorothy van Ghent, *The English Novel: Form and Function* (New York: Harper & Row), pp. 107-8, Litz, p. 111, and Wiesenfarth, p. 67.

13. *Pride and Prejudice,* p. 126.

14. *Pride and Prejudice,* p. 125.

15. The critic who comes down most severely on Austen for resorting to literary "grooves prepared . . . by hundreds of novels of sentiment and sensibility" is Mudrick, p. 120.

16. Wiesenfarth, p. 162. Samuel Kliger, on the other hand, would have it that this section shows Elizabeth learning to take class into account. In fact,

Elizabeth from the outset takes class into account, but it is never a matter of major importance to her and her attitude does not alter. This section shows Elizabeth changing her view, not about the class her family belongs to, but about her family's impropriety. See Samuel Kliger "Jane Austen's *Pride and Prejudice* in the Eighteenth Century Mode" in *University of Toronto Quarterly,* 16 (1945-6), 57-371.

17. Mary Lascelles, *Jane Austen and her Art* (London: Oxford Univ. Press, 1963), p. 162.

18. Butler, pp. 209-210. Yet while I agree with her that Elizabeth is in some respects like her father, and that we may attribute to his upbringing the fostering of her satirical disposition and consequent complacency, I see no evidence of Elizabeth's ever being in the least culpable of "irresponsible detachment" (p. 209).

19. See Mudrick, p. 120.

20. E. Halliday, p. 68.

21. Brower, p. 75.

22. Van Ghent, p. 111.

23. Brower, p. 75.

Anne Waldron Neumann (essay date fall 1986)

SOURCE: Neumann, Anne Waldron. "Characterization and Comment in *Pride and Prejudice*: Free Indirect Discourse and 'Double-voiced' Verbs of Speaking, Thinking, and Feeling." *Style* 20, no. 3 (fall 1986): 364-94.

[*In the following essay, Neumann studies the speech and thought of* Pride and Prejudice, *calling attention to Austen's use of "double-voiced verbs," or verbs that "conflate narration with reported discourse."*]

I. INTRODUCTION

Since so much of an Austen novel is *apparently* "shown" or dramatized rather than "told" or narrated, it becomes of particular interest not just to trace how Austen reports the speech and thought of her characters but also to consider when and how judgments on the characters' consciousnesses are implied as well as stated. The following study uses ***Pride and Prejudice*** to illustrate one aspect of how Austen creates consciousnesses for her characters by rendering and describing their speech and thought in what Mikhail Bakhtin, in his "Discourse Typology in Prose," calls "double-voiced utterances"—that is, sentences which combine a character's reported voice with the narrator's reporting voice, sentences in which the narrator can both render, and

comment on, the utterance reported (181). This study offers an improved taxonomy of reported discourse, applicable to other English novelists, and, in applying this taxonomy to Austen, it suggests a reading of her fiction.

Bakhtin's philosophy of language justifies close study of reported discourse because this study allows us to see how consciousnesses are formed and influenced: "What we have in the forms of reported speech," Bakhtin asserts, "is precisely an objective document" of the active, evaluative reception by one mind of the discourse of another (*Marxism* 117).[1] Austen's characters choose from the same modes of quotation and comment as are available to her narrator. Seeing what her characters remember and quote from what Henry Tilney in ***Northanger Abbey*** calls "social and literary intercourse" (*NA* 197), we learn how they assimilate that discourse *and* why they quote it—to satirize, moralize, or romanticize. How language expresses but also shapes judgment in Austen's view suggests how she believes consciousnesses are informed and—ideally—improved by social and literary discourse.

The assurance with which Austen's explicit narratorial comment employs Johnsonian abstract nouns for moral qualities is readily remarked. Much of Austen's characterization and comment is also implied by her telling choice of verbs of speaking and verbs of thinking or feeling, however. These verbs of communication, and of articulated and sometimes nonarticulated consciousness, are worth studying whenever they occur in Austen's narratives, but it is also significant *where* they occur—whether they originate in the actual discourse of a character, whether they form the narrator's introduction to quoted speech or thought, or whether they may seem to belong to narrator's and character's discourse *simultaneously*.

The special topic of the following study is such "double-voiced" verbs as these last, which conflate narration with reported discourse to combine concision with liveliness but sometimes also to confuse—intentionally—a character's subjective speech with the narrator's objective account of that character's thoughts or feelings. Ann Banfield claims that a "common assumption" of the "dual voice" view of indirectly reported discourse (which she attempts to refute) is that the inquit or parenthetical—the "he said" or "she thought" that may accompany and identify sentences of reported discourse—is the paradigmatic example of the narrator's contribution to a double-voiced utterance (189). I claim more for the "dual voice" position. I argue below that *sometimes*—in the "double-voiced" case—the inquit is *itself* an instance of double-voicedness.[2]

Since sentences with double-voiced verbs constitute, I suggest, a variation on free indirect discourse, identifying such verbs allows us better to recognize free indirect discourse in Austen's novels. And, because free in-direct discourse interweaves what could be a character's words into the narrator's discourse, but without explicitly attributing those words to the character in question, on the correct identification of free indirect discourse depends both *who sees* and *who speaks* in a given passage, the factors determining point of view in fiction. I shall suggest that Austen uses double-voiced verbs to distinguish characters whose point of view the narrator cooperates in reporting but also to identify characters who are left to speak their thoughts and feelings for themselves. That is, by means of this single device, Austen's narrator can not only share with her heroines the responsibility for articulating their reflections at the level of thought but can also satirize lesser characters who attribute thoughts and feelings to themselves in their speech—who moralize or romanticize, for example—without the narrator's cooperation and endorsement.

II. Free Indirect Discourse

In a recent reconsideration of free indirect discourse, Michael Peled Ginsburg notes that discussions of this narrative mode typically begin by presenting and refuting "definitions of FID offered by critics in the past" (133). Since, in analyzing verbs of speaking, thinking, and feeling in *Pride and Prejudice,* I also discuss what I identify as a variant of free indirect discourse, I too shall begin by briefly describing my model of how free indirect discourse reports speech and thought in Austen's novels.

Austen usually enlivens the *description* of instances of speech or thought by including words we feel might well partly *render* them. Free indirect discourse, I suggest, is that mode of indirectly reported speech or thought which quotes what we feel could be at least some of the words of a character's actual utterance or thought but which offers those words interwoven with the narrator's language (though not syntactically subordinated to it) *without explicitly attributing them to the character in question* (an interweaving that may necessitate certain grammatical transpositions described below). Ginsburg contests "the view that FID is simply the representation of the speech or thought of the characters. Even when the bivocality of the utterance in FID is acknowledged, its ambiguity is usually dismissed" (139). I define free indirect discourse as any sentence (or clause) containing words which (with the necessary grammatical transpositions) could plausibly be attributed to a character by the reader but which are not explicitly attributed to that character by the narrator. (For consistency, I define a sentence or clause without explicit attribution as free indirect discourse even when neighboring sentences contain the inquit which would imply that attribution.) Free indirect discourse in fiction is not *necessarily* the narrator quoting a character, ac-

cording to my definition (indeed, in a novel, we could seldom "know" this for certain). It need only read as though it *could* be quotation. My suggested definition thus *welcomes* ambiguity but also allows that not every instance of free indirect discourse is equally ambiguous.[3]

The usual sort of example can demonstrate typical differences between free direct and indirect speech or thought and tagged direct and indirect speech or thought:

> (Tagged) direct speech: He asked, "Shall I come here to see you tomorrow?"
>
> Free direct speech: Shall I come here to see you tomorrow?
>
> (Tagged) indirect speech: He asked if he should go there to see her the next day.
>
> Free indirect speech: Should he come here to see her tomorrow?
>
> (Tagged) direct thought: He asked himself, "Shall I come here to see her tomorrow?"
>
> Free direct thought: Shall I come here to see her tomorrow?
>
> (Tagged) indirect thought: He asked himself if he should go there to see her the next day.
>
> Free indirect thought: Should he come here to see her tomorrow?

"Tagged" (to mean "attributed"—quotation with a tag or inquit) is part of Seymour Chatman's terminology in "The Structure of Narrative Transmission" (230): "direct tagged speech," "direct free thought," "indirect free speech," "indirect tagged thought," and so on.[4] I retain the more familiar word order, omit *tagged* when possible, and use the general term *discourse* to refer to both "speech" and "thought." (Thus *free indirect discourse,* for example, includes free indirect speech and free indirect thought.)

By convention, direct discourse, tagged or free, preserves every word of the actual utterance reported—"actual," in the case of fiction. Tagged indirect discourse often (but not always) preserves *some* of them. Free indirect discourse, I suggest, in practice *usually* includes *some* of what *could be,* in Graham Hough's words, "the actual mode of expression, the *ipsissima verba* of a fictional character" (205)—with, perhaps, certain grammatical transpositions. If free indirect discourse did not preserve potential *ipsissima verba,* it would be the narrator's single-voiced utterance rather than quotation.[5] But determining which words may be quoted in a sentence interpreted as free indirect discourse is no harder than in a sentence of tagged indirect discourse, which may summarize or reorder or paraphrase or merely describe an utterance, as well as select from and in part quote it directly (compare Pascal 26). Again, if a sentence or clause can, in my opinion, plausibly be read as containing indirect quotation without attribution, I identify it as free indirect discourse. Readers may question the plausibility and reject the identification in specific instances. The category of free indirect discourse thus defined remains available, however, whether or not readers agree on particular instances of it.

Direct discourse does not assimilate and subordinate the reported clause to the reporting or attributing clause, if any—the "he said" or "she thought" or, as in the above example, "he asked." And, except for any reporting clause, this mode of reported discourse is single-voiced, a character's rather than the narrator's voice. In tagged or free *indirect* discourse, in contrast, one voice quotes and frames another, typically shifting any verbs or first- and second-person pronouns in what may be quotation to the narrative past and to the third person, as in the above examples.[6]

Tagged direct and indirect discourse explicitly identify the character who authored the utterance by means of the inquit (and tagged direct discourse also identifies exactly which words are quoted by means of quotation marks). Free indirect discourse, on the other hand, omits the inquit which announces quotation.[7] Because free indirect discourse lacks attribution, how do we recognize it as possibly reported discourse? That is, how does a novelist foreground the subjective language and viewpoint of a particular character against the usually more objective narratorial background? Or how does one character signal quotation of another character without being explicit? Like any form of irony—and free indirect discourse is often ironic—free indirect discourse must announce itself by some implicit means. We must be able to recognize that such sentences *could* be read as unattributed quotation of a character by the narrator, or of one character by another. At least, the *undecidability* of whether to interpret free indirect discourse as quotation should be recognizable.

The example displays the most explicit possible indicators of free indirect discourse. First, free indirect discourse usually preserves (as tagged indirect discourse typically does not) any deictic indicators of the *here* and *now* of the speaker's spatial and temporal perspective.[8] Second, tagged indirect discourse embeds a character's utterance as a subordinate clause—with subordinate-clause word order—in the narrator's utterance. But free indirect discourse—when it quotes a whole sentence—preserves (as does direct discourse) the word order and sentence form of the original utterance, most noticeably exclamations and questions (Pascal 9). Note, however, that when neither deictic indicators nor verbs and pronouns occur in a reported utterance—when, for example, only a fragment of a char-

acter's speech or thought is interwoven without attribution in, say, the narrator's language—we may not find *any* linguistically definable markers of quoted discourse. Paradoxically, in such a case, all quoted words would be unshifted from the character's "actual" words: we might equally well be reading free *direct* discourse.[9]

The most important markers of free indirect discourse are the most difficult to specify: we recognize content and often also diction and syntax particularly appropriate to a character, or particularly *in*appropriate to the narrator. Such discrepancies are especially apparent in Austen's satiric (rather than sympathetic) free indirect discourse (usually rendering speech in Austen's novels rather than thought) where the reporting and the reported voices seem to clash rather than cooperate.[10] Foregrounding what *deviates* in a character's speech from the narrator's normative background, satiric free indirect discourse in Austen's novels balances between morality and satire, between instruction and delight.

The study of reported speech and thought in fiction may necessitate reconstructing, or hypothesizing, what was "actually" *uttered* from what is *reported*. The *fabula,* as originally conceived by Russian Formalist critics like Boris Tomashevsky, is primarily a reconstruction by the reader of the events of a fiction in their "actual chronological and causal order" (Tomashevsky 67), in contrast to the order in which they may be recounted by the narrator in the *sjužet*. More generally, "the story [or *fabula*] is 'the action itself,' the plot [or *sjužet*], 'how the reader learns of the action,'" according to Tomashevsky (67n).[11] Thus the *fabula* can include reconstructions by the reader of the utterances of a fiction as they "actually" occurred—to whatever extent such reconstruction is possible—without the omissions, grammatical transpositions, or paraphrases with which utterances may be reported by the narrator in the *sjužet*. Double-voiced utterances are sentences in the *sjužet*. Interwoven in double-voiced utterances, however, are words "uttered" in the *fabula*. We may imagine that the narrator creates the *sjužet* (including the *report* of the characters' discourse) while Wayne Booth's "implied author" creates both *fabula* (including the imagined "actual" discourse of the characters) and narrator. This distinction, however artificial, is useful for talking about choices authors make in reporting discourse because it permits us to speak as though other choices were possible. "Narrator" and "implied author" are entities readers abstract from fictional texts; their abstract and necessarily artificial nature does not disqualify them—nor *fabula* and *sjužet*—from use by critics. This study freely hypothesizes what readers, if they paused to do so, *could* infer was said or thought in the *fabula* from what is written in the *sjužet*.

This reconstruction is particularly problematic—intentionally so—in the case of free indirect discourse, of course. As Austen wrote her sister after reading the page proofs of *Pride and Prejudice,* "a 'said he,' or a 'said she,' would sometimes make the dialogue more immediately clear," perhaps referring to her practice of omitting the inquit in free indirect discourse. "[B]ut," she continued, paraphrasing *Marmion,*

> I do not write for such dull elves
> As have not a great deal of ingenuity themselves.
>
> (***Letters*** 297-98)

To read a sentence as free indirect discourse, we must indeed use our ingenuity. We must infer who is quoted and which words of the sentence are quotation. And we are left to guess whether those words in the *sjužet* were uttered at the corresponding moment in the *fabula,* and even whether those words were spoken or thought. Nevertheless, we can often, if unconsciously, postulate answers to these questions. Clearly, more of who and which and when and how are defined by the context in some sentences of free indirect discourse. The first examples of free indirect discourse I shall cite from ***Pride and Prejudice*** are of this most "definite" type. And my very first example is—perhaps surprisingly—free indirect quotation by a character rather than by the narrator.

Mr. Bennet is one of those characters in ***Pride and Prejudice*** who is as capable of satire, including ironic quotation, as Austen's narrator. Mr. Bennet "would not give up Mr. Collins's correspondence for any consideration," for example, because its absurdities are so invaluable to quote and laugh at (364). When Mr. Bennet tells Elizabeth that the conclusion of a letter from Mr. Collins "is only about his dear Charlotte's situation, and his expectation of a young olive-branch" (364), we know Mr. Bennet is mimicking Mr. Collins. That is, the direct speech in which his remark to Elizabeth is reported contains Mr. Bennet's free indirect discourse: in describing Mr. Collins's letter, Mr. Bennet also quotes him. "Dear Charlotte" must be quoted from Mr. Collins's latest letter: Mr. Collins's bride was his "amiable Charlotte" in an earlier letter (128), and Mr. Bennet would not normally address her by her first name. The "young olive-branch," who will succeed Mr. Collins as heir to Mr. Bennet's entailed estate, is of course not described in these words in Mr. Collins's latest letter. But "olive-branch" quotes Mr. Collins's *first* letter to Mr. Bennet, transcribed earlier by the narrator, in which (Mr. Bennet evidently recalls) Mr. Collins offered himself as a matrimonial "olive branch" to make "every possible amends" to one of Mr. Bennet's daughters for inheriting Longbourn (63).[12]

Like Mr. Bennet, Austen's narrator too is skilled at the kind of free indirect discourse that makes words a character has previously said a vehicle for satire.[13] After Mr. Darcy's marriage to Elizabeth, the narrator tells us, Lady Catherine "condescended to wait on them at Pemberley, in spite of that pollution which its woods had re-

ceived" (388). This sentence is a *triple*-voiced utterance, genuinely polyphonic rather than merely dialogic. "Pollution" is not the narrator's opinion, of course; it quotes Lady Catherine "condescending" to visit Elizabeth to express in person her objections to a match between Elizabeth and her nephew: "Heaven and earth!—of what are you thinking? Are the shades of Pemberley to be thus polluted?" (357). "Condescend," in an amusing interweaving of points of view, is the verb Mr. Collins uses again and again to describe Lady Catherine. For example, in another of his letters to Mr. Bennet, Mr. Collins writes:

> "After mentioning the likelihood of [a marriage between Elizabeth and Mr. Darcy] to her ladyship last night, she immediately, with her usual condescension, expressed what she felt on the occasion; when it became apparent, that . . . she would never give her consent to what she termed so disgraceful a match."
>
> (363, and compare an earlier letter, 297)[14]

By Lady Catherine's "usual condescension," Mr. Collins—a sycophantic toady—*thinks* he means something like "graciousness" or "affability to one's inferiors"; *we* understand by it that Lady Catherine is displaying her usual abusive frankness and patronizing officiousness. Mr. Collins intends "condescension" in a positive sense; the narrator co-opts Mr. Collins's word to suggest its pejorative connotations.

Our first two examples of free indirect discourse quote words or phrases we have previously seen used by the characters in question—Mr. Collins's "olive branch," Lady Catherine's "pollution." We can answer whose words, which words, and when and how they were uttered (whether in speech or in thought) because we received all this information the first time the words were quoted. This is one extreme of free indirect discourse, which I call "definite" to reflect our certainty that it quotes "actual" utterances.[15]

If the contrast between the narrator's and a character's idiom and viewpoint is marked enough, however, we can readily identify what may be quotation without first having "heard" it, so to speak, from the character's own lips. We recognize mimicry without having experienced precisely what is mimicked. The devices by which Austen's narrator signals quotation of this type can be quite explicit. Sometimes we "know" by some means that there was an utterance by a particular character in the *fabula,* and a sentence at the appropriate point in the *sjužet* strikes us as translating back into the sort of thing that character would typically say in that situation. I call this kind of free indirect discourse, much the most common kind, "almost definite" free indirect discourse. My final introductory examples are of this not completely but very highly defined variety: that is, we have little doubt who uttered which words when and how (an "indefinite" type of free indirect discourse is discussed below). I do not imply that "almost definite" free indirect discourse is always *immediately* recognizable as possible quotation (though this is often the case) but merely that an argument for reading it as quotation can be very strongly made. The following examples suggest that, even when highly defined, free indirect discourse still retains a quality of distance and ambiguity.

In *Pride and Prejudice,* free indirect discourse is used very deftly to render conventional politeness, sometimes underlining how characters fail to *say* everything we suppose them to *think* and especially amusing when the characters speaking are at some level conscious of their own indirectness, when we see them attempting by indirections to find directions out. Free indirect discourse, which typically hovers between direct and indirect discourse in its linguistic characteristics, and adds a dimension of indirectness all its own by not being attributed, is a particularly appropriate medium to convey such coyness. We get an example of this kind of social fencing when Mrs. Bennet, "amid very complaisant smiles and general encouragement," cautions Mr. Collins against fixing his hopes of finding a mistress for his humble abode in Jane:

> —"As to her *younger* daughters, she could not take upon her to say—she could not positively answer—but she did not *know* of any prepossession;—her *eldest* daughter, she must just mention—she felt it incumbent on her to hint, was likely to be very soon engaged."
>
> (71)

The quotation marks in this passage—Austen did not know that free indirect discourse is supposed to omit them—ensure that we are reading Mrs. Bennet's "actual" reply to Mr. Collins (with the usual grammatical transformations): "As to my *younger* daughters, I cannot take upon me to say—I cannot positively answer," and so on. The syntax—coy hesitations and repetitions quickening toward her evident note of triumph at the end—reproduces Mrs. Bennet's imitation of elegant delicacy as she sets a trap for a second suitor without upsetting the snare in which she hopes an earlier suitor is about to become engaged.

Something the plot demonstrates Mrs. Bennet does well, after all, is to secure husbands for her daughters whether or not the gentlemen are "in want of a wife" (3). One of the novel's vindications of Mrs. Bennet is a scene in which Mr. Bingley, freed to resume his courtship of Jane by Mr. Darcy's tacit approval—and by Mr. Darcy's temporary absence—cooperates with Mrs. Bennet in her maneuvers to invite him to dinner. Mr. Bingley's complicity is also conveyed in almost definite free indirect discourse (but this time without quotation marks):

> Mr. Bingley called again, and alone. His friend had left him that morning for London, but was to return home in ten days' time. He sat with them above an hour, and was in remarkably good spirits. Mrs. Bennet invited him to dine with them; but, with many expressions of concern, he confessed himself engaged elsewhere.
>
> "Next time you call," said she, "I hope we shall be more lucky."
>
> He should be particularly happy at any time, &c. &c.; and if she would give him leave, would take an early opportunity of waiting on them.
>
> "Can you come to-morrow?"
>
> Yes, he had no engagement at all for to-morrow; and her invitation was accepted with alacrity.
>
> (344)

In this passage (the second sentence of which, incidentally, is also free indirect discourse), Mrs. Bennet understands that Mr. Bingley is near the point and that strategy no longer requires indirection; her share of the dialogue is in direct discourse. It is Mr. Bingley—still viewing with "half-laughing alarm" (340) Mr. Darcy's "concurrence" in his wooing (346)—who contrives with Mrs. Bennet for an invitation in that combination of directness and conscious indirection so deftly rendered—in the third paragraph of the passage quoted and in the first clause of its final sentence—in free indirect discourse.[16]

In both these last examples of free indirect discourse, whole sentences (or clauses) of the narrator's report coincide with whole sentences of the character's presumed utterance (except for the "&c. &c." summarizing Mr. Bingley's polite formulae). In our first two examples only a few words attributable to a character were interwoven in the narratorial background. The free indirect discourse which highlights selected words or phrases, and which usually reports speech in Austen's novels, is nearly always satiric because the contrast between the fragments of quoted language and the narratorial background (in particular, the rest of the words in the sentence)—and thus the implied discrepancy between narrator's and character's points of view—is especially marked. What we might call the free indirect discourse of whole sentences, on the other hand, often intersects with sympathetic rather than satiric free indirect discourse. Elizabeth's thought is typically reported in the free indirect discourse of whole sentences, frequently in language indistinguishable from the narrator's idiom, so that any "functional contrast" between narrator's and heroine's viewpoint is minimized.[17] But, in comic situations, whole sentences of a character's idiom stand out against the implied norm of the larger narratorial background. The free indirect discourse of whole sentences can be used to report speech satirically with little danger that readers will long confuse such sentences with narration.[18]

III. Double-voiced Verbs of Speaking, Thinking, and Feeling

The verbs of speaking, thinking, and feeling which introduce and identify sentences of tagged direct or indirect discourse originate with the narrator. But characters may also employ such verbs in their speech or thought (in Mrs. Bennet's speech to Mr. Collins quoted above, for example, "say," "answer," "*know,*" "mention," "felt," and "hint"). Some verbs of speaking that seem to belong equally well to narrator *or* character occur near the end of **Pride and Prejudice.** Here, after Jane and Mr. Bingley are finally engaged, what earlier seemed Mrs. Bennet's "schemes" and "invention" and "ill-judged officiousness" (345-46) have become, in Jane's words, "affectionate solicitude" (347). Now Austen demonstrates that even her favorite heroine—and even her stateliest hero—are not above similar happy contrivances, despite Mr. Darcy's earlier assertion that, especially in courtship, "'Whatever bears affinity to cunning is despicable'" (40). Here Mr. Darcy, after he has proposed to Elizabeth for the second time and been accepted, cooperates in free indirect discourse—like Mr. Bingley—with Mrs. Bennet's newest scheme. To leave Jane and Mr. Bingley alone together, Mrs. Bennet suggests Elizabeth and Kitty show Darcy Oakham Mount because "'It is a nice long walk, and Mr. Darcy has never seen the view.'" Elizabeth, who has not yet told her mother of her engagement, can "hardly help laughing at so convenient a proposal" (374) and "silently consent[s]" (375):

> Kitty owned that she had rather stay at home. Darcy professed a great curiosity to see the view from the Mount.

(374-75)

The self-consciousness of Mr. Darcy "profess[ing] a great curiosity to see the view" is heightened by a device which, once we remark it, we see constantly recurring in Austen's novels. I have suggested that Mr. Darcy's reply is free indirect speech although it may initially appear to be tagged. For instance, one could argue that Mr. Darcy's reply might have looked like this, rendered in tagged direct speech: "I have a great curiosity to see the view," Darcy professed. A rendering in tagged indirect speech might then have looked like this: Darcy professed that he had a great curiosity to see the view. Or, since indirect discourse can summarize any part of the reported clause as well as omit "that": Darcy professed a great curiosity to see the view. This is exactly the wording of the novel. Since *to profess* can mean *to make a pretense of,* we might infer that Mr. Darcy's duplicity is being announced by the narrator's choice of inquit. But *to profess* is also *to declare publicly,* and we might suppose that what Mr. Darcy "actually" said (in some *fabula* we may hypothesize behind Austen's *sjužet*) was, intending *to profess* in the sense of avowal: "I profess—or, I profess that I have—a great curiosity to see the view." The wording in the novel would then be free indirect discourse, but there is in fact no way to tell for certain whether we have before us an example of free or tagged indirect speech.

(Similarly, in the *fabula* we hypothesize behind Austen's *sjužet,* perhaps Kitty owned, "I had rather stay at home." But Kitty may equally well have *said,* "I *own* that I had rather stay at home.") Mr. Darcy's "profess" seems deliberately chosen to tease us into wondering how far his "anxious circumspection" (347) has bent in taking advantage of Mrs. Bennet's scheme for leaving Jane and Mr. Bingley alone together to contrive some privacy for Elizabeth and himself.

Such a verb as Mr. Darcy's "profess" or Kitty's "own," which might either be part of the narrator's inquit introducing tagged indirect discourse (that is, it originates with the narrator, in the *sjužet*) but which could equally well render part of the character's "actual" discourse (that is, it originates with a character, in the *fabula*), I call a "double-voiced verb of speaking." And I call the mode of discourse that results from using such verbs, though it may seem equidistant between tagged and free indirect discourse, "free indirect discourse with double-voiced verbs of speaking."

I classify sentences with double-voiced verbs as free rather than tagged because the double-voiced verb leaves it ambiguous whether narrator or character is responsible for the sentence. We cannot tell, that is, whether the above example is the narrator's summary of Mr. Darcy's statement, with all the objective endorsement—or perhaps the satiric coloration—this may imply, or whether it constitutes Mr. Darcy's own words, which, we presume, are neither so objective nor so satiric. Although a strong argument can often be made for reading sentences of free indirect discourse with double-voiced verbs as character's utterance, such an interpretation is not always immediate. Moreover, I shall suggest in a moment, with an example of Mr. Collins's discourse, that double-voiced verbs occur with differing degrees of probability of belonging to character or narrator: some double-voiced verbs are almost certainly the character's but just possibly the narrator's, some seem evenly balanced between the two possibilities, and some seem far more likely to belong to narrator than character. Thus the sentences such verbs introduce hover variously between narrator's and character's account, which justifies calling them "free" although they contain what looks like an inquit. Although a double-voiced verb is a *kind* of attribution, it only *associates* a sentence with a particular character but does not tell us whether to *attribute* it to him or her. Such ambiguity typifies free indirect discourse. Classifying these sentences as variations on free indirect discourse means that a simpler initial definition of free indirect discourse suffices.

Having once identified this device in Austen's novels, we see not only how often she uses it but also how much more "dramatized" her narratives become by the frequent *possibility* that what looks like narration, that is, an inquit, could instead be reported discourse. Again, such a phrase need not positively *be* reported discourse, according to my definition; indeed we can never "know" whether a double-voiced verb comes from character and *fabula* or narrator and *sjužet*. It need only sound as though it *could* be quotation.[19] By conflating inquit with possible reported discourse, double-voiced verbs of speaking, thinking, and feeling combine concision with liveliness. They also increase the flexibility of Austen's narratives by making transitions between passages of dialogue and narration—that is, between scene and summary—smoother because more gradual.

Because double-voiced verbs are sometimes verbs of thinking or feeling rather than verbs of speaking, sentences which first looked like the narrator's indirect report of a character's thoughts or feelings can seem on closer inspection to be free indirect discourse. (Double-voiced verbs must be *either* verbs of speaking, thinking, or feeling since they must be readable as the verb in an inquit.) An example of a double-voiced verb of feeling occurs in an exchange between Elizabeth and Mr. Darcy during the walk on which Mr. Darcy proposes a second time and is accepted:

> "What could [have] become of Mr. Bingley and Jane!" was a wonder which introduced the discussion of *their* affairs. Mr. Darcy was delighted with their engagement; his friend had given him the earliest information of it.
>
> "I must ask whether you were surprised?" said Elizabeth.
>
> (370; Austen's emphasis)[20]

The exclamation which begins this passage is another example of free indirect discourse with quotation marks. Although it is not explicitly attributed to her, it must render Elizabeth's speech (Mr. Darcy would have wondered about "Bingley and Miss Bennet"). We understand that what Elizabeth said was, "What *can* have become . . . ?" The second sentence could begin as tagged indirect thought, the narrator relating how Mr. Darcy feels about Bingley's engagement and thus implying what Mr. Darcy contributes to the ensuing "discussion." But it is more likely a free indirect report of Mr. Darcy's actual speech. That is, what resembles internal focalization on Mr. Darcy is more probably externally focalized,[21] the narrator's report of a speech in which Mr. Darcy partly anticipates Elizabeth's next question by reaffirming his direction of Mr. Bingley's affairs: "I am delighted with their engagement; my friend gave me the earliest information of it." Here a double-voiced verb *phrase*—"was delighted"—smooths a transition, from narration ("the discussion of *their* affairs") to dialogue. Note, however, that the opening exchanges of this dialogue have apparently already been rendered in free indirect discourse, demonstrating how flexibly Austen uses this narrative mode. I should again

emphasize that double-voiced verbs of thinking or feeling can introduce sentences that resemble tagged indirect *thought* but may render *speech*—if the character in question is speaking of his or her thoughts or feelings.

The formality of language in Austen's day as compared with our own multiplies the opportunities for free indirect discourse with double-voiced verbs of speaking, thinking, and feeling because conventional politeness affords a rich choice of potentially double-voiced verbs. In the following passage, for example, the Miss Bennets make an acquaintance:

> Mr. Denny addressed them directly, and entreated permission to introduce his friend, Mr. Wickham, who had returned with him the day before from town, and he was happy to say had accepted a commission in their corps. This was exactly as it should be; for the young man wanted only regimentals to make him completely charming.
>
> (72)

The opening sentence of this passage, if we omit "addressed them directly," is free indirect discourse with double-voiced verbs of speaking and feeling ("entreated" and "was happy to say"). It may well reproduce Mr. Denny's *ipsissima verba,* subject only to the usual transformational rules. Certainly the words of the sentence would be characteristic of Mr. Denny, and his "direct" "address" is reported by them. We cannot be *completely* certain that what Mr. Denny "really" said was, "I entreat permission to introduce my friend . . . who . . . I am happy to say has . . . ," but this is still an instance of what I called "almost definite" free indirect discourse.

The last sentence of the passage quoted above may also be free indirect discourse, however, or at least narration highly colored by a perspective foreign to the narrator's (and therefore constituting the narrator's ironic comment on that foreign perspective): it represents what the younger Bennet sisters *might* say to themselves privately, or perhaps *do* say to each other later—though not, presumably, what even Lydia would be bold enough actually *to* say to Mr. Wickham's face. That is, though the language and the sentiments are certainly characteristic of Kitty and Lydia, we cannot know whether the sentence renders an actual utterance of theirs or only reports the sort of thing they *would* say or think. Therefore, I call this narrative mode "indefinite" free indirect discourse because, although we can correctly identify the character to associate it with in the *sjužet* where it appears, its status as discourse in the *fabula* is uncertain. We can be almost entirely confident Kitty and Lydia have not exposed themselves by actually speaking this sentence, at least not in this scene. But neither can we be entirely certain that they think it.[22]

Indefinite free indirect discourse, which often hovers between speech and thought in this way, resembles in its ambiguity, but in another sense reverses, free indirect discourse with double-voiced verbs of speaking, thinking, and feeling. Indefinite free indirect discourse possibly quotes a character but may really be the responsibility of the narrator, while a typical example of free indirect discourse with double-voiced verbs looks like the narrator's tagged indirect report of a character's speech or thought but is more probably the character's own account of him- or herself.

The free indirect discourse reporting Mr. Denny's speech introducing Wickham is, however, perfectly straightforward: sympathetic rather than satiric. Interpreting this sentence as free indirect discourse (that is, reading its double-voiced verbs as belonging to Mr. Denny) does not clash with interpreting it as tagged indirect discourse (that is, reading the double-voiced verbs as the narrator's). Mr. Denny's politeness, his "entreat-[ing] permission" to perform an action and his being "happy" to be able to say something, we accept as plausible language for a character of Austen's day and Mr. Denny's rank. If he strikes a modern reader as wordy and overly formal, there are characters in *Pride and Prejudice* who are *genuinely* pompous and verbose—verbose, that is, according to the novel's norms. As with many of the narrative devices in *Pride and Prejudice,* double-voiced verbs of speaking, thinking, and feeling are worth special scrutiny in their satiric mode, where they suggest the origins and workings of both Austen's satire and her didacticism. If formality is a rich source of double-voiced verbs, and wordy formality even richer, we can predict that Mr. Collins's discourse will prove a gold mine of examples.

Mr. Collins's discourse is so larded with verbs of speaking and, especially, thinking, and the verbs selected are so characteristic of his diction rather than the narrator's, that we cannot, however, long mistake his free indirect discourse for tagged indirect speech or thought. The device of double-voiced verbs emphasizes an aspect of his personal style. Here is a brief sample of Mr. Collins's wordy formality when meeting Mrs. Philips:

> She received him with her very best politeness, which he returned with as much more, apologizing for his intrusion, without any previous acquaintance with her, which he could not help flattering himself however might be justified by his relationship to the young ladies who introduced him to her notice. Mrs. Philips was quite awed by such an excess of good breeding.
>
> (73)

The verbs of speaking and thinking associated with Mr. Collins in this passage could translate directly, we feel, into his actual discourse: "I apologize, Madame, for my intrusion, without any previous acquaintance with you, which I cannot help flattering myself, however, may be justified by. . . ." Because The verbs of speaking and thinking associated with Mr. Collins in this passage could translate directly, we feel, into his actual discourse: "I apologize, Madame, for my intrusion, without any previous acquaintance with you, which I cannot help flattering myself, however, may be justified by. . . ." Because "apologizing for his intrusion" *could* be tagged rather than free indirect speech, "apologizing" is indeed a double-voiced verb of speaking. But "flattering himself" is double-voiced only on first inspection. It is just barely possible that a sentence beginning "Mr. Collins could not help flattering himself that . . ." should be read as tagged indirect thought. But I have just suggested that a sentence which looks like Mr. Darcy's thought more probably renders his speech. We may begin to suspect that internal focalization through characters other than the heroine—even the hero—is rarer in Austen's novels than "first impressions" suggest since it so often conflates in this way with reported speech. Moreover, everything we know about Mr. Collins and his usual ecstasies of humility suggests that "flattering himself" is transformed from his actual speech ("actual" in the *fabula* we postulate). Indeed, Mr. Collins "flatter[s] himself" every time he opens his mouth. Even when he is "apologizing for his intrusion," or humbly attributing his flattering reception to his relationship with someone else (here the Bennet sisters, usually Lady Catherine de Bourgh, *occasionally* the Divinity), he gratifies his vanity by drawing attention to his humility.

Mr. Collins's wordiness consistently draws attention to himself, in fact. Another example of his attention-getting speech, demonstrating that verbs can be double-voiced in varying degrees, occurs as Mr. Collins escorts his cousins home from a second visit to Mrs. Philips:

> Mr. Collins, in describing the civility of Mr. and Mrs. Philips, protesting that he did not in the least regard his losses at whist, enumerating all the dishes at supper, and repeatedly fearing that he crouded [sic] his cousins, had more to say than he could well manage before the carriage stopped at Longbourn House.
>
> (84)

An amusing implication of this passage is that Mr. Collins sees praising and apologizing and entertaining his cousins as duties to "manage." But which of the four gerunds describing his duties in this passage might belong to both narrator and character, thus deserving to be called "double-voiced"? "Describing" is clearly not double-voiced at all; it can belong only to the narrator and not to Mr. Collins's discourse. The phrase it introduces is therefore tagged indirect speech, and very indirect at that (note, though, that Mr. Collins needlessly describes something flattering to himself to those who were there to observe it). "Protesting," on the other hand, might be double-voiced, that is, part of Mr. Collins's discourse ("I protest, my dear Miss Bennet, that I do not in the least regard . . ."). Though the verb may seem more likely to belong to narrator than character, this phrase is possibly free indirect discourse (Mr. Collins protests too much, however). "Enumerating" is another single-voiced verb: the phrase it introduces is the narrator reporting through the medium of tagged indirect speech that Mr. Collins talked about food (again a perfectly unnecessary "enumeration," given his audience, but food is another of his obsessions). "Fearing," finally, is unmistakably part of Mr. Collins's actual discourse (therefore he "repeatedly" fears). "Fearing" is thus near the other end of the double-voiced spectrum, belonging entirely to the character and not at all (or only as her joke) to the narrator.

"Fearing," however, is typical of Mr. Collins "repeatedly" drawing attention to himself and to how humble he is; that the main clause of his presumed utterance has himself and his mental condition for its topic ("I fear that . . .") rather than his cousins' physical condition (". . . that I crowd my cousins") testifies to his self-absorption. To "fear" something is not to exert oneself to avoid it. In particular, though we cannot "know" that Mr. Collins's actual utterance (in the *fabula*) was "I fear that I crowd my cousins," an utterance which fails to address his cousins—and the problem—directly, nonetheless, we presume (because free indirect discourse preserves questions) that his original utterance was *not* a question ("Am I crowding my cousins?" or perhaps, repeatedly, "Am I crowding you?"). A question would have implied a promise to rectify the situation, given an affirmative reply. Mr. Collins's free indirect discourse implies at most a *wish* to rectify the situation. Mr. Collins is all humility in the wish he expresses, all self-absorption in his actual behavior.

A brief recapitulation may be helpful here. The subject of double-voiced verbs of speaking, thinking, and feeling has led us to begin considering how much of Austen's characterization and comment is conveyed by her telling choice of verbs and verbals of speaking, thinking, and feeling, whether such verbs occur in the actual discourse of a character, whether they form the narrator's tag introducing direct or indirect discourse, or whether they are the double-voiced verbs we have been examining in passages of free indirect discourse. I suggested above that absence of attribution is the essential feature of free indirect discourse: that is, we must look for markers other than inquits to be sure we are not reading the narrator's language and viewpoint. It is tempting to speculate that double-voiced verbs are frequent in Austen's novels, that is, that they apparently emerge as a literary device at about the time that free indirect discourse emerges into prominence (especially the free indirect discourse reporting whole sentences), because they continue to supply, though in a more dramatized form, the inquits that free indirect discourse omits.

Free indirect discourse with double-voiced verbs of speaking, thinking, and feeling has a special dimension of ambiguity and satire, however. This mode of discourse may first resemble the narrator's objective account of a character but may equally appear to be the character's subjective account of himself. The sentence of Mr. Collins's presumptive discourse that we have been examining ("I fear that I crowd my cousins") is as typical of Austen's method of commenting by means of verbs of speaking, thinking, and feeling as it is of Mr. Collins's style. Mr. Collins's discourse is full of such apparently superfluous introductory tags ("I fear that"), which subordinate the ostensible matter of his sentences to his own state of mind and whose verbs are then available to become double-voiced. To convince ourselves how easy it would be to turn Mr. Collins's speech into this sort of free indirect discourse, a narrative mode which might almost have been invented with him in mind, we need only look at an example of his speech which the novel renders in tagged *direct* discourse. In the following passage—both the first part in free indirect speech (embedded in indirect thought describing Elizabeth's "surprise")[23] and the second part in direct speech—the verbs and verbals by which Mr. Collins refers to his own speech and thought are underlined:

> [Elizabeth] was rather surprised to find that [Mr. Collins] *entertained no scruple whatever on that head* [accepting Mr. Bingley's invitation to the Netherfield ball], and *was very far from dreading* a rebuke either from the Archbishop, or Lady Catherine de Bourgh, by *venturing* to dance.
>
> "I *am by no means of opinion*, I *assure* you," said he, "that a ball of this kind, given by a young man of character, to respectable people, can have any evil tendency; and I *am so far from objecting* to dancing myself, that I *shall hope to be honoured* with the hands of all my fair cousins in the course of the evening, and I *take this opportunity* of *soliciting* yours, Miss Elizabeth, for the two first dances especially,—a *preference* which I *trust* my cousin Jane will attribute to the right cause, and not to any *disrespect* for her."
>
> (87)

As in our previous example, where we inferred what Mr. Collins "actually" said from the rendering of his speech in free indirect discourse, in the latter part of this passage too, where we see his speech directly, we find a profusion of superfluous verb phrases purporting to express his precise state of mind. Of the eight clauses of his speech rendered in direct discourse, we note that "I" is the subject of six, including every one of the independent clauses. Other nouns and pronouns are consequently relegated to relatively subordinate syntactic roles: Mr. Collins's "fair cousins" are introduced by the synecdochal "hands," for example, and "my cousin Jane," who is actually the subject of her own dependent clause, appears to be the object of Mr. Collins's interpolated "I trust" and must give precedence to his "preference." We note also Mr. Collins's pedantic penchant for specifying to his listeners what he takes to be the exact degree to which he holds each of his opinions: "by no means of opinion" and "so far from objecting," for example, and, from the first part of his reply to Elizabeth rendered in free indirect discourse, "no scruple whatever on that head" (with its reminder of sermon-making) and "very far from dreading." Though such phrases promise information, they convey very little, other than Mr. Collins's endless self-absorption and the suspicion that he entertains no genuine self-examination on *any* head.

Let us examine one more example of Mr. Collins's direct discourse, again noting the many excuses Mr. Collins finds for referring to himself, but this time taking the liberty of editing his speech to see by one more means how much of his discourse is apparently superfluous:

> "If I," said Mr. Collins, "were so fortunate as to be able to sing [If I were able to sing], I should have great pleasure, I am sure, in obliging the company with an air [I should oblige the company with an air]; for I consider music as [for music is] a very innocent diversion, and perfectly compatible with the profession of a clergyman.—I do not mean however to assert that we can be justified in devoting too much of our time to music [We cannot, however, devote too much of our time to music], for there are certainly other things to be attended to. The rector of a parish has much to do."
>
> (101)

Since Mr. Collins begins this speech speculating aloud about his *hypothetical* ("If . . .") state of mind (". . . I"), a subject which can have little interest for his audience, his entire speech seems superfluous. We may begin to suspect that the purpose of Mr. Collins's discourse is very frequently to pronounce his own opinion, even when he is not asked for it, even when, as here, he was only one among "Others of the party . . . applied to" to entertain the company at the Netherfield ball (101). Mr. Collins's long and inappropriate homily on music and clerical duties becomes, ironically, his contribution to the entertainment of the assembled party—or at least to that of the satirical Mr. Bennet.

In Mr. Collins's readiness to volunteer his opinion, we see an imitation of Lady Catherine de Bourgh which may be the sincerest form of his flattery for his noble patroness. Not only does he always defer to Lady Catherine's opinions, but, as a snob who himself fills a position of authority, he lays down the law as much as she does, she from the eminence of her social and economic position, he from his clerical one. Mr. Collins's opinions are that clergymen may dance and sing, we have seen, and also that they must marry. Lady Catherine is Mr. Collins's authority on all these questions, especially the last: "Twice has she condescended to give

me her opinion (unasked too!) on this subject" (105). Like his patroness, Mr. Collins not only delights to give his opinion—"unasked too!"—he also, we have seen, habitually *announces* that he is giving an opinion: "I am by no means of opinion, I assure you . . ."; "I consider . . ."; "I do not mean however to assert. . . ." The effect is to draw attention to the pronouncement rather than to what his opinion is or how it was arrived at. The phrases Mr. Collins uses convey the *illusion* of someone who weighs his thoughts and arrives at judgments. Perhaps his studies at "one of the universities" (70) have taught him to adopt this tone. But the verbs of speaking and thinking associated with Mr. Collins all originate in his discourse and not with the narrator. Reported discourse always renders Mr. Collins's speech, never his thought. That is, Mr. Collins evidently renders his *own* thought (such as it is) in his speech, and we quickly learn to question the reliability of his report.

With Mr. Collins, free indirect discourse with double-voiced verbs of thinking consistently masquerades as *thought* but almost certainly renders *speech*. However we hypothesize a reader's probable response to such sentences—whether, for example, readers *first* interpret them as tagged indirect thought and only later as free indirect speech—in whatever order these two interpretations arise, and whatever probability we assign to each, the important points are, first, that the ambiguity remains undecidable, and, second, that the two interpretations clash satirically. In studying the consciousnesses created and the comments made on them in Austen's novels, we must also ask who renders each consciousness. In contrast to Mr. Collins's reporting his own consciousness, the narrator devotes many passages to *sharing* with Elizabeth the rendition of her thought—blending tagged indirect thought with the free indirect thought of whole sentences, often with double-voiced verbs—and we interpret such passages as sympathetic rather than satiric. The narrator honors Elizabeth, we feel, both by helping to report her thought and by trusting Elizabeth to articulate her *own* thought *in the form of thought*.

The verbs of speaking, thinking, and feeling used to render Elizabeth's thought suggest active engagement in ongoing reflection, not, as with Mr. Collins, empty talk about thought that never occurred. Mr. Collins's obsession with his own opinions makes him a burlesque, because extreme, version of the efforts at self-knowledge we admire in Elizabeth. Though he has no genuine opinions of his own, his compulsion to express his borrowed opinions suggests a self-absorption and opinion-atedness—suggests pride and prejudice, in short, rather than judgment and true self-awareness—which make Mr. Collins also Elizabeth's extreme *opposite* in the novel, a burlesque because a *false* version of the corrected judgment Elizabeth comes to represent.

IV. Characterization and Comment by Verbs of Speaking, Thinking, and Feeling

I have described in some detail in the case of Mr. Collins how Austen makes comic use of verbs of consciousness to characterize, both verbs from the character's own discourse and verbs chosen by Austen's narrator to report that discourse. To confirm that this kind of implied comment is frequently and deftly employed by Austen, we can briefly examine her treatment of several of the novel's other characters to see what we can learn about the quality of their thought from the verbs of speaking, thinking, and feeling associated with them, and from whether those verbs are double-voiced.

We remember that only Mary, of all the Bennet sisters, "might have been prevailed upon to accept" a proposal from Mr. Collins (124). Although she believes he should be "encouraged to read and improve himself by such an example as hers," she nonetheless appreciates his ponderous worth: "there was a solidity in his reflections which often struck her" (124). Her unexpected interest in the prospect of a ball at Netherfield resembles Mr. Collins's unexpected willingness to dance:

> [E]ven Mary could assure her family that she had no disinclination for it.
>
> ". . . I think it no sacrifice to join occasionally in evening engagements. Society has claims on us all; and I profess myself one of those who consider intervals of recreation and amusement as desirable for everybody."
>
> (87)

Like Mr. Collins, Mary "can assure" and "has no disinclination for" (double-voiced verb phrases), "thinks," "professes herself," and "considers." Cohn's two categories of quotation (see Note 9)—quoting satirically and quoting sympathetically—find their extremes in Mr. Bennet as contrasted with Mary and Mr. Collins. Mr. Bennet quotes the novel's other characters satirically. Mary, though we never learn from precisely which "great books" she laboriously "makes extracts" (7), cites her reading approvingly, as Mr. Collins echoes Lady Catherine, in order to moralize. If Mr. Bennet represents delight without instruction—two elements Austen's novels aim to *combine*—Mary and Mr. Collins represent instruction without delight. Mary's "observations of threadbare morality" (60) provide another burlesque—that is, an extreme (since unmediated by delight) and therefore a *false* version—of what Hough calls Austen's "language of judgement" (218).[24]

The verbs associated with Mary's mother, on the other hand, suggest an absence rather than a parody of judgment. Double-voiced verbs of *feeling* rather than thought are prominent in the report of her discourse. Incapable of rational reflection, Mrs. Bennet indulges in imaginings and fears:

> Mrs. Bennet was quite disconcerted. She could not imagine what business [Mr. Bingley] could have in town so soon after his arrival in Hertfordshire; and she began to fear that he might be always flying about from one place to another, and never settled at Netherfield as he ought to be. Lady Lucas quieted her fears a little by starting the idea of his being gone to London only to get a large party for the ball.
>
> (9-10)

Mrs. Bennet's fears are noisy ones, "quieted" by Lady Lucas. The second sentence of this passage, in other words, is not tagged indirect thought but free indirect *speech*, with double-voiced verbs of feeling and of not-quite-thinking ("fear" and "imagine"). Like Mr. Collins, whose speech implies—unreliably—that he thinks, Mrs. Bennet wrongly attributes to herself genuine hopes and fears. That she is "disconcerted" (perhaps another double-voiced verb) by Mr. Bingley's sudden departure and cannot "imagine" any rational explanation for such odd behavior recalls Stuart Tave's dictum that "Characters in Jane Austen who find things odd are usually simple-minded types" (44). Mrs. Bennet is apparently such a simple-minded character, who speaks—and "imagines" and "fears"—rather than thinks.

Mrs. Bennet's discourse, like Lady Bertram's letters recounting her son Tom's illness in *Mansfield Park,* is a "medley of trusts, hopes, and fears, all following and producing each other at hap-hazard . . . a sort of playing at being frightened" (*MP* 427), a stylistic description whose verbals suggest Austen was fully conscious of using verbs of thinking and feeling in discourse to define character and establish moral worth. As Mr. Collins burlesques Elizabeth's thoughtfulness, Mrs. Bennet's verbs are a moral shorthand contrasting her burlesque and self-attributed romantic susceptibility with Jane's genuine sensibility, and with Jane's steadfast efforts to regulate it.[25] However, though Mrs. Bennet lacks Elizabeth's judgment as well as Jane's sensibility, she sometimes has common sense: there *is* something odd about Mr. Bingley's second and apparently permanent departure from Netherfield, and Mrs. Bennet's comfortable prediction "that Mr. Bingley must be down again in the summer" and her faith in romance and in Jane's good looks are vindicated when Mr. Bingley returns to Netherfield in September.

Examining the verbs of speaking, thinking, and feeling associated with Mrs. Bennet, we see that, like Mr. Collins with his ostensible "thought," it is Mrs. Bennet, not the narrator, who reports her "feelings." Nevertheless, Mrs. Bennet is not the character in *Pride and Prejudice* lowest on the scale of true self-awareness. If, in our analysis of verbs of speaking, thinking, and feeling, Mrs. Bennet represents lack of judgment, her youngest daughter Lydia suggests a nearly total absence of *thought.* What characterizes Lydia is "high *animal* spirits, and a sort of *natural* self-consequence" (45; emphasis added), a "restless ecstacy" (230) and a "clamorous happiness" (235) that burlesque Elizabeth's sprightliness. And what typifies the narrator's depiction of Lydia is the extreme of external focalization: only her physical behavior and her speech are reported, usually in direct discourse, so, appropriately, double-voiced verbs cannot occur. The verbs that characterize Lydia have in any case nothing to do with judgment or sensibility; they are "talking" and, especially, "laughing":

> Lydia, in a voice rather louder than any other person's, was enumerating the various pleasures of the morning to any body who would hear her.
>
> "Oh, Mary," said she, "I wish you had gone with us, for we had such fun! . . . And then when we came away it was such fun! . . . I was ready to die of laughter. And then we were so merry all the way home! we talked and laughed so loud, that any body might have heard us ten miles off!"
>
> (222)

We might be surprised to stumble upon a sustained internally focalized view of Lydia in the course of the novel, but in fact there is just one. In the following passage, Lydia's anticipation of a visit to Brighton is described by the narrator, but still without double-voiced verbs of thinking or feeling because Lydia never articulates her own inner life:

> In Lydia's imagination, a visit to Brighton comprised every possibility of earthly happiness. She saw with the creative eye of fancy, the streets of that gay bathing place covered with officers. She saw herself the object of attention, to tens and to scores of them at present unknown. She saw all the glories of the camp; its tents stretched forth in beauteous uniformity of lines, crowded with the young and the gay, and dazzling with scarlet; and to complete the view, she saw herself seated beneath a tent, tenderly flirting with at least six officers at once.
>
> (232)

Such are the verbs defining Lydia's inner life: "She saw. . . . She saw. . . . She saw . . . ; and . . . she saw. . . ." What Lydia *sees* are large numbers of indistinguishable objects: a network of streets, tens and scores of officers, lines of tents, crowds of the young and gay in dazzling scarlet—all grouped in constellations radiating outwards from herself. "[B]eauteous uniformity" reminds us that Wickham "wanted only regimentals to make him completely charming" in Kitty's and Lydia's eyes (72). The attraction of uniforms suggests that—like men who when young are "captivated by youth and beauty, and that appearance of good humour, which youth and beauty generally give" (236; Colonel Forster and, alas, Mr. Bennet are two examples in the novel)—young women who chase officers are attracted only by what they *see* and are unlikely to dis-

criminate. Indeed, "never to be without partners" is all Lydia has "yet learnt to care for at a ball" (12), and Wickham is "by no means the only partner who could satisfy" her (87)—for dancing or for marriage.

Lydia's heedlessness, in thought and feeling, contrasts with Elizabeth's growing discrimination. While Lydia is daydreaming of breaking hearts in Brighton, Elizabeth has learned to judge the merits of Mr. Darcy and Lydia's worldly "angel" (291). To appreciate fully the paucity of verbs with which Lydia's inner life is rendered, we can contrast a passage two short paragraphs after Lydia's fantasy of Brighton, in which Elizabeth anticipates meeting Wickham for the last time before his regiment is transferred:

> Having been frequently in company with him since her return [from Hunsford], agitation was pretty well over; the agitations of former partiality entirely so. She had even learnt to detect, in the very gentleness which had first delighted her, an affectation and a sameness to disgust and weary. In his present behaviour to herself, moreover, she had a fresh source of displeasure, for the inclination he soon testified of renewing those attentions which had marked the early part of their acquaintance, could only serve, after what had since passed, to provoke her. She lost all concern for him in finding herself thus selected as the object of such idle and frivolous gallantry; and while she steadily repressed it, could not but feel the reproof contained in his believing, that however long, and for whatever cause, his attentions had been withdrawn, her vanity would be gratified and her preference secured at any time by their renewal.
>
> (233)

Contrasting with Lydia's vanity and undiscriminating flirtatiousness two paragraphs earlier is Elizabeth's realization that permitting Wickham's gallantry has deserved "reproof." Instead of passively daydreaming of attention, here—"in finding herself thus selected as the object of" it—Elizabeth "steadily represse[s] it." Without analyzing this passage in detail, we can note its rich variety of sentence structures, reflecting a discrimination that can recall gentleness which formerly delighted but now seems "an affectation and sameness" and gallantry which used to gratify but now appears "idle and frivolous." To make the contrast with Lydia as clear as possible, however, one need only note the many verbs of thinking and feeling either stated or implied in this passage and how many of them connote mental activity rather than passivity: Elizabeth is no longer agitated, no longer partial; she has learned to detect; she is no longer delighted; she is disgusted and wearied and has a fresh source of displeasure; Wickham's behavior testifies to her, and she had earlier marked it; now she is provoked; she loses all concern; she finds herself selected; she steadily represses; she cannot but feel the reproof; she infers what Wickham believes; her vanity is no longer gratified, and her preference not secured. We sense that narrator and character share responsibility for this passage, even though—in fact especially *because*—it is primarily tagged rather than free indirect discourse and its verbs are primarily single-voiced: the narrator compliments Elizabeth by choosing this rich variety of verbs and sentence structures to report her thought processes.

In an earlier, even more instructive passage, a transition is made to dialogue from Elizabeth's thoughts (rendered by the narrator in a very typical alteration between free and tagged indirect thought):

> It was generally evident whenever [Jane and Mr. Bingley] met, that he *did* admire her; and to *her* [Elizabeth] it was equally evident that Jane was yielding to the preference which she had begun to entertain for him from the first, and was in a way to be very much in love; but [Elizabeth] considered with pleasure that it was not likely to be discovered by the world in general, since Jane united with great strength of feeling, a composure of temper and a uniform cheerfulness of manner, which would guard her from the suspicions of the impertinent. She mentioned this to her friend Miss Lucas.

> "It may perhaps be pleasant," replied Charlotte, "to be able to impose on the public in such a case; but it is sometimes a disadvantage to be so very guarded."

> (21)

The substance of what Elizabeth "mention[s] . . . to her friend" is clear to us here because it has already been rendered in the form of Elizabeth's thoughts. But the economy of this transition from summary to scene is worth remarking. Moshe Ron notes that we do not infer that a single act or event is referred to when an instance of "knowing" is recounted in a narrative, though we do hypothesize such a single event for "perceiving" or "becoming known" (Ron 24). The above passage appears to open with a summary of knowledge Elizabeth has gained during several weeks of observing "the world in general" observing Mr. Bingley and Jane: "It was generally evident whenever they met, that. . . ." The second clause ("to *her* it was equally evident that . . .") may contain a double-voiced verb of thinking ("to *me* it is evident that . . .") and might thus be free indirect discourse (as might even the first clause): this is what a highly articulate character like Elizabeth could well say to herself in some single moment of thinking about Mr. Bingley and Jane. By the middle of the passage, we feel even surer that a specific moment of Elizabeth knowing that she knows is being evoked: although "She considered with pleasure" could describe repeated action ("Whenever she considered it, she felt pleasure"), it more probably describes a single though unspecified moment of reflection. Heroines often pause for such moments of reflection in Austen's novels.

Note, however, that the moment in which Elizabeth communicates those reflections to her friend, though clearly a single moment, is no more specified in time

and place than our hypothetical moment of reflection. What interests Austen, in other words, is what Elizabeth thinks and says about Jane's prudence and what Charlotte replies about policy, not whether they think and say these things while walking in the shrubbery after drinking tea, nor whether Charlotte is blonde and Elizabeth brunette. Whatever is not thought or speech is excised from Austen's narrative here. Thus, the moment of thought and the moment of speech are given the same ontological status in this passage—as perhaps thought and speech have nearly the same status for Austen in general. The transition also suggests that thought and speech are nearly equivalent to her heroines. Preoccupied with her thoughts, Elizabeth takes an early opportunity—no further specification of that moment is necessary—to speak them to her friend.

The transition further implies that Elizabeth will articulate her thoughts accurately in speaking them to Charlotte. It guarantees this by its assumption that to articulate Elizabeth's *spoken* words is unnecessary since the words she *thought* are already known. The highly articulated rendition of Elizabeth's consciousness—for which Elizabeth and the narrator share responsibility—can stand for Elizabeth's later account of her own thought to Charlotte, an utterance which is described but not otherwise rendered by "She mentioned this to her friend." Elizabeth's thought is already—at the level of thought—so highly articulated that Elizabeth is able to give the same articulate account of it to Charlotte as she gives to herself and as the narrator gives to us.

We are guaranteed not only that Elizabeth accurately articulates her own thoughts, however: we are also guaranteed that the narrator reports them accurately and sympathetically rather than satirically. We are guaranteed, in other words, that the blend of tagged and free indirect discourse, with double-voiced verbs, in which Elizabeth's thought is reported renders not merely the substance of her thought plus occasional snatches of language floating to the surface of her mind but also reflects how verbal Elizabeth's consciousness is. Chatman ("Narrative Transmission" 238) and Cohn (*Transparent Minds* 11) suggest that reported thought can seldom seem as mimetic as reported speech since it must often articulate what was originally unarticulated. Austen avoids this problem in the case of her heroines by the kind of thought she assigns them. She clearly views articulated consciousness as the highest form of thought, and she intends the above passage to render Elizabeth's thought as belonging to that highest kind.

At one point in ***Pride and Prejudice,*** Austen's narrator divides the circle of characters at Longbourn into "such as did think" and "such as did not" (348). With the above passages describing Elizabeth's thought before us, and with Lydia fresh in our minds as another extreme contrast to Elizabeth, we have a good idea of the range of consciousnesses Austen creates and how she comments on them by means of verbs of speaking, thinking, and feeling. We have also discovered, by close attention to double-voiced verbs, which consciousnesses are articulate and self-aware enough so that narrator and character share responsibility for rendering the character's thought *as thought,* or whether a character renders, in speaking, his or her own thoughts or feelings without the narrator's cooperation and endorsement.[26]

Notes

1. For evidence that the product of the Bakhtin circle published as V. N. Volosinov's *Marxism and the Philosophy of Language* was written substantially by M. M. Bakhtin, see Wehrle ix-xii. Bakhtin's "double-voiced utterances" and my own "double-voiced verbs" are convenient locutions in the context in which I shall use them but are not intended to exclude the possibility of *multi*-voicedness nor to ignore Bakhtin's interest in polyphony in the novel.

2. Since the following essay adheres to the double-voiced (and sometimes multi-voiced) interpretation of sentences of indirectly reported discourse, it opposes Banfield's "1 EXPRESSION/1 SELF" theory. Banfield insists that all expressive or evaluative elements in a sentence *must* originate with a single speaker or "SELF"—implying that narrators or characters cannot quote evaluative language and convey their own evaluation in the same sentence. I mention below other points of disagreement with Banfield. Banfield does, however, note that discourse parentheticals (roughly what I call inquits) can form part of represented speech or thought (what I call free indirect discourse) (Banfield 84). In this case, they might contain what I call double-voiced verbs. But Banfield's theory prevents her from reading such parentheticals as belonging potentially to *both* narrator and character.

3. Ginsburg rightly contends that free indirect discourse is not in general unambiguously attributable to a character. But sometimes, I suggest, free indirect discourse *is* intended to be read as filling the place of a character's utterance. Ginsburg calls for criticism showing how the "ambiguity and undecidability of FID" raise problems which are "central thematic preoccupations of the text" (146). I argue elsewhere (Neumann 63-78) that the absence of explicit attribution in free indirect discourse is particularly appropriate to a novel like Austen's, one of whose themes is gossip and prejudice. And I discuss below how the undecidability of free indirect discourse calls into question the articulateness and self-awareness of some of Austen's characters.

4. Chatman's terminology implies not only that reported discourse in its free and attributed forms differs only in the absence or presence of a tag, but also what direct as well as indirect discourse occurs free of attribution (Chatman cites examples of the former from *Ulysses*). He also emphasizes, in his "Structure of Narrative Transmission," that "discourse *features*" may "combine in various ways" and that these features should be the subject of study rather than "homogeneous and fixed" categories: "Variety . . . is thus accounted for in terms of various mixtures of independent features, not by an endless proliferation of categories or a Procrustean reduction of instances into normative types" (233-34). This freedom of features to recombine, independent of rigid categories, is also noted in their criticism of Banfield's theory of reported discourse by Dillon and Kirchoff 432.

   We nevertheless do well, as Chatman recognizes, to analyze the modes of reported discourse into which discourse features frequently coalesce because those modes derive their effect from the *constellation* of their features, not from the sum of the effects of their features individually. Positing which elements of the set of frequently cohering linguistic features generally identified as free indirect discourse are most characteristic of it, we can describe a paradigm case of free indirect discourse without expecting all sentences close to the paradigm to match it in every feature. Our inability to delimit a concept unambiguously does not mean we cannot usefully employ that concept and identify all but borderline instances of it. If we are aware how borderline cases compare and contrast with the paradigm, and how any ambiguity in them may function thematically, it matters little whether we identify them as instances of the type or not.

5. Such a sentence might, if its *content* were attributable to a particular character rather than the narrator, be what Hough calls "coloured narrative": not quoted discourse but narration colored by the point of view of a particular character, which coalesces into free indirect discourse, according to Hough, when it contains *ipsissima verba* (204-05). That is, in this "colored narration," as I shall call it, it is a character who "sees"—whose point of view is reported—but the narrator who "speaks"—in whose voice that viewpoint is narrated. In passages of pure narration, the narrator both "sees" and "speaks," and in directly quoted discourse, the character both "sees" and "speaks." In free and tagged indirect discourse, on the other hand (the double-voiced modes), character and narrator "see" and "speak"—in concert or disharmony—in the same sentence. In *Joyce's Voices,* Hugh Kenner's "Uncle Charles principle"—after Stephen

Dedalus's Uncle Charles whose actions are narrated in language he might *choose* if not language he actually *uses* (17-21)—designates passages in which the narrator's viewpoint is couched in an idiom borrowed from a character. It can thus cover the remaining case, in which the narrator "sees" while a character may be said to "speak."

Though in theory distinct, these narrative modes may in practice be indistinguishable. *Who sees* is not independent of *who speaks*. In separating style and point of view, we use "point of view" in a narrow sense: determined by *content,* not by the *form* in which the content is expressed. But point of view in a wider sense must comprise *both* what is seen and how it is spoken. In passages with separate sources of voice and viewpoint, the voice may import its own viewpoint and superimpose it on the content representing the first viewpoint. A clash between these two points of view can give rise to a third, authorial viewpoint which (as is usually the case in Joyce, for example) satirizes both the others.

6. By *free indirect discourse* I usually mean unattributed quotation of a character by a third-person narrator. On free indirect quotation of one character by another, however, see page 369 and note 13. And on free indirect discourse in first-person narration, see Stanzel (218-24). In untagged self-quotation, second-person pronouns—but not first-person pronouns—are shifted to the third person. In untagged quotation of another speaker by a first-person narrator or by a character, second- or third-person pronouns that refer to the quoting speaker are shifted to the first person.

7. As an instance of how discourse features recombine in practice, Austen sometimes uses quotation marks in sentences with every other feature of free indirect discourse: shifted tenses, third-person pronouns, and no inquit. See pages 371 and 375.

8. For many critics, including Pascal (9) and Fowler (102), here-and-now deixis typifies free indirect discourse. But critics disagree whether the absence of an embedding and attributing phrase is essential. Pascal argues that "'free' as it was originally used by [Charles] Bally, namely to indicate freedom from conjunctions [for example "that," as in "He said that . . ."] and from introductory verb," does not distinguish the device "in all circumstances and languages" (31). Fowler offers a typical example of free indirect discourse omitting the inquit (102), but a second example in a footnote retains it (102n). Dillon and Kirchoff note that

> Banfield deviates slightly from standard usage by classing stretches subordinate to a

verb of saying or consciousness as FIS if the stretches bear the other marks of FIS. Usually FIS is restricted to non-embedded sentences (as for example in Jesperson, Ullmann, Fillmore, and Bronzwaer).

(431n)

Thus as Chatman and most others now use the appellation "free," it means "free of attribution," "untagged" by an inquit. This seems to me the most useful sense. In particular, only when we define free indirect discourse as indirectly quoted discourse minus any inquit, can we readily recognize that some apparent inquits could equally be quoted discourse rather than narration.

9. "Present-tense" deixis is only one of *several* means—albeit the most visible—by which free indirect discourse foregrounds quotation so readers can recognize it without other attribution. Thus "free *in*direct discourse" seems an appropriate name because the "directness" of here-and-now deixis is not an essential feature. On the other hand, because free indirect discourse does apparently retain any here-and-now deixis occurring in the quoted material and also independent-clause word order—and thus seems to lie between direct discourse and indirect discourse on the scale of most direct or mimetic to least—this narrative mode might better be called "free *semi*-direct discourse." Matejka and Titunik translate Bakhtin's term for free indirect discourse as "quasi-direct discourse" (Bakhtin, "Discourse Typology" 141 ff.). Leo Spitzer proposed "halbdirekte Rede" (qtd. in Pascal 30). I suggest elsewhere, however, a taxonomy of indirect discourse according to the degree to which the "actual" words of the utterance reported seem either rendered exactly, or merely described, or both (Neumann 124-74). This taxonomy includes not only a variety of tagged indirect discourse which quotes or renders *some* of the "actual" utterance but also what I call a "highly rendered" variety which preserves *much* much of a speaker's "actual" or characteristic idiom, even, sometimes, here-and-now deixis. Thus, free indirect discourse could be viewed as a free version of highly rendered indirect discourse: at least, there exists a variety of indirect discourse which, with its inquit deleted, *would* resemble free indirect discourse. So Chatman seems justified that free and tagged indirect discourse differ theoretically only in the presence of a tag.

10. "Neutral" might be better than "sympathetic," which is not meant to imply the narrator's endorsement but simply that the two voices do not clash. Cohn identifies as the "two divergent directions open to the narrated monologue" (Cohn's name for free indirect thought) the "lyric" and the

"ironic," "depending on which imitative tendency prevails," either "fusion with the subject" or "distance from the subject, a mock identification that leads to caricature" ("Narrated Monologue" 111). McHale notes "a failure among stylisticians to push the analysis of irony and empathy in FID beyond merely naming these functions without specifying how FID actually gives rise to and sustains irony and empathy" ("Free Indirect Discourse" 275). I suggest one way free indirect discourse can be a vehicle for both irony and empathy when I show how the single device of the double-voiced verb—which mirrors how free indirect discourse itself functions—may or may not confuse the narrator's tagged indirect report of thought with whole-sentence free indirect speech, enabling the narrator either to share with the heroine in articulating her thought at the level of thought, or to satirize other characters who attribute thoughts and feelings to themselves in their speech without the narrator's cooperation and endorsement.

11. More recent close equivalents to *fabula* and *sjužet* include *story* and *discourse* (Chatman, *Story and Discourse* 19-20) and *diegesis* and *narrative* (Genette 25-27). Since this study uses the words *discourse* and *narrative* so frequently in other contexts, I retain the Russian Formalist terminology. Genette also employs a third term, *narrating,* to describe the producing narrative action and to answer the question "who speaks?," and his *focalization* describes whose point of view orients the narrative perspective, or "who sees?" (Genette 27 and 186ff.). In Mieke Bal's extension of Genette's theory, the narrator presents the words that form the text while the focalizor presents the content of those words. Since "narrating" and "focalization" thus often resolve into questions of reported discourse, and since this study deals explicitly with reported discourse, these terms are also omitted here.

12. A sentence beginning "The rest of his letter is only about . . ." might, one could argue, be Mr. Bennet's tagged rather than free indirect quotation because Mr. Bennet attributes what follows to Mr. Collins, the referent of "his." But this sentence has no inquit in the narrow sense, and it quotes without acknowledgment Mr. Collins's *first* letter, as well as describes his most recent one. So a case can be made that this sentence is indeed free. But should we perhaps view "olive-branch" as an example of Chatman's free *direct* discourse? Since Mr. Bennet not only mentions but also *uses* Mr. Collins's earlier locution, "olive-branch" would be assimilated to the grammar of Mr. Bennet's discourse were such assimilation necessary (as Mr. Collins's "*my* dear Charlotte's situation" has become Mr. Bennet's "*his* dear Charlotte's

situation"). We may therefore conclude that this sentence is closest to free *in*direct discourse, or we may decide that in practice such distinctions are not only frequently impossible but also unnecessary.

13. The free indirect discourse that re-quotes language previously quoted directly is very common in Richardson, Burney, and Edgeworth, and therefore presumably recurs in other eighteenth-century fiction. Italics often identify this re-quoted material (as today italics distinguish "foreign" locutions). That is, when a character in an eighteenth-century novel quotes another character's previous remarks, italics function like modern quotation marks within quotation marks to identify quoted discourse for the novel's readers—though not, of course, for the novel's other characters who cannot "see" this attribution. We imagine they *hear* it however: this kind of quotation is typically satiric, and the italics suggest the vocal intonation by which the quoter identifies and distances the quoted material.

Since satiric quotation is marked as quotation by the intonation of satire, it need not be explicitly attributed in order to be recognizable, suggesting that free indirect discourse—though not always satiric—may have *originated* in satire. And that characters in these novels quote without attribution in conversation—including the conversations recounted in the letters of Richardson's novels (that is to say, in imitations of communication within imitations of communication)—fully as much as narrators do in narration, strongly suggests that free indirect discourse may also have originated in everyday speech. This contradicts Banfield's central thesis that free indirect discourse is purely literary or written and cannot occur in communication or imitations of communication (239). Moreover, the convention of italics gives us a visible model of how the subjective and evaluative expressions of one character can be interwoven with the subjective and evaluative expressions of another, which supports a "dual-voice" theory as opposed to Banfield's "1 EXPRESSION/1 SELF" model of reported discourse. What Banfield sees as "problematic in the dual voice claim" is that the "second voice of the dual voice position is always the narrator's, never another character's" (188-89). But we *do* frequently find characters quoting other characters in free indirect speech (see Stanzel 222 for an example from (*Clarissa*). The way eighteenth-century characters quote without attribution suggests how we ought to read unattributed quotation by eighteenth-century narrators, *and* how we ought to read free indirect discourse in Austen and later novelists after the convention of italics has begun to disappear. (For an example in *Pride and Prejudice* retaining the italics of earlier novels, see *PP* 27 and 46, and Neumann 16-18.)

14. Readers can check DeRose's and McGuire's Austen *Concordance* for more examples of Lady Catherine's "condescension" in Mr. Collins's eyes (and see page 380 above) as well as to confirm that the *only* instances of "polluted" and "pollution" in Austen's novels are the two passages cited from *Pride and Prejudice,* making this latter instance of free indirect discourse even more certain to be quotation than the former.

15. As McHale remarks, context often has such a "disambiguating function." However, "this is knowledge that [Banfield's] theory cannot capture or reflect" ("Unspeakable Sentences" 32-33). Banfield's failure to take context into account—I would add to McHale's criticism—also means that she cannot permit free indirect discourse to *remain* ambiguous; for her there must always be linguistic markers which signal it unambiguously to readers. McHale suggests Banfield is "groping" toward a "contextual component" ("Unspeakable Sentences" 34). But in fact her theory again and again *forbids* such a component, perhaps the strongest argument against it.

16. Pascal notes that "the self-assertive 'I'" is omitted by this kind of free indirect discourse (51), which partly accounts for its flavor of indirectness.

17. Recall Bronzwaer's "more insightful" view of "the formal indications of FIS" than Banfield's "speaker-coherence model," according to Dillon and Kirchoff 434. As Dillon and Kirchoff suggest, following Bronzwaer, "the narrator's and character's point of view may not always be in 'functional contrast'—it is only when they are that it is important for the reader to distinguish them" (434). That is, it may sometimes not matter whether we attribute a given sentence of free indirect discourse to character or narrator. I would only add that it is important to distinguish when and with which characters this "functional contrast" occurs and when not.

18. In *Marxism and the Philosophy of Language,* Bakhtin distinguishes two fundamental tendencies in indirectly reported discourse. "Referent-analyzing" indirect discourse transmits and comments on the content or reference of an utterance; Bakhtin implies that it usually transmits the whole of the utterance in question. "Textur-analyzing" indirect discourse, on the other hand, "incorporates . . . words and locutions that characterize the subjective and stylistic physiognomy of the message viewed as expression . . . in such a way that their specificity, their typicity are distinctly felt" (130-

31). In Bakhtin's terms, whole-sentence, *lyric* free indirect discourse is referent-analyzing, and its markers occur in its reference: we recognize content more likely to belong to a character than to the narrator, or at least equally likely to belong to *either.* But *satiric* free indirect discourse is typically texture- no less than referent-analyzing, marked by form (diction or syntax) as well as by content.

19. If a sentence without attribution can plausibly be read as indirectly quoted discourse, then according to my definition it *is* free indirect discourse. That is, I *call* it free indirect discourse. I have begun to suggest, however, using Mr. Darcy's "profess," one function in Austen's novels of the at least temporary ambiguity of free indirect discourse.

20. Adding "have" is the usual emendation of this passage, according to R. W. Chapman (*PP* 397), but Chapman's suggestion that we instead read this sentence as "What could be come of . . ." (thus, in the *fabula,* "What *can* be come of . . .") does not change my reading of it as free indirect discourse.

21. Genette calls a narrative "internally focalized," or "focalized through" a character, when it is focused through the consciousness of that character (189).

22. Indefinite free indirect discourse resembles how we suppose a narrator might articulate what a character does not articulate, which is also one function of Hough's colored narration (see note 5 above). I distinguish these two modes in theory by insisting that indefinite free indirect discourse is *possibly* reported discourse because it contains what *could* be *ipsissima verba*: it *might* quote what a character *perhaps* articulated. Since colored narration, on the other hand—narration about a character's viewpoint but *in the usual narrative idiom*—is not quoted discourse, it should not contain *ipsissima verba*. It narrates and therefore articulates what a character perhaps could—but may well not—articulate (compare Chatman's "free indirect perception" [*Story and Discourse* 204] and Cohn's "psycho-narration" [*Transparent Minds* 11-12 and 21 ff]). My suggested definition of free indirect discourse as unattributed *ipsissima verba* thus implies that free indirect discourse cannot report non-reflective consciousness, though the category I call *indefinite* free indirect discourse contains in practice many ambiguous examples. Note too how closely indefinite free indirect discourse may in practice resemble Kenner's Uncle Charles Principle.

23. Does the narrator quote Elizabeth's thoughts *and* quote Mr. Collins's speech, or quote Elizabeth

who quotes Mr. Collins to *herself?* These possibilities (see note 17) are not in "functional contrast."

24. Samuel Johnson, for one, notes in *Rambler* 14 that authors both "improve" and "delight" their readers (78). Mary's and Mr. Collins's moralizing suggests that quoting—by analogy with John R. Searle's analysis of promising—may be defective or infelicitous if the quoter implicitly endorses what is quoted but does not sincerely intend to act on it. Mr. Bennet satirizes defectively if we assume that satire implies a promise *not* to act on what one quotes satirically (though satire, unlike moralizing, may imply no such promise). I suggest elsewhere (Neumann 235) that Elizabeth learns to combine delight with instruction by the end of the novel. She not only quotes the novel's other characters to her friends in order to satirize them; she also quotes them to herself to test her memory and judgment.

25. The romance-reading heroine of Charlotte Lennox's *Female Quixote* (1752) is "filled with the most extravagant Expectations, . . . alarmed by every trifling Incident; and kept in a continual Anxiety by a Vicissitude of Hopes, Fears, Wishes, and Disappointments" (1: 6). In 1807, Austen reread this novel with "very high" amusement: "I find the work quite equal to what I remembered it" *Letters* 173). In Mrs. Bennet's discourse too, the language of "trusts, hopes, and fears" represents what Austen described to one of her novel-writing nieces as "novel slang" (*Letters* 404): Mrs. Bennet flatters herself by quoting the literary heroines of her youth to attribute their romantic sensibility to herself.

26. I wish to thank Ann Banfield and Seymour Chatman for helpful conversations. And, to Avrom Fleishman and Jerome Christensen, I owe "gratitude and esteem" (*PP* 279).

Works Cited

Austen, Jane. *The Novels of Jane Austen.* Ed. R. W. Chapman. 3rd. ed. 5 vols. London: Oxford UP, reprinted with revisions 1943-69.

———. *Jane Austen's Letters to her Sister Cassandra and Others.* Ed. R. W. Chapman. 2nd ed. London: Oxford UP, reprinted with corrections 1959.

Bakhtin [Baxtin], M. M. "Discourse Typology in Prose." *Readings in Russian Poetics: Formalist and Structuralist Views.* Ed. Ladislav Matejka and Krystyna Pomorska. Cambridge: MIT P, 1971. 176-96.

———. [V. N. Vološinov]. *Marxism and the Philosophy of Language.* Trans. Ladislav Matejka and I. R. Titunik. New York: Seminar, 1973.

Bal, Mieke. *Narratology: Introduction to the Theory of Narrative.* Trans. Christine van Boheemen. Toronto: U of Toronto P, 1985.

Banfield, Ann. *Unspeakable Sentences: Narration and Representation in the Language of Fiction.* Boston: Routledge, 1982.

Booth, Wayne. *The Rhetoric of Fiction.* Chicago: U of Chicago P, 1961.

Chatman, Seymour. *Story and Discourse: Narrative Structure in Fiction and Film.* Ithaca: Cornell UP, 1978.

———. "The Structure of Narrative Transmission." *Style and Structure in Literature.* Ed. Roger Fowler. Oxford: Oxford UP, 1975. 213-57.

Cohn, Dorrit. "Narrated Monologue: Definition of a Fictional Style." *Comparative Literature* 18 (1966): 97-112.

———. *Transparent Minds: Narrative Modes for Presenting Consciousness in Fiction.* Princeton: Princeton UP, 1978.

DeRose, Peter L., and S. W. McGuire. *A Concordance to the Works of Jane Austen.* New York: Garland, 1982.

Dillon, George L., and Frederick Kirchoff. "On the Form and Function of Free Indirect Style." *PTL* 1 (1976): 431-40.

Fowler, Roger. *Linguistics and the Novel.* London: Methuen, 1977.

Genette, Gérard. *Narrative Discourse: An Essay in Method.* Trans. Jane E. Lewin. Ithaca: Cornell UP, 1983.

Ginsburg, Michael Peled. "Free Indirect Discourse: A Reconsideration." *Language and Style* 15 (1982): 133-49.

Hough, Graham. "Narrative and Dialogue in Jane Austen." *Critical Quarterly* 12 (1970): 201-29.

Johnson, Samuel. *The Rambler.* Ed. W. J. Bate and Albrecht B. Strauss. Vol. 1 of *The Works of Samuel Johnson.* 3 vols. New Haven: Yale UP, 1969.

Kenner, Hugh. *Joyce's Voices.* London: Faber, 1978.

Lennox, Charlotte. *The Female Quixote.* 1752. Facsimile rpt. 2 vols. Upper Saddle River: Literature House-Gregg, 1970.

McHale, Brian. "Free Indirect Discourse: A Survey of Recent Accounts." *PTL* 3 (1978): 249-87.

———. "Unspeakable Sentences, Unnatural Acts: Linguistics and Poetics Revisited." *Poetics Today* 4 (1983): 17-45.

Neumann, Anne Waldron. "Consciousness and Comment in Jane Austen's Novels." Diss. Johns Hopkins U, 1984.

Pascal, Roy. *The Dual Voice: Free Indirect Speech and its Functioning in the Nineteenth-Century European Novel.* Manchester: Manchester UP, 1977.

Ron, Moshe. "Free Indirect Discourse, Mimetic Language Games and the Subject of Fiction." *Poetics Today* 2 (1981): 17-39.

Searle, John R. *Speech Acts: An Essay in the Philosophy of Language.* Cambridge: Cambridge UP, 1970.

Stanzel, F. K. *A Theory of Narrative.* Trans. Charlotte Goedsche. Cambridge: Cambridge UP, 1984.

Tave, Stuart M. *Some Words of Jane Austen.* Chicago: U of Chicago P, 1973.

Tomashevsky, Boris. "Thematics." *Russian Formalist Criticism: Four Essays.* Trans. Lee T. Lemon and Marion J. Reis. Regents Critics Series. Lincoln: U of Nebraska P, 1965.

Wehrle, Albert J. Introduction. *The Formal Method in Literary Scholarship: A Critical Introduction to Sociological Poetics.* By M. M. Bakhtin/P. N. Medvedev. Trans. Albert J. Wehrle. Baltimore: Johns Hopkins UP, 1978. ix-xxiii.

Bruce Stovel (essay date winter 1987)

SOURCE: Stovel, Bruce. "'A Contrariety of Emotion': Jane Austen's Ambivalent Lovers in *Pride and Prejudice.*" *The International Fiction Review* 14, no. 1 (winter 1987): 27-33.

[*In the following essay, Stovel asserts that Austen's novel allows for the interpretation that Elizabeth and Mr. Darcy's relationship is an example of ideal love, as well as the view that it is an "immediate and magnetic attraction."*]

The *Oxford English Dictionary* defines "ambivalence" as "the coexistence in one person of the emotional attitudes of love and hate, or other opposite feelings, towards the same object or situation," and this concept would seem to apply precisely to *Pride and Prejudice.* During the first half of the novel, the central couple, Elizabeth and Darcy, are held together by just such contradictory feelings. Like Beatrice and Benedick in *Much Ado About Nothing,* each is the one the other loves to hate—and hates to love. And, like Beatrice and Benedick, the two lovers are matched in every way, including disdain for the other, and each finds the other a fascinating and inescapable object of attention. Yet that unwilling attraction to the other makes each hate the other as a threat to his or her pride and emotional independence. But one lover's expression of this hatred only increases the other's fascination; the power of the fascination increases the threat, which intensifies the expressions of hatred. This vicious circle can only be broken when the lovers fully accept their love and dismiss their hatred—that is, when their feelings for each other are no longer ambivalent.

Yet "ambivalence" is a word which entered the language only in this century, so it is well to be cautious in applying it to *Pride and Prejudice.* Not only was Jane Austen's novel composed almost 200 years ago, but in it she seems to attack love-as-attraction, a notion presupposed in the idea of emotional ambivalence. We know that the first version of *Pride and Prejudice,* written in 1796-97, was called "First Impressions"; though Jane Austen dropped the title before her novel was published in 1813 (another novel with that title had been published in 1801),[1] she suggests why she chose the original title late in the novel, after Elizabeth has seen the change in Darcy's manners at Pemberley and feels it can only be due to her influence: "If gratitude and esteem are good foundations of affection, Elizabeth's change of sentiment will be neither improbable nor faulty. But if otherwise, if the regard springing from such sources is unreasonable or unnatural, in comparison of what is so often described as arising on a first interview with its object, and even before two words have been exchanged, nothing can be said in her defence, except that she had given somewhat of a trial to the latter method, in her partiality for Wickham, and that its ill-success might perhaps authorize her to seek the other less interesting mode of attachment."[2] Like *Sense and Sensibility,* the one novel that precedes it in Jane Austen's career, *Pride and Prejudice* seems designed to discredit romantic love, or love at first sight, and to elevate instead "a less interesting mode of attachment": love grounded in a knowledge of the other's character.

Apart from the question of authorial intention, there is another reason for caution: many of Austen's most persuasive critics see no such ambivalence in the attitudes of Elizabeth and Darcy towards each other. True, many readers have clearly delighted in the lovers' ambivalence, whether or not the term was in existence to describe it. The anonymous reviewer of the novel in *The British Critic* for March, 1813, for instance, says of Elizabeth, "She is in fact the *Beatrice* of the tale; and falls in love on much the same principles of contrariety."[3] Writing in 1917, Reginald Farrer argued that, as in *Emma,* the heroine of *Pride and Prejudice* is "subconsciously . . . in love with" the hero from the start—but that in the earlier novel the author failed to make her heroine's real feelings clear.[4] And several modern critics consider Darcy's and Elizabeth's feelings towards each other as ambivalent, though none, to my knowledge, uses the term; David Monaghan, for example, notes that Elizabeth's acts of rudeness to Darcy "derive from an unconscious need to deny that, for all his faults, she finds Darcy attractive."[5] On the other hand, many acute modern commentators find no such depth psychology in *Pride and Prejudice.* Susan Morgan, for example, says, "For much of the story, Mr. Darcy cares for Elizabeth in spite of herself, and she does not care for him at all."[6] And Joseph Wiesenfarth says much the same: "Darcy comes to think that Elizabeth loves him whereas she could not care less for him because of the way she feels about his treatment of Jane and of Wickham."[7] Howard S. Babb says of Elizabeth that "the opposition of her whole nature to Darcy" brings about "the chief dramatic effect of the story: overwhelming surprise at his first proposal."[8] And Marilyn Butler, in her convincing account of Jane Austen's moral thinking, *Jane Austen and the War of Ideas,* suggests that Jane Austen meant to ridicule the whole notion of love at first sight by offering hate at first sight: "It is clear that to her love at first sight and hate at first sight are essentially the same. Both are emotional responses, built on insufficient or wrong evidence, and fostered by pride or complacency toward the unreliable subjective consciousness." Thus, she believes, the second half of the novel is necessarily drawn out: "Jane Austen has to allow time . . . for Elizabeth to change her emotional antipathy to Darcy into a predisposition to love him."[9]

Butler, Babb, Wiesenfarth, and Morgan are all primarily concerned with tracing the moral changes within Austen's protagonists; they analyze moral patterns embedded within Austen's plot, characters, and authorial commentary and show little interest in psychological analysis. But *Pride and Prejudice* is comic, and comedy has a both/and rather than an either/or vision. The novel invites us to see in its protagonists both a moral pattern and a psychological state, just as its plot shows Elizabeth and Darcy each combining, by the end, the apparent opposites of pride and humility, just as Elizabeth learns to combine her sister's charity with her own judgment, just as the marriage of Darcy and Elizabeth unites the unalloyed calculation embodied in the hasty and furtive union of Collins and Charlotte with the unalloyed impulse embodied in the equally hasty and furtive union of Wickham and Lydia. This harmonizing, inclusive vision has irony as its technical instrument. What is stated is less important than what is implied. Jane Austen was speaking of *Pride and Prejudice* when, in a letter to her sister, she adapted a couplet from Scott to describe her style: "I do not write for such dull elves / As have not a great deal of ingenuity themselves."[10] Thus any one act or speech in the novel may carry both a moral and a psychological sense, and each sense will then support the other. Elizabeth, for instance, tells Jane at the start of Volume Two that "There are few people whom I really love, and fewer still of whom I think well" (p. 135). Morally, Elizabeth is engaged in protecting herself from her own sharp intelligence: she has been humiliated by Charlotte's defection, but rather than asking why she has been so mistaken about Char-

lotte's character, she considers Charlotte's choice of Collins unaccountable and the world unsatisfactory. At the same time, she reminds us of her psychological predicament: she cannot think well of the people (Darcy included) whom she loves. The moral and psychological implications do not conflict, but illuminate and enrich each other.

Therefore, the question of authorial intention should be approached with this sense of the novel's comic and ironic inclusiveness in mind. Jane Austen may well be presenting in Elizabeth and Darcy's relationship both an ideal form of love, one grounded in a well-tested respect for each other's character, and a more immediate and magnetic attraction. If we think about the passage in which she defends Elizabeth's "less interesting mode of attachment," several counterbalancing implications emerge. For one thing, the novel shows that Bingley and Jane loved each other deeply and truly from their first meeting. "Oh! she is the most beautiful creature I ever beheld," the smitten Bingley says of Jane at the Meryton assembly (p. 11). Furthermore, Elizabeth did not actually give romantic love much of a trial in her partiality for Wickham, since he appeals to Elizabeth, not in himself, but as a weapon she can use in her merry war against Darcy. When we are told, "Elizabeth thought with pleasure of dancing a great deal with Wickham," the sentence continues, "and of seeing a confirmation of everything in Mr. Darcy's looks and behaviour" (p. 86). If her response to Wickham shows the unreliability of immediate physical attraction as a basis for love, it also shows the strength of the unacknowledged attraction that binds Elizabeth to Darcy. And if Jane Austen's defence of "the other less interesting mode of attachment" insists that the rational love between her central pair possesses dignity, serenity, and security, that does not preclude their having reached this plateau in Volume Three by a less than smooth and straightforward path during Volumes One and Two. Their attainment of rational love is all the more impressive when we realize the deeply irrational impulses from which it has grown.

In fact, virtually all of Jane Austen's pronouncements on Elizabeth's feelings towards Darcy occur in the second half of the novel: once his letter has been received, Darcy himself is largely absent—but Elizabeth's need to define her attitude towards him is pressing, and so we follow Elizabeth as she reviews "the whole of their acquaintance, so full of contradictions and contrarieties" (p. 279) and moves from credence to respect to approval to esteem to gratitude to affection and the realization that "he was exactly the man, who, in disposition and talents, would most suit her" (p. 312). But in the first half of the novel, Darcy, with all his dispositions and talents, is before Elizabeth, at least for the most part, and there is no occasion for her to define her feelings about him, since those feelings are of no real interest to her. If she notices during her stay at Nether-field that Mr. Darcy looks at her frequently, she as-sumes it must be caused by marked disapproval, and decides, "She liked him too little to care for his appro-bation" (p. 51). Apart from this one ironic summary—ironic because Elizabeth cannot see how much she does like Darcy, how much she does care for his approba-tion—the novel's hero remains during these scenes, to the heroine, simply *that* abominable Mr. Darcy" (p. 144).

In short, despite the novel's original title and the au-thor's comment upon the nature of love, nothing in the novel invalidates, and much encourages, the view that Jane Austen invites us to contemplate a hero and hero-ine who get to know each other by loving to hate and hating to love. When, halfway through the novel, Eliza-beth is forced by Darcy's letter to look back over her thoughts and actions, she castigates herself in very sug-gestive terms: "How humiliating is this discovery!—Yet, how just a humiliation!—Had I been in love, I could not have been more wretchedly blind. But vanity, not love, has been my folly" (p. 208). Elizabeth, it would seem, even in her great moment of self-recognition, is still protecting herself from full self-knowledge. A further clue to the presence of irony here lies in Elizabeth's self-accusation of vanity, and not pride. In the fifth chapter, Mary Bennet proudly distin-guishes between these two apparent synonyms: "Pride relates more to our opinion of ourselves, vanity to what we would have others think of us" (p. 20); Darcy con-tinues this distinction six chapters later, replying, when Elizabeth obliquely accuses him of vanity and pride: "Yes, vanity is a weakness indeed. But pride—where there is a real superiority of mind, pride will always be under good regulation" (p. 57). In short, Elizabeth should accuse herself of pride in her own superiority of mind, not vanity. Like Darcy, she is proud to be vain—and too proud to admit, at least yet, that she has been so wretchedly blind just because she *has* been in love.[11] Love, not vanity, has been her folly, but this fool will persist in her folly and become wise.

Elizabeth and Darcy, then, neither love nor hate at first sight, but fall quickly into a love/hate relationship which they do not recognize as such. Elizabeth admits some-thing of the sort when Jane asks her at the end of the novel how long she has loved Darcy: "It has been com-ing on so gradually, that I hardly know when it began" (p. 373). Darcy, by the way, makes the same confession to Elizabeth: "I was in the middle, before I knew I *had* begun" (p. 380). This ambivalence is highlighted by the symmetrical way in which each lover's feelings mirror the other's during the three main sections of the novel: the episodes leading up to Darcy's proposal; the pro-posal scene and ensuing letter (which together form the novel's center); and the whole second half of the novel, which follows from this central episode.

During the first section of the novel, the two lovers seem to be in different predicaments: Darcy is aware that he loves, and makes conscious advances toward Elizabeth; she is unaware of the love she feels for him, and her advances toward him are unintentional. At the same time, though, the lovers, as lovers, are mirror im-ages of each other: each loves and yet struggles to con-quer that love. If Darcy finds, after spending two days in Elizabeth's company at Netherfield, that "She at-tracted him more than he liked" (p. 60), Elizabeth has exactly the same divided response to him, although she does not realize it. And so she flirts with Darcy: she teases him, taunts him, quarrels with his statements, throws his past words in his face, points out his charac-ter defects, criticizes his treatment of his friends and his enemies, takes delight in vexing him—all without real-izing that her assumption of easy freedom and intimate concern encourages him to believe that she sees his love and welcomes it. Like Emma with Mr. Elton, Eliza-beth must make the humiliating discovery that she has led her suitor on to propose: "I believed you to be wish-ing, expecting my addresses," Darcy tells her at the novel's end (p. 396). There is ironic accuracy, then, in Darcy's statement to her at Rosings: "I have had the pleasure of your acquaintance long enough to know, that you find great enjoyment in expressing opinions which in fact are not your own" (p. 174). Jane Austen leaves Elizabeth's viewpoint frequently during Volume One to give us glimpses of Darcy's growing love and of his struggle against that love; these glimpses force us to see Elizabeth's comic ignorance, not only of Darcy's inner conflict, but, by implication, of her own as well.[12]

Darcy's proposal culminates and epitomizes this am-bivalent courtship. His offer of marriage is meant to ex-press his love, but unintentionally expresses hatred: he confesses that he proposes against his will, against his reason, and even against his character (p. 169). Eliza-beth, on the other hand, is vehement in her anger and intends to wound, yet her very vehemence is a sign that she feels more than she realizes. This is part of the point in Austen's careful paralleling of Mr. Collins' proposal to Elizabeth with Darcy's. Elizabeth feels no anger towards Collins, no matter how insulting he be-comes (and he does tell her that she is unlikely ever to receive another offer of marriage, since her expectations only amount to one thousand pounds in the four per cents). Collins is a fool, and Elizabeth knows that "His regard for her was quite imaginary" (p. 112). On the other hand, she realizes that Darcy is more worthy of her and does, in his way, love her, but with a love that undervalues her own, and this is why she is so hurt and vindictive in their great confrontation.

Elizabeth's accusations instigate Darcy to write his long letter to her. It is this letter and not Darcy's proposal which constitutes "the chief dramatic effect of the story" (to use the words of Babb quoted above): Elizabeth may feel overwhelming surprise when Darcy proposes, but we hardly do, since Jane Austen has prepared us for it by the narrative shifts to Darcy's viewpoint during Volume One and by an increasingly obvious serious of hints during the scenes at Rosings (a series something like those signs of Elton's intentions which Emma resolutely ignores). The letter, however, is completely unexpected, and creates a decisive change in the relationship of Elizabeth and Darcy. And, like the proposal, the letter epitomizes the ambivalent feelings of both the speaker and his auditor. Darcy begins in bitter hauteur—"Be not alarmed, Madam, on receiving this letter, by the apprehension of its containing any repetition of those sentiments, or renewal of those offers, which were last night so disgusting to you" (p. 197)—and the tone of wounded pride, of vindicating himself at her expense, is clear when he appeals to her justice and refers to the letter as "the explanation which is due to myself" (p. 197). But, despite appearances, Darcy's letter is really a love letter, as his candor, his scrupulous fairness, his respect for Elizabeth's judgment, the care with which he accounts for his actions, and the confidential revelation about Wickham's attempted seduction of his sister all confess. The letter ends with a sentence, "I will only add, God bless you," which Elizabeth considers to be "charity itself" (p. 368). If the letter is written out of divided feelings, Elizabeth responds to it with "a contrariety of emotion . . . Her feelings as she read were scarcely to be defined" (p. 204). At a first reading, "It was all insolence and pride" (p. 204); she is then indignant, incredulous, ashamed, humiliated in turn. After two hours of wandering in the Hunsford lane, "giving way to every variety of thought," she returns home, fatigued by "a change so sudden and so important" (p. 209). That change is summarized by Elizabeth's reflections after she meets Darcy again at Pemberley some four months later: "She lay awake two whole hours trying to make [her feelings] out. She certainly did not hate him. Hatred had vanished long ago, and she had almost as long been ashamed of ever feeling a dislike against him, that could be so called" (p. 265).

These last words suggest the change which occurs within both Elizabeth and Darcy during the second half of the novel: not only does hatred of the other vanish, but its place is taken by shame and humiliation, hatred turned inward. Elizabeth cries, "How despicably have I acted!" (p. 208), about her treatment of Darcy, and he says of his proposal to her, "I cannot think of it without abhorrence" (p. 367). In the first half of the novel, each directed hatred outward in order to protect a love turned inward, a self-love: what Darcy says in the closing pages is equally true of Elizabeth: "I was . . . allowed, encouraged, almost taught . . . to think meanly of all the rest of the world, to *wish* at least to think meanly of their sense and worth compared with my own" (p. 369). In the second half, each of them, by a painful act of will caused by the need to love and be loved, reverses this emotional balance, and loves outwardly and hates inwardly. Each finds that mutual love is preferable to self-love enjoyed in isolation. By an elegant homeopathy of the emotions, the expression of hatred has driven out hatred in each case. "How you must have hated me after *that* evening?" Elizabeth asks Darcy at the novel's end, and he replies, "Hate you! I was angry at first, but my anger soon began to take a proper direction" (p. 369). And Darcy says that his letter contained "some expressions which might justly make you hate me" (p. 368)—but, of course, Elizabeth learns Darcy's letter by heart, studies every sentence of it, reveals it to no one, and "her anger was soon turned toward herself" (p. 189). This inner redirection causes a change in behavior, and each lover moves, tentatively and indirectly, toward the other. Darcy's manners are transformed, and he rescues the Bennet family from disgrace, even becoming best man at Wickham's marriage to Lydia; Elizabeth allows herself to be taken to Pemberley and, after meeting Darcy there, instinctively seeks his sympathy and help by telling him of Lydia's elopement (a confession which parallels and answers his unprovoked confession about *his* sister's relations with Wickham). And, amusingly, as love replaces ambivalence in Elizabeth and Darcy, humility and diffidence supplant pride and prejudice, so that their sparkling duels of wit give way to tongue-tied, blushing, floor-scrutinizing encounters that would make Bingley and Jane seem brash and poised by comparison. At the novel's end, the two of them, and all of us, can be grateful, not only to Lady Catherine's attempts to separate them, but to the ambivalence which drew them together.

This psychology of ambivalence is not evident in *Sense and Sensibility*[13] or any of the obvious models for *Pride and Prejudice,* such as Fanny Burney's *Evelina.* Where did Jane Austen discover this new and rich conception? We will never know, of course, but it is interesting to speculate. The idea is consistent with the thinking of Samuel Johnson, Jane Austen's particular authority on moral and religious questions: "Inconsistencies," Imlac points out in Chapter Eight of Johnson's *Rasselas,* "cannot be right, but, imputed to man, they may both be true." Richardson's self-divided and self-contradictory lovers—particularly Lovelace and Clarissa—may have contributed something to Jane Austen's psychology of love. Perhaps the literary precursors of Elizabeth and Darcy are the wilful heroes and heroines of stage comedy: Shakespeare's Beatrice and Benedick, but also their progeny on the Restoration and eighteenth-century stage, such as Congreve's Mirabell and Millamant. The real source for Elizabeth and Darcy, however, was probably Jane Austen's observation of actual people. Just as many, perhaps most, readers of *Pride and Prejudice* are reminded of real-life counterparts of Mr. Bennet (whose character also lacks a clear literary precedent), so versions of the Elizabeth-Darcy mating dance abound in everyday life. It is a striking fact that the Beatrice-

Benedick plot of *Much Ado About Nothing* is the one story in all of Shakespeare's plays that has no known literary source. Similarly, Jane Austen might well have said of Elizabeth Bennet's contrariety of emotion what she says about her heroine at the end of ***Northanger Abbey.*** After explaining that Henry Tilney came to love Catherine Morland simply because he could see that she loved him, Jane Austen adds, "It is a new circumstance in romance, I acknowledge, and dreadfully derogatory of an heroine's dignity; but if it be as new in common life, the credit of a wild imagination will at least be all my own."[14]

Notes

1. See the Introductory Note in R. W. Chapman, ed., *The Novels of Jane Austen,* 3rd ed., II: *Pride and Prejudice* (London: Oxford University Press, 1965), pp. xi-xiii.

2. *Pride and Prejudice,* ed. Chapman, p. 279. All references are to this edition.

3. Cited from *Jane Austen: The Critical Heritage,* ed. B. C. Southam (London: Routledge, 1968), p. 44.

4. Farrer, "Jane Austen," *Quarterly Review,* 228 (1917), 1-30; cited here from *Pride and Prejudice,* Norton Critical Edition, ed. Donald J. Gray (New York: Norton, 1966), p. 344.

5. David Monaghan, *Jane Austen: Structure and Social Vision* (London: Macmillan, 1980), p. 66.

6. Susan Morgan, *In the Meantime: Character and Perception in Jane Austen's Fiction* (Chicago: University of Chicago Press, 1980), p. 82.

7. Joseph Wiesenfarth, *The Errand of Form: An Assay of Jane Austen's Art* (New York: Fordham University Press, 1967), p. 63.

8. Howard S. Babb, *Jane Austen's Novels: The Fabric of Dialogue* (Columbus: Ohio State University Press, 1962), pp. 136, 114.

9. Marilyn Butler, *Jane Austen and the War of Ideas* (Oxford: Clarendon Press, 1975), pp. 213, 209.

10. Letter of January 29, 1813, cited from *Jane Austen's Letters to Her Sister Cassandra and Others,* ed. R. W. Chapman (London: Oxford University Press, 1952), p. 298.

11. Andrew H. Wright has noted this irony. See *Jane Austen's Novels: A Study in Structure* (London: Chatto and Windus, 1961), pp. 113-14.

12. E. M. Halliday makes some important points about the effect of these changes in narrative viewpoint in his article, "Narrative Perspective in *Pride and Prejudice,*" *Nineteenth-Century Fiction,* 15 (1960),

65-71. The article is reprinted in the Norton Critical Edition of the novel and in *Twentieth Century Interpretations of Pride and Prejudice,* ed. E. Rubinstein (Englewood Cliffs, N.J.: Prentice-Hall, 1969).

13. A first version of *Sense and Sensibility,* entitled *Elinor and Marianne,* was completed before Jane Austen began *First Impressions* in late 1796. See Chapman's Introductory Note, p. xi.

14. *The Novels of Jane Austen,* 3rd ed., V: *Northanger Abbey* and *Persuasion* (London: Oxford University Press, 1965), p. 243.

Rachel M. Brownstein (essay date 1988)

SOURCE: Brownstein, Rachel M. "Jane Austen: Irony and Authority." *Women's Studies* 15, nos. 1-3 (1988): 57-70.

[*In the following essay, Brownstein focuses on several of Austen's novels, including* Pride and Prejudice, *to support her argument that Austen uses irony to convey a "discursive authority" from which women can derive pleasure in a patriarchal society.*]

It is a truth universally acknowledged, right now, that language is involved in giving and taking both power and pleasure. Whether we begin by asking if the pen is a substitute for the penis, or think about why we read stories of love and adventure, or consider, from any point of view, pornography or psychoanalysis, we end by analyzing ways people please themselves and assert authority over others by using words. (To observe that critics writing about pleasure and power have managed to get what measure of the good stuff they can is to state the merely inevitable.) Claiming that women writers are powerful—*i.e.* effective and influential—has been a focus of feminist critics concerned to dispute the canon, to rehabilitate forgotten writers, and to revise women's relation to the languages of power. That Jane Austen, unforgotten, canonized, and stunningly authoritative, has been a problem for feminists is not surprising: in the struggle for power between politically radical and conservative critics, she has for years been claimed by both parties. Her own interest in power is suggested as her uses of the word acknowledge there are different kinds: in ***Pride and Prejudice,*** for instance, Elizabeth says that "It is not in my power to accept" an invitation (211), and, "I do not know any body who seems more to enjoy the power of doing what he likes than Mr. Darcy," (183) and her friend Charlotte reflects that "all her friend's dislike [of Darcy] would vanish, if she could suppose him to be in her power." (181) Courtship as power play is the subject of all Austen's novels; playing with—or against—power is the substance of them. And through irony, by pointing to the limits of definitive and assertive language, Jane Austen suggests a powerful and pleasurable relation women in patriarchy may have to discursive authority.

The title page of *Sense and Sensibility,* the first novel Austen published, identified it as by "A Lady"; *Pride and Prejudice* is signed "By the Author of 'Sense and Sensibility,'" in other words by A Lady already published. The veiling signature insists on the dignity of femininity itself as "Currer Bell," "George Eliot," "Fanny Fern," or "Mrs. Humphry Ward" do not. It implies, as if modestly, that all ladies speak in the same voice—Austen was of course not the only one to write as one—, which with pointedly feminine obliqueness will avoid such blunt signifiers as proper names, and say precisely what one might expect it appropriately to say, and no more. "A Lady" insists like a post-modern critic on an author's gender and class, indeed identifies the writer simply as a representative, perhaps only a function, of gender and class. The word makes the titillating suggestion that sex is the subject, and also a promise that it will be avoided. (Austen obliges on both counts.) Finally, the signature indicates that the female author is an accepted kind of author, probably one who will make herself delightful and useful without going so far as to set up as an authority. As Mary Ellmann wrote decades before the body became a theme of cultural critics, "the male body lends credence to assertions while the female takes it away" (148). Signing herself "A Lady," even a published author promises to assert neither her (discreetly veiled) self nor any original idea of her own. This novelist will not, presumably, pit her literary capacity and performances against "the abilities of the nine-hundredth abridger of the History of England, or of the man who collects and publishes in a volume some dozen lines of Milton, Pope, and Prior, with a paper from the Spectator, and a chapter from Sterne, [which] are eulogized by a thousand pens;" she does not claim authority, merely, slyly, "genius, wit, and taste." (*NA,* 37)

On the other hand, precisely by coming on as A Lady the author is assuming a certain kind of authority: as Mary Poovey has argued, economic changes, together with anxieties about class and gender distinctions, created in eighteenth-century England the enthroned image of The Proper Lady, symbol of refinement and taste (and perhaps wit, if not genius), and with it, at considerable cost to themselves and their sex, some real power for ladies. It was largely limited to the drawing room. Austen's writing as such A Lady, her mode of assuming ladylike authority in ladylike language, provokes the questions about her social and political allegiances that have divided the critical authorities who have written on the most respected woman writer in English. Jane Austen's awesome respectability has alienated some of her readers, and inspired wrong-headed enthusiasm in

others. Does she want women's power confined to drawing rooms? Does she sanction or mock the image of the authoritative proper lady, which confines as it defines feminine power?

As A Lady, Austen seems now to represent and speak for British civility, perhaps even civilization, at its toniest. In *The Counterlife,* the American novelist Philip Roth introduces a representative traditional Austen fan, an Englishwoman who rereads the novels each year because, she says, "The characters are so very good." More explicitly, she continues, "I'm very fond of Fanny Price, in *Mansfield Park.* When she goes back to Portsmouth after living down with the Bertrams in great style and grandeur, and she finds her own family and is so shocked by the squalor—people are very critical of her for that and say she's a snob, and maybe it's because I'm a snob myself—I suppose I am—but I find it very sympathetic. I think that's how one would behave, if one went back to a much lower standard of living." (270) Mrs. Freshfield is pleased that the characters are fastidious, and that the author is—that both dislike squalor, quite as she does. It is not fair to lump such a reader with the so-called Janeites; she is no idealizer of a gentle, genteel Jane; what she is is a Jane Austen snob. She imagines Jane Austen has the same standards of embattled gentility she has, that like her Austen values those standards above everything. Readers of *Mansfield Park* will allow that Mrs. Freshfield's confusion of standards *for* living with standards *of* living is something Jane Austen tempts one toward; the serious question is whether Austen is accountable for attracting snobs like her and encouraging them in snobbishness. I think she is. When we thrill to the way Mrs. Bennet is dispatched as "a woman of mean understanding, little information, and uncertain temper," or to the translucent, transcendent tact with which Mr. Bennet tells his daughter Mary, in company, "You have delighted us long enough," (101), we respond with approval to a snob's ruthless high standards, and to her high-handedness. Austen's novels set us at a little, pleasant, critical distance from the actual, inelegant, disorderly world her letters reveal she herself lived in just as we do. Furthermore, the twentieth-century reader who, while not an authentic member of the English gentry, enjoys the sublime confidence of *Pride and Prejudice*—famously one of the world's impeccable masterpieces—can congratulate herself on her superior taste with a smugness very like Mrs. Freshfield's. I suspect that even morally serious readers able to list the shortcomings of Sir Thomas and Lady Bertram, and prove Jane Austen knew they are no better than Fanny Price's Portsmouth parents, enjoy their own complicity with Austen's sure, exclusive Lady's tone.

This tone is, wonderfully, so authoritative as to enable Austen to put down titled ladies. Those of us who are not complacent about being snobs enjoy noting that titled ladies are not among the most admirable characters in the novels: that hypercorrected Lady Middleton and empty Lady Bertram are portrayed as patriarchy's mere creatures, and conventional Lady Russell and authoritarian Lady Catherine de Bourgh as its wrongheaded police. Nevertheless, it is as a lady—an untitled member of the gentry, "a gentleman's daughter," which is how Elizabeth Bennet appropriates the term for herself—that Jane Austen condemns them. Austen carefully shows that Lady Catherine's manners are no more than her aspirations better than Mrs. Bennet's. To mock Lady Catherine's "authoritative manner," (84) she reports in unexceptionally calm and decorous ladylike tones that, for instance, after dinner and cards at Rosings, "the party . . . gathered round the fire to hear Lady Catherine determine what weather they were to have on the morrow. From these instructions they were summoned by the arrival of the coach. . . ." (166) Austen's special interest in exposing the pomposities of a great Lady or the pretensions of a couple of would-be ones—for example, the "two elegant ladies" (41) who are the Bingley sisters' maids—are signs, if we need them, that she signs herself with irony. There are ladies and ladies; "A Lady," as a signature, claims to be generic and claims at the same time a certain classy distinction. How are the claims related?

About being A Lady writing, which is to say about writing as a member of the group of women novelists, Austen's irony is even clearer, and also more complex. Her position on women's novels is spelled out in **Northanger Abbey**: they are more original than most of what's published, she declares. Even though their characters are very often stereotyped and their plots are commonly implausible, she says, they are both pleasurable and accurate, works "in which the greatest powers of the mind are displayed, in which the most thorough knowledge of human nature, the happiest delineation of its varieties, the liveliest effusions of wit and humour are conveyed to the world in the best chosen language." (*NA,* 38) The emphasis falls on "chosen language." Choosing language, commenting on the stereotypes and formulas of novelists, and the language available for use in social life, is always Austen's subject. Of Emma's response to Mr. Knightley's proposal, the narrator writes: "What did she say?—Just what she ought, of course. A lady always does." (*E,* 431). Writing as A Lady, Austen savors the discrepancy between being a stable sign in her culture as well as a user and analyst of its signs.

A letter to her niece Fanny Knight suggests her relish of a woman writer's peculiar position and power. Fanny, evidently, had regaled her aunt by recounting an adventure rather wilder than a fictional Austen heroine might have had, a visit to a gentleman's room. Intending to be charmed, indeed excited, there, poor Fanny had ended up disgusted, like Swift's gentleman in the lady's

squalid dressing room. Evidently she emerged with her sense of irony intact, and of this her aunt expressed approval: "Your trying to excite your own feelings by a visit to his room amused me excessively.—The dirty Shaving Rag was exquisite!—Such a circumstance ought to be in print. Much too good to be lost." (*Letters,* 412) A cluster of characteristic Austen values come together here: an appreciation of telling details; a pleasure in telling them, and in hearing tell; a clear sense of the connections between saying and feeling, and social and emotional life; and seriousness about getting into print. Austen admired women's novels that told stories like Fanny's, about the ironic self-awareness of a rational creature absurdly caught in a lady's place.

Her own novels, with their ostentatious embrace and sly mockery of the tropes of fiction for women, depend on her readers' familiarity with that fiction—on their having the thorough, easy knowledge of them that enables one to recognize social or literary conventions, and to relish them. The reader she counts on will respond to a turn of standard plot as if to the anthem of an outgrown school, and treasure a collegial allusion to such matters as the "telltale compression of the pages [that promises] . . . we are all hastening together to perfect felicity" (*NA,* 250)—all of us together, characters and narrator and readers assembled in the same linguistic craft. Austen presents herself as a daughter of the novelists who formed her vision and her readers', and continued to inform it. Condescending, mocking, competitive, this attitude is also defensively and devotedly filial. Far from struggling in a Bloomian agon with awesome precursors she aims to overthrow, Austen keeps her mother and sister novelists always in mind to measure the ways she is like and yet unlike them. If we must have a psychological hypothesis to "explain" this with, the paradigm of female development elaborated by Nancy Chodorow will be more useful than the Oedipal model.

Austen wrote first of all for her intimate family, "great Novel-readers & not ashamed of being so" (*Letters,* 38), as she put it; Austen fans tend like a very close family to be clubby and even a little apologetic about a very personal taste (as opposed to a liking for George Herbert, say, or George Eliot). We relish a sense of the choosiness and the exclusiveness (the sad accident of there being only six novels enhances it) of our little community. The pronoun in the title of Lionel Trilling's last essay, "Why We Read Jane Austen," reveals something more than a magisterial critic's traditionalist, universalist attitude: the feeling that the culture we share with Jane Austen is beleaguered or not enough valued, that powerful people on the outside don't take it seriously, serves to bind us more tightly together, "we" snobs like Mrs. Freshfield, "we" readers of women's novels, "we" humanists in a dehumanizing world, even "we" wary students of how language determines our pleasures and power. Those others who take the truth to be whatever is universally acknowledged remain ever in the corner of Jane Austen's eye: by their limitations we measure our own sagacity, and also our snugness. As Katherine Mansfield remarked, "every true admirer of the novels cherishes the happy thought that he alone—reading between the lines—has become the secret friend of their author." Wayne Booth, quoting this in *The Rhetoric of Fiction,* adds—losing the connection with words on the page, but avoiding Mansfield's "he"—that the Austen reader has an "illusion of travelling intimately with a hardy little band of readers whose heads are screwed on tight and whose hearts are in the right place." (266) The illusion depends on the way the confident, confidential tones of A Lady are deployed so as to mock the accents of authoritative patriarchal discourse in the universe that contains her universe and her fictions.

The literary tradition in which Jane Austen was placed and/or placed herself—the tradition of Jane West and Mary Brunton—was not the dominant tradition; one of the most arduous projects of feminist scholars has been to retrieve and reevaluate eighteenth-century fiction by women. Everything Austen wrote about the novel (and perhaps everything in her novels too) indicates that she knew quite as well as we do that the genre she chose or was constrained to choose (rather as her heroines choose their husbands) was not universally esteemed—that Catherine Morland is representative if not accurate in her assumption that "gentlemen read better books" than novels (*NA,* 106), works, presumably, of greater heft and seriousness. Logically enough, while portraying authority figures and their discourse as in general not exemplary, Austen mocked women's novels most for their moralizing. The maxims that articulate the attitude of patriarchal authority on sex and marriage, the main subject of such novels, are parodied in *Pride and Prejudice*: Elizabeth lifts up her eyes in amazement as her sister Mary moralizes, after Lydia runs away, "that loss of virtue in a female is irretrievable—that one false step involves her in endless ruin—that her reputation is no less brittle than it is beautiful." (*P & P,* 289) Pointedly, Austen does not write down: she will not preach like pedantic Mary. Her Mr. Collins comically echoes the stentorian tones of the "learned doctors" who spell out the moral meanings of romantic actions in novels by, for instance, Charlotte Lennox and Fanny Burney. In his final letter to Mr. Bennet he warns "my cousin Elizabeth, and yourself, of what evils you may incur, by a precipitate closure with [Darcy's] proposals," and declares his amazement at the "encouragement of vice" that occurred with Lydia and Wickham were received by her parents. (363-4) Mr. Bennet rightly observes that this clergyman's attitude is less than Christian, but he himself is no more a reliable authority than his heir is. He is as Elizabeth's meditations on his character point out considerably less than ineffectual, not only patheti-

cally hampered by the entail from disposing of his own patrimony, but worse than useless as a head of his household. Austen's shift from the explicit didacticism of her sister novelists is signalled by the absence of an authoritarian father figure from the novel: Mr. Gardiner, who has the tact to arrange some things, is a shadowy minor character. There is no one but the hero and heroine themselves to discuss, at the end, what "the moral" of their story might be (381). Hapless Mr. Bennet's comment on life itself meanwhile resonates: "For what do we live, but to make sport for our neighbours, and laugh at them in our turn?" (364) It is neither the moral of the whole novel nor one the whole novel repudiates.

Pride and Prejudice is about women's lives in relation to sexual roles and to marriage; therefore—that the connection is inevitable is Jane Austen's point—it is about power, and independence and authority. The novel opens, seductively, in the mode of the Johnsonian essayist: "It is a truth universally acknowledged that a single man in possession of a good fortune must be in want of a wife." On the face of it this sentence has an authoritative ring: as surely, it is the paradigmatic Jane Austen sentence, which was famously and enigmatically praised by Virginia Woolf as "a woman's sentence." Confronted by the sentence suitable for men writers, Woolf declared, Austen "laughed at it and devised a perfectly natural, shapely sentence proper for her own use and never departed from it." (80) The initiating philosophical-sounding premise of *Pride and Prejudice* is a good example. It laughs at authoritative sentence-making. As everyone has pointed out, it is full of logical holes: a truth universally acknowledged is probably less than true; the truth at issue here is not really that single men want girls (which "in want of" does not mean anyway) but that poor girls need husbands. And, far from describing the real state of things in society, the novel's first sentence expresses a gossip's fantasy that women exchange or traffic in men. The sentence acknowledges, by putting it first, Mrs. Bennet's view of things (or is it only what for her purposes Mrs. Bennet acts as if she believes?): that rich men want to be supplied with (even poor) wives. We are encouraged to reflect that although this is not the case, it may be operatively true when people act as if it's true. The power of discourse to determine action is suggested.

The last sentences of Chapter I, quite as authoritative as the first sentence is, complement it, by contrast. Far from entertaining Mrs. Bennet's point of view, the narrator here speaks from above, and decisively detaches herself from the woman: "She was a woman of mean understanding, little information, and uncertain temper. When she was discontented she fancied herself nervous. The business of her life was to get her daughters married; its solace was visiting and news." These dismissive declaratives crackling with the briskness that charms snobs are very different from the meditative voice that pronounces the ironic, pseudo-philosophical first sentence. But the conclusion of the chapter resembles its commencement in one important regard, that is, in claiming distance and authority—the authority a lady in a drawing room shares with a philosopher, a society epigrammatist shares with a judge. The reader is encouraged to reflect on the similarities and also the differences between ladies and philosophers, drawing rooms and the arenas of real power. And the limits of any authoritative statement are suggested when we look more closely and discover that the impressive balance and antithesis of the final sentence is factitious: Mrs. Bennet's solace, far from being a change from her business, is her mode of conducting that. "News," the narrator's last word on this first chapter, a simple word rather elaborately kinder to Mrs. Bennet than "gossip" might be, nicely labels the subject of the chapter. The cap suggests the chapter was substantive; but as Chapter 2 follows, the roundness and fullness the cap helps emphasize begin to seem illusory. We find that the scene between Mr. and Mrs. Bennet was by no means as crucial and conclusive as we thought when it turns out that Mr. Bennet visited Mr. Bingley before his wife asked him to.

The first sentence and the first chapter of *Pride and Prejudice,* integral, finished units in their different, equally forceful ways, mime so as subtly to mock the certainties of authoritative discourse; in the plot of the novel, such discourse becomes a theme. Proud Mr. Darcy sets the action going when he scrutinizes Elizabeth Bennet and pronounces her "Tolerable, but not handsome enough to tempt *me*!" To the feminist critic, that italicized pronoun recalls the sinister bar of the masculine "I" that Virginia Woolf described, in *A Room of One's Own,* as a shadow disfiguring male texts: as Darcy goes on to declare his opinions on female accomplishments and related matters, the egoism of the male authority is amusingly exposed. The action that devolves from his comment on Elizabeth proves his first judgment was false and the first step toward its own undoing. To begin with, Elizabeth mocks by repeating the line, telling the story on him; "she had a lively, playful disposition," the narrator explains, "which delighted in any thing ridiculous." (12) By talking so as to render him ridiculous she is deliberately manipulating her own psyche (rather in the manner of Fanny Knight visiting her gentleman's room); "he has a very satirical eye," she tells Charlotte, "and if I do not begin by being impertinent myself, I shall soon grow afraid of him." (24) In other words, by repeating his words to others she is talking for—in effect to—herself, choosing and using language not to express feeling but to create it, to make herself feel powerful. Darcy will accurately observe, much later, that she finds "great enjoyment in occasionally professing opinions which in fact are not your own" (174). Lest we think she does this just to

flirt, we find her, very much later in the novel, doing the same thing in the very private precincts of her own mind, as she thinks about the question of whether Bingley will propose to Jane. At the conclusion of that gentleman's visit to Longbourn, toward the novel's end, the narrator tells us that, "Not a word passed between the sisters concerning Bingley; but Elizabeth went to bed in the happy belief that all must speedily be concluded, unless Mr. Darcy returned within the stated time. Seriously, however, she felt tolerably persuaded that all this must have taken place with that gentleman's concurrence." (346) Here again, talky Elizabeth is enjoying herself by professing—silently, but nevertheless as if to a drawing-room audience, in well-constructed, carefully timed sentences—an opinion that is not seriously—not in fact—her own. The remarkable sentence that begins "Seriously, however," as it remarks on the non-seriousness of the sentence that precedes it, raises interesting questions about the power of positive assertions—highly subversive questions about the seriousness of all definitive statements and sentences, in what is after all a tissue of words, a series of sentences. Austen invites us to consider that words and sentences might not be signs or containers of meaning after all, that playfulness rather than meanings might be what they represent: "My dearest sister," Jane says once her affairs are settled and Elizabeth's are at issue, "'now *be* serious. I want to talk very seriously. Let me know every thing that I am to know, without delay. Will you tell me how long you have loved him?'" Elizabeth answers, "'It has been coming on so gradually, that I hardly know when it began. But I believe I must date it from my first seeing his beautiful grounds at Pemberley.'" Jane can tell she doesn't mean it: "Another intreaty that she would be serious, however, produced the desired effect; and she soon satisfied Jane by her solemn assurance of attachment." (373).

Elizabeth could tell herself Darcy might ruin her sister's happiness only because she knew he would not, being ready by now to have his friend marry Jane. As she also knows, he was long before conquered by her own "lively"—he does not call them "satirical"—eyes, "bewitched" by her powers, so much so as to ask her to understand—she would have had to be either an impossibly rational creature or a very smug witch to do so—that he fell in love with her against his better judgment. But she does not say these things. Many chapters later, when they finally can both with dignity agree to marry, it is after a long talk which ends with Elizabeth biting her tongue: on the verge of making a caustic observation, she "checked herself," for "she remembered that he had yet to learn to be laught at, and it was rather too early to begin." (371) Since people are comical, quite as Mr. Bennet says, dignity is precarious, and silence helps better than words to maintain it. Darcy will eventually be made to learn to laugh: in the novel's nearly penultimate paragraph, which begins to detail the bliss of the married life of the Darcys at Pemberley, we are told that Darcy's sister Georgiana "at first . . . listened with an astonishment bordering on alarm, at [Elizabeth's] lively, sportive, manner of talking to her brother. He, who had always inspired in herself a respect which almost overcame her affection, she now saw the object of open pleasantry. Her mind received knowledge which had never before fallen in her way. By Elizabeth's instructions she began to comprehend that a woman may take liberties with her husband, which a brother will not always allow in a sister more than ten years younger than himself." (388) In the happy end Georgiana will take the place at Elizabeth's side of Jane, the more feeling sister with whom Elizabeth shared the sisterly mockery of men Jane never could engage in either. She will be the female confidante and foil—the other woman to talk to—that is necessary to the happiness of even the mistress of Pemberley. Both Darcys, then, will be instructed by Elizabeth happily ever after. In other words, just as the marriage plot comes to triumphant closure it is neatly undercut: female bonding and women's laughter are elements of this novel's happy end. One woman will make a man the object of her pleasantries while another one listens and learns. This subtle subversion of the conventional romantic plot accords with the novel's attitude toward verbal tissues that appear to wrap things up once for all.

Like her heroine, Austen questions authoritative discourse through dialogue. Dialogue, Mary Ellmann wrote, "might be defined as the prevention of monologue" (xii); as such it is a critique of patriarchal absolutism in prose. There are many modes of dialogue in *Pride and Prejudice,* the first of which is ironic narrative. When Austen refers to the "two elegant ladies" who wait on the Bingley sisters she means that these women absurdly pretend, like their mistresses, to elegance. Irony is an efficient mode: the description of the maids serves for the mistresses. Like an impatiently rude interlocutor, irony questions a statement as it is made; a single sentence becomes in effect two, assertion cum contradiction.

Literal dialogue between characters in the novel may also be a process of assertion and contradiction, sometimes of opinions, sometimes of the authority to state them. Although we tend to remember *Pride and Prejudice* as chock full of witty exchanges, some of the most interesting dialogue is between talk and the lack of it. There dialogue is as much the subject as the mode of discourse. The first chapter is a case in point: "My dear Mr. Bennet," his lady begins the action by saying to him one day, "have you heard that Netherfield Park is let at last?", to which "Mr. Bennet replied that he had not." The switch to indirect discourse signals the man's taciturnity; he is not quite responding to his wife. One is reminded of this marital lack of exchange when Elizabeth and Darcy talk together later: "'It is *your* turn to

say something now, Mr. Darcy.—*I* talked about the dance, and *you* ought to make some kind of remark on the size of the room, or the number of couples.' He smiled, and assured her that whatever she wished him to say should be said." (19) Elizabeth is unlike her mother making deliberate, sophisticated conversation about conversing, but my point—aside from the small truths that voluble Elizabeth resembles her mother, and that Austen's egoistic young people both tend to italicize pronouns—is that Darcy is hardly a Benedick to Elizabeth's Beatrice, therefore that the real exchange is between talking and not talking, and that that is one way Austen suggests the limits of discursive authority.

In her Lady's voice, which combines an authoritative ring with flexible self-mocking undertones, Austen can comment with varying degrees of explicitness on the limits of rhetorical and human authority. Through self-reflexive irony she can keep her distance from the discourse of authority, the patriarchal mode of imposing oneself through language. Except for ladies in domestic and literary circumstances (drawing rooms and fictions) circumscribed by the world of men, women have been denied such authority. Writing as A Lady and considering the constraints that determine her persona—considering as a persona—, Austen reflected on the power of authoritative language. And on other kinds of power. When Elizabeth scrutinizes her third-volume feelings about Darcy, she acknowledges that it is she who has the power to provoke the words that will change her life: "She respected, she esteemed, she was grateful to him, she felt a real interest in his welfare; and she only wanted to know how far she wished that welfare to depend upon herself, and how far it would be for the happiness of both that she should employ the power which her fancy told her she still possessed, of bringing on the renewal of his addresses." (266) The rhythms are authoritative, magisterial. The novel reader knows the heroine must wait, and we with her, for a second proposal it is not in her power to make—but also that Elizabeth's struggle to turn fancy into knowledge and power is the significant action. The proposal, important though it is, will be a coda to the inner action of discriminating among thoughts and the words for them. Only if we ignore that sentence and its sisters can we read *Pride and Prejudice* as a mere romance. Which is not to gainsay the pleasure we take in the novelist's very romantically and conventionally uniting the lovers, in the very end—or, rather, in the Gardiners' having done so. Having been responsible for the mechanics of getting the couple together, Elizabeth's relatives are thrust forward in the novel's last sentence as the only legitimate claimants to agency. Does the emphasis fall on the fact that the hero and heroine are mere puppets of circumstances, or perhaps of the marriage plot? Are we meant to envy their prospect of happiness ever after in the paradise of Pemberley? Or to note with sly pleasure that these cultivated but rather dull middle-class Gardiners will be frequent guests at that monument to Lady Catherine's class? It is hard to decide, and this, I think, is what must be borne in mind when we write about Jane Austen, whose authoritative irony eludes, even mocks, our authoritative critical discourses.

Selected Bibliography

Austen, Jane. *The Novels of Jane Austen,* ed. R.W. Chapman (5 vols.) Oxford: Oxford University Press, 1933.

Austen, Jane. *Jane Austen's Letters,* collected and edited by R.W. Chapman. Oxford: Oxford University Press, 1979.

Booth, Wayne C. *The Rhetoric of Fiction.* Chicago: University of Chicago Press, 1961.

Chodorow, Nancy. *The Reproduction of Mothering.* Berkeley: University of California Press, 1978.

Ellmann, Mary. *Thinking about Women.* New York: Harcourt, Brace, Jovanovich, 1968.

Poovey, Mary. *The Proper Lady and the Woman Writer.* Chicago: University of Chicago Press, 1984.

Roth, Philip. *The Counterlife.* New York: Farrar, Straus, and Giroux, 1986.

Trilling, Lionel. "Why We Read Jane Austen." *The Times Literary Supplement,* 5 March 1976.

Woolf, Virginia. *A Room of One's Own.* New York and London: Harcourt Brace Jovanovich, 1957.

Jean Ferguson Carr (essay date 1991)

SOURCE: Carr, Jean Ferguson. "The Polemics of Incomprehension: Mother and Daughter in *Pride and Prejudice.*" In *Tradition and the Talents of Women,* edited by Florence Howe, pp. 68-86. Urbana: University of Illinois Press, 1991.

[*In the following essay, Carr analyzes the role of the mother in* Pride and Prejudice, *focusing on Mrs. Bennet's exclusion from the social world.*]

> She was a woman of mean understanding, little information, and uncertain temper.
>
> —Jane Austen, *Pride and Prejudice*

> Stupidity (incomprehension) in the novel is always polemical: it interacts dialogically with an intelligence (a lofty pseudo intelligence) with which it polemicizes and whose mask it tears away . . . at its heart always lies a polemical failure to understand someone else's discourse, someone else's pathos-charged lie that has appropriated the world and aspires to conceptualize it,

> a polemical failure to understand generally accepted, canonized, inveterately false languages with their lofty labels for things and events.
>
> —Mikhail Bakhtin, "Discourse in the Novel"

My first epigraph depicts the fictional mother, Mrs. Bennet in Jane Austen's *Pride and Prejudice* (1813), who is identified by her exclusion from the realms of sense and power, and is contained within her comic role.[1] As such, she stands in uneasy relationship to her daughter, Elizabeth, who both shares her mother's exclusion and seeks to dissociate herself from her devalued position by being knowing and witty where her mother is merely foolish.

My second epigraph, from Bakhtin's *The Dialogic Imagination,* raises questions about the social functions and effects of what is perceived as knowing discourse and what is perceived as meaningless babble.[2] What is usually identified as intelligence is the force that constructs the social order, creates canons, names names, and decides what is acceptable. It is central, focal, organizing. This "authoritative word," what Bakhtin terms "the word of the fathers," "permits no play with the context framing it, no play with its borders, no gradual and flexible transitions, no spontaneously creative stylizing variants on it. . . . One cannot divide it up—agree with one part, accept but not completely another part, reject utterly a third part" (pp. 342-43). Stupidity appears as a weakness that has no place in this proper order, that does the wrong thing and uses the wrong words, is unacceptable or embarrassing. Judged by the unity of the father's word, it seems incoherent or unproductive. Yet such "stupidity (incomprehension) in the novel is always polemical" (p. 403), interacting dialogically with authoritative discourse to disrupt its proper names and categories.

Incomprehension exposes the father's words to play, to jokes. The prototypical literary character who deploys such incomprehension is the fool, whose nonsense reveals gaps in the seamless authority of the father's word, for "by his very uncomprehending presence he makes strange the world of social conventionality" (p. 404). Yet as Freud argues in *Jokes and Their Relation to the Unconscious,* the naïve's "effect" depends on our conviction that he is unaware of (in Freud's terms, "it is not present in him" or he "does not possess") the inhibitions that govern most social discourse, or else he will be judged "not naïve but impudent." If we are not so convinced, "we do not laugh at him but are indignant at him."[3] The fool is a professional who plays the part of a naïve. His power is instrumental, defined not in terms of what he can "possess" for himself but by the effect he has on those in power. Fools exemplify what Freud calls a *"misleading [misverständlich] naïveté,"* representing "themselves as naïve, so as to enjoy a liberty that they would not otherwise be granted" (*Jokes,* p. 184). As long as liberty is something that is "granted," as long as fools do not expect to be made kings, the power of the father remains fundamentally intact.

Yet there is a type of incomprehension whose polemical effects are not finally so easily contained. Its social and literary prototype is the figure of the mother, who shares her child's exclusion from the languages of adulthood and power, and who has an interest in exposing the restraints imposed by patriarchy. A mother like Mrs. Bennet of *Pride and Prejudice* is not in a position to understand the polemics of her incomprehension. In the patriarchal culture in which Austen wrote, such an exposure must be indirect and guarded, or even unaware of its own threat and seriousness. The mother cannot afford to get her own jokes, nor can others accept the implications of her comedy. Her comedy hovers uncomfortably between unawareness and impudence, between triviality and threat. Unlike the fool, her "stupidity (incomprehension)" may not be sanctioned by the novel's explicit directives. It is often understood as simply ridiculous, even by the novel's other outsiders.

It is a critical commonplace to laud a fool's ability to "teach" authoritative speakers to laugh at their rigidity or to expose the faults and follies of a society's discourse.[4] But Mrs. Bennet is primarily defined not in such a direct relationship with authoritative speakers, not as "wife" who challenges "husband," but in her displaced role of mother who guides and restrains her children according to conventions that she herself need not comprehend and has not authorized. Her comedy is constrained by this dual role, by the effect of her foolishness on the children who must grow up under patriarchy. Yet stupidity is *always* polemical even when it is not explicitly understood, even when it is not incorporated into the novel's thematic designs. It may function not as a local challenge to individual failures of perception but as a sign of a general ideological confusion. The mother's position can be neither dismissed nor acknowledged. She persists at the margins of the novel as an irritating, troublesome, and yet indispensable figure.

In *Pride and Prejudice,* as in many nineteenth-century novels, the mother's function is misleadingly represented. Mrs. Bennet *is* a "woman of men understanding, little information, and uncertain temper," but this representation serves complex interests. To accept her as merely a figure of ridicule is to prevent any investigation of those interests, to ignore the ways in which this novel, in Pierre Macherey's words, is "haunted" by what it cannot say. We must, instead, conduct a double reading, attending not only to what Macherey describes as "that which is formally accounted for, expressed, and even concluded" but also to what is left unspoken or implicit.[5] We need to attend to the novel's resistances, to what is produced only to be quickly dismissed. We

thus "make strange" not only the ideology figured in the novel's social world but the ideology guiding the author's representations of social relations and conventions. We thereby consider tensions that remain tacit, that are neither authorized nor expunged, but that make the novel's resolution of social conflicts unfinished or overdetermined. Such a double reading extends our literary interests outside of the novel's social world to the exchanges between the novel and its formative culture. By reading doubly we question the insistence with which cues are delivered and the ways in which constructions are buttressed. We consider what is at stake when certain details are treated as error or as slips of the pen.

Mrs. Bennet is denied the prerogatives of a comic literary tradition: she does not win pleasure for her comedic scenes, forgiveness for her foibles, or credit for her effect on the social world. With an energy that seems excessive, given her slight role in the narrative, she is ridiculed both by powerful characters and the narrator. She is harshly criticized for a role she does not fulfill, for serious effects she does not achieve. She marks a lack of adult feminine power in the culture, a lack felt strongly by the young women she is supposed to educate and protect, and she is blamed for the excesses of the patriarchal culture. This essay explores what unspoken interests produce such a contradictory role for Mrs. Bennet. What interests are served by novelistic insistence that this character does not matter, that she is one-dimensional, that she has no effect? And how does such insistence coexist with the nagging, unsettling effect of the "trivial" character, with the threat she seems to pose to the social world of the novel, to her husband and daughters, to the possibility of women's discourse? Why should Mrs. Bennet's outbursts be found intolerable rather than humorous or socially productive?

Adrienne Rich calls the relationship between mothers and daughters in nineteenth-century fiction "the great unwritten story."[6] Mothers are thoroughly erased from these novels—rejected by their daughters, who wish to distance themselves from the socially conforming and repressed circumstances of their mothers, and disposed of by authors, who write them out of the story by imagining them as dead, bedridden, or left behind while the daughter journeys to Bath. They are, all too often, dismissed or ignored by critics who accept their marginalized status. The few mothers who do appear vanish into narrow stereotypes, both social and fictional. They are either dutiful and selfless or silly and self-indulgent, more likely to humiliate their daughters than to become role models or friends. They are not even given the dubious recognition afforded in twentieth-century fiction of being powerful, damaging adversaries.[7] Mothers are treated as wayward children, likely to say embarrassing things in front of company, needing to be cajoled and pampered, but not a very serious force—for good or ill.

As Nina Auerbach has argued, most nineteenth-century heroines strive to escape the "community of women," which "may suggest less the honor of fellowship than an antisociety, an austere banishment from both social power and biological rewards" (p. 3). They reject the more confined social world their mothers occupy to challenge the expectations of their fathers, brothers, or lovers. The great plot concerns not mothers and daughters but courtship,[8] which leads the heroine away from her mother and ends, conveniently, before marriage or childbirth, before the heroine must find a way to reconcile herself to that woman's world she earlier rejected. Through the ritual of courtship the heroine demonstrates her difference from her parents, especially her mother, whose concern with social rules, respectability, or safety is challenged, if not rejected. Yet the liberation of young, unmarried heroines leaves other women subject to patriarchy. The heroine (or the woman writer) is understood as the one woman who can negotiate the perils of the patriarchal world.

In *The Madwoman in the Attic*, Gilbert and Gubar discuss the "absence of enlightened maternal affection" in Austen's novels, which produces mothers "who fail in their nurturing of daughters" and daughters who are "literally or figuratively motherless." The relationship of mother and daughter is defined by "matrophobia—fear of becoming one's mother" (pp. 125-26). As a result, a mythical "mother-goddess" replaces the problematic social mother and becomes the figure of a feminine tradition that has been "dismembered, dis-remembered, disintegrated" under patriarchy (p. 98).[9] To "remember" and "become a member" of this "shattered tradition that is her matrilineal heritage" (p. 98), the nineteenth-century woman writer/heroine must "kill" the images imposed by patriarchy, the social mothers whom the dutiful daughter is supposed to reflect and reproduce.[10]

One of the ways the daughter seeks to liberate herself is through sharing the male characters' perception of the mother as comic. The situation could have been presented as tragic or wasteful—for the mother, who has no relationship with those around her, and for the daughter, who suffers from the lack of a significant guide. Imagining the mother as a "joke" seems to mitigate this loss and allows the daughter to move beyond what her mother desired or imagined. Yet Freud warns that there is no such thing as an innocent joke, that all jokes are tendentious.[11] Certainly the representation of the mother as comic is tendentious, ultimately working against the daughter's own interests. However much she gains by differentiating herself from a ridiculous mother, she cannot afford to trivialize the position she herself may occupy. Her own possibilities are finally implicated in the mother's position.

Mrs. Bennet occupies just such an uncomfortable position in her culture and in relation to her daughter Elizabeth. She is repeatedly characterized as trivial, static, or uninfluential, the antithesis of Lizzie's complexity and change. Modern readers have willingly accepted such cues and seen her as a dehistoricized trope, as "simply unformed matter," "the embodiment of the unthinking life-force that works through women," or "a transparently scheming boor" who, "like the life force, will persist, as foolishly as ever."[12] Mrs. Bennet holds none of the valued positions of mothers in her culture: she has little influence over the domestic realm and is absent from her daughters' scenes of confession and self-discovery. Elizabeth can "hardly help smiling" at Lady Catherine's concern that Mrs. Bennet has been "quite a slave to your education" (p. 199). Although Mrs. Bennet seems inescapable, constantly interrupting conversations and intruding where she is least wanted, she is ignored and countermanded by her husband and elder daughters. The narrator concludes the first chapter with an invitation to dismiss her as a static character of little interest. Having introduced Mr. Bennet as "so odd a mixture of quick parts, sarcastic humour, reserve, and caprice, that the experience of three and twenty years had been insufficient to make his wife understand his character," the narrator adds: "*Her* mind was less difficult to develope. She was a woman of mean understanding, little information, and uncertain temper. When she was discontented she fancied herself nervous. The business of her life was to get her daughters married; its solace was visiting and news" (p. 53). Although Mrs. Bennet is dismissed (p. 262) as a woman whose "weak understanding and illiberal mind" have lost her the "respect, esteem, and confidence" of her husband—and, by implication, of her daughter, the narrator, and readers—she is a constant enough force in the novel to evoke such strong criticism.[13] She is a serious handicap to her eldest daughters' romances and a serious instigator of her youngest daughters' folly.

Like Dickens's Mrs. Nickleby, who spoke "to nobody in particular . . . until her breath was exhausted,"[14] Mrs. Bennet's language reveals her self-absorbed inattention to her family's needs. She invariably misconstrues her effect on listeners, imagining specific insult from Darcy's general views about the country and city (p. 89) and missing the contempt with which the Netherfield ladies greet her comments (pp. 90, 144). She dwells in a land of "delightful persuasion" (p. 144), where she alone chooses how to interpret others' behavior. As when she bursts forth with her "exuberance" about Lydia's last-minute marriage, she cannot be shamed nor can her present feelings be disrupted with concern about the past or future.[15] Her well-rehearsed discourse on her "poor nerves" preempts her daughters' chances to complain or suffer publicly. After Lizzie rejects Mr. Collins, Mrs. Bennet recasts the entire episode as an attack on her. She does not imagine what the unpleasant scene may have cost Lizzie, nor does she consider how her daughter may have felt in rejecting a man her mother supports. Her complaints admit no cosufferers and need no audience: "nobody is on my side, nobody takes part with me, I am cruelly used, nobody feels for my poor nerves" (p. 153). Although she vows never to speak to her "undutiful children" again, she babbles on, lost in a self-contained grievance: "Not that I have much pleasure indeed in talking to any body. People who suffer as I do from nervous complaints can have no great inclination for talking. Nobody can tell what I suffer!—But it is always so. Those who do not complain are never pitied." Her complaints earn her no pity from her daughters, who "listened in silence to this effusion, sensible that any attempt to reason with or sooth her would only increase the irritation" (p. 154).

Although Lizzie is in some ways allied with her mother in a struggle with patriarchal powers, she does not willingly admit the allegiance. Embarrassed by her mother's failures and inadequacies, she can neither laugh her off as comic nor fully dissociate herself. Lizzie never speaks her criticism to her mother, treating her as someone beyond conversation or reform, beyond the improvement of sensibility evoked in the novel. Yet she clearly feels the burden of the association and struggles to convince others of their differences. Her mother has a surprising power to silence the heroine, who speaks out in every other situation. At Netherfield, in front of the critical audience of Darcy and Miss Bingley, Lizzie trembles "lest her mother should be exposing herself again. She longed to speak, but could think of nothing to say" (p. 90). She is all too aware of how powerful and final the response to such exposure can be; it is after such an outburst in front of the Netherfield set that "the mother was found to be intolerable" (p. 68). Physical distance does not shelter her from her identity as daughter of "such a mother" (p. 187),[16] and she suffers from the disturbing effects of Miss Bingley's reminders of their "dear friend's vulgar relations" (p. 83). It does not require her mother's presence, but only the "thought of her mother," to make her lose "confidence" in an argument with Darcy (p. 219). Lizzie's concern about exposure—her mother's and, more to the point, her own—shows her tenuous social position, her vulnerability to being judged by her rank or family rather than by her words, her fear that even her words will prove too daring, too revealing.

Lizzie's intense discomfort around her mother seems reciprocal: she is the "least dear" (p. 145) of Mrs. Bennet's children, the one chosen by Mr. Bennet to confound his opinion of women as "silly and ignorant" (p. 52). Such comments suggest that Lizzie has risen above the devalued position of her mother, both personally and socially. Yet Lizzie shares more with her mother than her father or the narrator acknowledges or than she herself can recognize. Her disvalued fictional role allows Mrs. Bennet to voice more radical discontents than can the heroine of the novel. She is "beyond the reach of reason" in her diatribe against entailing an es-

tate away from her daughters "in favour of a man whom nobody cared anything about" (pp. 106-7)—a complaint Elizabeth Bennet might well make if she were not too rational, too worldly wise. Lizzie shares her mother's shock at Charlotte's engagement to Mr. Collins, although she "recollected herself" (p. 165) in time to address her friend with guarded politeness. Like her mother, Lizzie allows herself "agreeable reflections" about what it would mean for Jane to marry Bingley, but whereas Lizzie keeps her dreams private, her mother speaks "freely, openly" (p. 140), causing her daughter to try "in vain . . . to check the rapidity of her mother's words, or persuade her to describe her felicity in a less audible whisper" (p. 141). Although Elizabeth has claimed she does not care what Darcy thinks of her, she "blushed and blushed again with shame and vexation" (p. 141) in watching his contempt for her mother's expressed social expectations. The aspiration of rising through marriage is thus displaced onto her mother's vulgarity, although Lizzie too has imagined Jane marrying into a fine house: "she saw her in idea settled in that very house in all the felicity which a marriage of true affection could bestow" (p. 140). Nor can Lizzie openly support her mother's eagerness to arrange for dinners or balls, contrivances necessary to promote the futures of five dependent girls. The calculation needed to achieve a secure marriage cannot be articulated except as comically disvalued speech.[17]

Mrs. Bennet, whose outbursts are a constant source of anxiety for her elder daughters, is regularly interrupted by her husband, her priorities ridiculed or diverted. Irked at her long tale about a ball and dancing partners, Mr. Bennet dismisses his wife's story and its mode of telling as designed only to irritate him (p. 60). That his daughters' futures depend on such slight details as who dances with whom and in what order, that they too must learn to read minute social signs, is of no concern to Mr. Bennet. As Nina Auerbach has argued, it is Mrs. Bennet who "forges her family's liaison with the outside world of marriage, morals, and money that eligible men embody. . . . While the mother builds connections, the father retreats from the business of marriage to his library" (p. 36).

Such nonchalance, such silence is the prerogative of the powerful, and in *Pride and Prejudice* it is permissible only for propertied men. Mr. Bennet regularly gains the upper hand by not answering his wife's addresses, and Darcy similarly maddens the importunate Miss Bingley. Mr. Bennet teases his family by postponing word that he has visited the new bachelors in town, and Darcy chooses when and how to impart the information he controls about Wickham and Georgiana. But when Jane or Lizzie is silent, the unusual behavior is noted and has serious consequences, causing Darcy, for one, to conclude that Jane is cold or Lizzie hostile. In her chapter on women's conversation in *The Women of England*

(1838), Sarah Stickney Ellis codifies the "uses of being silent" for women, suggesting that a woman's silence and speech are alike secondary, functioning "rather to lead others out into animated and intelligent communications, than to be intent upon making communications from the resources of her own mind."[18] Woman's silence is thus very different from the silence of authority which, as the inverse of Bakhtin's "word of the fathers," need not be repeated to make itself felt. The women in *Pride and Prejudice* work to fill up silences, to repair the suggestion that they have no purpose, no presence. At Netherfield, the ladies, whose "powers of conversation were considerable" when the men were out of the room, are reduced to nervous stratagems to persuade the men to break the silence they instill (pp. 99-102). The struggle is described as a contest, and Miss Bingley's failure to "win" Darcy "to any conversation" shows the imbalance between men and women speakers. Lizzie comments on this contest, suggesting that "our surest way of disappointing him, will be to ask nothing about it." She thus appears to control the situation, to have seen through and assumed for herself the power of silence that Miss Bingley, described as "incapable of disappointing Mr Darcy in any thing," cannot manage.

But Lizzie's silence is only an imitation of Darcy's power to withhold his words, since she must explain that she is doing it and must perform the very role in the scene she hopes to evade, that of speaker who waits for Darcy's response. When Darcy is "surprise[d] at her silence," Lizzie tries to validate her silence as something she has determined to enact, not merely a product of her social position. She does so with a complicated speech that she expects will "affront him": "Oh! . . . I heard you before; but I could not immediately determine what to say in reply. You wanted me, I know, to say 'Yes,' that you might have the pleasure of despising my taste; but I always delight in overthrowing those kind of schemes, and cheating a person of their premeditated contempt. I have therefore made up my mind to tell you, that I do not want to dance a reel at all— and now despise me if you dare" (p. 96). Lizzie claims her silence as a powerful privilege, affording her time in which to *determine, know, delight,* and *make up her mind.* Yet she must speak to defend her silence, and her actions all respond to expectations that are beyond her control to change. She can refuse to dance, but she cannot alter the nature of dancing and conversing, nor can she alter her position as one who must first be invited, who can only startle "in reply." The social discourse is preconstituted.

The less powerful speakers in such scenes are regularly marked as "crying" out their speech, as breaking the decorum of a scene in which Darcy's words need only be "said" to have impact and to gain attention. Women are thus required to speak in excess if they are to be heard at all, but such excess marks their speech as negligible. Mrs. Bennet is described by the narrator as "sharp" in defense of her five daughters, as indulging in "raptures" and "exaggeration." Although her words are necessary to safeguard a minimal social and economic standard for the Bennet girls, she must "rail bitterly" to make her point. And Lizzie has constantly before her the warning of Lydia, whose energies to procure her own desires are described by the narrator as "put[ting] herself forward," as full of "high animal spirits, and a sort of natural self-consequence," full of "assurance" that makes her "insist" rather than "cry," and "very equal therefore to address Mr Bingley on the subject of the ball, and abruptly remind[ing] him of his promise" (p. 91).

Lizzie can only differentiate herself from these censured women by explaining at length how her words are to be taken. She does not have Darcy's luxury of silence or her father's indulgence of privacy. As she experiences in her painful encounters with Lady Catherine and Mr. Collins, she is drawn into public discourse despite every attempt at resistance. When Mr. Collins dismisses her careful rejection of his proposal as "merely words of course," the "usual practice of elegant females," Lizzie cannot extricate herself from the social construction he has imposed. "I know not how to express my refusal in such a way as may convince you of its being one," she says. "Can I speak plainer?" Her only recourse is to refer him to her father, "whose negative might be uttered in such a manner as must be decisive" (pp. 148-50). Similarly, although she struggles to mark off some prerogatives for herself in her conversations with Lady Catherine (telling her, "*You* may ask questions which *I* shall not choose to answer"), she cannot end the scene. She can deny that Lady Catherine is "entitled" to know her mind and can refuse to be "explicit," but she must continue to speak to reject further attacks. Even as she insists, "I have nothing farther to say," she is provoked into a string of defensive replies ("I will make no promise of the kind"; "I must beg, therefore, to be importuned no farther on the subject"; "I have said no such thing"). Her defeated reaction afterward—"to acknowledge the substance of their conversation was impossible"—reflects more than an unwillingness to confide in her mother; it also suggests how powerless she is to control the "substance" of conversations (pp. 364-68).

Lizzie has been warned about the limits on women's discourse by an offhanded remark of Miss Bingley's. When Lizzie recommends that they "punish" Darcy by teasing or laughing at him, Miss Bingley protests that laughter would only serve to "expose ourselves . . . by attempting to laugh without a subject" (pp. 101-2). Lizzie rejects such an "uncommon advantage" for her male peer, refusing to allow him to conceal himself from the considerable power of her laughter. Yet, although Lizzie "wins" this scene by appearing to reject the conventions of male-female difference, Miss Bingley's comment raises a disturbing problem about women's discourse in Austen's realm. Lizzie's power to laugh depends on having a "subject"; without it her humor will seem as absurd and self-absorbed as her mother's. Although she seems more in control than her mother, Lizzie can neither end nor begin a scene of her own volition. If Darcy does not raise objections for her to correct or mock, her laughter will be seen as having no substance, no social effect; it will emerge not as valiant independence but, like her mother's, as ignorant blindness of serious realities.

The treatment of her mother as comic allows Lizzie, and Austen, to displace the implicit challenge against social limitations with a parental battle that is simpler to fight. The daughter challenges restrictions voiced by a mother who has had no role in creating those rules. Her resentment toward her mother suggests an inability to confront her father's authority and responsibility, but it also gives her the chance to practice rebellion in a less threatening context.[19] Mrs. Bennet's embarrassing outbreaks concern Lizzie partially because they proclaim what she must conceal and partially because the reception of these remarks shows Lizzie the contradictory proscriptions for women. Her mother has warned Lizzie (with a "cry") to "remember where you are, and do not run on in the wild manner that you are suffered to do at home" (p. 88). But Lizzie is caught in a bind: she must be guarded in her words and tactful in her wit if she is to win Darcy (she must always remember she is not "at home"), yet she can win him only by seeming independent and daring (by not allowing him to determine where her home shall be). She vacillates between an astute political analysis and a repression of such insights. When, for example, Darcy confesses he has been attracted by the "liveliness" of her mind, she suggests it might more accurately be termed "impertinence" (p. 388). But she is careful to teach her prospective sister-in-law how "impertinence" gets translated into a permitted or even valued quality: "[Georgiana's] mind received knowledge which had never before fallen in her way. By Elizabeth's instructions she began to comprehend that a woman may take liberties with her husband, which a brother will not always allow in a sister more than ten years younger than himself" (p. 395). Lizzie instructs Georgiana in a mild, affectionate version of sexual politics, but even such casual reminders indicate how careful women must be in determining what is allowed and what will be censured. Lizzie does not presume that Darcy's fondness raises her to a permanent position of "liberty"; even after they have declared their love, she is guarded in her speech, "check[ing]" her "long[ing]" to tease him by remembering "that he had yet to learn to be laught at, and it was rather too early to begin" (p. 380).

Lizzie is also cautious about making explicit the power relations between men and women. She counters her sister Jane's belief that "women fancy admiration means more than it does" with a caustic "and men take care that they should." But when Jane pursues the issue of what is "designedly done," Lizzie demurs from the extremity of her views—"without scheming to do wrong, or to make others unhappy, there may be error, and there may be misery"—and finally offers to be silent before she offends by "saying what I think of persons you esteem. Stop me whilst you can" (pp. 174-75). In the very next chapter, however, she rearticulates the political awareness to her aunt Gardener, who has attributed the failure of Jane's romance to "accident." "These things happen so often!" her aunt has concluded, and Lizzie sharply responds: "An excellent consolation in its way, but it will not do for *us*. We do not suffer by *accident*" (p. 178). She ultimately admits her father's complicity in Mrs. Bennet's ridiculed position, but even a private acknowledgment of this insight seems dangerous and must be carefully contained. Although she "had never been blind to the impropriety of her father's behavior as a husband" and "had always seen it with pain," she "endeavoured to forget what she could not overlook, and to banish [it] from her thoughts." It is only the public disaster of Lydia's seduction that allows her to blame her father as well as her mother for the "disadvantages which must attend the children of so unsuitable a marriage" (p. 262).

Lizzie is trapped between the equally unpleasant expectations of the "good" and "bad" daughter. The fall of Lydia, the bad daughter who is her mother's favorite, is instructive, since it reminds Lizzie of the danger of being judged as "fanciful" or "wayward." Mrs. Gardiner has warned Lizzie to be a good daughter, not of her mother but of her father: "you must not let your fancy run away with you. You have sense and we all expect you to use it. Your father would depend on *your* resolution and good conduct, I am sure. You must not disappoint your father" (p. 181). But Lizzie can see what society's "good sense" wins, what a good daughter can expect for herself. She is greatly unsettled by Charlotte's "sensible" marriage and has little sympathy with the "composure" with which both Jane and Charlotte repress their desires and observations. She also has the example of Miss Bingley, who has constructed herself as the perfect product of social rules, as exceedingly careful to do whatever it takes to win herself a powerful husband and house. In the fabulous world of *Pride and Prejudice,* it is Lizzie, the "bad" daughter, who succeeds and is allowed to laugh at her competitor and to outrank her sensible friend and sister. The happy ending rewrites the historically more likely outcome, the coopted marriage of Charlotte or the ridiculed position of her mother.[20] The heroine wins propriety and wealth through daring and rebellion made palatable to her world through her partial adherence to its rules. She succeeds by publicly being a "bad daughter" to her un-worthy mother, but she also succeeds by evading the sense and directives of patriarchal culture.

Pride and Prejudice marks the beginning of a time, as Judith Lowder Newton has argued, of "general ideo-logical crisis, a crisis of confidence over the status, the proper work, and the power of middle-class women" (p. 1). The ambivalent role of the mother, who in Austen's novel is both powerful and negligible, becomes a more conventional trope as it is codified and rationalized by a proliferation of advice books, novels about women's struggles, and treatises on the Woman Question. It is, therefore, productive to compare how the "foolish mother" is positioned in a novel in which the role is still implicit and how that position is solidified in a novel like Hardy's *Tess of the D'Urbervilles* (1891). By the end of the century, in *Tess,* Hardy presents a daugh-ter passionately condemning her foolish mother, blam-ing the mother for the daughter's tragedy. Such a scene is unmentionable in Austen, and not only because of the differing conventions of polite discourse.

By 1891 it was relatively uncontroversial to represent the mother as scapegoat for cultural disorder. When Tess discovers that there is "danger in men-folk," it is her "poor foolish mother" she blames for not having warned her.[21] The mother's failure in the personal realm is given broad-ranging cultural implications. Tess's mother has seen their fall from "nobility" as merely a "passing accident" rather than the "haunting episode" that ruins her child's expectations (p. 162). Her foolish-ness thus becomes a historical emblem—of the peasant-ry's failure to understand the threat of the aristocracy and of the urban world, of the failure of the "past" to understand the demands of "the modern age," of the failure of seeing "accident" or "nature" as a sufficient cultural explanation. And it apparently makes sense to trace all these powerful failures to a mother who has not taken her responsibilities seriously enough: "'O mother, my mother!' cried the agonized girl, turning passionately upon her parent as if her poor heart would break. 'How could I be expected to know? . . . Why didn't you warn me? Ladies know what to fend hands against, because they read novels that tell them of these tricks; but I never had the chance o' learning in that way, and you did not help me!' Her mother was sub-dued."

The implication is that ladies have an undue advantage over the daughter of a "poor foolish mother," an advan-tage which Tess sees as literary but which could more accurately be seen as the advantage of wealth and class. The mother's "simple vanity" becomes the focus for her daughter's anger, which cannot find its more appro-priate targets, both individual and cultural. But when the novel has Tess blame her mother for not "telling" her of worldly dangers, and when such an accusation

"subdues" the mother into a proper acceptance of guilt, there has been an important ideological manipulation of the role of mother. It is contradictory to locate the fault in not "telling"—in words—rather than in the "wrong doing" of men or the class inequities that make ladies better prepared to negotiate the perils of adult life. *Tess* thus provides a scapegoat for the powerful social trans-formations that affect the lives of women, for which daughters must be prepared. The mother, who is at best a commentator on the social realm, has taken the place of initiator, guardian, or betrayer.

Mid-nineteenth-century advice books, like the influen-tial series by Mrs. Ellis—*Wives of England, Daughters of England,* and *Women of England*—similarly imply that mothers are the source of broad cultural changes that disrupt the family and the lives of their daughters. They charge women with the responsibility for correct-ing and upholding moral standards for man, who is "confused by the many voices, which in the mart, the exchange, or the public assembly, have addressed them-selves to his inborn selfishness or his worldly pride [and . . .] stands corrected before the clear eye of woman, as it looked directly to the naked truth, and de-tected the lurking evil of the specious act he was about to commit" (*The Women of England,* p. 42). The blame for continued "selfishness" or confusion, for worldly pride or lurking evil, then rests not on the "confused" man but on the woman who fails to oppose him, to pro-vide him with a "clear eye" in which to see his faults. In an 1832 essay on the "Education of Daughters," Ly-dia Maria Child cites as a "true, and therefore an old remark, that the situation and prospects of a country may be justly estimated by the character of its women" and stresses the important transmission of such influ-ence from mother to daughter.[22] Such pronouncements suggest a cultural concern over what is perceived as women's and, more explicitly, mothers' responsibilities and failures. They also stress the narrow range of possi-bilities afforded mothers, in which the mother's behav-ior is always a failure, incapable of satisfying incom-mensurable demands. Deborah Gorham describes the mother-daughter relationships figured in Victorian lit-erature and art as inevitably producing two outcomes: "one in which the mother fulfilled her maternal func-tions, and one in which she would not or could not do so" (p. 47). To be a "good" mother according to the culture's proscriptions was to be a failure in her daugh-ter's eyes. But to be a "bad" mother was also to be a failure, to embarrass or commit her daughter to living outside the system of social rewards and approval only the father could bestow.

By working to institutionalize the "proper" discourses of women, to teach the emergent middle class how to be "good" mothers and "dutiful" daughters, nineteenth-century advice books suggest that the relationship be-tween mother and daughter was not seen as "natural" or as the province of individuals, but as requiring considerable institutional support and guidance. The aim was not to create self-fulfilled individuals but to acquire facility in approved social functions. In *Women of England,* Mrs. Ellis warned against encouraging young women to be too "striking" or to stray from their proper "station" as "relative creatures": "If, therefore, they are endowed only with such faculties, as render them striking and distinguished in themselves, without the faculty of instrumentality, they are only as dead letters in the volume of human life, filling what would otherwise be a blank space, but doing nothing more" (p. 108). To be part of social discourse, to avoid the marginality of being a "dead letter," a "blank space" in the "volume of human life," young girls must learn to function in predetermined ways, to fulfill the "instrumentality" established as their role and use in culture. Like their mothers, like Freud's child, they must learn to accept what is "granted" to them by an authority they work to uphold. It would be difficult for a mother to speak from such a proscribed position, and it would be painful for a daughter to hear such words. Austen's Mrs. Bennet makes the position and its restrictions visible and laughable; she "fails" to become an appropriate function and thus remains outside approved social practices. Her daughter "succeeds," but she too is implicated in her mother's exclusion from the social world. The novel "forgets" the bleakness of women's prospects in its exuberant ending, but at the cost of banning the mother from its view and of suspending the objections she voiced.

Notes

This essay is dedicated, with love and admiration, to my mother, Mary Anne Heyward Ferguson, who, unlike Mrs. Bennet, has been a wise comprehender and a supportive instigator of her daughters' efforts. An early version of this essay was presented at a Wellesley College symposium, "Mothers and Daughters in Literature," in February 1982.

1. Jane Austen, *Pride and Prejudice,* 1813 (New York: Penguin, 1972), p. 53.

2. Mikhail Bakhtin, *The Dialogic Imagination,* ed. Michael Holquist, trans. Caryl Emerson and Michael Holquist (Austin: University of Texas Press, 1981), p. 403.

3. Sigmund Freud, *Jokes and Their Relation to the Unconscious,* 1905, ed. and trans. James Strachey (New York: W. W. Norton, 1963), p. 182. Freud wrote: "weil eine solche bei ihm nicht vorhanden ist," "er besitze diese Hemmung nicht," and "lachen nicht über ihn, sondern sind über ihn enttrüstet" (Sigmund Freud, *Der Witz und Seine Beziehung zum Unbewussten* [Leipzig and Vienna: Franz Deuticke, 1905], p. 156).

4. Bakhtin locates the effect of incomprehension, not within the novel or in any specific character's ability to "teach" others, but in the novelist's awareness of multiple discourses: "A failure to understand languages that are otherwise generally accepted and that have the appearance of being universal teaches the novelist how to perceive them physically as *objects,* to see their relativity, to externalize them, to feel out their boundaries, that is, it teaches him how to expose and structure images of social languages" (*The Dialogic Imagination,* p. 404).

5. Pierre Macherey, *A Theory of Literary Production,* trans. Geoffrey Wall (1966; London: Routledge and Kegan Paul, 1978), pp. 80, 83. Macherey argues that such a double reading seeks "the inscription of an *otherness* in the work, through which it maintains a relationship with that which it is not, that which happens at its margins" (p. 79).

6. In *Of Woman Born: Motherhood as Experience and Institution* (New York: W. W. Norton, 1976), her influential analysis of American cultural attitudes toward motherhood, Rich claims: "This cathexis between mother and daughter—essential, distorted, misused—is the great unwritten story" (p. 225). See also Signe Hammer, *Daughters and Mothers: Mothers and Daughters* (New York: Quadrangle/New York Times Book Co., 1975); and Nancy Chodorow, *The Reproduction of Mothering: Psychoanalysis and the Sociology of Gender* (Berkeley: University of California Press, 1978). In her review essay on "Mothers and Daughters" (*Signs* 7 [1981], 200-222), Marianne Hirsch discusses the reasons for the historical "silence" and "the subsequent centrality of the mother-daughter relationship at this particular point in feminist scholarship" (p. 201). Her essay provides an extremely useful survey of recent studies that are "attempts to prove that the story of mother-daughter relationships has been written even if it has not been read, that it constitutes the hidden subtext of many texts" (p. 214). See also *The Lost Tradition: Mothers and Daughters in Literature,* ed. E. M. Broner and Cathy N. Davidson (New York: Frederick Ungar, 1980), a collection of essays on this issue. Studies that discuss the nineteenth-century scene in particular are: Patricia Meyer Spacks, *The Female Imagination* (New York: Avon Books, 1972); Françoise Basch, *Relative Creatures* (New York: Schocken Books, 1974); Ellen Moers, *Literary Women* (New York: Doubleday, 1976); Elaine Showalter, *A Literature of Their Own* (Princeton: Princeton University Press, 1977); Lynne Agress, *The Feminine Irony* (New York: University Press of America, 1978); Nina Auerbach, *Communities of Women* (Cambridge: Harvard University Press, 1978); Sandra M. Gilbert and Susan Gubar, *The Mad-*

woman in the Attic: The Woman Writer and the Nineteenth-Century Literary Imagination (New Haven: Yale University Press, 1979); Judith Lowder Newton, *Women, Power, and Subversion: Social Strategies in British Fiction* (Athens: University of Georgia Press, 1981; rpt. London: Methuen, 1986); and Deborah Gorham, *The Victorian Girl and the Feminine Ideal* (Bloomington: Indiana University Press, 1982).

7. In "The Female World of Love and Ritual: Relations between Women in Nineteenth-Century America," *Signs* 1 (1975), 1-29, Carroll Smith-Rosenberg suggests that "taboos against female aggression and hostility" may have been "sufficiently strong to repress even that between mothers and their adolescent daughters" (p. 17). But she also challenges the modern assumption that hostility between generations, "today considered almost inevitable to an adolescent's struggle for autonomy and self-identity," is an essential, ahistorical fact. Patricia Spacks explains the omission of mothers as a stylistic version of an unchanging resentment: "In nineteenth-century novels women express hostility toward their mothers by eliminating them from the narrative; twentieth-century fiction dramatizes the conflict" (*The Female Imagination,* p. 191).

8. Ellen Moers calls courtship "a dreadful word" in Austen, "for it implies something a man does to a woman, and can include adultery." She prefers "marriageship," and argues Austen saw marriage as "the only act of choice in a woman's life" (*Literary Women,* p. 70). Gilbert and Gubar concur that marriage is "the only accessible form of self-definition for girls in [Austen's] society" (*Madwoman in the Attic,* p. 127).

9. See Gilbert and Gubar, *Madwoman in the Attic,* pp. 97-104. Moers describes women writers as "an undercurrent" literary tradition (*Literary Women,* p. 42); Showalter discusses the "covert solidarity that sometimes amounted to a genteel conspiracy" between women novelists and readers in the nineteenth century (*A Literature of Their Own,* pp. 15-16).

10. Showalter discusses the "remarkable frequency" with which nineteenth-century women writers identified with the father at the "loss of, or alienation from, the mother" (ibid., p. 61). "[M]ost mothers in middle-class families were more narrow-minded and conventional than the fathers, who had the advantages of education and mobility. . . . The daughter's nonconformity would increase the strains in her relationship with her mother and lead her to make greater demands upon her father for love and attention" (p. 62). Susan Peck MacDonald argues that the "absence

of mothers" in Austen's novels derives "not from the impotence or unimportance of mothers, but from the almost excessive power of motherhood." The mother's power to "shield her daughter from the process of maturation" must be met by a "psychological rift" with the mother ("Jane Austen and the Tradition of the Absent Mother," in *The Lost Tradition,* ed. Broner and Davidson, pp. 58, 64). See also my discussion of Louisa Gradgrind's negotiation of her father's system and her mother's ineffectual resistance, in Jean Ferguson Carr, "Writing as a Woman: Dickens, *Hard Times,* and Feminine Discourses," *Dickens Studies Annual* 18 (1989), 159-76.

11. "Jokes, even if the thought contained in them is non-tendentious and thus only serves theoretical intellectual interests, are in fact never non-tendentious. They pursue the second aim: to promote the thought by augmenting it and guarding it against criticism. Here they are once again expressing their original nature by setting themselves up against an inhibiting and restricting power—which is now the critical judgment" (Freud, *Jokes,* pp. 132-33). See also Sigmund Freud, *A General Introduction to Psychoanalysis,* 1924, trans. Joan Riviere (New York: Washington Square, 1952), in which he discusses slips of the tongue and other comical errors: "They are not accidents; they are serious mental acts; they have their meaning" (p. 48).

12. The first two depictions are by Douglas Bush in his 1956 article "Mrs. Bennet and the Dark Gods: The Truth about Jane Austen," rpt. in *Twentieth-Century Interpretations of* Pride and Prejudice, ed. E. Rubenstein (Englewood Cliffs, N.J.: Prentice-Hall, 1969), p. 113, and the last two by Mark Schorer in his introduction to *Pride and Prejudice* (Cambridge: Houghton Mifflin, 1956), pp. xiii, xxi.

13. Nina Auerbach argues for the "equivocal" nature of Austen's discussion of "direct female power" and cites Harriet Martineau's "oblique apology" in *Society and America* (1837) that English girls would obey such a "foolish mother" (*Communities of Women,* p. 50).

14. Charles Dickens, *The Life and Adventures of Nicholas Nickleby* (London, 1838-39), ch. 11.

15. On Lydia's return, Austen describes Mrs. Bennet as "disturbed by no fear for her felicity, nor humbled by any remembrance of her misconduct" (p. 320). Nina Auerbach discusses Mrs. Bennet as curiously vague about the details of domestic life, but sees Lizzie as "beyond a certain point devoid of memory": "if she shares nothing else with her mother, her faculty of nonremembrance confirms

Mrs. Bennet's perception of the nonlife they have had together" (*Communities of Women,* p. 43).

16. In her essay on Charlotte's prospects, "Why Marry Mr. Collins?" in *Sex, Class, and Culture* (1978; rpt. London: Methuen, 1986), Lillian Robinson discusses Lady Catherine's harsh reminder that although Lizzie's father is a gentleman she is not "the daughter of a gentlewoman as well" (p. 185).

17. Judith Lowder Newton discusses *Pride and Prejudice*'s subversion of the issue of economic concerns by its association with Mrs. Bennet, "a woman whose worries we are not allowed to take seriously because they are continually undermined by their link with the comic and the absurd" (*Women, Power, and Subversion,* p. 70). See also Lillian Robinson's discussion of the economic difference the heroines would experience as daughters and as wives (*Sex, Class, and Culture,* p. 198).

18. In *The Women of England, Their Social Duties, and Domestic Habits* (London, 1838; rpt. Philadelphia: Herman Hooker, 1841), Mrs. Ellis begins her chapter on "the uses of conversation" with what she admits is the "somewhat paradoxical" discussion of silence, the "peculiar province of a woman" which derives "from her position in society" (p. 101). In *The Wives of England: Their Relative Duties, Domestic Influence, and Social Obligations* (London, 1843; rpt. New York: D. Appleton, 1843), she provides a fitting example of the authority of men's silence and the contingency of woman's speech. She advises men to leave the discipline of servants and children to their wives "because the master of a family with whom it rests to exercise real authority cannot so well unbend, and make himself familiar with the young people under his direction, the claims of this part of the community are strong upon the wives of England" (p. 235). The husband retains "real" power by being silent but allows his wife to "unbend" in speech; her exercise of domestic power is granted on the condition that she make herself "familiar" to a "part of the community" that remains "under" the "master."

19. A sociolinguistic study of mother-daughter relationships comments on the use of "indirection" by mothers to signal "to their children that a directive is meant more seriously than its surface structure suggests." They cite the view that "indirection occurs because mothers are less willing to demonstrate power openly than are fathers. They see in the mother's use of indirect means in controlling her children evidence of her discontent with the superordinate position of power which is available to her as a mother, but not elsewhere in her life." Their study suggests that such a doubled discourse both acknowledges and attempts to circumvent the disparity in social power of men and women, and its use arises from the mother's inexperience with power and her unwillingness to claim it openly. See Ruth Wodak and Muriel Schulz, *The Language of Love and Guilt: Mother-Daughter Relationships from a Cross-Cultural Perspective* (Amsterdam: John Benjamins, 1986), pp. 35-36. Wodak and Schulz discuss indirect means of control or instruction as a sign of the mother's need to domesticate her authority, to make it appear less intrusive or insistent, less like a usurpation of male prerogatives, but they also cite it as a manipulative practice which preserves the mother's power in a realm beyond critique, "because indirection denies the child a chance to respond" (p. 37). As is evident in the interviews, the mother's linguistic claim to power often arises from her borrowing of patriarchal languages. The signal to serious portent, or to powerful command, is achieved by moving outside the language used by mothers to children, by using those social discourses that remain the province of fathers—logic, proper language, or an approved state language. They provide many examples of such "metaphorical code switching (a switch from one register to another)": for example, American mothers' attempt to "convey seriousness by switching from a diminutive name to the child's full name" or Norwegian mothers' movement "from their local dialect into Standard Norwegian to emphasize a command" (p. 36).

20. See Lillian Robinson's discussion of the ending as improbable, "outside the realm of [Lizzie's] own and Jane Austen's imaginings" (*Sex, Class, and Culture,* p. 188).

21. Thomas Hardy, *Tess of the D'Urbervilles* (New York: W. W. Norton, 1979), pp. 69-70.

22. Lydia Maria Child, "Hints to Persons of Moderate Fortune," in *The American Frugal Housewife: Dedicated to Those Who Are Not Ashamed of Economy* (Boston, 1832; rpt. Worthington, Ohio: Worthington Historical Society, 1965), p. 1.

Joseph Litvak (essay date fall-winter 1992)

SOURCE: Litvak, Joseph. "Delicacy and Disgust, Mourning and Melancholia, Privilege and Perversity: *Pride and Prejudice.*" *Qui Parle* 6, no. 1 (fall-winter 1992): 35-51.

[*In the following essay, Litvak explores the ideas of disgust and pleasure in the various contexts in which they are presented in* Pride and Prejudice.]

> Let it be understood in all senses that what the word disgusting *de-nominates is what one cannot resign oneself to mourn.*
>
> —Jacques Derrida

In a well-known passage from one of her letters to her sister Cassandra, Jane Austen records her own response to *Pride and Prejudice* (1813):

> I had some fits of disgust. . . . The work is rather too light, and bright, and sparkling; it wants shade; it wants to be stretched out here and there with a long chapter of sense, if it could be had; if not, of solemn specious nonsense, about something unconnected with the story; an essay on writing, a critique on Walter Scott, or the history of Buonaparté [sic], or anything that would form a contrast, and bring the reader with increased delight to the playfulness and epigrammatism of the general style.[1]

That Austen can be driven to disgust not just by her own writing, but by its very *refinement,* by what is most "light, and bright, and sparkling" in it, comes as no surprise: the hyperfastidiousness she evinces here conforms perfectly with the venerable stereotype of gentle Jane, where the gentleness or gentility in question easily assumes a pathological or ideologically suspect character. Of course, what disgusts Austen is not so much her novel's "general style" itself as the lack of a "contrast" that would "bring the reader with increased delight to [its] playfulness and epigrammatism." In its belated wish to interpolate a certain differential heaviness, however, Austen's acute calculation of rhetorical effects bespeaks the characteristic work of an aesthetic of *distinction.*[2] Gagging on the stylistic consistency—that is, the *over*consistency—of *Pride and Prejudice,* getting sick from what amounts to too much of a good thing, Austen thus presents herself as her novel's ideal reader. For reading *Pride and Prejudice*—reading any Austen novel—means submitting, consciously or not, to a rigorous aesthetic *discipline,* undergoing subtle but incessant schooling in the ever-finer classifications, discriminations, and aversions that maintain Austen's exacting (because never quite explicit) norms of good manners and good taste, of "rectitude and delicacy," according to which anyone, even a distinguished hero or a delightful heroine,[3] or anything, even an unrelieved "playfulness and epigrammatism," can fall under the dreaded rubric of the disgusting.

But what if, instead of merely providing evidence of how well Austen has learned her own lessons, her "fits of disgust" signified a protest against that discipline? There is more than one way, after all, of being disgusted by *Pride and Prejudice*—indeed, by the very aesthetic properties that would seem to make it irresistibly appetizing. For if the novel functions discreetly and thus all the more efficaciously as a kind of conduct book, the good manners and good taste it works to implant operate in the service of a eugenic teleology of *good breeding*: that is, of the marriage plot, whereby the traditional novel idealizes heterosexuality and its reproduction. Much of the most adventurous recent Austen criticism, of course, has concentrated on uncovering just this ideological labor in her fiction. As a result, it has become possible not only to see how her novels serve up what D. A. Miller calls "social prescriptions that readers are palatably, even deliciously made to swallow," but also to begin to resist such dubious nourishment, spitting out—even spitting up—what no longer tastes quite so delicious.[4] In expressing her disgust on reading *Pride and Prejudice,* Austen may be doing something other than just voicing her fear of dulling (or offending) our palates with too much brilliance: she may in fact be seen as at once authorizing and enacting a resistant reading of her own text.

If *Pride and Prejudice* is disgusting because it is "too light, and bright, and sparkling," its seductive surface does not so much conceal a disciplinary core as constitute and convey a new and improved discipline of its own. The lightness of the style, I would argue, functions much like that of today's lighter, leaner cuisine, which, as we are constantly reminded not just by doctors and dietitians but, even more dishearteningly, by restaurant critics and cookbook authors as well, is both what we want and what's good for us. *Pride and Prejudice,* whose low-fat, low-cholesterol language positively makes our mouths water, begins to seem uncannily "modern," a prescient fictional precursor of our own food and drug administration.[5]

But the stylish askesis the novel purveys is not merely a question of style. In thematizing its *écriture minceur,* it articulates the strict moral regimen enforced by and upon what it would project as a whole interpretive community of weight watchers. The "easy playfulness" (70) of Elizabeth Bennet's manners is matched, not surprisingly, by her "light and pleasing" (70) figure, so that she serves as a fitting embodiment of the verbal ethos of the novel in which she stars. Thus streamlined, moreover, she can figure over and against characters like Mr. Collins, whose "heavy looking" (109) body almost automatically convicts him of the "stupidity" (163) with which he is soon charged, and which accounts for most of the rare morsels of "solemn specious nonsense" to be found in the text; or like the "indolent" (81) Mr. Hurst, whose vice is confirmed, and whose character irreversibly discredited, in the summary observation that "when he found [Elizabeth to] prefer a plain dish to a ragout, [he] had nothing to say to her" (81). If we haven't yet internalized the precept that less is more, those of us unfortunate enough to share Mr. Hurst's taste are reminded that the only appropriate response to a ragout is *dégoût.*

Even more telling, of course, is Elizabeth's moral superiority to the novel's various comically aberrant female characters, all of whom, in different ways, betray both an excessive appetite and an inability or an unwillingness to control it: Mrs. Bennet, who has never learned how to "hold her tongue" (305); Lydia Bennet, who has inherited not only her mother's shameless garrulity but also her none-too-discriminating taste for soldiers; Miss Bingley, who, with her invidious sarcasm (literally, a rending of flesh), repeatedly and haplessly bites off more than she can chew; Lady Catherine de Bourgh, whose similarly self-subverting freedom in "delivering her opinion" (198) more efficiently delivers proof of her "ill breeding" (207). Reduced—or rather, expanded—to comic types, these characters, paradoxically, can never really "grow": they can only repeat themselves. Even the notoriously "fast" Lydia is stuck in a one-joke role. Along with Collins, these "literary fat ladies," as Patricia Parker would call them, indeed provide whatever precious textual padding remains amid the general svelteness.[6] Modelled against the static backdrop they compose, the self-disciplined Elizabeth should seem to move even more sleekly through the novel's marriage plot, which, though it places obstacles in her path, does so, apparently, in order that we may marvel at the "liveliness" and general light-heartedness with which she negotiates them.

As Austen anticipated, however, the novel may not be sufficiently "stretched out" or larded to make us consume it with such "increased delight." Not every reader, at any rate, will choose to join the "admiring multitude" whom the marriage of Elizabeth and Darcy is destined to "teach . . . what connubial felicity really was" (325). What one hears as a certain sarcasm in this very phrasing may even bespeak *Austen's* distaste for the ideological project in which she finds herself enlisted. Of course, in carrying out this project, she is hardly unique among eighteenth- or nineteenth-century English novelists, and *Pride and Prejudice* is hardly the only one of her novels in which the exigencies of the marriage plot ultimately take precedence over every other claim for narrative interest. What makes *Pride and Prejudice* unusually hard to swallow, I have been suggesting, is not so much the marriage plot per se as the particular ideologico-aesthetic ruse that is supposed to make it go down so easily. For no matter how the novel's distinctive lightness (liteness?) gets glamorized, it remains a fetish in a symbolic economy of *privation*: indeed, it has to be turned into an object of *desire* precisely insofar as it represents—and requires—the systematic denial of *pleasure*.

For all its "Mozartean perfection," in short, *Pride and Prejudice* seems to me the least enjoyable of all of Austen's novels. Where the other novels offer us various juicy tidbits to sink our teeth into on the way to the wedding, *Pride and Prejudice,* though not *entirely* fat-free, generally exercises an almost stingy restraint in dispensing preclosural gratifications, withholding any that might tempt us to stray too far or too unproduc-

tively from its foreordained linear trajectory, catering only to those tastes whose indulgence will leave us, like the heroine, lithe and trim enough to be put through our paces.

Novels such as *Sense and Sensibility* and *Emma* obviously have to conduct their heroines (and their readers) toward the triumphant genital heterosexuality enshrined in the institution of marriage, but, as critics have shown, the very plotting of that development through a progression of proto-Freudian "phases" at least affords their heroines (and their readers) various perversely "pregenital" and/or nonprocreative excitations.[7] Faced with *Pride and Prejudice,* however, the reader who is not especially tantalized by the prospect of a wedding feast is going to be left feeling more than a little hungry.

In this situation, is there anything to do with one's mouth besides complain? As I have suggested, one way of resisting the heterosexist teleology of Austen's master plot is to cultivate—indeed, to *savor*—whatever perverse reader-relations that plot may permit, if only so as, precisely, to master them. To tease out the kinkiness of the interaction between Emma and Knightley, for example, or to play up the seductive theatricality of Mary and Henry Crawford, is fantasmatically to perpetuate a relation with a lost or occluded object: in the first example, a perversity *between* characters, which the normalizing narrative has to cover up; in the second, an energy more visibly located within characters themselves, who must therefore be dealt with more punitively, expelled from the text in a climactic paroxysm of moral revulsion. What a resistant reading of *Mansfield Park* may resist, then, is the pressure to reenact that expulsion: instead of casting the Crawfords out, as one is expected to do, one may try to keep them in, guarding them, perversely, in what French Freudian theory has helped us to picture as a crypt within—or upon—one's own reading body.[8]

In other words, if the disgusting "is what one cannot resign oneself to mourn," purgation is not the only response to it; what has been theorized as the fantasy of incorporation suggests an alternative form of non-mourning. The fantasy of incorporation promotes what Freud calls the work of melancholia, where the refusal to mourn signals a refusal of loss. Neither a mere throwing up and casting out nor, as in mourning, an idealizing, metaphorical introjection of the lost object, incorporation, as Derrida has suggested in his commentary on the work of Nicolas Abraham and Maria Torok, "involves eating the object . . . in order *not* to introject it, in order to vomit it, in a way, into the inside, into the pocket of a cyst."[9] Insisting on a certain literalization of the object, at once killing it and keeping it alive, incorporation is a fantasy not only of eating one's cake and having it, but also of *becoming* one's cake, of *identifying* oneself with it and thus of denying its absence, which the metaphorical substitutions characteristic of mourning would implicitly acknowledge.[10]

In view of what I've said about the slim pickings presented by *Pride and Prejudice,* however, the question would seem to be: how can one perpetuate a fantasmatic relation with something one never had in the first place? One possible answer might begin by recalling that, under the novel's terroristic regime of good taste, no one, not even Elizabeth Bennet, is immune from the charge of vulgarity. For example, Elizabeth's very athleticism—the clearest demonstration that hers is a *disciplined* body—provokes Miss Bingley's disgusted censure when, in a burst of unladylike impetuosity, Elizabeth undertakes the walk to Netherfield to visit her sister Jane and shows up in a dirty petticoat. If Miss Bingley's sneering assertion that this behavior displays "a most country town indifference to decorum" (82) testifies more damningly to her own bad moral taste, there might nonetheless be some advantages to not sanitizing Elizabeth too quickly by reading the passage "figuratively." That is, it might be useful to allow Elizabeth's dirtiness itself to maintain a certain insistent literality, a weight and density comparable to those enjoyed by the incorporated object in the work of melancholia.

And though, Lydia's worthy efforts notwithstanding, the novel as a whole may not satisfy one's appetite for certain perverse pleasures, Miss Bingley's ill-advised mudslinging, like Lady Catherine's later judgment that Elizabeth's marriage to Darcy constitutes a "pollution" (396) of the woods of Pemberley, has the oddly appealing effect of stigmatizing the heroine as not only a transgressor of class distinctions but also a sexual threat. However transparent a betrayal of her own jealousy, snobbishness, and sheer mean-spiritedness—that is, however disgusting in its own right—Miss Bingley's disgust suggests one way of cathecting what we might otherwise pass up as an excessively wholesome text: by recognizing that, through the very plotting of its heroine's upward mobility, of her inevitable ascent toward marriage, it affords us a way of articulating sex with class—specifically, of eliciting from it a certain *social* perversity, in which the older sense of "vulgarity" as social offense already anticipates or implies the newer one of "vulgarity" as sexual offense.

In fact, far from being adventitious or merely occasional, Elizabeth Bennet's implication in the disgusting to a great extent defines her. It is this very stance, moreover, that she takes (rather self-congratulatorily) to define herself. What she shares with her father, of course, and what qualifies the two of them to figure as the novel's most conspicuous author-surrogates, is a sophisti-

cated "delight . . . in any thing ridiculous" (59). Self-styled connoisseurs of the stupid and the vulgar, bemused practitioners of the art of treating the disgusting as a delicacy, these two characters demonstrate the classic middle-class technique, recently delineated by John Kucich, of making oneself look classier than the rest of the middle class.[11] But this raises a potentially unsettling question: to what extent are they therefore not only author-surrogates but critic-surrogates as well?

One reason for retaining a certain psychoanalytic frame of reference is that, inflected by an awareness of the politics of sophistication, it can help us not only to resituate the "easy" ironic "playfulness" that informs this lightest and liveliest of Austen's novels, but also to rethink our own way of consuming it. If the interesting characters in Austen's novels usually fall into two asymmetrical categories—the category inhabited primarily by the heroines, who can (or must) do the essentially interiorizing work of mourning; and the category of those who, endowed (or afflicted) with no such interiority, live exclusively in the nauseating vicariousness that, for Austen, virtually *is* the social—if, in short, the characters can be classified as either elegiac or emetic—what makes the jaunty Elizabeth Bennet *differently* interesting is that, oddly like the melancholic, she marks out a liminal zone between the interior and exterior. While she dwells exclusively neither among the disgusting nor among the mournfully refined, she effects a certain commerce between these two realms. As a refined consumer *of* the disgusting, she may have tastes more like those of a resistant critic than we might imagine, and more to teach us about our own refractory middle-class fantasies of incorporation than we already know.

That is, if *Pride and Prejudice,* more saliently than any of Austen's other novels, mobilizes the marriage plot in such a way as to legitimate the nascent social conjunction that has been called a "middle-class aristocracy,"[12] the concomitant middle-class sophistication embodied by Elizabeth Bennet has the capacity to signify more than just a binding of potentially unruly social energies: its overdetermination can provide an instructive context for the oppositional projects of contemporary bourgeois academic criticism. It is an irony worth remarking, in other words, that the discursive strategy impelling Elizabeth's success story—in which what really succeeds, more balefully, seems to be ideological containment itself—looks a lot like the discursive strategy whereby latter-day middle-class sophisticates would disrupt the very ideology in whose interest Elizabeth fares so well.

Much of the appeal of *Pride and Prejudice,* in any case, consists in its fulfillment of the wish that middle-class readers *can* be sophisticated. While the middle-class heroine of *Northanger Abbey* can only aspire to the sophistication epitomized by her aristocratic husband, Elizabeth Bennet not only possesses sophistication before the novel has even begun, but proves herself more charming than Prince Charming himself—more charming, more clever, more witty than all the Darcys and Bingleys and Hursts and de Bourghs put together. But what exactly *is* this middle-class sophistication that makes Elizabeth, according to her author, "as delightful a creature as ever appeared in print"? Just what is it in Elizabeth's "general style" that enables her not only to win Darcy but, in so doing, to outclass and infuriate snobs like Miss Bingley and bullies like Lady Catherine, making her the prototype of all those wisecracking comic heroines of literature and film, those avengers of their class against its supercilious would-be oppressors?

Consider the following exchange, in which Elizabeth attempts to recuperate her mother's embarrassing monologue about a suitor of Jane's who once wrote verses for her:

> "And so ended his affection," said Elizabeth impatiently. "There has been many a one, I fancy, overcome in the same way. I wonder who first discovered the efficacy of poetry in driving away love!"
>
> "I have been used to consider poetry as the *food* of love," said Darcy.
>
> "Of a fine, stout, healthy love it may. Every thing nourishes what is strong already. But if it be only a slight, thin sort of inclination, I am convinced that one good sonnet will starve it entirely away."
>
> Darcy only smiled; and the general pause which ensued made Elizabeth tremble lest her mother should be exposing herself again.
>
> (90)

Clearly framed as a diversionary tactic, Elizabeth's rather panicky "playfulness and epigrammatism" here work not just to take the spotlight away from her vulgar mother, but to establish Elizabeth's distinction over and against that vulgarity, with which she might otherwise seem too closely affiliated. But though Elizabeth may come off looking distinguished, the playful epigrammatism thanks to which she does so is not entirely distinct from the abjected discourse of the mother.[13]

For Elizabeth's wit obeys a chiastic logic, whereby Darcy's apparently refined, metaphorical defense of poetry as the "food of love" gets set up as a mere received idea, against which her own ironic, deidealizing reading, if it is to emerge as superior in analytic sophistication, must invoke a certain irreducible antimetaphorical insistence: that of the body and its appetites in their ineloquent, almost stupid, but strangely heroic materiality. While the "fine, stout, healthy" body in love can take poetry or leave it, such merely metaphorical food will hardly nourish what Elizabeth rather surpris-

ingly disparages as a "slight, thin sort of inclination." (Even if "stout," in Austen's day, may have meant "vigorous" rather than "thickset," we can indeed imagine here a happy prolepsis, not unlike that of "vulgarity," whereby the body for which this health-conscious novel secretly longs is neither slight nor even light, but perhaps best described by the distinctly un-Austenian adjective, *zaftig*.[14]) Indeed, so paradoxically offensive is the idealized metaphoricity of poetry as the food of love that it can have the literally disgusting effect of "starv[ing]" that weak inclination "entirely away." The savvy, down-to-earth Elizabeth advertises a robust middle-class materialism that—at once appealing to the debunking force of what a nicer aesthetic would find repulsive, and thereby evincing its own disgust vis-à-vis the latter—chokes on the spiritualizing clichés that the aristocratic Darcy, for one, has not been too proud to swallow.

This is not to say that Elizabeth has no saving interiority: her grief and humiliation in the wake of the disgrace caused by Lydia and Wickham, her anguished recognition that "never had she so honestly loved [Darcy], as now, when all love must be vain" (295), testify to her appetite for the work of mourning. But Elizabeth owes her success to more than just her refined and refining inwardness. If, on the one hand, what makes middle-class sophistication middle-class, as Norbert Elias suggests, is its displacement of merely exterior, superficial aristocratic *civility* into a psychologized *cultivation,* it just as constitutively distinguishes itself, on the other hand, by activating the resulting self-consciousness through an endless putting into quotation marks of its own lower stratum, of the vulgarity that thereby figures within it as an indelible prehistorical trace.[15] Through her witty remarks on poetry and love, Elizabeth distinguishes herself from Darcy and her mother alike, playing the high metaphorizing taste of the one off against the low literal-mindedness of the other—the terms in which she champions the body and literality, for instance, are themselves figurative—and thus exhibiting a rhetorical virtuosity that neither of them can claim.

Playing both sides against the middle—that is, against itself—middle-class sophistication vulgarizes mere (i.e., aristocratic) sophistication and sophisticates mere (i.e., lower-class) vulgarity. Elizabeth invites Darcy to acknowledge the charm of the latter tactic when, at the end of the novel, she asks him "to account for his ever having fallen in love with her":

> "My beauty you had early withstood, and as for my manners—my behaviour to *you* was at least always bordering on the uncivil, and I never spoke to you without rather wishing to give you pain than not. Now be sincere; did you admire me for my impertinence?"

"For the liveliness of your mind, I did."

"You may as well call it impertinence at once. It was very little less. The fact is, that you were sick of civility, of deference, of officious attention. You were disgusted with the women who were always speaking and looking, and thinking for *your* approbation alone. I roused, and interested you, because I was so unlike *them.*"

(388)

Resorting again to chiasmus, Elizabeth identifies her manner, as well as her "manners," in terms of an alluring "impertinence" as opposed to a disgusting "civility." Yet if she has "interested" Darcy where other women could not, this is not simply because of her difference from their "deference"—not simply because he finds refreshing what would otherwise seem disgusting—but because she has had the wit to *stylize* the vulgarity that keeps threatening to reclaim the rest of her family. "*Bordering* on the uncivil," Elizabeth's stylistic practice is a strategically displaced, ironically mannered version of what she has avowed in herself as a certain "coarseness of . . . *sentiment,*" itself bordering on the incorrigible Lydia's "coarseness of *expression*" (247; Austen's emphasis). And while Elizabeth by no means celebrates such contaminating contiguity with Lydia—or, for that matter, with any of the more disgusting members of her family, which is to say, just about everyone but Jane, the Gardiners, and perhaps her father—her remarks to Darcy above make disarmingly clear that she has grasped the rhetorical and social advantages of vomiting vulgarity into the inside, of incorporating it into a new, more capacious and more versatile class style.[16]

The evident upward mobility of this style might represent something of an embarrassment for those of us who recognize in it an uncanny precursor of our own would-be "impertinent" deployment of the "disgusting": if not unabashedly downward, the movement of oppositional criticism is supposed to be audaciously and unpredictably lateral, transgressing disciplinary divisions, cultural boundaries, and so forth. The point is not to unmask oppositional criticism as merely another mode of bourgeois careerism, but to mark the different, almost opposite, ethical and political valences with which strikingly similar strategies can be charged. For the fantasy of *incorporation,* which I have associated with an admirably perverse resistance to the normalizing (i.e., heterosexualizing) pressures of the marriage plot, bears a strong resemblance to the far less attractive operation of *containment*—more specifically, to "the endless 'rediscovery' of the carnivalesque within modern literature" (and criticism), which Peter Stallybrass and Allon White have demystified as "a counter-sublimation, a delirious expenditure of the symbolic capital accrued (through the regulation of the body and the decathexis of habitus) in the successful struggle of bourgeois hegemony."[17]

Perversely cultivating a taste for what the regime of "family values" demonizes as the disgusting, much recent gay, lesbian, and anti-heterosexist criticism could probably be historicized as a "counter-sublimation" of the kind Stallybrass and White describe. But less than the question of whether that criticism is "really" oppositional or "really" complicit in the success of bourgeois hegemony, what interests me is why the problematic of class and the problematic of sexuality so rarely engage each other in contemporary academic discourse. Not that our culture as a whole abounds in places where they can be found in dialogue; in this respect, the academy indeed mirrors the world from which it might be imagined to differ. While every television talk show nowadays strikes another blow against the poor old repressive hypothesis, what remains largely unspoken, in as well as out of the academy, is not sexuality but the class relations *around* sexuality. Yet, if this issue seldom gets addressed, it nevertheless—or for that very reason—gets acted out, generating powerful or even violent effects, as demonstrated currently by a whole range of attacks on "cultural elites," attacks launched most notoriously and most visibly in and through the mass media by right-wing politicians like Vice-President Dan Quayle, but also increasingly in evidence within the field of lesbian and gay studies itself, where a resentful activism sets itself up in opposition as much to a supposedly triumphant ivorytower mandarinate as to the aforementioned guardians of the Family.[18]

If the example of the impertinent Elizabeth Bennet confronts "perverse" criticism with a hypothetical narrative of its own class origins, it should go without saying that, far from constituting one more discrediting assault, this genealogy is designed to *promote* the cause of perversity. Instead of neutralizing "perverse" criticism by exposing its position of class privilege, it would suggest that "privilege"—or what gets stereotyped under that rubric—can itself have the dangerous force of the perverse. In a culture that tolerates the sophisticated even less than the disgusting—indeed, for which the sophisticated paradoxically represents the disgusting at its most egregious—and that constructs its middle class as the sacred repository of normality itself, the sophisticated middle-class connoisseur of the disgusting commits an offense that includes but is not limited to the sexual. Or rather, her sexual offense *counts* as a social offense, and vice versa. Not only has she developed unorthodox appetites, but she has the effrontery to flaunt them, as though looking down her nose at those members of her class who, less knowingly fluent than she in their command of the operative codes of good and bad taste, and therefore less adept at scrambling them, have to content themselves with merely upholding them. And since pride must always be met by prejudice, the bold infractions of elite criticism have to get recoded as *pathological,* as symptoms of sexual abnormality in its most repellent form, so that what might seem an enviable cosmopolitanism can take on instead the horrifying, abject alterity of what one avoids like the plague.

That this repellent form, especially in the age of "AIDS," is almost always male homosexuality reveals what we might call the other face of counter-sublimation: if the continuing success of bourgeois hegemony is best allegorized by the rising heroine of the marriage plot, her recasting in the homophobic image of the gay man reminds us how easily the privileged middle-class subject can turn into a scapegoat.[19] Rather than designate one figure or the other as the "true" embodiment of elite middle-class culture, we might try to imagine them as a telling composite, as an emblem of the dynamic interdependence of perversity *and* privilege in oppositional criticism. For if the former obviously inflames our culture's numerous arbiters of taste, the outrage that it signifies is scarcely separable from that of the latter. Privilege may not seem the most likely feature in the repertoire of an oppositional politics, but while its provocative potential may be hard to admit in theory, its provocative effects are everywhere legible in contemporary social practice.

Only if we presume to know that "privilege" can only mean one politically suspect thing does its intimate relationship with the perverse appear necessarily to give away the game of oppositional criticism—give it away, that is, as "nothing more than" a game, in which, for example, what is at stake is merely the familiar (or quasi-familial) antagonism between fractions of the dominant class, between, say, the Elizabeth Bennets and the Lady Catherine de Bourghs of the late twentieth century.[20] The pleasures of such sociological reduction are not to be denied; but privilege has its pleasures too, and if oppositional critics have not exactly denied them, neither have we been particularly eager to affirm them, whatever certain "activists" and "populists" would say to the contrary. By exhibiting our shameful "elitism" as tastelessly as our engrossed detractors like to accuse us of doing—as saucily, in other words, as we flaunt the sexual transgressiveness with which that "elitism" is symbolically interfused—we revolting critics might do more than just play into the hands of the enemy. By living up to our bad press, with the full insolence we are already thought to enjoy, we might find ourselves in an even more privileged position to repel sexual and aesthetic regimes that, as many people (not all of them middle-class academic critics) might say, are strictly from hunger.

This essay is an expanded version of a paper delivered at a special session entitled, "Austen's Manner," at the 1991 Modern Language Association convention. I would like to thank Mary Ann O'Farrell, who organized and chaired the session, and a fellow panelist, D. A. Miller, who has encouraged me to indulge my indelicate appetites. As always, Lee Edelman has provided invaluable nourishment, intellectual and otherwise.

Notes

1. *Jane Austen's Letters to Her Sister Cassandra and Others,* ed. R. W. Chapman, 2 vols. (Oxford: Clarendon Press, 1932), 2:299-300.

2. On this aesthetic (which, the author is at pains to show, is by no means *merely* an aesthetic), see Pierre Bourdieu, *Distinction: A Social Critique of the Judgment of Taste,* trans. Richard Nice (Cambridge: Harvard University Press, 1984). One of Bourdieu's central theses is that "Taste classifies, and it classifies the classifier. Social subjects, classified by their classifications, distinguish themselves by the distinctions they make, between the beautiful and the ugly, the distinguished and the vulgar, in which their position in the objective classifications is expressed or betrayed" (6).

3. The phrase "rectitude and delicacy" describes Jane Bennet (*Pride and Prejudice,* ed. Tony Tanner [Harmondsworth: Penguin, 1980], 168). Austen thought Elizabeth Darcy "as delightful a creature as ever appeared in print" (*Letters,* 2:297), but one does not have to endorse the snobbery of a Miss Bingley to notice in Elizabeth some of that "want of propriety" (228) that Darcy observes in almost everyone else in her family. As even a sympathetic critic like Claudia Johnson has to admit, "Elizabeth's wit is occasionally marked by an unabashed rusticity bordering on the vulgar" (*Jane Austen: Women, Politics, and the Novel* [Chicago: University of Chicago Press, 1988], 76); Johnson also remarks that Elizabeth's "celebrated liveliness" "verg[es] sometimes on unlady-like athleticism" (76). As for Darcy, it is significant that, while he makes a favorable first impression, before long "his manners gave a disgust which turned the tide of his popularity" (58).

4. D. A. Miller, "The Late Jane Austen," *Raritan* 10 (Summer 1990): 79. Miller's sumptuously suggestive reading of Austen's body politics has provided me with abundant food for thought. Other critiques of Austen's marriage plot include, for example, Joseph Allen Boone, *Tradition Counter Tradition: Love and the Form of Fiction* (Chicago: University of Chicago Press, 1987), 89-96; Franco Moretti, *The Way of the World: The "Bildungsroman" in European Culture,* trans. Albert Sbragia (London: Verso, 1987), 15-73; Mary Poovey, *The Proper Lady and the Woman Writer: Ideology as Style in the Works of Mary Wollstonecraft, Mary Shelley, and Jane Austen* (Chicago: University of Chicago Press, 1984), 194-207.

5. An example of the incoherences that occasionally beset this discourse of reduction appears in an article by Gina Kolata, entitled "Squeezing Fat, Calories, Guilt, and More Profits out of Junk

Food," on the "Ideas and Trends" page of the *New York Times* "Week in Review" section (Sunday, August 11, 1991, E5). On the one hand: "'It is very clear that the consumer wants low-fat and low-calorie foods—there is no question about that,' said Nomi Ghez, an analyst at Goldman Sachs who follows the food industry." On the other hand, several paragraphs later: "'We have been telling people for decades to give up most meats and dairy products, to eat vegetables, grains and fruits,' said Dr. Adam Drewnowski, the director of the human nutrition program at the University of Michigan. 'But this is not happening. People seem to be not entirely thrilled about eating naturally low-calorie foods like broccoli and grains. They turn up their noses and say, How about some chocolate chip cookies?'"

6. Patricia Parker, *Literary Fat Ladies: Rhetoric, Gender, Property* (New York: Methuen, 1987).

7. See, for example, Eve Kosofsky Sedgwick, "Jane Austen and the Masturbating Girl," *Critical Inquiry* 17 (Summer 1991): 818-37.

8. That, alternatively, one may cathect Fanny Price's oddly juicy neurosis itself, her "monstrosity," is suggested by Nina Auerbach, "Jane Austen's Dangerous Charm: Feeling As One Ought About Fanny Price," in her *Romantic Imprisonment: Women and Other Glorified Outcasts* (New York: Columbia University Press, 1986), 22-37.

9. Jacques Derrida, "Foreword: *Fors*: The Anglish Words of Nicolas Abraham and Maria Torok," trans. Barbara Johnson, in Nicolas Abraham and Maria Torok, *The Wolf Man's Magic Word: A Cryptonomy,* trans. Nicholas Rand (Minneapolis: University of Minnesota Press, 1986), xxxviii. This essay's epigraph, which I have just incorporated partially into the text, is from Derrida, "Economimesis," trans. Richard Klein, *Diacritics* 11 (Summer 1981): 23. The text, an analysis of Kant's aesthetics, informs my reference below to the relationship between disgust and vicariousness.

10. For a shrewd discussion of incorporation in terms of "the melancholia of gender," see Judith Butler, *Gender Trouble: Feminism and the Subversion of Identity* (New York: Routledge, 1990), 57-72. Butler's account is extremely helpful in its inflection of psychoanalytic theorizing toward a more searching analysis of the politics of gender and sexuality. My highly condensed remarks on incorporation owe much to her impressive synthesis and reorientation of a number of Freudian and post-Freudian texts.

11. See John Kucich, "Transgression in Trollope: Dishonesty and the Antibourgeois Elite," *ELH* 56 (Fall 1989): 593-618. In my thinking about the genealogy and the dynamics of middle-class sophistication, I am greatly indebted to Kucich's essay. See Poovey, 196-99, for an excellent account of the essentially defensive function of Elizabeth's "playfulness."

12. The term "middle-class aristocracy" comes from Nancy Armstrong, *Desire and Domestic Fiction: A Political History of the Novel* (New York: Oxford University Press, 1987), 160. See 134-60 for an account of Austen's role in articulating that "paradoxical configuration" (160). In his reading of *Pride and Prejudice,* Moretti also provides a helpful analysis of the symbolic marriage between the middle class and the aristocracy.

13. I allude here to Julia Kristeva, *Powers of Horror: An Essay on Abjection,* trans. Leon S. Roudiez (New York: Columbia University Press, 1982).

14. According to R. W. Chapman, *stout* in Austen "perhaps never = *fat*"; but he indicates one possible exception in her letters, and one could adduce others. See Chapman, ed., *Austen's Letters,* 2:Index VII ("Jane Austen's English"; no page number). As D. A. Miller would remind us, however, the economy of scapegoating virtually requires that any fat-affirmative gesture we glimpse here be accompanied by a compensatory violence against the "slight, thin" body: on "the aggression that the diminutive woman suffers in Austen no less than the large," see Miller, "The Late Jane Austen," 62-64. On the fat (female) body as "an alternative body-identity fantasy" in recent gay male culture, see Michael Moon and Eve Kosofsky Sedgwick, "Divinity: A Dossier, A Performance Piece, A Little-Understood Emotion," *Discourse* 13 (Fall-Winter 1990-91): 13. The notion of "chunks of literality" (36) elaborated in that essay has had a stimulating effect on my thinking about fatty residues in Austen. I am further indebted to Michael Moon for the felicitous term, "revolting criticism," which he used as the title for a session at the 1990 MLA convention, and which I echo at the end of this essay.

15. See Norbert Elias, *The History of Manners: The Civilizing Process, Volume I,* trans. Edmund Jephcott (New York: Pantheon, 1978). On the function of the lower bodily stratum in middle-class culture, see Peter Stallybrass and Allon White, *The Politics and Poetics of Transgression* (Ithaca: Cornell University Press, 1986).

16. For an acid and deliberately reductive reading of Derrida's sophisticated vulgarity, see Bourdieu, 494-500.

17. Stallybrass and White, 202, 201

18. On the activist/elitist binarism in gay studies, see Lee Edelman, "The Mirror and the Tank: 'AIDS,' Subjectivity, and the Rhetoric of Activism," in his *Homographesis: Essays in Gay Literary and Cultural Theory* (New York: Routledge, forthcoming). For an example of how this binarism gets framed and circulated, see Jeffrey Escoffier, "Inside the Ivory Closet," *Out/Look* 10 (Fall 1990).

19. For an extensive and richly nuanced analysis of how the homophobically constructed gay man can figure as the "other face" of the heterosexual woman, see Lee Edelman's essay, "Imag(in)ing the Homosexual: *Laura* and the Other Face of Gender," also forthcoming in *Homographesis*.

20. Readers of Bourdieu's *Distinction* will recognize that I allude here to his differentiation between dominant and dominated fractions of the dominant class, and to his elaboration of the conflict between those class fractions.

Gordon Hirsch (essay date winter 1992)

SOURCE: Hirsch, Gordon. "Shame, Pride, and Prejudice: Jane Austen's Psychological Sophistication." *Mosaic* 25 (winter 1992): 63-78.

[*In the following essay, Hirsch discusses* Pride and Prejudice *in the light of modern psychology, focusing on the role of shame in the novel.*]

Elizabeth Bennet's great moment of psychological insight in **Pride and Prejudice** comes soon after she reads Darcy's letter:

> She grew absolutely ashamed of herself. Of neither Darcy nor Wickham could she think without feeling that she had been blind, partial, prejudiced, absurd.
>
> "How despicably have I acted!" she cried. "I who have prided myself on my discernment. . . . How humiliating is this discovery!—Yet, how just a humiliation!—Had I been in love, I could not have been more wretchedly blind. But vanity, not love, has been my folly. Pleased with the preference of one [Wickham], and offended by the neglect of the other [Darcy], on the very beginning of our acquaintance I have courted prepossession and ignorance, and driven reason away, where either were concerned. Till this moment I never knew myself."
>
> (176-77; 2:13)[1]

Elizabeth's "prepossession" in favor of Wickham and against Darcy—her "prejudice," in other words—stems from her feeling slighted by Darcy, from her wounded "pride," from her sense of vulnerability. Her confidence, her "pride" in her own discernment, has collapsed, and she now reports feeling ridiculous, humiliated, ashamed.

In this way Jane Austen not only underlines the themes alluded to in her novel's title but also highlights their connection. Elizabeth's "pride" has driven her to be defensively "prejudiced." Although she once took satisfaction from her pride, it is now seen to be a response to threats to her self-esteem, a defense against feelings of inferiority, vulnerability and shame. Elizabeth understands her prejudice to be a product of her vulnerable pride, and beneath that pride—ready to return with a vengeance—is the feeling of shame.

With the notable exceptions of D. W. Harding and Bernard Paris, most critics of Jane Austen have not focused on the emotional content and concern with affect in her novels, preferring to concentrate either on her technical manipulations of tone and structure or on her moral thematics. This is particularly true of **Pride and Prejudice,** a novel which Austen herself referred to as possibly "rather too light, and bright, and sparkling" (**Letters** 299). Given that concern with appearing ridiculous is a major issue in the novel, however, the very nature of Austen's disclaimer invites one to look beneath the sprightliness of the performance. In doing so, one discerns not only the psychological acuity of her insights into the emotional dynamics of shame but also her sociological perceptiveness about the way a culture reinforces feelings of shame as a means of maintaining its hierarchies and control.

An instructive way to begin such a discussion is to note that about a century before Austen wrote her novel, David Hume had also investigated the relation between pride and shame, and stressed the importance of these two "passions" in the psyche. In his *Treatise of Human Nature,* Hume identified pride and humility as two fundamental, opposed feelings about the self—the first pleasant and the second painful. For Hume, as for Austen, pride is "not always vicious, nor [humility] virtuous" (297-98). Pride and humility are above all connected with "our idea of ourself" (277), though that idea is affected by the way others regard us; these emotions are, then, important regulators of human behavior in society. Like Austen, Hume was interested as well in the curious way pride attaches not only to our personal qualities but also to our family—"their riches and credit"—and to "any inanimate object which bears a relation to us"—a house, garden, region, or nation (307-08). Austen's study of pride and shame is, however, considerably more concrete and detailed than Hume's philosophical formulations, and the psychological issues she dramatizes are further illuminated by bringing the insights of modern psychology to bear.

The "Shame Experience," as Susan Miller calls it, or "Facing Shame," as Merle A. Fossum and Marilyn J. Mason entitle their book, is one of the subjects most intensively studied in recent years by psychoanalysts and psychodynamically oriented clinicians. Although such research includes a broad range of ideas, these studies have in common a particular emphasis on affect or felt emotions, and a view of shame as especially important and problematic in the development of identity, the sense of self. "Shame" is seen as encompassing a complex of associated affective and cognitive states, which include feeling ashamed, embarrassed, ridiculous, humiliated, dishonored, worthless, etc. Each term denotes a similar painful feeling about the self, though each suggests its own particular admixture of guilt, self-directed hostility, and other, related feelings.

One prominent clinician, Helen Block Lewis, offers this general description of the phenomenology of shame: "In shame, hostility against the self is experienced in the passive mode. The self feels not in control but overwhelmed and paralyzed by the hostility directed against it. One could 'crawl through a hole' or 'sink through the floor' or 'die' with shame. The self feels small, helpless, and childish" ("Shame" 19). Shame is a feeling of disgust, displeasure or embarrassment about some quality of the self, occurring typically at a moment of uncovering and exposure. It is connected with feelings of low-self esteem, and in some cases it may produce depression. Pride, identified with positive feelings about the self, is at the opposite pole of what the psychiatrist Donald Nathanson terms "the shame/pride axis." As is often the case in psychology, however, opposition at the poles may be more apparent than real. Frequently individuals attempt to master their shame through the development of an illusory, brittle pride. Shame is thus a "master emotion," one which is likely to trigger other affects and behaviors (such as rage or grandiosity) in response to deeply rooted feelings of personal inadequacy and inferiority. One reason for the importance of studies of shame in contemporary psychological research is the emphasis on observed, primary affect, and on a response to this affect which is also frequently evident on an emotional level, without an inordinate reliance on abstract psychological metatheory. These new, affect-based studies can be particularly useful in analyzing a novel like *Pride and Prejudice,* which seems to take feelings of pride and shame as its core psychological focus.

* * *

The heroine of Austen's novel, Elizabeth Bennet, appears at first glance to be witty, able and self-possessed; one recognizes, with Caroline Bingley, that "in her air altogether, there is a self-sufficiency" (226; 3:3). Nevertheless the basic situation of the novel explores Elizabeth's recurrent feelings of shame about her family, and the book tends to move from one shame-laden situation to another. Darcy's first proposal of marriage to Elizabeth and his letter of explanation after Elizabeth has rejected his proposal underline the importance of shame in the book. Even as Darcy proposes, "his sense of her

inferiority—of its being a degradation—of the family obstacles which judgment had always opposed to inclination were dwelt on" (161; 2:11). Elizabeth's mother, in particular, is only the daughter of a smalltown attorney, a station in life taken up by her brother-in-law, while her brother (Elizabeth's uncle) is, unfortunately, from the point of view of Darcy and his class, a London businessman who actually lives "within view of his own warehouses" (120; 2:2). "Could you expect me to rejoice in the inferiority of your connections?" Darcy pointedly asks (164; 2:11). Still worse than the "situation of your mother's family," Darcy notes, is "that total want of propriety so frequently, so almost uniformly betrayed by herself [Elizabeth's mother], by your younger sisters, and occasionally even by your father" (168; 2:12). Although Elizabeth begins Darcy's letter as a resisting reader, she grows increasingly distressed by what she feels to be the accuracy of his charges:

> The compliment to herself and her sister [Jane] was not unfelt. It soothed, but it could not console her for the contempt which had been thus self-attracted by the rest of her family; and as she considered that Jane's disappointment had in fact been the work of her nearest relations, and reflected how materially the credit of both must be hurt by such impropriety of conduct, she felt depressed beyond anything she had ever known before.
>
> (177; 2:13)

> In her own past behaviour, there was a constant source of vexation and regret; and in the unhappy defects of her family a subject of yet heavier chagrin. They were hopeless of remedy.
>
> (180; 2:24)

If the climax of the second volume, coming just at the midpoint of the novel, consists of Elizabeth's unflattering recognition of her vulnerability to shame and her understanding of what has motivated her behavior toward Darcy, the climactic chapter of the first volume, the description of the Netherfield ball, is a lengthy account of the way Elizabeth is racked by shame and embarrassment occasioned by one incident after another.

Elizabeth's two first "dances of mortification" with Mr. Collins, her clerical cousin, supply her with "all the shame and misery which a disagreeable partner for a couple of dances can give. The moment of her release from him was ecstasy" (78-79; 1:18). Next, Elizabeth dances with Darcy; they spar inconclusively on various topics, and end their dance in frosty taciturnity. Caroline Bingley then denounces Wickham to Elizabeth on the grounds that, "considering his descent, one could not expect much better" than "infamous" behavior from him (83; 1:18), an attack that particularly enrages Elizabeth because the Bennets' own rank in society is an issue. Collins again embarrasses Elizabeth by indecorously approaching and introducing himself to Darcy, who is vastly his social superior, justifying this breach of decorum to Elizabeth on the grounds that "I consider the clerical office as equal in point of dignity with the highest rank in the kingdom" (85; 1:18). Mary Bennet, "after very little entreaty . . . oblige[s] the company" with a song, followed by an encore, though it is obvious to all that "her voice was weak and her manner affected" (88; 1:18). Elizabeth's mother loudly proclaims her hopes that Jane will marry Bingley, as well as her indifference to Darcy's opinions. Through all of this, "Elizabeth blushed and blushed again with shame and vexation," and "was in agonies"; indeed, "to Elizabeth it appeared that had her family made an agreement to expose themselves as much as they could during the evening, it would have been impossible for them to play their parts with more spirit or finer success" (87, 88, 89; 1:18).

Reaching momentary peaks at the Netherfield ball and at the time she receives Darcy's letter, shame is the main affectual motif associated with Elizabeth throughout the novel. Sometimes she herself feels ashamed, worthless, humiliated; at other times, characters attempt to shame her. Whether they succeed or not depends on such things as the accuracy of their charges and the degree of her attachment to the shamer. Caroline Bingley, Mr. Collins and Lady Catherine de Bourgh are largely ineffectual in their attempts to play upon her shame; Darcy's criticisms are, in the long run, less easily dismissed. Elizabeth's characteristic response to feelings of shame is caustic wit. She defends against feelings of worthlessness and self-hate by attempting to gain the upper hand through witty and aggressive repartee.

This strategy is evident as early as the novel's third chapter, when Elizabeth overhears Darcy's remark at a ball that "she is tolerable; but not handsome enough to tempt *me*" (12; 1:3). Her effort to turn the tables and triumph over Darcy when recalling this incident is characteristic: "Elizabeth remained with no very cordial feelings toward [Darcy]. She told the story however with great spirit among her friends; for she had a lively, playful disposition, which delighted in anything ridiculous" (12; 1:3). Much later she recognizes the defensive and self-aggrandizing quality of her wit: "I meant to be uncommonly clever in taking so decided a dislike to [Darcy], without any reason" (190; 2:17).

Elizabeth grows increasingly angry and distraught as she learns of Darcy's efforts to dissuade Bingley from calling on Jane in London, which she attributes chiefly to Darcy's sense of the Bennets' "want of importance": "The agitation and tears which the subject occasioned brought on a headache; and it grew so much worse towards the evening that added to her unwillingness to see Mr. Darcy, it determined her not to attend her cousins to Rosings" for tea (159; 2:10). When Darcy, to her amazement, calls on her instead at the parsonage later that evening to propose marriage in a manner which she

Illustration from chapter three of Pride and Prejudice, *depicting the scene where Elizabeth Bennet overhears Mr. Darcy's remark at the ball.*

finds wounding, Elizabeth responds with a reactive humiliated fury, with what psychologists today would call "shame-rage" (Lewis, "Shame" 19): "She lost all compassion in anger. . . . 'If I could *feel* gratitude, I would now thank you. But I cannot. . . . The feelings which, you tell me, have long prevented the acknowledgment of your regard can have little difficulty in overcoming it after this explanation'" (161-62; 2:11). Darcy is able immediately to grasp some of what underlies Elizabeth's response: "[My] offences might have been overlooked, had not your pride been hurt by my honest confession of the scruples that had long prevented my forming any serious design" (163-64; 2:11). But Darcy's explanatory letter is required before Elizabeth can examine critically the origins of her own feelings.

Despite Elizabeth's conscious recognition, while reading Darcy's letter, of the role her vulnerable self-image played in the development of her "prejudice," her sister Lydia's later "infamy" in running off with Wickham reactivates her sense of shame, producing sleepless nights (250; 3:6). She sees Lydia's action as "such a proof of family weakness, such an assurance of the deepest disgrace" as certainly to foreclose any possible renewal of Darcy's proposal (232; 3:4): "From such a connection she could not wonder that he should shrink. The wish of procuring her regard, which she had assured herself of his feeling in Derbyshire, could not in rational expectation survive such a blow as this. She was humbled, she was grieved; she repented, though she hardly knew of what. She became jealous of his esteem, when she could no longer hope to be benefitted by it" (260-61; 3:8).

Lydia returns unashamed to her father's house after her marriage to Wickham (which has secretly been arranged by Darcy to preserve the honor of the Bennets), and Elizabeth is "disgusted" by "the easy assurance of the young couple. . . . Lydia was Lydia still; untamed, unabashed, wild, noisy, and fearless. . . . It was not to be supposed that time would give Lydia that embarrassment from which she had been so wholly free at first" (264-65; 3:9). Lydia has essentially followed in Elizabeth's footsteps: she has been attracted to and conned by Wickham. Worst of all, she is not even ashamed of acting on her wishes and running away with him! Lydia's impulsive behavior and lack of shame represent precisely what Elizabeth fears and represses in herself. Elizabeth is furious, too, that her mother is "more alive to the disgrace which the want of new clothes must reflect on her daughter's nuptials, than to any sense of shame at her eloping and living with Wickham a fortnight before they took place" (260; 3:8). When Darcy and Bingley revisit Longbourn, Elizabeth's "shame," "misery" and "wretchedness" all return as she listens to her mother brag about Lydia's marriage and single Bingley out for her attention while ignoring Darcy (282-83; 3:11).

At this critical moment of renewed low self-esteem, Lady Catherine de Bourgh reenters the novel and attempts to shame Elizabeth into promising not to marry Darcy. Lady Catherine's intervention backfires, of course, and this is certainly one example of the considerable strength and resiliency in the face of blatant and overt attempts to shame her which are also part of Elizabeth's character. She is restored to happiness when Darcy revives his marriage proposal, but at the end of the novel considerable attention is devoted to the continuing embarrassments of the courtship phase at home and to the question of who will and who will not be welcome at Elizabeth's new abode on Darcy's estate:

> The Collinses were come themselves to Lucas Lodge. . . . The arrival of her friend was a sincere pleasure to Elizabeth, though in the course of their meetings she must sometimes think the pleasure dearly bought, when she saw Mr. Darcy exposed to all the parading and obsequious humility of her husband. . . .

> Mrs. Philips's vulgarity was another, and perhaps a greater tax on his forbearance; and though Mrs. Philips, as well as her sister, stood in too much awe of him to speak with the familiarity which Bingley's good humour encouraged, yet, whenever she *did* speak, she must be vulgar. . . . Elizabeth did all she could to shield him from the frequent notice of either, and was ever anxious to keep him to herself, and to those of her

family with whom he might converse without mortification; and though the uncomfortable feelings arising from all this took from the season of courtship much of its pleasure, it added to the hope of the future; and she looked forward with delight to the time when they should be removed from society so little pleasing to either, to all the comfort and elegance of their family party at Pemberley.

(322-23; 3:18)

Of all the members of her family, the ones most truly welcome at Pemberley will be her uncle and aunt Gardiner, about whom Elizabeth had earlier said, "It was consoling that [Darcy] should know she had some relations for whom there was no need to blush" (213; 3:1). Throughout the novel, then, the family of emotions associated with shame—and Elizabeth's efforts to cope with these feelings by means of hostility or wit—constitute Elizabeth's leitmotif.

In fact, not only Elizabeth but one character after another, whether major or minor, is connected with feelings of shame, or attempts to shame another character, or related issues of self-esteem. Sir William Lucas, Charlotte's father, knighted during his mayoralty, takes "a disgust to his business and his residence in a small market town" and quits them both in favor of a more genteel existence in "Lucas Lodge" (17; 1:5). Caroline Bingley repeatedly tries to shame Darcy into giving up his interest in Elizabeth by calling attention to the woman who would become "your mother-in-law" should he win her (46; 1:10), or by remarking on Elizabeth's dirty stockings and petticoat "six inches deep in mud"—"such an exhibition"—when Elizabeth arrives at Netherfield after walking in the rain (32; 1:8). Mr. Collins's "mixture of servility and self-importance" (56; 1:13) expresses perfectly Austen's insight that grandiose fantasies and aggressive self-promotion may be a defense against threatened self-esteem. Intuitively knowledgeable about such matters himself, Collins pitches his proposal of marriage to Elizabeth in such a manner as to play upon her susceptibility to shame: "You may assure yourself that no ungenerous reproach shall ever pass my lips [about your want of fortune] when we are married" (93; 1:19); or, when his rejection appears likely, he warns Elizabeth that "it is by no means certain that another offer of marriage may ever be made to you" (95; 1:19). Wounded by Elizabeth's rejection, Collins, in a "state of angry pride" (100; 1:21), seeks revenge by rapidly turning his attention to Charlotte Lucas. Wickham, a confidence man usually able to defend against feeling by a display of "manners," nevertheless registers shame when he unexpectedly encounters Darcy in Meryton: "Both changed colour, one looked white, the other red" (63; 1:15). Lady Catherine de Bourgh tries to shame Elizabeth during the latter's visit to Rosings by expressing amazement that the Bennet daughters have had no governess and that all are "out" in society at once (142; 2:6). In her later, last-ditch effort to separate Elizabeth and Darcy, she castigates the "upstart pretensions of a young woman without family, connections, or fortune" (299; 3:14).

In particular Austen explores the role of shame in the makeup of four of the novel's more important characters—Charlotte Lucas, Mr. Bennet, Jane Bennet and Darcy. Elizabeth's relations with the first of these frequently touch on the expression of affect in this sense. Charlotte apparently feels less emotion but is readier to display her desire than Elizabeth. Though Elizabeth can scarcely believe her friend is serious about such tactics, Charlotte insists that "a woman had better show *more* affection than she feels" for a man, lest "she lose the opportunity of fixing him" (20; 1:6). When Charlotte acts on her beliefs and "fixes" the ridiculous Collins, Elizabeth sees Charlotte as "disgracing herself and sunk in her esteem"—"a most humiliating picture" (110; 1:22). Throughout her visit to Charlotte's new home at Collins's parsonage, Elizabeth studies Charlotte for signs of shame and embarrassment: "When Mr. Collins said anything of which his wife might reasonably be ashamed, which certainly was not seldom, she involuntarily turned her eye on Charlotte. Once or twice she could discern a faint blush; but in general Charlotte wisely did not hear. . . . When Mr. Collins could be forgotten, there was really a great air of comfort throughout, and by Charlotte's evident enjoyment of it, Elizabeth supposed he must be often forgotten" (134-35; 2:5). If "in general Charlotte wisely did not hear" what Collins says, the implication is that she does in fact "hear" it but chooses wisely to *ignore* it. The "faint blush" alone betrays her shame. Generally, Charlotte seems able to will to "forget" Collins altogether—at least so "Elizabeth supposed."

One of the problems readers experience in evaluating Elizabeth's visit with the Collinses is that nearly every perception of their marriage is filtered through Elizabeth's judgmental eyes, so that it is difficult to discern how critical Austen herself is of this marriage. Charlotte has, after all, attained the establishment she sought, however inadequate Collins may be as a spouse from Elizabeth's point of view. In fact, Elizabeth can scarcely see Charlotte as a person distinct from herself, with different needs and values. Elizabeth's parting thoughts about the couple suggest that the truth may be a bit more complicated than it had seemed at first: "Poor Charlotte!—it was melancholy to leave her to such society! But she had chosen it with her eyes open; and though evidently regretting that her visitors were to go, she did not seem to ask for compassion" (183; 2:15). Charlotte, in other words, may be at least a little less susceptible to feelings of shame, or perhaps a bit less threatened by them, than Elizabeth. Although alternative explanations are, of course, possible—for example, that Charlotte gives no indication of seeking compas-

sion precisely *because* she feels ashamed—it still remains clear that Charlotte has made her choice with a pretty good sense of the sort of person Collins is, and that Elizabeth would find such a choice more objectionable, and perhaps more threatening to her self-image, than Charlotte does.

Elizabeth's father is also defined largely in relation to shame, because he both humiliates his wife and fails to keep his younger daughters under sufficient control so as not to bring disgrace upon the whole family. "Captivated by youth and beauty," he has weakly married the ignorant and foolish Mrs. Bennet, and then has withdrawn both from her and from his family to his library (199; 2:19). When he is with his wife and family, he is guilty of "that continual breach of conjugal obligation and decorum which, in exposing his wife to the contempt of her own children, was so highly reprehensible" (200; 2:19). Furthermore, in failing to restrain his younger children, he is, as Elizabeth warns, compromising "our [family's] importance, our respectability in the world. . . . Oh! my dear father, can you suppose it possible that they [Kitty and Lydia] will not be censured and despised wherever they are known, and that their sisters will not be often involved in the disgrace?" (195; 2:18).

Of all the characters in the novel, Elizabeth's older sister, Jane, seems most identified with anxieties about harshly judging the self and others. Her principal trait is her reluctance to be critical of anyone. She is always ready to excuse and defend, or plead extenuating circumstances for whatever wrongs are done her by Mr. Bingley, his sister Caroline or Darcy. Jane would, for example, defend Charlotte's marriage to Collins, or argue that Darcy and Wickham have somehow simply misunderstood one another or been misinterpreted to one another. To some extent, her reluctance to judge is a tonic to Elizabeth's defensive rush to judgment, and some of the things the less critical Jane says turn out to be largely true. Yet Austen suggests that Jane's "steady sense and sweetness of temper" (202; 2:19) are also to be understood as what we would now describe as a reaction formation against critical feelings and even anger directed against her own self and others. These critical ideas and feelings, in other words, are replaced in her conscious awareness by their opposites—feelings of placidity and general benevolence. Jane's anger is a bit difficult to discern since she is "shut down," not capable of expressing it. If readers are not given much of an interior view of Jane's emotional life, we are, however, provided with a rather full portrait of the psychological dynamics at work within her family. Elizabeth's shame about and anger at both her parents are tangible, and it seems reasonable to suppose that some of these feelings are present in Jane, too, precisely because she has gone to the opposite extreme in her refusal to think ill of anyone.

Certainly in Jane's tendency toward depression, which emerges in the second volume of the novel, after she has apparently been dropped by Bingley, there is evidence that all is not well with Jane, that her "sweetness of temper" comes at a price. If Elizabeth occasionally gives way to a psychosomatic headache (159; 2:10), Jane seems to suffer longer-lasting "periods of dejection" (131; 2:4). When Elizabeth scans once more "all the letters which Jane had written to her since her being in Kent . . . in all, and in almost every line of each, there was a want of that cheerfulness which had been used to characterize her style. . . . Elizabeth noticed every sentence conveying the idea of uneasiness, with an attention which it had hardly received on the first perusal" (160; 2:11). "Jane had not written in spirits," Elizabeth decides (155; 2:10); "Jane was not happy" (192; 2:17). Jane is convinced that Bingley's failure to call on her in London can be explained only by his indifference to her, whereas Elizabeth more accurately suspects a conspiracy to keep Bingley away. Suspicions and critical feelings about others are in Jane's psyche, then, turned against the self. No one is unworthy except herself.

In fact, Jane seems to cope by attempting to suppress all kinds of uncomfortable affect, whether strongly negative or strongly positive—like her affection for Bingley. As Elizabeth sees it, "Jane's feelings, though fervent, were little displayed, and . . . there was a constant complacency in her air and manner, not often united with great sensibility" (177; 2:13). As a result, Darcy has a hard time discerning that Jane really is in love with Bingley, and we are similarly forced to deduce how sternly Jane judges herself. In both cases, however, the evidence is in the text. There is a restrained, depressive quality about Jane Bennet, an unmistakable sense of deficiency and diminished self-esteem. If a certain amount of self-restraint and humility are virtues for Jane Austen, she is also quite capable of demonstrating how these tendencies may be so pronounced as to become dysfunctional.

Of all the characters in the novel, however, Darcy represents perhaps the most interesting example of Austen's anatomy of shame—precisely because there seems to be an ambivalence on her part about the "pride" with which he is associated. If Elizabeth is the exemplar of the "prejudice" in the novel's title—by reason of the way she forms too readily and on insufficient information a judgment against Darcy and in favor of Wickham—Darcy is the exemplar of "pride." Of course, Austen characteristically complicates her thematic by showing that Elizabeth's prejudice arises from her wounded pride, and that Darcy is at various times associated with something very like prejudice. Yet the question the novel repeatedly poses is whether or not, given his immense fortune, grand estate and distinguished family, Darcy's pride—manifested particularly in his stiff and stand-offish manners—can be justified. Is there such a thing as "proper" pride, or is all pride to be seen as a kind of defense against shame or anxiety about shame?

For the first half of the novel, Elizabeth's criticism of Darcy's hauteur dominates, and Elizabeth appears to win her debates with the defenders of Darcy's pride—Charlotte Lucas, Mary Bennet, and Darcy himself. Elizabeth's antagonists repeatedly try to distinguish vanity from pride. Darcy "has a *right* to be proud," Charlotte thinks (18; 1:5); and bookish Mary Bennet, "who piqued herself upon the solidity of her reflections," as Austen puts it in a wry revelation of Mary's own vanity, offers this distinction: "Vanity and pride are different things, though the words are often used synonymously. A person may be proud without being vain. Pride relates more to our opinion of ourselves, vanity to what we would have others think of us" (19; 1:5). Thus Austen very early in the novel gives to two characters least likely to be identified as her spokespersons a certain grain of truth; a potentially strong defense of an appropriate pride is placed in weak hands. Can there be a sense of dignity and strength that is not riddled through with anxiety about shame, anxiety about the adequacy of the self? Can there be a pride which one has "a right" to feel?

The answer to these questions shifts gradually in Darcy's favor toward the center of the novel, particularly after he has a chance to defend himself and his behavior at length in his letter to Elizabeth; and the beginning of the third book, when Elizabeth and the Gardiners visit Darcy's home, Pemberley, tips the balance in Darcy's favor, when his housekeeper and Mrs. Gardiner weigh in on his side. As Mrs. Gardiner says, "There *is* something a little stately in him to be sure . . . but it is confined to his air, and is not unbecoming. I can now say with the housekeeper that though some people may call him proud, *I* have seen nothing of it" (215; 3:1). By the end of the novel, Elizabeth is able to declare flatly, "He has no improper pride"; those who, like her father, think him "a proud, unpleasant sort of man" simply "do not know what he really is" (316; 3:17).

This issue is complicated again, however, by Darcy's own, ashamed condemnation of his pride, which he describes as a defensive walling off of himself from others, something which cannot be justified on the grounds of either his personal character or his elevated social status:

> My behaviour to you at the time had merited the severest reproof. It was unpardonable. I cannot think of it without abhorrence. . . .
>
> I have been a selfish being all my life in practice, though not in principle. As a child I was taught what was *right,* but I was not taught to correct my temper. I

was given good principles, but left to follow them in pride and conceit. . . . I was spoiled by my parents . . . allowed, encouraged, almost taught to be selfish and overbearing, to care for none beyond my own family circle, to think meanly of all the rest of the world, to *wish* at least to think meanly of their sense and worth compared with my own. . . . You [Elizabeth] taught me a lesson, hard indeed at first, but most advantageous. By you I was properly humbled.

(308, 310; 3:16)

It is clear that Darcy could truly believe in his own distinction (and that of his family) only if he could "think meanly" of everyone else. Indeed, when one looks again at his original slighting of Elizabeth as "tolerable; but not handsome enough to tempt *me*" (12; 1:3), or of his response to Mrs. Bennet's chatter—"The expression of his face changed gradually from indignant contempt to a composed and steady gravity" (87; 1:18)—it is difficult not to give Darcy's self-criticism as much weight as other characters' later justifications of his behavior. They offer a defense in terms of behavior proper to one of his social rank; he offers a criticism based on knowledge of his own history and motivations. One assessment is social, the other psychological. Each has a kind of validity, and Austen never entirely settles the matter. Yet by opening up the issue to psychological investigation in this way, Austen raises the possibility that the less attractive components of Darcy's "pride"—his tendency to look upon others with contempt—derive from a potentially fragile image of self and family. These tendencies constitute what the psychologist Gershen Kaufman describes as a "defending script" to insulate the self against shame (101). Fond as she is of subtle definitions, Austen would find interesting Kaufman's attempt to differentiate between a desirable pride which affirms the self's accomplishments and personal qualities, and a more suspect version of pride, contempt, which elevates the self above others (224-25). Yet Austen would probably be skeptical about how readily this distinction can be maintained in practice. After all, her novel is not only about the vicissitudes of pride and shame, but also about their complicated relationship to one another.

By the end of the novel, Elizabeth has done a complete turnabout and now regards Darcy's behavior as entirely appropriate to one of his situation. This enables her to identify with his social rank and escape the shame of being associated with her own family. Of course, Elizabeth's marriage speaks to more than this; it represents the solution of a very complex human equation, for Elizabeth and Darcy are a suitable match in a number of ways. They *like* one another, each has a developed intellect, their temperaments are complementary, and their union is neither "imprudent" (as Elizabeth's with Wickham would have been) nor "mercenary" (like Wickham's pursuit of Miss King). The marriage of Elizabeth and Darcy represents, in other words, the

working out of Austen's thematic concerns about what constitutes a good marriage.

Yet it is also true that there is "upward mobility" in Elizabeth's marriage, and surely this improvement in her status will serve to minimize her anxieties about shame, her vulnerability to being disgraced by her family. To some extent, she will now be able to shut herself off from them. Lydia and Wickham will receive financial help, but neither Lydia nor her mother will be frequent guests at Pemberley. From Elizabeth's point of view, Darcy's social status and pride, now assimilated to herself, are very useful. In his study of the dynamics of shame, Leon Wurmser argues that love—as much as contempt, ridicule, envy, numbness and boredom—can be a screen affect for shame: "The one who loves wants to undo a basic disparity [a sense of deprivation or need] in himself and acquire in the fusion with the partner what he is lacking inside" (200). In this sense, Elizabeth is able to overcome her shame through her love and through her identification with Darcy.

On the one hand, Austen sees the painfulness of her young heroine's struggle with feelings of shame. Even when that shame is transformed defensively (reactively) into aggressive wit or anger, or into a kind of deadening repression of affect (as is at least partly the case with Charlotte Lucas and Jane), it is necessarily deforming. Shame may be associated with feelings of low self-esteem which become overwhelming, verging on depression. Jane Bennet is, as we have seen, depressed for much of the central part of the book, and Elizabeth, too, suffers self-hate and something very like depressive episodes after she receives Darcy's explanatory letter and again after Lydia runs off with Wickham.

On the other hand, Austen herself seems very much caught up in feelings of shame and acts of shaming. As a comic author and a satirist, she is concerned with ridiculing the ridiculous. Marvin Mudrick's well-known *Jane Austen: Irony as Defense and Discovery* is only one of many studies to focus on this crucial aspect of Austen's narrative technique—the way she takes a hardheaded, satiric look at all kinds of pretense, especially self-delusion, and engages in understated, implicit kinds of exposure. The author of these novels herself, then, exposes and shames. She does this, as Wayne Booth points out, not so much by having her narrator point and mock, as by coercing the reader in subtle ways to adopt her critical point of view toward her characters. Readers frequently express amazement at how they have been persuaded to see the action of the novel from Austen's point of view, how they have been seduced into sharing her values—values which they may not hold at all in real life—concerning the importance of class-consciousness, what constitutes a suitable marriage, the importance of rational control and emotional restraint, etc. As Bernard Paris has demonstrated, there is a connection between Austen's personal style and her writing style; in both she is a perfectionist (182-91). Attuned to the power relations between people in social life, and fascinated by the efforts of one person to dominate another, she is concerned to be in control of every word in her text, so as not to be found wanting. Her motto might be: "They are ridiculous, not I." For Austen as for Elizabeth Bennet, aggression is turned outward, away from the self. Yet, as one of the debates between Darcy and Elizabeth suggests, Austen is also aware that there are certain dangers in a consistently satiric stance toward life:

> "Mr. Darcy is not to be laughed at!" cried Elizabeth. "That would be an uncommon advantage, and uncommon I hope it will continue, for it would be a great loss to *me* to have many such acquaintance. I dearly love a laugh."
>
> "Miss Bingley," said he, "has given me credit for more than can be. The wisest and best of men, nay, the wisest and best of their actions, may be rendered ridiculous by a person whose first object in life is a joke."
>
> "Certainly," replied Elizabeth—"there are such people, but I hope I am not one of *them.* I hope I never ridicule what is wise and good. Follies and nonsense, whims and inconsistencies *do* divert me, I own, and I laugh at them whenever I can.—But these, I suppose, are precisely what you are without."
>
> "Perhaps that is not possible for any one. But it has been the study of my life to avoid those weaknesses which often expose a strong understanding to ridicule."
>
> (50; 1:11)

Elizabeth adopts the pose of the traditional satirist: I ridicule the ridiculous as a corrective measure, hoping to shape a better, more rational world. Yet Darcy knows that this attitude may be carried too far, that even the good may be turned into the ridiculous by an aggressively self-protective wit. Thus at the conclusion of this debate he suggests that Elizabeth's "natural defect . . . is wilfully to misunderstand" everybody (51; 1:11), to appropriate whatever anyone says in the service of her wit.

One way of putting Austen's own dilemma in this respect is to note that although she presents herself finally as a rationalist, committed to a corrective satiric vision, she is psychologically astute enough to know that the process of deciding what is "real," "true" and "rational" may have its unconscious and defensive determinants. Psychoanalyst Pinchas Noy links creativity with psychological insight in a way that Austen approaches intuitively, but also stops short of fully endorsing: "The main feature common to the process of creativity and the phenomenon of insight in psychoanalysis is the ability to transcend the rigid, reality-oriented frame of the intellect and transform it into a flexible apparatus suitable for dealing with the self in its needs, its de-fenses, and its striving for expression and contact with objects" (qtd. in Wurmser 284). On a rational level, Austen seems to think that the "reality-oriented frame of the intellect"—for her, reason and will—ought to dominate. Intuitively, however, she recognizes the power of an affect like shame and the role it might play in forming and shaping what an individual perceives as rational and correct.

In this context, the historical climate in which Austen composed her "novel of manners" becomes especially significant; *Pride and Prejudice* was written at the end of the Enlightenment—when the socially enforced religious sanctions used in earlier periods to keep personal behavior in check were being replaced by more secular, internalized, social sanctions. This is one reason why "manners," behavior that conforms to social norms, is such an important issue in the Austen world. Lewis argues that shame is, to some extent at least, a post-Enlightenment means of social control in a secular society: "An ethical system based on the premise that human nature is evil or aggressive [e.g., a system based on a premise of original sin] will emphasize guilt as its major control, whereas an ethical system that includes human sociability as a 'given' will also emphasize the shame (in one's own eyes) of losing the love of the 'other'" ("Shame" 3-4). If Calvin requires guilt, Rousseau must have shame for his social order.

Lewis, moreover, sees shame as a particular problem for women in Western society, since "our sexist and intellectual heritage contains an explicit devaluation of women and an implicit, insoluble demand that they accept their inferior place without shame" ("Shame" 4). While men are encouraged to be aggressive and dominating, women are raised to seek the approval of others (Lewis, *Sex* 203-19). Certainly this is the situation of the female characters in *Pride and Prejudice.* Their vulnerable place in the social order is underlined and maintained by their shame. Conversely, male characters like Darcy and Collins develop exaggerated forms of "pride" to express and maintain their social power and control. The characterization of Darcy is especially relevant in this respect, since here Austen also raises the question of whether this sort of pride can ever be anything but defensive and brittle in such a culture.

Accordingly, it is not surprising that the role of shame in cultural formation has drawn the attention of anthropologists and historians as well as psychologists. In their 1953 study, Gerhart Piers and Milton B. Singer provided an overview of the anthropological attempts to distinguish "shame cultures" from "guilt cultures." More recently, in a study entitled *Southern Honor,* the historian Bertram Wyatt-Brown points to the development of an ideal of personal honor, reinforced by episodes of shame and humiliation, as an essential element in the creation of the ideology and culture of the Old South.

Nor are we, at the close of the twentieth century, so remote from the shame culture that Austen and these other students of culture describe, for as Donald Nathanson notes: "The more I have studied shame and applied the results of this study to my work with patients, the more I am convinced that the overwhelming majority of our population lives in a state of chronic shame. This shame is either perceived as a sense of inadequacy relative to the ego ideal or denied and inverted as false pride" (191). As examples of "false pride" today Nathanson points to the pursuit of wealth and power, identification with sports teams, and the like—all in the interest of defending against "our (denied) fragility" (204). He might also have pointed to Cold War versions of American "patriotism," to the continuing tendency of the U.S. to resort to military intervention to work its will in the world, and to its recurrent need to proclaim its superiority, whether on the playing fields or in the international arena.

Shame and its "defending scripts" seem to play an important role in the academy as well. Academics tend to fall into two groups: those with narcissistic, grandiose images concerning the importance of their work and those who are convinced that they can never be good enough, that they are "impostors" who will be found out and perhaps driven from the academy. In their classic study of this "impostor syndrome," Pauline R. Clance and Suzanne A. Imes have analyzed the tendency of gifted professional women in particular to believe that they are really *not* bright and capable, that they have merely fooled anyone who thinks they are. Nor is the phenomenon limited to the female sex or to any specific professions. In society at large, the alternatives frequently seem to be a choice between, in Nathanson's words, "a sense of inadequacy relative to the ego ideal" and "false pride" (204).

The fact that shame and the defenses against it play such an important role in our own lives and culture thus suggests both how little things have changed and how much we have to learn from Jane Austen's exploration of these feelings nearly two centuries ago. Reading **Pride and Prejudice** in conjunction with modern discussions of the psychology of shame can help us better to understand not only Austen's novels but also some very important psychosocial forces that inform modern Western culture.[2]

Notes

1. All quotations from *Pride and Prejudice* are taken from the Signet New American Library edition. Since many modern editions of this novel are available, in my parenthetical citations I have provided not only page numbers but also, following the semicolon, book and chapter numbers.

2. My spouse, Elizabeth, and my colleagues, Michael Hancher and Joel Weinsheimer, gave this essay at-

tentive readings and offered helpful suggestions, for which I am most grateful.

Works Cited

Austen, Jane. *Pride and Prejudice.* 1813. New York: New American Library, 1980.

———. *Jane Austen's Letters to her Sister Cassandra and Others.* Ed. R. W. Chapman. 2nd edition. Oxford: Oxford UP, 1979.

Booth, Wayne C. "Control of Distance in Jane Austen's *Emma.*" *The Rhetoric of Fiction.* Chicago: U of Chicago P, 1961. 243-66.

Clance, Pauline R., and Suzanne A. Imes. "The Impostor Phenomenon in High Achieving Women: Dynamics and Therapeutic Intervention." *Psychotherapy: Theory, Research & Practice* 15 (1978): 241-47.

Fossum, Merle A., and Marilyn J. Mason. *Facing Shame: Families in Recovery.* New York: Norton, 1986.

Harding, D. W. "Regulated Hatred: An Aspect of the Work of Jane Austen." *Scrutiny* 8 (1940): 346-62.

Hume, David. *A Treatise of Human Nature.* 1739-40. Ed. L. A. Selby-Bigge. Oxford: Oxford UP, 1965.

Kaufman, Gershen. *The Psychology of Shame: Theory and Treatment of Shame-Based Syndromes.* New York: Springer, 1989.

Lewis, Helen Block. "Introduction: Shame—the 'Sleeper' in Psychopathology." *The Role of Shame in Symptom Formation.* Ed. Helen Block Lewis. Hillsdale, NJ: Erlbaum, 1987. 1-28.

———. *Sex and the Superego: Psychic War in Men and Women.* Rev. ed. Hillsdale, NJ: Erlbaum, 1987.

Miller, Susan. *The Shame Experience.* Hillsdale, NJ: Analytic P, 1985.

Mudrick, Marvin. *Jane Austen: Irony as Defense and Discovery.* Princeton: Princeton UP, 1952.

Nathanson, Donald L. "The Shame/Pride Axis." Lewis, *Role of Shame.* 183-205.

Paris, Bernard J. *Character and Conflict in Jane Austen's Novels: A Psychological Approach.* Detroit: Wayne State UP, 1978.

Piers, Gerhart, and Milton B. Singer. *Shame and Guilt: A Psychoanalytic and a Cultural Study.* Springfield, IL: Thomas, 1953.

Wurmser, Leon. *The Mask of Shame.* Baltimore: Johns Hopkins UP, 1981.

Wyatt-Brown, Bertram. *Southern Honor: Ethics and Behavior in the Old South.* New York: Oxford UP, 1982.

Matthew Schneider (essay date spring 1993)

SOURCE: Schneider, Matthew. "Card-playing and the Marriage Gamble in *Pride and Prejudice*." *Dalhousie Review* 73, no. 1 (spring 1993): 5-17.

[*In the following essay, Schneider argues that card-playing serves as an apt metaphor for the courtship ritual in* Pride and Prejudice.]

Henry Austen's casual observation that his novelist sister "was fond of dancing, and excelled in it" (*Pride and Prejudice* 308) has in recent years been invested by critics with a far-reaching metaphoric significance. Dancing, the argument goes, both figures the particular charm of Austen's style and provides an elegant symbolic matrix for much of the social interaction around which the novels are structured. A love of dancing was "the sort of thing one might expect," writes Stuart Tave, "that enjoyment and ability in moving with significant grace in good time in a restricted space" (1); and Langdon Elsbree observes that dancing provides a primary source for "action and speech in Jane Austen's fictional world and dramatize[s] the theme of courtship and marriage" (114). Celebrating the sexual passions in a ceremony that hints "at their power while keeping them safely contained in art" (Mansell 9), dancing embodies the tension between the struggle for individuality and polite society's prescribed gender identities and roles. As Henry Tilney tells Catherine Morland in *Northanger Abbey*:

> I consider a country-dance as an emblem of marriage. . . . [I]n both, man has the advantage of choice, woman only the power of refusal; that in both, it is an engagement between man and woman, formed for the advantage of each; and that when once entered into, they belong exclusively to each other till the moment of dissolution: that it is their duty, each to endeavour to give the other no cause for wishing that he or she had bestowed themselves elsewhere, and their best interest to keep their own imaginations from wandering towards the perfections of their neighbors, or fancying that they should have been better off with anyone else.
>
> (6)

While in most of Austen's six novels dancing serves as an unmatched metaphor for courtship and marriage, its aptness is less evident in *Pride and Prejudice.* Another frequently portrayed leisure activity, no less ubiquitous than dancing, seems better to represent in this novel the combination of behaviors and factors that enter into the complex process of matching nubile men and women with each other. Card-playing, a pastime of which the novelist was, to judge by her letters, at least as fond as she was of dancing, incorporates two important elements of the Austenian portrayal of courtship which dancing is less able to evoke: money and luck. For many women in the world of Austen's novels, marriage

was synonymous with economic survival: the narrator of *Pride and Prejudice* concurs with Charlotte Lucas's opinion that marriage "was the only honourable provision for well-educated women of small fortune, and however uncertain of giving happiness, must be their pleasantest preservative from want" (86). *Pride and Prejudice* concerns itself with how at least one well-educated woman of small fortune, Elizabeth Bennet, reconciles the conflicting demands of happiness and love with material subsistence. Card-playing, an activity which boils down to staking money—one kind of fortune—on the skilful manipulation of one's luck—another kind of fortune—incorporates these two indispensable elements of a successful marriage and thus symbolizes better than dancing the full range of factors that enter into marriage and courtship. No less ritualized than dancing, card-playing emphasizes the essential—even simultaneous—parts played by money and luck in Austen's depiction in *Pride and Prejudice* of engendering legitimate relations between the sexes.

If Jane Austen was fond of dancing and excelled at it, she was also fond of card-playing and other games that combined the elements of chance and skill. Letters to her sister Cassandra frequently describe both these games and Austen's chagrin at having been cajoled into playing and losing. Their mother seems to have been fond of the card-game commerce, in which players assume the roles of stock or commodities traders, offering to sell, barter, or trade their cards in order to acquire something like a winning hand in gin rummy. This game, which the Abbé Bellecour, author of a 1754 handbook of card game rules and strategies, calls "a very social Game, for as we have said, a dozen persons may play at the same time, and it is a Game of Commerce, as you win or lose in proportion as you estimate your Counters" (184), was not among Austen's favorites: on 7 October 1808 she wrote to Cassandra that the previous evening's diversion had consisted of "two pools of commerce, but I would not play more than one, for the stake was three shillings, & I cannot afford to lose that, twice in an even^g—" (*Letters* 215). Austen's favorite card game, at least through the autumn of 1808, was speculation: on 24 October she writes to Cassandra that "our evening was equally agreeable in its way: I introduced *speculation,* and it was so much approved that we hardly knew where to leave off" (229). Speculation's popularity with the Austen family seems to have ended with the coming of the new year, when it succumbed to a new game: brag. On 10 January 1809, Austen wrote to Cassandra that

> the preference of Brag over Speculation does not greatly surprise me, I believe, because I feel the same myself; but it mortifies me deeply, because Speculation was under my patronage; and, after all, what is there so delightful in a pair royal of Braggers? It is but three nines or three knaves, or a mixture of them. When one comes to reason upon it, it cannot stand its ground

against Speculation—of which I hope Edward [Cassandra's son] is now convinced. Give my love to him if he is.

(247)

Brag's ascendancy was even more short-lived than speculation's, however; only one week later, Austen again wrote to her sister:

I have just received some verses in an unknown hand, and am desired to forward them to my nephew Edwd at Godmersham.

"Alas, poor Brag, thou boastful Game!—
What now avails thy empty name?—
Where now thy more distinguish'd fame?—
My day is o'er, and Thine the same.—
For thou like me art thrown aside,
At Godmersham, this Christmas Tide;
And now across the Table wide,
Each Game save Brag or Spec: is tried."
"Such is the mild Ejaculation,
Of tender hearted Speculation.—"

(252-3)

Austen displays her wit in her response to this facetious family controversy; but the contest between brag and speculation also orients the surface moral distinctions implicit in the choice of card games in *Pride and Prejudice*. Though similar, the two games have, from the point of view of the novel, a significant difference, suggested by their names: whereas both are three-card betting games, in speculation, players bet "blindly"—that is, they wager on the face value of cards before they see them. Brag is identical to draw poker, but played with three instead of five cards. The dealer antes an opening blind bet, called the "dealer's edge," and the players bet both against the luck of the draw and each other, with each player knowing the value of the hand he holds. Speculation is thus a game of pure chance, while brag calls on its players to attempt to manipulate or outface their luck with their skill at bluffing—essentially deceiving—their opponents. As Edmund Hoyle put it, the ability to "deceive and distress your Adversaries" is a key to success in most card games, especially in betting and bluffing games like brag (ch. V).

Probably the relative decorousness of the names of the two games is enough to account for Austen's preference for speculation over brag. No doubt she was also less comfortable with brag's potentially more cutthroat tactics and competition. Ironically, however, her favorite novel depicts a world in which a woman's possession of the acumen and nerve of a good brag or poker player is directly proportional to her chances of making a successful marriage. A woman must be able to read faces, communicate her preferences wordlessly, and stimulate a man's interest while adhering to the strictures of decorum and modesty—in short, use everything in her power to influence the otherwise blindly bestowed dic-

tates of accident and luck. Ultimately, the economically and culturally disadvantaged position of women—a position taken as axiomatic by Austen—means that in courtship and marriage they must overcome the "dealer's edge" held by men through the exertion of greater skill at balancing self-disguise with tacit encouragement and persuasion.

Before Austen can chart the difficult process through which the heroine of *Pride and Prejudice* becomes a skilled player of the marriage-gambling game, however, the novelist must establish the association between money and marriage. She accomplishes this throughout the book by mixing the languages of love and economics. The novel's celebrated first sentence presents an example of this type of punning: "It is a truth universally acknowledged, that a single man in possession of a good fortune, must be in want of a wife" (1). The line's comic effect derives primarily from the incongruity between the lofty diction of the phrase "truth universally acknowledged" and the baldly mercenary sentiment with which the sentence ends. The humorous conflation of philosophic and monetary speculation continues through the first and into the second chapter, as Mr. Bennet misses no opportunity to amuse himself with repeated puns that portray the arrival of the Bingley party at Netherfield as a serendipitous investment opportunity for the families in the village. When, for example, Mr. Bennet tells his wife that he needn't call on Bingley, since their neighbor Mrs. Long has promised to introduce the Bennet girls to the rich young man at an upcoming party, Mrs. Bennet replies that Mrs. Long is a "selfish, hypocritical woman" who will do no such thing since she has "two nieces of her own" (3). In that case, replies Mr. Bennet, Mrs. Bennet herself should introduce the girls, justifying such a breach of decorum on the sound financial principle that he who hesitates is lost: "if *we* do not venture, somebody else will; and after all Mrs. Long and her nieces must stand their chance" (4). All financial ventures, from the stock market to marriage, entail an element of risk that one must expect and for which one must plan.

Elizabeth Bennet becomes aware of the social manifestation of this sound financial principle only after her disastrous first meeting with Darcy at Bingley's ball at Netherfield. At that same dance Jane Bennet meets and falls in love with Bingley; and, fittingly, the novel's first reference to card-playing arises in the post-mortem of the event conducted by Elizabeth and Charlotte Lucas. Convinced both of her sister's love for Bingley and his requiting Jane's affection, Elizabeth is thankful that their natural reserve has precluded any unseemly public display of passion:

It was generally evident whenever they met, that he *did* admire her; and to *her* it was equally evident that Jane was yielding to the preference which she had begun to entertain for him from the first, and was in a way to be very much in love; but she considered with pleasure that it was not likely to be discovered by the world in general, since Jane united with great strength of feeling, a composure of temper and a uniform cheerfulness of manner, which would guard her from the suspicions of the impertinent. She mentioned this to her friend Miss Lucas.

"It may perhaps be pleasant," replied Charlotte, "to be able to impose on the public in such a case; but it is sometimes a disadvantage to be so very guarded. If a woman conceals her affection with the same skill from the object of it, she may lose the opportunity of fixing him; and it will then be but poor consolation to believe the world equally in the dark. There is so much of gratitude or vanity in almost every attachment, that it is not safe to leave any to itself. We can all *begin* freely—a slight preference is natural enough; but there are very few of us who have heart enough to be really in love without encouragement. In nine cases out of ten, a woman had better shew *more* affection than she feels. Bingley likes your sister undoubtedly; but he may never do more than like her, if she does not help him on."

(13-14)

Charlotte's no-nonsense, statistical approach to courtship alarms Elizabeth, who finds herself forced to admit that though Jane and Bingley had spent four evenings together they knew little more about each other than "that they both like Vingt-un better than Commerce" (14). This exchange illustrates card-playing's primary level of signification in *Pride and Prejudice.* On the surface, taste in card games sounds the keynote of personality. Thus the stuffy and aristocratic Lady Catherine de Bourgh plays the skill-intensive and slow-moving game of quadrille, while the boisterous Lydia Bennet prefers lottery tickets, which the Abbé Bellecour calls "highly diverting," since "even those Players, whose vivacity prevents them from giving the least attention to their Game, may here play without any disadvantage, as it is altogether a Game of chance" (189). The motif also, however, serves, as Alistair M. Duckworth writes, "to expose elements of social conformity and individual freedom and to define a normative marriage of the moral self to a worthy society" (283). Lady Catherine's devotion to the old-fashioned game of quadrille foreshadows her reactionary opposition to the engagement of Darcy and Elizabeth. And Lydia's preference for games of blind chance both stems from her "always unguarded and often uncivil" (89) nature and portends the thoughtless elopement with Wickham that nearly ruins her family. Similarly, Jane's and Bingley's preference of vingt-un—in which chance predominates over skill—to commerce—which tests a player's skill at a relatively higher level—reflects the timidity that keeps her from making her feelings known and allows him to be swayed easily by his sisters and Darcy. Because both are relatively unskilled in manipulating the dealings of chance, they prefer merely to succumb to its dictates.

As Mr. Bennet tells them upon the occasion of their engagement, "You are both of you so complying, that nothing will ever be resolved on; so easy, that every servant will cheat you; and so generous, that you will always exceed your income" (239).

Though more sophisticated than her elder sister, Elizabeth Bennet at the beginning of the novel is also a relatively unskilled player of the social card game: just as Bingley misreads Jane, Elizabeth misreads Darcy's countenance and demeanor so utterly that his first proposal astonishes her "beyond expression" (130). As her accurate prediction of Jane's problems with Bingley demonstrates, Charlotte Lucas, at least at the beginning of the story, is the novel's canniest analyst of the courtship game. Charlotte is also, however, a skilled player, despite her disingenuous claim that "[h]appiness in marriage is entirely a matter of chance" (14). Her betrothal to the egregious Mr. Collins serves as more, however, than merely an illustration of marriage's unfortunate economic component or a primer for Elizabeth's initiation into the subtleties of the courtship game. Ultimately, the Charlotte-Mr. Collins subplot delineates the essential gender difference that underpins the rules of the marriage gamble.

Charlotte's engagement illustrates the extent to which accident and chance play vital roles in a great deal more than just the love affairs in *Pride and Prejudice.* Chance is in fact the tacit agent of most important plot events in the novel, as the history of Mr. Collins demonstrates. Despite his insufferable officiousness, this distant cousin of Mr. Bennet is the novel's luckiest character: the failure of Mr. and Mrs. Bennet to produce male offspring means that Longbourn, the Bennet estate, will upon the "melancholy event" of Mr. Bennet's demise pass to Collins. Mrs. Bennet observes to him that this will be "a grievous affair to my poor girls, you must confess. Not that I mean to find fault with *you*, for such things I know are all chance in this world. There is no knowing how estates will go when they come to be entailed" (45). The relatively modest income and home meantime enjoyed by Collins had arisen from the "fortunate chance" of his having been recommended to Lady Catherine de Bourgh "when the living at Hunsford was vacant" (48). Though unlucky at cards—he loses five shillings playing whist on his first night at Longbourn—Collins is lucky in love, securing Charlotte's hand only two days after Elizabeth's refusal of his ludicrous marriage proposal. But if Collins appears lucky in making the sensible Charlotte his wife, it is only because of the pains she takes to create such an impression. What appears as his luck may be at least equally attributed to her skill in manipulating what chance throws her way. The gender-based behavioral conventions of the world of *Pride and Prejudice* demand that women conceal even the relatively weak powers they possess to play the courtship game and influence its outcome. An artful or canny woman in the world of *Pride and Prejudice*—as elsewhere in Austen's novels—is an object of at best fun and at worst execration (think of *Emma*'s Mrs. Elton). Society demands that women who win in the marriage-game be thought of as the beneficiaries of accident or "beginner's luck." Elizabeth's refusal of Collins and the simultaneous departure of Bingley from Netherfield strikes Mrs. Bennet as an "exceedingly unlucky" (84) succession of events; but ill fortune for the Bennets means good fortune—in both senses of that word—for the Lucases. Sneaking away from the Bennet household before breakfast, Collins deals a hand which Charlotte has been preparing herself to play: "Miss Lucas perceived him from an upper window as he walked towards the house, and instantly set out to meet him *accidentally* in the lane. But little had she dared to hope that so much love and eloquence awaited her there" (85) (italics mine).

The engagement is a godsend for the Lucas family: they consider it "most eligible for their daughter, to whom they could give little fortune; and [Mr. Collins's] prospects of future wealth were exceedingly fair" (85-86). The sober Charlotte is "tolerably composed" by the event: "she had gained her point," we are told, and, being twenty-seven and "without ever having been handsome," she feels "all the good luck of it" (86). Elizabeth is stunned by her friend's acceptance of the buffoonish Mr. Collins as a life companion; but Charlotte explains her decision philosophically, and with a characteristic calculation of odds:

> "I am not romantic you know. I never was. I ask only a comfortable home; and considering Mr. Collins's character, connections, and situation in life, I am convinced that my chance of happiness with him is as fair, as most people can boast on entering the marriage state."
>
> (88)

Luckily, Elizabeth is spared by her relative attractiveness and youth from adopting wholesale Charlotte's harsh philosophy. As difficult as the marriage is for Elizabeth to accept—she "could not have supposed it possible" that Charlotte could sacrifice "every better feeling to worldly advantage" (88)—the significance of the episode is not lost on her. If Charlotte is the novel's most skilled and daring player in the marriage gamble and Jane the least, Elizabeth is, initially, the most reluctant. When Collins attempts to explain away her refusal of his proposal by declaring "it is usual with young ladies to reject the addresses they secretly mean to accept," Elizabeth replies that she is "not one of those young ladies (if such young ladies there are) who are so daring as to risk their happiness on the chance of being asked a second time" (75). Like Elizabeth, Darcy is reluctant to play the game; ironically, this shared trait results in both the attraction between them and the blunt-

ness which inflames the pride and prejudices to which both are particularly susceptible. In a telling exchange at Lady Catherine's garishly decorated home, Elizabeth jokingly proclaims herself "particularly unlucky" in having met Darcy, since he was able to "expose my real character, in a part of the world, where I had hoped to pass myself off with some degree of credit" (120-1). Darcy too finds himself singularly lacking what the novel's world exalts as the most valuable of social graces: "I have not the talent," he says, "of conversing easily with those I have never seen before. I cannot catch their tone of conversation, or appear interested in their concerns, as I often see done" (121).

Darcy's first unsuccessful proposal depicts how his "abhorrence of disguise of every sort" (133) initially matches and therefore clashes with Elizabeth's frankness and unwillingness to perceive non-verbal communications.

> More than once did Elizabeth in her ramble within the Park, unexpectedly meet Mr. Darcy.—She felt all the perverseness of the mischance that should bring him where no one else was brought; and to prevent its ever happening again, took care to inform him at first, that it was a favorite haunt of hers—.
>
> (125)

Elizabeth refuses Darcy's subsequent proposal because she thinks she perceives a contradiction between his words and demeanor:

> He concluded with representing to her the strength of that attachment which, in spite of all his endeavours, he had found impossible to conquer; and with expressing his hope that it would now be rewarded by her acceptance of his hand. As he said this, she could easily see that he had no doubt of a favourable answer. He *spoke* of apprehension and anxiety, but his countenance expressed real security.
>
> (131)

However accurate these observations appear, we cannot forget that they are filtered through Elizabeth's consciousness; and up to this point events have far more frequently surprised her than conformed to her expectations. Elizabeth has previously shown herself a rather poor reader of other people's looks. In spite of Elizabeth's conviction that the love between Jane and Bingley was written on their faces, what had once seemed to all concerned an imminent engagement had never materialized. And it is only Elizabeth's inability to find an ulterior motive for Darcy's account of Wickham that finally dispels her conviction that the latter's "countenance, voice, and manner . . . established him at once in the possession of every virtue" (142). Darcy's letter has an apocalyptic effect on Elizabeth, opening her eyes to the duplicity into which her pride and prejudice had unwittingly led her:

"How despicably I have acted!" she cried.—"I, who have prided myself on my discernment!—I, who have valued myself on my abilities! who have often disdained the generous candour of my sister, and gratified my vanity, in useless or blameable distrust.—How humiliating is this discovery!—Yet, how just a humiliation!—Had I been in love, I could not have been more wretchedly blind. But vanity, not love, has been my folly.—Pleased with the preference of one, and offended by the neglect of the other, on the very beginning of our acquaintance, I have courted prepossession and ignorance, and driven reason away, where either were concerned. Till this moment, I never knew myself."

(143-4)

It is telling that Elizabeth avoids card-playing throughout the novel; while she has, says Duckworth, "no Puritanical objection to cards" (284), she presumably intuits that she lacks the discernment that stamps a winning card-player. The revelation afforded her by Darcy's letter, however, grants Elizabeth that most valuable of the card-player's skills: the ability to read faces. Austen exhibits Elizabeth's new-found skill primarily in two subsequent scenes. The first occurs during her tour of Pemberley, Darcy's estate. In the family gallery, Elizabeth embarks on a "quest" for "the only face whose features would be known to her" (170). "Arrested" by Darcy's portrait, Elizabeth for the first time looks her future husband directly in the eyes, and is surprised to notice a "warmth" in his gaze that "softened its impropriety of expression" (171). The second scene is a great deal more dramatic, and occurs after Darcy has tacitly resolved the family crisis brought on by Lydia's elopement with Wickham. Aghast at rumors of an impending engagement between Darcy and Elizabeth, Lady Catherine rushes to Longbourn to "insist upon having such a report universally contradicted" (243). Elizabeth's demeanor toward her ladyship is perhaps best described as poker-faced: she both refuses to be intimidated by Lady Catherine's haughtiness and repeatedly insists on her right to conceal her thoughts and feelings. When, for example, Lady Catherine demands that Elizabeth admit there is no foundation for the rumors, she replies, "I do not pretend to possess equal frankness with your ladyship. *You* may ask questions, which *I* shall not choose to answer" (244). To Lady Catherine's declaration that she is "entitled to know" all of Darcy's "dearest concerns," Elizabeth responds, "But you are not entitled to know *mine*; nor will such behaviour as this, ever induce me to be explicit" (244). And when Lady Catherine demands that she promise "never to enter into such an engagement," Elizabeth answers with a sober and mature reminder that such a promise would have little effect in this world, ruled as it is by chance, accident, and the sometimes unfortunate tendency of people to do what they want:

"I am not to be intimidated into anything so wholly unreasonable. Your ladyship wants Mr. Darcy to marry your daughter; but would my giving you the wished-for promise, make *their* marriage at all more probable? Supposing him to be attached to me, would *my* refusing to accept his hand, make him wish to bestow it on his cousin?"

(246)

Elizabeth's deftness in handling Lady Catherine, a skilled but ultimately ineffectual player of the complicated game quadrille, demonstrates the extent to which her eye-opening experiences with Darcy end up, ironically, persuading her of the frequent necessity of concealing or disguising one's true feelings in order best to manage the decrees of luck and chance in social relations. With Lady Catherine, Elizabeth not only plays her cards close to her vest, she also refuses to be bluffed, to show her hand before the appropriate moment of the game. Unhampered by the impolitic frankness that had previously signalled her inexpertness at the social game, Elizabeth is finally ready to be united with Darcy. And after a brief penance during which she is repeatedly called on to bite her tongue while her unwitting family persists in abusing their savior, Elizabeth's happiness is completed by her engagement to Darcy. That her punishment is no more severe than this may perhaps be attributed to Austen's own tender feelings toward her favorite heroine.

If, as Richard Handler and Daniel Segal have observed, "each of Austen's novels concerns a young lady's movement from her natal family to the family created by her marriage" (1), *Pride and Prejudice* depicts the vital role played by chance and luck in that deceptively simple movement. That marriage in the world of Austen's novels is intimately connected with money offers further justification for the aptness of card-playing as a metaphor for the courtship, as this activity particularly requires its female participants to stake both their happiness and survival on both their ability to discern men's feelings from their looks and the willingness of men fully to disclose their character and "prospects." Of course, this is of particular importance to Elizabeth, seemingly the only member of her family to understand the tragedy of her parents' marriage and the destructive effects of the irony with which her father consequently approaches the world. His only sincere moment in the novel follows Elizabeth's announcement of her engagement to Darcy: Mr. Bennet pleads with his favorite child to "let me not have the grief of seeing *you* unable to respect your partner in life" (260).

It is the seriousness of this potential risk that prevents the card-playing metaphor from trivializing its referent. Mr. Bennet's plea to Elizabeth also highlights an aspect of marriage in *Pride and Prejudice* that the dancing metaphor tends to elide. This, of course, is the sometimes unlucky truth implicit in the state of affairs by which marriage affords many women their only respectable means of economic survival. As an image of the ideal marriage, replete with harmony and temperamental concord, dancing can hardly be improved upon. But even in the happy comic world of Austen's novels, few marriages live up to this ideal; of this sad fact the union of Mr. and Mrs. Bennet stands as an unmistakable reminder:

> Had Elizabeth's opinion been all drawn from her own family, she could not have formed a very pleasing picture of conjugal felicity or domestic comfort. Her father captivated by youth and beauty, and that appearance of good humour, which youth and beauty generally give, had married a woman whose weak understanding and illiberal mind, had very early in their marriage put an end to all real affection for her. Respect, esteem, and confidence, had vanished for ever; and all his views of domestic happiness were overthrown.
>
> (162)

By marrying Darcy, Elizabeth escapes her parents' fate. She does so only after recognizing, however, the degree to which the skills of the winning card-player correspond to the social skills needed to thrive in a society in which young women and men effectively compete for wealth and happiness. It is toward this somewhat grim truth that card-playing in *Pride and Prejudice* finally points, while illustrating for us at the same time the extent to which women in Austen's age were faced with staking their very existence on the skilful performance of ultimately competitive social rituals.

Works Cited

Austen, Jane. *Letters to her Sister Cassandra.* Edited by R. W. Chapman. Oxford: Clarendon, 1932.

———. *Northanger Abbey.* New York: Signet, 1965.

———. *Pride and Prejudice.* New York: Norton, 1966.

Bellecour, Abbé. *The Academy of Play.* London: printed for F. Newberry, 1754.

Duckworth, Alistair M. "'Spillikins, paper ships, riddles, coundrums, and cards': games in Jane Austen's life and fiction." *Jane Austen: Bicentenary Essays.* Cambridge: Cambridge UP, 1975.

Elsbree, Langdon. "Jane Austen and the Dance of Fidelity and Complaisance." *Nineteenth-Century Fiction* 15 (1960): 113-36.

Handler, Richard, and David Segal. *Jane Austen and the Fiction of Culture.* Tucson: U of Arizona P, 1990.

Hoyle, Edmund. *Mr. Hoyle's Games.* 12th ed. London: printed for Thomas Osborne, n.d.

Mansell, Darrell. *The Novels of Jane Austen: An Interpretation.* New York: Macmillan, 1973.

Tave, Stuart M. *Some Words of Jane Austen.* Chicago: U of Chicago P, 1973.

Julia Prewitt Brown (essay date 1993)

SOURCE: Brown, Julia Prewitt. "The 'Social History' of *Pride and Prejudice.*" In *Approaches to Teaching Austen's* Pride and Prejudice, edited by Marcia McClintock Folsom, pp. 57-66. New York: The Modern Language Association of America, 1993.

[*In the following essay, Brown discusses the ways in which Austen's novel depicts early nineteenth-century society, arguing that Austen explores the defining historical realities of her era.*]

In what sense are Jane Austen's novels historical? This is often the first question students ask when they read Austen. It may be posed in the form of the familiar question, Where are the Napoleonic Wars, the decisive historical event of her time? Or, more frankly, Why did Austen choose such limited subject matter? Why did she focus exclusively on personal relations? A reminder that "ordinary life" constitutes the blood and bone of the novel genre usually does not satisfy the eighteen-year-old who seeks in works of literature some grandeur of human purpose—and why should it? "Don't *begin* with proportion," urges a wise character in E. M. Forster's *Howards End.* "Only prigs do that. Let proportion come in as a last resource, when the better things have failed" (73). The student who begins by hating Jane Austen, I have discovered, usually ends by learning more from her than does the budding Janeite.

As for the historical content of the novels, students may not see it because they think of social history as "history with the politics left out," as G. M. Trevelyan once described it, rather than what it is: the essential foundation that gives shape to everything else. For the cultural historian Raymond Williams, for example, Austen's novels provide an accurate record of that moment in English history in which high bourgeois society most evidently interlocked with an agrarian capitalism. "An openly acquisitive society," writes Williams, "which is concerned also with the transmission of wealth, is trying to judge itself at once by an inherited code and by the morality of improvement" (*Country* 115). What is at stake here is not personal relations but personal *conduct*: "a testing and discovery of the standards which govern human behaviour in certain real situations" (113). Those situations arise from the unsettled world Austen portrays, with its continual changes of fortune and social mobility that were affecting the landed families of her time. Thus, although Darcy is a landowner established for "many generations," his friend Bingley has no estate and has inherited £100,000 from his father, who made money in trade; and although Mr. Bennet has an estate, he has married the daughter of an attorney who has a brother in trade, and his estate will not pass to his own children; and so on.

Readers may glimpse the "openly acquisitive society" in the heroine's first sight of Pemberley, Darcy's beautiful estate. Deeply impressed, even awestruck, by its elegance and grandeur, Elizabeth cannot but admit to herself that "to be mistress of Pemberley might be something!" (245). Later Elizabeth satirizes her own response when her sister asks her to explain when she first fell in love with Darcy: "It has been coming on so gradually," Elizabeth replies, "that I hardly know when it began. But I believe I must date it from my first seeing his beautiful grounds at Pemberley" (373). Elizabeth's wit distances her from herself, from the woman with the conventional response to Pemberley, just as the narrator's irony distances the reader from conventional responses. But before entering into a discussion of Austen's narrative irony, we may as well ask the conventional question, In what sense *would* being mistress of Pemberley "be something"?

In Austen's day England was still to a large extent an "aristocracy," or hierarchy based on property and patronage in which people took their places in a pyramid-like structure extending down from a minority of the rich and powerful at the top to ever wider and larger layers of lesser wealth to the great mass of the poor and powerless at the bottom. Together, the aristocracy and gentry owned more than two-thirds of all the land in England. In this largely agrarian society, government was conceived of as the authority of the locality, the government of parish, county, and town, whose officials were members of the gentry appointed by the Crown. In the course of the century, this system of local government was replaced by a modern bureaucracy of trained and elected administrators, but at the time Austen was writing, the gentry were the real governors of the countryside. Not until the commercial and political revolutions, accumulating full force in the eighteenth century, disrupted the solidarity of families founded on landed wealth did these ancient families, and the women who belonged to them, lose much of the power they had so long exercised. Only then did the state pass to the control of parliaments composed of men and elected by men.

Lady Catherine de Bourgh and her nephew Darcy are members of one such ancient family, and they are highly conscious of the power they possess. Both control the lives and incomes of scores of people on their estates, many of whom had no voting power until the Reform Bill of 1832. Even after that, until the secret ballot was passed in 1872, landlords could have a decisive effect on votes, since they were taken orally. Traditionally, the steward of an estate such as Darcy's would round up the tenants who could vote, take them to the polling place, and remain there while they called out their preference. A man such as Darcy, were he to run for a seat in the House of Commons, could then be sure of this built-in constituency of tenants. Wickham's chronic resentment, Austen implies, is a function of his having grown up as the son of the elder Darcy's steward, daily

observing so many more advantages accrue to Darcy than to himself.

Although women in the gentry had less authority than men, a matter I take up later, some had considerable power. The tradition of primogeniture established that, under the law, property was passed to the eldest son; and English matrimonial law stipulated that, through marriage, the husband became the owner of all his wife's property. But there were ways in which the gentry could and did protect its women. Mr. Bennet cannot alter the entail requiring that his estate go to the nearest male relation, but he can settle money on his daughters that, if proper legal measures are taken, will remain their own after marriage. Because Lady Catherine's estate is not entailed from the female line, she enjoys most of the advantages of her nephew. She is patroness of the living of Mr. Collins, for example, and he is only one of many people who are dependent on her and therefore must pay court to her. Elizabeth is right when she recognizes that to join Darcy's family and become mistress of Pemberley would indeed "be something." Family and marriage occupied a far more public and central position in the social government and economic arrangements of English society than they would later. In the novels of Austen, marriage is then accurately seen as an institution that both determines and is determined by history.

By the early nineteenth century, England was in the full swing of the first phase of the industrial revolution, which created the new class society of the Victorians. Vertical economic conflicts arose to challenge the horizontal layers formerly joined in agrarian dependency. Wide-scale competition among groups or classes with differing economic interests produced the vertical antagonism known as "class feeling." In *Pride and Prejudice* such tension is evident in the snobbery of the Bingley sisters, which disguises their sense of inferiority in having a parent who made money in trade, and in the way Lady Catherine looks down her nose at the Gardiners, who live in an unfashionably industrial section of London. (It is interesting to note how much more tolerant Austen is of the class of new merchants, revealed in her sympathetic portrait of the Gardiners, than some later novelists—Thackeray, for instance, in *Vanity Fair.*)

The common complaint against Austen then—that the novels are too narrow in their exclusive attention to the private marriage decisions of a single class—is based on a present-day conception of social organization, with its sharp division of the public and private domains. The word *private* is itself applied anachronistically to her world. What is its opposite? Is it perhaps *public*? Yet for much of the nineteenth century, the public authority of the state was only emerging; the public domain was in the process of extending its territory to include all that it would encompass in this century. For most people living in Austen's society, it could be argued that all of life was private, because it was centered in the private estate. In *Emma* Mr. Knightley talks about his responsibilities as a magistrate in the same breath as his deliberations about the plan of a drain. In *Pride and Prejudice* Darcy's virtues as a landlord are established by a dependent living within his own house, his housekeeper (248-49).

Perhaps we should define the opposite of *private* as *social* or *communal* and then see if we can locate this nonsocial, noncommunal presence in Austen's novels, especially within the institution that she places at the center of society: marriage. Austen permits us to overhear "private" conversations between husband and wife in several novels. The opening chapter of *Pride and Prejudice* is one such conversation, and there we notice that even when they are alone, Mr. and Mrs. Bennet address each other as "Mrs. Bennet" and "Mr. Bennet," suggesting a social and formal dimension within the "private" experience of marriage that has all but disappeared today. At the same time, the fact that Austen makes us privy to the conversation points to one of her greatest overriding themes: the growing privatization of marriage. In Austen's early novel, *Northanger Abbey,* marriage is linked to the general functioning of society and to the land; in her last, *Persuasion,* it is separated from the land and from stable community. In *Persuasion* particularly we see the origins of modern marriage, with its intense focus on the private "relationship" that a secular society imposes and its anticipation of the egalitarian marriage of companionship, represented by Admiral and Mrs. Croft (who, as the heroine notes, share the reins of their carriage—that is to say, marriage). This shift from marriage as a public, social institution to a private relationship is apparent in all the novels. That two of Austen's most famous scenes, in the opening chapters of *Sense and Sensibility* and *Pride and Prejudice,* point to the private hell she saw marriage could become suggests such a shift as well, and there is a telling difference between the scenes. In the earlier novel, Austen shows the public and formal structure of marriage determining a loathsome alliance: Mr. and Mrs. John Dashwood conspire to cheat their relations of their patrimony. In *Pride and Prejudice* we see more of the truly private misery of Mr. Bennet beneath the comedy. Actors who have played Mr. Bennet in film and theater have often failed to portray the darker side of his character—his debilitating weariness and boredom, his cynical inattention to his family—and in so doing have made the world of the novel seem weightless and insipid. The novel's "lightness," which Austen remarked on in her letters, cannot be appreciated if we do not feel its weight, and much of this substance is located in Austen's ever-increasing attention to the private self, most particularly in her rendering of the heroine's inner life.

Here again, the historical shift is apparent. In *Sense and Sensibility* the private experience of both Marianne and Elinor is almost always understood by means of a juxtaposition of their characters. When Marianne screams in misery at the center of the novel, her sister is there to hear it; the reader is given to understand the cry in its social context. But when Elizabeth Bennet reads Darcy's letter, she suffers alone: "Till this moment, I never knew myself" (208). When Emma realizes how much she has muddled and mangled her own and Harriet's emotions, "she sat still, she walked about, she tried her own room, she tried the shrubbery," yet no place will accommodate her; she cannot escape herself (323). And the heroine of Austen's last novel is consistently estranged in the way Austen represents her subjective life and role as observer.

The social historian Lawrence Stone calls this change the rise of "affective individualism," suggesting by the term an intrinsic relation between the democratization of society and the inner life. Austen shows her awareness and perhaps endorsement of this shift in culture by having Elizabeth Bennet declare her right to be happy; and it is interesting to note how frequently the word *happiness* appears in the novel. Elizabeth refuses Mr. Collins because he could not make her happy (107), although their marriage would secure her entire family economic protection for life. Later in the novel, when Lady Catherine attempts to appeal to Elizabeth's sense of social duty by insisting she agree not to marry her nephew, Elizabeth replies, "I am only resolved to act in that manner, which will, in my own opinion, constitute my happiness, without reference to *you,* or to any person so wholly unconnected with me" (358).

Stone's theory of social history suggests that only in a highly individualist society does happiness arise as an ideal: those who see themselves as living for themselves become interested in happiness. But if they view themselves as living for something beyond the self— say, the community—happiness loses its central place in human concern. That Austen reveals in almost every novel how difficult it is to negotiate a compromise between the drive for happiness and the necessity of a life of service all communities require of its citizens (most commonly in their role as parents) is not surprising. The question of happiness lies at the heart of the English tradition of liberal rationalism, particularly as it expressed itself in the works of Austen's contemporary Jeremy Bentham and later in the formulations of John Stuart Mill. One of Mill's major efforts was to reconcile a Benthamite faith in making happiness the supreme goal of human life with his communitarian belief in service, probably acquired through the classical education he received from his father (as Austen did from hers). In order to do so, Mill eventually insists on the existence of a private domain, set apart and separate from the demands of law and custom. This abstraction, the private domain, which we have difficulty imagining as an abstraction so much do we take Mill's ideas for granted, is the basis of the argument of *On Liberty* (1859). So little did Mill himself take it for granted, however, that a large section of *On Liberty* is devoted to establishing and defining its existence. Another example is that, until the secret ballot was passed, parliamentarians expressed their astonishment over the proposal on the grounds that no honorable person would have any reason to cast a vote in secret; the private domain was imagined only with difficulty.

These same ambiguities concerning the private self and its relation to custom and community make themselves felt in *Pride and Prejudice.* Austen tempers her affirmation of individual happiness as an ideal by means of a deep aesthetic vigilance over its possible excesses. The hero of the novel, for example, is as different in substance and temperament from the heroine as could be; he embodies the traditional self, one whose identity is based on a sense of his own position in the social hierarchy rather than on an evaluation of his inner worth. This is what Darcy means when he says to Elizabeth, after they have been united, that he was a good man in theory but not in practice. He accepted his own merit as given; until Elizabeth forces him to, he has no impulse to look critically inward. A traditional self with a strong sense of duty (as distinct from conscience), Darcy has before him a traditional—that is to say, arranged—marriage when the novel opens. Of course, contact with Elizabeth changes Darcy, but that Elizabeth ends by marrying so traditional a personality is perhaps the largest check on the modern drive for happiness (most intelligently represented by Elizabeth) in the novel.

Not all the self-seekers in the novel are as intelligent and virtuous as Elizabeth, however, which brings us to another way Austen tempers her affirmation of the pursuit of happiness. The novel continually juxtaposes to Elizabeth and Darcy's marriage the completely selfish marriage, such as the unions between Lydia and Wickham and between Charlotte and Mr. Collins, who live only for themselves and their own advancement. In contrast, Darcy and Elizabeth are envisioned at the conclusion of the novel as surrogate parents, moral guardians, and educators to Georgiana and Kitty, and as host and hostess at their ancient estate to members of the rising class of merchants, the Gardiners. The novel ends, then, on a note of affirmation of the power of marriage as an agent of constructive social change.

The last and most intimate qualification of the ideal of personal happiness concerns the way in which Austen treats Elizabeth's first involvement: her brief infatuation with Wickham. Whereas Darcy's presence at this point is a constant irritant to her, Wickham's presence makes her happy and is described as a "refreshment" (90). Today we would say that he makes her feel "comfortable"—that is, narcissistically contented with herself. Later Elizabeth comes to see that the pleasure she derived from his company had only to do with his silky talent for appealing to her vanity. The narcissistic *feeling* of happiness is thus not to be trusted, unless it has been earned, as it later is with Darcy, by means of vigorous criticism directed against oneself and the other. Plato wrote that we must learn to *bear* pleasure as well as pain, and it is this kind of vigorous joy that Elizabeth is experiencing when she writes to her aunt at the conclusion of the novel. "I am the happiest creature in the world. Perhaps other people have said so before, but not one with such justice. I am happier even than Jane; she only smiles, I laugh" (382-83).

With such qualifications and contrasts working off of and against the pursuit of individual happiness, it is easy to see why critics of the novel traditionally draw from it a moral emphasizing the classical value of living not for oneself but for community. The meaning of life in Austen, they would argue, is to be found not by focusing on ourselves, as Lydia and Wickham do, but in service, as Darcy and Elizabeth do at the conclusion of the novel. Some readers of Austen find this moral comforting; others (particularly feminist readers and critics) consider it objectionable because it appears to endorse patriarchal marriage and to be incompatible with the ideals of modern feminism. Insofar as feminism has been linked with the larger political shift toward liberal democracy over the past two centuries and has accepted unquestioningly the subjectivist premises of Mill, with their emphasis on the self and self-interest, such an interpretation may be justified. But Austen's seeming endorsement of the ideal of service is not incompatible with feminism at its roots, in the writings of her contemporary Mary Wollstonecraft. The author of the first major political treatise on behalf of women's rights, Wollstonecraft drew on Plato in centering her social philosophy outside the self and on the ideal of education; in *A Vindication of the Rights of Woman* she writes of women as "citizens" in whom we must expect "the conduct of an accountable being" (189; Oxford ed.)—a phrase that we can imagine encountering in an Austen novel.

We do not encounter it, however, although phrases like it are put into the mouths of characters; the ironic narrator rarely advances such bald moralities. It is all very well to say that, at the conclusion of the novel, Elizabeth and Darcy are living for something beyond themselves—the national community that Pemberley idealistically embodies, the younger persons they influence, eventually their own children—and that responsibility, rather than happiness, lies at the center of their concerns, but the ethos of *Pride and Prejudice* as a whole is one of pleasure. This is especially evident in the celebratory atmosphere of the closing chapters, which understandably have been compared to the conclusion of

Mozart's *Marriage of Figaro.* Is Austen having it both ways? Is she endorsing Elizabeth's admittedly selfish drive for happiness while at the same time condemning it in others? Elizabeth's words to Lady Catherine, in which she unabashedly asserts her right to think only of herself, make her no different *in theory* from Lydia. And in marrying the high-spirited individualist Elizabeth to such a traditional, community-minded man, is Austen having her cake and eating it too?

Of course she is. The spirit of **Pride and Prejudice** is one of pleasure, a high-minded joy in mastering contradictions not to be confused with regressive indulgence or romantic wish fulfillment. At no moment in the elegant and intense verbal combat between Elizabeth and Darcy is the moral attention relaxed. When they do come to an understanding, it is truly that, not the starry-eyed romantic business we see going on between Jane and Bingley. That Austen does marry off her heroine to one of the richest men in England, who is also about her age (no father figure), vigorous, attractive, intelligent, and obviously passionate, shows how reluctant Austen was to sacrifice the small independence Elizabeth already enjoyed as the daughter of an indulgent father to anything but the best and freest circumstances for a woman at that time. How free were such circumstances, one may ask? How challenging will life at Pemberley be for Elizabeth? How fulfilling could such a vicarious form of existence be by modern standards? Beyond bearing in mind, as I have already suggested, that family and marriage in the ruling class Austen wrote of occupied a far more decisive position in social organization than they would in a later, more democratic society, it would be a grotesque luxury to judge it by modern standards.

Feminist critics who have condemned Austen for not opening up any new vistas for the female spirit, for merely reaffirming the traditional option of marriage, may as well say to a starving person, "Man cannot live by bread alone." Like all her sisters, Elizabeth has only humiliating dependence on relations before her if she does not marry. No professions to speak of are open to her, and laws on every side are designed to restrict her independence. Within the privilege of the gentry class, wives had far less control over their lives than husbands did, and daughters had virtually none. Charlotte Lucas marries Mr. Collins because she does not wish to remain a daughter all her life; that marriage to Mr. Collins is seen as liberating by comparison with "spinsterhood" tells us all we need to know of the depth of Austen's irony on the subject of women.

What is remarkable about Austen's perspective on this subject is that she does not lapse into sentimental wish fulfillment but renders the crass, survivalist posture required of women with unfailing honesty and irony. The "honesty" and "irony" are interchangeable because of the fundamental contradiction in the gentry woman's situation: that she enjoyed tremendous privileges and relative comfort as a member of that class but that her ability to act independently within it was severely restricted. Elizabeth's refusal to marry Mr. Collins, for example, is not ponderously portrayed as an act of courage; it would take little courage to refuse so ridiculous a person as Mr. Collins. But given the situation of women and her own particular economic circumstances, to refuse him without giving way even for a moment to anxiety concerning the future shows an exceptional spirit. Elizabeth's sangfroid is again apparent when she refuses the far more imposing Darcy; she cannot be frightened by circumstance or intimidated by power. Popular women novelists writing at the same time as Austen often show heroines engaged in far more obvious acts of heroism and have been praised over Austen by feminists for portraying more adventurous women; in one such novel the heroine travels down the Amazon River. But Austen did not have to show Elizabeth traveling down the mighty river; she walks three miles in the mud to visit an ailing sister, and the society around her (including the hero) behaves as if she had (32-33). That Elizabeth remains unfazed by their exaggerated response to this most commonplace act—Darcy's admiration no more turns her head than Miss Bingley's visible contempt ruffles her—is not the least of her virtues. It is in Austen's ironic critique of her society, with its vulgar idolatry of the "lady" combined with its brute legal and economic restriction of her independence, together with her passionate endorsement of women who live within it and still manage to retain their self-possession (*dignity* is too lofty a word) that her feminism lies.

Nowhere is this passionate endorsement more complicated and subtle than in Austen's later work **Emma.** That Elizabeth Bennet must go through so much painful self-scrutiny to "earn" the happiness that is hers at the conclusion suggests perhaps the more youthful Austen's straightforward sense of justice. ("Justice," it will be remembered, is a word Elizabeth herself uses in connection with her own happiness in the letter to her aunt referred to earlier.) Austen was in her early twenties when she first drafted **Pride and Prejudice.** Within the brilliantly eccentric ironies of the more mature novel, Austen is far less concerned with reconciling the drive for happiness with the needs of the community. On the surface, however, Austen does make a deceptively good case for this theme, so good that many critics have read **Emma** as her most conservative novel from the point of view of social history, with the paternalistic landowner Mr. Knightley educating the young heroine in her responsibility to English community (an education most succinctly expressed in his lecture to her at Box Hill). Such a reading ignores the overriding irony of **Emma.** Entertaining the kind of massive reversal of sympathies and values that she had already shown herself capable of in **Mansfield Park,** Austen indulges Emma's caprices, amorality, and mistakes to the full, mourning before the fact the day she becomes Mrs. Knightley and can no longer afford to make mistakes—the way a parent might spoil a terminally ill child. By the time she wrote **Emma,** Austen's sense of "justice" to women had matured; and unless we appreciate her irony, it may seem bitter. In **Emma** Austen is secretly rejoicing over the passage of the old order, perhaps rejoicing all the more in knowing that many of her readers would feel it without knowing it, and that she was alone (or so she thought) in imagining a heroine "whom no one but myself will much like" (Austen-Leigh 157).

That Elizabeth Bennet is so easy to like makes **Pride and Prejudice** the less ironic novel. But Elizabeth's marriage to Darcy, as we have seen, is not without contradiction and irony. After they are united, Elizabeth "remembered that [Darcy] had yet to learn to be laught at" (371). Perhaps a juxtaposition of the two novels suggests more than anything else that no discussion of the social-historical context in which the heroines move can proceed without consideration of Austen's irony. The moral discrimination that forms the basis of that irony is so insistent, writes Raymond Williams, "that it can be taken as an independent value . . . which is in the end separable from its social basis." After making this profound observation, Williams goes on to attach that value to the democratic social agenda: "she provided the emphasis which had only to be taken outside the park walls, into a different social experience, to become not a moral but a social criticism," such as one finds in the Victorian moralists (*Country* 117). But we will leave it to the historical ideologists to determine the political direction Austen's emphasis would take later. Whatever one concludes, one cannot help but feel that Austen wrote more for later generations than for her own. This perception is apparent not only in her steady refusal to court the public attention she could so easily have gained but in the way the novels seem to feel themselves forward into time, articulating our own historical distance from her world by means of their irony. Historians have long been in the habit of claiming, as A. J. P. Taylor has written, that, among novelists, history began with Walter Scott, the historical novelist and contemporary of Jane Austen. But if history is a form of self-consciousness, perhaps history began with Jane Austen as well.

Works Cited and Consulted

Austen, Jane. *Emma.* Ed. R. W. Chapman. 3rd ed. London: Oxford UP, 1932, 1965.

———. *Jane Austen: Selected Letters 1796-1817.* Ed. R. W. Chapman. Oxford: Oxford UP, 1955. Rpt., with introd. by Marilyn Butler, 1985.

———. *Jane Austen's Letters to Her Sister Cassandra and Others.* Ed. R. W. Chapman. 2nd ed. London: Oxford UP, 1952.

———. *Mansfield Park.* Ed. R. W. Chapman. 3rd ed. New York: Oxford UP, 1932, 1966.

———. *Minor Works.* Ed. R. W. Chapman. Oxford: Oxford UP, 1954. Rev. ed. 1963.

———. *Northanger Abbey* and *Persuasion.* Ed. R. W. Chapman. 3rd ed. Oxford: Oxford UP, 1933. Rev. ed. 1965.

———. *Pride and Prejudice.* Afterword by Joann Morse. New York: Signet, 1961.

———. *Pride and Prejudice.* Ed. Donald J. Gray. Norton Critical ed. New York: Norton, 1966.

———. *Pride and Prejudice.* Ed. R. W. Chapman. 1932, 1967. London: Oxford UP, 1976.

———. *Pride and Prejudice.* Introduction by Mark Schorer. Riverside ed. Boston: Houghton, 1956.

———. *Pride and Prejudice.* Introduction by Tony Tanner. Harmondsworth, Eng.: Penguin, 1972.

———. *Sense and Sensibility.* Ed. R. W. Chapman. 3rd ed. New York: Oxford UP, 1933, 1967.

Austen-Leigh, J. E. *A Memoir of Jane Austen.* London: 1865, 1870, 1871; Oxford: Clarendon, 1926. Rpt. in *Persuasion.* New York: Penguin, 1965.

Austen-Leigh, William, and Richard Arthur Austen. *Jane Austen: Her Life and Letters—A Family Record.* New York: Dutton, 1913.

Forster, E. M. *Howards End.* New York: Random, 1921.

Stone, Lawrence. *The Family, Sex and Marriage: England, 1500-1800.* London: Weidenfeld, 1977.

Williams, Raymond. *The Country and the City.* New York: Oxford UP, 1973.

———. *The English Novel from Dickens to Lawrence.* London: Hogarth, 1984.

Wollstonecraft, Mary. *Collected Letters.* Ed. Ralph M. Wardle. Ithaca: Cornell UP, 1979.

———. *A Vindication of the Rights of Woman. English Romantic Poetry and Prose.* Ed. Russell Noyes. Oxford: Oxford UP, 1956.

William Christie (essay date 1997)

SOURCE: Christie, William. "Pride, Politics, and Prejudice." *Nineteenth-Century Contexts* 20, no. 3 (1997): 313-34.

[*In the following essay, Christie finds that in* Pride and Prejudice, *a novel deeply concerned with the pressing political issues of the day, Austen's compromise between conservatism and progressivism is ultimately a "collapse of the progressive position."*]

Progressively more preoccupied with the individual sensibility and with the individual as a morally autonomous consciousness, the social phenomenon of the novel reflected that ultimately indefinable manifold of changes in the details and structures of scientific, philosophical, and psychological thinking that is "universally acknowledged" to have altered the personal and social construction of the Self in the eighteenth century. The changes themselves invariably led to the question of authority: of who should rule over, or overrule, whom; of what entitled or empowered someone—more ethically, what qualified someone—to rule at all.

Once upon a time the answers, certainly to the first of these questions, had appeared self-evident: nominally, at least, men were to rule over women and parents to overrule their children; in society as a whole, "land was the most important single passport to social and political consideration," representing "not merely wealth, but stability and continuity, a fixed interest in the state which conferred the right to govern."[1] But throughout the eighteenth century the question of authority or "the right to govern" became progressively more vexed; by the 1790s—the years of Jane Austen's personal maturing and literary apprenticeship—it was not only vexed, but exigent.

I

It is no longer possible to assume that Jane Austen's achievement was contingent upon a disciplined, "classical" exclusion of the urgent political issues that occupied the more historically minded amongst her contemporaries; to argue, as George Steiner did in 1975, that it was precisely because of her indifference to "the fierce historical, social crises" which surrounded her that "the area defined for imaginative penetration could be superbly exploited."[2] On the contrary, this indifference is now recognized as artistic indirection, and Austen's novels are read as articulate forms of an historical awareness no less acute, and no less earnestly engaged with contemporary political issues, than *Political Justice* or *Lyrical Ballads*.

The titles alone of recent critical studies of Jane Austen's novels challenge the assumption of their decorous temporality and insularity: *The Improvement of the Estate; Jane Austen and the War of Ideas; Jane Austen and the French Revolution; Jane Austen and the State; Jane Austen in a Social Context; Jane Austen: Women, Politics, and the Novel*—amongst many others.[3] In their concern with authority in the face of new philosophies which brought all in doubt; in their concern with the relationship between the individual as an autonomous, ethically and emotionally motivated subject on the one hand, and the society to which that individual is somehow "contractually" related on the other—Austen's fictions have taken their place alongside the novels and

dissertations of contemporary ideologues, the articles and pamphlets and open letters of contemporary polemicists, and the dispatches of contemporary politicians.

As literary parodies, her novels show how popular, fictional distortions may reflect and even engender profound social (because moral) imbalances of the kind then under debate in the more overtly political arena. As comedies of manners, they are shot through with social and political nuances because for Austen, as for Edmund Burke, manners are no mere conventions (least of all literary ones) but "are more important than laws:"

> Manners are what vex or soothe, corrupt or purify, exalt or debase, barbarise or refine us. . . . They give their whole form and colour to our lives. According to their quality, they add morals, they supply them, or they totally destroy them.[4]

The identification of manners in Austen's novels with morals and with culture—in short, with ideology—charges with significance every character, every utterance, every gesture, every action, every social event. "A mind lively and at ease," as she comments in *Emma,* "can see nothing that does not answer" (Vol. II, ch. 9).[5] Far from being seen as cut off and self-contained, the world of her novels is now read as symbolic of English society in a revolutionary age—as symbolic, that is, in the Coleridgean sense that it "partakes of the Reality which it renders intelligible."[6]

It is one thing, however, for criticism to acknowledge her high-minded engagement with the urgent questions of authority and its mandate, it is quite another for it to achieve anything like clarity or consensus on what, precisely, Austen's position was on such issues as patronage, the place of women, the distribution of wealth, and parliamentary reform.

That the question of authority is at issue in ***Pride and Prejudice,*** for example, is apparent; it is explored through the elaborate pattern of dependence and independence, of decision and indecision, of control and license which constitutes the novel's moral design or "mapping." Indeed, authority is most often invoked in the novel by its abuse or its abrogation. We are witness to Mr Bennet's exercising no control over the destructive inanities of Mrs Bennet, or over the shameless and trivial behavior of his shallower daughters (or over his bank account, for that matter); to Sir William Lucas's opting out of bourgeois society in order to indulge his aristocratic fantasies and abandoning his daughters on the marriage market without a creditable dowry and a prey to the likes of Mr Collins; to Bingley's good-natured but whimsical irresolution, leaving him prey to the prejudiced certitude of Darcy; to the Colonel's and Mrs Forster's neglecting their role *in loco parentis,* leaving Lydia prey to Wickham (as well as to her own stupidity); to the Bingley sisters' self-serving representation of the polite world, vaunting its authority over good taste and correct behavior; to Mr Hurst's opting out of responsible, rational existence all together; and so on. What is less apparent, however, is the origin and precise political nature of this crisis of authority, or what the political solution might be.

The truth is that there are two political positions or perspectives in *Pride and Prejudice,* the discrepancy between which is strategic rather than merely unwitting or adventitious. The challenge of the novel lies in its representing *both* sides of what Marilyn Butler identifies in the novels of the 1790s as a "critical divide"

> between the advocates of a Christian conservatism on the one hand, with their pessimistic view of man's nature, and their belief in external authority; [and] on the other hand, progressives, sentimentalists, revolutionaries, with their optimism about man, and their preference for spontaneous personal impulse against rules imposed from without.[7]

What I propose is to explore the divided political allegiance of *Pride and Prejudice* by isolating and examining its two, discrepant positions or perspectives—one progressive and the other conservative—and to ask, among other things, how persuasive they are and whether their political implications are in co-operation or in conflict with each other in the novel.[8]

Between these positions or oppositions, made readily identifiable to her contemporaries by Austen's choice of certain words and objects and actions, *Pride and Prejudice* aspires to a critically well-documented compromise that takes its dialectical form from the characterization of Elizabeth (275, 338).[9] "Spontaneous personal impulse" is to be disciplined by assimilation into the prevailing order in the hope of giving that order new vigor and a more supple propriety; of humanizing its face without diminishing its authority; indeed, of extending and justifying the power of the ruling class by purging its gratuitous or purely self-serving prejudices, and thus restoring to it a function of which it could be genuinely proud. The energy and articulate individualism of Elizabeth Bennet is harnessed in a symbolic marriage, one that would enliven but (pre)serve the microcosmic order of a hierarchical society. Accommodation has thus arguably been made to genuine virtue and talent, though it has been made indirectly, by appropriation and mutual submission, rather than by direct political eruption, intervention, or reform. And it has been made only after a respect for "external authority" has been discovered or learned.

It is my contention that Austen's aspiring compromise is less a compromise than a capitulation or collapse of the progressive position. Indeed, so severe a sacrifice of progressive values is demanded, and so disingenuous

are some of the strategies of recognition and reversal used to effect the supervention of conservative values, that the "critical divide" in the novel is accentuated rather than resolved.

II

As it turns out, only the Gardiners are consistently responsible and "gentleman-like" (124), counselling and contributing without ever presuming to take over the affairs or the lives of others. And the Gardiners, significantly, are in trade, bringing to gentility the bourgeois virtues of (amongst others) expedition, industry, and an inobsequious humility. (Like all Jane Austen's variously prominent figures of ethical authority, the Gardiners— Aunt and Uncle; word and deed—represent a complex of complementarities.) Their being in trade is "significant" because *Pride and Prejudice* is an often spirited and occasionally acrimonious attack on the *status quo,* participating in "that tradition in English culture which has consistently, from the seventeenth century, opposed arbitrary aristocratic and patriarchal privilege."[10]

It is in Darcy's unapologetic and *aristocratic* assumption of control over Bingley's life and destiny, for example, that the pervasive social disease of authority abused can be seen most dramatically and most emblematically. "Why reverence a man because he happens to be born to certain privileges . . . ?," the radical William Godwin was asking in *Political Justice* (1793); must we "renounce our independence, in their presence?"

> in those cases of general justice which are equally within the province of every human understanding, I am a deserter from the requisitions of duty if I do not assiduously exert my faculties, or if I be found to act contrary to the conclusions they would dictate, from deference to the opinions of others.
>
> (Bk III, ch. 6)[11]

The attack on nobility in *Pride and Prejudice* is confined largely to the first half of the novel. By beginning with the progressive or "optimistic" impulse at work in the novel, I would thus preserve Austen's own, carefully calculated priorities (as throughout I would preserve oppositions that she herself sets up).

The potential for a radical critique is in fact established at the very opening of the novel by Austen's most famous utterance, on the face of it an ingenious and spirited satire on the inquisitiveness and acquisitiveness of the provincial gentry to which she belonged:

> It is a truth universally acknowledged, that a single man in possession of a good fortune, must be in want of a wife.

Amidst the "wealth" of implication of this single sentence, three extensive and disturbing social strictures formulate themselves—more extensive and more disturbing, that is, than we would expect of a mere flourish of local satire. First, there is the equivocal status of "truth," here attenuated or debased by its implicit and ironic identification with an equivocal, "universal" consensus. Accordingly, the verifying "universe" of the opening sentence shrinks to "a neighbourhood" in the second:

> However little known the feelings or views of such a man may be on his first entering a neighbourhood, this truth is so well fixed in the minds of the surrounding families, that he is considered as the rightful property of some one or other of their daughters.

The novel will go on to suggest just how capricious both public and personal "truth" can be, with the case of *Darcy v. Wickham* at the Meryton Assizes as exemplary: "All Meryton seemed striving to blacken the man, who, but three months before, had been almost an angel of light" (260).

The second and third strictures of the opening sentence are legally and linguistically inseparable; they are the socially constructed "truth" of the relationship between marriage and money on the one hand, and the dehumanization of women into property on the other. Both are established by a terminology of enormous suggestiveness: "in possession of" (owning) / "in possession of" (possessed by); "a good fortune" (wealth) / "a good fortune" (luck); "in want" (need) / "in want" (desire); "must" (of necessity) / "must" (imperative). Even the strictly hierarchical "man" and "wife" from the church ceremony is smuggled in. And what the sentence does *not* say—what it surely tempts without attempting—is "that a single man in want of a good fortune, must be in possession of a wife." Simply by reversing the adverbial phrases in the relative clause we have the predicaments of Wickham and of Colonel Fitzwilliam in a nutshell.

Such is the double-edged nature of possession, moreover, that the subtle political and emotional symbiotics captured in these opening lines is soon established, as the "single man" becomes "the rightful property" of the daughters of "the surrounding families." Seeking to extend his rightful property by marriage, the single man becomes the property of those he would appropriate!

The satire on the abuses of truth, marriage, and women in these lines anticipates the progressivist critique of society in *Pride and Prejudice* which is my first concern. As a critique, certain incidents or episodes are crucial, and the long episode of Elizabeth's visit to the newly-wed Collinses at Hunsford is a sensational example. Among other things, it is during this visit that Darcy discovers that the Lady Catherine de Bourgh is not qualified to assume the authority to which her position and wealth automatically entitle her. Yet when Darcy responds to Lady Catherine's treatment of Elizabeth at

Rosings by looking "a little ashamed at his aunt's ill-breeding" (154), he unwittingly anticipates the barbed accusation of failing to behave "in a more gentleman-like manner" (171) that Elizabeth is to level at him, not long after. In this, as in his meddling in Bingley's and Jane's affairs of the heart, Darcy proves himself his aunt Catherine's nephew. These signal failures in "that chastity of honour" characteristic of Edmund Burke's "age of chivalry" mark decisive moments in the novel as an allegorical "Pride's Progress," or remorseless humiliation of the aristocracy.[12]

Lady Catherine's style of patronage is, amongst other things, an anachronism. Although as a literary "character" she is immediately identifiable as the dictatorial dowager of the comedy of manners from Congreve to Coward, it is important also to recognize the historically specific impropriety of her behaviour. Patronage, as Lady Catherine exercises it, is rather a patronizing intrusion into the private lives, even into the thoughts and feelings, of individuals who have rights (to use an especially loaded word from the period)—rights, and the relative autonomy to think and to choose for themselves. "Mr Collins, you must marry. A clergyman like you must marry," she declares (echoing the confusion of necessity with the imperative that was anticipated in the opening sentence):

> "Chuse properly, chuse a gentlewoman for *my* sake; and for your *own*, let her be an active, useful sort of person, not brought up high, but able to make a small income go a good way. This is my advice. Find such a woman as soon as you can, bring her to Hunsford, and I will visit her."
>
> (95)

And for the gentlewoman's own sake? Lady Catherine's "interest," in the old sense—the things that concern her and that come under her aristocratic *aegis*—is extended comically but tellingly to include matters as trivial as the way in which her "serfs" grow their vegetables. "Nothing was beneath this great Lady's attention" (146).

It is hard to resist reading the exaggerated relationship between Lady Catherine and Collins, with his Tartuffian blend "of servility and self-importance" (56) while ultimately impotent and dependent, as a satirical reflection on the relationship between the State and a secularized, pusillanimous Church of England. What we can be certain of is that, in terms of the comic politics of Austen's allegory of the aristocracy, both Collins and Lady Catherine are anachronistic and marginal to a new and commendable spirit or spiritedness, the main expression or incarnation of which in *Pride and Prejudice* is the character of Elizabeth herself.

Central to the challenge that Elizabeth represents to the *status quo* is a brazen independence in the face of the intimidations of rank—specifically, in the face of Darcy and of his aunt. In the imposing, if vulgar context of Rosings, for example, when at last in the company of the sonorously portended Lady Catherine, Elizabeth's composure stands for the defiance of the individual, of individual intelligence and self-possession, in the face of arrogant authoritarianism (no less than, say, Caleb Williams's solitary resistance to the vengeful Falkland):[13]

> Elizabeth's courage did not fail her. She had heard nothing of Lady Catherine that spoke her awful from any extraordinary talents or miraculous virtues, and the mere stateliness of money and rank, she thought she could witness without trepidation.
>
> (144)

The first thing to note here is that for Elizabeth "money and rank" are merely stately, merely gratuitous. The second is that she can witness the merely stately "without trepidation," just as she has resisted Darcy's "fortune and consequence" with a comparable *in*trepidity (69).

Thirdly, she is prepared to defer only to talent and virtue, two values that, because they ignored or transgressed the artificial boundaries of class, were integral to every program for political revolution, reform, or revision. The radical Thomas Holcroft spoke through his eponymous heroine in *Anna St. Ives* (1792):

> It appears evident to my mind, at present, that we ought to consider whether an action be in itself good or bad, just or unjust, and totally disregard both our own prejudices and the prejudices of the world. Were I to pay false homage to *wealth* and *rank,* because the world tells me that it is right that I should do so, and to neglect *genius* and *virtue,* which my judgment tells me would be an odious wrong, I should find but little satisfaction in the applause of the world, opposed to self-condemnation.
>
> (Vol. VI, letter 100)[14]

Again, witness *Political Justice:* "the thing really to be desired is the removing as much as possible arbitrary distinctions, and leaving to *talents* and *virtue* the field of exertion unimpaired" (Bk II, ch. 3).[15] In 1808, the Whig *Edinburgh Review* was more uncompromising even than Holcroft and Godwin:

> Now, if any man thinks, that we should not extravagantly rejoice in any conceivable event which must reform the constitution of England,—by reducing the overgrown influence of the crown,—by curbing the pretensions of the privileged orders . . .—by raising up the power of real *talents* and *worth,* the true nobility of the country,—by exalting the mass of the community, and giving them, under the guidance of that *virtual aristocracy,* to direct the councils of England . . . must have read but few pages of this Journal.[16]

At Rosings, Elizabeth reserves her deference for such an aristocracy of virtue, and of genius or talents, alone.

It was John Wilkes's notorious demand for "a career open to talents" in the 1760s that made the concept and term "talent(s)" the catchcry of the radical challenge to the wholesale and unapologetic system of patronage and preferment—to the nepotism, that is—that had been institutionalized by, for, and within the ruling classes. Lady Catherine, for one, celebrates the power that she derives from the "privileges" she inherits and confers. Mr Bennet may convert Collins's toadying into broad humor when, at the end of the novel, he recommends that he hastily transfer his allegiance—"the nephew," he reminds Collins, "has more to give" than the aunt (340)—but the toadying itself is only symptomatic of the institution. His wife Charlotte's passing calculation of the benefits to be gained by the two of them from a marriage between Elizabeth and Darcy is too casually hard-edged even to be funny (161).

A comparably dark, less comic side of Lady Catherine's anachronism is revealed during her last encounter with Elizabeth at Longbourn, the encounter precipitated by Elizabeth's rumored engagement to her nephew. Lady Catherine's belated flourish reflects at once the crippling nostalgia, as well as the consequent panic, of the contemporary ruling classes of England in the face of a threatened attenuation of their power. The echo of her shrill insistence upon the priority and authority of her own and her sister's engagement of Darcy with her daughter Anne has a distinctly dying fall:

> "the engagement between them is of a peculiar kind. From their infancy, they have been intended for each other. It was the favorite wish of *his* mother, as well as of her's. While in their cradles, we planned their union: and now, when the wishes of both sisters would be accomplished, in their marriage, to be prevented by a young woman of inferior birth, of no importance in the world, and wholly unallied to the family? Do you pay no regard to the wishes of his friends? To his tacit engagement to Miss De Bourgh? Are you lost to every feeling of propriety and delicacy?"
>
> (315)

It would be difficult to exaggerate the importance of the implicit elegy for a dying order in this, and in other passages from the confrontation of Lady Catherine with Elizabeth—whose own replies, incidentally, often verge "on conceit and impertinence" (to quote Caroline Bingley in a different context [20]), and once or twice even upon the cruel. That the issue over which the two fall out should be marriage is no coincidence, for in marriage the question of authority, of the right to choose, bears directly upon both heart and holdings—almost exclusively so for most women of the period.

The complicity established in this exchange between author, heroine, and reader suggests Austen's approval of the supervention of the young couple's rights upon their parents' "interested" preferences, and of the romantic and comparatively recent assumption that affection and companionship were major concerns in the selection of a partner. In line with the growing autonomy of the individual, eighteenth-century England had witnessed a "marked shift in emphasis" in the motives for marriage: "away from family interest and towards well-tried personal affection."[17] As life imitated art, the forms and language of romantic love began to influence or constrain the behavior of all classes of society; "Without taking into account this powerful, widespread, and impelling passion at the heart of the marriage system, it is impossible to make sense of the other features."[18] "Husband and wife are always together and share the same society," remarked the astonished French tourist the Duc de Rochefoucauld in 1784, adding that "the Englishman would rather have the love of the woman he loves than the love of his parents."[19] Elizabeth is no Marianne Dashwood, but that she, too, accepts the change of priorities is evidenced by her guarded response to her Aunt Gardiner's prudence:

> ". . . since we see every day that where there is affection, young people are seldom withheld by immediate want of fortune, from entering into engagements with each other, how can I promise to be wiser than many of my fellow creatures if I am tempted, or how am I even to know that it would be wisdom to resist?"
>
> (129)

Romantic comedy offers such ample precedence for the obstruction of youthful love by superannuated "interest" that an historically specific, political reading of the scene between Lady Catherine and Elizabeth would seem perverse, were it not for the fact that Lady Catherine's patently anachronistic appeal to the priority of tradition and to the authority of her class highlighted the contemporary issues of social cohesion and individual rights: "Are the shades of Pemberley to be thus polluted?" she asks, rhetorically, in an unmistakably Burkean strain (317). Thomas Holcroft had the same political object in mind when in *Anna St. Ives* he had Anna resist her uncle Lord Fitz-Allen's demand that she marry the villain Coke Clifton:

> I immediately answered—If, sir . . . you understand any further intercourse between me and Mr. Clifton, I must not suffer you to continue in such an error. We are and ever must remain separate. Habit and education have made us two such different beings, that it would be the excess of folly to suppose marriage could make us one.
>
> Miss St. Ives—[my uncle collected all his ideas of rank and grandeur] Miss St. Ives, you must do me the honour to consider me as head of the family, and suffer me to remind you of the respect and obedience that are due to that head. The proposal now made you I approve. It is made by a man of family, and I must take the liberty to lay my injunctions upon you to listen to it in a decorous and proper manner.
>
> I answered—I am sorry, sir, that our ideas of propriety are so very opposite. But whether my judgment be

right or wrong, I am the person to be married to Mr. Clifton, and not your Lordship.

> (Vol. VI, letter 103)[20]

Like Holcroft, Austen is using a recognizably literary, even archetypal antagonism in an unequivocally political debate—a debate to which all the variously motivated marriages and all the romantic and comic incidents and motifs in *Pride and Prejudice* can be seen to contribute.

I want to go back now to the question raised by Lady Catherine as to who is most entitled or best qualified to marry Darcy. While the opening sentence leads directly to Bingley's arrival at Netherfield, it is with Darcy's "want of a wife"—again, both need and desire—that the novel and its politics are more concerned. Specifically, we need to go back to Rosings, and to the comic strategy of Ann de Bourgh's disqualification. If Lady Catherine's presumption of her daughter's priority is absurdly anachronistic, it appears as especially absurd when we think of Ann herself: "thin and small" according to Maria Lucas; "sickly and cross," according to Elizabeth (142). Again, later: "so thin and so small;" "pale and sickly; her features, though not plain, were insignificant" (145). The consensus amongst the various characters, to which Lady Catherine herself enthusiastically contributes, establishes Ann de Bourgh as "of a sickly constitution" (59); as chronically enervated and even mentally defective, quite apart from being taciturn, haughty, uninformed, and untalented. Her character reflects the satirical Austen at her most savage, recalling Swift/Gulliver on the aristocracy in the fourth part of *Gulliver's Travels*: "a weak diseased Body, a meager Countenance, and sallow Complexion, are the true Marks of *noble Blood*."

Indeed, Swift goes on—and it is on this idea that I want to expand—"a healthy robust Appearance is so disgraceful in a Man of Quality, that the World concludes his real Father to have been a Groom or a Coachman" (Part IV ch 6).[21] Swift's satirical construction of cross-class breeding as a variety of miscegenation, ironically displacing licensed incest, illuminates Austen's satirical technique in this episode of *Pride and Prejudice.* Using a later analogue, Ann de Bourgh's symbolic function in the novel as a socio-political allegory anticipates that of D. H. Lawrence's Lord (Clifford) Chatterly, the physically (sexually) disabled husband of *Lady Chatterly's Lover,* in which Swift's "groom" or "coachman" becomes the gamekeeper Mellors. Austen and Lawrence are admittedly strange bedfellows and Elizabeth is hardly prototypical of Mellors. Still, the fact that the anaemic Ann de Bourgh and the emasculated Clifford Chatterly should both figure the social, political, and spiritual inanition of a redundant aristocracy suggests a continuity between the two and confirms that continuity as more than literary.

And like Mellors, Elizabeth is nothing if not "healthy" and "robust," as "fine, stout, healthy" as the love that she wittily envisages as able to withstand the onslaught of a sonnet (39). Austen goes out of her way to enforce Elizabeth's physical and mental sanity, both at Rosings, where in direct contrast to the "sickly" Ann's hypothetical proficiency at the piano she performs with gusto and laughs "heartily," and elsewhere throughout the novel. Swiftian eugenics may not have entered consciously into Darcy's deliberations about marriage, but his attraction to Elizabeth is inspired by a sexuality in which both play and physical robustness feature prominently, even though her "easy playfulness" is originally found to be in "mortifying" contradistinction to the "manners . . . of the fashionable world" (19). It is Elizabeth who attends to Jane when she is bedridden at Netherfield; Elizabeth who, unlike the luxurious Mr Hurst, prefers "a plain dish to a ragout" (30); Elizabeth who supports the otherwise unfailing Mrs Gardiner in their walks around the extensive Pemberley estates (a full, active appreciation of which demands someone "healthy" and "robust"!). Indeed, Elizabeth is only rarely "overcome"—which is to say, only rarely succumbs to what was then the characteristically feminine reaction to physical or mental distress.

On this point, Jane Austen's "feminism" coincides with an historically recent (as well as characteristically rural) concept of female beauty; a concept of beauty which in its turn reflects the radical reorientation of the individual's relationship with the natural world and, correspondingly, with her own body—witnessed, for example, in the indignant protest of Mary Wollstonecraft:

> Fragile in every sense of the word, [women] are obliged to look up to man for every comfort. In the most trifling danger they cling to their support, with parasitical pertinacity, piteously demanding succour; and their *natural* protector extends his arm, or lifts up his voice, to guard the lovely trembler—from what? Perhaps the frown of an old cow. . . . I am fully persuaded that we should hear none of these infantine airs, if girls were allowed to take sufficient exercise, and not confined in close rooms till their muscles are relaxed, and their powers of digestion destroyed . . .
>
> I do not wish them to have power over men; but over themselves[22]

Wollstonecraft's is a salutary reminder of the politics of fresh air.

The extension to women of the vogue of walking and touring—like Rousseau, Elizabeth had "a love of solitary walks" (162)—meant a measure of bodily emancipation, the ideological significance of which is as evident as the ideological significance of Elizabeth Bennet's energy and independence:

> Elizabeth continued her walk alone, crossing field after field at a quick pace, jumping over stiles and springing over puddles with impatient activity, and finding herself at last in view of the house, with weary ankles, dirty stockings, and a face glowing with the warmth of exercise.
>
> (28)

Elizabeth is singled out by the novel and by its hero for her "animal spirits," expressed here in the "impatient activity" of present participles that might as appropriately be applied to her "liveliness" of mind and conversation (338): "crossing"; "jumping"; "springing"; "glowing." So later, she breaks from the unaccommodating order of Netherfield society *en courant* to run "gaily off, rejoicing as she rambled about" (46).

An unequivocally sexual energy informs and invigorates Elizabeth's ethical independence, as well as her intrepidity, her intellect and wit, and the anarchic sense of the bizarre that she inherits from her father: "I dearly love a laugh" (50). And the same energy would appear implicitly to promise to carry Elizabeth and all that she represents through the turmoil of the present, of "such days as these" (32).[23] Which is why she threatens the Bingley sisters:

> Miss Bingley began by abusing her as soon as she was out of the room. Her manners were pronounced to be very bad indeed, a mixture of pride and impertinence; she had no conversation, no stile, no taste, no beauty. Mrs. Hurst thought the same and added,
>
> "She has nothing, in short, to recommend her, but being an excellent walker. I shall never forget her appearance this morning. She really looked almost wild."
>
> "She did indeed, Louisa. I could hardly keep my countenance. Very nonsensical to come at all! Why must *she* be scampering about the country, because her sister had a cold? Her hair so untidy, so blowsy!" "Yes, and her petticoat; I hope you saw her petticoat, six inches deep in mud. . . ."
>
> "*You* observe it, Mr Darcy, I am sure," said Miss Bingley; "and I am inclined to think that you would not wish to see *your sister* make such an exhibition."
>
> "Certainly not."
>
> "To walk three miles, or four miles, or five miles, or whatever it is, above her ankles in dirt, and alone, quite alone! what could she mean by it? It seems to me to shew an abominable sort of conceited independence, a most country town indifference to decorum."
>
> (30-1)

Solitariness and independence—the sort of independence that consistently challenges decorum and wonders at the wisdom, not to say ethics of hastily legitimizing Lydia's and Wickham's doomed relationship, for example (269; 280); an "impulse of feeling" not always "guided by reason" that is correctly, if sententiously, identified by Mary (27); pedestrianism and unapologetic provincialism; an indifference to society's sanctions and conventions ("in her air altogether, there is a self-sufficiency without fashion" [239]); a "wild manner" (37); energy and excess—what do these represent but a configuration of values that can be identified as a version of Romantic radicalism? The censures that the Bingley sisters level at Elizabeth extend their own function beyond that of two ugly sisters in a Cinderella story to that of political conservatives, alarmed at Elizabeth's anarchic athleticism and individualism. Even Elizabeth's being tanned feeds a disgust that is characteristic both of a specifically urban refinement and of a more catholic snobbery. In short, the politics of *Pride and Prejudice* is in part at least a complex, sexual politics.[24]

The Bingley sisters' fear is only accentuated by their endeavors metaphorically to belittle (and so contain) Elizabeth's animal energy and its sexual attractiveness; her "crossing," "jumping," and "springing," it should be noted, are reduced to "scampering." On another occasion, they describe her eyes as "shrewish" (239). Darcy, on the other hand, more ingenuous in recognizing this attractiveness ("her fine eye . . . were brightened by the exercise"), seeks refuge in rigid, social interdictions, forcibly reminding both Bingley and himself that the Bennet sisters' inferior connections "must very materially lessen their chances of marrying men of any consideration in the world" (31), just as he reminds himself, later, "that were it not for the inferiority of her connections, he should be in some danger" (45).

Darcy's conservative propriety becomes a victim of his own passion, however, and he must learn through Elizabeth that it is "as ridiculous to attempt to fix the heredityship of human beauty, as of wisdom" (to quote Thomas Paine).[25] No prediction could be less accurate than Mr Collins's concerning Elizabeth's prospects: "Your portion is unhappily so small that it will in all likelihood undo the effects of your loveliness" (98). The effects of sexual attraction, it would appear, cannot be so easily undone. The apparently casual, occasional references to Darcy's "powerful feelings towards her" (84), to his being "in her power" (161), to "the power that she has over him" (234), reflect the hierarchical subversion effected by sexual attraction. "The beautiful expression of [Elizabeth's] dark eyes" (19) becomes the font and focus, so to speak, of an inordinate passion—literally in-ordinate: out of bounds, or out of the prescribed boundaries. With his proud unease and overcivilized repressions, Darcy has "never been so *bewitched* by any woman as he was by her" (45; my italics) and construes Elizabeth as a *femme fatale*:

> "In vain have I struggled. It will not do. My feelings will not be repressed. You must allow me to tell you how much I love and admire you." . . .
>
> His sense of her inferiority—of its being a degradation—of the family obstacles which judgment had al-

ways opposed to inclination, were dwelt on with a warmth which seemed due to the consequence he was wounding. . . .

> He concluded with representing the strength of that attachment which, in spite of all his endeavours, he had found impossible to conquer.
>
> (168)

In terms of *Pride and Prejudice* as an allegory of the ruling class brought literally and metaphorically to its knees, this is a powerfully symbolic moment. Darcy learns that the exclusive and arbitrary propriety of social rank that he invokes to strengthen his resistance is not only impotent, it is also iniquitous, and his own behavior arrogant. As he later recalls: "I was properly humbled" (328). Like Elizabeth, the novel is utterly unsympathetic and uncompromising throughout this first proposal, refusing to allow the honesty of Darcy's tortured confession "of the scruples that had long prevented my forming any serious design" to mitigate the offense given by his insensitivity to her moral and emotional individuality, an insensitivity surely understandable, if not "natural and just" (171). The novel would appear to countenance no excuses for Darcy's "pretensions" nor, abstracting, for such pride and presumption on the part of the ruling class.

And this is only the beginning of Darcy's ritual (self-)abasement. To be closeted with George Wickham in Gracechurch St, for example, where once Darcy would hardly have thought "a month's ablutions enough to cleanse him of its impurities" (127), and to be haggling with Wickham over the price of buying him off is, for Darcy, a punishment more sublimely fitted to the crime than anything W. S. Gilbert could invent. A self-confessed spoilt child of the aristocracy—"allowed, encouraged, almost taught . . . to think meanly of the rest of the world, to *wish* at least to think meanly of their sense and worth compared with my own"—Darcy ultimately emerges chastened and subdued, and willing to acknowledge rather as his savior, the woman with the "wild, wild eyes" whom he had once seen as *la belle dame sans merci*: "What do I not owe you! You taught me a lesson, hard indeed at first, but most advantageous. By you, I was properly humbled" (328).

The triumph of the new woman and of progressive individualism over an arrogant ruling class, reluctant to forego the unwarranted power that it inherited with its landed estates? On one level, certainly; there are complications, however.

III

The character in the novel most inclined to politicize Darcy's behaviour is Wickham, for example, and there is a certain danger in adopting the interpretative strategies of the novel's villain, as well as many of his specific political inferences regarding Darcy and Lady Catherine (69-75). High-minded political criticism in general, moreover, has much to learn from the fact that part of Wickham's "inducement" was an irrational resentment and "the hope of revenging himself" (180).

There is, however, plenty of less oblique evidence of the ultimate inadequacy of reading *Pride and Prejudice* exclusively as an allegorical "Pride's Progress." For one thing, there is almost the entire second half of the novel. After the heady episodes at Netherfield and Rosings, the reader is never again permitted such faith in Elizabeth's iconoclastic wit and energy. Her surprise at Darcy's proposal at Hunsford shifts the focus to her own self-ignorance, not to say hypocrisy, for not only has she chosen "wilfully to misunderstand" his manifest feelings (51)—fully apparent though they are to the reader (19)—but she has consciously or unconsciously solicited and encouraged those feelings with a provocative flirtatiousness from the beginning. Her later apology to Darcy represents the sustained reassessment that her values, and with them the values honoured by the novel, have undergone since the proposal: "My manners must have been at fault, but not intentionally I assure you. I never meant to deceive you, but my spirits might often lead me wrong" (328). Elizabeth, "virtual aristocrat," is required to suffer a humiliation—and "how just a humiliation" (185)—comparable with Darcy's own.

This humiliation and reassessment, along with the genuinely disturbing consequences of actions that at the time had seemed innocuous or "merely" irresponsible, demand a radical revision of many earlier incidents. "Follies" that had evoked Elizabeth's wit and satiric enthusiasm lose their "light, and bright, and sparkling"[26] appearance when Jane's happiness is seriously threatened by "the folly and indecorum of her own family" (190). More importantly, episodes that the reader has been encouraged to interpret as the triumph of rational individualism and natural candour over the narrow *hauteur* of rank can now be reread, in part at least, as exemplifying the threat posed by undisciplined "spirits" to polite or correct "manners." What for Darcy and the reader was "liveliness of mind" in Elizabeth, she herself now dismisses as "impertinence. It was very little less" (338)—"impertinence", tellingly, being an epithet used of her by the Bingley sisters (30; 45). Elizabeth's challenging Lady Catherine over Lydia's and Kitty's "coming out," for example, is to be radically revised as more forthright than just (148), as is her attitude generally. And along with the respect that Elizabeth belatedly discovers for Darcy's judgement comes the belated validity of what had once seemed a repressive formalism on his part, a validity that threatens to include even his disapproving comparison of Elizabeth's eruption into the lifeless rituals of Netherfield with the restrained behaviour of his sister Georgiana (30).

The novel's and Elizabeth's conservative renunciation of her wilfulness generally, and of her wilful interpretation of human motive in particular—a satiric habit itself satirized in the Elizabeth-like satire of the opening line?—belies Marilyn Butler's claim that, in the conservative novel, "there is seldom a hint that the impression the reader receives has been modified by the idiosyncrasies of the hero[/ine]'s vision". This is not to deny that "society is itself the real hero," rather to suggest that it is precisely the reader's complacent identification with Elizabeth's voice and vision, and of Elizabeth's voice and vision with author's own, that Austen sets out strategically to undermine.[27]

Pride and Prejudice in fact demands a more extensive and more radical revision of events in retrospect than any other Austen novel. So much so that if—like Darcy and unlike both Bingley and to a certain extent Elizabeth—we were to "remember at night all the foolish things that were said in the morning" (42), the delayed revelation of Elizabeth's improprieties might well leave the reader feeling betrayed and/or resentful at having been duped into enjoying and sharing her wit and gusto in the first place.

In spite of the revisionary strategies, however, an ineradicable sense remains of the novel's genuinely endorsing Elizabeth's earlier behavior. Nor is this simply willful misreading. Austen was a true poet and of the devil's party, with or without knowing it. The novel's allegiance to the more vital Elizabeth can only be renounced at the cost, not just of a large part of its appeal, but also of its coherence.

As it turns out, the strategically discrepant political positions assumed by the novel over the issue of Elizabeth's independence and iconoclasm are in unproductive, even destructive conflict. Elizabeth and the narrator have become *confused*—in their wit and irony, obviously; more tellingly perhaps in the "strong," sometimes ungenerous language of their censure (3; 62; 77; 121)—too confused certainly for so sudden a displacement of political and critical allegiance and so radical a conversion in Elizabeth as take place when she sees Pemberley for the first time:

> They gradually ascended for half a mile, and then found themselves at the top of a considerable eminence, where the wood ceased, and the eye was instantly caught by Pemberley House, situated on the opposite side of a valley. . . . It was a large, handsome, stone building, standing well on rising ground, and backed by a ridge of high woody hills;—and in front, a stream of some natural importance was swelled into greater, but without any artificial appearance. Its banks were neither formal, nor falsely adorned. Elizabeth was delighted. She had never seen a place for which nature had done more, or where natural beauty had been so little counteracted by an awkward taste. They were all of them

warm in their admiration; and at that moment she felt, that to be mistress of Pemberley might be something!

(215)

In one of the oldest of apocalyptic *topoi,* Elizabeth takes up a position atop "a considerable eminence" from where, like Blake's bard, she "past, present, and future sees." Her vision is of the power and continuity represented by the Country House, a power that (to quote Coleridge)

> reveals itself in the balance and reconciliation of oppo-site . . . qualities: of sameness with difference; of the general with the concrete; the idea, with the image; the sense of novelty and freshness with old and familiar objects; . . . and while it blends and harmonizes the natural with the artificial, still subordinates art to na-ture[28]

Pemberley functions as a synecdoche of patriarchal or-der and a metonym for Darcy himself: "a large, hand-some, stone building standing well on rising ground" belonging to one who "drew the attention of the room by his fine, tall, person, handsome features, noble mien" (7). It is, in fact, the second of a sequence of metonymic indices and icons through which Elizabeth comes to reconcile "the idea, with the image" of her future hus-band. (The first is the letter that Darcy wrote after his proposal at Hunsford.)

Following her apocalyptic vision of Pemberley, Eliza-beth will spend the remainder of the novel endeavoring to rationalize and to realize the instantaneous transvalu-ation that inspires her charged self-confession: "to be mistress of Pemberley might be something." Because the political implications are anomalous and the emo-tional implications unpleasant, the reader tends to gloss over this first episode at Pemberley. Not only is Eliza-beth's cherished independence sacrificed to a more pow-erful and spontaneous desire, but the desire itself—the desire to appropriate—is profoundly unromantic, if by romantic love we mean the disinterested affection of two individuals for each other, indifferent to social and political rewards and constraints. No identification of an ideological continuity between the abstract positions of what might be termed "the two Elizabeths" can obviate what presents as an ethical and emotional *dis*continuity or *volte face.*

In the subsequent tour through the House, index is con-firmed by index and icon. Elizabeth's third insight into Darcy comes through his furniture:

> The rooms were lofty and handsome, and their furni-ture suitable to the fortune of their proprietor; but Eliza-beth saw with admiration of his taste, that it was nei-ther gaudy nor uselessly fine; with less of splendour, and more real elegance, than the furniture of Rosings.

Again, the impulse to possess is spontaneous, and is underlined by the preponderance of first person pro-nouns:

"And of this place," thought she, "I might have been mistress! With these rooms I might now have been fa-miliarly acquainted! Instead of viewing them as a stranger, I might have rejoiced in them as my own."

(216)

Through the carefully generalized, metonymic charac-terizations of Darcy, the confident distinction that Eliza-beth could make at Rosings between "virtue and talent" and the "stateliness of wealth and rank" collapses dra-matically. Suddenly, wealth and rank are obscure ob-jects of desire that effect vital transformations; far from being *merely* stately, they have become very stately in-deed. And very compelling.

Longing "to explore its windings," Elizabeth returns to the garden only to suffer the "embarrassment . . . shame and vexation" of Darcy's joining them, as well as an unprecedented "discomposure" at the thought of being introduced at Pemberley again (221-2; 229). That her characteristic intrepidity should fail her, as it did not at Rosings, suggests both that a new appreciation of "wealth and rank" has been effected, and that the dis-tinction between good and bad taste is more significant than one might have imagined.

Elizabeth's final insight is mediated by the portraits of Darcy. The first portrait is by Reynolds (Mrs Reynolds, that is, not Joshua; Austen's joke, surely), and relates Darcy to his complex patronage. Its exaggerations and inaccuracies as an ideal imitation—"infidelities" ironi-cally attributed to Mrs Reynolds's faithfulness—end by ennobling her subject. The other two portraits are paint-ings, the one in the gallery further accelerating the revo-lution in Elizabeth's attitude:

> In the gallery there were many family portraits . . . and she beheld a striking resemblance of Mr Darcy, with such a smile over the face, as she remembered to have sometimes seen, when he looked at her. She stood several minutes before the picture, and returned to it again before they quitted the gallery . . .
>
> There was certainly at this moment, in Elizabeth's mind, a more gentle sensation towards the original, than she had ever felt in the height of their acquain-tance.

(220)

On an earlier occasion, when Elizabeth herself had threatened "to sketch" his character ("if I do not take your likeness now, I may never have another opportunity"), Darcy had doubted that the "perfor-mance" would reflect "credit on either" (84). It is all a question of perspective. The "more gentle sensation to-wards the original" that Elizabeth now experiences she does so, significantly and ironically, in the *absence* of "the original." Is this a reflection on the ingenuity, or on the duplicity of art?

Whichever is the case, the painting and especially the portrait has always had a complex nature: as art and as possession or commodity; as a symbol of mimetic and expressive quest and as a symbol of power (most often, like Darcy's library, inherited power):

> As a brother, a landlord, a master, she considered how many people's happiness were in his guardianship!— How much pleasure or pain it was in his power to bestow!—How much good or evil must be done by him!
>
> (220)

This passage would not be out of place in a Jacobin novel, except that the same "power" celebrated here by Elizabeth would be stigmatized as oppressive and unwarranted; as an encroachment upon the very lives that here comprise an awestruck list of Darcy's responsibilities. And yet Elizabeth's "trepidation" is recorded without manifest irony, heavily ironic though it is in the light of her previous confrontations—as heavily ironic as the "softening" that takes place as she gazes upon the portrait of one whose severity and arrogance has been, literally, "glossed over":

> As she stood before the canvas, on which he was represented, and fixed his eyes upon herself, she thought of his regard with a deeper sentiment of gratitude than it had ever raised before; she remembered its warmth, and softened its impropriety of expression.
>
> (220)

Mrs Reynolds, the painter, and Elizabeth are not the only ones guilty of faking their portraits (which in the euphemistic language of the novel has become "softening an impropriety of expression"). The narrator's reticence—*Austen*'s reticence—implicitly sanctions the precipitate and dubiously motivated reaction that Elizabeth experiences.

As a dramatic *anagnorisis,* the episode of Pemberley involves too sudden a renunciation of much that Elizabeth has felt and much that she has represented. It is just possible to accept that the power figured so seductively by Pemberley and by the portraits has a magic that could not have been conjured by the temporarily "dispossessed" Darcy himself, the Darcy with whom both the reader and Elizabeth have hitherto been familiar. (Though from the beginning there has been magic in Darcy's "consequence" for Charlotte Lucas, whose values are now achieving a belated, if unwitting sanction [81].) It is hardly credible, however, that it was only the bad taste of Rosings that failed to evoke from Elizabeth the intense longing for power and distinction that, when it becomes apparent at Pemberley, suggests a characteristic compulsion. To quote Jane Bennet: "I should be almost tempted to say, that there is a strong appearance of duplicity in all this" (133).

Pemberley stands an index of the "virtue and talent" of Darcy, not just as a individual—certainly not as a lover—but as a person of "wealth and rank"; as a "proprietor" and as an institution. This new synthesis involves the assumption that individuality means in large part the fulfillment of the responsibilities associated with one's function in society. It also involves Elizabeth's active acquiescence in the existing hierarchy, or rather patriarchy: "As a brother, a landlord, a master, she considered how many people's happiness were in his guardianship!" (220). As in Old Testament visions on mountains, where the assumption of divine authority involves a simultaneous submission to God as the highest order, so for Elizabeth "to be mistress of Pemberley"—to be "in possession of" Pemberley, like that "good fortune" of the opening sentence of the novel—is also to be mastered by both Darcy and Pemberley (as Darcy himself is admittedly mastered by Pemberley as a squirearchical responsibility involving historical continuity). "He for God only, she for God in him."[29]

Be that as it may, not only does a renewed respect for Darcy enter the novel *via* Elizabeth at this point, so too does a new sobriety and restraint. The young woman who knew "exactly what to think" (77), especially when provoked by false humility or polite doubt; the young woman who "loved absurdities" (136) and whose habitual tendency was to ironize and often, in liveliness of imagination, to misrepresent—becomes the woman who knows what she does not know and, with that, begins to know what she wants.

Here, too, there is a problem, however. Where in the past Elizabeth had chosen to ignore Darcy's passion and her own feelings towards him, what she now desires is contingent upon her identifying those feelings. Driven by her vision of patriarchal order and a very unromantic passion to appropriate, "jealous of his esteem" and thinking "of his regard with a deeper sentiment of gratitude" (275; 220), Elizabeth embarks upon an agonized search for elusive, possibly even non-existent feelings. The novel is more honest than its heroine on the issue of romantic love, as it turns out, and in some places more honest than its own authorial voice:

> If gratitude and esteem are good foundations of affection, Elizabeth's change of sentiment will be neither improbable nor faulty. But if otherwise, if the regard springing from such sources is unreasonable or unnatural, in comparison of what is so often described as arising on a first interview with its object, and even before two words have been exchanged, nothing can be said in her defence, except that she had given somewhat of a trial to the latter method, in her partiality for Wickham, and that her ill-success might perhaps authorise her to seek the other less interesting mode of attachment.
>
> (246)

"Gratitude and esteem," arguably, but the lady clearly protests too much. What of the latent ambition so dramatically invoked by Pemberley? And does satirizing the notion that none ever loved "that loved not at first sight" necessarily validate the "affection" or the "regard" to which it is (falsely) opposed? Is her "partiality for Wickham"—with whom, by her own confession, she had "never been much in love" (134)—really a valid measure? Can the rational preference for a love grounded on "gratitude and esteem" and of comparatively slow gestation actually create that love?

Moreover, the ironic appeal to experience in this passage is couched in such a way as to appear self-evident, and thus to disarm and even disdain opposition. But the reader's conscious or unconscious assent remains indispensable, and experience may tell us that "gratitude and esteem" are extremely *dubious* foundations of affection, especially of an affection between two mutually respectful, independent "rational creature[s] speaking the truth from [their] hear" (to adapt the definition with which a more spirited Elizabeth had challenged Mr Collins's patronizing obtuseness [98]). "Gratitude and esteem" form the basis only of the type of self-limiting or self-taming relationship in which Elizabeth "esteemed [her] husband" and "looked up to him" that Mr Bennet wishes upon Elizabeth on her own behalf (335). In this, too, a reactionary revision of the position adopted earlier by the novel is attempted: "for love and esteem are two very different things," Mary Wollstonecraft had written in *A Vindication of the Rights of Woman,* "esteem" only reinforcing "a degree of imbecility which degrades a rational creature in a way women are not aware of."[30]

Hard as she tries, Elizabeth proves unable convincingly to identify in herself or to invent for herself the love or passion required of her both by the comparatively recent phenomenon of the companionate marriage and by the more established literary genres of romantic comedy and romantic fairy tale. Barbara Hardy has argued that, on the contrary, it is not Elizabeth's love but her "self-analysis" that proves inadequate to the occasion: "the attempts at naming feeling, deny, frustrate, and defeat themselves", but the "very persistence of her reasoning shows the strength of feeling."[31] But there are other feelings besides love that compel us to rationalize, the "naming" of which we are more likely to repress: ambition, for example, or acquisitiveness. Elizabeth's frustrated endeavors to persuade herself only exaggerate the conservative impulse—even, arguably, darkly pragmatic or inadvertently cynical impulse—organizing the action of the novel. In her awkward conviction that Darcy "was exactly the man, who, in disposition and talents, would most suit her" (275) one hears a refracted echo of Charlotte Lucas: "I am convinced that my chance of happiness with him is as fair, as most people can boast on entering the marriage state" (113).

Accordingly, Elizabeth tends to construct herself rather as the object, than as the subject, of love: "she longed to know . . . in what manner he thought of her, and

whether, in defiance of everything, she was still dear to him" (222-3); "It is impossible that he should still love me" (225); "Her power [over him] was sinking; every thing *must* sink under such a proof of family weakness" (244-5); "How could I ever be foolish enough to expect a renewal of his love" (302); and so on, throughout some uncharacteristically tedious passages. It is in the long-awaited moment of their mutual "disillusionment" and betrothal that Elizabeth achieves the ultimate self-ratification and proves herself most alien to the spirited individualist of the first half of the novel:

> . . . he expressed himself on the occasion as sensibly and as warmly as a man violently in love can be supposed to do. Had Elizabeth been able to encounter his eye, she might have seen how well the expression of heartfelt delight, diffused over his face, became him; but, though she could not look, she could listen, and he told her of feelings, which, in proving of what importance she was to him, made his affection every moment more valuable.
>
> (325)

"Light, and bright, and sparkling" fade and sober with each new protestation of happiness that Elizabeth makes. And the comparatively few occasions upon which she exercises her wit in the latter half of the novel—her "spirits soon rising to playfulness again" (337)—can too easily be read as designed to protect herself from an unacceptable truth. Like the plea for a willed amnesia in response to Jane's reminding her of how much she dislikes Darcy:

> *That* is all to be forgot. Perhaps I did not always love him so well as I do now. But in such cases as these, a good memory is unpardonable. This is the last time I shall ever remember it myself.
>
> (331)

The real joke here is the one that Austen covertly addresses to the reader, asking for "that willing suspension of disbelief that constitutes poetic faith" in the full and certain knowledge that only that can obviate the inconsistencies![32] And Elizabeth's dating her love of Darcy from the moment of her "first seeing his beautiful grounds at Pemberley" (332) is also a joke—is it not?

There is no magic solution for the self-tamed shrew: "Elizabeth, agitated and confused, rather *knew* that she was happy, than *felt* herself to be so" (331). If this is designed to elevate a love based upon esteem and understanding above a love based upon feelings, it is curiously self-defeating, serving instead only to render her commitment to Darcy the more doubtful. Elizabeth's respectful and grateful feelings on the one hand, and Darcy's romantic passion on the other, remain categorically distinct, leaving an ironic gulf between the circumstantial details of the novel and its fairy-tale structure. Here is a version of the perennial Cinderella fantasy indeed, but without the perfunctory mutual love of the hero and heroine.

Austen was not alone in seeing the solution to the *impasse* that England had reached in the early years of the nineteenth century in a strategic alliance between an enterprising but respectful middle and lower orders on the one hand, and, on the other, an equally respectful nobility and gentry at once responsible and yet responsive to challenge and to qualified changes within the existing order of things. But the sacrifice that is the price of that order in **Pride and Prejudice,** the sacrifice of that romantic and feminist individualism whose energy and excess enlivened the action and conversation of the first half, is unconvincing. For the symbolic marriage of Darcy and Elizabeth to matter or be meaningful, Elizabeth's belated prostration before "wealth and rank" cannot be fully assimilated. **Pride and Prejudice** is uncompromising, and cannot negotiate the "critical divide" between progressivism and conservatism that it constructs, other than by repressing the former ("a good memory is unpardonable"). But the Elizabeth who will ever retain the reader's allegiance is irrepressible.

Notes

1. J. V. Beckett, *The Aristocracy in England 1660-1914* Oxford: Blackwell, 1986, 43.

2. In "Eros and Idiom," in his *On Difficulty and Other Essays* Oxford and New York: OUP, 1978, 95-136 (131).

3. Alastair M. Duckworth, *The Improvement of the Estate: A Study of Jane Austen's Novels,* Baltimore: Johns Hopkins UP, 1971; Marilyn Butler, *Jane Austen and the War of Ideas,* Oxford: Clarendon, 1975; Warren Roberts, *Jane Austen and the French Revolution,* Basingstoke and London: Macmillan, 1979; Mary Evans, *Jane Austen and the State,* London and New York: Tavistock, 1987; David Monaghan (ed.), *Jane Austen in a Social Context,* Basingstoke and London: Macmillan, 1981; Claudia L. Johnson, *Jane Austen: Women, Politics and the Novel,* Chicago and London: U Chicago P, 1988.

4. In the first of "Four Letters on a Regicide Peace;" as quoted in Terry Eagleton, *The Ideology of the Aesthetic,* Oxford: Blackwell, 1990, 42.

5. *Emma,* eds. James Kinsley and David Lodge, The World's Classics, Oxford and New York: OUP, 1980, 210.

6. In *Statesman's Manual; Lay Sermons,* Ed. R. J. White, Bollingen Series LXXV, Princeton, NJ: Princeton UP, 1972, 30.

7. *Jane Austen and the War of Ideas,* 164-5.

8. All references to *Pride and Prejudice* included in the text are to the World's Classics edition, Eds James Kinsley and Frank W. Bradbrook, Oxford and New York: OUP, 1980.

9. Though criticism sometimes follows Elizabeth in seeing this compromise as emotional and moral only, the political significance is invariably implicit, the classic treatment being Lionel Trilling's dialectic of "female vivacity" and "strict male syntax" in his *The Opposing Self,* London: Secker and Warburg, 1955, 222. For a selection of more recent "documentation," see Mary Evans, *Jane Austen and the State,* 24; Claudia L. Johnson, *Jane Austen: Women, Politics and the Novel,* 93; Laura G. Mooneyham, *Romance, Language and Education in Jane Austen's Novels,* London and Basingstoke: Macmillan, 1988, 68; Patricia Meyer Spacks, *The Female Imagination,* New York: Knopf, 1975, 121; Jane Spencer, *The Rise of the Woman Novelist,* Oxford: Blackwell, 1986, 172.

10. Mary Evans, *Jane Austen and the State,* 65.

11. *Enquiry Concerning Political Justice,* Ed. Isaac Kramnick, Harmondsworth: Penguin, 1976, 245.

12. *Reflections on the Revolution in France* [1790], Ed. Conor Cruise O'Brien Harmondsworth: Penguin, 1968, 170.

13. "The mind is master of itself; and is endowed with powers that might enable it to laugh at the tyrant's vigilance" (Vol. II, ch. 13); William Godwin, *Caleb Williams* [1794], Ed. David McCracken, London: OUP, 1970, 188.

14. *Anna St. Ives* [1792], Ed. Peter Faulkner, London: OUP, 1970, 343. My italics.

15. *Political Justice,* 184. My italics.

16. In a review by Francis Jeffrey and Henry Brougham of Don Pedro Cevallos, *Exposition of the Practices and Machinations which led to the Usurpation of the Crown of Spain,* Edinburgh Review XIII, no. 25 (October 1808), 215-234 (233-4). My italics.

17. Lawrence Stone, *The Family, Sex and Marriage in England 1500-1800* [1977], abr. Ed. Harmondsworth: Penguin, 1979, 183.

18. Alan Macfarlane, *Marriage and Love in England: Modes of Reproduction 1300-1840,* Oxford: Blackwell, 1986, 208.

19. As quoted in Stone, *The Family, Sex and Marriage,* 220.

20. *Anna St. Ives,* 358.

21. *Gulliver's Travels,* Ed. Paul Turner, World's Classics, Oxford and New York: OUP, 1976, 261.

22. *Vindication of the Rights of Woman* [1792], Ed. Miriam Kramnick, Harmondsworth: Penguin, 1975, 153-4.

23. "When Darcy goes on to say, 'I cannot comprehend the neglect of a family library in such days as these,' we see that he regards himself as a guardian of his ancestral inheritance and views the present age as particularly threatening," Laura G. Mooneyham, *Romance, Language and Education in Jane Austen's Novels,* 53.

24. For Jane Austen on sexuality, though not sexual politics, see Alice Chandler, "'A pair of Fine Eyes': Jane Austen's treatment of Sex," *Studies in the Novel* VII (Spring, 1975), and Daniel Cottom, *The Civilized Imagination: A Study of Ann Radcliffe, Jane Austen, and Sir Walter Scott,* Cambridge, London, New York: Cambridge UP, 1985, 71 ff.

25. *Rights of Man* [1791-2], Ed. Henry Collins, Harmondsworth: Penguin, 1969, 197.

26. Jane Austen, of *Pride and Prejudice,* to her sister Cassandra, 4 Feb. [1813]; *Jane Austen's Letters to Her Sister Cassandra and Others,* ed. R. W. Chapman, 2 vols in 1, London, 1952, 299.

27. *Jane Austen and the War of Ideas,* 124.

28. *Biographia Literaria,* Eds James Engell and W. Jackson Bate, in 2 vols, Bollingen Series LXXV, Princeton, NJ: Princeton UP, 1983, II, 16-17.

29. *Paradise Lost,* IV, 299.

30. *Vindication of the Rights of Woman,* 154.

31. *A Reading of Jane Austen,* London: Peter Owen, 1975, 51.

32. On the "deliberately deflationary" endings of Austen's novels, see Daniel Cottom, *The Civilized Imagination: A Study of Ann Radcliffe, Jane Austen, and Sir Walter Scott,* 94. Robert Garis is more bluntly critical: "Elizabeth learns to love a man whom she has detested on first acquaintance, doesn't know very well and rarely sees," in "Learning Experience and Change," *Critical Essays on Jane Austen,* Ed. B. C. Southam, London, Boston, Melbourne and Henley: RKP, 1968, 60-82 (72).

Sandra Peña Cervel (essay date 1997-98)

SOURCE: Cervel, Sandra Peña. "*Pride and Prejudice*: A Cognitive Analysis." *Cuadernos de Investigación Filológica,* nos. 23-24 (1997-98): 233-55.

[*In the following essay, Cervel analyzes* Pride and Prejudice *from the perspective of Cognitive Linguistics, a conceptual model for reality that, Cervel argues, Austen's novel exhibits.*]

1. Introduction

An analysis of literary works can be carried out from different points of view which will vary with the critic's aims and ideology. An analysis along the lines provided by specific linguistic theories has seldom been attempted. I shall try to show that this type of analysis sheds light on the understanding of a literary work. In this connection, this paper attempts to be a demonstration of the applicability of an analysis of literary works by means of some of the conceptual tools provided by Cognitive Linguistics[1]. This linguistic school appeared around the mid 1970s. Since its inception, studies on the way our conceptual systems are organized have been given special prominence. With the mentioned aim in mind, it is our intention to analyze from a cognitive perspective some of the aspects of Jane Austen's 18th century novel *Pride and Prejudice*[2].

According to Cognitive Linguistics, we conceptualize reality in terms of a number of cognitive constructs called Idealized Cognitive Models or ICMs. Among these, metaphor and image-schemas are prominent. I shall attempt to show that Jane Austen makes use of them in an unconscious way. Lakoff (1989, 1990) and other proponents of Cognitive Semantics have shown that metaphors and image-schemas pervade our experience to such an extent that we make unconscious use of them in our everyday life. There is evidence in the novel of these pervasive phenomena and we shall attempt to make them explicit. For instance, the analysis of the characters and their interrelationships will reveal the underlying presence of some of these constructs.

In order to carry out our task, we shall take as our basis the work carried out by such leading cognitive linguists as Lakoff (1987, 1989, 1990, 1993, 1996), Lakoff and Turner (1989), Lakoff and Johnson (1980), Johnson (1987), Taylor (1989), as well as the interesting insights in Fornés and Ruiz de Mendoza (1996), Ruiz de Mendoza (1996), Pérez (1997) and even some ideas I have already put forward in previous work on Cognitive Semantics (see Peña 1996, 1997a, 1997b). First, we shall proceed to define such notions as prototype, image-schema, schematic enrichment, metaphor, idealized cognitive model and others, which will prove invaluable for our purposes. The application of this terminology to the novel shall provide the grounds for the construction of the main characters and shall shed new light on the explanation of the relationships which hold between the main characters. We shall devote the second part of our paper to such an explanation bearing in mind the context and structure of the novel under consideration. We shall see the application of the notion of image-schema and of some metaphors like the DIVIDED PERSON, the TRUE SELF, the SELF AS SERVANT, and the SCATTERED and SPLIT SELF metaphors, which have been postulated by Lakoff (1996). Finally, we shall attempt to reach some conclusions regarding *Pride and Prejudice* and, more precisely, concerning the relationships among its characters. Hopefully, the overall result will be a somehow innovative analysis of some aspects of *Pride and Prejudice.*

2. Some theorical notions for the understanding of *Pride and Prejudice.*

According to Lakoff (1987: 68) Idealized Cognitive Models (ICMs) are the way in which human beings organize our knowledge. ICMs may be defined as cognitive structures whose purpose is to represent reality from a certain perspective, in such a way that they result in a process of idealization of reality (see Lakoff 1987, 1989, and Peña 1996). Lakoff (1987: 68) states that "each ICM . . . uses four kinds of structuring principles":

—propositional structure

—image-schematic structure

—metaphoric mappings

—metonymic mappings

He also adds that "category structures and prototype effects are by-products of that organization". In this connection, we shall proceed to define prototypes. According to Lakoff (1987) many categories are understood in terms of ideal abstract cases. There exist different prototypes of the same concepts depending on the time and society under consideration. As a matter of fact, a great part of our cultural knowledge happens to be organized in terms of prototypes. We must take into account that the context of the work we will try to analyze is the 18th century England and, no doubt, 20th century readers will regard many 18th century prototypes as too farfetched. However, they are not, or, at least, they were not, if we bear in mind the context in which Jane's novel is situated. We must not lose sight of the fact that societies, in the same way as customs and cultural features, change considerably with the passage of time. This is the obvious reason why we cannot expect the prototype of the 18th century husband to coincide with the one we have in the 20th century.

Let us consider now two of those structuring principles used by each ICM. We shall proceed in two stages. First, we shall study image-schemas. Second, we shall focus our attention on metaphor.

The notion of image-schema shall shed light on some aspects of the novel we are analyzing. It is defined as a generic-level conceptual construct. Image-schemas have been found to structure several semantic domains and to lie at the base of a great number of metaphorical constructions, as shall be shown later on. These constructs have been studied in detail, among others, by such authors as Johnson (1987) and Lakoff (1989, 1990, 1993) who define them as abstractions or generalizations over spatial concepts. Among the clearest examples of image-schemas we may include the CONTAINER, the PATH and ORIENTATION schemas. On this occasion, we would also like to place emphasis on the so-called LINK schema, since it plays an important role in the novel. Each image-schema consists of a number of structural elements and a basic logic which can be applied to abstract reasoning. For instance, the CONTAINER schema consists of an interior, an exterior and a boundary; it also has a basic logic according to which entities may be either inside or outside a container, and if A is inside container B, and B inside C, then A is inside C (see Lakoff, 1989: 116, and Peña, 1997a for a critical revision).

In a recent paper (see Peña 1997b), I postulated the existence of two different kinds of image-schema: basic and subsidiary. There is evidence that all image-schemas do not possess the same status. For instance, FORCE does not exist as an independent image-schema but as subsidiary to the PATH schema. We must also bear in mind that there exist different levels of dependency, as will be shown below.

The process of *schematic enrichment,* as postulated by Fornés and Ruiz de Mendoza (1996), will also constitute a notion of crucial importance in our analysis. According to these authors, the criterion of cognitive economy involves that at least in great part of our metaphorical processing some image-schemas, which are given priority over other non-generic cognitive models, are activated and that, when the activation of another cognitive model is unavoidable, such an activation takes place in a partial way as guided by the basic structure of the image-schema. This guided activation is what they call *schematic enrichment.* Such a process makes use of cognitive models of all sorts: image-schemas (either basic or subsidiary), metaphor, metonymy, and propositional models. It needs to obey the Invariance Principle[3] and it is usually a source of numerous contextual implications[4].

Let us analyze an instance of an image-schema. Taking as a basis Johnson's (1987: 45-48) commentary on the most common force structures that are usually found in our experience, we shall begin our discussion of the FORCE schema by providing a more detailed version of it[5].

Lakoff, when talking about the PATH schema, distinguishes the following structural elements: a starting point, an end point and a direction. These elements constitute the most basic form of this image-schema. Related to the PATH schema and depending on it for its development, we have the FORCE schema, which Johnson (1987:45ff) has studied in great detail. But other image-schemas such as COMPULSION, OBSTACLE, COUNTERFORCE, DIVERSION, REMOVAL OF RESTRAINT, ENABLEMENT, ATTRACTION and REPULSION depend on the FORCE image-schema, which is in turn dependent on the PATH schema for their understanding and development. Let us see them in detail.

1. COMPULSION. On several occasions, we get the impression that we are moved by some internal or external force. Some metaphorical examples include: *I was moved by the poem, I was pushed into depression, He let himself be carried away by the song.* The interpretation of these expressions involves a starting point, a path, a destination or end point, a direction and some kind of force, either internal or external, which involves movement. Let us analyze the example *I was pushed into depression*: the starting point coincides with a non-depressive mood, even though nothing else is specified; the destination is a depression; there also exists some force, which on this occasion is an external one which involves some forced movement toward the destination. The subject is passive and that is the reason why it does not move on its own. Bearing in mind this metaphor and its definition, we could state that the source domain is represented by a path which includes the following correspondences:

—The traveller is a passive subject.

—The path leads the subject to a depression.

—The end point or destination is the depression, which is conceptualized as a container.

—The force involves movement and is external, as suggested by the verb.

2. OBSTACLE. This construct could be regarded as an image-schema in itself. However, it depends on the FORCE schema which is 'enriched' by its activation. In some cases, there exists some kind of obstacle which prevents us from reaching our goal or destination. For instance: *Her accident was an enormous setback to her career, The failure of the experiment put us back at square one.*

Analysing in detail the example *Her accident was an enormous setback to her career,* which belongs to an important metaphorical system named A CAREER IS A JOURNEY (which is related to others such as LOVE IS A JOURNEY or LIFE IS A JOURNEY) (see Ruiz de Mendoza, 1995), we realize that the career is conceptualized in more concrete terms, like a journey, which implies the PATH schema and the existence of some kind of force which makes the movement possible. Nevertheless, any unavoidable obstacle, which prevents us from moving forward and reaching our goal, can appear. In the proposed example, the obstacle is an accident, which at least for some time, will prevent the subject from reaching her goal or destination.

3. COUNTERFORCE. Johnson (1987: 46) defines such a force gestalt as "two equally strong, nasty and determined force centers which collide face-to-face, with the result that neither can go anywhere". This concept is interrelated to OBSTACLE, since in some way both force centers which collide are an obstacle which prevents someone or something from reaching a goal or destination. For instance, in the example *He was wrestling with his emotions* we conclude that there are two forces which counteract and cancel each other out. This is the reason why the movement along the path is interrupted and the goal cannot be reached.

4. DIVERSION. According to Lakoff (1987: 46) this is "a variation on the previous force gestalt". As a matter of fact, two forces collide face-to-face and one of them, which is weaker than the other one, is diverted. A clear example of this would be: *The insufficiency of the welfare system led me to explore pornography.* The passive subject is under the influence of two forces, each of them leading him to different destinations. But one of the forces is not strong enough and thus it is the other one that leads and controls the subject.

5. REMOVAL OF RESTRAINT. When an obstacle disappears, any kind of force can move along a path, since there exists no counterforce or diversity of opinions regarding the goal or destination to be reached. For instance, *As soon as segregation disappeared, black children proved that they could reach the same goals as white ones.* The implication which stems from this example and similar ones is that there existed an initial obstacle which prevented something or someone from reaching a goal, because there was no movement. However, the movement caused by any force can make someone or something move and reach the goal, since such a person or thing is able to avoid the counterforce or obstacle. However, on some occasions, the obstacle does not seem to be easily removed and thus, we find such examples as: *The solution is very far, We are not near the solution.*

6. ENABLEMENT. This construct takes place when people become aware that they have some power to carry out some action because there exists no obstacle or counterforce to control it. Examples: *I think we are on the right track, Let's follow this line of thought.*

7. ATTRACTION. In relation to the PATH image-schema, attraction takes place when there exist two or more forces which try to approach each other. Examples: *We are getting closer, Those two lovers are inseparable, Something in me pulls me toward the wrong kind of man.* It is required that the forces tend to move along the same path which leads them to the same goal so that attraction takes place. On the other hand, the opposite force, REPULSION, involves some diversity of opinions. For instance: *They are far from each other.*

As we shall later see in our analysis of *Pride and Prejudice,* the NEAR-FAR image-schema, which as far as Lakoff is concerned is basic, is actually dependent on the subsidiary ones of ATTRACTION and REPULSION. In a few words we could conclude that the former construct depends on some kinds of FORCE, which are dependent on the FORCE schema, which is here postulated to depend on the PATH one. NEAR would imply ATTRACTION and FAR would imply REPULSION.

Furthermore, it should be noted here that the LINK image-schema, which is involved in cases of ATTRACTION, depends on the PATH schema and, more precisely, on ENABLEMENT and REMOVAL OF RESTRAINT, which are dependent on the FORCE image-schema. The structural elements included in the LINK schema are, according to Lakoff (1989: 119) the following: two entities, A and B, and a link which joins them. For instance, in the case of ATTRACTION, A and B can be two subjects and the link joining them the force of attraction between them.

Another theoretical aspect we would like to consider concerns the nature of metaphor. Lakoff, Johnson and Turner, among others, have been able to unravel many of the intricacies of the English metaphorical system within the frame of Cognitive Linguistics. They have postulated metaphor to be a conceptual rather than merely a linguistic phenomenon. According to these scholars, metaphor is a conceptual mapping of a source domain to a target domain, where aspects of the source are made to correspond with the target. These correspondences enable us to reason about the target domain by using our knowledge about the source domain (see Lakoff & Johnson, 1980; Lakoff & Turner, 1989; Lakoff, 1993, 1996). Let us take some metaphorical systems which will later prove useful to study some aspects of the construction of the characters in the novel. Lakoff (1996) postulates the conceptualization of the human being in terms of the CONTAINER image-schema. Since our childhood we are fully aware that our bodies are like three-dimensional containers. The basic structural elements contributing to the building of such a construct are postulated to be an interior, an exterior and a boundary. In this connection, the notion of human being, which is an abstract term, is conceptualized in spatial terms, which happen to be more concrete than the former one. Following up this line of thinking, Lakoff (1996) states that the concept of human being could be understood as an ensemble of a Subject and a Self. The Subject represents reason, conscience and subjective experience. The Self, which is controlled by the Subject, represents our body and emotions. These ideas give way to the DIVIDED PERSON metaphor, from which Lakoff derives a series of entailments. For instance, on some occasions, the Subject loses control over the Self, situation from which the LOSS OF THE SELF metaphor stems. Furthermore, the same person's different interests and concerns may be conceptualized as different people in conflict or as people in different places, giving way to the SPLIT SELF or SCATTERED SELF metaphors[6]. Lakoff (1996) also mentions that another entailment from the DIVIDED PERSON metaphor is the TRUE SELF metaphor, in which the Self and the Subject share the same space. Moreover, the Self can show two different aspects, as will be evidenced in the analysis of the novel under consideration: they are the private and the public self; the former represents the interior self, and the latter stands for the exterior self, which is possible through the metaphorical conceptualization of the human being as a container (see Lakoff, 1996). The final entailment Lakoff (1996) points out is the SELF AS SERVANT metaphor, according to which the Subject is the master and the Self its servant.

Once we have dealt with two basic cognitive constructs, let us consider an instance of an ICM which will be of crucial importance for the analysis of some aspects of Austen's novel. We shall label this ICM 'the Control ICM'. Part of it contains the following entailments[7]:

1) Any entity, either a person or an emotion, has an area of influence within which the entities found there are controlled. However, if the entities within such an area of influence are more powerful than the former entity, this entity may be controlled by them. For instance, in the example *I fell into a deep depression,* the depression, which is conceptualized as a container, is the powerful entity which controls the subject. However, in the sentence *I emerged from the catatonic state I had been in,* the subject, which was controlled by an emotional state described as a container, proves more powerful than it. As a result, such a subject controls this state and is able to escape its influence.

2) The area of influence created by a container is the inside of the container. Such a container will comprise either people or emotions in the form of fluids. It is usually the case that the intruder entity is the active one affecting the entity or entities within the container, which are thought to be passive, either positively or negatively, but the opposite is also possible. In the sentence *I am full of pain* the intruder and active entity is 'pain', which affects the subject, conceptualized as a container, negatively. However, in the example *I entered a state of euphoria* the intruder entity, the subject, is passive and it is the emotional state, seen as a container, that affects such a subject.

3) Even though the area of influence of a container is the inside of it, by virtue of the process of *schematic enrichment,* as postulated by Fornés and Ruiz de Mendoza (1996), such an area is liable to be enlarged by means of an implicit PATH schema, either horizontal or vertical, in which control generally decreases in proportion to physical distance. In other words, we can draw a vertical path with an UP-DOWN orientation within a container when dealing with the PEOPLE ARE CONTAINERS metaphor. The more liquid in the container, the farther away the liquid is from the bottom and the less control a person will have over the fluid. When there is too much pressure within the container and the fluid makes the container explode, the greater the distance between the source (bottom of the container) and the end of the

path (top of the container) is created. As a result, the loss of control becomes greater. This is due to the fact that the fluid (the emotion or emotions) has crossed the limit beyond which control decreases more and more. For instance, if we say that someone burst with joy, that person will be in a situation in which he or she has no control of this emotion any longer.

Moreover, if we imagine the drawing of a horizontal path where the source is the centre of the container, the further we move away from the centre, the more we approach the periphery, and the further the entity is from the centre of the container, the less control it will have over the emotion.

4) The reason for the fact that control generally decreases in proportion to physical distance is that forces usually lose power little by little when they are far from their starting point and this is the case with emotions.

The insights into conceptualization provided by Cognitive Linguistics may apply to many aspects of the construction of a novel such as *Pride and Prejudice.* In what follows I shall examine the characters and the relationships which are established between them. This will be the starting point for the analysis of the characters' changes and relationships in the novel.

3. COGNITIVE ANALYSIS OF JANE AUSTEN'S *PRIDE AND PREJUDICE*

It is our intention in this section to apply the cognitive mechanisms and concepts which we have just described in order to shed new light on the way Jane Austen built the characters involved in the novel and on their inter-relationships.

To begin with, let us focus on the notion of prototype. We shall analyse two main prototypes: the ideal man and the ideal woman or rather, the ideal husband and the ideal wife. To begin with, the novel clearly reflects the division between high and low social classes of 18th century England. In fact, the novel is but a parallel of the realworld social situation in the 18th century. *Pride and Prejudice* shall reveal both societies, as will be made evident by means of this analysis. No doubt, the prototypical man and woman of the 18th century differ from the prototypes which are observed nowadays, since some cultural differences are the by-products of the passage of time. Looking for evidence in this respect, the novel explicitly describes the following prototypes:

—Prototypical woman:

> p.32: "A woman must have a thorough knowledge of music, singing, drawing, dancing, and the modern languages, to deserve the word; and besides all this, she must possess a certain something in her air and manner of walking, the tone of her voice, her address and expressions, or the word will be but half deserved.

"All this she must possess", added Darcy, "and to all this she must yet add something more substantial, in the improvement of her mind by extensive reading".

—Prototypical man:

> p.318: "Good gracious! Lord bless me! only think! dear me! Mr Darcy! Who would have thought it? And is it really true? Oh, my sweetest Lizzy! How rich and how great you will be! What pin-money, what jewels, what carriages you will have! Jane is nothing to it—nothing at all. I am so pleased, so happy! Such a charming man!—So handsome! so tall! . . . Dear, dear Lizzy! A house in town! Everything that is charming! Three daughters married! Ten thousand a year . . ."

As shown above, it was important for women to be able to get a good husband, which meant a man belonging to the highest social class. Marriage was thought to be a necessity for both men and women and that was the goal pursued by most people in 18th century England. Furthermore, the so-called marriage of convenience was the usual practice, by virtue of which both husband and wife's fortunes were joined. Let us see how marriage is regarded as a necessity for both men and women when Jane Austen has scarcely begun to write her novel.

> p.1: "It is a truth universally acknowledged, that a single man in possession of a good fortune must be in want of a wife.

> However little known the feelings or views of such a man may be on his first entering a neighbourhood, this truth is so well fixed in the minds of the surrounding families, that he is considered as the rightful property of some one or other of their daughters".

As may be seen from the excerpt above, to be in possession of money was extremely important. Even the people in the low social class aimed to obtain possessions, property and wealthy husbands for their daughters to marry.

Nevertheless, some characters in *Pride and Prejudice* (Jane and especially her sister Elizabeth) do violence to the prototype. These two characters do not belong to a noble family but marry two high-ranking men. Bingley and Darcy represent the high social class, whereas Jane and Elizabeth stand for the low layers of society. In this connection, the former characters entail goodness, whereas the latter ones imply evilness. This is explainable in terms of the metaphors GOOD IS UP (OR HIGH) and BAD IS DOWN (OR LOW) (see Lakoff?). That is the reason why Jane and Elizabeth Bennet are looked down on by such high-ranking people as Mr Bingley's sisters and other people belonging to the same social class (for instance Lady Catherine, whose daughter was expected to marry Mr Darcy). At that time people's incentive for marriage used to be money and social status. Jane Bennet and Mr Bingley, the same as Elizabeth Bennet and Mr Darcy, will encounter a series of obstacles in their way to happiness. These obstacles originate in the violation by the characters of the norms associated with the accepted cultural prototypes we have mentioned. Later on, we shall make evident the reason for the fact that at the end Jane and Elizabeth Bennet are able to marry Mr Bingley and Mr Darcy respectively. Such an explanation shall be given from a cognitive point of view.

Another purpose in this section is to reveal how the cognitive mechanisms at work in the novel shed new light on the relationships which the characters themselves establish among one another. Such relationships which exist are extremely complex. I would like to stress the expression *between pairs,* since the relationships within the frame of the novel are usually established between two people or between the two social classes involved. Because of space limitations it is not possible to cover all the characters and their relationships. However, I shall emphasize those which are more important for the understanding and development of the novel. To begin with, I shall attempt to study the couple formed by Elizabeth's parents so as to go on to analyse their relationship and how these two characters evolve throughout *Pride and Prejudice.*

Nevertheless, before going into more detail, I would like to point out that relationships in general are established by virtue of the LINK image-schema. A study of this schema sheds light on the nature of relationships in the novel. For instance, the relationship between the Bennet couple could be understood in terms of the force of ATTRACTION. The relationship between such characters is complex to such an extent that they constitute one of the main sources of irony in *Pride and Prejudice.* At first sight, the division of roles of husband and wife matches the division between the Subject and the Self. Mr Bennet represents the Subject, whereas his wife stands for the exterior or public Self, since her main aim in life is to think about social conventions. She is always in want of hobnobbing with people belonging to the high social class and of marrying her daughters at all costs. She always bears in mind the future husband's wealth and property. However, irony is at work when we readers realize that in fact the one who has control over the other member of the couple is Mrs Bennet. Mr Bennet does not represent the Subject but the Servant of the SELF AS A SERVANT metaphor. In this way, Mrs Bennet would play the role of Subject and her husband would remain loyal to his wife. At the beginning of the novel, there exists evidence in favour of this view. For instance, Mrs Bennet wants her husband to go and visit Mr Bingley as soon as he arrives at the village. Even though Mr Bennet refuses to do it at his wife's request, showing his reason and behaviour as a Subject, eventually he ends up doing it.

p.2:—Mrs Bennet: "But it is very likely that he (Mr Bingley) may fall in love with one of them, and therefore you must visit him as soon as he comes".

—Mr Bennet: "I see no occasion for that. You and the girls may go, or you may send them by themselves, which perhaps will be still better, for as you are as handsome as any of them, Mr Bingley might like you the best of the party".

. . . "They have none of them much to recommend them" replied he; "they are all silly and ignorant, like other girls; but Lizzy has something more of quickness than her sisters".

At the end, however, Mr Bennet surrenders unconditionally and visits Mr Bingley. This is the reason why I have mentioned his role as one of the main sources of irony all through the novel because at the beginning it was Mr Bennet that seemed to be guided by reason and consciousness. However, we can prove that his role is reduced to what his wife orders him to do. Moreover, a great degree of irony is provided by the fact that it is the external Self, represented by Mrs Bennet—who would have to submit herself to the dictates of reason—that controls the one who was supposed to be the Subject in principle.

As the plot develops, Mrs Bennet does not change in character and she will stand for some mixture of outer Self and Subject. She even rejoices at her daughter Lydia's marriage with an officer called Wickham, a dishonest man who only intends to marry her because that is his only way out. Mrs Bennet's jubilant expressions reveal that she is superficial, an outer Self who only tries to adapt herself to the conventions belonging to the high layers of society. In fact, her main aim is to marry her daughters with high-ranking men because in that way they will possess much money and property, love being disregarded as the main objective for marriage. However, Mr Bennet undergoes some change as the novel develops. After his daughter Lydia's marriage with Wickham he realizes he has been too benevolent and he decides to change in character. In this way, he becomes a real Subject and thus, has some control over those who surround him. Let us consider the following example:

p. 250:—"You go to Brighton!—I would not trust you so near it as East Bourne for fifty pounds!. No, Kitty, I have at least learnt to be cautious, and you will feel the effects of it. No officer is ever to enter my house again, nor even pass through the village. Balls be absolutely prohibited, unless you stand up with one of your sisters. And you are never to stir up out of doors, till you can prove, that you have spent ten minutes of every day in a rational manner".

As a matter of fact, the relationship which is established between Mr and Mrs Bennet is so distant in nature that it may be interpreted in terms of a PATH image-schema. In it REPULSION, a kind of FORCE, plays a prominent role, because they try to be far from each other since their aims and goals in life are very different. We could even talk about some COUNTER-FORCE. None of them manages to impose his or her viewpoint on the other member of the couple. We could even go as far as to say that they do not have a defined aim or goal. For instance, let us analyze the following example:

> p.5: ". . . and, as he spoke, he left the room, fatigued with the raptures of his wife".

In this example and all through the novel under consideration, we reach the conclusion that Mr Bennet does not help being within the same place, which in cognitive terms abides by the container logic as his wife. Thus his main shelter is the library, since he is clever enough to know that his wife will not enter this room. The farther he is from her, the less control Mrs Bennet will have over him by virtue of one of the points of the basic logic of the Control ICM. By applying the CONTAINER image-schema, we can think of a person as a container endowed with an area of influence. The closer Mr Bennet is to his wife, the more he will by affected by her. This is due to the fact that she seems to be more powerful than him, at least until he changes in character and becomes a true Subject.

Another relationship which, from my point of view, is worthy of special emphasis is that which is established between Jane and Elizabeth, the two eldest sisters. Throughout the novel, readers become aware that they differ in character to a great extent. However, a cognitive analysis will shed some light on their characters and behaviour. Their relationship is established by virtue of ATTRACTION, a kind of FORCE subsidiary to the PATH image-schema. The LINK image-schema (dependent on ATTRACTION, subsidiary in turn to the PATH schema) applies in the understanding of the relationship between Jane and Elizabeth. Even though they differ in character, as pointed above, at heart they share the same goal or aim at the end of that imaginary PATH image-schema: happiness, which is equivalent to marriage all through *Pride and Prejudice.* They seldom happen to be far from each other and when some separation takes place, for instance when Jane travels to London or when Elizabeth goes to Derbyshire with the Gardiners, they always keep in touch by means of letters. By virtue of the CONTAINER image-schema, we characterize both sisters as containers. In the schema, Elizabeth's area of influence affects Jane. Elizabeth may be regarded as the Subject, whereas Jane would stand for the inner Self. Elizabeth is frequently engaged in meditation. An example of Elizabeth's (the subject's) influence on Jane (the inner Self) is the following one:

> p.188: "What a stroke was this for poor Jane! who would willingly have gone through the world without believing that so much wickedness existed in the whole race of mankind, as was here collected in one individual . . . Most earnestly did she labour to prove the probability of error, and seek to clear one without involving the other.

—"This will not do", said Elizabeth, "you never will be able to make both of them good for any thing. Take your choice, but you must be satisfied only with one. There is but such a quantity of merit between them; just enough to make one good sort of man; and of late it has been shifting about pretty much. For my part, I am inclined to believe it all Mr Darcy's, but you shall do as you chuse".

—"I do not know when I have been more shocked", said she (Jane). "Wickham so very bad! . . .".

Nevertheless, it is of the utmost importance to emphasize that even though Elizabeth is described as a Subject in cognitive terms, she also partakes of some characteristics belonging to the inner Self. This is so to such an extent that she sometimes shows her feelings and emotions, even though this happens more frequently at the end of Austen's novel. However, she never partakes of the characteristics of the outer Self. Let us consider an example in which Jane shows her feelings, her inner Self, of which Elizabeth seems to be devoid:

> p.188: (Jane): . . . "It is really too distressing. I am sure you must feel it so".
>
> (Elizabeth): "Oh, no, my regret and compassion are all done away by seeing you so full of both".

This example shows the PEOPLE ARE CONTAINERS FOR EMOTIONS metaphor. In this way, Jane is regarded as a container in whose interior there is some fluid, represented by the emotions of regret and compassion. However, Elizabeth denies that she is endowed with such feelings. As a result, she stands for a container whose interior is empty. Nevertheless, as postulated before, above all at the end of the novel, Elizabeth undergoes an important change in character. As a result, she reveals her emotions, her inner Self. For instance, let us mention this example:

> p.156: "Elizabeth made no answer, and walked on, her heart swelling with indignation".

In this example, Elizabeth is seen as a container. In cognitive terms, the PEOPLE ARE EMOTIONS metaphor can give way to such a metaphorical system as DIFFERENT PARTS OF THE BODY ARE CONTAINERS FOR EMOTIONS[8], which is the case which concerns us at this moment. By virtue of the notion of *perspectivization* postulated by Taylor (1989: 90), we can pay attention to some parts of the body and disregard others. Thus we focus our attention on Elizabeth's heart, which is a container that holds an emotion in the form of a liquid in its interior and there is such a quantity of such a fluid that the container is swelling, even though it could also explode. *Pride and Prejudice* abounds in this kind of expressions.

In this vein, we could wonder why Elizabeth makes her feelings and emotions (her inner Self) prominent above all at the end of the novel. By virtue of a non-cognitive explanation we could postulate that this process has been the by-product of a change undergone by the character. However, the cognitive interpretation leads one to think that from the very beginning Elizabeth possessed this inner Self. However, those characteristics with which she was endowed and which made her a Subject were more prominent than those which characterized her as an inner Self. Furthermore, the area of influence created by Jane affects her to such an extent that if at the end we can say that Jane partakes of some features of the Subject, Elizabeth can be said to possess some characteristics belonging to the inner Self.

The proximity which exists between Jane and Elizabeth makes them influence each other. This reflects part of the logical entailments generated by the NEAR-FAR image-schema, which is subsidiary to FORCE OF ATTRACTION (which in turn depends on the PATH schema (see Peña, 1997b)), since, as we have mentioned above, both sisters have the same goal or aim in life: the happiness provided by marriage. Not even their marriage separates them because they will live very near each other:

> p.324: "The darling wish of his sisters was then gratified; he bought an estate in a neighbouring county to Derbyshire; and Jane and Elizabeth, in addition to every other source of happiness, were within thirty miles of each other".

Finally, I shall consider the love relationship between Jane and Mr Bingley before going into that between Elizabeth and Mr Darcy. Even though both relationships have several points in common, they are far from being similar to each other, since the nature of these relationships is very different.

As far as Jane and Mr Bingley are concerned, their relationship is possible thanks to their affinity of characters. Let us see how clearly Mr Bennet describes such an idea:

> p.292: "You are a good girl", he replied, "and I have great pleasure in thinking you will be so happily settled. I have not a doubt of your doing very well together. Your tempers are by no means unlike. You are each of you so complying, that nothing will ever be resolved on; so easy that every servant will cheat you; and so generous, that you will always exceed your income".

In a few words, their tempers characterize them as inner Selves. There exist many instances throughout the novel under consideration in which both Jane and Mr Bingley stand for the inner Self. As a result their feelings and emotions, which they freely indulge, are of the utmost importance. Their temper is benevolent, this fact resulting in an apparent weakness of character since they seem to be guided by feelings rather than by their reason.

The relationship between Elizabeth and Mr Darcy is comparable to that between Jane and Mr Bingley. There is evidence all through the novel that Darcy and Bingley respond to the requirements of the CONTAINER schema. In this way, the area of influence created by Darcy affects Bingley, the latter representing the inner Self, the former standing for the Subject and especially for pride. In this connection, Jane Austen mentions Darcy's pride on several occasions throughout her novel. However this feature, which stands out from the rest in his character, is made less and less prominent as the plot develops. The reason for this fact may be that Bingley's inner Self affects him, in the same way as Elizabeth undergoes a considerable change by virtue of the area of influence created by her sister Jane. This latter character, just like Bingley, stands for that part of the body which is guided by feelings and emotions.

Furthermore, the relationship held between Jane and Bingley is very complex until the time when they marry. In this connection, the LOVE IS A JOURNEY metaphor[9] must be mentioned. This metaphor has been described as a system of correspondences: the two lovers are travellers who travel along the same path towards the same destination. In the novel, Jane and Bingley are seen as travellers who have a common goal which is happiness or love. However, they will encounter many obstacles in their way, the most prominent of them being their different social class. Due to this, Jane is thought to be inferior to Bingley because of the money and property possessed by each of them. Nevertheless, these two characters do not let themselves be carried away by the conventions imposed by the outer Self, by those social conventions which guide the world where they live. As a result, they do not let these obstacles interpose their way to happiness. They will decide to travel together all along this path in spite of difficulties since both are looking forward to reaching their destination. The kind of force named ATTRACTION between Jane and Bingley will be evident throughout *Pride and Prejudice.* A prominent impediment in their relationship is the fact that Bingley lets himself be controlled by his friend Darcy, who thinks that Jane does not love him and persuades him to travel to London. This is the reason why their relationship is interrupted for some time due to the distance which separates them, even when Jane travels to London.

As postulated before, the relationships which are held between the characters of the novel are conceptualized in terms of proximity. In this respect, those characters belonging to the low social class will gradually enter the area of influence created by high-ranking people. In such a way that the former will approach the latter more and more. The most important settings throughout the novel are those in which high-ranking people live such as Pemberley, Netherfield and Rosings. In this connection, we could talk about schematic enrichment of the PATH image-schema. Those characters who belong to the low social class, such as the Bennets, live in Longbourn, which can be conceptualized both as a container and as the beginning of a path. On the other hand, those places inhabited by high-ranking people will stand for the end of the path, which can also be regarded as a container where balls and important meetings take place. People belonging to the low social class will consider their main destination to reach the other container, that is to say, those places where the high aristocracy lives. In this way, they will be able to enter their area of influence. This is the reason why at the beginning of the novel Mrs Bennet is looking forward to hobnobbing with members of the aristocracy. For instance, she asks her husband to pay a visit to Mr Bingley as soon as possible. This is the way in which Mrs Bennet manages to approach high-ranking people. These places inhabited by rich people will be the setting in which Bingley's love towards Jane and Darcy's love towards Elizabeth will have their origin. Nevertheless, such a path in which there exists some obvious schematic enrichment, will be endowed with several obstacles or impediments, for instance, Bingley's sisters. Or, for example, at the beginning of *Pride and Prejudice,* Darcy despises those people who belong to a social class which is inferior to his own. When he talks to Sir William Lucas, a character who plays a secondary role in the novel, the following conversation takes place:

> p.20: "What a charming amusement for young people this is, Mr Darcy!—There is nothing like dancing after all—I consider it as one of the first refinements of polished societies".

> "Certainly, sir;—and it has the advantage also of being in vogue amongst the less polished societies of the world. Every savage can dance".

In relation to the relationship established between Bingley and Jane, as postulated before, distance is a prominent impediment in their common way towards love. This is due to the fact that nearness causes some force of ATTRACTION between them[10]. When Jane receives the news that Bingley has left Netherfield, she gets disappointed.

> p.99: "The whole party have left Netherfield by this time, and are on their way to town, and without any intention of going back again".

Another obstacle or impediment on Jane and Bingley's way to love is Bingley's sisters, who want their brother to marry a high-ranking woman and they persuade him to travel to London and leave Netherfield. Nevertheless, when Darcy tells him the truth about Jane's feelings towards him, Bingley comes back to Netherfield and the relationship held between him and Jane is established again due to their proximity. Moreover, at this moment the kind of force named REMOVAL OF RESTRAINT

is at work since Bingley ignores his sisters. As a consequence, he decides to come back to Longbourn and the novel will develop in the Bennets' house at the end. The reason for this fact is that Bingley enters the area of influence created by the Bennets, since he acts regardless social conventions. Bingley is guided by feelings and nothing prevents him from marrying Jane. We shall notice that the relationship between Jane and Bingley is possible due to Darcy and Elizabeth's influence. But it is also a fact that the relationship between Bingley and Jane makes possible the one established between Darcy and Elizabeth.

I shall also shed new light on the relationship between Elizabeth and Darcy by applying the tools provided by Cognitive Linguistics. In the first place, we must bear in mind that this relationship is even more difficult than the one we have just analyzed. This relationship can also be defined by means of the LOVE IS A JOURNEY metaphorical system. In this way we shall encounter more obstacles or impediments than in the previous relationship. To begin with, the two characters' tempers constitute the first obstacle. Both Elizabeth and Darcy tend to influence other people, the former influencing Jane, her sister, and the latter, Bingley, his friend. Therefore, we could postulate some affinity of characters at first sight. However, at the beginning of *Pride and Prejudice* Elizabeth stands for prejudice and Darcy for pride. Hence, the title of the novel. The COUNTER-FORCE schema, which is subsidiary to the PATH image-eschema, allows the reader to interpret the clash between these two obstinate characters. They represent two force vectors which point at two different directions. Elizabeth and Darcy seem to differ in their goals, and this is the reason why they travel along different paths in most part of the novel. We have already set an example in connection with Darcy's pride when talking to Sir William Lucas. Another instance is provided by the following sentence:

> p.15: "Everybody says that he is ate up with pride".

By means of this example, Darcy is conceptualized as a container full of pride. On the other hand, Jane could be said to be filled with prejudices, as the following example shows:

> p.18: "But no sooner had he made it clear to himself and his friends that she had hardly a good feature in her face, than she began to find it was rendered uncommonly intelligent by the beautiful expression of her dark eyes . . . Of this she was perfectly unaware; to her he was only the man who made himself agreeable no where, and who had not thought her handsome enough to dance with".

As the novel develops, Darcy begins to like Elizabeth but she does not change her mind since she already has some opinion of him guided by her prejudices and does not pay any attention to him. Moreover, the first time he asks her to marry him, her prejudices lead her to reject his proposal. The first time Darcy proposes marriage to Elizabeth, he does it in the Bennets' house, in the same way Bingley proposed marriage to Jane. This is a reason for Elizabeth to reject such a proposal. Houses were the usual places for people to make marriage proposals and they can be conceptualized as containers. Elizabeth does not let herself be guided by conventions whereas Darcy pays great attention to them, at the beginning above all, due to his pride. The second time Darcy proposes marriage to Elizabeth, she accepts such a proposal since it has taken place outdoors. Their love shall only be disapproved by Lady Catherine because she wanted Darcy to marry her daughter in order to join their large fortunes. Both Elizabeth and Darcy could be defined in terms of independence and decision since they both are Subjects and do not let themselves be controlled. Therefore, the main impediment in their relationship is Elizabeth's prejudice and Darcy's pride, of which they get rid of at the end of the novel. In cognitive terms, we could say that once the type of force named REMOVAL OF RESTRAINT is at work, their path towards love is guided by ATTRACTION. But Elizabeth shall reject her cousin's (Mr Collins) proposal and her relationship with Wickham in this imaginary path towards love. Furthermore, on many occasions Elizabeth hesitates. Thus we could talk about her as conceptualized as the SPLIT OR SCATTERED SELF, even though she hates people who act guided by the postulates it implies:

> p.114: "The more I see of the world, the more am I dissatisfied with it; and every day confirms my belief of *the inconsistency of all human characters*"
>
> (italics added)

Mrs Gardiner also defines Bingley in terms of the SCATTERED SELF metaphor, when the truth has not been revealed yet:

> p.118: "A young man, such as you describe Mr Bingley, so easily falls in love with a pretty girl for a few weeks, and when accident separates them, so easily forgets her, that this sort of inconsistencies are very frequent".

As far as the relationship established between Elizabeth and Darcy is concerned, Darcy's pride reaches such a degree that the first time he proposes to Elizabeth, he talks about the obstacles which exist in their path towards love. In such a way that there are not only impediments but also some kind of inner conflict between his reason and his feelings within him. Let us see how he mentions these obstacles:

> pp.158-59: "In vain have I struggled. My feelings will not be repressed [i.e., he cannot control his feelings since there exists some kind of COMPULSION which

makes him love her, as well as some obvious ATTRACTION]. You must allow me to tell you how ardently I admire and love you".

> Elizabeth's astonishment was beyond expression. She stared, coloured, doubted, and was silent. This she considered sufficient encouragement, and the avowal of all that he felt and had long felt for her, immediately followed. He spoke well, but there were feelings besides those of the heart to be detailed, and he was not more eloquent on the subject of tenderness than of pride. His sense of her inferiority—of its being a degradation—of the family obstacles which judgement had always opposed to inclination, were dwelt on with a warmth which seemed due to the consequence he was wounding, but was very unlikely to recommend his suit".

Darcy is still guided by the features which belong to the outer Self, which corresponds to the prejudices and social conventions of the society in which he is living. He cannot ignore these facts. Thus, in their way towards love conventions will constitute an obstacle because Elizabeth belongs to the low social class.

On another occasion, Darcy adds more impediments in their way towards love, which affect his relationship with Elizabeth:

> p.166: "My objections to the marriage were not merely those, which I last night acknowledged to have required the utmost force of passion to put aside, in my own case; the want of connection could not be so great an evil to my friend as to me.—But there were other causes of repugnance; causes which, though still existing, and existing to an equal degree in both instances, I had myself endeavoured to forget, because they were not immediately before me.—These causes must be stated, though briefly.—The situation of your mother's family, though objectionable, was nothing in comparison of that total want of propriety so frequently, so almost uniformly betrayed by herself, by your three sisters, and occasionally even by your father.—Pardon me.—It pains me to offend you. But amidst your concern for the defects of your nearest relations, and your displeasure at this representation of them, let it give you consolation to consider that, to have conducted yourselves so as to avoid any share of the like censure, is praise no less generally bestowed on you and your eldest sister, than it is honourable to the sense and disposition of both".

When Darcy writes Elizabeth a letter where he tells all the truth, she experiences a series of feelings which can be conceptualized as OBSTACLES or even COUNTERFORCES which prevent their relationship from going on. Her prejudices cannot leave her mind and she cannot avoid thinking about what has happened and she even regrets having let herself be guided by prejudice, which can be described in terms of COMPULSION. In the past, she was led to feel what her prejudices dictated her and was not guided by the reason which had always characterized her.

Once REMOVAL OF RESTRAINT is at work, that is to say, when both Darcy's pride and Elizabeth's prejudice disappear, their relationship becomes possible.

Through the mediation of the interaction between the NEAR-FAR and ATTRACTION schemas, which are subsidiary to the PATH image-schema, ATTRACTION grows. Due to this fact the relationships between Jane and Bingley on the one hand, and between Elizabeth and Darcy (both of them conventionalized in terms of a journey), on the other hand, are likely to take place. All their obstacles have disappeared and there is nothing or nobody that can stop them. People also change their minds with respect to Darcy, who acknowledges his pride and decides to abandon this attitude.

The relationship between Elizabeth and Darcy is also possible. As mentioned before, both characters let themselves be guided by reason on most occasions. This is evident above all at the end of *Pride and Prejudice,* where they are not guided by pride and prejudice, the main impediments in their relationship, any longer. This is the way in which Darcy conveys this fact:

> p.320: "How unlucky that you should have a reasonable answer to give, and that I should be so reasonable as to admit it!".

4. CONCLUSION

The present paper has attempted to offer the potential reader a new viewpoint of the novel through the analysis of the main characters. This has been done in terms of some cognitive constructs such as image-schemas or conceptual metaphors (for instance, the DIVIDED PERSON metaphor). They have shed new light on the relationships among the characters in the novel. Furthermore, we could go as far as to state that the whole novel is summarized in terms of the LOVE IS A JOURNEY metaphor. The title of the novel itself: *Pride and Prejudice,* points to some impediments in this journey towards love. However, they disappear, the end of the novel being the typical comic happy ending.

Apart from reducing the novel to a single metaphorical system, an analysis in cognitive terms provides the grounds for the construction of the main characters and for the overall interpretation of the work. Furthermore, this kind of analysis is visual to such an extent that the work is wholly understood without the aid of abstractions. There is evidence that within this framework the changes undergone by the characters and the relationships which hold between them are explained on the basis of what we readers see and experience every day. This is one of the main reasons why the present paper is devoid of abstract explanations. For instance, the conceptualization of people as containers is tremendously visual since it is something which pervades our perception of reality. Moreover, this helps us to understand that the Subject and the Self are two parts which integrate a whole: the human being, and the reason why relationships such as the one established between Jane and Bingley on the one hand and between Elizabeth and Darcy on the other are likely to exist.

Finally, we have seen that Jane Austen has made use of a series of universal constructs as the grounds for the construction of her novel. She has done this unconsciously because they are engraved on our mind in such a way that we use them automatically.

Notes

1. One example of the possibility of applying this linguistic theory to the analysis of literary works has been carried out by Pérez (1997). This author has applied some of the tools provided by Cognitive Linguistics to the analysis of some aspects of Bowles's *The Sheltering Sky.* Such an analysis has proved invaluable for our purposes.

2. In the novel, Mr Bingley, his sisters, Mr Darcy and some other high-ranking people arrive in Longbourn, the place where the Bennets and other characters belonging to the low social layers live. As the plot develops, Mrs Bennet, a superficial character, shall attempt to approach aristocratic people more and more so that her daughters may marry rich men. At the beginning, there exist some difficulties in the relationships established between Mr Bingley and Jane Bennet, on the one hand, and between Mr Darcy and Elizabeth, on the other. This is due to the fact that the Bennets are low-class members, whereas the two gentlemen possess great fortunes thanks to their position in society. The clash between social classes is evident. Finally, impediments will disappear and the end is the typical happy ending, even though Lydia Bennet marries a dishonest officer called Wickham. Jane and Elizabeth will be able to marry Mr Bingley and Mr Darcy respectively.

3. Ruiz de Mendoza (1996) provides an Extended version of the Invariance Principle. Lakoff (1990, 1993) defines what he has termed the Invariance Principle as follows: "Metaphorical mappings preserve the cognitive topology (that is, the image-schema structure) of the source domain, in a way consistent with the inherent structure of the target domain". The Extended Invariance Principle, as postulated by Ruiz de Mendoza (1996), says as follows: "All contextual effects motivated by a metaphoric mapping will preserve the generic level-structure of the source domain and of any other input space involved, in a way consistent with the inherent structure of the target domain".

4. Contextual implications are the result of inferential activity in which ICMs and information from other sources, like the context of situation, are used. Fornés and Ruiz de Mendoza (1996) seem to have drawn this concept from Sperber and Wilson (1995).

5. For a detailed discussion of the FORCE schema as a subsidiary image-schema, see Peña (1997b).

Former versions of the analysis of this image-schema may be found in Peña (1996, 1997a).

6. At this point, I would like to state that the SPLIT SELF and the SCATTERED SELF metaphors could be postulated to be a single metaphor. Lakoff (1993: 5) refers to the former as a situation in which "inconsistent aspects of oneself are conceptualized as different selves" and to the latter (1993: 11) by stating that "when different aspects of the Self are attending to different concerns, the Self is divided into parts that are in different places". No doubt, both metaphors make reference to a single situation: the Self is split into several parts, which entails that these parts are in different places.

7. Former versions of the description of this ICM may be found in Ruiz de Mendoza (1996) and Peña (1996).

8. For more details on this metaphorical system, see Peña (1997a).

9. For details on this metaphor, see Lakoff (1993).

10. As postulated in Peña (1997b), the NEAR-FAR image-schema, which Johnson (1987: 126) regards as basic, is subsidiary to the kinds of force ATTRACTION-REPULSION respectively, the FORCE schema being in turn dependent on the PATH image-schema.

References

Austen, J., 1963. *Pride and Prejudice.* London: Dent.

Fornes, M. & Ruiz De Mendoza, F. J., 1996. "Esquemas de imágenes y construcción del espacio", *RILCE,* Universidad de Navarra; en prensa.

Johnson, M., 1987. *The Body in the Mind: the Bodily Basis of Meaning, Reason and Imagination.* Chicago: Chicago University Press.

Lakoff, G., 1987. *Women, Fire and Dangerous Things: What Categories Reveal about the Mind.* Chicago: Chicago University Press.

Lakoff, G., 1989. "Some empirical results about the nature of concepts", *Mind and Language,* 4, 123-129.

Lakoff, G., 1990. "The Invariance Hypothesis: is abstract reason based on image-schemas?". *Cognitive Linguistics* 1-1: 39-74.

Lakoff, G., 1993. "The contemporary theory of metaphor". Ortony, A. (ed.), *Metaphor and Thought,* 2nd ed. Cambridge University Press.

Lakoff, G., 1996. "The internal structure of the Self". G. Fauconnier & E. Sweetser, (eds.), *Spaces, Worlds, and Grammar.* Chicago: Chicago University Press.

Lakoff, G. & Johnson, M., 1980. *Metaphors We Live By.* Chicago: Chicago University Press.

Lakoff, G. & Turner, M., 1989. *More than Cool Reason. A Field Guide to Poetic Metaphor.* Chicago & London: Chicago University Press.

Peña, M. S., 1996. "The role of the Control ICM and of image-schemas in metaphors for emotions", *Penas, B* (ed.) *The Pragmatics of Understanding and Misunderstanding.* Universidad de Zaragoza, Servicio de Publicaciones Forthcoming.

Peña, M. S., 1997a. "The role of the event structure metaphor and of image-schematic structure in metaphors for happiness and sadness". *Miscelánea. A Journal of English and American Studies.* Universidad de Zaragoza; vol 18, pp. 253-266

Peña, M. S., 1997b. "Esquemas de imagen básicos y subsidiarios: análisis del esquema de camino". *Los distintos dominios de la Lingüística Aplicada desde la perspectiva de la Pragmática.* Zaragoza: Anubar Ediciones.

Pérez, L., 1997. "A Cognitive Analysis of Pawl Bowles's The Sheltering Sky", Universidad de La Rioja; unpublished draft.

Ruiz De Mendoza, F. J., 1995. "Perspectives on metaphor", *Proceedings of the 13th Congress of AESLA,* Castellón, Jaume I University; forthcoming.

Ruiz De Mendoza, F. J., 1998. "On the nature of blending as a cognitive phenomenon", *Journal of Pragmatics*; 30/3, pp. 259-274, North-Holland, Amsterdam.

Sperber, D. & Wilson, D. 1995. *Relevance. Communication and Cognition.* Oxford: Basil Blackwell.

Taylor, J. R., 1989. *Linguistic Categorization. Prototypes in Linguistic Theory.* Oxford: Clarendon Paperbacks. (2nd ed. 1995).

Susan Reilly (essay date April 2000)

SOURCE: Reilly, Susan. "'A Nobler Fall of Ground': Nation and Narration in *Pride and Prejudice.*" *Symbiosis* 4.1 (April 2000): 19-34.

[*In the following essay, Reilly stresses that, through her portrayal of the ideal and picturesque private estate at Pemberley, Austen reinforces English nationalism and decries the "dangerous enthusiasms of New World democratic ideals."*]

Elizabeth, as they drove along, watched for the first appearance of Pemberley Woods with some perturbation; and when at length they turned in at the lodge, her spirits were in a high flutter. The park was very large, and contained great variety of ground. They entered it at one of its lowest points, and drove for some time through a beautiful wood, stretching over a wide extent. Elizabeth's mind was too full for conversation, but she saw and admired every remarkable spot and

Jane Austen, 1775-1817.

point of view. They gradually ascended for half a mile, and then found themselves at the top of a considerable eminence, where the woods ceased, and the eye was instantly caught by Pemberley House, situated on the opposite side of a valley, into which the road with some abruptness wound. It was a large, handsome, stone building, standing well on rising ground.

—*Pride and Prejudice,* Volume III, Chapter I.[1]

Pemberley Woods is a likely enough spot from which to explore Austen's views on English nationalism and domestic tourism. It stands perhaps as one of her most univocal representations of Englishness and gentrified taste. Yet it may seem a strange landing from which to launch a survey of the author's views on America. Austen's descriptions of the landscape on which Pemberley House is situated, and her narrative style in the novel in which it makes its appearance, however, take on new meaning when viewed in the light of the North American topographical narrative, a genre which during the last decades of the eighteenth century put forward enticing descriptions of a wilderness frontier and brave new world that lured or threatened to lure Southey and Coleridge, among thousands of others, to American shores. Austen's Burkean response to the rhetoric of these narratives, along with the ways that response highlights the relation between novel, empire, and nation, is

the subject of this essay.[2] Austen's was a response crafted through the deployment of a fierce nationalism which is inscribed, using the principles of the picturesque, in the landscape, plot, and narrative style of *Pride and Prejudice*—a work whose very title, as we shall see, was taken from a piece of early anti-American satire.

A great deal of critical effort centring on the Age of Revolution has been directed towards theories of landscape and towards landscape's connection to textual narrative. Austen has been the subject of a number of such studies, or has been pointed to by-the-way as the exemplar of the Tory idealism of the landed gentry. John Barrell stands behind most views of Austen's heroines as displaying a 'correct taste' in landscape with an 'almost ostentatious virtuosity'.[3] Yet even earlier critics like Walton Litz had observed that only in Austen's later novels does she move from 'man-made landscapes' which rely on the theory and descriptions of Gilpin to the relatively more 'natural landscapes' of *Mansfield Park, Emma,* and *Persuasion.*[4] Indeed Austen's early landscapes are so much centered on the country residences of English society and so blind to the life of the less fortunate around them that Kenneth Clark goes so far as to characterize them as fantastical.[5] But whatever claims they may make for the later works, few critics would disagree that Austen's early novels are steeped in rhetorical imitations of the picturesque aesthetic which define, reinscribe, and codify standards of gentrified taste and decorum.

In such works as *Observations on the River Wye* Gilpin privileged domestic tourism and elevated it as a conduit to taste and sublimity. Austen adopted Gilpin's prescriptions for grouping and for presenting figures and scenes in perspective and shadow and imported his emphasis on the beauties of domestic landscape.[6] Editors are quick to gloss the references to his theories in Austen's early works. Mavis Batey in particular among Austen's commentators links notions of 'Taste and Feeling' to the picturesque in Austen, and to the ways they connect to matters of aesthetic appreciation in landscape and the cult of sensibility.[7]

But Austen's adoption of the ideals of 'the picturesque decade'[8] has itself come under critical scrutiny. Carole Fabricant, Raymond Williams, and Tim Fulford have argued that the picturesque ideals of tourism and the prospect view circulated in the works of aestheticians and poets were used by Thomson, Austen, and others to naturalize the suffering of the poor and keep the rhetoric of landscape exclusive to the English landed class. It is especially noteworthy, however, that fiction and theory begin to promote the domestic beauty of the *English* countryside over and against the primal and Edenic spectacles of North America represented in travel and topographical literature, or in response to accounts of antique and artistic glories on the Continent, at precisely the time such narratives were beginning to gain a toehold on the English imagination.

Marilyn Butler argues that during the 'alarmist years'—1795-1817—when Austen wrote her six novels 'about and addressed to the gentry', journals, newspapers, and sermons, along with pamphlets, novels, and satirical verse, were filled with Loyalist sentiment and preached the 'old-fashioned values of piety and patriotism.'[9] Authors like Austen, Gilpin and Burke threaded those values through the narrative tapestry of their works using landscape as their canvas. But the North American travelogue which proliferated during the same period put forward an ideology of human happiness and fellowship which valorized wildly beautiful American land and linked it to revolutionary ideals of liberty and equality. Many were written, in fact, prior to the American Revolution and helped sparked the drive to 'wilderness' embodied by America itself.

One influential practitioner in the genre was Gilbert Imlay, perhaps better known as the father of Mary Wollstonecraft's daughter Fanny and the recipient of a series of letters, written by Wollstonecraft, from Sweden, Norway, and Denmark.[10] Imlay's *Topographical Description* (first published 1794) was presented as a collection of unsigned 'letters' and included Filson's Boone narratives, *The Adventures of Colonel Daniel Boon* and *The Discovery of Kentucky,* works critical in establishing the farmer-hero of American myth.[11] Describing the 'extent of fine land' in the Ohio River Valley, Imlay incorporated picturesque prose to connect views of the American countryside to feelings of rapture and brotherhood, and to promote an ideal of a landscape over which even the lowliest creature could be 'lord':

> While the setting sun gilds those extensive plains, the mild breezes of a summer's eve, playing upon the enraptured senses, softens the heart to love and friendship. Unperceived, upon some eminence, you may enjoy the sport of wild animals, which here rove unconcerned lords of the field. Heavens! what charms there are in liberty![12]

Echoing Rousseau, the passage goes on to elevate North American geography, illuminated by the light of reason, as the 'empire' of freedom:

> Man, born to enslave the subordinate animals, has long since enslaved himself. But reason at length, in radiant smiles, and with graceful pride, illuminates both hemispheres; and FREEDOM, in golden plumes, and in her triumphal car, must now resume her long-lost empire.
>
> (36)

After offering up a list of American 'civil liberties,'[13] Letter VIII stresses the amazing fact that 'foreigners [. . .] may purchase and hold lands on the day of their arrival' (220).

It was just this sort of 'un-English' and libertine view of emigration and parceled-out land in works written by English, American, and French authors that Burke and Austen reacted so strongly against. Travel, even in the pages of a book, which promoted the 'vice' of Pantisocratic ideals of accessible or communal land was a threat to Englishness, for by offering foreign landscapes of liberty it weakened an ideal of domestic stability bound to Tory notions of moral fitness and intimately linked to private and paternal control of land. In ***Pride and Prejudice,*** as in many of Austen's novels, no one ever stirs abroad. In an age when travel writings, especially those concerning North America, were crisscrossing the Atlantic, the Arcadian countryside of Hertfordshire, augmented by a 'tour to the Lakes' and 'the celebrated beauties of Matlock, Chatsworth, Doverdale, and the Peak' (Gray 153, 154) seems universe enough for the travelling delights of Austen's characters.

Yet, as Park Honan has shown, Austen had heard or read a good deal about America from her family and their friends.[14] And she seems to have developed an aversion to foreigners and foreign travel which bordered on xenophobia. After reading Southey's *Dom Espirella's Letters,* a travelogue purporting to have been written from England by a young Spaniard offering a lively account of life and manners in that country, Austen characterized the work as 'Horribly anti-English' and as despicable as the 'foreigner' whose character Southey assumes.[15] Still, Austen was an inveterate reader of travel writings, and hers was an age in which such narratives flourished.[16] She read Carr's *Travels in Spain,* either Buchanan's *Researches in Asia* or his *Christianity in India,* (and possibly both) and one of Baretti's accounts of Italy, and owned a duodecimo copy of Bell's *Travels from St. Petersburg.*[17] Though she deemed it faulty, one of her most frequently-mentioned travel narratives was Mrs. Grant's account of Catalina Schuyler, a Dutch emigrant to America, entitled *Memoirs of an American Lady,* published 1808.[18] The work contains the usual litany of sites of natural American beauty. Though its author was at pains to position early Dutch settlers as 'persecuted loyalists' in their motherland and to recall and date the beauty of the American landscape to pre-revolutionary times, the work characterizes the Hudson River Valley as 'fertile and beautiful', a land of 'luxuriant harvest', and noted that the early Dutch settlement contained 'boundless liberty of woods and pasturage' (Grant 11, 13, 178). For Grant, as for so many other writers in the genre, America was a field of liberty, a bountiful Eden to which those who had been persecuted and dispossessed of their lands could flee for refuge while being assured of the promise of expansive and fertile ground.

For Austen, however, the ideal landowner embraces not the revolutionary ideals of equality and freedom, but the rural paternalism which assures the stability of the landed class. By acting as 'landlord and master'—a 'disinterested' 'guardian' of his estate (Gray 158, 159)—Darcy insures against corruption from within the upper gentry. By his 'attentive kindnesses' as a governing steward who is 'affable to the poor' (Gray 158), he wards off the threat of 'democratic opinions' and peasant unrest.[19] As Carole Fabricant has observed, the tour of Darcy's estate by Elizabeth and the Gardiners, like the country-house tourism it reflected, effectively advertises the values of the gentry. Yet while domestic tourism promoted nationalism and offered the poor controlled access to the estates of wealthy landowners, foreign tourism, and the literature that recorded it has been seen as serving very different ideological ends, of encouraging 'the illusion of cultural diversity while permitting' and even 'reinforcing the continued ethnocentricity of English culture'. The ongoing wars with France and America rendered travel even more perilous than crude transportation methods already dictated. But foreign tourism represented other dangers as well—a profligate and wanton access to land which was tied to ideals of classless liberty, and which threatened English culture just as menacingly as did the taste for the bizarre and the primitive which critics have argued it satisfied.[20] The attention to the 'perils of the free spirit' which form the subject of the 'persistent theme' (Litz 220, in Spacks) of Austen's works manifests itself in an aversion to travel and to the freewheeling libertarianism it represented, both on the Continent and across the Atlantic. Austen may never have forgiven Southey his early Jacobin aspirations and she dismissed his early writing as the ravings of a turncoat and a radical; but she read his 1816 *The Poet's Pilgrimage to Waterloo* with 'much approbation',[21] for after his early Pantisocratic fervour he depicted 'the nature of foreign peoples' in a manner 'which helped define British imperialist ideology'.[22]

Austen was inclined to see the worst in foreigners, and even her treatment of the landowning immigrant Lady Catherine de Bourgh is tinged with disdain.[23] In this essay I would like to examine another direction in which Austen's distrust of foreigners and foreign ideals was directed: towards the American continent. Her earliest-published novel, *Pride and Prejudice,* first drafted in the aftermath of the American War and in the shadow of the specter of the French Revolution, uses rising ground not only to figure the moral, cultural, and ethnic elevation of its principal model of Englishness—Fitzwilliam Darcy—but also the ways in which English soil was to be kept safe from the corruption and physical invasion threatened by democratic ideals. As Tim Fulford has persuasively argued, landscapes often reinscribed the ideals of conservative gentry through the use of the prospect view,[24] to which Austen frequently alludes throughout *Pride and Prejudice.* Because they were gained from a commanding position, such views afforded a means for the propertied classes to represent their political dominance as confirmed by the natural scene. Bishop Berkeley had argued in 1712 that the prospect view offered the observer a panorama in which all 'parts' of the landscape were viewed in equal proportion.[25] An overhead vista offered the capacity 'to take a distant, extensive and detached view of the scene, to be above self-interest' (Fulford 3) and thus was a trope of the landowner's disinterestedness, a concept Austen uses over and over in her novels. Disinterestedness, the *sine qua non* for 'wise government' (Fulford 8), is consistently linked, like the prospect view, with moral probity and applied as the crowing virtue in *Pride and Prejudice.*[26]

Mr. Darcy, as he was aptly portrayed in an early anonymous piece in the *Critical Review,* is 'a man of high birth and great fortune.'[27] The very paragon of English virtues, the 'model landlord and master' (Fabricant 254) is heir to Pemberley House, which itself sits on an 'eminence' commanding a prospect of Pemberley Woods, whose every vista provides the viewer at each step with a 'nobler fall of ground.' The 'rising' language of the Pemberley Woods scene is impossible to miss. The purview Pemberley House affords from its windows establishes the classic verbal prospect view—a vista from the sublime summit of the 'vertical empire' attained via 'paths of glory' retold in English art, poetry, and expedition.[28] From the dining room window Elizabeth sees that

> Every disposition of the ground was good; and she looked on the whole scene, the river, the trees scattered on its banks, and the winding valley, as far as she could trace it with delight.

Immediately after taking the view from Pemberley, Elizabeth's thoughts proceed to its governance—to ruling the estate via a match with Darcy: 'And of this place,' thought she, 'I might have been mistress!'[29]

Darcy's character is inextricably bound to the type of heritable land he both controls by ownership and admires and prefers. He suffers, for example, from a 'great curiosity' to view the prospect from Oakham Mount (241). Elizabeth's eventual entrée to the 'noble' estate (52) of Pemberley, accomplished by the marriage which permits unlimited access to those grounds, 'strengthens and affirms', as Fabricant observes, the elevated social class into which the heroine ascends (Fabricant 255). She rises, like the ground at Pemberley, in a 'much-naturalized version' of what Butler has called the 'anti-jacobin fable' (Butler 100) into the elevated realm of Darcy and his ancestors, ironically poised to eradicate the polluting French influence of Lady Catherine and restore true English taste and gentility to the land.

The prospect view is inscribed even in the narration of the novel itself. Richard Whately, early Austen critic and supporter, remarked that Austen had 'not been forgetful of the important maxim, so long ago illustrated by Homer, and afterwards enforced by Aristotle, of saying as little as possible in her own person.'[30] Character is revealed with a crafted 'disinterest' as though impartially from above and outside. There are no diegetic intrusions of the author's voice until the end, and the plot is unfolded partially through letter and dialogue. The Pemberley scene itself rises like a peak to the centre of the novel.

Representation of landscape in *Pride and Prejudice* is rooted, too, in the work of another author beloved of Austen—Edmund Burke—and the novel is permeated by Burkean anti-revolutionary rhetoric which expresses itself, as it does in Burke's *Reflections,* through land-linked representations of England and Englishness. Austen may have known and capitalized on the connection between Burke and his aristocratic patron, Lord Fitzwilliam, when she applied the name to her hero. The 'decay and corruption' which for Burke threatens the 'treasure of [English] liberty' is the same imminent corruption which threatens the Bennets and the 'decent regulated pre-eminence [. . .] given to birth', the 'principle of hereditary property and hereditary distinction'.[31] Both Burke and Austen seek to exorcise foreign and libertine ideals through a discourse of English nationalism which both authors linked to the soil itself and to a class of Englishmen who controlled it. As these representations strengthened nationalism, they pointed at the same time to the imagined horrors of a world in which landscape was out-of-control—due partly to the moral laxity of its aristocratic owners—and in the hands of rebels and revolutionaries abroad. The principles of political democracy which Burke critiqued come under attack in his *Reflections,*[32] especially as they were applied to the confiscation 'to the last acre' of aristocratic land in France. Burke compared the hordes of democratic 'money-jobbers' who implemented seizure of property to the 'barbarous' Roman 'confiscators' and their 'auctions of rapine' (Burke, 215, 216-17). The 'Barbarism' which would succeed a revolution in England was to be guarded against by avoiding waste and indiscretion, through a 'consecration' of the land which Burke is careful to link in part to the stewardship of the clergy. 'Wild'ness in Austen is unfavorably linked to uncontrolled behavior, and by extension to the wild*erness* of North America. Darcy's housekeeper Mrs. Reynolds warns Lizzy and the Gardiners that the profligate and parasitical Wickham has turned out 'very wild.' Lydia and Kitty Bennet are characterized as 'wild.' The Bingley sisters consider it a serious malign to remark to their brother that Elizabeth 'looked almost wild.' For the Bingleys, the wild state is connected not with Edenic harmony and plenty, but with an uncultivated lack of taste which threatens to divide landowners from their estates.

The wild, fertile, and unsettled North American landscape was itself a trope for the democratic liberty which in England threatened to spell the end of estate life. Indeed, Burke's *Reflections on the Revolution of France* (published 1790) was provoked by the sermons and pamphlets of the radical preacher Richard Price—himself, like the young Burke, a supporter of the American Revolution. By 1790 Burke was arguing that revolutionary 'grasshoppers' like Price 'made the field ring' from under a fern with their 'importunate chink'[33] while the proper masses of Englishmen, whom Burke portrays as 'thousands of great cattle', are content to repose 'beneath the shadow of the British oak', and silently 'chew the cud' (Andrews 74-75). For Austen, as for Burke, patriotic Englishmen wanted nothing more than to stay at home, touring and grazing on English countryside.

In 1893, Frederick Jackson Turner wrote the classic academic statement of the myth of the American frontier. European immigrants, he argued, moving onto the wild lands of North America, were seen as gaining the liberty and creativity that were the sources of American democracy. That myth depended on free and available land—on wilderness.[34] In the England of Austen's time, topographical narratives spread the craze for North American exploration. American geographical and travel narratives were highly politicized, and offered relief from the general oppression generated by the class system in Europe. Though in 1784 Benjamin Franklin had tried to correct the widespread assumption that emigrants from Europe would be given 'land gratis'[35] in America, the belief that land was to be had almost for the asking was promulgated through works by Imlay, Williams, Cooper, Morse, Crèvecoeur and Brissot. In 1795, the year the Pantisocracy scheme was hatched, Southey had been reading Williams's *Farther Observations on the Discovery of North America,* a work which would provide him with the eponymous hero of his 1805 poem *Madoc.*[36] Thomas Poole echoed the sentiments of Coleridge and Southey when he wrote that the America of the 1790's offered 'the only asylum of peace and liberty.'[37] Coleridge had read Thomas Cooper's, Gilbert Imlay's, and Jean-Pierre Brissot's accounts of travel in America in 1794. Cooper was the son of a wealthy Manchester industrialist who emerged in 1787 at the age of twenty eight as a friend of liberal causes with the publication of his *Letters on the Slave Trade* in *The Manchester Chronicle.* He has been characterized as 'the land agent of liberty', for he 'crossed the Atlantic to reconnoiter a suitable refuge for what Joseph Priestley called 'the friends of liberty'' (Andrews 94). The works of Cooper, Imlay, and Brissot, as Coleridge wrote to Southey, commended the eastern shores of the continent as sites of 'excessive beauty.'[38]

Brissot, born near Chartres in 1754, abandoned the legal profession for a career in journalism. Later a revolutionary politician who was present at the storming of the Bastille, he was guillotined in 1793 along with twenty other Girondists. Brissot's 1791 *New Travels in America* sparked tremendous interest in Europe and abroad. A translation was completed in Paris by the American Joel Barlow and was published in London in 1792. It was immediately republished in pirated editions in New York and Dublin in the same year, and in Boston in 1797. Five publications of the work appeared in German between 1792 and 1795, one was published in Dutch in Amsterdam (1794), and one in Swedish appeared in Stockholm in 1797.³⁹ Though there had been numerous land scams in New England (especially in Rhode Island) about which he was aware,⁴⁰ and although the price of land in New England was rising, Brissot still talked of 'free Americans' ('Amèricains libres') and of the purchase of land as the project by which a public could be organized 'according to the lessons taught by experience, [. . .] common sense and reason, and comformable to the principles of fraternity and equality which ought to unite all men.'⁴¹

American soil was portrayed as especially fertile:

> It would seem logical that all the large land areas of the world are equally fertile. It is, however, possible that the soil of America may be much more productive and contain proportionately many more natural resources.
>
> (Brissot 34)

Connecticut is described as the Paradise of the United States, the Ohio River Valley and Louisiana as rich, fertile, and beautiful. Brissot pointed out in his preface that at the time of his writing, France had already 'won' its liberty, but that the French needed to learn from Americans how to preserve that 'blessing.'

Yet while these narratives were enormously popular and influential, their rhetoric was refuted in works like Burke's *Reflections,* which proposed that Englishmen ought to be as docile and content to graze on English countryside as a herd of cattle.⁴² Though born in Dublin, Burke used English landscape as the ground upon which sublimity was reaped and sown. His Tory representations of the English nation 'as a landed estate which needed to be protected' so that it could 'handed down to the next generation' (Sales 88) was one which Austen handled in miniature through the central conflict surrounding the entailment of the Bennet estate in *Pride and Prejudice.* An early friend and ally of Charles Fox against the folly of the British government's American policy, Burke's later horror of the revolutionary confiscation of property in France caused him to aver in 1790 that property must be 'predominant in the representation' and 'represented in great masses of accumulation, or it is not rightly protected' or 'safe' from 'invasion.' Breaking up the ownership of the land, allowing it to be 'divided among many', meant weakening its defensive power and rendering it subject to foreign attack (Burke 140). Burke, an 'erstwhile friend of liberty'⁴³ but by now a large estate owner himself, wrote that 'the power of perpetuating our property in our families is one of the most valuable and interesting circumstances belonging to it' (Burke 140). 'Liberty' for Burke was a 'social' and 'practical' liberty to maintain private property and to be free of 'trespass' against his estate of Gregories, at Beaconsfield, in Buckinghamshire, a 'costly establishment' purchased in 1768.⁴⁴

Austen grew up in the wake of the separation of American land from England. The United States were declared independent in the first year of her life. She was weaned on Anti-American rhetoric that spewed forth from the pulpit and was heard even in the words of her father, vicar of the parish of Steventon, who beginning three days before his daughter's birth held extra services, and read out prayers against the American rebels.⁴⁵ Austen's brother Francis, while at naval school in the 1780's, kept careful notes on American geography.⁴⁶ It should not be surprising, therefore, that 'the "American War"', as Park Honan observes, 'was one household topic at the rectory as Jane Austen first learned to talk, to read, and to interpret adult opinions;' (Honan 185) yet the influence of America and the American Revolution on Austen has been curiously understudied.

Anti-American sentiment was long-lived. Americans were thought to lack taste, the essential quality for the 'wise government' of the Tory gentry. Honan offers a general statement that they were 'known to be indelicate or tasteless' (Honan 187); on the home front, at least one anti-American contribution in the Austen brothers' production *The Loiterer* implied as much and even provided Austen with her final title. In November 1789, five months after the fall of the Bastille, James Austen printed a story by a St. John's College friend which 'satirizes the American ideal of a classless democracy by investing two moral abstractions, *pride* and *prejudice,* with Tory values.'⁴⁷ The hero is ruined by Washington's American Revolution.

Washington himself had by this time been crafted into a powerful revolutionary symbol—one which was tied to representations of 'free' available, and 'natural' land in the works of Imlay, Brissot, and others. The French-born Crèvecoeur, who after having traveled through Canada, the Great Lakes Region, and Pennsylvania settled on a farm in the colony of New York, dedicated his *Voyages* to the American general, who would be portrayed by Byron and others as a wild child of the mountains and cataracts in narratives of the period. Thomas Poole kept a lock of his hair which was given to him by American friends. Coleridge, during one of his famous walking tours, proposed 'an American toast to General Washington' at Bala in 1794.⁴⁸ Washington was also the subject of a prospect poem in the style of Thomson and Cowper, published during Austen's teenage years: William Crowe's 1788 topographical poem *Lewesdon Hill* had made Washington's Mt. Vernon a landscape of liberty, upon which its owner 'rests after having delivered his country from British imperialism.'[49]

Austen's sentiments tended towards anti-Americanism and persisted even beyond the publication of *Pride and Prejudice* in 1813. On 2 September 1814, when England was again at war with America, she wrote to her sister-in-law Martha Lloyd that in the continuing British-American conflict ('War of 1812') her country was entitled to 'the protection of Heaven', and she placed her hopes on England 'as a Religious Nation, a Nation *in spite of* much Evil improving in Religion, which I cannot believe the Americans to possess' [emphases mine].[50] For Austen, the belief that God was on the English side in the 'just war' against America only confirmed and supported her notion of the propriety of class-controlled English land as a defense against further trouble from the upstart, classless and rebellious American child with its well-advertised and alluringly open wilderness. 'Nobility' for Austen is literally inscribed on English land: Darcy's 'nobler fall of ground', bestowed on 'disinterested' and deserving gentlefolk, displays its lordly 'eminence' in a nature Providentially arranged, its taste, and the moral fitness to govern enjoyed by its owners. And it keeps the English nation a nation by displaying the class-determined and land-linked solidarity of the country of which it is a part.

Pemberley House for Austen is the pinnacle of English taste and landed power. Commanding a view of the valley below, Pemberley Woods is not only figured as lofty but as situated in a position from which to survey and enjoy the many 'charms' of the territory below. After entering the woods and 'bidding adieu to the river for a while', Lizzy and the Gardiners

> ascended some of the higher grounds, whence, in spots where the opening of the trees gave the eye power to wander, were many charming views of the valley, the opposite hills, and the long range of woods overspreading many, and occasionally part of the stream.
>
> (161)

Prospects like these offered a way to 'tour' without movement. Such views brought the country, as it were, to the viewer's feet. Austen's blending of landscape and nation in the Hertfordshire countryside literally lies at the foot of Pemberley, whose eventual governance by Darcy and Elizabeth will pool, as it does in Burke, resource with virtue.

For Burke, 'the outrage on all the rights of property', 'the act of seizure of property', was the most noxious of the poisoned effluvia which flowed from the fountainhead of democracy, which itself was in his eyes 'the most shameless thing in the world' (Burke 207, 206 191). 'The very idea of the fabrication of a new government', he wrote, 'is enough to fill us disgust and horror' (117). The National Assembly was portrayed as 'mixed mob of ferocious men, and of women lost to shame', who had 'inverted order in all things' (161).

Austen adopts a set of remedies strikingly similar to Burke's in *Pride and Prejudice*'s denouement. Darcy's fortune is certain to be protected by the modesty and prudence of the heroine, one who amidst a luxury-loving circle is so frugally represented that she trims her own hats and travels on her two feet. To allow waste and indiscretion to creep into the landed class, to countenance the 'wild' and savage behavior associated both with American landscape and its native inhabitants is to risk both losing the riches gained in Austen by inheritiance and maintained by moral rectitude, and, as in Burke, the dangerous spread of mob-generated 'wild' revolutionary ideals.

Fears of domestic insurrection among the English poor (fuelled by the examples of the French and American Revolutions) threatened to overturn the stable world of Austen's Hertfordshire gentry.[51] Travel narratives created and inflamed the passion for liberty-through-land which was so attractive for Englishmen with democratic sympathies, and which offered them a prospect, however flawed, for freedom and prosperity. But Austen, as Raymond Williams argues, sees land as linked to issues of class-bound moral worth, cultivation, and taste, which is figured by an inherited code and the country estate—and not to democratic ideals of individual and political liberty displayed in land's easy availability and accessibility in America.[52] Austen's English stay in England; Austen's countryside, like the landscape paintings of her British contemporaries, in some sense 'stands for the nation'[53]—a nation attempting to maintain an uneasy balance between private property, opening of controlled domestic sites for touring, and the discontent of the growing numbers of poor and opposers of the class system. Austen's 'omnipotent' narrator sees all, says all, and hears all in the 'disinterested' mode which is in reality the mode of the English gentry. By settling her heroine, through the long-established and inherited land of the hero Mr. Darcy, in a private estate, situated on a prospect, Austen positions her stationary, domestic novel against the perambulatory and peripatetic travel narrative from North America. She limits the spread, by limiting the mobility, of her characters' exposure to the dangerous enthusiasms of New World democratic ideals. 'Liberty' for Austen is Bingley's 'liberty of a manor' at Netherfield—Burke's 'social' liberty applied to the Hertfordshire estate provided by 'inherited property' (Gray 11).

Notes

This paper was delivered on 12 December 1999 at the Twenty-Third Annual Conference of the Northeast American Society for Eighteenth-Century Studies, University of New Hampshire, Durham, New Hampshire, USA.

1. All Quotations from *Pride and Prejudice* are taken from the Norton Critical edition prepared by Donald Gray, (hereinafter cited as Gray) the 1993 edition.

2. For a discussion of the connection between the sentimental novel in England and America, and their use of the captivity narrative, see introduction to Deidre Lynch and William B. Warner, eds., *Cultural Institutions of the Novel* (Durham and London: Duke University Press, 1996) and Michelle Burnham, 'Between England and America: Captivity, Sympathy, and the Sentimental Novel' in *Cultural Institutions,* 47-72.

3. John Barrell, *The Idea of Landscape and the Sense of Place, 1730-1840: An Approach to the Poetry of John Clare* (Cambridge: Cambridge University Press, 1972) 5.

4. A Walton Litz, 'New Landscapes,' from *Jane Austen: A Study of Her Artistic Development* (New York Oxford University Press, 1965) 150-60; hereinafter cited as Litz. Excerpted and reprinted in Patricia Meyer Spacks, ed. *Persuasion* (New York and London: W. W. Norton, 1995) 217-23.

5. See Litz, in Spacks, 217. The Clark phrase which Litz quotes is 'landscapes of fantasy.' Spacks fails to note the source.

6. On Gilpin's influence in Austen's work see Christopher Gillie, *A Preface to Jane Austen* (London: Longman, 1974), 87-88, passim.

7. Mavis Batey, *Austen and the English Landscape* (London: Barn Elms, 1996) 8.

8. From the title of chapter two, Ann Bermingham, *Landscape and Ideology: The English Rustic Tradition, 1740-1860* (Berkeley: University of California Press, 1986).

9. See Marilyn Butler, *Romantics, Rebels, and Reactionaries: English Literature and its Background, 1760-1830* (Oxford: Oxford University Press, 1982) 96, 97, and 100.

10. *Letters Written During a Short Residence in Sweden, Norway, and Denmark* was first published by Johnson in 1796. See also *The Love Letters of Mary Wollstonecraft and Gilbert Imlay* (Norwood, PA: Norwood editions, 1978), a reprint of the 1908 edition; and *Mary Wollstonecraft: Letters to Gilbert Imlay* (London: C. Kegan Paul, 1938), reprinted from 1879 edition.

11. For a discussion of the evolution of the American hero, see Richard Slotkin, 'Evolution of the National Hero,' in *Regeneration Through Violence: The Mythology of the American Frontier, 1600-1860* (Middletown, Connecticut: Wesleyan University Press, 1973), 313-68.

12. Gilbert Imlay, *A Topographical Description of the Western Territory of North America,* facsimile copy of the third edition (London: J. Debrett, 1797), ed. Joseph J. Kwiat (Duluth: University of Minnesota Press, 1968) 35-36.

13. Among these are trial by jury and the freedom to practice trades and employment without molestation.

14. See Park Honan, 'Jane Austen and the American Revolution,' *University of Leeds Review* 28 (1985-86) 181-95.

15. See David Nokes, *Jane Austen: A Life* (New York: Farrar, Straus, and Giroux, 1997) 335. The letter, in which Austen offers her remarks, was written from Southampton to Cassandra at Godmersham Park on 1 October, 1808, and is printed in *Jane Austen's Letters,* ed. R. W. Chapman (Oxford: Oxford University Press, 1979) 209-14.

16. Burke himself penned a clear-eyed contribution to the genre which was relatively free from grand claims and rhetorical flourishes many years before his *Reflections,—An Account of the European Settlements in America. In Six Parts* (London: Dodsley, 1757), possibly the joint work of Edmund and William Burke. My copy text is the second edition, (London: Dodsley, 1758).

17. See Chapman, *Letters,* vol. II, 292 (letter to Cassandra, 24 January 1813). In 1807 Austen was reading either Baretti's 1768 *Account of the Manners and Customs of Italy* or his *Journey from London to Genoa* (Chapman I, 185, letter to Cassandra, 20 February, 1807). On Buchanan see Chapman II, 292 (letter to Cassandra, 24 January, 1813). For an description of Austen's copy of Bell, see Gilson, 'Jane Austen's Books,' *The Book Collector* 23, (1974), 27-39, 31.

18. Anne Macvicar Grant, *Memoirs of an American Lady: With Sketched of Manners and scenery in America, as They existed Previous to the Revolution.* (London: Longman, Hurst, Ress and Orme, 1808). Austen had read the work by 1809, see letter to Cassandra 10 Jan. 1809, Chapman I 248.

19. Uvedale Price, *Essay on the Picturesque As Compared with the Sublime and the Beautiful* (1794), quoted in Bermingham 67, 68. Price, like Richard

Payne Knight, sought to craft a theory of the picturesque based on Gilpin's practical ideas.

20. See Carole Fabricant, 'The Literature of Domestic Tourism and the Public Consumption of Private Property' in *The New Eighteenth Century: Theory, Politics, English Literature,* eds. Felicity Nussbaum and Laura Brown (New York:: Methuen, 1987) 254-75. The quote is from page 257.

21. *Letters,* Chapman II 476 (letter to Alethea Bigg, 24 January, 1817).

22. Timothy Fulford, 'Heroic Voyagers and Superstitious Natives: Southey's Imperialist Ideology', *Studies in Travel Writing* 2 (Spring 1998) 46-94, The quote is from page 46.

23. The matter of Lady Catherine's origins is unsettled in the novel. I am grateful to Richard Gravil for pointing out the nuances and implications of French and Norman ancestry, and for suggesting the possibility that Austen's critique of the 'Norman yoke,' if it were in play, would have been allied with Jacobin as much as Tory principle.

24. See Timothy Fulford, *Landscape, Liberty, and Authority: Poetry, Criticism, and Politics From Thomson to Wordsworth* (Cambridge: Cambridge U Press, 1996); Introduction and passim. Subsequent references are provided in parentheses in the text.

25. Berkeley, *Passive Obedience,* in *The Works of George Berkeley, Bishop of Cloyne,* ed. T. E. Jessop, 9 vols. (London: 1948-57) vol. VI, 32-33, cited in Fulford 3-4.

26. See, for one example among many in the novels, Elizabeth Bennett to her sister, Jane: 'Your sweetness and disinterestedness are really angelic' (Vol. II Chapter I).

27. Review: (unsigned), *Critical Review* March 1813. 4th series, iii, 18-24. Reprinted in B.C. Southam, vol I, page 45.

28. See Simon Schama, *Landscape and Memory* (New York: Knopf, 1995) 463-78, on the importance of 'mountainous Britain' to the ideology of empire in the eighteenth century. Quotations are from chapter heading, 463, and 464. For a discussion of the prospect poem, see Fulford, *Landscape, Liberty, and Authority,* introduction and passim, and William Richey, 'The Politicized Landscape of *Tintern Abbey,' Studies in Philology* 95:2 (Spring 1998) 197-213.

29. Citations from Volume II chapter I, 156-157 in Gray.

30. See Richard Whately, unsigned review in *Quarterly Review* (January 1821), xxiv, 352-76; excerpted and reprinted in Patricia Meyer Spacks, ed., *Persuasion,* 197-205, and in B.C. Southam, *Jane Austen: The Critical Heritage,* 87-105. Quote is from Southam, 97.

31. Edmund Burke, *Reflections on the Revolution in France and the Proceedings in certain Societies relative to that Event* (Harmondsworth: Penguin, 1986) 143, 141.

32. The problem of whether Burke's critique of the French Revolution is inconsistent with his former support of the revolution by the American colonies is a vexed and complex one. I am grateful for suggestions on this matter from Timothy Fulford and Richard Gravil. For a discussion of the matter of how far Burke's critique of the French was taken up by Cooper see also Gravil, 'James Fenimore Cooper and the Spectre of Edmund Burke,' *Romanticism on the Net* 14 (May 1999).

33. Stuart Andrews, *The Rediscovery of America: Transatlantic Crosscurrents in an Age of Revolution* (New York: St. Martin's; Basingstoke: Macmillan, 1998) 74.

34. Frederick Jackson Turner, *The Significance of the Frontier in American History,* from an address delivered at the forty-first annual meeting of the State Historical Society of Wisconsin, December 14, 1893. On American landscape painting and its connection to national mythmaking see Stephen Daniels, *Fields of Vision* (Princeton: Princeton University Press, 1993), chapters 5 and 6, 146-99.

35. Benjamin Franklin, *Information to Those Who Would Remove to America,* in *Two tracts: Information to Those Who would remove to America, and Remarks Concerning the Savages of North America,* third edition, (London: Stockdale, 1784), 5.

36. Williams's work attempts to prove that America was discovered by Prince Madoc, about the year 1170.

37. See Vol. I, 98, *Thomas Poole and his Friends,* by Margaret Poole Sandford, 2 vols (London and New York: Macmillan, 1888).

38. It is Andrews who characterized Cooper as 'and agent of liberty', 94. Coleridge quotation is from a letter his letter to Southey, cited in Andrews, 185, and taken from Griggs, *Collected Letters* I 99.

39. Brissot de Warville, Jacques Pierre, *Nouveau Voyages dans les Etats-Unis* (Paris: Buisson, 1791). Translated from the French as *New Travels in the United States of America. Performed in 1788.* By Joel Barlow London: J. S. Jordan, 1792. On the publication and translation history, see the Harvard edition, ed. Echeverria, (1964), xxvi-xxviii.

40. See, for example Brissot's chapter on Rhode Island, 129-33 in 1964 translation. Fraudulent land-agents like 'The Atherton Company' would not only bilk Indians, with the help of the colonial government, out of thousands of acres of land, but sell the title to these lands to more than one group of settlers, for example the Huguenots and veterans of King Philip War.

41. Quoted from Brissot, *New Travels in the United States,* 29 and 41. For a fuller discussion of Brissot's representations of America see Andrews, chapter 9, 109-20.

42. Burke, *Reflections,* cited in Stuart Andrews, *The Rediscovery of America: Transatlantic Crosscurrents in an Age of Revolution* (New York: St. Martin's; Basingstoke Macmillan: 1998).

43. Simon Schama, *Landscape and Memory,* (New York: Knopf, 1995), 248.

44. Quotations from Burke are from letter of 'Oct 1789' referred to in prefatory title, reprinted in *Correspondences* VI, 39-50, and from Conor Cruise O'Brien, ed., Burke's *Reflections on the Revolution in France,* 19. Cobban and Smith, however, established that it was written in November, and probably not forwarded before the end of that year. See Conor Cruise O'Brien, notes to Penguin edition of *Reflections,* 15.

45. Tomalin, 19. Such sermons were apparently not uncommon, and anti-American pamphlets were published under the guise of the sermon. Coleridge's father John privately printed his own political statement, *A Fast Sermon,* which deplored the outbreak of American War of Independence, in 1776. Exactly one year after Revd George Austen's sermon, The Reverend John Coleridge preached another of his anti-American sermons in support of divine right at Ottery St. Mary, Devon. It was printed for the author the next year as 'Government Not Originally Proceeding from Human Agency but Divine Institution' in London, and sold by Rivington, Buckland, Richardson, and Urquhart at two bookseller's shops in the city.

46. See page 188 in Park Honan, 'Jane Austen and the American Revolution,' *University of Leeds Review* 28 (1985-86): 181-95.

47. Quotation is from Honan, 189. The story appeared in *The Loiterer,* no 41, 7 November 1789.

48. Richard Holmes, *Coleridge: Early Visions* (London: Penguin, 1989) 63.

49. Quote is from Fulford, *Landscape, Liberty, and Authority,* 226. For representations of Washington see, e.g., Byron (Childe Harold's Pilgrimage Canto IV, stanza 96, ll. 856-64), and William Crowe, *Lewesdon Hill.*

50. R. W. Chapman, ed., *Jane Austen's Letters,* page 508. Jane Austen to Martha Lloyd, 2 September, 1814.

51. For a discussion of the relation of landowners to the rural poor, see Bermingham, 'The Picturesque Decade' in *Landscape and Ideology.*

52. See Raymond Williams, 'Three Around Farnham,' 108-19 in *the Country and the City* (London: Hogarth, 1973).

53. Michael Rosenthal, Christiana Payne, and Scott Wilcox, eds., *Prospects for the Nation: Recent Essays in British Landscape, 1750-1880* (New Haven: Yale University Press, 1997) 15.

Barbara K. Seeber (essay date 2000)

SOURCE: Seeber, Barbara K. "We Must Forget It: The Unhappy Truth in *Pride and Prejudice.*" In *General Consent in Jane Austen: A Study of Dialogism,* pp. 85-92. Montreal: McGill-Queen's University Press, 2000.

[*In the following essay, which applies Mikhail Bakhtin's linguistic theory of dialogism to Austen's works, Seeber concludes that* Pride and Prejudice *remains "haunted" by the narrative of Wickham and Georgiana despite the main narrative's repression of this material.*]

Pride and Prejudice, Austen's "own darling Child" (Austen 1995, 201), is often considered the quintessential Austen novel, certainly the most widely read and most widely taught in schools and at the undergraduate level. As Marilyn Butler points out, "the general public has liked ***Pride and Prejudice*** the best of all Jane Austen's novels, and it is easy to see why" (1987, 217). Susan Morgan agrees that the novel "has a charmed place as the most popular of Austen's novels" (1980, 78). In criticism, too, the novel has held a privileged position: A. Walton Litz, for example, calls it "a summing up of her artistic career, a valedictory to the world of ***Sense and Sensibility*** and a token of things to come" (1965, 99).

In this discussion ***Pride and Prejudice*** has been far less central, giving way to the novel often considered its diametric opposite: ***Mansfield Park.*** Elizabeth triumphantly claims that Jane "only smiles, I laugh" (Austen 1988, 2:383), but Fanny Price does neither. For Lionel Trilling, "no small part" of ***Mansfield Park***'s "interest derives from the fact that it seems to controvert everything" that ***Pride and Prejudice*** "tells us about life": the latter "celebrates . . . spiritedness, vivacity, celerity, and lightness," while "almost the opposite can be said" of ***Mansfield Park*** (1955, 211). Time has proven Austen right: "I am very strongly haunted by the idea that to those Readers who have preferred P&P. it will appear inferior in Wit, & to those who have preferred MP. very inferior in good Sense" (Austen 1995, 306). Austen's famous remark to her sister Cassandra that **Pride and Prejudice** is "rather too light & bright & sparkling;—it wants shade" has often been read without its irony:

> It wants to be stretched out here & there with a long Chapter—of sense if it could be had, if not of solemn specious nonsense—about something unconnected with the story; an Essay on Writing, a critique on Walter Scott, or the history of Buonaparte—or anything that would form a contrast & bring the reader with increased delight to the playfulness & Epigrammatism of the general stile.—I doubt your quite agreeing with me here—I know your starched Notions.
>
> (Ibid., 203)

That **Pride and Prejudice** is considered Austen's best or most perfect novel has a lot more to do with preconceived assumptions about Austen than with the novel itself. As Claudia Johnson points out, "We will certainly misrepresent her accomplishment if we posit this singular novel as the typical one against which the others are to be judged" (1988, 93).

In the case of Elizabeth and Darcy, love conquers all. Their union, critics argue, is achieved by displacing class and economic realities onto secondary characters and plots. For Mary Poovey, "the realistic elements" are "carefully contained" (1984, 202). The love between Darcy and Elizabeth "not only overcomes all obstacles; it brings about a perfect society" by the end of the story (201): "With Darcy at its head and Elizabeth at its heart, society will apparently be able to contain the anarchic impulses of individualism and humanize the rigidities of prejudice, and everyone—even Miss Bingley—will live more or less happily in the environs of Pemberley, the vast estate whose permanence, prominence, and unique and uniquely satisfying fusion of individual taste and utility, of nature and art, symbolize Jane Austen's ideal" (202). According to Judith Lowder Newton, "For all its reference to money and money matters, for all its consciousness of economic fact and economic influence, **Pride and Prejudice** is devoted not to establishing but to denying the force of economics in human life. In the reading of the novel the real *force* of economics simply melts away" (1981, 61). Common to these interpretations is the idea that Austen displaces her social realism and social criticism in order to present a utopian ending "with an air of credibility which lends force to the spell of the fantasy upon us" (85).[1]

Indeed, **Pride and Prejudice** presents a particular challenge. Of all the novels, it comes closest to reconciling the individual with society, the very project with which Austen is usually associated. Even a critic like Johnson, whose readings seek to redeem Austen from charges of conservatism, is somewhat baffled by **Pride and Prejudice.** Agreeing with Poovey that the "markedly fairy-tale-like quality" (1988, 74) of the novel is "almost shamelessly wish fulfilling" (73), she struggles to argue that the novel is not, therefore, "politically suspect" (74): "Austen consents to conservative myths, but only in order to possess them and to ameliorate them from within, so that the institutions they vindicate can bring about, rather than inhibit, the expansion and the fulfilment of happiness" (93). Yet in her conclusion Johnson admits that the novel is "a conservative enterprise, after all" (92): it is "profoundly conciliatory . . . and of all Austen's novels it most affirms established social arrangements without damaging their prestige or fundamentally challenging their wisdom or equity" (73-4). We can, however, uncover some disturbances to a novel often considered "categorically happy" (73) by bringing the cameo narrative to the fore.

The challenges of the past are displaced or resolved only if we read **Pride and Prejudice** monologically and ignore the dialogism facilitated by the cameo. The main narrative requires characters and readers to forgive and forget, but the cameo vengefully offers a reminder of the past. In his introduction to Bakhtin's *Problems of Dostoevsky's Poetics,* Wayne Booth admits that he has "often scoffed about modes of criticism that care so little about formal construction that they would be unaffected if the works discussed had been written backward"; yet much of Bakhtin's criticism "would not be affected if we discovered new manuscripts that scrambled the order of events, or the handling of flashbacks and foreshadowings, or the manipulations of point of view. It is not linear sequence but the touch of the author at each moment that matters. What we seek is what might be called the best *vertical* structure, rather than a given temporal structure and its technical transformations" (1984, xxv). If we refuse to follow the main narrative's linearity and temporal progression towards reconciliation and instead place the "handling of flashbacks" in the foreground, then we arrive at a very different text, a dialogic text, in which the narrative cameo holds equal weight with the main narrative. Such an interpretation, which could be construed as reading **Pride and Prejudice** as if it "had been written backward," registers the novel's dialogism. The main narrative is based on a reconciliation of the past and the present, but if the reader refuses to become co-opted into this monologic narrative, then **Pride and Prejudice**'s happy ending emerges as fragile and conditional indeed.

In his letter of vindication to Elizabeth, Darcy tries to explain his interference in Jane and Bingley's relationship, and he gives a history of Wickham: "My character required it to be written and read" (Austen 1988, 2:196). Darcy's narrative is, of course, in direct contrast to the one circulated by Wickham earlier in the novel. Darcy reveals the profligate behaviour of Mr Wickham, culminating in his attempt to seduce Georgiana, then only fifteen years old: "Mr Wickham's chief object was unquestionably my sister's fortune, which is thirty thousand pounds; but I cannot help supposing that the hope of revenging himself on me, was a strong inducement." Georgiana confided in her brother, who fortunately averted the crisis: Mr Wickham "left the place immediately" (202).

This past, rather than being contained in the cameo, repeats itself. Wickham reincurs massive debts and seduces and elopes with Lydia. Again Mr Darcy rescues the situation and bribes Wickham to marry Lydia. The cameo narrative points out the vulnerability of the heroine. Like Marianne Dashwood and Anne Elliot, who closely escape the villains of their respective novels, Elizabeth narrowly avoids the dangerous consequences of her flirtation with Wickham.

Moreover, the cameo brings out the anxieties surrounding the marriage of Elizabeth and Darcy. The plot of Wickham, the fortune-hunter in pursuit of Georgiana and Pemberley, presents an unflattering parallel to Elizabeth's aspirations towards Pemberley: "She felt, that to be mistress of Pemberley might be something!" (245). As Susan Fraiman points out, there is an "element . . . of crass practicality": "Elizabeth is appalled by Charlotte's pragmatism, and yet, choosing Darcy over Wickham, she is herself beguiled by the entrepreneurial marriage plot" (1989, 182). Lady Catherine de Bourgh would agree. The narrative cameo aligns Elizabeth and Wickham and almost sets them in competition with one another. Wickham's failed attempt to win Georgiana's fortune and his consolation prize (Lydia) shed an interrogative light on Elizabeth's success. The main narrative insists that Elizabeth's motives are noble, but the cameo contaminates this purity, since ultimately Elizabeth gets the very thing to which Wickham has aspired. Darcy states that Wickham was motivated by greed and "the hope of revenging himself on me" (Austen 1988, 2:202). In a sense, Elizabeth achieves the ultimate revenge. Once considering Elizabeth "not handsome enough to tempt *me*" (12), Darcy finds himself "tortured" (367) into humility and love. The relationship and confidence between Wickham and Elizabeth in the first half of the novel should not be dismissed or underestimated. In the end Wickham, too, profits by Elizabeth's infiltration of Pemberley. The cameo raises Lady Catherine's question (357): "Are the shades of Pemberley to be thus polluted?"

Mr Darcy is remarkably possessive of the information the narrative cameo contains. Indeed, he has a lot at stake—the sanctity and mystique of Pemberley and its inhabitants: "To no creature had it been revealed, where secrecy was possible, except to Elizabeth." Darcy is "particularly anxious to conceal it" from Bingley due to his "wish which Elizabeth had long ago attributed to him" (270) of joining Georgiana's and Bingley's fortunes. Darcy needs to erase any memories of Georgiana's misconduct and any memories that suggest the gullibility of the Pemberley residents (Darcy's father, sister, and, finally, himself). In the light of Darcy's succumbing to Elizabeth—"In vain have I struggled" (189)—this is particularly important. Thus Wickham's behaviour in the cameo has to be forgotten, because it brings up the very questions that the main narrative has to elide in order to achieve its "fairy-tale-like quality." This applies equally to Darcy and to Elizabeth; he needs to maintain his image as a responsible and discriminating estate owner, and Elizabeth needs to present herself as marrying "only" for love. The cameo narrative's presence, however, continually disrupts these constructions and the main narrative's closure. Fraiman interprets Darcy as an author whose letter "monopoliz[es] the narrative" (1989, 176) and "in a play for literary hegemony (to be author and critic both), tells us how to read him" (176-7), leaving Elizabeth vanquished and humiliated: "Against the broad chest of Darcy's logic, Elizabeth beats the ineffectual fists of her own" (177). Elizabeth, however, has an equal stake in regulating the letter.

There are constant reminders of the past throughout the novel. Georgiana's presence is a case in point. At a gathering at Pemberley, Miss Bingley "took the first opportunity of saying with sneering civility" to Elizabeth, "Pray, Miss Eliza, are not the————shire militia removed from Meryton? They must be a great loss to *your* family." Elizabeth sees the unintended effect on Darcy and Georgiana: "An involuntary glance showed Darcy with an heightened complexion, earnestly looking at her, and his sister overcome with confusion, and unable to lift up her eyes." "Had Miss Bingley known what pain she was then giving her beloved friend, she undoubtedly would have refrained from the hint" (Austen 1988, 2:269), but "not a syllable had ever reached her of Miss Darcy's meditated elopement" (269-70). This episode registers the inherently disruptive power of the past, which cannot be contained in "secrecy."

Like Mr Elliot in *Persuasion,* Wickham is a family member who is permanently married to the main narrative. Despite Mr Bennet's initial opposition, the prodigal son-in-law is received at Longbourn. Lydia visits Pemberley, and both Lydia and Wickham stay at Netherfield, "frequently . . . so long, that even Bingley's good humour was overcome, and he proceeded so far as to *talk* of giving them a hint to be gone." Darcy "for Elizabeth's sake . . . assisted . . . [Wickham] farther in his profession," and both Elizabeth and Jane are regularly "applied to, for some little assistance towards discharging their bills" (387). Although they are "banished to the North" (314), they are an integral part of the family circle. This is very different from *Mansfield Park,* in which no attempt is made to "rescue" Maria Bertram, whose banishment is permanent: Sir Thomas does not grant her visitation rights.

To accomplish *Pride and Prejudice*'s family reunion, Wickham's past has to be erased. Jane is "thankful . . . that we never let them know what has been said against him; we must forget it ourselves" (274). Although Elizabeth argues that "'Their conduct has been such . . . as neither you, nor I, nor any body, can ever forget'" (305), she firmly avoids the topic: "Come, Mr Wickham, we are brother and sister, you know. Do not let us quarrel about the past" (329). Johnson argues that the novel's "conclusion preserves the heroines' friendships and promises the mutual regard of husbands and relations": "The band of good friends is all related by marriage in the end, but they are not good friends because they are related—as conservative apologists would have it—rather they are good relations because they were good friends first" (1988, 92). Johnson clearly overlooks the presence of Wickham, but Austen goes out of her way to include him.

At the end of the novel, Elizabeth and Darcy discuss Darcy's letter. Elizabeth reassures him that all is forgiven: "The letter, perhaps, began in bitterness, but it did not end so. The adieu is charity itself. But think no more of the letter. The feelings of the person who wrote, and the person who received it, are now so widely different from what they were then, that every unpleasant circumstance attending it, ought to be forgotten. You must learn some of my philosophy. Think only of the past as its remembrance gives you pleasure" (368-9). *Pride and Prejudice* itself functions like this letter; the novel's memory is highly selective. Wickham, however morally bankrupt, is no longer a threat and is recuperated into a highly comic ending, becoming Mr Bennet's "favourite" (379) son-in-law. Similarly, when Jane, expressing concern for Elizabeth's acceptance of Darcy, says, "I know how much you dislike him" (372), Elizabeth replies: "*That* is all to be forgot. Perhaps I did not always love him so well as I do now. But in such cases as these, a good memory is unpardonable. This is the last time I shall ever remember it myself" (373). The novel follows the structure of comedic reversal: "The Bennets were speedily pronounced to be the luckiest family in the world, though only a few weeks before, when Lydia had first run away, they had been generally proved to be marked out for misfortune" (350). Like *Persuasion, Pride and Prejudice* is a novel about second chances, but neither Elizabeth nor Jane nor Lydia suffer in the way Anne Elliot does.

Austen points out the selective memory that is required to believe that at the end of the novel we have a "perfect society" (Poovey 1984, 201). "Though Darcy could never receive *him* at Pemberley" (Austen 1988, 2:387), Wickham and the remembrance of the past cast a shadow over Pemberley. Like the narrative cameos in *Sense and Sensibility* and *Persuasion,* the tale of Wickham and Georgiana is a vehicle for dialogism, for it reminds us of material that the main narrative represses. *Mansfield Park* and *Northanger Abbey* are similarly haunted by tales of violence.

Note

1. Two notable exceptions to the readings of *Pride and Prejudice* as a "happy" novel of reconciliation are Susan Fraiman's "The Humiliation of Elizabeth Bennet" and Paula Bennett's "Family Plots." Fraiman discusses the homosocial trading of Elizabeth between Mr Bennet and Darcy. Bennett draws on family systems theory to explore the dysfunctional nature of Elizabeth's family.

Bibliography

Austen, Jane. *Jane Austen's Letters.* Edited by Deirdre Le Faye. 3d ed. Oxford: Oxford University Press, 1995.

———*The Novels of Jane Austen.* Edited by R. W. Chapman. 6 vols. 3d ed. Oxford: Oxford University Press, 1988.

Bennett, Paula. "Family Plots: *Pride and Prejudice* as a Novel about Parenting." In *Approaches to Teaching Austen's* Pride and Prejudice, edited by Marcia McClintock Folsom, 134-9. New York: Modern Language Association, 1993.

Booth, Wayne C. Introduction. In Mikhail Bakhtin. *Problems of Dostoevsky's Poetics.* Edited and translated by Caryl Emerson, xiii-xxvii. Minneapolis: University of Minnesota Press, 1984.

Butler, Marilyn. *Jane Austen and the War of Ideas.* 1975. Oxford: Clarendon, 1987.

Fraiman, Susan. "The Humiliation of Elizabeth Bennet." In *Refiguring the Father: New Feminist Readings of Patriarchy,* edited by Patricia Yaeger and Beth Kowaleski-Wallace, 168-87. Carbondale: Southern Illinois University Press, 1989.

———"Peevish Accents in the Juvenilia: A Feminist Key to *Pride and Prejudice.*" In *Approaches to Teaching Austen's* Pride and Prejudice, edited by Marcia McClintock Folsom, 74-80. New York: Modern Language Association, 1993.

Johnson, Claudia L. *Jane Austen: Women, Politics, and the Novel.* Chicago: University of Chicago Press, 1988.

Litz, A. Walton. *Jane Austen: A Study of Her Artistic Development.* New York: Oxford University Press, 1965.

Morgan, Susan. "Emma Woodhouse and the Charms of Imagination." *Studies in the Novel* 7 (1975): 33-48.

————*In the Meantime: Character and Perception in Jane Austen's Fiction.* Chicago: University of Chicago Press, 1980.

Newton, Judith Lowder. *Women, Power and Subversion: Social Strategies in British Fiction, 1778-1860.* New York: Methuen, 1981.

Poovey, Mary. *The Proper Lady and the Woman Writer: Ideology as Style in the Works of Mary Wollstonecraft, Mary Shelley, and Jane Austen.* Chicago: University of Chicago Press, 1984.

Nora Foster Stovel (essay date 2002)

SOURCE: Foster Stovel, Nora. "Famous Last Words: Elizabeth Bennet Protests Too Much." In *The Talk in Jane Austen,* edited by Bruce Stovel and Lynn Weinlos Gregg, pp. 183-203. Edmonton, Canada: University of Alberta Press, 2002.

[*In the following essay, Foster Stovel examines Elizabeth's first impressions of Mr. Darcy, claiming that the reader knows they are destined for each other from the beginning because of Austen's "classic comic structure."*]

"I believe, Ma'am, I may safely promise you *never* to dance with him" (*PP* 20). So Elizabeth Bennet declares to her mother in *Pride and Prejudice.* These are famous last words indeed. The astute Austen reader suspects the lady protests too much and anticipates witnessing her eat her words. The fact that she does protest too much, however, suggests that Elizabeth is impressed with Darcy from the outset, a theory that we will see borne out later in the book.[1] In fact, I suggest that we know all along that Darcy and Elizabeth are destined to be united at the end of the novel because the reader recognizes classic comic structure and Janeites recognize Austen's methods.[2] In order to make the plot intriguing, however, the author must place obstacles in the lovers' primrose path. So our pleasure lies in observing the skill with which the novelist overcomes these obstacles.

The occasion of this foolhardy promise is, of course, the famous, or infamous, snub that Darcy directs at Elizabeth on their first meeting at the Meryton Assembly. Charles Bingley interrupts his dance with Jane Bennet to urge Darcy to dance with her sister Elizabeth, who is languishing for want of a partner. Looking around until he catches her eye, Darcy withdraws his own and replies coldly, "She is tolerable; but not handsome enough to tempt *me*; and I am in no humour at present to give consequence to young ladies who are slighted by other men" (12).

Admirers of Darcy have long been at pains to account for his rudeness: supposing that he must be aware that she *can* overhear him, since he *does* overhear him, his

barb seems to be deliberately launched. Why is he so cruel? Shyness will not suffice to exonerate him. Nor will his dislike of dance or small talk. I suggest that he is offended: first, his friend has preempted him in monopolizing the most beautiful and eligible woman in the room, and, second, Elizabeth has had the effrontery to catch his eye, as if "to beg for a partner" (26). After all, "the single man in possession of a good fortune" (3) may not be Charles Bingley, but his friend, Fitzwilliam Darcy, his superior in birth, position, and fortune. We need only think of Miss Bingley's fawning flattery to see how Darcy must constantly repel advances from single women in want of a good fortune. I suggest that Darcy is attracted to Elizabeth and is resisting the attraction in the pattern of the eminently eligible single man of fortune—a theory borne out by subsequent developments. Colin Firth, who plays Darcy in the BBC/A&E TV adaptation of *Pride and Prejudice,* cites in an interview "a very helpful saying: 'A man who is eligible needs to entertain no one,'" and adds, "So out of both shyness and a lack of necessity [Darcy] remains aloof" (Birtwistle 102).

Whatever Darcy's reasons, Elizabeth imputes the worst possible interpretation to his words. But her "lively, playful disposition" (12) turns the slight into an amusing story. Mrs. Bennet, outraged by the snub, declares, "I quite detest the man" (13), and advises, "Another time, Lizzy, . . . I would not dance with *him,* if I were you." Elizabeth goes one better by promising "*never* to dance with him" (20). Mrs. Bennet is scarcely the type for rational behaviour, and so, by allying herself with her mother, Elizabeth has put herself beyond the realm of reason. Just as Mrs. Bennet is said to be "beyond the reach of reason" (62) on the subject of the entail of the Longbourn estate, so Elizabeth has put herself beyond the reach of reason on the subject of Fitzwilliam Darcy.[3]

This phenomenon is, of course, the prejudice of Austen's title—a title one of my students referred to as *The Pride and the Prejudice.*[4] As Fanny Burney says in *Cecilia,* "The whole of this unfortunate business . . . has been the result of PRIDE and PREJUDICE" (930). Modern psychology employs another term for this phenomenon: it is referred to as *mental schema,* whereby an individual forms a rigid mental framework that influences the interpretation of all data.[5] Elizabeth is a classic case of such schema: Darcy's snub, combined with her pride in her own perspicacity—what Walton Litz terms "Elizabeth's pride of her own quick perceptions" (102), a pride fostered by her doting father—results in an inflexible prejudice against Darcy that will require three volumes to dismantle.

Let us remember the original title of the novel—*First Impressions.*[6] What I might call "love at first impression" may inspire their prejudice. Darcy and Elizabeth, I argue, fall in hate, or, rather, fall into a love/hate relationship, as a result of offended pride. As Colin Firth explains, "[Darcy] hates [Elizabeth] because he fancies her" (100). Elizabeth acknowledges, "I could easily forgive *his* pride, if he had not mortified *mine*" (20). Mary, the pedantic Bennet sister, offers a useful definition: "Vanity and pride are different things. . . . Pride relates more to our opinion of ourselves, vanity to what we would have others think of us" (20). This definition applies perfectly to Darcy and Elizabeth: he is proud while she is vain. Darcy refines this distinction further: "Yes, vanity is a weakness indeed. But pride—where there is a real superiority of mind, pride will be always under good regulation" (57). He acknowledges that his temper is unyielding, even resentful: Elizabeth concludes, "*Your* defect is a propensity to hate every body," to which he replies with ironic accuracy, "And yours . . . is wilfully to misunderstand them" (58). Much of the reader's delight consists of witnessing Elizabeth being obliged to dismantle her prejudice and Darcy his pride—a process that provides the impetus for the novel.

Elizabeth proves as good as her word, and the fast-stepping that she is forced to execute to avoid dancing with Darcy, before he manages to outmanoeuvre her, affords the reader considerable entertainment—especially since the perverse author contrives to construct Volume I in terms of a series of dances. As Henry Tilney explains to Catherine Morland at the Bath Assembly in *Northanger Abbey,* in both matrimony and dancing "man has the advantage of choice, woman only the power of refusal" (77). As Elizabeth later notes to Colonel Fitzwilliam, who has been recounting Darcy's success in saving his friend Bingley from a most imprudent match, Darcy takes "great pleasure in the power of choice" (183). Whereas Darcy enjoys exercising his power of choice, Elizabeth can only exercise her right to refuse.

The second dance occurs at the gathering at Lucas Lodge, when Sir William flaunts his courtly manners by urging Darcy to dance with Elizabeth. Although Darcy has just expressed his disdain for the amusement, declaring, "Every savage can dance" (25), he is not unwilling to partner her.[7] But she remonstrates, "Indeed, Sir, I have not the least intention of dancing.—I entreat you not to suppose that I moved this way in order to beg for a partner" (26). Why, then, *has* she moved towards them, if not to seek a partner? Elizabeth is steadfast in refusing to accede either to Darcy's polite propriety or to Sir William's persistent persuasion, however. When the latter asks rhetorically, "Who would object to such a partner?" (26), Elizabeth "looked archly, and turned away" (26). Austen adds, "Her resistance had not injured her with the gentleman" (26-27). As Colin Firth notes, for once Darcy is "the pursuer rather than the pursued: it's irresistible" (Birtwistle 102).

Let us not fail to accord credit to Caroline Bingley for helping to dismantle Darcy's resistance to Elizabeth, for I suggest that he uses Elizabeth to protect himself from Miss Bingley's advances. He is hoist with his own petard, as the saying goes, however, for in attending to Elizabeth in order to offend Caroline, he falls under Elizabeth's spell. Upon Caroline's confronting him, he responds, "I have been meditating on the very great pleasure which a pair of fine eyes in the face of a pretty woman can bestow" (27). Darcy is learning the language of looks: the very glance that offended him at the Meryton Assembly now enchants. As Colin Firth says, "That's when he first notices her eyes. What starts off as intriguing becomes profoundly erotic for him" (Birtwistle 102). The glossary of glances is a vocabulary that Austen will pursue.

Darcy has further opportunity to admire Elizabeth at Netherfield when she goes to visit Jane, who, thanks to her mother's ingenuity, has fallen ill after getting soaked through while riding on horseback to Netherfield and must therefore remain there for a week to recover. Darcy persists in gazing intently at Elizabeth, who persists in misinterpreting his steadfast gaze:

> Mr. Darcy's eyes were fixed on her. She hardly knew how to suppose that she could be an object of admiration to so great a man; and yet that he should look at her because he disliked her, was still more strange. She could only imagine however at last, that she drew his notice because there was a something about her more wrong and reprehensible, according to his ideas of right, than in any other person present. The supposition did not pain her. She liked him too little to care for his approbation.
>
> (51)

The fact that men do not usually stare at women because they do *not* like the way they look serves to emphasize Elizabeth's rigid mind-set that will not admit any data that does not fit her schema.

When Elizabeth arrives with her petticoat inches deep in mud as a result of walking three miles to see her sister, Caroline Bingley attempts to denigrate her by observing, "She has nothing . . . to recommend her, but being an excellent walker" (35). But being an excellent walker is a giant step towards being an exquisite dancer. When Miss Bingley attempts to call Darcy's attention to herself by playing "a lively Scotch air," he surprises Elizabeth by asking, "Do not you feel a great inclination, Miss Bennet, to seize such an opportunity of dancing a reel?" She is so surprised that she remains silent, provoking him to repeat his question, to which she replies, "I do not want to dance a reel at all—and now despise me if you dare." He replies, "Indeed I do not dare" (52). As Austen notes, "Darcy had never been so bewitched by any woman as he was by her. He really believed, that were it not for the inferiority of her connections, he should be in some danger" (52). Thus, Austen reinforces the idea that Darcy is resisting his attraction to Elizabeth because of his prejudice against her class. Her technique has the opposite effect from what is intended, however. Later Darcy acknowledges, "I believed you to be wishing, expecting my addresses" (369). Perhaps, at some level of which she is wilfully ignorant, she deliberately piques his admiration with her playful teasing. As she later declares, "Had I been in love, I could not have been more wretchedly blind" (208). Such passion may be at the root of her prejudice.

The grand finale of Volume I is, of course, the Netherfield ball on November 26. The Elizabeth—Darcy duo has by now become a trio and the antagonism rendered more complex by the arrival of George Wickham to join the———shire Militia stationed near Meryton. In short, the plot thickens. Besides his handsome face, fine figure, easy manners, and *appearance* of virtue (Austen is always careful to include the word "appearance" to suggest that Elizabeth cannot see beyond surfaces), Wickham has the added advantage of being able to fuel Elizabeth's anger at Darcy. So blinded is she by her bias against Darcy that she cannot see the impropriety of Wickham's confidences to a virtual stranger nor the impudence of his vilifying his patron behind his back. Jane's tolerant nature provides the perfect foil for Elizabeth's intolerance: when she says, upon hearing Wickham's history of Darcy, "One does not know what to think," Elizabeth retorts, "I beg your pardon;—one knows exactly what to think" (86): "Attention, forbearance, patience with Darcy, was injury to Wickham" (89).

Anticipating "the conquest of all that remained unsubdued of [Wickham's] heart" (89) at the Netherfield ball—for "to be fond of dancing was a certain step towards falling in love" (9), as Austen reminds us at the outset—Elizabeth is crushed to discover that Wickham has avoided the ball by going to town, and her animosity towards Darcy is exacerbated accordingly. Consequently, she is so surprised by his voluntarily inviting her to dance that, "without knowing what she did, she accepted him" (90)—suggesting that her impulses are right, but her head in the form of her mental schema is at war with her heart. But when Charlotte Lucas remonstrates, "I dare say you will find him very agreeable," Elizabeth retorts, "Heaven forbid!—*That* would be the greatest misfortune of all!—To find a man agreeable whom one is determined to hate!—Do not wish me such an evil" (90). Austen suggests that Elizabeth is well aware of her prejudice: Darcy is the man she loves to hate.

Elizabeth, "amazed at the dignity to which she was arrived in being allowed to stand opposite to Mr. Darcy," employs first silence, then talk to torment him. Initially she maintains a steadfast silence, until, after they had "stood for some time without speaking a word," and "fancying that it would be the greater punishment to her partner to oblige him to talk" (for Darcy is taciturn, while Elizabeth is talkative), she speaks, adding, "It is *your* turn to say something now, Mr. Darcy.—*I* talked about the dance, and *you* ought to make some kind of remark on the size of the room, or the number of couples," provoking him to ask, "Do you talk by rule then, while you are dancing?" (90-91). She replies, "Sometimes. One must speak a little, you know. It would look odd to be entirely silent for half an hour together, and yet for the advantage of *some,* conversation ought to be so arranged as that they may have the trouble of saying as little as possible" (91). She adds, "We are each of an unsocial, taciturn disposition, unwilling to speak, unless we expect to say something that will amaze the whole room, and be handed down to posterity with all the eclat of a proverb" (91). Her catechism continues as she provokes Darcy by inquiring about his quarrel with Wickham, asking whether he never allows himself to be "blinded by prejudice": "It is particularly incumbent on those who never change their opinion, to be secure of judging properly at first" (93). Ultimately she succeeds in her design of offending him, and they separate in silence. What Reuben Brower terms "the poetry of wit" or "*jeux d'esprit*" (168, 171) Andrew Davies, screenwriter of the BBC/A&E adaptation, labels "a fencing match caught in dance" (Birtwistle 71). Indeed, Darcy and Elizabeth do resemble that reluctant couple, Beatrice and Benedick, from Shakespeare's comedy *Much Ado About Nothing,* who love to hate and hate to love, and who, in turn, inspired warring couples like Mirabel and Millamant in Congreve's *The Way of the World.*[8]

No sooner has she achieved her object, however, than circumstances conspire to challenge her complacency. Her admirer, Mr. Collins, on learning that he is in the presence of a relative of his patroness, Lady Catherine de Bourgh, announces to Elizabeth his intention of introducing himself to Darcy. Elizabeth is appalled at his effrontery in accosting a man so much his social superior and observes with embarrassment as Collins courts Darcy's contempt. A "most unlucky perverseness" (with the initials J.A.) seats Darcy where he can overhear Mrs. Bennet's insulting comments, just as Elizabeth overheard Darcy's insults at the Meryton Assembly: "What is Mr. Darcy to me, pray, that I should be afraid of him? I am sure we owe him no such particular civility as to be obliged to say nothing *he* may not like to hear" (99). After dinner, Mary regales the company with her songs. Finally, Collins displays his partiality for Elizabeth by monopolizing her in the dance, where he "gave her all the shame and misery which a disagreeable partner . . . can give" (90). Austen concludes, "To Elizabeth it appeared, that had her family made an agreement to expose themselves as much as they could during the evening, it would have been impossible for them to play their parts with more spirit, or finer success" (101). It is Darcy's disapproval that she fears the most, of course, for she does not wish to fuel his prejudice against her connections, indicating that his opinion is of the utmost importance to her. In short, she desires his approbation.

Collins's invitation to the dance proves to be a prelude to his proposal of marriage to Elizabeth. Recall Henry Tilney's comment to Catherine Morland at the cotillion ball in *Northanger Abbey*: "I consider a country-dance as an emblem of marriage" (76); so it proves in *Pride and Prejudice*. After cataloguing his reasons for marrying—not the least compelling being that it is the recommendation of his patroness, Lady Catherine de Bourgh—and assuring her "in the most animated language of the violence of [his] affection" (106), he is incapable of accepting her refusal, assuming that it is her natural delicacy that leads her to refuse, plus the coquetry of an elegant female who wishes him to repeat the offer. Finally, she is forced to insist: "I do assure you that I am not one of those young ladies (if such young ladies there are) who are so daring as to risk their happiness on the chance of being asked a second time" (107)—famous last words again. Remember them, for these are additional words that she will be obliged to eat. She then declares categorically, "Do not consider me now as an elegant female intending to plague you, but as a rational creature speaking the truth from her heart" (109)—a good example of self-deception, for Elizabeth is anything but rational at this point and has little interest in learning the truth, especially where Fitzwilliam Darcy is concerned.

Collins is, of course, a comic counterpart to Darcy, anticipating him first in dancing with, and then in proposing marriage to, Elizabeth. Even their proposals are parallel in some ways, as both detail their reasons for or against marrying. While Collins changes the object of his attentions and proposals with alacrity, however, Darcy stands firm in both his affections and his intentions.

Volume I ends with the overthrow of all Mrs. Bennet's dearest hopes of seeing her two eldest daughters well married—well, married. Elizabeth rejects the proposal of Mr. Collins, who redirects his attentions towards her friend, Charlotte Lucas, almost as readily as he redirected his intentions from Jane to Elizabeth. Jane's hopes are dashed by the news that the Bingley party is returning to London with no prospect of revisiting Netherfield. As a cheerless Christmas season approaches, Mrs. Bennet wallows in the winter of her discontent. Only the visit of the Gardiners consoles the Bennet women. When Aunt Gardiner hears of Elizabeth's preference for Wickham, she cautions her against encouraging such an imprudent attachment: "You have sense, and we all expect you to use it" (144). Elizabeth takes

this appeal to her intelligence to heart, and, although she does allow herself one outburst—"Oh! *that* abominable Mr. Darcy!" (144)—she promises to "do [her] best" (145). When her aunt suggests a tour of the Lakes, she greets the prospect eagerly, exclaiming rhetorically, if disingenuously, "What are men to rocks and mountains?" (154).

Volume II does take the Bennet women far afield: Jane accompanies the Gardiners to London, where she is ignored by the Bingleys and left to languish alone; Elizabeth accepts Charlotte's urgent invitation to visit her new establishment at Hunsford Parsonage in Kent, where Elizabeth is able to admire Collins's conjugal felicity and the condescension of his patroness, Lady Catherine de Bourgh—all delights that she might have been able to call her own: "Words were insufficient for the elevation of his feelings; and he was obliged to walk about the room, while Elizabeth tried to unite civility and truth in a few short sentences" (216).

No sooner is Elizabeth established in Kent, however, than Darcy arrives at Rosings Park with his cousin, Colonel Fitzwilliam. The intercourse between the Park and the Parsonage provides many opportunities for Elizabeth to tease Darcy about his taciturn temperament: she even twits him about snubbing her at the Meryton Assembly. His excuse of shyness and dislike of small talk may impress the reader, who credits him with being "the strong silent type," but not the intolerant Elizabeth. As Darcy observes, "We neither of us perform to strangers" (176). Interestingly, this is the first time Darcy refers to himself and Elizabeth as *we*, suggesting a new level of intimacy.

The Rosings episode constitutes a turning point in Darcy's feelings for Elizabeth. I suggest that there are several reasons for this development. First, Darcy sees Elizabeth for the first time in isolation from her family. Secondly, he realizes that rank is no guarantee of good manners, for he is as embarrassed by the behaviour of his aunt, Lady Catherine de Bourgh, as Elizabeth could be by her own relations. Lastly, Colonel Fitzwilliam admires Elizabeth, and, although he makes it clear to her that he cannot afford to entertain any serious intentions towards her, his admiration must carry weight with his cousin, if only to arouse his jealousy.

Easter brings a renewal of Darcy's admiration of Elizabeth. Charlotte Lucas, unblinded by pride, prejudice, or passion, is able to interpret his "earnest, steadfast gaze" (181) and concludes, "My dear Eliza, he must be in love with you" (180). She is convinced that "all her friend's dislike would vanish, if she could suppose him to be in her power" (181). But Fitzwilliam's account of the decisive part played by Darcy in vanquishing all her sister Jane's hopes of happiness arouses Elizabeth's resentment: "If [Darcy's] own vanity . . . did not mislead him, *he* was the cause, his pride and caprice were the cause of all that Jane had suffered" (186). Then, "as if intending to exasperate herself as much as possible against Mr. Darcy" (188), she rereads Jane's letters. It is in this mood of resentment that she greets Darcy's proposal of marriage.

"In vain have I struggled. It will not do. My feelings will not be repressed. You must allow me to tell you how ardently I admire and love you" (189). The reader, like the heroine herself, is in shock. The effect is as if a singer had changed register, moving from musical comedy to grand opera. The polite social mask is off. Darcy has long been the classic strong silent type, but still waters run deep indeed, and he is, unlike Collins, run away with by the violence of his affection. But where Austen allowed Collins to articulate his reasons for marrying in his own words, she wisely represses Darcy's reasons against marrying, summarizing them in the omniscient narrative. We can assume that his eloquence on the subject of his pride and her inferiority renders him just as rude, however, as did Bingley's initial invitation to partner Elizabeth in the dance, for he provokes her to incivility and accusations of his officious interference with regard to Bingley and Jane and his vicious behaviour to Wickham. Darcy cuts to the quick when he accuses: "These offences might have been overlooked, had not your pride been hurt by my honest confession of the scruples that had long prevented my forming any serious design" (192). The gloves are off, and the wigs are on the green. She responds, "You could not have made me the offer of your hand in any possible way that would have tempted me to accept it" (192-93). These are famous last words, Volume II, and Elizabeth will devote all of Volume III to attempting to eat them. She expands her rejection eloquently:

> From the very beginning, from the first moment I may almost say, of my acquaintance with you, your manners impressing me with the fullest belief of your arrogance, your conceit, and your selfish disdain of the feelings of others, were such as to form that ground-work of disapprobation, on which succeeding events have built so immoveable a dislike; and I had not known you a month before I felt that you were the last man in the world whom I could ever be prevailed on to marry.
>
> (193)

The lady does indeed protest too much and in the process reveals, ironically, that she *has* considered marriage to Darcy. However, she does, as a result of this direct attack, achieve the last word. Darcy retires in defeat (or so it appears), leaving Elizabeth in a tumult of emotion, as she cries for half an hour—a torrent of tears that alerts the reader to the emotions Elizabeth refuses to acknowledge.

How curious it is, then, that, although she intends to avoid Darcy, her morning walk the next day takes her to the gates of Rosings Park, whence he emerges to give her a letter that the reader scans with almost as much impatience as the heroine herself. The missive provokes the process that his proposal failed to effect, namely the dismantling of her bias or schema. Darcy achieves this feat by appealing to her *reason* and her sense of *justice*, just as her Aunt Gardiner appealed to her *sense*. And a challenge to her reason and sense of justice must be answered:

> With a strong prejudice against every thing he might say, she began his account of what had happened at Netherfield. . . . His belief of her sister's insensibility, she instantly resolved to be false, and his account of the real, the worst objections to the match, made her too angry to have any wish of doing him justice. He expressed no regret for what he had done which satisfied her; his style was not penitent, but haughty. It was all pride and insolence.
>
> (204)

However, his desire to exonerate himself of blame and deserve her approbation by humbling his family pride to confess the scandal of his sister's intended elopement with Wickham ultimately has the desired effect. Like the figure of Justice herself, she "weighed every circumstance with what she meant to be impartiality" (205), in a manner that Reuben Brower calls her "judicial process" (176). Her eyes are opened, and she realizes that "she had been blind, partial, prejudiced, absurd":

> "How despicably have I acted!" she cried.—"I, who have prided myself on my discernment!—I, who have valued myself on my abilities! who have often disdained the generous candour of my sister, and gratified my vanity, in useless or blameable distrust.—How humiliating is this discovery!—Yet, how just a humiliation!—Had I been in love, I could not have been more wretchedly blind. But vanity, not love, has been my folly.—Pleased with the preference of one, and offended by the neglect of the other, on the very beginning of our acquaintance, I have courted prepossession and ignorance, and driven reason away, where either were concerned. Till this moment, I never knew myself."
>
> (208)

This epiphanic moment constitutes the turning point in Elizabeth's character development. Only when she achieves self-knowledge is she able to perceive Darcy's true character.

> Mr. Darcy's letter, she was in a fair way of soon knowing by heart. She studied every sentence: and her feelings towards its writer were at times widely different. When she remembered the style of his address, she was still full of indignation; but when she considered how unjustly she had condemned and upbraided him, her anger was turned against herself; and his disappointed feelings became the object of compassion. His attachment excited gratitude, his general character respect; but she could not approve him; nor could she for a moment repent her refusal, or feel the slightest inclination

ever to see him again. In her own past behaviour, there was a constant source of vexation and regret; and in the unhappy defects of her family a subject of yet heavier chagrin.

(212)

Her reaction to his letter is a lesson in reading and interpretation.[9] It clarifies her continuum of reactions as she admits the justice of Darcy's prejudice against her relations' and her own defects.

Reunion with Jane tempts Elizabeth to "gratify whatever of her own vanity she had not yet been able to reason away" (218) by communicating Darcy's proposals to her sister. But, for once, she exercises restraint, until they are at leisure at Longbourn, where she reveals "Darcy's vindication" (225) in relation to Wickham. She concludes, "One has got all the goodness, and the other all the appearance of it" (225). She burlesques her bias in accounting for it to her more tolerant sister:

And yet I meant to be uncommonly clever in taking so decided a dislike to him, without any reason. It is such a spur to one's genius, such an opening for wit to have a dislike of that kind. One may be continually abusive without saying any thing just; but one cannot be always laughing at a man without now and then stumbling on something witty.

(225-26)

Here she acknowledges her desire to employ her prejudice against Darcy as an opportunity to exercise her wit.

Volume II ends with the effective dismantling of both Darcy's pride and Elizabeth's prejudice. But it also ends with the renewed disappointment of both elder Bennet sisters' marital hopes, and only the prospect of the Gardiners' tour of the Lakes cheers Elizabeth until a change of schedule limits their tour to Derbyshire, the site of Darcy's country estate. "To Pemberley, therefore, they were to go" (241).

While Volume I staged the meeting of Elizabeth and Darcy in her home county of Hertfordshire, and Volume II reunited the pair on the relatively neutral ground of Kent, Volume III reunites them initially on Darcy's own turf of Derbyshire and finally in Hertfordshire once again, bringing their journeys full circle. Elizabeth is suitably impressed by Darcy's estate and thinks, "to be mistress of Pemberley might be something!" (245). The testimony to Darcy's good nature by his housekeeper, Mrs. Reynolds, makes an impression, and, upon viewing his portrait in the gallery, she "thought of his regard with a deeper sentiment of gratitude than it had ever raised before" (251). To her great surprise, no sooner does she view his portrait than she meets the man himself. Embarrassed by the perverseness of the meeting and amazed at the alteration in his manner, she is im-

pressed by his civility to the Gardiners and his wish to introduce her to his sister. Elizabeth remains puzzled, but the Gardiners perceive his admiration for their niece and feel "the full conviction that one of them at least knew what it was to love. Of the lady's sensations they remained a little in doubt; but that the gentleman was overflowing with admiration was evident enough" (262). Even Elizabeth is impressed by the alteration in his behaviour and is obliged to adjust her attitude accordingly: "Such a change in a man of so much pride, excited not only astonishment but gratitude—for to love, ardent love, it must be attributed" (266). Her gratitude inspires her to review her feelings:

She respected, she esteemed, she was grateful to him, she felt a real interest in his welfare; and she only wanted to know how far she wished that welfare to depend upon herself, and how far it would be for the happiness of both that she should employ the power, which her fancy told her she still possessed, of bringing on the renewal of his addresses.

(266)

Collins is vindicated, for Elizabeth wishes for the very thing she assured Collins she would never desire—namely, to invite a man to repeat his proposals. Fate in the form of the novelist intervenes, however: no sooner is Elizabeth well on the way to a reconciliation with Darcy than her hopes are dashed in the cruellest manner by a letter from Jane informing her that her youngest sister, Lydia, has eloped with none other than George Wickham. A further perversity brings Darcy to wait on Elizabeth at the very moment when the shock of this catastrophe has thrown her into a tumult of emotions; in the heat of the moment, she confesses her sister's shame to Darcy—a striking example of both her trust in his discretion and the level of intimacy that they have attained. His silence and hasty departure, the result of his apparent disapprobation, dash her nascent hopes of reconciliation:

As he quitted the room, Elizabeth felt how improbable it was that they should ever see each other again on such terms of cordiality as had marked their several meetings in Derbyshire; and as she threw a retrospective glance over the whole of their acquaintance, so full of contradictions and varieties, sighed at the perverseness of those feelings which would now have promoted its continuance, and would formerly have rejoiced in its termination.

(279)

Given the perversity of Elizabeth's nature, it is not surprising that the disgrace brought on the entire Bennet family by Lydia's shame ironically makes Elizabeth aware for the first time of her true feelings for Darcy, for it is human nature to value what we possess only when we have lost it. The achievement of Lydia's marriage to Wickham makes her regret that she ever informed Darcy of the affair (311). It also makes her realize that now "there seemed a gulf impassable between them" (311), for Darcy, even if he could overcome his repugnance at an alliance with the Bennet family, would never connect himself with a family that would make him brother-in-law of the man he so justly despised:

> What a triumph for him, as she often thought, could he know that the proposals which she had proudly spurned only four months ago, would now have been gladly and gratefully received! . . .
>
> She began now to comprehend that he was exactly the man, who, in disposition and talents, would most suit her. His understanding and temper, though unlike her own, would have answered all her wishes. It was an union that must have been to the advantage of both; by her ease and liveliness, his mind might have been softened, his manners improved, and from his judgment, information, and knowledge of the world, she must have received benefit of greater importance.
>
> But no such happy marriage could now teach the admiring multitude what connubial felicity really was. An union of a different tendency, and precluding the possibility of the other, was soon to be formed in their family.
>
> (312)

The reader, however, thanks to the author's narrative skill, is a better judge than Elizabeth of Darcy's character. Not until after Lydia's wedding does Elizabeth learn from her sister's foolish loquacity that Darcy was a witness to her marriage to Wickham. Petitioning Aunt Gardiner prompts a letter revealing all that Darcy has done to effect the marriage, from hunting down the couple to bribing Wickham to marry Lydia by offering to settle his debts and purchase his commission. The motive Darcy professes is regret that "his mistaken pride" led him to conceal Wickham's real viciousness (322). Elizabeth's vanity may be equally to blame, for publication of the truth would have rendered her previous preference for Wickham risible. But she begins to suspect his real motive: "Her heart did whisper, that he had done it for her" (326).

Finally Elizabeth listens to her heart. This Janus-faced heroine has often been led towards Darcy by her heart—at the Meryton Assembly, the Lucas Lodge ball, the Netherfield ball, and at Rosings Park—but has been driven away from him by her head, in the form of her mental schema. Elizabeth's own pride is finally humbled by Darcy's generosity; in a satisfying reversal, she is proud of *him*:

> They owed the restoration of Lydia, her character, every thing to him. Oh! how heartily did she grieve over every ungracious sensation she had ever encouraged, every saucy speech she had ever directed towards him. For herself she was humbled; but she was proud of him. Proud that in a cause of compassion and honour, he had been able to get the better of himself.
>
> (326-27)

The fact that Darcy proves himself to be not only generous, but also masterful in effecting this felicitous resolution of the situation may also, I suggest, influence Elizabeth's feelings.

September, surprisingly, brings the return of Bingley to Netherfield for the hunting season—to Mrs. Bennet's delight and Jane's distress. He comes to call, bringing that "tall, proud man" whom Mrs. Bennet so detests (334). Elizabeth is mortified by her mother's rudeness to their benefactor:

> To Jane, he could be only a man whose proposals she had refused, and whose merit she had undervalued; but to her own more extensive information, he was the person, to whom the whole family were indebted for the first of benefits, and whom she regarded herself with an interest, if not quite so tender, at least as reasonable and just, as what Jane felt for Bingley.
>
> (334)

The words "reasonable and just" counter "proud and prejudiced." Elizabeth's sense of shame as her mother boasts about Lydia's marriage is such that years of happiness could not compensate her, as she sees her own prejudice burlesqued in her mother's behaviour. Darcy's determined silence inspires her despair: "A man who has once been refused! How could I ever be foolish enough to expect a renewal of his love? Is there one among the sex, who would not protest against such a weakness as a second proposal to the same woman? There is no indignity so abhorrent to their feelings!" (341). Collins would be gratified at such a vision of hubris humbled.

Jane is more fortunate: with a little help from Mrs. Bennet, Mr. Bingley renews his addresses, and an understanding is reached between this well-suited, good-natured pair—but not until the influential Darcy has confessed to Bingley his subterfuge in concealing from him Jane's presence in London the previous winter and has communicated his approval of the match.

Elizabeth despairs of achieving equal felicity. But help comes from a most unexpected quarter. Lady Catherine de Bourgh proves to be an unlikely *dea ex machina* whose insolent interference backfires: descending on Longbourn in her chaise and four with the aim of exacting Elizabeth's promise to give up all pretensions to Darcy's hand in marriage in favour of her own daughter, her ladyship underestimates her antagonist's obstinacy, and her efforts achieve the opposite of their intended effect. "Are the shades of Pemberley to be thus polluted?" (357), Lady Catherine inquires rhetorically. The answer, apparently, is "Yes, they are," for Elizabeth resolutely refuses to refuse to marry Darcy. Ironically, her ladyship's complaints of Elizabeth's obstinacy lead Darcy to dare to hope (367). He returns to Longbourn to renew his addresses, but remains steadfastly silent.

Since, as Henry Tilney explained, woman does not have the advantage of choice but only the power of refusal, Elizabeth is driven to subterfuge to bring on the renewal of Darcy's addresses. She forms "a desperate resolution" to invite a proposal by thanking him for his kindness to Lydia: "Mr. Darcy, I am a very selfish creature; and, for the sake of giving relief to my own feelings, care not how much I may be wounding your's. I can no longer help thanking you for your unexampled kindness to my poor sister" (365). He responds, "If you *will* thank me, . . . let it be for yourself alone. That the wish of giving happiness to you, might add force to the other inducements which led me on, I shall not attempt to deny. But your *family* owe me nothing. Much as I respect them, I believe, I thought only of *you*" (366). He accepts her invitation: "You are too generous to trifle with me. If your feelings are still what they were last April, tell me so at once. *My* affections and wishes are unchanged, but one word from you will silence me on this subject for ever." How different is this diffident address from his previous arrogant proposal! For once, Elizabeth is inarticulate, as she "immediately, though not very fluently, gave him to understand, that her sentiments had undergone so material a change, since the period to which he alluded, as to make her receive with gratitude and pleasure, his present assurances" (366). Austen writes, "The happiness which this reply produced, was such as he had probably never felt before; and he expressed himself on the occasion as sensibly and as warmly as a man violently in love can be supposed to do . . . he told her of feelings, which, in proving of what importance she was to him, made his affection every moment more valuable" (366). Austen declines to repeat Darcy's words to the avid reader. Elizabeth learns that passion is more likely to render a man speechless than eloquent. Later, when she taxes Darcy with taciturnity, he has a ready reply: "You might have talked to me more when you came to dinner," she protests, and he responds, "A man who had felt less, might" (381).

Only when they have reached an understanding can they confess their previous prejudices; Elizabeth explains "how gradually all her former prejudices had been removed" by his letter (368). Colin Firth says, "He is so profoundly challenged by her that his old prejudices cannot be upheld" (Birtwistle 105). Their competition in conceit becomes a contest in contrition, a contest Darcy clearly wins. He then confesses, "What will you think of my vanity? I believed you to be wishing, expecting my addresses." Elizabeth replies, "My manners must have been in fault, but not intentionally I assure you. I never meant to deceive you, but my spirits might often lead me wrong." (369) This exchange suggests what the reader has suspected, namely that Elizabeth, unconsciously, was attempting to attract Darcy's addresses all along, but her prejudice or schema prevented her from interpreting his attentions and her own

emotions correctly. She also offers a rational account of Darcy's falling in love with her that bears out our original theory:

> The fact is, that you were sick of civility, of deference, of officious attention. You were disgusted with the women who were always speaking, and looking, and thinking for your approbation alone. I roused, and interested you, because I was so unlike them. Had you not been really amiable you would have hated me for it; but in spite of the pains you took to disguise yourself, your feelings were always noble and just; and in your heart, you thoroughly despised the persons who so assiduously courted you.
>
> (380)

In *Cecilia*, Fanny Burney writes: "Yet this, however, remember; if to PRIDE and PREJUDICE you owe your miseries, so wonderfully is good and evil balanced, that to PRIDE and PREJUDICE you will also owe their termination" (930). Tony Tanner observes, "During a decade in which Napoleon was effectively engaging, if not transforming, Europe, Jane Austen composed a novel in which the most important events are the fact that a man changes his manners and a young lady changes her mind" (103). But changing her mind has always been a lady's prerogative, and, in this case, the reader approves Elizabeth's change of heart. She is such an attractive heroine that the reader wishes to see her rewarded by marital happiness. As Austen writes to her sister Cassandra in 1813, "I must confess that *I* think her as delightful a creature as ever appeared in print" (I. 201). Generations of readers have agreed.

Austen does not let Elizabeth off the hook so easily, however. She must run the gauntlet of family and friends, as each points to her well-known prejudice, and she is forced to eat her words repeatedly. First Jane remonstrates, "Oh, Lizzy! do any thing rather than marry without affection" (373). When her father protests, "Lizzy . . . what are you doing? Are you out of your senses, to be accepting this man? Have not you always hated him?" (376), Austen comments, "How earnestly did she then wish that her former opinions had been more reasonable, her expressions more moderate!" (376). When he says, "We all know him to be a proud, unpleasant sort of man; but this would be nothing if you really liked him," she replies, with tears in her eyes, "I do, I do like him. . . . I love him. Indeed he has no improper pride. He is perfectly amiable" (376). But the worst is to come: Mrs. Bennet's former fulminations against Darcy are nothing to her effusions once he has been accepted. Loquacity is a sure sign of foolishness in Austen's books. Mrs. Bennet's raptures, sprinkled with exclamation marks like a teenage girl's letter, are a comic inversion of her previous prejudices as she gushes:

> Good gracious! Lord bless me! only think! dear me! Mr. Darcy! Who would have thought it! And is it really true? Oh! my sweetest Lizzy! how rich and how great

you will be! What pin-money, what jewels, what carriages you will have! Jane's is nothing to it—nothing at all. I am so pleased—so happy. Such a charming man!—so handsome! so tall!—Oh, my dear Lizzy! pray apologise for my having disliked him so much before. I hope he will overlook it. Dear, dear Lizzy. A house in town! Every thing that is charming! Three daughters married! Ten thousand a year! Oh, Lord! What will become of me. I shall go distracted.

(378)

Just as Lady Catherine is a parody of Darcy, so Mrs. Bennet is a caricature of Elizabeth, and, just as Lady Catherine absorbs all Darcy's conceit, freeing him to be courteous, so Mrs. Bennet absorbs all Elizabeth's folly, freeing her to be rational, so that the couple can live happily ever after. As Elizabeth assures Jane, "It is settled between us already, that we are to be the happiest couple in the world" (373). One suspects that their union will be more interesting than Jane and Bingley's, however, for, although Darcy has no improper pride, he "had yet to learn to be laught at" (371). Elizabeth, however, *has* learned to avoid uttering famous last words.

Elizabeth Bennet is not the only Austen protagonist who protests too much, however. Emma Woodhouse insists to Harriet Smith, "I am not only, not going to be married, at present, but have very little intention of ever marrying at all" (*E* 84). Not until Harriet herself sets her cap at Mr. Knightley does Emma realize that "Mr. Knightley must marry no one but herself!" (408). But that is another story—and another essay.

Notes

1. Farrer, for example, thinks that Elizabeth is "subconsciously . . . in love with" Darcy from the outset (17).

2. Juliet McMaster, in "Talking about Talk in *Pride and Prejudice,*" states that skill in language "marks Darcy out from the beginning as a man of intelligence, and a fit mate for Elizabeth" (82).

3. Reuben Brower foresees the conclusion in this beginning: "As all ambiguities are resolved and all irony is dropped, the reader feels the closing in of a structure by its necessary end, the end implied in the crude judgment of Darcy in the first ballroom scene" (179).

4. I wish to thank my students for many opportunities to discuss *Pride and Prejudice.* I also wish to thank my husband, Bruce Stovel, for discussing the novel with me over the years.

5. David Miall writes, "Within psychology, the analysis of narrative has been directed by an information processing approach, in particular by different versions of schema theory" (55).

6. See the Introductory Note in R. W. Chapman's edition of the novel (xi).

7. For a fuller discussion of this subject, see my essay, "'Every Savage Can Dance': Choreographing Courtship in the Novels of Jane Austen."

8. Interestingly, the anonymous reviewer of the novel in the *Critical Review* for March 1813 writes of Elizabeth, "She is in fact the *Beatrice* of the tale; and falls in love on much the same principles of contrariety" (Southam 13). For more on this, see Bruce Stovel, "'A Contrariety of Emotion': Jane Austen's Ambivalent Lovers in *Pride and Prejudice.*"

9. This idea is developed in Gary Kelly's essay "The Art of Reading in *Pride and Prejudice.*"

Works Cited

Austen-Leigh, James Edward. *A Memoir of Jane Austen.* 1870. Ed. R. W. Chapman. Oxford: Clarendon, 1926.

Birtwistle, Sue, and Susie Conklin. *The Making of* Pride and Prejudice. London and New York: Penguin, 1995.

Brower, Reuben A. "Light and Bright and Sparkling: Irony and Fiction in *Pride and Prejudice.*" *The Fields of Light: An Experiment in Critical Reading.* New York: Oxford University Press, 1951. 164-81.

Burney, Frances. *Cecilia, or Memoirs of an Heiress.* 1782. Ed. Margaret Anne Doody and Peter Sabor. Oxford and New York: Oxford University Press, 1988.

Farrer, Reginald. "Jane Austen." *Quarterly Review* 228 (1917): 1-30.

Kelly, Gary. "The Art of Reading in *Pride and Prejudice.*" *English Studies in Canada* 10 (1984): 156-71.

Litz, A. Walton. *Jane Austen: A Study of Her Artistic Development.* New York: Oxford University Press, 1965.

McMaster, Juliet. "Class." *The Cambridge Companion to Jane Austen.* Ed. Edward Copeland and Juliet McMaster. Cambridge: Cambridge University Press, 1997. 115-30.

———. "Talking about Talk in *Pride and Prejudice.*" *Jane Austen's Business: Her World and Her Profession.* Ed. Juliet McMaster and Bruce Stovel. London: Macmillan and New York: St. Martin's, 1996. 81-94.

Miall, David. "Beyond the Schema Given: Affective Comprehension of Literary Narratives." *Cognition and Emotion* 3.1 (1989): 55-78.

Pride and Prejudice. Dir. Simon Langton. Wr. Andrew Davies. With Colin Firth and Jennifer Ehle. BBC/A& E mini-series, 1995.

Stovel, Bruce. "'A Contrariety of Emotion': Jane Austen's Ambivalent Lovers in *Pride and Prejudice.*" *International Fiction Review* 14 (1987): 27-33.

Stovel, Nora Foster. "'Every Savage Can Dance': Choreographing Courtship in the Novels of Jane Austen." *Persuasions: The Jane Austen Journal* 23 (2001): 29-49.

Southam, B.C., ed. *Jane Austen: The Critical Heritage.* London: Routledge and Kegan Paul and New York: Barnes and Noble, 1968.

Tanner, Tony. *Jane Austen.* Cambridge, MA: Harvard University Press, 1986.

FURTHER READING

Bibliographies

Clark, Robert. "Further Reading." In *Sense and Sensibility,* edited by Robert Clark, pp. 213-15. New York: St. Martin's Press, 1994.
    Offers a reading list on Austen arranged by topic.

Wright, Andrew H. "Annotated Bibliography." In *Jane Austen's Novels: A Study in Structure,* pp. 197-205. London: Chatto & Windus, 1953.
    Provides an annotated bibliography of secondary sources dating from the earliest critical responses to Austen's work through the early twentieth century.

Biography

Bloom, Harold. "Chronology." In *Jane Austen's* Pride and Prejudice, edited by Harold Bloom, pp. 127-28. New York: Chelsea House Publishers, 1987.
    Provides a useful chronology of Austen's life and career.

Criticism

Anderson, Walter E. "Plot, Character, Speech, and Place in *Pride and Prejudice,*" *Nineteenth-Century Fiction* 30, no. 3 (December 1975): 367-82.
    Succinctly summarizes Austen's development of dramatic action, which determines this work's essential form, power, and interest.

Damstra, K. St John. "The Case against Charlotte Lucas." *Women's Writing* 7, no. 2 (2000): 165-74.
    Posits that Charlotte Lucas deceptively manipulates Elizabeth and Darcy into marrying for reasons that work to her benefit.

Deresiewicz, William. "Community and Cognition in *Pride and Prejudice.*" *ELH* 64, no. 2 (1997): 503-35.
    Discusses the various ways in which a sense of community defines the plot of *Pride and Prejudice* and produces the character of Elizabeth Bennett.

Fergus, Jan. "The Comedy of Manners." In *Jane Austen's* Pride and Prejudice, edited by Harold Bloom, pp. 107-26. New York: Chelsea House Publishers, 1987.
    Treats the novels of Austen and her contemporaries as comedies of manners, focusing on *Pride and Prejudice* and the conventions it reinforces.

Gamble, David E. "Pragmatic Sympathy in Austen and Eliot." *The College Language Association Journal* 32, no. 3 (March 1989): 348-60.
    Compares the epistemological concerns of *Pride and Prejudice* and George Eliot's *Adam Bede,* arguing that their main characters both resort to sympathy as a "practical necessity for dealing with others and the world."

Goldstein, Philip. "Feminism and Poststructuralist Criticism: The Reception of *Pride and Prejudice.*" In *Communities of Cultural Value: Reception Study, Political Differences, and Literary History,* pp. 83-112. Lanham, Md.: Lexington Books, 2001.
    Evaluates the efforts of various schools of criticism to analyze *Pride and Prejudice,* contending that poststructuralist feminist critics acknowledge Austen's forceful social criticism in the novel but fail to "consistently accommodate the fragmented character of modern culture."

Greene, Donald. "The Original of Pemberley." *Eighteenth-Century Fiction* 1, no. 1 (October 1988): 1-23.
    Examines evidence to determine whether Chatsworth House—the country seat of the Cavendishes, Dukes of Devonshire—was the real-life prototype for Austen's Pemberley.

Harris, R. Allen. "Social Definition in *Pride and Prejudice*: An Exercise in Extensional Semantics." *English Studies in Canada* 17, no. 1 (March 1991): 163-75.
    Analyzes extensional semantics in *Pride and Prejudice* through Austen's use of pronouns.

Hopkins, Lisa. "Mr. Darcy's Body: Privileging the Female Gaze." *Topic* 48 (1997): 1-10.
    Discusses the ways in which Andrew Davies' 1995 television adaptation of *Pride and Prejudice* presents Mr. Darcy as an object of female desire.

Newman, Karen. "Can This Marriage Be Saved: Jane Austen Makes Sense of an Ending." *ELH* 50, no. 4 (winter 1983): 693-710.
    Analyzes the ending of *Pride and Prejudice* in terms of feminist theory, highlighting Austen's satirical and ironic commentary on the socioeconomic realities of early nineteenth-century women.

Rainbolt, Martha M. "The Likeness of Austen's Jane Bennet: Huet-Villiers' 'Portrait of Mrs. Q.'" *English Language Notes* 26, no. 2 (December 1988): 35-42.
    Analyzes textual and historical sources as evidence

that Austen meant for her character Jane Bennet to physically resemble the subject of a portrait by the artist Jean Francois Marie Huet-Villiers.

Simpson, David. "The Cult of 'Conversation.'" *Raritan* 16, no. 4 (spring 1997): 75-85.

Examines the value of conversation in contemporary society, using *Pride and Prejudice* as an example of a novel in which the purpose of the plot is to establish the basis for a conversation between the hero and the heroine.

Trevor, William. Introduction to *Pride and Prejudice,* pp. iv-xii. Oxford: Oxford University Press, 1999.

In his introduction to the Oxford World's Classics edition of *Pride and Prejudice,* Trevor grounds the reader in the contextual setting of the novel and draws attention to Austen's major themes.

Tsomondo, Thorell. "Representation, Context and Cognition; and Jane Austen." *Theoria* 64 (May 1985): 64-74.

Discusses the representational framework in Austen's works, analyzing Austen's "system of signs" in *Pride and Prejudice.*

Walder, Dennis, and Pam Morris. "Reading *Pride and Prejudice.*" In *The Realist Novel,* edited by Dennis Walder, pp. 31-60. London: Routledge, 1995.

Interprets *Pride and Prejudice* as a realist novel, using Mikhail Bakhtin's linguistic theory of dialogism to analyze the structure of the work and its relation to society.

Wiesenfarth, Joseph. "The Case of *Pride and Prejudice.*" *Studies in the Novel* 16, no. 3 (fall 1984): 261-71.

Argues that during the period of civic urgency that characterized the Napoleonic Wars, Austen's novel presents an ideal value system of social prosperity founded on individual happiness.

Wiltshire, John. "Jane Austen, Health, and the Body." *Critical Review* 31 (1991): 122-34.

Reads Austen's novels in terms of the body and health, comparing her portrayal of physical health with moral health and exploring the body's relationship to culture.

Additional coverage of Austen's life and career is contained in the following sources published by Thomson Gale: *Authors and Artists for Young Adults,* **Vol. 19;** *Beacham's Guide to Literature for Young Adults,* **Vol. 3;** *British Writers* **Vol. 4;** *British Writers: The Classics,* **Vol. 1;** *British Writers Retrospective Supplement,* **Vol. 2;** *Concise Dictionary of British Literary Biography, 1789-1832; Dictionary of Literary Biography,* **Vol. 116;** *DISCovering Authors; DISCovering Authors: British* **and** *Canadian; DISCovering Authors Modules: Most-studied Authors* **and** *Novelists; DISCovering Authors 3.0; Exploring Novels; Literary Movements for Students,* **Vol. 1;** *Literature and Its Times,* **Vol. 2;** *Literature and Its Times Supplement,* **Vol. 1;** *Literature Resource Center; Nineteenth-Century Literature Criticism,* **Vols. 1, 13, 19, 33, 51, 81, 95, 119;** *Novels for Students,* **Vols. 1, 14, 18;** *Twayne's English Authors; World Literature and Its Times,* **Vol. 3;** *World Literature Criticism;* **and** *Writers for Young Adults Supplement,* **Vol. 1.**

Sophia Peabody Hawthorne
1809-1871

(Born Sophia Amelia Peabody) American travel writer and diarist.

INTRODUCTION

Sophia Hawthorne, generally remembered as the wife of the celebrated nineteenth-century American author Nathaniel Hawthorne, is regarded by modern commentators as an accomplished writer of travel sketches, descriptive letters, and journals. The only original work of Hawthorne's to be published during her lifetime was the journal she kept during her European travels, *Notes in England and Italy* (1869). Since that time, as her letters and diaries have become available to the general public, scholars have come to recognize Hawthorne's exceptional writing talents. Collections of her letters have been reproduced in literary journals, and contemporary scholars consider her compositions as irreplaceable primary sources for the study of Nathaniel Hawthorne's home life, periods of creativity, and personality, as well as valuing them for the firsthand view they provide of the Victorian era both in America and abroad.

BIOGRAPHICAL INFORMATION

Hawthorne was born in Salem, Massachusetts, into a prominent family, the female members of which would rise to the forefront of the nineteenth-century movement for the equal rights of women. Her mother Eliza was a teacher and supported her children with the income she received from a series of schools run from her home. The elder of Sophia's two sisters, Elizabeth, was an active member of the New England Transcendentalists, a group that included such well-known and influential writers as Ralph Waldo Emerson, Henry David Thoreau, and Margaret Fuller. Sophia's other older sister, Mary, was also a writer and wife of educational reformer Horace Mann. Hawthorne's place in this dynamic family was that of youngest daughter and invalid. From the age of nine she suffered violent, debilitating headaches that often confined her to her room for days at a time. She was nonetheless well educated at home by her mother, father, and sister Elizabeth. In her youth, Hawthorne learned to read Latin, Greek, Hebrew, French, German, and Italian and studied a broad range of academic disciplines from natural science to religion. A woman of high intellect and learning, she

was also a skilled painter. In 1833, Hawthorne accompanied her sister Mary to Cuba in the hopes that the subtropical climate would lessen the pain of her headaches. The sisters remained there for two and a half years, and during that time Sophia wrote long, descriptive letters to her family. These letters were passed from hand to hand among family, friends, and acquaintances and form the body of *The Cuba Journal*. Passages from these letters enchanted a Peabody family friend, Nathaniel Hawthorne, and he later used some of them as the basis for his own stories. Elizabeth had discovered that the young writer was a near neighbor and struck up an acquaintance with him. When he finally met Sophia, he found that she had illustrated one of his short stories in its magazine appearance and was immediately taken with this talented young woman. Their courtship lasted from 1837 until 1842 and included a voluminous exchange of letters. (Nathaniel Hawthorne burned his wife's letters to him in 1853, but Sophia preserved all of his correspondence.) According to the letters that Hawthorne wrote after her wedding, her marriage was blissful, and she dedicated herself to being the perfect wife to a gifted genius. The Hawthornes had three children, Una, Julian, and Rose, to whom Hawthorne was as passionately devoted as to her husband. During these years, Nathaniel supported the family through his position as surveyor of the Salem Custom House, a government appointment. He lost that job in 1849 after a change of political administration, and afterward Sophia helped support the family by hand-painting lampshades and fire screens while her husband wrote, in quick succession, *The Scarlet Letter, The House of the Seven Gables,* and *The Blithedale Romance* in the early 1850s. In 1853, Nathaniel was appointed U.S. Consul to Liverpool, and the family moved to England. He resigned in 1857, and the family subsequently settled in Italy for a year before returning to England, where they lived for another year. While in Italy, Hawthorne, delighted to finally be in the presence of great artistic masterpieces, was at pains to introduce her husband to the glory of art. For the first time, she was able to see and study the originals of many works that she had copied and knew only from reproductions. She concluded that her own artistic skills were only mediocre, though her husband was inspired by her drawings to write *The Marble Faun.* The Hawthornes returned to America in 1860 and moved into the Wayside in Concord, Massachusetts, which they had purchased from Bronson Alcott before they left. The next four years were difficult for them. Una had been so ill in Rome that she had nearly died, and she experienced repeated relapses after returning home. The Civil War had begun, and in 1864, after a protracted period of poor health, Nathaniel died. Hawthorne was left in difficult financial straits and began a lengthy and frustrating correspondence with Nathaniel Hawthorne's publisher, James Fields, about the royalties due her from the money earned by her husband's books. Fields suggested that she could make some money by releasing his journals, and she at last agreed on the condition that she could edit them. In an effort to reduce her expenses, Hawthorne moved her family to Dresden, Germany, in 1868. While living in Dresden, she copied and edited her own journal, which was published as *Notes in England and Italy* in 1869. A year later, she and her daughters Una and Rose moved to London. Hawthorne died there of pneumonia in 1871.

MAJOR WORKS

Hawthorne was a devoted diarist and letter-writer throughout her life. Her letters from Cuba, which sometimes extend to the length of twenty pages or more, describe the country and its people as well as documenting unfolding social and political events. These letters make up *The Cuba Journal,* kept as private correspondence until they were edited and published in 1985. In addition to compelling accounts of Caribbean plantation

life, Spanish colonialism, and the vigorous mercantile and slave trades in Havana, Hawthorne's overseas correspondence contains samples of the writing that her husband undoubtedly read before they actually met, which later was used as inspiration for several of his short stories. Hawthorne's first and only publication during her lifetime, *Notes in England and Italy,* is a combination of letters she wrote in England, while her husband served as U.S. Consul to Liverpool, and extracts from journals she kept during the succeeding years when the family lived as tourists in Italy. The text offers reflections on the landscape and, especially in Italy, on renowned masterpieces of classical and Renaissance art. In the years after her husband's death, Hawthorne edited Nathaniel's notebooks for publication. These include three of Nathaniel Hawthorne's journals: *Passages from the American Notebooks* (1868), *Passages from the English Notebooks* (1870), and *Passages from the French and Italian Notebooks* (1872). In editing these works, Hawthorne made extensive alterations according to her taste and the custom of the time, freely deleting many passages, including any mention of herself or her children, and emending numerous portions of the text she thought offensive to Victorian sensibility.

CRITICAL RECEPTION

Unwilling to make her writings public, Hawthorne made only one exception, publishing her *Notes in England and Italy* in direct response to mounting financial pressures in the late 1860s. Despite the vogue for travel literature at that time, Hawthorne remained one of only very few women who published book-length travel accounts during this period. The collection was well received, and eight editions were printed within thirteen years of its first appearance. At the time of her death, a family friend, Henry Bright, wrote to Hawthorne's son Julian, "No one has yet done justice to your mother. Of course, she was overshadowed by *him,*—but she was a singularly accomplished woman, with a great gift of expression . . . she was, too, an artist of no mean quality." In the contemporary era, critics have come to recognize Hawthorne's contributions as a travel-writer and diarist. Her editorial acumen, however, remains controversial. Regarding Hawthorne's editing of her husband's journals for publication, her substantial excisions and changes have generally been viewed with contempt by twentieth-century scholars. This opinion has since been tempered as commentators have come to understand that Hawthorne's editing style was common to the era.

PRINCIPAL WORKS

Passages from the American Note-Books. 2 vols. [editor] (journal) 1868

Notes in England and Italy (journal) 1869

Passages from the English Note-books. 2 vols. [editor] (journal) 1870

Passages from the French and Italian Note-books. 2 vols. [editor] (journal) 1872

*"A Sophia Hawthorne Journal, 1843-1844" (journal) 1975

The Cuba Journal, 1833-1835 (journal) 1985

†"With Hawthorne in Wartime Concord: Sophia Hawthorne's 1862 Diary" (journal) 1988

‡"Sophia Hawthorne's Diary for 1861" (journal) 1989

Selected Literary Letters of Sophia Peabody Hawthorne, 1842-1853 (letters) 1992

§"Sophia Peabody Hawthorne's *American Notebooks*" (journal) 1996

*Published in periodical *The Nathaniel Hawthorne Journal.*

†Published in periodical *Studies in the American Renaissance.*

‡Published in periodical *Nathaniel Hawthorne Review.*

§Published in periodical *Studies in the American Renaissance.*

CRITICISM

Claire M. Badaracco (essay date spring 1981)

SOURCE: Badaracco, Claire M. "Pitfalls and Rewards of the Solo Editor: Sophia Peabody Hawthorne." *Resources for American Literary Study* 11, no. 1 (spring 1981): 91-100.

[*In the following essay, Badaracco places Hawthorne's editorship of her husband's journals in historical context and reflects on the process of editing Hawthorne's own* Cuba Journal.]

When I began to edit the *Cuba Journal* as a solo editorial project, I recall describing in blithe naivete my aspirations and goals. I told a distinguished colleague that because the collection which housed the document permitted neither microfilm nor typewriters, I was planning to transcribe in pencil the three-volume, one-thousand-page holograph during the day, type a transcript from the handwritten copy in the evenings, eventually proofread typescript against holograph, and perform the necessary tasks of annotation, apparatus, and introduction. My friend looked at me squarely enough—man to man, so to speak—and admitted sympathetically: "My dear, you will need a wife." Indeed, in a discussion of the pitfalls and rewards of the solo editor, the labor of more than a few of the wives of literary and historical men, who have delved in, proofed and indexed, done what-

ever tasks were necessary, would have to be acknowledged. For without their careful work, many editorial projects never would have been accomplished.

Sophia Peabody, who wrote the *Cuba Journal,* was the wife, sometime muse, and amanuensis of Nathaniel Hawthorne; and after his death in 1864, left with little other than her husband's papers, she was a "solo editor."[1] Though best known in this century for the omissions in her 1868 edition of Hawthorne's *Notebooks,* and as the model for Hilda in *The Marble Faun,* Sophia was a minor painter of some ability, well-educated for a female of that day, and an able writer.[2] Hawthorne called her "The Queen of Journalizers" and admired her Cuba Journal.[3] Because they shared an understanding of his literature during their twenty-two-year marriage, Sophia was possibly the best person to act as Hawthorne's editor. But as it developed, the edition was one upon which she was too heavily dependent financially, and too closely allied with emotionally.

Sophia's rationale for editing Hawthorne's Notebooks was entirely typical of the late nineteenth century's Victorian attitude toward editing, which regarded the process as a business of "cutting out" rather than one which entailed search and discovery, selection and arrangement, "adding in" through annotation, and "reporting fully" the circumstances of every emendation.[4] The late-nineteenth-century editor tried to protect or "veil" the author from the rudely inquisitive reader who might "pry," in some cases extending the veil to cover editorial identity. It might be said that their scrupulous concern about authorial intention led them to edit for a posthumous audience rather than for their contemporaries, and in contrast with our own time, where editing has been described as "providing the protein in the Nation's diet for all time to come," the nineteenth-century editor was at heart retrospective.[5] During the last century, a posthumous edition was regarded as having slightly less literary merit than a biography, and as being a bit more ambitious than a memoir or an elegy. Further, editing the papers of a great public man— whether author, minister, or statesman—frequently was the occupation of widows.

When James Ticknor Fields asked Sophia to write a biography of her late husband, some ten months after his death, she said she did not feel the "call," but admitted "trembling" at the thought of entering the world again.[6] In the spring of 1865, she recorded her first reading of Hawthorne's notebooks.[7] That fall she began editing the papers out of sentiment: one day she copied three pages from an early journal of their married life, at another time twelve pages from the Brook Farm Journal, then several pages from his American Notebook, and random passages from "Footprints on the Sea Shore."[8] Deeply contented, happy for the chance to "live once again all day" with her "Gorgeous Flower of Time,"

Sophia was soon copying from nine a.m. until nine p.m., "taking time only for a walk to the post."[9]

Soon she no longer deferred to Fields's editorial judgment, and began to develop her own, particularly with regard to selection and arrangement. Without discussion, they agreed that contemporary names should be deleted.[10] Sophia began copying a steady twenty pages a day, "driven by a sort of iron necessity to keep copying," her sense of mission complete.[11]

By late November, 1865, she was working straight through until midnight, correcting the first printer's copies, returning proof with long letters of her own, sometimes several in one day. In one she listed fifteen points of editorial disagreement with Fields, including capitalization, placement of quotation marks and accuracy of word transcription, paragraph structure, reliability of dates, and the proper title for the whole edition:

> This book, dear Mr. Fields, is not truly a Diary because by no means is there a daily record. It is, as Mr. N says a *note-book*. So should not the title be "Passages from Hawthorne's Notebooks." There are such long intervals—sometimes a months intervals—that it is in no wise a diary. And it is especially desirable that all these brackets should be "expunged"—and the lines put between the sentences as I have put them, and as they are put in the MSS by Mr. Hawthorne himself—thus—For otherwise I think the breaths of all the readers would be taken away, and they would be all dead men—for brackets cause one to suspend breath, as it were, in reading, and if this suspension continue too long, mortal life ceases.[12]

Sophia began to think of her role as editor in an increasingly defensive posture when the proofreaders of Fields's publishing house began to make unauthorized changes upon the printer's copy:

> The "S" in Revelations must be retained. Why is it crossed out?

> The expression 'dreadful earnest' . . . must remain . . . unless we undertake to improve Mr. Hawthorne's english, which I think cannot well be done, for he uses words very thoughtfully and conscienciously.

> My dear Mr. Fields—That pathetic and interesting sentence "In this dismal chamber *Fame* was won"—should not be put as a part of a paragraph. It is in the manuscript quite by itself, and a page or two removed from the sentence about choosing wives. Pray have that altered. . . .[13]

Since 1829, when Sophia had been given arsenic as a part of a series of heroic cures administered by Dr. Walter Channing, her health had not been strong.[14] It was poor health which sent Sophia south to Havana in the winter of 1833. In January of 1866, again her health was a problem: she was unable to work because of a perennial winter cough, which would lead to an early death within five years.[15] Stating that she had mastered the difficult skill of "leaving myself out" of the transcription, she acknowledged several months later, "I have grown wiser and look at the manuscript from a less inward point of view," yet in the next breath she exploded: "I lost my head copying the Old Manse Journal—all the heavenly spring time of my married life comes back in these cadences—so rich and delicate—and what I cannot copy is of course sweeter than the rest."[16] The winter of 1867 brought Sophia again the expected ill health—which was expensive, she reminded Fields—as she vacillated about whether or not to publish a piece she had found about her "children's doings" called *Twenty Days*.

With the American Journal completed by the winter of 1866, there were "six and a half volumes of English notes left to copy, plus all the Italian Notebooks which had not been absorbed in *The Marble Faun*"; Sophia was on the brink of bankruptcy, lacking money for coal and food.[17] With the coming of June, Sophia worried about July's bills. She had copied over four hundred pages of the English Journals and decided against publishing the memoir titled *Twenty Days* because it was "too domestic."[18] With "no money left," she was "aghast" to learn from Fields that he was claiming she had spent the $10,000 payment for transcription and in addition owed him $700. She immediately relinquished the disputed article *Twenty Days* and put the remainder of Nathaniel's private papers in his hands, hoping the "publishment" would "bail her out."[19]

At the same time she worried about her insolvency, the inevitable sale of The Wayside and move to board at Salem, she was occupied correcting proof. Five months later, Sophia had not yet sold the family home, but walked the garden paths in bitterness, long separated from the fashionable literary circles of Fields's drawing room, recovering from another winter illness which apparently left her in partial physical paralysis and losing her hair. She longed for Europe, for "the other side of the sea," far away from "meddlesome Concord."[20]

When Sophia's $10,000 plus copyright income apparently had been used, and Fields offered her 12% royalty rather than the 15% which Hawthorne customarily received, Sophia became hysterical, offering to give Fields the Norway Spruce trees on her property if he would pay her as much money as he could for her edition. Though she relented eventually, Sophia at first refused to complete an index.[21] When the edition was finished, she sold The Wayside and moved to Dresden, then to England, where after another winter bout of influenza, she died in London in February, 1871. Coincidentally, about the same time, Fields sold a Hawthorne autograph manuscript for the benefit of the Boston Consumptives' Home. In a letter dated the same day as Sophia's death, he insisted to the seller that if the manuscript did not fetch $25, it should be returned to him.[22]

When the full text of Hawthorne's *American Notebooks* appeared, edited by Randall Stewart, some sixty years after Sophia's work had been completed, the *New York Times Book Review* managed the announcement with indignation, exulting on Christmas Day, 1932, in bold-face banner headlines, that "nice Nellieism" had been replaced at last by the "bite and tang" of Hawthorne's "elemental rusticity," and the author himself was no longer a "victim" of "too loving an editor."[23] Though the zealous quality of that well-known review was later tempered by Stewart and by Claude Simpson, evidence of the same tone persists today among scholars who continue to write in the Victorian vein about Sophia as an "emasculating" editor.[24]

Like their brethren of the previous century, the literary scholars of the "new critical" school were scrupulous about textual matters, eager to derive moral lessons from language, a bit pious about the significance of their labor, and, I submit, oblivious to the external evidence provided by history. Sophia Peabody Hawthorne's edition should be regarded in the historical light of the circumstances under which it was accomplished. Clearly, the Widow Hawthorne produced the 1868 edition out of financial necessity rather than excessive love.

Similarly, for editors to regard Sophia's editorial work other than within the framework of the history of nineteenth-century women in New England would be shortsighted.[25] Sophia belonged to that last generation of the women of pre-industrial American society who were not admitted to public schools, but who had access to the schoolrooms only in the evening or summer, when the boys were resting or playing.[26] Within that tradition, where girls were educated in front parlors, "reading" was commonly understood to mean *elocution,* "composition" was *making copies,* and "writing" was primarily an exercise in journals and copy-books. Certainly one could talk also about the rhetorical proprieties of the female dame school which were typical of the age, and in addition, about the role of journals, diaries, and letters as surrogates for women's artistic achievements in the nineteenth century as well as in our own time; but these are other subjects.

Sophia's *Cuba Journal* was written as an exercise in her continuing self-education, upon the prescription of her painting teacher, Washington Allston; her minister, Rev. William Ellery Channing; her doctor, Walter Channing; and her sister, Elizabeth Palmer Peabody.[27] She wrote self-consciously, keeping well within the proprieties of the travel letter genre, and she had Lord Chesterfield as well as Mrs. Jameson in mind as models.[28] Sometimes this had the happy effect of producing an interesting narrative, but more generally, the result was one which attempted to please several expectations of genre at once. Allston expected to read a painter's note-

book, Channing an invalid's prayerbook. Elizabeth anticipated a conversational Record such as the one she kept in 1834 for A. B. Alcott's Temple schoolroom.[29] Sophia's sense of her audience's expectations overwhelmed her at times, and she possessed virtually no authorial intention which was distinguishable from that which she perceived her audience would demand. This point is fundamental to an understanding of Sophia's 1868 edition, because her rationale there was a maturation of her earlier stance as a journalist.

When considering Sophia as an editor, it is also useful to examine the extent to which her own journals were edited and the characteristics of these changes. Although her *Cuba Journal* letters were addressed to her mother, as any good daughter's might be, they were sent to her sister Elizabeth, through her brother George, care of Searle and Upham, in Boston. When Elizabeth received the letters, she distributed some singly, some in small packets, among twenty-five eminent Bostonians, including A. B. Alcott and George Emerson.[30] During the year 1834, Elizabeth held seven-hour "reading parties" in Boston for the girls of Judge Charles Jackson and the Burroughs-Rice families, where she read aloud the first volume of Sophia's *Cuba Journal,* deleting verbally any passages which she thought might cause her sister embarrassment, such as all references to slavery and enthusiasm for Cuba.[31] After being read among the Bostonians, the letters were forwarded to Mrs. Peabody in Salem, who recopied those she sought to improve and invented letters for those which had been lost. As a result, nearly one-third of the extant first volume of Sophia's *Cuba Journal* exists only as copies in the hand of Mrs. Peabody.

Within the year after the sisters' return from Cuba in the spring of 1835, the Peabody women had handsewn and bound the fifty-seven letters plus an "Appendix" into three volumes of identical size and color, with the title "Letters from Cuba" embossed in gilt upon leather spines. When the volumes were given to Nathaniel Hawthorne in 1837 or 1838, he probably read only the second and third. They are superior to the first in narrative interest and literacy, and copies by Mrs. Peabody occur infrequently. In any case, Nathaniel Hawthorne copied sixteen passages from the second and third volumes of Sophia's *Cuba Journal* into his first American Notebook.[32] Those passages were among those which Sophia deleted from her 1868 edition of his papers.

Hawthorne would have been aware when he was given Sophia's Cuba Journal that he was not reading a private diary or notebook such as his own. (Indeed, a comparison of the journal style of Sophia and Nathaniel during the 1830s is startling and instructive—and also another subject.) When Hawthorne read the *Cuba Journal,* he read a homemade book, a family's edition of the letters of a young woman who had not sullied herself with authorial ambition, but who was, nonetheless, intensely literate. He would have known or guessed, one would like to conjecture, how lovingly the Peabody women had selected and arranged the contents, how carefully considered had been the copies, how proud the entire family was of Sophia's illustrations and of the entire three-volume production.[33]

In January of 1976, when I began editing the *Cuba Journal,* and my distinguished colleague said that I would need a wife, I regarded my situation historically. The proposed work was to be an edition of an edition, written by a woman best known as Hawthorne's editor, who had been taken to task severely by early twentieth-century editors for having censored the "best parts" of Hawthorne's papers. Yet it was more than probable that the most interesting part of the document called the *Cuba Journal* had been destroyed in the process of having been edited by Sophia's family.

While I knew I was not without company in my solo endeavor, and was merely one more hand in a long history of those who had read and copied and edited the document, still this remained: one hundred and fifty years after the fact, the document was inaccessible to most readers. What was available in print were several dubious critical commentaries by Hawthorne scholars and two sentimental biographical accounts.[34] The document had suffered by being read only in its narrowest literary context: in the shadow of Hawthorne's "manly" production, Sophia's seemed "thin and melodic."[35] Despite the valid claims for the literary interest of the *Cuba Journal,* traditionally the document had been read with more attention to internal, textual criteria than regard for external evidence.

Like Sophia's 1833 Journal, consideration of her 1868 solo editorial endeavor, in its own way a period piece, profits by an examination of the external evidence. The Widow Hawthorne's edition was not only typical of the day, it might have been produced by any number of other Victorian editors. Sophia's experience as a solo editor serves well as an example of the pitfalls which any editor might encounter. Though the pitfalls of solitary editorial work might emerge from too intimate an association with one's materials, and one's effectiveness might diminish in proportion to one's reliance upon the edition for income, an editor's rationale, whatever it might become eventually, should proceed from a policy of inclusiveness rather than exclusivity. The document ought to be considered authentic, that is, worth including, until proven otherwise by evidence or circumstance. The pitfalls of any edition are determined by the kind of document one has chosen to edit. Whether or not one edits literature or history is less important, finally, than whether the document is public or private, and whether or not the author of the document led a public life.[36]

I submit that there is a kind of edition which is well suited to the solo scale: one where editors regard themselves contentedly as "mere" scribes, involved in a non-canonical, non-corporate project, dealing with anonymous documents, or with documents by authors who led non-public lives. Motivated by investigative rather than critical, interpretive or curatorial instincts, this hypothetical solo editor would perceive herself to be more archeologist than archivist and would treat the document as if it were a shard, regarding the burden of her scholarship to be reporting on the state of an artifact, rather than describing, interpretively or critically, proceedings of an artistic or evidential nature. This would dispose the editor to prefer to work from holographs, providing a close reading of the physical properties of the original in introductory materials which would precede the text.

Hypothetically, the editor would embrace the possibility that the document might be of greater interest than its author; this would place the editor in the position of the connoisseur. By that I mean the editor's rationale would be determined more by her conception of authority and authenticity than by audience. For if an audience is considered to be more fundamental than the document, or is thought to be posthumous, as it was commonly misunderstood to be in the late nineteenth century, there is the temptation to suppress or reveal or confess or, in some way, to alter the original. Yet if one edits for the future, one tends to oversay; this thrusts the editor into an ungainly defensive posture, inherently off-balance, pitting apparent necessity against the unpredictable, what might be read eventually as pedantry or bias. One edits for one's own time; that is all an editor is able to do. For this editor, albeit "solo," is in very good company, and the rewards of the unrelieved holographic association which solitary scholarship provides are very great indeed.

Notes

1. The Cuba Journal, 1833-1835, is a letter series in three-volume holograph, from the Papers of Sophia Peabody Hawthorne, Berg Collection, New York Public Library. Volume III, edited by Claire Badaracco, will be published by the Essex Institute, Salem, Massachusetts, in 1983. Correspondence pertaining to Sophia's editorial work is among her papers in the Boston Public Library, some of which have been published by Randall Stewart and Edward Wagenknecht in the *Boston Public Library Quarterly.*

2. See Sophia Peabody Hawthorne, ed., *Passages From The American Notebooks of Nathaniel Hawthorne,* 2 vols. (Boston: Ticknor & Fields, 1868); Randall Stewart, *The American Notebooks of Nathaniel Hawthorne* (New Haven: Yale University Press, 1932); Nathaniel Hawthorne, *The*

Marble Faun (Boston: Ticknor & Fields, 1860). Sophia's painting teachers were Thomas Doughty, the early leader of the Hudson River School, and Washington Allston. Her ability as a painter is displayed in her oil portrait of Allston, copied after Chester Harding, which hangs in the Massachusetts Historical Society. See also Mrs. E. F. Ellet, *Women Artists* (New York: Harper, 1859), p. 316.

3. See John D. Gordan, "Nathaniel Hawthorne, the Years of Fulfillment" (Catalogue for the Berg Collection Exhibition, New York Public Library, 1954), p. 18.

4. Lester J. Cappon, "A Rationale for Historical Editing Past and Present," *William and Mary Quarterly*, 23 (January 1966), 59-60; Lyman H. Butterfield, "Editing American Historical Documents," *Proceedings of the Massachusetts Historical Society*, 78 (1966), 94.

5. Haskell M. Monroe, Jr., "Some Thoughts for an Aspiring Historical Editor," *American Archivist*, 32 (April 1969), 159.

6. Sophia Hawthorne to James Ticknor and Annie Adams Fields, July 29, September 14, 1864. Boston Public Library.

7. Sophia Hawthorne to James T. Fields, April 18, 1865. Boston Public Library.

8. Sophia Hawthorne to James T. Fields, October 1, October 8, 1865. Boston Public Library.

9. Sophia Hawthorne to Annie Adams Fields, January 19, 1865; Sophia Hawthorne to James T. Fields, October 13, 1865. Boston Public Library.

10. Sophia Hawthorne to James T. Fields, October 12, 14, November 20, December [16], 1865. Boston Public Library.

11. Sophia Hawthorne to James T. Fields, October 20, 1865. Boston Public Library.

12. Sophia Hawthorne to James T. Fields, November 20, 1865. Boston Public Library.

13. Sophia Hawthorne to James T. Fields, November 20, 1865. Boston Public Library.

14. 1829 Diary of Sophia Peabody. Peabody Papers, Berg Collection, New York Public Library.

15. Sophia Hawthorne to Annie Adams Fields, January 4, 1866. Boston Public Library.

16. Sophia Hawthorne to James T. Fields, July 24, 1866. Boston Public Library.

17. Sophia Hawthorne to James T. Fields, February 25, March 23, March 28, 1867. Boston Public Library.

18. Sophia Hawthorne to James T. Fields, June 10, July 7, 1867; January 30, 1868. Boston Public Library.

19. Sophia Hawthorne to James T. Fields, October 8, 27, November 3, 1867; May 20, 24, 1868. Boston Public Library.

20. Sophia Hawthorne to James T. Fields, May 2, 10, 1868. Boston Public Library.

21. Sophia Hawthorne to James T. Fields, June 2, 7, 12, July 28, August 2, 1868. Boston Public Library.

22. James T. Fields to an unknown correspondent, February 27, 1871. Houghton Library, Harvard.

23. Herbert Gorman, "Hawthorne's Notebooks Are Rescued From Distortion," *New York Times Book Review*, December 25, 1932, p. 3.

24. Randall Stewart, *Regionalism and Beyond*, ed. George Core (Nashville: Vanderbilt University Press, 1968); Lyman H. Butterfield and Julian P. Boyd, "Historical Editing in the United States," *Proceedings of the Amerian Antiquarian Society*, 72 (1962), 315; Hyatt H. Waggoner, "A Hawthorne Discovery: The Lost Notebook, 1835-1841," *New England Quarterly*, 49 (December 1976), 623-25.

25. See Ann Douglas, *The Feminization of American Culture* (New York: Alfred A. Knopf, 1977).

26. Thomas Woody, *A History of Women's Education in the U.S.* (1929; rpt. New York: Octagon, 1966); Elizabeth Palmer Peabody, "Female Education in Massachusetts," *Barnard's American Journal of Education*, 30 (1880), 584.

27. While an invalid, Sophia assisted Elizabeth with her translation of *Self-Education, or the Means and Art of Moral Progress*, by M. Le Baron De Gerando (Boston: Carter & Hendee, 1830).

28. Lord Chesterfield's *Letters* to his son and Mrs. Jameson's *Diary of the Ennuyeé*.

29. Elizabeth Palmer Peabody, *Record of a School: Exemplifying the General Principles of Spiritual Culture* (Boston: J. Munroe, 1835); A. Bronson Alcott, *Conversations with Children About the Gospels* (Boston: J. Munroe, 1836-37).

30. Among the Cuba Journal readers I have identified are the families of Rev. William Ellery and Dr. Walter Channing, Martha Cochrane, Amelia and Caroline Ethridge, Sally Gardiner, Rev. F. W. P. Greenwood, Elizabeth Hibbard, the Charles Jackson family, Mrs. Lee and her six daughters, Thomas B. Park, Sophia Pickman, Mrs. Rice, Sophia Ripley, the Rodman family, and Fanny Searle.

31. Elizabeth Palmer Peabody to Mary Tyler Peabody, October 24, 31, November 21-26, 1834. Peabody Papers, Berg Collection, New York Public Library.

32. See *Hawthorne's Lost Notebook, 1835-1841,* facsim. from the Pierpont Morgan Library (University Park: Pennsylvania State University Press, 1978), pp. 62-64.

33. See Claire Badaracco, "The Night-Blooming Cereus/A Letter from the Cuba Journal 1833-35 of Sophia Peabody Hawthorne/With a Check List of Her Autograph Materials in Amerian Institutions," New York Public Library *Bulletin of Research in the Humanities,* 81 (Spring 1978), 56-73.

34. Newton Arvin, *Hawthorne* (Boston: Little, Brown, 1929); Randall Stewart, *Nathaniel Hawthorne: A Biography* (New Haven: Yale University Press, 1948); Julian Hawthorne, *Nathaniel Hawthorne and His Wife* (Boston: Little, Brown, 1950).

35. Arvin, p. 79.

36. G. Thomas Tanselle, "External Fact as An Editorial Problem," *Studies in Bibliography,* 32 (1979), 32-33.

Thomas Woodson, James A. Rubino, and Jamie Barlow Kayes (essay date 1988)

SOURCE: Woodson, Thomas, James A. Rubino, and Jamie Barlow Kayes. "With Hawthorne in Wartime Concord: Sophia Hawthorne's 1862 Diary." *Studies in the American Renaissance* (1988): 281-84.

[*In the following excerpt, Woodson, Rubino, and Kayes consider the background to Hawthorne's journal of 1862.*]

In addition to her considerable correspondence, Sophia Hawthorne left behind several notebooks, journals, and diaries—documents that will allow scholars to follow the incidents of her life in much more consistent detail than can be done for her husband's. He often tried to efface documents of a merely biographical interest, allowing survival much more frequently to notebooks that retained the value of providing brief, generalized subjects or incidents for stories than to anything that savored of the autobiographical or confessional.

During her last years she made use of the format of the Pocket Diary, apparently following Nathaniel's lead. In England in 1856 he had kept such a record, giving a brief, telegraphic report to each day usually on the day itself. Beginning at Paris in 1858, and again in Rome in 1859, he had continued the practice, recording many names and places that did not get into the very full notebooks he was also keeping in preparation for writing *The Marble Faun.* At that time Mrs. Hawthorne journalized at greater length, but less frequently. She

wrote with special detail on visits to museums and galleries. This writing eventually also found print, as *Notes on England and Italy.*

Upon their return to America in 1860 Hawthorne seems to have abandoned both the notebook and the diary as forms of expression, except for during his trip in March and April 1862 to Washington and the scenes of war in Virginia; but this document's survival is very doubtful. What is now available are a few paragraphs from a moment during his vacation in Maine that same summer, where he sketched some communal preparations for war, many hundreds of miles from the battlefields.

His wife's records were, as often before, more consistent. During a brief visit to Boston in late January 1861 she bought a diary, and set to work to keep a really daily record. This book, in which she wrote entries for slightly more than half of the days of that year, came later into the possession of her son Julian, and is preserved, with many of his papers, in the Bancroft Library of the University of California, Berkeley. For 1862 she bought a new book, and kept a more complete record of that year; there are substantial entries for 350 days. This second Civil War diary, which is here published for the first time, became the property of her daughter Rose, who used it in the closing part of her *Memories of Hawthorne,* but only in a selective and fragmentary way. In 1980 this book, along with many letters from the 1860s by Mrs. Hawthorne, and a few by her daughters, became part of the manuscript collection of the Pierpont Morgan Library, New York. It is by the kind permission of the Morgan Library, and the generous assistance of its curator of manuscripts, Herbert Cahoon, that we are able to publish the diary, and to make use of the related letters in our notes.

While it is natural that one's first curiosity about this diary should be for what it tells us about Nathaniel Hawthorne's life and writing, there is much else of interest. Hawthorne seems to have spent most of his time in his tower study at the Wayside, more or less detached from—but probably very much aware of—the many comings and goings of the rest of the household. Una, at eighteen years old, and Rose, at eleven, did not attend formal schools, but took lessons in art and music and languages with other girls of their ages, at home and in the several other intellectually alert residences of Concord. Julian was sixteen years old and trying to catch up with those boys who were like him preparing to enter Harvard in two years. He attended the famous experimental school conducted by Franklin Benjamin Sanborn in the center of the village.

Julian Hawthorne wrote an essay, "Hawthorne's Last Years," for a centenary celebration of his father's birth. "Concord," he recalled, "in those days, was after all a homely old place, and the folks were hospitable. Here were the cordial Manns and Aunt Lizzie Peabody, and Mr. Bull, the grape-grower, and the benign light of Emerson's countenance, and white-locked, orphic Mr. Alcott, blinking as though dazzled by the light of his own inspiration; and hook-nosed, bearded, stealthy Thoreau, and Ellery Channing, stalking in, downcast and elusive, but with a substantial man inside, could you but catch him; and Judge Ebenezer Rockwood Hoar, with his lovely, spiritual sister; and other kindly people." Many of these names had achieved legendary dimensions by 1904, but Julian's recollections correspond pretty closely with the data in his mother's diary. The Emerson and Hoar children have their place, along with youngsters from such other prominent Concord families as the Bartletts and the Keyeses, and the offspring of Bostonians who boarded with Sanborn, the Higginsons and Stearnses and Wards. Julian's three teenaged cousins, the sons of Mary Mann, are quite important, as is his less glamorous cousin Ellen Peabody, who had married a young man of Concord, George Phineas How, and was as much a neighbor as the widowed Mrs. Mann.

Sophia Hawthorne's relations with her sisters Mary and Elizabeth, always a source of information about her husband and children, were particularly interesting in 1862. Throughout the previous decade the abolition of slavery had been a point of frustration and contention among them, with both Elizabeth in Boston and Mary as wife of the president of Antioch College in Ohio following the struggles of Sumner and Garrison and even John Brown with devoted admiration, while the Hawthornes, indebted to the proslavery politics of Franklin Pierce for their opportunity to spend seven years in Europe, wished the American social upheaval were only an unpleasant dream. By 1860 the sisters were close together again, Mary bringing her sons to Concord immediately after her husband's death, and the Hawthornes returning to the Wayside. Elizabeth travelled considerably, but kept a residence in Boston, and came to stay at Mary's for holidays and vacations. Now the war brought them together emotionally and spiritually, since the fervor of patriotism transcended dissension over the timing and tactics of emancipation. They all welcomed—apparently including Hawthorne himself—Lincoln's Emancipation Proclamation, announced finally on New Year's Day of 1863.

For Nathaniel Hawthorne probably the most important new acquaintances of the year 1862 were Edward Dicey, the British journalist, and Rebecca Harding, the novelist from Wheeling, West Virginia. For Sophia, Ethan Allen Hitchcock, a soldier turned philosopher and Transcendental psychologist, held the same role. He, like Dicey and Harding, came to Concord during the summer, at the invitation of Mary Mann, who had first discovered his books. He came soon to feel, his diary reveals, the unique intensity of Sophia's appreciation.

The other people outside of Concord most important to her were her husband's publishers, James and Annie Fields, and William D. Ticknor. Ticknor was Hawthorne's indispensable companion for his month in the South in March and April. Mrs. Fields is certainly Sophia's most frequent correspondent, her hostess in Boston, hostess also to Una and Julian, and to Nathaniel. James T. Fields, in addition to entertaining each member of the family in the most appropriate manner, provided costumes for parties and winter clothing or spending money if needed. He also gave books. The Hawthornes were already receiving each volume as it appeared of the new Ticknor & Fields edition of the Waverley novels of Sir Walter Scott, and in both 1861 and 1862 diaries her most frequent mention of "my husband" is for reading aloud in winter evenings from these: ten titles during the first year, and five more in 1862. Judging from the books the diary records Sophia as reading, Fields provided a copy of each new publication of the firm that might interest one of the Hawthornes. This was in response to Sophia's letter to Annie of 21 January 1861 about the depression that came on Hawthorne from the lack of variety and size of his library: "He is really getting demoralized you perceive." Nathaniel read a few of the ensuing flood of books, but she read them all, and also the *Atlantic Monthly,* edited by Fields, from cover to cover.

She also followed closely in the newspapers the military progress of the war, hoping in vain, as were many Northerners, for the decisive victory that would give an early end to the conflict. The same sharp interest can be detected in her husband's writing of 1862—of course in his reports on his journey to the war zone, "Chiefly about War-Matters" and "Northern Volunteers: From a Journal"—but also in his papers on England for the *Atlantic,* and his fiction about Concord during the Revolution, "Septimius Felton" and "Septimius Norton." . . .

Patricia Dunlavy Valenti (essay date 1990)

SOURCE: Valenti, Patricia Dunlavy. "Sophia Peabody Hawthorne: A Study of Artistic Influence." *Studies in the American Renaissance* (1990): 1-21.

[*In the following essay, Valenti highlights the importance of Hawthorne's painting and appreciation of art and the influence these had on others around her, including her husband.*]

"Sophia, wife of Nathaniel Hawthorne" is the simple inscription which marks the grave of a woman remembered for her marriage to one of the foremost men in American letters. However, she deserves to be remembered among the earliest women in American painting. The flawlessness of her copies could have provided her with a comfortable living, but she aspired with the intensity and seriousness of a professional to surpass the status of an amateur or copyist to become a painter of original canvases. Her aspirations were affirmed by the leading painters of the day who became her mentors. Influenced as she was by Chester Harding, Washington Allston, and Thomas Doughty, she then exerted an influence upon her husband as his mentor in understanding the visual arts and the place they held in his fiction, a fact perhaps recognized by their son, Julian who, entitling the biography of his father *Nathaniel Hawthorne and His Wife,* wrote that "in drawing, painting, and sculpture she showed a loving talent not far removed from genius. Thus she was able to meet at all points her husband's meditative and theoretic needs with substantial and practical gratification."[1]

Born on 21 September 1809, Sophia Amelia Peabody was the third daughter of Nathaniel and Elizabeth Peabody.[2] Her older sisters were Elizabeth Palmer Peabody and Mary Tyler Peabody, who married Horace Mann; the Peabodys had three sons after Sophia's birth. Her early education, subjected to Elizabeth's enormous intellectual curiosity, was atypical of the education of females in Massachusetts in the first half of the nineteenth century and included the study of Greek, Hebrew, Latin, and French.[3]

In 1824 drawing was added to Sophia's studies, an event which coincided almost exactly with the onslaught of debilitating headaches; but it was not until the Peabody family moved to Boston that Sophia's artistic apprenticeship began in earnest.[4] The intellectual and artistic environment in Boston stimulated Sophia's mind and talents tremendously. Her notebooks for the years 1829 and 1830 reveal almost daily commentaries on her reading of classical writers and her reflections on theological matters. One of the contemporary writers whom she enjoyed was Coleridge, and his work tempted Sophia to "poetize."[5]

Soon, however, the practice of visual arts rather than the writing of poetry dominated her attention. This concentration was fostered by several male mentors whose presence cannot be overestimated for, as Linda Nochlin in her essay "Why Have There Been No Great Women Artists?" asserts, the absence of mentors had been one of the social and cultural factors which kept women from artistic achievement. The world's "great" painters, Nochlin points out, participated in the life of the academies, where, for example, the painting of nudes (an exercise forbidden to women although women were allowed to pose nude) was part of the acquisition of artistic skills. Male artists thus had an environment in which to exchange ideas; they obtained mentors, patrons, power, and self-confidence. In contrast, Nochlin remarks,

> to [this] single-mindedness and commitment . . . we might set the image of the "lady painter" established

by nineteenth-century etiquette books and reinforced by the literature of the times. It is precisely the insistence upon a modest, proficient, self-demeaning level of amateurism, the looking upon art, like needlework or crocheting, as a suitable "accomplishment" for the well-brought-up young woman, who naturally would want to direct her major attention toward the welfare of others—family and husband—that militated against any real accomplishment on the part of women.[6]

Nochlin further points out that those women artists who did not conform to this image were "all almost without exception . . . the daughters of artist fathers, or generally later, in the nineteenth and twentieth centuries, had a close personal connection with a stronger and more dominant male artistic personality."[7]

Sophia had been led to believe that her chronic, severe headaches would render her an invalid, unable to marry.[8] Therefore, she never considered painting a genteel, temporary accomplishment, but rather a potential, hopefully remunerative, profession. However, more than her presumed invalidism would have prompted Sophia to see herself as a professional painter rather than as an amateur. The attention of the most important painters of her day afforded her mentorial support and the aforementioned "close personal relationship with a stronger and more dominant male artistic personality" which could confirm her desire to become a painter of stature. Aware of Sophia's talent, these mentors appear to have sought her out and granted her special privileges not accorded all aspiring artists. This represents especially compelling evidence that Sophia should be considered among the earliest serious female painters in America because the only other recognized contemporary women painters acquired their mentors, initially at least, because they were related to them.

Anna Claypoole Peale (1791-1878) and Sarah Miriam Peale (1800-85), for example, were the daughters of James Peale and the nieces of the portrait painter Charles Willson Peale, whose encouragement and criticism particularly influenced Sarah, a noted portrait painter in Baltimore between 1825 and 1829. Jane Stuart (1812-86) was the youngest child of Gilbert Stuart. Although he refused to instruct his own children, Jane furtively observed him and when Stuart died in poverty in 1828, Jane opened her own studio in Boston to support her family. Although she began by copying her father's work, a review of the 1833 exhibit at the Academy of Fine Arts praised her in her own right as "among the best portrait painters in our city, so far as color and keeping go."[9]

While Jane Stuart and Sarah and Anna Peale were able to cultivate their talent within the domestic sphere and could initially obtain recognition because of their relatives who were established artists, Sophia's talent was recognized and fostered by those outside her family, thus suggesting the high degree of its merit in a culture where women were rarely recognized outside the domestic sphere. Indeed, the nature of Sophia's relationship towards her mentors was somewhat ambivalent. She seems to have enjoyed a comfortable, personal (at times almost flirtatious) relationship with these mentors while holding them and their work in awe. Although they cultivated her taste and technique, she had the confidence in her own opinions to differ with them on occasion. Although she was their devout pupil, they repeatedly urged her beyond copying and encouraged her to create her own canvases.

Sophia's first mentor was Francis Graeter, a German illustrator of early American children's books who was then working at Elizabeth Peabody's school. Sophia learned from him the techniques of copying.[10] Graeter also instructed Sophia in German and accompanied her to the Boston Athenlvum where they would view and evaluate paintings. They admired Salvatore Rosa's "Landscape with Cattle" and Claude Lorraine's "Seaport" while they disapproved of Allston's picture, "Mother and Child," because they thought the attitude of the child unnatural. However, their opinion differed on another of Allston's paintings. Sophia liked a painting she referred to as "The Doomed Bride," but Graeter "denounced it utterly" saying that the expression of the bride was solely for effect, and that a spectator "always ought to be able to imagine how the countenance would look afterwards." Sophia and Graeter seem to have shared many enjoyable outings at the Athenlvum, and when Graeter failed to arrive to escort her to the Athenlvum on one occasion, Sophia noted coyly in her diary that "the perfide came not."[11]

However, Sophia's more significant mentors were Chester Harding, Thomas Doughty, and Washington Allston. They formed a triumverate of influence upon her style, technique, and ability. Chester Harding, a self-taught portrait artist, was as surprised as he was gratified by the "Harding Fever" which flourished in the artistic market place in the 1830s. Thomas Doughty, like Harding, had had little formal training in painting, but his sojourn in Paris had exposed him to the French landscape painters. The early 1830s were the most prosperous of his career, and his relatively small, delicately toned landscapes, which inevitably contained woodlands and simple river scenes, were, for that brief period of time, very popular. Washington Allston was, however, the most important painter to emerge from this period in American art, for his talent was acclaimed internationally as well as at home. Coleridge called Allston "a man of . . . high and rare genius . . . whether I contemplate him in the character of a Poet, a Painter, or a Philosophical analyst"; and Coleridge's theory of the fine arts in the area of "the Graphic" was developed by "continual reference to Allston."[12] Allston's typical landscape, depicting the grandeur of nature contrasted against a dwarfed figure in the foreground, brought the English Romantic influence to the Hudson River School of painters. Furthermore, he was one of the few painters of his time who drew heavily upon literary texts for his subjects and themes.[13]

Sophia was directly influenced by each of these painters. She went to the studio of portrait-painter Chester Harding to watch him work. Harding, who painted Sophia's portrait in 1830, asked to see her paintings. She recorded his reactions thus: "Mr. Harding wanted to see my picture and politely praised it—and offered to teach me to paint heads—said I should copy his portrait of Allston which he would not suffer any body else in Boston to do. . . . He is a noble souled man—I like him exceedingly." Sophia was very impressed with Harding's rendition of Allston on canvas, with "The head erect—in the attitude of a receiver of supernatural communion with something up and beyond—the eye looking through things temporal with the piercing fire (Promethean) of inspiration."[14]

Sophia's relationship with Harding, like her relationship with Graeter, was comfortable, friendly and unintimidated. It was Sophia who suggested that Harding name his newly born son Allston, a suggestion which her mentor accepted with greater enthusiasm than did his wife. Harding visited Sophia frequently, once prompting her to call to him through her window asking "when he wanted a vision of my sweet face over his throne," and Sophia followed Harding to his studio and painted even when the July heat seemed to be "purgatory" to her; but Harding was "as agreeable as he could possibly be all the time I was doing penance."[15]

Because Sophia was sometimes confined to bed on account of her severe headaches, she could not avail herself of Thomas Doughty's advertised offers, such as the following one in the *Boston Evening Transcript,* to give classes in his studio: "The following branches will be taught, viz Landscape in Oils and Water Colors, Pencil Drawing, Drawing on stone, Flowers, Fruits, etc., etc."[16] Rather, through the maneuvering of Elizabeth, Doughty paid Sophia the enormous compliment of coming to her home to instruct, and Elizabeth recorded her sister's lessons with Doughty thus: "She would lie on the bed, and he had his easel close by. Every day, in the interval of his lessons, she would imitate on another canvas what he had done. And her copy of his landscape was even better than the original, so that when they were displayed side by side, everybody guessed her copy to be the one that Doughty painted."[17]

Sophia's brother, Wellington, had originally introduced the painter as "Mr. Dowdy," a misnomer which coincided with Sophia's initial impression, for she felt that he did not look like a genius, yet presumed that he might have "times of illumination when he is in the act." Indeed, Doughty more than fulfilled Sophia's hopes. When he brought Sophia a picture of his to sketch, she recorded that her "whole internal organization underwent an agitation at the sight of him—it seemed as if he had the power of my life and death." Watching Doughty paint and copying his paintings caused Sophia to experience intense emotional and physiological reactions: "Ye Powers! how my heart beat. It seemed as if he embodied the art in some way so that I was in its immediate presence and I felt consequently awe struck. He looked very smiling and pleasant however, not in the least fearful, and painted an hour and then left me to copy. . . . The instant he departed I began my own operations and found that the portion of his art which he had left on the board possessed the same aweful power as he brought with him, and before I put my brush to the picture, I trembled from head to foot. Certainly I never felt so much about any such thing before—I did not know what to make of it. . . . I was afraid to be alone with the—what? I am sure I cannot tell."[18]

So important was copying Doughty's work and receiving his praise that Sophia was able to overcome her physical complaints when she knew that Doughty would be arriving for a lesson. Furthermore, with Doughty as her mentor, Sophia felt probably for the first time the overwhelming desire to create her own compositions. She recorded this burgeoning desire in the following journal excerpt: "the violent commotions of my heart were a little quieted by his pronouncing my work very well done, better than he expected. It was extremely interesting to see him create. It filled me with a sensation quite suffocating. What an intense feeling of delight it gives me to think that I may ever create too."[19] Yet notwithstanding the awe with which she regarded Doughty, she was able to maintain a critical view towards some of his techniques. Doughty is "rather too purple in his heavenly taste," she recorded, and when he failed to arrive at the appointed time for one of their lessons, she chastized the "scamp" who had gone for a ride with his wife instead.[20]

Sophia's relationship with Washington Allston, with whom she was acquainted through the family of the Reverend William Ellery Channing, had the most significant impact on her artistic career for a number of reasons. Allston showed great interest in Sophia's talent and lent her a copy of Flaxman's Herod and Aeschylus so that she could trace the engravings. More important must have been his statement that one could make a living through landscape painting in the United States,[21] a fact which certainly bolstered Sophia's confidence that she would be able to make a living as a professional painter. He further suggested that she go to Europe where she could devote herself to art, and he exhorted her to "copy only masterpieces,—nothing second rate," as Elizabeth put it.[22]

Copying Allston's own work was an emotionally charged experience for Sophia because it occasioned "an intense enjoyment almost intoxicating. It was an emotion altogether too intense for my physicals. A most refined torture did it work and has it worked . . . upon my head—accompanied with a deathly sickness. . . . Every faculty of my mind and every thing of which I thought was tinged with a burning splendor which was almost terrible and I did not let my imagination excurse."[23] However, the turmoil produced by copying Allston's paintings was productive even if painful for Sophia. In Dedham, Sophia copied prodigiously, and Elizabeth was able to obtain fifty dollars per canvas for her sister.[24] Her health eventually improved, her confidence flourished, and in January 1832 Sophia wrote to Elizabeth:

> What do you think I have actually begun to do? Nothing less than create and do you wonder that I lay awake all last night after sketching my first picture. I actually thought my head would have made its final explosion. When once I began to excurse, I could not stop. Three distinct landscapes came forth in full array besides that which I had arranged before I went to bed and it seemed that I should fly to be up and doing. I have always determined not to force the creative power but wait til it had mastered me and now I feel as if the time has come and such freedom and revelry does it bring![25]

In May 1832 Sophia reported that she had finished her own landscape which she brought to Boston where Allston, who then had several paintings on exhibit at the Athenlvum, came to see it. "It does you great credit," he said, "I have found no fault with it." His reaction to a copy of a French landscape was not so positive; Sophia recorded that "He thought I might find pictures enough to copy but he wished that I might copy nature." Thus Sophia continued in the most creative period of her life, and by September 1832 she recorded that she had completed in just seventy-two hours her fourth original painting.[26] Sophia's landscapes, housed at the Essex Institute, may possibly be two of these originals. These landscapes demonstrate a high degree of technical competency and are similar to the compositional elements of Doughty's work. In both of Sophia's landscapes, a figure in the foreground treads a winding path and is dwarfed by overhanging trees. The background in these landscapes is of mountains fading into the distance against a sky of muted tones.[27]

Sophia's artistic successes were mixed blessings for they coincided with severe emotional turmoil. Whether Sophia's emotional upheaval was the cause of her creativity or the result of it, painting sometimes left her with "the unalloyed agony of overstretched nerves." She recorded somewhat elliptically: "then I understood the majesty—the beauty—the sublimity with startling clearness. Visions of landscapes and scenes such as never rose upon other than mental eyes—ideal beauty—marble starting into curved lines of grace." Elsewhere she questioned, "Why am I so privileged to exercise this divinest art?" and again she recorded that she made a "desperate effort . . . to be myself in my occupation. I wonder if there are many people who live life thus as it were by drawing up buckets of life with hard labor from the well of the mind."[28]

This intensity of her artistic experiences and sensitivity regarding questions about her art may have been, in some measure, drug induced. Cantwell characterizes her responses as "the feverish intensity of a convalescent or habitual user of drugs"; she was given narcotics, first opium and then hyosycamus, which produced a twilight sleep. Undoubtedly the drugs and the head pains for which they were prescribed intensified her emotional responses to situations, both artistic and personal. However, the degree of emotion in these responses may have been attributable in part to the fact that painting was such an intensely important activity for Sophia. She wanted to be a painter of the caliber of her mentors, an aspiration which, while motivating her, caused tremendous anxiety and might have contributed a pyschogenic basis for the debilitating headaches.[29]

In 1833 Elizabeth Peabody was attempting to publish a volume of "Grecian Theology and Mythology" and had decided that Sophia should illustrate it with lithographs. Sophia had no training in this method, and her efforts to comply with commitments Elizabeth had made for her led to work which was far below Sophia's standards. The blinding headaches were accompanied again by dreadful nightmares—one was of Elizabeth dead in a coffin in the Peabodys' parlor—and culminated in Sophia's complete physical and emotional collapse. The Peabodys truly feared for Sophia's life, and decided that, accompanied by her sister Mary, she should take a trip to Cuba to restore her health. On 6 December 1833, the sisters sailed for Cuba where they spent the next two years. Dr. Channing's only advice to her upon her departure was: "Don't think!"[30]

Sophia's Cuban sojourn was just what the doctor ordered. She was removed from the pressures of Boston, her family, and the highly stressful influence of her artistic mentors. While Mary acted as governess to wealthy Cuban planters, Sophia enjoyed the leisure to ride horseback, socialize with young men at parties and balls, observe tropical flora and fauna, read, and pursue various aspects of her art in a relaxed manner. Lacking mentors or classes, Sophia developed her skill in portraiture, sculpted, reflected upon her art work, and experimented in some new forms including restoration and decorative art. Her headaches abated, and the sisters returned to Massachusetts in 1836. The entire experience was recorded and preserved through the letters Sophia and Mary sent to their family in what they called *The Cuba Journal.*

However, Sophia's return to Salem brought a return to the headaches and the copying notwithstanding the fact that Elizabeth was now able to fetch one hundred dollars per canvas for her sister. This represented a significant sum for Sophia's art, as indicated by its relative market value when compared with the prices Doughty received for his paintings. In 1837 Doughty obtained his highest prices ever for his paintings—$250.00 to $350.00. However, during his most productive and lucrative period, 1832-37, his canvases sold for as little as thirty dollars.[31]

On 16 November 1837, perhaps the most decisive event in Sophia's life occured, even though it took place while she was bedridden with a severe headache. The Peabodys had moved to Boston, and Elizabeth arranged for her sisters to meet their new neighbor, Nathaniel Hawthorne. In lieu of meeting Nathaniel in person on this occasion, Sophia sent him two artistic emissaries: a copy of Flaxman's Greek poets from which she had been copying drawings and her "Cuba Journal."[32]

Nathaniel probably recognized a kindred spirit through certain aspects of Sophia's depiction of her Cuban experiences. In one of her accounts she described an attempted portrait of a host, Don Fernando, which she recorded in her journal thus: "It was the most beautiful, soul-beaming face I have ever produced, but a touch of the pencil is omnipotent and a false one banished the living soul from the features and changed a high noble look into an expression of utter stupidity and ordinariness."[33] These comments, like those cited earlier about Harding's portrait of Allston, indicate Sophia's belief that a painting, specifically a portrait, had almost magical properties and could convey something beyond that which was strictly pictorial. Perhaps in Sophia's sketch of Don Fernando "her mistake was the reality," demonstrating the artist's uncanny ability to depict "truth" even unwittingly.[34] Whatever the relationship between Don Fernando's "real" character and Sophia's depiction of him, Hawthorne undoubtedly realized that this incident bore an uncanny similarity to the experience of the painter in "The Prophetic Pictures" which he composed some time before meeting her and had published in 1837.

Hawthorne also read Sophia's record of her attempts to restore a painting which had been obscured by age. Sophia had dipped her fingers in some aromatic oils and "touched the corners of the picture. A gorgeous crimson tint was revealed, [as was] the golden glory of the floating hair, the majesty of contrition in the upraised brow and lustrous eye."[35] This incident gave Hawthorne his inspiration for "Edward Randolph's Portrait," which he published in 1838.[36] Perhaps Hawthorne was describing Sophia when he wrote of Alice Vane, the heroine of "Edward Randolph's Portrait," that she was "a pale, ethereal creature, who, though a native of New

England, had been educated abroad, and seemed not merely a stranger from another clime, but almost a being from another world. . . . It was said that the early productions of her own pencil exhibited no inferior genius, though, perhaps, the rude atmosphere of New England had cramped her hand, and dimmed the glowing colors of her fancy."[37]

While "Edward Randolph's Portrait" was the first of Hawthorne's fictional works directly influenced by Sophia, her influence upon Hawthorne's understanding of the visual arts was far more profound and pervasive than the obvious supplying of prototypes for plot and character. Sophia was for Hawthorne a congenial spirit with whom he could discuss literature, painting, and the relationship between the two. Indeed, Sophia functioned as Hawthorne's mentor, helping him to verbalize his inchoate ideas about pictorial expression, for nothing recorded about Hawthorne's life prior to his relationship with Sophia indicates that he had any exposure to the visual arts. His course of study at Bowdoin had neglected history, modern languages, and literature, as well as anything related to the pictorial arts such as art history or painting, emphasizing instead the classics, philosophy, and mathematics.[38] Hawthorne does not seem to have compensated for this omission in his education by attending the annual art exhibits at the Boston Athenlvum since no mention of these exhibits is made in his early journals. Sophia, however, seems to have whetted Nathaniel's interest in attending the exhibits for on 23 June 1839, Elizabeth wrote to Sophia that Hawthorne went to Allston's exhibit at the Athenlvum "and was eager to know what [Sophia was] going to paint."[39]

Sophia and Nathaniel came to regard each other as predestined soul-mates. Although her letters to him during their courtship were destroyed, Nathaniel's letters to Sophia record an intense relationship which grew on physical, spiritual, intellectual, and artistic levels. Because Sophia's recovery from illness was the prerequisite for their marriage, Hawthorne responded in distress when Sophia wrote that the price of her art was sometimes her good health; but notwithstanding the fact that Sophia continued to paint, her health did improve during their courtship. Envisioning their future as one in which they each would pursue their respective arts, Hawthorne wrote her: "Oh, beloved, if we but had a cottage, somewhere . . . and have a place to Bᴇ in. . . . And you should draw and paint, and sculpture, and make music, and poetry too, and your husband would admire and criticize; and I, being pervaded with your spirit, would write beautifully, and make myself famous for your sake."[40]

Hawthorne sought out Sophia's opinion of his work, and their discussion of those stories which contain specifically pictorial elements illuminates the visual nature of Hawthorne's imagination. For example, he wrote to Sophia commenting on her evaluation of two of his stories, "Monsieur du Mirroir" and "The Man of Adamant," and lamenting that he had "failed in giving shape and substance to the vision which I saw."[41] "The Man of Adamant" foreshadows the particular use of sculpture which Hawthorne developed more extensively in *The Marble Faun,* his last completed work of fiction. There, the works of the sculptor Kenyon are used to reflect Hawthorne's notion that statues appear to possess an ability to preserve a person from the ravages of time and decay. However, this is an idea Hawthorne had discussed explicitly with Sophia many years before he wrote *The Marble Faun.* In writing about a clay bas-relief of Charles Chauncey Emerson which she had completed, he said, "thou hast achieved mighty things. Thou hast called up a face which was hidden in the grave—hast re-created it, after it was resolved to dust—and so hast snatched from Death his victory."[42]

Nathaniel also felt that he and Sophia would create joint productions which would blend her visual and his verbal talents: "I never owned a picture in my life," he wrote to her, "yet pictures have always been among the earthly possessions (and they are spiritual possessions too) which I have most coveted. . . . When we live together in our own home, belovedest, we will paint pictures together—that is our minds and hearts shall unite to form the conception, to which your hand shall give the material existence. I have often felt that I could be a painter, only I am sure that I could never handle a brush;—now my Dove will show me the images of my inward eye, beautified and etherealized by the mixture of her own spirit."[43]

Their first collaboration occured within a year after Nathaniel and Sophia met. A wealthy Salem resident and friend of Sophia's, Miss Susan Burley, financed a special, limited printing of "The Gentle Boy," Nathaniel's short story which had originally been published anonymously in *The Token* in 1832. Miss Burley evidently wished to provide a vehicle for publishing Sophia's drawings, but the illustration did not please Sophia entirely for the engraver "changed the position of the eyes of Ilbrahim, darkened the brows, [and] turned the corners of the mouth downward instead of the original curve." This must have been a disappointment for Sophia, who wrote enigmatically to Elizabeth: "So much for the Word uttering itself through my fingers in the face of Ilbrahim."[44] Sophia was apt almost to deify Nathaniel in her letters, referring to him as Apollo, for example. Thus the "Word" may have been her synonym for Nathaniel. However, the sentence also suggests her real attempts to render the verbal in a visual medium, a notion which is echoed by Nathaniel's dedication of this special edition of "The Gentle Boy" to

"Miss Sophia Amelia Peabody, This Little Tale, To which Her Kindred Art has Given Value, is respectfully inscribed." Hawthorne continues along this vein in the preface:

> No testimony in regard to the effect of this story, has afforded the Author so much pleasure as that which brings out this present edition. However feeble the creative power which produced Ilbrahim, it has wrought an influence upon another mind, and thus given to imaginative life a creation of deep and pure beauty. The original sketch of the Puritan and the Gentle Boy, an engraving from which now accompanied the Tale, has received what the artist may well deem her most attainable recompense—a warm recommendation of the first painter in America. If, after so high a meed, the Author might add his own humbler praise, he would say that whatever of beauty and pathos he had conceived but could not follow forth in language, has been caught and embodied in the few simple lines of this sketch.[45]

Undoubtedly the "first painter in America" refers to Washington Allston, whose enthusiastic review in 19 January 1839 *Christian Register and Boston Observer* encouraged "the young artist . . . to go on in the beautiful work and put into 'simple severe lines' more of Mr. Hawthorne's exquisite fancies."[46]

Another example of Sophia's illustration of Nathaniel's work is housed in the Pierpont Morgan Library and is identified by a note in Rose Hawthorne Lathrop's hand: "Said by Aunt Lizzie P[almer] P[eabody] to be drawn by Mamma as illustration for Papa's story." This pencil-sketch portrait of Judge Pyncheon, bearing the inscription "The Portrait, House of Seven Gables, page 39," renders perfectly the verbal description of Judge Pyncheon found on that page of the first edition of the novel.

Not only did Nathaniel have Sophia illustrate specific works, but he also composed verbal descriptions of himself and his surroundings which he hoped she would translate into pictures:

> I wish you would make a sketch of me, here in our own parlor; and it might be done without trusting entirely to imagination, as you have seen the room and the furniture—and (though it would be the least important item of the picture) you have seen myself. I am writing now at my new bureau, which stands between the windows; there are two lamps before me, which show the polished shadings of the mahogony panels to great advantage. A coal fire is burning in the grate—not a very fervid one, but flickering up fitfully, once in a while, so as to remind me that I am at my own fireside. I am sitting in the cane bottomed rocking chair . . . and another hair cloth arm-chair stands in front of the fire.[47]

In this passage Nathaniel displayed a particular sensitivity to the pictorial elements of balance and light. Seated betweeen two windows with two lamps in front

of him, he thus implied that he was the focus of the picture though he protested that he would be its least important element. He was also explicit about the type of light in the room, produced by the flickering of two lamps and the firelight.

In another letter, Nathaniel discussed the effects, both physical and psychological, of the play of lights upon a painting. Citing Sophia's paintings entitled "The Menaggio" and "The Isola," Hawthorne said: "I gaze at them in all sorts of light—daylight, twilight, and candlelight; and when the lamps are extinguished, and before getting into bed, I sit and look at the pictures in the flickering of the fire-light. They are truly an infinite enjoyment."[48]

This pair of paintings was especially important to Sophia and Nathaniel. They are landscapes of Lake Como done after the manner of Doughty and similar in compositional elements to those landscapes cited earlier in this essay. Nathaniel wrote to Sophia that he "actually trembled as [he] undid" the wrappings when he received the pictures, and he identified the figures which are depicted as Sophia and himself. "The Isola" contains a lone female figure in the foreground whose back is to the viewer; "The Menaggio" depicts two figures standing on a bridge.[49] "Yes," wrote Nathaniel, "it must be my very self; and from henceforth it must be held for an absolute and indisputable truth. It is not my picture but the very I; and as my inner self belongs to you, there is no doubt that you have caused my soul to pervade the figure. Thus we are, unchangeable. Years cannot alter us, nor our relation to each other."[50]

Like Sophia's trembling reaction to Doughty's art, "The Menaggio" and "Isola" produced a physical effect upon Nathaniel and for much the same reason. Both Sophia and Nathaniel evinced a belief in the almost magical ability of a painting to capture a person's essential character and transmit it immutably through time. This is a theme which Nathaniel sounded at various points in his literary career, most obviously in "The Prophetic Pictures," "Edward Randolph's Portrait," *The House of the Seven Gables,* and *The Marble Faun,* but nowhere had he stated these ideas more explicitly than in his correspondence with Sophia. In a letter to Sophia dated 11 December 1839, he reflected upon daguerreotype, an invention which had only that year been announced in America.[51] "I wish there were something in the intellectual world analogous to Daguerreotype (is that the name of it?) in the visible—something which should print off our deepest, and subtlest, and delicatest thoughts and feelings as minutely and accurately as the above mentioned instrument paints the various aspects of Nature."[52]

Perhaps the painting that Sophia produced which "printed off" the young couple's "deepest" and "delicatest" thoughts most significantly was completed early in their marriage, just two months before the birth of their first child.[53] Sophia began copying a painting of a bas-relief of Endymion with the intention of selling it, hopefully to someone she knew so that one day she might buy it back. The price would be one hundred dollars; "if it be worth one cent, it is worth that," Sophia wrote her mother. But as Sophia worked, she felt that the painting had "come out of my soul. What a record it is of these happy, hopeful days! The divine dream shining in Endymion's face, his body enhanced in sleep, his soul bathed in light, every curve flowing in consummate beauty—in some way it is my life."[54] The painting represented Sophia as the moon goddess and the sleeping Endymion as Nathaniel himself. When the picture was finished, neither Nathaniel nor Sophia could part with it. "I always go through the valley of the shadow of death in painting every picture," Sophia wrote, "and the more worth the picture has, the more dismal my journey. But at last I stand on the delectable mountains and now I seem to be there with Endymion."[55]

Unfortunately this picture cannot be found, for Rose Hawthorne has described it as "a picture in pale brown monochromes, of the most remarkable finish and beauty of draughtmanship."[56] However, the subject that Sophia chose and the identifications that she made of its figures shed enormous light upon both Nathaniel and Sophia's life and art. The theme of Keats' lengthy poem, the spiritualization of Endymion through his immersion in the physical, sexual nature of experience, suggests obvious parallels to Nathaniel's life. Indeed, this affirmation of the union of the spiritual and physical is a recognition to which he had come through his relationship to Sophia. "My breast is full of thee; thou art throbbing throughout all my veins," he wrote her; "Never, it seems to me, did I know what love was, before. . . . But our hearts are new created for one another daily, and they enter upon existence with such up-springing rapture as if nothing ever existed before—as if, at this very *now,* the physical and spiritual world were but first discovered, and by ourselves only."[57]

Indeed, Sophia's influence upon Nathaniel's understanding and use of the visual arts is a rich, subtle, and pervasive one. At the most obvious level she seemed to have provided him with prototypes for plot and character in his fiction. Yet even this facet of her artistic influence is subtle and complex. In *The Marble Faun,* for example, the reader will observe, as was noted above, Nathaniel's use of sculpture in a manner similar to that which he had discussed with Sophia years earlier. Critics of *The Marble Faun* have consistently remarked that Hilda, the gentle, virginal copyist of that work, resembles Sophia. The assumption has then been made that Miriam, the mysterious, sensuous, original artist, represents a kind of woman that Hawthorne would not affirm, notwithstanding the fact readers generally find her the more attractive of the two women. Knowing,

however, that Nathaniel encouraged all aspects of Sophia's art, not just her copying, and that their relationship had a clearly sensual element, as is evinced through many of his letters and her treatment of Endymion, one can see aspects of Sophia in Miriam as well as in Hilda.

Sophia also provided for her husband a sympathetic critic of his works, one with whom he shared formerly inchoate notions of pictorial representation and its function in fiction. Nathaniel responded to Sophia's art as she did to the art of Doughty and Allston, with awe and reverence which produced physical agitation. Both Sophia and Nathaniel regarded pictures as an almost magical, definitely spiritual, artistic medium which could capture ineluctable qualities of a subject's psyche that eluded verbalization. Similarly, sculpture was for both Sophia and Nathaniel a means of defying time.

Although Nathaniel's literary career, specifically in his use of the visual arts, flourished in his relationship with Sophia, her marriage to Nathaniel coincided with a shift in her artistic career. She virtually abandoned oil painting after Una's birth, but she demonstrated her flexibility as an artist by making inlaid hand fire-screens and painted lampshades for five dollars each. Her family benefited from Sophia's industry, for the Hawthornes were never financially secure, and this was never truer than upon Nathaniel's loss of his position at the Custom House. The $150.00 that Sophia had saved from the sale of her decorative arts kept the family afloat while Hawthorne wrote *The Scarlet Letter.* Perhaps Nathaniel had some foreknowledge of his wife's economy when he wrote about his dismissal to Hillard: "The intelligence has just reached me; and Sophia has not yet heard it. She will bear it like a woman—that is to say better than a man."[58]

In the final analysis, the mentorial relationships threaded through Sophia's life reflect a network of influence among the leading figures in American arts and letters in the first half of the nineteenth century. Sophia's mentors were the foremost artists of her day, and from them, at the most obvious level, she learned to copy. Her skill in portraiture, landscape painting, and the use of literary texts as subjects for her art can be traced directly to the influence of Harding, Doughty, and Allston. She learned from their direction and incorporated their methods while she enjoyed comfortable, personal relationships with them, relationships which, perhaps, tempered the awe in which she held them and their work. While she could assert opinions different from theirs in matters of taste and technique, she nonetheless reacted with extreme emotional intensity to their influence. Her Cuban sojourn seemed to have provided her with the respite necessary to coalesce her artistic strength. Unbeknownst to her, the Cuban sojourn provided a buffer between her experience with great artists as mentors and her experience as the mentor to a great artist. Heretofore she has been remembered only as the wife of Nathaniel Hawthorne; clearly she deserves to be remembered as one of the earliest female painters in America and as one who influenced, as well as was influenced by, the great artists of her era.

Notes

1. Julian Hawthorne, *Hawthorne and His Wife: A Biography,* 2 vols. (Boston: Houghton, Mifflin, 1884), 1:41-44. Josephine Withers includes Sophia Hawthorne in her study of nineteenth-century American women artists, "Artistic Women and Women Artists," *Art Journal,* 35 (Summer 1976): 331-34. Although Withers believes that Sophia's "ambitions and accomplishments lay somewhere between the amateur and the professional," Withers acknowledges that Sophia's marriage to Nathaniel and "her interest in art had a profound, if indirect, effect on their lives" (331).

2. Julian Hawthorne, in *Hawthorne and His Wife* (1:46), gives his mother's date of birth as 21 September 1811; Louisa Hall Tharp, *The Peabody Sisters of Salem* (Boston: Little, Brown, 1950), pp. 17, 342, cites the Salem records of the date of Sophia's birth, given two years earlier.

3. Tharp, *Peabody Sisters,* pp. 37-38. Joan Maloney's essay, "Mary Toppan Pickman: The Education of A Salem Gentlewoman, 1820-1850," *Essex Institute Historical Collections,* 123 (January 1987): 1-28, demonstrates that while the education of most women during that period emphasized the acquisition of "ornamental accomplishments," a classical education was possible for Salem's young ladies in "at least one segment of society" (28).

4. Tharp, *Peabody Sisters,* pp. 37-38.

5. Unpublished manuscript journal, 16 and 20 July 1830, NN-B. All citations to Sophia Peabody's unpublished manuscript journals or diaries are from NN-B and will be documented as fully as possible. Some documentation is partial where entries are not fully dated or lack page numbers. The fruits of the desire to "poetize" are very probably Sophia's Continuation to "Christabel" published in an essay by Patricia Valenti in the *Nathaniel Hawthorne Review,* 13, no. 1 (Spring 1987): 14-15.

6. Linda Nochlin, "Why Have There Been No Great Women Artists?" in *Art and Sexual Politics,* ed. Thomas Hess and Elizabeth Baker (New York: Collier, 1973), p. 27. Withers in "Artistic Women" also discusses the conventional nineteenth-century expectation that artistic "accomplishments were intended to be distracting, not engrossing; a diversion, not a preoccupation"; however, she cites

Sophia as one of the women artists "who move around this stereotype" (331).

7. Nochlin, "No Great Women Artists," p. 30.

8. Tharp, *Peabody Sisters,* p. 46.

9. Ann Sutherland Harris and Linda Nochlin, *Women Artists: 1550-1950* (New York: Alfred A Khopf, 1976), pp. 220-21; Elsa Honig Fine, *Women and Art: A History of Women Painters and Sculptors from the Renaissance to the Twentieth Century* (Montclair, N.J.: Allanheld & Schram LVPrior, 1976), pp. 100-104. Fine cites another exception to the rule of the mentorial relative in the case of Sarah Gooderidge (1788-1853). Known as "Goode," she painted Gilbert Stuart who sat for her to have "his effigy made" although he allowed no one else that honor (pp. 99-100).

10. Tharp, *Peabody Sisters,* p. 46.

11. Unpublished manuscript journal, 11 [n.m.] 1832 and 9 [n.m.] 1830, NN-B. Robert F. Perkins, Jr., and William J. Gavin III, in their edition of *The Boston Athen\vum Art Exhibition Index: 1827-1874* (Boston: The Library of the Boston Athen\vum, 1980), confirm that Allston's "Mother and Child," Rosa's "Landscape with Cattle," and Lorraine's "Seaport" were exhibited at the Athen\vum in 1830 (pp. 11, 35, 119). It is more difficult to identify the painting Sophia called "The Doomed Bride" because no such painting by Allston was exhibited at the Athen\vum that year, nor—more puzzling still—do William H. Gerdts and Theodore E. Stebbins, Jr., in *A Man of Genius: The Art of Washington Allston, 1779-1843* (Boston: The Museum of Fine Arts, 1979), cite any of Allston's paintings by that title.

12. Samuel Taylor Coleridge, *Biographia Literaria,* ed. J. Shawcross, 2 vols. (Oxford: Oxford University Press, 1967), 1:304.

13. Gerdts and Stebbins, in *A Man of Genius,* provide the most useful reference on Washington Allston. Similar references for Harding and Doughty, respectively, are Leah Lipton, *A Truthful Likeness: Chester Harding and His Portraits* (Washington: The National Portrait Gallery, Smithsonian Institution, 1985), and Frank H. Goodyear, Jr., *Thomas Doughty 1793-1856, An American Pioneer in Landscape Painting: A Selection and Catalogue* (Philadelphia: Pennsylvania Academy of the Fine Arts, 1973). Also very helpful is Howard N. Doughty's unpublished manuscript, "A Biographical Sketch of Thomas Doughty" (New-York Historical Society, 1941).

14. Unpublished manuscript journal, 12 July 1830 and 14 July 1830, pp. 188, 191-92, NN-B. Lipton

points out that Sophia's copy of Harding's 1830 portrait of Allston is housed at MHi. This portrait is reproduced by Lipton in *A Truthful Likeness* (p. 98), as is Harding's portrait of Sophia herself (p. 95).

15. Unpublished manuscript journal, 22 July 1830, pp. 202-203; 18 July 1830, p. 195; 14 July 1830, pp. 191-92, NN-B.

16. Quoted in Goodyear, *An American Pioneer,* p. 17.

17. Quoted in Julian Hawthorne, *Hawthorne and His Wife,* 1:64-65.

18. Unpublished manuscript journal, [n.d.] [n.m.] 1830; [n.d.] [n.m.] 1830, pp. 123-24, NN-B.

19. Unpublished manuscript journal, 15 [n.m.] [n.y.], p. 134; 12 [n.m.] 1830, NN-B.

20. Unpublished manuscript journal, 5 and 6 June 1830, pp. 157, 161, NN-B.

21. Elizabeth Palmer Peabody to Sophia Peabody, 1835 and 1838, NN-B.

22. Julian Hawthorne, *Hawthorne and His Wife,* 1:65-66.

23. Unpublished manuscript journal, 10 January 1832, NN-B.

24. Tharp, *Peabody Sisters,* p. 54.

25. Quoted in Tharp, *Peabody Sisters,* p. 55.

26. Quoted in Tharp, *Peabody Sisters,* pp. 57, 59.

27. Tharp has pointed out that Sophia was careful to give credit to the original if one of her paintings was a copy, and thus concludes that paintings without such citations are probably originals. Tharp says because these paintings are not identical to those of Doughty or Rosa, whose manner they appear to imitate, they are probably original canvases (*Peabody Sisters,* p. 346). However, because much of Doughty's work has been lost, it is impossible to accept Tharp's reasoning that one of Sophia's paintings is an original simply because Doughty's extant work does not contain an exact duplicate. Perkins points out that Sophia's Landscape was exhibited at Boston Athenlvum in 1834 (*Exhibition Index,* p. 108).

28. Unpublished manuscript journal, 10 January 1832, 20 January 1830, 15 February 1832, NN-B.

29. Robert Cantwell, *Nathaniel Hawthorne: The American Years* (New York: Rinehart, 1948), p. 244. Sophia's maladies initially suggest those of nineteenth-century American gentlewomen which B. Ehrenreich and D. English discuss in *Complaints and Disorders: The Sexual Politics of Sickness* (Old Westbury, N.Y.: Feminist Press, 1973). These authors surmise that fainting, headaches, and the need for bed-rest were probably the only acceptable way such women could escape the stresses of socially imposed domestic roles. However, the pattern of Sophia's condition defies facile identification with this historical generalization. First of all, her symptoms exceeded the socially acceptable limits of genteel invalidism. Furthermore, her illness did not provide her with escape from a circumscribed domestic role, for that role had never been presumed for her, nor did she assume that role for herself. Her family believed that her art must be her means of self-support because her illness would render her unfit for marriage and childbearing; nonetheless, Sophia's illness sometimes interferred with her pursuit of what she wanted most—to be a painter of original canvases.

30. Tharp, *Peabody Sisters,* p. 70; quoted in Cantwell, *Hawthorne,* p. 240.

31. Tharp, *Peabody Sisters,* p. 107; Howard N. Doughty, *A Biographical Sketch,* pp. 32, 56, 62.

32. Tharp, *Peabody Sisters,* pp. 115-16.

33. Quoted in Cantwell, *Hawthorne,* p. 253.

34. In *Hawthorne,* Cantwell develops this notion at some length through a discussion of the corruption of the Cuban social system in which Sophia was participating though without, perhaps, understanding on a conscious level its ramifications (pp. 253-54).

35. Quoted in Tharp, *Peabody Sisters,* pp. 97-98.

36. Sophia Peabody to Elizabeth Palmer Peabody, J. Hawthorne, *Hawthorne and His Wife,* 1:185.

37. "Edward Randolph's Portrait," *The Centenary Edition of the Works of Nathaniel Hawthorne,* ed. William L. Charvat et al., 20 vols. to date (Columbus: Ohio State University Press, 1962-), vol. 9, *Twice-Told Tales* (1974), p. 259.

38. Randall Stewart, *Hawthorne: A Biography* (New Haven: Yale University Press, 1948), pp. 16-17.

39. Rose Hawthorne Lathrop, *Memories of Hawthorne* (Boston: Houghton, Mifflin, 1897), p. 28. Norman Holmes Pearson, introduction to Hawthorne's French and Italian notebooks (Ph.D. dissertation, Yale University, 1941), 1:xii, is one of the few critics who has recognized Sophia's influence, concluding that were it possible to trace with precision the source of Hawthorne's artistic development "the field would doubtless lie in the particular interest in art on the part of his wife."

40. *Centenary Edition,* vol. 15 *The Letters, 1813-1843,* ed. Thomas Woodson, L. Neal Smith, and Norman Holmes Pearson (1984), p. 339.

41. *Letters,* pp. 572-73.

42. *Letters,* p. 442.

43. *Letters,* pp. 397-98.

44. Quoted in Lathrop, *Memories,* p. 24; Tharp, *Peabody Sisters,* p. 119. In *Hawthorne,* Cantwell describes this illustration, which was apparently drawn after the manner of Flaxman, as "a frail, haunting, shadowy drawing, characteristic of her work. Her art was distinctive, personal, . . . a century later it would have been fashionable" (p. 289).

45. Preface to *The Gentle Boy: A Thrice Told Tale* (Boston: Weeks, Jordan; New York and London: Wiley and Putnam, 1839).

46. Washington Allston, "The Gentle Boy," *Christian Register and Boston Observer,* 19 January 1839, p. 4, col. 6.

47. *Letters,* p. 362.

48. *Letters,* p. 404.

49. John Idol, "Hawthorne on Sophia's Paintings of Lake Como," *Nathaniel Hawthorne Society Newsletter,* 10, no. 2 (Fall 1984): 11.

50. *Letters,* p. 402.

51. Benjamin Lease, "Diorama and Dream: Hawthorne's Cinematic Vision," *Journal of Popular Culture,* 5 (Fall 1971): 316.

52. *Letters,* p. 384.

53. Tharp, *Peabody Sisters,* p. 161.

54. Quoted in Lathrop, *Memories,* pp. 72-73.

55. Quoted in Tharp, *Peabody Sisters,* p. 181.

56. Lathrop, *Memories,* p. 72.

57. *Letters,* p. 620.

58. *Centenary Edition,* vol. 16 *The Letters, 1843-1853* (1985), p. 620.

T. Walter Herbert (essay date 1993)

SOURCE: Herbert, T. Walter. "The Queen of All She Surveys." In *Dearest Beloved: The Hawthornes and the Making of the Middle-Class Family,* pp. 37-58. Berkeley: University of California Press, 1993.

[*In the following essay, Herbert analyzes the inner fears and sadness of Hawthorne's early life and summarizes her spiritual and social thought.*]

Sophia Hawthorne is the most vilified wife in American literary history, after having been in her own time the most admired. Elizabeth Shaw Melville has been blamed for not having measured up to Fayaway, and although Lidian Emerson was eminently presentable, like her short-lived predecessor, Ellen Louisa Tucker, neither woman is credited with having a vital relation to her husband's imagination. Thoreau, Whitman, and James did not marry, and Henry Adams's wife, Clover Hooper, is omitted—a gasping silence—from the story of his education. Sophia Hawthorne, by contrast, was hailed as indispensable to the flowering of her husband's genius, a role that Hawthorne himself fervently celebrated and impressed upon his friends and his children. "Nothing seems less likely," Julian affirmed, "than that he would have accomplished his work in literature independently of her sympathy and companionship" [Julian Hawthorne, *Nathaniel Hawthorne and His Wife,* 2 vols. Hereafter: *NHW,* 1:39].

Scholars in our own time have found Sophia a force to be reckoned with. When Randall Stewart discovered how extensively she had edited the English Notebooks, he noted "the Victorian ideal of decorum" that guided her and concluded that her interferences cannot fairly be judged against twentieth-century standards of editorial scholarship [Nathaniel Hawthorne, *The English Notebooks,* ed. Randall Stewart. New York: Russell & Russell, 1962, p. xxi]. Yet compared with Nathaniel's genius for undermining the decorums of Victorian life, Sophia's temperament seems an epitome of moralistic hypocrisy. Frederick Crews has noted the zealous minute care with which her revisions purify Hawthorne's language, observing that many of her alterations draw attention to indecent meanings that would pass unnoticed if she had not marked them. Crews condemns this as "the work of a dirty mind" [*The Sins of the Father: Hawthorne's Psychological Themes,* 1966, 12-14]. Not only is Sophia peculiarly alert to what she considers nasty, but the whole course of her censoring impulse runs counter to the openness of Hawthorne's imagination. It has become hard to understand how the man who wrote Hawthorne's works could have married Sophia at all, to say nothing of pronouncing her an indispensable source of spiritual sympathy and support.

The commonly accepted picture of Sophia conceals her playful warmth, her intellectual fervor, and the fierce independence of her spirit. Sophia was a maker of manners; and she continues to stir involuntary loathing because she remains a powerful avatar of a perishing god. (It is not hard to show disinterested curiosity in a divinity one has never worshiped, by whose adherents one has never been injured or aided.) The domestic angel had a primal religious force in the nineteenth century that she no longer enjoys, yet something of the awesome old energy still haunts us.

The growing sadness of Sophia's life, like the growing shrillness of her moralism, results in good measure from a paradox at the heart of her achievement. She pioneered a convention of womanhood that obliged her to deploy her creative powers vicariously, through Nathaniel. Among women who have sought to fulfill themselves through the achievements of a man, few have succeeded better than Sophia. She chose a man bound for greatness, in whom her own ambitions could be realized and to whom she was truly indispensable. The ironies of that triumph and its fearful price will occupy us to the end of her story; and they are already evident at the outset, where the inner meanings of her illness took form.

The "female malady" that harassed and interrupted the lives of other Victorian women became for Sophia an embracing idiom of selfhood.[1] Her primary symptom was a disabling headache typically tripped off by unexpected noises, at times so slight as the clinking of silverware. Sophia found a spiritual portent in these agonizing experiences and persistently sought their meaning.

> All day yesterday my head raged, and I sat a passive subject for the various corkscrews, borers, pincers, daggers, squibs and bombs to effect their will upon it. Always I occupy myself with trying to penetrate the mystery of pain. Sceptics surely cannot disbelieve in one thing invisible, and that is *Pain*. Towards night my head was relieved, and I seemed let down from a weary height full of points into a quiet green valley, upon velvet turf. It was as if I had fought a fight all day and got through.[2]

A mythological haziness surrounds accounts of the onset of Sophia's problem, in which one nonetheless finds clear assertions of her having been remarkably vigorous and healthy in girlhood ([*The Cuba Journal, 1833-1835,* ed. Claire Badaracco, 1981. Fascimile, Ann Arbor, Mich.: University Microfilms, 1985. Hereafter *Cuba,* xxx]; Tharp, 24). At the age of twenty-four Sophia spent a year in Cuba, hoping that relaxation and the warm climate would cure her; she wrote home that "it would be utter folly to expect a rooted pain of fifteen years or more to be expelled in 'one little month'" (*Cuba,* 25). Taken as a key to chronology, this remark would indicate that the illness began when Sophia was nine years old or younger; but we are not dealing here with chronological time. This "rooted pain" was deep in the self and thus is felt to be deep in the past. Julian traces the trouble even closer to the sources of Sophia's identity; his version of the family story blames her dentist father, who "incontinently" dosed her with allopathic drugs when she was teething (*NHW* 1:47).

Louise Tharp's *Peabody Sisters of Salem* [1988] sketches a still earlier myth of origins that suggests why it seemed plausible to blame her father's ineptitude. At the heart of Sophia's illness was an anti-patriarchal impulse that is visible in the tradition of womanly character from which she sprang.

The Peabody family was among the most distinguished in New England during Sophia's girlhood; but the Palmers—her mother's family—figured largest in the claim to high status that the women of the family asserted. Sophia's mother—Elizabeth Palmer Peabody—retained worshipful memories of a grandfather, General Palmer, who was a pre-Revolutionary aristocrat. He made his home at Friendship Hall, a splendid mansion set in the midst of extensive landholdings, where Elizabeth in childhood stretched out on the floor of the library to read Shakespeare and Spenser from leatherbound volumes.

Sophia's crisis of health at her entry into adulthood replays that of General Palmer's daughter Mary.[3] She too possessed unusual physical vigor and was a crack shot and a fearless rider. So intrepid was she, in fact, that her father consented to a test of nerve proposed by her fiancé, who crept up on her while she was reading in the garden and fired a pistol close by her head. Mary Palmer forthwith went into hysterics, broke the engagement, and secluded herself in her bedroom as a nervous invalid unable to endure sudden noises.

Alexis de Tocqueville observed that the transition from girlhood to womanhood in democratic America was a drastic change, and while he tried to put an attractive face on it, his description makes clear it was a change for the worse. "The independence of woman is irrecoverably lost in the bonds of matrimony." She leaves her father's house, an "abode of freedom and of pleasure," to live "in the home of her husband as if it were a cloister" (2:201). This typical crisis may have become more pronounced in the 1830s, when Tocqueville came to America, than it was when young Miss Palmer took to her bed fifty years earlier. Yet the plight of a strong-minded young woman facing the limitations of marriage is a time-honored theme of family relations. It is a staple of Shakespeare's plays—as with Hermia, Portia, Juliet, and Cordelia—where the father's tyrannical command brings on the conflict.

The "joke" played on General Palmer's spirited daughter was a joint enterprise, carried out together by the two men, and it seems evident that her nervous ailment was a protest against the servitude that the gunshot announced, matrimony as a state of subjection to her husband, fully authorized by her father. General Palmer, it seems, yielded to his daughter's protest: he was stricken with remorse and gave orders that members of the household observe silence within earshot of her bedroom.

The rebellious spirit that goes into such a protest strongly characterized Sophia Peabody's foremothers. Her grandmother Betsey Hunt—also brought up in luxury—secretly taught herself to read because her father forbade instruction; and she eloped with young Joseph Palmer, the general's son, who had been willing to supply her with books.

Elizabeth Palmer Peabody, Sophia's mother, inherited a full share of this womanly valor; she struggled all her life to retain some purchase on the social prominence that was jeopardized following the loss of General Palmer's fortune. Having an "earnest wish to gain for herself a decent independence," Elizabeth accepted menial employments in her early twenties, but she also published poems in vigorous heroic couplets on political topics, prominently including the rights of women [Megan Marshall, "Three Sisters Who Showed the Way." *American Heritage* 38, no. 6 (Sept.-Oct. 1987) 58-66]. For a time she set her hopes on her husband, Nathaniel Peabody, but his medical practice yielded only fitful success, and the family's circumstances did not markedly improve when he decided to try his hand as a dentist. Elizabeth developed a significant career of her own as a writer and an educator; her children grew up amid the bustle of the household schools that she established, for which she wrote class materials that were subsequently published as *Sabbath Lessons; or, an Abstract of Sacred History* and *Holiness; or, the Legend of St. George*. But this career did not bring financial security, so that her oldest daughter, Elizabeth, was encouraged to begin work as a schoolteacher at the earliest possible date, as was Mary, the next oldest.

Mrs. Peabody pursued these high-minded undertakings in a social situation that riddled them with contradictions. The vision of social eminence she derived from her memories of Friendship Hall was unrealizable in the turbulent economy of the early nineteenth century. The "unbought grace of life" that the colonial gentry transferred to America from the traditional aristocracy of Great Britain became impossible to sustain as the boom-and-bust cycles of an unregulated capitalism recurrently discomposed the status hierarchy. The New England gentry, responding to this threat by attempting to close ranks, asserted a new form of solidarity, centered on the possession and conservation of wealth as opposed to the maintenance of kin connections cutting across lines of economic difference. The separation of social groupings by levels of affluence meant that the prestige earlier attaching to names like Peabody and Palmer began to drain away [Anne Rose, *Transcendentalism as a Social Movement*, 1981, 5-12, 19-22].

For men, the freedom from mercenary struggle that earlier had marked social prominence was now replaced by the claim of having succeeded in that very struggle. Dramas of leisured cultivation were increasingly enacted by the wives of wealthy men, not by the men themselves. Instead of a manorial Friendship Hall presided over by a venerable old gentleman, the new emblems of status were the great McIntire mansions on the residential streets of Salem that were paid for by the profits of shipping ventures and managed by ladies of refinement.

Struggling to keep a school going and prodding her husband to greater efforts was unlike any such life. Because Mrs. Peabody was a married woman (unable to sign a contract, own property, or vote) there was no possibility that the life she led would one day be seen as a temporary encampment on the hard road to a splendid demesne. One of the lessons of Mrs. Peabody's adulthood was that a woman's self-reliant efforts, no matter how intelligent or vigorous, could not be rewarded with economic success.[4] Yet in her fierce commitment to education as a path to moral and cultural attainment, Mrs. Peabody explored alternative avenues to womanly triumph available in the rising middle-class order.

Sophia Peabody was proud to believe that the Peabodys were descended from Boudicca, the queen of the Britons, who led a bloody revolt against Roman overlordship (Tharp, 19). All three of Elizabeth Peabody's daughters—Elizabeth, Mary, and Sophia—were indomitable warriors; Sophia's distinctive armor was the identification of womanhood itself with an aristocratic spirituality, to be kept defiantly aloof from the squalor of mercenary preoccupations.

It seems that Mrs. Peabody assigned to Sophia the task of embodying what she herself had glimpsed in girlhood, the *otium cum dignitate* that was incompatible with the relentless striving of her adult years. On numerous occasions Mrs. Peabody declared that Sophia, because of her "delicate" nature, was unable to make a journey, or pay a visit, or take a job that Sophia herself was quite eager to accept. When Sophia was fourteen, her sisters were teaching in wealthy households in Maine, and Elizabeth wrote home in great excitement over meeting a woman who was personally acquainted with Madame de Staël. "Madame de Stael made no distinction between the sexes," she wrote to Sophia. "She treated men in the same manner as women. She knew that genius has no sex" (Tharp, 33). Mrs. Peabody would not allow Sophia to visit her sisters in Maine.

Splitting headaches are not the same thing as aristocratic leisure, and the feminine spirituality Sophia cultivated was a virtue enshrined by the rising American middle class, not by the landed gentry of the late eighteenth century; yet in Sophia's illness these divergent themes were fused, the symbolism of elite status being refashioned in a pattern that ascribed childlike innocence and purity to women while making them exemplars of unworldly cultivation. She lay abed, able to eat no foods except those of the purest white—white bread, white meat, and milk—and, like General Palmer's daughter, suffering dreadfully at the slightest noise. Yet she also deployed her extraordinary energy and ability in the study of literature, geography, science, European and American history, Latin, French (and later Greek, Hebrew, and German), and drawing.

The special treatment accorded Sophia did not set Mrs. Peabody at odds with the two older daughters, at least not overtly. Sophia's care, as well as her education and religious training, was a project in which both sisters cooperated, and in which her sister Elizabeth took a strong hand. The whole family worked together to treat Sophia as having a distinctive quality rightly demanding the utmost solicitude from those who cared about her and appreciated who she was. All her life Sophia expressed heartfelt gratitude for the selfless devotion that had been lavished on her.

The new democratic ethos offered strong incentives to women of gentry origins who carried high abilities and ambitions into the society of post-Revolutionary America. Even as the Constitution was being drafted, Abigail Adams, recognizing that the doctrine of equal rights should apply to herself, wrote the famous letter asking her husband to "remember the ladies." The grounding of human dignity in individual striving, especially where directed toward the public good, inspired women of talent and pride to dream of high achievement; and in the generation of Sophia's mother there was little contradiction between running schools and writing about education while being a wife and mother.

Trained to boldness and independence of mind, Sophia and her sisters expected to have "careers," lives of significant activity directed by their own choices.[5] Like men who are indoctrinated with this ideal, they faced the problem of making such lives their own, as distinct from obeying the precepts of their indoctrinators. How was Sophia to lead her own life, rather than live out a compensatory feature of her mother's? The Peabody sisters also faced additional dilemmas as the chasm deepened in their early years between a woman's domestic occupations and the world in which public achievement was possible. The undertakings that were united in their mother's life came under divergent pressures, so that the daughters were forced to choose: Elizabeth remained single as she pursued a public career; Sophia and Mary made marriages. But in the early nineteenth century these were not choices between clearly defined alternatives; each possibility was impregnated with the energies of its opposite. Like these rivalrous devoted sisters, the available possibilities were both united and at odds; and the tensions among them were at stake in the interior conflict that devastated and animated Sophia.

* * *

Sophia, whose interest in her inner life never waned, typically idealized her descriptions of formative experiences, celebrating the selfless maternal love that trained her in womanly spirituality. But when her own children were approaching maturity, she recalled a childhood experience that was "slightly bitter" and wrote it up for them in circumstances that indicate the attendant status anxieties.[6]

In March 1860, when the Hawthornes were preparing to return from England, the family made an expedition to Bath. On arriving at the railway station, they were directed to a hotel much finer than Sophia thought they could afford. A single night in such a place, Sophia wrote her sister, might consume a whole year's income. The family's sitting room was "hung with crimson," and the dining service featured the "finest cut crystal, and knives and forks with solid silver handles, and spoons too heavy to lift easily." Once they discovered that the expense was not prohibitive, the Hawthornes made the most of the occasion. Nathaniel and Sophia styled themselves "the Duke and Duchess of Maine" while Julian became "Lord Waldo," Una "Lady Raymond," and Rose "Lady Rose" [Ramona E. Hull, *Nathaniel Hawthorne: The English Experience 1853-1864,* 1980, 187], titles recalling the Hawthorne family legend of a vast manorial establishment near Raymond, Maine. Thus fortified with emblems of high place, Sophia drafted her story as told by "the Countess of Raymond" to "the Duchess Anna."

When Sophia was four or five years old, she was playing outdoors on a visit to her grandmother's house and picked up a fat puppy that squirmed too hard for her to manage, slipped from her grasp and dropped to the pavement with a loud squeal. Sophia's aunt rushed from the house, shook her violently by the arm, and gave her a severe scolding. The aunt was "tall, stately, and handsome," Sophia recalled, "and very terrible in her wrath. I felt like a criminal, and as it had never yet occurred to me that a grown person could do wrong, but that children only were naughty, I took the scolding, and the earthquake my aunt made of my little body, as a proper penalty for some fault which she saw, though I did not."

The victim of an injustice that she could not articulate, Sophia is sent off to her grandmother's upstairs bedroom and there, looking out the window, she beholds her nemesis:

> I saw a beggar girl, sitting on a doorstep directly opposite, and when she caught sight of me, she clenched her fist and uttered a sentence, which, though I did not in the least comprehend it, I never forgot. *"I'll maul you!"* said the beggar girl, with a scowling, spiteful face. I gazed at her in terror, feeling hardly safe, though within stone walls and half-way up to the sky, as it seemed to me. I was convinced she would have me at last, and that no power could prevent it, but I did not even appeal to my Grandmamma for aid, nor utter a word of my awful fate to anyone.

Sophia felt compelled to keep secret this terrifying image of her own fury. The beggar girl's wanton unprovoked rage is a perfect opposite to the speechless submission Sophia herself was then suffering, and a replication in small of the attack on her by her aunt. The threat of being "mauled" by the beggar girl could not be excluded by the bedroom walls, nor could Sophia's grandmother dispel it, and Sophia remained certain that this curse would pursue her until it was fulfilled.

It is possible that young Sophia associated the tyranny of her grandmother and her aunt with the minute supervisory attention lavished on her by her mother and sisters. But it is hardly likely that—in her little-girlhood—she connected the beggary of the urchin with the economic dependence of women and secretly sympathized with the beggar girl's defiant fury (and felt all the more threatened by it) because it symbolized a rebellion against the humiliating necessities that prompted her mother and sisters to treat her as they did. But we are not dealing here with a five-year-old's account. Sophia wrote this story after the years of puberty, in which the restriction of her life became fixed, and after seventeen years of marriage. An elaborate pattern of meaning had crystallized around the original incident, and Sophia describes an earlier encounter with the beggar girl that relates directly to her mother and includes broader themes of psychic and social subjugation.

Sophia reports that the advent of the beggar girl banished all thought of her aunt's anger; and as she gazed on the little hobgoblin, she realized they had met before. This had happened

> when I had escaped out of the garden-gate at home, and was taking my first independent stroll. No maid nor footman was near me on that happy day. It was glorious. My steps were winged, and there seemed more room on every side than I had heretofore supposed the world contained. The sense of freedom from all shackles was intoxicating. I had on no hat, no walking dress, no gloves. What exquisite fun! I really think every child that is born ought to have the happiness of running away once in their lives at least,—it is so perfectly delightful. I went up a street that gradually ascended, till, at the summit, I believed I stood on the top of the earth. But alas! at that acme of success my joy ended, for there I confronted suddenly this beggar-girl,—the first ragged, begrimed human being I had ever seen.

The encounter with the urchin again takes place against the background of confinement, not at the hands of her wicked aunt, but in her beloved mother's home. The hat, gloves, and outdoor dress are paraphernalia of the genteel nurture that shackled Sophia, and her escape is an exercise of inner strength, the discovery of a larger space, the prospect of climbing to the top of the world. Yet her jubilant freedom leads straight to the encounter with a much more desperate enslavement.

What happened next was a grotesque parody of her lessons in genteel propriety: "She seized my hand, and said 'Make me a curtsey!' 'No!' I replied, *'I will not!'*, the noble blood in my veins tingling with indignation. How I got away, and home again, I cannot tell; but as I did not obey the insolent command, I constantly expected revenge in some form, and yet never told mamma anything about it."

The story presents Sophia as having her choice of shackles, and choosing with great energy. Fearlessly defying the "insolent" girl, she retains the dignity of her class position as a young lady. But in fleeing home she is fleeing to a world of curtsies, not enforced with rough commands, but enforced nonetheless.

As she amalgamated the two incidents, Sophia became fascinated by the word *mauled*. "What was that? Something doubtless, unspeakably dreadful. The new, strange word cast an indefinite horror over the process to which I was to be subjected. Where could the creature have got the expression?" Not only does the beggar girl know about curtsies, but she has also acquired somewhere a relatively sophisticated vocabulary. As her years unfolded, Sophia had good reason to dread the prospect of collapsing, with all her education and sensibilities, into poverty. She knew she did not have family wealth by which to bankroll a life of genteel invalidism, and when the time came for her to scramble for her own living—by way of editing Hawthorne's notebooks after his death—she proved fit for the task. Other New England women of her class and generation did not fare so well and suffered the degradation of carrying their cultural attainments into circumstances of financial ruin and of watching their children grow up in squalor.[7]

The conventional recourse for a woman in Sophia's circumstances was to uphold the standard of womanly refinement whose imperatives were as harsh as those of the beggar girl but which served as the regalia of the emerging middle class. If a growing girl failed to attain the selfless delicacy of a "true woman," she risked falling into the working class, or beneath, where beggars and bullies lived out their desolate lives and sought occasions for taking futile vengeance on their social superiors, or on the working-class women who often served as vicarious targets. For a woman to unsex herself by asserting her aggressive impulses (to say nothing of her erotic impulses) was to invite consignment to this outer darkness, which was the sharpest social terror now assailing the old New England gentry, that of failing to negotiate the transition into the new elite and falling into laboring-class degradation.

Sophia's story is a parable of the cross-pressures inherent in the ideal of womanhood she sought to make her own. The beggar girl polices the genteel "feminine" order by reduplicating its commands with harsh clarity and by reminding the potential rebel of what lies out-side. She is thus the object of the policing action she herself executes. The story invests the beggar girl with two opposed impulses, both of structural significance to the emerging gender arrangement as Sophia came to embody it: violence exploding in opposition to the stan-dard of womanhood that was set before her as manda-tory, and violence exerted to support the same standard.

The horror Sophia felt at the prospect of being "mauled" by this figure was generated by the psychosocial contra-diction grinding away in her own personality. Her life was conditioned permanently by a psychic autoimmune reaction in which, spontaneously and with fierce dedi-cation, she sought to rid herself of the very qualities of fierce spontaneity that were built into the reaction itself. A feedback loop of inner conflict was established that could be set in motion by a slight external irritation and would then, under its own self-driven dynamic, cre-scendo to a mind-splitting roar. The experience of being ripped apart, of being made into an "earthquake," of be-ing "mauled," of being "destroyed": all these were im-posed on her by the inherent contradictions of a social situation that both cultivated and repressed the direct exercise of her native force.

* * *

Sophia managed to place her conflicts—and the illness to which they led—in the service of her own initiative, wresting a degree of mastery from the conditions of her victimization. She became a careful student of her own condition, and as one doctor after another proved un-able to "cure" her, she emerged as an authority on the treatment she required. "This morning I awoke very tired," she writes in her journal, "& as if I must take some exercise to change the nature of the fatigue—so although it snowed & Molly [her sister Mary] thought it 'absurd'—I took a drive with Mamma for half an hour & as I expected was relieved of the vital weari-ness, though I acquired physical." Noting that Mary considers her "wilfully & foolishly imprudent," Sophia insists that she is herself the only judge because the knowledge of her pain is incommunicable. "Heaven grant," she piously concludes, "that none may *through experience* understand the excruciating sensation I per-petually feel."[8]

Sophia found one avenue toward mastering her condi-tion in the conviction that it offered spiritual insight. Having disposed of Mary's claim that the sleigh ride was "absurd," Sophia turns to comment on the opinion of a physician she admired: "Dr. Shattuck was right when he so decidedly declared I never should be re-lieved 'till I heard the music of the spheres'—in other words—till I had put off corruption." Sophia here is not anticipating her own death but referring to a mystical transaction in which her miseries are sublimated in a communion with the divine. The inner conflicts that threatened her with psychic disintegration also gave her experiences of transcendent harmony.

Sophia cherished throughout her life a girlhood dream that portrayed this process, recounting it to her children and to intimate friends as an emblem of her essential spirituality. The dream—as Julian described it—was "of a dark cloud, which suddenly arose in the west and ob-scured the celestial tints of a splendid sunset. But while she was deploring this eclipse, and the cloud spread wider and gloomier, all at once it underwent a glorious transformation; for it consisted of countless myriads of birds, which by one movement turned their rainbow-colored breasts to the sun, and burst into a rejoicing chorus of heavenly song" (*NHW* 1:49).[9]

This is not a dream about a silver lining, or about the sun bursting through a cloud, but of the whole cloud in-stantly transformed into a heavenly chorus. Sophia would certainly have agreed that the process depicted here is "sublimation," inverting the post-Freudian sense of the term, in which the earthy desires sublimated are considered to be real. Sophia's inward experience at-tested a central axiom of romantic Neoplatonism, that sublimation gives access to the sublime, the movement from earthly murk into radiant spiritual truth taking place at a single step. As her son declared, the transcen-dental ontology of Sophia's dream was "among the firmest articles of her faith" (*NHW* 1:49).

Sophia's experience of redemptive communion with the divine meant that her agonizing sensitivity counted as a moral litmus, unerringly reactive to earthly evils. Since freedom from nervous headaches required "putting off corruption," she acquired a command post within the consciences of all who knew and understood her. Her sister Elizabeth remarked on the voluntary acquiescence Sophia's needs inspired. "All these years mother was her devoted nurse,—watching in the entries that no door should be hard shut, etc. . . . I had a school of 40 scholars, and she became interested in them, and they would go into her room; and the necessity of keeping still in the house so as not to disturb her, was my means of governing my school: for they all spontaneously governed themselves" [Norman Holmes Pearson, "Elizabeth Peabody on Hawthorne," *Essex Institute His-torical Collections* 94 (1958): 272-73].

Elizabeth was one of the most forceful and accom-plished American women of the century, accustomed at an early age to managing her own life and to setting plans for others to follow. After opening a school in Brookline in 1825, she became a friend and disciple of William Ellery Channing, with whose endorsement she enlarged her school and took on as partner a prominent teacher of elocution named William Russell. By 1828 the whole family had moved from Salem to Boston, and Elizabeth's long career of educational and cultural leadership in that city commenced. Elizabeth knew a struggle for dominance when she saw one, and she was frankly astonished at Sophia's successes. "I never knew any human creature who had such sovereign power over everybody—grown and child—that came into her sweet and gracious presence. Her brothers reverenced and idolized her" (Pearson, 273).

Sophia found it virtually impossible to act frankly in her own behalf because self-assertion invited a "nervous" attack. At age thirteen she discovered, for example, that she had an exceptional talent for drawing and painting, yet the first dawning of this realization brought on a bout of incapacity. "She was thrown into a sickness," her sister observed, "from which she never rose into the possibility of so much excitation again; and by a slight accident was disabled in the hand and could not draw" (Pearson, 272). When Sophia returned to drawing and painting several years later, she sought to resolve this dilemma by becoming a copyist instead of creating her own pictures.[10] She soon became so skillful that knowledgeable observers could scarcely distinguish her work from the originals, and her copies of pictures by Washington Allston, Chester Harding, and other leading painters were much in demand.

Sophia was both fascinated and repelled by Elizabeth's public enterprises. Sophia sent letters home from Cuba, which her sister circulated among friends in Boston, and before the year was out, Sophia's *Cuba Journal* had made a name for itself. Word got abroad that Sophia's "effusions" were "ravishing," so that Elizabeth was able to organize readings for invited guests that on some occasions ran as long as seven hours (*Cuba,* xxxviii). Sophia professed herself "aghast": "I do not like at all that my journal should be made such public property of—I think Betty is *VERY* naughty. . . . I assure you I am really provoked. I shall be ashamed to shew my face in the places that knew me—for it seems exactly as if I were in print—as if every body had got the key of my private cabinet & without leave of the owner—are appropriating whatever they please" (249, 470-471). Elizabeth in reply urged Sophia to publish in *The Atlantic Monthly,* which Sophia refused to do. Early in their courtship, however, she offered the journal to Nathaniel Hawthorne, who—doubtless pleased at being handed the key to her private cabinet—copied sections of it into his own notebook. From him she received a recognition suited to the sovereign aloofness she wished to maintain: he called her the "Queen of Journalizers" (xxxix, xli).

Elizabeth and Sophia present a contrast of spirits deeply alike. The pressure Elizabeth exerted against the conventions of domesticity in her public undertakings was felt by Sophia as an inner imperative, as was the pressure of those conventions themselves. Sophia's psychic

struggle was an internalized version of the conflict Elizabeth waged outwardly, so that the drama and danger of Elizabeth's public career were recapitulated as a subjective experience by her younger sister.

Sophia describes her artistic endeavors in the winter of 1832 in language that indicates the blend of overpowering excitement and overpowering dread that accompanied the effort to put her talent to work. "Yesterday I began copying Mr. Allston's picture," she begins.

> It was intense enjoyment—almost intoxicating. It was an emotion altogether too intense for my physicals. A most refined torture did it work & has it worked today upon my head—accompanied with a deathly sickness. After a ride yesterday the sickness passed away in a degree & left . . . [a] headache which seemed to exalt every faculty of my mind & everything of which I thought was tinged with a burning splendor which was almost terrible & I did not dare to let my imagination excurse.[11]

Observe the fusion of seemingly contradictory emotions. The ecstasy that she expresses in sustaining "a refined torture" is masochistic, yet at the heart of this ravishment is the purposeful exercise of her talent. To "excurse" is to play with fire, a daring and passionate adventure of the mind along the borders of insanity. "What do you think I have actually begun to do?" she writes to Elizabeth on another occasion. "Nothing less than *create* and do you wonder that I lay awake all last night after sketching my first picture. I actually thought my head would have made its final explosion. When once I began to excurse, I could not stop" (Tharp, 55).

* * *

Sophia's effort to comprehend her experience took the path marked out by her Neoplatonic faith. Instead of examining the concrete dilemmas of being a woman, and of being Sophia Peabody, she undertook a meditative exploration of transcendental realities. Here is a journal entry from her twentieth year:

> A dubious morning. I felt rather as if a tempest had passed over & crushed my powers when I awoke—for such a violent pain—while it is on me, gives me a supernatural force—combined with an excessive excitement of all my tenderest nerves, which nearly drives me mad. Yesterday whenever a door slammed or a loud voice made me start throughout in my powerless state—I could not keep the tears—burning tears from pouring over my cheeks. . . . Oh how mysterious is this unseen mighty agent. There is evident reason why a murderous instrument should cause anguish—but how is this inward-invisible agony caused? It seems as if a revelation had passed in my head & that I can no more mingle with the noisy world.[12]

Sophia sustains a supernatural revelation that would not have seized her if she were free of her malady. On the journey to Cuba, undertaken in hopes of a cure, she commented on the spiritual loss entailed by getting well: "I believe I understand in a degree the very great blessing of sickness. . . . Coming years of 'Health' never can be so dear to me as the past years of suffering—I shall go back to them as I would enter the inner chamber of the tabernacle where the throne & the ark—were filled with the presence & commands of the Invisible GOD" (*Cuba,* 250).

Sophia's pain exalts her from the earthly to the divine by making her preternaturally aware of the intricacy of her psychic and physical organization, and thus of her own miraculous character as a creation of God. If she were merely a "nervous" woman, she affirms, her mind would have collapsed under the pressure; instead, she is a visionary prophet.

> We are indeed fearfully & wonderfully made, & no one can know *how* fearfully till they are sensitive in the nicest parts of this wonderful machinery—If I had been *nervous* in the common acceptation of the term, I think I should not only have been *mad,* but afraid to move or feel. . . . In the extremity of my suffering when I was conscious of a floating off of my senses—a resolute fixing of my mind upon immutable, never changing essence . . . has enabled me to regain my balance so entirely that I feel as if I had had direct revelation to my own mind of the existence of such a Being.

> (*Cuba,* 252-253)

This interior experience opened Sophia's mind to the Godhead spiritually immanent in the creation, not merely to the rational order that natural theologians like William Paley found in it. Sophia's romantic ecstasy testified directly to the great soul pervading nature, the local syntax of her ego dissolving into the universal discourse. "When the omnipresent beauty of the universe comes & touches the cells of Memory," she wrote home from Cuba, "& has an answer from all our individual experiences of the beautiful in thought & act during the Past—& blending with the Present—in symphonious oneness—carries us on to the future by the power of that trust or faith which is nobler because more disinterested than any other attitude of the mind, connecting all. . . . There is no need of logic to convince the hearkening spirit that there is a GOD—Knowledge by intuition is the unerring truth" (*Cuba,* 585).

If Elizabeth had succeeded in publishing the *Cuba Journal* in 1833, Sophia Peabody would be numbered among the earliest public exponents of transcendentalist spirituality. Both sisters were caught up in the ferment among young Unitarian clergymen who were inspired by Wordsworth, Coleridge, and Carlyle and who published articles in the *Christian Examiner* seeking to articulate the new consciousness.

Elizabeth had taken charge of her younger sister's education when Sophia was five years old and had inculcated Unitarian convictions regarding rational virtue

and the perfectibility of human nature, scrupulously shielding her from the "terrible doctrines" of Calvinism (Pearson, 270). By the time Elizabeth moved the family to Boston in 1828, she was already attuned to the themes in William Ellery Channing's teaching that encouraged the development of transcendentalism and caused the leaders of the new movement to look on him as a spiritual father. Elizabeth is best known for the practical support she provided for transcendentalists, for her role in Alcott's Temple School, and for establishing the West Street Bookstore, where *The Dial* was published and Margaret Fuller held her conversations. But Elizabeth was intellectually active as well; she published a series of articles titled "The Spirit of the Hebrew Scriptures" in the *Christian Examiner* for 1834—grounded on her own reading of the Hebrew and of German criticism. Her ideas greatly alarmed Professor Andrews Norton of Harvard, a defender of Unitarianism against the new movement, so that he ordered the cancellation of Elizabeth's series after the third of her six articles had been published (A. Rose, 54). When Frederic Henry Hedge formed the Transcendental Club in 1836, Elizabeth Peabody (and Margaret Fuller) were invited to join (Edwin Hariland Miller, *Salem Is My Dwelling Place: A Life of Nathaniel Hawthorne,* 1991, 106).

Sophia quickly accepted the transcendentalist doctrine most alarming to orthodox Unitarians, namely that spontaneous impulses of the soul could serve as a guide to truth, replacing the cold conclusions of reason. Unitarians were especially touchy on this point because their Calvinist opponents had claimed all along that liberal worship of reason would lead in the end to wanton irrationalism, and the transcendentalists appeared to fulfill this prophecy. Because it advanced the claims of religious intuition, an 1833 article on Coleridge by Frederic Henry Hedge was seen by proponents of transcendentalism as the *"first word"* uttered in public in behalf of the new spirituality [Miller, 67].

Sophia started reading Coleridge in 1830 and attempted a conclusion to the unfinished "Christabel."[13] On the journey to Cuba three years later she was ready to articulate the relationship between Coleridge's romantic ontology and her own aesthetic raptures. "A forest always seems to me to have intelligence—a soul—The trees seem a brotherhood—Especially when they are all motionless—It must be the 'intellectual breeze' of which Coleridge speaks, that wakes that feeling within us, in the presence of nature, or 'the intense Reply of hers to our Intelligence' & we are the 'harps diversely framed'" (*Cuba,* 480).

In reply, Elizabeth sounded a note of caution that echoes the Unitarian resistance to transcendental teaching and serves as yet another reminder of the way issues of the public controversy were also fought out within the partisans. "Sentiments about Beauty," Elizabeth declared, "do not constitute Religion" (*Cuba,* xxxiii).

Early in 1835 Sophia drafted a meditation in her personal notebook concerning Coleridge and Plato, exploring the union of self-knowledge with knowledge of the transcendent: "To study our own Life is to study all Life—since in this Life of ours are emblems and representations of every form and power and spirit of life. And this is Life—to apprehend . . . the IDEAL that images itself in our Being, wherein by self study & self representation, sustained and purified by the Actual not less than by the Speculative powers, we find the Absolute, All Representing One, and finding Him we know & in Him image ourselves."[14]

The purity of soul required for such knowledge, Sophia explained, was possible only for those unsullied by traffic with this world. Far from lamenting her lengthy postponement of conventional adult responsibilities, she celebrated childlikeness. "In the heart of Infancy do I hope for that Light & Life to spring that shall regenerate the Philosophy and Life of future Time, when Literature shall flourish in the greenness of youth . . . when Language shall become the transcript and representative of the unshadowed Life of Childhood."[15]

Sophia rejected the suspicion that her childlike consciousness was merely naive and that her convulsive recoil from the "earthly" might blind her to realities that deserve to be taken seriously. "My meditations turned upon my habit of viewing things through the *'coleur de rose'* medium," she wrote, "when suddenly, like a night-blooming cereus, my mind opened, and I read in letters of paly golden green, words to this effect. The beautiful and good and true are the only real and abiding things, the only proper *use* of the soul and Nature. Evil and ugliness and falsehood are *abuses,* monstrous and transient. I do not see *what is not,* but what *is,* through the passing clouds."[16]

Sophia thus adopted an understanding of evil as nonbeing that found expression in the romantic religion diversely articulated in Massachusetts by Emerson and Mary Baker Eddy. To Sophia, as to Emerson and Eddy, the perception of evil is a defect of spiritual sight that leads people to mistake the transient clouds of earth for the eternal sunlight passing through them. But the essential quality of Sophia's mind is not in the conclusions she reached, but in the vigor with which she pursued her spiritual excitements. Well before Emerson issued to the Phi Beta Kappa society at Harvard College his dictum that "the one thing in the world, of value, is the active soul" [*Selections of Ralph Waldo Emerson,* edited by Stephen E. Whicher, 1957, 68], Sophia was living it out.

She was Woman Thinking, and she laid claim to the poetic power of vision according to which the ennobled spirit is able to refashion reality itself. Yet the plastic power of her eye and its expression in language were only subordinate modes—romantic doctrine equally affirmed—of her personal presence, which brought this creative force to bear on other souls. "Natures apparently far sturdier and ruder than hers depended upon her, almost abjectly, for support," Julian declares. "She was a blessing and an illumination wherever she went; and no one ever knew her without receiving from her far more than could be given in return. Her pure confidence created what it trusted in" (*NHW* 1:48).

* * *

Sophia's piety retained a strongly social meaning. Like those throughout New England who responded to transcendentalist doctrines, Sophia felt a desire to buttress an elite identity that was increasingly threatened in the rising commercial economy. Without inherited wealth to defend, transcendentalists asserted an aristocracy of intellect and virtue against whose lofty standards of taste and moral cultivation the rude multitude could plausibly be scorned or made targets of "improving" enterprises. In *Transcendentalism as a Social Movement* Anne Rose discusses the defensive consolidation of wealth that split the old elite class into affluent and penurious sectors, and she ably portrays the radical critique of contemporary social developments that the transcendentalists provided; but Rose does not notice the reactionary and defensive impulses arising from the transcendentalists' own elite identity, which they shared with doctrinal antagonists among the Unitarians and Calvinists, as against vulgarian Methodists, Baptists, and the Roman Catholic Irish.

Sophia was aware that the economic instability of American society was forcing a revision in the way elite status was marked. "In America," she wrote in her commonplace book, "greatness can never be predicated of a man on account of position—but only of character, because from the nature of our institutions, place changes like the figures of a kaleidoscope—and what is a man profitted because he *has been* a President—a Governor, or what not. This comes near to showing how factitious is all outward rank and show and especially American rank & show. In the old world birth, culture, permanence and habit give more prestige and Quality."[17] Sophia's yearning for the "Quality" conferred by Old World position carries over into the vocabulary she uses to describe the greatness of character that distinguishes superior persons in the New World: they are a nobility whose station is permanent because it is rooted in the eternal.

The transcendental ecstasy in which Sophia gazes out over the Cuban landscape vindicates her claim to aristocratic pre-eminence: "I felt like an eagle & like the Queen of all I surveyed." Sophia was well aware of speaking here for a community of moral sentiment. She articulates what Emerson and Thoreau were to establish as a commonplace of romantic revolt, namely that the true possession of property is enjoyed by those who respond to its inherent poetry, not those who hold the deeds to it. "We who enjoy it, not in proportion to the revenue of gold it yields to our coffers, but in the infinite proportion of unappropriating & immaterial pleasure it pours into our hearts. . . . We it is who possess the earth. It was mine that morning—I was the queen of it all" (*Cuba,* 566-567).

Sophia was painfully aware that she was not rich: her life of leisure on the Cuban coffee plantation was purchased through the efforts of her sister Mary, who worked in the household as a governess. Sophia realized that cultivated persons may be placed at the mercy of vulgar souls who have the money to hire and fire them. She writes home from Cuba sympathizing with the effort of a Mr. Gardiner to find a teaching job where his "disinterested, uncalculating, elevated soul" would be properly appreciated, and she lashes out at Salem, where the leaders of society are indifferent to Mr. Gardiner's value, because in Salem "the God Mammon decides all ranks & degrees." Sophia detested the formation of a new moneyed class from which she was excluded: "Oh mean & pitiful Aristocracy! even more despicable than the pride of noble blood & of bought titles!" (*Cuba,* 305).

Sophia thinks of herself as a queen set apart from the corrupt British aristocracy yet also distinct from the American high priesthood of Mammon. Her response to the troubles of yet another noble-souled teacher—Francis Graeter, who had been her drawing instructor—displays the humiliation and fury at stake in her claim to exalted status:

> When you speak of the treatment of our friend Mr. G by the purse-proud mean-souled aristocracy of Salem, my soul is just like a volcano spouting fire & flame. . . . I wonder when the day will come that man will consider money as nothing but a trust for the good of others—instead of making a throne of base metal to sit thereon & look down with disdain upon the far nobler, far more exalted crowd below, who have not the pitiful & dangerous advantage of dollars & cents—but nevertheless are the true & unacknowledged nobility of God's kingdom.
>
> (*Cuba,* 410)

Sophia envisions a nobility consisting of persons like herself, and she now had a system of religious ideas to account for her own experience and that of her spiritual kindred. The cruel fate of such exalted spirits is to live perforce in a materialistic self-seeking society. Their sufferings appeared to Sophia—like her own sufferings—to be evidence of exceptional stature. "I do not realize how coarse & rough the world is till I see the crushing & bruising of an exquisitely attuned nature un-

der its trampling foot." The victims of this rude world should not give way to despair, she declares, but should remember that vindication is in the hands of God.

Francis Graeter's difficulty in making a living reminds Sophia of her own brother Nathaniel, who seemed unable to find a purpose in life. The idea strikes her "with *overwhelming* force" that Nathaniel is at heart an artist:

> I thought of his contemplative, gentle, uncalculating—solitary disposition—his love of being by himself—his abhorrence of bustle & noise—his fits of abstraction—his purity and singleness of mind—his difficulty in realizing that there could be cheating & falsehood in the world, & it struck me as with a flash of lightning that a great mistake had been made, that God designed him for an artist & that we had been pushing & urging him against his organization & natural gifts.
>
> (*Cuba,* 411-412)

Sophia imagines here a fit companion for herself, and her imagination races forward to picture their working together. "Nothing must be done rashly," she tells her mother,

> but I want to fly home, put the pencil into his hand, & see what he would do at once, giving him the idea that he could do any thing. . . . How delightful to think of having a bona fide brother artist—I could colour & he, with his exquisite truth of eye, could draw & we could be all to one another that each is wanting in. He could illustrate story books—& help me draw my men and women in my landscapes—& we should be as happy as a king and queen in fairy land with creating wands in their hands.
>
> (*Cuba,* 413-414)

It had long been understood that Sophia would never marry, principally because she looked on herself—so her sister Elizabeth remarked—"as a little girl" (Pearson, 267). Sophia's disabilities rendered her incapable of keeping house with her mother, and marriage would surely entail the added burdens of rearing children. The obstacles to marriage, however, were not only practical. What mate could be found for such an extraordinary being, deep within whose character there lay a violent conflict in which "submission" embraced a vehement self-assertive ambition? Her ambition, moreover, reached out to include projects that could be paid for only by a well-to-do husband.

Sophia envied an elderly Mrs. Kirkland in Salem, doubtless one of the aristocracy of Mammon, who had taken an exciting trip to the Near East. "Shall I ever stand upon the Imperial Palace of Persepolis? Who knows but when I am dried to an atomy like Mrs. Kirkland. . . . And when I go, perhaps my husband will not be a paralytic. Oh! I forget. I never intend to have a husband. Rather, I should say, I never intend any one shall have me for a wife" (*NHW* 1:185-186). Sophia puts her finger exactly where the central problem lay, not in "having a husband" but in being "had." Subordination to the authority of a man seemed inseparable from marriage, especially if the man—unlike her father—were capable of achieving worldly success sufficient to pay for a journey to the East. In erecting a transcendental philosophy on the sublimation of her inner torment, however, Sophia had opened a way to find a suitable kindred spirit.

The tenuousness of Sophia's membership in the "nobility of the Kingdom of God" comes through clearly in the manic excitement with which she claims it. Was it a nobility only of spiritual communion, or could it be perpetuated on this earth through a noble marriage? How many young men were available who had kept themselves in childlike innocence, unspoiled by the world, and could also manage to support a wife? These were urgent issues of Sophia's experience when she discovered in 1837 that just a few streets away, in her own home town of Salem, there had lived for years in quiet seclusion a man of unearthly beauty writing great works of literature.

Toward such a figure the yearnings of Sophia's royal soul could be directed: her desire for a life of heroic sacrifice, in which her achievements would be selfless because they were the achievements of another, and her wish to exercise her spiritual influence, strengthening the divine spirit in the artist as he struggled to keep his own supernal vision undimmed by earthly distractions. Here was a relation in which the deepest submission, the most reverent obedience, could lead to a spectacular triumph.

As they were just becoming acquainted, Sophia made the following remarks: "Mr. Hawthorne said he wished he could have intercourse with some beautiful children,—beautiful little girls; he did not care for boys. What a beautiful smile he has! . . . He said he had imagined a story, of which the principal incident is my cleaning that picture of Fernandez. To be the means, in any way, of calling forth one of his divine creations, is no small happiness, is it? . . . He has a celestial expression. It is a manifestation of the divine in the human."[18]

As her wedding approached, five years later, Sophia rejoiced that her membership in the nobility of the kingdom of God would soon be sealed for all eternity, by way of marriage to the King. "I marvel how I can be so blessed among mortals—how that the very king & poet of the world should be my eternal companion henceforth. . . . Time is so swallowed up in Eternity now that I have found my being in him, that life seems all one—now & the remotest hereafter are blended together. In the presence of majestic, serene Nature we shall stand transfigured with a noble complete happiness."[19]

Notes

1. See the discussions of "neurasthenic" illness as disclosing the predicament of women in works by Elaine Showalter, Jean Strouse, Ruth Bernard Yeazell, and Kathryn Kish Sklar. . . .

2. Sophia Peabody to her sister Elizabeth Palmer Peabody, journal-letter of 24 April-1 June 1838 (Bancroft). Entry for "27th Friday Morning."

3. I am indebted to Megan Marshall for information that corrects Louise Hall Tharp. Here, for example, Tharp identifies the invalid daughter of General Palmer as Elizabeth. Although Marshall's forthcoming biography of the Peabody sisters will shed new light on their character and relationships, Tharp's interpretation of the impulses at work within the family remains plausible in general outline, in keeping with the social transformation taking place during this period. For an illuminating recent discussion see Bruce Ronda, Introduction to *Letters of Elizabeth Palmer Peabody.*

4. For a fine discussion of Mrs. Peabody's youthful struggle to express her remarkable talents see Megan Marshall, "Two Early Poems by Mrs. Elizabeth Palmer Peabody." During her adulthood as in her youth Mrs. Peabody's contemporaries noted disapprovingly her "determination to be independent and self-supporting." See Ronda, Introduction to *Letters of Elizabeth Palmer Peabody,* p. 9.

5. See Burton J. Bledstein, *The Culture of Professionalism,* on the "career" as a creation of middle-class culture.

6. Sophia Peabody Hawthorne, "Remembrance of a visit to her grandmother, written in story form" (Berg). Julian's use of the narrative confirms its autobiographical character (*Nathaniel Hawthorne and His Wife,* 1:51).

7. Lydia Sigourney offers a parable of such womanly desperation in *Letters to Mothers* (215-216): she relates the experience of a "young girl, brought up in comparative affluence," who becomes impoverished after the death of her father and perishes soon after, when ill-paid and degrading work destroys her health.

8. Sophia Peabody [Hawthorne] Journal, Boston, 1 April-8 August 1829, with entries for 1831 (Berg). Entry for 19 March 1831.

9. Sophia cites this dream at the time of her husband's death, in a letter to Annie Fields, 30 May 1864, that indicates she had told Annie about the dream earlier, when their intimate friendship was taking form. See Letters to Annie Fields, (Boston).

10. Hilda, in *The Marble Faun,* is similarly a copyist. Her divine selflessness permits her to comprehend paintings of male masters from their point of view (56-57).

11. Sophia Peabody [Hawthorne] Journal, Boston, January-18 February 1832 (Berg). Entry for 10 January.

12. Sophia Peabody [Hawthorne] Journal, Boston, 1 April-8 August 1829, with entries for 1831 (Berg). Entry for "Monday 28th."

13. See Patricia Valenti, "Sophia Peabody Hawthorne's Continuation to 'Christabel,'" 14-15.

14. Sophia Peabody [Hawthorne], Holograph Notebook, January-June 1835 (Berg).

15. Sophia Peabody [Hawthorne], Holograph Notebook, January-June 1835 (Berg).

16. Sophia Peabody to her sister Elizabeth Palmer Peabody, journal-letter of 24 April-1 June 1838 (Bancroft). "Entry for April 24th."

17. Sophia Peabody [Hawthorne] Commonplace Book, 1835 (Berg).

18. Sophia Peabody to her sister Elizabeth Palmer Peabody, 26 April-1 May 1838 (Berg).

19. Sophia Peabody to Mary W. Foote, 19 June 1842 (Berg).

Works Cited

ARCHIVAL SOURCES

Bancroft

Bancroft Library, University of California, Berkeley. Hawthorne Family Papers (72/236 z).

Hawthorne, Elizabeth Manning. Letters, manuscript copies.

[Hawthorne,] Sophia Peabody. Letter in journal form to Miss Elizabeth Peabody, April-May 1838.

Berg

New York Public Library, Astor, Lenox and Tilden Foundations. Henry W. and Albert A. Berg Collection.

Hawthorne, Elizabeth Manning. Letters.

[Hawthorne,] Sophia Peabody. Commonplace Book, 1835.

———. Letters.

———. Holograph Notebook, January-June 1835.

———. Journal, Boston, 1 April-8 August 1829, with entries for 1831; January-18 February 1832.

Hawthorne, Sophia Peabody. Journal, Rome, 14 February-15 March 1858.

———. Journals, Italy. 5 vols, 17 March-21 October 1858.

———. Letters.

———. Remembrance of a visit to her grandmother, written in story form.

Hawthorne, Una. Holograph Notebook, January-June 1835.

WORKS BY NATHANIEL HAWTHORNE

The English Notebooks. Ed. Randall Steward. New York: Russell & Russell, 1962.

The Marble Faun; or, the Romance of Monte Beni. Ed. Matthew J. Bruccoli and L. Neal Smith. Vol. 4, Centenary Edition, 1968.

OTHER SOURCES

Bledstein, Burton J. *The Culture of Professionalism: The Middle Class and the Development of Higher Education in America.* New York: Norton, 1978.

Hawthorne, Sophia Peabody. *The Cuba Journal, 1833-1835.* Ed. Claire Badaracco, 1981. Fascimile, Ann Arbor, Mich.: University Microfilms, 1985.

Marshall, Megan. "Two Early Poems by Mrs. Elizabeth Palmer Peabody." *Massachusetts Historical Society Proceedings* 100 (1988): 40-59.

Peabody, Elizabeth Palmer. *Letters of Elizabeth Palmer Peabody: American Renaissance Woman.* Ed. Bruce A. Ronda. Middletown, Conn.: Wesleyan University Press, 1984.

Pearson, Norman Holmes. "Elizabeth Peabody on Hawthorne." *Essex Institute Historical Collections* 94 (1958): 256-276.

Showalter, Elaine. *Women, Madness, and English Culture, 1830-1980.* New York: Pantheon Books, 1985.

Sigourney, Lydia H. *Letters of Mothers.* New York: Harper and Brothers, 1845.

Sklar, Kathryn Kish. *Catharine Beecher: A Study in American Domesticity.* New Haven, Conn.: Yale University Press, 1973.

Strouse, Jean. *Alice James: A Biography.* Boston: Houghton Mifflin, 1980.

Valenti, Patricia. "Sophia Peabody Hawthorne's Continuation to 'Cristabel.'" *Nathaniel Hawthorne Review* 13 (1987): 14-16.

Patricia Dunlavy Valenti (essay date 1996)

SOURCE: Valenti, Patricia Dunlavy. "Sophia Peabody Hawthorne's *American Notebooks*." *Studies in the American Renaissance* (1996): 115-28.

[*In the following excerpt, Valenti discusses Hawthorne's editing of her husband's journals, contrasting entries written by Sophia and by Nathaniel in the family note-books from which the published Hawthorne journals were derived.*]

Within months of Nathaniel Hawthorne's death, James T. Fields suggested to Sophia Hawthorne the publication of a series of extracts from her husband's journals. Sophia initially rejected this overture, but her financial situation quickly dictated that she accept the enticing offer of $100.00 per installment for the publication of "gems" from her husband's notebooks. Sophia thus began the work of selecting, editing, and copying pages from these notebooks. The first installment, an excerpt from Nathaniel's earliest journal,[1] appeared in the January 1866 issue of the *Atlantic Monthly*. Fields then suggested that Sophia further mine the journals to produce a book, and she agreed. In late 1868, Sophia's work culminated in the two volume publication of *Passages from the American Note-Books of Nathaniel Hawthorne* (*Centenary Edition, [CE]* 8:682-84, 693).

Sophia's editorial procedures were influenced by several factors. First of all, she attempted to assume her husband's wishes in editing for correctness. Therefore, she silently corrected Nathaniel's lapses in grammar and spelling. Sophia was also guided in various ways by Fields, although she developed and enforced her own judgments against his, particularly when these involved fidelity to her husband's text. Finally, she enacted conventional Victorian editing practices. She toned down Nathaniel's words and phrases that might have then seemed crude; she dressed up language that might have seemed familiar or colloquial, and she cut sections (sometimes excising sizable portions of the manuscripts) which seemed to her overly intimate or domestic. In short, to protect Nathaniel from embarrassment before public exposure, she excised and emended his text as any late-nineteenth-century editor might have.

But it was Sophia's own revulsion from public exposure combined with her self-deprecation as a writer that prompted a major editorial decision: she deleted entirely those portions of the notebooks which she had written. Beginning within days of their marriage, Sophia and Nathaniel had kept a common journal in two separate notebooks sold in 1909 by Stephen H. Wakeman, a wealthy collector, to the Pierpont Morgan Library, where the notebooks are housed today. The first, designated MA580, contains entries dating through the fall of 1843. The second, designated MA569, commences with entries following Una's birth and continues through 1852, with several entries in Una's hand and one interpolated entry (Sophia's transcription of a verse-like composition by Julian), dated 1854. The Centenary Edition perpetuates Sophia's deletions by publishing only Nathaniel's portions of MA580 as section vi and his portions of MA569 as section vii of volume eight,

The American Notebooks. This "considerable fraction," as it is referred to in the Centenary Edition (8:687), deserves greater attention than endnotes and notes on textual variants acknowledging Sophia's extant 30,000 words. Her contribution is essential to our understanding of the composition of these two sections of the *American Notebooks;* furthermore, Sophia's presence illuminates Nathaniel's character in light of the transcendental discourse of the woman who was his wife.

Although these two notebooks were a joint venture of husband and wife, the extant manuscripts present themselves primarily as Sophia's texts. The first words of MA580—Sophia cut out the preceding pages of this notebook—are a fragment of her now and forever enigmatic words: "wife. I could not comprehend why." Sophia's entry ends this notebook, and her entries begin and end the second notebook as well.

The physical condition of MA580—the "honeymoon journal" as it might well be called—demonstrates Sophia's effort to keep her record of private moments just that. Pages or parts of pages have been excised, sometimes causing entries to be chopped off, to begin mid-sentence, or to appear without a date. These excisions weakened the binding of the octavo leaves, necessitating Deborah Evetts', Book Conservator at the Pierpont Morgan Library, skilful repair of pages in order to keep the notebook intact. During this conservation of MA580, Evetts numbered only the rectos of leaves or parts of leaves, with numbers in the right corner. The editors of the Centenary Edition, however, number every page, part of a page, and stub of the octavo leaves; therefore, the pagination of Nathaniel's published portion of MA580 does not correspond to the pagination found on the manuscript.

Neither Sophia's nor Nathaniel's entries follow a regular pattern in MA580. Sometimes weeks go by without an entry from either spouse, while on other occasions both spouses contribute an entry for the same day. Sometimes spouses contribute several entries, followed by a single entry from the other spouse. Sometimes the spouses alternate entries day by day. Despite these irregularities, there is an antiphonal quality to the entries. One spouse calls, the other answers. Topics raised by one spouse initiate further commentary, direct or oblique, by the other. At other times, one spouse communicates messages or requests to the other, and on several occasions Sophia and Nathaniel used the journal in lieu of letters during the other's absence, Sophia sometimes directly addressing her husband on these pages.

The pattern of the spouses' entries in MA569—the "Family Notebook," as T. Walter Herbert has dubbed it—differs markedly from that in MA580. Gone is the antiphonal quality of the earlier notebook. Although MA569 spans a ten-year period, the spouses alternate only eleven times, sometimes allowing a year or more to elapse between entries or sets of entries. Sophia makes a total of five lengthy contributions, with one brief remark concluding Nathaniel's entry for 23 March 1848, followed by her unfinished paragraph dated 26 March of that year. Following her initial entry is Nathaniel's brief transcription of Una's words on 20 June 1847 (published as the first entry of *CE*, 8, section vii). In addition to this five-line transcription, Nathaniel makes four substantial contributions to the notebook, his last, entitled "Twenty Days with Julian & Little Bunny," beginning on 28 July 1851 when Sophia departs for West Newton with Una and the infant Rose. The last entry, which begins approximately a year later, is Sophia's and might well be entitled "Eighteen Days with Una, Julian, Rose and Little Turtle and Puss." In fact, Sophia makes explicit the comparison—or perhaps it would be more correct to say the contrast—between her record of events and Nathaniel's. She remarks with some chagrin, "I wish I had leisure to daguerreo-type & paint the hours as they go as my husband did while I was away from Lenox—but I have not a moment all day & it is late at night before I can sit down to write & then I scrawl as fast as my pen can go & write nothing & that illegibly. My dear husband will be disappointed I am sure" (MA580, p. 133).

The physical description and condition of MA569 also differs from that of MA580 in several ways. Pagination, again in Evetts' hand, is found on the outside corner of both the rectos and versos of this notebook, and this pagination corresponds to that used in the Centenary Edition. Although Sophia did cross out some words or passages, MA569 contains no excisions. Therefore, this notebook does not evince the damage to the binding obvious in MA580. At various points, however, Una and Julian drew and scribbled on the notebook, an example of which—an illustration of the inside cover of MA569—is reproduced on p. xv of Herbert's *Dearest Beloved: The Hawthornes and the Making of the Middle-Class Family*. The children's pencil and ink drawings, scribblings, and ink blots appear with greatest frequency on pages 140 through 149, the last pages of the notebook. Upon these pages Sophia kept the aforementioned account of daily life while Nathaniel travelled to Bowdoin and the Isle of Shoals. Although it appears that Sophia generally wrote around the children's scribblings and drawing—occasionally striking through a word or phrase, microscopic examination suggests that on occasion the children may have scribbled over their mother's writing. Nathaniel's entries are always found on clean pages.

More significant than the physical differences between the manuscripts are the telling differences between the spouses which are revealed by their entries. Nathaniel's entries appear to be more deliberately crafted around what the editors of the Centenary Edition describe as "portraits of striking character, and other exercises in minute observation" (8:678)—the Concord River, his garden, a visit from Ellery Channing or Thoreau, his time alone with Julian. As if writing to an audience beyond the intimate and immediate one of his wife, Nathaniel frequently identifies persons by first and last names; he is careful, for example, to identify Louisa as his sister. Nathaniel's entries indicate a degree of self-consciousness and formality not seen in Sophia's extant entries which seem more spontaneously a record of their day-to-day life—their meals, their walks, their visitors.[2]

Although the shared general subject of Nathaniel and Sophia's observations in MA580 is nature and the general environs of the Old Manse, tonal and philosophical differences between the spouses are conspicuous.[3] In Sophia's first entry, she records a walk with her husband of a few weeks. Nathaniel chides her that she has "transgressed the law of right in trampling down the unmown grass," and therefore, he "punish[es]" her by not joining her to climb a hill. "This I did not like very well," Sophia writes. In her next description, undisturbed by fluctuations between sunlight and shade, she employs an oxymoron: "We penetrated the pleasant gloom & sat down upon the carpet of dried pine needles." Then Sophia—not Nathaniel—initiates the physical contact which leads to a sexually suggestive position: ". . . I clasped him in my arms in the lovely shade, & we laid down a few moments on the bosom of dear mother Earth. Oh how sweet it was!" This embrace is followed by "a slight diamond shower—without any thunder or lightening, & we were happiest." As they observe the surrounding landscape, Sophia notes that without wind, "the stillness was profound. There seemed no movement in the world but that of our pulses." She concludes this entry with her awareness that "the rapture of my spirit was caused more by knowing that my own husband was at my side than by all the rich variety of plain, river, forest, & mountain around & at my feet" (MA580, p. 2). Displacing descriptions of sexual arousal from her body onto nature, Sophia's comparative structure yokes her responses to the natural world with her responses to her husband. Both produce "rapture."

In this notebook, Sophia frequently describes her responses to nature in terms suggestive of sexual experience. For example, writing about the first spring of her married life, Sophia compares her love for Nathaniel to the rushing waters of melting snow and ice: "I can rush into my husband with all my many waters & sing & thunder with all my waves in the vast expanse of his comprehensive bosom" (MA580, p. 41). In a 23 April 1843 entry, she writes: "Sunday . . . soft & sunny after a misty dawn, & the birds sang without end—I felt inclined to respond 'Yes, yes, yes—I know it I know it!'" (MA580, p. 30).

Nathaniel was incapable of these euphoric responses to nature, however, and he laments this disposition in one entry dated 4 September 1842: "Oh that I could run wild!—that is, that I could put myself into a true relation with nature, and be on friendly terms with all congenial elements" (8:358). Nathaniel similarly remarks upon his inability always to view nature as beneficent. He records that on 24 September 1843, a "glorious" autumn day, "it is impossible not to love Nature; for she evidently loves us. At other seasons she does not give me this impression; or only at rare intervals" (8:393).

In Nathaniel's descriptions, the elements of nature are apt to be unpleasant or even noxious. In the second entry in MA580, dated 5 August 1842 (the first to appear in *CE,* 8, section vi), he writes: "A rainy day—a rainy day—and I do verily believe there is no sunshine in this world, except what beams from my wife's eyes" (8:315). Frequently relying on biblical allusions, Nathaniel describes the Old Manse as a Paradise where he is Adam, and Sophia is Eve. But this Eden is made less so by its lack of "water fit either to drink or to bathe in." In this paradise, "Providence does not cause a clear, cold fountain to bubble up at our doorstep" (8:317).

Even Nathaniel's allusions to the Old Manse as "Paradise" suggest his anxiety about temporal happiness in that or any other garden. If Eve represents the first woman, untainted in the innocence of Eden, she also represents the temptress whose offer of forbidden fruit precipitates eviction from that very domain of strifeless bliss. And just as the Garden of Eden had its serpent, the grounds of Old Manse contain a potential contaminant—the foul water source from which the Concord River does not, to Nathaniel's mind, offer immediate relief.

Indeed, in the 6 August 1842 entry, Nathaniel moves swiftly from one paragraph about "the bewitched" new cistern at the Old Manse which stubbornly "remains almost empty" to the next paragraph about the Concord River, "the most sluggish stream that I was ever acquainted with." Nathaniel continues: "Owing to this torpor of the stream, it has nowhere a bright pebbly shore, nor is there so much as a narrow strip of glistening sand. . . ." The eel which he catches in the Concord "has the prominent flavor of mud" and the river is "fit to compare" only with "torpid earthworms" (8:318, 320). Nathaniel understands how the putrid yellow lily with "its unclean life and noisome perfume" can come from this river, but he "marvel[s] whence [the white] pond lily derives its loveliness and perfume, sprouting from the black mud over which the river sleeps . . ." (8:318).

This choice of detail is rife with sexual symbolism. As Herbert rightly points out, Nathaniel views "the river as a domain of sexual filth." The lilies in Concord River, invoking conventional associations of flowers with vagina, are categorically divided, pure from impure.[4] For Nathaniel, proximity to the real river's overwhelming sexual symbols—the contradictory female symbols of the noisome yellow and pure white lilies (the flowers Sophia wore in her hair during their marriage ceremony) and univocally repulsive male symbol of flaccid eel and worm, cannot give "the ideality which the soul always craves" (8:321).

For Nathaniel, a re-vision of the Concord River is possible only when he distances himself from it. On 7 August 1842 he writes that, from the top of a hill he can recognize:

> some injustice in my remarks. . . . At a distance, [the river] looked . . . so etherealized and idealized that it seemed akin to the upper regions. . . . every tree and rock imaged with a distinctness that made them even more charming than the reality. . . . All the sky, too, and the rich clouds of sunset, were reflected in the peaceful bosom of the river; and surely, if its bosom can give such an adequate reflection of Heaven, it cannot be so gross and impure as I described it yesterday.
>
> (8:320-21)

Nowhere are the differences between Sophia and Nathaniel more telling than in their contrasting descriptions of the Concord River, for on 24 August 1842, Sophia records her returning from a visit with the Alcotts to the Old Manse via the river thus:

> [We] floated down the shining stream. It was utterly still, so that it was impossible to tell where the tangible ended & the reflected began on the margin—excepting that the reflected was more beautiful. . . . The purple pickerel flower & the gorgeous cardinal & spirea of all colors & arrowhead & pond lilies all seemed rejoiced to be in that fairy world beneath the earth. And the clouds of fleecy whiteness floated through the blue ether down far below us—as if we were sailing in midair between two firmaments & all the emerald garniture of earth were poised by the power of counter-forces around us. The yellow water of the river turned all the plants that grow in its bed into pure gold—One might imagine it the golden river of Pactolus & the plains beside it those of the enchanting Greece.

In contrast to her husband's view, Sophia's vision endows the river with positive values. Where Nathaniel sees yellow, she sees gold; what for him was sluggish is for her still. While Nathaniel sees but two types of flower—one which represents purity and one which represents impurity—Sophia sees myriad flowers, all of which seem to rejoice in their beauty. Most significant is the fact that immanence—the very act and moment of floating down the Concord—fosters Sophia's rapturous vision. Nathaniel, however, can achieve some degree of appreciation for the Concord only at a distance from it. For Sophia, opposing elements—earth and sky, real and ideal—create a "power of counter-forces" which cause all of nature to be "poised," balanced, and held together. A true Transcendentalist, Sophia sees the river as an emblem of the commingling of the real and the ideal. For Nathaniel, opposing elements bifurcate, unbalance, and threaten his vision of the natural world. Thus Nathaniel's descriptions of nature, which engender disturbing sexual metaphors, seem all the more discordant when intoned beside Sophia's clear, sensuous harmonies of nature's bounty and love for her husband.

The shared subject of nature in the first notebook yields to the couple's observations of their children in the second; but Nathaniel and Sophia again differ significantly in their depiction of the childhood antics of Una and Julian. Sophia begins this journal exactly one month after Una's birth, recording her delight in putting Una to her breast. Nursing Una is both a joy and a "privilege" (MA569, p. 1c). Sophia extols the infant's great size, her graceful shape, her serenity, and her exceedingly good health. Even the baby's method of eliminating gas causes maternal pride, for Una "suffers less from wind & colic than most babies—She has so much strength that she disposes of the wind by various indescribable noises—I did not know a baby's voice could utter such sounds—" (MA569, p. 2). Una's sounds are elsewhere described as "bird-notes & warbles" (MA569, p. 9), and the infant evokes praise from family, friends, and visitors as "the most beautiful, majestic, queen like reposeful of babies—a picture—a statue—a born lady—a princess—a dream baby—an ideal child—& every fine name that could be applied" (MA569, pp. 7-8).

Sophia's litany of praise for Una makes Nathaniel's litany of contempt for this child all the more conspicuous. The first item in Nathaniel's hand in this notebook is his transcription of Una's expression of ennui: "I'm tired of all sings" (8:398). Significantly, this entry is paralleled by Julian's similar sentiments which Sophia transcribed at the end of her 23 July 1849 entry: "All the world / seems dreary / every where / I go all the / world seems / dreary . . ." (MA569, p. 46). Thus the father records the daughter's unseemly world-weariness; the mother records the same sentiments in the son.

Nathaniel's first substantial entry records one day's observation of his children, observations cast in the singularly detached mold of a spectator taking notes on someone else's family. This distance is created by a number of rhetorical strategies. At times he refers to himself in the passive voice or in the third person as "the father." In a similarly formal manner, Julian is "the little boy," Sophia, "their mother." As if witnessing a drama he writes "enter Mamma," and he repeatedly refers to their lives as a history, one which warrants his clarification of the children's ages. Using the present tense, Nathaniel creates a moment-by-moment account— "Now Una offers. . . . Now Una proposes . . . ," which highlights his removal from their activities: he is

writing about the lives his wife and children are living. So accustomed must Una be to his stance as writer that when she asks, "Where is little Julian?" she is inquiring, "where is the place of little Julian, that you've been writing about him" (8:399-406 passim).

Una endures a catalogue of her father's displeasure. Her "looks [are] cloudy; her aspect is ominous." Her talk is "babble," her requests "exceedingly ungracious," her objections the "harsh and [ill-bred] little croak of a voice." Although Nathaniel is troubled by what he sees as her lethargy and laziness, her animated movements are disdained as "sudden jerks, and . . . extravagant postures;—a very unfortunate tendency that she has; for she is never graceful or beautiful, except when perfectly quiet. Violence—exhibitions of passion—strong expressions of any kind—destroy her beauty" (8:403-20 passim).

Even when Nathaniel grants Una a good disposition, she is "as troublesome as a little fly, buzzing around people." Her quieting after initial resistance at bedtime is "the blessedness and kindliness of a euthanasia." And his occasional praise is tainted by oxymoron or understatement as when Nathaniel finds Una in a "strangely complaisant mood" or when "[s]he looks not altogether unpretty" (8:407, 418). Nathaniel's only sustained praise for Una comes in the repeated pleasure he takes in her legs which are "praiseworthy," "the only handsome legs I ever knew a child to have," or, at the very least, "serviceable." Yet when Una attempts to make "her leg . . . a standing joke," her father remarks without much enthusiasm that "she is rather apt to repeat a witticism that has once been successful" (8:399, 415, 418, 420). Nathaniel's antipathy toward Una, coupled with his singular attention to her legs, suggest that his hostility masks an inappropriate sexual attraction.[5]

Nathaniel's responses to Una and Julian are decidedly gendered. While Nathaniel castigates Una for volatility, he admires Julian's "sturdy and elastic life; there never was a gait more expressive of childish force and physical well-being . . ." (8:415). When Una complains of being warm and "opens her breast," Nathaniel interprets her gesture as "the physical manifestation of the evil spirit" (8: 420), but when Julian runs about nude, Nathaniel perceives that his son "enjoys the felicity of utter nakedness." Nathaniel records that Sophia's attempts to dress Julian on this occasion are greeted with "cries of remonstrance" (8:402), but when—on another occasion—Nathaniel attempts to dress his naked daughter, he describes her resistance as "a terrible struggle— and she gets almost into a frenzy; which is now gradually subsiding and sobbing itself away, in her mother's arms" (8:406).

Sophia's responses to Una are also gendered, but the mother *praises* the child for her tranquil, graceful ways while the father *condemns* the child for her lack of these qualities. And Nathaniel recognizes that he differs from Sophia in their perceptions of their daughter: "When Una is mischievous—which is not often—" (a curious remark from Nathaniel considering that his portrait of her is so unremittingly negative) "there seems to me a little spice of ill-nature in it, though I suppose her mother will not agree to this" (8:407).

This "ill-spice" and "manifestation of the evil spirit" seemed all the more apparent to Nathaniel when the family lived in the Mall Street house while Mrs. Hawthorne was dying. To occupy their days, Julian and Una invented various imaginary scenarios in which they alternately pretended to be the doctors, their grandmother, and the family members who nursed her: "The shouts, laughter, and cries of the two children had come up into the chamber, from the open air, making a strange contrast with the death-bed scene." Though both children create this incongruity between playfulness and dying, vitality and decrepitude, it is Una upon whom Nathaniel projects these dichotomies of nature. In Una, he writes, "there is something that almost frightens me . . .—I know not whether elfish or angelic, but, at all events, supernatural. . . . I cannot believe her to be my own human child, but a spirit strangely mingled with good and evil, haunting the house where I dwell. The little boy is always the same child, and never varies in his relation to me" (8:429, 430-31).

Nathaniel's ruminations on this mysterious commingling of good and evil in his female child are reminiscent of his earlier musings upon the Concord River's coexisting symbols of feminine purity and impurity: "It is a marvel whence [the white pond-lily] derives its loveliness and perfume, sprouting as it does from the black mud over which the river sleeps, and from which, likewise, the yellow lily draws its unclean life and noisome perfume" (8:318). His male child may possess a "tenderness, love, and sensibility in his nature" as well as a "disposition to make use of weapons"(8:424, 434) without provoking Nathaniel's misgivings about his son's character or doubts about his own paternity.

Sophia, however, is much more even in her responses to her children. She is far more apt to narrate without excessive judgment the routines of their daily lives— their progress in history and arithmetic, for example. But she does not stint in her expressions of pride over their acquisition of Christian scripture and its application to their moral life. Self-sacrifice and self-control are the hallmarks of this morality for both children. Una learns that her kindness and generosity to Julian prompt the same behavior from him toward her, and these are virtues both children are expected to demonstrate (MA580, pp. 63-64).

Although Sophia writes with hyperbole, "Never were there such divine children," she concludes this remark with the paradox that they are "far diviner than if more

spotless of blame—" (MA580, p. 112). While she celebrates their virtues, she can also qualify her praise by noting the "singular perception [Julian] often or perhaps *sometimes* manifests" (MA580, p. 117). Una's putting burrs in Julian's hair and Julian's calling Rose "ugly thing" do not disintegrate her perceptions of these children.

Sophia's last entry in MA580 creates an interesting symmetry with the first in that notebook. In her first entry, she recorded beginning to nurse Una; in her last, she records weaning Rose. While the first set of entries reflected the euphoria of the new mother, this last entry reflects the weariness of the mother of three young children who tends to domestic duties while her husband vacations. But the record that Nathaniel kept of his trip to the Isle of Shoals, published in section eight of volume eight of the Centenary Edition (510-43), suggests that he gave little thought home during that period. He makes only one brief remark—"a letter from Ticknor, but none from home" (8:534-35)—regarding his family. Rather, as Rita Gollin has shown, Nathaniel's record of this trip demonstrates him to be "a man who played cards, sang 'glees,' drank appletoddy, and believed in ghosts; a frustrated but persistent fisherman; and an aficionado [*sic*] of storms."[6] He is not man who hangs upon the receipt of news from home. Nor does he seem to be a man preoccupied in mourning for a sister who had died but one month earlier.[7] Rather, he seems a man who easily disassociates himself from the emotional claims of being a father, a husband, and a grieving brother.

Sophia, meanwhile, is "prostrated" from the heat and nights of sleep interrupted by a wakeful baby. She acknowledges feeling "rather skittish" and anxious, with "a heavy responsibility" (MA569, pp. 115, 110). Yet added to her responsibilities is her husband's injunction that she keep a journal during his absence, an effort which produces no gratification for she judges it so poorly executed. "It is not of much use to write such skeletons," she concludes (MA569, p. 148). Indeed, the physical condition of these last pages paint a telling portrait of Sophia's life. Sophia's dutiful, detailed, daily record is written around and on top of Una's and Julian's drawing, writing, scribbling, and ink blots. Her very sentences are surrounded and superseded by these children.

The appearance of these last pages demonstrates graphically Sophia's lack of control over her life, just as the content of these pages show her reaching for a relationship with her husband which eludes her grasp. His absence creates a vacuum which "All the grace & loveliness & beauty & goodness & radiant intellect of these children cannot make up at all" (MA569, p. 119). She laments that his letters do not arrive frequently, and when a letter does arrive, it causes a pleasurable physical reaction—"awakening, resting, soothing, thrilling"—followed by bitter weeping. Although she rationalizes that her sobbing is "an offset to my blessedness in having such a husband & such children," she continues, "but yet it is also because I am not better, more beautiful, more worthy to be his wife & to sun in his love. It should be a celestial angel to deserve him—& I am not" (MA569, p. 121).

If Edwin Haviland Miller is correct to assert that Nathaniel swore off sexual relations with his wife at about this time,[8] Sophia may here be expressing her grief over the loss of their conjugal relations. Because she is not "celestial" but sensual—the spontaneous lover of nature, the woman physically bound to her children—she feels intensely her husband's physical and emotional absence. And she may well have interpreted his various distancing strategies as his rejecting her because she was not sufficiently good, worthy, or beautiful. The loss of her husband's presence and attention affected her profoundly.

Notes

1. This notebook was thought to be lost or no longer extant at the time *The American Notebooks* was edited by Claude M. Simpson and published as volume eight of *The Centenary Edition of the Works of Nathaniel Hawthorne* (Columbus: Ohio State University Press, 1972). Barbara S. Mouffe subsequently discovered and published *Hawthorne's Lost Notebook: 1835-1841* (University Park: Pennsylvania State University Press, 1978).

2. In introductory remarks on his edition of "A Sophia Hawthorne Journal, 1843-1844," John MacDonald makes a similar observation: ". . . Nathaniel Hawthorne's journals rarely afford that sort of detailed attention to daily activity which allows reconstruction of those specific conditions which so much determine the mood of individual life. . . . His wife's journals are different. They revel in detail, often becoming the kind of diaries which Hawthorne never kept. . . . They are simply a record of day-to-day events made in an attempt to capture, the joy and the pain of life as immediately as it was being lived" (*Nathaniel Hawthorne Journal 1974*, ed. C. E. Frazer Clark, Jr. [Englewood, Col.: Microcard Editions, 1975], p. 1).

3. In August of 1842, Margaret Fuller also noticed "a striking contrast of tone between a man and a woman so sincerely bound together by one sentiment" (Joel Myerson, "Margaret Fuller's 1842 Journal: At Concord with the Emersons," *Harvard Library Bulletin*, 21 [July 1973]: 328). Nathaniel and Sophia had responded quite differently to Ellery Channing's request that he and his bride,

Ellen (Margaret's sister), board with the Hawthornes. Nathaniel seemed aghast at the suggestion that he might share his home under any condition; Sophia's response, presumably less horrified by these prospects, is lost.

4. T. Walter Herbert, *Dearest Beloved: The Hawthornes and the Making of the Middle Class Family* (Berkeley: University of California Press, 1993), pp. 144, 122.

5. Part four of Herbert's *Dearly Beloved* is an elaborate analysis of Hawthorne's autobiographical deployment of the Beatrice Cenci narrative. Although I do not concur with the line of his argument here, I do agree with Herbert that the tone of attraction-repulsion which colors Nathaniel's relation to his eldest child may suggest an unconscious incestuous fascination.

6. Rita Gollin, "Hawthorne on the Isle of Shoals," *Nathaniel Hawthorne Review*, 13 (Spring 1987): 7.

7. Hawthorne's sister Louisa had died on 27 July 1852 when the steamer *Henry Clay* caught fire on the Hudson River near New York City. Louisa had jumped overboard and drowned. This tragic incident clearly had not affected Nathaniel's travel plans or made him fear travel by ship.

8. Edwin Haviland Miller, *Salem is My Dwelling Place: A Life of Nathaniel Hawthorne* (Iowa City: University of Iowa Press, 1991), p. 397.

Luanne Jenkins Hurst (essay date 1999)

SOURCE: Hurst, Luanne Jenkins. "The Chief Employ of Her Life: Sophia Peabody Hawthorne's Contribution to Her Husband's Career." In *Hawthorne and Women: Engendering and Expanding the Hawthorne Tradition*, edited by John L. Idol, Jr. and Melinda M. Ponder, pp. 45-54. Amherst: University of Massachusetts Press, 1999.

[*In the following essay, Hurst concentrates on Hawthorne's indefatigable support of her husband in his literary pursuits.*]

Sophia Hawthorne once wrote to her sister Mary Mann: "If I could help my husband in his labors, I feel that that would be the chief employ of my life. But all I can do for him *externally* is to mend his shirts & socks—spiritually, it is another thing" (6 Apr. 1845, ms., Berg Collection).[1] Ironically, she seems not to have realized how much she did do to help Nathaniel Hawthorne "in his labors." Sophia was always Nathaniel's most devoted admirer, and in her letters she consistently promoted him as the greatest and most creative artist alive. These letters also reveal her reactions to his stories and romances as he finished them and read them to her (her reactions being clearly important to him), and they reveal her fierce loyalty to him—sometimes leading to a strong rebuke of a beloved sister who dared to criticize her husband's social aloofness or leading her to chastise her mother for failing to send books for Nathaniel to read. Perhaps her greatest contribution to her husband's literary career was her concern for the sanctity of his study. When they moved to a new home, one of her first occupations was making Nathaniel's study as physically comfortable and visually pleasing as possible. She also established a pattern in the early years of their marriage of never interrupting him when he was writing and did her best to keep the children and even visitors from intruding. Her letters reveal the Hawthornes' daily life, and the person who made everything run smoothly was clearly Sophia Hawthorne. She shielded her husband from social contracts he would have found trying, including contact with the "busy & confused" Peabody household (13 Apr. 1843), defended him against criticisms made by professional reviewers or family and friends, and insulated him from the children's noise as much as she could. Though she did not recognize it, Sophia Hawthorne made a major contribution to the success of her husband's career as one of America's great men of letters.

For Sophia Amelia Peabody, who grew up in a very sociable family, marriage to Nathaniel Hawthorne must have required some adjustment in her expectations about the social interaction she would have with others. She not only adapted but did her best to shield her husband from others when he wished to avoid them, and she defended him vigorously when she perceived a need. She made many obligatory social calls on her own and did her best to account innocuously for her husband's obvious avoidance of her parents' noisy, crowded, and matriarchal household. When she had to write her mother (three months after her marriage) to change the date of a proposed visit, she was careful to explain that it had been *her* mistaken assumption that she and Nathaniel would come at the earlier time; "for my husband says he never thought of going as soon as I had planned" (9 Oct. 1842). She also emphasized his mother's being "in an ecstacy of impatience" to see him as the reason for his leaving her in Boston and going right on to Salem. Already she had begun to smooth the way for him socially and to shield him from contacts that he would find unpleasant.

Her sister Mary's criticism of Nathaniel caused Sophia to write: "His abomination of visiting also still holds strong, be it to see no matter what angel—I do not care to perplex him with entreaties for this end." Later in the same letter, she continued:

> I wish my darling May would not express surprise or displeasure any more for his not doing this & that with regard to visits—It does not good, & only makes me feel uncomfortable that she should not let this point go, & think of him in other regards. Of what moment will it be a thousand years hence whether he saw this or that person? Whereas, it is of great account that he should not be constantly disturbed by the presentment of this question. If he had the gift of speech like some others, Mr Emerson & Wm Greene, for instance, it would be different, but he evidently was not born for mixing in general society. His vocation is to observe & not to be observed.
>
> (9 Oct. 1842)

Here, her tone was kinder and more conciliatory than it would be almost a year later when Mary raised the issue again:

> Mary Mann has not the smallest notion of him. What she regards as weakness in him is but a very *strong* resolution & an Idea. I have myself hardly come near the depth & riches of his intellect & its laws after six years of intimate communion—& then how can any one judge him who has seen him hardly six times & then never intimately? But I spoil my subject by trying to write about it.
>
> (3 Sept. 1843, to Mrs. Elizabeth Peabody)

In both letters Sophia emphasized Nathaniel's hospitality when others visited him and said it was his calling to observe: "His vocation is that of a poet, of the highest grade—who must stand apart & observe, & not be mingled up with the petty, though often genial & graceful little ceremonies & etiquettes of life" (3 Sept. 1843, to Mrs. Peabody). Though her husband could make himself "approach other persons," she asked indignantly,

> But why should he? Why, in the name of common sense & reason should he? Are not there enough persons to pass their days or a portion of them in social intercourse with men & women? Does it not take all sorts of people to make a world—? & why should not each one fulfill his calling? He has not the gift of tongues—he is not a talker like Mr Emerson—He was not born to chat nor converse. Words with him are not 'airy nothings' nor even of little weight as with most people—Words with him are worlds—suns & systems—& cannot move easily & rapidly—
>
> (3 Sept. 1843, to Mrs. Peabody)

Sophia Hawthorne soon became so accustomed to living in the "retirement" that Nathaniel found necessary that she was overwhelmed by a visit back to her parents' home and requested:

> Tell my sistreen that I do not want them to make another beautiful party for me. I have promised my husband to go to bed at ten o'clk while I am in Boston, & I had rather see each person separately. It is much more satisfactory, for I am like a bewildered bee among choice flowers when so many rare people are all present, attracting me.
>
> (22 Feb. 1843, to Mrs. Peabody)

In a later letter she referred to how "busy & confused" everything was during her visit (13 Apr. 1843, to Mrs. Peabody). These requests and reactions show how completely Sophia had adjusted to and come to understand her husband's disposition. This understanding also led her to treat his study as the most important room in their home, no matter where they lived.

When they were newlyweds, Sophia carefully decorated Nathaniel's study at the Old Manse and learned not to interrupt him when he was writing. In addition to hanging her own paintings of Lake Como, she adorned the study with reproductions of famous works by European masters and gave an honored place to a bust of Apollo. After she had a miscarriage in February 1843, she made a special point of having Nathaniel's study cleaned so that it would not remind him of the "sad Scenes enacted there," and Nathaniel deviated from his usual practice to have her sit with him while he wrote (22 Feb. 1843, to Mrs. Peabody). Generally, however, Sophia did not interrupt Nathaniel while he was writing. One of the few times when she did, she described to her mother what happened: "I went into the orchard & found my dear husband's window was open, so I called to him, on the strength of the loveliness [of the spring day], though against rules. His noble head appeared at once & a new sun & dearer shone out of his eyes on me, but he could not come then because the Muse had him entrapped in a gold net—so I was obliged to be content with Mary [the maid]" (20 Apr. 1843).

Though her description was poetic, Sophia made it clear that she knew better than to argue with the Muse. She respected Nathaniel's privacy as an artist so much that she never asked him what he was working on. She once explained to her mother, "I can comprehend the delicacy & tricksiness of his mood when he is evolving a work of art by a small degree of the same in my own case—And his must be far greater, because he is so much greater, & his thoughts go far out of sight" (9 Jan. 1844). She waited for him to discuss his creations in his own time. He often read them to her before sending them to the publisher, but occasionally she did not see them until they were in print (as was the case with his *Life of Franklin Pierce*).

When they left the Old Manse and moved in with Nathaniel's mother and sisters, Sophia feared that their family of three would not be able to stay together and prayed earnestly about their new situation. Even at that time of inner turmoil, one of her main concerns was that Nathaniel have a study: "He & Una are my perpetual Paradise, & I besieged Heaven with prayers that we might not find it our duty to separate, whatever privations we must outwardly suffer in consequence of remaining together. All I asked for was for them, & for a quiet spot in which he might write. Heaven has answered my prayers most bounteously—" (7 Sept. 1845, to Mrs. Peabody).

In later accommodations, Sophia continued her preoccupation with Nathaniel's study. When they lived at 18 Chestnut Street in Salem (1847), she lamented the fact that her husband had no separate place for writing. While visiting her parents, Sophia wrote to Nathaniel:

> Thou, beloved, oughtst not to be obliged to undergo the wear & tear of the nursery—It is contrary to thy nature & to thy mood—Thou wast born to muse & to be silent & through undisturbed dreams, to enlighten the world—I have suffered only for thee in my babydom—When I can once shut thee away in thy study, & shew thee our jewels only when they are shining—then it will be unalloyed delight day by day—
>
> (16? July 1847)

Not surprisingly, when they moved to 14 Mall Street two months later, Nathaniel's study was on the third floor with his mother's and sisters' living quarters located on the second floor to insulate him from the noise of the children on the first floor. Sophia did spend most of her time with the children, and as they grew, she conducted her own school for them. (Being from a family of educators, she was better qualified than many who taught in more formal situations.) In the Mall Street house, Sophia made it possible for Nathaniel to have the seclusion he needed to write *The Scarlet Letter.*

After the Hawthornes moved to Lenox in May 1850, Nathaniel, as was his custom, took the summer off from writing. This summer he especially needed to recover from the strain of the previous year when he had been dismissed from the Salem Custom House, his mother had died, and he had written *The Scarlet Letter* in a few intense months. When the autumn arrived, however, Sophia's letters once more reflected her concern that Nathaniel have an appropriate retreat for writing. They had arranged a study for him in the summer, but she was concerned that it would not be warm enough in the winter. She wrote to her mother for advice on a special way of heating a small room with hot water in a tin container. She also mentioned the possibility of his "taking the guest-chamber for his study. It will be the most quiet room unless the wind blow all its trumpets louder on that side of the house than upon any other. But he would not have the sun there" (29 Sept. 1850). What he did have was the situation he needed to write *The House of the Seven Gables* that winter and *A Wonder Book for Girls and Boys* in the following months.

When the Hawthornes rented the Manns' home in West Newton (Nov. 1851 to May 1852), Sophia made special arrangements for "Mr Hawthorne's house-comfort," requesting that her father, who lived nearby, "make his visits to me . . . in the morning while Mr Hawthorne is writing, so that our afternoons & evenings may be en famille." She added, "I want my time to teach the children, . . . & we do not want any body at all but our five selves—" (2 Oct. 1851, to Miss Elizabeth Peabody). During this time of what Sophia called "*complete* retirement," Nathaniel wrote *The Blithedale Romance*.

After they bought the Wayside in Concord, Sophia seems to have paid even more special attention to Nathaniel's study—his first in his own house. She wrote to his sister Louisa: "The study is very pleasant & quite high studded & I purpose to have it the best adorned of any room in the house. Apollo reigns there, & the Transfiguration & Endymion & the Comos hang on the walls—And there are to be two book cases—one already is up" (17 July 1852). In a letter to her mother, she described the new carpet on the study floor, noting that it "looks like rich velvet" (6 June 1852). Sophia may have had in mind a remark that Nathaniel had made almost two years earlier when they were arranging his study in Lenox. He described his ideal study, and she resolved to help him have it one day:

> Mr Hawthorne said this morning that he should like to have a study with a soft, thick Turkey carpet upon the floor & hung round with full crimson curtains, so as to hide all rectangles. I hope to see the day when he shall have such a study. But it will not be while it would demand the smallest extravagance, because he is as severe as a stoic about all personal comforts, & never in his life allowed himself a luxury. It is exactly upon him therefore that I would like to shower luxuries—because he has such a spiritual taste for beauty. It is both wonderful & admirable to see how his taste for splendor & profusion is not the slightest temptation to him—how wholly independent he is of what he would like, all things being equal—
>
> (29 Sept. 1850, to Mrs. Peabody)

Nathaniel had recently published his third major novel (*The Blithedale Romance*) when he purchased the Wayside. He must finally have felt secure enough financially to permit himself a little bit of luxury in his new study, for he would have had to approve the expenditures, though it was Sophia who chose the carpet, paint, wallpaper, and other supplies and supervised the improvements to the whole house. She went to the house a day or two ahead of Nathaniel and was pleased to have many of the carpets down before he and Julian arrived—"So that he had quite a civilized impression of the house at first glance. & was delighted with it, not having seen it since his first visit in snow-time, when it was desecrated . . . with all sorts of abominations, & it seemed fit only for a menagerie of cattle" (6 June 1852, to Mrs. Peabody). In the study at the Wayside, Nathaniel wrote his biography of Pierce as well as *Tanglewood Tales* before leaving for England. When the Hawthornes returned to the Wayside seven years later, they added the famous tower to house Nathaniel's study. Perhaps because of her experience as an artist in her own studio in the years before her marriage, Sophia always recognized the importance of her husband's having a sanctu-

ary for his work, and she made it possible for him to withdraw from ordinary life to produce extraordinary art.

Before the Hawthornes had been married a year, they had established what was to be a lifelong pattern (interrupted only by the times when Nathaniel held public office) of Nathaniel's writing in the mornings without interruption and coming out of his study by afternoon (or sometimes evening) for time with his family. When Nathaniel was working on a romance or other long work, he would sometimes write all day. At such times Sophia would not interrupt him even to get needed supplies from his study. While he was writing *The Scarlet Letter,* she wrote her mother,

> Will you ask Father to buy half a ream of good letter paper for us as cheap as possible. I have no paper. And I want some yellow envelopes[.] I have no ink down stairs & cannot disturb Mr Hawthorne. He writes immensely—I am almost frightened about it—But he is well now & looks very shining—
>
> (27 Sept. 1849)

When he was working on *The House of the Seven Gables,* Sophia apologized for not writing often to her sister Mary Mann and explained: "I have very little time to write at all—because the children are always about me, you know. I have no Antonia [Mary's maid], & Mr Hawthorne is writing & I do not like to put them into his care even in the afternoon, because he still is mentally engaged when out of his study" (9 Sept. 1850). Clearly, she was making sure the children were well cared for, but she was also giving Nathaniel the necessary time and space for his writing. After he finished the romance, she wrote to her mother, "Papa now descends from his study at noon, instead of at night, & this causes a great rejoicing throughout his kingdom—" (12 Feb. 1851).

When Nathaniel had finished a story or romance, he often read it to Sophia, and she often passed on her reactions to his works in her letters to her mother and sisters. She wrote to her sister Elizabeth in February 1850:

> Mr Hawthorne read to me the close of the Scarlet Letter last evening. If I may compare the effect of the Moral Sublime of the Great Stone Face to the distilling of the dew of Hermon—(for such seemed my tears) I must liken that of the Scarlet Letter to a Thunder Storm of Rain—& forked lightning leaping from the black cloud to write with its finger of fire on the darkness. . . . The omnipotence of the Moral Sentiment here triumphs over the world—The human being is rent in twain to give egress to this irresistible Power—Earth dwindles before it—all the ceremonies & pomps of common life pale at its Sovereign urgency—I really thought an ocean was trying to pour out of my heart & eyes—but I had the magnetic power upon me of Mr Hawthorne's voice also—swaying me like a mighty wind—(spirit means wind) tremulous with the pathos of GOD's Word speaking through him.
>
> (4 Feb. 1850)

After he read the end of *The House of the Seven Gables* to her, Sophia wrote to her mother:

> There is unspeakable grace & beauty in the conclusion, throwing back upon the sterner trajedy of the commencement an etherial light & a dear home-loveliness & satisfaction—How you will enjoy the book,—its depth of wisdom, its high tone, the flowers of Paradise scattered over all the dark places, the sweet wall-flower scent of Phoebe's character, the wonderful pathos & charm of old Uncle Venner. I only wish you could have heard the Poet sing his own Song as I did; but yet the book needs no adventitious aid—It makes it[s] own music, for I read it all over again to myself yesterday, except the last three chapters.

> (27 Jan. 1851)

Three weeks later she wrote a more extensive critique to her sister Elizabeth:

> "The House of the Seven Gables" is a totally different book from the "Scarlet Letter". I might quote the words which Little Bun used to the mountain.

> "Talents differ: all is well & wisely put." It is, I think, a great book. While I listened I was in enchantment from the wisdom, the depth of insight, the penetration into the reality of things, the tragic power, the pathos, the delicate grace, the jewels of rarest beauty scattered throughout, like flowers over broad prairies—And you know his wonderful reading! . . . I always feel, when my husband is reading his own works that it is impossible they can ever seem just so when any one else reads them. Yet I find they bear the test, & so I found with this. For I read it all over to myself before it went to the Publishers. The Rosebud Phoebe blooms on the darker picture as Juliet shone on the night, like a jewel in an Ethiop's ear. And Alice's pale, stately head bends like a regal white lily before a rough gale. I am charmed by the simplicity of the plot. It is as simple as a Greek tragedy, & certainly the diamond purity, the marble severity & perfection of the style never has been, never can be surpassed. A foolish book written in such a style would have a worth—but when it is but the setting of a rich jewel of Truth, how must it be?

> (16 Feb. 1851)

In this same letter Sophia gave some insight into Nathaniel's feeling about a work after it was published as well as her awareness that he was likely to discount her praise as coming from someone who loved him and was not objective. As positive reviews vindicated her opinion, she indulged in the luxury of saying, "I told you so." She also gave a perceptive explanation for why her husband's works might not appeal to the broadest segment of the public and predicated a greater fame for him in the future than in his own time:

> For himself, he is tired to death of the book. It seems to him at present perfectly inane; but so it is, I think, every time—I am rather shy of commendation—because it is too much like striking the same note—I am too near—But I venture roundly to assert my impression & then wait humbly till there be a reverberation

from remoter spheres. Then I triumphantly say "So *I* said." The absolute freedom from caricature, even from the most airy, tricksy caricature in all he writes perhaps is one reason why the popular ear may not be as quickly arrested as by a writer of far less truth & power,—just as the common eye would prefer a striking painting a little exaggerated to a pure marble statue that is more beautiful & true at the end of a thousand years to the one who contemplates it aright than when first it appears among men. . . . And he who rises to such a lofty point of view as to see unclouded emanations from the source of Light, & then is so simple as most simply to record his visions, Such an one is not often recognized in his day & generation as the Seer he will afterwards prove.

> (16 Feb. 1851)

A more controversial work than his romances was Nathaniel Hawthorne's campaign biography of Franklin Pierce. The defensive tone of Sophia's reaction to it reflected her awareness that even her own family might respond negatively to what her husband had done:

> I have just now finished reading the little Biography which I did not see in manuscript. It is as serene & peaceful as a dream by a green river, & such another lily of testimony to the character of a Presidential candidate, was, I suspect, never before thrown upon the fierce arena of political warfare. Many a foot & hoof may trample on it, but many also will preserve it for its beauty. Its perfect truth & sincerity are evident within it, to say nothing of the moral impossibility of Mr Hawthorne uttering any but words of truth & good faith. As no instrument could wrench out of him a word he did not know to be veracious in spirit & letter—so also no fear of whatsoever the world may attribute to him as motive would weigh a feather in his estimation. He does the thing he finds right, & lets the consequences fly—They are nothing to him—

> (10 Sept. 1852, to Mrs. Peabody)

As this quotation shows, Sophia often idealized Nathaniel's character. She also could not resist defending him and his writings against various critics. One especially telling passage occurs in a letter to her sister Elizabeth in reference to *The Scarlet Letter*:

> Mr Hawthorne does not know why Mr Channing should think his book the using up of "stormy gasses." He is not conscious of it—Mr Bellows seems to have also an idea that he has purified himself by casting out a legion of devils into imaginary beings. But it was a work of the imagination wholly & no personal experience, as you know very well. Mr Channing has a wonderful comprehension of Mr Hawthorne, but he is mistaken in supposing him to be gloomy in his nature. Not Ariel is more pervaded with light & airy joy for himself; but he sees men & he sees passions & crimes & sorrows by the intuition of genius, & all the better for the calm, cool, serene height from which he looks. Doubtless all the tendencies of powerful, great natures lie deep in his soul; but they have not been waked, & sleep fixedly, because the noblest only have been called into action—In no person have I ever known the spiritual

practically so predominant—& the Right so supreme over the wrong, the intellectual—over the physical. Mr Bellows is singularly obtuse about the tone & aim of the "Scarlet-Letter". This questioning of its morality is of all criticisms the funniest—especially this notion some short sighted persons have about the author's opinion of the crime! when the whole book is one great tragic chorus of condemnation—when such terrible retribution follows—when even the retribution lives & breathes in Pearl from beginning to end. It is curious, is it not? I think ministers are peculiarly exercised by the book—They have some singular fear of it.

(21 June 1850)

Sophia insisted again in a later letter that Nathaniel was *not* gloomy. She was referring to Cornelius Mathews's calling her husband "Mr. Noble Melancholy" in his account of a famous picnic of literary men in the Berkshires (published in the *Literary World* on 31 Aug. 1850). She admitted, "He is pensive, perhaps—as all contemplative persons must be . . . because he sees & sympathizes with all human suffering—" Then she continued (and once more showed her idealized view of him): "He has always seemed to me, in his remote moods, like a stray Seraph, who had experienced in his own life no evil, but by the intuition of a divine Intellect saw & sorrowed over all evil—As his life has literally been so pure from the smallest taint of earthliness—it can only be because he is a Seer, that he knows of crime" (4 Sept. 1850, to Mrs. Peabody).

Being married to a woman who thought so highly of him and was so clearly happy to be his wife and to do whatever she could to make his life comfortable and his circumstances conducive to his chosen career had to be a major factor in the success of Nathaniel Hawthorne as an author. The fact that she was clearly an intelligent and thoughtful admirer must have also been encouraging to her husband. Before her marriage Sophia Peabody was recognized in Salem and in Boston as a gifted artist, and modern scholars are not the first to wonder if she ever regretted giving up her art to become Mrs. Nathaniel Hawthorne. When a visiting friend raised a similar question in 1850, asking why Sophia "did not paint & draw & hire people to take care of the children," her private response (which she later reported to her sister Elizabeth) was that her children were "the best pictures I ever painted, the finest poetry I ever could write, better poetry than I ever can write" (16 Feb. 1851). Though this declaration does not address her relationship with Nathaniel, it reflects her happiness in her domestic situation in general and harmonizes with other, more direct remarks about her joy in being his wife. She wrote to him in 1847: "*I* do not need to stand apart from our daily life to see how fair & blest is our lot. . . . Every mother is not like me—because indeed no other mother has such a father of her children, & such a husband to herself—. . . . This I tell thee all the time, but thou canst not believe it." Later in the same letter, she continued:

The beauty & loveliness & nobleness & grace which possess me in the shape of these fairest children which enchant all peoples—these lay hold on the basis of being—these are permanent & immortal—my mind & heart dwell on them—Above all, beyond them is thyself—who art my everlasting satisfaction—my ever present felicity—my pride & glory & support—my sufficiency—I ask no more—GOD has poured out his horn of beneficence upon my head—into my cup—I am the happiest of women—

(16? July 1847)

Note

1. All of the original manuscripts of Sophia Peabody Hawthorne's letters that are cited in this essay are located in the Henry W. and Albert A. Berg Collection of English and American Literature of the New York Public Library, Astor, Lenox and Tilden Foundations, and are quoted by permission.

Bettina L. Knapp (essay date March 2002)

SOURCE: Knapp, Bettina L. "But It Is Impossible in Such Hurried Visits to Immortal Works, to Give an Adequate Idea of Their Character." *Journal of Evolutionary Psychology* 22, no. 1-2 (March 2002): 47-58.

[*In the following essay, Knapp explores Hawthorne's responses to Italian Renaissance art as contained in the "Roman Journal" portion of her* Notes in England and Italy.]

"Character," upon which Sophia Hawthorne's art appraisals focused, spawned many of the critical responses . . . imprinted in her **"Roman Journal"** (1858). Not only did her probings reveal an ingrained sense of esthetics, a historical understanding of the artists and the periods treated; but most intriguing were her glimpses into her inner topography: her idealizations, happy, and somber mood swings. Understandably, then, did her verbal distillations range from rationally and meticulously controlled to flamboyant, lyrical, and excitable assessments. Her melding of ethics paved the way for ideological strayings which, on occasion, took her far afield from the constricting guidelines of her time. Such flights encouraged her to *see into* line, form, and rhythmic sequences, transforming her **"Roman Journal"** into a living document of the soul.

Sophia's art critiques disclosed a uniquely personal *feel* for figures and objects, which not only expanded the scope of her original intent, but endowed the segments of the canvas that caught her eye with life and breath. It may be averred that when deeply moved by a visual image, she became possessed by it, unleashing a flow of insights which struck deep into the heart of the artist's creative impulses—and by extension her own spirited energies.

NOTES

IN

ENGLAND AND ITALY.

By MRS. HAWTHORNE.

NEW YORK:

G. P. PUTNAM & SON.
1869.

Title page of Notes in England and Italy, *1869.*

Immensely qualified to pursue a vocation of art criticism, Sophia who had been drawing and painting since the age of eleven, accomplished her undertaking with exactitude and dexterity. Indeed, Thomas Doughty and Washington Allston had been so impressed with the copies she had made of their canvases, that the latter artist suggested she go to Europe and "devote herself to art" (J. Hawthorne, 1968. *Nathaniel Hawthorne and his Wife.* I, 64ff.).

Significant as well was the joy she seemed to have in the composition of the **"Roman Journal."** Orchestrated within these pages were her finely trained pictorial talents, her complex, and at times confidential ideological notions, and, yes, her bodily reactions to the sensory experience aroused in her by the art object per se. "How I like to write down the illustrious names of what I have all my life long so much desired to see! I cluster them together like jewels, and exult over them" (S. Hawthorne, 1869, *Notes in England and Italy,* 98)[1]. Indeed, the power of Sophia's projections onto an image may even have helped her come to terms with certain

latent, but troubling feelings that the work had constellated in her psyche.

CHARACTER AND THE ARCHETYPAL IMAGE

The word character derives from the Greek—*charakter,* to engrave, indicating a distinctive sign. Sophia's art appreciations encompassed not only the beauty, ugliness, and drama she saw in the linear forms before her, but the behavioral patterns locked into the artists' designs and tonalities as well. In this regard, her typological assessments may be identified with C. G. Jung's *archetypes* (from the Greek, *archi,* beginning, and *typos, stamp,* or original form in a series of variations). Archetypal or primordial images, which emerge from the profoundest layers of the unconscious, are contained in the "suprapersonal and non-individual" collective unconscious. Although "inaccessible to conscious awareness," the contents of the collective unconscious are the archetypes and their specific symbolic representations, archtypal images" (E. Edinger, *Melville's Moby-Dick,* 147). Archetypes are experienced in universal motifs, such as the Great Mother, the Spiritual Father, and so forth.

To be noted in our discussion of Sophia's **"Roman Journal"** are her annotations and frequent emphases on archetypal images revolving around the *anguish of martyrdom,* and various types of *mother, father,* and *maiden/ parthenos* figures. In many cases, her reactions seem to strike a powerful note with her, disclosing certain magnetic fields and/or energy centers in her psyche, which in turn cause her to *project* more intensely onto the images under scrutiny. The increase in fascination or revulsion garnered from the picture(s) under scrutiny, serve to heighten her pulsations, which she then decants in her verbalizations. For example, her depictions of Cesare Borgia or Beatrice Cenci, are notable not only for the vigor of Sophia's shifting emotions, but for their catalytic impact on an ensuing inner transformatory process: change from an abstract unconscious assessment to an electrically charged conscious appraisal injected into the written word. In that the impact of this type of *rite of passage,* may be compared to the "eruption of an inner, but active volcano," its aftermath could be destabilizing (J.Jacobi 1957, *Complex, Archetype, Symbol,* 48).

The word *projection,* as used above, implies an act of thrusting forward "a process whereby an unconscious quality or ontent of one's own is perceived and reacted to in an outer object" (E. Edinger, 1987, 147). To project, then, is to attribute characteristics we love or hate onto others, or to ascribe to images and forms those that seem to answer an unknown or unrealized inner need of the observer. While Sophia believed in many instances that the qualities she assigned to an individual, or to a group, in an art work belonged to the beings represented in the painting before her, they frequently were her own. While possibly unaware of their existence in her unconscious, accounting for her inability consciously to understand their reverberations in her life, they nonetheless lodged inchoate in her psyche.

That Sophia projected so freely onto the art works she examined allowed this demure, well educated New England lady to imbue her writings with *fervor, passion, poetry,* and/or, *dislike and contempt.* Her impressions, for examples, of Domenichino's canvas, "The Chase of Diana," featuring this Roman deity and her maidens running through nature's bountiful fields, imbued her writings with a mood redolent with girlish glee, revealing her deep-seated needfulness of abandon, release from concern, constriction, and the coercive guidelines of her existence. Only via the word, catalyzed by form, colorations, and rhythm could Sophia, the *voyeuse,* feel free to express the hiddenness of her yearnings.

Archetypal Anguish/Pain

That Sophia should have singled out physical torment in the canvases she described is not surprising, given the emphasis on the subject in Italian religious painting. Her highly empathetic reactions to crucifixions and to various types pf ascetic practices are equally understandable. Having suffered debilitating head pains throughout her childhood and adolescence, and having taken daily doses of "poison" prescribed by doctors to assuage her distress, enabled her to *feel into* the discomfort of others (Hawthorne, 1968, 63). One might aver that her verbalizations of pain triggered by visual images offered her some form of solace, if only the comfort of knowing that she was not the sole recipient of physical hurt.

Sophia's extended and ingrained experience with corporal torment was lived on both a personal and a religious level, repentance, atonement, and sacrifice living at the heart of Christianity. Understandably did she experience an *imitatio Christi* of her own, which served not only to trigger her already well formed "religious instinct," but, in so doing, heightened for her the numinosity of the moment (Jung, C. W. 10, 659).

Domenichino's "Martyrdom of St. Sebastian"

Constellated in Sophia's detailed, and ironically, lyrical depiction of Domenichino's (1582-1647) "Martyrdom of St. Sebastian," was the inner resonance the ecstatic experience afforded her. Her *projection* on to his suffering not only allowed her still living and searing memories of pain to surface, but triggered an increase in her own already deeply compassionate, nonetheless unconscious, attraction for martyrdom as well.

While the eye contact she made with the emotive figure of Domenichino's saint Sebastian elevated her to more spiritual climes, it also succeeded in glorifying, insofar

as she was concerned, his suffering through the silent agony of his "divine patience" (204). Unlike other depictions of this type, she indicated that Domenichino

> has succeeded in making the triumph over pain complete, and instead of the distressing horror, I felt only a peace which passes all understanding. The longer I looked, the more profoundly I was affected by the sublimity of the sacrifice, for St. Sebastian looks delicately organized, and full of tender susceptibility, as if pain to him were pain indeed, and as if he were conscious, perfectly, of the agony he endured, and should endure. . . . His gentle might is inflexible, and controls the quivering sensations of anguish into resignation; and his countenance is becoming celestial, as I said as the heavens open upon him, with the sound of trumpets, the golden crown, and above all, the Lord Jesus, not represented bleeding and wounded, and as "a man of sorrows," but with serene joy beaming like a pearl on his forehead. His aspect says to the sufferer, "Come unto me, my beloved, my brother, and I will give you rest. . . .
>
> (S. Hawthorne, **"Roman Journal,"** 206)

Sophia's uncanny insights into Domenichino's forms, tones, and patternings also seemed to have brought into the open certain hidden characteristic traits of her own, namely, those identified with her ascetic Puritanical cultural canon. Her keenly felt understanding of the saint's "sorrow" and "torment" mirrored her own relatively well defined, but unconscious ontological patterns and modes of sensing. Key to her search, she explained, was her desire "to know all about Domenichino, and whether he painted *unconsciously* in a religious devotion, or whether personal experience of sorrow and torment had revealed so much to him as this" (206). While the answer to such a question was and is elusive, she concluded by shunning the personal, and opting for the collective *divine* sphere, indicating that

> we generally take a masterpiece as if directly from the hand of God, and do not consider the character or idiosyncrasies of the artist. But it seems as if the soul must be pure, and the instrument clean, by means of which the Creator delineates such a scene as is represented here.
>
> (206)

While attempting to conserve and preserve her own emotional anonymity, Sophia nonetheless descended ever more deeply into her subliminal world, confronting in so doing a whole pain-ridden cataclysmic past. Let us recall that Sophia's years of illness, she asserted at the time, had only made her ill-equipped to "fulfil the duties of married life," but would have "dangerously agitated Madame Hawthorne," Nathaniel's mother, thus forbidding wedlock. Whereupon, the heroic and self-sacrificing Sophia took it upon herself to stipulate that only if she were cured of her illness would she marry her beloved. "If God intends us to marry. . . . He will let me be cured; if not, it will be a sign that it is not best" (J. Hawthorne, 199). The likelihood that she would remain an invalid may have precipitated her entry during those difficult years into her own harrowing and psychologically abysmal domain. As sometimes occurs in psychosomatic diseases, "the cure was actually accomplished; and the lovers were justified in believing that Love himself was the physician" (Ibid).

Reminiscent of a hierogram or sacred representation, "The Martyrdom of Saint Sebastian" seemed to have aroused Sophia's long forgotten emotions of awe, fear, terror, divine reverence and beatitude. Yet, and of great interest to the reader of her **"Roman Journal"** while she would identify with "the sublimity of the sacrifice" as an abstraction, she was unable to accept its brash viscerality in the reality of the blood and gore Dominichino had set onto his canvas. For this reason, perhaps, she was increasingly drawn to the statue of Saint Bruno by Jean Antoine Houdon (1741-1828). Reflecting the ideals of the Enlightenment, he featured his man of religion in a dignified pose, "looking down in reposeful thought, with his hands crossed, and a face of sincere benignity" (207).

Reni's Beatrice Cenci

Sophia's visible empathy for Beatrice Cenci, the protagonist of Guido Reni's (1575-1642) tableau, was deeply moving. This masterpiece that hung in the Barberini Palace "baffles words," our critic indicated. What touched Sophia most deeply were the tragic circumstances surrounding this young girl's fate and the resulting intensity of her suffering (212). That her father, the vice-ridden Francesco Cenci, had imprisoned both his daughter and her stepmother, Lucrezia, in a lonely castle, had encouraged these women to elicit help—to see to his murder—from the former's brothers, and perhaps from her lover as well. Tried and convicted in 1599, the conspirators were put to death.

Rather than focusing on the pathology of Beatrice's eyes, Reni's authentic depiction of "indefinite desolation," and "unfathomable grief" emerged exclusively from the "perfect beauty of her face, without one line of care, or one shadow of experience—translucent and pure as marble." Sophia's use of the word "translucent" (L. *trans,* through, and *lucere,* shine) and "pure" (L. *purus*), endowed Beatrice with *immaculateness* of purpose and deed: thus untouched by any and all pollutants, she was free from sin. Nontheless, that Sophia analogized her with "marble," a hard, smooth, and cold substance, implied an ambiguity in the young girl's character (213). Could her stone-like impassibility, her extreme control over all facets of her body-mind complex, be looked upon as a saving attribute to an otherwise agonized personality? Might she have been instrumental in her father's murder? Yet have the inner strength to obliterate all visible facial signs of such a

deed? "Night is gathering in her eyes, and the perfect face is turning to stone with this weight of voiceless agony" (213).

Sophia's reference to "an expression in her eyes" may have been intended to dramatize the dangers awaiting one so innocent of crime. Or, had Beatrice unconsciously invited her crushing fate? Had her eyes transformed themselves into audible, and forever questioning instruments: "Oh, what is it—what has happened—how am I involved?" (213) Unique among human countenances, Beatrice's had been divested of everything save the "ruin of hope, joy, and life; but there is unconsciousness still, as if she did not comprehend how or why she is crushed and lost" (213). To convey the stifling nature of the young girl's turmoil, Sophia had recourse to the silence of facial pantomime. "The rosebud lips, sweet and tender, are parted slightly, yet with no cry, nor power to utter a word. Long-past words is the misery that has banished smiles forever from the blooming flower of her mouth" (213).

Most admirable, and most tellingly in terms of Sophia's approach to the art object, was her awareness concerning Beatrice's sense of submission to and acknowledgement of her suffering. Her ability to *accept* her earthly lot had opened up Sophia, as observer, to the young girl's soul power: the breadth and depth of her spirit of atonement, of her brand of moralism—factors uppermost in our New Englander's psychological experience. "The white, smooth brow is a throne of infantine, angelic purity, without a visible cloud or a furrow of pain, yet a wild, endless despair hovers over it. . . . The delicate, oval cheeks are not flushed not livid, but marble-pale, unaffect by the torrents that have bathed them, as if it were too hard an agony to be softened by tears . . ." (213).

Although never overt, the impact of Beatrice's emotional lapidation in Reni's portrait was experienced more intensely by Sophia than, for example, Domeninchino's "The Matryrdom of St. Sebastian." That Sophia had projected onto Beatrice's world of torment had ignited in her a connection between object and subject, enabling her to convey her seeing feelings by verbally palpating the young girl's agony. Devoid of murmurs, cries, even whimpers, Sophia greeted Beatrice's walled-in silence as a closure, an inner journey into the very *livingness* of Reni's canvas. No need of blood and gore to activate an observer's emotions. Reni's miracle resurrected Beatrice's unforgettable countenance via the brush stroke, the interplay of light and shadow, the exquisite immobility of phenomena in the universal significance of its own mutism. Her reverence for Beatrice's agony lived in on its transcendence.

Like Emerson, Sophia trusted her *feelings*. Like her mentor, she experienced the mind as a creative instrument, responsive to its own cosmogony. As Emerson wrote in his "Over-Soul": "We live in succession, in division, in parts, in particles. Meantime within man in the soul of the whole; the wise silence, the universal beauty, to which every part and particle is equally related; the eternal One" (R. W. Emerson, 1980," *Norton Anthology.* 322).

THE MOTHER ARCHETYPE

Much admired by Sophia was Francesco Francia's (1450-1517) painting of "A Holy Family" hanging in the Barberini Palace.

FRANCIA'S "A HOLY FAMILY"

Francia's early experiences had first been a goldsmith and coin-maker endowed his canvases with a down-to-earth quality with which Sophia undoubtedly identified. Eliciting her most powerful projections were Francia's Madonnas. Unlike those of other artists, namely Raphael, his Madonnas, Sophia indicated, featured older women, still beautiful, but nontheless giving the impression of having lived through years of disquietude and inner conflict. Because Francia's deft palette and linear markings highlighted matronly, rather than simply esthetic facial qualities, they spoke directly to Sophia, and on her terms. Incised in the Madonna's facial contours were life's disheartening and difficult moments. Rather than singling out her exquisiteness alone, he underscored a mother's life experience, her "matronly, pure and intellectual qualities" (209).

A homebody adhering to a daily routine, Sophia tried her best to understand and to deal with the variety of problems arising during a householder's daily trajectory. Equally siqnificant in her purview was the Madonna in her role as *archetypal* Mother: a divine, eternal, and universal collective figure, who lived as an ideal presence in Sophia's heart. Most impressive in her viewing of Reni's Madonna was her ability to unify dual images: that of *personal* "MOTHER, with a perfect sense of all her responsibilities—and the *archetypal* sacred mother, who "has the Christ for her son" (209).

CORREGGIO'S "NATIVITY"

Mention must be made of Corregio's "Nativity," displayed at Sant' Andrea. Underscored by Sophia are sequences of patterned luminosities in this canvas: "the light comes from the child, irradiating the Madonna with white effulgence, and dazzling all who stand near" this inviolable image (223). That the Mother is the recipient of cascading lucency, and the child even more dazzling, so serves to set them apart from others, thereby indicating Jesus's godliness and Mary's significance (223).

As a collective and vibrant image embedded in Sophia's unconsious, the Mother figure in Corregio's "Nativity" may have symbolized for her one of countless birthing women endowed with ultimate feelings of inner plenitude. A figure of authority, lest it be forgotten, the Madonna was also the vessel by means of which the "divine child" came into being. As an archetypal infant, common to many cultures—Christ for the Christians, Moses for the Jews, Dionysus-Bacchus for the Greeks, Buddha for Buddhists—the newborn symbolizes futurity for some, innocence for others, and god and/or messiah figure able to redeem humanity's ills. For Sophia, he was looked upon, understandably, as Jesus, the savior!

Deeply moving for this reader are Sophia's allusions throughout her **"Roman Journal"** to "sacred Madonnas, mothers with tender, anxious care and noble expression, and divine babes and holy saints" (239). Her need for such an understanding, protective, and assuaging maternal presence seems to highlight her yearning for such a presence in her world: the *Mother* being the one to forever dispense *indispensable* tenderness and love to her children. As a soul force or anima image, the *Mother* is the bearer and nourished of life. Identified with *Eros,* she functions as the relating principle which brings things together in nature and in the human psyche as a spiritually and intellectually unifying force in the mind. She is feminine *logos,* upon which Sophia relied so deeply throughout her life.

THE FATHER ARCHETYPE

The positive archetypal father, looked upon by Sophia as protector and spiritual director of the family—the usual *pater familias*—was identified for the most part with the moral precepts of social and religious traditions, that is, courage, loyalty, and the male *logos.* Nowhere are these characteristics visible in Raphel's (1483-1520) portrait of Cesare Borgia (Borghese Gallery).

RAPHAEL'S CESARE BORGIA

Raphael's canvas "fixed" Sophia's attention for its comingling of "excessive handsome" outer traits, as opposed to incredibly vivious inner characteristics, revealing him as a "monster of humanity" (237). The son of Pope Alexander VI, Cesare Borgia (1476-1507), an unscrupulous warrior and politician, an artful killer of those who threatened his rise to power, was imprisoned in Spain, and finally died fighting for the French king of Navarre who had befriended him. This Man of the Renaissance, looked upon as the living incarnation of Niccolò Machiavalli's Prince, is remembered for his cruelty and his ruthlessness.

> For his figure is stately, graceful, and commanding, and his head turns upon his shoulders in a princely way, and his features are high and perfectly chiselled. . . . But soon one discovers that out of the fine sculpture of form and face looks a cold, dark, cruel, and vindicative

soul. The black eyes are especially terrible. They do not send forth any beams, but are introspective, secret and evil. They reminded me of the eyes of the sullen vulture in the Zoological Gardens in London, who sits on his perch, and looks vicious and designing, and above all, cold and indifferent. . . . The cold lips are closed firmly, with an immutable fixedness of fell purpose. He has ceased to be aware that there is a conscience, and there is no longer any tender sensibility in him to suggest to himself that he is a monster.

(237)

Well aware of humankind's behavioral swings, Sophia sought to, and sucdeeded in, reconciling extremes; the darkness of Borgia's soul in contrasts to the many beatitudinous figures she had noted during the course of her visits to Roman museums. Although taken with the beauty of martyrs, as yielders of compassion and givers of love and comfort, she was accepted as well that other, sinister, side of living beings. The latter, reminiscent of the earliest stage of the alchemists' scientific experiments—the *nigredo,* or blackening process, is equivalent to the state of chaos, existing prior to the separation of the elements, and in the psychological terminology, prior to the birth of consciousness. Aware of human propensity for intemperate acts, Sophia knew from experience that heights do not exist without depths, nor light without darkness, nor good without evil. Borgia, the supreme arbiter of the *nigredo* phase, was primal darkness!

The destructive father archetype as detailed in Sophia's vision of this ominous creature was incised in her sharp detailing of such specific features as his eyes, lips, and fixedness of intent. Such emphasis served not only to underscore the portentous dissonances embedded in his personality, but to expose the wiliness of this highly intelligent, but manipulative being, whose inner climate was directed by venal impulses.

Sophia's mention of Borgia's "black eyes" (eyes for the Platonist being the gateway to the soul), which she analogized to those of "the sullen vulture," endowed our Renaissance man with the attributes of a great bird of prey, while also underscoring his remoteness, unfathomableness, and anthropophagous instincts. His physical, social, and spiritual aberration aroused Sophia's sense of the dramatic, inviting her to highlight his fixed, closed and "curved lips," which this reader associated with a prison cell into which no one had access. Sophia's verbal canvas revealed a man cut off from his feelings, amoral in every sense of the word, an arch pragmatist whose ends justified his means. "He has ceased to be aware that there is a conscience" (237). Demarcations between good and evil never having been made conscious, encouraged the religiously oriented Sophia to proclaim him an exile from humanity living in a kind of limbo of his own manufacture.

That Borgia was possessed of a "cold, dark, and vindictive soul" encourages a connection with Cronos/Saturn, a Titan who not only castrated his father, but devoured his children for fear of being overthrown by them. So, too, was Borgia a virulent killer. Secluded in his inwardness, as Saturn was in the distant heavens, humans, human and divine acted in parallel fashion when faced with a threat to their power. Indeed, Borgia, Sophia wrote, had "made a pact with the Son of the Morning beautiful once like himself, but fallen, fallen now" (237). With a touch of naiveté, she wondered how Raphael could have borne "to study and dwell upon such a countenance, and then render it so sincerely, as to create another Cesar Borgia, to live during the world's forever?" (238)

THE ARCHETYPAL VIRGIN/PARTHENOS

Sophia's feelings of wishful thinking, particularly those centering on the *parthenos*—the unmarried maiden—seem implicit in her idealization of Graeco-Roman culture. The freedom, abandon, sense of release, and unmitigated joy elicited in her verbal animation of Domenichino's "The Chase of Diana" evidences her thrilling encounter with this canvas at the Borghese Gallery.

DOMENICHINO'S "THE CHASE OF DIANA"

Sophia's attunement to nature—her probably unfulfilled yearnings to run, hop, gambol, and dance in open meadows in consort with other *parthenoi*—lend a wistfulness to her depiction of Domenichino's canvas.

Lovely maidens are grouped all about. A wreath of three is rejoicing over the fight of an arrow just sped by one, while a bouquet of two is looking on with animated faces. Diana, in the centre, stands eminent, with arms uplifted over her head, and limbs elastic ans swift for the chase. Two children are lying in the water in the foreground, taking the *fresco* and the *dolce farniente.* The picture overflows with bounding, eager, rosy, pure life, splendid as morning; and the children balance the quiet sky, in their pause from play.

(236)

Which were the attributes of Diana that encouraged Sophia to verbally thresh her breathless admiration for this divinity? As an earth archetype, she represented everything that Sophia's outward existence was not. Diana, who quested her prey freely, vigorously and fearlessly in raw nature, had earned the title of "the Wild One." Unlike the beautiful, determined, but gentle New Englander, the uninhibited huntress and archer coursed over hill and dale, into forested and mountainous lands with her pack of maidens, knowing no stops, no limitations. In contrast were the behavioral patterns of the staid, constricted Sophia, whose morality was both unbending and unyielding. How best could she experience such pleasures? By *fantasizing*! She virtually transfixed as she gazed at the frolicking and spiraling nymphs joying endlessly in the greenness of the open meadows and undefined spaces before her.

Sophia and Diana were paradoxical figures. As Moon goddess, the latter was identified with the mysteries revolving around the waxing, waning, and disappearing moon, and the punishments or euphoric experiences meted out to those who served her cult. Similarly did Sophia retain her inward secrets, decanting them slowly and thoughtfully at appropriate times, as verbal flickerings in signs, metaphors, anaphoras, alliterations, and tonal dissonances. Her light, born of darkness shone and lived in the strictly defined contours of her social world, and was experienced for the most part in the luster of her projections, or by lavishing love on those she touched. Unlike Diana *parthenos,* however, our Roman visitor was neither autonomous, nor independent, nor accountable to herself alone. A helping figure, she was forever ministering to her husband, children, and friends, transposing on Diana's euphoria for life to the authenticity of her acts and values.

VERONESE'S "THE RAPE OF EUROPA"

Pleasure and sensuality were embedded in Sophia's depiction of Paolo Veronese's (1528-88) "The Rape of Europa," which hung in the Palace of the Conservatori. In sharp contrast to solid/stolid puritanical values, the delight and gusto of her verbal distillations reached incandescent proportions in the array of "stuffs of silk and gold, shining with jewels and brimmed with the rapture that perfect, material well-being gives" (246).

Singing a virtual hymn to the Earth, Sophia was unsparing in her detailed depiction of the painter's finely tuned forms and dynamically graded palette. "It is a glory of earthly felicity, without divine or ethereal in it" (246). She marveled as well at the luxury and splendor of rich womanly beanty in the form and face of Europa. The highlighting of material elements served to enhance the voluptuousness of the soon-to-be-raped young girl (246). Might the excitement of the scene have unconciously *entranced* this New England mother to the point of eliciting in her a touch of envy? (Europa, so giving in sexual matters, was, nontheless, antipodal to Sophia's sexually repressed environment. Why else would Sophia have been so mesmerized by the enactment of a rape? Why her dithyrambs concerning the *bull*? "The complete comeliness of the white bull—the large, soft eyes and mild aspect of subdued strength, with the radiant garland of flowers across its brow, are quite in harmony, and the creature seems as high-toned as Europa—nor more nor less" (246).

Nor were sensual/sexual details wanting in Sophia's following three-dimensional verbal orgy:

> A little Cupid holds him with a slight wreath, quite securely, and stands with one tiny foot on his leg, as if the bull were a lamb. It is a sumptuous, glowing reality—no dream or vision. There are velvets, brocades, precious stones, and Europa is a queenly woman. The white bull is lying down in the foreground, and Europa sits upon his back, while her maidens finish her toilet . . . Her eyes and head are raised, and a little thrown back . . . Over a thicket the head of another bull, or of a cow, is thrust out, the eyes flashing fury and amazement (ox-eyed Juno, perhaps).

> (246)

Although *rape* may be sumptuously and thrillingly evoked by the male painter who increasingly projects on to his increasingly painterly delineations, it is not necessarily so in the empirical world. Could Sophia's sensual commentary of such a crucial event have possibly evoked personal memories of her wedding night? The visceral joy and excitement garnered from the coupling experience she depicted seemed to have invited her, as *voyeuse* to ponder such an event in retrospect, to relive the thrill of these forbidden joys and bounties of earthly existence. Or was it a momentary lapse on Sophia's part? A desire to rekindle the doctrine of a fourth century Sicilian philosopher, Euhemerus, who believed gods to have once been human beings, thus fostering the ancient belief in the cohabitation between Gods and humans!

Sophia's archetypal Europa, alive as sign and symbol in her psyche, was a living incarnation of the rites and rituals of a whole counterculture for her, one which must have conjured distant and lavish fantasy lands, antipodal to the stark universe of emotional deprivation into which destiny had so precipitiously submerged Sophia

> Europa is Venice, as she was in the days of the Doges, when all her palaces were alight with refulgent life and state, and looked like jewels studding the rim of her water-courses, when the air was heavy with fragrant sighs and perfumes, and delicious tones from harp and dulcimer overflowed from gondola and balcony, till the senses could bear no more enjoyment.

> (247)

Born of Sophia's secreted personal world, her **"Roman Journal"** was not simply an intellectual rendition of the multiple art listings she had seen, but an organ, or instrument, of her collective unconscious. Rather than prosaic, it distilled a whole psychic field, born from a remarkable attunement to her cultural canon as well as to the broadening experience of Emersonian transcendental thought. Many of her remarks in her **"Roman Journal"** may be considered breakthroughs, stepping-stones taking her beyond the traditional and so-called acceptable notions of her day. Is this to say that she felt alienated from her environment? Her emphases, for example, on the sensual side of life, its lavishness, and the joy and abandon of tactile pleasures, might so indicate. By contrast, she may have used these devices as mediating and indefinable powers to help her gain entry into an expanded consciousness that would offer her creative and emotional plenitude.

Sophia's ability to both differentiate and diffuse emotions via linear forms, tonalities, and scenic escapes, only to knit them together moments later in verbally vibrant synthetic mixtures, suggests a unique resulting from her fundamentally open and giving nature. That she allowed her inner voice to flow forth in lyrical, sometimes girlish glee, interspersed with vibratos ushered in by terrifying lower tones, fired and flamed the *magic* of her verbal artistry, releasing her from what might have been the fate of an emotional shut-in: the aridity and destitution of that very livingness to which she responded so dramatically before the paintings she saw. No, Sophia's world remained rich with warmth and sentience until her end.

As bespeaks her namesake, *Sophia,* the name given by the Valentinian Gnostics to their intangible *Soul,* So our New England lady was "a world soul," born of the original *Sophia's* "smile" (E. Neumann, 1959, *Art of the Creative Unconscious,* 56).

Note

1. Sophia Hawthorne, *Notes in England and Italy,* 308.

Bibliography

Edinger, Edward, 1968, "An Outline of Analytical Psychology. New York: C. G. Jung Foundation for Analytical Psychology, pp. 1-12.

———. 1978, *Melville's Moby-Dick: A Jungian Commentary.* New York: A New Directions Book.

Franz, Marie-Louise von, 1988, *Projection and Re-Collection in Jungian Psychology.* London: Open Court.

Hawthorne, Julian, 1968, *Nathaniel Hawthorne and his Wife.* Archon Books.

Hawthorne, Sophia, 1869, *Notes in England and Italy.* New York: G. P. Putnam & Son.

Jacobi, Yolande 1957, *Complex Archetype Symbol in the Psychology of C. G. Jung.* Princeton: Princeton University Press.

Jung, C. G. 1990, *Collected Works,* 6. Translated by H. G. Baynes. Revised by R. F. C. Hull. Princeton: Princeton University Press.

Neumann, Erich 1959, *Art and the Creative Unconscious.* New York: Pantheon.

Norton Anthology of American Literature, 1980. Shorter Edition. New York: W. W. Norton & Co.

Julie E. Hall (essay date 2002)

SOURCE: Hall, Julie E. "'Coming to Europe,' Coming to Authorship: Sophia Hawthorne and Her *Notes in England and Italy.*" *Legacy* 19, no. 2 (2002): 137-51.

[*In the following essay, Hall portrays Hawthorne's transformation from amanuensis and editor for her husband to professional writer as the author of* Notes in England and Italy.]

With the publication of *Notes in England and Italy,* a volume based on letters and journals she wrote while the Hawthorne family lived abroad from 1853 to 1860, Sophia Peabody Hawthorne for the first and last time in her life put herself "into a pair of book covers," as she once described it, and presented herself before the public gaze as an author. Although the nineteenth century was fairly afloat in travel literature, with Italy "taking the lead in eliciting memoirs" (Buzard 159), Hawthorne's *Notes* made a place for itself in the crowded market. Appearing serially in *Putnam's Magazine* in 1869 and then in book form in both England and the United States later that year, Hawthorne's volume was in its eighth edition with Putnam and Sons in 1882, fourteen years after its first appearance. The publication of *Notes* also marked Hawthorne's entrance into a rather elite club, for while some eighteen hundred writing Americans published travel books before 1900, only about two hundred of these were women, and fewer than fifty American women had published book-length travel accounts by the time Hawthorne's volume appeared.[1]

Despite these facts, Sophia Hawthorne is seldom thought of or treated as an author. Indeed, her entrance into the public world of print is a part of her story that is usually forgotten, ignored, or dismissed, for it co-exists only uneasily with accepted views of Hawthorne as the quintessential Victorian woman, content to live her life within the confines of nineteenth-century gender codes. In his famous 1884 biography of his parents, *Nathaniel Hawthorne and His Wife,* Julian Hawthorne drew the outlines of a life from which few have departed. "She lived for her husband," Julian writes of his mother, and when he gives an account of Sophia's considerable literary activities after Nathaniel's death, which included both the editing of her husband's journals and the publication of her own book, Julian mentions only her editorial work. In one of the latest revisionings of the Hawthorne family, *Dearest Beloved: The Hawthornes and the Making of the Middle-Class Family,* T. Walter Herbert goes further than previous biographers in recognizing Hawthorne as a complex woman (and he does mention *Notes*), but he ultimately endorses established opinion when he contends that Hawthorne "pioneered a convention of womanhood that obliged her to deploy her creative power vicariously, through Nathaniel. Among women who have sought to fulfill themselves through the achievements of a man, few have succeeded better than Sophia" (38). Nina Baym concurs in "Again and Again, the Scribbling Women," writing that Sophia "had given up whatever public ambition she might have had in exchange for drawing her life's meaning from Hawthorne's life" (24). And Luanne Jenkins Hurst, in an examination of

Sophia's contributions to Nathaniel's career, foregrounds a line from a Sophia Hawthorne letter—"If I could help my husband in his labors, I feel that that would be the chief employ of my life"—but fails to note two cases of true literary influence: Nathaniel's use of Sophia's journal-writing as a source for "Edward Randolph's Portrait" and "Drowne's Wooden Image" (Hall).

I argue that the standard, accepted picture of Sophia Peabody Hawthorne is but a half-truth. Certainly, she embraced her life as wife to America's "great romancer" and mother of three children. Indeed, as we have seen, she herself helped foster the impression that these roles, with their requisite subordination of self, brought her total fulfillment ("If I could help my husband in his labors . . ."). However, the publication of her book testifies to quite another impulse—the impulse to speak with her own voice, to tell her own story, to claim authority and authorship for herself. As Mary Kelley notes in *Private Woman, Public Stage,* entering "the public realm," for a woman, was "a testing of the limits imposed upon a woman's life, and it suggested the will or the desire on the woman's part to test or resist those limits. It suggested a new assertion of a woman's being . . ." (125). I contend that the publication of *Notes* was just such a "new assertion" for Sophia Hawthorne, that it was a triumph of her will to create and a telling transgression of her culture's gender codes.

Like women before and after her, Hawthorne's coming to authorship was characterized by ambivalence and struggles not just with "cultural constraints" but also "between herself and herself" (Gilbert and Gubar 17)—the artistic self that desired expression, and the socialized self that had internalized its culture's dictums and valuations of women. Indeed, Hawthorne's 1869 book venture was not the first but rather the third time Hawthorne had been presented with the opportunity to publish. Her famous sister Elizabeth Peabody had urged her to "go public" with letters she wrote from Cuba, 1833-35, and both Elizabeth and James T. Fields, Nathaniel Hawthorne's editor and partner in the powerful Ticknor and Fields publishing house, approached Hawthorne on the subject of her English letters and Italian journals in 1859. She refused all proposals. Sophia and Nathaniel responded to Fields's 1859 proposition in separate letters but with one voice. Nathaniel declared that Fields was "quite right in wanting Mrs. Hawthorne for contributress; . . . I have never read anything so good as some of her narrative and descriptive epistles to her friends; but I doubt whether she would find sufficient inspiration in writing directly for the public" (18: 203).[2] The letter echoes another written some two years earlier to William Ticknor, in which Nathaniel proclaims, "Mrs. Hawthorne altogether excels me as a writer of travels. Her descriptions are the most perfect pictures that ever were put on paper" (18: 63). Sophia's response to

Fields's 1859 request was more adamant than her husband's. "I am very sorry indeed," she writes,

> that you should ask me to do any thing for you which I cannot possibly do. I assure you most earnestly that nothing less urgent and terrible than the immediate danger of starvation for my husband and children would induce me to put myself into a magazine or a pair of book covers. You forget that Mr Hawthorne is the Belleslettres portion of my being, and besides that I have a repugnance to female authoresses in general, I have far more distaste for myself as a female authoress in particular.
>
> (18: 202)

The passage is rich and suggestive. When she denotes "Mr Hawthorne" as "the Belleslettres portion" of her being, Sophia Hawthorne simultaneously lays claim to and displaces a "self" that is literary and productive/creative. Yet the statement is literally inaccurate, for throughout her life Hawthorne was an avid letter writer and journal keeper: some fifteen hundred of her letters and portions of at least nineteen diaries and journals, dating from 1829-1871, are housed in various collections today. Hawthorne also constructs an intriguing physical/sexual metaphor when she refers to authorship as "putting [her]self into a pair of book covers," voicing the vulnerability, discomfort, even shame she would feel in coming before the public. The most disturbing line in the passage, though, is certainly the expression of what can only be called loathing—Hawthorne uses the word "repugnance"—for other women and that part of her self that might aspire to or attempt authorship.

However, a letter by Sophia Hawthorne to her sister Elizabeth Peabody about the 1859 proposal sounds a very different note indeed, speaks another part of Hawthorne's divided self, and articulates the desire upon which she would act almost ten years later. Unlike the Hawthornes' letters to Fields, this missive portrays the couple in conflict and suggests that the united front they presented outside the family circle was just that: a front. "I see," Hawthorne writes,

> that it is my plain duty not to argue the matter any further with Mr. Hawthorne. I perceive what his cool reason prescribes for him. . . . You know I have to postpone all my own possibilities in the way of art. But I have always had a vast fund of patience and devoutly believe I shall have a scope and field for all I can do in another world, if not in this. . . . Oh there is often so much richer a return for giving up than having—that to have seems to me far the lesser boon.[3]

This passage contains no hint of the "distaste" for female authoresses or artists that Hawthorne professed in her letter to Fields. Instead, even as it endorses the nineteenth-century ideals of "true womanhood"—duty, subservience, and self-sacrifice—that worked to keep women confined in the home and the domestic, it refers overtly to Hawthorne's artistic "possibilities," and it writes an afterlife in which dreams and ambitions are realized.

It seems clear, then, that despite the praise Nathaniel often had for his wife's writing, when it came to publication, he enforced his society's restrictive gender codes.[4] Indeed, the rather casual tone of Nathaniel's November 28, 1859, remark to Fields—"I doubt whether she would find sufficient inspiration in writing for the public"—is belied in a letter penned one day later to Francis Bennoch:

> Mrs. Hawthorne had a note from Fields, yesterday, requesting her to become a contributor to the *Atlantic Monthly*! I don't know whether I can tolerate a literary rival at bed and board; there would probably be a new chapter in the "Quarrels of Authors." However, I make myself at ease on that score, as she positively refuses to be famous, and contents herself with being the best wife and mother in the world.
>
> (18: 204)

The exclamation point at the end of the first sentence communicates the level of Nathaniel's agitation. His figuring of Sophia Hawthorne, author, as a rival "at bed" is even more telling, suggesting that for Nathaniel, a publishing wife was an emasculating threat.[5] Nor was this the first time Nathaniel had considered the possibility, or inscribed it in sexual terms. In 1856, he wrote to his wife about a new issue of the *Little Pilgrim,* Grace Greenwood's magazine for children:

> In Grace Greenwood's last "Little Pilgrim," there is a description of her new baby!!! . . . I wonder she did not think it necessary to be brought to bed in public, or, at least, in presence of a committee of the subscribers. My dearest, I cannot enough thank God, that, with a higher and deeper intellect than any other woman, thou hast never—forgive me the bare idea!—never prostituted thyself to the public. . . . It does seem to me to deprive women of all delicacy; it has pretty much such an effect on them as it would to walk abroad through the streets, physically stark naked.
>
> (17: 456)

How was it, then, that Sophia Peabody Hawthorne, a woman who had throughout her life practiced the art of writing but who had never crossed the threshold into the public realm—how or why was it that in 1869 she did just that? Certainly, the factors leading to this moment were many and various, including the financial problems Hawthorne and her children experienced after Nathaniel's death in 1864. In this respect, Sophia's 1859 letter to Fields was all too prescient. Yet we can also note that in penning the phrase, "nothing less terrible and urgent than immediate starvation . . . would induce me to put myself into a magazine or a pair of book covers," Hawthorne was leaving herself an opening, constructing the conditions under which she would find publication permissible; she was, in essence, allowing for the possibility. Indeed, for many nineteenth-century women, entering the literary marketplace was easier when it was done under the banner of home and family—it was, to borrow a phrase from Dennis Porter, to "conflate the opposition, to make a duty of desire" (11). Mary Kelley remarks on this fact in her study of those nineteenth-century American writing women she terms "literary domestics." "From their literary income," Kelley notes,

> [these women] supported or contributed to the support of themselves and their families, yet felt compelled to justify that support on the basis of domestic need. . . . [T]heir need to rationalize [their actions] in domestic terms underlined the fact that they were women of the home who simultaneously came to assume the male roles of public figure, economic provider, and creator of culture. They became hybrids, a new breed, or . . . literary domestics.
>
> (xi, 111)

Sophia Peabody Hawthorne was one of this "new breed."

Some scholars believe that financial need alone motivated Sophia Hawthorne to publish *Notes.* Mary Suzanne Schriber contends that "only the dire financial straits that pertained in 1869 when she gathered together her *Notes* could drive Sophia Hawthorne to publish" (*Writing Home* 122-23). Thomas Woodson likewise maintains, in the "Historical Commentary" to the Centenary edition of *The English Notebooks, 1853-1856,* that "for Sophia, the eventual publication of her letters . . . was much more an act of economic necessity than the expression of a 'literary rivalry' of any kind. Her final emergence as what her husband might have called a 'female scribbler' occurred for the same reasons and at the same time as her editing of his notebook" (Woodson 733-34). I disagree with this argument for several reasons. First, indications are that by 1868-69, the severe financial problems that beset Hawthorne after her husband's death—and that seem to have been most acute in 1866-67[6]—were diminishing. Hawthorne's editing began to bring in money in 1866, when the *American Notebooks* appeared in twelve installments in the *Atlantic Monthly,* for which Sophia was paid one hundred dollars each. When *Passages from the American Notebooks* appeared in late 1868, Hawthorne received at least five hundred dollars from the English publishers alone (Simpson 694). That same year, Hawthorne moved her family to Dresden, Germany, where Julian planned to enroll in the famous Dresden Realschule, or Polytechnic, to study engineering (Bassan 45), and where Hawthorne believed the family could live more economically. Early entries in Hawthorne's 1869 Dresden journal show careful and precise accounting of financial outlays. . . .

[Such entries], though, become scarce as the months pass, suggesting that Hawthorne was less careful with and less anxious about money. Records of piano lessons for Rose and German lessons for Julian; of ceilings being white-washed and walls papered; and of tickets purchased to symphony and opera performances indicate that the family was not living on a shoe-string.

Additionally, the timeline of Hawthorne's editorial and authorial work itself argues that *Notes* was more than just a financial enterprise for its author and that Hawthorne did harbor authorial ambitions. As I have noted, *Passages from the American Notebooks,* the first of the three sets of Nathaniel's journals that Hawthorne edited and published, appeared in late 1868. As early as December 1867, Hawthorne had also begun work on the *English Notebooks* (Woodson 736-37), but in 1869 she laid them aside and turned to a new project and one that was wholly her own. From January to May of that year, she records in her journal that she is steadily working on the manuscript for *Notes*; it was published later the same year. In June 1869, she returned to Nathaniel's *English Notebooks,* re-reading copy written earlier, making additional revisions, and transcribing another volume of the Notebooks that she found "after I thought I had done all."[7] *Passages from the English Notebooks* was published in England and the United States in 1870; *Passages from the French and Italian Notebooks* followed in 1871-72. The question the timeline poses is this: with the *English Notebooks* almost complete and the *French and Italian Notebooks* awaiting her attention as well, why would Hawthorne interrupt her editorial work to produce her own book, if money was her sole concern? If the image of Sophia Hawthorne, author, was indeed as "repugnant" to her as she had once claimed, why not save her own letters and journals until she had absolutely no other options, or at least until she had published all of her husband's notebooks? I believe the answer is that Hawthorne was motivated by more than money; that she did, in fact, long to be recognized not just as an editor/preserver of her husband's writing and creations, but as a creator and a word crafter herself. Notably, too, the impulse that produced *Notes* was not a lone one. On June 26, 1869, Hawthorne records in her journal that she is reviewing her *Cuba Journal*—those letters from Cuba that Elizabeth Peabody had encouraged her to bring out some thirty years earlier—to determine if they are fit to publish. Although she decided they would not do—"There is so much about people in them,"[8] she writes—it is interesting to speculate that Hawthorne might have published again, had she not died in 1871. And, finally, we must add that even if Hawthorne did publish primarily to fill an empty pocketbook, she is certainly not the first or only woman *or* man to do so, nor does the fact negate Hawthorne's achievement or the historical and literary value of her text.

Another element in Hawthorne's life that helped pave the way for her eventual appearance in print was the exceptionally strong tradition of writing in her family of origin. In fact, every member of the Peabody family who survived early adulthood became a published author. Hawthorne's mother, Elizabeth Palmer Peabody, published original poetry in a local newspaper early in her life (Bailey 553); brought out a textbook entitled *Sabbath Lessons: or, An Abstract of Sacred History* in 1810; and authored a children's version of Spenser, *Holiness: The Legend of St. George,* in 1836—accomplishments all the more notable because they occurred so early in the century.[9] Dr. Nathaniel Peabody, Sophia's father, authored *The Art of Preserving Teeth* (1828), and her only surviving brother, Nathaniel, wrote a history of the family that appeared in *Grandmother Tyler's Book* (1925). Mary Peabody Mann, the youngest of the three Peabody sisters, published with her older sister Elizabeth *Moral Culture of Infancy, and Kindergarten Guide* (1863); co-edited with Elizabeth the *Kindergarten Messenger* (1873-75); wrote a three-volume biography of her husband, *Life and Works of Horace Mann* (1865-68); and two decades later published a novel entitled *Juanita: A Romance of Real Life in Cuba Fifty Years Ago* (1887).

The most important of Sophia Hawthorne's familial influences, though, was likely her older sister, Elizabeth. A pioneering educator, member of the Transcendentalist group, publisher, and book-seller, Elizabeth was also an author many times over. *Key to History: First Steps to the Study of History* (1832), *Record of a School* (1835), *Aesthetic Papers* (1849), *Reminiscences of Reverend William Ellery Channing, D. D.* (1880), and *Last Evening with Allston* (1886) are some of the works that issued from her pen. When Elizabeth enlisted Sophia's help on her second record of Bronson Alcott's experimental Temple School, *Conversations with Children on the Gospels* (1836), she likely provided Sophia with her first experience producing a text. As I have noted, it was also Elizabeth who encouraged Sophia to publish both her Cuba letters in the 1830s and her European travel writings in 1859. Sophia testified to Elizabeth's importance in her life and her development as a writer when she dedicated her one published work not to her famous husband, nor to her children, but "To Elizabeth P. Peabody, by her Sister, S. H." Elizabeth was, for Sophia Hawthorne, "a female precursor who . . . [proved] by example that a revolt against patriarchal literary authority [was] possible" (Gilbert and Gubar 49).

Hawthorne's experiences with writing and, particularly, the business of publishing continued during her marriage to Nathaniel. It was not uncommon for Sophia to correspond with Nathaniel's publishers for him, and she regularly read—or heard Nathaniel read—his manuscripts before he sent them off for publication. In the case of at least one novel—*The House of the Seven Gables*—Sophia read proof sheets as they came back from the printer,[10] and, as the editors of the Centenary

Edition *Marble Faun* have shown, with this the last of Nathaniel's novels, Sophia served as a kind of copy-editor, clarifying hard-to-read passages in the fair copy, systematizing pagination, and marking and making factual and stylistic changes, many of which her husband adopted.[11]

Another stage of what we could call Sophia Hawthorne's "inadvertent, unstructured . . . apprenticeship" in writing—the "only type there could have been for a woman," Mary Kelley maintains (122)—began after her husband's death, when she edited Nathaniel's notebooks for publication. Probably no single other fact of Sophia Hawthorne's life is as well-known, or as excoriated. The criticism began when Randall Stewart discovered, upon gaining access to Nathaniel's original manuscript journals, that language in the published *Notebooks* had been changed, and passages in the manuscript had been inked out, even excised. His treatment of Sophia in his Introduction to *The American Notebooks* (1932) was scathing. He branded Sophia the "bowdlerizer" of Nathaniel's journals, condemning what he termed the "prudishness or false delicacy" that led to the changing of words like "bellies" to "paunches," and "dung" to "excrement," and "the artificial taste and cultivation" that led to the substitution of "ill" for "sick" and "drinking" for "swilling" (xv, xvi). He charged that "the published version [of the journals] seriously misrepresents [Hawthorne's] character and literary genius" (xiii).

Much less well-known, unfortunately, are Stewart's later findings, based upon his study of the correspondence between Sophia Hawthorne and James Fields while Hawthorne was at work on the *Notebooks*. That correspondence, Stewart wrote, threw "new light on Mrs. Hawthorne's editing and the extent of her responsibility in the early editions of Hawthorne's journals," revealing that "Fields exerted an important influence upon her editorial work." And he concluded that "[i]f [Hawthorne] had had an entirely free hand, her editions would doubtless have been less unfaithful to the originals" ("Editing" 314-15). Although Stewart still found Hawthorne guilty of what he terms "editorial sins," he also noted that in some cases it was Sophia who argued strongly for the retention of Nathaniel's original words. In one instance, for example, Sophia went to bat for Nathaniel's use of the words "dreadful earnest," crossing swords with the proofreader, Mr. Nichols, in the process:

> The expression "dreadful earnest" is the one Mr. Hawthorne uses with great force—far more force it has than "dreadfully earnest." He uses the word *earnest* as a noun—and the epithet dreadful as meaning *full of dread*—not in the hackneyed way. In this I disagree with Mr. Nichols. It must remain I think "*dreadful ear-*

nest"—unless we undertake to improve Mr. Hawthorne's English, which I think cannot well be done, for he used words very thoughtfully and conscientiously.

(qtd. in "Editing" 305)

At another time, Hawthorne wrote Fields that "I often am obliged to fight about *moods of verbs*—about which Mr. Hawthorne was very nice—. . . . These happy words are a peculiarity and specialty of Mr. Hawthorne's style, and must always be retained" (qtd. in "Editing" 314). Hawthorne also realized, with the instincts of an artist herself, the value of Nathaniel's journals. "My first idea," she once wrote Fields, "was that the journals were very rapid sketches—mere outlines, cartoons of the great pictures he meant to paint fully out"; at another time she compared them to the "pen and ink and pencil sketches of the pictures of the old masters, in the contemplation of which we come so very near the creative soul of the artist" (qtd. in Stewart, "Editing" 300, 301). Stewart concludes that Hawthorne spotted the "germ of Pearl," the "first idea of the grand Procession of Life," and seems to have been in favor of printing the journal account of a young woman's drowning, which Nathaniel drew upon for his rendering of Zenobia's death in *The Blithedale Romance* ("Editing" 302, 309, 311).

Subsequent editors of Nathaniel Hawthorne's *Notebooks* agree with Stewart's later assessment. In his balanced treatment of the subject, Claude M. Simpson notes the "gentility and propriety [that] motivated [Sophia] consistently" in her editorial changes, but maintains as well that "in effect, [Fields] taught her how to edit according to contemporary standards" (685-86). Thomas Woodson observes, too, Sophia's penchant for suppressing "references to tobacco and alcoholic beverages, accounts of sexual actions and bodily functions," and names of living persons, but allows that many of her alterations were those "any copy editor would make" (738-41).

What I argue for here is that, whatever we may think of Hawthorne's editorial principles, work on her husband's notebooks and journals gave her valuable first-hand experience in all that was involved in transforming private writings into a published book: from selection of material to grammatical clean-ups, from the discipline of copying to experience dealing with publishers and proofreaders. It was, you might say, a dress rehearsal, for immediately after she finished editing the *American Notebooks,* she began work on her own. In her 1869 journal, Hawthorne records that on January 3 she "wrote Preface to the 2d Ed. of [Nathaniel Hawthorne's] Am Notes"; on January 14 she put a bundle of manuscript into the mail; and on January 15 she "copied [the] cathedral letters [the name by which she designated her letters written from England, and which make up the first section of *Notes*] all PM till 12 at night."[12] Moving from Nathaniel's manuscripts to her own, she hardly missed a beat. Copying and editing her letters and journals as she had her husband's, Hawthorne this time produced a text that would bear her name. Her sureness of purpose reveals the confidence, gained through experience, with which she approached this new task. Her "apprenticeship" was complete.

An additional factor in Hawthorne's coming to authorship, I believe, was the influence of Europe itself. For it was within the "foreign" contexts of England and Italy that she composed the works she would later publish; and it was in Dresden, Germany, where she moved with her children in 1868, four years after her husband's death, that she revised her letters and journals to produce *Notes*.[13] As William W. Stowe writes in *Going Abroad: European Travel in Nineteenth-Century American Culture,* "Americans . . . used Europe as a setting for personal liberation and the fulfillment of desire," as "a stage for independent self-definition, for establishing personal relations with culture and society that did not necessarily fit the conventional patterns prescribed by hometown and family standards" (xii, 5). One of the most famous examples of a nineteenth-century American woman artist who used Europe as a means of escaping the confining cultural patterns of her native land, and of exploring, even re-making herself, was transcendentalist writer Margaret Fuller. Several other notable American women were part of the expatriate artists' community in Rome while the Hawthornes were there, such as Harriet Hosmer, Maria Lander, Edmonia Lewis, and Margaret Foley. In fact, as William H. Gerdts notes, the United States alone, among other nations, "knew a collective feminine presence" of artists in Italy in the mid-nineteenth century (69). For Sophia Hawthorne as for these other women, Europe was a site for re-creating or re-visioning the self and for fulfilling forbidden desires. As she wrote her letters and journals during her initial European tour (1853-1860), she also wrote a self that was empowered—by virtue of her experiences and adventures—to "[claim] the authority of a writer and guide," to act as teacher and interpreter (Stowe 12). When she returned to Europe in 1868 and set about preparing her manuscript for publication, another desire was enacted, another self fashioned, and in 1869 she presented herself to the world as Sophia Hawthorne, author.

So how does Hawthorne write herself in the pages of *Notes*? What kind of persona does she create against the backdrop of Europe? She is an American woman with democratic principles who nevertheless betrays class-consciousness and a desire for importance when she notes that she and her family regularly stay in first-rate accommodations. She is wife to an American writer acclaimed abroad as well as at home, whose status ensures the family extraordinary treatment. Although

Nathaniel is most often referred to in the text as "Papa," we are yet sure to know his identity, for on the title page of *Notes* our author identifies herself as "Mrs. Nathaniel Hawthorne." She is also the mother of three children, referred to in the text by the initial letters of their first names—U. (Una), J. (Julian), and R. (Rose, or "baby")—and she extols the role. In describing one picture of the holy family, by Francia, Hawthorne muses on Mary as mother: "Mary's face is extremely beautiful, matronly, pure and intellectual . . . as if her experience were deep and wide. It is a MOTHER, with a perfect sense of all a mother's responsibilities" (209). She is educated and literary, quoting readily from a host of authors such as Wordsworth, Burns, Byron, Scott, Herbert, Smollett, Dante, and Virgil. And she aligns herself especially, and not surprisingly, with the Romantic tradition when she devotes chapters of her book to Newstead Abbey, home of George Gordon, Lord Byron, and pilgrimages through Burns's and Sir Walter Scott's country.

With a quick wit, a ready pen, and an eye for detail and description, as her husband so often noted, Hawthorne gives us characterizations worthy of a novelist and metaphors both apt and clever in the pages of *Notes*. One elderly caretaker encountered at Bolton Priory in England is described as a "bundle of wrinkles, held together by a velvet jacket and small-clothes [sic], [who] rested on his spade, and gazed at me out of his queer little eyes, but spoke never a word. He resembled one of the gothic gurgoyles [sic] which are carved on the cloisters and at the springing of the arches of cathedrals" (17). A cabman in York has "a face exactly like dough just beginning to become bread, still quite white" (23); and the shop of an antiquarian collector is, Hawthorne tells us, "about as big as one division of a walnut" (56). Skillful representations of dialect add to some portraits. In Scotland, after touring Inversnaid, Hawthorne writes that "it was all in harmony to hear the Scotch dialect and accent on every side. Mothers calling out to their bairns 'Take care, noo! Sit doon or ye'll fa.' 'Dinna put the roup in her mou, it's nae gude' and so on" (169).

Often, too, of course, Hawthorne is tour guide and historian. The following passage, recounting a visit to the mausoleum of celebrated Scottish Romantic poet, Robert Burns, is exemplary in its blend of description, subjective response, and objective fact:

> [The mausoleum] is round, with a dome, and formerly was open to the air. . . . The sculpture is by Turner-elli, in very high relief. Burns stands with the plough, and Scotland's Muse hovers in the air, about to wrap him in her mantle. . . . [T]he face is said to be a perfect likeness. The figure is stout and well made, and the head large and compact, with clustering hair, large eyes and mouth, and the whole expression pleasant. . . . He died on the 22d of July, 1796, when but

thirty-seven years old, sixty-one years ago; and in 1815, . . . his coffin was removed to its present abiding place. . . .

(125)

Perhaps more than anything else, though, Sophia Hawthorne sees herself and inscribes herself within her text as an artist and an art connoisseur. For, in fact, Hawthorne was an artist. She had studied with Washington Allston, Thomas Doughty, and Chester Harding, some of the most prominent figures in the nineteenth-century American art world; had exhibited her paintings professionally in the 1830s; and had commanded, at one time, up to fifty dollars apiece for her fine, reputedly flawless copies (Valenti n27 p. 18; 6).[14] Like other American artists, she had dreamed of touring Europe and seeing the masterpieces she had long admired, studied, and, in not a few cases, copied. As she wrote when she visited the Pitti Palace in Florence, "To-day I saw Michel Angelo's Three Fates; and I needed more than one pair of eyes to gaze, for I had all my life wished to see it" (360). The Preface to *Notes* announces Hawthorne's predilection, the purpose of her work, and the design that helps unify a book composed of letters written from England and Scotland and journals kept in Italy, penned over a period of years. "If," she writes, *Notes* "will aid any one in the least to enjoy, as I have enjoyed, the illustrious works of the Great Masters in Architecture, Sculpture, and Painting, I shall be well repaid for the pain it has cost me to appear before the public." The structure of *Notes* bears out the emphasis in the Preface: while the Hawthorne family lived in England for over five years, "our old home" occupies only 117 pages of Hawthorne's text, with a trip to Scotland receiving an additional seventy-seven pages. Italy, however, the great land of art, where the Hawthornes sojourned for one year and four months, receives 352 pages, and of those 352, Florence, birthplace of the Renaissance, occupies 163.

In *Writing Home,* Mary Schriber also identifies art as the dominant concern of Hawthorne's text and finds that Hawthorne most fully "lives in those passages in *Notes* that record visits to galleries and critiques of art" (117). Schriber and I disagree fundamentally, however, in our readings of the book. Schriber believes that *Notes* is an example of autobiographical "self-destruction" and that in it, Hawthorne attempts to portray herself as her culture's ideal of Woman and "erase those aspects of herself that are other" (93, 109). One of those "other" selves, according to Schriber, is Hawthorne as artist, who is "compellingly articulate" in the "several stunning descriptions of art works that punctuate her account" (117). As I point out, though, *Notes* is predominantly given over to descriptions of art, and there are far more than "several stunning accounts" in its pages. I argue, in opposition to Schriber, that *Notes* is rather a testament to and expression of Hawthorne's creative

spirit, and that in its pages, Sophia Hawthorne—wife, mother, and nineteenth-century woman—figures herself as well as artist and writer.

In Part I, "Notes in England," great architectural works take the stage. York Minster, Lincoln and Peterboro Cathedrals, and St. Botolph's Church each head up a chapter; indeed, as I have mentioned, in her 1869 journal Hawthorne customarily refers to the letters that make up this section as her "Cathedral letters." Hawthorne's account of her visit to Peterboro Cathedral is characteristic:

> After dinner we took a walk. Peterboro is a very small town gathered in front of its glorious minster. . . . As we entered the Close, the world seemed shut out, as it always does inside these monastic retreats . . . upon me the effect of the three vast arches of the western facade was more sublime and magnificent than that of any architecture I have yet seen in England. . . . I did not know before what a grand power lay in a lofty curve, and words can never convey an idea of it. The first impression was that those arches had more to do with heaven than earth. Though the line returns again to the same level from which it rises, yet it seems to have been transfigured as it soared and sang in its circuit. They are the emblem of a saint's soul, whose visible form still exists. He stands on the earth, but his spirit has ascended into another world, and remains there, in truth, though he is yet with us in mortal guise. They are an image of endless aspiration in constant rest. . . .

(71-72)

Here as elsewhere in *Notes,* Hawthorne, a true aesthete, is inspired to beautiful prose by the beauty she beholds. The "lofty curve" becomes an "emblem" and an "image" of earthly aspiration and of the human spirit that, like an arch, would soar heavenward, only to return (during this life) again to earth. The power of the form transmutes it into something that is almost alive, that "soars" and "sings." And its paradoxical nature—although it is fixed and static, it seems, as the eye follows the curve of the line, to be motion itself—represents to Hawthorne the marriage of other opposites: heaven and earth, aspiration and rest.

Artist and interpreter, Hawthorne turns instructor and art historian in succeeding paragraphs on the Cathedral:

> [F]rom the Lady-chapel, all along the aisles to the west front, on the walls beneath the windows, are the intersected arches, which first suggested the pointed arch. I took great pains to draw you some of them, to show you the transition steps from Norman to the early English or pointed style. The Norman arch is a perfect semicircle, heavy and massive. Doors, windows, and arches were all rounded, and the pillars were very thick, and the sculptured ornaments bold and rude. By degrees the style was enriched with zigzag adornments and the chevron; and then came the intersected arch.

(76-77)

This passage retains many qualities of the original letter, written to Hawthorne's oldest child Una,[15] such as the use of the familiar "you," which creates a sense of immediacy and intimacy and carries the audience of *Notes* into the scene. Hawthorne also refers to a sketch that accompanies her explanation of the Norman, the early English, and the intersected arches. It was her habit, observable in some of her earliest preserved letters and journals, to accompany her writing with sketches, and it was her habit as well to take a sketch-book with her while she toured, at once practicing her artistic skills and capturing, in images as well as words, for herself and others, the sights and scenes of Europe.

Hawthorne's emphasis on art is only intensified in the Italian portion of *Notes*. Many accounts of individual works occupy two to three pages of printed text, like the description of Guido Reni's Archangel Michael slaying the dragon, a portion of which is quoted below. I include lengthy passages of text here because *Notes* is not readily available, having long been out of print, and because it is important to an understanding of what Hawthorne aspired to do, and what she succeeded in doing, as a result of her unique combination of gifts. With the knowledge of a working artist and the skill of a practiced writer, Hawthorne captures and recreates in words some of the world's greatest masterpieces. Notable in the following passage are the care with which Hawthorne denominates color—the corselet is "sapphire," not blue, the mantle is "crimson," not red; the frequency of figurative language, especially simile and metaphor; and the coherence and completeness of the description:

> The armory of heaven seems to have been exhausted to furnish forth the splendor of his array. His corselet is of sapphire, and identical with the curves and lines of the glorious form. A crimson mantle floats around him, like the red band in the rainbow let loose for his adornment, a symbol of his flaming love; and from his brow waves backward light spirals of pale gold hair. The sandals are bound upon his feet with lacings of azure and gold, and fastened high with large rubies that burn like fire. How can any one describe the aerial tread of those angelic feet? The left one is planted upon the head of the dragon, who looks up at the seraphic vision with the face (it is said) of [Pope] Innocent Tenth, an evil-eyed old demon, and now powerless beneath the ethereal touch. The right foot rests upon a rock, with as little effect of weight as the alighting of a bird upon a tree. It is the insubstantial yet immutable firmness of divine power. . . . One hand, the left, holds the chain with which the dragon is to be bound, and which already secures him. The right is uplifted, grasping a sword, in act to strike. The glitter and flash of the inevitable stroke dazzle as it descends. Out-spread wings of pencil-color, just the hue of the shaded side of a cloud near the moon, hold poised this celestial Leader of the Hosts of God. The downcast white lids, with dark lashes, the untroubled brow, the curves of the closed lips, without disdain or pride, but tender and sweet, though resolute without effort, show the messen-

ger of Our Father. What endless worlds of meaning are evolved from this master-piece. A perfect work is a unit of Truth, and all truth is one.

> (277-78)

"Outspread wings of pencil-color, just the hue of the shaded side of a cloud near the moon"—certainly only an artist could conceive such a color-description, but only a writer with an artist's sensibility could translate a seen object so completely into a "word picture." Indeed, Hawthorne's word pictures sometimes move into the realm of pure poetry, as in the following description of the famous Campanile, or bell-tower, in Florence, designed by Giotto Di Bondone:

> Giotto must have diffused his spirit through the stones and lines. One of its bells sang out as we passed—a deep, round, liquid sound. . . . It was music, dropped through water. . . . It was as if the great dome itself had rolled from the soul of its artist, a pure globe of melody, and dropped singing into the sea of space.

> (341)

Another sustained passage of highly imaginative prose is found in Hawthorne's description of the famous—one might say notorious—portrait of Beatrice Cenci, which also figures prominently in her husband's last novel, *The Marble Faun*. As T. Walter Herbert notes, "The Cenci" was "a central icon of the Anglo-American fascination" with Rome, and "the Hawthornes were among those who found it endlessly absorbing" (219). Believed in the nineteenth-century to be the work of Guido Reni, the painting portrays the woman at the center of a sensational and tragic tale. Allegedly the victim of an incestuous relationship perpetrated by her step-father, Beatrice Cenci was later convicted of conspiring in his murder and was executed. Hawthorne takes the portrait as her text and reads there a story of innocence overcome, yet somehow untainted, by evil. Beatrice's is a woe surpassing words as "she passes to her doom":

> At last, at last! . . . And now we sat down before Beatrice Cenci! . . . Never from any human countenance looked out such ruin of hope, joy, and life; but there is unconsciousness still, as if she did not comprehend how or why she is crushed and lost. The white, smooth brow is a throne of infantine, angelic purity, without a visible cloud or a furrow of pain, yet a wild, endless despair hovers over it. The lovely eyes, with no red nor swollen lids, seem to have shed rivers of crystal tears that have left no stain—no more than a deluge of rain stains the adamantine arch of heaven. It is plain that the fountains are exhausted, and she can no longer obtain any solace from this outlet of grief. The delicate, oval cheeks are not flushed nor livid, but marble-pale, unaffected by the torrents that have bathed them, as if it were too hard an agony to be softened by tears. The mouth is unspeakably affecting. The rose-bud lips, sweet and tender, are parted slightly, yet with no cry, nor power to utter a word. Long-past words is the mis-

ery that has banished smiles forever from the blooming flower of her mouth. Night is gathering in her eyes, and the perfect face is turning to stone with this weight of voiceless agony. She is a spotless lily of Eden, trailed over by a serpent, and unable to understand the desecration, yet struck with a fatal blight. Her gaze into the eyes of all human kind, as she passes to her doom, is pathetic beyond any possibility of describing. One must *see* that backward look to have the least idea of its power, or to know how Guido [Reni] has been able to express . . . a sorrow that has destroyed hope, and baffles the comprehension of its victim.

(212-14)

While it was as an artist that she saw herself, Hawthorne also was a writer, as she reveals over and over again in the pages of her manuscript, in her skillful portraits of people and lands and in her masterful descriptions and interpretations of art and architecture. But not until 1869—a full ten years after she wrote the last of her European journals—was Hawthorne ready to re-envision herself as a professional writer, a publicly known and recognized author. In late 1868, as I have noted, Hawthorne made the bold decision to move her family to Dresden, Germany. The move was opposed by many Hawthorne family friends,[16] and it has been viewed by modern tellers of the Hawthorne tale as "a final flight" (Tharp 314), a "venture as ill conceived and pathetic as Clifford's train ride in *The House of the Seven Gables*" (Miller 524-25). But perhaps it was something else—perhaps it was a strike for freedom. In *Haunted Journeys: Desire and Transgression in European Travel Writing*, Dennis Porter writes that

> at one level, most forms of travel at least cater to desire: they seem to promise or allow us to fantasize the satisfaction of drives that for one reason or another is denied us at home. As a result, not only is travel typically fueled by desire, it also embodies powerfully transgressive impulses. If, as anthropologists have long since taught us, borders of all kinds are perceived as dangerous as well as exciting places, and are associated with taboos, this is no less true of territorial borders, of tribal or national frontiers.

(9)

Indeed, perhaps some of the resistance to Hawthorne's decision arose from an awareness of its implications: she was moving out of her "cultural confinement within domestic and local boundaries and . . . into national and international spaces, seizing for [herself] the freedom of movement that has been the historical prerogative of the male" (Schriber, Introduction xvi). Freedom of movement; freedom of mind: Hawthorne was transgressing borders "psychological and geographical" (Schriber, Introduction xvi). Almost immediately after her arrival in Dresden, she began work on her forthcoming book. Hawthorne had entered a "new realm of being" (Kelley 125)—she had become Sophia Hawthorne, author.

Thus, I believe, Europe played a major role in Sophia Hawthorne's transformation from private writer to public author. In England and Italy in the 1850s, Hawthorne defined herself as an artist among artists, but also, importantly, as an artist who wrote. Art critic and connoisseur, she was simultaneously the teller of her own travels, the narrator of her own tale. Returning to Europe in 1868, Hawthorne cast herself in another role—that of professional writer. Possessed of a purpose—to "aid any one in the least to enjoy . . . the illustrious works of the Great Masters," as she writes in her Preface—motivated by need, and fueled by desire, Hawthorne summoned the courage and the will to transgress external and internal boundaries and risk what she called "the pain it cost me to appear before the Public" (Preface, *Notes*). In coming to Europe, Sophia Hawthorne had come into herself.

Notes

1. Some of the American women who preceded Hawthorne into print were Fanny Hall, *Rambles in Europe* (1836); Catharine Maria Sedgwick, *Letters from Abroad to Kindred at Home* (1841); Lydia Sigourney, *Pleasant Memories of Pleasant Lands* (1842); Margaret Fuller, *Letters from Europe* (1846-50); Caroline Kirkland, *Holidays Abroad; or Europe from the West* (1849); and Harriet Beecher Stowe, *Sunny Memories of Foreign Lands* (1854). See Harold F. Smith, *American Travellers Abroad: A Bibliography of Accounts Published Before 1900*.

2. All references to Nathaniel Hawthorne's fiction, letters, and journals, and certain of Sophia Hawthorne's letters, are to the *Centenary Edition of the Works of Nathaniel Hawthorne* and are cited by volume and page number in the text.

3. Letter to Elizabeth Peabody [1860], Henry W. and Albert Berg Collection, New York Public Library, Astor, Lenox and Tilden Foundations, hereafter referred to as B-NYPL.

4. Mary Schriber concurs. See *Writing Home* 120-23.

5. Indeed, this attitude may have extended to any *woman* in his family, for Rose Hawthorne records an incident in which Hawthorne commanded her, while she was still quite young, "'Never let me hear of your writing stories! I forbid you to write them!'" See Lathrop 422-23.

6. See Randall Stewart, "Mrs. Hawthorne's Financial Difficulties," especially pages 45-52.

7. Holograph journal, Dresden, Germany, 1869, B-NYPL.

8. Holograph journal, Dresden, Germany, 1869, B-NYPL.

9. Hawthorne's mother, Elizabeth Palmer Peabody, also testifies to the personal cost of taking up the pen in a letter quoted by Bruce A. Ronda in the Introduction to a collection of daughter Elizabeth Palmer Peabody's letters. "I mean to do all I can to keep peace," Peabody writes, "and have determined never to write anything again, excepting letters, and as few of them as possible; never to touch a book, except upon the Sabbath, and to devote every moment to work of some kind. I am convinced that my attempts to write poetry have gained me more ill will than any actions of my life" (9).

10. Hawthorne's entry for "Sunday [February] 9th" in her 1851 journal reads, "Two proofs came of House of Seven Gables—I read them with pert interest. There never was such perfection of style."

11. See Introduction to the Centenary Edition of *The Marble Faun* (Simpson xxv) and "Textual Introduction" of the same volume (Bowers lvi and lxv-lxx).

12. Holograph journal, Dresden, Germany, 1869, B-NYPL.

13. Mary Schriber also notes the "impact of European travel on an American woman" in her discussion of Hawthorne's *Notes* (*Writing Home* 123). She does not, however, comment at any length on Hawthorne's return to Europe in 1868.

14. Several examples of Hawthorne's work survive today: an illustration by Sophia serves as the frontispiece for a special edition of Nathaniel's "The Gentle Boy," published in 1837; a drawing of Horace Mann can be found in Mary Peabody Mann's biography of her husband; a copy of Chester Harding's portrait of Washington Allston hangs in the Massachusetts Historical Society; a bas-relief of Charles Emerson, probably executed by Hawthorne after Charles's death for her friend and Charles's fiancée, Elizabeth Hoar, is in the Emerson House in Concord, Massachusetts; and two oil paintings are housed in the Peabody Essex Institute, Salem, Massachusetts.

15. See pages 722-34 of the "Historical Commentary," volume 21 of the *Centenary Edition* of Hawthorne's works. Una and the couple's youngest child, Rose, remained with a nurse during three 1857 excursions taken by Nathaniel, Sophia, and Julian. The letters that make up Parts I and II of *Notes*, "Notes in England" and "Notes in Scotland," were written during that time. As the editors remark, letters were always, in the Peabody family, a semi-public performance; Sophia likely knew at the time she wrote these letters that they would find their way to her sister Elizabeth, and

thence to other family members and friends. She may thus have had several audiences in mind when she composed them (see 21: 729).

16. Louise Hall Tharp records that both General Franklin Pierce and George Hillard, the Hawthorne's attorney, opposed the plan (314).

Works Cited

Bailey, Sarah Loring. *Historical Sketches of Andover, (Comprising the present towns of North Andover & Andover) Massachusetts.* Boston: Houghton, 1880.

Bassan, Maurice. *Hawthorne's Son: The Life and Literary Career of Julian Hawthorne.* Columbus: Ohio State UP, 1970.

Baym, Nina. "Again and Again, the Scribbling Women." *Hawthorne and Women: Engendering and Expanding the Hawthorne Tradition.* Ed. John L. Idol, Jr., and Melinda M. Ponder. Amherst: U of Massachusetts P, 1999. 20-35.

Bowers, Fredson. Textual Introduction. *The Marble Faun.* By Nathaniel Hawthorne. *The Centenary Edition of the Works of Nathaniel Hawthorne.* Ed. William Charvat, et al. Vol. 4. Columbus: Ohio State UP, 1968. xlv-cxxxii.

Buzard, James. *The Beaten Track: European Tourism, Literature, and the Ways to "Culture," 1800-1918.* Oxford: Clarendon, 1993.

Gerdts, William H. "Celebrities of the Grand Tour: The American Sculptors in Florence and Rome." *The Lure of Italy: American Artists and the Italian Experience, 1760-1914.* Theodore E. Stebbins, Jr. Museum of Fine Arts, Boston, with Abrams Publishers, New York, 1992. 66-93.

Gilbert, Sandra M., and Susan Gubar. *The Madwoman in the Attic: The Woman Writer and the Nineteenth-Century Literary Imagination.* New Haven: Yale UP, 1979.

Hall, Julie. "A Source for 'Drowne's Wooden Image' and Hawthorne's Dark Ladies." *Nathaniel Hawthorne Review* 16 (1990): 10-12.

Hawthorne, Julian. *Nathaniel Hawthorne and His Wife: A Biography.* 2 vols. Boston: Houghton, 1884.

Hawthorne, Nathaniel. *The Centenary Edition of the Works of Nathaniel Hawthorne.* Ed. William Charvat, et al. 23 vols. Columbus: Ohio State UP, 1962-97.

Hawthorne, Sophia Peabody. Holograph Journal. Lenox, Massachusetts, December 26, 1850-[March] 14 [1851]. Henry W. and Albert Berg Collection, The New York Public Library, Astor, Lenox and Tilden Foundations (B-NYPL).

———. Holograph Journal. Dresden, Germany, January 3, 1869-December 31, 1869. B-NYPL.

———. Letter to Elizabeth Peabody [1860]. B-NYPL.

———. *Notes in England and Italy.* New York: G. P. Putnam & Son, 1869.

Herbert, T. Walter. *Dearest Beloved: The Hawthornes and the Making of the Middle-Class Family.* Berkeley: U of California P, 1993.

Hurst, Luanne Jenkins. "The Chief Employ of Her Life: Sophia Peabody Hawthorne's Contribution to Her Husband's Career." *Hawthorne and Women: Engendering and Expanding the Hawthorne Tradition.* Ed. John Idol, Jr., and Melinda Ponder. Amherst: U of Massachusetts P, 1999. 45-54.

Kelley, Mary. *Private Woman, Public Stage: Literary Domesticity in Nineteenth-Century America.* New York: Oxford UP, 1984.

Lathrop, Rose Hawthorne. *Memories of Hawthorne.* Boston: Houghton, 1897.

Miller, Edwin Haviland. *Salem Is My Dwelling Place: A Life of Nathaniel Hawthorne.* Iowa City: U of Iowa P, 1991.

Porter, Dennis. *Haunted Journeys: Desire and Transgression in European Travel Writing.* Princeton: Princeton UP, 1991.

Ronda, Bruce A. Introduction. *Letters of Elizabeth Palmer Peabody.* By Elizabeth Peabody. Ed. Bruce Ronda. Middletown: Wesleyan UP, 1984. 1-46.

Schriber, Mary Suzanne. Introduction. *Telling Travels: Selected Writings by Nineteenth-Century American Women Abroad.* Ed. Mary Suzanne Schriber. DeKalb: Northern Illinois UP, 1995. xi-xxxi.

———. *Writing Home: American Women Abroad, 1830-1920.* Charlottesville: U of Virginia P, 1997.

Simpson, Claude M. Historical Commentary. *The American Notebooks.* By Nathaniel Hawthorne. *The Centenary Edition of the Works of Nathaniel Hawthorne.* Ed. Claude M. Simpson. Vol. 8. Columbus: Ohio State UP, 1972. 677-98.

———. Introduction. *The Marble Faun.* By Nathaniel Hawthorne. *The Centenary Edition of the Works of Nathaniel Hawthorne.* Ed. William Charvat, et al. Vol. 4. Columbus: Ohio State UP, 1968. xix-xliv.

Smith, Harold F. *American Travellers Abroad: A Bibliography of Accounts Published Before 1900.* Carbondale: Southern Illinois UP, 1969.

Stewart, Randall. "Editing Hawthorne's Notebooks: Selections from Mrs. Hawthorne's Letters to Mr. and Mrs. Fields, 1864-1868." *More Books, Bulletin of the Boston Public Library* Sept. 1945.

———. Introduction. *The American Notebooks.* By Nathaniel Hawthorne. Ed. Randall Stewart. New Haven: Yale UP, 1932.

———. "Mrs. Hawthorne's Financial Difficulties: Selections from Her Letters to James T. Fields, 1865-1868." *More Books, Bulletin of the Boston Public Library,* Feb. 1946.

Stowe, William W. *Going Abroad: European Travel in Nineteenth-Century American Culture.* Princeton: Princeton UP, 1994.

Tharp, Louise Hall. *The Peabody Sisters of Salem.* Boston: Little, Brown, 1950.

Valenti, Patricia Dunlavy. "Sophia Peabody Hawthorne: A Study of Artistic Influence." *Studies in the American Renaissance* (1990): 1-19.

Woodson, Thomas. Historical Commentary. *The English Notebooks, 1853-1856.* By Nathaniel Hawthorne. *The Centenary Edition of the Works of Nathaniel Hawthorne.* Ed. Thomas Woodson and Bill Ellis. Vol. 21. Columbus: Ohio State UP, 1997. 709-48.

FURTHER READING

Biographies

Cowley, Malcolm. "The Hawthornes in Paradise." *American Heritage* 10, no. 1 (December 1958): 30-5, 112-15.

> Recounts the courtship and early married life of Sophia and Nathaniel Hawthorne, interspersed with excerpts from their journals and letters.

Hawthorne, Julian. "Sophia Amelia Peabody." In *Nathaniel Hawthorne and His Wife,* pp. 39-81. Cambridge, Mass.: The Riverside Press, 1884.

> A chapter from Julian Hawthorne's biography of his parents in which he describes his mother, her upbringing, the role she played in the family, and her influence on his father.

Marshall, Megan. "Three Sisters Who Showed the Way." *American Heritage* 38, no. 6 (September-October 1987): 58-66.

> Examines the role of the Peabody sisters in the nineteenth-century American women's liberation movement.

Miller, Edwin Haviland. "A Calendar of the Letters of Sophia Peabody Hawthorne." *Studies in the American Renaissance* (1986): 199-204.

> A list of Hawthorne's letters preceded by a biographical sketch.

Tharp, Louise Hall. *The Peabody Sisters of Salem,* Kingsport, Tenn.: Kingsport Press, 1950, 372 p.

> Biography of Hawthorne and her sisters Mary and Elizabeth, significant portions of which are devoted to Hawthorne's Cuba sojourn and married life.

Criticism

MacKay, Carol Hanbery. "Hawthorne, Sophia, and Hilda as Copyists: Duplication and Transformation in *The Marble Faun.*" *Browning Institute Studies* 12 (1984): 93-120.

> Considers Hawthorne's resemblance to the character of Hilda in her husband's novel *The Marble Faun.*

McDonald, John J. "A Sophia Hawthorne Journal, 1843-1844." *Nathaniel Hawthorne Journal* (1975): 1-30.

> Reprint of a portion of Hawthorne's journal preceded by a brief introduction.

Norko, Julie M. "Hawthorne's Love Letters: The Threshold World of Sophia Peabody." *American Transcendental Quarterly* 7, no. 2 (June 1993): 127-39.

> Uses the letters Hawthorne's husband wrote to her during their courtship to examine his image of her as the embodiment of their shared ideals and aspirations.

Person, Leland S., Jr. "Hawthorne's Love Letters: Writing and Relationship." *American Literature* 59, no. 2 (May 1987): 211-27.

> Explores Nathaniel Hawthorne's idealized vision of his wife and her profound influence on his writing.

Additional coverage of Hawthorne's life and career is contained in the following sources published by Thomson Gale: *Dictionary of Literary Biography*, Vols. 183, 239; and *Literature Resource Center.*

Alfred de Musset
1810-1857

(Full name Louis Charles Alfred de Musset) French playwright, poet, novelist, essayist, and short story writer.

The following entry presents critical discussion of Musset from 1969 to 2003. For further information on Musset's life and career, see *NCLC,* Volume 7.

INTRODUCTION

Considered one of the leading figures of the French Romantic movement, Musset produced numerous distinguished works of lyric poetry and several esteemed plays, including his outstanding historical tragedy *Lorenzaccio* (1834). Musset's verse cycle *Les nuits* (1835-37; *The Nights*), inspired by his love affair with French writer George Sand, is typically regarded among his preeminent poetic compositions. This brief, tumultuous relationship with Sand also found expression in Musset's only novel, *La confession d'un enfant du siècle* (1836; *Confession of a Child of the Century*). In these works drawn from his personal life, Musset sought to universalize his experiences of failed passion and emotional suffering, constructing a persona of the prototypical Romantic artist. Likewise, the protagonists in many of his remaining works, including a series of comic plays that pioneered the tradition of "armchair theater"—dramatic works designed to be read rather than staged—are also frequently viewed as projections of Musset himself. Unlike the dramatic works of his contemporaries, however, Musset's plays continue to be staged with regularity well over a century after his death. His lyric poems, especially those he composed during the years 1833 to 1837, are generally viewed as some of the finest in the French language.

BIOGRAPHICAL INFORMATION

Musset was born in Paris in 1810. His parents were both descended from cultured families and provided an intellectual environment for their child. A brilliant though undisciplined student, Musset pursued medicine, law, and painting at the Collège Henri IV in Paris before choosing a career in literature. This decision was influenced in part by his acquaintance with Victor Hugo, who introduced him to the Romantic *cénacle,* or literary society, which included Hugo, Alfred de Vigny,

Charles Augustin Sainte-Beuve, Charles Nodier, and Prosper Merimée. Musset's earliest literary work was a free translation and redaction of Thomas De Quincey's *Confessions of an English Opium Eater.* Published before De Quincey's work became well known, *L'Anglais mangeur d'opium* (1828) received little attention from Musset's contemporaries. His next work, a collection of short plays and narrative poems entitled *Contes d'Espagne et d'Italie* (1830; *Tales of Spain and Italy*), however, was an immediate popular success that introduced the young author to all of Paris. In 1830, Musset's first play *La nuit vénitienne; ou, Les noces de Laurette* (*A Venetian Night*) was staged. Its infamous public failure prompted the author to compose most of his subsequent plays to be read, not produced. Musset's next volume of plays *Un spectacle dans un fauteuil* (1833-34; *Scene in an Armchair*), lent its name to a form of drama known as "armchair theater" and would later be recognized as among his most enduring literary creations. In 1833, Musset met the French novelist George Sand at a dinner in honor of contributors to the

Revue des deux mondes. Their ensuing affair, though brief, provided the passion that he felt his poetry lacked. After spending several months together in Paris, they traveled to Venice for the winter. Musset became ill, and, while nursing him back to health, Sand fell in love with his doctor, Pietro Pagello. Devastated, Musset left Italy. Upon Sand's return to Paris, they resumed their tempestuous love affair, which continued intermittently until early 1835. Despite its disastrous effect on his physical and emotional health, Musset's relationship with Sand proved an unequalled inspiration; beginning in 1833, and during the next several years, Musset composed what are generally considered to be his greatest works of drama and poetry. In 1847, Musset's comedy *Un caprice* (1840; *A Caprice*) was successfully produced at the Comédie-Française, the French national theater in Paris. Emboldened by this achievement, Musset revised several of his armchair dramas for the stage during the late 1840s and early 1850s and composed new works. By this time, however, Musset's literary powers had entered a period of radical decline. Elected to the prestigious Académie Française at age forty-two after two unsuccessful nominations, Musset had nevertheless surpassed the pinnacle of his career. As editions of his collected works appeared in the 1850s, increasing bouts of depression and rapidly deteriorating physical health, abetted by the dissolute lifestyle he had led since his youth, culminated in Musset's death in 1857.

MAJOR WORKS

Comprised of four separate poems—"La nuit de mai," "La nuit de décembre," "La nuit d'août," and "La nuit d'octobre"—Musset's *Les nuits* cycle chronicles the poet's gradual recovery from the intense suffering and bitterness caused by the end of a love affair, capturing this process over four disparate nights. All but "La nuit de décembre" take the form of a conversation between the poet and his Muse. In that work, an evocation of winter that depicts loneliness and desperation, a black-clad figure of death appears. Through the poems of *Les nuits,* Musset affirmed his belief in the importance of love and its relationship to art. In the last of the series, "La nuit d'octobre," the poet rests after reconciling with his past. Musset's other notable poetic works composed in the same period as *Les nuits* include his outstanding Romantic lyrics "Lettre à M. de Lamartine" and "Souvenir," which were anthologized in the collection *Poésies nouvelles, 1836-1852* (1852). This volume, along with *Poésies complètes* (1840), reflects the bulk of Musset's mature poetic output and includes numerous examples of his later poetry. In these works, Musset frequently adopts a tone of witty, light, and graceful detachment that contrasts with the passionate anguish and longing of his earlier poetry. While they differ from *Les nuits* and the Romantic lyrics of the 1830s in terms of mood and subject, these pieces nevertheless share certain stylistic qualities with their predecessors, including striking imagery, natural speech, and varied patterns of meter, rhythm, and rhyme. Among Musset's dramas, *Lorenzaccio, Fantasio,* and *On ne badine pas avec l'amour* (*No Trifling with Love*), all of which were composed during the writer's affair with Sand and published in the collection *Un spectacle dans un fauteuil,* are generally categorized among his finest works. In the historical drama *Lorenzaccio,* Musset portrays a sixteenth-century attempt by Lorenzo de' Medici to liberate the republic of Florence from foreign dominion, concentrating on the gradual disillusionment and surrender of his hero to treachery and deceit. Set in a fantastical projection of late medieval Germany, the comedic *Fantasio,* a work noted for its effective use of Romantic irony, follows its title figure as he disguises himself by employing the garb and mien of a jester in order to enter the court of the Bavarian king. Acting the role of the sardonic clown, Fantasio saves the king's daughter Elsbeth from an unwanted marriage. *On ne badine pas avec l'amour,* as well as the later play *Il faut qu'une porte soit ouverte ou fermée* (1845; *You Can't Have It Both Ways*), are examples of Musset's *proverbs dramatique,* short comic sketches designed to illustrate their aphoristic titles with wit and a characteristic lightness of touch. Musset's only complete novel, *La confession d'un enfant du siècle* is an autobiographical work that chronicles its protagonist's search for pleasure following a failed love affair. The novel also depicts the Romantic *mal du siècle,* a term that describes the malaise of the generation that was born after the fall of Napoleon, too late to take part in the glories of either the French Revolution or the Napoleonic Empire. A life-long essayist and reluctant but accomplished writer of short prose fiction, Musset composed the noted *Lettres sur la littérature* (*Letters of Dupuis and Cotonet*), a series of four articles that first appeared in the *Revue des deux mondes* between 1836 and 1837 and satirize the excesses of the Romantic movement; his short stories, collected in *Nouvelles* (1848) and *Contes* (1854), were largely written for financial reasons but nevertheless include several works of merit.

CRITICAL RECEPTION

In an unfinished novel entitled *Le poète déchu,* Musset describes his semi-autobiographical protagonist as a "fallen poet." Likewise, during his own lifetime, Musset was forced to accept with a certain degree of irony the fact that his prose works, rather than the poetry and dramas on which he prided himself as a writer, would form the basis for his popular acclaim. Indeed, the notoriety surrounding Musset's affair with George Sand, coupled with his alluring persona as a troubled, suffering artist contributed to the success of his novel *La confession d'un enfant du siècle.* Since his death, however, scholars have asserted that Musset's enduring reputation rests upon his lyric and dramatic compositions. Remarking on his collected poetry, twentieth-century critics largely have moved beyond a prior focus on the personal nature of these works in order to appreciate both Musset's stylistic luminosity and the inventive means by which he evokes themes of suffering and love as they relate to artistic creation. In regard to his plays, Musset's outstanding works of the 1830s continue to elicit the greatest share of scholarly interest, with contemporary critics acknowledging that *Lorenzaccio* and the plays of *Un spectacle dans un fauteuil* form the basis of his fame as a Romantic playwright. In examining these works, ranging from tragedy to light drama, critics have praised Musset's brilliant use of dialogue as well his balance of stylistic delicacy and emotional power. While biographical assessments of Musset's highly personal works, thought to embody his descent into debauchery and search for innocent, exalted love, broadly persist, scholars of the contemporary period generally attribute the continuing popularity of his work to the universality and passion of his poetic expressions of love and loss.

PRINCIPAL WORKS

L'Anglais mangeur d'opium [translator; from the autobiography *Confessions of an English Opium Eater* by Thomas De Quincey] (autobiography) 1828

†*Contes d'Espagne et d'Italie* [*Tales of Spain and Italy*] (play and poetry) 1830

La nuit vénitienne; ou, Les noces de Laurette [*A Venetian Night*] (play) 1830

‡*Un spectacle dans un fauteuil.* 3 vols. [*Scene in an Armchair*] (plays) 1833-34

La confession d'un enfant du siècle [*Confession of a Child of the Century*] (novel) 1836

§*Comédies et proverbes* (plays) 1840

‖*Poésies complètes* (poetry) 1840

Nouvelles (short stories) 1848

#*Poésies nouvelles, 1836-1852* (poetry) 1852

**Comédies et proverbes* (plays) 1853

††*Contes* (short stories and essays) 1854

Oeuvres posthumes (plays, poetry, and letters) 1860

Oeuvres complètes de Alfred de Musset. 10 vols. (plays, poetry, novel, short stories, essays, and letters) 1866

Correspondance de George Sand et d'Alfred de Musset (letters) 1904

The Complete Writings of Alfred de Musset. 10 vols. (plays, poetry, novel, short stories, essays, and letters) 1905

Correspondance (1825-1857) (letters) 1907

*Most of Musset's works were originally published in the periodical *Revue des deux mondes* and first translated in 1905 in *The Complete Writings of Alfred de Musset.*

†This work includes the verse *contes* "Don Paez," "Portia," and "Les Marrons du feu."

‡This work contains the dramas *Les Caprices de Marianne* (*The Whims of Marianne*), *Fantasio, Lorenzaccio* and *On ne badine pas avec l'amour* (*No Trifling with Love*).

§This work includes the drama *Un caprice* (*A Caprice*).

‖This work includes the poetic cycle *Les nuits.*

#This work includes the poems "Lettre à M. de Lamartine" and "Souvenir."

*This work includes the dramas *Il faut qu'une porte soit ouverte ou fermée* (*You Can't Have It Both Ways*) and *On ne saurait penser à tout.*

††This work includes the essays *Lettres sur la littérature* (*Letters of Dupuis and Cotonet*).

CRITICISM

Russell S. King (essay date May 1969)

SOURCE: King, Russell S. "Alfred de Musset: Some Problems of Literary Creativity." *Nottingham French Studies* 8, no. 1 (May 1969): 16-27.

[*In the following essay, King highlights the theme of creative lassitude in Musset's life and writings.*]

Baudelaire describes Musset disparagingly as "*un paresseux* à effusions gracieuses."[1] Like all writers who believe in, or rely on, artistic inspiration for composing their works, Musset and his critic, Baudelaire, frequently if not permanently feared lest their inspiration might "dry up." Sometimes this fear is expressed explicitly, sometimes it is transformed into something more subtle, such as we find in, for example, Mallarmé's sonnet beginning *Le vierge, le vivace et le bel aujourd'hui.* Sartre's condemnation of Baudelaire—whether it be valid or otherwise is irrelevant at this point—could more appropriate be directed against Musset. Musset's refusal to accept responsibilities and act positively would make him an easier target for an existentialist critic. The portrait his brother gives us,[2] though fascinating in some of the detail, is that of a dull and motiveless existence.

Despite his not inconsiderable output, Musset was always tormented by the notion that he was a literary impotent. It is interesting to examine how this flaw in his personality, if flaw it is, pervades his writings, particularly his more serious writings between the years 1833 and 1838. Long before La Rochefoucauld, in his *Maximes* (no. 266, and compare no. 630), had recognized the influence of "la paresse":

"C'est se tromper que de croire qu'il n'y ait que les violentes passions, comme l'ambition et l'amour, qui puissent triompher des autres. La paresse, toute languissante qu'elle est, ne laisse pas d'en être souvent la maîtresse: elle usurpe sur tous les desseins et sur toutes les actions de la vie; elle y détruit et y consume insensiblement les passions et les vertus."

A paralysing inertia prevented Musset from writing the works of art which he believed it to be his destiny to compose. Herein lies the conflict which he elaborated in the *Nuits* cycle of poems; it is a trait common to almost all his heroes, albeit indirectly; and it is the mainspring of Musset's own special *mal du siècle*. Moreover, the action of many of his imaginative writings springs from attempts to overcome this inactivity.

The poem **"La Nuit de Mai"** provides a clear illustration of Musset's difficulty in composing. This poem takes, typically for Musset, the form of a debate, between the Muse and the Poet, that is, more exactly, between Musset-Poet and Musset-Man, both more or less equal representations of Musset himself. The muse urges the Man to write, enumerating reasons why he should devote himself more fruitfully to his art and even suggests possible subjects. She endeavours to entice the Man away from his present neglect of her, using the combined charm of Mother, Mistress and Sister:

> O paresseux enfant! regarde, je suis belle.
> Notre premier baiser, ne t'en souviens-tu pas,
> Quand je te vis si pâle au toucher de mon aile,
> Et que, les yeux en pleurs, tu tombas dans mes bras?[3]

Nonetheless, the Man fabricates unconvincing pretexts for not satisfying the Muse by actual composition and creative activity:

> Je ne chante ni l'espérance,
> Ni la gloire, ni le bonheur,
> Hélas! pas même la souffrance.
> La bouche garde le silence
> Pour écouter parler le cœur.[4]

Of course, the Muse, and Musset himself, fails to be convinced: the "bouche" is more reliably productive than the heart. Such reasoning echoes the defiant concluding stanzas of **"La Nuit d'Août:"**

> J'aime, et je veux chanter la joie et *la paresse* . . .
> Aime et tu renaîtras; fais-toi fleur pour éclore.
> Après avoir souffert, il faut souffrir encore;
> Il faut aimer sans cesse, après avoir aimé.[5]

Such is the philosophy Musset chose to follow, alas! during much of his life. He was not persuaded by it, being aware that such an existence, for an artist, leads too easily to sterility, instead of giving the artist a richer background on which to draw in order to enlarge the scope of his art.

Love and suffering are valuable to the poet only when subsequently transformed into art. They are a means to an end, part of a creative process not an end in themselves, a distinction which Musset preferred to ignore after about 1838. The Muse urges:

> L'herbe que je voulais arracher de ce lieu,
> C'est ton oisiveté; ta douleur est à Dieu.[6]

Significantly the Muse follows these lines by others more celebrated and all too frequently misinterpreted:

> Rien ne nous rend si grands qu'une grande douleur
> Mais, pour en être atteint, ne crois pas, ô poète,
> Que ta voix ici-bas doive rester muette.[7]

Observe the punctuation: there is not as much as a comma between the first and second lines. The first line is considered too often in isolation to reinforce certain almost masochistic tendencies in Musset to wallow excessively in grief, with no reference to the all-important qualifying lines. The poet's suffering cannot, in itself, give the poet greatness. In **"La Nuit de Mai,"** the Muse fails to convince the Man who, ironically, has the last word:

> Mais j'ai souffert un dur martyre,
> Et le moins que je pourrais dire,
> Si je l'essayais sur la lyre,
> La briserait comme un roseau.[8]

Nevertheless the Muse is the victor in that a poem has been produced, even if it is an "art-poem," that is, a poem about poetry and its creation. The struggle to compose is the subject of the poem, with Musset playing, in the form of a debate, the rôle of the self-conscious artist. **"La Nuit de Mai"** is a poem about poetry just as Gide's *Les Faux-Monnayeurs* is a novel about the/a novel.

"La Nuit d'Août" is similarly conceived. It too is concerned with the inert poet reluctant to practise his art. Further fruitless pretexts are tentatively put forward:

> O ma Muse, ne pleurez pas!
> A qui perd tout, Dieu reste encore,
> Dieu là-haut, l'espoir ici-bas.[9]

But Musset had little or no faith in God and even less hope "ici-bas."

In **"La Nuit d'Août,"** the Muse uses an argument dearer, and more disturbing, to Musset: the destructive and paralysing effect on the artist of corruption, pleasure, love, and life and experience in general. The Muse asks:

> Que fais-tu loin de moi, quand j'attends jusqu'au jour?
> Tu suis un pâle éclair dans une nuit profonde.
> Il ne te restera de tes plaisirs du monde
> Qu'un *impuissant mépris* pour notre honnête amour.[10]

Cynicism and scorn are the inevitable result of close contact with, and experience of, life. Nonetheless a parade of cynicism suited Musset, and others of his age, but he was aware of its contaminating effect on the creative powers of the artist. An increasing awareness of this, along with a refusal to accept it fully and honestly, accounts in some measure for the gradual falling off of Musset's artistic career. The more one loves, he feels, the more one loses sight of love; similarly the more one becomes acquainted with life and its complexities, the more one loses faith and hope in one's own life. For Musset, innocence, youth and enthusiastic fervour are essential to the poet. In the apostrophe addressed by the poet to the Muse at the end of **"La Nuit d'Août,"** the poet defies the Muse:

> J'aime, et pour un baiser je donne mon genie.[11]

If the poet so acts, he soon has little further to relate in his art but the analysis and description of the ensuing conflict between his artistic life and his ordinary experiences:

> J'aime, et je veux chanter la joie et la paresse,
> Ma folle expérience et mes soucis d'un jour.[12]

The conflict between these two selves is of central significance in his mid-career writings. Before this defiance of the Muse, for example, in the *Contes d'Espagne et d'Italie* (1830), Musset is a more optimistic, enthusiastic and less personal writer. After about 1833, a dominant theme in his works is, directly or indirectly, the problem of creation, and, by extension, action.

For this reason, **"La Nuit d'Octobre"** is a very fitting sequel to **"La Nuit d'Août."** In **"La Nuit d'Octobre,"** the Muse is summoned to console the repentant, neglectful poet returning after some wounding experience. Just as Gide, amongst others, was to conclude that happiness lies in the search for happiness, Musset is able only to depict the return to the Muse, not what he is capable of achieving after his return. Here, temporarily at least, the poet recognizes the superiority of the Muse, of artistic creation, unlike the conclusion of **"La Nuit d'Août."** "Jours de travail! seuls jours où j'ai vécu! O trois fois chère solitude! Dieu soit loué, j'y suis donc revenu, à ce vieux cabinet d'étude."[13]

What has he to sing about?

> Dieu soit loué, nous allons donc chanter! . . .
> Oui, je veux vous ouvrir mon âme,
> Vous saurez tout, et je veux vous conter
> Le mal que peut faire une femme.[14]

Here the poem draws to a close. Such subject-matter, though of course legitimate, is far from the visionary and imaginative purpose Musset once believed essential to poetry. Once the Muse has successfully consoled the poet, the latter declares:

> Maintenant, Muse, à nos amours!
> Dis-moi quelque chanson des beaux jours.[15]

Musset is cheating, in pretending that the "affair" with the Muse is beginning. The affair, meaning creation, has already been exhausted.

In the *Nuits* cycle, the apparent theme is "love." According to one critic, the "secret" of the *Nuits* poems and the *Confession* is Musset's "instabilité en amour": "son impuissance d'aimer longtemps et fidèlement, d'aimer comme il faut aimer."[16] By extension and by implication the theme is also Musset's "instabilité en art." Much attention is paid to the Poet who is weak, generally incapable of sustained creative activity. The reader tends to equate Musset himself with the Poet rather than with the Muse. But the Muse voices more clearly and directly the artistic aspirations of the true, free artist, hampered by the weakness and often invalid arguments expressed by the Poet.

Reasons for his inability to apply himself to his art, to allow his superior artistic nature to dominate his other less worthy instincts, are complex and difficult to distinguish. There is a lack of faith in society, and in French art of the 1830s. At the age of seventeen, in 1827, in a letter to his school friend, Paul Foucher, the brother-in-law of Victor Hugo, he wrote of his uneasiness and sense of futility: "Je t'écris donc pour te faire part de mes dégoûts et de mes ennuis; tu es le seul lien qui me rattache à quelque chose de remuant et de pensant; tu es la seule chose qui me réveille de mon néant et qui me reporte vers un idéal que j'ai oublié par impuissance."[17] Paul de Musset reports a conversation he had with his brother complaining of judgements made of him: "Ce reproche de paresse est une invention nouvelle qui sent d'une lieue le siècle des manufactures . . . Parmi ceux qui m'appellent paresseux, je voudrais savoir combien il y en a qui répètent ce qu'ils ont entendu dire, combien d'autres qui n'ont jamais lu un seul de mes vers, et qui seraient bien attrapés si on les obligeait à lire autre chose que *Les Mystères de Paris.* Le roman-feuilleton, voilà la vraie littérature de notre temps."[18] Quantity too easily became the yard-stick by which an established writer's reputation was maintained and enhanced. An artist who does not produce or who produces rarely, is too easily condemned for neglect of his art. Of course, in one respect, Musset is putting into the mouths of a philistine public a notion which he himself held much of his life.

If only he could apply himself regularly to his work, like a George Sand or a Balzac. Baudelaire, too, was conscious, and more honestly and lucidly so, of the therapeutic value of regular and dedicated effort: "Une nourriture très substantielle, mais régulière, est la seule chose nécessaire aux écrivains féconds. L'inspiration est décidément la sœur du travail journalier. Ces deux contraires ne s'excluent pas plus que tous les contraires qui constituent la nature. L'inspiration obéit, comme la faim; comme la digestion, comme le sommeil. Il y a sans doute dans l'esprit une espèce de mécanique céleste, dont il ne faut pas être honteux, mais tirer le parti le plus glorieux."[19] This same theme is re-expressed in a more frenzied, extreme manner towards the end of his

Mon Cœur mis à nu. The difficulties in being a "part-time" writer are considerable. It is for this reason that Rimbaud has puzzled and attracted so many readers: when he finally decided to abandon literature, he did so completely.

Rolla and *La Confession d'un Enfant du Siècle* reflect a philistine society incapable of appreciating art. Esteem for a living artist, especially a living poet, was largely diminished. Already in **"Les Vœux Stériles,"** published in the *Revue de Paris,* as early as October 1830, Musset bemoans the purposelessness and unimportance of the modern poet, in comparison with his counterpart in Ancient Greece and Renaissance Italy:

> Temps heureux, temps aimés. Mes mains alors peut-être,
> Mes lâches mains, pour vous auraient pu s'occuper;
> Mais aujourd'hui pour qui? dans quel but? sous quel maître?
> L'artiste est un marchand, et l'art est un metier . . .[20]

For the artist of the 1830s fulfilment was possible only when, and if, the artist could translate his art into action. Chateaubriand, Lamartine, Hugo, Stendhal, Mérimée . . . all were, or became, in some measure, "public figures" or men of action. There was never any prospect of Musset following suit.

> Heureux, trois fois heureux, l'homme dont la pensée
> Peut s'écrire au tranchant du sabre et de l'épée! . . .
> Qui que tu sois, enfant, homme, si ton cœur bat,
> Agis! jette ta lyre; au combat, au combat!
> Ombre des temps passés, tu n'es pas de cet âge.[21]

Like Verlaine, Musset was not generally tormented by public incomprehension; but awareness of the vast gulf separating him and those he was supposedly writing for filled him with a sense of paralysing futility. Gide was able to overcome this by addressing his works to the "lecteur de demain." Those near to Musset were only partially and occasionally capable of understanding this feeling. Paul de Musset, forever urging his brother to write, recognized some validity in his brother's argument:

> "Il m'a battu sur tous les points, qu'il a cent fois raison, que ses ennuis, son silence, ses dédains ne sont que trop justifiés, que s'il voulait les exprimer, il ferait rentrer sous terre ceux qui se mêlent de le blâmer ou de le plaindre, et que tôt ou tard, son immense supériorité sera reconnue par tout le monde."[22]

Such an explanation of his inertia can be only partially valid. Had this pretext been either completely true or completely untrue, Musset, who was basically honest, could more easily have faced up to the reality of the problem. Musset was sincere, even if idle. Believing, in 1838, that a new Golden Age was approaching for the arts, he felt fired with enthusiasm, but this was short-lived. This renascent faith is in part explained by the recent success of the Opera singer Maria Garcia (La Malibran). His enthusiasm was again roused, in 1847, when his plays were rediscovered and first produced in Paris. Despite these temporary changes of fortune, the need for an appreciative, intelligent public is not totally valid. All great writers have complained of being misunderstood. Indeed, to be misunderstood is almost a "prerequisite" of the modern writer, and certainly of the Romantic and post-Romantic poet.

Musset's disharmony with his age and contemporaries is manifested in his identification with a past society. In the *Contes d'Espagne et d'Italie,* Musset was doing little more than following a trend in giving his poems an Italian or Spanish backdrop. Nonetheless Musset already felt an attraction towards other vaguely conceived and vaguely known countries.[23] When not specifically concerned with his own problems and those of the society in which he lived, as in the *Confession* and *Rolla,* he preferred to turn to other societies in which the artist was happier, enjoying a more fruitful and appreciated existence. Paul de Musset clearly recognized this preference in his brother:

> "S'il fût né dans le siècle de Louis XIV, Alfred de Musset eût été de la cour, admis dans l'intimité du Roi; il aurait eu tous les privilèges réservés alors à la noblesse et au génie . . . Il aurait pris une part active aux plaisirs délicats du seul souverain qui ait jamais connu le grand art de grouper autour de soi tous les talents et de les absorber au profit de sa gloire. Homme du monde par excellence il serait devenu un véritable grand seigneur."[24]

Politically and socially, Musset was probably unable, in 1835, to envisage such a society as a desirable alternative to the July Monarchy. Nevertheless, this does not prevent him from wishing that he had been born a century earlier, and feeling resentment that he had not been. "Je suis venu trop tard dans un monde trop vieux," he exclaims in *Rolla.*

Predictably, Musset liked to associate himself with people who also would have been of the court in pre-Revolutionary France. This tendency was already apparent in Musset at the age of eighteen:

> "Il ne manqua pas de se lier avec des jeunes gens plus riches que lui, et de vouloir les suivre dans leur train de vie. Les premiers tailleurs de Paris eurent seuls l'honneur d'approcher de sa personne, et il leur donnait de l'occupation. Les promenades à cheval étaient à la mode parmi ses amis; il loua des chevaux. On jouait gros jeu; il joua. On faisait les nuits blanches; il veilla."[25]

It would be dishonest to deny an element of vanity and pretentiousness in Musset; but it is only part of the truth. The middle-class society of Musset's writings differs enormously from that of Balzac, Hugo and Sand. His society resembles more closely that of pre-Revolutionary France.

This escape in time is especially evident in his theatre, with the emphasis on Italy, and particularly Renaissance Italy. *André del Sarto* is set in fifteenth-century Florence; *Lorenzaccio* in sixteenth-century Florence; *Les Caprices de Marianne* in Naples at the time of Francis I; *Carmosine* goes further back to an earlier age, whilst *La Nuit Vénitienne* and *Bettine* are of a more contemporary, though indeterminate Italy; *Fantasio* and *Barberine* are set in a distant Munich and Hungary.[26] These are all places in which Musset felt that he would have been, as an artist, more in harmony with society.

It is not original to draw close parallels between Musset's heroes and his own character. One turns perhaps too readily to the anecdote, or to the second chapter of the *Confession* and several of the plays. The source of much of his *malaise* is not to be related to society but to his own character, to his "non-commitment." At school he had been a good pupil, but for egotistical motives. Later, he was unable to pursue any course of studies: he soon abandoned Law; he gave up Medicine after his first dissection; he tried his hand at painting for which he had some talent; he held an administrative post (an "entreprise de chauffage militaire"), for ten months in 1829, which he was happy to relinquish. For ten years after 1838 he held a Librarianship at the Ministry of the Interior, which was in reality little more than a sinecure. Another librarianship at the Ministry of Public Instruction failed to materialize.

No pattern or sense of regularity was ever imposed on his life. His brother's biography of him is in parts taken up with arguments concerning broken contracts with Buloz, the director of the recently-founded *Revue des Deux Mondes,* to whom he had promised *Contes, nouvelles* and other writings. After the failure of *La Nuit Vénitienne*—the failure was partly brought about by technical mishaps—Musset, unable to bear such humiliation, quickly renounced writing for the theatre.

This picture of an indecisive Musset, unemployed and probably for the most part unemployable, but unable to cope with a life of leisure, is, as it were, the blueprint of all Musset's heroes, whether it be Fantasio, Rolla, Lorenzo or Perdican/Camille in *On ne badine pas avec l'amour.*

The second section of *Rolla* gives a remarkably detailed portrait of such a man. Though the anecdote is not based on Musset's personal experience, the poem takes on a vividly personal tone. Clearly influenced by Byron, *Rolla* is the analysis of Musset's own *mal du siècle.*

> En sorte que Rolla, par un beau soir d'automne,
> Se vit à dix-neuf ans maître de sa personne,—
> Et n'ayant dans la main ni talent ni métier.
> Il eût trouvé d'ailleurs tout travail impossible;
> Un gagne-pain quelconque, un métier de valet,
> Soulevait sur sa lèvre un rire inextinguible.
> Ainsi, mordant à même au peu qu'il possédait,
> Il resta grand seigneur tel que Dieu l'avait fait.[27]

Habit was a quality he despised, the mark of lower enslaved classes. He was "débauché jusques à la folie, et dans les cabarets vivant au jour le jour." His education and position in society are incompatible with the financial means at his disposal. He decides to lead the life he prefers, not, like Valentin in **"Les Deux Maîtresses,"** on alternate days, but for three years; then he will commit suicide, when his fortune is exhausted. The attraction for Musset of such an anecdote lies in Rolla's dilemma: not having the means to lead the only life he can or desires to lead. Valentin has an occupation, "un avocat sans causes"—a vague profession matching Musset's equally vague profession as a writer: but Rolla had no "talent ou métier."

The hero of *Fantasio* is a happier, less bitter brother of Rolla, though he has "le mois de janvier sur le cœur, . . . solitaire dans la foule . . . désireux d'être ailleurs . . ." Most particularly he is "affamé d'action." In this play one sees Fantasio with his friends Spark and Hartman pleasantly whiling away their time in cafés, cabarets, like Musset who spent much of his life playing chess. Their lives are dominated by boredom, inaction and monotonous repetition:

> "Quelle admirable chose que les *Mille et une Nuits*! O Spark, mon cher Spark, si tu pouvais me transporter en Chine! Si je pouvais seulement sortir de ma peau pendant une heure ou deux!"[28]

They spend their time imagining new ways to occupy themselves and new ways to escape. "Remarques-tu une chose, Spark? C'est que nous n'avons point d'état; nous n'exerçons aucune profession . . . Il n'y a point de maître d'armes mélancolique." Absence of a real occupation leads to introspection. "Cette ville n'est rien auprès de ma cervelle. Tous les recoins m'en sont cent fois plus connus; toutes les rues, tous les trous de mon imagination sont cent fois plus fatigués; je m'y suis promené en cent fois plus de sens, dans cette cervelle délabrée."[29] When, by ruse, he becomes clown at the court of the King of Bavaria, he is happier than before. In part, he, a *bourgeois de Munich,* is flattered at belonging to a court with its glamour and excitement. This post too must be temporary: "J'aime ce métier plus que tout autre; mais je ne puis faire aucun métier." Ironically when war is declared between Bavaria and the Prince of Mantua, Fantasio observes: "Eh Madame, si la guerre est déclarée, nous saurons quoi faire de nos bras; les oisifs de nos promenades mettront leurs uniformes; moi-même je prendrai mon fusil de chasse, s'il n'est pas encore vendu."[30] Baudelaire, Vigny, not to mention Stendhal's Julien Sorel, were all much troubled by the vacuum left by the absence of military activity in the post-Napoleonic era. Possibly one of the reasons for the inferior quality of literature during the Revolutionary period and Napoleonic age was that men were able to achieve fulfilment in action.

Much has been said about *On ne badine pas avec l'amour,* its origin, and parallels have often been drawn between the hero Perdican and Musset on the one hand, and Camille and George Sand on the other. In his plays, especially in *Les Caprices de Marianne,* often more than one character is a projection of Musset's own character. The "pragmatic" Perdican here corresponds with the poet of the *Nuits* poems, and the idealist Camille with the Muse. The play is a bitter one. There is no fulfilment for the heroine and the hero proceeds along his haphazard way, from one flirtation to another. Perdican is an angrier Fantasio; of course, he is not prepared, unlike Camille, to make the sacrifice—suicide—of Rolla. Perdican has successfully completed his studies (unlike Musset); he is now, at the age of twenty-one, "Docteur à quatre boules blanches," of the University of Paris. Perhaps, like his ludicrous father, he is destined to become some vague "homme d'état" . . . for six months of the year. There is no further reference to an occupation or career for Perdican. He has led a life in the capital similar to that of Musset:

> "Vous avez commencé l'expérience de la vie, says Camille. Je sais quel homme vous êtes, et vous devez avoir beaucoup appris en peu de temps avec un cœur et un esprit comme les vôtres."[31]

Camille instinctively knows that this "métier de jeune homme" is part of the process which will eventually corrupt and contaminate their relationship. Perdican and Musset have become, with experience, too cynical and scheming to be able to achieve the love so much sought by the heroine. Although *On ne badine pas* is essentially the story of a thwarted idealist, the heroine is thwarted not so much by the impossibility of her ideal, but because Perdican is weak.

Ever since Sarah Bernhardt played the title rôle in *Lorenzaccio* in 1896, critics have turned with more enthusiasm to this play then to any other of Musset's writings. It has proved the most baffling and rich in interpretations of all. Rolla, Perdican, Fantasio, Valentin and Octave are, in varying degrees, portraits of the inactive Musset. In Lorenzo Musset portrays a hero, like the others, idle, indolent, partially idealistic, but submitting himself to an easy, empty life of pleasure. All Musset's heroes have been in search of an occupation, whether they were aware of it or not. Musset now turns directly to his question.

Lorenzo was once a studious, innocent, young man who preferred his books and solitude, "un rêveur, un philosophe." He has become ironic, scornful and strangley melancholic; he has lost faith in man, society and all progress whether social or human. The only occupation open to a distinguished member of the Medici family is at the court, where Lorenzo becomes the boon companion of his cousin Duke Alexander de' Medici.[32] What is relevant to this essay is the solution which Musset attempts to put forward. The occupation (action) needed to stabilize the mind of Lorenzo, which would be of lasting effect, has here been reduced to a single act, as in Sartre's *Les Mouches.* This is the attempt of a lazy, weak man: Lorenzo wants to become a man of action, by committing one act. For this reason Lorenzo realizes long before he commits the deed that it will be in vain. He cannot become a man of action; indeed, far from integrating the various facets of his personality by action, and giving expression to it, the act of assassination betrays and destroys his personality. Lorenzo seeks too easy a solution: a life of action requires a continuous effort. Such a solution is no more likely to satisfy than that found by Valentin in **"Les Deux Maîtresses,"** and even Fantasio's temporary employment as court-clown.

What is interesting in this aspect of *Lorenzaccio* is that it has similarities with other of Musset's works. In **"Croisilles,"**[33] for example, the son of a goldsmith endeavours to recover the fortune which his industrious father has lost through no fault of his own. He immediately, and not surprisingly, turns to gambling; and when he loses all, he blames fate. Later he invests all his money in a single cargo, and of course the ship is lost at sea. The hero, like Lorenzo, seeks to achieve by one act—gambling—what normally requires time, effort and determined application.

The parallel is even more obvious in **"Le Fils du Titien."**[34] What is significant is not the manner in which Musset transformed his relationship with Aimée d'Alton (later Madame Paul de Musset) into that of Beatrix Donato and Pomponio Tiziano. The essence of the anecdote is more relevant: the hero proves himself a painter of genius with one creation. Why should he continue?

> "Alfred," writes his brother, "ne manqua pas . . . de soutenir cette thèse: qu'un chef d'œuvre suffit à la gloire d'un homme, et que l'artiste de génie, quand il a prouvé une fois ce qu'il sait faire, devrait s'en tenir là et ne point s'exposer au reproche de radotage, comme il est arrivé à Corneille, au Guide et au Titien lui-même."[35]

Musset has tried unsuccessfully, if we pay close attention to the last lines of the work—"Il resta ainsi jusqu'à sa mort *fidèle à sa paresse*"—to argue that Titian's son was a great artist because he had created a great masterpiece. Nonetheless, if only he, like Emily Brontë with *Wuthering Heights,* could be considered an artist of genius for so little! Why should he be obliged to create so much, so often, to prove himself so frequently? Musset envied such easy fame.

Action, application, method, inspiration are all parts of the creative process. Problems of literary creation must be faced by all serious writers. Paul Verlaine even devoted occasional poems to the subject:

> Ce qu'il nous fait, à nous, c'est aux lueurs des lampes,
> La science conquise et le sommeil dompté,
> C'est le front dans les mains du vieux Faust des estampes.
> C'est l'Obstination et c'est la Volonté.[36]

André Gide used his *Journaux,* and Baudelaire his *Journaux Intimes* to voice and debate the numerous problems besetting the artist. Hugo, like other Romantics had a passion for Prefaces and Manifestos. Musset disdained these methods, preferring to incorporate his personal problems into his art.

Behind much of the writing of Musset lurks the yearning for action, meaningful action. For Sartre, literary creation is a "deed"; Musset was not really convinced. His weakness and indecision, produced in some measure by his lack of trust in contemporary art and himself, is manifested, directly and indirectly, in numerous ways: his nostalgic escape into past ages in which he felt his role as an artist would have been less demanding on him and more widely appreciated; the debate, not only on love and experience but on art and its creation, of the *Nuits* cycle; and it is essentially the common trait of most of his heroes. Constantly, throughout his writings, the theme of action, sustained action, and creation are worked out; but never with a lasting or effective solution.

Notes

1. Baudelaire, *L'Art Romantique: Théophile Gautier,* Edition de la Pléiade, 1954. Interestingly, elsewhere, Baudelaire refers to himself as a "paresseux nerveux," p. 1028.

2. Paul de Musset, *Biographie de Alfred de Musset,* Alphonse Lemerre, Paris.

3. Alfred de Musset, "La Nuit de Mai," in *Poésies Nouvelles,* Garnier Frères, 1962, p. 36.

4. *Ibid.,* p. 38.

5. "La Nuit d'Août," p. 50.

6. "La Nuit de Mai," p. 38.

7. *Ibid.,* p. 39.

8. *Ibid.,* p. 40.

9. "La Nuit d'Août," p. 49.

10. *Ibid.,* p. 47.

11. *Ibid.,* p. 50.

12. *Ibid.,* p. 50.

13. "La Nuit d'Octobre," pp. 52-3.

14. *Ibid.,* p. 53.

15. *Ibid.,* p. 59.

16. Alphonse Bouvet, *Musset, l'amour, l'érotisme et le messianisme de la souffrance,* in *Revue des Sciences Humaines,* April-June, 1968.

17. Alfred de Musset, *Correspondance.* Edited by Léon Séché. Letter to Paul Foucher, dated 23 September 1827, p. 12.

18. Paul de Musset, *op. cit.,* p. 286.

19. Baudelaire, *op. cit.,* p. 946.

20. Alfred de Musset, "Les Vœux Stériles," in *Premières Poésies,* p. 119.

21. *Ibid.,* p. 120.

22. Paul de Musset, *op. cit.,* p. 290.

23. Musset had not left France before his ill-starred and over-dramatized journey to Italy with Sand in December 1833.

24. Paul de Musset, *op. cit.,* p. 4.

25. *Ibid.,* p. 81.

26. The other plays, *contes* and *nouvelles* tend to be embroidered anecdotes set in a contemporary Paris.

27. *Rolla,* in *Premières Poésies,* p. 6.

28. *Fantasio,* in Volume I, of *Comédies et Proverbes,* Garnier Frères, p. 238.

29. *Ibid.,* p. 239.

30. *Ibid.,* p. 273.

31. *Ibid., On ne badine pas avec l'amour,* p. 300.

32. Bernard Masson had dealt very lucidly in an article, *Lorenzaccio ou la difficulté d'être, Archives des Lettres Modernes,* 1962, with many psychological elements in the play. Others have elucidated what we would call the modern, existentialist implications of the work.

33. This *nouvelle* was published in the *Revue des Deux Mondes* in February 1839.

34. A *conte* published in the *Revue des Deux Mondes* in May 1838.

35. Paul de Musset, *op. cit.,* p. 189.

36. In the second section of the *Epilogue* in Verlaine's *Poèmes Saturniens*. There is something more than topical, Parnassian sentiments in these lines.

Russell S. King (essay date October 1969)

SOURCE: King, Russell S. "Indecision in Musset's *Contes d'Espagne et d'Italie.*" *Nottingham French Studies* 8, no. 3 (October 1969): 57-68.

[*In the following essay, King surveys Musset's* Contes d'Espagne et d'Italie, *examining this work as a product of the writer's early literary apprenticeship.*]

In the early and middle years of French Romanticism, few writers and fewer critics succeeded in defining the movement clearly and positively. Hugo's *Préface de Cromwell,* published in 1827, the most prominent of Romantic manifestos, is seen to be inadequate when one examines its validity in so far as even Hugo himself was concerned. What relevance does the *Préface* have in such disparate works as *Les Orientales* (1829), *Le Dernier Jour d'un Condamné* (1829), *Hernani* (1830), and *Les Feuilles d'Automne* (1831)? Earlier, Stendhal, in his *Racine et Shakespeare,* had argued on much safer grounds, by declaring that being Romantic meant being "modern," being of one's age, but this says little.

Despite the manifestos, despite *Hernani,* despite the *Cénacle,* Sainte-Beuve, *Le Globe,* despite Chateaubriand and Lamartine, Romanticism meant different things for different writers. In England, the role and significance of *imagination* binds together the principal exponents of Romanticism, with the glaring exception of Byron. In France no one quality or characteristic unifies the writers of the 1820s and 1830s. There were many strands and many short-lived fashions. Apart from experimentation and innovation in form, versification and vocabulary, Romanticism was manifested in a predilection for the Orient, Spain, the Middle Ages and the Renaissance; for England, Shakespeare, Ossian, Byron; for *Werther* and René's *mal du siècle;* for the glorification and even sanctification of nature and love; for liberalism, political opposition, Republicanism, monarchy, socio-political awareness. . . .

For a nineteen-year-old writer, in 1829, striving to be both original and modern, such a picture was indeed bewildering. Musset's ***Contes d'Espagne et d'Italie*** can be seen as a product of this bewilderment. . . .

The poems [of the ***Contes d'Espagne et d'Italie,***] were first read before a large audience of the *Cénacle* on Christmas Eve, 1829, an occasion which Dumas describes in his *Mémoires.* The reception must have been

pleasing to a young débutant who had just celebrated his nineteenth birthday. Although all did not rush to acclaim the new poet, he was attentively heard, the young ladies blushed, the "orthodox" Romantics were scandalized by some of the liberties in his versification. Once the *Contes*[1] were published, critics felt impelled to review the work at length; an aunt, the "Chanoinesse de Vendôme," disinherited him, and Harel, the Director of the Odéon theatre, begged him to write a play, "la plus neuve et la plus hardie possible."[2]

This collection represents for the most part Musset's earliest literary efforts. In 1828, he had published a free translation of De Quincey's *Confessions of an English Opium Eater,* and, on 31 August 1828, his first poem, **"Un Rêve,"** was printed. Earlier poems are known, including a song written for his mother when he was fourteen; another, dated Le Mans, October 1826, is addressed to a Mademoiselle Zoé le Douairin, whilst yet another **"La Nuit"** was written at about the same time.

Attention seems to have been focussed almost excessively, in the case of Musset, on a half-dozen poems and as many plays. Other works have been neglected. The ***Contes d'Espagne et d'Italie*** have been passed over, rightly perhaps more than wrongly, for several reasons: they bear manifest traits of immaturity, and, as a collection, a seemingly defiant lack of unity. It is interesting to observe an apprentice-writer, however clumsy he may be, practising his new "métier." Even if a young writer is more susceptible to strong influences, much of the future writer can already be discerned. Mérimée, in the *Théâtre de Clara Gazul,* Verlaine in *Poèmes Saturniens,* Gide in *Les Cahiers d'André Walter,* are especially interesting to the student of these authors: the artist can be seen struggling to master his art, before he slips into formula or routine writing during his later and more successful career.

The *Contes* comprise fifteen pieces, almost all possessing a different form. The first, **"Don Paez,"** a narrative poem, with some dialogue inserted, is the Spanish *conte;* this is followed by **"Les Marrons du Feu,"** a poem similar in subject-matter, set possibly in Venice, and written throughout in dramatic form; the third is **"Portia,"** the Italian *conte;* to balance the "exotic" poems, the final poem, **"Mardoche,"** is set in contemporary Paris. Between the three early poems and **"Mardoche,"** there are eleven poems, with the more or less general heading of *Chansons à mettre en musique et fragments.*[3]

"Don Paez," the opening poem of the collection, with its Spanish title, followed by an epigraph, untranslated, from *Othello,* is at once recognizable as a work of the late 1820s. *Othello* is the archetypal study of jealousy, the theme of this long narrative poem. The ever-increasing legend surrounding the writings and life of Byron is the major influence on the young Musset, more than Shakespeare, despite frequent translations of his work and the successful visit to Paris, in 1828, of an English Shakespearian Company. It is the satirical realism of Byron, the violent action and sentiment, and blasphemy, . . . dramatic and exaggerated. Don Paez leaves his mistress to return to sentry duty; fellow officers all claim that their mistress is the most fair. Don Etur's mistress turns out to be the same as that of Don Paez, Juana d'Orvado. A duel is fought, and whosoever wins must avenge her treachery by killing her too.

> Tu vois, prit don Paez, qu'il faut qu'un de nous meure.
> Jurons donc que celui qui sera dans une heure
> Debout, et qui verra le soleil de demain,
> Tuera la Juana d'Orvado de sa main.
> —Tope, dit le dragon, et qu'elle meure, comme
> Il est vrai qu'elle va causer la mort d'un homme.[4]

The dual is described with enthusiastic and vigorous detail. Don Paez is victorious and purchases from an old woman a philtre which he takes and gives to his mistress; they die together.

The outward passion, especially associated with Spain, was a new preoccupation of French writers. In **"Don Paez,"** Musset is creating in verse what attracted Mérimée in some of the playlets of the *Théâtre de Clara Gazul.* Romantic eyes were turned away, temporarily, from the contemporary Parisian scene.

Not unexpectedly, the emotions of Don Paez—Musset was only eighteen at the time of composition—are of an equally violent nature. Attempts to analyse motives and sentiments are absent. Description of Don Paez and his mistress are generally of a physical nature, superficially realistic, stressing dark eyes, pale skin, dainty feet. . . . There is no real impression of inner conflict, apart from the hesitation of Don Paez concerning the most effective way of avenging his betrayal. The passion is uncomplicated, and is soon transformed into hatred: "Je n'ai plus maintenant d'amour que pour ma haine." One of the few attempts in the **Contes** to offer moral or psychological explanation occurs towards the end of Part Two:

> Amour, fléau du monde, exécrable folie,
> Toi qu'un lien si frêle à la volupté lie, . . .
> Plutôt que comme un lâche on me voie en souffrir,
> Je t'en arracherai, quand j'en devrais mourir.[5]

This is not yet the conflict between love and passion: love has not yet made its appearance.

The Romanticism, in content, of **"Don Paez"** is very marked, though limited. It is "exterior," an exaggerated exoticism: frequent references to Spain and Madrid, and other Spanish embellishments, and the vigour of language and action, were "modern" in 1829. Note the mock-heroic tone of these lines:

> En y regardant bien, frère, vous auriez pu,
> Dans l'ombre transparente, entrevoir un pied nu.
> —Certes, l'Espagne est grande, et les femmes
>   d'Espagne
> Sont belles mais il n'est château, ville ou campagne,
> Qui contre ce pied-là, n'eût en vain essayé
> (Comme dans Cendrillon) de mesurer un pied.[6]

Hints of another variety of Romanticism, the more personal variety, are not altogether absent: the poverty of the old woman who sold the philtre to Don Paez was beginning to trouble writers: 1829 is the year of Hugo's *Le Dernier Jour d'un Condamné.* The frequent use of *frère* is an attempt to identify the reader more personally, albeit facetiously, with the action, in a less sophisticated manner than Baudelaire's "hypocrite lecteur, mon semblable, mon frère."

The second poem of the collection is not really a *conte,* but is written in verse dialogue throughout. It is set in Italy, probably Venice. The proverbial title, meaning a catspaw, comes from La Fontaine's Fable, *Le Singe et le Chat* The violence and vigour of **"Don Paez"** now becomes flagrant melodrama, similar in tone and subject-matter to Mérimée's *Une Femme est un Diable* and *Le Ciel et l'Enfer.* An actress with a fiery temperament, La Camargo, uses a gallant, admiring priest to seek revenge on a wealthy young man, Rafael Garuci, who has abandoned her. Rafael is murdered but the heroine refuses to "reward" the priest.

This melodramatic brand of Romanticism, with gallant, lecherous priests, murders (there are two in **"Marrons"**), crudity of language, is more typical of the secondary literature of the eighteenth century, though, in the hands of some more serious writers, it was in vogue again in the 1820s.

Like **"Don Paez,"** **"Marrons"** is intended as a study of woman's treachery. Ironically, it is the hero, Rafael, who is unfaithful, but as La Camargo herself observes, love and moral standards for man and woman differ considerably:

> Il est sûr qu'une femme
> Met dans une âme aimée une part de son âme.
> Sinon, d'où pourrait-elle et pourquoi concevoir
> La soif d'y revenir, et l'horreur d'en déchoir?
> Au contraire un cœur d'homme est comme une marée
> Fuyarde des endroits qui l'ont mieux attirée . . .
>   . . . La pensée
>
> D'un homme est de plaisirs et d'oublis traversée;
> Une femme ne vit et ne meurt que d'amour;
> Elle songe une année à quoi lui pense un jour![7]

A greater attempt is made at characterization than in **"Don Paez."** Rafael is a somewhat less melancholy prototype of Fantasio:

> Que voulez-vous? moi, j'ai donné ma vie
> A ce dieu fainéant qu'on nomme fantaisie.

C'est lui qui, triste ou fou, de face ou de profil,
Comme un polichinel me traîne au bout d'un fil; . . .
                     . . . L'année
Dernière, j'étais fou de chiens d'abord, et puis
De femmes. Maintenant, ma foi, je ne le suis
De rien.[8]

The play is a rather simple dramatic exercise. Thematically, there is little that is typical of Musset. The heroine and the priest, with their exaggerated and superficial sentiments, display little more than Musset's precocious mastery in manipulating a plot and characters. The irony and wit which pervades this poem and much of the earlier writings of Musset spring from certain contradictions, notably the contradictions between the passions sincerely felt by an adolescent and the grotesque and melodramatic manner in which they are manifested. Nonetheless the source of cynicism in Musset, as in Byron, is manifold and complex.[9]

As in **"Don Paez"** and **"Les Marrons du Feu,"** the action of **"Portia"** revolves around a triangle, again one woman and two men. **"Portia,"** however, represents a step closer to the maturer Romanticism of Musset. This poem contains keener psychological insight, and its characters, though quite humourless, are more recognizable Musset types. An ageing Florentine count marries, suspects his young wife of infidelity, discovers her and her lover, a mysterious young man. The lover kills him in a duel. The couple take flight, but the mysterious young man reveals that he is nothing but a penniless fisherman. Although the anecdote is melodramatic, the pace is slower than in the earlier works. Musset is now a little more intent on describing the sentiments and even characterization. The husband, Onorio Luigi, though ageing, is of the same family as Rolla, Fantasio and Lorenzo:

Débauché par ennui, mais triste par nature,
Voyant venir le temps, il s'était marié.

His wife, unlike the passionate heroines of the two earlier *contes,* is less exaggerated and more subtly portrayed.

Mariée à quinze ans, noble, riche, adorée,
De tous les biens du monde à loisir entourée,
N'ayant dès le berceau connu qu'une amitié,
Sa femme ne l'avait jamais remercié;
Mais quel soupçon pouvait l'atteindre? Et qu'était-
  elle,
Sinon la plus loyale et la moins infidèle
Des épouses?[10]

The mysterious lover clad in a black cloak is a figure of melodrama, a common element in Romantic drama. Little attempt is made to analyse his motivations. He remains mysterious. Providence is alluded to when his tale is related. This spares undue psychological explanation, a "short-cut" to which Musset often resorted.

Yet another path Romanticism was taking, and one which achieved greater prominence in the later decades of the nineteenth century, is to be glimpsed in **"Portia"**: the significance of environment:

Venise! ô perfide cité,
A qui le ciel donna la fatale beauté,
Je respirai cet air dont l'âme est amollie,
Et dont ton souffle impur empesta l'Italie![11]

With their histories and atmosphere of vice and crime, Venice, in **"Portia,"** Paris, in **"Rolla,"** Florence, in *Lorenzaccio,* all contaminated their inhabitants.

Clearly, in **"Portia,"** many strands of Romanticism are present: the local colour, Venice, though less exaggerated, is little more than a backdrop. The setting could almost be Paris.

"Don Paez" is the *conte d'Espagne,* **"Portia,"** the *conte d'Italie,* and now, to fill out a volume which the publisher had considered rather slim, Musset added **"Mardoche,"** a contemporary French *conte.* **"Mardoche"** is long—590 lines of ten-lined, numbered stanzas like Byron's *Don Juan*—racy, bearing all the signs of rapid composition, lacking the condensation and crystallization of a more carefully conceived and composed work.

Once again there is, as in **"Portia,"** the triangle of the ageing husband, the young wife and the ardent, and temporarily successful, lover. Although the jealous husband discovers his wife's betrayal and threatens to send her to a convent, the focus is on the "apprenticeship" in love of the young Mardoche.

More than any earlier hero, Mardoche is the prototype of most of Musset's heroes; his portrait is in a large measure autobiographical. Young, only twenty years old, alone because he has no money, he immediately launches into a life of fashionable elegance and mild debauchery after inheriting a small fortune. Musset is here concerned with Mardoche's first "affair." Intelligent, precocious insight into depraved human nature, blasphemous, yet with a sensitive yearning for a great passion, aloof, forever posing, displaying, and perhaps possessing, a violent disposition—these are some of the essential traits of Musset's early Romantic hero. The debt to Byron is manifest.

Despite the obvious criticism levelled against **"Mardoche,"** this poem is not a bad one. Indeed, its very raciness and humour, sustained throughout, are allied to what was, fundamentally, a serious theme: the need for love, in conflict with the contaminating, destructive effect of experience.

In **"Mardoche,"** Musset deliberately burlesques a serious theme, not so much to destroy the seriousness as to give the poem an added dimension. Similarly, André

Gide never presented his reader with a portrait of a perfect individualist hero, but rather a burlesqued one, as in *Les Caves du Vatican,* or a failed individualist as in *L'Immoraliste* and *Les Faux-Monnayeurs;* only in *Les Mouches* does Sartre present some kind of real existentialist hero. Their art would be debased if it solely sought to present, directly, portrayals of their ideas and philosophies. Subtlety is needed. In **"Mardoche,"** Musset imprints his own originality—his humour, his fantasy, including a certain touch of naïve cynicism—to make the work something more than a mere portrait of a young, apprenticed Romantic hero. Such skilled use of wit is a new development in Musset.

The eleven short poems, *chansons, stances,* a sonnet, a ballad, present a somewhat different picture. Three of the songs, **"L'Andalouse," "Madrid,"** and **"Madame la Marguise"** are addressed to an Andalusian woman, probably the same one. The first two are predominantly descriptive, listing her charms, particularly her Spanish physical features and dress. The first,

> Avez-vous vu, dans Barcelone,
> Une Andalouse au sein bruni,[12]

became one of the most celebrated songs of the age, set to music by Hippolyte Monpou.[13] The second, **"Madrid,"** continues the description, but is less colourful and somewhat less complimentary. **"Madame la Marquise"** introduces a new note: here, the Andalusian, though she falls asleep, plays the rôle of the comforting "muse" of the later *Nuits* poems.

> Oh! viens! dans mon âme froissée
> Qui saigne encor d'un mal bien grand,
> Viens verser ta blanche pensée
> Comme un ruisseau dans un torrent! . . .
> Donne-moi, ma belle maîtresse,
> Un beau baiser, car je te veux
> Raconter ma longue détresse,
> En caressant tes beaux cheveux.[14]

These three poems are essentially simple, playful, descriptions of exotic love.

In the shorter poems, the deeper note is not confined to **"Madame la Marquise."** A sincere heart-felt despair after the betrayal by his mistress pervades the short, twelve-lined, untitled poem beginning *Quand je t'aimais.* This poem effectively illustrates Musset's attraction to the sentimental brand of Romanticism, to lyricism, characterized by Lamartine and much of Hugo, with the emphasis on love, betrayal or separation and death of the beloved.

Likewise, the **"Sonnet,"**

> Que j'aime le premier frisson d'hiver! le chaume,
> Sous le pied du chasseur, refusant de ployer!

describes the return to Paris for the winter, but to a Paris deprived of the mistress who once loved him and who loves him no longer. The first eleven lines are conventional enough, describing oncoming winter, and invoking Paris with its Louvre, smoke, postilions, grey skies, Seine, lights. . . .

"A Ulric G." introduces yet another aspect of the theme of love and suffering. It is a poem dedicated to Ulric Guttinguer, whom Musset met in 1829, and who invited him to stay at his country home at Honfleur, in Normandy. Musset envied the extensive, amorous experience and suffering of his host. The psychological dualism of Guttinguer, like that of the ageing husband in **"Portia,"** though rudimentary in these two poems, attracted Musset.

> Tu portes dans ta tête et dans ton cœur deux mondes,
> Quand le soir, près de moi tu vas triste et courbé.[15]

The Romantic hero's psychological interest springs from inner conflict: *Marion de Lorme,* the prostitute with the pure heart, Fantasio, with "le mois de mai sur les joues et le mois de janvier dans le cœur," Lorenzo, torn in the conflict between vice and purity.

The same poem introduces, for the first time explicitly in the *Contes,* a note of masochistic pleasure in suffering, destined to be, later, one of the principal targets of invective against Musset.

> Toi, si plein, front pâli sous des baisers de femme,
> Moi si jeune, enviant ta blessure et tes maux.

This vein of Romantic literature points the way to some of Verlaine, and some, if not much, of Baudelaire.

"Stances" is the almost Parnassian evocation of the remains of a Pyrenean monastery, reflecting the passion, in 1830, for medieval and Renaissance backgrounds. **"Venise,"** later set to music by Gounod, is a description of the Venetian scene and life; **"Le Lever,"** the portrait of a huntswoman, and **"Au Yung Frau,"** a "conceit" comparing the heart of a pure young maiden with the unattainable, snow-clad peak of the Jungfrau. These poems are largely pictorial, with minimal human interest. They reflect a fashionable trend in literature, bearing several resemblances to Hugo's *Les Orientales.*[16]

Interestingly, the most celebrated piece of the collection in the **"Ballade à la Lune,"** which achieved instant celebrity and notoriety, in 1830. A glance at the critics of the period would give the impression that this was the only poem of note in the volume. The point of departure is the comparison of the moon, glimpsed above the spire of a steeple, with the dot over an i.

> C'était, dans la nuit brune,
> Sur le clocher jauni,

La Lune,
Comme un point sur un i.[17]

The moon is mocked mercilessly and wittily. The description of the moon is followed, but not in the original version, by several brief descriptive scenes of a rather scabrous nature. Was Musset poking fun at fashionable Romanticism? Musset warns the reader, in **"Les Secrètes Pensées de Rafaël,"** against treating this poem seriously:

O vous, race des dieux, phalange incorruptible,
Electeurs brevetés des morts et des vivants;
Porte-clefs éternels du mont inaccessible, . . .
Sans partialité, sans malveillance aucune,
Sans vouloir faire cas ni des ha! ni des ho!
Avez lu posément—la Ballade à la lune!!![18]

Musset was right to give such a warning. He was not mocking Romantic literature but some of its exaggerations. The humour adds another dimension to the work; it is Musset's original contribution to the school. The poem also represents in a small way his plea for artistic independence. No sooner was he introduced to the *Cénacle* than he began to break away. As in **"Mardoche,"** and many of the other pieces, including **"Don Paez,"** Musset was reacting against the humourless earnestness of many writers and critics of the era. All were too intent on legislating, writing prefaces, and passing judgement. The very brief Preface to the *Contes d'Espagne et d'Italie* can almost be called an Anti-Preface.

It is indeed as much in the tone of the *Contes* as in their subject-matter that Musset's groping bewilderment is discernible. Was the modern writer, of 1830, to strike a note of tragedy, comedy, tragedy mingled with comedy, as Hugo advised, banter, militant didacticism or intimate lyricism? In 1829, Musset was an uncommitted artist, not yet certain which art form to choose; some (painting, for example) had already been discarded. Writing was still to be considered "un passe-temps our se désennuyer."[19] In *Le Poète déchu,* published posthumously, Musset wrote:

A dix-huit ans j'hésitais encore sur l'état que j'embrasserais, lorsque le hasard me lia avec quelques jeunes gens qui s'occupaient de littérature. Ils faisaient des vers, j'en fis comme eux, et mes premiers essais réussirent. Cependant, je ne songeai pas à me livrer à la poésie qui ne me semblait qu'un passe-temps.[20]

Art was something not to be treated too seriously; this suited the adolescent Musset bent on "living," yearning as much for a "passion dévorante" as for literary fame.

The tone of the *Contes* is for the most part one of vigorous comedy tinged with persistant cynicism. For Maurice Souriau, "le romantisme des *Contes d'Espagne et d'Italie* n'est qu'un costume de carnaval."[21] For Kathleen Butler, "these poems scandalized conservative critics . . . who could not fail to perceive that in the **"Ballade à la Lune"** and several passages of **"Mardoche"** their youngest recruit was poking fun at them."[22] Nonetheless, the variations in tone cannot be easily categorized. Although **"Portia"** is serious, and the **"Ballade à la Lune"** is mockingly comic, the tone is often mixed. As Jasinski has rightly stated: "Il mêle en proportions indéfinissables l'ironie à la sincérité. Ses outrances mêmes tournent au pastiche et souvent à la parodie."[23] Musset's cynicism comes naturally; but it is also designed to conceal an over-sensitive and vulnerable mind. He preferred to mock rather than be mocked, even if it meant mocking himself:

Les louanges me furent prodiguées et la vanité me monta au cerveau. J'étais paresseux et insouciant; il me parut agréable d'être un génie en herbe, par boutades, à ma fantaisie, et sans avoir l'air d'y penser. Je jouais d'un air d'indifférence avec ma petite gloire naissante; je me fis une muse de mon caprice, et les femmes trouvèrent que j'avais raison.[24]

Musset's cynicism in the *Contes* and his attitude to this work is distinct from, but in some measure related to, the cynicism which resulted from his "experience" and precocious insight into human motivations and behaviour. In the *Confession d'un Enfant du Siècle* Musset studies the impulsion one sometimes has to destroy what one loves and cherishes. This theory can be applied to his early collection of poems: he prefers to mock the artistic beliefs he held at the time of composition. Immaturity must count for something here.

The comic and the serious apart, the dominant tone of the longer *contes* is one of violence: this is an important element of the Romanticism of the 1820s. "But the Romanticism of 1830 also suggests supercharged passions, jealousy, revenge, and sudden death; Byronic impertinence and Satanic laughter concealing the heart-felt sob."[25] Understandably, this brand of Romanticism is more likely to attract a young, barely mature writer: it is the Romanticism of Mérimée's *Théâtre de Clara Gazul* (1825), Hugo's *Han d'Islande* (1823) and the first three pieces of Musset's *Contes.*

As much as in the subject-matter and tone, the form of the *Contes* reflects the indecision of the adolescent Musset. All the poems are different. Experimentation, evident at every turn, was the order of the day: songs, ballads, narrative poems, a short play entirely in verse, complete with stage directions.[26] Epigraphs from Shakespeare and Schiller introduce the *Contes,* reflecting the dominant influence on French literature of foreign literatures.

For some critics, the predominant feature of the *Contes* is Musset's handling of versification: a deliberately daring use of rhymes, a displacement of the caesura, a frequent breaking-up of the alexandrine into a trimeter for effect; and enjambement, a reaction against the Romantics' preoccupation with "rime riche" which was intended to compensate for the other liberties which had been recently claimed for poetry. These are all significant for the student of versification and poetry.

In subject-matter, in tone, and in form and versification, the *Contes* seem indecisive, experimental and lacking in unity. This need not imply condemnation. Musset was groping, dazzled by the many directions which art was pursuing in 1829, and the many manifestos and doctrinaire prefaces writers were urged to follow and illustrate in their writings. Many of the elements of early, middle and late Romanticism are discernible. The principal omission is the absence of any preoccupation with artistic creation, perhaps the dominant theme of the *Nuits* poems, and indirectly of much of Musset's later writings. His art had not yet turned in on itself at this early stage. It is a joyful work for the most part. Musset must have derived pleasure in its composition.

The *Contes* are in most respects different from the major works which one most readily associates with Musset, and which the modern reader tends not to appreciate. In his celebrated letter addressed to Paul Demeny, Rimbaud wrote:

> "Musset est quatorze fois exécrable pour nous, générations douloureuses et prises de visions,—que sa paresse d'ange a insultées! O! les contes et les proverbes fadasses! . . . Tout garçon épicier est en mesure de débobiner une apostrophe Rollaque, tout séminariste en porte les cinq cents rimes dans le secret d'un carnet. . . . Musset n'a rien su faire; il y avait des visions derrière la gaze des rideaux: il a fermé les yeux."

Rimbaud and modern critics alike bemoan the absence of real originality and penetrating vision in Musset. Modern scholarship has concerned itself almost exclusively with, firstly, *Lorenzaccio,* secondly, the Musset-Sand episode, and, thirdly, the sources of the plays. In the *Contes* it is probably not the exageratedly personal note of *On ne badine pas avec l'amour* and the *Nuits* which is to be regretted, but the lack of it.

The more authentic Musset was not to emerge until after the publication of the *Contes.* One tends to divide Musset's career a little too easily into two parts, separated by the Venetian episode. Today, particularly since Jean Pommier and others have shown that *Lorenzaccio* was written before the end of 1833, this division is no longer acceptable. The publication of the *Contes d'Espagne et d'Italie* marks a more significant change in the development of Musset the artist. The work was written for, under the influence of, and in some measure against, the Hugo-Nodier school.

However, the *Contes* as an exercise in versatility represent an impasse. Little was written in the following three years, from 1830 to 1832. What works were written are among the more original and authentic of Musset's writings: **"Les Secrètes Pensées de Rafaël," "Les Vœux Stériles,"** and **"La Coupe et les Lèvres."** In these writings and the more celebrated plays of 1833, one sees Musset examining certain metaphysical, philosophical and æsthetic questions. His personality is more clearly engaged in an almost existential search for identity. The play-acting of the *Contes* is over. He is no longer the dilettante described in **"Les Secrètes Pensées de Rafaël."**

Nevertheless, the psychological complexities of this dilettante are not altogether absent from the *Contes.* Musset, the 'chérubin vicieux,' is already apparent. The commonly held notion that Musset was basically innocent and idealistic until George Sand arrived on the scene is simply not valid. The writer of **"Mardoche"** and **"Rolla"** may well be the same as the writer of the pornographic **"Gamiani."** Interestingly, the 'chérubin vicieux' period can only be short-lived: continued, it would be simply "vicieux." It would perhaps be dishonest not to admit that some of the attraction of the *Contes d'Espagne et d'Italie* lies in the rather delicate balance between naïve, exuberant youthfulness and the almost scabrous tone and detail of some of the work.

Though a work of experimentation and apprenticeship, its success was dazzling for such a young writer. Harel's request for a play to be produced at the Odéon, numerous lengthy reviews, an attentive and largely enthusiastic reception at the Cénacle, the number of musical renderings,[27] all contributed to make this, Musset's first original publication, an auspicious success.

The *Contes d'Espagne et d'Italie* are not only an exercise in versatility, as they first appear, but also a product of indecision. They are the product of an adolescent yearning to write, but not yet sure what to write nor how to write.

Notes

1. This abbreviated title is not to be confused with the six *contes* published in 1854, which include *Histoire d'un Merle Blanc* and *Mimi Pinson.*

2. There is some doubt about whether Harel approached Musset, or Musset Harel.

3. Bizet, Gounod and Monpou (Hippolyte Monpou, 1804-1841, composed light operas, and set to music poems by Béranger and Hugo) are but three of many composers to set some of these poems to music.

4. Musset, "Don Paez," in *Premières Poésies,* Edition Garnier Frères, Paris: 1962, p. 11.

5. *Ibid.,* p. 12.

6. *Ibid.* p. 6.

7. *Op. cit.,* "Les Marrons du Feu," pp. 34-35.

8. *Ibid.* pp. 36-37.

9. There is an interesting chapter entitled *L'Ironie de Musset* in *Ames et Thèmes Romantiques,* Pierre Moreau, Librairie José Corti, 1965.

10. *Op cit.* "Portia," 58.

11. *Ibid.,* p. 68.

12. Musset, it appears, believed Barcelona to be in Andalusia. He had not yet travelled out of France.

13. See note 3.

14. *Op cit.,* "Madame la Marquise," pp. 77-78.

15. *Op cit.,* p. 80.

16. G. Brereton, in his *Introduction to the French Poets,* calls the *Contes d'Espagne et d'Italie* Musset's *Orientales.*

17. *Op cit.,* "Ballade à la lune," p. 86.

18. In *Premières poésies,* p. 125.

19. See *Namouna,* in *Premières Poésies,* p. 260.

20. Musset, *Le Poète déchu,* Edition de la Pléiade, *Prose,* p. 307.

21. Maurice Souriau, *Histoire du Romantisme en France,* Volume II, Editions Spes, Paris, 1927, p. 13.

22. Kathleen T. Butler, *History of French Literature,* Volume II, Methuen & Co. Ltd, London, 1923, p. 95.

23. René Jasinski, *Histoire de la Littérature Française,* Volume II, Boivin et Compagnie, Paris, 1947, p. 455.

24. "Le Poète déchu,"*op. cit.,* p. 307.

25. P. E. Charvet, *A Literary History of France. The Nineteenth Century,* Ernest Benn Ltd, London, 1967, p. 135.

26. Herbert S. 'Gochberg has written an interesting book on the developing dramatic technique of Musset: *The Stage of Dreams: the dramatic art of Alfred de Musset,* Droz, Geneva, 1967.

27. In 1891, the Viscountess de Janzé had counted 150 musical renderings of Musset's poems, by composers including Gounod, Bizet, Delibes, Offenbach, etc.

Adele King (essay date fall 1971)

SOURCE: King, Adele. "The Significance of Style in *Fantasio*." *Language and Style* 4, no. 1 (fall 1971): 301-10.

[*In the following essay, King analyzes various modes of language—poetic, prosaic, and sentimental—employed in Musset's drama* Fantasio, *describing the characters and themes associated with each.*]

The way we use language often reveals our basic attitudes towards life. In Musset's **Fantasio** there are three styles of language, three ways of looking at life. Fantasio and his friends are spontaneous and playful. Their sense of values is not predetermined by fixed ideas, but is discovered in the process of living. The language they use is witty, metaphoric, and nuanced. We might call this language poetic, since it contains shades of feeling and insight only expressible through word-play. Contrasted to Fantasio and his friends is the court, which represents responsibility, duty, and the fixed values of society. Those aligned with the values of the court speak in clichés, dead expressions, and pompous diction. We might call this language prose, since it limits the expression of possible responses to life. A third language is that of the governess, who speaks in images drawn from romances and sentimental stories. She represents a false romanticism of fixed, stylized illusions. A central theme of **Fantasio** is the battle for the soul of Elsbeth. Although her use of language and her sensibility are similar to those of Fantasio and his friends, Elsbeth is at first willing to sacrifice her natural spontaneity to the obligations of the "prose" world. It is by way of the insight offered her through Fantasio's "poetry," as much as by his actions, that she is saved.

Fantasio presents his vision of life to Elsbeth while playing the role of court fool. Assuming another identity is natural to Fantasio because for him all life is a game, all social roles are play-acting. The role of court fool is particularly appropriate to his purposes. Traditionally the fool or jester uses playful language as an indirect way of conveying truths which, if stated directly, would be unacceptable.[1] Even before he dons the fool's costume, Fantasio is a natural jester with words, a creator of spoken poetry. He disdains writing poetry and prefers the spontaneity of life to fixing feelings permanently in artistic form: "un verre de vin vaut mieux qu'un sonnet" (288); "Ah! si j'étais poète, comme je peindrais la scène de cette perruque voltigeant dans les airs! Mais celui qui est capable de faire de pareilles choses dédaigne de les écrire" (318). Words are, however, important to him as he shows by his numerous comments about the use of language.[2] He will not write a sonnet, but he will express his feelings through the way he speaks.

The poetic element in Fantasio's use of language can be seen in his concern for the sound of words. He loves to play on words, to make puns: "Pourquoi voulez-vous que je vous en veuille?" (313). Here he plays on two senses of a word ("vouloir" as "to wish" and "en vouloir à" as "to bear a grudge against") in a single sentence with a humorous repetition of *vs.* Fantasio puns in order to reveal his feelings:

Spark:

Tu me fais l'effet d'être revenue de tout.

FANTASIO:

> Ah! pour être revenu de tout, mon ami, il faut être allé dans bien des endroits.
>
> (286)

"Revenir de quelque chose" means "to lose one's fascination with something," i.e., "to go back, to return to a normal, unemotional state"—thus, "revenir de tout," "to be disgusted with everything," "to sink into a dull normality," as it were. Fantasio takes "revenir" literally as a verb of movement and uses it to define his state of mind. How can he come back to the norm if he hasn't been away? Boredom, *le mal de siècle* of which he complains, is not the result of being disillusioned with experience; it results from never having had the energy or the faith to set forth towards any experience. Through a pun Fantasio defines his particular depression, a feeling that there is no point in going somewhere from which one might then "revenir."

Puns are often taken up and developed in conversation from a remark of another person. The poetic use of language is, for Fantasio, a social activity; he has a sharp wit, a quick sense of repartee. His comments often take the form of a suggestive expansion of, or parallel to, a remark made to him. He turns Spark's suggestion that he travel into lighthearted mockery of the large number of English tourists in Europe:

SPARK:

> Va en Angleterre.

FANTASIO:

> J'y suis. Est-ce que les Anglais ont une patrie? J'aime autant les voir ici que chez eux.
>
> (288)

Such banter is also a means of expressing Fantasio's boredom with life, which travel could not relieve. When Fantasio arrives, rather drunk, to meet his friends, Hartman comments, "Tu as le mois de mai sur les joues" (i.e., his face is flushed from drinking). Fantasio replies, "C'est vrai; et le mois de janvier dans le coeur" (282). He takes up Hartman's metaphor and mocks its banality; but he also expands the image in order to show the discrepancy between his appearance and his feelings.

Fantasio uses many metaphors and images, including a number of commonplace comparisons: "muet comme la tombe" (293); the prince as "un animal immonde" (317); he and Elsbeth as "deux roues qui ne suivaient pas la même ornière" (312); Elsbeth as "cette pauvre brebis" (306). Evan a poetic nature cannot always avoid the commonplace: "Cela est si difficile quelquefois de distinguer un trait spirituel d'une grosse sottise! Beaucoup parler, voilà l'important" (300). When depressed Fantasio even longs for "un calembour usé" (282). But,

when speaking of something that touches his emotions or his self-awareness, he is capable of admirable poetic imagery, often tinged with irony directed both towards its object and towards himself. He compares his head to "une vieille cheminée sans feu" (282). He then reverses the comparison, imagining the houses of the city as heads, to be covered by a nightcap from heaven:

> Je voudrais que ce grand ciel si lourd fût un immense bonnet de coton, pour envelopper jusqu'aux oreilles cette sotte ville et ses sots habitants.
>
> (282)

In the expression of disgust with the city (one of whose "houses" or "heads" is his own "cheminée sans feu"), there is also a feeling of disgust with himself, because of his lack of energy. Later he returns to this image, and extends it, by comparing the dull, familiar streets of the city with the dull, familiar paths of his own imagination (286).

Fantasio would like to escape from his feeling of boredom and gain some faith. As he tells us in another extended poetic comparison, he can believe neither in love nor in religion:

> L'amour n'existe plus, mon cher ami. La religion, sa nourrice, a les mamelles pendantes comme une vieille bourse au fond de laquelle il y a un gros sou. L'amour est une hostie qu'il faut briser en deux au pied d'un autel et avaler ensemble dans un baiser; il n'y a plus d'autel, il n'y a plus d'amour.
>
> (290)

The strategy involved is complex. Love is compared to religion; but religion has become an old hag, an undesirable woman. Each of Fantasio's possible faiths is undermined by being compared to the other. The violence of the tone, the disagreeable imagery ("mamelles pendantes comme une vieille bourse") are signs that the clever word-play is a way of mocking and perhaps of controlling his despair. Fantasio can only conjure up a possible love through a series of metaphors:

> quelque belle fille toute ronde comme les femmes de Miéris; quelque chose de doux comme le vent d'ouest, de pâle comme les rayons de la lune; quelque chose de pensif comme ces petites servantes d'auberge des tableaux flamands. . . .
>
> (289)

As his choice of metaphors indicates, he despairs of finding a true object of love in this world; he can only envisage a mistress as an impossible combination of disparate qualities from paintings and from the natural world.

Fantasio's words are often ironic and mock his lack of real feeling. His love affairs will inspire no real passion:

je fredonnerai des solos de clarinette dans mes rêves,
en attendant que je meure d'une indigestion de fraises
dans les bras de ma bien-aimée.

(285)

His occasional displays of energy are meaningless: "je
danse comme Jésus-Christ sur le vaste Océan" (288).
This is not a serious comparison of himself to Divinity;
it is an exaggerated metaphor through which he laughs
at his own pretensions and at the limitations of his own
power. At the end of the play, his witty explanation of
his situation is filled with self-mockery: "mon oncle
. . . me laisse mourir de faim dans tous les cabarets du
royaume" (321); "si je mens, je consens à les payer [les
dettes]" (321). He starves only in "cabarets"; he could
pay his debts if he wanted to. Even his offer to fight for
Elsbeth's father is, he wittily acknowledges, of little
use: "moi-même, je prendrai mon fusil de chasse, s'il
n'est pas encore vendu" (322).

Fantasio's world is an incomprehensible jest, provoking
both laughter and tears, and the only valid response to
this world is the witty and the ironic. His language is a
reflection of his view of reality, a view strikingly modern in its emphasis on the incomprehensibility of the
universe:

> Un calembour console de bien des chagrins, et jouer
> avec les mots est un moyen comme un autre de jouer
> avec les pensées, les actions et les êtres. Tout est cale-
> mbour ici-bas.

(302-303)

"In the beginning was the Word"; but, to Fantasio, the
Word which creates the universe is not to be taken seriously; it is a pun. God's Word has created a meaningless world, from which He is effectively absent, not caring what happens to His creatures: "Dieu laisse faire les
hommes . . . il ne fait guère plus de cas de nos plaintes
que du bêlement d'un mouton" (297). Even nature is
"pitoyable": "Comme ce soleil couchant est manqué"
(283). The artist is free to create his own vision of life,
by playing with words and stretching their meanings;
his words mock the meaningless Word of the Divine.[3] If
the world is a pun, one asserts oneself by punning
against it; one defends oneself from believing in anything seriously by making life into a play on words: "Je
suis en train de bouleverser l'univers pour le mettre en
acrostiche" (300). Language is play, a means of creation, a joke to counteract the cruel joke which is the
world. With no faith in any absolute, man is reduced to
his own vision; style of life and style of language become his only values.

Fantasio's comrades share his playful view of life and
are also masters, if lesser masters, of word-play and
wit. They occasionally indulge in puns and clever replies. Hartman puns on the double meaning of "sentir":

FACIO:

> Il sent l'espion d'une lieue.

HARTMAN:

> Il ne sent rien du tout.

(281)

The play on "sent" ("smells like," "has the appearance
of," or "smells out," "is conscious of") denigrates
Marinoni's stupidity while showing Hartman's cleverness. He had earlier mocked Marinoni's pretentious
speech:

MARINONI:

> C'est une belle femme, à ce que je présume?

HARTMAN:

> Comme vous êtes un bel homme, vous l'avez dit.

(280)

and Marinoni's slowness in comprehension:

MARINONI:

> . . . vous avez dit fantasque?

HARTMAN:

> Je l'ai dit, cher inconnu, je me suis servi de ce mot.

(281)

Hartman also uses many metaphors and images, often
for purposes of mockery: "Il faut que je carillonne un
jour de fête" (279); "fantasque comme un bergeron-
nette" (281); "il se dandine comme un conseiller de justice" (281). Spark is less clever and less malicious. He
creates, however, the most striking metaphor of the
play:

> L'éternité est une grande aire, d'où tous les siècles,
> comme de jeunes aiglons, se sont envolés tour à tour
> pour traverser le ciel et disparaître; le nôtre est arrivé à
> son tour au bord du nid; mais on lui a coupé les ailes,
> et il attend la mort en regardant l'espace dans lequel il
> ne peut s'élancer.

(289)

Fantasio is most creative in his word-play when he is
trying to express his boredom, or when he is trying to
convert Elsbeth. He sees life as a game; but he has become bored with the game because it has no purpose.
By chance he finds not only a new role to play, in which
he can demonstrate his verbal agility, but also an opportunity to convince someone else of the value of spontaneity and playfulness. In doing this, he finds energy and
joy in living. Saving Elsbeth from sacrificing happiness
to politics gives him, if only temporarily, a purpose in
life to replace his lost faith in religion and love. To accomplish this purpose, he must keep his identity secret.

When she discovers him in her garden, Elsbeth asks, "Que faites-vous là, à cueillir ces fleurs?" He replies, "Je suis un brave cueilleur de fleurs" (299). In a quick and clever reply, he seems to answer her question, while in fact merely repeating her words. At first, he attempts a direct statement of his point of view, the only wit of which lies in his repetition of the constructions that she used:

ELSBETH:

> Pauvre homme! quel métier tu entreprends! faire de l'esprit à tant par heure! N'as-tu ni bras ni jambes, et ne ferais-tu pas mieux de labourer la terre que ta propre cervelle?

FANTASIO:

> Pauvre petite! quel métier vous entreprenez! épouser un sot que vous n'avez jamais vu!—n'avez-vous ni cœur ni tête, et ne feriez-vous pas mieux de vendre vos robes que votre corps?

> (300-301)

Her reply (Voilà qui est hardi, monsieur le nouveau venu!") perhaps shows him the inadvisability of such a frontal attack. He immediately changes his tactics. When she remarks, "Tu es laid, du moins; c'est certain," he replies, "Pas plus certain que votre beauté" (303). Her insults are returned as compliments. His display of wit also suggests that cleverness is more important than beauty.[4]

Fantasio demonstrates his wit by creating extended analogies. He compares Elsbeth to a mechanical bird, only able to sing a music-box theme:

> C'est un serin de Cour; il y a beaucoup de petites filles très bien élevées qui n'ont pas d'autres procédés que celui-là. Elles ont un petit ressort sous le bras gauche, un joli petit ressort en diamant fin, comme la montre d'un petit-maître;

> (311)

or to an unnaturally cultivated flower, untrue to its own nature:

> Cette tulipe que voilà s'attendait bien à être rouge; mais on l'a mariée; elle est tout étonnée d'être bleue: c'est ainsi que le monde entier se métamorphose sous les mains de l'homme.

> (302)

To further this comparison, Fantasio puns on two senses of "greffe," which can mean either a horticultural graft or the registration of a legal document: "les jardiniers et les notaires font des greffes si extraordinaires" (301-302). The implication is that Elsbeth's marriage (primarily a social act, to be legally registered for the sake of peace) is as unnatural as the grafting of fruit trees.

Fantasio's puns are an indirect means of persuasion. When Elsbeth says, "Si tu as écouté ma conversation avec ma gouvernante, prends garde à tes oreilles," he replies: "Non pas à mes oreilles, mais à ma langue. Vous vous trompez de sens; il y a une erreur de sens dans vos paroles" (302). Elsbeth immediately recognizes the pun on "sens" ("sense organ" and "meaning"): "ne me fais pas de calembour." Through his pun Fantasio corrects Elsbeth; she spoke of ears when she meant tongue, giving a wrong meaning to her sentence. (She obviously wants him not to tell others what he has heard.) There is also a subtle suggestion that Elsbeth's words, including those he overheard (her announcement to the governess that she will, reluctantly, marry the Prince) lack "sens" as "common sense." Fantasio not only puns on her mistaken use of "oreilles," but he also suggests the folly of her decision to marry. Later, Elsbeth queries whether Fantasio is what he seems to be, since he understands her so well; or are his words merely the effect of chance? "Est-ce à moi que s'adressent tes folies, ou est-ce au hasard que tu parles?" He replies: "C'est au hasard, je parle beaucoup au hasard: c'est mon plus cher confident" (312). In the pun on "au hasard" ("at random," but also "to chance"), Fantasio gives Elsbeth's words a deeper meaning. Yes, he speaks *to* chance, to the universe as accidental, not governed by law; he does not believe in that deterministic universe into which she has been thrust, and in which her marriage is a necessary condition for the peace of her father's kingdom. The pun is a way of suggesting more to Elsbeth than Fantasio will permit himself to say directly. Like a Shakespearean clown, he dispenses wisdom through word-play.

Contrasted to Fantasio and his friends are the exponents of a prose view of life. They are incapable of wit and spontaneity. The Prince de Mantoue is unable to see beyond his own immediate interests and consequently to understand any nuances of feeling or language. At his first entrance he admits his inability to comprehend the spoken word: "Ecris cela; je ne comprends clairement que les écritures moulées en bâtarde" (293). He cannot understand that Elsbeth rejects him. Because he imagines other people to be as unable to comprehend nuances as himself, he unnecessarily explains everything he says: "Oui, mon ami (je t'ai accordé ce titre)" (294). The Prince's need to see everything in writing is the opposite of Fantasio's preference for speech.[5] For Fantasio language is living and vital; for the Prince language is unspontaneous and fixed. Despite his intellectual limitations and pomposity, the Prince would like to be a poet. He thinks he speaks in "mots à double entente" (308). Like Fantasio, he dons a costume; he appears as Marinoni, an aide-de-camp. The Prince, however, is too prosaic to be an actor. He cannot remember the role he is supposed to play. He is never equal to inventing the appropriate language; he continually complains that words fail him: "Qu'il serait difficile de trouver des paroles" (305).

Those who accept their place in society are concerned with their dignity; their language is often pompous. "J'ai parcouru les alentours du palais, et ces tablettes renferment les principaux traits des conversations différentes dans lesquelles je me suis immiscé" (293-94) is Marinoni's longwinded way of saying he has copied down some remarks he heard about Elsbeth. The Prince's declaration of love is filled with inflated rhetoric: "Heureux les grands de la terre! ils peuvent vous épouser" (305); "un coeur pur et sans tache bat sous ce modeste uniforme" (305). Even the King, although he has enough sense of humor to laugh at the wig flying through the air, is, as the representative of social stability, appropriately inclined to pompous exclamation: "Que les bénédictions de mon peuple te rendent grâces pour ton père!" (309). The metaphors and images prose characters use are clichés. The King speaks of politics as a spider's web (278), a commonplace image, as is his comparison of the "aide-de-camp" to the Prince's shadow: "Quel est donc cet aide de camp qui vous suit comme votre ombre?" (304). The Prince, pleased with his own appearance, can think of no more interesting metaphor than: "Il me semble que je suis poudré comme un homme de la dernière classe" (294). Language is, for most people, as Fantasio knows, primarily a way of expressing banalities which mask the secrets of the heart:

> tout ce que les hommes se disent entre eux se ressemble; les idées qu'ils échangent sont presque toujours les mêmes dans toutes leurs conversations; mais, dans l'intérieur de toutes ces machines isolées, quels replis, quels compartiments secrets!
>
> (284)

But the prose characters prefer to suppress any secrets or emotions which upset their ordered universe.

The governess represents a third life-style to Elsbeth, neither the prosaic nor the witty. She represents self-indulgent sentimentality which sees reality through the banalities of romantic literature: "On dit que c'est un Amadis" (296); "C'était un vrai Triboulet" (299); "le roi serait un véritable Jephté" (299); "C'est un vrai conte de fées" (313). She speaks of having "pleuré un torrent du ciel" (296) and compares Elsbeth to "un vrai agneau pascal" (298). Such romantic clichés falsify the truth. Elsbeth is sometimes tempted to see life through such false categories: "Je ne suis qu'une pauvre rêveuse; peut-être la faute en est-elle à tes romans" (297). The facile romantic becomes dominant in Elsbeth when she vainly imagines that Fantasio is the Prince: her mind becomes filled with "tant de fleurs étranges et mystérieuses" (318).

Elsbeth's use of language is closer to Fantasio's than to that of the court; it is perhaps the awareness revealed in such word-play which finally saves her both from her romantic tendencies and from sacrificing herself to her social role. She is quick to turn Fantasio's comments into her own images. When he says "je cueille modestement des fleurs en attendant qu'il me vienne de l'esprit," she cleverly replies, "Cela me paraît douteux, que vous cueilliez jamais cette fleur-là" (300). While denying that Fantasio has any wit, she shows her own wit. She quickly takes up a casual remark of Fantasio's about his shadow, using the word as the basis of a clever, if cruel, suggestion that he is not comparable to her former jester: "Vous avez raison de parler de votre ombre; tant que vous aurez ce costume, elle lui ressemblera toujours, je crois, plus que vous" (300). She compares Fantasio's search for wit to tilling an infertile soil: "ne ferais-tu pas mieux de labourer la terre que ta propre cervelle?" (301). When he compares himself to a "oiseau en liberté," she replies that he is rather a "oiseau en cage" (309). Elsbeth's wit, mainly revealed through repartee with Fantasio, shows a mental agility that allows her eventually to embrace his view of the world. At the end of the play she recognizes that life is not a romance; Fantasio is not the Prince and she cannot marry him. She also understands that the peace of her father's kingdom is not worth sacrificing herself in an unwanted marriage. She pays Fantasio for having prevented her marriage; her illusions and her sense of responsibility destroyed, she gives Fantasio the key to her garden so that he can return to play the court fool from time to time.[6] Elsbeth, we feel, is beginning to see life as a game.

Fantasio is a criticism of systems of language which impose order on life. The world is not a chivalric romance as the governess would have it; neither is the world rational and "prosaic," requiring social duties and a sense of dignity. Instead, we accept Fantasio's view of the world. *Fantasio* is perhaps the most "modern" of Musset's plays in its refusal to impose order and values on life. In Musset's later plays, verbal wit is less important, because the view of life offered is less "absurd." There are fixed values, love in particular; consequently wit becomes a barrier to fulfilment. As the title *On ne badine pas avec l'amour* suggests, an irresponsible or trifling use of language leads to tragedy. Fantasio himself might be a hero from *Le Mythe de Sisyphe,* a court fool to set beside the Don Juan or the revolutionary. He is without illusions; he will play out his life, with the aid of puns and metaphors, as a series of roles, without ever believing that any role is meaningful.[7]

Notes

1. Fantasio's clowning obviously owes much to Musset's reading of Shakespeare. See notes, p. 1364, of Alfred de Musset, *Théâtre Complet,* ed. Mau-

rice Allem (Paris, 1958). Quotations from Musset are taken from this edition.

2. One might say that Musset points to the thematic significance of language in the play by the number of characters who mention it.

3. See Camus's discussion of the Romantic aesthetic in *L'Homme Révolté,* where he calls the Romantics "des créateurs solitaires, rivaux obstinés d'un Dieu qu'ils condamnent." (*L'Homme Révolté* [Paris, 1951], p. 74.)

4. The words are ambiguous, as Allem points out (p. 1365). They may mean "Just as certain," i.e., "I am ugly and you are beautiful," or "No more certain," i.e., "I am perhaps not ugly and perhaps you are not beautiful." If read in the latter sense, the reply reinforces the superiority of wit, since beauty is seen to be a relative quality.

5. Musset seems to have been particularly amused by the stodgy character who needs to see things written down. In *On ne badine pas avec l'amour,* the Baron says: "j'avais même écrit, noté—sur mes tablettes de poche—que ce jour devait être le plus agréable de mes jours" (337).

6. We might see the repartee as a kind of courtship and the key as a sexual symbol. However, the text of the play does not allow us to assume any happy ending in the offing.

7. Interestingly, Fantasio, like Camus's Caligula, wishes he could catch hold of the moon (287). The realization that man cannot attain the absolute is, for both characters, the beginning of their play-acting.

Russell S. King (essay date May 1972)

SOURCE: King, Russell S. "Romanticism and Musset's *Confession d'un enfant du siècle.*" *Nottingham French Studies* 11, no. 1 (May 1972): 3-13.

[*In the following essay, King acknowledges that* La Confession d'un enfant du siècle *is a decidedly Romantic work featuring Musset's projection of the post-Napoleonic social malaise in France and comments on the novel as it analyzes a young libertine who succumbs to a lack of faith in his society and its ideals.*]

Musset published his only novel, **La Confession d'un Enfant du Siècle,** in 1836. Professor Grimsley is right to complain that the work is too infrequently examined for its intrinsic literary merits.[1] Readers and critics have tended to concentrate on two aspects of this work. Firstly they have seen the novel in an autobiographical light, comparing the hero with Musset himself and the heroine with George Sand, emphasizing similarities and discrepancies between the real relationship and the version of the novel, measuring it against the other accounts of the celebrated liaison. Secondly students of the Romantic movement have limited their study to Chapter Two of the first book, which had already been published separately in the *Revue des Deux Mondes* on 15 September 1835 and which gives a clear analysis of the *mal du siècle* interpreted largely in a historical context.

In this article I propose to ignore almost totally the biographical aspect and concentrate on the nature of the Romantic *mal du siècle.* I hope to show that the historical explanation of the Romantic malady, fascinating and plausible though it is, only partially explains the malady of the hero as he is presented in the novel which follows.

Despite the richness and frequency of the imagery, the analysis of the Romantic *mal du siècle* in the first twenty pages of the novel is clear and explicit. The writers and poets of 1830 had been born at the height of Napoleon's career. "Les mères inquiètes avaient mis au monde une génération ardente, pâle, nerveuse" (p.1).[2] Their childhood had been a time of excitement amidst the turmoil. "Et pourtant jamais il n'y eut tant de joie, tant de vie, tant de fanfares guerrières, dans tous les coeurs" (p.2). After 1815 France was exhausted and desired only peace and sleep:

> De même qu'un voyageur, tant qu'il est sur le chemin, court nuit et jour par la pluie et par le soleil, sans s'apercevoir de ses veilles ni des dangers; mais, dès qu'il est arrivé au milieu de sa famille et qu'il s'asseoit devant le feu, il éprouve une lassitude sans bornes et peut à peine se traîner à son lit: ainsi la France, veuve de César, sentit tout à coup sa blessure. Elle tomba en défaillance, et s'endormit d'un si profond sommeil, que ses vieux rois, la croyant morte, l'enveloppèrent d'un linceul blanc. La vieille armée en cheveux gris rentra épuisée de fatigue, et les foyers des châteaux déserts se rallumèrent tristement.
>
> (pp. 3-4).

What was there now for the youth to do? They had been bred for war and had dreamed of Moscow and the Pyramids:

> Ils n'étaient pas sortis de leurs villes; mais on leur avait dit que, par chaque barrière de ces villes, on allait à une capitale d'Europe. Ils avaient dans la tête tout un monde; ils regardaient la terre, le ciel, les rues et les chemins; tout cela était vide, et les cloches de leurs paroisses résonnaient seules dans le lointain.
>
> (p. 4).

The only occupation which remained for them was to enter the Church, like Stendhal's Julien Sorel. Political involvement, the intoxication felt in the pursuit of liberty, brought back memories of 1789 and the Terror, and the young men knew that in the immediate future any attempts to pursue some ideology would be doomed to failure. This was the lesson of July 1830. Faith in monarchy and religion, gradually eroded during the eighteenth century, collapsed more or less with the revolution, the Terror and Napoleon. It is this collapse of faith and the failure to replace the ancient values which lie at the source of Musset's view of the French Romantic age. Voltaire, whom he attacks at the end of the first book, as he had done three years earlier in **"Rolla,"** is symbolically blamed for the void which so many felt within them and in their lives. What was a young man to do but turn to a life of debauchery, using sensual pleasures to fill or disguise the void:

> Un sentiment de malaise inexprimable commença donc à fermenter dans tous les jeunes cœurs. Condamnés au repos par les souverains du monde, livrés aux cuistres de toute espèce, à l'oisiveté et à l'ennui, les jeunes gens voyaient se retirer d'eux les vagues écumantes contre lesquelles ils avaient préparé leurs bras. Tous ces gladiateurs frottés d'huile se sentaient au fond de l'âme une misère insupportable. Les plus riches se firent libertins; ceux d'une fortune médiocre prirent un état, et se résignèrent soit à la robe, soit à l'épée; les plus pauvres se jetèrent dans l'enthousiasme à froid, dans les grands mots, dans l'affreuse mer de l'action sans but.
>
> (pp. 10-11).

Not only did the political situation contribute to the steady erosion of faith, but the literature of the period, too, particularly from abroad, infected the youth of France, the major culprits being Goethe and Byron. Why, Musset wonders, could poets no longer write of happiness?

> Que ne chantiez-vous le parfum des fleurs, les voix de la nature, l'espérance et l'amour, la vigne et le soleil, l'azur et la beauté? Sans doute vous connaissiez la vie, et sans doute vous aviez souffert, et le monde croulait autour de vous, et vous pleuriez sur ses ruines, et vous désespériez.
>
> (p. 13).

These aspects, though, are merely the individual elements which are to be seen in a historical context. This is the point which Musset stresses most emphatically on four occasions. The period, presumably the Restoration and July Monarchy, was a period of transition, during which the institutions and values of the past had been overthrown but temporarily put together again, though with little conviction. The future was still a distant dream:

> Le siècle présent, en un mot, qui sépare le passé de l'avenir, qui n'est ni l'un ni l'autre et qui ressemble à tous deux à la fois, et où l'on ne sait, à chaque pas qu'on fait, si l'on marche sur une semence ou sur un débris.
>
> (p. 7).

L'astre de l'avenir se lève à peine; il ne peut sortir de l'horizon; il reste enveloppé de nuages, et, comme le soleil en hiver, son disque y apparaît d'un rouge de sang, qu'il a gardé de 93. Il n'y a plus d'amour, il n'y a plus de gloire. Quelle épaisse nuit sur la terre! Et nous serons morts quand il fera jour.

> (p. 15).

Towards the end of the second chapter, Musset summarizes this historical view which has, it seems, become one of the most celebrated definitions of the French Romantic *mal du siècle:*

> Toute la maladie du siècle présent vient de deux causes; le peuple qui a passé par 93 et par 1814 porte au coeur deux blessures. Tout ce qui était n'est plus; tout ce qui sera n'est pas encore. Ne cherchez pas ailleurs le secret de nos maux.
>
> (p. 20).

This interpretation is plausible, clearly described, and usually taken as an explanation of much of Musset's pessimism. When it is applied to the novel which it introduces, its validity must in some measure be questioned.

The question of faith, however, or rather lack of it, is consistent with the historical explanation. Octave, the hero, does not believe; he has never been taught to believe. There are, at times, suggestions that Octave is groping to regain, or perhaps, gain for the first time, his faith:

> O Dieu! je l'ai vue là sur ses genoux, les mains jointes, inclinée sur la pierre. . . . Je la soulevai dans mes bras. "O mon unique amie! m'écriai-je, ô ma maîtresse, ma mère et ma soeur! demande aussi pour moi que je puisse t'aimer comme tu le mérites. Demande que je puisse vivre; que mon coeur se lave dans tes larmes; qu'il devienne une hostie sans tache, et que nous la partagions devant Dieu."
>
> (pp. 212-213).

He is unable to pray himself, but he can ask Brigitte, his mistress, to pray for him. Without faith, which extends far beyond a simple faith in God, but a faith in goodness, hope, and life itself, Octave's life becomes empty, vain, a process leading to ever deeper disillusionment. Towards the end of the novel the hero pathetically asks:

> A quoi bon? pourquoi tant de luttes? qui donc est là-haut qui regarde et qui se plaît à tant d'agonies? qui donc s'égaye et se désoeuvre à ce spectacle d'une création toujours naissante et toujours moribonde?
>
> (p. 310).

Octave suggests that he was born in a century in which faith no longer existed. The previous century had already achieved its goal, as Musset suggests here and in **"Rolla,"** before the hero Octave was born: "Et toi Jésus, qui l'as sauvée, pardonne-moi, ne le lui dis pas. Je suis né dans un siècle impie, et j'ai beaucoup à expier. Pauvre fils de Dieu qu'on oublie, on ne m'a pas appris à t'aimer" (p. 313). Faith seems impossible to Octave. When he desperately turns for guidance to the Bible, he simply finds further reason for doubt, as did Vigny in his poem *Le Mont des Oliviers*. When Octave later turns to Christ for comfort, it is the suffering of Christ, particularly on the Cross, which partly explains the attraction.

Octave, unlike his friend Desgenais, requires faith of some sort. Faith in God is now replaced by faith in love. There is something almost religious in the love Octave has for his first mistress and later for Brigitte: "Ma Maîtresse, créature que j'idolâtrais . . ." (p. 22). "Je sentais la piété de son sourire" (p. 139). "Notre amour montait à Dieu" (p. 172). "C'était un culte que j'avais pour Brigitte" (p. 233). This vague, almost mystical love which he feels for his mistresses occupies his whole world:

> Je sentais que mon amour était ma perte, mais que vivre sans elle était impossible.
>
> (p. 28).

> Je n'avais vécu que par cette femme; douter d'elle, c'était douter de tout; la maudire, tout renier; la perdre, tout détruire. Je ne sortais plus, le monde m'apparaissait comme peuplé de monstres, de bêtes fauves et de crocodiles.
>
> (p. 38).

> L'espace renfermé entre les quatre murs de votre jardin est le seul lieu au monde où je vive; vous êtes le seul être humain qui me fasse aimer Dieu. J'avais renoncé à tout avant même de vous connaître.
>
> (p. 157).

It is love which brings Octave closer to God with its intensification of feeling which, somehow, is perhaps to be interpreted as a reflexion of divine love: "Vivre, oui, sentir fortement, profondément, qu'on existe, qu'on est homme, créé par Dieu, voilà le premier, le plus grand bienfait de l'amour." (p. 147).

Even Desgenais acknowledges the religious aspect of love, but dismisses it as an illusion, an unattainable ideal:

> L'amour, c'est la foi, c'est la religion du bonheur terrestre; c'est un triangle lumineux placé à la voûte de ce temple qu'on appelle le monde. Aimer, c'est marcher librement dans de temple, et avoir à son côté un être capable de comprendre pourquoi une pensée, un mot, une fleur font que vous arrêtez et que vous relevez la tête vers le triangle céleste.
>
> (p. 50).

There is doubt, though, in the novel whether Musset or his hero, Octave, really consider love as a reflection of divine love, or a replacement for divine love which no longer is possible. Perhaps it is merely a means of escape from the misery, drabness and futility of his existence. There are suggestions elsewhere in Musset's writings that in fact this last interpretation is the right one.

Desgenais, who represents the voice of experience and reason in Musset himself, seems to share essentially the same yearnings as Octave, but experience has taught him that perfection in this world is impossible, for all, even life itself, is illusion. For this reason he prefers prostitutes and accepts physical love for what it seems to be.

> La perfection n'existe pas; la comprendre est le triomphe de l'intelligence humaine; la désirer pour la posséder est la plus dangereuse des folies. . . . L'insensé veut posséder le ciel; le sage l'admire, s'agenouille et ne désire pas. La perfection, ami, n'est pas plus faite pour nous que l'immensité. Il faut ne la chercher en rien, ne la demander à rien, ni à l'amour, ni à la beauté, ni au bonheur, ni à la vertu.
>
> (pp. 40-42).

One may consider Octave, and Musset, as idealists in that they seem to be in search of perfect love. However, it is important to remember that Musset makes his hero a young man of nineteen at the beginning of the novel when he is betrayed by his mistress. There is consequently something rather adolescent in his love, which has little or no firm basis in experience or knowledge. His idealism is adolescent. Like Musset's own experience at a young age, Octave's despair springs from wounded vanity: "Ce que je ne pouvais concevoir, ce n'etait pas que ma maîtresse eût cessé de m'aimer, mais c'était qu'elle m'eût trompé" (p. 26). Jealousy and vanity count for as much as the disillusionment felt when he discovered the imperfection of his love and the worthlessness of his mistress.

Of course, one of the reasons for the failure of Octave and Desgenais to retain their faith in love as a substitute for religious faith is that they have no faith at all in the women they choose to love. The mistress who betrays Octave earlier in the novel is a young widow who is "fort libre". Octave is so concerned with his own reactions that her attempt to justify herself is limited to one paragraph. His egocentricity prevents him from ever understanding the female point of view. He appears neither interested in her nor in her love for him. He seems interested only in his own love. Desgenais warns him against confusing the wine with the intoxication it produces: but this advice makes little difference to Octave, for he appears to confuse the two. In the second part of the novel, in which the hero does all he can to destroy the love he has finally won, Octave seems to be punishing Brigitte firstly for his past disappointments which he suffered at the hands of another woman, and secondly because she ceases to be compatible with the strange sort of love which he desired.

The most important aspect of the *Confession* is the ambivalence of Octave's spiritual, platonic love. Below the surface there are signs that the novel is very much in the tradition of the libertine novel of the previous century, and that the hero, and one often suspects the same of Musset, is more interested, despite all, in sexual love and cerebral titillation than in platonic love.

When we first meet Octave, in Part I chapter iii, he is attending dinner after a fancy dress ball, in the company of his fashionable friends, and excited because he is about to spend the night with his mistress:

> J'étais à table, à un grand souper, après une mascarade. Autour de moi mes amis richement costumés, de tous côtés des jeunes gens et des femmes, tous étincelants de beauté et de joie; à droite et à gauche, des mets exquis, des flacons, des lustres, des fleurs; au-dessus de ma tête un orchestre bruyant, et, en face de moi ma maîtresse, créature superbe que j'idolâtrais.
>
> (pp. 21-22).

Five pages later we learn in an aside that Octave, since his first disappointment, has been in love many times. We also discover early in the narrative that nature for him serves principally as an aphrodisiac. "Le spectacle de la nature ayant toujour été pour moi le plus puissant des aphrodisiaques" (p. 34). So one begins to suspect that in fact Octave, even before the discovery of his mistress's infidelity, was more excited by the sexual aspect of the relationship. Just as at the beginning of the story we are introduced to an Octave happy because his mistress has invited him to spend the night with her. . . .

There are further suggestions in the novel which reveal an Octave excited by the sight of any woman:

> Dans quelque lieu que je fusse, quelque occupation que je m'imposasse, je ne pouvais penser qu'aux femmes; la vue d'une femme me faisait trembler. . . . Mais il en résultait que toute idée de plaisir des sens s'unissait en moi à une idée d'amour; c'était là ce qui me perdait. Car, ne pouvant m'empêcher de penser continuellement aux femmes, je ne pouvais faire autre chose en même temps que repasser jour et nuit dans ma tête toutes ces idées de débauche, de fausses amours et de trahisons féminines, dont j'étais plein. Posséder une femme, pour moi, c'était aimer; or je ne songeais qu'aux femmes, et je ne croyais plus à la possibilité d'un véritable amour.
>
> (pp. 59-60).

This is not the only reference to such an obsession. Later when he lifts the sheet to behold a naked Brigitte he is equally, and quite naturally, excited: "A cette vue, tous mes sens s'émurent. Etait-ce de douleur ou de désir? Je n'en sais rien" (p. 305). Earlier he was excited, too, at the sight of Brigitte undressing: "Je rentrais alors dans la chambre et je trouvais Brigitte se disposant à se déshabiller. Je contemplais avidement ce corps charmant, ces trésors de beauté, que tant de fois j'avais possédés" (p. 254).

On other occasions too, Musset seems to stress the actual possession. When Octave decides to console himself with a waitress, he makes her undress partly, then sets about lighting the fire and recreating the atmosphere of an evening he has spent with his first mistress. At the end of Part III, originally intended as the end of the narrative, sexual possession is considered the ultimate in human happiness: "Celui-là mourra sans se plaindre: il a possédé la femme qu'il aimait" (p. 174).

It is not surprising that, in the second part of the novel, Octave's debauchery should come to the fore, driving him to destroy what he loved and cherished most. He boasted of being a rake. The analysis of Octave's debauchery is explained, apparently, because of the total faith Octave has in love, faith in anything else being impossible in the age he lived in. When this faith is betrayed, and love, like all else, is shown to be an illusion, his cynicism leads to the uncontrollable desire to destroy the love which he seemed to cherish. However, one might very well question whether Octave ever really believed in some pure, overwhelming kind of love which gave life, his life, meaning and occupation. One may conclude that Octave, like Perdican in *On ne badine pas avec l'amour,* was always a potential rake. . . .

. . . [We] begin to approach the standpoint of *Lorenzaccio,* where debauchery and evil are seen to be fundamental forces in mankind which time and a little experience suffice to bring to the surface. In other words, Octave is a libertine, but, at nineteen, he is still an apprentice libertine.

Like all Musset's heroes, Octave is a special case, but a special case which is not necessarily a product of Musset's own time. Fundamentaly there is something universal about the writer, as Baudelaire suggests when he wrote that "Alfred de Musset, féminin et sans doctrine, aurait pu exister dans tous les temps et n'eût jamais été qu'un paresseux à effusions gracieuses."[3]

The first, most surprising admission, at the beginning of the narrative, is that Octave had not suffered at all until the day he discovered the treachery of his mistress. "J'ai à raconter à quelle occasion je fus pris d'abord de la maladie du siècle . . . J'avais alors dix-neuf ans; je n'avais éprouvé aucun malheur ni aucune maladie; j'étais d'un caractère à la fois hautain et ouvert, avec toutes les espérances et un coeur débordant" (pp. 21-22). What then, one may wonder, was the reason for the long analysis of the Revolution and Empire into which the generation of 1830 had been born? He was happy and full of hope then till this fatal day.

There are ample suggestions that Octave's *mal,* though, like Musset's own, did in fact have an almost physical manifestation and probably origin, including, for example, nervous disorders and fevers:

Tant les nerfs de mes orteils étaient crispés.

(p. 24).

La fièvre me reprit avec une telle violence, que je fus obligé de me mettre au lit.

(p. 29).

Une grande faiblesse s'empara de moi; j'étais épuisé de fatigue. Je m'assis dans un fauteuil; peu à peu mes idées se troublèrent; je portai la main à mon front, il était baigné de sueur. Une fièvre violente faisait trembler tous mes membres.

(p. 152).

Et mon mal empirait sans cesse. . . . J'avais, au milieu de mes folies, de véritables accès de fièvre qui me frappaient comme des coups de foudre; je m'éveillais tremblant de tous mes membres et couvert d'une sueur froide.

(pp. 226-227).

At frequent intervals Octave refers to his experience and case as an illness, using terms like *mal* and *maladie*. He speaks of his "coeur si malade" (p. 99). Brigitte tells him that he is nothing more than an "enfant malade, défiant ou mutin" (p. 212).

The common characteristic which binds together almost all Musset's heroes, Rolla, Fantasio, and Lorenzo, is that they are all idle young men, with apparent potential and talent, but no ambition or ability to find an outlet for their superior gifts. They are unemployed and unemployable, yet they hanker after some occupation which might give their lives a semblance of purpose and some stability. When Octave is betrayed, he comes face to face with the emptiness of his idle life:

Que faire à présent? Je n'avais point d'etat, aucune occupation. J'avais étudié la médecine et le droit, sans pouvoir me décider à prendre l'une ou l'autre de ces deux carrières; j'avais travaillé six mois chez un banquier avec une telle inexactitude, que j'avais été obligé de donner ma démission à temps pour n'être pas renvoyé. . . . Mon seul trésor, après l'amour, était l'indépendance.

(p. 33).

He refuses to listen to any suggestion that he might find some useful occupation: "Lorsqu'on me parlait d'une autre occupation, je ne répondais pas" (p. 37). Reproaches from Brigitte have no effect on him: "Je m'arrêtais à tout moment pour me jeter aux genoux de Brigitte, qui me traitait de paresseux, disant en riant qu'il lui fallait tout faire et que je n'étais bon à rien" (p. 234). At the end of the novel, Octave has found nothing to replace the faith he had in love, and the sense of heroism he feels in his final sacrifice will not sustain him for long.

Octave is not so much a romantic hero, but he plays at being one. The influence of the earlier tales of Byron, particularly *Lara,* which Musset admired, is in evidence

in this novel. Often in the **Confession** one may detect a false, posturing stance adopted by the hero, who seems to watch himself act out his role of a suffering, betrayed hero and lover:

Je criais à faire retentir toute la maison, et en même temps les larmes me coupaient parfois la parole si violemment, que je tombais sur le lit pour leur donner un libre cours.

(pp. 27-28).

Tantôt je lui peignais ma vie passée sous les couleurs les plus sombres, et lui donnais à entendre que, s'il fallait me séparer d'elle, je resterais livré à une solitude pire que la mort; je lui disais que j'avais la société en horreur, et le récit fidèle de ma vie, que je lui avais fait, lui prouvait que j'étais sincerè.

(p. 161).

At times the note struck seems a false one. For example when Octave discovers his betrayal, he at first wants to possess her once more and then kill them both (p. 28). When his friend Desgenais asks him if it is his first mistress, he cries out melodramatically that it is his last (p. 30). He later wants to be like the wounded bull in the ring which is left to retire to a corner and suffer and die in peace (p. 39). There are frequent references throughout the book to weeping willows, a tree which is associated with Musset himself and his grave at the Père-Lachaise cemetary. At the end of the novel Octave withdraws to leave Brigitte and Henri Smith together, and he will be free to continue to suffer alone. There are certain adjectives which become almost predictable: "profond désespoir" (p. 32), "profonde tristesse" (p. 120), "tristesse inexprimable" (p. 52), "affreuse tristesse" (p. 64).

What is indeed surprising about this novel is that the posturing seems an act signifying nothing in particular. In **"Rolla,"** *Fantasio* and *Lorenzaccio,* the heroes all choose roles to play for some reason or other, and the role is a product of the psychological and metaphysical side of the hero himself. But Octave, preoccupied with watching himself acting out his role, comes to few metaphysical conclusions. Is it perhaps because he is cast in the role of lover, unlike the others mentioned above? In the second part of the novel, Octave merely examines why he seems bent on destroying what he loves, and why he wishes to become or appear a rake. He does not examine the force of evil latent in mankind in the way that Lorenzo does. Nor does he have the lucidity of Fantasio who knows that the post of court jester is merely a mask to disguise the futility not only of his existence but of all existence.

Octave is essentially a weak person. He blames his youth for his predicament: "La grande raison qui m'empêchait de guérir, c'était ma jeunesse" (p. 59).

One of the attractions of Brigitte is that she is older, and can act as a mother, whom Octave has apparently never known: "O ma maîtresse, ma mère et ma soeur" (p. 212).

The major sign of his weakness, if it is weakness, is his constant reference to fate and to forces outside him to explain his conduct. It seems that he probably does not believe in fate in any religious sense, but it is a useful way of explaining what appears inexplicable: "Je ne sais quelle force désespérée m'y poussait" (p. 28); "Laissez-moi croire . . . qu'un bon ange est quelque part, qui unit parfois à dessein les faibles mains tremblantes tendues vers Dieu" (p. 54); "Il faut me laisser à ma destinée" (p. 61); "Pourquoi m'ôter le seul rayon de soleil que la Providence m'ait laissé?" (p. 157); "Ce fatal amour qui me dévore et qui me tue" (p. 168); "Faire le mal! tel était donc le rôle que la Providence m'avait imposé!" (p. 299). In *Lorenzaccio,* Musset also uses providence partly as a picturesque way of suggesting something which is psychologically too complex for the hero to understand, partly because he does not wish to penetrate the psychology of his heroes to any greater depth.

The other psychological explanation to which Musset resorts, as he does in many of his writings, is that each man is really made up of two different men pulling in opposite directions. This reflects, no doubt, an influence of Musset's own autoscopia, a kind of hallucinatory experience in which one can see a projection of oneself outside of oneself: this is an experience which perhaps inspired the famous **"Nuit de Décembre."** Octave concludes that he comprises two men, "un homme qui riait et un autre qui pleurait" (p. 101). It is only in this light that he can begin to understand the vacillations between extreme joy and depression: "Je m'étais couché sur cette parole avec des transports de joie, mais, en sortant de chez moi, j'éprouvai, au contraire, une tristesse invincible" (p. 166). His life seemed to alternate between good and bad days: "Pendant longtemps les bons et les mauvais jours se succédèrent presque régulièrement; je me montrais alternativement dur et railleur, tendre et dévoué, sec et orgeuilleux, repentant et soumis" (p. 198).

It is also possible to consider Octave and Desgenais, in the early part of the novel, as two projections of the author, a device used by Musset elsewhere in *Les Caprices de Marianne.* In *On ne badine pas avec l'amour* Musset puts as much of himself in the heroine as in the hero. In *Lorenzaccio,* one may consider many of the characters, including Lorenzo himself, Philippe Strozzi and Julien Salviati, as projections of their author. In the *Confession,* Desgenais represents in some measure the voice of experience, reason, and subdued cynicism. When, in the second part of the novel, Octave comes to share many of his views, Desgenais disappears from the scene.

In some respects Octave is an early decadent, just as Musset foreshadows many of the writers of the later part of the century. Octave has no faith in the present, and never thinks of the future. "Notre siècle n'a pas de formes. . . . En sorte que nous ne vivons que de débris, comme si la fin du monde était proche" (p. 35). When he sees the weather as a reflection of his own mood, it is a mood of desolation and death which it reflects: "C'était par une de ces sombres soirées où le vent qui siffle ressemble aux plaintes d'un mourant; une pluie aiguë fouettait les vitres, laissant par intervalles un silence de mort" (p. 39).

Experience is seen in terms of art, particularly literature. It is not so much that life is an imitation of art, as it became later in the century, but life and experience are always seen, unfavourably, in comparison with art. Octave, like René and all the early romantic heroes, has read voraciously, giving them, as Chateaubriand notes, a second-hand experience and desires which reality could not satisfy. Desgenais criticizes Octave for wanting a kind of love which is found only in old novelists and poets. Octave compares his orgies and experiences with those of the Roman Empire and Petronius and finds them wanting. He reads Virgil in the country. On his first encounter with Brigitte he discusses literature and music. It is therefore not so much that art replaces life for Octave, but art has a greater reality for the passive, sensitive hero, and stands in the way to his enjoyment of real experiences, leaving him constantly in need of more inaccessible remedies and sensations.

It is in some measure in this light that Octave's attraction to suffering is to be explained. When he is wounded in a duel, he feels a kind of pleasure at the sight of his blood. His mistress gave him a medallion to which he attached claws which would hurt and scar him: "Ces clous, qui m'entraient dans la poitrine à chaque mouvement, me causaient une volupté si étrange, que j'appuyais quelquefois ma main pour les sentir plus profondément. Je sais bien que c'est de la folie; l'amour en fait bien d'autres" (p. 37). Later when he is falsely courted by another woman who endeavours to win him by posing as a fellow-sufferer, he is almost conquered. When he falls in love with Brigitte it is the contrast between her serene beauty accompanied by suffering, not her own but that of an ill woman she is tending. It is this juxtaposition of beauty and suffering which appeals to Octave. No sooner is their love shared than Octave tries to destroy it, because failure and suffering are the only states with which he is able to live. As he himself realizes, he is trifling with suffering: "Tu badines avec la souffrance" (p. 216). Perhaps the many examples of sadism and the tendency to cultivate suffering are to be considered as a desire to punish himself for his failings in real life.

What is most noticeable therefore is the gulf which separates the historical explanation of the *mal du siècle* and the actual portrait of Octave. Octave never hankers after the excitement of the Napoleonic wars. He is uninterested in politics. He seems neither to support nor oppose the Restoration or July monarchy. His glorification of love and mysticism have an only apparent religious significance, for the *Confession* is in part a disguised libertine novel with a contemporary idealistic, mystic veneer. The metaphysical crisis is less profound than in *Lorenzaccio* and **"Rolla,"** and the result of the hero's inability to find some worthy stable love. The *mal du siècle* derives from a combination of the hero's weaknesses: weakness in his human relations, weakness in his ability to persevere in anything for long. The novel does not relate these manifestations of his weakness to the age in which Octave lived.

The age was indeed and age of declining faith, but for Octave to blame the age for his particular failures is but a further sign of his weakness. It is weakness which is the key to all Musset's heroes. Nonetheless, the **Confession** is a Romantic novel, a typical product of the Romantic age, with a hero who belongs to the same family as Werther, René, and countless others. But this is not sufficient to justify Musset's historical explanation of the romantic *mal du siècle.*

Chapter Two promises an analysis of a young man who has no faith in his age, his society, its ideals, a young man paralysed by this lack of faith, a hero we detect to a certain extent in **Lorenzaccio** and **Fantasio.** In the **Confession** we are shown a young apprentice libertine involved in his first two liaisons, who decides that life is futile because his love-affairs are short-lived, and because he is an idle, rather weak young man.

Notes

1. Ronald Grimsley, "Romantic Emotion in Musset's Confession d'un enfant du siècle", *Studies in Romanticism,* Volume IX, Spring 1970, Number 2.

2. All page references are to the Garnier edition of the novel. A new edition with a preface by Claude Duchet, 1968, has the same pagination.

3. Baudelaire, *Œuvres Complètes,* Bibliothèque de la Pléiade, p. 682.

Donald W. Tappan (essay date spring 1974)

SOURCE: Tappan, Donald W. "Musset's Murderous Rose." *Romance Notes* 15, no. 3 (spring 1974): 430-32.

[In the following essay, Tappan explicates the thematic function of the rose in Musset's "La nuit de mai," linking it with the poem's representation of fecundity and procreative union.]

> La rose, vierge encor, se referme jalouse
> Sur le frelon nacré qu'elle enivre en mourant.

This image from the second speech of the Muse in the early lines of **"La Nuit de mai"** has been the subject of several explanatory footnotes by editors of texts destined for students. Most agree that it is the "frelon" who is dying. Steinhauer and Walter, for example, in their anthology translate the second line: "on the pearly drone which it intoxicates as he dies."[1] French editors generally agree with the interpretation; Chassang and Senninger explain "en mourant" as "tandis qu'il meurt."[2] Others justify it by attempting to explain away the "unusual" grammatical structure. Thus Lagarde and Michard inform the student that "en mourant" "se rapporte à *frelon* (construction archaïque),"[3] and the editor of the Classiques Larousse selections explains: "Dès le XVIIIe siècle, le gérondif ne peut plus se rapporter qu'au sujet. Or, ici, c'est bien le frelon qui meurt. Archaïsme ou solécisme."[4] Morris Bishop offers the same interpretation but with some reservations as to the acceptability of the meaning: "while [the hornet] dies. (This murderous behavior of the rose is very surprising.)."[5] François Denoeu, for grammatical reasons, proposes to the contrary that the rose dies: "which she enraptures as she dies; as he dies, *referring to* le frelon, *makes as much sense but runs counter to the phrasing.*"[6]

We may agree with Bishop that the rose as murderess is indeed "surprising," and we may doubt Denoeu's assertion that a dying hornet "makes as much sense" as a dying rose in the situation. Not only is it grammatically indefensible to read "en mourant" as modifying the direct object "que [le frelon]," but such a reading results in a preposterous picture, while the syntactically accurate death of the rose produces a richly suggestive image in perfect harmony with the tone and content of the passage.

From the very first line of the poem, "Poète, prends ton luth, et me donne un baiser," an equation is set up between the process of artistic creation and the act of love, of procreation. Referring to the surging life forces all about them on a spring evening ("sent ses bourgeons *éclore;* le printemps *naît;* les vents vont *s'embraser;* aux *premiers* buissons verts"), the Muse repeats her double invitation at line 6. As the poet remains oblivious to her presence, the Muse becomes increasingly more fervent in tone and more lavish, even bold, in her allusions to fecundity. Just after the image of the rose, she says:

> Ce soir, tout va fleurir: l'immortelle nature
> Se remplit de parfums, d'amour et de murmure,
> Comme le lit joyeux de deux jeunes époux.

(vv. 21-23)

As the poet, with awakening consciousness, experiences a vague uneasiness in body and soul, the Muse's invitation becomes overt and blatantly erotic:

Poète, prends ton luth; le vin de la jeunesse
Fermente cette nuit dans les veines de Dieu.
Mon sein est inquiet, la volupté l'oppresse,
Et les vents altérés m'ont mis la lèvre en feu.
O paresseux enfant! regarde, je suis belle.

                                        (vv. 34-38)

Upon close scrutiny, the image of the rose is revealed as the aspect of the May evening which most directly introduces the theme of procreation and leads into the Muse's further allusions to fecundity. The phrase "vierge encor" immediately suggests sexuality. The rose welcomes the hornet's presence within her petals; she has desired him and jealously seeks to detain him: "se referme jalouse / Sur le frelon nacré." He will be the agent of fertilization, of the desired end to her virginity, of the fulfillment of her function as a flower. In a mutual satisfaction of sensual appetites, she "intoxicates" him with the nectar he has come to gather as he plays his inadvertent role in the process of pollination. The rose, as a blossom, dies, not tragically, but simply because her role in the cycle of life has been played. After the consummation brought about by the visit of the hornet, she will cease to be a flower and take new form as a fruit, bearing the seeds that assure the continuity of life. The rose undergoes a metamorphosis rather than death. Read in this way, the image can be seen as entirely consistent with the ambiguous theme of productive union with which Musset begins **"La Nuit de mai."**

Notes

1. Harry Steinhauer and Felix Walter, *Omnibus of French Literature* (New York, 1941), II, 325.

2. A. Chassang and Ch. Senninger, *Recueil de textes littéraires français: XIXᵉ Siècle* (Paris, 1966), p. 214.

3. André Lagarde and Laurent Michard, *XIXᵉ Siècle* (Paris, 1965), p. 213.

4. Bernard Lalande, ed., *Pages choisies: Poésie,* par A. de Musset (Paris, n.d.), I, 54.

5. Morris Bishop, *A Survey of French Literature* (New York, 1965), II, 64.

6. François Denœu, *Sommets littéraires français* (Boston, 1957), p. 324.

Russell S. King (essay date April 1974)

SOURCE: King, Russell S. "Linguistic and Stylistic Clues to Characterization in Musset's *Fantasio.*" *Neophilologus* 58, no. 2 (April 1974): 187-94.

[*In the following essay, King concentrates on Musset's depiction of the title figure in his drama* Fantasio *as a faithless young man, examining this character's extensive use of exclamation, rhetorical questioning, conditional phrases, and similar ironic or manipulative forms of speech.*]

The playwright does not enjoy the novelist's more obvious advantages in portraying and analysing characters, for the benefits obtained from a multiplicity of modes of narration are largely closed to him. The playwright, unlike the third person narrator in the novel, is unable to pause to describe and analyse the emotions of a character; and, in most drama, the soliloquy is used more sparingly than interior monologue or free indirect speech, at least in modern writings. Character indications—age, temperament, etc.—in the *dramatis personae* or at the beginning of an act or scene are intended primarily for the casting producer or actor, rather than for the public for whose entertainment the work is composed. Of course the reader-spectator of dramatic writings has always—and rightly—been encouraged to pay particular attention, firstly, to what a character says about himself, and, secondly, to what other characters say about him. However characters discuss each other more fully and satisfactorily in the novel than on the stage.

Another approach to character analysis is to examine some of the linguistic and stylistic features with which a playwright chooses to endow the various characters in his play. Indeed a playwright's function is, in a sense, to write speech for a certain number of people, and to differentiate between them in their speech patterns. The author's creation is not the play we see enacted on a stage as much as the text he writes, representing dialogue lasting a certain period of time.

Each of his characters may well be distinguished and defined by certain features: lexical idiosyncrasies, sentence variation and complexity, a preference for certain grammatical forms or combinations, and a frequent or periodic use of tropes.

If we examine Musset's short play, *Fantasio,* written in 1833, a play about a young "man about town" who becomes court jester in the Bavarian court, four features—not necessarily the principal ones—distinguish, either in frequency or in use, the protagonist's speech from that of the other characters: the use of the exclamation mark, rhetorical questions, conditional sentences, and rhetorical repetitions of grammatical forms. Though frequency counts of some of these features in Fantasio's speech can be measured against that of the other characters, it must be remembered that, for example, the speech of the protagonist, a round character, will almost invariably be richer in stylistic and linguistic features, than other flat characters, and only some of the features, and in certain contexts, will provide clues to character.

Fantasio's exclamatory style is explicitly signalled by the author's liberal use of exclamation marks. They occur not only after interjections but at the end of sentences. In Act I alone Fantasio utters many different interjections: Oh!, Ouf!, Allons, voyons!, Hélas!, Ah!,

Ah!, ah!, Ah! mon Dieu!, Eh bien donc!, Eh bien!, Tiens! Tra la, tra la!, Ohé!, and Hé! The *gouvernante*'s speech too is characterized by a number of interjections: En vérité!, Seigneur!, (twice), Seigneur mon Dieu! (twice), Eh bien! (twice), Tiens (without the exclamation mark), Tu crois! and Ah!

The use of the exclamation mark at the end of a sentence varies more considerably still. The author's use of the exclamation mark may appear arbitrary, for some sentences have one whereas others which appear to justify one equally are without. In Act I, 25 per cent of Fantasio's sentences contain an exclamation mark;

> Que cela m'ennuie que tout le monde s'amuse!
> Comme ce soleil couchant est manqué!
> Quelle admirable chose que les Mille et une Nuits!
> C'est tout un monde que chacun!
> Vive la nature!

This graphic use of the exclamation mark, which could have been used more liberally in the speech of Fantasio but not elsewhere, contrasts sharply with the speech of his boon companion, Spark (8 per cent), and Elsbeth (11 per cent), though less so with the *gouvernante* (14.5 per cent) and the King (12 per cent). But, unlike Fantasio, the King and the *gouvernante* are more witnesses to difficult situations and more complex characters, and their function is to react with predictable surprise and bewilderment:

> Comme vous parlez tristement!
> Le Prince de Mantoue!
> Comme vous voilà émue sur la pointe de vos petits
>   pieds!

Closely related to the exclamatory style is the rhetorical question (including the related ratiocinative question) which, too, accounts for 13 per cent of the sentences in Fantasio's speech. A definition of the rhetorical question is complicated by certain idiosyncratic uses by the author. A favourite device is for a speaker to ask a question, which ordinarily would solicit a reply, and instead of pausing for the reply, to continue with a further statement, which tends to free the addressee from an obligation to reply directly:

> Ohé! braves gens, qui enterrez-vous là? Ce n'est pas maintenant l'heure d'enterrer proprement.

> Qu'importe qu'il fasse une malheureuse? Je laisse mon bon père être un bon roi.

Likewise there is difficulty in determining the status of a cluster of questions, where one answer alone may be expected:

> Saint-Jean est mort? le bouffon du roi est mort? Qui a pris sa place? le ministre de la Justice?

The absence of capital letters in the second and fourth questions reveal that they are essentially expansions of the first and third[1]. Other rhetorical questions are explicitly signalled by the use of an exclamation mark rather than a question mark:

> Ah! Mon Dieu! qu'est-ce que tu vas imaginer là!
> Est-il possible que le prince de Mantoue soit parti sans que je l'aie vu!

The ratio of rhetorical questions to all sentences varies considerably from one character to another. Fantasio's use of the rhetorical question (13 per cent) is only a little above average for the work as a whole because it is a feature of some of the other minor characters' speech. One in four of Spark's sentences takes the form of a question, but, with one possible exception, none of these is rhetorical, for his function is to serve as a "feed", to use the modern jargon, to Fantasio:

> Où coucheras-tu ce soir?
> Veux-tu ma bourse?
> Qui, par exemple?

The high incidence of rhetorical questions in the other characters too, in the king whose questions are more rhetorical, in that the principal aim is to express a point of view in a more polite form, and in the heroine, would suggest that it is a characteristic also of the work as a whole, and, possibly, of the author. Nonetheless in the speech of Fantasio it becomes a form of question-answer debate he has with himself to generate further speech, rather than with other characters with whom, on evidence, he is disinclined to converse, despite what he declares on the subject of communication:

> Où veux-tu que j'aille? Regarde cette vieille ville enfumée; il n'y a pas de places, de rues, de ruelles, où je n'aie rôdé trente fois; il n'y a pas de pavés où je n'aie traîné ces talons usés . . .

> Quel plaisir pourraient me faire vos chagrins?, quel chagrin pourraient me faire vos plaisirs? Vous êtes ceci, et moi cela. Vous êtes jeune et moi je suis vieux; belle, et je suis laid; riche, et je suis pauvre.

This usage, sometimes known as the ratiocinative question, is not a true rhetorical question but can be considered as a sub-category.

The third related feature to be examined is the high incidence of conditional sentences. On occasion the protasis takes a disguised form, rather than the conventional "si":

> Dussé-je me faire battant de cloche . . .
> Nous aurions beau nous marier tous, il n'y aurait . . .

On five occasions, four of them in the speech of Fantasio, the protasis becomes an exclamation, with the apodosis omitted:

> Si tu pouvais me transporter en Chine! Si je pouvais seulement sortir de ma peau pendant une heure ou deux! Si je pouvais être ce monsieur qui passe!

In the play, which comprises only 1125 lines[2], there are 68 conditional sentences, of which 27 occur in the speech of Fantasio, an incidence of 1 conditional sentence in every 14. In the majority of cases, especially in Fantasio's speech, the protasis precedes the apodosis, giving it therefore greater emphasis, as the linear line of thought and utterance—statement followed by qualifying condition—is usually broken, which results in a foregrounding of the hypothesis.

The use of the conditional sentence must be examined in context. In the case of the *aide-de-camp,* Marinoni, it serves to underline his subordinate relationship to his Prince and his excessive deference:

> Si mon souverain l'exige, je suis prêt à mourir pour lui.
>
> Si mon souverain le commande, je suis prêt à souffrir mille tortures.
>
> Permettez-moi de baiser cette main charmante, madame, si ce n'est pas une trop grande faveur pour mes lèvres.

Elsbeth's use (14 times) reflects her dilemma, in that she hesitates in marrying for political reasons, to please her father and avoid war between the two states:

> Si je refusais le prince, la guerre serait bientôt recommencée.
>
> Il me plaît, s'il vous plaît; il me déplaît, s'il vous déplaît.
>
> Je pense qu'il est prince de Mantoue, et que la guerre recommencera demain entre lui et vous, si je ne l'épouse pas.

In the case of Fantasio, the conditional sentence reflects his desire to argue and even quibble, and his perpetual debate about the present, and the future, and about life in general:

> Si je n'avais pas d'argent, je n'aurais pas de dettes.
>
> S'il y avait un enfer, comme je me brûlerais la cervelle pour aller voir tout ça!
>
> Si je n'étais dans cette prison, je serais dans une autre.
>
> Si vous me rendez la liberté, on va me prendre au collet.

This use serves an entirely different purpose from that of the comically urbane *aide-de-camp.*

Though sentence length—a simple word count shows that Fantasio's speech contains the longest sentences—is partly a result of extensive subordination and embedded word groups, it is determined more by the grammatical parallelisms of forms, which characterize the speech of all the characters. Such syntactic repetitions have already been illustrated in the quotations showing the peculiar use of rhetorical questions in Fantasio's speech. Often sentences are subdivided into smaller sentences by the use of a semi-colon:

> Quelque belle fille toute ronde comme les femmes de Miéris; quelque chose de doux comme le vent d'ouest, de pâle comme les rayons de la lune; quelque chose de pensif comme . . .
>
> Buvons, causons, analysons, déraisonnons, faisons de la politique; imaginons des combinaisons de gouvernement . . .
>
> Il faut que je me grise, que je rencontre l'enterrement de Saint-Jean, que je prenne son costume et sa place, que je fasse enfin la plus grande folie de la terre . . .

This is description for the sake of description, speech for the sake of speech. One word or syntactic structure immediately engenders another parallel one. The communication to others of metaphysical ideas or further information is of secondary importance.

Ideas are attractive to Fantasio because they afford him the opportunity to juggle with words. Indeed a *particular* incident or detail or word uttered by another character serves as a pretext to display his talent in expressing some epigrammatic comment on life or experience in *general:*

SPARK:

> Va donc au diable, alors!

FANTASIO:

> Oh! s'il y avait un diable dans le ciel! s'il y avait un enfer, comme je me brûlerais la cervelle pour aller voir tout ça! Quelle misérable chose que l'homme! ne pas pouvoir seulement sauter par sa fenêtre sans se casser la jambe! . . .

SPARK:

> Si tu étais amoureux, Henri, tu serais le plus heureux des hommes.

FANTASIO:

> L'amour n'existe plus, mon cher ami. La religion, sa nourrice, a les mamelles pendantes comme une vieille bourse au fond de laquelle il y a un gros sous . . .

ELSBETH:

> Ce palais en est une assez belle (une = une cage); cependant c'en est une.

FANTASIO:

> La dimension d'un palais ou d'une chambre ne fait pas l'homme plus ou moins libre. Le corps se remue où il peut; l'imagination ouvre quelquefois des ailes grandes comme le ciel dans un cachot grand comme la main.

Often a simple statement provides a pretext for developing a metaphor, comparing the human brain to the streets of a city, or a princess to a toy canary operated by a spring.

The high incidence of exclamations, rhetorical questions and conditional sentences in Fantasio's speech compared with a lower incidence of these combined features in other characters, suggests that Fantasio uses speech for special effects, not to solicit and impart information, but to argue and debate. In this, rhetorical questions, to which he often provides some answer himself, and conditional sentences are closely allied in that they reflect his desire to debate with himself, though aloud, in the presence of others. He enjoys manipulating words and thoughts.

Indeed what is becoming apparent is not so much his profundity on metaphysical questions, but his verbal dexterity, his use of words and grammatical constructions for effect, less to express deep thought but to entertain his audience by the manner in which he manipulates words and thoughts. In Act I, his audience comprises his boon companions, and, more appropriately, perhaps symbolically, in Act II, the court where he has assumed the post of court jester and punster. In the form-content relationship, the emphasis is on form, inasmuch as the two can be distinguished.

A brief description of the principal distinctive stylistic and linguistic traits of Fantasio's speech, his exclamatory, rhetorical style with interjections, questions, complex subordination of sentences, an extensive use of conditional sentenecs, his use of any pretext to express some aphoristic generality or protracted metaphor, all constitute not so much his character and beliefs, but clear clues to them.

With such verbal versatility, he displays qualities which suggest to his friends and himself that he should be a writer. His friend Spark, for example, recommends that he becomes a "journaliste ou homme de letters" for "c'est encore le plus efficace moyen qui nous reste de désopiler la misanthropie et d'amortir l'imagination". Later, Fantasio states, perhaps only in jest, that he is writing "une élégie qui décidera de mon sort". On two occasions he expresses admiration for the *Thousand and One Nights,* and imitates the escapist fairy-tale language when he first speaks in Act I and again later:

> Il était une fois un roi de Perse . . .

> Il y avait une fois un roi qui était très sage, très sage, très heureux, très heureux . . .

Elsewhere he refers to Jean-Paul, to a "romance portuguaise", which in fact comes from Byron, and to Pope and Boileau, all of whom use a style of language which is consistent with Fantasio's.

However Fantasio is not a writer. Indeed he has no profession:

> Remarques-tu une chose, Spark? c'est que nous n'avons point d'état; nous n'exerçons aucune profession.

> J'aime ce métier (de bouffon) plus que tout autre; mais je ne puis faire aucun métier.

A knowledge of other writings of Musset (especially **"Rolla"** written in the same year) and the author's biography would suggest that Fantasio is probably a victim of an education which prepares a man for a life of leisure which financial circumstances no longer permit. But this is an extra-literary explanation. The text itself suggests that Fantasio believes in nothing; the political expediency he opposes is typified by a marriage of convenience, and political leaders who are essentially buffoons. War alone may provide some activity to disguise the monotony of daily existence: "Si la guerre est déclarée, nous saurons quoi faire de nos bras".

Literature, on the other hand, which promises to be a worthy escape, is shown to be only a substitute, and therefore vain and contemptible. How can we believe in art, if we fail to believe in life, experience, love, human communication, on which art is based, Fantasio seems to ask. Spark points out to him this function of art to "désopiler la misanthropie et d'amortir l'imagination". Wine, not artistic creativity, is the only escape: "Un sonnet vaut mieux qu'un long poème (because it's shorter), et un verre de vin vaut mieux qu'un sonnet". Towards the end of the play, Fantasio explicitly expresses the inferiority of art to action: "Ah! si j'étais poète, comme je peindrais la scène de cette perruque voltigeant dans les airs! Mais celui qui est capable de faire de pareilles choses dédaigne de les écrire". Since life, and, in consequence, art can offer nothing new, Fantasio expresses his horror of new novels and demands an "old worn-out pun". Art is degraded into a kind of acrostic, he declares, in which the poet juggles with words and difficult rhymes.

Fantasio who does not believe in action, though he welcomes the prospect of war, and not only appears to hold creative art in contempt, but also to lack the necessary application to complete a work of art, is left with his linguistic skills and verbal wit with which he cloaks an array of fashionably pessimistic comments on life, art, love, to entertain his friends and the court.

> Beaucoup parler, voilà l'important; le plus mauvais tireur de pistolet peut attraper la mouche, s'il tire sept cent quatre-vingts coups à la minute, tout aussi bien que le plus habile homme qui n'en tire qu'un ou deux bien ajustés.

> Un calembour console de bien de chagrins; et jouer avec les mots est un moyen comme un autre de jouer avec les pensées, les actions et les êtres.

In a sense these last lines reflect part of the romantic dilemma; the dynamic experimentation of form and linguistic possibilities and an overwhelming belief in the value of art (which Fantasio does not share) combined with a profoundly negative cosmic view. The artist can only devote his writing (and the jester Fantasio his speech) to giving expression to it. Like the writer, Fantasio is an entertainer who does not impart or solicit information, but who thinks aloud, to impress his audience with his verbal wit and sombre thoughts, on whatever topic that presents itself.

Musset's hero is affected by the *mal du siècle,* but the spoken word provides a strong antidote. The use of the exclamation, rhetorical questions and repetitions, and conditional sentences provide a clue to one major aspect of his character, which would be less fully understood and elucidated by a more general psychological and philosophical approach. The psychologist would almost certainly seek to show that Fantasio becomes a court jester *because* of his *mal du siècle,* an escape into irony, fantasy and mechanical existence. Indeed there are statements in the text to substantiate this interpretation, which one critic has fully analysed[3]. Nonetheless his assumption of the role of court jester is surely not explained solely because circumstances happen to provide that outlet. His temporary employment as jester is a symbolic representation of the poet for whom words replace acts. Just as no action is found with any real value or significance, words too are empty, and destined for the entertainment of a listening audience, rather than for a reader, for Fantasio, a potential writer, has no faith, no application, no consistent vision, to encourage him to translate his rich linguistic talents into a written work of art.

Notes

1. In this case, one might conclude, as I have done, that there are two "ordinary" questions, and two rhetorical questions.

2. Numbered in the Bordas edition.

3. David Sices, "Musset's *Fantasio*: The Paradise of Chance", The Romanic Review, Volume 58, 1967, pp. 23-37.

Louise Fiber Luce (essay date spring 1977)

SOURCE: Luce, Louise Fiber. "The Mask of Language in Alfred de Musset's *Proverbes.*" *Romance Notes* 17, no. 3 (spring 1977): 272-80.

[*In the following essay, Luce studies Musset's skilled application of language as a medium of disguise, deception, and equivocation in his short theatrical pieces, or* proverbes.]

An appropriate arena to observe the problematic role of language in Musset's theater is with that group of plays belonging to the subgenre, the *proverbe.* According to its formal rules, dialogue itself holds center stage in the *proverbe;* language is the "main character." The plot, what little there is, serves merely as a foil for a dazzling display of repartee, for discourse characterized by wit, refinement and elegance. Yet the dramatic tradition we find in Musset's *proverbes,* with their liberal dose of the *précieux* conventions, veils more serious considerations. The verbal dialectic between speaker and receiver, where words can serve as obstacle or mediator, casts language in a problematic and very contemporary light.

Three of Musset's *proverbes,* ***Il faut qu'une porte soit ouverte ou fermée, Un Caprice,*** and ***On ne saurait penser à tout,*** ably demonstrate the thesis that language can play an essential role in man's search for self-realization. In these plays, words become an externalization of the self, or what Leo Spitzer calls "the psychological etymon of the soul." Yet language is also a social act, a sharing of this *moi profond,* and one of means by which the hero strives to achieve integration with society. Unfortunately the moment the message (charged with personal significance) leaves the speaker, it takes on an autonomy of its own, for it must in turn be interpreted by a receiver whose own view of reality is as complex as that of the sender. Words then do mean more than they say. Co-substantial to the speaker, yet independent of him, to what degree can communication be established through language?

In Musset's ***Il faut qu'une porte soit ouverte ou fermée,*** considered one of his finest *proverbes,* the verbal charade game is at its best. Here, language is a purely formal ritual where badinage has become part of the aristocratic code of two *gens d'esprit.* An important consequence of any sophistication, however, is that it breeds distance. In the case of ***Il faut qu'une porte soit ouverte ou fermée,*** the distance is reinforced by the artificiality, or obstacle, of language. There is a real hindrance to effective communication in the play because language is so formalized that the message it transmits has lost all meaning. The Marquise realizes this, yet the greater the boredom caused by the ceremonies of her milieu, the more she clutches at words.

The Marquise is especially aware of the vacuity of the language of love. Just as she associates worldliness with the emptiness of her life, she equates the banalities of elegant conversation with the insincerity of love. From a general condemnation of courtship, "cette éternelle, insupportable cour, qui est une chose si inutile, si ridicule, si rebattue," the Marquise then names its components: "*Quelques phrases bien fades,* un tour de valse et un bouquet, voilà pourtant ce qu'on appelle faire la cour."[1] She refers to the litany of empty compliments as "balivernes," "niaiseries," and "fadaises." As for the gallants who proffer them, she categorically states: "Vous autres hommes à la mode, vous n'êtes que des confiseurs déguisés" (p. 162).

Although the Marquise is indeed attracted to the Count, the only tool at her disposal to test his sincerity is the same badinage she has just condemned. One realizes the paradox of her situation: in spite of the fact that she is "raisonnable," or that the Count has "le sens commun," they are both trapped in the vain platitudes which make up the language of love. So she will have to play the game, but this time *en pleine connaissance de cause.* As Pierre Moreau says, badinage supposes "un parti-pris de ne pas prendre au sérieux ce qui nous tient le plus au cœur. Il est une défense contre la souffrance du *moi* et contre la pompe du siècle. Le *moi* est indiscret; il n'est pas permis de le mettre en scène qu'à condition de le déguiser, et même de mentir."[2] This, certainly, explains the Marquise's use of verbal masking. With the caution of an *avertie,* she will continue her dialogue with the Count, covering her true feelings with the spirited banter so familiar to her.

One must see an extended exchange between the Marquise and the Count in this verbal sparring match to admire Musset's skill in maintaining rapidity and lightness on the one hand, and at the same time intimating only too well the Marquise's use of words as a weapon to parry any possible hypocrisy on the part of the Count:

LA MARQUISE:

—Ah! ciel! vous allez faire une phrase.

LE COMTE:

—Pas du tout. Si vous ne voyez rien, c'est qu'apparement vous ne voulez rien voir.

LA MARQUISE:

—Voir quoi?

LE COMTE:

—Cela s'entend du reste.

LA MARQUISE:

—Je n'entends que ce qu'on me dit, et encore pas des deux oreilles.

LE COMTE:

—Vous riez de tout; mais, sincèrement, serait-il possible que depuis un an, vous voyant presque tous les jours, faite comme vous êtes, avec votre esprit, votre grâce et votre beauté . . .

LA MARQUISE:

—Mais, mon Dieu! c'est bien pis qu'une phrase, c'est une déclaration que vous me faites là. Avertissez au moins: est-ce une déclaration ou un compliment de bonne année?

LE COMTE:

—Et si c'était une déclaration?

LA MARQUISE:

—Oh! c'est que je n'en veux pas ce matin. Je vous ai dit que j'allais au bal, je suis exposée à en entendre ce soir; ma santé ne me permet pas ces choses-là deux fois par jour.

(p. 161)

Even *en fauteuil,* the pleasure the spectator derives from this scene comes principally from its internal dynamics. Indeed, throughout the play, this sprightly cross-fire constantly enchants the listener. Moreover, in a genre like the *proverbe,* where there is so little plot, the risk of the play remaining static is always present. With his usual apparent ease, Musset has succeeded admirably in avoiding this inertia.

At the same time, however, Musset is also telling the spectator: "Look here! Look what we have done to ourselves. We are buried in words; gay, fanciful words, to be sure; but they have eventually blocked any true communication. They are hollow and counterfeit, and no longer say what we want them to say." The Marquise and the Count never do put aside this level of language. The verbal mask is never dropped. Nevertheless, painfully and hesitatingly, they do manage to reach an understanding and let their true feelings be known. In the case of *Il faut qu'une porte soit ouverte ou fermée,* communication has been achieved in spite of the obstacle, or mask, of language.

Un Caprice, a *proverbe* whose original title was *Un jeune curé fait les meilleurs sermons,* continues Musset's preoccupation with verbal masking.[3] Now, however, a new dimension is added because of Madame de Léry's innate sense of *l'esprit de finesse.* Quite unlike Mathilde, the spokesman of the naïve who have not yet learned to parry with words, Madame de Léry moves unerringly through any compromising conversation.

Thus, *l'esprit de finesse* is a certain type of intelligence which applies to the problems of practical psychology. It could appropriately be called *l'esprit d'à propos.* The speaker has the ability to conform verbally to the demands of a given situation, to understand the conventions and needs of a given moment, and, more importantly, to understand his own motives as well as those of the persons involved. He is intuitively aware, in control, and consequently at ease. The ensuing self-confidence places him in a position of psychological authority which can be used to manipulate others—for their own good or not, as the case may be.

L'esprit de finesse, then, is one step above preciosity with its empty glitter for its own sake. To be sure, *l'esprit de finesse* is still a social game; yet more important considerations are involved. In the case of *Un Caprice,* the very happiness of Chavigny and Mathilde is at stake. At this point, language is no longer an inno-cent game. It still functions at the social level as a pat-tern of *bienséances,* frivolous and engaging; at the hu-man level, however, language becomes an arm which protects or attacks.

The conflict of **Un Caprice** involves two categories of language: *la langue du cœur* and *l'esprit de finesse.* Mathilde, who uses only the former, lacks the experi-ence to protect herself with *l'esprit de finesse.* She is frank and open, and almost loses her husband because of this. She makes no effort, uses no wiles to success-fully control his potential philandering. Since she speaks her heart in unequivocal terms, there is no room for her to retreat, to advance, or to manipulate others. It is not only her lack of subtlety which troubles Chavigny, but also her utter vulnerability.

Left to her own resources, Mathilde would have been unable to save the situation. Madame de Léry, however, who immediately and intuitively understands the prob-lem, functions as a *deus ex machina* to bring about a successful dénouement. Chavigny is quite correct when he says to Mathilde that "Madame de Léry est votre oracle" (p. 135).

Older than her young protégée, more experienced, Ma-dame de Léry never falters in her conversation; the *mot juste* is always ready. Her caustic comparisons of cer-tain *grandes dames* whom she knows to "une madone au bout d'un bâton," "un grand balai pour épousseter les araignées," or "une cigale, avec un gros corps et de petites pattes," must have thoroughly delighted Henri Bergson. Her disabused comments on the change purse ("Je l'ai vue traîner depuis des siècles . . . c'est un vrai héritage que vous avez fait.") always stop on the gra-cious side of impertinence. Her precious description of a cup of tea ("de l'eau chaude, avec un soupçon de thé et un nuage de lait") is so much froth to hide more seri-ous matters.

Chavigny is charmed with this double register of mean-ing, with the equivocal sentences where no direct an-swer would be fitting. He understands that "il peut ar-river qu'un homme marié ait *deux façons de parler,* et, jusqu'à un certain point, *deux façons d'agir*" (p. 151). This comment is all the more interesting because it es-tablishes a complicity between language and action (i.e., to act, to play a role). The same complicity of lan-guage and role playing can be heard in another observa-tion by Chavigny: "Un homme marié n'en reste pas moins homme; la bénédiction ne le métamorphose pas, mais elle l'oblige quelquefois à *prendre un rôle* et à en *donner les répliques*" (p. 151). He knows that "il ne s'agit que de savoir, dans ce monde, à qui les gens s'adressent quand ils vous parlent, si c'est *au réel ou au convenu, à la personne ou au personnage*" (p. 151). Language is inextricably bound to disguise and can

cover as effectively as the mask of carnival, role play-ing, or the multiple personality. Chavigny knows this, and like Madame de Léry he moves easily in the world of badinage.

L'esprit de finesse, therefore, is the key to a successful resolution of **Un Caprice.** Madame de Léry, because of her expertise, stays within the limits of badinage and adroitly leads Chavigny to a realization of his wife's worth. One understands her frequent appeals to Mathilde to "se fier à moi." She is a mediator, and lan-guage itself, through *l'esprit de finesse,* is the touch-stone of a harmonious integration with others. Yet, de-spite the reconciliation achieved in both **Un Caprice** and **Il faut qu'une porte soit ouverte ou fermée,** cer-tain distinctions must be made between the two *prover-bes.* First, the Marquise, whose happiness depends on the outcome of her dialogue with the Count, is too per-sonally involved to have the emotional self-confidence of Madame de Léry. Secondly, the Marquise saves only herself, while Madame de Léry has gone one step fur-ther. Like Fantasio, she has performed the altruistic act.

In the *proverbe,* **On ne saurait penser à tout,** another important aspect of verbal masking is encountered. It would be frankly difficult to decide which of the main characters of the play is the most madcap—the Mar-quis, the Baron, or the Countess. One thing is certain however. All three characters think incoherently, con-verse incoherently, and act incoherently.

Conversation, of course, is the mainstay of the action. The central question debated in the *proverbe* is whether the Countess will marry the Marquis. Yet the use of language in this play has taken on a surprising new di-mension since the sleek badinage of **Il faut qu'une porte soit ouverte ou fermée.** Musset seems to have gone the last possible step and destroyed even the ex-ternal logic of conversation. In **On ne saurait penser à tout,** although the message being transmitted may have its own inner logic, its meaning has been shattered and lost somewhere between the sender and the receiver. As two people speak, the signs become distorted and garbled. The result is a conversation where the words of each speaker ricochet off each other and never reach their intended target.

Perhaps the play **Fantasio** is a reasonable starting point to analyze the disintegration of words. Fantasio, too, wanders in his own verbal labyrinth of equivocal speech, allusions, and *non sequiturs.* Such disordered thought and speech are fitting for a person who feels alienated from others, as he does, and trapped by the emptiness of his existence. If his language is incoher-ent, it is because his existence is incoherent. . . .

It is the language of "non-sense" which prevails in **On ne saurait penser à tout.** Consider first of all the char-acters. The Marquis is subject to "les égarements déplorables." He is continually in a world of his own, with its own rules and significance. The Marquis' valet, Germain, is quite generous in his explanation of the Marquis' actions: "Ce n'est pas qu'il oublie, c'est qu'il pense à autre chose" (p. 222). As for the Baron, he quickly labels his nephew's condition as "une maladie." According to his standards, the young man is abnormal, unwell, not like others. The uncle seriously doubts the Marquis' ability to be an envoy for the King: "Crois-tu qu'un pareil extravagant est capable d'aller à Gotha?" (p. 224). He even pleads with his nephew to be attentive to conventions: "Il faut donc que vous me promettiez de tenter sur vous-même un effort salutaire, de vaincre ces petites distractions, ces faiblesses d'esprit parfois fâcheuses, afin de conduire sagement les choses" (p. 226). The Baron's advice falls on deaf ears, however.

The Countess herself is "une autre cervelle fêlée," according to the Baron. Even the Marquis concedes that "quand vous lui parlez, elle semble vous écouter, et elle est à cent lieues de là." As for the Marquis' residing so close to her estate, the Baron mockingly says that it is "un beau voisinage pour un fou" (p. 223).

In the above comments concerning both the Marquis and the Countess, the pattern of withdrawal becomes insistent: they are "ailleurs," "à cent lieues d'ici," "égarés." Theirs is a world apart where they are not only physically isolated from Paris on their country estates, but also psychologically remote from the norms of society.

Moreover, one must also consider the role of the Baron in this *proverbe*. Although he is the one who has furnished the most devastating comments on the comportment of the Marquis and the Countess, is there a more pompous, absurd character than the Baron himself? He is another superb example of Musset's *pantins,* as mechanical as the clocks which guide his life. Yet he is also a representative of the norm, of the *ordre établi.* This, of course, is Musset's *tour de force.* . . . It is delightful to hear the Marquis with his "egarements" admit to the Countess with her "cervelle fêlée," that his uncle "n'a pas la tête parfaitement saine; entre nous, il radote un peu!" (p. 246). Such a judgment from the Marquis, who is a master of incoherence, not only produces a comic effect, but it also forces us to ask who really are the unstable in society.

In *On ne saurait penser à tout,* therefore, two characters search for the reality of love. We have already seen the restraints that badinage has placed on expressing true emotion in *Un Caprice* and *Il faut qu'une porte soit ouverte ou fermée.* It would seem that verbal masking is not enough now, that the hero must go outside the conventions of badinage. Consequently a verbal car-

nival explodes in *On ne saurait penser à tout,* just as the literal event did in *Fantasio* . . . with the same disruption of the norm.

Among the variants which Musset develops to maintain an incoherent world are dialogues where one party either does not hear or does not remember what has already been said. Musset also uses the technique of two people talking on a bias, each one mistaking the other's point of reference. The Baron's comments, for example, will refer to a trip to Gotha for the King, while the Marquis, thinking his uncle is referring to a legal contract, develops the conversation from this point of view. We find as well that the normal association of objects (black/white, cream/sugar) has been destroyed. A lone sheet of music, rather than clothes, is packed in a trunk; tobacco is put on a dish of strawberries; a hostess is left a tip for serving her guest a cup of tea. The illogical climate of the Marquis' environment culminates in the final scene of the play where the Marquis and the Countess pack a trunk for their wedding trip. All of the preceding verbal "non-sense" is resumed in the incongruous assortment of objects placed in the trunk: "un cor de chasse, du thé, un violon, un fusil." This is hardly the staple fare of orthodoxy.

Undoubtedly, *On ne sauarit penser à tout* offers an intriguing option in the verbal dialectic revealed in the *proverbes.* When it is joined with *Un Caprice* and *Il faut qu'une porte soit ouverte ou fermée,* three general categories of language emerge: *la langue du coeur,* badinage with its possible *esprit de finesse,* and finally, the collapse of speech into incoherence. As happens frequently in Musset's theater, there is no consistent guarantee in any of the three levels of language that the individual will integrate with society. Yet the *proverbes,* whose generic premise rests on language and communication, add immeasurably to the *corpus* of Musset's dramatic production. Considering the persistence of the mask metaphor in Musset's plays, where plot, characters, and setting coalesce under the aegis of the mask, it is not surprising to find that language will also integrate itself into this dominating metaphor.[4] Although Henri Lefebvre discounts the *proverbes* as a genre apart and quite unrelated to the thesis found in Musset's major works, the three *proverbes* we have just examined seem to belie this critical assessment.[5] From Lorenzaccio to Fantasio, the mask of language is always present, and the greater the hero's failure to integrate with others, the more intense the verbal mask becomes. Because of the problematic nature of language, the distance between Madame de Léry and Fantasio is not that great. Indeed, masking with words eventually imposes itself as a dynamic current in Musset's theater and part of its lifeblood.

Notes

1. Alfred de Musset, *Théâtre,* II, ed. Maurice Rat (Paris, 1964), p. 162. All references in my article are to this edition and volume. Emphases are my own.

2. "L'Ironie de Musset," *Revue des Sciences Humaines,* Facs. 108 (October-December, 1962), p. 505.

3. The question of whether to designate various Musset plays as *proverbes* will not be treated in this discussion. Those plays labeled as *proverbes* by Musset will be referred to in this manner in the article.

4. For a discussion of the masked event, see my article in *French Review,* XLV (1972), Special Issue, 85-94.

5. Henri Lefebvre, *Alfred de Musset, dramaturge* (Paris, 1955), pp. 39, 78.

Marie Maclean (essay date January-April 1979)

SOURCE: Maclean, Marie. "The Sword and the Flower: The Sexual Symbolism of *Lorenzaccio.*" *Australian Journal of French Studies* 16, no. 1 (January-April 1979): 166-81.

[*In the following essay, Maclean probes the masculine and feminine symbolism of Musset's drama* Lorenzaccio *in relation to its tragic theme of sexual defilement.*]

The world of *Lorenzaccio* is a world of striking, almost stylized contrast. Night and day, male and female, purity and debauchery, are shown in a type of Manichean opposition. These basic oppositions are, however, subject to a pattern of reversal. In Musset's Florence, under the corrupt Alexandre de Medicis, an inversion of values appears to have become the norm. Musset often deliberately negates or perverts the traditional meaning of symbolism and imagery in order to impress on his audience this distortion of values. For the Medici court:

> Faire du jour la nuit et de la nuit le jour, c'est un moyen commode de ne pas voir les honnêtes gens.
>
> (I.2)[1]

The hero is subject to the same process. His mission of "righting the wrong" is invalidated by ambiguities and flaws in his motivation. The highly conscious process of deceiving others blinds him to the fact that unconsciously he is deceiving himself.

A study of the ambiguities inherent in the paradigmatic structure of the play, and indeed in the syntagmatic pattern of inversion already noted by Masson,[2] requires a

thematic focus. As the symbolism of the play is dominated by the dark ritual of the blood wedding, it would appear that sexual relationships and sexual imagery, which occurs in sometimes bewildering variety, are most likely to repay close attention. Constellations of motifs grouped around the themes of virility and femininity rely not only on polarisation but on a series of mirror effects, some reflecting, some distorting, some reversing. The light cast on motivation and situation by symbols and images which at times complement and at times directly contradict one another produces a series of psychological and intellectual shock effects which are inherently dramatic, as well as inherently romantic in their use of the grotesque and in their debt to Shakespeare. One outcome of this study will be to show that the sexual symbolism is all-pervasive and coherent enough to engender a code of its own, and to invest the tragedy with a latent "message". An understanding of this process complements traditional interpretations of the play.

In tracing this use of theme and motif only occasional mention will be made of the plot of *Lorenzaccio* with its three strands of intrigue: Lorenzo's planning and execution of the murder of his cousin, Duke Alexandre, the to and fro between impotent idealism and self destructive vendetta among the republican Strozzi, and the endeavour by the machiavelian Cardinal Cibo to use his sister-in-law's adultery with the duke to further his own power. Attention will rather be centered on the portrayal of the hero, Lorenzo de Medicis, in all his different guises and disguises, and of the "heroine", who, as I hope to show, is Florence herself, the Great Mother in her multifarious aspects. Both are characterised by ambivalence and diversity, both are linked with sexually oriented archetypes.

Lorenzo's mother draws two portraits of her son, as sharply divided as day and night; the virginal student of the past, that Lorenzino linked with the positive masculine images of the rising sun and the waiting crown of gold (I.6) and the *spectre hideux,* the corrupt treacherous cynical Lorenzaccio of the present. Lorenzaccio is basically a creature of the night with its feminine connotations: he first appears at night, he rarely goes to bed before day-break (II.4), he is haunted by his own double, the dark shadow of his former self, and reveals yet another double as he plays the part of the effeminate Lorenzetta, the Duke's *mignon.* The real Lorenzo is none of these figures and yet contains something of all of them. He feels himself caught in the trap of his own planned but irreparable inversion, aware that the self he has divided can never permanently be made whole. However it is gradually shown that the feminine element in Lorenzo preceded his double life at Alexandre's court. Hints, such as his youthful love of "les fleurs, les prairies et les sonnets de Pétrarque" (IV.3),

Poster promoting Musset's play Lorenzaccio, *performed circa 1896.*

and the night setting given the decision which altered his life, suggest Lorenzo's early awareness of a strongly female component in himself. This component he has endeavoured to deny by assuming it as a mask.

If the hero of the play appears and acts under the feminine sign of the moon (I.1 and IV.9), the "heroine" Florence, that other "divided self", is constantly under the influence of the sun, traditionally masculine. The Florentines are forced by their nature to extremes:

> . . . c'est le sang qui coule violemment dans ces veines brûlantes, c'est le soleil étouffant qui nous pèse

> (III.6)

Florence, the flowering city, is essentially personified as female throughout the play. All the women characters represent aspects of Florence herself, the *mater dolorosa* Marie, the sacrificial virgin Louise, the rare combination of brain and beauty, Catherine, the budding courtesan sacrificing honour to pleasure, Gabrielle, and the patriotic adultress, Ricciarda. Similarly, the crest of Florence is neither the white lily of purity, nor the golden *fleur de lis* bestowed by the Valois on the Medici, but the scarlet *fleur de lis,* symbol of passion, and yet she embodies them all.

The eternal feminine, the great mother renewed through the blood of her sons, Florence survives both honour and disgrace, both orgy and penitence. She is not only a harsh mother (witness the curse of the banished which ends act I) but a city violated and corrupted, in degraded contrast to her glorious history, her passions diverted to petty and unworthy ends, and yet still beloved and still beautiful. The dark streets may be stained with wine and blood, the flowers broken and scattered, the free republic subjected to a succession of tyrants, yet both past and present history lend significance to an act of violence which is part of the self-destruction of the once great Medici. As the bastard Alexandre is an unworthy descendant of [*Côme*], *le père de la patrie,* so the city he rules is:

> Florence la bâtarde, spectre hideux de l'antique Florence.

> (I.6)

In the *fange* of the present, church and state, town and countryside sink together.

Given the central importance of Florence in ***Lorenzaccio,*** we must ask why, in the final version of the play, Musset introduced the present first scene, giving it precedence over the cross-section of Florentine society and opinion on the night of the Nasi ball (now scene 2) which was originally to have opened the play. The present scene I not only presents the hero immediately, but by its tightly condensed mixture of symbolism and ironic allusion, serves as an introduction to the major themes of the play and both their direct and their latent connotations.

Generally the theme of nature, and especially of trees and gardens, has positive associations in ***Lorenzaccio.*** Natural scenes, however, are nearly always distant in either time or space (Lorenzo's youth in Cafagguiolo, the Cibo country estate) and mostly represent dreams or ideals of peace, security and virtue which are bitterly contrasted with the actual state of Florence. A real garden is used as the setting to scene I where it represents the *hortus conclusus* of virginity, about to be violated and laid open by the seducer already within its barriers. The cold moonlight which lights the scene is the *face livide* (IV.9) of evil rather than the chaste rays of the virgin goddess. The time is midnight, the witching hour, but the ghost which walks is the all too real form of the Duke's latest victim already wearing the jewels which are the price of her virtue.

Lorenzo's long speech in praise of seduction is a masterpiece of *double entendre,* referring not only to the pleasures of corrupting this particular girl but to his own initiation into vice at the duke's court and, at yet another remove, to his counter-infiltration of the duke's confidence. Its three key words are *étudier, ensemencer, infiltrer.* The whole build-up to his plan of murder is contained in:

> [. . .] tout dire et ne rien dire [. . .] habituer doucement l'imagination qui se développe à donner des corps à ses fantômes, à toucher ce qui l'effraye, à mépriser ce qui la protège! Cela va plus vite qu'on ne pense; le vrai mérite est de frapper juste.
>
> (I.1)

The last two images at the end of Lorenzo's speech are particularly effective and significant. Not only are they deliberate ironical devaluations of two of the favourite images of romanticism, the hidden river and the flowering tree, but the metaphor of the violent surge of passion under a thin layer of ice refers much better to Lorenzo himself than to the girl. The flower (thanks to the semantic link with Florence) is, with the night, a major feminine archetype of the play. Here the picture of the flowering tree and its rare harvest links with the invasion of the garden to produce the first suggestion of *defloration,* which is the theme that connects all the sexually significant constellations of the play together. *L'arbuste en fleurs,* Gabrielle, is to be deflowered as many others have been. More specifically Lorenzo himself has been deflowered by Alexandre, both literally, by his introduction to sodomy, and metaphorically, as he acquired a taste for vice. We will see how his planned revenge is also a defloration, but by the sword.

The pregnant undertones of the whole scene lead into Maffio's prophetic exclamation:

> Ah! massacre! ah! fer et sang! j'obtiendrai justice de vous.
>
> (I.1)

In fact the murder by steel and blood, which gives the Duke the justice he deserves, will be meaningless to Florence because *fer et sang* are wrongly valued and wrongly used by the republicans as well as by the Medici court.

An element in this scene, easily neglected, but most important because of its rôle in the psychological development of the play, is the fact that Maffio's sister is portrayed as a willing victim, her principles not strong enough to resist her sensuality and greed. She is already redolent of the *exquise odeur de courtisanerie.* The same element of perverted enjoyment is present in Lorenzo's later reminiscence:

> j'aurais pleuré avec la première fille que j'ai séduite, si elle ne s'était mise à rire.
>
> (III.3)

This attitude which he considers typically feminine, is what Lorenzo most fears and resents in himself: his own propensity to satisfaction in the rôle he claims to have assumed as mask. The same easy-going yielding to temptation, this sliding into acceptance of corruption and tyranny has also been the reaction of Florence to *her* recent defloration by pope and emperor. Like Gabrielle, *fille publique en une nuit* (II.1) Florence is now *une catin* (II.2).

Scene 2 takes place at the end of the same night and shows the pattern of inversion and corruption on a broader scale. Only seven scenes of the play are set at night, but they are all vitally important, and show the beginning and the end of the pattern of defloration, both public and private. In scene 2, while the Duke and his court waste their substance in drunken orgies, we see the people held in check either by their fear of the German garrison, their preferring profit to liberty, or more insidiously their fascinated enjoyment of the carnival atmosphere, the lights, the music, the dancing, the reversal of social norms and moral values. Only a few patriots like the goldsmith realise with disgust that Florence seems to have adopted the dubious popular maxim: "If you must be raped, lie back and enjoy it." The use of the fancy dress ball in this scene enables a concrete presentation of the reversal of norms. Here too the inversion of male and female is shown as homologous to that of day and night. The nun's costume assumed by Alexandre, Lorenzo and Salviati flaunts not only their pleasure in degrading what others hold sacred but the bisexuality which, together with sadism, lends variety to the satiation of drunkenness and orgy.

The fact that this costume is both female and religious points forward to the use made in the play of the sexual ambivalence of the clergy. Cardinal Cibo's praise of the Duke's costume:

> Bon, bon! le duc est jeune, marquise, et gageons que cet habit coquet des nonnes lui allait à ravir.
>
> (I.3)

indicates the moral difference between the public and private face of the clergy. In all of them, from the Pope downwards, the ambiguity of church vestments is reflected in licentiousness (both hetero- and homosexual in the Medici and the Farnese) and moral double-dealing. Cardinal Cibo's red robes are equated with the androgynous power of the devil:

> César a vendu son âme au diable: cette ombre impériale se promène affublée d'une robe rouge, sous le nom de Cibo.
>
> (IV.4)

The suggested transvestism represents his opportunism and moral prostitution, expressed openly in:

Pour gouverner Florence en gouvernant le duc, vous
vous feriez femme tout à l'heure, si vous pouviez.

(IV.4)

Just as the actual change of dress precedes the metaphorical development of the theme, so too the ball is
held to celebrate a real wedding, followed presumably
by a real consummation, and this foreshadows the variations and inversions of the event which are to follow.
Prophetic too is the play on the different meanings of
faire la noce:

Que le diable emporte la noce, ceux qui y dansent et
ceux qui la font!

(I.2)

Throughout the first act of the play the moral inversion
is constantly stressed not only by the contrast with fidelity, love and virtue (all symbolically linked with
nature), but by the reversal of the "natural" order
whereby Alexandre, a bastard of mixed blood, sits self-
confidently on the throne, while his cousin Lorenzo, legitimate and noble on both sides, plays the rôle of intriguing sycophant and pander which would in the
"normal" order of things belong to the bastard (e.g. Edmund in *King Lear*).

However, one traditional symbol of Florentine society
is not generally inverted, though frequently misused.
One belief is held in common by *every* character in the
play (with the possible exception of Cardinal Cibo) and
that is the mystique of the sword as the ultimate expression of virility.[3] The over-estimation of virility is all-
pervasive and gives coherence to the *décor mythique* of
Lorenzaccio as well as being the starting point for the
pattern of sexual imagery found therein. Not only are
real swords almost continuously present, but the language of the play is filled with them to saturation point.
The actual noun *épée* is used 51 times and with the
other members of its paradigm, *couteau, stylet, pique,*
etc. 81 times. As well verbal and adjectival expressions
of cutting, striking and piercing are constantly present.
The "beau idéal" of this society appears to be Pierre
Strozzi, who, having wiped out the insult to his sister in
Salviati's blood, says:

Je me promènerais volontiers l'épée nue, et sans en es-
suyer une goutte de sang.

(II.5)

The correlative to this use of the sword as virility symbol is the remarkable number of images of castration,
mutilation and impotence present in the play. I have
counted some forty, and they run through from act I, sc.
1 (with the disarming of Maffio) to act 5, sc. 7 (the
poor man with "une espèce de couteau long comme une
broche" who cannot bring himself to stab Lorenzo).
The castration images range from the lecher Salviati's

quite concrete loss of a leg through to allusions to the
transcendental mutilations of the crucifixion which is
remembered by the thorns, the nails, the lance, that is,
the *act* of crucifying. It is no accident that the protagonists swear so often by *la mort de Dieu, le corps du
Christ, le sang du Christ.*

Virility and castration are the main themes of Act I sc.
4, which is dedicated to the sword. It was the first scene
of George Sand's *Une conspiration en 1537,* the starting point for Musset's play.[4] Her ending of this scene,
Lorenzaccio, Castrataccio, c'est cela, sums it up fairly
well, though Musset presents both symbolism and character with somewhat more subtlety. The tree has now
reverted to use as a masculine image and the scene
opens with the Papal nuncio's suggestion that in the
"forest" of Florence, and particularly from the family
tree of the Medici, "il y a encore quelques mauvaises
branches à élaguer". Doubly ironic in view of the play's
outcome, the specific branch whose pruning is requested
by the pope is Lorenzo, and his crime is—"castration"
(the beheading of the statues of the Arch of
Constantine). Alexandre, instead of saying:

Moi, je trouve cela drôle d'avoir coupé la tête à tous
ces hommes de pierre

(I.4)

might well ponder the significance of the act.

The two public faces (or masks) of Lorenzo are shown:
Lorenzaccio, the traitor and lecher whose vile weapon
is the *épée acérée* of his wit, and Lorenzetta, the Duke's
mignon:

une femmelette, l'ombre d'un ruffian énervé! un rêveur
qui marche nuit et jour sans épée, de peur d'en aper-
cevoir l'ombre à son côté!

(I.4)

Unlike the true *men,* who bare or brandish their sword
at the slightest provocation, Lorenzo, when challenged
to a duel, pretends to faint, thus showing himself a
coward and a eunuch:

La seule vue d'une épée le fait trouver mal. Allons,
chère Lorenzetta, fais-toi emporter chez ta mère.

(I.4)[5]

In contrast to the concrete presence of the sword, and
the real if negative power of its masculine symbolism,
made clear by the fact that even Lorenzo's pious mother
is more horrified by his refusal to take up a challenge
than by all his other sins, the "feminine" ideals associated by Musset with the flower, which include hope,
liberty, beauty and purity, are generally conspicuous by
their absence. The only times that flowers appear on
stage they symbolise adultery (III.5) and death (IV.5).

This clash between positive and negative symbolism is analogous to the clash between dreams and reality, so basic to the tragedy.

Only two characters, in the bloom of youth, seem to personify hope for the future. One is Catherine, Lorenzo's young aunt, who succeeds in being beautiful, intelligent *and* chaste. The earlier images of mother Florence denying milk to her children are contrasted to Lorenzo's hope of redemption by:

> une goutte de lait pur tombé du sein de Catherine, et qui aura nourri d'honnêtes enfants
>
> (IV.5)

The other is the young painter Tebaldeo. Tebaldeo is a dreamer, although as an artist he has some hope of making dreams come true. Masson[6] seems to me right in stressing the importance of Act II, sc. 2, and in seeing Tebaldeo as a younger version of Lorenzo, another Lorenzino, but I do not think that Tebaldeo's views on art can be accepted unreservedly as the positive message of the play. The case is rather the same as elsewhere, that the positive messages are undercut by their cynical manipulation and ironically distanced by their negative counterparts; in other words, feminine *images* are also subject to defloration. They are, in Lorenzo's words, *parfaitement vrai et parfaitement faux.*

Take Tebaldeo's long metaphor of imagination as the flowering tree producing perfect fruit. The fruit of art is said not to lose its *poussière virginale,* but the metaphor certainly has. We first met it in Sc. I applied to the budding courtesan about to be deflowered by lust. In the same way the young artist's resolute love of his mother, Florence, will soon be set against the picture of Florence as a ghoul lapping up the blood of her sons as it is spilt in her streets, a picture drawn by that other dreamer and lover of the republic, Philippe Strozzi (II.5). Lorenzo will not be long in giving us a more cynical version of the fertilising power of suffering. In fact everything Tebaldeo says must be evaluated in the light of the desolate disillusionment of Lorenzo's estimate of humanity and human ideals in Act III, sc. 3. Certainly Musset here affirms the value of art, but he also shows us bitterly that if the artist wades through the dung-heap to pluck the flower of art, the flower may be divine but the artist will go on smelling of dung. Experience must be bought at a price, and the only adequate retort to Tebaldeo's facile remark:

> Les champs de bataille font pousser les moissons, les terres corrompues engendrent le blé céleste.
>
> (II.2)

is the one Lorenzo makes:

> Les familles peuvent se désoler, les nations mourir de misère, cela échauffe la cervelle de monsieur! Admirable poète! Comment arranges-tu tout cela avec ta piété?
>
> (II.2)

In fact we later see Tebaldeo losing his virginal naïveté as, listening in horror to his patron's views on murder for fun, he conceals his distress and forces a polite remark (II.6). The picture he is painting is, after all, what matters.

Special comment is needed on the statement Tebaldeo makes which is most significant for the purposes of this study:

> Une blessure sanglante peut engendrer la corruption dans le corps le plus sain. Mais des gouttes précieuses du sang de ma mère [Florence] sort une plante odorante qui guérit tous les maux. L'art, cette fleur divine, a quelquefois besoin du fumier pour engraisser le sol et le féconder.
>
> (II.2)

The lily, symbol of Florence, grows from the swamp (*la fange* of I.6), and stands for the rebirth of glory and beauty from darkness and chaos. The *fleur de lis* specifically has the same hermetic significance as the pentangle; with the upper part, the pistil, representing the male principle and the lower petals, the female principle, it incorporates the magical power of androgyny. It is because Florence has the same compelling power of regeneration and creation as is attributed to her symbol, and the same beauty, that she plays the central rôle in the drama. This is why she can be both *stérile* and *féconde,* and her blood both *précieux* and *corrompu.* To the artist too are frequently attributed some of the resources of the androgyne. Tebaldeo, who often wears "une robe blanche et une calotte rouge" and yet carries a stiletto in his belt, has the same rather ambivalent sexuality as Lorenzo, who says "Je me ferais volontiers l'alchimiste de ton alambic [. . .]". This question of the *coniunctio oppositorum* must be considered again in the discussion of Lorenzo's "wedding". It is interesting that he makes the first direct reference to *le jour de mes noces* to Tebaldeo.

The "wedding day" is next mentioned in Act III sc. 1 where Lorenzo's murderous intentions are made explicit and the killing is rehearsed with the devoted Scoronconcolo. Here a plethora of extravagantly masculine symbolism shows how thoroughly Lorenzo, as well as his servant, adheres to the virile mystique of the period. However, just as Lorenzo has convinced the court of the truth of his play-acting, so now what will be truth is disguised as a game: "Tu as inventé un rude jeu, maître," says Scoronconcolo.

But the player loses control of the game. Lorenzo, the "public eunuch" is privately affirming his virility in his swordsmanship and evoking murder in a series of imperatives which proceed pathologically from striking and piercing to disembowelling, tearing and gnawing. As he moves into uncontrollable hysteria the sovereign masculine symbol of the sun is three times invoked, but it is a sun as parched and frustrated as Lorenzo himself.

The murder-wedding is here first seen as a ritual in which blood will both quench the thirst for vengeance and revitalise the masculine principle:

> O jour de sang, jour de mes noces! O soleil! soleil! il y a assez longtemps que tu es sec comme le plomb; tu te meurs de soif, soleil! son sang t'enivrera.

> (III.1)

This not only makes explicit the notion of murder as defloration and as sexual satisfaction, but conveys a curiously double prophecy. Alexandre is in fact murdered at midnight under the sign of the moon; it is *Lorenzo* who will be stabbed by daylight.

The scene functions in this way as *mise en abyme*. Another aspect of this function is the repetition here in earnest of the pretended faint at the Duke's feet. This genuine loss of consciousness, shown to be quite common by his companion's reaction, is one obvious source of Lorenzo's constant doubts of his own masculinity. It is his fear of impotence which drives him repeatedly into wild over-estimation of virility. The best example is the soliloquy (IV.3) which begins:

> De quel tigre a rêvé ma mère enceinte de moi?

This long speech shows Lorenzo's self-doubt in a series of rhetorical questions and ends in a remarkable image of "active" impotence:

> Quand j'entrerai dans cette chambre, et que je voudrai tirer mon épée du fourreau, j'ai peur de tirer l'épée de l'archange et de tomber en cendres sur ma proie.

> (IV.3)

Lorenzo's private adherence to the code of virility has been shown by Masson to be symbolised in on-stage action as well as imagery. He very discreetly notes the phallic significance of the contrast between the *horizontal* "Lorenzetta" fainting at the Duke's court (I.4) and the *vertical* Lorenzo of (II.5):

> A cette humiliation répond un premier redressement. Redressement, au sens physique du terme, puisque le poète l'exprime en un jeu de scène symbolique.[7]

This *jeu de scène* is the moment when Lorenzo, till then recumbent, rises in exaltation to his feet on seeing Pierre's sword stained with Salviati's blood and cries:

> Tu es beau, Pierre; tu es grand comme la vengeance.

From then on, says Masson:

> L'homme étendu devant l'épée n'est plus; c'est à un homme debout que nous avons affaire.

> (ibid.)

However, if we are to accept this interpretation, it cannot end there. In III.1, as we have seen, Lorenzo, genuinely unconscious, is once more horizontal at Scoronconcolo's feet and will in fact go through more self-betrayals and doubts before the one climactic moment of triumphant verticality.

Scoronconcolo, guessing at his master's hatred and need for revenge, voices the *reductio ad absurdum* of the masculine code:

> Est-ce que sur deux hommes au soleil il n'y en a pas toujours un dont l'ombre gêne l'autre? Ton médecin est dans ma gaine; laisse-moi te guérir. (Il tire son épée.)

> (III.1)

But this would be "marriage by proxy" and would merely reinforce Lorenzo's sickness. Lorenzo reasserts his determination to kill his own enemy, and so that no element of the ritual wedding may be missing, he swears to use a virgin sword:

> Mais pour lui je ne me servirai pas d'une épée qui ait servi pour d'autres. Celle qui le tuera n'aura ici-bas qu'un baptême, elle gardera son nom.

> (III.1)

The necessity for this ritual self-vindication is made clearer by its being shown in its social context, epitomised by the Strozzi-Salviati vendetta. The overconfident masculinity of Pierre Strozzi, whose true worth is soon to be made clear when he sells his sword, together with his much-vaunted honour, to a foreign King, lends especial irony to the final words of his appeal to his father to join in a coup against the Medici:

> Venez voir marcher au soleil les rêves de votre vie. La liberté est mûre; venez, vieux jardinier de Florence, voir sortir de terre la plante que vous aimez.

> (III.2)

Here is Tebaldeo's "feminine" imagery seen in a new and ironic light. Exposed to the harsh sun, dreams will prove to be mere illusions. The only garden Philippe will tend will be the grave of his murdered daughter. Liberty and virginity will stay buried together.

". . . une république, la plus belle qui ait jamais fleuri sur la terre", the Florence imagined by such idealists as Philippe Strozzi and Marquise Cibo, is evoked in Act III, sc. 3, only to be denied. This long scene shows, as part of Lorenzo's self-revelation, the relationship between the "hero" and "heroine" of the play. Lorenzo has studied Florence, observed her every face, "comme un amant observe sa fiancée en attendant le jour de ses noces! . . .". He claims that Florence, like himself, has learned to enjoy her defloration, has indeed, like himself, courted it. The two colours of the lily, white and gold,[8] are here used by Musset to represent the lost purity of Lorenzino, the lost honour of the Medici, whose crest proudly featured the gold *fleur de lis,* and by association the lost liberty of Florence.

The actual presence of death on-stage, the poisoning of Louise Strozzi, prepares us for the intensification of negative feminine symbolism. In Act IV stage action and imagery concentrate towards the ritual act of murder and its ritual space, the bed. It opens with Lorenzo arranging the fatal assignation:

> Dans ma chambre, seigneur; je ferai mettre des rideaux blancs à mon lit et un pot de réséda sur ma table; [. . .] ma tante sera en chemise à minuit précis [. . .]
>
> (IV.1)

White for purity, white for death, white for the marriage bed, red for the blood on it and for the sun which will rise, "curieux des nouvelles que cette nuit te dira demain" (IV.1). The remarkable ambiguity of Lorenzo's soliloquy (IV.3) contains as only certainty, *cette joie brûlante comme un fer rouge* which the thought of the coming night brings.

While Lorenzo decks his room as funeral chamber with flowers at the foot of the bed, and begins an evocation (which extends through four scenes) of Othello's marriage bed murder with a wish that Alexandre may have prayed before coming to the rendez-vous, we see the imagery made concrete with the actual burial of Louise Strozzi:

> Avant de la mettre dans son dernier lit, laissez-moi l'embrasser. Lorsqu'elle était couchée, c'est ainsi que je me penchais sur elle pour lui donner le baiser du soir.
>
> (IV.7)

The antithesis of bed as grave and grave as bed, of the murder of the chaste female and that of the debauched male, and of the evening embrace of innocence and the midnight *baiser* of lust, all work to enhance the impact of the final scene.

Scene 9 of Act IV is the *réplique* to scene 1 of Act I and is played outside in the cold night. We see Lorenzo preparing himself for the murder of the Duke as he prepared the Duke for the defloration of Gabrielle. Presiding once again is the pale moon, the goddess who conjoins light and darkness, red and white, blood and water, Eros and Thanatos.[9] The *lanterne sourde* carried by the seduced girl is echoed in Lorenzo's monologue by the repeated question of whether to put out the torch or leave it burning (a symbolic question if ever there was one):

> [. . .] j'emporterai la lumière—cela se fait tous les jours—une nouvelle mariée, par exemple, exige cela de son mari pour passer dans la chambre nuptiale. [. . .]
>
> (IV.9)

Having thus established the suggestion of defloration and of the bridal night Musset then reverses Lorenzo's decision to "put out the light":

> Non! non! je n'emporterai pas la lumière.—J'irai droit au cœur; il se verra tuer . . . Sang du Christ! on se mettra demain aux fenêtres.
>
> (IV.9)

The echo of Othello's "I think my wife be honest, and think she is not" (III.3) (Est-elle bonne fille?) leads into imagining a victim *en chemise* like Desdemona. Thoughts of virginity and purity merge in a dream of the gentle flowering of white beauty against the peace of nature.[10] The memory of the white washing, purified in the simplest way, drying against the green grass, contrasts with his earlier despair of self-purification: "je ne puis [. . .] me laver les mains, même avec du sang." (IV.6).

Another light, another train of association, bring his thoughts back to the purification by blood. Earlier suggestions of the act of crucifixion,[11] especially Scoronconcolo's "Pour toi, je remettrai le Christ en croix!" (III.1) take shape in a gruesome vision of cutting, nailing and penetration:

> on taille, on remue des pierres. Il paraît que ces hommes sont courageux avec les pierres. Comme ils coupent! comme ils enfoncent! Ils font un crucifix; avec quel courage ils le clouent! Je voudrais voir que leur cadavre de marbre les prit tout d'un coup à la gorge.
>
> (IV.9)

The rapid swings between contrasting visions, as between elation and apprehension, culminate in an almost uncontrollable state of physical and mental excitement. One thought predominates, the reversal of the humiliating feminine rôle he has been forced to play. At this point Alexandre, Lorenzaccio's *mignon,* is still cast as bridegroom in the coming ritual, a groom who should wear new clothes for the sacrifice of virginity, but the bride is already assuming a curious duality:

> Eh, mignon! eh, mignon! mettez vos gants neufs, un plus bel habit que cela; tra la la! faites-vous beau, la mariée est belle. Mais, je vous dis à l'oreille, prenez garde à son petit couteau.
>
> (IV.9)

Whereas, in his cynical picture of Lucretia:

> Elle s'est donné le plaisir du péché et la gloire du trépas. Elle s'est laissé prendre toute vive comme une alouette au piège, et puis elle s'est fourré bien gentiment son couteau dans le ventre.
>
> (II.4)

the knife merely repeated and completed the act of rape in the self-violation of suicide, now *la mariée* is not only armed but ready to attack. Lorenzo, in fact, in his hour of triumph, has succeeded in temporarily reintegrating his divided self. As the monologue ends he is both male and female, both the sacrifice and the sacrificer, both the flower and the sword.

The final consummation of the sacrifice is short and swift. The Duke, fatuous in his self-satisfaction, is symbolically castrated, stripped of his sword which is then so entangled in its buckler that it cannot be unsheathed. As he climbs into the white bed, he sees himself in his customary rôle of seducer, little realising that the reversal is now complete. In this moment of climax, his heavy male figure plays the female part, waiting for defloration. Lorenzo enters sword in hand, acting at last the male rôle in their *hideuse comédie*. As he repeatedly stabs the thrashing body of Alexandre he consummates their blood-wedding and acquires its lasting token:

> Regarde, il m'a mordu au doigt. Je garderai jusqu'à la mort cette bague sanglante, inestimable diamant.

> (IV.11)

In the satisfaction of sexual triumph, in the masculine revenge he has exacted for his own degradation and that of Florence, his joy seems to recreate the unity, beauty and purity he has lost forever. The dark night streets of the sordid city, chilled by a cold wind, are lost in a momentary vision of a feminine world at peace with itself:

> Que le vent du soir est doux et embaumé! Comme les fleurs des prairies s'entr'ouvrent! O nature magnifique! ô éternel repos!

> (IV.11)

However, Florence is no longer the flowering city, neither she nor Lorenzo is free, and neither is unified or purified by the ritual sacrifice. The very success of the murder, qua sexual revenge, means Lorenzo's destruction as a person. In killing the Duke, as his social background and the mystique of the sword demanded, he has asserted his virility but destroyed the feminine side of his own nature. The murder is, he knows, unrepeatable: "J'étais une machine à meurtre, mais à un meurtre seulement." (V.6). He knows he will never be whole again, he is now "plus creux et plus vide qu'une statue de fer-blanc" (V.6). Conversely the very failure of the murder, qua act of liberation, was inevitable. The republicans could not have believed Lorenzo's triple warning of the Duke's death because of the finality with which he had assumed the mask of vice and cowardice. He has punished them for their contempt by rendering them impotent, but he has also punished himself.

Lorenzo's failure to reconcile the masculine and feminine elements in himself, except in the moments of power immediately before the murder, is expressed by the change from the nocturnal setting of the end of Act IV to the daytime setting of Act V. Night and day have been the positive and negative poles of the play, now the night and the moonlight have ended and only the sun, drunk with blood, remains.

So the vicious circle of inevitable failure, expressed in the *gageure* of Act III sc. 3, comes to pass. Florence remains *noyée de vin et de sang* (III.3), willing victim to a new tyranny, while Lorenzo dies, unresisting, by a paid assassin's knife and finds a watery and nameless grave in a Venetian lagoon. This last pathetic and ironic reversal of rôles in the long sequence of treachery, lust and murder is counter-pointed by Philippe's useless exhortation: *Redevenez un homme*. Similarly the Florentines' willing cheers for their new duke are counterpointed by two cliché'd verses from an execrable poet:

> Chantons la Liberté, qui refleurit plus âpre
> Sous des soleils plus mûrs et des cieux plus vermeils.

> (V.5)

So, in their last pitiful metamorphosis, the sword of virility becomes a kitchen knife stabbed into an exile's back, and the flower of art and liberty two lines from a second-rate anthology.

Three versions of a motif grotesquely linked with the dramatic parody of the ritual of marriage may finally serve to typify the many-faceted variations and inversions, the interplay between negative and positive and between male and female which give ***Lorenzaccio*** its particular character. Three rings symbolise unions planned for Duke Alexandre. The first ring, metaphorical and concrete at the same time, is the token of the blood-wedding of the two Medicis, the *bague sanglante* left by the Duke's teeth on Lorenzo's finger. The second ring, sign of his marriage to Florence, is not only metaphorical but a delusion, part of the dream of Marquise Cibo which has already led her to betray her own marriage:

> Le jour [. . .] où tu [Alexandre] seras la tête d'un corps libre, où tu diras: Comme le doge de Venise épouse l'Adriatique, ainsi je mets mon anneau d'or au doigt de ma belle Florence, et ses enfants sont mes enfants. . . .

> (III.6)

The third ring is metaphorical and yet most real, the ring of power which stands in cynical contrast to both the first ring which is the sign of melodramatic action and the second which is the sign of idealistic inaction. This is the ring with which Cardinal Cibo intended to bind Alexandre and with which he now binds Côme at the play's end:

> [. . .] je serai l'anneau invisible qui l'attachera, pieds et poings liés, à la chaîne de fer dont Rome et César tiennent les deux bouts.

> (II.3)

So Florence is finally subject to another Medici. Nothing seems changed. The only immediate option open to Musset's "heroine" is yet another rape, this time at the hands of Pierre Strozzi and his new employer the king of France. Pierre sums this up with brutal realism:

> Le roi de France, protégeant la liberté de l'Italie, c'est justement comme un voleur protégeant contre un autre voleur une jolie femme en voyage. Il la défend jusqu'à ce qu'il la viole.

(IV.4)

The tragedy of **Lorenzaccio** is epitomised by the perversion of the theme of defloration, which should be an initiation leading into a new life, a beginning not an end, a birth not a death. But for Florence this tragedy is the end of only one life in a series of lives. Though subject to rape and vendetta, Florence remains the Great Mother, everchanging and unchanging.[12] Only history, however, can remind us of this. Musset offers no final words of hope to redeem the bleak cynicism of the coronation of Côme de Médicis, the marriage of Florence to her new "bridegroom".

Notes

1. References are given only to acts and scenes. The text used is that established by Dimoff in *La Genèse de Lorenzaccio,* Paris, Droz, 1936.

2. Gratitude is owed to Bernard Masson by all students of *Lorenzaccio*. His monumental *Musset et le théâtre intérieur: nouvelles recherches sur "Lorenzaccio"*, Paris, Colin, 1974, contains groundwork essential to the present article.

3. The social background with its emphasis on masculine honour agrees with the main contemporary sources used by Musset: Benedetto Varchi's *Storia Florentina* and Benvenuto Cellini's *Autobiography*.

4. Although Musset follows the main lines of Sand's scene, sometimes using it verbatim, he puts much more emphasis on the word *épée,* using it 11 times to her 5.

5. Musset's own society still subscribed to this myth. While he was actually writing *Lorenzaccio,* Musset had to defend himself against a charge of avoiding a duel, having failed to call out a journalist who defamed George Sand. He wrote to a friend "Si [. . .] on vous adressait quelques questions à ce sujet, vous voudriez bien répondre que mon intention était de me battre, et que j'ai été prévenu". Letter dated *Fin août, 1833* from G. Sand—A. de Musset, *Correspondance,* Monaco, Rocher, 1956.

6. Masson op. cit., p. 196 ff.

7. ibid., p. 165. See also his *Lorenzaccio ou la difficulté d'être,* A.L.M., 46, 1962.

8. As well as the numerous other references to the 1830 revolution found in Act III by critics, we should include the double attribution of the *fleur de lis*. As the ideals of Florence were betrayed by the Medici, so the ideals of France were betrayed by Charles X: "mais le silence continuait toujours, et l'on ne voyait flotter dans le ciel que la pâleur des lis". *Confession d'un enfant du siècle,* Chap. 1.

9. See Chevalier et Gheerbrant, *Dictionnaire des Symboles,* Paris, Laffont, 1969.

10. Compare the use of nature in the "Willow Tree" song (*Othello* IV. 3).

11. The link in Musset's mind between sexual passion and the crucifixion is shown in a letter to George Sand dated *février 1835*. "Une main invisible m'amenait à toi, l'ange de tes douleurs m'avait mis dans les mains une couronne d'épines et un linceul blanc, et m'avait dit: va lui porter cela; tu lui diras que c'est moi qui les lui envoie. Moi je croyais tenir une couronne de fleurs et le voile de ma fiancée; ainsi je suis venu et je te les ai donnés." from *Correspondance,* op. cit.

12. A great variety of studies of archetypal patterns and clusters have resulted from the growth of hermeneutics, but acknowledgement should be made to the seminal position of the works of Mircea Eliade and Gilbert Durand.

Vivien L. Rubin (essay date April 1979)

SOURCE: Rubin, Vivien L. "The Idea of the Clown in Musset's *Fantasio*." *French Review* 52, no. 5 (April 1979): 724-30.

[*In the following essay, Rubin underscores Musset's ironic evocation of Fantasio as a court jester figure associated with ennui, futility, and disenchantment rather than light-hearted comedy.*]

As David Sices has commented, "*Fantasio* is a play that seems to generate misunderstandings."[1] One misunderstanding which persists and which is shared by a number of distinguished commentators is, I believe, a crucial one. It is, to put it briefly, the belief that, alone among the plays of Musset's most creative dramatic period, *Fantasio* is a work "in which for once everything works out for the best."[2] To read *Fantasio* in this way is to fail to recognize fully the use that Musset makes here of the idea of the clown and hence is to miss one of the fundamental ironies of a play which proposes as hero the figure of the court jester.

Let us look first at the picture that we are given of Saint-Jean, the dead jester whose place at court Fantasio briefly fills, for Saint-Jean is essential to the play, even though we never meet him. We are alerted at once to his importance for he is first spoken of in the very opening exchange of the play where, in a conversation between the king and his secretary, we learn both that the buffoon is dead and that his death has caused the princess sorrow. The strength and unexpectedness of the princess's attachment are underlined by the king's blunt expression of surprise:

RUTTEN:

La mort de Saint-Jean l'a contrariée.

LE ROI:

Y penses-tu? la mort de mon bouffon? d'un plaisant de cour bossu et presque aveugle?

RUTTEN:

La Princesse l'aimait.[3]

It is, of course, the death of Saint-Jean which provides the occasion for Fantasio's escapade and hence for the play itself. Moreover, in a play concerned with a brief meeting or two and a few insignificant events, where we know next to nothing of the past lives of the characters and, when we leave them, nothing specific of what their future will be, the memory of Saint-Jean has the effect of opening a shadowy door into the past, just as the deliberately inconclusive ending invites us to peer at the dim forms of what is yet to be. More important, however, is the fact that the personality of the dead Saint-Jean, his relationship with the princess and the affection which she felt for him, help to determine the quality and tone of the relationship which is established between Elsbeth and Fantasio. No doubt Fantasio's own wit and charm count for much, but we are not allowed to forget Saint-Jean. The princess herself says at one point: "Tu me parles sous la forme d'un homme que j'ai aimé, voilà pourquoi je t'écoute malgré moi. Mes yeux croient voir Saint-Jean" (II, 5). Finally, and very important in a play in which pairing, both contrasting and complementary, is an essential feature of the structure, much of the complexity and suggestiveness of *Fantasio* is expressed through the identifications and oppositions which Musset establishes between Saint-Jean as he is revealed to us by those who knew him, and Fantasio himself. The evocation of the dead clown gives us a sharper perception of the living one.

Saint-Jean is clearly intended to represent the natural, not merely the professional, fool, for he possessed both the sharp wit and the physical deformities so often associated with the idea of the buffoon. But however physically deformed he may have been, his spirit was whole. His gaiety made his hearers forget his ugliness so that, as Elsbeth's governess recalls, "les yeux le cherchaient toujours en dépit d'eux-mêmes!" (II, 1). Faced with the prospect of the princess's marriage to a foolish prince, both Elsbeth and her governess feel his lack sorely: "Si Saint-Jean était là!" laments the governess, while Elsbeth sighs, "Ah! Saint-Jean, Saint-Jean!" He loved the princess and she admired and loved him in return. Elsbeth speaks of him, in this same conversation with her governess, as having been "un diamant d'esprit" and confesses that "son esprit m'attachait à lui avec des fils imperceptibles qui semblaient venir de mon cœur." She recalls how much she appreciated his bracing reaction to her own romantic inclinations and muses, "Sa perpétuelle moquerie de mes idées romanesques me plaisait à l'excès, tandis que je ne puis supporter qu'avec peine bien des gens qui abondent dans mon sens." Deformed and nearly blind though he was, his position was a secure and established one, accepted without question by all. But there was more to Saint-Jean than a witty jester who teased the princess with grace and warmth: there was also Saint-Jean, the man of creative imagination. This nearly blind man could make others see. The princess is still speaking: "C'était un homme bizarre; tandis qu'il me parlait, il me passait devant les yeux des tableaux délicieux; sa parole donnait la vie, comme par enchantement, aux choses les plus étranges." Thus, in this retrospective evocation of Saint-Jean, Musset proposes the image of an ideal fool type whose station, though lowly, was secure, who loved and inspired love, and who was creative as well as sharply perceptive: a poet as well as a punster.[4]

If we now take a look at Fantasio himself as he first appears to us in the long second scene of act one, we shall discover, as other commentators have noted, that Fantasio is also a fool, even before he assumes the dead jester's wig and hump.[5] But the dissimilarities between Fantasio and Saint-Jean are, it becomes clear, as significant as the resemblances. For Fantasio is a modern fool. He is the fool who has no roots, no settled, accepted place in the world. He wears no livery and has no physical deformity, but he is nonetheless a prisoner of his role, for his ailment is spiritual.

As soon as we meet Fantasio, it becomes apparent that, like the court jester, his main occupation is the exercise of his wit upon every subject which catches his attention. His conversation, in colorful and picturesque language, moves with facility from one subject to another as he passes in rapid review the major questions which are wont to exercise man's mind and feelings. Contrary to Gochberg's assertion that Fantasio speaks on frivolous topics, Fantasio in fact trivializes the serious.[6] For, whereas we understand that Saint-Jean's wit sprang from a certain mental and spiritual health, Fantasio's is symptomatic of a pervasive malaise. Fantasio is not merely mocking the ways of the world but is expressing his own disenchantment, his sense of the emptiness of life, while transposing his distress into an acceptably frivolous key. Fantasio is as disenchanted with himself as with the world around him and the holiday mood serves only to bring into relief his sense of alienation from himself and others: "Que cela m'ennuie que tout le monde s'amuse." His constant introspection has made him unutterably weary of himself. Life, whether it be of the senses, the emotions or the intellect, has lost its savor. Lacking the discipline or dedication which would enable him to apply himself to some purpose, he sees man in terms of limitations rather than potentialities: "Quelle misérable chose que l'homme! ne pas pouvoir seulement sauter par sa fenêtre sans se casser les jambes!" The sense of the uniqueness of the individual is felt by Fantasio but turns easily into a sense of his isolation: "Quelles solitudes que tous ces corps humains!" Fantasio casts around for some escape from his ennui: if only he could *do* something, if only he could feel some enthusiasm, if but for superficial pleasures; if only he could be someone else, be somewhere else; if only death held out some prospect of interest: "Oh, s'il y avait un diable dans le ciel! S'il y avait un enfer, comme je me brûlerais la cervelle pour aller voir tout ça!" If only he could achieve complete mental and emotional surcease: "Tiens, Spark, il me prend des envies de m'asseoir sur un parapet, de regarder couler la rivière et de me mettre à compter un, deux, trois, quatre, cinq, six, sept, et ainsi de suite jusqu'au jour de ma mort."

In his chapter on *Fantasio,* Gochberg defines Fantasio's melancholy as "not a deep, constant agony of boredom, but rather a light-hearted impatience, revealing an ebullient imagination waiting for events to grace it with a theater and an audience" (p. 157). Certainly, to use Starobinski's expression, Fantasio still has wings.[7] His verbal brilliance and command of imagery reveal that he, too, represents the poetic imagination. Like Saint-Jean, he has the poet's touch and can play magically with words. But "play" is the operative term: ideas, feelings, actions are become for him a mere game of words in a world without true meaning. In his conversation with Spark, his restless review of impossible alternatives serves only to underline how incapable he is of constructive action. His sallies, however colorful and witty, harp insistently on the same themes: the empty weariness of life, the futility of effort.

The same sense of isolation and impotent desire for something different informs the long and important passage in which Fantasio imagines the scene of a woman offering a stirrup cup to a stranger at her door. In the course of his conversation with Spark, and with a characteristic non-sequitur, Fantasio breaks into a Portuguese love song, declaring that when he hears it, it always makes him want to fall in love. When Spark asks with whom, Fantasio replies airily that he has not the faintest idea and, in order to answer the question, launches into an evocation of a type of woman found in the works of a Flemish painter, thereby removing the

question of falling in love from the realm of life and possibilities into that of art and the ideal. This evocation of an ideal type then develops into a more detailed description. The image of the woman is progressively intensified in terms of feeling, charity, responsibility, as she also grows older. She begins as "quelque belle fille toute ronde," then becomes "quelque chose de pensif comme ces petites servantes d'auberge"; midway she is "une jeune femme sur le pas de la porte," with the fire alight within, supper ready and the children asleep; and finally she is "la bonne femme," who watches for a moment the lonely traveler as he pursues his journey and who, as she returns to her hearth, lets fall "cette sublime aumône du pauvre: 'Que Dieu le protège!'" A lesser but similar intensification takes place with the figure of the rider. By the end of the passage, Fantasio is gazing not so much at the mental picture of an ideal woman with whom he could fall in love, but at that of a kind of reality into which he cannot enter. For both the man and the woman symbolize participation and commitment, the woman with her domestic ties and responsibilities, who can yet still offer up a compassionate prayer for a stranger and the rider who, already having traveled far, is still pressing on through a long and hazardous night. Fantasio, meanwhile, has no commitments and his adventures, all in the imagination, have apparently been only self-destructive, for he already feels too overcome by lassitude to wish to continue. True, in this at least, to the essential nature of the buffoon, he remains an observer, uncommitted—except to self-indulgence of an irresponsible and frivolous kind.

It is just such an irresponsible self-indulgence which leads Fantasio to take the place of the royal jester. When he appears at court we see him entering gleefully into his role, declaring: "Quel métier délicieux que celui du bouffon!" (II, 3). As Starobinski comments, Fantasio represents the mind which, bored with itself, recovers a certain temporary vitality by assuming a disguise, playing a masquerade (p. 271). Fantasio appears, almost miraculously, to have solved several of his problems. Characteristically, he does not content himself with just any suitable jester costume, but needs must have a replica of the livery that Saint-Jean had worn, complete with hump and large red wig; he does not contemplate creating an entirely new personage, but depends on the tangible props of another's life to give himself the illusion of leaving his own.

The external transformation which Fantasio now undergoes not only dramatizes his tendency to escape from responsibility but also illustrates the question of the contrast between appearance and reality. We have already spoken of the glaring contrast between Saint-Jean's outwardly deformed person and his clear spirit, between Fantasio's youth and inventive wit and his sense of imaginative death, to give but two examples. Fantasio himself is ever conscious of the disparity between appearance and reality and strikes this note early on: "Tu as le mois de mai sur les joues," cries a friend, while Fantasio retorts, "C'est vrai et le mois de janvier dans le cœur." The play is compact with ironic disparities and dualities of this kind. Now, the handsome godchild of the dead Queen becomes the ugly jester, while the Prince of Mantua will shortly don his aide-de-camp's "simple frac olive," as Marinoni prepares to array himself in the glorious uniform of his prince. These different exchanges of costume all warn against accepting appearance for reality and they are, also, examples of that process of man-made metamorphosis which can compound the deceptive nature of appearances. For while appearances may be misleading by their very nature, at times they are so because, as Fantasio explains to Elsbeth, "le monde entier se métamorphose sous la main de l'homme" (II, 1). Yet the problem is further complicated by the fact that, though many artful transformations may be wrought by the hand and mind of man, these metamorphoses may be doubly illusion. In the two most glaring examples of metamorphosis in the play, that of Fantasio into fool and the prince into aide-de-camp, the change of costume has in fact the effect of bringing into clear relief existing aspects of their characters: the prince's ineptitude declares itself more clearly and immediately than might otherwise have been the case, while for Fantasio the adoption of the jester's wig confirms how at home he is in the part.

Fantasio's transformation then is, as Gochberg noted, more apparent than real. However, when he moves into the court, he is moving into a context where the role of the buffoon is legitimate, even necessary: "Il nous faudra absolument un bouffon," says Elsbeth in the final scene. Fantasio suddenly finds himself with a certain harmony established between himself and his context. Nothing will be asked of him and he need ask nothing of himself. As a result, we are conscious of a change of emphasis or of mood, to use Sice's word. Fantasio's conversation is no longer recording an absence, an undefined but strongly felt desire for something different; instead, he speaks of the pleasures of his situation. Whereas before he had complained of the wearisome limitations imposed by the town and, more effectively, by his own ennui, he now chides the princess for comparing the castle to a gilded cage. And he who had earlier been tantalized by the illusory promises of metamorphosis, whatever the form it might take, now warns the princess that not all such changes are equally felicitous and attacks her, however charmingly, for accepting her forthcoming marriage. Finally, because he has inherited, along with the costume, the dead jester's legitimacy and therefore also the creative possibilities of the role, Fantasio is able by a curious dispensation to achieve a positive good.[8] Having adopted his disguise to serve his own purposes, he is able by chance to serve another, as he perpetrates the practical joke which quite unexpectedly brings all plans for the wedding to an end.

Yet, after all, Fantasio is *not* the admirable Saint-Jean; he is not the legitimate poet-jester, at one with his role and therefore fulfilled by it. Just as he underwent no essential change when he donned his jester's costume, so will this brief interlude in his life bring no change when his charade is discovered. Once outside the context of the court and without the suggestive powers of the legitimate role, he will return to his former condition where buffoonery is both an expression of his isolation and a substitute for something more positively creative of which he is incapable. Starobinski comments, "Fantasio . . . n'a pas d'avenir et ne veut pas en avoir. Musset nous le montre courant à sa propre perte dans un bruit de flacons et de grelots . . ." (p. 275). Fantasio is aware of the incapacitating effects of his ennui. He rejects every proposal, whether his own or someone else's; he rejects, however humorously, the notion of composing a comic poem on the events of the day; and he also refuses the princess's offer of the jester's job, in revealing terms: "J'aime ce métier plus que tout autre, mais je ne puis faire aucun métier." The fact that the part of the buffoon is a veritable metaphor for his own personality means that, with the discovery by the princess of his true identity, the element of impersonation or masquerade, already slim enough, would be reduced to the vanishing point, if he stayed, and he would no longer be playing Saint-Jean, but himself. Inevitably, he would soon be saying restlessly, "Si je pouvais seulement sortir de ma peau pendant une heure ou deux! si je pouvais être ce monsieur qui passe!" When his impersonation is over, we are conscious of a subtle dispersion of the magic and authority which he had generated in his buffoon's coat and wig. Having been wittily and delicately on the offensive, he now becomes rather absurdly, almost awkwardly, on the defensive. Thanks to the princess's generosity, he will return to the aimless life of a young man who on principle never pays his debts. The futility of the existence that he is contemplating is underlined anew in this, his last speech in the play: "Si vous trouvez que cela vaille vingt mille écus de vous avoir débarrassée du prince de Mantoue, donnez-lesmoi, et ne payez pas mes dettes. Un gentilhomme sans dettes ne saurait où se présenter. Il ne m'est jamais venu à l'esprit de me trouver sans dettes."

What of Elsbeth's present of the key and her invitation to him to retreat to the garden whenever the pressures of the world weigh too heavily? Does this represent a solution to Fantasio's existential difficulties, as Sices suggests (pp. 87-88)? Significantly, Elsbeth receives from Fantasio no response to this invitation. Just as Fantasio cannot remain, so he could surely not return, and for the same reasons. Besides, the castle is now known to him. How could this creature of whim, for whom the spontaneous, unpremeditated act represents a temporary escape from himself and his ennui, choose to return to this now familiar place? How could he contemplate a repeat performance? This short play is full of parallels and contrasts, echoes and reverberations, and here, at the end, Elsbeth and Fantasio act out a variation on the scene which Fantasio had imagined earlier, of the woman at the inn offering a benediction for the traveler bound for the unknown. Elsbeth, secure in her castle and her garden, holds out to Fantasio a helping hand, while Fantasio, who has stopped only for a moment's respite, moves on. For him, also, we must feel, "la nuit est profonde là-bas, le temps menaçant, la forêt dangereuse" (I,2).

Thus, Musset's originality in **Fantasio** lies not only in his wit and inventive fantasy but also, in part, in the use that he makes of the idea of the clown to explore that state of "disenchantment" which he saw as new and critical and which he was to describe so eloquently in the second chapter of his **Confession d'un enfant du siècle.** Musset is also the first to make that identification of clown and poet which, as Starobinski points out, was soon to become familiar and which already expresses here the poet's sense of loss and isolation (pp. 270-71). Through his brilliantly suggestive use of pairing and juxtaposition, Musset creates in this play a nostalgic perspective which suggests a past in which the poet, though often no doubt perceived as a strange and lowly creature, yet had an accepted and creative place in society; now, however, the poet is a prisoner of his premature disillusionment and no longer feels that he has a legitimate—and necessary—part to play. Saint-Jean, however grotesque his appearance, remained whole to the end. It is the handsome Fantasio who is deformed and it is he who succumbs to the temptations of inertia and self-destruction. And so, in this supposedly light-hearted comedy, Musset in fact develops themes of alienation and failure which, in various guises, inform his other major plays and which, though typical of the Romantic period, still have meaning for us today.

Notes

1. *Theater of Solitude: The Drama of Alfred de Musset* (Hanover: University Press of New England, 1974), p. 66.

2. Herbert S. Gochberg, *Stage of Dreams: The Dramatic Art of Alfred de Musset (1828-1834)* (Geneva: Librairie Droz, 1967), p. 151.

3. All quotations from Musset's play are taken from his *Œuvres complètes,* edited by Philippe Van Tieghem (Paris: Editions du Seuil, 1965).

4. Charles Affron, in *A Stage for Poets: Studies in the Theatre of Hugo and Musset* (Princeton: Princeton University Press, 1971), p. 161, sees Saint-Jean as "a metaphor for art, the particular art of Musset."

5. See, for example, Henri Lefebvre, *Musset,* 2nd ed. (1955; rpt. Paris: L'Arche, 1970), p. 68; Gochberg, p. 152.

6. "His conversation moves wittily and often incoherently from one trivial subject to another" (p. 152).

7. Jean Starobinski, "Note sur le bouffon romantique," *Cahiers du Sud,* 61 (1966), 271.

8. Starobinski comments, "Derrière la modernité romantique du caractère de Fantasio, nous voyons subsister l'une des fonctions archétypales du clown: il fait tourner, presque innocemment, la roue de fortune" (p. 274). It should perhaps be noted that the positive good which Fantasio achieves is an immediate, personal one for the princess. From the larger view, and granted that any alliance with the Prince of Mantua would seem to be of dubious long-term benefit, the resumption of the war, which is spoken of in the last scene, can hardly be considered an altogether happy outcome.

Lloyd Bishop (essay date spring-summer 1979)

SOURCE: Bishop, Lloyd. "Romantic Irony in Musset's 'Namouna.'" *Nineteenth-Century French Studies* 7, nos. 3-4 (spring-summer 1979): 181-91.

[*In the following essay, Bishop regards Musset as the first practitioner of Romantic irony in French poetry and drama and evaluates his use of this mode in the long poem "Namouna."*]

Since romantic irony, as Henri Peyre has pointed out, has been studied chiefly by German scholars and has received relatively little attention by specialists of French Literature, a definition or two may be in order at the outset.[1] In *A Dictionary of Literary Terms* (Barnet *et al*) we are told that "The romantic ironist detaches himself from his own artistic creation, treating it playfully or objectively, thus presumably showing his complete freedom."[2] Henri Peyre stresses the crucial point that this ironic detachment comes not after but during the creative performance itself: "Through that irony, the creator stressed his independence of his own creation precisely as he was accomplishing it."[3] A well-known example is Byron's Don Juan on shipboard bidding farewell to Spain and to his beloved Julia, vowing never to "think of anything, excepting thee" and suddenly growing sea-sick. One impetus to this particular form of irony was no doubt the desire to avoid the embarrassing sentimentality, bathos and hyperbole that marred so much Romantic literature. A more profound impetus was the modern tendancy to see man not as the classical *homme absolu* but as a complex network of contradictory impulses, wavering between idealism and cynicism, between altruism and solipsism, between reason and emotion and, for the orthodox, between good and evil.

Historically, it was Victor Hugo who first asked his fellow Romantics in France to ponder the esthetic implications of man's dualism. One can therefore take 1827 and the *Préface de Cromwell,* not as the actual starting point (for reasons that will be discussed immediately), but as the initial springboard of or "call for" romantic irony in France. It is Alfred de Musset who is its first real practitioner in poetry and in drama.

In his influential Preface, Hugo argues for a Shakespearean mixture of the comic and tragic because such a mixture is found in the very heart and soul of man and therefore at the very center of the human experience. Robert Penn Warren, explaining the importance of the coarse humor of Mercutio in *Romeo and Juliet* says that "the poet wishes to indicate that his vision has been earned, that it can survive reference to the complexities and contradictions of experience."[4] But Shakespeare's vision is "earned" not simply through this rather facile structural device but chiefly through the density of his characterization and his style. Hugo, rather naively, thought that the mere juxtaposition of the comic and the tragic, the sublime and the grotesque, would guarantee that the Romantic Drama would achieve this earned vision and that it would capture life in its very complexity. But Hugo's *mélange des genres* is mere antithesis not ambivalence or paradox. There is no romantic irony to be found in the Hugolian Hero. He may rub elbows with bufoons in comic scenes tacked on to the main business at hand, but his attitude toward himself remains essentially simple: he takes himself seriously and even tragically.

Alfred de Musset's heroes on the other hand often give off a sense of romantic irony not just because one can feel *within the same character* a tension between opposite impulses, but especially because the author's attitude toward his characters as well as their own attitude toward themselves seems ambivalent. These characteristics are found in **"Namouna,"** one of Musset's longest but least understood poems. What little attention has been given to the poem has been directed mainly at the Don Juan figure that the poet sketches in the second canto. Nowhere is there a discussion of the romantic irony that informs the poem from beginning to end and that provides the key to an understanding of the poem's total impact.

. . . . .

Irony in Musset is basically a tendency to deflate, often at the expense of his fellow Romantics, often at his own expense. When the irony is directed at certain tendancies of the Romantic movement, this, of course, is, *not* romantic irony since the author is not identifying in the least with what he is mocking. For example, when Musset irreverently likens the moon shining over a belfrey to a trivial dot over an i, he is not deflating his own style but the clichés of his contemporaries. Similarly when Musset, in **"Namouna"** (I, xxiii–xxiv), apologizes for the lack of local color in this "oriental tale," because, as he says, he has never been to the Orient and has "never stolen anything from a library," this is not romantic irony etiher since it is really directed at the superficial local color of Hugo's *Orientales.* In a passage such as the following, taken from the *dédicace* to *La Coupe et les Lèvres:*

> Vous me demanderez si j'aime ma patrie.
> Oui;—j'aime fort aussi l'Espagne et la Turquie.
>   . . . . .
> Vous me demanderez si je suis catholique
> Oui;—j'aime fort aussi les dieux Lath et Nésu.
>   . . . . .
> Vous me demanderez si j'aime la sagesse.
> Oui;—j'aime fort aussi le tabac à fumer.

the last line, on first reading may seem to be deflating the author's own ego, but the context and the parallel structure of the couplets make it clear that the irony is still being directed outward at conventional wisdom—just as it is against patriotism and catholicism—rather than Musset's supposed hedonism and anti-intellectualism. It is conventional life not the poet himself that is not being taken seriously just as in Byron's lines

> I say—the future is a serious matter—
> And so—for God's sake—hock and soda water![5]

However, in **"Namouna"** we witness a curious mixture of irony-at-the-expense-of-Romanticism and romantic irony, the latter directed against Hassan, the very hero of Musset's poem. Consider the following passage:

> Il n'avait ni parents, ni guenon, ni maîtresse.
> Rien d'ordinaire en lui,—rien qui le rattachât
> Au commun des martyrs,—pas un chien, pas un chat.
> Il faut cependant bien que je vous intéresse
> A mon pauvre héros.—Dire qu'il est pacha,
> C'est un moyen usé, c'est une maladresse.
> Dire qu'il est grognon, sombre et mystérieux,
> Ce n'est pas vrai d'abord, et c'est encor plus vieux.[6]

Musset is poking fun at the hackneyed hero of Romanticism: the orphan, the outcast, the pariah, solitary both in his *état civil* and in his moral-intellectual superiority, the *beau ténébreux,* somber, mysterious, misanthropic and melancholy. But at the same time he is deflating his own hero. First, he dashes the reader's hopes of encountering a more flamboyant hero and, more importantly he abruptly halts the narrative to ponder the technical problem of enlisting the reader's sympathy. Throughout the entire poem, as here, the narration of Hassan's story is interrupted thematically by the intrusions of the author and structurally by the intrusion of the present tense upon the regular narrative tenses. The reader is constantly shuttled between the past exploits of Hassan and the present preoccupations of his creator.

The intrusion of the present tense begins as early as the poem's second stanza:

> Hassan avait d'ailleurs une très noble pose,
> Il était nu comme Ève à son premier péché.
> Quoi! tout nu! n'avait-il pas de honte?
> Nu, dès le second mot!—Que sera-ce à la fin?
> Monsieur, excusez-moi,—je commence ce conte
> Juste quand mon héros vient de sortir du bain.
>
> (I, i-ii)

The description of Hassan's *entrée en scène*—deflating in itself is interrupted first by the anticipated exclamations of the scandalized reader and later by the vocative and imperative of the penultimate line. Then the narrative completely breaks down as Musset switches to the present of the narrative act: "Je commence ce conte / Juste quand. . . ."

In the eighth stanza the weeping of Hassan's latest victim is prefaced and thus negated by the present tense:

> Un silence parfait règne dans cette histoire.
> Sur les bras du jeune homme et sur ses pieds d'ivoire
> La naïade aux yeux verts pleurait en le quittant.
>
> (I, viii)

The effect of ironic detachment is reinforced by the pseudo-conventional epithets, "d'ivoire" and "aux yeux verts."

Musset constantly uses the present tense to express his independence of his own hero:

> Au fait, s'il agit mal, on pourrait rêver pire.—
> Ma foi, tant pis pour lui:—je ne vois pas pourquoi
> Les sottises d'Hassan retomberaient sur moi.
>
> (I, xxx)

> —Je rappelle au lecteur qu'ici comme là-bas
> C'est mon héros qui parle, et je mourrais de honte
> S'il croyait un instant que ce que je raconte
> Ici plus que jamais, ne me révolte pas.
>
> (I, xxxix)

In his brilliant analysis of a passage from Rousseau's *Confessions* Jean Starobinski has shown how the author achieves subtle ironic effects by shifting from the narrative past to the present as "qualitatively privileged

tense."[7] The present of the narrative act conveys not only a foreknowledge of what is going to be related (and is thus invested with Sophoclean irony) but also the superior wisdom and experience of the writer writing *now*, so that the relation of author to character (or, in Rousseau's case, of author-past vs. author-present) is one of amused condescension. We are dealing with romantic irony because Musset, like Rousseau, does identify with the character he is mocking. It must be borne in mind that romantic irony is a double irony, it works in two opposite directions at once: the poet will declare himself alienated from his hero, but this alienation itself is also ironic—it masks the author's limited but genuinely sympathetic identification. Despite his many (ironic) declarations of independence and detachment, Musset offers Hassan, as we shall see, as an important incarnation of his *Weltanschauung*. The role of Hassan, no less than that of Rolla, Octave, Fantasio, Franck or Lorenzaccio, has serious implications that have been consistently overlooked by the critics.

By stanza xxxii the romantic irony shifts from the hero to the poet himself who despairs of being able to finish his rambling poem. In stanza lxi Musset admits having digressed so long that he has forgotten where he has left his story. Then he will apologize to the reader for a hiatus here, a barbarism there, and so forth. What we really have here is romantic irony in triplicate: first, the poet pokes fun at his hero; then at himself and his poem; and finally the reader is constantly discouraged from identifying with Hassan by being made self-conscious through the many vocatives directed at him by the poet. Hassan is constantly wedged between the reader and the writer:

> Tu vois, lecteur, jusqu'où va ma franchise,
> Mon héros est tout nu,—moi, je suis en chemise.
>
> (I, lxxv)

Another source of romantic irony in **"Namouna"** is the poem's overall structure. Musset keeps promising his reader to get on with the story but keeps putting it off. The narrative proper does not begin until the third and final canto—a mere fourteen stanzas compared to the fifty-five stanzas of the second canto and the seventy-eight stanzas of the first. The poet even devotes the first four of the final fourteen stanzas to still another apology for rambling off the subject, leaving only the last sixty lines (out of a total of 882) to the actual plot of this "oriental tale." Thus the hero of the story and the story itself are treated with ironic detachment from beginning to end. The obvious fact is that we are not dealing with narrative poetry at all—even to mock the heroic would require more narrative than we are given—but with the poetry of ideas. The poem must be read not only on its comic level (brilliantly done in itself) but on a deeper one.

. . . . .

The second canto is devoted not to Hassan at all but to Musset's idea of the perfect Don Juan. Musset's Don Juan has none of the vulgarity, the gratuitous cruelty, the cynicism, the hatred of both God and man found in many of his illustrious predecessors:

> C'est qu'avec leurs horreurs, leur doute et leur blasphème
> Pas un ne t'aimait, Don Juan; et moi, je t'aime.
>
> (II, xxxix)

He is rather the "candide corrupteur" loving and leaving three thousand women in his search for an ideal one. It is important to note that the hyperbolic figure, tripling the usual number of Don Juan's conquests is serious rather than comic in effect. Although his thirst—which is of a moral as well as esthetic and erotic nature—is never quenched, Don Juan never gives up hope:

> . . . tu mourus plein d'espoir.
> Tu perdis ta beauté, ta gloire et ton génie
> Pour un être impossible et qui n'existait pas.
>
> (II, liii)

Maurice Allem misreads Musset's Don Juan: "Cet homme privilégié, que la nature avait fait inaccessible aux soucis vulgaires et qu'elle avait formé d'une essence presque divine, en arrive, dans sa marche désespérée de femme en femme, de déception en déception, à mettre son bonheur dans une cruauté sadique envers les pauvres créatures coupables de ne lui avoir point donné le bonheur qu'il attendait de l'amour."[8] There is no sadism in Don Juan's dealings with women, only a fierce optimism urging him on in his quest.

The relationship between this idealized Don Juan and Hassan is crucial for an appreciation of the total impact of the poem. This relationship is expressed in the last two lines of the canto:

> Ce que don Juan aimait, Hassan l'aimait peut-être.
> Ce que don Juan cherchait, Hassan n'y croyait pas.

Thus Don Juan goes from woman to woman because of an impossible dream, a quixotic quest, whereas Hassan goes from woman to woman since, knowing such a quest is hopeless, one woman is as good as another.[9] Here, Hassan is misread by Philippe Van Tieghem: "La femme est pour lui simple passe-temps . . . Et, cependant, ses amours rapides le bouleversent jusqu'au cœur, jusqu'à l'âme, il se laisse conduire sans crainte 'du plaisir au bonheur'; il conserve l'illusion de pouvoir vivre sur la terre le rêve idéal qui l'habite."[10] It is Don Juan who is love's martyr, not Hassan; the latter, as we have just seen, "n'y croyait pas." Although Musset is stressing the difference between the two types of Don Juan in the lines quoted above, they are nevertheless linked not only by the parallel syntax but also by the tentative "peut-être" suggesting a latent idealism in

Hassan: he would gladly remain faithful to a perfect woman if such a woman existed. Hassan's doubt links him to the author ("un être impossible . . . qui n'existait pas.") In fact there can be no doubt that Hassan, no less than Musset's other heroes, is a projection of the poet himself, a point that is important to keep in mind when judging the causes and effects of romantic irony.

On its deepest level the poem, despite its comic surface, must be read as a somber meditation on the ethical implications of a world devoid of a perfect being in heaven as well as on earth and denied self-delusion by virtue of its new-found skepticism. The only response to such a bleak situation is Hassan's quantitative ethic: since the spiritual longings of man will never be satisfied, the modern Don Juan (Hassan) must live within the confines of the senses deriving what consolation from them he can and prolonging his pleasure as long as he can.

One of the curious effects of the second canto is that while Hassan does not even figure in it sympathy is indirectly built up for him. We have mentioned the latent idealism: it is only Hassan's superior lucidity (Voltaire's men have by now been born) that prevents him from being as naively idealistic as Don Juan. (Philippe van Tieghem thinks Hassan even "more idealistic" than Don Juan another misreading). There is also the suggestion of a certain courage, for Hassan as well as for Don Juan, to live in the face of ugly Reality. And the absence of self-pity, automatically precluded by the romantic irony, makes Hassan more sympathetic than many another Romantic Hero.

But the romantic irony also prevents Hassan from being inflated into an idealized creation. The chief source of irony directed against him is the fact that he is not only obliged to compete with but is overshadowed by the Don Juan of the canto-long digression. But Don Juan, too, is a victim of romantic irony: he is treated seriously but is wedged between the Hassan of the first and final cantos which are, furthermore, written basically in a comic vein. The final irony is that neither hero is given the title role, which belongs to an inconsequential servant girl whose plight is described in less than thirty lines. The total effect of the poem—and this seems to have escaped all the critics—is an irony directed at modern man: with our disabused cynicism and scientism, our unredeemed sensualism, Hassan is the only Don Juan figure we deserve.

. . . . .

There is a significant passage at the beginning of **"Namouna"** that throws light not only on the romantic irony of the poem itself but also on the particular kind of vision that impels the poet to use it.

> Vous souvient-il, lecteur, de cette sérénade

Que don Juan, déguisé, chante sous un balcon?
—Une mélancholique et piteuse chanson,
Respirant la douleur, l'amour et la tristesse.
Mais l'accompagnement parle d'un autre ton.
Comme il est vif, joyeux! avec quelle prestesse
Il sautille!—On dirait que la chanson caresse

Et couvre de langueur le perfide instrument,
Tandis que l'air moqueur de l'accompagnement
Tourne en dérision la chanson elle-même,
Et semble railler d'aller si tristement.
Tout cela cependant fait un plaisir extrême.—

(I, xiii-xv)

This "extreme" esthetic pleasure, produced by the ironi-cal counterpoint in *Don Giovanni* is based on the spec-tator's recognition of a psychological and moral truth:

C'est que tout en est vrai,—c'est qu'on trompe et
    qu'on aime;
C'est qu'on pleure en riant;—c'est qu'on est innocent
Et coupable à la fois;—c'est qu'on se croit parjure
Lorsqu'on n'est qu'abusé; c'est qu'on verse le sang
Avec des mains sans tache, et que notre nature
A de mal et de bien pétri sa créature:
Tel est le monde, hélas! et tel était Hassan.

(I, xv-xvi)

Thus, just as convincingly and much more succinctly than the *Préface de Cromwell*, this mini-manifesto urges a *mélange des genres* based on a new kind of ironic vi-sion which, in its turn, is based on a view of man not as a smooth, uniform monolith but as a creature of am-bivalence and paradox, what Laforgue will call "l'innombrable clavier humain." Musset's description of Hassan, which immediately precedes this passage, provides an illustration:

Il était très joyeux, et pourtant très maussade.
Détestable voisin,—excellent camarade,
Extrêmement futile,—et pouvant très posé,
Indignement naïf,—et pourtant très blasé,
Horriblement sincère,—et pourtant très rusé.

(I, xiii)

Romantic irony is more than a stylistic device used in the service of a limited context: it is a mode of vision with psychological and philosophical implications. The author's ambivalent attitude (alienation—identification; antipathy—sympathy) toward the hero of his story stems from a moral agnosticism informed by a view of the human psyche as *fundamentally* unstable, contradic-tory and unpredictable or, as Montaigne and Gide would put it, *ondoyant et divers.* The pseudo-scientific fore-sight of an earlier generation of *idéologues* and, for that matter, the more modest hindsight of our own genera-tion's *caractérologues,* are summarily dismissed by a skeptical irony directed not only outward at the incom-prehensible Other but also at the elusive, slippery Self. This instability, this multiple-changing ego or, if you

prefer, this existential freedom, will be studied exten-sively in the twentieth century by writers as different as Proust, Pirandello, Eugene O'Neill and Nathalie Sar-raute. The originality of Musset's paradoxical vision in **"Namouna,"** especially within the historical context of the Romantic movement, is pointed out by Philippe van Tieghem: ". . . pour la première fois, Musset, dans ce poème, a trouvé son domaine propre: le point de jonc-tion de la vie sentimentale et de la vie morale, le carre-four de l'idéal et de la corruption, du plaisir et du dés-espoir. Un pareil motif d'inspiration est plus dramatique que lyrique, parce que la position de l'auteur est éminemment instable et contradictoire; elle s'oppose à la position statique de l'idéalisme de Lamartine et au dynamisme optimiste de Hugo."[11]

Thus nineteenth-century French Literature is given a new kind of comic vision, tinged with sadness and seri-ousness, but not taking the seriousness too seriously. It started with Musset in poetry and in drama and, in a much more attenuated form, with Stendhal in the novel and will have distinguished variations performed by Flaubert, Charles Cros and Laforgue. The twentieth century will take romantic irony and turn it into *hu-mour noir*: the playfulness will still be there, but the tragic overtones will be emphasized. With romantic irony we are still dealing with skepticism and disillu-sionment leading to a comic sense of life.

Notes

1. Henri Peyre, *Literature and Sincerity* (New Ha-ven: Yale University Press, 1963), p. 141.

2. Sylvan Barnet et al, *A Dictionary of Literary Terms* (Boston: Little, Brown and Company, 1960), pp. 51-52.

3. Henri Peyre, ibid.

4. Robert Penn Warren, "Pure and Impure Poetry," *The Kenyon Review* (Spring, 1943), 252.

5. Lord Byron, fragment on the back of the poet's manuscript of the first canto of *Don Juan.*

6. Alfred de Musset, *Poésies* (Paris: Gallimard, 1962), pp. 244-45. All subsequent quotations from "Namouna" are taken from this edition.

7. Jean Starobinski, *L'Œil vivant,* II (Paris: Galli-mard, 1961), p. 115.

8. Maurice Allem, *Alfred de Musset,* édition revue et corrigée (Paris: Arthaud, 1947), p. 54.

9. See Maurice Allem, footnote 37 in Musset's *Poé-sies,* pp. 705-706.

10. Philippe van Tieghem, *Musset* (Paris: Hatier, 1969), p. 47.

11. Van Tieghem, p. 47.

Joseph Lowin (essay date December 1979)

SOURCE: Lowin, Joseph. "The Frames of *Lorenzaccio.*" *French Review* 53, no. 2 (December 1979): 190-98.

[*In the following essay, Lowin describes Musset's structural framing of action, character, and theme in* Lorenzaccio.]

Were one to view a full-length play, not as one observes a stage production, through perception of its temporal, linear development, but, spatially, as one views a painting, with an immediate impression of a static whole, one would perceive the most "important" scene of the play at or near the center of the canvas, receiving the greatest concentration of light. It would be less clear but no less true that the first and last acts of the play would be at or near the margins of the canvas in a subtle play of darkness, shadow, and diffused light. One might find as well, embedded in works of art of considerable technical subtlety and nuance—for example in *Las Meninas* by Velázquez or in *Hamlet*—a structure which, by its mirroring of the whole of the work of art, reveals its unity.

In what ways does the play—as a *literary* text—circumscribe itself so that it may best posit a created world within its limits? How does the play reveal what it is that is going on? If many plays lend themselves to such "frame analysis," few lend themselves to such an analysis more fully than Musset's **Lorenzaccio.**[1]

The central scene of **Lorenzaccio,** the one receiving the greatest concentration of light, is, of course, the enormous third scene of the third act of the play, containing an extended dialogue between Philippe Strozzi and Lorenzo in which Lorenzo realizes and expresses for the first time his true motives for the proposed tyrannicide. The action of the play revolves around this moment of self-revelation and affirmation of consciousness.[2] This essay will focus on the ways the action of the play frames the central scene, making two main points. The first point concerns the correlation between "marginal" characters and structural "marginality." It stresses the significance of formal and thematic symmetry and shows that the margins of the play are not necessarily finite. One finds in the play a recurrent insistence on an "elsewhere" which expands the given space. The second point builds on the first and takes up where the first leaves off. It concerns the more meaningful of the dilations of the scenic space, the ones which are contractions as well as expansions and which are reduced models of the play. Emphasis is placed on the thematics of the frame, which embraces either a *paysage* or a *portrait,* either virtue or corruption, or which conceivably might embrace a void.

The analyses of Hassan el Nouty[3] and Bernard Masson[4] and the *mise en scène* of the director of the Za Branou Theatre in Prague, Otomar Krejca (discussed in Mas-

son, pp. 337-91) pay particular attention to the opening and closing of the play. According to Nouty, although the situation at the beginning and at the end of the play is static in appearance only, there is enough of a similarity between the initial and final situations to allow for the view that the architecture of the piece is circular, even helical; viewed thus, the play has no true ending. Although Nouty's analysis affirms the vagueness of its ending, he seems to deny that Musset's work has any borders. As our analysis will show, they are there and they play an important role in the esthetic wholeness of the work. Bernard Masson analyzes the play with even more attention to detail. He notes that scene for scene and sometimes decor for decor the last act returns us to the point of departure. History is like nature; a tyrant replaces a tyrant the way one night follows another. According to Masson, the fifth act of the Za Branou production of the play, which took place in Prague in 1969, is a complete annihilation of the action of the play. In Krejca's *mise en scene,* according to Masson, "la pièce de Musset n'aura été après tout qu'un long, tumultueux et fertile entracte" (Masson, p. 389).

Unclosed circle, spiral, or broad intermezzo, the play, though it may have no ends, does have margins. The first and fifth acts are what permit the viewer to distinguish the play from what is non-play, much as a frame on a painting permits one to distinguish between the painting and the wall. Although a part of the work, the framework is definitely a limit of the work. And it is a limit in a very positive sense.

In **Lorenzaccio,** above all, the first and fifth acts insist on their own marginality. It is evident that the intrigues played out in act I and mirrored in act V are peripheral not only to the main action of the play but also to the political life of the Florence of 1537.

The quarrel between the Strozzi and Salviati families, for example, is a personal one and, finally, has no wider repercussions. One might have thought at the beginning of the play that since the Strozzi name appears to stand for virtue and the Salviati name for vice, this strand would have been woven more prominently into the text. In act V the Strozzi-Salviati quarrel is reduced to a quarrel between children, who fight not only because that is what their families do, but because that is what children do. By the end of the play as well, Philippe, the only Strozzi who might have been called on to play a central role, has abdicated that position and has placed himself outside even the periphery of the intrigue.

Another pattern which serves as a framework around the main action of the play is that of the episode of the marquis and marquise Cibo. Like Philippe, the marquise, although peripheral, attempts to have some effect on the central action. Like Philippe, she fails abysmally and is relegated finally to the margins of the play where she belongs. She belongs there not at all uselessly but because Musset gave her a role to play which carries with it much of the significance of the structure of the play. More than any of the male characters, she mirrors the essence of Lorenzo's dilemma.

The movement of the scene in which the Cibo couple makes its first appearance is directed outward, away from the main stage. Laurent Cibo takes leave of his wife the marquise to inspect his properties on the outskirts of Florence and will be gone for the duration of the central action of the play. He is totally outside the framework. The marquise is left behind ostensibly to make an attempt at centrality: an adulterous affair with Alexandre will save Florence. Before she plunges in, however, she follows her husband visually, away from the scene, away from Florence. She breaks through the framework of the play by opening a window and seeing, with her mind's eye only, the vast expanses of freedom and purity that are represented by the Cibo domain at Massa, where, we are told, she has spent idyllic hours. What is far away, what is off-stage, what is past, is good.

The window of the marquise represents the first instance in the play of what Masson calls dilation of scenic space. He makes much of the proliferation of windows in *Lorenzaccio*: "Musset suggère un au-delà du décor, qui fait du microcosme scénique la cellule d'un univers plus vaste qui le contient. Tel est le sens premier de ces fenêtres qui ouvrent sur un envers du décor et évoquent un ailleurs où les personnages en scène ne sont pas, mais où ils pourraient être" (Masson, p. 124). It is not only windows, however, which create the possibility of infinite expansion.

In another instance, Catherine, Lorenzo's aunt/cousin/ sister/beloved, and Marie, Lorenzo's mother, are seated on the banks of the Arno. Like the marquise, who "sees" Massa, Marie sees another *locus amoenus,* the Cafaggiuolo of Lorenzo's youth and purity. She sees a mirror of Florence—and its opposite. Again, not only are the bounds of space overcome but those of time as well. For with Marie, we are privileged to gain a glimpse of the *Lorenzino d'autrefois.* Marie's lament presents us with another para-text: the story of a potentially different unfolding of events. Had Lorenzo remained where he belonged by birth, at the center, he would not be today what for Marie has become "un spectre hideux." The marginality of the scene between Marie and Catherine on the banks of the Arno is further emphasized at its conclusion when the two women become witnesses to the departure of citizens who have been banished from Florence by the duke. The movement of the scene is a generalized, structured, impersonal, mannered, almost choral one, away from the center toward the periphery and beyond, leading out of the view of those on stage. This movement away from the center is mirrored

in the scene of the reconciliation of the marquis and marquise Cibo in the last act. They have once again become the idyllic lovers of act I, as though the adultery had not taken place. The manner of Musset's presentation of the reconciliation is significant. Not a word is spoken onstage by the lovers. Rather, two anonymous gentlemen, in six simple *répliques,* describe the happy couple, oblivious to the tumult surrounding them, passing hand in hand through the stage. For all their presence contributes to the effect of the scene, they might as well be in the wings.

Probably the most important scene of the first act which is subsequently reduplicated in the last takes place between the silk merchant and the goldsmith. Masson remarks that the scene itself is a "spectacle dans un spectacle: il y a ceux qui se divertissent et ceux qui regardent se divertir" (Masson, p. 188). The people are spectators of their own political and social destiny. But they are more than just spectators; they are witnesses, commentators, critics of the scene they are observing and about which they bear solemn testimony. The stylized language of their testimony is significant. The *orfèvre* delivers a discourse in which the political life of Florence is transformed metaphorically into architectural life. Substance becomes structure; the tableau becomes its framework. The language of the goldsmith is crucial. His speech appears unnatural, contrived, stilted, as though read from a text. To the silk merchant, his interlocutor, it appears to have come from a script: "Vous avez l'air de savoir tout cela par cœur." The formal nature of the goldsmith's speech rises to consciousness in the mind of the merchant and is subjected to analysis or criticism within the play itself.

In the final act of the play, these two peripheral characters, the merchant and the goldsmith, reappear. Their roles now are reversed. Whereas previously it was the goldsmith who indulged in prolixity, he now remains relatively silent, and it is the merchant's turn to be garrulous as he delivers himself of the famous speech of the six Sixes. His language is so contrived as to appear absurd and is dismissed as such by the goldsmith. Abruptly, with almost no transition, the two bourgeois disappear from the scene to be replaced by another couple, the Preceptors, accompanied by the Strozzi and Salviati children. It is as though the bourgeois had dissolved into the Preceptors. Even the language remains the same; it is the language of caricature. It is outrageously affected, pedantic, *précieux.* The two Preceptors appear to be influenced neither by the macrocosmic political upheaval which has just taken place nor by its microcosmic reflection which appears before their eyes in the actions of the contentious children. The Preceptors themselves are a mirror, reduced to the absurd, not only of the Cibo couple, but of the artist Tebaldeo. Like Tebaldeo, they are interested only in the work of art that results from the revolution. One of the Preceptors has, in fact, written a sonnet describing the events as he perceives them, and is parading it before his colleague for commentary and appreciation. Because of the scuffling of the scamps only a two-line fragment of the sonnet is recited. These two lines are sufficient to show that we are in the presence of an antiphrastic interior reduplication of the larger work:

> Chantons la liberté qui refleurit plus âpre,
> Sous des soleils plus mûrs et des cieux plus vermeils.
>
> (V,5, p. 198.)

If the reflowering at the end is more harsh than the situation at the beginning, the liberty of which the poet/pedant speaks is ironic. Liberty is the one thing which is decidedly not the result of the action of the play.

Undramatic language, produced by undramatic, peripheral characters, leads away from the action of the text in the direction of its limits. The structure of repetition constitutes a framework around the main action of **Lorenzaccio.** Grouped in the framework of the play, at its margins, are the spectators, the commentators, and the inefficacious actors. Theme and structure play off against each other in the diffused light as the distinction between the two is blurred at the point of their conjuncture. Paradoxically, by alluding to an "elsewhere," the framework states poetically but clearly that the limits of the text may be transcended, both by expansion and contraction.

It is at the point where expansion and contraction occur simultaneously that Musset's contribution to the poetics of framing is most striking. The notion of simultaneous expansion and contraction is embodied in what is the most peripheral set of *répliques* in the first act. It relates to the non-appearance of Benvenuto Cellini on stage and to his presence as potential story-teller in the wings. The content of Cellini's "bonne histoire" is never recorded in the play and will remain an unknown paratext, an abstract possibility. The peripherality of Cellini, the artist who "appears" in the wings, is reflected by the peripherality of Tebaldeo, the artist who does actually appear on stage.[5]

Of the thirty-eight scenes of **Lorenzaccio,** none is more peripheral than the one in which Tebaldeo appears so prominently. Of the forty-four-odd characters in the play, few are more unnecessary. None of Musset's characters illustrates more forcefully Musset's technique of literary framing.

In act II, scene 2, Lorenzo notices that Tebaldeo is carrying a painting in his hands. He calls attention to it metonymically: "Vous avez, il me semble, un cadre dans les mains" (II,2, p. 89). The ensuing conversation has as its subject the contents of the frame. From Tebaldeo we learn that his painting of the Campo Santo is an "esquisse bien pauvre d'un rêve magnifique." This humble statement provokes a number of assertions by Lorenzo which reveal the true function of Tebaldeo's "frame." What is crucial is not what is on the canvas but *what might be put inside the frame.* "Vous faites," says Lorenzo, "le portrait de vos rêves? Je ferai poser pour vous quelques-uns des miens." Tebaldeo's frame, therefore, serves a function similar to that of the unseen canvas in Velázquez's painting, *Las Meninas.* Not only might it reflect the scene being painted, but it might also reflect a scene *outside* the borders of the work of art.

Lorenzo, in fact, declines to see the painting at all. His taunting remarks, "Est-ce un paysage ou un portrait? De quel côté faut-il regarder, en long ou en large?" appear to be the tasteless appreciation of a philistine. This blurring of the distinction between a *paysage* and a *portrait* has far-reaching significance, however. The marquise Cibo, when she feels the need to escape from the suffocating atmosphere of her adultery, does not go to a window for relief from the dramatic tension; instead, she contemplates a portrait of her husband. What is crucially important about the picture is that the marquise transforms the *portrait* into a *paysage*: the marquis becomes Massa. She sees in the portrait something that is not there, or rather something that is evoked by it and which results in its expansion. This distortion of the contents of the frame is central to Musset's handling of interior framing, where the reduced model is transformed into a structure even larger than the main body, where concentration leads to expansion.

For Lorenzo, as well, what is in a frame is far less important than *what might be there.* For Lorenzo, Tebaldeo's frame *could* contain the portrait of a courtesan (whom Tebaldeo would decline to paint) or it *could* contain a view of Florence. These two options, the *portrait* and the *paysage,* are qualitatively different microcosmic reflections of Lorenzo's own corruption. Tebaldeo's refusal to paint "la Mazzafirra toute nue" (II,2, p. 90), coupled with his enthusiastic willingness to paint corrupt Florence, appears to irritate Lorenzo keenly. As long as the contents of Tebaldeo's frame do not make a severe distinction between Lorenzo's corruption and that of society, Lorenzo can see himself as a mere reflection of the corrupt society, as a mirror—or as a work of art. As soon as the artist, however mediocre, insists on a severe distinction between personal and social corruptions, Lorenzo is threatened. Is his criminal life a reflection of the portrait of a lowly courtesan or is it the reflection of a noble city which has become like a whore? "Est-ce un paysage ou un portrait? De quel côté faut-il regarder, en long ou en large?" Tebaldeo's frame is important for what it might contain, the mirror of Lorenzo's moral dilemma. It is *both* a scale model *and* a dilation of the scenic space. The insight provided by the frame applies an unbearable pressure on Lorenzo. The only issue from the abyss represented by the frame is to attempt to corrupt the artist, to make him an accomplice in a political act. After his confrontation with Tebaldeo, Lorenzo is challenged by another incarnation of virtue, Catherine. She proposes to read from a book on Roman history. Lorenzo interrupts and "reads" *his own version of the text*: "Il y avait une fois un jeune gentilhomme nommé Tarquin le fils" (II,4, p. 100). Lorenzo changes the "histoire de sang" into a "conte de fées," rewriting the text, as the marquise has repainted the portrait.

Tebaldeo, a reflection of what Lorenzo once was, and Brutus, a model for what he wishes to become, are only two of the many doubles of Lorenzo in the play. In fact, all the male characters in the play who display individuality, with the exception of Cardinal Cibo,[6] mirror Lorenzo. All are virtual incarnations of Lorenzo, either past or future, either probable or at least remotely possible.

The case of Philippe is especially instructive. In the central scene of the play, the one receiving the greatest concentration of light, Philippe challenges Lorenzo directly, the way Tebaldeo had challenged him only obliquely. It is in this scene (III,3) that Lorenzo is led, by a mysterious process which lacks both logical and chronological development, to his self-revelation. The scene itself only seems to lack internal coherence. It is held together in fact by the repeated use of framing metaphors, devices which focus on the surface of things and on the inexorable forces—from both inside and out—which cause a puncturing of the surface.

Philippe, using the metaphor of the container, demands that Lorenzo exhibit its contents. "Que l'homme sorte de l'histrion! Ne m'as-tu pas parlé d'un homme qui s'appelle aussi Lorenzo, et qui se cache derrière le Lorenzo que voilà?" (III,3, pp. 128-29). And then he throws down the gauntlet. "Es-tu au dedans comme au dehors une vapeur infecte? Toi qui m'as parlé d'une liqueur précieuse *dont tu étais le flacon,* est-ce là ce que tu renfermes?" (III,3, p. 132, my italics). Philippe demands a change of perspective from inside to out.

Lorenzo rises to the challenge with deliberation. His answer is not a direct one, however. He notes that there is a danger in looking beneath the surface, beyond mere reflection, or even beyond a complex system of reflections. Lorenzo sees himself as having once been an admirer of surfaces. He claims to have been able to penetrate the surfaces of things, to reach their essences, and to have found them corrupt. He even uses the architectural metaphor the goldsmith had proposed in describing the political life of Florence, comparing life itself to a city. Lorenzo claims to have looked through the windows of the city, not outwardly to Massa or Caffagiuolo, but inwardly at evil, and, having done so, even though protected by a *cloche de verre,* to have become tainted.

The surfaces, both of the macrocosm represented by the corrupt city whose windows are its limits and of the microcosm represented by the *Lorenzino d'autrefois* who contains virtue's precious liqueur and who is himself contained in a protective bell-jar, have been hopelessly intertwined. As Lorenzo reviews the text and texture of his life, he sees that there have been other surfaces as well, which have been more than mere surfaces. At one time Lorenzo was able to externalize the virtue he knew he contained. He would even walk around with his good *fantôme* at his side. He takes seriously his mother's fantastic vision of the spectre of the *Lorenzino d'autrefois*. He records as well that, in order to execute his "political" plan, he chose still another surface identity, the theatrical mask of vice. Lorenzo fully realizes now that this mask has stuck to his skin. And yet, it is not the interfusing of surfaces which is, finally, important.

What Lorenzo has come to fear is not that the interior of the *flacon* be *infecte,* not that the interior of the frame be vicious, but that it be empty. He is concerned lest the bell-jar house a vacuum. The enigma of Lorenzo's life is not solved by the assassination; it is merely expressed, externalized, exhibited, mirrored in the larger world of the play. Lorenzo has been the scaffolding in which there existed a scale model of the larger-than-life Lorenzo. The expressed Lorenzo is, although not the political savior of Florence, a man of virtue, a witness to virtue—and its prophet. His action is his text, and it is given to be read.

What remains after the writing of the text is a void. In Venice, outside the stage of Florence, Philippe remarks that after all that has taken place, Lorenzo has not changed. Lorenzo concurs, but with one caveat: "Il n'y a de changé en moi qu'une misère—c'est que je suis plus creux et plus vide qu'une statue de fer-blanc" (V,6, p. 200). Lorenzo, in realizing his act, in realizing his mother's dream, has realized at the same time his greatest fear: he has lost his potentiality. Both the "Lorenzaccio" and the "Lorenzino" spectres are now externalized. "Lorenzo," however, remains, metaphorically, an empty frame, a frame that contains neither *paysage* nor *portrait*.

The ending of *Lorenzaccio,* the play, is parallel to the end of Lorenzo the person: it is neither good nor bad; it is neither progress nor change. Côme's inauguration speech is a text read off-stage which renders ambiguous the action which has taken place on stage. Indeed, we may question whether *Lorenzaccio* as a whole is a *portrait* or a *paysage*. "De quel côté faut-il regarder, en long ou en large?" As in the case of Tebaldeo's painting, one can only speculate about what the frame might contain. As in the case of Lorenzo, what we actually see is only a frame.

Outer and inner framing are functions of an esthetic system. By the use of a complex network of frames, Musset expands the work of art beyond its material limits. His contribution in **Lorenzaccio** is that he was able to expand the limits without transgressing the strict bounds of the genre in which he wrote. He was able to fashion the frame out of the painting.

Notes

1. A theory of "frame analysis" as an interdisciplinary methodology can be found in Erving Goffman, *Frame Analysis* (New York: Harper & Row, 1974). Among literary critics, see Boris Uspensky, *A Poetics of Composition* (Berkeley: University of California Press, 1973), and Jurij Lotman, *The Structure of the Artistic Text* (Ann Arbor: Michigan Slavic Contributions, 1977).

   All references to *Lorenzaccio* will be taken from the following edition and will be made in the text: Alfred de Musset, *Théâtre complet,* Bibliothèque de la Pléiade (Paris: Gallimard, 1958).

2. Apparently, Anne Ubersfeld (in "Révolution et topique de la cité: *Lorenzaccio*," *Littérature* 24 (1976), 41 sees the regicide as the center of the play. The present analysis, by its very method, excludes such a perspective. It agrees wholeheartedly, however, with Ubersfeld's general statements concerning the rest of the action: "S'il se passe beaucoup de choses dans la pièce, elles sont toutes marginales par rapport au régicide." Many, she says, "n'ont aucun caractère de nécessité dramatique."

3. Hassan el Nouty, "L'Esthétique de *Lorenzaccio*," *Revue des Sciences Humaines,* 108 (1962), 589-611.

4. Bernard Masson, *Musset et le théâtre intérieur. Nouvelles recherches sur "Lorenzaccio"* (Paris: Amand Colin, 1974). Subsequent references to this work will be made in the text. One might agree fully with Masson's well-developed argument that for Musset a *spectacle dans un fauteuil* is not so much a *théâtre de lecture* as it is a *théâtre intérieur;* one might insist, however, that it is interior theatre to the extent that it demands of the spectator, at the theatre or in the armchair, that he look at the work with closer attention to both detail and perspective than a mere reading or stage production permits.

5. Masson comments at length on the central role Cellini was to have played in *Lorenzaccio.* He shows convincingly (pp. 13-31) how Cellini's *Vita,* more than any other work, might have served the function of intertext for the play. Masson also enunciates a hypothesis for Musset's relegation of Cellini to the wings and for his replacement in the text by the non-historical painter Tebaldeo Freccia.

6. The cardinal is neither central nor peripheral to the action of *Lorenzaccio.* At most, he is peripheral to the peripheral story of the marquise, encircling her like a vulture. He is a shadow of a much larger political intrigue, that of the Pope and the emperor, being played elsewhere. He is not merely peripheral to the text; he is foreign to it.

Lloyd Bishop (essay date summer 1984)

SOURCE: Bishop, Lloyd. "Musset's 'Souvenir' and the Greater Romantic Lyric." *Nineteenth-Century French Studies* 12, no. 4 (summer 1984): 119-30.

[*In the following essay, Bishop maintains that Musset's poem "Souvenir" fits the structural, thematic, and narrative mode of the "greater Romantic lyric" as defined by Meyer Abrams and exemplified in poetic works by William Wordsworth, John Keats, Victor Hugo, and others.*]

The earliest formal invention produced by Romantic poets is a genre that Meyer Abrams has called the "greater Romantic lyric," a genre that evolved out of eighteenth-century loco-descriptive poetry and that includes such well known poems as Coleridge's "The Eolian Harp" and "Fears in Solitude," Wordsworth's "Tintern Abbey," Shelley's "Stanzas Written in Dejection," Keat's "Ode to a Nightingale" and Schiller's "Der Spaziergang."[1] It is only recently that the genre has been shown to include French poems as well, specifically "Tristesse d'Olympio" and "Le Lac."[2] That **"Souvenir"** is very similar thematically to "Le Lac" and to "Tristesse d'Olympio" is a cliché of literary history; that it is an important exemplar of the greater Romantic lyric is a fact that needs to be demonstrated. The purpose of this essay is to provide such a demonstration by placing Musset's poem in this larger context.

The greater Romantic lyric, as described by Abrams, is an extended poem involving a description of a natural setting, an interaction or interinvolvement between the setting and the observing subject modulating into a sustained meditation that interweaves perceptual, personal and philosophical elements and that produces thus a *paysage moralisé*. It presents a determinate speaker in a particularized setting, whom we overhear as he carries on a sustained colloquy either with himself, with the outer scene or with a silent human auditor, present or absent. It exhibits in particular two basic patterns of experience and formal thematic development with a third pattern often present:

The speaker begins with a description of the landscape; an aspect or change of aspect in the landscape evokes a varied but integral process of memory, thought, anticipation, and feeling which remains closely interinvolved with the outer scene. In the course of this meditation the lyric speaker achieves an insight, faces up to a tragic loss, comes to a moral decision, or resolves the emotional problem. Often the poem rounds upon itself to end where it began, at the outer scene, but with an altered mood and deepened understanding, which is the result of intervening meditation.[3]

As Abrams asserts, this controlled and shapely lyric is of great interest not only because it was the first Romantic formal invention, but also because it was so very prevalent during the Romantic period and because it engendered so many successors. Variations on the mode were performed by Matthew Arnold, Walt Whitman, William Butler Yeats and more recently by Wallace Stevens and W. H. Auden.[4] Since the concept of the greater Romantic lyric is relatively new, the list of exemplars and of variants will undoubtedly be lengthened considerably by literary scholars during the next decade or two, especially, we hope, in French literature. This essay is presented as one effort in that direction.

Let us look closely at **"Souvenir"** to see how well it fits into the mould of the greater Romantic lyric.

1. *An extended poem involving a description of a natural setting, an interaction or interinvolvement between the setting and the observing subject modulating into a sustained meditation that interweaves perceptual, personal and philosophical elements.*

"Souvenir" is an extended lyric consisting of 45 quatrains, nearly three times the number in "Le Lac," and begins with the narrator's reaction to a revisited natural setting.

> J'espérais bien pleurer, mais je croyais souffrir,
> En osant te revoir, place à jamais sacrée . . .[5]
>
>   (1-2)

As in "Tintern Abbey," "Le Lac" and "Tristesse d'Olympio" the scene is associated with a beloved female companion, and the secluded scene ("cette solitude")—just as in "Tintern Abbey"—impresses "thoughts of more deep seclusion." The narrator's friends fear that the revisitation will prove too wrenching an experience for him.

> Que redoutiez-vous donc de cette solitude,
> Et pourquoi, mes amis, me preniez-vous la main?
>
>   (5-6)

Perceptual and personal elements are immediately interwoven: Nature becomes a "shrine" [*tombe*] where sleeps a memory." The setting immediately evokes the image of a former mistress.

> Les voilà, ces coteaux, ces bruyères fleuries,
> Et ces pas argentins sur le sable muet,
> Ces sentiers amoureux remplis de causeries,
>   Où son bras m'enlaçait.
>
>   (9-12)

The rest of the poem is a philosophical meditation, compelled by the natural scene, on the evanescence of human happiness and, as we shall see, on the essence of human life.

2. *A determinate speaker in a particularized outdoor setting, whom we overhear as he carries on a sustained colloquy either with himself, with the outer scene or with a silent human auditor, present or absent.*

"Souvenir" is anchored to a specific time and place as Patricia Ward has said of "Tintern Abbey" and "Tristesse d'Olympio." Musset's brother Paul has related to us the particular circumstances under which the poem was written: the revisitation at Fontainebleau of a natural scene that Musset had shared seven years earlier, in 1833, with George Sand shortly before their fateful trip to Italy; the unexpected meeting with her, several months after the revisitation, at the Théâtre Italien; the feverish writing of **"Souvenir"** that very night.

The narrator's colloquy is carried on in the first stanza with the outer scene—

> En osant te revoir, place à jamais sacrée

in the second stanza with silent human auditors ("mes amis") and in the third and fourth stanzas with himself. At the end of the fifth stanza the poet apostrophizes Nature once again:

> Lieux charmants, beau désert qu'aimait tant ma
>   maîtresse,
>   Ne m'attendiez-vous pas?
>
>   (19-20)

The imperative of the sixth stanza seems addressed simultaneously to Nature and to the poet's worried friends addressed earlier.

> Ah! Laissez-les couler, elles me sont bien chères,
> Ces larmes que soulève un coeur encor blessé!
> Ne les essuyez pas, laissez sur mes paupières
>   Ce voile du passé!
>
>   (21-24)

3. *The speaker begins with a description of the landscape; an aspect or change of aspect in the landscape evokes a varied but integral process of memory, thought, anticipation and feeling which remains closely interinvolved with the outer scene.*

In **"Souvenir"** the sight of the heather and hillocks, the "silvery" sound of footsteps in the sand, activate the involuntary memory and produce a varied reaction. First, sweet nostalgia: the poet recalls the "fair days" of his youth; then his mistress's intense love of this particular setting; but the recollection of her subsequent betrayal brings tears to his eyes. However, a stoic pride, worthy of Vigny, prevents the poet from indulging in self-pity and recrimination.

> Je ne viens point jeter un regret inutile
>
> (25)

> Que celui-là se livre à des plaintes amères,
> Qui s'agenouille et prie au tombeau d'un ami.
>
> (29-30)

> Loin de moi les vains mots, les frivoles pensées,
> Des vulgaires douleurs linceul accoutumé,
> Que viennent étaler sur leurs amours passées
>   Ceux qui n'ont point aimé!
>
> (53-56)

All these varied feelings remain closely intervolved with the outer scene. In fact, the intervolvement is so close that the pathetic fallacy comes into play. The very *sentiers* which witnessed the lovers' embrace become, through a transferred epithet, *amoureux* themselves (11); and the poet's stoic pride is reinforced by the fact that Nature herself sets the example:

> Fière est cette forêt dans sa beauté tranquille,
>   Et fier aussi mon coeur.
>
> (27-28)

4. *In the course of the meditation the lyric speaker either achieves an insight, faces up to a tragic loss, comes to a moral decision or resolves the emotional problem.*

All these thematic elements are present in **"Souvenir."** The first insight gained is that Time is not only the great destroyer, as Hugo and Lamartine had complained, but also and more importantly, the greater healer.

> O puissance du temps! ô légères années!
> Vous emportez nos pleurs, nos cris et nos regrets;
>
> (45-46)

This thought leads the poet to pick a philosophical quarrel with Dante—

> Dante, pourquoi dis-tu qu'il n'est pire misère
> Qu'un souvenir heureux dans les jours de douleur?
> Quel chagrin t'a dicté cette parole amère,
>   Cette offense au malheur?
>
> (57-60)

and to achieve another insight. For him the memory of a happy experience is more real than the original experience itself:

> Un souvenir heureux est peut-être sur terre
>   Plus vrai que le bonheur.
>
> (67-68)

It is more durable; it is purer in an almost chemical sense of being unalloyed with baser instincts and motives or bitter feelings like jealousy and revenge.

> Ainsi de cette terre, humide encor de pluie,
> Sortent, sous tes rayons, tous les parfums du jour;
> Aussi calme, *aussi pur,* de mon âme attendrie
>   Sort mon ancien amour.
>
> (37-40; italics added)

Here the purity of love experiences, transformed into what Robert Denommé calls "crystallized recollections,"[6] is associated with the vibrant purity of the earth after a gentle rain, just as the "souvenir heureux" of stanza 17 is associated with the *pur flambeau* of the moon. Indeed it is Nature's "natural purity" that impels thoughts of moral purity (cf. the *vallon pur* observed by Olympio). In "Tintern Abbey" Wordsworth tells us that he finds "In nature and the language of the senses"

> The anchor of my *purest* thoughts, the nurse,
> The guide, the guardian of my heart, and soul
> Of all my moral being.
>
> (italics added)

The original experience, then, is maintained through memory in its pristine, "natural" purity and also escapes the ravages of Time. Another pre-Proustian insight is that man is not the sum of all his experiences, as Malraux and the existentialists have told us, but of the privileged moments.

> Ce fugitif instant fut toute votre vie.
>
> (99)

This is a position diametrically opposed to the one taken by Hugo's persona at one point in "Tristesse d'Olympio":

> N'existons-nous donc plus? Avons-nous eu notre
>   heure?
>   . . . . .
> L'air joue avec la branche au moment où je pleure;
> Ma maison me regarde et ne me connaît plus.
>
> (77-80)

At this point a bitter Olympio sees human existence as an insignificant speck in Space and Time, but he too will ultimately resolve the problem by invoking the *sacré souvenir.*

Musset arrives at this insight at the very beginning of his poem. At first he fears that the memory educed by the revisited scene will not be "pure" but bitter-sweet; this is the meaning of the *pleurer/souffrir* nuance of

"J'espérais bien pleurer, mais je croyais souffrir / En osant te revoir. . . ." But he notes with relief that no bitterness has surfaced: he can face up now to the greatest loss in his life with equanimity. The emotional problem, already under control at the beginning of the poem, is definitively resolved, and the poet will affirm a moral decision: he will forgive his unfaithful mistress and will remember the good days without bitterness.

5. *Often the poem rounds upon itself, to end where it began, at the outer scene, but with an altered mood and deepened understanding which is the result of the intervening meditation.*

After stanza 10 and for the length of 31 successive stanzas the outer scene in **"Souvenir"** is totally forgotten and yields to the abstract meditation. In stanza 42 the poet finally addresses Nature once again, then becomes aware once again, in the penultimate stanza, of the scene before him ("ces vastes cieux") and in the concluding stanza interweaves the setting ("ce lieu") with the treasured memory. The poem ends where it began: at the outer, "sacred" scene.

> Je me dis seulement: "A cette heure, *en ce lieu,*
> Un jour, je fus aimé, j'aimais, elle était belle.
> J'enfouis ce trésor dans mon âme immortelle,
>   Et je l'emporte à Dieu!
>
> (177-180; italics added)

The fact that the poem rounds upon itself is confirmed also by the sudden change in rhyme schemes at the end. Nearly all (41 out of 45) of the poem's quatrains have *rimes croisées,* but the final two stanzas return to the *rimes embrassées* used in the initial stanza. Nearly all (43 out of 45) of the quatrains begin with a feminine rhyme, but the final stanza returns to the initial masculine rhyme of the first stanza.

Musset's insistent use of the demonstrative adjective when describing or alluding to the natural scene, both at the beginning of the poem and at the end—

> ces vastes lieux
> ce lieu
> ces coteaux
> ces buissons
> cette solitude
> cette terre
> ces pas argentins

recalls that of Wordsworth in "Tintern Abbey."

> these waters
> these steep and lofty cliffs
> these orchard-tufts
> this dark sycamore
> these hedge-rows
> these pastoral farms
> these beateous forms

> this fair river
> this delightful stream

These demonstratives establish the dependence of the objects perceived upon the subjective experience of the perceiver. As Richard Haven explains:

> But of course in "Tintern Abbey" we can separate setting from speaker only by a conscious effort that violates the poem. Gray's verbs [In "Elegy Written in a Country Courtyard"] relate noun to noun; Wordsworth's relate noun to first person pronoun: "I hear," "I behold," "I view," "I see." Even when the subject of the verb is not "I," the construction still conveys a subjective relation: "cliffs, / That on a wild secluded scene *impress / Thoughts*" and "*connect* the *landscape* with the *quiet* of the sky" (5-8; italics added). The pattern is described as one which cannot exist independently of the perceiver, and it is this which constitutes the particularity of both speaker and setting. . . . The emphasis is on the demonstrative pronouns [sic.] (*these* waters, *these* cliffs, *this* dark sycamore) which relate the nouns to the pronoun ("these where I am, which I see") rather than on the nouns themselves.[7]

The demonstratives in **"Souvenir"** act as shifters as well as pointers: they shift the emphasis to subjective experience. The natural objects, inventoried more than described, denote not so much the outer scene in itself as events in consciousness. (The thing itself is a sign, says Derrida, and the sign itself is an absence, says Blanchot). To the Romantic nature poet the ontological status of natural objects is dual, and the two components of the duality are not usually equal. Things stand there initially, but only initially, in (a) their noumenal presence, their independent and transcendent being, as things-in-themselves to be admired in themselves, disinterestedly, [but this admiration already contaminates the transcendence with the presence of the admiring observer]; however their true being resides foremost in (b) their function as pointers to human feelings and to human relationships. Here for instance is the end of "Tintern Abbey":

> *these* steep and lofty cliffs
> And *this* green pastoral landscape, were to me
> More dear, both (a) for themselves, and (b) for thy sake.

The spatial contours in **"Souvenir"** are vague, not because Musset, any more than Lamartine, is an inadequate Nature poet, but because this is not a true descriptive poem but one of revery and meditation—a greater Romantic lyric. Georges Poulet has noted (*Les Métamorphoses du Cercle*) that Lamartinian space is only initially and imperfectly the locus of material and concrete things. Ultimately, inevitably, in poem after poem, things retreat. This is also true of **"Souvenir"** in which after stanza 10 the numerous objects focussed on earlier effect a strategic withdrawal in order to allow the ideas, for which the things are mainly signs, to occupy stage center. And this is why Musset, like Wordsworth and Lamartine, attaches vague, general epithets to his nouns even when, at the beginning and at the end of his poem, he does focus on the natural objects. The demonstrative adjectives are as operative as the vague descriptive ones, and properly so.

"Tintern Abbey"

THESE *pastoral* farms
THIS *dark* sycamore
THESE *beauteous* forms
THESE *steep* and *lofty* cliffs
THIS *delightful* stream

"Le Lac"

rocs *sauvages*
noirs sapins
beau lac
CES roches *profondes*
riants coteaux
CETTE pierre *où* tu
la vis s'asseoir

"Souvenir"

CES bruyères *fleuries*
CES sapins à la *sombre* verdure
CETTE forêt dans sa *beauté*
tranquille
CETTE gorge *profonde*
CES sentiers *amoureux*
CETTE vallée *amie*

If Wordsworth, Lamartine and Musset had filled their poems with sharp detail, with the perfervid precision of an amateur botanist, this would have detracted, in my view, from the meditative mood. Nature, again, is not being admired, it is being examined philosophically. The demonstrative adjectives, for instance, point not to the beauty of the natural objects perceived by an admiring subject but to an essential and mysterious coalescence of subject-object.

. . . . .

One can also speak of an altered mood or deepened understanding at the very end of **"Souvenir"** because of the sudden and somewhat surprising religious note. If one discounts the figurative (i.e., *seemingly* secularized) epithet "sacré" of the first stanza and the angry expletive "juste Dieu" of stanza 21 it is not only the sole religious one but also the very last one sounded in the poem, occupying thus a singularly privileged position. A man's treasured memories remain with him, Musset tells us, not just for the length of his mortal days but throughout a God-governed eternity. Memories of privileged moments form, then, not only the very center of worldly existence but of the other-worldly paradise, the soul's immortal consciousness.

Ton âme est immortelle, et va s'en souvenir.

(**"Lettre à M. de Lamartine"**)

This is quite different from the treatment that God receives in "Tristesse d'Olympio" from Hugo, who a bit later in his career will conceive of himself as the poet *vates* and who will write "sous la dictée d'en haut" (Sartre). In Hugo's poem God is not depicted as the guardian of sacred memory but as the very instrument of oblivion.

Dieu nous prête un moment les prés et les fontaines
Les grands bois frissonnants, le rocs profonds et
   sourds,
Et les cieux azurés et les lacs et les plaines,
Pour y mettre nos coeurs, nos rêves, nos amours;

Puis il nous les retire. Il souffle notre flamme.
Il plonge dans la nuit l'antre où nous rayonnons;
Et dit à la vallée, où s'imprime notre âme,
D'effacer notre trace et d'*oublier* nos noms.

(italics added)

Why in **"Souvenir"** this sudden reference to God from a writer who in poetry, fiction and drama expresses a metaphysical anguish arising from his age's loss of faith—and his own—and who at bottom is much less a religious soul than Hugo? Surely it is not a facile device designed to elicit from the reader a stock response of the only-God-can-make-a-tree type. This is simply not Musset's style. I think the best answer may be found in Georges Poulet's discussion of the romantic consciousness. If the first impulse of the man of sensibility is to be receptive to new sensations *from* the outside (despite the centrality of the self in Romantic literature, consciousness of objects precedes self-consciousness, especially and necessarily when the emotion experienced is Romantic love), his second impulse is to communicate these feelings *to* the external world: the movement now is from the center, the self, to the periphery.

L'âme humaine est conçue comme un foyer d'impressions qui rayonnent au-dehors . . . Tout sentiment cherche à s'épandre et à se communiquer. Comment sentir, sans éprouver le besoin de faire partager à toutes les sensibilités périphériques les émotions ressenties d'abord au centre.[8]

Chaque heure de l'existence, chaque lieu, si ténu qu'il soit, occupé par la moindre présence, devient un centre d'énergie irradiante, qui, comme dit Saint-Martin, "croît à la fois et dans tous les sens; occupe et remplit toutes les parties de sa circonférence."

Chaque point de la création, chaque moment particulier de la durée, révèle [for Romantics like William Blake just as for the poets of the Renaissance] une capacité d'expansion véritablement infinie.[9]

For Musset, not every but *any* hour of existence, any privileged moment or "sacred" place, can become an irradiating center capable of infinite expansion:

Ce fugitif instant fut toute votre vie.

. . . . .

To see a World in a Grain of Sand
And a Heaven in a Wild Flower,
Hold Infinity in the palm of your hand
And Eternity in an hour,

This is basically a religious idea, which links Musset (despite certain critical clichés to the contrary) to the mainstream of European romanticism.

> Presque simultanément, en France, en Allemagne, en Angleterre, les romantiques découvraient ou retrouvaient le caractère essentiellement religieux de la centralité humaine: "Je suis le point central, la source sainte" chante Astralis dans le roman de Novalis. L'homme est source, et source sacrée. Dans la profondeur de sa centralité se mêlent de façon indescriptible le mystère de son être propre et celui du Dieu qui s'y veut associé.[10]

What Poulet calls "the explosion of the center" suggests not only the sacredness of the Self, but an ever-widening periphery, the Romantic quest for the Absolute. But there is also in **"Souvenir,"** I think, an idea of implosion, a bursting inward to the center's center, to its mysterious, essential and sacred core. This is why Olympio too will cry out that his memory is "sacred." One must read Musset's *place à jamais sacrée* as presenting not simply a conventional epithet used as a trite compliment to a former mistress, but as expressive of a genuine if unorthodox religious feeling. The God of many a Romantic is not the transcendent God but the one within—

> . . . non pas un Dieu extérieur, objectif, travaillant au bon fonctionnement de sa Providence externe, mais le Dieu plus intérieur à nous-mêmes que nous-mêmes et plus central que nous ne le pourrions jamais devenir.[11]

. . . . .

Our conclusion is brief and obvious. We have not forced Musset's **"Souvenir"** into the mould of the greater Romantic lyric: we are dealing here, just as much as with "Tintern Abbey," "Tristesse d'Olympio" and "Le Lac," with a perfect fit.

Notes

1. For Coleridge, Wordsworth, Keats and Shelley, see M. W. Abrams, "Structure and Style in the Greater Romantic Lyric," in *From Sensibility to Romanticism: Essays Presented to Frederick A. Pottle,* eds. Frederick W. Hilles and Harold Bloom (New York: Oxford University Press, 1965), p. 527. Reprinted in *Romanticism and Consciousness,* ed. Harold Bloom (New York: Norton, 1970). References are to the original edition. For Schiller, see Abrams, *Natural Supernaturalism: Tradition and Revolution in Romantic Literature* (New York: Norton, 1971), pp. 453-57.

2. For "Tristesse d'Olympio," see Patricia A. Ward, "Tristesse d'Olympio and the Romantic Nature Experience," *Nineteenth-Century French Studies,* 7 (1978-79), 4-16. For "Le Lac," see Lloyd Bishop, *"Le Lac* and the Greater Romantic Lyric,"; in circulation, copies sent upon request.

3. Abrams, "Structure and Style in the Greater Romantic Lyric," 527-28.

4. For Yeats, see George Bornstein, "Yeats and the Greater Romantic Lyric," in *Romantic and Modern: Revaluations of Literary Tradition* (Pittsburgh: University of Pittsburgh Press, 1977), pp. 91-110. For the others, see Abrams, p. 529.

5. Alfred de Musset, *Poésies complètes,* ed. Maurice Allem (Paris: Gallimard, 1962), p. 404. All subsequent quotations and references to line numbers are based on this edition.

6. Robert T. Denommé, *Nineteenth-Century French Romantic Poets* (Carbondale: Southern Illinois University Press, 1969), pp. 134 and 149.

7. Richard Haven, "Some Perspectives in Three Poems by Gray, Wordsworth, and Duncan," in *Romantic and Modern,* pp. 176-77.

8. Georges Poulet, *Les Métamorphoses du cercle* (Paris: Plon, 1961), p. 133.

9. Poulet, *Les Métamorphoses du cercle,* p. 139.

10. Poulet, *Les Métamorphoses du cercle,* p. 138.

11. Poulet, *Les Métamorphoses du cercle,* p. 138. Musset, like so many Romantics espoused—at least at times—a vague pantheism and his belief was—at times—as strong as his unbelief. (Cf. his letter to the duchesse de Castries: "Vous me dites que ce qui me manque c'est la foi. Non, Madame. J'ai eu ou cru avoir cette vilaine maladie du doute, qui n'est, au fond, qu'un enfantillage, quand ce n'est pas un parti pris, ou une parade . . . La croyance en Dieu est innée en moi; le dogme et la pratique me sont impossibles. . . .") Quoted by Gilbert Ganne, *Alfred de Musset: Sa Jeunesse et la nôtre* (Paris: Librarie Académique Perrin, 1970), p. 135. The religious note at the end of "Souvenir" is also announced by the lengthy poem, "L'Espoir en Dieu" (1838). For a good recent study of *Souvenir* that discusses some of the issues treated in this essay, see P. J. Siegel, "Musset's *Souvenir*: Hugo or Dante?," *Les Bonnes Feuilles,* 8, 1, 3-16.

James F. Hamilton (essay date May 1985)

SOURCE: Hamilton, James F. "From *Ricochets* to *Jeu* in Musset's *On ne badine pas avec l'amour*: A Game Analysis." *French Review* 58, no. 6 (May 1985): 820-26.

[In the following essay, Hamilton examines the motif of game-playing and display of structural, thematic, and

psychological tensions between spontaneity and calculation in Musset's On ne badine pas avec l'amour.]

> Des ricochets! Ma tête s'égare; voilà mes idées qui se bouleversent. Vous me faites un rapport insensé, Bridaine. Il est inoui qu'un docteur fasse des ricochets.
>
> (1, 5)[1]

Our understanding of Musset's masterpiece on love has progressed from the study of parallels between the couples Perdican-Camille and Musset-George Sand to the examination of conflicting bipolarities, psychological and temporal.[2] To this approach must be added structural and ideological dimensions capable of elucidating the play's dramatic mechanism. Only then can motivation, time, and space be grasped as a dynamic whole. The generative principle of this expanded interpretation derives from the verb *badiner* in the title to Musset's tragi-comedy. The implied motif of *jeu* goes to the heart of Romantic drama, its psychology and metaphysics.[3] The complementary image, *ricochets,* appears four times at the end of Act 1 and is metaphorized to convey the spontaneous breakdown of order. Stones are thrown by a university doctor and noble, Perdican, who courts a peasant girl, Rosette; and, village rascals follow them to the chateau, all to the horror of the Baron. In short, I contend that the images of *ricochets* and *jeu* reflect two contrary modes of behavior. The first—unreflective, spontaneous, and natural—characterizes Perdican's conduct up to the second fountain scene. Here, he joins Camille by operating on the basis of calculation, strategy, and artifice—the behavioral mode of *jeu.*

"Ricochet" explains repeated movement in the play. It occurs when Perdican's advances toward Camille are thwarted. His desires are deflected in the direction of Rosette where they dissolve in frustration. Then, he rebounds to Camille and the next "ricochet" takes effect. This dynamics is made apparent upon the reunion of Perdican and Camille. Rebuffed by his cousin who refuses a kiss and an invitation to take a walk, Perdican goes alone to the village. The unreflected quality of Perdican's "ricochet" from Camille to Rosette is illustrated by his trance-like state of mind the morning after his argument with Camille on religion: "Où vais-je donc?—Ah! je vais au village" (3, 1). The kiss intended for Camille is given to Rosette who is identified by the chorus: "C'est Rosette, la sœur de lait de votre cousine Camille" (1, 4). A few lines later, Perdican links the two women in his inquiry: "Ta sœur Camille est arrivée. L'as-tu vue?" Similarly, Perdican defends his kisses: "Quel mal y trouves-tu? Je t'embrasserais devant ta mère. N'es-tu pas la sœur de Camille? ne suis-je pas ton frère comme je suis le sien?" (2, 3). Perdican's confused images of the two women points to the level of rich psychological meaning in *On ne badine pas avec l'amour.*

Structurally, the "ricochet" effect is based upon the commonplace of a romantic triangle, but it establishes a trajectory whose terminal points constitute bipolarities. A confluence of meanings—temporal, spatial, psychological, and philosophic—is associated with each set of points. When traumatized by Camille's transformed personality and her concomitant rejection of him, Perdican is forced to redefine himself. Upon returning to his country estate after completion of doctoral studies in Paris, he appears to journey back into time in the search of enduring values.[4] Perdican finds his emotional roots among the peasants of the village. There, in spite of his ten-year absence, he retrieves his ideal self in the eyes of those who, less corrupted and blinded by prejudice and social rank, see him both as child and man: "Que Dieu te bénisse enfant de nos entrailles! Chacun de nous voudrait te prendre dans ses bras; mais nous sommes vieux, monseigneur, et vous êtes un homme" (1, 4). Moreover, the peasants take joy in the reunion of a loved one, without regard to his legal status as inheritor, and liken his return to a rebirth: "Votre retour est un jour plus heureux que votre naissance. Il est plus doux de retrouver ce qu'on aime que d'embrasser un nouveau-né."

Chateau and village, present and past, form a temporal-spatial network around which Perdican careens in his "ricochets" from Camille to Rosette. Foster sisters, playmates, beautiful young women, such images overlap in the troubled mind of Perdican. Rebounding from a cold, critical Camille, he finds not only Rosette but a reflection of his cousin in the past. However, on one occasion, the illusion becomes translucent to Perdican. He is moved by the reflection of his memories in Rosette, the village folk, and the setting, but he is also disconsolate because of their meaninglessness for Camille. The contrast strikes a painful emotional chord, and Perdican mourns the past, as Rosette naively observes: "Regardez donc, voilà une goutte de pluie qui me tombe sur la main, et cependant le ciel est pur" (2, 3). He begs Rosette's pardon, but she does not understand: "Que vous ai-je fait, pour que vous pleuriez?". The fault is not hers but that of Perdican who seeks the impossible, the unification of the past and the present, the village and the chateau in the recaptured joy and innocence of childhood.

The bipolar structure of the plot has a parallel psychological component that provokes Perdican's "ricochets" and promotes game playing. He sees in himself a continuum from the past to the present, a child in the man. However, Maître Bridaine views him as a learned doctor; the Baron suspects him of seducing "les filles du village en faisant des ricochets"; Camille regards him as an experienced man of the world (1, 5). In confessing a number of love affairs and in rejecting the sanctity of marriage, Perdican gives evidence of a double identity. He is a libertine (philosopher-seducer) and a Romantic hero (lover-child). This principle of characterization, *dédoublement,* is manifested by oscillation and ambiguity and renders self-knowledge problematic.[5] The same psychological principle motivates Camille. In addition to being a lover-child, she is a coquette (casuist-tease) in the tradition of Molière's Célimène but with a premature *pruderie*. Their double identities, libertine/lover and coquette/lover, expose the childlike qualities of Perdican and Camille and verify the extent to which, despite appearances, they are indeed cousins. At crucial moments in the conflict, each doubts not only the sincerity of the other but is unsure also of his own feelings. Because of this inherent instability, psychology in *On ne badine pas avec l'amour* cannot serve as a vantage point from which to elucidate its dramatic structure. The motifs of *ricochets* and *jeu* derive their meaning from the philosophic substance of the play.

Game playing and its preparatory stage of unreflected trajectory, *i.e., ricochets,* along the chateau-village circuit (in its spatial, temporal, and psychological dimensions) can hardly be understood without recourse to ideology in general and to Rousseauist doctrine in particular. Structural bipolarity in *On ne badine pas avec l'amour* corresponds to the ideological opposition between art and nature. Introduced at the opening of the play, it provides the philosophic touchstone upon which all successive actions are judged. The joint arrivals of Maître Blazius and Dame Pluche oppose corpulence, fresh wine, and good cheer to sterility, vinegar, and piety. This opposition of nature and anti-nature, reinforced by stylistic effects, evokes a positive and a negative reaction from the peasant chorus and is continued in the movements of Camille and Perdican. For example, after refusing to kiss Perdican, Camille turns her back to him and focuses on an object which encompasses her values—a portrait of a great aunt devout and never married: "Oh! oui, une sainte! c'est ma grand-tante Isabelle. Comme ce costume religieux lui va bien" (1, 2). In contrast, Perdican lingers before a pot of flowers which he appreciates solely for its beauty and scent and he subsequently waxes lyrical: "Voilà donc ma chère vallée! mes noyers, mes sentiers verts, ma petite fontaine" (1, 4). Not only are the cousins situated in the opposite worlds of nature and art, color symbolism places Rosette and Camille at opposite ends of affectivity. Rosette's name promises passion, fecundity, and spontaniety while Camille's name conveys cold purity, sterility, and contrivance.[6]

Bipolarity—structural, psychological, and philosophic—creates the tension necessary to dramatic conflict and opens the possibility of a reconciliation of opposites in the union of lovers. Steps in this direction are taken in a site where past and present, village and chateau, nature and art converge—"à la petite fontaine." In the first fountain scene, Perdican remains on the "ricochet" projectory of uncalculated movement from chateau to village. Although Camille operates on the level of *jeu* (in the sense that her actions are premeditated, that she

wears a mask and has set the stage), the outcome of their meeting still offers hope. Perdican reacts truthfully to her queries, and, in the heat of mutual anger but heartfelt emotions, she removes her mask to confess a fear of love and its sufferings. The nature principle seems to overcome art, interpreted as deceit and false piety, to promise liberation for her and the possibility of union. However, an event intervenes which removes Perdican from nature and makes him an actor with a mask. Intercepting a secret letter from Camille to Sister Louise, he learns that Camille's conduct had been prearranged so as to deceive him. Feeling victimized by her boasts of having driven him to despair, he promises himself revenge: "je n'ai pas le poignard dans le cœur, et je te le prouverai. Oui, tu sauras que j'en aime une autre avant de partir d'ici" (3, 2).

When pride prevails in Perdican's conduct, he leaves the unmediated level of *ricochets* to compete with Camille on that of *jeu*. The second meeting at the fountain results in the profanation of nature that separates Perdican from the truest part of himself, *l'enfance*, the spiritual source of his being. From the Rousseauist perspective, pride leads to corruption—thought for the purpose of dominance—which makes Perdican liable to evil.[7] Moreover, by imitating Camille's game-playing, he abandons the past, the village, and nature. Morally, Rosette is deserted to become an object of exploitation, the only unmasked and unconscious player of a game which is imposed without her consent.[8] Structurally, the play's bipolar principle becomes so imbalanced in favor of art that any reconciliation of opposites is rendered highly improbable. Resolution of conflict through union would require a miracle.

Once the "game" is set into motion—triggered by fear and unconscious hostility—it escalates through reprisal, denial of aggression through repression, and further emergence in unforseen ways. This spiral of escalating psychological warfare eludes control to threaten the social peace of its community. Two questions emerge from this dilemma, a moral and a pragmatic one: who is at fault and how does one stop the "game"? The first question is broader than the more obvious one: who started the "game"? To this it suffices to reply that the social aspect of games requires that more than one person play. Although Camille is at fault in the first instance, her conduct adheres consistently to the bipolar principles of château and art. Moreover, her free will is severely circumscribed by the negativity of her convent experience. In contrast, Perdican reverses allegiance from nature to art through an apparently free decision, although provoked and made in anger. He defiles the fountain place of his childhood. Although the peasant chorus has nothing positive to say about Camille, its attitude toward Perdican changes from paternal warmth to distrust. The voice of village and nature, a veritable social conscience, sides with Rosette against Perdican who is portrayed no longer as a child returned as a man but as a libertine: "Hélas! la pauvre fille ne sait quel danger elle court en écoutant les discours d'un jeune et galant seigneur" (3, 4).

The theoretical question of culpability and the pragmatic one of stopping the "game" are closely associated. A series of critical moments occurs in the conflict and offers this possibility: Camille's momentary dropping of her mask with the ventilation of anger ("O Perdican! ne raillez pas, tout cela est triste à mourir") which opportunity is thwarted by Perdican's rage (2, 5); the exposure of Perdican's duplicity to Rosette, hidden behind the tapestry, which is misused by Camille to belittle Perdican and to drive him into a marriage which neither wants: "Eh bien! apprends-le de moi, tu m'aimes, entends-tu; mais tu épouseras cette fille, ou tu n'es qu'un lâche!" (3, 6); the meeting of the three in the village where Rosette tries to withdraw by returning her necklace to Perdican. The gesture is accepted by a patronizing Camille but rebuffed by her proud cousin who walks off with Rosette. Shortly thereafter, Camille sends for Perdican but is unable to verbalize her feelings and she retreats: "Non, non—O Seigneur Dieu!" (3, 7). No clear picture of culpability emerges from these missed opportunities. The "game" is out of control.

The failure to stop the "game" serves to elucidate the character traits of Perdican and Camille, but psychoanalysis must yield to philosophy in explaining the improbability of their reconciliation. Three ways of bringing the "game" to a halt come to mind, and two of them apply to the play. They are "return to nature," magnanimous self-sacrifice, and spiritual elevation. Musset adheres faithfully to the Rousseauist inspiration of his thought in *On ne badine pas avec l'amour.* At an abstract level, Perdican and Camille cannot return to the innocent happiness of childhood. They resemble the majority of people in the social state "dont les passions ont détruit pour toujours l'originelle simplicité.'" In particular, his studies and love affairs in Paris and her indoctrination by forlorn women in the convent condemn the cousins to live in the social state where *paraître,* mask, vanity, and class consciousness prevail.

No synthesis is possible for Perdican between château and village, art and nature, present and past. Camille and Rosette can never become one woman. However, the social state does permit radical reversals in character and conduct. Through the Old Regime system of values propagated by Corneille, a noble person can demonstrate a generosity of such magnitude as to elicit a corresponding self-sacrifice of ego on the part of one's opponent, albeit a lover. Unfortunately, the nobility of Perdican and Camille remains on the level of *orgueil* rather than *fierté.* For example, in their argument on religion and love, Perdican warns Camille: "Tu es une orgueilleuse; prends garde à toi" (2, 5). Likewise, she charges him with pridefulness in the exposure of his lies to Rosette: "Je m'étais vantée de t'avoir inspiré quelque amour, de te laisser quelque regret. Cela t'a blessé dans ton noble orgueil?" (3, 6). Hence, their noble pride impedes their rising above roles in a childish but fatal game, a microcosm of a corrupt social state.

Since the bipolar world of Perdican does not offer resolution either through a "return to nature" or noble magnanimity, he has no recourse but withdrawal in despair or transcendence of the conflict through spiritual elevation. His communal confession in the chapel of the chateau removes the psychological obstacle to the union of adversaries. He rises above his role: "Orgueil, le plus fatal des conseillers humains, qu'es-tu venu faire entre cette fille et moi?" (3, 7). Tragic irony brings the libertine to his knees in prayer at the end of the play while the would-be nun finds herself unable to pray. The lie of her vocation is made manifest while Perdican's "sentiment de la nature" is shown to have a spiritual foundation, in true Rousseauist fashion. This revelation of truth exacts a price greater than the personal pain of humiliation. Instead of purging their pride through commitment in full responsibility for their actions, Perdican and Camille sacrifice a third party. Rosette witnesses their reconciliation and dies. Separated from village and nature through their game-playing, she is also cut off from the world of the château and art. Deprived of her place in life, she falls prey also to a fictitious temporality, Perdican's desire to unite past and present, and Camille's dissolution of the future through fear.

The question of culpability proceeds to the forefront. Camille is rendered silent before her god and returns to the convent. Her increasing isolation toward the end of the play foretells her fate, the regret of love lost and never enjoyed. At the same time, Perdican imagines blood on his hands. In a patriarchal society where young men are free to be educated and have experiences, while young women are protected, he bears the responsibility of opening up life to Camille with patient persuasion and sensitivity. Unfortunately, he forfeited the possibility of playing the role of preceptor-lover in the manner of Rousseau's Saint-Preux. He takes the initiative in their debate only to overpower Camille by his intellectual, secularized view of the world. The idealism of love ("mais il y a au monde une chose sainte et sublime, c'est l'union de ces êtres si imparfaits et si affreux") is not made accessible to the young novice (2, 5). Perdican makes an ideological point and spurns his would-be student ("Adieu, Camille, retourne à ton couvent") just when she starts to open up: "J'ai eu tort de parler; j'ai ma vie entière sur les lèvres." Literary tradition has Perdican returning to a libertine life in

Paris. However, having known love and with a guilt accentuated by an awakened spirituality, he seems destined to be lonely and misunderstood in the world.

The motif of game playing, of consciously assuming a role, culminates in Musset's **Lorenzaccio** and reflects the alienation of Romantic writers from post-revolutionary France.[10] The play ends with confessions for sins wrought by "des enfants gâtés" and "deux enfants insensés," an image used in his description of a lost generation, *La Confession d'un enfant du siècle* (1836). The pervasive guilt and sense of perdition at the ending to *On ne badine pas avec l'amour* would seem to reflect the cosmology of sin without redemption.[11] If institutions and sexual roles constitute secondary factors in social disharmony, its primary cause is found in a human nature made defective by pridefulness, a principle of social fragmentation and self-alienation. However, the images of *jeu* and *ricochets* reflect a dialectic beyond despair. Implicit in *On ne badine pas avec l'amour* and explicit in Musset's lyrical poetry, the cure for *orgueil* comes from a commitment to life through love and brave acceptance of suffering in-the-world without transcendence.[12] The interplay of pride and love as a closing and opening to life is set forth by Musset as a Romantic social pact in the final stanza of **"La Nuit d'août"** (1836):

> Dépouille devant tous l'orgueil qui te dévore,
> Cœur gonflé d'amertume et qui t'es cru fermé.
> Aime, et tu renaîtras; fais-toi fleur pour éclore;
> Après avoir souffert, il faut souffrir encore;
> Il faut aimer sans cesse, après avoir aimé.

Notes

1. Musset, *Théâtre I* (Paris: Garnier-Flammarion, 1964), p. 298. All quotations refer to this edition and are indicated by act and scene.

2. See David Sices, "Multiplicity and Integrity in *On ne badine pas avec l'amour*," *French Review*, 43 (1969-70), 443-51, and Robert Lorris, "Le Côté de Perdican et le côté de Camille," *Australian Journal of French Studies*, 8 (1971), 3-14.

3. See M. Crouzet, "Jeu et sérieux dans le théâtre de Musset," *Journées d'Études sur Alfred de Musset* (Clermont-Ferrand: SER Faculté des Lettres, 1978), p. 35, who characterizes *le jeu* as: "un déchirement manichéen qui est sans doute la métaphysique générale du romantisme. . . . Le jeu est le négatif d'un sérieux absolu, le détour par le néant qui affirme l'absolu de l'homme."

4. See the thesis of David Sices, p. 447.

5. See Jean-Pierre Richard, *Etudes sur le romantisme* (Paris: Editions du Seuil, 1970), p. 208.

6. See Pierre Gastinel, *Le Romantisme d'Alfred de Musset* (Paris: Hachette, 1937), p. 424, who

stresses Rosette's incarnation of nature and adds: "Ne reconnaît-on pas là l'influence de Rousseau vers qui Sand a ramené Musset pour un temps?"

7. See Rousseau's "Discours sur l'inégalité" in *Du Contrat social* (Paris: Garnier, 1962), p. 68. Rousseauist pride is not to be confused with the Christian admonition to humility. Rousseau identifies "le premier mouvement d'orgueil" as initiating the separation of man from nature; he sees himself as being superior to other species.

8. Metaphorically, Rosette relives the plight of "natural man" who, upon emergence from nature, is forced into a social pact with prescribed roles, none of his choosing and against his will. See James F. Hamilton, *Rousseau's Theory of Literature: The Poetics of Art and Nature* (York, South Carolina: French Literature Publications Co., 1979), p. 83.

9. See Rousseau, p. 105.

10. For recent studies, see Naomi Schorr, "La Pérodie dans *Lorenzaccio*," *Michigan Romance Studies*, 2 (Winter 1981), 73-86, and James F. Hamilton, "Mimetic Desire in *Lorenzaccio*," *Kentucky Romance Quarterly*, in press.

11. See Richard, p. 208, who characterizes Musset's plays as "psychodrames" and perceives in Musset "un vœu secret d'auto-punition."

12. In the moral landscape of Musset, *l'horizontalité* prevails. Transcendence is limited to "l'éternité de chaque moment de vie." See Georges Poulet, *La Distance intérieure II* (Paris: Plon 1952), p. 248.

James F. Hamilton (essay date 1985)

SOURCE: Hamilton, James F. "Mimetic Desire in Musset's *Lorenzaccio*." *Kentucky Romance Quarterly* 32, no. 4 (1985): 347-57.

[*In the following essay, Hamilton elucidates patterns of imitative desire in Musset's* Lorenzaccio, *linking these structural elements with the drama's themes of disillusionment, futility, and sexual ambivalence, as well as with character motivation in the work.*]

> "Pour comprendre l'exaltation fiévreuse qui a enfanté en moi le Lorenzo qui te parle, il faudrait que mon cerveau et mes entrailles fussent à nu sous un scalpel."
>
> (III, 3)[1]

In the above passage, the hero challenges us to probe the motives of his obsessive desire. Lorenzo de Médicis dedicates his life to the accomplishment of one feat, the murder of his cousin and constant companion, Alexandre, the Duke of Florence. Musset's insistence upon the sexual exploits of the Medici scions and the underlying tension of their sibling rivalry pushes the text beyond a historical accuracy assured by his travels to Italy and research in Renaissance chronicles. The Lorenzo portrayed by Musset is inspired by a madness akin to the creative impulse of the poet and artist. Lacking ideological conviction, he is not taken seriously as a political assassin.[2] He represents a type of Romantic hero and embodies an aesthetics of action.[3] His denial of convention points not only to a search for identity but to a quest for immortality.[4] However, the contradiction between his "exaltation" and his degenerate conduct invites a psychological analysis; he seems to be driven by an inferiority complex.[5] These insights need to be integrated within a comprehensive theoretical model, one characterized by a broad understanding of myth. From this perspective, the insatiable pride of the Medicis puts them on a par with the ancient Greek house of Atreus.[6] Similarly, the city of Florence is cast as a fallen woman like the decadent Athens, the corrupt Rome, and the whore of Babylon as cited in *Revelations*.

From every angle—historical, psychological, and mythical—the city of Florence constitutes the focus of attention. For example, Emperor Charles V and the Pope intervene militarily and politically in the affairs of Florence, while King Francis I seeks eagerly to find a pretext to do so. The city is viewed as a prize, an object of desire, which is alternately loved and hated by those who compete for its possession. Fallen from its liberty as a republic and bearing a feminine name, Florence embodies the contrary symbolism of mother and harlot. This contradiction imposes an extreme tension upon the psyche of Lorenzo, the originally pure and idealistic student of Florence as a model republic.

The images of republican Florence and his mother, Marie Soderini, merge in Lorenzo's mind. As a child, he absorbs maternal affection and partisan ideology in the same embrace. This subtle indoctrination is confessed by Marie to her younger sister: "Et cette admiration pour les grands hommes de son Plutarque! Catherine, Catherine, que de fois je l'ai baisé au front en pensant au père de la patrie" (III, 3). The associated images of mother and city are reciprocal; Marie imagines the accusatory cries of citizens betrayed by Lorenzo: "Tu es la mère de nos malheurs!" (I, 6). A few lines later, the parting curses of exiles reinforce the overlapping identities of Marie, Florence, and mother: "Adieu Florence, peste de l'Italie! Adieu mère stérile, qui n'a plus de lait pour tes enfants!" Sterility in a mother betokens the lack of love for a child. This is the drama of Marie, who identifies herself as a mother but rejects her son. Only an alienated mother can see her son objectively as being ugly, and she dreams of him with revulsion, "dans les bras d'un spectre hideux." In contrast, Catherine rationalizes the cowardice of Lorenzo; she

blames Florence for his excesses and defends his essential goodness: "Je me dis malgré moi que tout n'est pas mort en lui."

Without attempting to draw a strict cause/effect relationship between a mother's feelings and a son's behavior, several rather obvious points can be made. First of all, the images of city, mother, and aunt fuse within the mind of Lorenzo. When republicans disregard Lorenzo's nocturnal announcement of his impending assassination of the Duke, he cries out in despair: "Pauvre Florence! pauvre Florence!" (IV, 7). Shortly afterwards, he uses similar language in a reflection that links mother and aunt: "—Pauvre Catherine! Que ma mère mourût de tout cela, ce serait triste" (IV, 9). Contrary to historical fact, Lorenzo receives notice of Marie's death after the failure of his assassination. More important but less easy to prove, the images of Florence, mother, and aunt generalize to all women within a Madonna/prostitute syndrome. His prevailing scorn of women is challenged by Catherine. In reply, he makes only two exceptions to his misanthropy, Catherine and Marie: "Je vous estime, vous et elle. Hors de là, le monde me fait horreur" (II, 4). Hence, from the standpoint of structure, Florence heads the triangular conflict in *Lorenzaccio* and is accompanied at its apex by a number of female surrogates.

The base angles of the triangle are occupied by Lorenzo and Alexandre. In a conventional plot, the two cousins would compete for the attention and favor of a beloved situated graphically in the projection of their desires at the apex of the "eternal" triangle. In fact, a number of conditions place Lorenzo and Alexandre de Médicis in positions of mutual envy, resentment, and admiration. First, the Duke also suffers from a sense of inferiority, as is shown in the duel scene.[7] When Lorenzo faints or pretends to faint at the sight of a naked sword blade, the sibling rivalry and latent antagonism explode on the part of Alexandre: "Fi donc! tu fais honte au nom de Médicis. Je ne suis qu'un bâtard, et je le porterais mieux que toi, qui es légitime" (I, 4). Lacking the refinement, education, and imagination of his more noble-minded cousin, Alexandre emphasizes his masculine superiority. He delights in humiliating his effeminate cousin, "une femelette," and calls attention to "ce petit corps maigre," "ces mains fluettes et maladives," etc. Despite such disparaging remarks (provoked partly by jealous courtiers), Alexandre takes a protective stance toward his cousin and shows more loyal affection to him than to any of his mistresses: "J'aime Lorenzo, moi, et, par la mort de Dieu! il restera ici."

The rivalry of Lorenzo and Alexandre does not function according to literary convention, for they are locked in a degrading relationship. Its dynamic of repulsion and attraction constitutes a "mimetic rivalry" which goes to the heart of much human behavior. Basically, the theory of "mimetic rivalry" holds that others' desires teach us what we want. However, the imitative character of desire takes a deviated form in *Lorenzaccio.* Rather than considering Alexandre as an obstacle to the attainment of a prize, a woman, or a mutual ambition, Lorenzo becomes dependent on him. Lorenzo needs the brute desire of his cousin in order to legitimize and sustain his own desire.[8] For instance, Lorenzo portrays himself as enjoying the women cast aside by Alexandre, "les restes de ses orgies," most of whom he was in the habit of procuring (III, 3). At the same time, he is troubled by the ghost of his pure youth and filled with self-hatred. The destabilizing aspect of this kind of mimetic triangle results from its ambivalence. Desire transfers from the object to its obstacle but is capable of returning to its original orientation. In the case of Lorenzo, he idealizes Florence, is enthralled by the uninhibited sensuality of Alexandre, and intends always to return to the "woman" of his youth. This love of a reflection from a rival feeds upon itself with overtones of a homosexuality permeated with masochism and guilt.[9]

The situation becomes clear if one visualizes a triangle with the object, Florence, at its apex (A) and the rivals, Lorenzo and Alexandre, at its base angles (ABC and ACB). The projection of Lorenzo's desire through Alexandre to the idealized Florence (from B to C to A) becomes dormant. The horizontal plane at the base of the triangle (BC) intensifies to carry the action in reflected images of mutual admiration and disgust. Unlike the traditional love triangle, desire is blocked and turns inward. It becomes incapable of striving upward to attain the ideal in an ennobling quest.

The mimetic triangle in *Lorenzaccio,* with its distinguishing character of sexual ambivalence, takes form in the opening scene of abduction. With Lorenzo and a squire, Alexandre awaits the departure of a maiden from a Florentine home. The darkness of midnight hides corrupt actions which harbor even darker motives in an ambiance of evil. Their shadowy figures mask an ignoble conduct which situates them outside of the law and society. Through the mediation of Lorenzo, the Duke reaches back into time to practice the ancient right of a ruler, "le droit du seigneur," to deflower virgins in his kingdom (III, 3). To be sure, this primordial ritual of fertility has political significance in Renaissance Florence. Alexandre rules the city through force, and the phallus complements the sword to humiliate and to undermine the morale of noble republican families that resist. So, too, seduction as the preference for wealth and pleasure over principle is shown to characterize bourgeois society in the persons of merchants who profit from the Duke's profligate expenditures. More importantly, the opening scene serves to illuminate the peculiar relationship of Lorenzo and Alexandre which is central to the conflict in *Lorenzaccio.*

The triangle of Alexandre, Lorenzo, and the maiden incorporates sexuality, violence, and the metaphysical. These levels of meaning are felt by the maiden's brother, Maffio, who confuses reality and illusion when waking from a dream to surprise the abductors. After being disarmed, he refers to "des lois à Florence" and "ce qu'il y a de sacré au monde" but finds a culprit in the person of Alexandre rather than a defender (I, 2). A more basic confusion of roles occurs between Alexandre and Lorenzo. Little passion is shown by the Duke; his preoccupation with the cold night air and matter-of-fact remark about another social commitment give the impression of performing a princely duty out of habit. His amorous motivation depends upon Lorenzo, who depicts in a long speech the exquisite sensual delight and domination awaiting the Duke in his despoiling of a fifteen-year-old girl. He promises a total possession of body and mind through "le filon mystérieux du vice," and he demeans her as a sexual object with images such as *trésor, chatte, fruits plus rares, exquise odeur.* Verbs of force and penetration convey a vicious violence. The interplay of Lorenzo and Alexandre points to a mimetic mechanism: Lorenzo uses the maiden to excite the Duke, to satisfy his own sexual needs, and to control the behavior of his male superior.

The apex of the mimetic triangle can now be defined with greater comprehension. It represents Florence as an absolute ideal whose profane embodiment, within the rivalry of Lorenzo and Alexandre, includes the maiden in the opening abduction scene as well as Marie and Catherine. So, also, the base angles of the triangle can now be defined vis-à-vis the secondary plots in *Lorenzaccio.* The relationship of Lorenzo with Alexandre as a mimetic rival on plane BC of the triangle degenerates into lust, and it is mirrored on two parallel tiers by competing rivalries. If the sides of the mimetic triangle (AB and AC) are extended for greater complexity, the triangular relationship of Tebaldeo, Alexandre as hero, and Florence (B'C'A) takes shape. Its plane of B'C' operates on the level of art. The third competing rivalry in the extended mimetic triangle includes the Marquise, Alexandre as hero, and Florence (B"C"A). Its plane of B"C" represents love. Tebaldeo and the Marquise compete with Lorenzo in trying to reveal the republican essence of Florence through idealized images of Alexandre in oil color and in sweet whisperings of grandeur. Artist and mistress seek to immortalize an idealized Florence in the person of Alexandre. Their attempts to incarnate the ideal demonstrate the abstract level of motivation prevailing in the play, and, more importantly, the deviated character of Lorenzo's struggle.

Lorenzo experiences not only the suffering of a mistress in his feeling of self-betrayal but also the more abstract frustrations of an artist. His interrogation of Tebaldeo (the painter who is commissioned to do a portrait of

Alexandre) matches the intensity of his heartfelt conversations with Philippe Strozzi. Certain similarities make the bright young men fellow spirits, but one major difference sets them worlds apart. Each has experienced a vision of the absolute which is referred to by Tebaldeo as "une extase sans égale" (II, 2) and as "l'exaltation fiévreuse" by Lorenzo (III, 3). Each has dedicated his youth to realizing a higher reality of transcendent values through what Tebaldeo describes poetically as "l'enthousiasme sacré" and "ce feu divin" (II, 2). Moreover, each is inspired by an ideal of Florence, which is called "ma mère" by Tebaldeo and "une catin" by the taunting Lorenzo.

The artist and the assassin part company on their vision of the absolute. Whereas descent symbolizes Lorenzo's vision of the sacred, images of ascent in rising organ music, hymns, incense, pale smoke, and perfume characterize Tebaldeo's view of art which serves "la gloire de l'artiste" and that of God (II, 2). Tebaldeo shows himself to be a man of the Renaissance by seeing evil within a humanist perspective ("les terres corrompues engendrent le blé céleste"), and he is able to reconcile his carnal nature with the quest for perfection: "Je suis artiste; j'aime ma mère et ma maîtresse" (II, 2). The psychoanalytic distinction between the creative artist and the compulsive neurotic applies here.[10] By reconciling his conflicts through art, Tebaldeo magnifies his humanity. In contrast, Lorenzo appreciates only the evil in man and seeks through a highly ritualized conduct to elevate a deviation from the norm to the level of art. His dream, born out of despair rather than courage, lacks authenticity and necessarily takes a destructive direction.

The illusory aspect of Lorenzo's creative enterprise is dramatized by another idealist. The Marquise de Cibo seeks to rival the influence of Lorenzo by supplanting him in her role of ideological muse. She also experiences an ambivalence between political ideal and amorous means: "Est-ce que j'aime Alexandre? Non, je ne l'aime pas, non assurément. . . . Pourquoi y a-t-il dans tout cela un aimant, un charme inexplicable qui m'attire? Que tu es belle, Florence, mais que tu es triste!" (II, 4). Her appeals to the heroic imagination of Alexandre ("j'ai de l'ambition, non pas pour moi—mais pour toi! toi et ma chère Florence") serve only to cool his ardor, and he abandons her for another woman, Catherine (III, 6). However, failure does not result in tragedy. The Marquise frees herself from an illusory ambition and a degrading role through an act of courage. She confesses everything to her husband in front of her temptor, the Cardinal. Thus, the Marquise reconciles symbolically the dual identity of Florence, mother and woman, when threatened by the loss of her freedom and soul.

The struggle between the flesh and the spirit experienced by the Marquise parallels that of Lorenzo but on a less exalted plane. A metaphysical thrust prevails in his desire from its inception in the Roman Coliseum. This very private moment during Lorenzo's student life in Rome holds the key to his personality transformation, and its confession is provoked by a political incident. The sons of Philippe Strozzi, patriarch of Florentine republicans and father figure to Lorenzo, are arrested. Paternal hysteria and cries of revenge imperil the hero's assassination plan and force him to reveal his secret motives.

The Coliseum scene narrated by Lorenzo takes place in this emotional context, and his story has a dreamlike quality which further complicates analysis. Nevertheless, a few factual observations can be made. First, having no rational explanation for his experience, Lorenzo pictures himself in a trancelike state of mind: "une certaine nuit que j'étais assis dans les ruines du Colisée, *je ne sais pourquoi* je me levai; je tendis vers le ciel mes bras trempés de rosée, et je jurai qu'un des tyrans de la patrie mourrait de ma main . . . *il m'est impossible de dire* comment cet étrange serment s'est fait en moi" (III, 3; italics mine). Second, the inspiration takes place in a very special site of heroic grandeur, the Roman Coliseum. Third, a radical change in outlook occurs on the part of Lorenzo, who turns his back on the contemplative life of a scholar and the likelihood, as a Medici, of high office in the Church or the state. Finally, the upheaval is accompanied by a euphoria which Lorenzo likens to the exaltation of falling in love.

The turning point in Lorenzo's life, acted out in a highly symbolic fashion, points to the religious experience of revelation and conversion to a new view of the world. Through a combination of fortuitous circumstances and formative influences, Lorenzo transcends the profane worlds of society and nature to catch a privileged glimpse into the realm of absolute values which promise immortality. This metaphysical level of meaning authorizes the use of myth and ritual. From these interpretative vantage points, Lorenzo's momentary transcendence is facilitated by the Roman Coliseum, which acts as a cosmological point in the planes of time and space where heaven, earth, and hell converge, a "center of the sacred."[11]

Lorenzo undergoes the eternally repeated experience of the *homo religiosus,* an initiation into the sacred, whose various cultural configurations show certain consistent tendencies. Lorenzo's actions deviate from the general pattern of ritual only in their spontaneous occurrence outside of the communal safeguards of tribe, clan, family, or sex group. Traditionally, initiation into the secrets of the sacred takes place upon the reaching of manhood, and the ritual requires the separation of a young man from his mother. This induction into the warrior's group symbolizes the passage from the profane to the sacred worlds, which implies a death and a rebirth into a higher order of values. The ritualized initiation into manhood and its responsibilities is often followed by a physical trial designed to humiliate the flesh and fortify the spirit.[12]

Because the spiritual character of his adventure defies rational discourse, Lorenzo utilizes the language of metaphor. For example, he compares his vision to "une statue qui descendrait de son piédestal pour marcher parmi les hommes" (III, 3). Through this image (which is reaffirmed subsequently in Lorenzo's beheading of royal statues in the Constantine Arch), he defines himself vis-à-vis the gods and heroes of antiquity.[13] The descent of the statue, comparable to that of Orpheus, is enacted by Lorenzo, who descends symbolically from purity into vice, a hell of his own making, in order to gain immortality.[14] In a mimetic rivalry with the Duke (whose power as a ruler confers automatically the love/hate ambivalence of taboo), Lorenzo immerses himself in carnal pleasure. This perverted ritual of baptism continues his initiation into the sacred by humiliating the flesh through debauchery rather than denial. Political purpose is foresworn by Lorenzo ("Je ne voulais pas soulever les masses"), and he situates his struggle on the allegorical plane of individual combat with "la tyrannie vivante" (III, 3). The tension between his desire to be godlike and his debasing roles as procurer and court jester results in a psychopathological crisis of near madness which, as in the case of shaman priests, verifies mythically his supernatural election.[15]

Lorenzo is caught in "a double bind" between his exalted mission of gaining immortality in the persona of Florence and a blinding fascination for Alexandre.[16] Metaphysically, he is trapped in the initiatory, apprentice stage of the sacred, unable to forget his vision and unable to reverse the effects of his trial by the flesh: "si je pouvais revenir à la vertu, si mon apprentissage du vice pouvait s'évanouir, j'épargnerais peut-être ce conducteur de boeufs. Mais j'aime le vin, le jeu et les filles; comprends-tu cela?" (III, 3). Theoretically, the ambivalence of Lorenzo could have persisted indefinitely. His mimetic rivalry with Alexandre tends to self-perpetuate through the reinforcing of images reflected between cousins. Lacking the Marquise de Cibo's courage and Tebaldeo's humanity, the ability of Lorenzo to break out of an impasse between the dual fascination of an object and its obstacle remains questionable. Paradoxically, the reciprocal character of mimetic rivalry triggers a crisis which, releasing Lorenzo from his ambivalence, allows him to pursue the sacred through an act of violence.

The interaction of Lorenzo and Alexandre undergoes a reversal which casts an ironic light on the ensuing tragedy. For the first time within the dramatized intrigue, Alexandre takes the initiative in a love affair without the help of Lorenzo or someone else such as the Cardinal. The reversal in procedure (as set in the opening abduction scene) is possible within a mimetic rivalry, but the Duke chooses an object of passion repugnant to Lorenzo. Because Lorenzo identifies Catherine with Marie, calling her "la sœur de ma mère," he cannot reflect the lust of Alexandre (III, 3). To be sure, force of habit tempts Lorenzo to repeat his mimetic role as participant in seduction, but he cannot: "J'allais corrompre Catherine; je crois que je corromprais ma mère" (III, 3). His impotence reflects more than the taboo of incest prohibition, for Catherine's image is elevated to the region of pure ideals. She is pictured by Lorenzo as a mother figure nursing future generations, "une goutte de lait pur tombé du sein de Catherine, et qui aura nourri d'honnêtes enfants" (IV, 6). Hence, the ideal of Florence, the original object of his desire, regains its hold upon Lorenzo. The tension between his initiation into the sacred and his degrading friendship for Alexandre increases to the point of madness and can be released only in a ritual whose action bypasses the conscience to purge aggression through violence as in primitive times.[17]

During the rehearsal of Alexandre's assassination, Lorenzo attains a level of delirium capable of breaking through the civilized barrier of reason. His language transcends politics as he calls for a sacrificial murder which would include eating of human flesh: "Ouvre-lui les entrailles! Coupons-le par morceaux, et mangeons, mangeons!" (III, 1). References to blood, wedding, the sun, arid sterility, and baptism point to the unconscious reenactment of a primordial archetypal pattern of behavior. Pagan rituals required the periodic sacrifice of the king, the king's first son, and then a ram to assure continued fertility.[18] A similar process of transferring evil to an individual or to a group, the scapegoat victim, reappears in the holocaust of modern times.[19]

Lorenzo's murder of the Duke is so immersed in symbolism that the form of his crime overshadows and explains the act itself. First, a complex reversal of sexual roles occurs. Lorenzo takes the place of Catherine, who is supposed to be seduced by the Duke. Pretending to play his habitual role of *entremetteur,* Lorenzo breaks out of his mimetic reflection to identify with Catherine and, indirectly, with Florence. Second, Alexandre is murdered in bed. Symbolically, justice demands that the beast be sacrificed on the altar where so many maidens had yielded their virtue in tribute to his power. The association of nuptials and blood ("jour de sang, jour de mes noces") thus takes on a double meaning. Third, the sword thrust repeatedly into Alexandre assumes the ironic character of revenge against rule by military and sexual imposition. Fourth, Lorenzo experiences an exaltation of the senses and the spirit, a total release from the contingencies of time and place: "Que le vent du soir est doux et embaumé! comme les fleurs des prairies s'entr'ouvrent! O nature magnifique, ô éternel repos!"

(IV, 11). In the solitude of grandeur, Lorenzo seeks to make known the sacred by spreading chaos. His metaphysical aim of destruction for the purpose of awakening mankind to the truth of his evil places Lorenzo closer to the Caligula of Camus than to Shakespeare's Hamlet.[20]

Lorenzo's murder of the Duke fails politically as an assassination and metaphysically as a tragic sacrifice. The citizens of Florence and their foreign allies are not motivated to restore the republic. This failure can be explained mythically by the absence of a valid scapegoat ritual. In order to unite the community against a sacrificial victim, there must be a collective transfer of guilt and a violence carried out anonymously or in the name of widely spread beliefs.[21] To the contrary, Lorenzo imbues the murder with the symbolic significance of his private world and his personal search for immortality. At most, the murder of Alexandre provokes a political crisis which entails the reenactment of the origins of society in a hypothetical primordial murder.[22] Faced by the fearful prospect of open-ended violence, people opt for the reestablishment of order despite its injustice. Ironically, Lorenzo's murder by a mob carries overtones of scapegoat violence: "Ne voyez-vous pas tout ce monde? Le peuple s'est jeté sur lui. Dieu de miséricorde! on le pousse dans la lagune" (V, 6). The guilt of cowardice for not revolting is transferred to Lorenzo, whose death reestablishes public order.

The failure of Lorenzo is tied to the question of guilt for his death. Who is at fault? Lorenzo? Society? The gods? The bourgeoisie? From the standpoint of mimetic desire, Lorenzo is doomed to failure. Caught in the double fascination for an object and its obstacle, he cannot overcome pride to see his predicament. However, the success of the Marquise in regaining her freedom after degradation makes Lorenzo's status as a tragic hero problematic at best. He dies with his heroic pride apparently intact without understanding his failure and arrogantly defiant until the end. Hence, little catharsis is generated by his fall. Blame is shifted implicitly from a Romantic type of "innocent criminal" to an insensitive society wherein selfish merchants and corrupt politicians prevail in a "business as usual" manner. By identifying with the hero's moral superiority and the few university students who did revolt upon Alexandre's death, the reader is in his pride also left unchallenged and intact.

The Romantic myth of the "misunderstood genius" and his alienation from the ascending bourgeoisie of early nineteenth-century France would seem to blunt the attainment of tragic emotion in *Lorenzaccio*. Confronted by the materialistic values which denied the poet's mission, as dramatized in Vigny's *Chatterton* (1835), Romantics could illustrate national history or even play political roles like Lamartine, Balzac, Stendhal, and

Hugo in order to defend their dignity. In contrast, *Lorenzaccio* epitomizes the dangers of a Romantic idealism which confused a personal microcosm and a political macrocosm in the preference for martyrdom over collective action. Lorenzo wrongly identified evil as being primarily a metaphysical question rather than one of actions, and the anonymity of his murder gives the lie to a Romantic's absolute value of differentiation.

The incapacitating disillusionment of Musset's generation is often termed "le mal du siècle." As explained in the opening chapter to *La Confession d'un enfant du siècle* (1836), it arises from the collective despair of failure, that of the Napoleonic Empire and its foundation in the French Revolution. In a frantic attempt to fill the void of lost idealism and boredom, a generation of young men threw itself into libertinage, action without purpose, and materialistic ambition. Disbelief in politics, art, and human nature prevails in Musset's identification of evil as the only remaining source of inspiration: "Au lieu d'avoir l'enthousiasme du mal, nous n'eûmes que l'abnégation du bien; au lieu du désespoir, l'insensibilité."[23] For a generation of Frenchmen, despair is embodied in a historical figure of Renaissance Italy to create not only the most complex hero in the Romantic Theatre of France but also a timeless character whose conflicts are played out in a mythic dimension. The dramatization in *Lorenzaccio* of ritualized violence with heavy sexual overtones strikes chords of universal meaning which yield profound insights into the troubled mind and the origins of motivation.[24]

Notes

1. Musset, *Oeuvres complètes,* ed. Philippe Van Tieghem (Paris: Editions du Seuil, 1963), p. 348. All references to *Lorenzaccio* are taken from this edition and are indicated by act and scene.

2. See Herbert S. Gochberg, *Stage of Dreams* (Genève: Droz, 1967), p. 171, who characterizes the murder as being "completely without political consequence"; David Sices, *Theatre of Solitude* (Hanover, New Hampshire: The University Press of New England, 1974), p. 134, who calls it "a pure act of revenge"; Naomi Schor, "La Pèrodie: Superposition dans *Lorenzaccio,*" *Michigan Romance Studies*, 2 (Winter 1981), 73-86, who theorizes as to an attempted literary parricide of Shakespeare.

3. See Anne Ubersfeld, "Le Portrait du peintre," *RSH,* 42 (1977), 48.

4. See David Baguley, "Le Mythe de Glaucos: l'expression figurée dans *Lorenzaccio* de Musset," *RSH,* 41 (1976), 259-69.

5. See Bernard Masson, *Lorenzaccio ou la difficulté d'être* (Paris: Minard, 1962), pp. 5-19. His psy-

chological thesis is developed further in *Musset et le théâtre intérieur* (Paris: Minard, 1974) and *Musset et son double: Lecture de Lorenzaccio* (Paris: Minard, 1978).

6. The comparison is made by Lorenzo while questioning his motives for killing Alexandre: "Pourquoi cela? Le spectre de mon père me conduisait-il, comme Oreste, vers un nouvel Egisthe? M'avait-il offensé alors?" (III, 3).

7. In his application of Adler's concept of inferiority, Bernard Masson concentrates exclusively on Lorenzo.

8. See René Girard, *"To Double Business Bound": Essays on Literature, Mimesis, and Anthropology* (The Johns Hopkins University Press, 1978), p. 67. While emphasizing Freud's failure to understand the mimetic mechanism, he states, "The subject needs the desire of his rival to sustain and legitimize his own desire."

9. See René Girard, *"To Double Business Bound,"* whose theory on "the mimetic formation of 'neurotic' desire" holds that latent homosexuality and masochism denote a single phenomenon, the rival's predominance over the object and the fascination he exercises (p. 54). The implicit homosexuality in *Lorenzaccio* is verified by a discarded scene involving an audience given to Cellini by the Duke while in bed with Lorenzo. See Paul Dimoff, *La Genèse de Lorenzaccio,* reprint of 1936 edition (Paris: Société des textes français modernes, 1964), p. 169.

10. See Otto Rank, *The Myth of the Birth of the Hero,* ed. Philip Freund (New York: Vintage Books, 1936; rpt. 1964; translation of 1914 text in German), p. 273.

11. See Mircea Eliade, *Images and Symbols* (New York: Sheed & Ward, 1952), p. 75.

12. See Mircea Eliade, *Rites and Symbols of Initiation,* trans. from French (New York: Harper & Row, 1958), pp. 8-9, 96.

13. See David Baguley, "Le Mythe de Glaucos," who compares Lorenzo to the son of Sisyphus who threw himself into the sea to prove his immortality.

14. See Eliade, *Rites and Symbols of Initiation,* p. 125, who asserts: "By assuming such risks of suggested perilous descents to Hell, the Hero pursues the conquest of immortality."

15. See Eliade, *Rites and Symbols of Initiation,* pp. 90-101.

16. See René Girard, *Des choses cachées depuis la fondation du monde* (Paris: Grasset, 1978), p. 358.

17. For the origins of blood rituals, see James G. Frazer, *The Golden Bough. A Study in Magic and Religion* (New York: MacMillan, 1955), I, 329-41, and an opposing view in René Girard's *La Violence et le Sacré* (Paris: Grasset, 1972), pp. 36, 353, 396. For the origins of ritualized conduct, see the summary of research on the brain from an evolutionary perspective in Mary Long, "Ritual and Deceit," *Science Digest,* Nov./Dec. 1980, pp. 87-91, 121. The reptilian part of the brain, the R-complex, controls the unthinking behavior of violence, ritual, and imitation.

18. See Frazer, p. 340.

19. René Girard, *"To Double Business Bound,"* pp. 226-28.

20. The connection is made by Catherine Muder Huebert, "The Quest for Evil: *Lorenzaccio* and *Caligula," Romance Notes,* 18 (Fall 1977), 66-72.

21. René Girard, *"To Double Business Bound,"* pp. 226-28.

22. See Freud's hypothesis as to the slaying of God the Father as the original crime in *The Complete Psychological Works (1917-1919),* ed. James Strachey (London: Hogarth, 1955), 17:261. While Eliade sees the myth of the "murdered divinity" as the basis of ritual, Girard views the original act of violence as a historical reality. See *Myth and Reality* (New York: Harper & Row, 1963), p. 99 and *"To Double Business Bound,"* p. 208.

23. See Musset, *La Confession d'un enfant du siècle,* ed. M. Allem (Paris: Garnier, 1968), p. 16.

24. I should like to thank two colleagues, Professors Richard Grant of the University of Texas and Laurence Porter of the Michigan State University, for their close readings of this study.

Barbara T. Cooper (essay date winter 1986)

SOURCE: Cooper, Barbara T. "Breaking Up/Down/ Apart: 'L'Eclatement' as a Unifying Principle in Musset's *Lorenzaccio." Philological Quarterly* 65, no. 1 (winter 1986): 103-12.

[*In the following essay, Cooper explores the principle of fragmentation in* Lorenzaccio, *suggesting that the play is "a prototype of modern French drama."*]

In act 3, scene 3 of Musset's **Lorenzaccio,** Lorenzo de Médicis tries to convince Philippe Strozzi that his idealized, optimistic vision of life and humanity is the product of a (self-) delusion—an illusion.

> Ah! vous avez vécu tout seul, Philippe [Lorenzo tells his aged friend]. Pareil à un fanal éclatant, vous êtes resté immobile au bord de l'ocean des hommes, et vous

avez regardé dans les eaux la réflexion de votre propre lumière. . . . Mais moi, pendant ce temps-là, j'ai plongé; je me suis enfoncé dans cette mer houleuse de la vie; j'en ai parcouru toutes les profondeurs, couvert de ma cloche de verre; tandis que vous admiriez la surface, j'ai vu le débris des naufrages, les ossements et les Léviathans.[1]

Where Philippe sees a smooth, radiant surface, Lorenzo perceives a turbulent sea whose every wave can be counted. While Philippe stands immobile on the banks of the ocean of life, Lorenzo dives to its bottom and explores its murky depths which he finds littered with the debris of ships and bodies and inhabited by not one, but several sea monsters.[2] Lorenzo's vision, then, is of a world that has broken up, broken down, broken apart. Yet from the fragments of men and their ambitions that he has seen, Lorenzo creates a whole: a world view. In the pages that follow, I shall attempt to show how Musset's text, like Lorenzo's underwater vision, is composed of fragments that unite to form a whole. In the end, I hope to be able to demonstrate that the fragmentation of the text, the characters, and their fictional universe makes *Lorenzaccio* a forerunner of many of the twentieth century's most modern dramas.

In recent years, *Lorenzaccio* has been the object of intense critical scrutiny. Practitioners of structuralism, socio-criticism, and semiotics—to name only a few of the theoretical orientations represented in current Musset scholarship—have all contributed to our understanding of the play in some significant way.[3] Yet, as Bernard Masson already predicted in 1974:

> Quel que soit, en effet, l'abord choisi, il est frappant que la pièce nous offre à peu près toujours le même visage ambigu: d'une part, la rupture des scènes, les changements de lieux, l'entrecroisement des intrigues, la multiplicité des personnages figurent un univers de la discontinuité . . . mais, dans le même temps, il n'est pas une scène, pas un décor, pas une intrigue, pas un personnage . . . qui ne témoignent, en quelque façon, pour un univers continu, homogène, intelligible, clos sur lui-même et ordonné à sa propre nécessité.[4]

Masson, of course, was right. However one approaches *Lorenzaccio,* one is inevitably struck by the coherence, the underlying unity of this work whose surface is so obviously fragmented. Much has already been written about the temporal and spatial discontinuities and the plural, seemingly disjunctive plot line of the play. The failure of dialogue to convince, to communicate, and to inspire action has also received much attention. I shall not, therefore, repeat those demonstrations here (see note 3). Instead, I shall assume that the breakdown of language, the breaking up of the plot, and the breaking apart of time and space represent a deliberate attempt to create the appearance of a fragmented, disordered, chaotic universe. To go beyond that appearance, to reveal the fundamental unity of Musset's piece, however, one

must supplement these analyses of the play's physical components (plot, dialogue, time and space) with an examination of the political, social, and psychological dimensions of the text.

If Florence is a fragmented physical space—and the multiplicity of decors in Musset's drama suggests that it is—it is also a political entity that has broken apart. As the goldsmith tells the silk merchant in act 1, scene 2 (p. 339):

> Florence était encore (il n'y a pas longtemps de cela) une bonne maison bien bâtie; tous ces grands palais, qui sont les logements de nos grandes familles, en était les colonnes. Il n'y en avait pas une, de toutes ces colonnes, qui dépassât les autres d'un pouce; elles soutenaient à elles toutes une vieille voûte bien cimentée, et nous nous promenions là-dessous sans crainte d'une pierre sur la tête.

The harmony, the unity, indeed the very integrity of this political edifice has since been destroyed, the goldsmith goes on to tell his interlocutor. "L'empereur a commencé par entrer par *une assez bonne brèche* dans la susdite maison" and the once protective republican shelter has now become a towering citadel—"un gros pâté informe fait de boue et de crachat"—from which the "bâtard/butor" Alexandre de Médicis and his German troops sweep down on the people of Florence (all quotes p. 339; emphasis mine).[5] Alexandre exercises his illegitimate authority by means of brute, and brutal, force, the goldsmith claims. The city-home has been destroyed and pillaged. While the vandal Duke Alexandre "couche dans le lit de nos filles, boit nos bouteilles [et] casse nos vitres" (p. 339), many of those who once lived in peace, harmony, and safety have been forced to leave the erstwhile republic.

These exiled citizens—"pauvres bourgeois," "pères de famille chassés de leur patrie," republicans reduced to "des ombres silencieuses . . . sur la route" (1.6, p. 335)—stand as further evidence of the fragmentation of the body politic that was Florence. Dispersed to the four corners of Italy (Pisa, Rome, Venice, Ferrara), they curse the motherland from which they have been expelled ("adieu, mère stérile, qui n'as plus de lait pour tes enfants") and which they do not recognize as theirs ("adieu, Florence la bâtarde, spectre hideux de l'antique Florence"—both p. 357). Florence, of course, is no longer theirs. It is Alexandre's, or rather, it is the Holy Roman Emperor's and the Pope's, both of whom seek to manipulate their puppet Duke from behind the screen of Cardinal Cibo's red robes.

Were *Lorenzaccio* a play written in accord with the rules of neo-classical composition, one might expect all of the action to occur in the antechamber to the throne room of the Duke's palace. Even as late as 1825 when Alexandre Soumet wrote his neoclassical tragedy *Jeanne d'Arc,* unity of place, although expanded to encompass all of Rouen, nonetheless focussed on conventional sites of power—a prison, a hall of justice, a place of execution. *Lorenzaccio* does not so much break with this dramatic tradition as give shape to a more diffuse, more invasive type of political power that will not be confined or defined by its buildings. The tyranny and debauchery of Alexandre's reign are felt everywhere—in the streets, the marketplaces, the homes of the humble and the palaces of the grand, as well as the Duke's court—and thus all of these spaces are represented in the text. Once united by the ties that link all citizens of a republic to one another, these multiple sites now stand as mute testimony to the shattering, yet perversely binding power of oppression.[6]

Alexandre's rule shatters more than the political unity of Florence, however. It also breaks up families. Mothers sell their daughters (1.1, p. 334 and 3.3, p. 394) and wives sacrifice their honor (2.5, p. 372) to the lustful Duke and his procurers. (See, too, 3.5, p. 398 where Lorenzo's mother accuses her son of trying to prostitute his aunt Catherine and 4.5, p. 416 where Lorenzo declares: "J'allais corrompre Catherine; je crois que je corromprais ma mère, si mon cerveau le prenait à tâche. . . .") On those rare occasions when brothers seek to avenge the insults to their sisters' virtue, they are punished by exile (Maffio) or arrested (Pierre and Thomas Strozzi), thus leaving the family even more fragmented than before.

After his sons ("deux enfants de mes entrailles") have been taken off to prison, Philippe Strozzi assures Lorenzo in 3.3 (p. 389) that "On m'arracherait les bras et les jambes, que, comme le serpent, les morceaux mutilés de Philippe se rejoindraient et se lèveraient pour la vengeance." What his words express is not so much the intensity of his desire for vengeance as the sense of dismemberment, of radical separation from his children that he experiences as a result of their arrest.[7] Clearly, the vigor of his assertion is belied by his drooping posture (he has collapsed on a bench) and his repeated references to his advanced age. Nonetheless, Philippe does soon assemble the Strozzi clan of which he is both the patriarch and the head (see 3.7, p. 404: "Je suis le chef de la famille" which, in addition to its literal meaning, can be read as an extension of the body-family image first advanced in scene 3). He chides his family on its willingness to be dominated by the Médicis and asks the meaning of his sons' arrest. "Est-ce à dire qu'on abattra d'un coup de hache les nobles familles de Florence, et qu'on arrachera de la terre natale des racines aussi vieilles qu'elle?" (p. 404) Yet, when his daughter dies after having drunk poisoned wine, Philippe's spirit breaks down under the weight of his accumulated despair and suffering. Refusing to pursue the revenge he had called down on the Médicis only moments before, Philippe now tells his family:

Liberté, vengeance, voyez-vous, tout cela est beau; j'ai deux fils en prison, et voilà ma fille morte. Si je reste ici, tout va mourir autour de moi. L'important, c'est que je m'en aille, et que vous vous teniez tranquilles. . . . Je m'en vais de ce pas à Venise.

(3.8, p. 407)

Morally "abattu" and physically "arraché de la terre natale," Philippe will never again be able to reconstitute his once-whole being nor his family. Even after he has been reunited with his sons, Philippe discovers that his paternal authority has been eroded and that Pierre no longer treats him with filial respect. (See Pierre's outburst in 4.6, p. 419: "Vieillard obstiné! inexorable faiseur de sentences! vous serez cause de notre perte" which leads Philippe to reflect: "Ton jour est venu, Philippe! tout cela signifie que ton jour est venu.") Thus family solidarity has been fragmented as irremediably as political unity and freedom.

Like the Florentine republic and the Strozzi family, Lorenzo, too, breaks down under the weight of tyranny. He, however, is not so much the victim of Alexandre's rule (Lorenzo notes in 4.3, p. 411 that "[Alexandre] a fait du mal aux autres, mais il m'a fait du bien, du moins à sa manière") as of his own hubris (3.3, pp. 391-392) and ambition. "Cela est étrange," Lorenzo reflects, "et cependant pour cette action j'ai tout quitté; la seule pensée de ce meurtre a fait *tomber en poussière* les rêves de ma vie; je n'ai plus été qu'une *ruine,* dès que ce meurtre . . . s'est posé sur ma route et m'a appelé à lui" (p. 411, emphasis added). When he thinks back to the time when he loved ". . . les fleurs, les prairies et les sonnets de Pétrarque, le *spectre* de [s]a jeunesse se lève devant [lui] en frissonnant." When he thinks forward to the moment when he will kill Alexandre, ". . . [il a] peur de tirer l'épée flamboyante de l'archange, et de *tomber en cendres* sur [s]a proie" (both p. 411, emphasis added). Clearly, what Lorenzo is risking is both his moral and his physical integrity, the unity and whole(some)ness of his mind and body.

Scholars have already insisted on the importance of the many forms of Lorenzo's name used in Musset's play (see, for example, the articles by Bem and Thomas in note 3). What we need most to derive from their analyses is an awareness that the fragmented signifier Lo/renz/acci/o is not the reflection of a plurality of signifieds, but rather of an absent signified. To prove this point, one need only recall the frequency with which Lorenzo is decribed as "une ombre" (1.4, p. 347 and 3.3, p. 397), "une fumée malfaisante" (1.6, p. 355), "une vapeur infecte" (3.3, p. 390), "un spectre" (several places, but especially 2.4, p. 369), "un fantôme" (3.3, p. 395)—that is, a thing without substance. To give shape to his being, Lorenzo has had to put on "[un] masque de plâtre" (3.3, p. 393) and "[les] habits neufs de la confrérie du vice" (3.3, p 394; 4.5, p. 416). He has become an effigy—"un homme de cire," "une statue"—an empty shell. The uncertainty of Lorenzo's being and identity is further emphasized by the repeated use of interrogative and conditional sentences. In 2.4 (p. 370), for example, Lorenzo's uncle Bindo asks him: "Etes-vous des nôtres, ou n'en êtes-vous pas? voilà ce qu'il nous faut savoir." In 3.3 (p. 388), Philippe insists: ". . . Si la hideuse comédie que tu joues m'a trouvé impassible et fidèle spectateur, que l'homme sorte de l'histrion. Si tu as jamais été quelque chose d'honnête, sois-le aujourd'hui." In the end, Lorenzo is nothing more than his act (see 4.10, p. 426: "C'est toi, Renzo?—Seigneur, *n'en doutez pas*." Emphasis added.) It is an act without consequence and thus without duration; it is as ephemeral as it is unsubstantial. Having accomplished his goal, Lorenzo likewise disappears without a trace.

Lorenzo's death (5.6, p. 441) provides a reverse image of the assassination of the Duke. It is an image marked by dispersal. Night becomes day; a closed space is replaced by an open space; a known and seen assassin is replaced by one who is unknown and unseen; and the bed, a place of stillness and repose, is replaced by the lagoon, a place of movement and flux. What is more, Lorenzo's wounds and his watery grave point to his physical disintegration. Set upon by a vicious populace ("des Léviathans"?), Lorenzo is shoved into the lagoon where his body will no doubt be transformed into an "ossement," the anonymous debris of his all too human ambition.

Whereas earlier studies of Musset's play have emphasized the fragmentation of time, space, and the plot line, or the divorce between word and deed, saying and doing, I have tried to show here how the principle of "l'éclatement"—of breaking up/down/apart—operates in the spheres of politics, society, and psychology, on the levels of theme, characterization, and image. One could, of course, multiply the examples given here. A study of the notion of legitimacy would reveal the links among family, state, and psyche that underlie the passages cited above and at the same time would extend our examination of the images of fragmentation even further. Thus when Lorenzo trembles at the sight of a sword in 1.4, the Duke mockingly chides him: "Fi donc! tu fais honte au nom des Médicis. Je ne suis qu'un *bâtard*, et je le porterais mieux que toi, qui es *légitime*?" (p. 348, emphasis added). Alexandre's illegitimacy is more than a fact of his birth, however. "Un bâtard, une moitié de Médicis," as the goldsmith describes him in 1.2 (p. 339), Alexandre is also the illegitimate ruler of Florence. Imposed on the populace by the Emperor and the Pope, he is neither the rightful heir to the throne nor the freely-elected (or consented) choice of "les grandes familles." Lorenzo, on the other hand, might properly have governed the city. "Sa naissance ne l'appelait-elle pas au trône? . . . Ne devais-je pas m'attendre à cela?"

asks his mother (1.6, p. 355). But if Lorenzo's youthful beauty and noble ambitions once led Marie Soderini to kiss her son on the forehead "en pensant au *père* de la patrie," she now judges that ". . . il fait tourner à un infâme usage jusqu'à la glorieuse mémoire de ses *aïeux*" (1.6, pp. 354 and 355; emphasis added). Agitated and uncertain as he prepares to assassinate his cousin Alexandre (4.3, p. 411), Lorenzo himself questions the legitimacy of his act ("Que m'avait fait cet homme?"), his motivation ("Le spectre de mon père me conduisait-il, comme Oreste, vers un nouvel Egiste?"), his birth and his humanity ("De quel tigre a rêvé ma mère enceinte de moi? . . . De quelles entrailles fauves, de quels velus embrassements suis-je donc sorti?").[8] The turmoil of his mind is reflected in the repeated use of interrogative sentences and the breakdown of logical progression from one thought to the next. Like these thoughts, illegitimacy is marked by a failure, a breakdown of the principles of succession. It will be recalled that Musset's contemporaries considered this very lack of logical, temporal, and physical succession to be the principal defect of the play. By now, however, it should be obvious that the underlying similarities between the "forme" and the "fond" of the text are in fact the primary source of its aesthetic unity. Having said that, it is time to turn our attention to the broader issue posed by Musset's pervasive use of the themes and techniques of "l'éclatement," that is, to the question of the play's modernity.

In Part 2, chapter 5 of his book *Théâtre et pré-cinéma* (Paris: Nizet, 1978), Hassan El Nouty suggested that **Lorenzaccio,** however disconcerting it might have been for Musset's contemporaries, appeals to the modern reader/viewer because of its cinematographic qualities. Professor El Nouty is right, of course. The cutting and editing techniques, the varied camera angles and distances that are the stock in trade of contemporary filmmakers can all be found in Musset's play. Nonetheless, if we are to discover the connections between **Lorenzaccio** and the modern French theater, we might do well to look beyond these purely technical devices and examine the way Musset's armchair drama casts its "hero" into the world.

Certainly, Musset's alienated, corrupt hero is a product of his age and of the influence of English and German romanticism on his creator. Yet it is also true that Lorenzo resembles those twentieth-century protagonists who have lost touch with or become disconnected from a collectivity (humanity) which they frequently despise. Like them, Lorenzo is both victimizer and victim, director and dupe of the absurdity of existence, the irrationality of evil. His radical Otherness, like theirs, is underscored by logical discontinuities, verbal incongruities, and spatial and temporal disjunctions. More than anything else, perhaps, it is this "éclatement," this breakdown of causality and personality, of communica-

tion and community that makes *Lorenzaccio* a prototype of modern French drama.

In *L'Ecole du spectateur* (Paris: Editions sociales,
1981), Anne Ubersfeld has written at length about the
discontinuities that mark the contemporary theater. It
seems appropriate, then, to turn to her for a salutary
word of caution before arriving at a conclusion. Ubersfeld notes (p. 302) that

> Dans tous les cas la discontinuité n'a pas toujours le
> même sens ou la même fonction; elle peut: a) donner
> des images de la dislocation du monde et avoir sur ce
> point valeur et fonctionnement référentiel; b) montrer
> chez l'énonciateur la destruction (subjective) d'une vue
> cohérente du monde, l'impossibilité de penser le monde
> et surtout de le penser comme représentable; c) elle
> peut marquer le dégagement par rapport à un *sujet* cen-
> tralisé, que ce sujet soit l'énonciateur, le personnage ou
> le comédien.

Ubersfeld's distinctions are pertinent to our discussion
of the modernity of *Lorenzaccio* precisely because they
allow us to perceive the continuities and discontinuities
that mark the *Weltanschauung* of nineteenth- and
twentieth-century French dramatists. Thus, although
Musset's world may have been different from that of,
say, Artaud, Ionesco, or Beckett, one can, I think, defend the thesis that *Lorenzaccio,* like their works, stands
in part as a referential reflection of the dislocations each
dramatist observed in the world around him. (Our readings of Musset's play and, for example, of *Le Rhi-
nocéros* would be as much impoverished by ignoring
their referential allusions as by limiting our interpretations of those texts to ideas supported by historical
analogies.)

Similarly, Musset may be seen as precursor of modern
drama to the extent that his play shows signs of a nascent "dégagement par rapport à un *sujet* centralisé"
(emphasis in the original quote, cited above). To be
sure, in typical early nineteenth-century fashion, Lorenzaccio gives his name to Musset's piece. Yet Lorenzo is
neither the sole nor always the central subject of the
drama. As Atle Kittang and others have convincingly
shown (note 3, *supra*), Lorenzo shares the actantial role
of subject with other protagonists in the play just as, on
a thematic level, he shares the title of subject with the
city of Florence. Musset, however, does not go as far as
his twentieth-century counterparts in exploring the problems of subjective unity or unity of subject. However
much his work forecasts our modern preoccupations
with these problems, it is nonetheless true that Musset's
views are firmly rooted in the romantic literature, philosophy, and psychology of his age.

It is doubtless this same romantic vision of the universe
that keeps Musset from sharing twentieth-century dramatists' belief that the world is no longer a coherent

whole, that it is impossible "de penser le monde et
surtout de le penser représentable" (see quote above).
On the contrary, as I argued at the very beginning of
this study and as I hope to have shown in the pages that
followed, the fragmentation that marks Musset's text
does not so much render the dramatized world unrepre-
sentable as differently representable—or as the French
might say, "représentable autrement." Just as Lorenzo
constructed a unified vision of the world from the underwater debris he poetically equated with humanity
and human ambitions, so, too, has Musset created a
unified fiction from his fragmented text. As Ubersfeld
writes in *L'Ecole du spectateur*: "A travers le discon-
tinu, il y a toujours quelque part le fil de la
continuité . . ."(p. 302). To my mind, her statement at
once describes Musset's play and its relation to modern
French drama.

Notes

1. Alfred De Musset, *Théâtre 1,* Texte intégral (Paris:
   Garnier-Flammarion, 1964), 3.3, p. 393. Further
   references to *Lorenzaccio* will be noted in my
   text. For a recent study of the image of the ship-
   wreck in the nineteenth century, see ch. 10: "Perils of the Deep" in Martin Meisel, *Realizations:
   Narrative, Pictorial, and Theatrical Arts in
   Nineteenth-Century England.* (Princeton U. Press,
   1983).

2. In her article "Révolution et topique de la cité:
   Lorenzaccio," *Littérature* 24 (1976): 49, Anne
   Ubersfeld identifies the Leviathan not with the
   Biblical monster, but with its Hobbesean descen-
   dant, "L'Etat qu'il définit comme le pouvoir de
   créer et de *casser* toute loi." (This definition of
   Hobbes's Leviathan is not Ubersfeld's but that of
   Le Petit Larousse illustré [Paris: Larousse, 1982],
   p. 1466 and the emphasis is mine.) As will be
   seen, I share her conviction.

3. It would be impossible to list all the recent studies
   of *Lorenzaccio* here. Some of the most significant
   for this examination of Musset's play include
   Jeanne Bem, "*Lorenzaccio* entre l'Histoire et le
   fantasme," *Poétique* 11, no. 44 (1980): 451-61;
   Claude Duchet, "Théâtre et sociocritique: La Crise
   de la parole dans deux pièces de Musset," pp.
   147-56 in Duchet et al. eds., *Sociocritique* (Paris:
   Nathan, 1979); Atle Kittang, "Action et langage
   dans *Lorenzaccio* d'Alfred Musset," *Revue ro-
   mane* 10, no. 1 (1975): 33-50; Bernard Masson,
   Musset et le théâtre intérieur (Paris: Colin, 1974);
   Walter Moser, "*Lorenzaccio*: le Carnaval et le Cardinal," *Romantisme* 19 (1978): 94-108; Jean-
   Jacques Thomas, "Les Maîtres-mots de Musset:
   Peuple et *pouvoir* dans *Lorenzaccio,*" pp. 179-96
   in Michel Glatigny and Jacques Guilhaumou, eds.,
   Peuple et pouvoir: Etudes de léxicologie politique

(Lille: Presses Universitaires de Lille, 1981); Anne Ubersfeld, "Le Portrait du peintre," *Revue des sciences humaines* no. 165 (1977): 39-48 and "Le Moi-statue ou le discours auto-réflexif chez Musset," pp. 63-79 in *Journées d'études sur Alfred de Musset* (Clermont-Ferrand: SER Faculté de lettres/ Société des Etudes Romantiques, 1978).

4. In *Musset et le théâtre intérieur,* p. 122.

5. Lorenzo's uncle Bindo Altoviti will take up this image again when he declares in 2.4 (p. 370): "Toutes les grandes familles voient bien que le despotisme des Médicis n'est ni juste ni tolérable. De quel droit laisserions-nous s'élever paisiblement cette maison orgueilleuse sur les *ruines* de nos privilèges?" (emphasis added). On a more personal level, Lorenzo's mother Marie compares her dreams to a fairy palace that has turned into a dilapidated shack. She complains in 1.6 (p. 355): "Cela est trop cruel d'avoir vécu dans un palais de fées, où murmuraient les cantiques des anges, de s'y être endormie, bercée par son fils, et de se réveiller dans une *masure* ensanglantée, pleine de *débris* d'orgie et de *restes* humains, dans les bras d'un *spectre* hideux qui vous tue en vous appelant encore du nom mère" (emphasis added).

6. A similar argument can be made regarding unity of time. Time can be regulated and harmonious like the workings of a benevolent government or it can be as inexorable and unpredictable as tyranny.

7. Writing about a certain type of modern literature in an article entitled "La Déliaison," (*Littérature* 3 [1971]: 48), André Green has suggested that ". . . il s'agit moins de représenter le corps que de le faire vivre en éclats, fragmentés et morcelés." It seems to me that this is precisely the effect achieved by Philippe's words.

8. For a recent analysis of the psychological dimension of the play and the theme of the absent father, see Jules Bedner, "*Lorenzaccio* ou Oedipe à Florence," *Neophilologus* 67, no. 1 (1983): 42-54 and Naomi Schor, "La Pèrodie: Superposition dans *Lorenzaccio*," pp. 73-86 in Ross Chambers, ed., *Discours et pouvoir* (Dept. of Romance Langs., U. of Michigan, 1982).

Anthony Zielonka (essay date fall-winter 1986-87)

SOURCE: Zielonka, Anthony. "Images of the Poet in Musset's *Le Poèt déchu.*" *Nineteenth-Century French Studies* 15, nos. 1-2 (fall-winter 1986-87): 87-93.

[*In the following essay, Zielonka centers on distinctions Musset makes between the qualities of a poet and those of a prose writer in his unfinished novel* Le poète déchu.]

Musset est quatorze fois exécrable pour nous, générations douloureuses et prises de visions,—que sa paresse d'ange a insultées! O les contes et les proverbes fadasses! ô les nuits! ô Rolla, ô Namouna, ô la Coupe! tout est français, c'est-à-dire haïssable au suprême degré; [. . .] Musset n'a rien su faire: il y avait des visions derrière la gaze des rideaux: il a fermé les yeux. Français, panadif, traîné de l'estaminet au pupitre de collège, le beau mort est mort, et, désormais, ne nous donnons même plus la peine de le réveiller par nos abominations!![1]

Alfred de Musset is an author who is studied predominantly as a writer of plays (his greatest work being *Lorenzaccio*), and, to a lesser degree, of poetry. Of his prose writings only the major novel *La Confession d'un enfant du siècle* has attracted anything like the amount of critical attention that it deserves. Ever since the virulent attacks that were made on Musset's reputation by the Symbolists, of which the passage from Rimbaud's second "Lettre du Voyant," quoted above, is a prime example, the importance of Musset as a poet and as a writer who reflected seriously on the function and purpose of poetry has tended to be undervalued.

The subject of the present article, *Le Poète déchu,* is a fascinating though brief and fragmentary work of fiction by Musset, which has not hitherto been commented upon in any detail by critics of his writings.[2] The principal interest of this work does not lie in its narrative or plot. In many respects the story is made up of faint echoes of the plot of *La Confession d'un enfant du siècle.* It is, however, an interesting text, especially when considered from an autobiographical point of view. Musset, who was prompted by the death of his father in 1832 to write a large number of works which might easily be published, in order to support himself and his family, here expresses his frustration with this state of affairs. Given the high ideal that he had set himself as a poet, he shows why he cannot be satisfied with his self-imposed role as a writer of prose fiction which is destined for a popular readership.[3]

The most interesting aspect of *Le Poète déchu,* however, is that it gives a clear insight into Musset's vision of what a genuine and sincere poet really is or should be. The main categories of images by which a poet may be defined appear here. Firstly, there are many evocations of the inauthentic and ultimately worthless poet that the narrator considers himself to have been in the past, in spite of the popularity that he had once enjoyed. Secondly, Musset describes the kind of poet that the narrator has struggled to become. He aims to make use of his personal experience and of the problems that he has encountered to achieve and express a fully mature appreciation of the world and of life in general.

The discussion of the differences between the poet and the writer of prose, in the concluding section of *Le Poète déchu,* partly accounts for the presence in most of Musset's writings of a division or opposition, as his own personality predisposed him, at different times, to write poetry and fictional, dramatic or critical prose.[4] Speaking, here, through the voice of his first-person narrator, Musset seems to regret that he is himself unable to live up to his high ideal, a fact which is underlined by the title that he eventually chose to give to his work.[5]

The aim of this article is to analyze the various images of the poet and the ideas concerning his role and development that are presented in *Le Poète déchu.* The first-person narrative begins with a declaration of purpose which is reminiscent of the opening of *La Confession.* The narrator speaks of the liberating and healing effects that his work will have: "Je porte un fardeau qui m'écrase, en vous en parlant, je le secoue avant de m'en délivrer pour toujours" (306). This is immediately followed by a declaration of regret that, judged by his own standards, he cannot claim to be a true poet. Interestingly, Musset comments on the paradoxical fact that he is writing about poetry in prose—in a literary form that he despises. Instead of standing on the edge of a cliff, as Byron might have done: "c'est dans une chambre d'auberge qu'il me convient de parler; et il est juste que je me serve d'un langage que je méprise, d'un grossier instrument sans cordes dont abuse le premier venu" (306).

He accepts that—"C'est mon métier de parler en prose [. . .]" (306)—and decides to use this inferior form to express his dissatisfactions. He uses several striking images to evoke this enterprise: "Il me plaît même qu'il en soit ainsi; j'aime à revêtir d'un haillon le triste roman qui fut mon histoire, à jeter dans le coin d'une masure le tronçon d'épée brisé dans mon cœur" (306).

In the second section,[6] the narrator voices his dislike of the type of successful poet that he was in his youth. He realizes that in the first phase of his career, when he wrote verse with great ease and merely for the pleasure of doing so, he was, in fact, an egotistic, naïve and inauthentic poet:

> [. . .] mes premiers essais réussirent. Cependant, je ne songeai pas à me livrer à la poésie qui ne me semblait qu'un passe-temps. [. . .] je venais à Paris presque tous les jours et je m'amusais à chercher des rimes en marchant au bord de la rivière.
>
> (307)

Having led an easy life of vain pursuits and pleasure, he sees that he could create no genuine poetry but only what he calls "cette toile d'araignée" (308). The narrator believes that since he had still not felt any genuine emotion and had no ideas to express, his writing of poetry was simply an empty game. This view of the naïve and false poet who participates in the fashionable poetic controversies of the Romantic movement is revealed in an extended simile of a player of dominoes:

> [. . .] je m'avisai de jouer avec les mots, et de me faire des hochets de ces symboles qui représentent tout, les passions, les êtres et les choses. Je les retournais au hasard comme un étudiant désœuvré remue des dominos sur la table d'un café; je les jetais à croix ou pile pour les entendre résonner; le plus sonore et le plus bizarre, le plus nouveau surtout, était le meilleur; [. . .]
>
> (309)

He regards his early poetic activities with a considerable degree of irony: "amoureux fou d'un vers baroque, d'une phrase gothique, d'un sonnet gaulois, criant qu'on avait pêché une perle . . ." (310).

It is the intense emotional suffering that he experiences after the unhappy ending of his love affair, when the woman he loves leaves him, that provokes a radical change in his outlook. During the temporary isolation which he imposes on himself after this crisis he reflects, for the first time, on the meaning of his life. He begins to view life much more seriously than he used to and describes the change in his behaviour as a stage in the process of growing up. In order to be a poet he must first become a mature human being: "On ne devient pas homme en un jour" (311).

The next step that he takes towards becoming a genuine poet is to realize the full extent of the potential and power of the human mind, of the capacity of human emotions and of the value of experience. He had not previously noticed that the human mind and soul is a kind of perfect musical instrument:

> N'en doutez pas, c'est une chose divine que cette étincelle fugitive enfermée sous ce crâne chétif. Vous admirez un bon instrument, un piano d'Erard, un violon de Stradivarius, grand Dieu! et qu'est-ce donc que l'âme humaine? Jamais, depuis trente ans que j'existe, je n'ai usé aussi librement que je l'aurais voulu de mes facultés; jamais je n'ai été tout à fait moi-même qu'en silence. Je n'ai encore entendu que les premiers accents de la mélodie qui est peut-être en moi. Cet instrument va bientôt tomber en poussière; je n'ai pu que l'accorder, mais avec délices.
>
> (312)

The narrator gives an example of the enhanced sensitivity and increased emotional capacity that he now had for the first time and which he believes are the attributes of a true poet. He focuses on the experience of the joyful anticipation of returning to the object of one's love, whether this be one's country, a woman, a friend, a room, or even, quite simply, a bed. The true poet experiences such an emotion of unrestrained joy not merely in respect of one individual or object, but of the whole world:

> Supposons que vous revenez d'un voyage, que vous rentrez dans Paris, que vous êtes à la barrière, arrêté par l'octroi. Si vous êtes capable d'une émotion, ne

sentez-vous pas quelque plaisir, quelque impatience, en pensant que vous allez retrouver cette maison, cette chambre? Le cœur ne vous bat-il pas en tournant la rue, en approchant, en arrivant enfin? Eh bien! ce plaisir naturel, mais vulgaire, cette impatience du lit et de la table que vous sentez pour ce qui vous est connu et familier, supposez maintenant que vous l'éprouvez pour tout ce qui existe, noble ou grossier, connu ou nouveau; supposez que votre vie est un voyage continuel, que chaque barrière est votre frontière, chaque auberge votre maison, que, sur chaque seuil, vos enfants vous attendent, que dans chaque lit est votre femme; vous croyez peut-être que j'exagère; non, c'est ainsi qu'est le poète; c'est ainsi que j'étais à vingt ans!

(312)

He refers to his poetic capacity as a flower, which he has carefully cultivated and watered (313). It is at this point in his story, just as he is ready to express his ideas in poetry, that his father dies and that he is obliged to write the popular novels which enable him financially to support his family. He accepts the constraints of what he refers to as "ce travail forcé" (314), with extreme reluctance. As a poet, he finds the idea of writing a fixed number of pages a day and of working to a deadline very stifling.

The realization that he has been misusing his talents by doing such work occurs when he compares the novels that he has been writing, the main theme of which is love, with the Francesca da Rimini episode in Dante's *Inferno*. After re-reading this passage, which consists of a mere twenty-five lines, he is moved to tears. The poetic genius of Dante is confirmed by the fact that a reader can still react to his poem in this way after five centuries. This thought prompts Musset's narrator to say that a poet should not misuse the fruits of his experience by writing sterile literature which he does not feel deeply inspired to write. He should utilize his personal experience of life to give his work meaning, inspiration and dynamism. The image of the tear-drop is developed further:

C'est donc l'habitude du chagrin et du travail, c'est donc l'infortune, sinon la misère, qui fait jaillir la source; et qu'une goutte en reste, c'est assez, n'est-ce pas? Et si, au lieu de cela, travail et chagrin, misère et habitude se réunissent pour dessécher la source, pour dégrader l'homme, l'amoindrir et l'user, cette goutte qui fût peut-être tombée, cette larme, que deviendra-t-elle? Elle coulera sur le carreau pendant que l'homme tient sa tête entre ses mains et pleure de rage et de fatigue.

(316)

In the eighth and final section of the text, Musset discusses the differences that separate a poet from a writer of prose. According to Musset, the poet uses rhyme and, since he writes in verse, a more demanding form than prose, he must have an even more precise idea of what he wants to say than the prose-writer. He must also spend a longer time perfecting his writings and adapting his ideas to suit the literary form that is being employed. The art of the poet consists, to a large degree, in concentrating the various aspects of an idea into as small a space as possible:

Ces corollaires sont plus ou moins bons, brillants, justes, séduisants; ils détournent, ramènent, expliquent, enchantent; pour le prosateur, ce sont des veines, des minerais; pour le poète, les reflets d'un prisme. Il faut au poète le jet de l'âme, l'idée mère; [. . .]

(316)

Poetry is the art of condensing all the facets of a subject in such a way that they may stimulate the reader's imagination: "Dans tout vers remarquable d'un vrai poète, il y a deux ou trois fois plus que ce qui est dit; c'est au lecteur à suppléer le reste, selon ses idées, sa force, ses goûts" (316-317).

Poetry is also essentially musical. Musicality and melody are present in poetry rather than in prose: "la prose n'a pas de rythme déterminé, et sans le rythme, la mélodie n'existe pas" (317). The fundamental principles of poetry are: "le rythme et la mesure" (317). The prose-writer must simply write what he thinks. As the following image makes clear, he does not need to stress the musical or melodic quality of what he writes: "Que dirait-on d'un homme qui, ayant une affaire pressée, s'imposerait l'obligation de ne marcher dans les rues qu'en faisant des pas de bourrée comme un danseur?" (317).

There is, according to Musset, a clear contrast between writers of prose and poets, and, although he claims that he does not wish to place the poet above the prose-writer or to think of one as a horseman and of the other as a pedestrian (317), he does refer to them as two different species:

Je veux dire que ce sont deux natures entièrement différentes, presque opposées et anti-pathiques l'une à l'autre. [. . .] Le romancier, l'écrivain dramatique, le moraliste, l'historien, le philosophe voient les rapports des choses; le poète en saisit l'essence.

(317-318)

The poet has a natural and intuitive response to the essentials of life, and his mind is able to transcend the contingent affairs of the world: "Son génie, purement natif, cherche en tout les forces natives; sa pensée est une source qui sort de terre. [. . .] il ne connaît qu'un homme, celui de tous les temps" (318).

Musset clearly expresses the belief that poets can come to a closer appreciation of the essential mysteries of life than prose-writers. Goethe is cited as an example of a true poet who could contemplate a pebble for hours and who could see the divine aspects that exist within the simplest of objects (318).

Le Poète déchu testifies to Musset's obsessive and sincere search for genuine principles of poetry. The originality of his enterprise is stressed by Philippe Van Tieghem, who regrets that Musset did not go on to write poems of his own in accordance with the principles that he set out in this text:

> En somme, selon ces pages, écrites vers 1839, le poète tel que le conçoit Musset est fort semblable au "voyant" de Rimbaud. [. . .] Il [Musset] a dépassé de bien loin les conceptions poétiques qui étaient les siennes autour de 1830 et celles des romantiques plus âgés qui étaient encore en pleine période de création. Mais sa conception ne s'est présentée à lui qu'à une époque où sa verve créatrice première était tarie et où sa force nerveuse n'était plus assez grande pour soutenir l'effort intense que demande chez le poète la poésie qu'il imaginait alors.[7]

As one reads the last lines of Musset's detailed and fascinating poetic program, which projects an image of a poet who can establish a wholly dynamic and intuitive relationship with life, one cannot but conclude that Rimbaud's judgement of Musset's achievement was unjustifiably negative:

> Regarder, sentir, exprimer, voilà sa vie; tout lui parle, il cause avec un brin d'herbe; dans tous les contours qui frappent ses yeux, même dans les plus difformes, il puise et nourrit incessamment l'amour de la suprême beauté; dans tous les sentiments qu'il éprouve, dans toutes les actions dont il est témoin, il cherche la vérité éternelle. Tel il est né, tel il meurt, dans sa simplicité première; arrivé au terme de sa gloire, le dernier regard qu'il jette sur ce monde est encore celui d'un enfant.

(318)

Notes

1. Arthur Rimbaud, *Œuvres complètes,* ed. A. Adam (Paris: Gallimard, Bibliothèque de la Pléiade, 1972) 253 (letter to Paul Demeny, 15 May 1871).

2. References are to the Pléiade edition of the *Œuvres complètes en prose* (Paris: Gallimard, 1971). *Le Poète déchu* appears on 306-318 of this edition. See also the notes by M. Allem and P. Courant and the variants (1093-1103). Written in 1839, *Le Poète déchu* is an incomplete work which remained a series of eight unpublished fragments until Paul de Musset published one section (VIII) in February 1859, in *Le Magasin de Librairie.* He subsequently included four of the remaining parts in his *Biographie d'Alfred de Musset.* For the full history of the text's publication, see the note on 1095. For a valuable and recent re-assessment of the poetic achievement of Musset, see Patricia J.

Siegel's article "Musset, protagoniste de l'avenir," *Nineteenth-Century French Studies,* 4 (1975-1976): 220-232.

3. See the notes in the Pléiade edition for a summary of the autobiographical elements present in the text. Parallels include: the subjects studied by Musset, his reactions to the unhappy ending of his love affair with George Sand and to the death of his father. Musset evidently shared the feelings that are expressed by the poet: "Un jour, il conçut la pensée de chercher un remède à sa souffrance dans sa souffrance même, en faisant le récit des tortures d'un poète condamné par la nécessité à un travail qu'il méprise. Il écrivit sur ce sujet quarante pages d'un pathétisme déchirant, et qui surpassait en éloquence *la Confession d'un enfant du siècle* elle-même. [. . .] Je ne vois dans aucune littérature un équivalent de cette œuvre étrange" (Paul de Musset, quoted on 1094).

4. The theme of the duality of the self or of the divided personality was one of Musset's most fundamental preoccupations. It appears, notably, in *Lorenzaccio, La Confession* and "La Nuit de décembre."

5. Musset was initially undecided about whether to call the work *Le Rocher de Sisyphe* or *Le Poète déchu.* See the note on 1094.

6. It is not possible to ascertain whether the numbering and ordering of the sections were made by Musset himself. See 1095 of the Pléiade edition.

7. Philippe Van Tieghem, *Musset,* new ed. (Paris: Hatier, 1969) 121.

Donald Gamble (essay date spring-summer 1987)

SOURCE: Gamble, Donald. "Developing Drama: The Earliest *contes en vers* of Alfred de Musset." *Dalhousie French Studies* 12 (spring-summer 1987): 3-18.

[*In the following essay, Gamble evaluates the narrative and dramatic structure of Musset's early verse works "Don Paez," "Portia," and "Les marrons du feu," published collectively as* Contes d'Espagne et d'Italie *in 1830.*]

Les Contes d'Espagne et d'Italie, Musset's first collection of verse, was completed in late 1829 and published in January, 1830. With the exception of an accomplished sonnet, ten *chansons* still found in anthologies and **"Mardoche,"** a long poem in the manner of Byron expressly written to round out the volume, the collection contains three *contes en vers*: **"Portia," "Don Paez"** and **"Les Marrons du feu."** Characterised as they are by intrigue, violent passion and Mediterranean exoticism, these three poems clearly reflect the literary fashions of their time; that is probably a reason why they are so rarely read in our own, and still less often discussed. As is frequently the case, however, this first collection of the author reveals many of the themes and attitudes that would inform much of his later work; and it is no less significant for questions of style: in the pages that follow I hope to show that it was with these early poems that Musset began his career as a dramatist, and that the origins of his highly individualistic theatrical technique are to be found not in the first volume of *Un Spectacle dans un fauteuil,* but in the three *contes en vers* of *Les Contes d'Espagne et d'Italie.*

The theatricality of the collection was noted even by some of Musset's first critics,[1] and its preface abounds with references to drama and the theatre:

> Il est certain que la plupart de nos anciennes pièces de théâtre, à défaut de grands acteurs, demeurent sans intérêt; Molière seul, inimitable, est resté amusant.
>
> Le moule de Racine a été brisé; c'est là le principal grief: car, pour cet adultère tant discuté du fou et du sérieux, il nous est familier: les règles de la trinité, de l'unité, établies par Aristote, ont été outrepassées. En un mot, les chastes Muses ont été, je crois, violées.
>
> (813)[2]

Even a preface is, according to the young author, "presque toujours, sinon une histoire ou une théorie, une espèce de salutation théâtrale" (813). That modern critics have devoted so little attention to the dramatic aspects of these *contes* is, therefore, all the more surprising. The tendency to dialogue in particular has been mentioned, however briefly; but this is only one aspect of the theatricality of these poems; others are equally noteworthy: the settings, or tableaux, into which the dialogues are fitted, the acute psychological insight which will constitute a major strength of subsequent dramatic characters, the generally rhetorical and theatrical nature of the language and, finally, the particular role of the narrative voice. Because **"Don Paez"** and **"Portia"** illustrate the evolution to a dramatic form, while **"Les Marrons du feu"** is in effect already a play, it is the first two *contes en vers* in particular which will be examined here, although **"Les Marrons du feu"** will also be considered toward the conclusion.

One of the most interesting aspects of **"Don Paez"** and **"Portia"** with regard to Musset's later dramatic production is to be found in what may be termed the tableaux. Originally intended as mere background description to support the main themes in accordance with the Cénacle's advocation of the picturesque, these details in fact remain quite separate from the rest of the narration and are much less subordinate to the action that was no doubt first intended. Although too lengthy and too fre-

quent—there are, on balance, two per canto—to be quoted in their entirety here, these passages are easily located, often as distinct units, within the body of each poem.

The first tableau in **"Don Paez"** comes just after the narrator's introduction, beginning "Un mardi, cet été . . ." and continues for twenty-one lines to: "En y regardant bien, frère, vous auriez pu, / Dans l'ombre transparente, entrevoir un pied nu" (48). Further glimpses of the beautiful Juana's dwelling and a view of the lovers themselves are provided in the same division, in the fourteen and one-half lines from: "Cependant les rideaux, autour d'elle tremblant, / La laissaient voir pâmée aux bras de son galant" (48). The second canto starts with a scene, thirty-two lines long, of Don Paez walking about the battlements while the other soldiers pass their night in camp gambling and telling tales (49). A second tableau vividly depicts the attitudes of Don Paez and his rival Don Etur as they begin their fight to the death over the capricious Juana; it continues for twenty-six lines from: "Comme on voit dans l'été, sur les herbes fauchées, / Deux louves, remuant les feuilles desséchées, / S'arrêter face à face . . ." (50). The first fifteen lines of the third canto are devoted to a description of the house of the sorceress Belisa (50); soon after, its interior and Belisa herself are portrayed in the lines starting "Point de lit au dedans," and ending just before the narration breaks into formal dialogue (50/51). The last tableau of this *conte* is found in the twenty lines at the beginning of the fourth canto: Juana eagerly prepares herself to receive Don Paez as Madrid is transformed by the magic of the night (52).

With no narrative introduction, **"Portia"** is begun with a tableau, similar in its organisation to the first one in **"Don Paez:"** eleven and one-half lines introduce two of the three main characters, the noble Onorio Luigi and his young wife Portia, and establish a time and setting (65). Another, briefer descriptive passage of approximately eight lines from "Cependant que, debout dans son antique salle, / Le Toscan sous sa lampe inclinait son front pâle . . ." prepares the entry of the mysterious Dalti (66). The second canto of **"Portia"** is divided between two scenes: one, in the interior of a dark church, is set in the first eleven lines (66); the next, in a remote summer-house on Luigi's estate, is introduced shortly after (66). There is only one tableau in the last canto of this poem, describing the still beauty of Venice by night and the rapid movement of the lovers' gondola over the lagoon; two passages, however, are devoted to it: the first is found in the twenty-four lines which begin the canto (68); another, much shorter, is placed almost at the end of the *conte:*

> L'horizon était vide, et les flots transparents
> Ne reflétaient au loin sur leur abîme sombre,
> Que l'astre au pâle front qui s'y mirait dans l'ombre.
>
> (69)

The outstanding traits of these tableaux are their generality and the apparent rapidity with which they are sketched: for they are not so much detailed pictures as broad scenes; they do not so much further the plot as furnish a backdrop and create an atmosphere. As the list above demonstrates, the mood, even within a single scene, may be changed; in this case the tableau is altered to express it. This is especially noteworthy in the second canto of **"Don Paez,"** where the portrayal of the hero is as dramatic as the situation in which he is involved: "A le voir, on dirait à coup sûr / Une pierre de plus dans les pierres gothiques / Qu'agitent les falots en spectres fantastiques" (50)—quite a change from the image he presented at the beginning of the canto: "Seul, en silence, il passe au revers des créneaux" (49). The same development is found in the last division of **"Portia"** where, to convey the seriousness and even tragedy of her final position, the character of the scenery around Portia is entirely transformed: after the light and playful aspect of the start—"Les pieds dans la rosée, et son masque à la main, / Une nuit de printemps joue avec le matin" (68)—comes the stark and forbidding impact of the conclusion: "L'horizon était vide . . ." (69). This is, of course, pathetic fallacy for dramatic effect. If we look beyond the tableaux themselves to consider their position within the context of the poems, we find that, like the scenarios and stage settings of a play, they create a colourful background and specific atmosphere to introduce a whole episode of the action or new developments within that action. In conjunction with the quite definitely theatrical cast of much of the remaining structure of these *contes,* such broad tableaux can be considered to be fulfilling a dramatic function.

The tableaux provide, therefore, an atmosphere in which the action and the dialogue placed after them can be exercised to maximum effect; in fact they are so important that the development of the *contes* is organised around them: in both **"Don Paez"** and **"Portia,"** a separate canto is devoted to each individual tableau-setting, as if it were, in effect, a separate act. If we consider the basic organisation of Musset's earliest plays, we see that it results directly from the technique used in these poems. A most noteworthy example is his first drama in prose, *La Quittance du diable,* written in April, 1830, only four months after the appearance of the *Contes d'Espagne et d'Italie.* This short play is divided not into acts or scenes, but rather into tableaux, designated as such: "Premier tableau: Un jardin au pied d'une colline"; "Deuxième tableau: Un cimetière. Plusieurs tombeaux"; "Troisième tableau: Un appartement dans le château, éclairé par une lampe" (483; 489; 490). The same dramatic technique is found in *La Coupe et les Lèvres* and *A quoi rêvent les jeunes filles.* In describing the décor of this last *comédie,* another critic, Steen Jansen, has written that

> ce qu'on remarque d'abord, c'est la relative indépendance de chaque scène. Elles sont fortement séparées les unes des autres par les changements de décor qui interviennent à chaque nouvelle scène (sauf en deux cas: I, 3-4 et II, 3-4. . . .). . . .
>
> Il y a donc un vide—spatial et temporel—entre chaque scène, et le lecteur/spectateur a l'impression de voir défiler une succession d'images qui forment chacune une unité. Si ces images forment pourtant aussi un ensemble, c'est qu'elles illustrent toutes la vie d'un même groupe de personnages.[3]

This independent scenic structure is one of the main characteristics of what Jansen describes as "une nouvelle technique dramatique";[4] as I hope to have shown, it is evident in its earliest stages in the longer poems of the *Contes d'Espagne et d'Italie.*

The single instance in either **"Don Paez"** or **"Portia"** where one tableau does not provide the setting for an entire division of the poem, that is, where there is a change of lieu within a single canto, is found in the second part of **"Portia,"** in which we move from the deserted church of the beginning to an intimate summerhouse for the lovers' meeting. This transfer in mid-canto involved a number of structural difficulties: Musset had not only to find a means of successfully uniting the second scene with the first within the framework of a single division—a problem which solved itself when the two settings each had an individual canto—but he had to do this, if possible, without losing the mood of dramatic suspense which he was evidently intent on creating in preparation for the lovers' tryst and their subsequent discovery by the jealous husband, Luigi. How was the tension to be maintained through a change in setting, when it usually emanated in large part from the nature of the setting itself? A series of direct questions, rapidly piled one upon the other, not only continues the suspense, but also serves to relocate us in the new décor which, in quite characteristic fashion, is presented first:

> Où donc, noble jeune homme, à cette heure où les ombres
> Sous les pieds du passant tendent leurs voiles sombres,
> Où donc vas-tu si vite? . . .
> . . . . .
> Jeune homme, où donc vas-tu? qui te pousse ou t'appelle?
> Pourquoi comme un fuyard sur l'arçon te courber?
> . . . . .
> Mais, près de ce palais, pourquoi ton oeil errant
> Cherche-t-il donc à voir et comme à reconnaître
> Ce kiosque, à la nuit close entr'ouvrant sa fenêtre?
> . . . . .
> Pourtant au pied du mur, sous les arbres caché,
> Comme un chasseur, l'oreille au guet, tu t'es penché.
> D'où partent ces accents? et quelle voix s'élève
> Entre ces barreaux, douce et faible comme un rêve?
>
> (66/67)

In this way another tableau, suitably adapted to the lovers' encounter that will follow, is presented through the rapid questions which successfully link the two scenes and even develop the dramatic tension introduced in the first ("'Le ciel / Les garde!' dit la vieille en marchant à l'autel," etc., 66). We note, however, that Musset achieved this scenic transition only through his manipulation of the dialogue, and it is to the dramatic character of this second that we must now turn our attention.

Describing the nature of the lyricism in Musset's first collection, Pierre Gastinel noted that it possessed distinctly theatrical overtones, explaining that "chez Musset, le lyrisme tourne toujours au dialogue. Partout le poète trouve moyen de mener une conversation."[5] Gastinel considers as dialogue not only the lines attributed to imaginary characters within the framework of the *contes*, but also the many interjections by the narrator himself. These last will be examined elsewhere in a separate consideration of the rôle of the narrative voice; even disregarding for the moment, however, the presence of this narrator, what remains in **"Portia"** and **"Don Paez"** after the tableaux are drawn is for the most part dialogue.

The drift of such dialogue to a purely dramatic form is less evident in **"Portia,"** where conversation between the characters never works itself beyond the limits imposed by the narrative structure; in **"Don Paez,"** too, the dialogue is included for as long as is possible within the body of the poem. A statement by the "dragon jaune et bleu" in the second canto, for example, appears as follows:

> Lui, bâillant à moitié: "Par Dieu! c'est l'Orvado,
> Dit-il, la Juana, place San-Bernardo".
>
> (49)

But this careful inclusion of the conversation within the framework of the *conte* grows somewhat confused in the dialogue between Don Paez and his rival Don Etur (II), and finally breaks down altogether in the third division, where Musset begins to introduce each segment of the discussion by the speaker's name:

> Don Paez, cependant, hésitant à sa vue,
> Elle lui tend les bras, et sur sa gorge nue,
> Qui se levait encore pour un embrassement,
> Elle veut l'attirer.
> > DON PAEZ:
> > Quatre mots seulement,
> Vieille.—Me connais-tu? Prends cette bourse. . . .
>
> (51)

This technique is continued in the last canto (IV): Musset no doubt felt he would be correcting any ambiguity for his readers; by the same alteration, however, he also went a long way in changing the viewpoint of his poem, for in labelling each element of speech separately, he was able to develop the independent expression of individual figures to an even greater degree. At this point

responsibility for the evolution of the *conte* is in large measure transferred to the characters themselves: it is the beginning of real drama.

The brief descriptions frequently included in the middle of the dialogues are also noteworthy; carefully placed as they are, such indications could almost be mistaken for stage directions:

> Dieu fit que Don Paez l'entendit; et la fièvre
> Le prenant aux cheveux, il se mordit la lèvre.
>
> (49)

> Comme, à cette parole, il montrait son sein nu,
> Don Paez, sur son coeur, vit une mèche noire. . . .
>
> (49)

> —Madame," dit Luigi s'avançant quatre pas,—
> Et comme hors du lit pendait un de ses bras,
> De même que l'on voit d'une coupe approchée
> Se saisir ardemment une lèvre séchée,
> Ainsi vous l'auriez vu sur ce bras endormi
> Mettre un baiser brûlant,—puis tremblant à demi:
> "Tu ne le connais pas, ô jeune Vénitienne!
> Ce poison florentin qui consume une veine. . . .
>
> (**"Portia"** 65)

In an assessment of the dramatic potential of the dialogue in these poems we must also note Musset's frequent use of certain linguistic devices, such as the rhetorical question:

JUANA:

> M'oubliez-vous, Paez, et l'endroit où nous sommes?
>
> (52)
> Mais quand tu m'as noyé de baisers et de larmes,
> Dis, qui peut m'en défendre, ou qui m'en guérira?
> Tu m'as fait trop heureux; ton amour me tuera!
>
> (**"Portia"** 67);

apostrophe and hyperbole:

JUANA:

> Dieu! vrai Dieu! quelle folie étrange
> Vous a frappé l'esprit, mon bien-aimé! mon ange!
>
> (52)
> "Le ciel
> Les garde!" dit la vieille en marchant à l'autel
>
> (**"Portia"** 66);

and dramatic irony:

JUANA:

> Qu'avez-vous, mon amour? pourquoi fermer la porte
> Au verrou? don Paez a-t-il peur que je sorte?
>
> (52)

Accepting the modern preference for Musset's plays at the expense of his poetry, Henri Lefèbvre has written that Musset's poetic style is in any case best suited to a theatrical audience; his reasons for this judgement are of especial interest here in a consideration of the dramatic attributes of the *Contes d'Espagne et d'Italie*:

> Les mouvements oratoires qui passaient par-dessus la tête du lecteur vont au théâtre passer la rampe. Le don d'éloquence, nuisible au lyrisme, devient sur scène une qualité primordiale. Le personnage qui parle éloquemment à l'autre personnage s'adresse, à travers celui-ci, au spectateur; il le vise et l'atteint.[6]

Although another critic has noted an absence of "l'épaisseur du vécu" in **"Les Marrons du feu,"**[7] there are in these early *contes* solid indications of what would prove to be one of the most compelling features of Musset's theatre: his acute, almost intuitive understanding of human psychology.[8] This is particularly evident in **"Portia";** Musset managed to strike just the right chord in his portrayal of the young heroine whose childish naïveté and lack of experience are the source of real tragedy in the story; the figure of her much older husband, Onorio Luigi, is also convincing. It would have been easy to make out of him a conventional Romantic villain, but already such exaggeration was prevented by the instinct to nuance and truth which would lead, one year later, to the subtleties of *La Nuit vénitienne*. Instead of a jealous monster in the manner of Hugo, we have, in the second canto, a broken-hearted and almost pathetic old man for whom one must feel more than a little pity:

> Les amants regardaient, sous les rayons tremblants
> De la lampe déjà par l'aurore obscurcie,
> Ce vieillard d'une nuit, cette tête blanchie,
> Avec ses longs cheveux plus pâles que son front.
>
> (67)

Melodrama is approached with the sudden greying of Luigi's hair, but rarely elsewhere, for in **"Portia"** especially Musset was moving beyond the dimensions of the usual Romantic stereotypes into the human density of his theatrical characters. At the same time, it is to be noted that the rather simpler psychologies of the figures in **"Don Paez"** reflect the less complicated mechanism of the plot: in themselves, the characters are not badly drawn.

Further evidence of Musset's knowledge of human nature is found in the observations of the narrator, who comments on these characters and their circumstances even as the *contes* unfold. In **"Don Paez,"** his introductory passage itself contains brief but perceptive sketches of certain kinds of women: "Ces bégueules / Qui ne sauraient aller au Prado toutes seules," and, still worse, "celles / Dont le temps se dépense en intrigues nouvelles" (48). Here again, as in the tableaux, we find Mus-

set's characteristic use of carefully selected detail to convey an impression which is both general and richly evocative:

> Celles-là vont au bal, courent les rendez-vous,
> Savent dans un manchon cacher un billet doux,
>
>   . . . . .
>
> Suivre l'imbroglio de ces amours mignons,
> Poussés en une nuit comme des champignons.
>
> (48)

A more profound understanding of women is revealed in the fourth canto, when the narrator describes Juana's mood as she awaits her lover:

> —Oh! Comme à cet instant bondit un coeur de femme!
> Quand l'unique pensée où s'abîme son âme
> Fuit et grandit sans cesse, et devant son désir,
> Recule comme une onde, impossible à saisir!
> Alors, le souvenir excitant l'espérance,
> L'attente d'être heureux devient une souffrance.
>
> (52)

An equal perception is found in his comments in **"Portia:"**—Quel homme fut jamais si grand, qu'il se pût croire, Certain, ayant vécu, d'avoir une mémoire . . ." (68). It was this understanding which enabled Musset to go to the heart of a personality, or type of personality, and faithfully portray it; the strength of the highly individual figures which resulted is one of the outstanding qualities of his theatre where, in contrast to those of many Romantic dramatists, the characters once again assume their necessary rôle as the source and focus for the action and development of the plot.[9]

Beyond the psychological insights afforded by its frequent intrusions, the dramatic implications of the rôle assigned to the narrative voice in these *contes* may be less evident. We must remember, however, that the narrator in both poems is endowed, directly in **"Don Paez,"** rather more indirectly in **"Portia,"** with a separate identity: the first word in **"Don Paez"** is "je," and this chronicler has a character and opinions, as his introduction to the poem makes quite clear: "Je n'ai jamais aimé, pour ma part, ces bégueules / Qui ne sauraient aller au Prado toutes seules . . ." (48). Everything that occurs in these two *contes* is bracketed by the narrative voice; nor are we allowed to forget it, for the presence of this narrator is everywhere evident: in his apostrophes to the reader through personal address (such as "vous" and "frère" in **"Don Paez;"** "vieillards décrépits," etc. in **"Portia"**), imperatives, and direct questions, and also in his references to what has already been related ("'Messieurs,' cria d'abord notre moustache rousse . . ."—**"Don Paez,"** 49). These devices, together with the frequent intrusions considered above, continue the development of an independent narrative personality in each of the poems to the point where it addresses not only readers, but characters within the *contes* as well—Juana, for example, in **"Don Paez:"**

—Voyez-vous, le long de cette rampe,
Jusqu'au faîte en grimpant tournoyer une lampe?

(52);

or Dalti in **"Portia:"**

Tes voeux sont-ils si haut et si loin avancés?
Jeune homme, songes-y; ce réduit, tu le sais,
Se tient plus invisible à l'oeil, que la pensée
Dans le coeur de son maître, inconnue et glacée.

(66)

Ultimately, therefore, the narrator himself becomes physically present in his drama as an onlooker; this evolution of the narrative voice from omniscience to questioning presence is entirely in keeping with the gradual movement of these poems to a more dramatic form. For the paradox involved in this broad use of direct address is that the very technique which consciously brings the reader into the work also, applied to fictive characters, excludes the narrator from it, that is, maintains between him and his creation, his own imaginary world, a certain distance. The narrator is observer. This division between him and what he narrates is exactly parallel to that between the dramatist and his drama; and as can be seen, the results obtained are rather similar: such distancing is an essential ingredient of traditional dramatic expression. That an autonomous narrator appears later (in the fourth canto) in **"Don Paez"** than in **"Portia"** (in the second of three divisions) would indicate—both date from 1829, but there is no exact chronology—that the latter was written first: in **"Portia,"** this device is used; in **"Don Paez,"** found as it is toward the end of the *conte,* wholly integrated into what seems to be the natural progression of the poem, it is used more dramatically.

Because of their importance for the structure of some of Musset's first plays, two functions of the narrative voice within these *contes* must be especially considered: lending direction and general unity to the poems, and providing comments on the people, places, and situations within them. In **"Portia,"** and particularly in **"Don Paez,"** it is the narrator who is one of the most important elements in the general organisation of the *conte*: linking the various tableaux together, he is in large measure responsible for the structural harmony of the whole. Variations of this initial method are found in some of the plays written shortly afterward, most notably in the *Spectacle dans un fauteuil.*[10] In the loose arrangement of the very different tableaux of *La Coupe et les Lèvres* through the figure of Frank, whom events befall, in the broad orchestration of the plot of *A quoi rêvent les jeunes filles* by Laerte, even in the loose unity of *Lorenzaccio* centred, according to one critic at least, around the lone figure of the Duke,[11] we find traces of the structural pattern which underlies the organisation of the longer *contes* of Musset's first collection.

In my examination of the tendency to dialogue in these poems, I have written that drama begins at the point where separate speeches are assigned to individual characters, as in the third canto of **"Don Paez."** The narrator consequently becomes less significant, and were this to continue, his characters, capable of independent expression, would be endowed with life of their own and grow beyond the framework of the *conte*. In this case, the structurally autonomous narrative voice would be limited to a semi-independent secondary rôle, that is, reduced to a chorus. This is precisely what occurs in *La Coupe et les Lèvres* (1832) and *On ne badine pas avec l'amour* (1834); the information supplied by the omniscient narrator in, for instance, the broad tableaux of **"Don Paez"** is provided in *On ne badine pas avec l'amour* by the speeches of the chorus, his structural descendant:

Cependant, les rideaux, autour d'elle tremblant,
La laissaient voir pâmée aux bras de son galant;
Oeil humide, bras morts, tout respirait en elle
Les langueurs de l'amour, et la rendait plus belle.
Sa tête avec ses seins roulait dans ses cheveux. . . .

(**"Don Paez,"** 48)

LE CHOEUR:

Doucement bercé sur sa mule fringante, messer Blazius s'avance dans les bluets fleuris, vêtu de neuf, l'écritoire au côté. Comme un poupon sur l'oreiller, il se ballotte sur son ventre rebondi, et les yeux à demi fermés, il marmotte un *Pater noster* dans son triple menton. Salut, maître Blazius, vous arrivez au temps de la vendange, pareil à une amphore antique.

(*On ne badine pas avec l'amour* I/1, 299).

Additional examples would demonstrate the similarity of the preceptive tones of the narrator of **"Portia"** and the chorus of *La Coupe et les Lèvres*.

To this point **"Les Marrons du feu"** has not been mentioned because its form is clearly dramatic: there is less need to discuss its dialogue, the distinctive psychology of its characters, and its dramatic effects, now all completely legitimate. One might well wonder, however, what place the narrative voice and tableaux which figure so prominently in the other early *contes* have found in it, and it is these two aspects of the play which will be very briefly examined here.

In his analysis of **"Les Marrons du feu,"** Herbert Gochberg has written that "the form is strictly dramatic. The speaking parts are indicated in the traditional manner and the division into scenes is quite clear."[12] There still remains, however, a visible trace of the narrative voice of the other poems in the short *Prologue* to the play: in the first place, the "jeune auteur" who delivers it addresses us no less directly than did the narrators of **"Don Paez"** and **"Portia,"** secondly, this initial presentation establishes a *cadre*, an imaginative framework, which is just as fictitious—given the original appearance of this play in a published collection—as the narrator's introduction to **"Don Paez:"**

> Messieurs et mesdames, c'est une comédie,
> Laquelle, en vérité, ne dure pas longtemps;
> Seulement que nul bruit, nulle dame étourdie
> Ne fasse aux beaux endroits tourner les assistants.
> . . . . .
> N'allez pas nous jeter surtout de pommes cuites
> Pour mettre nos rideaux et nos quinquets à bas.
> Nous avons pour le mieux repeint les galeries.
>
> (53)

Traces of a narrative presence also surface in the last lines of this play:

> L' ABBÉ
>
> Mais . . .—Elle est partie, ô Dieu!
> J'ai tué mon ami, j'ai mérité le feu,
> J'ai taché mon pourpoint, et l'on me congédie.
> C'est la moralité de cette comédie.
>
> (65)

Although this *conte* is presented in a form which is essentially dramatic, the characters who appear within it are still the puppets of a narrator, or "jeune auteur," who arranges them in their fantastic postures as he wishes, at will; regardless of the distancing, this is precisely what we have observed in both **"Don Paez"** and **"Portia."** The abbé's final reference to the framework within which he appears—"cette comédie"—underlines it: his actions have been directed to an end, to a "moralité" determined by another; his rôle has merely been to illustrate them, and it is over.[13]

In **"Les Marrons du feu,"** brief indications for the setting and explicit stage directions largely replace the tableaux and short intra-dialogue descriptions found in **"Don Paez"** and **"Portia."** It is interesting to note, however, that minor changes were made, consisting mostly of additions, in specifications for the décor in editions of this *conte* which appeared after 1830[14]—proof of an increased concern with the suitability and precision of the theatrical form in which it had been cast. For all that, longer, set descriptions, which compose the tableaux of the other two poems and reflect the young Musset's response to the Cénacle's call for the picturesque, are still included in **"Les Marrons du feu;"** but such broad scenes now spring from the mouths of the characters themselves, as part of the dialogue, rather than from the narrative voice. The vista included in the long monologue of the abbé after he has murdered Rafael is particularly notable; it conveys, as do the most important tableaux of **"Don Paez"** and **"Portia,"** a mood as well as a scene: "Maintenant le hibou tourne autour des falots. / L'esturgeon monstrueux

soulève de son dos / Le manteau bleu des mers . . ." (64). The general but penetrating psychological observations elsewhere expressed by the narrative voice are likewise still present, but they too are now presented as the comments of single characters:

comments of single characters:

> RAFAEL:
>
> C'est l'historie du coeur.—Tout va si vite en lui!
> Tout y meurt comme un son, tout, excepté l'ennui!
>
> (54)

> CAMARGO:
>
> —C'est la règle, ô mon coeur!—Il est sûr qu'une femme
> Met dans une âme aimée une part de son âme.
> . . . . .
> Au contraire un coeur d'homme est comme une marée
> Fuyarde des endroits qui l'ont mieux attirée.
>
> (57)

That Musset's intuitive understanding of human nature is still being expressed in the words of his characters rather than through their actions indicates, no doubt, that the transition to a purely theatrical form is not complete; at the same time, however, it is important to remember that everywhere in Musset's work is to be found the tendency to precept and maxim of the best classical tradition.

It can be seen, therefore, that if the form of **"Les Marrons du feu"** is more evidently dramatic than that of the other two *contes,* it clearly reflects the fundamental organisation of **"Portia"** and **"Don Paez"** through the lingering presence of the narrative voice and the descriptive tableaux. In this it resembles most of the plays from the first period of Musset's career, the period in which he wrote, one after another, many of his best works: *A Quoi rêvent les jeunes filles* (1832), *On ne badine pas avec l'amour* (1834), *Lorenzaccio* (1834) . . . All these plays contain the structural and dramatic elements of the earliest *contes en vers*. It would be difficult to exaggerate their importance for, refined and reapplied, these elements formed the basis of Musset's innovative dramatic technique: as a result of the cohesion assured by the central narrative voice or single character who replaced him, these plays could be organised around different tableaux and so could become much less traditional, much more flexible; it was this flexibility, this freedom from a more conventional dramatic structure, which in turn made it possible for Musset to express himself entirely as he wished, spontaneously and poetically. It was the dramatic technique that originated with the composition of his first *contes en vers* which enabled Musset fully to reveal his delicate fantasy and fragile dreams in some of the most enduring dramas of nineteenth-century France.

Notes

1. See Pierre Gastinel, *Le Romantisme d'Alfred de Musset,* Diss. Paris 1931 (Paris: Hachette, 1933), pp. 139 and 145.

2. All page references are to the Seuil edition (Collection l'Intégrale) of Musset's *Oeuvres complètes,* edited by Philippe van Tieghem (Paris, 1966). This is the best edition of Musset's complete works now available; van Tieghem, unlike Allem in the Pléiade volume of the theatre, has very rightly preserved the original form of Musset's plays rather than present the subsequent versions adapted for the stage and cut for the censor.

3. Steen Jansen, "Alfred de Musset, dramaturge: *A quoi rêvent les jeunes filles* et la technique dramatique d'*Un Spectacle dans un fauteuil,*" *Orbis Litterarum,* 21 (1966), p. 229.

4. See Jansen, p. 238.

5. Gastinel, p. 103.

6. Henri Lefèbvre, *Musset: Essai,* 2ᵉ éd. (Paris: L'Arche, 1970), p. 102.

7. See Eric Gans, *Musset et le "drame tragique": Essai d'analyse paradoxale* (Paris: Corti, 1974), p. 62.

8. It surfaces, however rapidly, even in the preface to the collection when Musset compares the young author who pays tribute to those who have come before him to "un provincial qui, en entrant au bal, s'incline à droite et à gauche, cherchant un visage ami" (813).

9. There can be very little doubt about the importance Musset assigned even from the outset to intimate psychological description; in the examples I have quoted above from the *Contes d'Espagne et d'Italie* is already to be found ample illustration of the tendency which would be expressed as theory only with the "Dédicace" of *La Coupe et les Lèvres* two years later in 1832:

> L'un comme Calderon et comme Mérimée
> Incruste un plomb brûlant sur la réalité,
>
> . . . . .
>
> L'autre comme Racine et le divin Shakespeare,
> Monte sur le théâtre, une lampe à la main,
> Et de sa plume d'or ouvre le coeur humain.
>
> . . . . .
>
> Mais s'il m'était permis de choisir une route,
> Je prendrais la dernière . . .

> (101/102)

10. And later in the intimate first-person optic of many of his *contes* and *nouvelles.*

11. In his discussion of the dramatic technique of *A quoi rêvent les jeunes filles,* Steen Jansen has noted "l'absence d'action principale et unifiante; enfin le rôle dévolu à un personnage central [Laerte] qui—sans être le pôle d'une opposition dynamique entraînant une action—assure l'unité de la pièce, c.-à-d. ici la liaison entre les scènes successives" (p. 238); in the same article he has written of *Lorenzaccio* that

> de la relative indépendance des actions, il résulte qu'il n'y en a pas une dont on puisse dire sans discussion qu'elle est la principale, et que les autres lui sont subordonnées. Elles forment pourtant un tout cohérent, parce qu'elles sont toutes—sauf une qui oppose Lorenzo et sa mère— déclenchées par des oppositions où l'un des antagonistes est le duc. Le duc est donc le personnage central qui assure l'unité de la pièce. . . . C'est par cette qualité de lien unifiant seule et non par son caractère propre qu'il acquiert d'abord une fonction dans la pièce".

> (p. 247)

12. Herbert Gochberg, *Stage of Dreams: The Dramatic Art of Alfred de Musset (1828-1834)* (Genève: Droz, 1967), p. 33.

13. This view of the theatre as a fantastic personal universe governed only by the caprice of its creator may explain the fascinating fragment which follows, composed by Musset toward the end of his life:

> Dieu dort et le monde est son rêve.

> Dieu dort et . . . toutes les créations successives ou simultanées qui amusent son sommeil ne sont que des apparences. Le Monde est le rêve de Dieu. Quand Dieu s'éveillera . . . les apparences retomberont dans leur néant primitif; les simulacres de créations et d'êtres, de globes et de planètes, de systèmes et de vies, s'évanouiront à jamais. Dieu finira de rêver.

> (930/931)

14. See Allem's footnotes (numbers 8, p. 611; 29, p. 614; and 78, p. 617) to *Les Marrons du feu* in the Pléiade edition of Musset's *Poésies complètes* (Paris: Gallimard, 1957).

Phillip A. Duncan (essay date fall-winter 1987-88)

SOURCE: Duncan, Phillip A. "Patterns of Stasis and Metamorphosis in Musset's First Sonnet." *Nineteenth-Century French Studies* 16, nos. 1-2 (fall-winter 1987-88): 78-83.

[*In the following essay, Duncan interprets Musset's sonnet that begins "Que j'aime le premier frisson d'hiver," emphasizing themes of equilibrium and cyclic change in the poem.*]

The complexities and subtle resonance of Musset's first sonnet justify multiple readings of this densely woven poetic statement. A recent analysis by Lloyd Bishop virtually exhausts one approach, emphasizing the theme and imagery of inconstancy and examining the poet's ambivalence toward change. "Images of inconstancy, impermanence and change," he finds, "are coextensive with the text; they provide its formal constant."[1] An earlier, and likewise very valuable, commentary by James Hewitt stresses also the centrality of the theme of inconstancy, arguing that the poem celebrates "a change of season and a change of heart" and that its "images of inconstancy . . . combine to threaten any possible permanence."[2] These two are the only scholars who have examined carefully Musset's first sonnet:

> Que j'aime le premier frisson d'hiver! le chaume,
> Sous le pied du chasseur, refusant de ployer!
> Quand vient la pie aux champs que le foin vert embaume,
> Au fond du vieux château s'éveille le foyer;
>
> C'est le temps de la ville,—Oh! lorsque l'an dernier,
> J'y revins, que je vis ce bon Louvre et son dôme,
> Paris et sa fumée, et tout ce beau royaume
> (J'entends encore au vent les postillons crier),
>
> Que j'aimais ce temps gris, ces passants, et la Seine
> Sous ses mille fallots assise en souveraine!
> J'allais revoir l'hiver.—Et toi, ma vie, et toi!
>
> Oh! dans tes longs regards j'allais tremper mon âme;
> Je saluais tes murs.—Car, qui m'eût dit, madame,
> Que votre cœur sitôt avait changé pour moi?

References to change are, indeed, insistent in some stanzas. In the second quatrain and the first tercet the narrator perceives a world in ceaseless transformation; however, although impermanence suffuses these lines and, as an inevitable human reality, may be integral to much of Musset's vision of human relations, it does not follow that the poet concedes the flux of nature without protest. Indeed, in the **"Lettre à Lamartine," "Souvenir,"** and elsewhere Musset finds consolation in certain absolute and eternal prizes of human experience: memory and the soul, for example. Not surprisingly, much of his art reflects a determination to resist the erosion characteristic of human experience, to establish secure places and a state of temporal grace which allow the heart and mind to exorcise, briefly at least, existential nausea. Rather than a playful acceptance of the fickle heart, what the reader might well expect in this sonnet, given Musset's anguish over all manner of loss (with **"Tristesse"** an excellent example), is an expression of the poet's "double" vision of the world which opposes stasis to change—a contest which ends here in the tragedy of change victorious.

The references of the first quatrain are to renewal and static mass. More important to the "frisson" in the first line than notions of tentativeness or change is its announcement of a revolution in the seasonal cycle: the reappearance once more of winter in its endless return. The inalterable rotation of the seasons is as easily understood as a phenomenon of permanence or equilibrium as the contrary and, indeed, here, the approach of winter is represented as a perpetual beginning, a pseudo-spring. It is a time when, in the poem, the magpie comes into the fields as though it were a migratory bird in springtime arriving for the rituals of a mating season and new life. The countryside is fragrant and green. That these attributes are nominally assigned to harvested hay is overwhelmed by the impression created of youthfulness and sexuality ("vert"). Certainly, this line serves as a preamble to the anticipated renewal of passion in the arms of the Parisian lover, as does the heat of the "foyer" in line four. The annual relighting of the fire in the château in the last line is the final affirmation of return in the quatrain. Its comfortable warmth, centripetal, reassuring, emphasizes continuity and harmonizes with the previous cyclical references of these verses.

A second theme introduced is material density and solidity. The stubble on which the hunter treads in the first couplet is unyielding. The narrator has transformed an image of debilitation and decay, the debris of the pastures, into one of endurance and stability. The architectural mass of the château further contributes to a sense of immutability in the scene. At the same time, its ancient presence ("le vieux château") underscores continuity in the situation. The accumulation of these indices of permanence, eternal return, and inalterable density establishes a condition of timelessness in the initial panorama and with its emotional increment of hope (incongruously), plenitude and reassurance, constitutes an ambiance which the narrator expects to perpetuate in the arms of the lady in Paris.

Finally, in stanza one the narrator underscores uniqueness. The huntsman is alone, the magpie is solitary and fire beckons from a single hearth in the depths of the château. The unique phenomena at the beginning of the poem reinforce the integrality and metaphorical unity of quatrain one and are related to the theme of constancy in the stanza, for the concomitant of permanence is oneness. Singularity suggests the unchanging, not becoming other, and contrasts with the multiplicities and ephemerae of stanzas two and three.

The circular motifs of the first stanza predict the structure of the sonnet as a whole which juxtaposes two cycles expressing alternately rest and motion. To stanza one's static terms stanzas two and three oppose metamorphosis. The final tercet offers a summation of the conflicting forces and a resolution in favor of change.

The first half of the last tercet echoes the theme of the first quatrain, the second half decisively rejects the inertia of the opening and plunges on to an altered state in a return to the fluid conditions of the middle stanzas. The narrator expects to come full circle and to recover in love the state of completeness evoked in the first quatrain's pastoral retreat. However, in the central verses the original stasis dissolves and the changeability of the new, Parisian environment serves as a psychological and metaphorical preparation for the fickleness of the mistress. The architecture of this sonnet associates it with other works of Musset such as **"Nuit de mai"** which demonstrate, in the argument of Russell King, the conflict between the poet's Apollonian (disciplined, creative) and his Dionysian (pessimistic, chaotic) aspects.[3] It is in the Dionysian segments of the first sonnet that the inconstancy and impermanence noted by Bishop and Hewitt are emphatic.

The first couplet of quatrain two is transitional, opening with this work's second overt architectural reference: the "Louvre et son dôme." That the Louvre seems to extend the motif of architectural stability established in the first quatrain is deceptive. Monumental as the palace is, it differs in that it reflects not the singularity of previous references, but multiple associations. It evokes the transit of multifarious historical events, dynasties, thousands of inhabitants and visitors. It is a public structure unlike the private one of the first quatrain. A transitional phenomenon, such a locus implies continuity but simultaneously introduces characteristics of manifoldness and change.

The six lines following the second quatrain's introductory couplet develop the theme of motion, variety and dissolution that it insinuates. Paris turns to smoke; the call of the coachman is dissipated and lost; the passersby, legion and faceless, disappear; the street lamps flicker, uncertain. The ceaseless flow of the Seine, sovereign, epitomizes the flux of the metropolis whose winter color, grey (a color void), contrasts with the ripe green of the pseudo-spring in the country. The narrator calls the kaleidoscopic city "ce beau royaume . . . que j'aimais . . . ," but the fabric of images subverts the assertion. The city is a shadow world without substance or fixity, a mirage where the only purchase is the rampart sheltering (the narrator believes) imperishable love.

The final tercet presents some affinities with the opening stanza. In its first line there is a return to the immobilities of the beginning of the poem. The "longs regards" in which the narrator intended to immerse his soul return the reader to the temporal extensions of the initial exposition. And the walls which he greets recall the "vieux château"; both walls and château represent possible sanctuaries offering the promise of renewal as well as continuity.

In the end the narrator is undeceived: the mistress is false. The narrator's sortie from a place of security to reach the keep of steadfast love has failed. The mistress has been lost to the contagion of the city's vacillations. Bishop argues, on the contrary, that a Don Juan narrator has been given his just desserts, relating him to the magpie interpreted as frivolous and thieving, and that the shift at the end of the poem from familiar to formal address is an expression of the narrator's abrupt coolness and imminent indifference. However, the narrator's final statement is just as probably an expression of pain and of the unbridgeable distance which his mistress has opened between them.

The sonnet recounts a tragedy. The narrator issues from a site of order and certainty, where frail and failing vegetation is made as dense as stone, where winter is spring, and light and warmth animate a structure that leaves an impression of enduring mass and timelessness. Filled with the anticipation of absolute love, corollary of his own hermetic and unchanging domaine, he seeks in a vacuous metropolis the fastness of the lover's retreat evoked symbolically earlier by the château and its central fire. In the course of the narrator's quest the reader encounters the affirmative signs of the first quatrain in the later, corrupted forms of the opposing cycle: the frozen pavement of stubble becomes the flowing track of the Seine; the single hunter becomes the multitudinous passersby; the green of the fragrant hay becomes the grey of the city's atmosphere; the single hearth and its fire becomes a thousand trembling, uncertain lamps. Finally, the narrator believes that he has reached asylum: the walls shielding the mistress that promise a return to the security of the locus in stanza one, but within he finds only the same absence experienced in the city streets.

Bishop considers the "deep structuring" of the poem to be "the narrator's ambivalence toward the sudden change in his relationship with this particular woman and in a broader and more significant sense, his ambivalence toward change in general" (456). There is ambivalence in the narrator's attitude toward his mistress on the one hand, says Bishop, because "one can easily imagine him as a lover framiliar with evanescent love affairs" (456). This might be the case were the narrator and Musset one and the same, but the text does not authorize such an identity. There is insufficient evidence in the poem to support the argument that the narrator is the equivalent of a mercurial Don Juan. Even his "love" for the animation and volatility of the capital could legitimately be discounted as his ardent anticipation of the refuge of constant love that the city's seductive aura masks. As for the narrator's "ambivalence toward change in general," the thrust of Bishop's remarks is to demonstrate that, as he states it, "the images of inconstancy . . . are coextensive with the text; they provide its formal constant" (457). His emphasis is on the absence of ambivalence.

The first verses speak of permanence and equilibrium, of ancient halls and natural cycles. The poet initially establishes an ambiance of stability. The poem is cyclic—a structure promised by the return of the seasons, return of the magpie, return of fire to the hearth, and "return," finally, as the narrator returns, to another place of stability: the walls isolating ostensibly timeless love from the flux of the city. Recognizing this structure of continuity and return as primary, but in opposition to a cycle of chaos that defeats order, it is difficult to acknowledge Bishop's concept of the narrator with his "enjoyment of change for its own sake" (456). More plausibly, he is a seeker after absolutes who, presuming to complete one plenitude with another, is tragically defeated.

Notes

1. Lloyd Bishop, "Musset's First Sonnet: A Semiotic Analysis," *Romanic Review,* LXXIV (1983): 457.

2. James R. Hewitt, "The Tropes of Self in the Poetry of Alfred de Musset," Diss. New York University, 1973: 161-2.

3. Russell King, "Musset, The Poet of Dionysius," *Studies in Romanticism,* 13 (Fall 1974): 326.

Lloyd Bishop (essay date 1987)

SOURCE: Bishop, Lloyd. "After 1830: A Poet of Many Styles and Genres." In *The Poetry of Alfred de Musset: Styles and Genres,* pp. 17-52. New York: Peter Lang, 1987.

[*In the following excerpt, Bishop presents a survey of Musset's poetic genres and styles, including his short lyric poetry, narrative and dramatic verse, and* Les nuits *cycle.*]

Shorter Poems

Musset's shorter pieces are written in many different genres: elegy, sonnet, rondeau, madrigal, *chanson,* romance, ballad, epigram, epistle, *billet, impromptu.* Some, like **"Un Rêve,"** his first published poem, and **"Une Vision,"** another early work, deal with the fantastic; others (e.g., **"Charles-Quint," "Jeanne d'Arc," "Napoléon"**) with the historical. They offer a wide variety of moods, from the very grave (**"Sur la Naissance du Conte de Paris"**) to the light and humorous (**"Le Songe du Reviewer"**). The theological seriousness of the long poem **"L'Espoir en Dieu"** was immediately followed by the brief and frivolous **"A la mi-Carême,"**

showing, as his brother Paul tells us, the "mobility" of a young and impressionable mind. Stylistically, the shorter pieces are characterized on the whole by a simplicity that contrasts sharply with the flamboyant manner of the *Contes.* The vocabulary is ordinary, there are few learned allusions and few bold images. A sustained repetition here and there is the only rhetorical device consistently used. Many poems are little more than rhymed prose. Many others are quite charming or witty: Musset was the only major French romantic poet with a sustained sense of humor.

From the point of view of versification, these shorter pieces reveal that Musset has given up his romantic taste for experimentation. The most notable feature is the frequent use of *vers mêlés.* In **"Adieu"** the octosyllable is used with the decasyllable; in **"Rappelle-toi"** the decasyllable is used with the alexandrine as well as with lines of 6 and 4 syllables. In some pieces the length of a line is just half that of the preceding one: 8+4 in **"Mimi Pinson"** and **"Adieux à Suzon,"** 10+5 in **"Conseils à une Parisienne."** The uneven line is occasionally used: seven syllables in **"Le Rideau de ma voisine,"** for instance, and five syllables in **"La Nuit."**

A good number of the shorter pieces, as one would expect, are merely occasional poetry—tokens of thanks, fits of pique, etc. Most of the *épîtres* are addressed to friends, mistresses, ex-mistresses and would-be mistresses. The most noteworthy of these deal with the various forms and stages of love and friendship. Several pieces (**"A Pépa," "A Juana," "A Ninon," "A Aimée d'Alton"**) express a charming, superficial infatuation, usually in an unaffected tone and unmannered idiom.

> Quand le sommeil sur ta famille
> Autour de toi s'est répandu,
> O Pépita, charmante fille,
> Mon amour, à quoi penses-tu?
>
> Qui sait? Peut-être à l'héroïne
> De quelque infortuné roman:
> A tout ce que l'espoir devine
> Et la réalité dément;
>
> Peut-être à ces grandes montagnes
> Qui n'accouchent que de souris;
> A des amoureux en Espagne,
> A des bonbons, à des maris;
>
> Peut-être aux tendres confidences
> D'un coeur naïf comme le tien;
> A ta robe, aux airs que tu danses;
> Peut-être à moi,—peut-être à rien.

(**"A Pépa"**)

The tone changes with the George Sand cycle, seven short pieces written between August 1833 and January 1835, published posthumously, and which belong to the mainstream of the serious love lyric. The first poem celebrates the triumphant return of love to a heart that for three years had thought itself cured and hardened. In another the poet contrasts true love and the true happiness it brings with the vain "comédie humaine." But the last three pieces record the end of the stormy love affair.

> Il faudra bien t'y faire à cette solitude,
> Pauvre coeur insensé, tout prêt à se rouvrir,
> Qui sait si mal aimer et sait si bien souffrir.
>
> **("A George Sand"** V)

> Et cet amour si doux, qui faisait sur la vie
> Glisser dans un baiser nos deux coeurs confondus,
> Toi qui me l'as appris, tu ne t'en souviens plus.
>
> **("A George Sand"** VI)

To the woman who thus not only rejected the poet's love but erased the happy times from her memory the final piece sends a desperate plea for remembrance.

> Fais riche un autre amour et souviens-toi du mien.
> Laisse mon souvenir te suivre loin de France;
> Qu'il parte sur ton coeur, pauvre bouquet fané,
> Lorsque tu l'as cueilli, j'ai connu l'Espérance,
> Je croyais au bonheur, et toute ma souffrance
> Est de l'avoir perdu sans te l'avoir donné.
>
> **("A George Sand"** VII)

The cycle is noteworthy for its sober tonality which prevents the frequent rhetorical devices (apostrophe, hyperbole, personification, anaphora and the ornamental epithet) from weakening the convincing expression of genuine love and genuine sorrow.

Vladimir Nabokov has said that French romanticism has given us the poetry of love and German romanticism the poetry of friendship. But Musset is a poet for whom friendship too was important both personally and poetically: A good proportion of his opus is addressed to close friends and near-friends. In **"A Ulric G."** and **"A mon ami Edouard B",** for example, he commiserates with two friends who have suffered disappointments in love. He envies the former for his "blessure" and his "maux;" to the latter he expresses a romantic aesthetics:

> Ah! frappe-toi le coeur, c'est là qu'est le génie.
> C'est là qu'est la pitié, la souffrance et l'amour.

In **"A mon ami Alfred T."** Musset praises Alfred Tatet for not being a fair weather friend, for staying with him through adversity; the theme then develops into that of pain, just as it was for love, being the true measure of friendship.

> Mais du moins j'aurais pu, frère, quoi qu'il m'arrive,
> De mon cachet de deuil sceller notre amitié,

> Et, que demain je meure ou que demain je vive,
> Pendant que mon coeur bat, t'en donner la moitié.

In another poem addressed to Tatet, Musset celebrates the sybaritic pleasures of youth and the more lasting joys of friendship.

> —Oui, la vie est un bien, la joie est une ivresse;
> Il est doux d'en user sans crainte et sans soucis;
> Il est doux de fêter les dieux de la jeunesse,
> De couronner de fleurs son verre et sa maîtresse,
> D'avoir trente ans comme Dieu l'a permis.
> Et, si jeunes encore, d'être de vieux amis.

For Victor Hugo Musset entones a ringing tribute to friendship winning out over a literary quarrel. To Charles Nodier he expresses, years later, his nostalgia for the friendship of the Cénacle days. To his brother Paul returning from Italy he expresses with touching sincerity his deep affection.

> Ami, ne t'en va plus si loin.
> D'un peu d'aide j'ai grand besoin.
> 　　Quoi qu'il m'advienne,
> Je ne sais où va mon chemin,
> Mais je marche mieux quand ma main
> 　　Serre la tienne.

Of the other short pieces the most successful are the *chansons* and the sonnets, the former for their often Verlaine-like musicality, . . . the later for their formal perfection. . . . Partly because of the flexibility of his rhyme schemes and partly because of his natural talent, there is never any feeling of strain in the sonnets. Their moods range from extreme joy ("Qu'il est doux d'être au monde . . .") to extreme sorrow, that for example, of the well known **"Tristesse."**

> J'ai perdu ma force et ma vie,
> Et mes amis et ma gaieté;
> J'ai perdu jusqu'à la fierté
> Qui faisait croire à mon génie.
>
> 　　. . . . .
> Le seul bien qui me reste au monde
> Est d'avoir quelquefois pleuré.
> 　　. . . . .

NARRATIVE POETRY

During the still formative years that followed the publication of the *Contes,* Musset was groping for a style of narrative poetry that would be truly his own, in the sense of being in accord with his temperament and in the sense of finding his unique voice. **"Suzon"** and **"Octave,"** both written in 1831, continue the flippant Byronic manner and the Italo-Hispanic atmosphere of the *Contes.* They are minor works and hastily written, as evidenced by the somewhat confused plots and the sloppy versification (some lines do not even have a rhyme). **"Suzon"** is a licentious and sacrilegious tale of two debauched and atheistic priests who stop at nothing, including murder, to seduce an unwilling woman. **"Octave,"** as a drama of jealousy and vengeance, does not represent an advance in the quality of Musset's writing, it is in fact inferior to **"Portia"** and to **"Don Paez."**

It was also during this early period that Musset wrote most of the long "fragment," **"Le Saule,"** which marks a new poetic manner in its great length, its sustained seriousness and its oratorical style. The piece abounds in apostrophes, ornamental periphrases, rhetorical questions, personification of abstractions and classical clichés like "le manteau de la nuit." The tale is basically a melodrama in which Georgette, the idealized heroine, is sent off to a convent by her father to protect her chastity from the advances of the young Tiburce. (Tiburce is a composite of several types of romantic hero: He has the blond hair and delicate, "effeminate" features of the author himself; his eyes however have the hardness and severity of the Byronic hero; like many another romantic hero, he was born in poverty and is an orphan; like Coelio of *Les Caprices de Marianne,* his voice is sad, and like Coelio again, Tiburce is the bookish, studious type; like Manfred and Faust he is a solitary seeker of Life's mystery but soon discovers that human knowledge is vanity.) Georgette languishes in the absence of her lover, who finally arrives, disguised as a monk. But too late: she dies of grief and he in turn will die by his own hand.

The two most famous passages are the invocation to the Evening Star and the Hymn to the Sun, which are not directly related to the narrative. Some critics have exclaimed over these "morceaux choisis;" others have complained of "passages passe-partout." One critic (Maurice Grammont) has shown that they are "suggestively" related to the plot and theme. In any event we are at the farthest remove from the casual style of **"Mardoche."**

> Pâle étoile du soir, messagère lointaine,
> Dont le front sort brillant des voiles du couchant,
> De ton palais d'azur, au sein du firmament,
>   Que regardes-tu dans la plaine?
>
> Etoile, où t'en vas-tu, dans cette nuit immense?
> Cherches-tu sur la rive un lit dans les roseaux?
> Ou t'en vas-tu, si belle, à l'heure du silence,
> Tomber comme une perle au sein profond des eaux?
>
> Ah! si tu dois mourir, bel astre, et si ta tête
> Va dans la vaste mer plonger ses blonds cheveux,
> Avant de nous quitter, un seul instant arrête;—
> Etoile de l'amour, ne descends pas des cieux!

"Namouna" was originally intended as a filler to add volume to the first "livraison" of *Un Spectacle dans un fauteuil.* The poem is an ironic treatment of the Don Juan myth. There are in fact two Don Juans here: the idealized hero of the second canto and Hassan, the cyni-

cal hero of the first and final cantos. The latter is a cheerful débauché with a repressed *Weltschmerz,* a creature of paradox and ambivalence. The two Don Juan types are an expression of Musset's contradictory personality and of his contradictory attitudes toward love. Despite the basically comic presentation, the poem treats obliquely of the poet's disarray: One senses tears at times behind the laughter, "signals of a heart of pain," as Pushkin said of the "motley" chapters of his half-sad, half-mirthful *Eugene Onegin.* And the poem's romantic irony makes it denser than a cursory reading would suggest. . . .

Musset's most important narrative poem is **"Rolla."** The story is well known. The hero is a young nobleman whom an improvident father has left with a modest inheritance which must last Rolla a lifetime since he has too much aristocratic pride to consider assuming a profession or learning a trade. He abhors the habits and routine of everyday life and looks with misanthropic scorn upon kings and paupers alike. A romantic hero, he walks "naked and alone in this masquerade called Life." Since the future holds no promise of happiness or meaningfulness, he sets out systematically to squander his small fortune on three years of debauchery; when he is down to his last few pennies, he will spend them on a prostitute and kill himself.

On the surface Rolla is a Don Juan of the Mardoche-Hassan mould. But he possesses neither their flippancy nor their caddishness, and the poet insists on his good qualities rather than his failings. He is, for instance, "loyal, intrépide et superbe" and "naïf . . . comme l'enfance." And despite his wayward ways, his heart remains pure. *Pur* is the most important and, with its synonym, *chaste,* the most frequently used epithet in the poem; it points up the pathos of Rolla's situation. It is his nostalgia for the purity of childhood and the very vestiges of that purity that make his situation tragic. He is not a wicked young man but rather an *enfant du siècle,* that is, a victim of the philosophical disarray of his times.

The poem does not end on a note of total despair. The prostitute with whom Rolla spends his last night on earth, Marie, is even younger than he—she is 15, he 20—and her heart, like his, is still virginally pure. In Musset's casuistry the "heart" is not contaminated by the vile actions of the body: everything seems to depend on "the direction of intention." Through the long night the two young people experience, not love but "the specter of love." At the very end they do experience—if only a brief moment—the ecstasy of real love. The poem leaves the reader with the suggestion that if a new, viable Faith arose it would find ready adherents even among the cynical and degenerate youth of modern times. The suggestion is prepared by an earlier passage:

Penses-tu cependant que si quelque croyance,
Si le plus léger fil le retenait encor,
Il viendrait sur ce lit prostituer sa mort?

Generically, **"Rolla"** is as much an ode as a narrative poem. The slender plot serves as pretext for a series of lyrical fragments, more or less directly related to it, that express in sustained oratory the philosophical implications of the story.

Rolla does not appear at all in the first canto. The narrator, who is both a persona of the poet and a kindred spirit of the hero, represents especially the youth of Musset's time. The tone is one of high seriousness; there is not a trace of irony or nonchalance here or in any of the cantos. The first movement begins with no fewer than twelve successive rhetorical questions. The first one introduces the general theme—"Do you miss the days when the gods were alive and life was young?." The eleven others serve as anaphorical (i.e., musical) amplifications. The canto ends with seven more rhetorical questions developing musically the theme "Where is there a Savior, a saint for us? Where is hope?"

A noteworthy feature of the poem's overall structure is the rapid juxtaposition of fragments, which are not linked by explicit transitional material but which do contribute to the whole. The poet passes from one fragment to another at a breathless pace, which is at times disconcerting. This aspect of Musset's style has been observed by Philippe Van Tieghem: "Musset . . . procède par raccourcis . . . Les images sont comme des hallucinations rapides, des 'illuminations' instantanées, que le poète n'a pas le temps d'expliquer, mais qui suppose toute une scène symbolique" (*Musset,* p. 61) and by Emile Montégut: "Rapide, primesautière, l'inspiration de Musset procède par bonds qui, aussi rapprochés qu'ils soient, laissent toujours entre eux un certain intervalle" (*Nos Morts,* p. 260).

The second canto finally introduces Rolla, describing him as the greatest débauché of the world's most libertine city. But an extended metaphor immediately qualifies the hyperbole.

> . . . son corps était l'hôtellerie
> Où s'étaient attablés ces pâles voyageurs;
> Tantôt pour y briser les lits et les murailles,
> Pour s'y chercher dans l'ombre, et s'ouvrir les en-
> trailles,
> Comme des cerfs en rut et des gladiateurs;
> Tantôt pour y chanter, en s'enivrant ensemble,
> Comme de gais oiseaux qu'un coup de vent rassemble,
> Et qui, pour vingt amours, n'ont qu'un arbuste en
> fleurs.

Rolla is pictured here not as a man of sinful intentions but simply as a passive creature indolently watching his passions perform (cf. the simile that precedes the long metaphor: "il les [ses passions] laissait aller / Comme un pâtre assoupi regarde l'eau couler.") The image of the *hôtellerie* supports the body/heart antimony that allows Musset's hero to retain his essential purity while his body is the mere locus of unseemly actions. The passage offers an excellent example of Musset's animating imagery—passions presented as drunken, raucous travelers in a tavern—his pictorial gifts, and the appropriateness of imagery to theme, qualities that characterize most of the poet's work. The metaphor is unusual because of its length and because it is fed by two similes the latter of which is itself extended.

The rest of the second canto switches back and forth from Rolla to a series of digressions only tangentially related to the plot but which do bear on Rolla's moral and metaphysical situation. By way of contrast we move from Rolla's lack of worldly, professional and moral ambition to Hercules choosing, in a happier time, "Vertu" over "Volupté"; then we move from a one-line restatement of Rolla's dissipated life—

> Rolla fit à vingt ans ce qu'avaient fait ses pères.

—to an eleven-line digression on the sinfulness of large modern cities; then from Rolla's haughty pride and noble heart to the famous digression on *la cavale sauvage.*

> Lorsque dans le désert la cavale sauvage,
> Après trois jours de marche, attend un jour d'orage
> Pour boire l'eau du ciel sur les palmiers pou-
> dreux. . . .
>
> . . . . .
>
> Elle cherche son puits dans le désert immense.
>
> . . . . .
>
> Alors elle se couche, et ses grands yeux s'éteignent,
> Et le pâle désert roule sur son enfant
> Les flots silencieux de son linceul mouvant.
>
> Elle ne savait pas, lorsque les caravanes
> Avec leurs chameliers passaient sous les platanes,
>
> Qu'elle n'avait qu'à suivre et qu'à baisser le front
> Pour trouver à Bagdad de fraîches écuries.

While there is no explicit link made between the *cavale* and Rolla, implicit analogies abound: the noble race, the proud thoroughbred; the "savage," untamed nature of both horse and hero; the tragic death after three days of anguished wandering in the desert, an objective correlative of Rolla's three years of aimless and anguished wandering in the *vaste désert d'hommes* called Paris; and finally the refusal to join the herd to trade freedom for safety and comfort.

> Si Dieu nous a tirés tous de la même fange,
> Certe, il a dû pétrir dans une argile étrange
> Et sécher aux rayons d'un soleil irrité
> Cet être, quel qu'il soit, ou l'aigle, ou l'hirondelle,

Qui ne saurait plier ni son cou ni son aile,
Et qui n'a pour tout bien qu'un mot: la liberté.

Canto III is an ode to purity, that of childhood and early adolescence, as exemplified paradoxically by Marie, the young prostitute. It is especially while she sleeps that she retains her virginal purity: For Musset the dreams of youth are not fulfillments of repressed erotic wishes but, rather, a healthy regression back to the primordial innocence of man before the first sin. A short digression on Eve obliquely reinforces the theme.

This romantic narrative is expressed in a predominantly neo-classic style: The entire poem is studded with rhetorical questions and apostrophes; regular alexandrines predominate; and in the main the imagery is unobtrusive and traditional (snow is paler, marble less sparkling white than the milky skin of this sleeping child, etc.)

Also interesting stylistically is the way the numerous digressions are woven musically into the narrative; they come not as simple restatements but as variations on a theme. In Canto IV for example Musset interweaves contrapuntally the passionate love-making of Rolla and Marie with equally passionate invective against Voltaire, who is used as a synecdoche for all the "démolisseurs stupides" of the Enlightenment. The counterpoint itself expresses, without the need of explicit statement, the cause and effect relationship the poet is trying to establish:

Dors-tu content, Voltaire, et ton hideux sourire
Voltige-t-il encor sur tes os décharnés?
. . . . .

Il est tombé sur nous, cet édifice immense
Que de tes larges mains tu sapais nuit et jour.
. . . . .

Entends-tu soupirer ces enfants qui s'embrassent?
. . . . .

Des sanglots inouis, des plaintes oppressées,
Ouvrent en frissonnant leurs lèvres insensées.
En les baisant au front le Plaisir s'est pâmé.
Regarde!—ils n'aiment pas, ils n'ont jamais aimé.

The interweaving of narrative and apostrophe is effective here, it produces density thanks to the philosophical overtones: The demise of Christianity means not only that the thirst for the ideal and the absolute will never be satisfied, but also that men have lost their faith in each other; human love is now an empty simulacrum of true love. In desperation, modern man, for whom Rolla is a symbol, replaces the ancient hope for life and joy eternal with a grudging acceptance of the ephemeral, an anguished hedonism.

. . . . .

DRAMATIC POETRY

It was also during his early period that Musset made his theatrical debut, which was traumatically unsuccessful. *La Nuit vénitienne* (December 1, 1831) was greeted with hoots and whistles and had to be withdrawn after just two performances, partly because of a staging accident, partly because the romantics were disappointed to find that the play was a throwback to Marivaux rather than an experimental drama constructed along Hugolian lines, and partly too because the classicists had not forgiven the irreverent author of the *Contes*. Humiliated, Musset renounced the legitimate theater until as late as 1847. But he did devote his considerable dramatic gifts to the creation of an Armchair Theater, *Un Spectacle dans un fauteuil,* poetic dramas designed not for the live stage and a live audience but for readers of dramatic poetry and prose.

His first contribution to the Armchair Theater, *La Coupe et les Lèvres* (1832) is a "dramatic poem," a genre that Musset was the first to introduce into French literature and modeled on Goethe's *Faust* and Byron's *Manfred.* It is also a "tragedy" because it presents us with a tragic hero in the same sense that Goethe and Byron's heroes are tragic. The protagonist, Charles Frank, is a young man of twenty filled with both a deep appetite for and an even deeper hatred of life. He rejects the society of his fellow Tyrolian hunters, and in a rage burns down his father's house, thus severing symbolically all ties with humanity. His bitter nihilism is explained in the soliloquy that ends act 4. Frank, like Rolla, describes himself as the child of an impious age that believes in nothing. Musset alludes to the pernicious legacy of the materialist philosophy of the previous century.

Je renierai l'amour, la fortune et la gloire;
Mais je crois au néant, comme je crois en moi.
Le soleil le sait bien, qu'il n'est sous la lumière
Qu'une immortalité, celle de la matière.

He also curses the nefarious "analyseurs" of the Enlightenment. The result of this intellectual legacy is disaster.

L'amour n'existe plus; la vie est devastée.
Et l'homme, resté seul, ne croit plus qu'à la mort.

This statement anticipates one of Malraux's: The death of God will bring on the death of man since the latter will be able to define himself "vertically" only in terms of the one remaining absolute: Death.

After knowing fame, wealth and sensual love, Frank soon learns to despise them, concluding like Pushkin's Boris Gudonov that

Glory, luxury and the devilish love
Of women seem beautiful from a distance.

He returns at the end of the play to his native village and to the childhood sweetheart, Déidamia, he had left behind. Déidamia is a symbol not only of hope for the future but of the lost purity and innocence of Frank's youth. Just moments before the nuptials are to be performed, just before the cup touches the lips, Déidamia is murdered by Frank's former mistress, Belcolore, symbol of the dangers of debauchery but, on another level, of Frank's—and modern man's—incurable doubt.

The overall thematic structure of **La Coupe,** like that of Rolla, is loosely integrated. Musset seems to switch emphasis mid-way through the poem. As Jean d'Aquitaine explains: "On croirait que le poète a voulu d'abord faire la tragédie de l'orgueil et de la puissance qu'il peut développer dans une âme, mais soudain il tourne court sur une autre donnée et fait le procès de l'inconduite, qui s'arme d'un poignard et termine le drame, malgré l'idylle du cinquième acte, par un assassinat" (*Musset le poète,* p. 65). Perhaps a determined reader could find a central unifying theme (the impossibility of happiness in a hypersensitive soul, or the impossibility of transcendence), but it is true that the author has not clearly focussed his major point.

The plot of **La Coupe** is arranged by Chance, not because of a technical flaw but for the desired philosophical implications. Frank calls himself "fils du hasard," and it is indeed Chance that throws him into the path of the beautiful and treacherous courtesan, Belcolore; it is Chance that makes him wealthy through luck at the gambling table; and it is Chance that brings him military glory rather than almost certain death in battle. The point is that since the age of Voltaire and the *philosophes* of the Enlightenment, divine providence no longer rules the universe.

> La poussière est à Dieu;—le reste est au hasard.
>
> *(Rolla)*

The style of **La Coupe** is declamatory, marked by long and loud monologues, rhetorical flourishes, artificial eloquence. The sentences are often periodic in structure, epic in tonality. Musset pulls out all the stops: magnification and the marvelous (if a universe ruled by Chance can be said to partake of the supernatural), repetitions, enumerations, apostrophes, extended laudations and imprecations. Let one example, a Faustian imprecation, suffice:

> Malheur aux nouveau-nés!
> Maudit soit le travail! maudite l'espérance!
> Malheur au coin de terre où germe la semence,
> Où tombe la sueur de deux bras décharnés!
> Maudits soient les liens du sang et de la vie!
> Maudite la famille et la société!
> Malheur à la maison, malheur à la cité,
> Et malédiction sur la mère patrie!

The declamatory style is appropriate to the genre: Musset is not striving for psychological realism but philo-sophical lyricism, something new in French poetry, and refreshing when compared to Vigny's prosaic philosophical poems.

The second contribution to the Armchair Theater is a comedy, and like many comedies it has no real hero since the idealistic, shy and self-effacing Silvio, as M. P. Van Tieghem puts it, is "nullement un caractère mais une manière d'aimer" (*Musset,* p. 44) that is, almost an abstraction. While lacking a real hero, the play is the first study of the *jeune fille* in French dramatic literature. It is a delightful comedy of fanciful plot and poetic atmosphere in the Shakespearean manner. There is no attention paid to the historical or geographical setting ("La scène est où l'on voudra"), or to authentic costumes, there is no satire on contemporary mores, no complicated imbroglio, no clever marivaudage, no bravura passages or even any *mots d'auteur* (see Van Tieghem, p. 43-44). Musset insists not on the ridiculous (although the ridiculous Irus serves as foil to Sylvio) but on the charming world of two naive adolescent girls, the twin sisters, Ninon and Ninette, who at fifteen are in love with love. With A quoi rêvent les jeunes filles? Musset introduces another genre new to French literature, the *comédie de fantaisie.*

The basic style of the play can be characterized as poeticized conversation. The dialogues in several scenes are contrapuntally arranged. In the following passage for instance the sisters are "on stage" together but are in two different parts of the garden; unaware of each other's presence, they are engaged not in dialogue but in a lyrical duet.

NINON

> Toi dont la voix est douce, et douce la parole,
> Chanteur mystérieux, reviendras-tu me voir?
> Ou, comme en soupirant, l'hirondelle s'envole,
> Mon bonheur fuira-t-il, n'ayant duré qu'un soir?

NINETTE

> Audacieux fantôme à la forme voilée,
> Les ombrages ce soir seront-ils sans danger?
> Te reverrai-je encor dans cette sombre allée,
> Ou disparâtras-tu comme un chamois léger?

NINON

> L'eau, la terre et les vents, tout s'emplit
>   d'harmonies.
> Un jeune rossignol chante au fond de mon coeur.
> J'entends sous les roseaux murmurer des génies
>   . . .
> Ai-je de nouveaux sens inconnus à ma soeur?

NINETTE

> Pourquoi ne puis-je voir sans plaisir et sans peine
> Les baisers du zéphyr trembler sur la fontaine,
> Et l'ombre des tilleuls passer sur mes bras nus?
> Ma soeur est une enfant,—et je ne le suis plus.

NINON

    O fleurs des nuits d'été, magnifique nature!
    O plantes! ô rameaux! l'un dans l'autre enlacés!

NINETTE

    O feuilles des palmiers, reines de la verdure,
    Qui versez vos amours dans les vents embrasés!

The theme of the passage is of course the awakening of the senses: Nature is seen for the first time in its sexual aspect ("baisers du zéphyr;" "rameaux enlacés;" "vents embrasés"). Seldom have Musset's charm and delicacy of touch been as effective as here.

Silvio, although more a flat than a round character, is nearly as charming in his youthful naiveté as the sisters. Like Perdican he has just recently graduated from the university; unlike Perdican he is tongue-tied when first meeting the girl he is supposed to marry. (The girl's romantic father, Laërte, an interesting character in his own right, gives Silvio his choice of fiancée and even trains his shy son-in-law in the art of seduction!) But when alone his tongue is loosened and offers experimental (for him) images ranging from clichés

    Frêles comme un roseau, blondes comme les blés . . .

to preciosity

    On dirait que l'aînée est l'étui de sa soeur.

And at the end of the play he indulges in a veritable flood of similes when addressing his fiancée (Ninon).

    Vos yeux sont de cristal,—vos lèvres sont vermeilles
    Comme ce ciel de pourpre autour de l'occident.
        . . . . .

    Votre taille flexible est comme un palmier vert;
    Vos cheveux sont légers comme la cendre fine
    Qui voltige au soleil autour d'un feu d'hiver.
    Ils frémissent au vent comme la balsamine;
    Sur votre front d'ivoire ils courent en glissant,
    Comme une huile craintive au bord d'un lac d'argent.
    Vos yeux sont transparents comme l'ambre fluide
    Au bord du Niemen;—leur regard est limpide
    Comme une goutte d'eau sur la grenade en fleurs.
        . . . . .

    Le son de votre voix est comme un bon génie
    Qui porte dans ses mains un vase plein de miel.
    Toute votre nature est comme une harmonie. . . .

Frank of *La Coupe* and Silvio of *A quoi rêvent* present the two basic and contrasting types of hero found in Musset's fiction and drama as well as his narrative and dramatic poetry. The first is cynical and corrupt, disillusioned with life, with his fellow man, with love, and finally with himself. The second is inexperienced, pure in body and in mind, tender, trusting, and expecting much, in fact everything, from love. It is a commonplace of Musset criticism that the two types are reflections (stylized refractions, rather) of Musset's dual personality.

    . . . . .

EXTENDED LYRICS

Musset's famous Night Cycle, which includes in addition to the four *Nuits* the **"Lettre à Lamartine,"** **"L'Espoir en Dieu"** and **"Souvenir,"** presents extended lyrics written between 1835 and 1841. Until this cycle Musset's longer poems had been narrative and dramatic, that is, impersonal. The cycle presents the poet's thoughts and feelings on poetry, love, religion, memory and life in general, but the theme that gives the cycle its profoundest unity is that of the role of suffering in the life of a poet.

The *Nuits* are usually considered elegiac *cris de coeur* (hostile critics speak of gush and mush) but in the main they explore *ideas* thanks especially to the Poet/Muse dialectic. The principal theme is not the poet's suffering per se but the relationship between suffering and poetic creativity and the relationship between suffering and love. The cycle forms an organic, if loosely knit, unit, but critics have paid scant attention to the contribution of each poem to the whole and their relationship with each other. The **"Nuit de Mai"** is an unresolved debate between the Poet and his Muse. The latter, who represents Musset's more energetic and positive side, insists that suffering is inspiration, the very stuff of great poetry.

    Rien ne nous rend si grands qu'une grande douleur.
        . . . . .

    Les plus désespérés sont les chants les plus beaux.
    Et j'en sais d'immortels qui sont de purs sanglots.

Her final argument takes the form of the famous parable of the Pelican, who lets its young feed on his heart, just as the lyric poet sacrifices his privacy and bears his soul for the spiritual and aesthetic nourishment of the public. The Poet (Musset's passive, pessimistic side—but the capital letter enlarges the debate beyond the scope of a mere personal problem), insists on the contrary that intense suffering stifles the poet's voice.

    La bouche garde le silence
    Pour écouter le coeur.
        . . . . .

    L'homme n'écrit rien sur le sable
    A l'heure où passe l'aquilon.

Although it is the poet who has the last word in **"La Nuit de Mai"** and who speaks alone in **"La Nuit de Décembre,"** it is the Muse's theory that is put into practice in the latter: The Poet enumerates—and in verse!—his many sorrows, thus effecting a catharsis that will eventually liberate him from sterile passivity and melancholy. At the time he wrote **"La Nuit de Mai"** Musset's state of mind was no doubt closer to that of the Muse than that of his persona. The Muse invites the Poet to imitate the springtime—

> Poète, prends ton luth et me donne un baiser;
> La fleur de l'églantier sent ses bourgeons éclore,
> Le printemps naît ce soir; les vents vont s'embraser.

Similarly, just before writing the **"Nuit de Mai"** Musset himself felt as if a new poetic phase was about to blossom forth. His brother Paul tells us that having written nothing during the Winter months of 1835 his friend Alfred Tatet asked him what would be "the fruit of his silence." Musset allegedly replied: "Aujourd'hui j'ai cloué de mes propres mains, dans la bière, ma première jeunesse, ma paresse et ma vanité. Je crois sentir enfin que ma pensée, comme une plante qui a été longtemps arosée, a puisé dans la terre des sucs pour croître au soleil. Il me semble que je vais bientôt parler et que j'ai quelque chose dans l'âme qui demande à sortir."[1] (Note in passing that Musset refers to his poetry as *pensée,* a point brought up a moment ago and one that I shall bring up again shortly. . . . Musset then wrote the **"Nuit de Mai"** in a state of exaltation, setting candles at his writing table for the Muse, and upon completing it he felt that his mental anguish had been cured.

For the cure thus effected to be a lasting one Musset needed to confront directly the anguish only hinted at in **"La Nuit de Mai."** The next stage was that recommended by the Muse: *épanchement,* that is, the cathartic role of **"La Nuit de Décembre."** In this second poem of the cycle most of the poet's traumatic experiences and *blocages* are made explicit: the cruel disappointments in love (three especially: his first one Mme Beaulieu, his greatest one, George Sand, and his most recent one, Mme Jaubert), the death of his father, the *hantise du double,* and the central theme, solitude.

The self-portrait presented in **"La Nuit de Décembre"** is that of an authentic romantic hero: We see not just the solitude, but the thirst for the absolute and the unknown ("la soif d'un monde ignoré"), the misanthropy and cynicism ("La face humaine et ses mensonges"), the eternal boredom ("le boiteux Ennui"), the death wish ("Partout où j'ai voulu mourir"). Musset's double, who haunts him at every grievous moment in his life, is described as "Un orphelin vêtu de noir"—two topoi constantly attached to the romantic *beau ténébreux.*[2]

The **"Nuit de Décembre"** is an elegy—the only one, incidentally, of the four *Nuits* that is a true elegy—but his grief, having come out into the open, can now be put behind him or at least faced up to. In the rest of the

cycle the poet is not going to indulge in sorrow for sorrow's sake, as is often claimed or implied; he is going to try to come to grips with it. The third *Nuit* ("d'Août"), thanks to the second one, will be written in a serene mood, "son coeur guéri," according to his brother. "Ouvre tes bras," the poet joyously cries to the Muse, "je viens chanter."

In the **"Nuit d'Août"** the Poet is ready to deal with his greatest emotional crisis, the George Sand affair, and to work his way toward psychological liberation: He will seek love elsewhere. The poem captures the poet's frame of mind at this point in his emotional career as expressed to Sand herself (now only "a friend") in his correspondence.

> J'aurai cependant d'autres maîtresses; maintenant les arbres se couvrent de verdure et l'odeur des lilas entre ici par bouffées: tout renaît et le coeur me bondit malgré moi. Je suis encore jeune, la première femme que j'aurai sera jeune aussi.
>
> (***Correspondance,*** p. 59.)

> Plus je vois de choses crouler sous mes pieds, plus je sens une force cachée qui s'élève, et se tend comme la corde d'un arc . . .

> C'est le printems . . . ce sont les fleurs et toute cette verdure qui m'appellent à la vie.
>
> (Ibid., p. 68)

> Peut-être les élégies dont mon coeur est plein vont se changer en hymne. Il me semble que la nature entière l'entonnerait avec moi . . . Je ne sais si c'est de peur ou de plaisir que je frissonne. Je vais aimer.
>
> (Ibid., p. 72)

As in these letters it is "immortal Nature" that teaches the poet that life and love must go on after tragedy.

> Puisque l'oiseau des bois voltige et chante encore
> Sur la branche où ses oeufs sont brisés dans le nid;
>   . . . . .
>
> Puisque, jusqu'aux rochers, tout se charge en poussière;
> Puisque tout meurt ce soir pour revivre demain;
>   . . . . .
>
> Après avoir souffert, il faut souffrir encore;
> Il faut aimer sans cesse, après avoir aimé.

The fourth and final *Nuit* ("d' Octobre") expresses this same feeling of expectation and renewed confidence in life and in himself, but only after the poet has vented his spleen. The Muse must convince him that grief is instructive

> L'homme est un apprenti, la douleur est son maître.

and that hatred is beneath his dignity

> Tu dis vrai: la haine est impie.

He will forgive and forget the betrayals of former mistresses and think only of his new one (Aimée d'Alton).

From the polyvalent figure of the first *Nuit* the Muse becomes progressively more maternal in the **"Nuit d'Août"** and the **"Nuit d'Octobre,"** "signe évident", says Bernard Masson, "d'une remise en ordre de la psyché perturbée ("Relire les *Nuits,*" p. 197). The *Nights,* collectively, tell the story of a debilitating crisis followed by an intermittent but finally successful convalescence, indeed a rebirth, the resurrection of a poet who had thought himself dead. The last verb of the last *Night* is *renaître.*

The year before he wrote **"La Nuit d'Octobre"** Musset began but never completed a fifth poem, **"La Nuit de Juin."** Only four lines are known to us, but they are enough to indicate clearly the central theme and tone:

> Muse, quand le blé pousse, il faut être joyeux.
> Regarde ces coteaux et leur blonde parure.
> Quelle douce clarté dans l'immense nature!
> Tout ce qui vit ce soir doit se sentir heureux.

One has only to compare the bright joyous imagery of these lines with the darker hues of the first two *Nuits* to see how far Musset has evolved during the course of the cycle.

> Comme il fait noir dans la vallée!
>
> **("Nuit de Mai")**

> Un malheureux vêtu de noir
> Qui me ressemblait comme un frère.
>
> **("Nuit de Décembre")**

The basic style of the night cycle can be called oratorical lyricism. Repetitions, apostrophes, long enumerations and anaphoras, rhetorical questions and exclamations abound. The poet is not even averse to using what he has often decried: the ornamental periphrasis. The month of June for instance, is presented thus:

> Depuis que le soleil, dans l'horizon immense,
> A franchi le Cancer sur son axe enflammé . . .

and the moon becomes "l'astre cher au voyageur." The oratory, which at times borders on the declamatory, does not derive from any lack of spontaneity and sincerity. On the contrary, declamation and intense emotion, as the Muse knows well, often go hand in hand.

> Leurs déclamations sont comme des épées.
> Elles tracent dans l'air un cercle éblouissant,
> Mais il y pend toujours quelques gouttes de sang.
>
> **("Nuit de Mai")**

Spontaneous, not studied, eloquence is indeed one of the marks of Musset's style.

There are two reasons why the *Nuits* do not degenerate into maudlin sentimentality. The first is the dramatic form they are given. The dark brooding of the Dionysian poet is countered, writes Russell King, by the restraint of the Apollonian Muse; or, as Bernard Masson puts it, the darker side of the poet's Jungian *Selbst* is confronted by his *Anima.* The long, well constructed and harmonious sentences of the Muse give a sense of controlled emotion, of clarity and logic. She speaks in stately alexandrines while the tense, impulsive Poet often speaks in shorter lines and shorter sentences punctuated by anguished questions and exclamations and uneven or staccato rhythms created by an enjambement, a displaced caesura, a seven-syllable line ("Honte à toi qui la première") or a six-syllable line followed by an octosyllable. Upon rereading the *Nuits* Alphonse Bouvet was struck by "leur apparent décousu et leurs contradictions." However the Muse/Poet debate, which inhibits perfect unity of theme and tone, and the sudden changes of mood within the Poet himself are but other aspects of the dramatic nature of these highly original lyrics.

The second reason is the surprising emphasis on general ideas rather than on the unique situation of Alfred de Musset. When the Poet alludes to his sorrow in **"La Nuit de Mai"**

> Mais j'ai souffert un dur martyre

the specific nature of the *martyre* is not explained. And in the other *Nuits* the culpable women remain anonymous and tend to be presented on an abstract level: *la femme* rather than *cette femme.* The Poet too is depersonalized by the capital P and by the abstract tenor of most of his argument.

> *L'homme* n'écrit rien sur le sable
> A l'heure où passe l'aquilon.

> *La* bouche garde le silence
> Pour écouter *le* coeur.

> *Leurs* déclamations sont comme des épées

> Rien ne *nous* rend si grands qu'*une* grande douleur.

> *Il faut* aimer sans cesse . . .

> Muse, quand le blé pousse, *il faut* être joyeux.

This generalized, intellectualized and depersonalized lyric stance escaped the notice of nineteenth-century critics. To René Doumic goes the honor of having first discovered or at least elaborated on the *flou voulu* of the *Nuits.* Writing in 1897 he establishes an important fact:

> Le plus frappant, dans les *Nuits,* c'est de voir comment
> le poète y dépouille son émotion de tous les éléments
> particuliers, de tous les détails qui l'auraient faite étroite

et précise . . . Les personnes, les noms, le décor ex-
térieur, le lieu, la date, autant de détails que nous sommes libres d'imaginer à notre gré . . . Telle est pour la
poésie lyrique elle-même, la condition de vie et de la
durée: il faut qu'elle dépasse les émotions d'un homme
et l'expression des sentiments d'un jour, pour arriver
jusqu'à ce fond immuable et commun où, par delà les
individus et les temps, toutes les souffrances humaines
se reconnaissent et se répondent.

> (Quoted by P. Gastinel, *Romantisme de Musset*, p.
> 493)

Thus Doumic sees Musset striving for universality.
Joachim Merlant thinks rather that it is a sense of delicacy that impels poets like Musset to speak in general
rather than specific terms: "l'expression verbale jette
toujours une lumière trop nette, trop crue sur les sentiments. Aussi les poètes de la vie intérieure, Musset,
Vigny, Lamartine, Verlaine, se sont-ils de plus en plus
préoccupés de trouver une forme indécise, flottante, qui
parle aux seuls initiés; c'est à la fois un scrupule de
délicatesse morale et de probité artistique. A vouloir
dire complètement certaines choses on les trahit"
(*Musset: Morceaux choisis*, p. 101). Margaret Rees
(*Musset*, p. viii) is impressed with how much "food for
thought" there is to be found in Musset's work and sub-
mits (p. 65) that the important role of ideas in the *Poésies nouvelles* has been soft-pedaled by the critics. Philippe Van Tieghem (*Musset:* p. 21) is convinced that the
most striking characteristic of the *Nuits* is the primacy
of the intellectual, and Patricia Siegel ("Structure et
thématique," chapter 2) calls them the apogee of Musset's thought.

The style of the other three poems in the cycle is similar to that of the four *Nuits*. The **"Lettre à M. de
Lamartine"** (1836) is addressed, with considerable rhetorical flourish, to the Christian poet and especially the
poet of sorrow with whom Musset now identifies thanks
to his new feeling that great pain is providential (**"Nuit
d'Octobre"**). As with nearly all the poems in the cycle
the movement is from autobiographical allusions (here
the second and final *rupture* with Mme Jaubert, mingled
as usual with his first disappointment in love) to more
general considerations, from the particular to the universal. Musset affirms his belief in a vaguely perceived
God and in the immortality of the soul, which will eventually triumph over its transient grief and preserve for
eternity the memory of true love. This final theme is
expressed in oratory that has been both praised for its
"incomparable" forcefulness and damned for its grandiloquence.

> Tu te sens le coeur pris d'un caprice de femme,
> Et tu dis qu'il se brise à force de souffrir.
> Tu demandes à Dieu de soulager ton âme:
> Ton âme est immortelle, et ton coeur va guérir.
>
> Le regret d'un instant te trouble et te dévore;
> Tu dis que le passé te voile l'avenir.

> Ne te plains pas d'hier; laisse venir l'aurore:
> Ton âme est immortelle, et le temps va s'enfuir.
>
> Ton corps est abattu du mal de ta pensée;
> Tu sens ton front peser et tes genoux fléchir.
> Tombe, agenouille-toi, créature insensée:
> Ton âme est immortelle, et la mort va venir.
>
> Tes os dans le cercueil vont tomber en poussière;
> Ta mémoire, ton nom, ta gloire vont périr,
> Mais non pas ton amour, si ton amour t'est chère:
> Ton âme est immortelle, et va s'en souvenir.

"L'Espoir en Dieu," despite the title and apparent
theme, expresses an anguish more than a faith. The de-
liberative monologue and the fluctuating feelings that
develop as the poem progresses are dramatic, not dog-
matic. The poem registers the musings of a doubter
who "wants" to believe. There are Pascalian echoes: the
anguish before the infinite—

> Malgré moi l'infini me tourmente..
> Je n'y saurais songer sans crainte et sans espoir.

and a theological wager of sorts—

> Pour que Dieu nous réponde, adressons-nous à lui.
> . . . . .
>
> Si le ciel est désert, nous n'offensons personne:
> Si quelqu'un nous entend, qu'il nous prenne en pitié!

The final section, however, presents almost accusatory
questions

> Pourquoi fais-tu douter de toi?
> Quel triste plaisir peux-tu prendre
> A tenter notre bonne foi?
>
> Pourquoi donc, ô Maître suprême,
> As-tu créé le mal si grand?

and a challenge

> Soulève les voiles du monde
> Et montre-toi, Dieu juste et bon!

"Souvenir" offers the cycle's final statement on the
problem of ephemeral love. It is a development of the
optimism expressed in the **"Lettre à Lamartine."**
Life's rare privileged moments do endure: in the
memory, in poetry, and in the soul's immortal consciousness. The poem belongs to a genre that Meyer
Abrams has called the greater Romantic lyric. . . .

Two other extended lyrics of note are **"A la Malibran"**
(1838) and **"Souvenir des Alpes"** (1852). The first
holds little interest for the reader of the late twentieth
century for two reasons: the subject and the style. Musset himself explains in the elegy that while great painters and poets live eternally through the works that survive them, the art of a great singer is lost to posterity.

The magnificent voice of La Malibran could not be recorded then as now, and so her fame gradually died out with the passing generations. Another thematic problem is the idealization of an undoubtedly dedicated artist who died prematurely; she died, in fact, not so much the victim of her dedication to her art and her public, and not the victim of her fiery genius, as the poem claims, but from a fall off a horse. And the 25 rhetorical questions (more than 46% of the poem's sentences and more the 64% of the sentences in the middle section—stanzas 8 to 24-) become tiresome to the modern reader. **"Souvenir des Alpes,"** like the more famous **"Souvenir,"** is another good example of the greater Romantic lyric. . . .

The originality of Musset's lyricism should be stressed. Despite the poetics of the **"Nuit de Mai"** (which will be put in its proper perspective in the next chapter), Musset's extended lyrics are *not* simple *cris de coeur,* mere developments of an exclamation. They move consistently from the personal to the general and belong as much to the poetry of ideas as to traditional lyricism. One critic, Yves Le Hir, has noticed the high frequency of maxims and aphorisms in Musset's love lyrics. Even in the many exclamatory and interrogative sentences it is usually an *idea,* not a complaint, that is being developed lyrically.

Notes

1. Valentine Brunet (*Le Lyrisme d'Alfred de Musset*) finds evidence that Musset's sorceress, Belisa (in *Don Paez*), may have been influenced by *La Celestina* of Fernando de Rojas. See Brunet for a more detailed account of Musset's Spanish sources.

2. Alfred de Musset, *Poésies complètes,* ed. Maurice Allem (Paris: Gallimard, 1957), p. 36. All subsequent quotations from Musset's poetry are taken from this edition. References to line numbers are given only for the detailed stylistic analyses in Part Two. Purely documentary information following quotations from secondary sources are placed in the text rather than in notes. The information includes only the name of the author, a short or shortened title and page number. For full bibliographical information, including name of publisher, date and place of publication, consult the Bibliography.

Bibliography

Abrams, Myer W. "Structure and Style in the Greater Romantic Lyric." in *From Sensibility to Romanticism: Essays Presented to Frederick A. Pottle,* eds. Frederick W. Hillis and Harold Bloom. New York: Oxford University Press, 1965, pp. 527-560.

Aquitaine, Jean d.' *Alfred de Musset: l'oeuvre, le poète.* Paris: Gaillard, 1907.

Doumic, René. "Le classicisme de Musset." *Revue des Deux Mondes,* 15 June 1907, 923-24.

Gastinel, Pierre. *Le Romantisme d'Alfred de Musset.* Paris: Hachette, 1933.

Grammont, Maurice. *Le Vers français: ses moyens d'expression, son harmonie.* Paris: Delagrave, 1967.

King, Russell S. "Musset: the Poet of Dionysus." *Studies in Romanticism,* 13 (1974), 323-32.

Le Hir, Yves. "L'Expression du sentiment amoureux dans l'oeuvre poétique d'Alfred de Musset." *Le Français Moderne,* 23 (1955), 176-190 and 275-279; 24 (1956), 15-34.

Masson, Bernard. "Relire les *Nuits* de Musset sous la lumière de Jung." *Revue d'Histoire Littéraire de la France,* 76, 192-210.

Merlant, Joachim, ed. *Musset: Morceaux choisis.* Paris: Didier, 1924.

Montégut, Emile. *Nos Morts contemporains.* Paris: Hachette, 1893.

Musset, Alfred de. *Poésies complètes.* Ed. Maurice Allem. Paris: Gallimard, 1957.

Rees, Margaret. *Alfred de Musset.* New York: Twayne, 1971.

Siegel, Patricia J. "Structure et thématique dans la poésie d'Alfred de Musset." Diss. Yale, 1970.

Van Tieghem, Philippe. *Musset.* Paris: Hatier, 1969.

Alain Piette (essay date fall 1989)

SOURCE: Piette, Alain. "Musset's *Lorenzaccio.*" *The Explicator* 48, no. 1 (fall 1989): 17-20.

[*In the following essay, Piette contends that the protagonist of Musset's drama* Lorenzaccio *is an ironic figure associated with chaos, self-destruction, and futility, rather than a tragic hero.*]

Lorenzaccio is usually considered Musset's most original contribution to world literature and drama. Yet, although most critics agree on the play's literary quality, history shows us few successful productions. As was the case with most of his plays, Musset did not write this drama for the stage. Musset's plays are primarily meant to be read, as the title of one of his collections, *Armchair Theatre* (**Un Spectacle dans un fauteuil,** 1832, 1834) indicates. But the trouble with the play lies chiefly in the enigmatic character of its protagonist: the complex, almost obscure motivation for his climactic act is the substance of the play. Lorenzaccio's characterization is a delicately woven texture, whose threads seem to converge toward the murder in act IV, scene 8.[1] Yet the murder does not solve anything: in view of its final result—the immediate coronation of another tyrant—and Lorenzaccio's own indifference, our general comprehension of the play's "hero" is confused, and we are left with more questions than answers.

I would like to suggest that *Lorenzaccio* is not the tragedy of a misunderstood or unappreciated hero: there is little or no evidence in the text that points to a noble motive in Lorenzaccio. The most ambitious, if not completely successful, definitions of Lorenzaccio's character have been thematic and historic. Many critics espouse the optimistic view of the historian F. Schevill,[2] to the effect that Lorenzaccio's murder of Alessandro is designed to free his country from a monstrous tryanny. In this interpretation, Lorenzaccio is a disillusioned young aristocrat fallen from innocence, a man bone-weary of a debauchery to which he had meant only to pretend in order to win Alessandro's confidence. Herbert Hunt[3] and Paul Dimoff[4] adopt a biographical point of view: they see in Lorenzaccio the reflection of Musset's own disgust with society after the failure of the 1830 revolution, which he had wholeheartedly supported, and the deterioration of his relationship with George Sand.

More satisfying perhaps is Robert Denommé's interpretation.[5] He views Lorenzaccio as an early version of what Verlaine called the "poète maudit," the Romantic hero par excellence, who deliberately alienates himself from the society he lives in, and whose predicament puts him above the petty laws of a tedious and hypocritical universe. Inherent in the posture of the Romantic hero is a deep-rooted disgust with the world. In *Lorenzaccio,* this feeling takes on ironical overtones, inasmuch as the protagonist, because of his privileged position at court as the Duke's minion and informer, is not only a part of the society he loathes but an instrument of its survival. This irony is the key to Lorenzaccio's character. It elicits an attitude of self-contempt that is present throughout the play, but which becomes prominent in Lorenzaccio's last scene. He is subject to a strong self-destructive impulse, which finally overwhelms him when he willfully surrenders to the blows of his assassin.

Lorenzaccio's tendency toward self-annihilation is a corollary of his predicament as "poète maudit." It arises from his awareness of his own dual nature: unable to reconcile his life of debauchery at the court of Florence with the loftier ideals of his Romantic youth, he chooses to evaporate into nothingness. His murder of Alessandro has no other purpose than itself, and it is nothing short of suicide. On a political level, it achieves nothing. Far from inciting the people of Florence to revolt, as the partisans of the Strozzi would have it at the beginning of the play, it simply reaffirms the rule of the Medici over the city. Lorenzaccio himself is conscious of the gratuitousness of his act from the start. To Filippo Strozzi, who asks him why he is going to commit the murder if he believes it useless, Lorenzaccio replies:

> I'll make a wager with you. I am going to kill Alessandro. Once my deed is accomplished, if the republicans act as they should, it will be easy for them to establish a republic, the finest that ever flourished on this earth. Let's say they may even have the people with them. I wager that neither they nor the people will do anything.
>
> (61)

The murder will not change anything, and Cardinal Cibo knows it; he quotes *The Aeneid*:

> The first golden bough torn down is replaced by another,
> And as quickly there grows a similar branch of a similar metal.
>
> (84)

Alessandro is like one of the statues that Lorenzaccio beheaded at the Arch of Constantine in Rome in a fit of iconoclastic frenzy. Indeed, in his last scene, Lorenzaccio strongly suggests that he himself could be one of them when he confesses to Filippo Strozzi after the murder that "I am hollower than a tin statue" (91). Alessandro's murder is a mere act of vandalism, and, as in vandalism, the emphasis in *Lorenzaccio* is on an individual's act: Musset is concerned only with *what* is done rather than with *why* it is done. The private and public significance of the action are explored, not its motivation.

The murder scene further emphasizes Lorenzaccio's suicidal tendencies. As Marie MacLean noted,[6] it has all the aspects of a tumultuous wedding night; the stabbing has the connotations of a monstrous copulation, whose orgasmic culmination ends in the death of one of the lovers. Ironically, it is Lorenzaccio who is "laid to rest." Transfixed in front of the Duke's dead body, he mutters as Scoronconcolo drags him away: "O magnificent nature! O eternal tranquility!" (82). He realizes that by killing Alessandro he has sealed his own doom. He is not a praying mantis but a wasp, and he has just lost his sting. His actual demise is only a matter of days. By killing the Duke, Lorenzaccio has no other purpose than to realize his own nature, whose essence he tries to explain to Filippo Strozzi in a beautiful moment of shrewd self-definition:

> You ask me why I'm going to kill Alessandro? Do you want me to poison myself or jump in the Arno? . . . Do you realize that this murder is all that's left of my virtue? . . . If you honor anything in me, it is this murder which you honor.
>
> (61-2)

Lorenzaccio *is* this murder.

His own death, which is eagerly called for, is deprived of any tragic dimenson: it has nothing to do with tragic retribution. In fact, it occurs almost unobtrusively in a most undramatic scene. Lorenzaccio rushes out on the street despite Filippo Strozzi's warning and almost immediately thereafter is reported dead by one of the servants. The whole takes only a few seconds, and the killing is off-stage. The play closes on the image of the new duke taking the oath of office, and we realize that Lorenzaccio's crime has been useless. As he himself has maintained since the beginning of the play, he is not invested with a messianic mission. He is merely trapped in a world he cannot call his own. His urge toward self-consumption and the gratuitousness of his act can be seen as Romantic prefiguring of the existentialist cry of the burned-out Meursault in Camus' *Stranger.*

As we see then, Lorenzaccio's murder of his cousin Alessandro de Medici, Duke of Florence, is little else than the culmination of a series of selfish, malevolent acts, the logical outcome of a life of corruption. Lorenzaccio is the Romantic hero par excellence. As Shaw observed in his review of the play in 1897, "In the Romantic school horror was naturally akin to sublimity."[7] Lorenzaccio is the monster whose otherworldliness puts him above the petty laws of a tedious and hypocritical society. The representative of a perversely superior race of giants, as the Medici view themselves, he is an outlaw in the true sense of the term, and his life is governed by a single non-principle: chaos.

Notes

1. Alfred de Musset, "Lorenzaccio," *The Modern Theatre,* vol. 6., ed. Eric Bentley (Gloucester Mass.: Peter Smith, 1974). Hereafter referred to by page number in the text.

2. Ferdinand Schevill, *The Medici* (New York: Harcourt, Brace, 1949).

3. Herbert J. Hunt, "Alfred de Musset et la Révolution de Juillet: la leçon politique de *Lorenzaccio,*" *Mercure de France* 251: 1934.

4. Paul Dimoff, *La Genèse de Lorenzaccio* (Paris: Droz, 1933).

5. Robert T. Denommé, "The Motif of the 'Poète Maudit' in Musset's *Lorenzaccio,*" *L' Esprit créateur* vol. 5, no. 2 (1965): 138-46.

6. Marie McLean, "The Sword and the Flower: The Sexual Symbolism of *Lorenzaccio,*" *Australian Journal of French Studies* 16(1979):166-81.

7. G. B. Shaw, "Lorenzaccio," *Dramatic Opinions and Essays with an Apology by Bernard Shaw* (New York: Brentano's, 1922):295.

D. R. Gamble (essay date fall-winter 1989-90)

SOURCE: Gamble, D. R. "Alfred de Musset and the Uses of Experience." *Nineteenth-Century French Studies* 18, nos. 1-2 (fall-winter 1989-90): 78-84.

[*In the following essay, Gamble discusses Musset's artistic application of life experience to his literary works.*]

"Alfred de Musset, féminin et sans doctrine, aurait pu exister dans tous les temps et n'eût jamais été qu'un paresseux à effusions gracieuses. . . ."[1] No one, of course, can be right all the time, and Charles Baudelaire was no exception: originally offered in his essay on Gautier of 1859, this embarrassing estimation of the character and contribution of Musset has since been successfully challenged by the studies of a number of scholars and literary critics. It is true that Musset disliked prefaces and literary manifestoes and so wrote very few; his attitude to theory and theoretical discussion in general is best revealed in the remarks he made in a letter to his brother during the summer of 1831:

> Chacun de nous a dans le ventre un certain son qu'il peut rendre, comme un violon ou une clarinette. Tous les raisonnements du monde ne pourraient faire sortir du gosier d'un merle la chanson du sansonnet.[2]

Through the study, however, of the critical remarks found in his correspondence, newspaper articles, short stories, plays and poems, it has been convincingly demonstrated that Musset did indeed have a coherent theory of poetry to which he consistently adhered, and moreover that it was, in its constant emphasis on the moods and impressions of the poet himself, considerably influenced by the fashions and attitudes of his own time. It is not my intention here to review at length what has already been revealed of Musset's theory of poetry,[3] but rather to discuss one central aspect of it that has not yet been fully explored and the consequences it had, not only for Musset's verse, but also for his short stories and, perhaps most important of all, for his theater. I wish to discuss the place and importance of experience for Musset in literary creation; and by "experience," I mean the poet's actual experience of life, his acquaintance with the broad world around him.

To appreciate the significance of this aspect of his literary theory, it must first of all be understood that at the center of Musset's poetic lay the emotions of the poet himself: ". . . Joie ou douleur / Tout demande sans cesse à sortir de ton coeur," Musset wrote of the poet in **"Les Voeux stériles"** (1830);[4] through its moods and discoveries his own heart was not only to furnish the thematic material for his verse, it was also to generate the inspiration and enthusiasm necessary for its composition. Subjects like politics and nature, that had such appeal for poets like Hugo and Lamartine, were completely excluded; this left Musset free to interpret the spirit of his own time through the feelings it aroused in that contemporary whom he knew best: himself. Not surprisingly, Musset insisted on the absolute sincerity of such verse; and since it was this individual veracity that alone justified its expression, there was no need to fashion it to the demands of any particular style, be it Romantic or classical.

These, then, in barest outline, are the central tenets of a poetic whose primary objective was intimate and unrestrained self-expression. Its origins lay in the literary attitude stressing personal feeling prevalent during Musset's early youth, in the example of personal revelation characteristic of authors whom he especially admired like de Quincey and Byron, and in his commitment in literature almost from the outset to what has been termed "la poursuite de la vérité humaine."[5] These various ideas coalesced into a definite theory of poetry, however, only after Musset had already gained some notoriety as a poet with the publication of his first volume of verse, *the Contes d'Espagne et d'Italie,* in December, 1829. In the exotic and slightly fantastic popular image of Spain and Italy he had found the perfect setting for the expression of his youthful dreams. This early volume, in fact, contained the most extensive poetic vision Musset would know; it was followed by a disappointing series of abortive fragments. Musset then realized that conscious literary creation—and the career he had chosen for himself as a poet—would require a more serious effort. In this way began the meditation that resulted in the composition of **"Les Secrètes Pensées de Rafaël, gentilhomme français"** (1830), **"Les Voeux stériles"** (1830), and **"La Dédicace de la Coupe et les lèvres"** (1832): in the poems, that is, which first stressed the importance of the poet's own emotions and so established the core of the poetic I have described.

Even as this verse was being written Musset adopted a quite different style of life. The distance between him and Hugo's *Cénacle* had been growing since 1830, and he now replaced that group with a new circle of wealthier and more urbane acquaintances centered around the dandy Alfred Tattet. With them Musset satisfied his penchant for a more aristocratic existence. It was also much more worldly. Musset's early life had in fact been somewhat sheltered, and this was his first contact with the harsher realities of the materialistic Paris of Louis-Philippe. Within a short time, however, Musset was thoroughly familiar with "les moeurs de ce pays étrange qu'on a nommé le boulevard de Gand" (896). "C'est un des points rares sur la terre où le plaisir s'est concentré" (896).[6] Musset's prolonged exploration of the Parisian underworld has often been ascribed to his immaturity, to his desire to live free of social constraint, and to his considerable appetite for sensual pleasure; but these reasons offer only a partial explanation. If Musset's radical change of life-style followed the formulation of his poetic as closely as it did, it was

that the two were linked: because his conception of poetry had become so intimate, so focused on his own personality, Musset had concluded that in order to go on composing it he would have to broaden his own experience to have sufficient new material to express: in late 1831, he deliberately began to seek out the new adventures he now felt necessary for the poetry he hoped to write. The testimony left by those closest to him corroborates this view. In a commemorative article published on 11 May 1857—just nine days after Musset's death—Sainte-Beuve, his old friend and the literary critic who knew him best, clearly referred to what might be termed Musset's "theory of experience":

> Alfred de Musset, comme plus d'un des personnages qu'il a peints et montrés en action, s'était dit qu'il fallait tout voir, tout savoir, et, pour être l'artiste qu'il voulait être, avoir plongé au fond de tout. Théorie périlleuse et fatale![7]

And in the biography of his brother he published in 1877, Paul de Musset lends credence to Sainte-Beuve's words with his own recollections of his younger brother's activities in 1831:

> Sous le prétexte d'acquérir de l'expérience, il menait, d'ailleurs, une vie assez dissipée. Les jeunes gens à la mode se réunissaient le soir au Café de Paris. On y organisait des parties de plaisir sur une grande échelle.[8]

If Paul de Musset appears to have had reservations about Alfred's explanation for his behavior, it should be borne in mind that he was writing almost half a century later, well aware that his brother's theory of experience had eventually led to results rather different from those that were initially envisaged.

But all began well. Musset made his most ambitious early attempt to exploit his newly-acquired experience in **"Rolla"** (1833), whose realistic detail—the rapid sketch of "les restes d'une orgie" (141), the graphic description of child prostitution—would have been unthinkable in the idealized visions of his first collection. The influence of this experience is also clearly evident in the charged metaphors of other poems he wrote at this time: **"A Julie"** (1832), for instance, or **"Namouna"** (1832). Needless to add, Musset's debauchery during these years also made possible his slim contribution to erotica, **"Gamiani ou deux nuits d'excès,"** first published in 1833 but probably written, according to the most recent article on the subject,[9] in late 1831 or early 1832. With obvious exceptions, however, most of this work is minor, for even as its pleasures became addictive, Musset soon came to find less and less inspiration in what he was discovering of the world around him.

This contradiction lies at the source of Musset's greatest play, *Lorenzaccio,* completed in draft before he left for Italy with George Sand and possibly revised further on his return before it was published in August, 1834. But even by the time Musset began the drama in late 1833 his experience of the Parisian underworld had made him realize the limitations of his theory and what practising it had cost him. It was this knowledge that fuelled his disenchantment with his own life and so enabled him to identify as closely as he did with his unhappy historical protagonist: just as Musset's ambitious love of art had led him to adopt a theory of experience that had unexpectedly wedded him to debauchery and excess, so too had Lorenzo dei Medici's love of liberty and noble dream to restore the republic to Florence led him to adopt the mores of its corrupt and corrupting Duke; and Lorenzo's sacrifice, of course, was to be no more successful that Musset's own. The parallel between them is too great for there to be any doubt: it was Musset's own unhappy experience as an artist, his early dream and its unfortunate consequences, that allowed him to recreate his central character as successfully as he did. Like Lorenzo, lost irrevocably to cynicism and lust, Musset in his darker moments might even then have confessed: "Il est trop tard. Je me suis fait à mon métier. Le vice a été pour moi un vêtement, maintenant il est collé à ma peau (Act III, scene 3: 341). Elsewhere in *Lorenzaccio,* too, there are significant references to the theory of art by which Musset had lived, most notably in the discussions between Lorenzo and the young painter Tebaldeo (in Ac II, scene 2). Excusing as he can the corruption of Florence, it is Tebaldeo who suggests that "l'art, cette fleur divine, a quelquefois besoin du fumier pour engraisser le sol et le féconder" (327), that "les terres corrompues engendrent le blé céleste" (328). Musset's changing attitude toward his view of experience, however, is clear from the character he chose to express it, for as sympathetic as Tebaldeo may be, the young artist is essentially portrayed as idealistic, and even naïve.

Musset's awareness of the limitations and dangers of his theory, however, brought about no immediate change in his approach to literary creation, as he now looked more and more to love, to his experience of this emotion at its most intense, as the greatest source of poetic inspiration. Hence the remarks that Musset had made in a a brief poem to his friend Édouard Bocher in 1832:

> Tu te frappais le front en lisant Lamartine,
> . . . . .
> Ah! frappe-toi le coeur, c'est là qu'est le génie.
> C'est là qu'est la pitié, la souffrance et l'amour;
> C'est là qu'est le rocher du désert de la vie,
> D'où les flots d'harmonie,
> Quand Moïse viendra, jailliront quelque jour.
>
> (90-91)

This attitude accounts for the resonance of his affair with George Sand, which began in June, 1833: for Musset the episode had a professional as well as a personal significance. This view of love also explains the intensity of the *Nuits,* begun in the spring of 1835, shortly after Musset had broken with Sand for the last time. For whatever else he had written during their liaison— and many of his best plays date from that period— Musset's passion for his mistress had not produced the great lyric poetry that he had earlier felt must result. It was Musset's contemplation of this unalterable fact that finally led him to reassess completely the value of experience in literary creation. This reassessment of his theory, of course, is expressed through the *Nuits* cycle, which is an inner dialogue between Musset and his Muse about his difficulties in poetic creation. Accordingly, through the cycle the discussion of love is limited essentially to its influence on his creativity as a poet— however much may have been written about the identify of the women in the various poems. Musset's passion for Sand had overwhelmed and stifled him: "L'homme n'écrit rien sur le sable / A l'heure où passe l'aquilon" (152), the poet protests to his disappointed Muse in **"La Nuit de mai"** (1835). In **"La Nuit d'août"** (1836), from a theoretical viewpoint the most important poem of the cycle, the Muse reveals the result of Musset's meditation on the relationship between poetry and experience, art and life:

> De ton coeur ou de toi lequel est le poète?
> C'est ton coeur, et ton coeur ne te répondra pas.
> L'amour l'aura brisé.
>
> (156)

In this way Musset acknowledged that his theory of poetry based upon emotional involvement had been a mistake, his attempt to channel personal experience directly into creative expression a failure; and worse: by diverting his interests and energy, by increasing his awareness of reality, his earlier search for new experience had only weakened his imaginative powers. Toward the end of **"La Nuit d'août"** is found a line that expresses the ultimate consequence of Musset's meditation on his theory: "J'aime," wrote the poet, "et pour un baiser je donne mon génie" (156). Feeling he must choose between the pleasures to which his earlier pursuit of stimulating experience had accustomed him and the reflextion and constant dedication he now concluded were necessary for great art, Musset in the end chose life: and love.

In a manner, therefore, that he can hardly have foreseen, Musset's theory of experience brought about the composition of the *Nuits* cycle; and whatever we may think of it today as a whole, its poems contain some of his most accomplished and best-known verse. The impact of this theory and the experience it entailed was such, however, that it led not only to *Lorenzaccio* and the *Nuits,* but to one of Musset's most memorable short stories as well.

Some two years after he had announced his decision to live for himself rather than his art in **"La Nuit d'août,"**

Musset illustrated and to some extent vindicated his choice in the short story **"Le Fils du Titien,"** published in the spring of 1838. By a convincing transposition, it is the great Venetian painter's young son Pippo, himself very gifted, who is forced to choose between his artistic career and his personal desires: forced to choose because the disciplined life he would have to live as an artist and the carefree existence he wishes to enjoy with his wealthy patrician mistress are not compatible. As the narrator explains:

> . . . Il est certain que ce qui est véritablement beau est l'ouvrage du temps et du recueillement, et qu'il n'y a pas de vrai génie sans patience.

(701)

In spite of his unique talent and the encouragement of the woman he loves, in the end the young painter feels that the intense dedication his art requires is a price too high for him to pay: "Et avec sa gaieté habituelle, il concluait en s'écriant: 'Au diable la peinture! la vie est trop courte'" (701).

As I have already suggested, the sobering realizations that accompanied Musset's experience of life are reflected in lesser works as well: directly in short stories like **"L'Histoire d'un merle blanc"** (1839) and *Le Poète déchu* (1842), rather more obliquely in the realistic character of some of his later plays and the wistful depths of his last poems. What I hope already to have shown here, however, is the way in which Musset's approach to poetry and the experience to which it led marked indelibly the course of his development as an artist. In itself his theory of experience can hardly be considered a success; its ultimate effect, in fact, was Musset's almost complete abandonment, after 1838, of serious poetic endeavor.

But nor was this theory entirely abortive. For if Musset's experience robbed him of his illusions and made him aware of his limits as an artist, it also finally acquainted him with the paradoxes that lay hidden deep within his own character. In this way it provided him, even as it failed, with the personal material he sought: responding to his intense introspection and sense of loss, the gifted but facile writer of the *Contes d'Espagne et d'Italie* struck a new chord, and so was able briefly to transform the debris of his own unhappy life into consoling personal monuments of lasting art.

Notes

1. Charles Baudelaire, *Oeuvres complètes,* éd. Claude Pichois, 2 vols., Bibliothèque de la Pléiade (Paris: Gallimard, 1976) 2: 110.

2. Alfred de Musset, *Correspondance: Tome 1/1826/ 1839,* éd. Marie Cordroc'h, Roger Pierrot, Loïc Chotard (Paris: Presses Universitaires de France, 1985) 48.

3. See, for example, chapter 11 ("Les Idées littéraires de Musset") of Philippe van Tieghem, *Musset,* 2e éd. (Paris: Hatier, 1969), for a well-organized and in the main reliable account of his views.

4. Alfred de Musset, *Oeuvres complètes,* ed. Philippe van Tieghem, Collection l'Intégrale (Paris: Éditions du Seuil, 1966) 85. Further references within the body of the text are made to this edition.

5. Pierre Gastinel, *Le Romantisme d'Alfred de Musset,* diss. Paris 1931 (Paris: Hachette, 1933) 201.

6. From the long introduction that Musset wrote for, but never included in, his short story *Les Deux Maîtresses* of 1837. In Philippe van Tieghem's edition of Musset's *Oeuvres complètes* used here it has been published on pages 896-97 as the fragment it remains and entitled *Le Boulevard de Gand.*

7. Charles-Augustin Sainte-Beuve, *Causeries du lundi* 16 vols. (rpt. Paris: Garnier, 1926) 13: 367.

8. Paul de Musset, *Biographie d'Alfred de Musset: sa vie et ses oeuvres,* 4e éd. (Paris: Charpentier, 1877) 100.

9. Simon Jeune, *"Gamiani*: poème érotique et funèbre d'Alfred de Musset," *Revue d'Histoire Littéraire de la France* 6 (1985): 990.

James F. Hamilton (essay date fall-winter 1991-92)

SOURCE: Hamilton, James F. "Reversed Polarities in the *Nuits*: Anatomy of a Cure." *Nineteenth-Century French Studies* 20, nos. 1-2 (fall-winter 1991-92): 65-73.

[*In the following essay, Hamilton offers a psychoanalytic reading of Musset's* Les nuits *as poems based on the polarity of projected ego and* anima.]

Musset structures his series of lyrical poems as a dialogue between the Muse and the Poet and, in one instance, between the implied poet and his alter ego, "qui me ressemblait comme un frère."[1] The two voices or roles in the poems are linked with Musset's "duality of temperament."[2] In the *Nuits,* personality and biography lend themselves to his romantic technique of *dédoublement,* the projected splitting of self and the feeling that one contains dual and usually opposed identities.[3] Polarity in the *Nuits* (1835-37) arises from the emotional aftermath of Musset's two-year love affair with George Sand that ended in March 1835. Through the self-therapy of poetry, he attempts to come to terms with his conflicting feelings.[4]

My interpretation focuses on the internal dynamics of Musset's *Nuits* in order to shed light on the creative process. I see the Poet and the Muse not only as projections of Musset, but more specifically, from the stand-point of Jungian psychology, as his dramatized ego and *anima.* They evolve in a dynamic relationship away from "sickness," defined as reversed polarity, toward a "cure" or stabilized self, reflected in a realignment of the polarized interlocutors. The theme of "guérison," constituting a psychological as well as a structural criterion of success in the *Nuits,* also benefits from Musset's insight into dramatization. Just as Jungian psychology opens up the dynamic mechanism of dialogue in the poems to reveal characterization, phenomenological analysis shows how their setting evolves in relation to the poet's state of mind.

The dramatized selves of Musset act out his conflicts within the dimensions of space, time, and materiality of opposing world views. Introduced in the opening stanzas of **"La Nuit de mai"** (15 June 1835) the two selves confront one another on an unequal footing. That of the Muse is verbalized first and is associated with the spatial qualities of expansion, exteriorization, and verticality. She announces the rebirth of spring with its burgeoning wild roses, greening bushes, and flowering trees. All of nature opens, and the Muse's insistent entreaties are garbed in the barely disguised language of seduction as seen in her repeated imperative: "Poète, prends ton luth et me donne un baiser" and in the urgent imagery of a rustic setting transformed into a perfumed boudoir: "Comme le lit joyeux de deux jeunes époux" (23). Indeed, the Muse's blatant imagery can be justified by its elevated intention of externalizing the Poet's need to create, to be artistically productive. Moreover, the visualization of fecundity, passion, and joyful love does not restrict the Muse to terrestrial values. As the source of her being, she identifies with the elements of fire, air, and sky and, in so doing, lays claim to mythical elements associated with the masculine.[5] Born on the warm winds of spring sweeping down from above, she threatens to return: "Mon aile me soulève au souffle du printemps / Le vent va m'emporter; je vais quitter la terre" (125-26).

The second, opposing world is experienced by the Poet who has retreated into himself. Characterized by contraction, interiorization, and horizontality, his existence lacks light, perspective, and openness. Preoccupation with his inner space distances him from personal contact, and he is slow in responding to the Muse. Indeed, overshadowed by her verbal energy and passionate vitality, he feels threatened by her insistent invitation to life and to the stirrings within himself: "Qu'ai-je donc en moi qui s'agite, / Dont je me sens épouvanté?" (25-26). In contrast to nature's fecundity, the Poet laments his separation from life through loneliness and sterility: "Je suis seul; c'est l'heure qui sonne; / 0 solitude! 0 Pauvreté!" (32-33). He is chided by the Muse for his laziness and, indirectly, for his "impuissance" (121). Little wonder that he rebels in the concluding stanza: "O

Muse! spectre insatiable, / Ne m'en demande pas si long" (192-93). Limited to the terrestrial, horizontal plane of existence, he is unsure of his feelings and is cut off from the outside world by his lack of confidence.

The opposing worlds of the Poet and the Muse can be explained by the concept of polarity that has considerable standing in literary criticism, science, myth, and in Jungian psychology. The concept of *dédoublement* has been referred to, and this romantic theme enjoys an intuitive insight into human nature. The brain is divided into two hemispheres, unequal but complementary, which work side by side and have some bearing as to gender.[6] Myth also sees polarity as being of central importance to life and speculates that the sacred, when entering the field of time, provides transcendent energy by breaking "into pairs of opposites."[7] Between experimental science and mysticism stands Jungian psychology. It maintains that all energy and life are born of the tensions of opposites such as good and evil, day and night, life and death. etc., and that balance is made possible by the self-regulating system of the psyche.[8] In the attempt to understand the function of polarities in the unconscious mind, the seat of creativity, Jung has set forth theoretical models based on contrasexual factors. Each gender incorporates, in addition to an ego and its shadow, tendencies of its opposite. The *anima* represents the woman within man and the *animus,* the man within woman. Each contrasexual factor has a positive and a negative potential. Development requires the integration of opposites in the process of individuation.[9]

In the *Nuits,* polarity is reversed in the sense that Musset's projected *anima* in the Muse overwhelms the Poet through her power of movement across time, space, and matter. For his part, the Poet appears to be mired in a present not of his choice, unable to reflect upon the past or project himself into the future. To be sure, some unconscious "bad faith" may be involved, for the shadow aspect of Musset's dramatized ego projects upon the Muse an aura of possessive and emasculating, if not devouring, maternalized figure of beloved.[10] Indeed, both the Poet and the Muse show evidence of ambivalence between negative and positive aspects of personality, as in a dramatic character. In other words, the conflicts of Musset are acted out through opposing forces on complex levels of meaning radiating from his self.[11]

The major symptom of reversed polarity in the *Nuits,* passivity, is featured in the first half of the next poem, **"La Nuit de décembre"** (1 December 1835). Lacking an assertive ego, the Poet undergoes the stages of life— schoolboy, lover, libertine, exile—as if he were a neutral observer of life without the personal responsibility to shape his world through values and actions. Indeed, a latent guilt surfaces periodically. This contradiction between his illusion of innocence and identity as a libertine literally explodes in the confrontation of his internal and external realities: "Et mon verre, en touchant le sien, / Se brisa dans ma main débile" (47-48).

The Poet's passivity seems to be fueled by guilt which culminates at the deathbed of his father where time is reversed to reveal the stranger as "un orphelin vêtu de noir" (53). The inability to cope with the loss of his father as an adult reflects the extent to which his ego has receded. Hence, without a counterbalancing force, the Poet's feelings race out of control: "Partout où le long des chemins, / J'ai posé mon front dans mes mains / Et sangloté comme une femme" (97-99). Frustrated by his passivity, he feels violated by life: "Partout où j'ai comme un mouton / Qui laisse sa laine au buisson, / Senti se dénuer mon âme."

As the passive partner of the implied dialogue in **"La Nuit de décembre,"** the Poet is tempted to transfer responsibility for failure onto his absent counterpart, the Muse (poetic surrogate, woman or beloved, as well as his projected *anima*): "Et je songeais comme la femme oublie, / Et je sentais un lambeau de ma vie / Qui se déchirait lentement" (133-35). Temporally, he is torn between the past with its "eternal" promises of love and an empty present. His fear is reflected in the maternal element of water which threatens the loss of self by dissolution in the other: "Comme un plongeur dans une mer profonde, / Je me perdais dans tant d'oubli" (150-51).[12] However, fear of the other is overcome by anger's purging images of "faible femme, orgueilleuse insensée" (158) and "ce coeur de glace" (167). The ego of the Poet becomes unblocked but remains in a regressed state of resentment against dependency.

With a realignment of ego and *anima,* an integration of the Poet's self and a more balanced view of the world become possible. The first indication of victory over psychic imbalance can be seen in the Poet's distinction between the beloved or *la femme* and nature: "Partez, partez! la nature immortelle / N'a pas tout voulu vous donner" (172-73). Musset's persona starts reconciling itself to the necessary presence of the feminine principle without fear of absorption into it. Hence, he avoids the misogyny of Vigny's "La Colère de Samson" where woman, portrayed as leopard and viper, is associated with the weakness of man—affective and carnal—that originates in nature but is ministered to by woman. Moreover, Musset's distinction makes possible the painful process of emotional separation from the "other" who not only bears resemblance to the maternal Muse but to the divinity as well: "Eternal Dieu! toi que j'ai tant aimée / Si tu pars, pourquoi m'aimes-tu?"

Frustration ventilated in the absence of the Muse's overbearing presence reflects the assertion of his ego. The activation of this principle in the Poet's world is prepared by the scene with his father, "mon père" (51),

and it is confirmed by an elevated reappearance in the concluding "vision": "—Ami, notre père est le tien" (199). With a semblance of balance between his *anima* and ego, the Poet feels less urgency for completion in the "other" and shows less fear of separation from the beloved and its resulting loneliness. His double reveals his mission of guardianship in a message of hope: "Viens à moi sans inquiétude, / . . . Ami, je suis la Solitude." Another reason for progress in the poem goes to the core of Musset's personality. A profound love of life moves his being, and it (together with a continuing realignment of his projected *anima* and ego) comes to the forefront in the next poem, **"La Nuit d'août."**

With the self-nurturing insight of "La Vision," that loneliness is not a condemnation, "un mauvais destin," but a necessary part of the human condition, images of fear and despair—drowning and suicide—give way to expanded being through a normalization of existential polarities. Although the Muse opens **"La Nuit d'août"** (15 August 1836), she does so with quiet discretion: "J'attends en silence." With ideas of the past and image of the Poet as child, she is greeted by a vigorous interlocutor come of age who vies with her to gain control of their dialogue. His strategy puts distance between them. By hailing her as "ma mère et ma nourrice," the Poet de-eroticizes and objectifies their relationship. For her part, the Muse seems to resent the loss of her title as object of passion, "ma maîtresse," and she stoops to control through manipulation: "Il ne te restera de tes plaisirs du monde / Qu'un impuissant mépris pour notre honnête amour" (25-26). The attempt to control through an appeal to fear and guilt continues in her assertions about his inconstancy, loss of vocation, and waste of self in loving: "Hélas! mon bien-aimé, vous n'êtes plus poète. / Rien ne réveille plus votre lyre muette" (57-58).

Closure is now represented by the Muse whose *animus* degenerates into the possessive love of a dethroned matriarch. Opening to life experience becomes, then, the posture of the Poet who announces the rebirth of nature and the continuity of life. At the same time, he sees death in the valley. This opposition of horizontality and verticality, nature and the Creator ("Dieu là haut, l'espoir ici-bas") reflects an incipient balance between his own *anima* and ego that permits the harmonious view of existence in the conclusion.

In a final distancing from the Muse (who threatens the forfeiture of his genius by the gods) the Poet takes control of **"La Nuit d'août"** and the series of poems. In turning his back on the "heavens" of the Muse to focus on the earth, the Poet makes life rather than art the generating center of his existence. However, horizontality does not end in the cult of pleasure for its own sake. Love is located on the plane of continuity that opens out to infinity. Closure falls before the necessity of repeated exposure to experience. Suffering and love combine as human functions of immeasurable capacity to participate in the immortality of continuing creation: "Aime, et tu renaîtras."

The exaltation of his ego released in a credo of love and its expanded being within the inexhaustible continuum of life make possible new gains in self-confidence and creative thinking. However, one is justified in wondering how much of this psychological progress is retained. Musset's internal drama—as played out in the next poem, **"La Nuit d'octobre"** (15 October 1837)—stabilizes the realignment of his projected selves and furthers his self-integration on a deeper level of consciousness. For the first time in a poem based on an explicit dialogue, the Poet begins. A scanning of the stanzas reveals an approximate equality in the length of roles. For her part, the Muse's own ego gains equal footing with her previously dominant *animus*. She recognizes the Poet not as an appendage of herself but as a separate being, a "friend" rather than a dependent child. They engage in a balanced dialogue with sufficient distance and mutual respect: "Muse, sois donc sans crainte; au souffle qui t'inspire / Nous pouvons sans péril tous deux nous confier" (45-46).

Only by working together in harmony can the Muse and the Poet, projections of Musset's *anima* and ego, cure his broken heart and heal his fragmented self. The theme of "cure" dominates **"La Nuit d'octobre"** and constitutes a criterion of success by which the whole series of poems can be interpreted. At first, the Poet claims to be cured in answer to the Muse's concerned query: "O poète? en es-tu guéri? . . . Je suis bien guéri de cette maladie" (34, 41). His return to work ("Jours de travail! seuls jours où j'ai vécu") sounds promising but, paradoxically, psychological progress compounds his suffering. With emotional distance, he realizes the extent of his previous enslavement: "C'est une femme à qui je fus soumis" (73). Regrets as to time lost lead him to relive his former madness, jealousy, against which he struggles: "Va-t'en, retire-toi, spectre de ma maîtresse" (148). Peace of mind lies not in trying to forget her (as proposed by the Muse) but in admitting "une blessure / Qui jamais ne guérira" (191-93). The cure must be found, he intuits, in the faculty that made the experience possible, his heart.

Regression into offended sensibilities ("Ton souvenir abhorré") is checked by the firm but caring counsel of the Muse who reasserts the Poet's own credo of suffering as the necessary condition to moral expansion: "Les moissons pour mûrir ont besoin de rosée; / Pour vivre et pour sentir l'homme a besoin des pleurs" (222-23). Through the willingness to reexperience his pain, the Poet is helped by the Muse to attain a broader view of his former beloved. She becomes a fellow being created as his equal, the companion who opened life to him, a concerned friend who saw his "wound" but was unable to "close" it (260-67).

Sensitive enough to feel deeply and strong enough to confront his feelings, the Poet commits himself to the reconstruction of his world. His commitment takes the form of an oath to ban hate, to free himself from the past, and to reaffirm life. Its condition of fulfillment rests upon forgiveness of himself and the beloved: "L'instant suprême où je t'oublie / Doit être celui du pardon. / Pardonnons-nous—je romps le charme / Qui nous unissait devant Dieu" (296-99). Images of rebirth, exalted in the ending to **"La Nuit d'août,"** conclude this series of poems on a sounder foundation. There is a more equal balance between his *anima* and ego in a stabilized self and a hopeful view of the world: "Viens voir la nature immortelle / Sortir des voiles du sommeil; / Nous allons renaître avec elle / Au premier rayon du soleil!".

Polarized dialogue in the *Nuits,* now defused and regularized, extends as a meditation in **"Souvenir"** (15 February 1841). Although this major poem is presented traditionally as Musset's answer to Lamartine's *Le Lac* (1817) and Hugo's *Tristesse d'Olympio* (1837), it functions internally as a sequel to the *Nuits*.[13] A basic change in form tends to confirm resolution of psychological conflict. Dialogue structure and the technique of *dédoublement* in fictionalized personae yield to a first person speaker. Hence, **"Souvenir"** offers a vantage point from which to appraise the outcome of Musset's self-healing through the therapy of poetry.

Progress made in the *Nuits* is retained and solidified in **"Souvenir."** For example, the implied poet continues to reject the illusion of an absolute cure by admitting "un coeur encore blessé," and he upholds the humanizing value of its pain, "sa cicatrice . . . si douce à sentir" (22, 51-52). Similarly, he preserves the affective distinction between his beloved and the setting of their love in nature: "Je ne viens point jeter un regret inutile / Dans l'écho de ces bois témoins de mon bonheur" (25-26). More important than the dimension of space, he separates the past self of his beloved from her present self. The moral victory on this level of temporality allows the Poet to transcend anger and to visualize objectively the "death" of his relationship, the transformation of a beloved mistress into "une femme inconnue" while preserving the wonder and value of his feelings.

The Poet's conversion to a religion of love in **"La Nuit d'août"** and his discipleship in **"La Nuit d'octobre"** develop into love's apostleship in **"Souvenir."** He charges Dante and unidentified poets (presumably romantics) with shortsighted vanity and "blasphemy" in decrying love's "misery" (66). In his conclusion, the object of love is transcended by an integrated view of the world that reconciles horizontality and verticality in the dimensions of earth and heaven, and temporality in the present and past. The essence of life, pure love, is preserved in a private world beyond contamination of anger, time, and space:

> Je me dis seulement: A cette heure, en ce lieu,
> Un jour, je fus aimé, j'aimais, elle était belle.
> J'en fouis ce trésor dans mon âme immortelle,
> Et je l'emporte à Dieu!

Despite progression in the *Nuits* that leads to the seemingly solid integration of self in **"Souvenir,"** a cloud hangs over the outcome of Musset's therapy through poetry. In the sonnet, **"Tristesse"** (14 June 1840), which predates **"Souvenir"** by eight months, a behavioral problem is expressed that puts into doubt the possibility of a lasting "cure" to his broken heart and a viable readjustment to life. In this highly confessional sonnet heavy with guilt, the faculties of reason and feeling are brought into harmony to know a higher "truth" ("Quand je l'ai comprise et sentie"), but the habits of a disorderly life nullify the poet's freedom to undertake a personal reform ("J'en étais déjà dégoûté").

Musset's acute awareness of his failure to harmonize reason and sentiment, action and feeling, situates his personal struggle in the broader context of generation. Disappointment in love reflects the search for meaning in life typical of French romantics living in the aftermath of the Enlightenment's aborted revolutionary idealism and the fall of imperial grandeur. Musset's mourning for the lost love of his life figures in "le mal du siècle" and its sense of anguished disillusionment. Loss of love and a fragmented self are part of a collective loss of destiny and betrayal of youthful revolutionary ideals. This confluence of personal time and history receives eloquent form in the opening to *La Confession d'un enfant du siècle* (1836) where a young generation born in war and for war, "des neiges de Moscou et du soleil des Pyramides," is faced with absorption into bourgeois materialism or desperate dissipation.[14] For Musset and his projected personae in the *Nuits,* war is internalized in an impossible love where the self is set against itself leading to a fragmentation of being. His polarized projections strain toward the "cure" of harmony through integration, but he never succeeds through the therapy of poetry to resolve a historical dislocation.[15]

Notes

1. See Musset's "La Nuit de décembre," *Premières Poésies, Poésies nouvelles* (Paris: Gallimard, 1976) 249. All quotations are to this edition. Numbers in parentheses refer to verses in the poem under consideration.

2. See Gérard Milhaud, "Psychopathologie de Musset," *Europe* (nov.-déc. 1977): 5-16, whose thesis

of duality in Musset's life and works derives from Alfred's "double tempérament."

3. See James Smith, "The 'homo duplex' in Nineteenth-Century French Literature," *Studies in Honor of A. G. Engstrom,* ed. Robert T. Cargo and Emmanuel Mickel (Chapel Hill: University of North Carolina Press, 1972) 127-38.

4. Some progress in this direction is usually acknowledged by critics. See Pierre Odoul, *Le Drame intime d'Alfred de Musset* (Paris: La Pensée universelle, 1976) 19 who contends: "Ainsi Musset, longtemps avant Freud, avait pressenti le rôle essentiel de la psychanalyse et tenté, par elle, de se guérir."

5. See Georges Bachelard, *La Psychanalyse du feu* (Paris: Gallimard, 1938) 100-101.

6. See Linda Garmon's summary of Norman Geschwind's theory of brain development, "Of Hemispheres, Handedness and More," *Psychology Today* (November 1985): 40-48.

7. See Joseph Campbell, The Power of Myth (New York: Doubleday, 1988) 28.

8. See Carl G. Jung, "On the Psychology of the Unconscious: The Problem of the Attitude-Type," Two Essays on Analytical Psychology (1956; rept. Cleveland and New York: The World Publishing Co., 1965) 64.

9. See M.-L. von Franz, "The Process of Individuation," *Man and his Symbols,* ed. Carl G. Jung (New York: Dell, 1964) 186-207.

10. See Graham Padgett, "Bad Faith in Alfred de Musset: A Problem of Interpretation," *Dalhousie French Studies,* 3(1981): 65-82, who applies Sartre's ideological definition of commitment and whose conclusion remains external to Musset's world in its reductionist thrust. For the negative *anima* figures, see L. Franz, *Man and his Symbols* 187.

11. See Georges Poulet, *Les Métamorphoses du cercle* (Paris: Plon, 1961) 136.

12. For the psychology of water symbolism, see Georges Bachelard, *Water and Dreams,* trans. from 1942 ed. by Edith R. Farrell (Dallas: Institute of Humanities and Culture, 1983) 15.

13. See Lloyd Bishop, "Musset's *Souvenir* and the Greater Romantic Lyric," *Nineteenth-Century French Studies* 12.4-13.1 (Summer-Fall 1984): 119-30.

14. See Alfred de Musset, *La Confession d'un enfant du siècle* (Paris: Garnier, 1968) 4.

15. For a study on the psychology of "le mal du siècle," see James F. Hamilton, "The Anxious

Hero in Chateaubriand's *René, Romance Quarterly* 34 (November 1987): 415-24.

Jeanne Fuchs (essay date 1991)

SOURCE: Fuchs, Jeanne. "George Sand and Alfred de Musset: Absolution through Art in *La Confession d'un enfant du siècle.*" In *The World of George Sand,* edited by Natalie Datlof, Jeanne Fuchs, and David A. Powell, pp. 207-16. Westport, Conn.: Greenwood Press, 1991.

[*In the following essay, Fuchs appraises Musset's novel* La Confession d'un enfant du siècle, *illuminating its religious qualities as confessional literature.*]

The love affair between George Sand and Alfred de Musset is probably the best-documented liaison in nineteenth-century letters. Musset was the first to publish an account of their romance in his novel, ***La Confession d'un enfant du siècle,*** which appeared in February, 1836—one year after the lovers' final separation. Actually, parts of the novel had been published as early as September 1835 in *La Revue des deux mondes.*[1]

Before turning to the specific analysis of this novel, it would be helpful to recapitulate briefly what had happened between Sand and Musset during the one year and nine months that their relationship lasted. George Sand and Alfred de Musset first met in June 1833 at a dinner party given by François Buloz, publisher of *La Revue des Deux Mondes.* Charles-Augustin Sainte-Beuve introduced them. She was twenty-nine; he was twenty-three. Both were already famous. She had published *Indiana* in 1832; he had published ***Contes d'Espagne et d'Italie*** in 1829 (at age nineteen), and, at the time they met, his ***André del Sarto*** and ***Les Caprices de Marianne*** had just been released.[2]

Both were also notorious: she for her amorous and sartorial eccentricities; he as a dandy, a libertine, and a skeptic. In retrospect, it seems inevitable that this pair of "enfants terribles" of the early nineteenth century should fall in love. Consequently, it should not be surprising that, according to all the most reliable sources, six weeks after the now-famous Buloz dinner party, Sand and Musset were lovers (Adam, 53).

Musset was delicate, gracious, nervous, and effeminate. He felt reinvigorated by Sand, and believed that with her he had found the grand passion of his life (Adam, 57). Sand was the virile one in the relationship; she was charmed by Musset's wit, his manners, his exquisite delicacy, and his freshness (Adam, 59). Most of all, he was what she wanted more than anything else—a child—her "bon enfant" (Adam, 59). She preached the New Testament and wanted him to become a disciple of

Jean-Jacques Rousseau. Feeling as if he were reborn, Musset left his debauched companions and let himself be "converted" (Adam, 60).

From August to October, the pair was madly in love; they worked together and were both productive during this period. Musset wrote the masterpiece of nineteenth-century French theater—***Lorenzaccio;*** Sand wrote *Lélia.* Because of the lifestyles both had established previously, the lovers had difficulty being alone, and, of course, there was the usual quota of skeptics and scandalmongers who wished the lovers ill. Consequently, they decided to take a trip to escape the troublemakers and be alone. They left Paris for Italy on December 12, 1832.

On January 2, 1833, Sand and Musset arrived in Venice. During the course of what was then a long journey, both had been ill off and on, and soon after their arrival in Venice, Sand became seriously ill. Musset left her alone to go out on the town with the French consul. He began drinking again and frequented the dancers and singers from La Fenice (Adam, 100).

A doctor was finally called to attend to Sand; his name was Pietro Pagello. Thanks to this first innocuous "house call," Pagello was catapulted to a rather dubious fame. Sand recovered, but by February 4, it was Musset who was now desperately ill. He went through what most critics call a "crise de folie," although it was more likely delirium tremens coupled with some sort of viral infection. Once again, Dr. Pagello was summoned. His prognosis was more than gloomy: he told Sand that Musset might die. Sand nursed Musset through weeks of fever, ravings, and illness, but was not faithful. By February 12, she had become Pagello's mistress.

Musset recovered by early March and left Venice alone on March 29 for Paris. He arrived home on April 12 and promptly retreated to his room, where he remained for weeks reading *La Nouvelle Héloïse* and *Werther.*

Sand returned to Paris on August 14 with Pagello. There is much evidence that she was by then already bored with him, for she escaped almost immediately to Berry to see her children, leaving Pagello in Paris. On October 23, Pagello packed and left for Venice; Sand paid the fare. In the interim, Sand and Musset went through a series of violent ruptures and reconciliations. The definitive break came in March 1835.

While Musset's novel does not follow the above events in a factual way, it captures the ecstasy, the tension, the turmoil, the disillusionment, and the ultimate devastation that their love affair encompassed. Written just at the end of the relationship, ***La Confession d'un enfant du siècle*** emerges as a distillation of the pleasure and pain lovers inflict on one another, transposed into a glorious prose poem by one of the most delicate and graceful writers of the age. Musset's talent as both playwright and poet combined to produce a work at once lyric and dramatic, which possesses much of the force of the many literary confessions that precede his, and to which he was no stranger.

The word "confession" in the title serves to underscore the religious framework within which Musset chose to tell his tale. It is rare to ascribe a religious interpretation to any of Musset's works. As a whole, his oeuvre rests comfortably in the profane category. Nonetheless, even a casual reading of *La Confession d'un enfant du siècle* reveals an intensity of feeling that goes far beyond the simple recounting of a failed love affair. The vocabulary, the imagery, the tone, the structure—in short, all the literary devices used by Musset—point to a profound desire by the author for catharsis, for transcendence, and, to use the religious term, for absolution.

La Confession d'un enfant du siècle remains without doubt its author's *De Profundis Clamavi;* it is masterpiece of its genre, and it was Musset's last major work. Although he lived for twenty-one years more, it is clear he believed that his love affair with George Sand had ruined what was left of his life (*Confession,* 241).

While Sand was also deeply affected by their ruined romance, she was essentially a far more resilient person than Musset. Her life, sustained as always by her work, proved to be long and productive. In the tradition of Romantic poets, Musset died relatively young at forty-seven; Sand lived to the "unromantic" age of seventy-two.

Art as exorcism, confession, or catharsis is not a new idea. Consciously or unconsciously, this beneficent aspect of art is present in most, if not all, works of art. Musset's literary influences in this regard are many; he knew his Rousseau well: In fact, his father, Victor-Donatien Musset-Pathay, had written the standard biography of Rousseau of the period. In addition, Musset had not only read but had also translated Thomas De Quincey's *Confessions of an Opium Eater* into French (*Confession,* xl). However, most important for Musset was Saint Augustine, whom he venerated, and who is mentioned in *La Confession d'un enfant du siècle* itself as "the most manly man who ever was" (*Confession,* 97).

Musset's devotion to St. Augustine is suggested by the religious overtones of the title he chose: ***"Confession."*** It is the religious aspect of this work that will be examined in this study. Confession, whether private or public, presupposes private or public absolution, and that is precisely what Musset sought to achieve in this novel through the protagonist, Octave.

Two aesthetic decisions underscore Musset's intentions; each complements the other and enhances Musset's gifts as a dramatist. First is the use of a grandiose historical panorama in which to situate his novel, and second is the complex structure of the work itself.

In general, Musset's work is not characterized by grandness. He was not and did not wish to be a Victor Hugo or an Honoré de Balzac. He never desired to say everything about everybody. In describing his own work, Musset wrote, "My glass is not large but I drink from my glass."[3] Even in *Lorenzaccio,* which is set in Renaissance Florence, Musset concentrates on the individual dilemma of the main character—the political and historical elements become of interest only as they relate to the fate of the protagonist.[4]

It is uncharacteristic, therefore, that Musset begins *La Confession d'un enfant du siècle* on a grand scale. Octave's fate is a metaphor for the moral dilemma of the entire generation of young men that followed the Napoleonic era. The idea of depicting the flaws of an entire generation through one character is clearly announced in the novel's title. It is a confession, yes, but it is the confession of a child of the century, of his own time. The individual and the universal are artfully combined throughout the narration. Therefore, any absolution sought would be for all those who shared the same sins with Octave.

Because of the Napoleonic wars and the promises of glory and empire in which they were enveloped, the fathers of Musset's generation are depicted as perpetually absent. Musset describes the children of this era as having been "conceived between battles"—as remembering their fathers riding off on horseback (*Confession,* 2). He sees Napoleon as "invincible and immortal," and says that "death herself was then, so grand, so magnificent in her smoking purple" (*Confession,* 3). France had become "the widow of Caesar" (*Confession,* 3), and the "children of those absent fathers dreamed of the snows of Moscow, of the sun on the Pyramids" (*Confession,* 4). In the world of disillusionment that followed Napoleon's ignominious defeat, these children would wait in vain; they were left in the ruins. Musset says that if they spoke of glory, ambition, hope, love, or life, they were told, "Become priests" (*Confession,* 5). The immense horizon of the future loomed before them. They were weak, passionate, nervous—figuratively emasculated. An "inexplicable malaise" overcame them, and love became an illusion like glory and religion (*Confession,* 12). There was universal doubt, and French youth believed in nothing. For Musset, the greatest geniuses to come after Napoleon were Goethe and Lord Byron; he calls them "colossuses of sadness."

Musset's analysis of the state of Octave's soul (his *état d'âme*) and that of his contemporaries is meticulous and unsparing—truly Flaubertian in the delight taken in the dissection of feelings. Octave incarnates not the "Everyman" of the Napoleonic era, but rather the "Everychild" as survivor of that era. Although the remainder of the novel is played out in a more private setting, the origin of Octave's malady is never forgotten, and is reintroduced regularly at crucial moments. Society is indicted not just for what it has done to men, but also for ruining women.

The second aesthetic element that stresses Musset's intentions in the novel is its structure. Musset's theatrical gifts and his rich sense of the dramatic come to the fore in the way in which he has constructed the novel. The structure parallels that of classical tragedy. In fact, one critic likened this work to Greek tragedy because of the pity and terror it arouses.[5] It has also been viewed as a decadent *Romeo and Juliet* because of the unbearable intensity of some of the scenes (Rees, 53). Musset divided **La Confession** into five parts or acts. Each part has a varying number of chapters or scenes. Parts 1 and 2 are given over to exposition and the peripeteias of the protagonist. The heroine is not introduced until Part 3, which also contains the climax of the novel. Parts 4 and 5 trace the inevitable destruction of the ideal love so longed for by the protagonist. Furthermore, this destruction is brought about by a flaw in Octave's character—ironically, by his inability to love. By using a classical framework, the author not only highlights the seriousness of the tale for himself, but also reveals that he seeks the catharsis that all tragedy requires.

Thus catharsis is to art what absolution is to religion. By studying Octave's development throughout the work, it becomes apparent that Musset was seeking not just to unburden himself through his confession but also to transcend his experience by receiving absolution.

From the novel's declamatory opening, the reader is whisked into an intimate scene of betrayal. It is a key moment. Seated at an elegant dinner table, Octave gazes dreamily at his beautiful mistress as he contemplates their rendezvous for later that evening. Accidentally, his fork drops from the table and, as he bends to retrieve it, he sees his mistress's leg entwined with that of the young man seated next to her. Neither of their faces reveals the slightest sign of this intimacy; in fact, both are engaged in conversation with others. Stunned, Octave, nonetheless continues to observe the pair with unbearable fascination throughout the remainder of the meal.

The mistress who betrays Octave is never given a name; thus, she becomes the incarnation of the unfaithful and capricious female. She leaves an indelible mark on Octave's soul. The rest of Part 1 traces the stages of jealousy and despair through which the hero passes, and his self-disgust at still being attracted to a woman who could betray him so casually. Octave remains permanently traumatized by her deception.

A literary device often employed by Musset in his poetry and theater is the *Doppelgänger*. In **La Confession d'un enfant du siècle,** the doppelgänger for Octave, who at the outset is idealistic and vulnerable, is a character named Desgenais. He is a bit older than Octave—blasé, skeptical, and cerebral. After Octave's first mistress betrays him, Desgenais, in parts 1 and 2 of the novel, undertakes a kind of sentimental education of his friend.

The concluding chapters of Part 1 and all of Part 2 are given over to long and brilliant, though pessimistic, philosophical discussions about love, virginity, fidelity, marriage, motherhood, and the role of civilization in ruining women. There are successive indictments of literature, the eighteenth century, and society in general. Once again, the narrative alternates between the universal and the particular.

Seeking the absolute is dangerous business, Desgenais informs his friend. Octave has been duped by what poets write about love, which, for Desgenais, has nothing to do with reality. Desgenais uses the example of Praxiteles to make his point: He says that the Greek sculptor created his Venus from a composite of all the beautiful women in Athens, and omitted their faults (*Confession,* 41). He adds, "Wanting to find in real life loves equal to those found in antiquity is like looking for Venus in a public square or wanting nightingales to sing Beethoven symphonies" (*Confession,* 41). Desgenais concludes that human reason can heal illusions but cannot control or stop the torment that one feels because of them (*Confession,* 73). In true Romantic fashion, Desgenais treats love as an illness, and spends all of Part 2 attempting to cure Octave of it. If love is an illusion, one remedy for its loss is debauchery. Part 2 of the novel contains a detailed description of debauchery as well as Octave's personal determination to become a libertine and to develop a blasé attitude toward life in general.

In the culminating scene of Part 2, the course of the novel is abruptly changed by the terrible news of the death of Octave's father. Stricken by this unexpected turn of events, Octave retires to his father's country home—the place where his father had died. In the solitude of this retreat, Octave undertakes an examination of conscience. He compares his father's orderly and virtuous existence with his own dissolute life. He feels remorse and shame, and determines to mend his ways.

Thus has Musset, the master playwright, carefully prepared the moment for the arrival on stage of his heroine. In the George Sand role we have Brigitte Pierson. Up to this point in the novel, the love depicted has been profane. Now, at the very heart of the narration, the first and only example of sacred love is introduced, and seems to have been waiting in this idyllic setting to redeem or, at least, to rehabilitate the deeply scarred protagonist.

Brigitte is a young widow who lives quietly in the country with her aunt. She is ten years older than Octave. The widow is known in the region for her piety and her good works: She has become a sister of mercy in caring for the poor and the ill in the countryside. From the moment she appears in the novel, Brigitte is depicted in intensely religious terms: "ange," "soeur de charité," "rosière," and "Brigitte la rose." In this pure and rarefied atmosphere, Octave sees the chance to lead a virtuous life. That he might achieve his goal through Brigitte's intercession is implied from their first meeting. Octave is impressed with Brigitte's simplicity, her intelligence, and her infectious gaiety. He feels a return to innocence when he walks through the fields with her (*Confession,* 139). Indeed, in this wholesome setting, Octave begins to recuperate and to regain a sense of inner worth. Crediting Brigitte with this change, he says to her, "God sent you like an angel of light to pull me out of the abyss" (*Confession,* 162).

This, of course, is precisely what Sand had done for Musset. Alfred, like Octave, met George after a failed love affair followed by a period of debauchery (Adam, 45-48). Just about everyone who has written about Sand and Musset—both their contemporaries and later critics—agree that she had, at least at first, a salutary effect on him. Henri Lefebvre goes so far as to assert that it was thanks to Sand that Musset became a man and an authentic writer.[6] Lefebvre goes on to analyze the qualities found in Sand that aided Musset in his own development: "George Sand united the contradictory qualities that Musset demanded from a woman and from love. Genial and sensual, amorous and maternal, pure and impure, experienced and naive, George was able for some time to effect a reconciliation between dream and reality, between him and himself" (*Confession,* 62).

By making the age difference between Octave and Brigitte greater than that between him and George (ten years as opposed to six), Musset stresses the feminine qualities cited by Lefebvre, and thus heightens the fatal nature of the couple's love in the novel.

Part 3 of *La Confession* is suffused with a religious aura, and traces the growth of love between Octave and Brigitte. As long as their love for each other stays on a spiritual plane, there is peace. Brigitte seems to intuit this, for, when she realizes that Octave has fallen in love with her and she with him, she runs away. First she leaves the village to visit relatives, and then she persuades Octave to leave the village for several months. Of course, none of these ploys works and, eventually she confesses her love to him in an intensely

voluptuous and romantic scene as they are riding horseback through the forest.

The final chapters of Part 3 rise in a magnificent crescendo—an ode to love written with an intensity of passion not found in the earlier descriptions of profane love. Octave feels that "a hymn of grace was coming from his heart and that their love was rising up to God" (*Confession,* 172). The vocabulary is markedly religious: There is a blending of Octave's passionate feelings, which have left him in a state akin to religious ecstasy, and sensual delight. Love becomes "a principle of the universe . . . [a] precious flame which all nature, like an uneasy vestal, surveys incessantly in the temple of God" (*Confession,* 172). He speaks of those who have "blasphemed" using the name of love, and of love finding its true "apostles" united in a kiss; he evokes the first timid signs of love with cherubs hovering above the lovers; and he recalls their "divine dreams," and their "serenity of happiness." He bemoans his own sense of powerlessness to capture his feelings about love when he explains, "What human word can ever describe the weakest caress?" (*Confession,* 173).

Paul de Musset tells us, in his biography of his brother, that Alfred considered ending the novel with Part 3. Indeed, Sainte-Beuve thought that he should indeed have concluded on this delirious note. Sainte-Beuve speaks of the "exquisite and irreproachable voluptuousness" of the last chapter, and compares it with "passionate and intoxicating" passages in *Adolphe* and *Obermann.* He says that Musset's passage is like "a warm breeze in May" or "the first scent of lilacs."[7]

Obviously, however, Musset did not opt for the deliriously harmonious ending that Part 3 would have afforded him. Modern critics celebrate his decision.[8] The exultation of Part 3 is short-lived, and Part 4 shifts to an even more confessional tone as the relationship between the lovers begins to deteriorate. Octave becomes suspicious of Brigitte almost immediately: His suspicion is triggered by a white lie she tells him. Brigitte often plays the piano for her lover. One particular piece that he appreciates was written by Brigitte herself, but she has told Octave that it was composed by the Italian composer Stradella. One day, after she finishes playing it for Octave, she laughs and calls him a "dupe," and says that she has "tricked" him, that he has been "deluded" by her because it is she who has written the piece. This one miscalculation costs Brigitte dearly. It brings back to Octave a flood of unhappy memories of the deceitfulness of women and his betrayal by his first mistress. He sees himself sinking into an abyss of suspicion and jealousy, but he is powerless to stop his descent.

The romance between Octave and Brigitte follows the same downward trajectory as Octave's mood. He begins questioning people about Brigitte's behavior before he knew her. His suspicions drive him to become sadistic toward her. Even though he feels remorse over his actions, he willfully pursues his destructive course. Brigitte's reaction, at first, is one of complete astonishment, but little by little, she realizes that Octave's attitude and the change that has come over him are beyond her powers to reverse. She begins to treat him like a sick child and to resign herself to the pain caused by his illness.

In the meantime, Brigitte's reputation is tainted because it is obvious to all in the village that Octave is her lover. A further blow is dealt when her aunt dies. Shunned and alone, Brigitte resigns herself to her now-unhappy life with her lover. At the same time, she realizes that she can no longer endure life in the village, and so the lovers leave for Paris in a highly charged scene that ends Part 4.

It is clear that once physical possession has occurred, Octave reverts to the Octave of Paris, the libertine. The suffering caused by unconsummated love is replaced by a cerebral, self-inflicted suffering, rooted in suspicion and jealousy. Happiness eludes Octave, and by extension, Brigitte, because of his own perversity and willfulness. Ultimately incapable of reconciling spiritual and physical love—the sacred and the profane—Octave becomes determined to destroy any relationship between himself and Brigitte.

While the change to Paris in Part 5 has, at first, a positive effect on the couple, their happiness evaporates quickly. Paris, in the novel, recaptures in large part the tension of the real-life drama of Sand and Musset in Venice. The lovers escape the pain of the present by planning trips and projects for the future. Paradoxically, Octave and Brigitte's desire to flee is juxtaposed with their inability to act. On the figurative plane, they cannot depart for the "promised land." In fact, they had left behind any hope of attaining it when they abandoned the original setting in which their love blossomed. Religious imagery abounds in these passages. Octave envisions their trip as containing the "terrors of exile" and "the hopes of a pilgrimage" (*Confession,* 237). When Octave watches Brigitte sleep, he longs for purification through "repentance." He wishes that a temple, consecrated to love, existed where he might be baptized (*Confession,* 233). He compares himself to St. Thomas, doubting and adoring. Curiously, when Octave evokes St. Thomas, it is the St. Thomas in a portrait by Titian that he has in mind. Musset's choice here produces a mirror effect between the Titian portrait and his own work of art, his novel: Just as Musset's portrait of the love affair between Octave and Brigitte has become more intense, and more "real" than the actual love affair between George and Alfred, so too Titian's rendering of St. Thomas had been filtered through that artist's sensibilities and goes beyond whatever reality it originally represented. Because of the immediacy and universality of the work of art, it transcends the moment it depicts, and fixes it on another plane. Musset's choice of St. Thomas is of further interest in that it supports the thesis that the author was seeking absolution for his hero (it also is an oblique reference to Venice). Musset equates Octave with an apostle, a man who overcame his doubts and became a saint.

The catalyst necessary to break the lovers' impasse arrives in the person of a young man, a distant relative of Brigitte. The Pagello character is named Smith in the novel. It seems curious that Musset chose such an innocuous and British Protestant name to designate his rival, Pagello, an Italian Catholic and self-styled Don Juan. The vagueness of the name, as well as the character, reveal Musset's intention in choosing it: He did not blame Pagello for what happened in Venice; he blamed himself. Besides, Pagello had afforded an escape from what had become an intolerable situation. Smith is described in simple, noble terms, and when Brigitte falls ill, he begins to visit the couple daily. Once well, Brigitte hesitates about leaving Paris, and their departure is repeatedly delayed, sometimes by Brigitte and sometimes by Octave.

Octave begins to observe Smith and Brigitte when they are together, and he is struck by their sadness. With no evidence of intimacy, he concludes that they are in love. The only indication he can uncover of a link between them is a single, empty teacup, from which he suspects they both have drunk (*Confession,* 343 n.215).

Octave begins to dwell on his former debauchery; he believes that he is permanently tainted because of it, and decides that he and Brigitte are doomed if they stay together. Even after this insight, he is unable to let go of her, and a series of violent scenes follows. The turning point comes one evening, as he stands over the sleeping Brigitte with a knife in his hand. When he uncovers her bosom and sees a crucifix there, he falls to his knees and repents. During this scene, Octave speaks to Christ, and acknowledges that it was through suffering that Christ became God (*Confession,* 314). At dawn, Octave finally resolves to let Brigitte go. The final chapter depicts Brigitte and Octave exchanging tokens of friendship—rings—just before they part forever. She goes off with Smith, and Octave remains alone.

Musset places the blame for the failed love affair on Octave; he exculpates Brigitte and Smith completely. The text reveals Musset's understanding of himself and a deep sense of guilt about his behavior. The suspicion and jealousy that Octave feels about Brigitte are imaginary, but they were not imaginary in the real-life drama. Sand betrayed Musset in Venice. There was no question about it. By putting all the blame on his protagonist, Musset makes Octave the sacrifice, the victim in the tragedy and its most arresting figure. Octave's flawed character has caused him to lose the woman who might have saved him from himself. Nonetheless, his suffering, coupled with the realization of his faults, ennoble him.

Brigitte emerges as a more mundane figure. She leaves Octave for someone else, while he remains solitary. The heroine echoes the sentiments of George Sand, when she tells Octave that he is not capable of love (*Confession,* 279). Musset reiterates this idea in both the novel and his letters. What he could not attain in his own life, in his relationship with Sand or with any other woman, Musset achieves through art. The difference is that *La Confession d'un enfant du siècle* seeks purification for the protagonist and attains it after a painful examination of conscience and confession.

Musset's novel represents a supreme effort to resolve, on the aesthetic plane, what had become irreconcilable for him in reality. Through confession, the poet seeks, at least, a laicized form of absolution. The reader may serve as the surrogate priest, as the protagonist repents and asks for absolution for his overburdened soul.

Notes

1. Alfred de Musset, *La Confession d'un enfant du siècle* (Paris: Garnier Frères, 1968); all translations are those of the author.

2. Antoine Adam, *Le Secret de l'aventure vénitienne: La Vérité sur Sand et Musset* (Paris: Librairie Académique Perrin, 1938), 51.

3. In *A Survey of French Literature,* ed. Morris Bishop (New York: Harcourt Brace and World, 1965), 2:61.

4. *Théâtre de Musset,* ed. René Clair (Paris: Gallimard, 1964), 1:347-490.

5. Margaret Rees, *Alfred de Musset* (New York: Twayne, 1971), 23.

6. Henri Lefebvre, *Musset: Essai* (Paris: L'Arche, 1955), 62.

7. Charles-Augustin Sainte-Beuve, *Portraits contemporains* (Paris: Calmann-Lévy, 1891), 2:211.

8. Joachim Merlant, *Le Roman personnel de Rousseau à Fromentin* (Geneva: Slatkine Reprints, 1970), 393.

Warren Johnson (essay date winter 1995)

SOURCE: Johnson, Warren. "Capricious Exuberance: Gender and Mediation in Musset's Comedies." *Dalhousie French Studies* 33 (winter 1995): 27-34.

[*In the following essay, Johnson cites the relationship between language and desire portrayed in such works as* Fantasio, Les caprices de Marianne, *and* On ne badine pas avec l'amour.]

When Count Almaviva disguises himself as the music teacher in *Le barbier de Séville,* his mask allows him to penetrate a space previously interdicted. The role reversal of *Le jeu de l'amour et du hasard* likewise permits entry into a privileged space of observation. The mask in these two eighteenth-century precursors of Musset creates the possibility of contact between spheres that have been socially constructed as separate, whether they be physical places or social classes.

Musset's reworking of the master-servant inversion in *Fantasio* exemplifies his shift in emphasis from the transgression of social obstacles to a questioning of the nature and value of the individual. Whereas disguise in these plays of Beaumarchais and Marivaux implies an exercise of power by occluding identity and motives in order to control the way the Other perceives the self, such attempts to manipulate one's image in Musset are frequently doomed to failure. But equally unsuccessful are the efforts to inspire feeling by the simple assertion of existence or love. The men who prove attractive to women in several of his *comédies et proverbes* have a verbal exuberance that goes beyond the simple imperative declaration of desire. To be appreciated, the seductiveness of a discourse that breaks free of self-absorption to suggest the aleatory nature of the universe through its flights of fancy needs to be highlighted by comparison with the banality of another's less imaginative language. The value of this facility with language, which reflects the speaker's notion of reality as comically doubled and driven by caprice and chance, requires a counterpoint whose more strictly representational discourse will prove incapable of inspiring either desire or affection.

The repeated motif of the mask in Musset has been sometimes seen as a liberation of the self at the price of an irreconcilable splintering or alienation.[1] The frequent use of doubled characters, one critic observes, parallels this internal division of the individual.[2] Musset's would-be lovers frequently have recourse to doubles or intermediaries, as Cœlio in *Les caprices de Marianne* uses the services of Ciuta and Octave.[3] Rather than focusing on the tertiary or mediating figure's role as proxy, I would like to discuss his function as an implicit point of comparison that underlines the superior attractiveness of expressive extravagance.[4]

Four of Musset's shorter plays are structured around this pivotal transfer of interest from one man to another on account of the mediating figure's verbal dexterity. In other comedies where the mediating figure does not become an object of the woman's passionate attachment, she experiences a heightened sensitivity in response to the mediator's rhetoric. I would like to focus in particular on the ways that women respond to a "capricious" or fanciful language because it allows them to negotiate around the constraints placed on their identity by figures of male authority. Finally, I will suggest how the resistance to defined roles by both men and women characters, generalized throughout the comedies, as well as desire itself depend on some form of mediation.

Personal identity in Musset derives from social interactions. As David Sices observes, for Musset the individual is defined by encounters with external reality and the subjective appraisal of others based on roles the individual plays (133).[5] His characters find the mask sticking to their skin because the notion of personality as independent of the influence of others turns out to be an illusion. Yet whereas Lorenzaccio's awareness of himself as a hollow man impels the tragic end despite the loss of faith in his plans, in the comedies the characters' imperfect sense of the forces constituting them sounds a subtending ironic note.

The triangular situation of a young woman pursued by both an overly sincere young swain and a more enticing prospect forms the mediation in the earliest plays. Razetta of *La nuit vénitienne* (1830) is bested by the Prince d'Eysenach, who wishes to marry Laurette even though he realizes she does not love her. Like Elsbeth of *Fantasio,* the heroine of this early comedy initially feels compelled to accede to the marriage arranged for her. But she finds the Prince more charming because of his dazzling evocation, in the longest speech of the play, of the total freedom he promises her in order to satisfy her every whim:

> Ne faites pas surtout un rêve sans le réaliser; qu'un caprice, qu'un faible désir n'échappe pas à ceux qui vous entourent, et dont l'existence entière est consacrée à vous obéir.
>
> (25)

Razetta's attempts to coerce his beloved to kill the Prince by pathetically and hyperbolically threatening suicide if she fails him, exemplify the self-obsession and will to control others that will repeatedly be rejected in Musset's later works.

The rivalry between Cordiani and André del Sarto in the play of 1833 that bears the latter's name pits a sexually experienced man discovering love for the first time against the dispassionate colder eye of the artist. André confesses of himself: "Je suis un homme sans caractère" (65). It is precisely the nondescript language of this amorphous and flaccid "Mann ohne Eigenschaften" that leads to a splitting of the self and an introspective obsession with the way everything appears to be drifting away from him. By contrast, the instinctive understanding that grows between Cordiani and André's wife arises from the expression of the spontaneous overflow of powerful feeling in André's friend. If we see little direct contact between the male and female characters in the play, it is clear nevertheless from Cordiani's dia-

logue in the opening scene that the lover is capable of lyrical bursts that contrast sharply with André's world-weariness.

The situation of *Bettine* (1851) retains the triangular structure of a verbally adroit mediating figure who wins out over a self-absorbed lover, though here the success of the former becomes possible through the elopement of the latter with another woman. Steinberg, the bridegroom-to-be, is distracted on his wedding day by financial troubles, thus allowing the Marquis Stéfani with his knack for well-turned compliments and his enthusiasm for Rossini to win the heart of the heroine.

Of Musset's best-known comedies, *Les caprices de Marianne* (1833), chronologically the third of those Musset published, follows most closely the pattern of mediation established in *La nuit vénitienne* and *André del Sarto.* Cœlio's use of intermediaries in order to gain access to a supposedly prudish Marianne, first the old woman Ciuta and then his friend Octave, is unsuccessful because Octave's superior eloquence in pleading for Cœlio ignites Marianne's feelings for the go-between. In describing Cœlio's suffering at the unrequited love, Octave lyrically evokes the "pain" she has caused:

> Un mal le plus cruel de tous, car c'est un mal sans espérance; le plus terrible, car c'est un mal qui se chérit lui-même, et repousse la coupe salutaire jusque dans la main de l'amitié; un mal qui fait pâlir les lèvres sous des poisons plus doux que l'ambroisie, et qui fond en une pluie de larmes le cœur le plus dur, comme la perle de Cléopâtre; un mal que tous les aromates, toute la science humaine ne sauraient soulager, et qui se nourrit du vent qui passe, du parfum d'une rose fanée, du refrain d'une chanson, et qui suce l'éternel aliment de ses souffrances dans tout ce qui l'entoure, comme une abeille son miel dans tous les buissons d'un jardin.
>
> (77-78)

Cœlio's initial intermediary Ciuta, by contrast, only echoes his plaintive urgings and so fails to enchant Marianne who threatens to tell her husband if Cœlio persists. Toward the end of the play, when he realizes that Marianne's affections seem to be turning in Octave's favor, Cœlio recognizes that his own lack of rhetorical gifts is to blame:

> Je sais agir, mais je ne puis parler. Ma langue ne sert point mon cœur, et je mourrai sans m'être fait comprendre, comme un muet dans une prison.
>
> (92)

Ironically, though Octave's boisterous joviality pleases Marianne more than Cœlio's melancholic sighing, she has to defend herself against Octave's opinion of women, not unique in the nineteenth century, that makes them either "abjecte" (a whore) if she gives in, or a statue if she refuses. While Octave dismisses Marianne's remarks on his insensitivity to her position, his verbal panache makes her prefer him to a more sincere and respectful admirer. Unadorned expressions of love fail to communicate to her. As Marianne remarks:

> Il faut croire que sa passion pour moi était quelque chose comme du chinois ou de l'arabe, puisqu'il lui fallait un interprète, et qu'elle ne pouvait s'expliquer toute seule.
>
> (85)

It is revealing that when Octave remarks, while discussing with Cœlio various means to get at Marianne, "Si tu en aimais une autre? Viens avec moi chez Rosalinde" (76), the literal-minded lover assumes that his friend is suggesting that he change the object of his affections, rather than use the woman as a way of inciting Marianne's jealousy the way Perdican does Rosette in *On ne badine pas avec l'amour*. Deception, provided it is artfully concealed, and disrespect, Cœlio fails to realize, are not necessarily barriers to appealing to Musset's women, as long as the man possesses a certain grandiloquence.

The scenario of desire being deflected onto the intermediary appears *en abyme* in the account that Hermia, Cœlio's mother, gives to her son of how she came to fall in love with his father. The seductiveness of the father's discourse when he came pleading the case for another led to her preferring the emissary to the man he represented, who subsequently committed suicide upon learning what had happened. The pleading itself, Hermia explains, killed off the slight affection inspired in her by months of assiduous declarations (81).

The title of the play, to a reader unfamiliar with Musset's theatre, would suggest that Marianne, like the women in the comedies discussed above, is flighty and her irresponsibility directly the cause of Cœlio's death. However, *caprice,* like the frequent adjective *fantasque,* the noun *fantaisie,* and the suggestive name Fantasio, carries a quite different connotation in the world of the armchair spectacles. Musset's women tend to see in the assiduous attentions of their admirers a form of entrapment into the impossible role of Madonna, if they are to avoid the equally uncomfortable labels of whore or statue. The restrictions imposed by these extremes are more objectionable, because more insidious, than an open insensitivity. Even a character as unsympathetic to the feminist cause as Octave appears preferable because his verbal embellishments leave her free to indulge in a fantasy that redefines Octave as her true object of desire, just as Cœlio's mother fell in love with her suitor's intermediary. Personal identity, a product of social interactions, depends on language. The most appealing male figures are those whose imaginative language allows women to construct masculine desire according to their own wishes. Caprice and fantasy in Musset designate the resistance to socially defined roles, whether they be cherished doll, long-suffering wife (*Un caprice*), or one who pays his debts (*Fantasio*).

As with *Fantasio* (1834), in *Le chandelier* (1835) the seductiveness of the mediating figure's discourse leads not to a romantic relationship but rather to a sort of maternal affection, though in this play the positive and negative characteristics are intermixed within the same person. Fortunio, who, as his name suggests, blunders onto his mediating role, is sought out to act as cover or "candlestick" (a term whose delicate scabrousness encapsulates the *fantaisiste* speech that proves seductive). The dragoon Clavaroche, who explains the term to his mistress Jacqueline, has the skill of a practiced *beau parleur*. His soliloquy in II.i, significantly spoken in front of a mirror, reveals that he views his toying with married women as a diverting game that he refuses to take too seriously. Fortunio, in contrast, has a naïve ardor that pleases Jacqueline ("Puis-je être bon à quelque chose? Veuillez parler avec confiance. Quoique bien jeune je mourrais de bon cœur pour vous rendre service" [343]). Yet he verges on committing the same mistake of being too direct in expressing his puerile gallantry that thwarted Cœlio in *Les caprices de Marianne*. Nevertheless, his impact on Jacqueline is significant, turning her from a brazen hussy in confronting her eternally ridiculous husband to a woman with a softened heart content with a *ménage à trois*. When she tells Fortunio, "Sais-tu que je t'aime, enfant que tu es . . ." (374), she is responding to his self-sacrificing if gushing devotion that manages to touch even so hard a heart as hers. Though the opposition between verbal skill and sincerity is internalized in the character of Fortunio and his rival also has a knack for language, the contrast remains clear between a discourse driven by self-centeredness and one that expresses verbal expenditure for its own sake.

Elsbeth, who finds a kindred soul in the most eloquent of Musset's capricious figures, Fantasio, is herself described as "fantasque" by both Hartman (106) and Marinoni (114). She delighted in the wit of the late buffoon Saint-Jean, even though the jester made fun of her romantic ideas. Conversely, like Marianne and other Musset heroines, she rejects the Prince of Mantua when he, in disguise as his valet, expresses too directly his utter devotion.

Fantasio's attractiveness, at least as a verbal sparring partner for Elsbeth, derives from his desire to escape from himself, his socially defined role as "bourgeois de Munich" (134) who would satisfy his creditors. He exclaims toward the beginning of the play: "Si je pouvais seulement sortir de ma peau pendant une heure ou deux!" (108). The mask of the buffoon, with its consequent discursive liberation, allows for the creation of an alterity that satisfies both Fantasio and the Bavarian princess beyond its practical utility as disguise. The closing scene, where he refuses the twenty thousand crowns as a price of his remaining outside of the banal system of monetary exchange, indicates clearly that he prefers the capricious world of chance to economic security and the marginalized position his disguise offers to being firmly ensconced in a social identity.

Fantasio's remark about Elsbeth's arranged marriage, "que le hasard est capricieux!" (124), encapsulates his world view that endears him to her. Verbal caprice responds to the constraints of a world that limits freedom, either through financial obligations or social dictates. Fantasio mocks the upbringing imposed on young women that makes them sound like little more than canaries stuffed with a hurdy-gurdy (127-28). The playfulness of his language is a reflection of his notion of reality and a compensation for its inadequacies:

> Un calembour console de bien des chagrins; et jouer avec les mots est un moyen comme un autre de jouer avec les pensées, les actions et les êtres. Tout est calembour ici-bas . . .
>
> (121)

Our perceptions are colored by the lenses of our prejudices, without our being able to understand their distorting effects. Since access to reality, including the nature of the self, is problematic if not impossible, since we are constantly subject to pressures to conform to others' ideas of ourselves, verbal ebullience is a way of freeing ourselves and embracing the aleatory through producing a form of it. Fantasio, in liberating Elsbeth from the choice of accepting the Prince of Mantua or being responsible for war, promises to take up arms so that "si vous entrez jamais à Mantoue, ce sera comme une véritable reine" (135) and not simply as the consort of a figure of male authority.

Camille of *On ne badine pas avec l'amour* (1834) likewise instinctively resists the marriage arranged for her and Perdican. In her language and behavior, she resembles her capricious sisters elsewhere in Musset. Moments after telling Perdican that she does not want to marry either him or anyone else, she refers to him in her conversation with Dame Pluche as her fiancé (268). Her affectionate behavior when she meets Perdican at the rendez-vous she has requested, belies her earlier refusal of him. "Je suis d'humeur changeante," she admits (273). Her coldness despite these expressions of interest in him leads Perdican to accuse her of having a mask of devotion imposed on her by the nuns to whom she intends to return (280).

The ultimate failure of their relationship is due not so much to Perdican's lack of verbal skill as to the defective mediation of his too-transparent (and thus obviously manipulative) ruse to inspire her jealousy by feigning to court Rosette. Like other Musset heroines, Camille searches for liberation from the constraining circumstances imposed on her, and so the resentment at Perdican's trickery overshadows her feelings of mimetic desire. Inasmuch as Perdican attempts to coerce her interest in him, he falls victim to the same mistake as those male characters who assume that it is sufficient to declare their desire for it to be reciprocated.[6] But the near success of his stratagem underlines the importance of mediation, for were it not for Rosette's somewhat enigmatic death, their reconciliation would presumably have been consummated.

Camille's perception of Perdican's insincerity in wooing her foster sister recalls the dramatic ironies recurrent throughout Musset's theatre. Perdican's mask of attraction toward Rosette parallels the scenes of deception and misunderstanding touched on before. But these ironies inspired by deliberate manipulation tend to give way to an unexpected, hence ironic, reversal. The best-laid plans come unraveled, revealing once again the uncontrollable, contingent order underlying and subverting human intention. The comedy of Musset's *comédies et proverbes* is based on the sense of a world ultimately out of control and a human impulse to free oneself from restrictions, an "imp of the perverse" liable to counteract every deliberate scheme. The unanticipated turns arising out of the mediated circumstances of the plays are products of this tendency, especially in the women characters, to resist the intentionality of those who wish them to conform to certain images. For such minds, a subjectivity that expresses its liberation from the will to power over others through verbal exuberance inevitably proves the more desirable.

To say that identity depends on social interactions, one of my starting points in this discussion, is to recognize that not only desire but being itself is mediated. But for it to prove attractive, this mediation must either be, or at least appear to be, a spontaneous effect of chance juxtapositions. Exuberant language creates a verbal mask that is necessary for the self to be recognized at all. This language itself becomes a form of mediation that creates the meeting ground on which male desire can successfully negotiate the female resistance to control and restraint. Like all value, the attractiveness of the verbal sublime and grotesque[7] depends on difference and contrast, which implies the necessity of mediation for the distinctions to be appreciated. Desirability arises from the intersection of differences at a given moment in time, and thus Musset's cherished image of the couple blended together and eternally sufficient unto themselves[8] reveals its essential incompatibility with the more sober-minded recognition of the aleatory. The masking of exuberant language reveals in fact the essential emptiness of the self in those figures who understand instinctively the illusory nature of the statements

"I am" and "I want." Those who persist in clinging to their tattered sense of individuality are doomed to be unmasked, ironized as self-deluded and naïvely unaware of the nature of the world as governed by happenstance. Unlike the rigid *fantoches* and the banally sincere, the living characters in Musset are in dynamic flux, creations of values projected onto them by the Other, a mechanism dependent on exchange and comparison. The juxtaposition of the woodenly ingenuous with the authenticity of the verbally adroit clarifies to what extent these often somber plays can be called comedies.

Notes

1. Bernard Masson claims that Musset's theatre always tells the same story of a young man in quest of himself, of his interior unity, of his rootedness in the universe, and of his communication with others. Masking, according to Masson, is necessary to advance in a world of appearances and in order to be sincere with oneself. But Lucienne Serrano points out how Fantasio's mask of a buffoon, even though it gives him freedom, leads to an interior split, and this split links him to Lorenzaccio.

2. The motif of the double has attracted the interest of several critics. Robert Mauzi sees it generalized in Musset either as a pathological symptom or lyrical or tragic theme. Bernadette Bricout notes how the double is used as a sort of protective mask. Disguise, she argues, is a public face that allows others to label the self, a process at once reductive and reassuring because it protects the inner self and gives a measure of power by allowing the masked individual to observe from a position of security. We can see, however, from the hair-raising fate of the Prince of Mantua in *Fantasio* that masking can just as easily lead to a subversion of the Other's esteem.

3. J. Beauverd has catalogued these intermediaries of love and notes that the amorous plans fail or death results from "*une atteinte à la personnalité du médiateur*" (11-12, his emphasis).

4. In stressing the element of chance, I want to move away from Rachel Wright's emphasis on the positive mentoring role of the male figures to show how women acquire much greater awareness of their power through their interactions with certain men.

5. Before Sices, Henri Lefebvre also observed that there is no inaccessible interiority in Musset, but rather each person "finds" his thoughts in talking with another.

6. James Hamilton's analysis of the movement from aleatory game to premeditated "ricochet" in the play highlights this conflict between chance and intention.

7. I am of course using *grotesque* in the positive sense given to it by Hugo in the Préface to *Cromwell* (1827). The grotesque—that is, the exuberance combined with the sublime that characterizes the modern and the real, according to Hugo—marks the language of Musset's positive figures. The Romantic grotesque, a reprise of the delight in embellishment of the pre-classical baroque, valorizes the irregular, the unanticipated, the excessive. It contrasts precisely with the controlled *marivaudage* that constitutes a regulated social game.

8. Jean-Pierre Richard in his indispensable pages on Musset in *Études sur le romantisme* discusses how this vision of union in love is often torn apart by doubt.

References

Beauverd, J. 1978. "L'entremise d'amour dans l'œuvre de Musset: action et disparition d'une structure." *Journées d'études sur Alfred de Musset*. Clermont-Ferrand: Faculté des lettres, Société des études romantiques. 3-28.

Bricout, Bernadette. 1977. "Le visage des masques dans le théâtre de Musset." *Europe* 583-84:69-82.

Hamilton, James F. 1985. "From *Ricochets* to *Jeu* in Musset's *On ne badine pas avec l'amour*: A Game Analysis." *French Review* 58:820-26.

Lefebvre, Henri. 1955. *Alfred de Musset, dramaturge*. Paris: L'Arche.

Masson, Bernard. 1962. "Le masque, le double et la personne dans quelques comédies et proverbes." *Revue des sciences humaines,* n.s. 108 (oct.-déc.):551-71.

Mauzi, Robert. 1966. "Les fantoches d'Alfred de Musset." *Revue d'histoire littéraire de la France* 66:257-82.

Musset, Alfred de. 1990. *Théâtre complet*. Éd. Simon Jeune. Bibliothèque de la Pléiade. Paris: Gallimard.

Richard, Jean-Pierre. 1970. *Études sur le romantisme*. Paris: Seuil.

Serrano, Lucienne. 1977. *Jeu de masques: essai sur le travesti dérisoire dans la littérature*. Paris: Nizet.

Sices, David. 1974. *Theatre of Solitude: The Drama of Alfred de Musset*. Hanover, NH: University Press of New England.

Wright, Rachel L. 1992. "Male Reflectors in the Drama of Alfred de Musset." *French Review* 65:393-401.

Susan McCready (essay date fall 1997)

SOURCE: McCready, Susan. "Performing Stability: The Problem of Proof in Alfred de Musset's *Un Caprice* and *La Quenouille de Barbérine*." *Romance Notes* 38, no. 1 (fall 1997): 87-95.

[In the following essay, McCready regards the theme of fidelity and its proof in two of Musset's comedies of the 1830s.]

A husband is unsure of his wife's fidelity and hatches a scheme to prove that she is unfaithful; a wife worries that her husband is about to stray and enlists the help of her maid to spy on him; a young man promised in marriage to a young woman wants to test her to prove that she will be faithful before he says "I do." Disguises are worn; letters are intercepted; conversations overheard, but in the end, the lovers always recognize each other's true, essential value and are united. This is a standard comic plot: some sort of conflict (a doubt about fidelity) is introduced into a once-stable system (a happy marriage) and the conflict is resolved through "negotiations," which, in the end, uphold the (slightly altered) status quo.[1] The traditional comic resolution eliminates a sometimes sinister indeterminacy, through a performance of stability—usually the promise of the marriage of the young protagonists to the "correct" partner or the reunion of husband and wife. The lovers in such traditional comedies are exemplary figures whose negotiations about fidelity or marriage can be read in general terms as meditations on the collectively imagined value of love, fidelity and marriage in society. The happy resolution of the conflict is a "making real" (to use Elaine Scarry's term) of these abstract values, which are now anchored for the audience in the theatrical performance and for the characters by some performance *within* the play.

Elaine Scarry shows in *The Body in Pain* how anxieties about indeterminacy (what she calls "unanchored claims"—such as the claim of the realness of God) lead to the complex, collective psychological project of *analogical verification,* which consists of anchoring those claims in a physical body and usually in physical pain. For example, according to Scarry, in the Old Testament, scenes of wounding are meant to substantiate, to "make real" the existence of God; the marks on the bodies of the Israelites are to be read as "proof" of the power of God, who has no body. This process is what "grounds" the claim of God's realness, a claim on which an entire social order is based. We can also see this process at work in the theater, in plays in which the conflict centers on the need to prove something (and in comedies it is often love or fidelity that is in question). The need for *physical* evidence (of love, of fidelity) drives the action of the play until the characters are satisfied, and in plays in the most traditional mode, satisfaction comes only with the happy marriage (performed or renewed) of the protagonists. At the same time, the play itself serves the function of analogical verification for its audience, whose unanchored claims about love and fidelity are embodied in the physical performance of the play.[2]

Many of Musset's plays conform to this basic structure as characters rehearse a variety of strategies to arrive at some sort of "proof." The strategies are the traditional comic devices such as secret, disguise (and recognition), and *dédoublement,* which at first heighten the indeterminacy (and the comic effect). In the end, however, the negotiation of values played out in these strategies reaches a resolution, a collective agreement about value(s) which (re)stabilizes the system. Thus artificial indeterminacy (disguise, etc.) is a pretext to a performance of stability.[3] In his *Confession d'un enfant du siècle,* Musset as social critic suffers precisely from his "contemporary indeterminacy," a malaise, which according to Musset is endemic to his rudderless generation as it drifts between the past and the future. He describes the situation of the French youth in the 1830s thus:

> . . . derrière eux un passé à jamais détruit, s'agitant encore sur ses ruines, avec tous les fossiles des siècles d'absolutisme; devant eux l'aurore d'un immense horizon, les premières clartés de l'avenir; et entre ces deux mondes . . . quelque chose de semblable à l'Océan qui sépare le vieux continent de la jeune Amérique . . . le siècle présent, en un mot, qui sépare le passé de l'avenir, qui n'est ni l'un ni l'autre et qui ressemble à tous deux à la fois, et où l'on ne sait à chaque pas qu'on fait, si l'on marche sur une semence ou sur un débris.
>
> (*Prose* 85)

Un Caprice and *La Quenouille de Barbérine,* two comedies from the 1830s are both meditations on this indeterminacy and attempts to establish new exchange values through which the individual and the society might become "grounded" once more.

Both of these plays (and several others in Musset's œuvre) embody concerns about exchange, value, and power, but they do so within a system that presents the value of marriage and fidelity as a given. While the fidelity of specific characters may be put into question in some of these plays, the value of fidelity is always agreed upon in the happy ending which (re)unites husband and wife. Certainly the most well-known of these comedies is *Un Caprice,* a one-act play in eight scenes. First published in 1837, *Un Caprice* had a successful run at the Théâtre-Français beginning in 1847 and has been one of Musset's most performed plays ever since. *Un Caprice* is particularly illuminating as it opens with the proof of conjugal devotion (the purse Mathilde is making for her husband) and the proof of adultery (the *other,* "counterfeit" purse accepted by the husband from another woman). The rest of the play is a series of manipulations that will "set things right" again, negotiating an agreement about the essential value of fidelity.

The opening scene of *Un Caprice* finds Mme Chavigny (Mathilde) placing the finishing touches on a red purse she has made in secret as a surprise for her husband. Urged on by affection for her husband and her fear of losing him to another, Mathilde plans to offer the purse to her husband as a mark of her own fidelity. She has worked in secret, she explains, to avoid the appearance of a reproach: "Cela aurait eu l'air de lui dire: 'Voyez comme je pense à vous' . . . tandis qu'en lui montrant mon petit travail fini, ce sera lui qui se dira que j'ai pensé à lui." (*Théâtre* 422). She goes on to address an affectionate apostrophe to the purse in which it becomes clear that the real value of the purse is not in any intrinsic worth as an object, but in its offering. "Pauvre petite! tu ne vaux pas grand-chose, on ne te vendrait pas deux louis. Comment se fait-il qu'il me semble triste de me séparer de toi!" (*Théâtre* 422). In fact, Mathilde has great difficulty in separating herself from the purse. Not only is she already clearly projecting her identity onto the purse, confounding herself psychologically with it,[4] but the act of offering the purse will be physically deferred and finally performed only through the mediation of Mme de Léry.

The first obstacle to offering the purse comes from Mathilde herself, who has not finished it when her husband enters. He proudly (one might say sadistically) displays another purse, a blue purse given to him as a gift. Mathilde's friend and confidante Mme de Léry then enters and immediately identifies the author of the blue purse as a Mme de Blainville, confirming Mathilde's suspicions. Mme de Léry's teasing remarks about the purse show a clear continuity with Mathilde's attitude toward her own purse. That is, here, a purse is not just a purse. "On a mis sept ans à la faire et vous jugez si pendant ce temps-là elle a changé de destination. Elle a appartenu en idée à trois personnes de ma connaissance. C'est un vrai trésor que vous avez là" (*Théâtre* 426). While the specific item exchanged is not necessarily meaningful, the exchange itself has meaning within the societal context.[5] In this case, the exchange is inscribed in the courtly tradition of the love token, in which accepting a gift or wearing clothing in the lover's color is part of a "code" which signifies the lovers' constancy (or infidelity). Both Mme de Léry and Mathilde (and presumably Mme de Blainville) immediately understand this, but Chavigny refuses to accept the purse's "meaning." He makes much of Mathilde's nonsensical question on first seeing the purse: "De quelle couleur est-elle?" (*Théâtre* 425). But, in fact, in the context of the courtly code, the color signifies the purse's author and so to ask "What color is it?" is really to ask "Who gave it to you?" Chavigny likewise

sees (or claims to see) only nonsense in Mathilde's displeasure that he should display the purse in public, replying "La montrer! Ne dirait-on pas que c'est un trophée?" Of course, that is precisely what it is: the purse represents his (imminent) conquest of Mme de Blainville and his denial of this fact makes his intentions all the more clear. When Mathilde begs Chavigny to give up the blue purse, the subtext is just as clear, but he again refuses, preferring to take everything literally in order to deny its signification.

It is Mme de Léry who, once apprised of the situation between the spouses, is able to turn Chavigny's refusal against him. She has Mathilde's purse presented to him anonymously, then teases him to guess its author. This time, it is she who remains (at least in appearance) in the realm of the literal as Chavigny (convinced that the purse is a gift from Mme de Léry, herself) attempts to seduce her. In an inversion of his earlier scene with Mathilde, Chavigny begs to know who made the red purse, then gladly exchanges the blue one for it. The exchange made, Mme de Léry reveals that the red purse was made by Mathilde. With this moment of recognition everything falls back into place: Chavigny now understands the true value of Mathilde's love and plans to confess his faults to her and in so doing to restore conjugal felicity.

Musset's 1849 verse play *Louison* follows a similar storyline, in which a would-be unfaithful husband is corrected through a series of substitutions, and when the dust settles, rediscovers the true value of his faithful wife. Neither comedy ever puts into serious question the "value" of fidelity; rather in both cases the husband simply needs to be reminded of it. In *La Quenouille de Barbérine,* first published in 1835, the *value* of a wife's fidelity is so evident that Ulric wagers "tout ce qu['il] possède sur terre" (*Théâtre* 313) on Barbérine's fidelity. In this case, her fidelity must be (and, of course, is) proven, but its worth is made explicit. In the 1851 play *Bettine,* the unfaithful fiancé Steinberg uses the *appearance* of Bettine's infidelity as a pretext to break their engagement, after she has sacrificed all of her belongings to pay his debts. He determines value only in economic terms, and since Bettine is no longer able to support him financially, she is no longer of value to him. Her abandonment leads Bettine in turn to recognize the true worth of the Marquis, her erstwhile suitor, and the play concludes with their happy marriage. Again, value is not put into question; it only needs to be recognized.[6]

In *Un Caprice,* the obstacle to Chavigny's recognition of Mathilde's value is his own desire to have it both ways. In refusing to admit that his having accepted a purse from Mme de Blainville "means" anything, he is able to keep both possibilities (fidelity or infidelity) in play. He is able to do this because he himself is not engaged in the exchanges taking place. We have spoken of the purse as an "arbitrary object" in the system of exchange, but in the realm of literature it is anything but arbitrary. As a metonymy for the woman who offers it, the purse has obvious sexual connotations and becomes the object of "analogical verification" of which Elaine Scarry speaks. Not only, as we have seen, do the two purses "make real" certain claims (Mathilde's stands for fidelity, while Mme de Blainville's stands for proof of infidelity), they illustrate the power imbalance inherent in the relationships of the characters. That is, they stand for the radical embodiment of the women as opposed to the un-embodied power of Chavigny who is able to refuse their signification as long as it is convenient because he is not himself embodied in the exchange. Scarry opposes the vulnerable, physical body to the powerful, un-embodied voice, and so it is no surprise if here the power exercised by the un-embodied Chavigny is discursive.

When in her scene iv confrontation with her husband, Mathilde falls on her knees to beg him to give up the blue purse (intending, unbeknownst to Chavigny, to replace it with the red one), the engagement of her body in this action exemplifies the degree to which she is already physically engaged in the exchange of the purses. Chavigny's reply and his immediate exit demonstrate his power; he is able to enforce his will discursively by naming Mathilde's action "un enfantillage" (*Théâtre* 430) and physically by cutting off all discussion in leaving. In a way, Chavigny is already absent before his exit as he is not really "in" the negotiation that Mathilde is attempting to operate. In scene viii, the analogous scene between Chavigny and Mme de Léry, the power imbalance is corrected. This time, Mathilde is physically absent from the stage (although metonymically figured in the presence of the red purse) and acting only as her proxy, Mme de Léry is not herself implicated in the exchange she successfully operates; that is, she is all voice. In contrast, Chavigny goes through a process of "embodiment" over the course of the scene, as Mme de Léry (by withholding the name of the author of the red purse) is able to reverse the power dynamic of the earlier scene. Chavigny, himself, begs on bended knee to know the name of his admirer, as Mathilde had done earlier.

When Mme de Léry destroys the blue purse, however, the exchange is not complete, since Chavigny believes that Mme de Léry is the author of the red purse. Another substitution must be made before Chavigny recognizes his error. Significantly, the correction is discursive. As Chavigny had done earlier with Mathilde, after a scene peppered with verbal sparring, Mme de Léry simply states the literal facts: "Si vous trouvez que Mathilde a les yeux rouges, essuyez-les avec cette petite bourse que ses larmes reconnaîtront, car c'est votre bonne, brave et fidèle femme qui a passé quinze jours à la faire" (*Théâtre* 448). Turning his own discursive

strategy against him, Mme de Léry forces Chavigny to recognize the significance of the situation he himself created. The resolution, the return of Mathilde and Chavigny's pledge to tell her of his attempted seduction of her friend, underscores the importance of discourse in this play and in systems of exchange in general. Here word-play can be used to create a sort of indeterminacy (as in the failed seduction of Mme de Léry) or it can be used to diffuse indeterminacy by a cold statement of fact.

La Quenouille de Barbérine presents an even clearer example of the double use of discourse and the power imbalance of embodiedness vs. un-embodiedness. Here a young knight, Rosemberg, wagers that Ulric's wife Barbérine will be unfaithful during his absence. Infuriated by this slander and sure of his wife's fidelity, Ulric accepts the wager and Rosemberg journeys to Ulric's chateau to attempt to seduce Barbérine. From the outset, Rosemberg is "all voice"; his only proof of Barbérine's faithlessness is the commonplace "on dit" about the faithlessness of all women. "Je n'ai pas médit d'une femme," he explains, "j'ai exprimé mon opinion sur toutes les femmes en général" (*Théâtre* 312). But like Chavigny, Rosemberg will undergo an embodying transformation, as the wise Barbérine pretends to be seduced in order to administer a particularly humiliating punishment to Rosemberg: imprisoned in her tower, he is forced to spin to earn his board. "Si vous voulez boire et manger, vous n'avez d'autre moyen que de faire comme les vieilles femmes qui gagnent leur vie en prison, c'est-à-dire de filer. Vous trouverez une quenouille et un rouet tout préparés dans cette chambre" (*Théâtre* 322). Barbérine, speaking from off-stage is now all voice and all powerful. At her mercy is Rosemberg who falls prey to his own bodily need for food and is forced to spin. Foregrounded in this play is, of course, the issue of gender: Rosemberg's punishment is humiliating because he is not only embodied (made vulnerable) but feminized.

While discourse seems to be a sort of double-edged sword, what Scarry refers to as something that is both a tool and a weapon, in this play there is always an external, verifiable truth to which discourse refers. In *Un Caprice,* under the watchful eye of Mme de Léry, husband and wife are reunited. The essential superiority of Mathilde is recognized, as is the essential value of fidelity. The same is true of the other plays we have mentioned: they are all about coming "to terms'" in different relationships, but they all rely on artifice (play-acting, disguise) within the play to arrive successfully at their ends. As we have seen, the *mises en scène* manufactured by the characters within the plays correspond narrowly to an essentially unquestioned (though temporarily challenged) "real," which is the value they are "proving" ("embodying," "substantiating," "demonstrating") and whose proof makes its self-perpetuation possible.

Notes

1. This is basically the plot of Marivaux's *L'Epreuve* and *Le Jeu de l'amour et du hasard,* among others, but it is not limited to comedy. It is also the plot of *A Winter's Tale* and Chaucer's clerk's tale (which is Perrault's "Griselidis") and with the minor variation of an unhappy ending (in which the value of the spouse is recognized too late) becomes the basic plot of *Othello.*

2. Anne Ubersfeld has shown convincingly that the spectator of a theatrical performance does not simply "believe in" the reality of what is enacted on stage, but undergoes a complex negotiation to discern the referential relationship of *two* real spaces, that of the concrete ("real") space of the stage and that of quotidian reality, "celui où s'exerce son action, celui où il n'est pas spectateur" (Ubersfeld 11).

3. Albert Smith has nonetheless argued convincingly that at least in *Les Caprices de Marianne,* Musset subverts this traditional comic structure, and transforms it into something new and distinctly Romantic precisely by refusing to banish all instability. The same might also be said for other plays in Musset's œuvre, in which comedy and tragedy share the stage, either through comic structure turned tragic, or, as in *La Nuit vénitienne,* tragic conflict diffused into masked comedic gaiety.

4. For example, after failing to present the purse to him, Mathilde is about to throw it on the fire and then stops herself and addressing the purse says: "Mais qu'as-tu fait? . . . Il n'y a pas de ta faute; tu attendais, tu espérais aussi" (*Théâtre* 431). She is clearly projecting her own intentions onto the purse.

5. I follow Marcel Mauss's analysis in his "Essai sur le don," in which the gift's importance lies not in the object itself but in its contextualized function as "total social fact." Of course, in the case of *Un Caprice,* the choice of a purse is not arbitrary, but deeply significant, as well will see.

6. We might compare this to the typical fairy tale, in which virtue is hidden or not recognized (Perrault's "Peau d'âne" is an example) until some especially virtuous prince or king reveals the true identity of the mistreated heroine. As in the plays we are discussing, virtue or value is a "given" but appearance is deceiving (sometimes intentionally so) and it can be mistaken. Usually in fairy tales it is an authority figure who "sets things right." We should remark that in the more "psychologized"

theater of Musset, it is often up to the individual to recognize his/her mistake and to make amends.

7. This is perhaps clearest in *Bettine,* which opens with the arrival of the *notaire* with marriage contracts for Bettine and Steinberg ready. By the end of the play, after having been put off on several occasions, he will be invited to stay and preside over the signing of marriage contracts by Bettine and the Marquis.

Works Cited

Mauss, Marcel. "Essai sur le don," in *Sociologie et anthropologie,* Paris: Presses Universitaires Français, 1973.

Musset, Alfred de. *Œuvres complètes en prose,* Paris: Gallimard, 1951.

———. *Théâtre complet,* Paris: Gallimard, 1990.

Scarry, Elaine, *The Body in Pain,* New York: Oxford University Press, 1985.

Smith, Albert. "Musset's *Les Caprices de Marianne*: A Romantic Adaptation of a Traditional Comic Structure," *Nineteenth Century French Studies,* Vol. 20 No. 1-2 (1991-2 Fall-Winter): 53-64.

Ubersfeld, Anne. "Notes sur la dénégation théâtrale," in Régis Durand (ed.) *La Relation théâtrale,* Lille: Presses Universitaires de Lille, 1980.

David Sices (essay date 1997)

SOURCE: Sices, David. Introduction to *Historical Dramas of Alfred de Musset,* translated by David Sices, pp. 1-6. New York: Peter Lang, 1997.

[*In the following excerpted introduction to his translations of Musset's historical tragedies, Sices briefly summarizes the contexts and content of* Lorenzaccio *and* Andrea del Sarto.]

FILIPPO

Would you deny the history of the entire world? . . .

LORENZO

I don't deny history. I just wasn't there.

Lorenzaccio, V, 2

Alfred de Musset's literary work abounds in contradictions: his abiding reputation as one of the major French Romanticists, vs. his attack on the romantic æsthetic in the name of classical tradition, constitutes only the most pervasive of them. But another significant contradiction can be found in his historical tragedies. It is true that he managed to complete only two of them, quite early in his career; but one of those—*Lorenzaccio*—is probably the most successful and enduring of the entire genre, certainly the most frequently produced on the French and international stage.[1] Its ultimate message, however, is, paradoxically, the meaninglessness of history.

The major practitioners in France of Romantic historical drama—Ludovic Vitet, Alexandre Dumas *père*, Victor Hugo—had essentially a dual purpose: to bring the Romantic historical vision inspired notably by the example of Sir Walter Scott onto the stage as well as into the novel, and to create a serious new theater, capable of displacing from the stage of the Comédie-Française the traditional French "classical" tragedy, whose neo-Aristotelean rules, perfected by Corneille and Racine, had been brought forward into those times by numerous epigones. The Romantics' aim was a tribute to the importance of the official French theater in their day. The 1830 début of Hugo's *Hernani* in that temple of classicism, celebrated in Théophile Gautier's *Les Jeunes-France* and Albert Besnard's famous painting, and recounted ever afterward in French manuals of literary history, marked the triumph and perhaps the high-water mark in France of the Romantic movement. But Musset had a different end in view, particularly following the fiasco of his **La Nuit vénitienne** in performance at the Odéon later that same year. So when he wrote his two completed historical tragedies, **Andrea del Sarto** and **Lorenzaccio,** in 1832 and 1833, he did not have stage performance in mind: their inclusion in a volume entitled **Un Spectacle dans un fauteuil,** "An Armchair Show," makes it clear that, at least for the moment, Musset was thinking in terms of an ideal stage, more flexible, more intimate, and in the final analysis more spectacular than anything then conceivable at the Comédie-Française or in the French theater in general. His imagination, both poetic and dramatic, was thus freed from the limitations of contemporary stage practice and resources. On the other hand, however, unlike a Shakespeare, a Racine or a Molière, he was not granted the possibility of seeing his plays take shape in their natural medium, of modifying them on the basis of their audiences' response, of developing his own dramatic instinct in the give-and-take of the theater. When the time came to produce **Andrea del Sarto** in 1848, those revolutionary days were not right for politically "irrelevant" drama, and Musset himself, who had lost the freshness of vision that led him to create his greatest plays in his early twenties, was tempted into modifications to suit the requirements of the "real" stage. As for **Lorenzaccio,** it was not to be mounted until 1896, almost forty years after the author's death, and even then in a severely altered version commissioned by Sarah Bernhardt as an addition to her list of travesty roles: the reduction from five to four acts, with a far smaller cast and the elimination of most subplots, denatured Musset's original dramaturgy.

Musset's conception of historical drama is situated somewhere between those of Ludovic Vitet's *Scènes historiques,*[2] which attempted to dramatize real historical events and thereby render them accessible to a broader public, and historical tragedies like Victor Hugo's *Hernani* and *Ruy Blas,* which used historical characters and events as a background for essentially fictional heroes. **Andrea del Sarto,** which, according to Musset's brother, Paul, was derived from "the abridged notices accompanying the engravings in the *Musée Filhol,*"[3] takes the celebrated Italian renaissance painter as its artist-hero or anti-hero. **Lorenzaccio,** drawn from Benedetto Varchi's 16th-century chronicles, *Storia fiorentina,* via a historical sketch by George Sand, uses historical personages as its primary characters, although it interprets those characters, as well as the events they were involved in, according to Musset's own notion of history.

It is perhaps not surprising that two dramas written at such proximity in Musset's creative development, both drawn from events in the life of renaissance Florence, should share a common historical perspective, even though they are very different in scope and realization. **Andrea del Sarto** is about half **Lorenzaccio**'s length and has proportionally even fewer characters; more importantly, it lacks the complexity of plot, characterization, and theme to be found in the latter play. Dealing with the artist as failure because of love, a common theme throughout Musset's work (its best example is perhaps to be found in the short story, **"Le Fils du Titien"**[4]), **Andrea del Sarto** tells the story of the artist's final days. Like Robert Browning's well-known poem dating from over a decade later, Musset's play takes its view of the painter, directly or indirectly, from the one propagated by Giorgio Vasari in his *Lives*: most notably that the artist squandered his talent and misused funds given him by the King of France because of excessive infatuation with his wife, Lucrezia del Bene, and a lack of will-power. Musset treats Lucrezia more sympathetically than does Browning, and invents a disciple and friend of the artist, Cordiani, who betrays him with Lucrezia and, at the end of the play, flees with her from Florence as news comes of Andrea's suicide (also invented by the Romantic Musset, in place of the artist's later premature death from the plague). Balancing this more sympathetic treatment of Lucrezia and her lover, Musset views Andrea as the survivor of a glorious generation—that of Leonardo, Michelangelo[5] and Raphael—whose heroic example is giving way to the mannerists' petty imitations. In fact, modern scholarship has tended to see Andrea del Sarto as a master of the rising mannerist generation, rather than the morally and artistically decadent heir of earlier artists, and to emphasize the appreciation that he and his work benefitted from in contemporary Florence, not to mention

Italy, France, and the rest of Europe, rather than the inglorious penury and oblivion alleged by Musset, in conformity with Vasari.

From the point of view of the twenty-two-year-old Musset, Andrea del Sarto's fortyish age at death must have seemed rather advanced, making Lucrezia's betrayal of him with a younger man understandable, if not forgivable. In any case, love and betrayal more often than not go together in the author's works. The conflict between love and artistic creation is another that informs a great number of those works, as well. Anticipation of failure became Musset's most characteristic literary theme; in fact, it extended even to the circumstances of his life. We cannot help remembering Flaubert's epistolary comment to Louise Colet, twenty years later: "Musset will have been a charming youth, and then an old man."

Lorenzaccio, as I have said, is a far more complex work. Like **Andrea del Sarto,** it takes an historical figure as its protagonist; also like the earlier work, it treats history with considerable liberty in pursuit of its themes. But it is far less single-minded: apart from the increased number of characters—about thirty-five—and scenes—thirty-eight—in its five acts, involving a large number of different sets, it is marked by greater psychological complexity in its principal characters; its action, centering around the historically factual assassination of Duke Alexander de' Medici by his cousin, Lorenzo de' Medici, in 1536,[6] is in reality a multiple, interwoven set of three main plots and several subordinate ones.[7] The story of Lorenzaccio's[8] conspiracy to murder his cousin, in order to restore a republican form of government, is mingled with two related plots (in both senses of the term): one by Filippo Strozzi and his family to avenge an insult made to his daughter, Luisa, and incidentally to restore the oligarchic form of republic that had formerly existed in Florence; and one by Ricciarda Cibo to win Duke Alexander over by her love to a more enlightened, less despotic and brutal form of rule. Through these various plots, which culminate, in the fourth act, in Lorenzo's murder of the Duke, followed by the inactivity on the part of the "republicans" that he had foreseen, are entwined the successful machinations of Cardinal Cibo, Ricciarda's brother-in-law, to maintain control over the city; the impotence of Florentine noblemen and churchmen in the face of Alexander's despotism and death, and of his succession by Pope Paul III's instrument, Cosimo de' Medici; the vain imprecations of Florentine exiles as they set out for life elsewhere; commentaries on all these events by two Florentine burghers, as well as by two poet-tutors who are willing to celebrate whatever form of government seems to be in power; the futile efforts of young students to reclaim their traditional political rights (this has been seen as a reflection of recent events in France, during the Revolution of 1830); and the fright of an idealistic young painter at the bloodthirsty language he hears Alexander

and his bodyguard use as he is painting the Duke's portrait.[9] The artist-as-hero was in vogue at that time—Balzac had published his *Chef d'œuvre inconnu* in 1831—but Musset's artists, in both **Andrea del Sarto** and **Lorenzaccio,** already express a broadly autumnal, disillusioned view. That Musset was deliberately "dedramatizing" his story, and emphasizing thereby the lack of political or moral significance of Lorenzo's act, is made clear at the end of the play, where he chooses to conclude his action with a disappointing, prosaic address, submissive to the real powers, translated almost verbatim from Varchi's chronicle, and spoken "in the distance" toward the populace massed offstage.

Musset's great historical drama, **Lorenzaccio,** can still speak eloquently to the modern reader or playgoer, beyond its important dramatic innovations, through its very contemporary themes: both the denial of historical meaningfulness that permeates it, expressed succinctly in the epigraph at the head of this introduction, and its political and psychological analysis of a city occupied by foreign forces, represented in the play by the German soldiers who hold the Citadel and control Florence in the name of the Emperor and the Pope. The latter may provide an explanation for both increased French interest in the play at the end of the second World War and its choice for a major production by the Za Branou Theater of Prague following the invasion of Czechoslovakia by Soviet tanks in 1968. Although the play offers little hope of meaningful political action in the face of despotism, it is one artist's moving representation of and response to tyranny, and its "unheroic" hero possesses thereby a certain tragic grandeur in the face of power and men's willingness to bow to it.

Lorenzaccio thus goes well beyond Musset's elegiac vision of the artist in society in **Andrea del Sarto.** The two historical dramas taken together, however, represent a considerable artistic achievement, particularly on the part of so young an author, and deserve to be better known outside the linguistic borders of their nation . . . .

Notes

1. As for *Andrea del Sarto,* it has been set to music by the composer Daniel-Lesur, first (in 1947) as incidental music, then as a symphonic poem and finally as a lyric drama, premiered by the Marseilles Opera in 1969.

2. Paul Dimoff analyzed *Lorenzaccio*'s debt to the unfinished *scène historique* of Musset's lover, George Sand, "Une Conspiration en 1537," in *La Genèse de Lorenzaccio,* Paris, 1964.

3. See Paul de Musset, *Biographie d'Alfred de Musset,* in Musset, *Œuvres complètes,* Paris, 1963, p. 28.

4. First published in *Revue des deux mondes,* 15 May 1838, then collected in Musset's *Nouvelles* in 1848.

5. Since Andrea's dates are 1486-1530, Michelangelo, who died in 1564, was still alive at the time of Musset's protagonist's death.

6. Not in 1537, as in George Sand's title for her *scène historique.*

7. See my *Theater of Solitude. The Drama of Alfred de Musset,* chapter 6, for a more complete analysis of the play's action.

8. The Italian suffix *-accio* traditionally applied to Lorenzo is pejorative. Curiously, Alexandre Dumas *père* entitled his play on the same subject *Lorenzino,* emphasizing, as does Musset, Lorenzo's small stature, which—along with Lorenzo's apparent sexual ambivalence and his lack of "masculine" courage—may explain why the role was played by female actors, starting with Sarah Bernhardt, for over half a century.

9. I do not share the view expressed in Bernard Masson's otherwise exemplary study, *Musset et le théâtre intérieur* (see in particular p. 394), that the painter, Tebaldeo, as well as other young figures is in some way spared from the general cynicism of the play and represents a triumph of art over crass political realism.

John Le Vay (essay date summer 1999)

SOURCE: Le Vay, John. "Musset's 'La Nuit d'octobre.'" *The Explicator* 57, no. 4 (summer 1999): 209-12.

[*In the following essay, Le Vay observes mythic patterns and imagery of rebirth and redeemed love in Musset's* Les nuits *poems.*]

According to myth, in the fall (October), Attis/Adonis is slain. He goes underground in winter (December), is reborn in spring (May), and attains heroic strength in summer (August).[1] There is something of that pattern in the four "Nights" (*Les Nuits*) of Alfred de Musset. But the May rebirth is abortive: "le printemps naît" (line 3), but the frozen poet remains in suspended animation: "who can write on the sand / in the teeth of the north wind?" (194-195).[2] December conforms to the underworld archetype, being dominated by a melancholic, ghostly visitant clad all in black. August begins with a lovelorn, girlish goddess and a world-weary, slightly patronizing poet who has not yet recovered the power of song—one who is not reborn poetically.

For Adonis-Musset, October, or autumn, serves two symbolic functions: It is indeed the time of the slaying of Adonis by the black boar (George Sand), but it is also the time of harvest, and at the end of **"La Nuit d'Octobre"** the poet gathers a modest golden harvest of poetical sensibility from his love-harrowed heart.

What the wise Muse in the poem tells the petulant poet in the culminating Night is, roughly, that the experience of the emotion of love is what is important; the object of love is, so to speak, immaterial. It is the *chagrin d'amour* (not the *plaisir*) that allows one, in hard won serenity (all passion spent), truly to appreciate deep friendship (232), the beauties of the green world (234), "les sonnets de Pétrarque, Michel-Ange et les arts, Shakespeare et la nature" (235-36), and "ineffable harmonie des cieux" (238).

"Couldst thou [she asks] love so well thy new true blue-eyed mistress, hadst thou not been grieved and tormented by the brown-eyed traitoress?" (242-45). The poet, in short, is told that his youthful agon with the *femme fatale* was good for him:

> Pourquoi veux-tu haïr ta jeune expérience,
> Et détester un mal qui t'a rendu mielleur?
>
> (255-56)

George Sand, six years his senior had much to teach him:

> Elle savait la vie, et te l'a fait connaître;
> Une autre a recueilli le fruit de ta douleur.
>
> (264-65)

She, the brown-eyed one (in that bygone "mystérieuse et sombre histoire" [293]), by flaying his heart, had made him a better lover of young blue-eyes, and, much more important, a better poet. The dark one had been appointed by Fate (263) to inspire him by breaking his heart (and she was presently performing the same function for Chopin, though of course Musset does not tell us this).

Magnanimity, says the Muse, is the name of the love game. "When thou findest thou canst weep for her ("plains la" [260]), the perfidious one, then thou wilt be ready for love; then "tu sais aimer" (269).

In the final strophe of **"La Nuit d'Octobre,"** the poet comes to agree with the Muse: Hate is no good—there is no poetry of hate. So he will banish for good the hateful dark woman; the moment she is erased from his memory will be the moment she is forgiven. But that is not quite what the Muse had in mind: "Do not destroy those days [the Muse says] when thou wast in love with her—they were good days, if brief" (200-01). The dark women, even in her malign aspect, serves a positive purpose in the poet's psychic life. "She is not a devil, she is a woman, and God has caused thee, through her, to divine," "en suffrant, le secret des heureux" (260-61).

The poet is not quite as magnanimous as the Muse would have him be, but he does profess to have reached the point of "pardon" (297), and is even able to say "let us pardon each other" (298), but only as a prelude to expunging her from his memory. Immediately after the moment of forgiving and forgetting the "femme à l'œil sombre" (166), the east brightens with the rosy glow of dawn, and the poet invites his soul, the Muse,

> Viens voir la nature immortelle
> Sortir des voiles du sommeil;
> Nous allons renaître avec elle
> Au premier rayon du soleil!
>
> (310-13)[3]

And so Musset-Adonis, who missed rebirth in the spring, finds it in the autumn.

It appears, *apres tout,* that the *nouvelle* "belle maîtresse" (242), *avec* "les yeux bleus" (276) *et, apparement, les cheveux* "blonds" (302), *et, bien-heureusement,* "le sourire divin" (245), is a straw woman, a fair scarecrow set up to ensure the banishment of that *oiselle noire,* the black baroness, George Sand. She would, in fact, appear to be an incarnation of the angelic Muse, the "blonde rêveuse" (302), and thus is a kind of pious fiction.

This conclusive **"October Night"** (1837) is, in fact, the third anniversary of the night (1834) when the poet banished the dark lady of his sonnets:

> Va-t'en, retire-toi, spectre de ma maîtresse!
> Rentre dans ton tombeau, si tu t'en es levé.
>
> (148-49)

The first October night (described in lines 104-51) had, as far as we can see, no dawn. On the **"Night of May"** (**"La Nuit de Mai,"** 1835), in spite of the erotic pulsations of the balmy, perfumed late night and the Muse's dulcet and seductive tones, the still chilly poet cannot rise to her bait.

Once again, the flowerlike (48), blond (51), golden-robed (54) Muse stands in antithesis to the somber baroness (not directly addressed in May), who has engendered in the dejected poet ("triste et silencieux" [57]) "ennui" (60), "melancholie" (96), "pleurs" (141), "sanglots" (152), "douleur" (141), "blessure" (146), "malheur" (187), and even "horreur" (172). The Muse is "his true mistress" (52) and his "dearest sister" (128). In spite of his continuing high regard for her, the poet is able to give her only one rather limp kiss, before she flies (miffed) back to heaven. He excuses himself from singing, saying in parting: "I have suffered a dire martyrdom, and if I were to put it to the lyre, every string would break" (200-02). He has not, we should say, sufficiently distanced his material.

On the **"Night of December"** (**"La Nuit Decembre,"** 1835) the golden goddess does not appear, for this is the winter/underworld canto, and Musset spends it in the company of his sable-suited doppelganger. This is his inner self, his blood brother, the personification of his melancholy from which arises his poetry (on the brother's brow is a wreath "of withered myrtle" [45], at his foot "a fallen lute" [58]).

Although the dark brother appears to the poet throughout his life at moments of high sorrow (and, early on, at a moment of "misère d'amour" [27]), he does not appear during the affair of the dark lady until far into the "nuit sombre" (181), when he comes upon the poet mooning over a mesh of black/brown hair (148) and a clutch of love letters. But the dark "inward companion" makes no mention of the dark lady; he simply says, "When thou art in sorrow, come thou with confidence to me" (213-14). Tacitly, he brings the same message as does the Muse: that "melancholie" (111) is the wellspring not only of tears but of poetry. At the end, he does not call himself Melancholy but says: "Je suis la solitude," which, for a poet, is the same thing.

In the sultry **"Night of August"** (**"La Nuit d'Aout,"** 1836) the immortal Muse begins like a naive, lovelorn girl pining for her errant (roué?)[4] poet; but when the renegade enters (a little hangdog) and says, "Yes, my dear, I'm back, and I'm ready to sing to thee" (18), she quickly regains authority. Although ignorant of the details, she knows that while he has been away from her he has been "yielding to his evil destiny in darkness" (30) and indulging in the kind of fleshly love that "dissipates the treasures of the soul" (61). "Well, yes," says the poet, "I came to grief, but I shall sing out of my grief" (67). "Ah," says the Muse, "but thou has damaged thy heart, and "ton coeur est le poète" (81).

Again the fair goddess, a nymph of the wildwood (85), bearing a blue flower (32), directing the poet's gaze "aux cieux" (38), is pitted against the dark harlot, the chain-bearing "fière beauté" (31), bent on dragging the poet down "dans l'ombre" (30). And the poet with the damaged heart, whom the Muse looks so sadly on, must speak the words of wisdom to himself: "Cast out pride from thy bitter heart, and rediscover love: having once loved, one must love without cease" (133-37). Like Dante, he knows he must write "according to the dictates of Love."[5] And that brings us back to the conclusion of **"La Nuit d'Octobre,"** where the Angel of Love is called "ma blonde rêveuse."

Notes

1. As for any four part work (especially one with a four seasons context), a four elements assignation is indicated: as, for example, May (spring) = air; August (summer) = fire; October (autumn) = earth; December (winter) = water.

2. All translations are my own.

3. These lines echo the opening lines of *La Nuit d'Octobre,* which predict that his "disastrous" (70) love will vanish like the mist at sunrise.

4. Musset's commerce with harlots may be seen as an adjunct (or reflex) to the black baroness affair.

5. *Purgatorio,* 24.54, also *La Vita nuova,* 13.2.

Work Cited

Berthon, H. E., ed. *Nine French Poets 1820-1880.* London: Macmillian, 1950.

Yifen Beus (essay date spring-summer 2003)

SOURCE: Beus, Yifen. "Alfred de Musset's Romantic Irony." *Nineteenth-Century French Studies* 31, nos. 3-4 (spring-summer 2003): 197-209.

[*In the following essay, Beus considers the ironic mood of Musset's collected drama and poetry, characterizing the writer as an outstanding proponent of nineteenth-century French Romantic irony.*]

The year of 1797, though somewhat arbitrary in terms of historical significance in German and French drama, marks German philosopher and theorist Friedrich Schlegel's initial efforts to establish irony as a philosophical as well as literary concept. The concept of irony was then being rediscovered and redefined by the early Romantics and is now considered by scholars of Romanticism essential to the understanding of the Romantic doctrines. As Friedrich and his brother August Wilhelm Schlegel drew inspiration from the early (Shakespeare and Cervantes) as well as the contemporary moderns (Sterne, Diderot, and Goethe) in analyzing and theorizing modern art and literature, the French also noticed the dominance of Shakespeare in English and German literary criticism as well as of eighteenth-century sentimentality. Sterne's *A Sentimental Journey* and *Tristram Shandy* were widely read in France and gave him a near celebrity status during his visits to numerous literary salons in Paris. Diderot deliberately copied Sterne's model when writing his *Jacques le fataliste* and prompted the French literary circles to reflect on the use of humor and the role of the author in the creative process and the relation to his work and audience. The transition from the classic to the modern is most notably fostered by Mme de Staël and her group at Coppet. Under the impact of eighteenth-century sentimentality, the promotion of German literary theory by the Coppet Group as well as the anti-classicist sentiment developed within the French literary circle, a number of writers, such as Hugo, Stendhal, Musset, and Vigny, produced works that recognize the merits of the new Romantic ideals and advocate what their German counterparts had done decades before. In this article, I will examine the dramatic works of Musset in the light of Romantic irony, an irony that synthesizes conflicting forces to produce a universal type of poetry and reveals the nature of artistic creation by a self-critical writing process of the author while preserving the art work's function to describe the author's duty to the society and to reflect his own time.

Among the French Romantic dramatists, the theories of Hugo, Vigny, and Musset on "modern drama" and the role of the author bear most striking resemblance to that of Friedrich Schlegel. This is in no way accidental. The Schlegels' discussions of humor, irony, and poetry are not unfamiliar in the French literary circle thanks to translations of the Schlegel brothers' works, the Schlegels' debates with the French literary and publishing circles about the Romantic/classic contrast, and the publications, Staël's *De l'Allemagne* in particular, and literary discussions of the Coppet group. Nor has the subject gone altogether unnoticed.

At the time when Hugo and Vigny were primarily poets, the younger Musset also started his career writing poetry. However, he found himself lacking passion as a poet, and after the indifferent reception of his first staged play, *La Nuit vénitienne* in 1830, he also lost enthusiasm for writing plays for the stage. Instead, as the title of *Un Spectacle dans un fauteuil* (1832) indicates, he went on to write plays for reading. Most of these were not meant to be performed at the time of their writing, though they were staged later, thanks to the advancement of stage technology. Quite ironically, his place as one of the greatest dramatists of his time was established through these then unstageable works. These works, along with those of Hugo and Vigny, are generally considered the best exemplars of Romantic irony in nineteenth-century French drama.

Some personal traits of Musset group him with Hugo and Vigny, while others distinguish him from the latter. On one hand, Musset belongs to a younger generation of the French Romantics (with Gautier, Nerval, and others) than that of Hugo and Vigny (who are his seniors by eight and thirteen years respectively). Yet, though only in his twenties, he produced, contemporaneously with them and all in the short span of two years (1833-34), such brilliant dramatic works as *Les Caprices de Marianne, Fantasio, On ne badine pas avec l'amour* and *Lorenzaccio.* Secondly, his affair with George Sand, though brief, had a profound impact upon his view on the nature of the poet and his creative process, one that made several of his poetry collections and prose writings (*Les Nuits, Le Poète déchu,* and *"Le Fils du Titien"*) more intensely biographical than theirs. Thirdly, despite their ideal to bring forth a harmonious yet critical synthesis of the duality of their personal life and their experience as poets and dramatists, Hugo and Vigny fell short of realizing their theories—Hugo often had to compromise his ideals to accommodate the contemporary stage and audience,[1] and Vigny practically withdrew from the theatre after *Chatterton,* the only dramatic work that reflects a real attempt to use the stage to advocate his criticism and to attack a society responsible for stifling poetic genius. Musset also turned away from the contemporary theatre after the failure of **La Nuit vénitienne** in 1830, only to create the closest French exemplars of Romantic irony in drama in the Schlegelian sense. His armchair drama literally freed him from the restraints and demand of contemporary theatrical conventions and practice. The power of his poetic imagination and youthful passion overflows in his plays, an exalted creative state which he was not able to reach in his earlier poetry.

The modernity of Musset's dramas was not to be recognized until the twentieth century when they could be produced in their original versions without the modifications dictated previously by the limits of nineteenth-century stage, where such techniques and design as swift scene changes and poetically colorful landscape were not possible. Inspired by Musset's comedies, Jacques Copeau, one of France's most innovative directors in the 1920s and 30s, published a manifesto for a new theatre where the director's duty is to faithfully translate the dramatist's work into a "poetry of the theatre," using complex composition of lighting and stagecraft to convey such an effect. In an introduction to an edition of Musset's **Comédies et Proverbes** (Paris, 1931), he describes the playwright as one of the greatest of dramatic authors who have an intuition of the laws that govern a play. Speaking of Musset's craftsmanship as a dramatist, Copeau writes:

> He possesses the secret of light composition. I do not mean something mawkish or weak by that. But an agility, a joyousness. True power in art is delicate and explosive. It abolishes real duration at one stroke. . . . There he [Musset] is in command of everything. An image, an allusion, a passage, a break, a balancing of scenes or speeches, and perhaps even less, is enough for him to stir up the powers of illusion, to awaken a desire in the imagination and to satisfy it at the same moment.

> (qtd. in Sices 241-42)

Musset's comedies have also been referred to as "cinematic":

> The "cinematic" quality of Musset's drama, which was noted as early as the 1920s, makes it apparent that motion picture was not so much a device which revolutionized the concept of dramatic structure as the necessary realization of an evolving theatrical vision in search of its technological means.

> (Sices 241-42)

Thus the shifting perspectives of **Les Caprices de Marianne** provided a dramatic base for Jean Renoir's film technique in *La Règle du jeu.* These distinct qualities of his dramas are ahead of their time in terms of dramaturgy and audience appeal, for the nineteenth-century stage was not equipped to manage the shift of perspectives within a short time, and such changes often created inconsistency in the plot and thus disoriented the audience. "His mind leaps from idea to idea, image to image almost too quickly to provide his reader with the logical links between," comments Margaret Rees (128). Only a modern stage or else the cinema, where advanced machinery and technology are available, can match the speed of Musset's mind at work to realize the visions expressed in his plays.

Though Musset is considered one of the most important figures of the French Romantics, his attitude towards the practice, particularly in drama, of his contemporaries is more suspicious than readily agreeing. Musset's fundamental attitude toward the contemporary Classical and Romantic debate appears to be an ironic one in that Musset mocks both the haughty self-important posture of cultural superiority of the French with their pride in their classicism and the Romantics' idealistic yet naive attempt to revolutionize the literary tradition with its expressive lyricism; notwithstanding, both classicism and the new Romantic development gave inspiration to Musset's own youthful eccentricities. This attitude is reflected in his own dramatic style, which interestingly combines the wit and cynicism of seventeenth-century French classicism with Shakespeare's method of describing characters, settings, and costumes through dialogue rather than detailed stage directions at the beginning of each scene, as is common in nineteenth-century drama. Uncompromising in his views of a theatre that concentrates on the development of the characters' minds and motives as well as revealing the playwright's idealistic yet cynical attitude toward his work, Musset was not a popular success as a dramatist like Dumas or Hugo, who, despite their attempt to realize the ideals of the new genre "drame," often succumbed to stage conventions of exotic local color, ornate setting, and melodramatic manipulation of emotions. Many critics[2] agree that Musset's dramas come closest among their peers to the realization of the ideals developed, in the Romantic manifesto "Preface to Cromwell," by the poet who had served him as a mentor and introduced him into the Romantic circle. Unlike Hugo and Dumas, who enjoyed a great degree of popularity but, at the same time, needed to constantly deal with theatre managers, scene/costume artists, technical staff, and cast during productions, Musset, after giving up writing for the stage, had greater freedom to realize the poetic ideals fostered by the Romantics.

Musset had always been concerned with defining the role of poetry and the poet. A number of his poems and prose writings reveal this concern. *Les Nuits* (1835) consists of dialogue-like stanzas between the Poet and the Muse. *Le Poète déchu,* a fragmentary narrative written in 1839, can be read like a *Bildungsroman* or portrait of a young artist who discovers the true poet's function after going through mental trials and suffering—a biographical overtone of his wrenching relationship with George Sand. I. G. Daemmrich summarizes Musset's conception of the poet:

> He must have suffered an emotional crisis which reveals to him the fundamental importance of genuine feeling for his creativity; he must sacrifice his most intimate feelings to his art; he must renounce political activism in order to concentrate on the general human condition; and his work must touch his readers. In order to create truly significant poetry, he should attain both a state of exaltation and one of detachment from his emotions. Finally, he should face the bitter reality that his high calling will lead to his rejection by a materialistic and politically oriented society.
>
> (5-10)

The end of Musset's relationship with George Sand produces the "emotional suffering" for him to mature as a poet, argues Daemmrich. This experience also becomes the raw material for his poetry. But while expressing such emotional agony in his writing, Musset treats his works with a certain degree of detachment. In order to achieve this, it would be necessary for him to become isolated from his society, to free himself from social, political, and even personal concerns. This detachment will serve the true poet as a purifying stage leading to the state of spiritual "exaltation." But, this antagonistic view towards society often leads him to a state of complete self-absorption and to a self-isolation with no escape, like that described in Vigny's *Chatterton.*

Musset's ironic affection for and detachment from his work are reflected through a juxtaposition of sarcastic and comic attitudes. A central aspect of the Schlegelian irony, the author's overall tone of being serious while at the same time appearing comic and critical, is thus also present in Musset's "comédie." Most of the heroes and situations in his plays clearly embody such irony—the seriousness of Musset's attitude is often conveyed with and disguised in laughter, and a surprising tragic denouement is common in his "comedies." This Shakespearean mixture of tragic/comic (as in *Lear* and *Hamlet*) and Socratic irony expressed through seeming lightness make his aesthetic practice closer to the Schlegelian aesthetic than that of his peer dramatists. The striking resemblance between Musset's own philosophy of art and poetry and his love affairs and those of his protagonists/antagonists reflects his commitment to the poet's personal experience as the subject matter for poetry. And yet, this identification with his hero is often juxtaposed with an attitude of critical cynicism toward

him. Using **"Namouna,"** one of Musset's longest poems, which exhibits a "curious mixture of irony-at-the-expense-of romanticism and romantic irony," Lloyd Bishop points out this general characteristic of Musset's irony. In dealing with Musset's irony, he says, we must bear in mind that

> romantic irony is a double irony, it works in two opposite directions at once: the poet will declare himself alienated from his hero, but this alienation itself is also ironic—it masks the author's limited but genuinely sympathetic identification. Romantic irony commits itself to what it criticizes.
>
> (98)

Musset's hero often speaks in elegant classical style with lyrical images to express ideas, emotions, and desires in serious situations when such mannerism seems comically out of place. As Célio, for example, expresses his frustration in courting the heroine of *Les Caprices de Marianne,* his pitiful lovesickness makes his metaphors trite and Octave's unsympathetic response sarcastic and yet reasonable:

CÉLIO:

> Qui pourrait dire: ceci est gai ou triste? La réalité n'est qu'une ombre. Appelle imagination ou folie ce qui la divinise. Alors la folie est beauté elle-même. Chaque homme marche enveloppé d'un réseau transparent qui le couvre de la tête aux pieds; il croit voir des bois et des fleuves, des visages divins, et l'universelle nature se teint sous ses regards des nuances infinies du tissu magique. Octave! Octave! Viens à mon secours! . . . Fais ce que tu voudras, mais ne me trompe pas, je t'en conjure. Il est aisé de me tromper; je ne sais pas me défier d'une action que je ne voudrais pas fairemoi-même.

OCTAVE:

> Si tu escaladais les murs?

CÉLIO:

> A quoi bon, si elle ne m'aime pas?

OCTAVE:

> Si tu lui écrivais?

CÉLIO:

> Elle déchire mes lettres ou me les renvoie.

OCTAVE:

> Si tu en aimais une autre?
>
> (I: iv)

This dialogue displays a typical dichotomy between two protagonists—one appears strong and rational while the other is weak and sentimental. In this plaint from Célio, Musset presents his agony in a poetic statement full of symbolism and at the same time as a comic result of Célio's hopeless cowardice. Octave's simple suggestions only make Célio's lovesickness an apparent theme for a love comedy and occludes the tragic element through Octave's ironically comic indifference toward the heroine. However, this jest-like tone turns out to be antithetical to the tragic development of the story. The Schlegelian irony of seriousness and jest at the same time is manifested here in Musset's detached humor and cynicism toward his protagonist.

Although his sarcastic attitude toward his contemporary Romantics distinguishes his manner from that of other French Romantics, Musset shares the characteristic of a socially detached Romantic hero in his profession as a dramatist/poet. Goethe's *Werther* was the first German work that expressed the developing "mal du siècle" pessimism through its suicidal theme and attracted immense popularity in France. Ever since, suicide, one of the many forms of the Romantic hero's agony of alienation, became a common motif in Romantic literature, and many Romantics expressed this alienation complex in their own lives by remaining silent or by softening their critical tone. Their choice of silence or conciliation led to withdrawal (in the case of Vigny), or to compromising their ideals in order to conform with public taste and maintain popularity (Dumas, a typical and very successful example, and Hugo, to a lesser degree). In Musset's case, his silence and ceasing to be an active dramatist for the contemporary stage takes a different turn—he becomes a voice for his own youthful zeal and imagination by liberating them from social concerns and by producing works that require tremendous imaginary participation on the reader's part. He turns the reader's closet into a world of imagination and jest, often setting his plays in foreign lands and at times without any chronological reference (such as Naples in *Les Caprices de Marianne,* Florence in *André del Sarto,* Munich in *Fantasio,* and Venice in *La Nuit vénitienne*), creating incoherent story lines (a potential love interest begins in *Fantasio,* but ends without any result, or a war is declared without particular effects) providing anti-dramatic denouements (Octave refuses the love of Marianne in *Les Caprices de Marianne*), using disguised identities of characters (Fantasio disguises himself as a jester, and the prince as his own aide-de-camp) to confound theatrical reality. All these devices that draw the spectator's attention to an intentional "break of theatrical illusion" are essential to create an irony that highlights the self-reflexivity and fictionalization of the work itself.

Musset's techniques of irony can be broken down into the following areas, all of which in fact are interwoven with each other in the structure of the play to contribute to the total ironic effect of the work: using dialogues for lyrical yet humorous descriptions of set, costume, and characters, use of disguise (personification, masks, etc.) to manipulate the ambiguities of reality and illu-

sion, and finally, perception of love as the overarching theme of his drama. Writing for the closet without all the production-related hassles and by embedding these techniques of irony in his work, Musset was able to rely on his lyricism and the reader's imagination to create dramas at his will.

Les Caprices de Marianne, ironically the only major play performed during Musset's lifetime, can best represent his youthful burst of poetry and freedom of imagination. All of his techniques interwoven to create an irony can be seen in this comic-tragedy. The plot turns around Célio's desire to gain Marianne's love. Célio, a shy, timid, and good-natured young man, is frustrated by his failure in courting Marianne, wife of judge Claudio. He asks the brave and outspoken Octave to win her heart in his behalf. As Octave stirs up Marianne's passion, he also arouses jealousy in her husband. Claudio issues a warning that whoever steps into their garden to meet with Marianne will be killed. As Célio hastens to the rendezvous arranged by Octave, Marianne's note to Octave about the trap comes too late to Célio, who consequently dies believing that Octave has betrayed him. At Célio's grave site, Marianne confesses her love for Octave, but the latter reveals the truth to her: "Je ne vous aime pas, Marianne; c'était Célio qui vous aimait" (274).

At the beginning of *Les Caprices de Marianne,* the only description of the two men, Octave and Célio, both dressed up in carnival attires is through their dialogue, which also contrasts the two personalities by their costumes:

OCTAVE:

> Comment se porte, mon bon monsieur, cette gracieuse mélancolie?

CÉLIO:

> Octave! . . . Ô fou que tu es! Tu as un pied de rouge sur les joues. D'où te vient cet accoutrement? N'as-tu pas de honte, en plein jour?

OCTAVE:

> Ô Célio! Ô fou que tu es! tu as un pied de blanc sur les joues. D'où te vient ce large habit noir? N'as-tu pas de honte, en plein carnaval?

(I: iv)

As the characters ask each other what their costumes mean, the reader is shown this contrast between the two characters, though the contrast is quite obvious—an aspect common in Musset's comic irony and a sort of mocking attitude of Musset toward the audience's ability to interpret the play. The polarization of the characters (Octave: lively, daring, and outspoken; Célio: reserved, timid, and passive), emphasized by the use of repetition and symmetry, in fact underlines the spiritual kinship between Octave and Célio and their structural relationship in the play—they are sort of mirror images that reflect each other and two sides of the same soul—indeed, Musset's own—in reaction to the world (Sices 35).

In another conversation between Octave and his cousin Claudio, Musset's reliance on wordplay rather than acting and stage movement, displays an ironic twist:

OCTAVE:

> Ah! Cousin Claudio, vous êtes un beau juge; où allez-vous si vite?

CLAUDIO:

> Qu'entendez-vous par là, seigneur Octave?

OCTAVE:

> J'entends que vous êtes un podestat qui a de belles formes.

CLAUDIO:

> De langage ou de complexion?

OCTAVE:

> De langage, de langage. Votre robe est pleine d'éloquence, et vos bras sont deux charmantes parenthèses.

(II, vi)

As in the scene describing the traits of Octave and Célio, the humor and irony arise from the play of metaphor and meaning during the dialogue. Characterization as well as the plot are developed through such play of language—by Musset as well as characters in the play. Octave uses his witty and symbolic language to court Marianne in Célio's behalf, acting as the double of the latter, while this intrigue and illusion in fact produce comic effects, but also lead to the play's tragic ending. The duplicity of the signifying process reveals the fictionality of the play itself—it's a product of the author's wordplay. This irony is further complicated by the contrast of the use of language between male and female characters. While buffoonery and wit appear in conversations among male characters, lyricism typifies expressions of views of love and the admiration/criticism of the heroine in these two passages by Octave addressed to Marianne at different times:

> Vous êtes comme les roses du Bengale, Marianne, sans épine et sans parfum. . . . Qu'y trouvez-vous qui puisse vous blesser? Une fleur sans parfum n'en est pas moins belle; bien au contraire, ce sont les plus belles que Dieu a faites ainsi. . . .

(II: iv)

> Elle n'en vaut ni plus ni moins. Elle sait qu'elle est bonne à boire et qu'elle est faite pour être bue. Dieu n'en a pas caché la source au sommet d'un pic inabor-

dable, au fond d'une caverne profonde; il l'a suspendue en grappes dorées sur nos brillants coteaux. Elle est, il est vrai, rare et précieuse, mais elle ne défend pas qu'on l'approche. Elle se laisse voir aux rayons du soleil, et toute une cour d'abeilles et de frelons murmure autour d'elle matin et soir. Le voyageur dévoré de soif peut se reposer sous ses rameaux verts; jamais elle ne l'a laissé languir, jamais elle ne lui a refusé les douces larmes dont son cœur est plein. Ah! Marianne! C'est un don fatal que la beauté . . . puisse Célio vous oublier!

(II: viii)

In the first passage, Octave uses a simple metaphor (roses of Bengal) to describe Marianne's beauty and indifferent attitude (without hate or love), while in the next, he not only uses much more complex and suggestive images, hinting at a contrast between the unapproachable Marianne and easily accessible good wine that quenches any thirsty and fatigued travelers, but he also presents bitter criticism of her beauty and indifference as a fatal attraction to Célio. On one hand, his descriptions flip back and forth between ambiguous compliments (without thorns/without perfume; nonetheless beautiful) and vigorous criticism (unlike thirst-quenching wine), for he only intends to court her on Célio's behalf, but his metaphors appear double-edged and even embarrassing, yet honest to Marianne. On the other hand, he also senses a potentially tragic outcome that will spring from their plot and genuinely hopes that Célio will simply forget her. The mixture of sensuality in his words and indifference in his intention produces a near comic oddity in a tragic triangular relationship between Célio, Marianne, and Octave. These images also disturb the flow of the plot, for their power of symbolism overshadows the story and heightens the contrast between Octave's strength and the passiveness of Marianne and Célio.

As with characterization, the treatment of love—the main theme in most of Musset's dramas—is in the same manner of wit and sarcasm. Some contemporaries might have viewed his treatment of love affairs as a cliché for the Romantic poetic ideal. However, the fact that he wrote most of his plays in his early twenties when youthful passion and free imagination would dominate his writing distinguishes his style from that of the other Romantics. In fact, love relationships became the very source of his creativity and originality during this prolific period.[3] Shakespeare also served as an obvious inspiration for using love themes (intrigues, betrayals, and mismatches) combined with humor to create comic irony. However, Musset's love stories are never an *All's Well That Ends Well*. The audience's expectation of a happy ending in comedies is subverted by the bitter, even tragic denouement and the non-resolution of the plot: Célio dies believing that Octave has betrayed him, and the latter rejects Marianne's love only to confess to her that it was Célio who loved her; Fantasio's life is spared and freedom regained, but the ending is not the happy and predictable one of a romance between Fantasio and Esbeth; Lorenzo succeeds in assassinating Alexander, but falls victim to a hired killer; after an apparent reunion of Camille and Perdican in *On ne badine pas avec l'amour,* Camille abruptly bids farewell to Perdican upon Rosette's death. Musset toys with the very concept of comedy, using it as an antithetical term to undermine theatrical conventions and definition of the genre. Like most Romantic dramas, Musset's "comedies" are also full of intrigues, themes of revenge and betrayal, disguise or exchange of identities, but the subject of love is neither sublime nor trifling; instead, it is Musset's source of irony and illusion, for man's grotesque nature is brought forth in its forms of duplicity (jest, disguise, and concealment of intention) when man is trapped in love.

Musset's use of intrigue and disguise to confound dramatic illusion and reality complements the apparently superficial themes of love and complicates the fictive reality in the reader's reading process. The pride of Perdican and Camille conceals their true feelings for each other and motivates their role-playing in order to make the other suffer. Perdican delights in making others believe what is other than his true intention as he expresses to Rosette his determination to marry her against the wishes of his family and all the townspeople: "Je trouve plaisant qu'on dise que je ne t'aime pas quand je t'épouse" (III: vii). The irony of this statement lies in the fact that what Perdican is telling Rosette is but an intrigue to punish Camille, while the townspeople are right about his pretending to love Rosette. His initial satisfaction of misleading Camille and eventually his agony of losing her affection originate from this role-playing that not only conceals his true intention from others, but also confounds himself. Only toward the end does he realize that it is his pride that has led to all the pretense and misunderstanding between him and Camille:

> Orgueil, le plus fatal des conseillers humains, qu'es-tu venu faire entre cette fille et moi? . . . Elle aurait pu m'aimer, et nous étions nés l'un pour l'autre; qu'es-tu venu faire sur nos lèvres, orgueil, lorsque nos mains allaient se joindre?
>
> (III: viii)

However, as Perdican has always believed (or been tricked into believing by his pride?), he justifies vanity, revenge, and pride as but human nature: "Il a bien fallu que nous nous fissions du mal, car nous sommes des hommes" (387). Musset uses "pride" as the deciding factor to set up the role-playing parallel for both protagonists in developing the plot and to manipulate characterization. He turns it into a disguise to create a double illusion for the audience, making the role-playing a drama within the drama.

Another instance of disguise appears in the double-natured court jester in *Fantasio.* The intricate mixture of comic and serious elements in the fool's character provides the author a convenient means for manipulating the dramatic illusion through sporting with the meaning of words and appearances. While *The Arabian Nights* signifies to Fantasio magical transportation to fantasy lands to elude reality, he longs to discover interior reality of individuals concealed under their appearances:

> Quelle admirable chose que les Mille et Une Nuits! Ô Spark! Mon cher Spark, si tu pouvais me transporter en Chine! Si je pouvais seulement sortir de ma peau pendant une heure ou deux! Si je pouvais être ce monsieur qui passe! . . . Je suis sûr que cet homme-là a dans la tête un millier d'idées qui me sont absolument étrangères; son essence lui est particulière. Hélas! Tout ce que les hommes se disent entre eux se ressemble; les idées qu'ils échangent sont presque toujours les mêmes dans toutes leurs conversations; mais, dans l'intérieur de toutes ces machines isolées, quels replis, quels compartiments secrets! C'est tout un monde que chacun porte en lui! Un monde ignoré qui naît et qui meurt en silence!
>
> (I: ii)

Fantasio's desire to uncover what is truly inside every man's head is materialized through the ironic concealment of his own identity by disguising himself as the jester. The character of jester prescribes a double nature in his words and deeds and thus obscures others' vision in seeing his true intention: can he be only joking, or can he be serious? And in fact, most likely, the jester reveals truth through his jokes; thus the role of jester serves as a natural disguise of truth, and at the same time a means to discover truth. Fantasio provides an omniscient perspective in the development of the story and allows the reader/spectator to see the dramatic irony created through this very character.

Fantasio's playing the fool also raises a question about the act of representation for the character as well as for the author:

> Quel métier délicieux que celui de bouffon! J'étais gris, je crois, hier soir, lorsque j'ai pris ce costume et que je me suis présenté au palais; mais, en vérité, jamais la saine raison ne m'a rien inspiré qui valût cet acte de folie.
>
> (II: iii)

Is this monologue speaking only for Fantasio, or for the author as well? That is the question. Since most of Musset's plays were not staged till much later, this technique addresses the reader and his imaginative ability to paint a picture of the two realities—the fictional and the one disguised within the fictional. Like the fool in *King Lear,* Fantasio has the liberty to speak truth through jest or to joke in order to deceive. This self-reflexive disguise invites the audience/reader to investigate the nature of the narrative, or the illusion on the stage. It turns the play into a meta-theatre for the theatre, questioning the art of drama as a form of representation and expression through the character's very act of acting.

This (con)fusion of characters and realities leads further to a philosophical question about truth, about reason, and unreason. As in *King Lear,* the intermingling of truth and untruth, sanity and madness, reality and illusion, is presented through the character of the fool, whose profession as master of sarcastic wordplay and double identity as the king's jester and confidant best suit Musset's artistic intention in creating Romantic irony. Musset's use of disguised personalities (Octave acting on Célio's behalf as Marianne's suitor in order to win her hand for Célio, Fantasio as the clown to conceal his love for Elsbeth, Lorenzo in ***Lorenzaccio*** concealing his true self in order to gain the trust of the Duke—and even various male leads in his plays being played by actresses)[4]—reveals to the reader the very nature of theatre: reality depends on the manipulation of perspectives by the author as well as the reader's imaginative involvement in the viewing process. It is a technique of authorial control similar to that of the German ironist Ludwig Tieck. And as with Tieck, Musset's only option to create such drama is to free the dramatist from the physical restraints of the theatre. Only thus can drama express the self-reflexivity of Romantic irony to its fullest.

Notes

1. Lloyd Bishop comments that Hugo's heroes appear to be "mere antithesis, not ambivalence or paradox" as the dialectic prescribed in the "Preface" hoped to achieve (94).

2. W. D. Howarth points out that there is usually cynicism and idealism united in handling the dramatic situation with a bitter intensity that "seems to belie the label 'comédie' in Musset (Charlton 235-38). David Sices recounts the numerous Romantic theoretical treatises and manifestos that call for a new theatre (Stendhal's *Racine et Shakespeare,* Hugo's "Preface to Cromwell," and Vigny's "Dernière nuit de travail"), and argues hat the dramatic works corresponding to these statements seldom live up to their promises due to practical theatre affairs. Lloyd Bishop criticizes Hugo's characters for lacking psychological depth in terms of his ideal of the grotesque/sublime paradox.

3. For instance, Octave's descriptions and praises of Marianne have an overtone of Musset's view of George Sand.

4. Although not prescribed by Musset, these male leads played by actresses became standard at the Comédie. Madame R. Debrou played Fortunio in the 1848 *Le Chandelier* at the Théâtre Historique,

while in 1916 Mlle Piérat revived the tradition of the female Fortunio and became Comédie Française's first female Lorenzaccio. See Sices, 180.

Works Cited

Bishop, Lloyd. *Romantic Hero and His Heirs in French Literature.* New York: Peter Lang, 1984.

———. *The Poetry of Alfred de Musset: Styles and Genres.* New York: Peter Lang, 1987.

Charlton, D. G., ed. *The French Romantics.* Cambridge: Cambridge UP, 1984.

Daemmrich, I. G. "Alfred de Musset's View of the Poet." *Revue des Langues Vivantes* 39.1 (1973): 5-10.

Musset, Alfred de. *Théâtre complet.* Paris: Gallimard, 1958.

———. *Œuvres complètes en prose.* Paris: Gallimard, 1960.

Rees, Margaret A. *Alfred de Musset.* New York: Twayne, 1971.

Sices, David. *Theater of Solitude: the Drama of Alfred de Musset.* Hanover, NH.: UP of New England, 1974.

FURTHER READING

Criticism

Callen, A. "The Place of *Lorenzaccio* in Musset's Theatre." *Forum for Modern Language Studies* 5, no. 3 (July 1969): 225-31.
    Claims that *Lorenzaccio* demonstrates the unity of Musset's dramatic vision.

———. "Dramatic Construction in Musset's *Lorenzaccio.*" *Forum for Modern Language Studies* 9, no. 2 (April 1973): 182-91.
    Concentrates on Musset's break with classical dramatic structure in *Lorenzaccio.*

Collister, Peter. "Taking Care of Yourself: Henry James and the Life of George Sand." *Modern Language Review* 83, no. 3 (July 1989): 556-70.
    Mentions Musset's use of his real-life relationship with George Sand in his *La confession d'un enfant due siècle* within the context of Henry James's literary perceptions of Sand and her writing.

Cooper, Barbara T. "Staging a Revolution: Political Upheaval in *Lorenzaccio* and *Léo Burckart.*" *Romance Notes* 24, no. 1 (fall 1983): 23-9.

Compares treatments of historical, political, and rhetorical themes in Musset's *Lorenzaccio* and Gérard de Nerval's *Léo Burckart.*

Cox, Jeffrey N. "Melodrama, Monodrama and the Forms of Romantic Tragic Drama." In *Within the Dramatic Spectrum: The University of Florida Department of Classics Comparative Drama Conference Papers,* Volume VI, edited by Karelisa V. Hartigan, pp. 20-34. Lanham, Md.: University Press of America, 1986.

Includes a brief discussion of Musset's *Lorenzaccio* as part of a survey devoted to the Romantic redefinition of eighteenth-century tragic drama.

Denommé, Robert T. "Chatterton, Ruy Blas, Lorenzaccio: Three Tragic Heroes." *Laurels* 61, no. 1 (spring 1990): 55-67.

Studies the title figures of Alfred de Vigny's *Chatterton,* Victor Hugo's *Ruy Blas,* and Musset's *Lorenzaccio* as modern protagonists dramatized in accordance with the social and political changes precipitated by the French Revolution.

Grayson, Jane. "The French Connection: Nabokov and Alfred de Musset. Ideas and Practices of Translation." *Slavonic and East European Review* 73, no. 4 (October 1995): 613-58.

Centers on Vladimir Nabokov's translations of Musset's "La nuit de décembre" and "Lettre à M. de Lamartine," remarking on the potential influence of the French writer on the Russian-born Nabokov.

King, Russell S. "A Crisis in Romantic Writing: Fantasio's Words vs. Chatterton's Silence." *Orbis Litterarum* 31 (1976): 59-71.

Focuses on a preoccupation with the uncertainty of language in Musset's *Fantasio* and Alfred de Vigny's *Chatterton.*

———. "Byron and France: Mademoiselle Byron or the Case of Alfred de Musset." *Renaissance and Modern Studies* 32 (1988): 70-9.

Affirms the profound literary influence of Lord Byron on Musset.

Leach, Laurie F. "Lorenzo and the Noblest Roman: The Nobel Assassins of *Lorenzaccio* and *Julius Caesar.*" *Romance Notes* 28, no. 3 (spring 1988): 241-45.

Appraises the protagonist of Musset's drama *Lorenzaccio* alongside Marcus Brutus of Shakespeare's *Julius Caesar.*

Lemettais, Michèle. "'Courtly Love': An Ancient Initiation Rite and a Nineteenth-Century Reality." *Cincinnati Romance Review* 3 (1984): 56-65.

Asserts the validity of the critical conception of courtly love by drawing evidence from Musset's short play *Les caprices de Marianne.*

MacInnes, John W. "*Lorenzaccio* and the Drama of Narration." In *Text and Presentation: The University of Florida Department of Classics Comparative Drama Conference Papers,* Volume III, edited by Karelisa Hartigan, pp. 137-45. Lanham, Md.: University Press of America, 1988.

Considers the discursiveness of Musset's *Lorenzaccio* as it dramatizes the tensions inherent in self-expression.

Mandelker, Amy. "The Haunted Poet: Esenin's *Man in Black* and Musset's 'La nuit de décembre.'" In *The Supernatural in Slavic and Baltic Literature: Essays in Honor of Victor Terras,* edited by Amy Mandelker and Roberta Reeder, pp. 226-45. Columbus, Ohio: Slavica Publishers, 1988.

Identifies Musset's "La nuit de décembre" as a source of Sergej Esenin's poem *The Man in Black.*

Nurnberg, Monica J. "Inspiration and Aspiration: Gautier's 'La Diva' and Musset's 'Une soirée perdue.'" *Australian Journal of French Studies* 15, no. 5 (September-December 1978): 229-42.

Compares Théophile Gautier's "La Diva" and Musset's "Une soirée perdue," commenting on the shared setting, atmosphere, and theme in these poems.

Roussetzki, Rémy. "Theater of Anxiety in Shelley's *The Cenci* and Musset's *Lorenzaccio.*" *Criticism* 42, no. 1 (winter 2000): 31-57.

Argues that in *The Cenci* and *Lorenzaccio* Shelley and Musset attempt to modernize the antique genre of dramatic tragedy by staging the internal anxieties of their respective central figures.

Salines, Emily. "The Figure of the Innocent Prostitute in Two French Versions of Thomas De Quincey's *Confessions of an English Opium Eater.*" *Women in French Studies* 5 (1997): 205-14.

Analyzes the character of Ann, a child prostitute, as variously rendered by Musset and Charles Baudelaire in their French translations of De Quincey's autobiographical *Confessions of an English Opium Eater.*

Sices, David. "Multiplicity and Integrity in *On ne badine pas avec l'amour.*" *French Review* 43, no. 3 (February 1970): 443-51.

Comments on Musset's ironic use of grotesque minor characters as structural elements and exponents of theme in *On ne badine pas avec l'amour.*

———. Introduction to *Alfred de Musset: Comedies and Proverbs,* pp. ix-xv. Translated by David Sices. Baltimore, Md.: Johns Hopkins University Press, 1994.

Summarizes the enduring appeal of Musset's short, comic dramas.

Szogyi, Alex. "Musset's *Lorenzaccio*: George Sand's Ultimate Gift." In *Woman as Mediatrix: Essays on Nineteenth-Century European Women Writers,* edited by Avriel H. Goldberger, pp. 89-98. Westport, Conn.: Greenwood Press, 1987.

Examines George Sand's drama *A Conspiracy in*

1537 as an illuminating companion piece to Musset's *Lorenzaccio.*

Terdiman, Richard. "The Mnemonics of Musset's *Confession.*" *Representations* 26 (spring 1989): 26-48.

Discusses the theme of confessional memory in Musset's novel *La confession d'un enfant du siècle.*

Additional coverage of Musset's life and career is contained in the following sources published by Thomson Gale: *Dictionary of Literary Biography,* Vols. 192, 217; *European Writers,* Vol. 6; *Guide to French Literature, 1789 to Present*; *Literature Resource Center*; *Nineteenth-Century Literature Criticism,* Vol. 7; *Reference Guide to World Literature,* Eds. 2, 3; and *Twayne's World Authors.*

How to Use This Index

CMW = *St. James Guide to Crime & Mystery Writers*
CN = *Contemporary Novelists*
CP = *Contemporary Poets*
CPW = *Contemporary Popular Writers*
CSW = *Contemporary Southern Writers*
CWD = *Contemporary Women Dramatists*
CWP = *Contemporary Women Poets*
CWRI = *St. James Guide to Children's Writers*
CWW = *Contemporary World Writers*
DA = *DISCovering Authors*
DA3 = *DISCovering Authors 3.0*
DAB = *DISCovering Authors: British Edition*
DAC = *DISCovering Authors: Canadian Edition*
DAM = *DISCovering Authors: Modules*
   DRAM: *Dramatists Module;* *MST:* *Most-studied Authors Module;*
   MULT: *Multicultural Authors Module;* *NOV:* *Novelists Module;*
   POET: *Poets Module;* *POP:* *Popular Fiction and Genre Authors Module*
DFS = *Drama for Students*
DLB = *Dictionary of Literary Biography*
DLBD = *Dictionary of Literary Biography Documentary Series*
DLBY = *Dictionary of Literary Biography Yearbook*
DNFS = *Literature of Developing Nations for Students*
EFS = *Epics for Students*
EXPN = *Exploring Novels*
EXPP = *Exploring Poetry*
EXPS = *Exploring Short Stories*
EW = *European Writers*
FANT = *St. James Guide to Fantasy Writers*
FW = *Feminist Writers*
GFL = *Guide to French Literature,* Beginnings to 1789, 1798 to the Present
GLL = *Gay and Lesbian Literature*
HGG = *St. James Guide to Horror, Ghost & Gothic Writers*
HW = *Hispanic Writers*
IDFW = *International Dictionary of Films and Filmmakers: Writers and Production Artists*
IDTP = *International Dictionary of Theatre: Playwrights*
LAIT = *Literature and Its Times*
LAW = *Latin American Writers*
JRDA = *Junior DISCovering Authors*
MAICYA = *Major Authors and Illustrators for Children and Young Adults*
MAICYAS = *Major Authors and Illustrators for Children and Young Adults Supplement*
MAWW = *Modern American Women Writers*
MJW = *Modern Japanese Writers*
MTCW = *Major 20th-Century Writers*
NCFS = *Nonfiction Classics for Students*
NFS = *Novels for Students*
PAB = *Poets: American and British*
PFS = *Poetry for Students*
RGAL = *Reference Guide to American Literature*
RGEL = *Reference Guide to English Literature*
RGSF = *Reference Guide to Short Fiction*
RGWL = *Reference Guide to World Literature*
RHW = *Twentieth-Century Romance and Historical Writers*
SAAS = *Something about the Author Autobiography Series*
SATA = *Something about the Author*
SFW = *St. James Guide to Science Fiction Writers*
SSFS = *Short Stories for Students*
TCWW = *Twentieth-Century Western Writers*
WLIT = *World Literature and Its Times*
WP = *World Poets*
YABC = *Yesterday's Authors of Books for Children*
YAW = *St. James Guide to Young Adult Writers*

Literary Criticism Series
Cumulative Author Index

al-Hariri, al-Qasim ibn 'Ali Abu Muhammad al-Basri
1054-1122 .... **CMLC 63**
See also RGWL 3

Ali, Ahmed 1908-1998 .... **CLC 69**
See also CA 25-28R; CANR 15, 34; EWL 3

Ali, Tariq 1943- .... **CLC 173**
See also CA 25-28R; CANR 10, 99

Alighieri, Dante
See Dante

Allan, John B.
See Westlake, Donald E(dwin)

Allan, Sidney
See Hartmann, Sadakichi

Allan, Sydney
See Hartmann, Sadakichi

Allard, Janet .... **CLC 59**

Allen, Edward 1948- .... **CLC 59**

Allen, Fred 1894-1956 .... **TCLC 87**

Allen, Paula Gunn 1939- ..... **CLC 84; NNAL**
See also AMWS 4; CA 112; 143; CANR 63, 130; CWP; DA3; DAM MULT; DLB 175; FW; MTCW 1; RGAL 4

Allen, Roland
See Ayckbourn, Alan

Allen, Sarah A.
See Hopkins, Pauline Elizabeth

Allen, Sidney H.
See Hartmann, Sadakichi

Allen, Woody 1935- .... **CLC 16, 52, 195**
See also AAYA 10, 51; CA 33-36R; CANR 27, 38, 63, 128; DAM POP; DLB 44; MTCW 1

Allende, Isabel 1942- ... **CLC 39, 57, 97, 170; HLC 1; SSC 65; WLCS**
See also AAYA 18; CA 125; 130; CANR 51, 74, 129; CDWLB 3; CLR 99; CWW 2; DA3; DAM MULT, NOV; DLB 145; DNFS 1; EWL 3; FW; HW 1, 2; INT CA-130; LAIT 5; LAWS 1; LMFS 2; MTCW 1, 2; NCFS 1; NFS 6, 18; RGSF 2; RGWL 3; SSFS 11, 16; WLIT 1

Alleyn, Ellen
See Rossetti, Christina (Georgina)

Alleyne, Carla D. .... **CLC 65**

Allingham, Margery (Louise)
1904-1966 .... **CLC 19**
See also CA 5-8R; 25-28R; CANR 4, 58; CMW 4; DLB 77; MSW; MTCW 1, 2

Allingham, William 1824-1889 ...... **NCLC 25**
See also DLB 35; RGEL 2

Allison, Dorothy E. 1949- .... **CLC 78, 153**
See also AAYA 53; CA 140; CANR 66, 107; CSW; DA3; FW; MTCW 1; NFS 11; RGAL 4

Alloula, Malek .... **CLC 65**

Allston, Washington 1779-1843 .... **NCLC 2**
See also DLB 1, 235

Almedingen, E. M. .... **CLC 12**
See Almedingen, Martha Edith von
See also SATA 3

Almedingen, Martha Edith von 1898-1971
See Almedingen, E. M.
See also CA 1-4R; CANR 1

Almodovar, Pedro 1949(?)- .... **CLC 114; HLCS 1**
See also CA 133; CANR 72; HW 2

Almqvist, Carl Jonas Love
1793-1866 .... **NCLC 42**

al-Mutanabbi, Ahmad ibn al-Husayn Abu al-Tayyib al-Jufi al-Kindi
915-965 .... **CMLC 66**
See also RGWL 3

Alonso, Damaso 1898-1990 .... **CLC 14**
See also CA 110; 131; 130; CANR 72; DLB 108; EWL 3; HW 1, 2

Alov
See Gogol, Nikolai (Vasilyevich)

al'Sadaawi, Nawal
See El Saadawi, Nawal
See also FW

Al Siddik
See Rolfe, Frederick (William Serafino Austin Lewis Mary)
See also GLL 1; RGEL 2

Alta 1942- .... **CLC 19**
See also CA 57-60

Alter, Robert B(ernard) 1935- .... **CLC 34**
See also CA 49-52; CANR 1, 47, 100

Alther, Lisa 1944- .... **CLC 7, 41**
See also BPFB 1; CA 65-68; CAAS 30; CANR 12, 30, 51; CN 7; CSW; GLL 2; MTCW 1

Althusser, L.
See Althusser, Louis

Althusser, Louis 1918-1990 .... **CLC 106**
See also CA 131; 132; CANR 102; DLB 242

Altman, Robert 1925- .... **CLC 16, 116**
See also CA 73-76; CANR 43

Alurista .... **HLCS 1**
See Urista (Heredia), Alberto (Baltazar)
See also DLB 82; LLW 1

Alvarez, A(lfred) 1929- .... **CLC 5, 13**
See also CA 1-4R; CANR 3, 33, 63, 101, 134; CN 7; CP 7; DLB 14, 40

Alvarez, Alejandro Rodriguez 1903-1965
See Casona, Alejandro
See also CA 131; 93-96; HW 1

Alvarez, Julia 1950- .... **CLC 93; HLCS 1**
See also AAYA 25; AMWS 7; CA 147; CANR 69, 101, 133; DA3; DLB 282; LATS 1:2; LLW 1; MTCW 1; NFS 5, 9; SATA 129; WLIT 1

Alvaro, Corrado 1896-1956 .... **TCLC 60**
See also CA 163; DLB 264; EWL 3

Amado, Jorge 1912-2001 ... **CLC 13, 40, 106; HLC 1**
See also CA 77-80; 201; CANR 35, 74; CWW 2; DAM MULT, NOV; DLB 113, 307; EWL 3; HW 1, 2; LAW; LAWS 1; MTCW 1, 2; RGWL 2, 3; TWA; WLIT 1

Ambler, Eric 1909-1998 .... **CLC 4, 6, 9**
See also BRWS 4; CA 9-12R; 171; CANR 7, 38, 74; CMW 4; CN 7; DLB 77; MSW; MTCW 1, 2; TEA

Ambrose, Stephen E(dward)
1936-2002 .... **CLC 145**
See also AAYA 44; CA 1-4R; 209; CANR 3, 43, 57, 83, 105; NCFS 2; SATA 40, 138

Amichai, Yehuda 1924-2000 .. **CLC 9, 22, 57, 116; PC 38**
See also CA 85-88; 189; CANR 46, 60, 99, 132; CWW 2; EWL 3; MTCW 1

Amichai, Yehudah
See Amichai, Yehuda

Amiel, Henri Frederic 1821-1881 .... **NCLC 4**
See also DLB 217

Amis, Kingsley (William)
1922-1995 ...... **CLC 1, 2, 3, 5, 8, 13, 40, 44, 129**
See also AITN 2; BPFB 1; BRWS 2; CA 9-12R; 150; CANR 8, 28, 54; CDBLB 1945-1960; CN 7; CP 7; DA; DA3; DAB; DAC; DAM MST, NOV; DLB 15, 27, 100, 139; DLBY 1996; EWL 3; HGG; INT CANR-8; MTCW 1, 2; RGEL 2; RGSF 2; SFW 4

Amis, Martin (Louis) 1949- .... **CLC 4, 9, 38, 62, 101**
See also BEST 90:3; BRWS 4; CA 65-68; CANR 8, 27, 54, 73, 95, 132; CN 7; DA3; DLB 14, 194; EWL 3; INT CANR-27; MTCW 1

Ammianus Marcellinus c. 330-c. 395 .... **CMLC 60**
See also AW 2; DLB 211

Ammons, A(rchie) R(andolph)
1926-2001 ...... **CLC 2, 3, 5, 8, 9, 25, 57, 108; PC 16**
See also AITN 1; AMWS 7; CA 9-12R; 193; CANR 6, 36, 51, 73, 107; CP 7; CSW; DAM POET; DLB 5, 165; EWL 3; MTCW 1, 2; PFS 19; RGAL 4

Amo, Tauraatua i
See Adams, Henry (Brooks)

Amory, Thomas 1691(?)-1788 .... **LC 48**
See also DLB 39

Anand, Mulk Raj 1905-2004 ...... **CLC 23, 93**
See also CA 65-68; CANR 32, 64; CN 7; DAM NOV; EWL 3; MTCW 1, 2; RGSF 2

Anatol
See Schnitzler, Arthur

Anaximander c. 611B.C.-c. 546B.C. .... **CMLC 22**

Anaya, Rudolfo A(lfonso) 1937- ...... **CLC 23, 148; HLC 1**
See also AAYA 20; BYA 13; CA 45-48; CAAS 4; CANR 1, 32, 51, 124; CN 7; DAM MULT, NOV; DLB 82, 206, 278; HW 1; LAIT 4; LLW 1; MTCW 1, 2; NFS 12; RGAL 4; RGSF 2; WLIT 1

Andersen, Hans Christian
1805-1875 .... **NCLC 7, 79; SSC 6, 56; WLC**
See also AAYA 57; CLR 6; DA; DA3; DAB; DAC; DAM MST, POP; EW 6; MAICYA 1, 2; RGSF 2; RGWL 2, 3; SATA 100; TWA; WCH; YABC 1

Anderson, C. Farley
See Mencken, H(enry) L(ouis); Nathan, George Jean

Anderson, Jessica (Margaret) Queale
1916- .... **CLC 37**
See also CA 9-12R; CANR 4, 62; CN 7

Anderson, Jon (Victor) 1940- .... **CLC 9**
See also CA 25-28R; CANR 20; DAM POET

Anderson, Lindsay (Gordon)
1923-1994 .... **CLC 20**
See also CA 125; 128; 146; CANR 77

Anderson, Maxwell 1888-1959 .... **TCLC 2, 144**
See also CA 105; 152; DAM DRAM; DFS 16, 20; DLB 7, 228; MTCW 2; RGAL 4

Anderson, Poul (William)
1926-2001 .... **CLC 15**
See also AAYA 5, 34; BPFB 1; BYA 6, 8, 9; CA 1-4R; 181; 199; CAAE 181; CAAS 2; CANR 2, 15, 34, 64, 110; CLR 58; DLB 8; FANT; INT CANR-15; MTCW 1, 2; SATA 90; SATA-Brief 39; SATA-Essay 106; SCFW 2; SFW 4; SUFW 1, 2

Anderson, Robert (Woodruff)
1917- .... **CLC 23**
See also AITN 1; CA 21-24R; CANR 32; DAM DRAM; DLB 7; LAIT 5

Anderson, Roberta Joan
See Mitchell, Joni

Anderson, Sherwood 1876-1941 .. **SSC 1, 46; TCLC 1, 10, 24, 123; WLC**
See also AAYA 30; AMW; AMWC 2; BPFB 1; CA 104; 121; CANR 61; CDALB 1917-1929; DA; DA3; DAB; DAC; DAM MST, NOV; DLB 4, 9, 86; DLBD 1; EWL 3; EXPS; GLL 2; MTCW 1, 2; NFS 4; RGAL 4; RGSF 2; SSFS 4, 10, 11; TUS

Andier, Pierre
See Desnos, Robert

Andouard
See Giraudoux, Jean(-Hippolyte)

Baraka, Amiri 1934- .... **BLC 1; CLC 1, 2, 3, 5, 10, 14, 33, 115; DC 6; PC 4; WLCS**
See Jones, LeRoi
See also AFAW 1, 2; AMWS 2; BW 2, 3; CA 21-24R; CABS 3; CAD; CANR 27, 38, 61, 133; CD 5; CDALB 1941-1968; CP 7; CPW; DA; DA3; DAC; DAM MST, MULT, POET, POP; DFS 3, 11, 16; DLB 5, 7, 16, 38; DLBD 8; EWL 3; MTCW 1, 2; PFS 9; RGAL 4; TUS; WP

Baratynsky, Evgenii Abramovich
1800-1844 .... **NCLC 103**
See also DLB 205

Barbauld, Anna Laetitia
1743-1825 .... **NCLC 50**
See also DLB 107, 109, 142, 158; RGEL 2

Barbellion, W. N. P. .... **TCLC 24**
See Cummings, Bruce F(rederick)

Barber, Benjamin R. 1939- .... **CLC 141**
See also CA 29-32R; CANR 12, 32, 64, 119

Barbera, Jack (Vincent) 1945- .... **CLC 44**
See also CA 110; CANR 45

Barbey d'Aurevilly, Jules-Amedee
1808-1889 .... **NCLC 1; SSC 17**
See also DLB 119; GFL 1789 to the Present

Barbour, John c. 1316-1395 .... **CMLC 33**
See also DLB 146

Barbusse, Henri 1873-1935 .... **TCLC 5**
See also CA 105; 154; DLB 65; EWL 3; RGWL 2, 3

Barclay, Alexander c. 1475-1552 .... **LC 109**
See also DLB 132

Barclay, Bill
See Moorcock, Michael (John)

Barclay, William Ewert
See Moorcock, Michael (John)

Barea, Arturo 1897-1957 .... **TCLC 14**
See also CA 111; 201

Barfoot, Joan 1946- .... **CLC 18**
See also CA 105

Barham, Richard Harris
1788-1845 .... **NCLC 77**
See also DLB 159

Baring, Maurice 1874-1945 .... **TCLC 8**
See also CA 105; 168; DLB 34; HGG

Baring-Gould, Sabine 1834-1924 ... **TCLC 88**
See also DLB 156, 190

Barker, Clive 1952- .... **CLC 52; SSC 53**
See also AAYA 10, 54; BEST 90:3; BPFB 1; CA 121; 129; CANR 71, 111, 133; CPW; DA3; DAM POP; DLB 261; HGG; INT CA-129; MTCW 1, 2; SUFW 2

Barker, George Granville
1913-1991 .... **CLC 8, 48**
See also CA 9-12R; 135; CANR 7, 38; DAM POET; DLB 20; EWL 3; MTCW 1

Barker, Harley Granville
See Granville-Barker, Harley
See also DLB 10

Barker, Howard 1946- .... **CLC 37**
See also CA 102; CBD; CD 5; DLB 13, 233

Barker, Jane 1652-1732 .... **LC 42, 82**
See also DLB 39, 131

Barker, Pat(ricia) 1943- ...... **CLC 32, 94, 146**
See also BRWS 4; CA 117; 122; CANR 50, 101; CN 7; DLB 271; INT CA-122

Barlach, Ernst (Heinrich)
1870-1938 .... **TCLC 84**
See also CA 178; DLB 56, 118; EWL 3

Barlow, Joel 1754-1812 .... **NCLC 23**
See also AMWS 2; DLB 37; RGAL 4

Barnard, Mary (Ethel) 1909- .... **CLC 48**
See also CA 21-22; CAP 2

Barnes, Djuna 1892-1982 .... **CLC 3, 4, 8, 11, 29, 127; SSC 3**
See Steptoe, Lydia
See also AMWS 3; CA 9-12R; 107; CAD; CANR 16, 55; CWD; DLB 4, 9, 45; EWL 3; GLL 1; MTCW 1, 2; RGAL 4; TUS

Barnes, Jim 1933- .... **NNAL**
See also CA 108; 175; CAAE 175; CAAS 28; DLB 175

Barnes, Julian (Patrick) 1946- . **CLC 42, 141**
See also BRWS 4; CA 102; CANR 19, 54, 115; CN 7; DAB; DLB 194; DLBY 1993; EWL 3; MTCW 1

Barnes, Peter 1931-2004 .... **CLC 5, 56**
See also CA 65-68; CAAS 12; CANR 33, 34, 64, 113; CBD; CD 5; DFS 6; DLB 13, 233; MTCW 1

Barnes, William 1801-1886 .... **NCLC 75**
See also DLB 32

Baroja (y Nessi), Pio 1872-1956 .... **HLC 1; TCLC 8**
See also CA 104; EW 9

Baron, David
See Pinter, Harold

Baron Corvo
See Rolfe, Frederick (William Serafino Austin Lewis Mary)

Barondess, Sue K(aufman)
1926-1977 .... **CLC 8**
See Kaufman, Sue
See also CA 1-4R; 69-72; CANR 1

Baron de Teive
See Pessoa, Fernando (Antonio Nogueira)

Baroness Von S.
See Zangwill, Israel

Barres, (Auguste-)Maurice
1862-1923 .... **TCLC 47**
See also CA 164; DLB 123; GFL 1789 to the Present

Barreto, Afonso Henrique de Lima
See Lima Barreto, Afonso Henrique de

Barrett, Andrea 1954- .... **CLC 150**
See also CA 156; CANR 92

Barrett, Michele .... **CLC 65**

Barrett, (Roger) Syd 1946- .... **CLC 35**

Barrett, William (Christopher)
1913-1992 .... **CLC 27**
See also CA 13-16R; 139; CANR 11, 67; INT CANR-11

Barrie, J(ames) M(atthew)
1860-1937 .... **TCLC 2**
See also BRWS 3; BYA 4, 5; CA 104; 136; CANR 77; CDBLB 1890-1914; CLR 16; CWRI 5; DA3; DAB; DAM DRAM; DFS 7; DLB 10, 141, 156; EWL 3; FANT; MAICYA 1, 2; MTCW 1; SATA 100; SUFW; WCH; WLIT 4; YABC 1

Barrington, Michael
See Moorcock, Michael (John)

Barrol, Grady
See Bograd, Larry

Barry, Mike
See Malzberg, Barry N(athaniel)

Barry, Philip 1896-1949 .... **TCLC 11**
See also CA 109; 199; DFS 9; DLB 7, 228; RGAL 4

Bart, Andre Schwarz
See Schwarz-Bart, Andre

Barth, John (Simmons) 1930- ... **CLC 1, 2, 3, 5, 7, 9, 10, 14, 27, 51, 89; SSC 10**
See also AITN 1, 2; AMW; BPFB 1; CA 1-4R; CABS 1; CANR 5, 23, 49, 64, 113; CN 7; DAM NOV; DLB 2, 227; EWL 3; FANT; MTCW 1; RGAL 4; RGSF 2; RHW; SSFS 6; TUS

Barthelme, Donald 1931-1989 ... **CLC 1, 2, 3, 5, 6, 8, 13, 23, 46, 59, 115; SSC 2, 55**
See also AMWS 4; BPFB 1; CA 21-24R; 129; CANR 20, 58; DA3; DAM NOV; DLB 2, 234; DLBY 1980, 1989; EWL 3; FANT; LMFS 2; MTCW 1, 2; RGAL 4; RGSF 2; SATA 7; SATA-Obit 62; SSFS 17

Barthelme, Frederick 1943- ...... **CLC 36, 117**
See also AMWS 11; CA 114; 122; CANR 77; CN 7; CSW; DLB 244; DLBY 1985; EWL 3; INT CA-122

Barthes, Roland (Gerard)
1915-1980 .... **CLC 24, 83; TCLC 135**
See also CA 130; 97-100; CANR 66; DLB 296; EW 13; EWL 3; GFL 1789 to the Present; MTCW 1, 2; TWA

Bartram, William 1739-1823 .... **NCLC 145**
See also ANW; DLB 37

Barzun, Jacques (Martin) 1907- ..... **CLC 51, 145**
See also CA 61-64; CANR 22, 95

Bashevis, Isaac
See Singer, Isaac Bashevis

Bashkirtseff, Marie 1859-1884 .... **NCLC 27**

Basho, Matsuo
See Matsuo Basho
See also PFS 18; RGWL 2, 3; WP

Basil of Caesaria c. 330-379 .... **CMLC 35**

Basket, Raney
See Edgerton, Clyde (Carlyle)

Bass, Kingsley B., Jr.
See Bullins, Ed

Bass, Rick 1958- .... **CLC 79, 143; SSC 60**
See also ANW; CA 126; CANR 53, 93; CSW; DLB 212, 275

Bassani, Giorgio 1916-2000 .... **CLC 9**
See also CA 65-68; 190; CANR 33; CWW 2; DLB 128, 177, 299; EWL 3; MTCW 1; RGWL 2, 3

Bastian, Ann .... **CLC 70**

Bastos, Augusto (Antonio) Roa
See Roa Bastos, Augusto (Antonio)

Bataille, Georges 1897-1962 .... **CLC 29; TCLC 155**
See also CA 101; 89-92; EWL 3

Bates, H(erbert) E(rnest)
1905-1974 .... **CLC 46; SSC 10**
See also CA 93-96; 45-48; CANR 34; DA3; DAB; DAM POP; DLB 162, 191; EWL 3; EXPS; MTCW 1, 2; RGSF 2; SSFS 7

Bauchart
See Camus, Albert

Baudelaire, Charles 1821-1867 . **NCLC 6, 29, 55; PC 1; SSC 18; WLC**
See also DA; DA3; DAB; DAC; DAM MST, POET; DLB 217; EW 7; GFL 1789 to the Present; LMFS 2; PFS 21; RGWL 2, 3; TWA

Baudouin, Marcel
See Peguy, Charles (Pierre)

Baudouin, Pierre
See Peguy, Charles (Pierre)

Baudrillard, Jean 1929- .... **CLC 60**
See also DLB 296

Baum, L(yman) Frank 1856-1919 .. **TCLC 7, 132**
See also AAYA 46; BYA 16; CA 108; 133; CLR 15; CWRI 5; DLB 22; FANT; JRDA; MAICYA 1, 2; MTCW 1, 2; NFS 13; RGAL 4; SATA 18, 100; WCH

Baum, Louis F.
See Baum, L(yman) Frank

Baumbach, Jonathan 1933- .... **CLC 6, 23**
See also CA 13-16R; CAAS 5; CANR 12, 66; CN 7; DLBY 1980; INT CANR-12; MTCW 1

Benavente (y Martinez), Jacinto
1866-1954 .... **HLCS 1; TCLC 3**
See also CA 106; 131; CANR 81; DAM
DRAM, MULT; EWL 3; GLL 2; HW 1,
2; MTCW 1, 2

Benchley, Peter (Bradford) 1940- .. **CLC 4, 8**
See also AAYA 14; AITN 2; BPFB 1; CA
17-20R; CANR 12, 35, 66, 115; CPW;
DAM NOV, POP; HGG; MTCW 1, 2;
SATA 3, 89

Benchley, Robert (Charles)
1889-1945 .... **TCLC 1, 55**
See also CA 105; 153; DLB 11; RGAL 4

Benda, Julien 1867-1956 .... **TCLC 60**
See also CA 120; 154; GFL 1789 to the
Present

Benedict, Ruth (Fulton)
1887-1948 .... **TCLC 60**
See also CA 158; DLB 246

Benedikt, Michael 1935- .... **CLC 4, 14**
See also CA 13-16R; CANR 7; CP 7; DLB
5

Benet, Juan 1927-1993 .... **CLC 28**
See also CA 143; EWL 3

Benet, Stephen Vincent 1898-1943 ... **SSC 10;
TCLC 7**
See also AMWS 11; CA 104; 152; DA3;
DAM POET; DLB 4, 48, 102, 249, 284;
DLBY 1997; EWL 3; HGG; MTCW 1;
RGAL 4; RGSF 2; SUFW; WP; YABC 1

Benet, William Rose 1886-1950 ...... **TCLC 28**
See also CA 118; 152; DAM POET; DLB
45; RGAL 4

Benford, Gregory (Albert) 1941- ..... **CLC 52**
See also BPFB 1; CA 69-72, 175; CAAE
175; CAAS 27; CANR 12, 24, 49, 95,
134; CSW; DLBY 1982; SCFW 2; SFW
4

Bengtsson, Frans (Gunnar)
1894-1954 .... **TCLC 48**
See also CA 170; EWL 3

Benjamin, David
See Slavitt, David R(ytman)

Benjamin, Lois
See Gould, Lois

Benjamin, Walter 1892-1940 .... **TCLC 39**
See also CA 164; DLB 242; EW 11; EWL
3

Ben Jelloun, Tahar 1944-
See Jelloun, Tahar ben
See also CA 135; CWW 2; EWL 3; RGWL
3; WLIT 2

Benn, Gottfried 1886-1956 .. **PC 35; TCLC 3**
See also CA 106; 153; DLB 56; EWL 3;
RGWL 2, 3

Bennett, Alan 1934- .... **CLC 45, 77**
See also BRWS 8; CA 103; CANR 35, 55,
106; CBD; CD 5; DAB; DAM MST;
MTCW 1, 2

Bennett, (Enoch) Arnold
1867-1931 .... **TCLC 5, 20**
See also BRW 6; CA 106; 155; CDBLB
1890-1914; DLB 10, 34, 98, 135; EWL 3;
MTCW 2

Bennett, Elizabeth
See Mitchell, Margaret (Munnerlyn)

Bennett, George Harold 1930-
See Bennett, Hal
See also BW 1; CA 97-100; CANR 87

Bennett, Gwendolyn B. 1902-1981 .... **HR 2**
See also BW 1; CA 125; DLB 51; WP

Bennett, Hal .... **CLC 5**
See Bennett, George Harold
See also DLB 33

Bennett, Jay 1912- .... **CLC 35**
See also AAYA 10; CA 69-72; CANR 11,
42, 79; JRDA; SAAS 4; SATA 41, 87;
SATA-Brief 27; WYA; YAW

Bennett, Louise (Simone) 1919- .... **BLC 1;
CLC 28**
See also BW 2, 3; CA 151; CDWLB 3; CP
7; DAM MULT; DLB 117; EWL 3

Benson, A. C. 1862-1925 .... **TCLC 123**
See also DLB 98

Benson, E(dward) F(rederic)
1867-1940 .... **TCLC 27**
See also CA 114; 157; DLB 135, 153;
HGG; SUFW 1

Benson, Jackson J. 1930- .... **CLC 34**
See also CA 25-28R; DLB 111

Benson, Sally 1900-1972 .... **CLC 17**
See also CA 19-20; 37-40R; CAP 1; SATA
1, 35; SATA-Obit 27

Benson, Stella 1892-1933 .... **TCLC 17**
See also CA 117; 154, 155; DLB 36, 162;
FANT; TEA

Bentham, Jeremy 1748-1832 .... **NCLC 38**
See also DLB 107, 158, 252

Bentley, E(dmund) C(lerihew)
1875-1956 .... **TCLC 12**
See also CA 108; DLB 70; MSW

Bentley, Eric (Russell) 1916- .... **CLC 24**
See also CA 5-8R; CAD; CANR 6, 67;
CBD; CD 5; INT CANR-6

ben Uzair, Salem
See Horne, Richard Henry Hengist

Beranger, Pierre Jean de
1780-1857 .... **NCLC 34**

Berdyaev, Nicolas
See Berdyaev, Nikolai (Aleksandrovich)

Berdyaev, Nikolai (Aleksandrovich)
1874-1948 .... **TCLC 67**
See also CA 120; 157

Berdyayev, Nikolai (Aleksandrovich)
See Berdyaev, Nikolai (Aleksandrovich)

Berendt, John (Lawrence) 1939- ...... **CLC 86**
See also CA 146; CANR 75, 93; DA3;
MTCW 1

Beresford, J(ohn) D(avys)
1873-1947 .... **TCLC 81**
See also CA 112; 155; DLB 162, 178, 197;
SFW 4; SUFW 1

Bergelson, David (Rafailovich)
1884-1952 .... **TCLC 81**
See Bergelson, Dovid
See also CA 220

Bergelson, Dovid
See Bergelson, David (Rafailovich)
See also EWL 3

Berger, Colonel
See Malraux, (Georges-)Andre

Berger, John (Peter) 1926- .... **CLC 2, 19**
See also BRWS 4; CA 81-84; CANR 51,
78, 117; CN 7; DLB 14, 207

Berger, Melvin H. 1927- .... **CLC 12**
See also CA 5-8R; CANR 4; CLR 32;
SAAS 2; SATA 5, 88; SATA-Essay 124

Berger, Thomas (Louis) 1924- .. **CLC 3, 5, 8,
11, 18, 38**
See also BPFB 1; CA 1-4R; CANR 5, 28,
51, 128; CN 7; DAM NOV; DLB 2;
DLBY 1980; EWL 3; FANT; INT CANR-
28; MTCW 1, 2; RHW; TCWW 2

Bergman, (Ernst) Ingmar 1918- ...... **CLC 16,
72**
See also CA 81-84; CANR 33, 70; CWW
2; DLB 257; MTCW 2

Bergson, Henri(-Louis) 1859-1941 . **TCLC 32**
See also CA 164; EW 8; EWL 3; GFL 1789
to the Present

Bergstein, Eleanor 1938- .... **CLC 4**
See also CA 53-56; CANR 5

Berkeley, George 1685-1753 .... **LC 65**
See also DLB 31, 101, 252

Berkoff, Steven 1937- .... **CLC 56**
See also CA 104; CANR 72; CBD; CD 5

Berlin, Isaiah 1909-1997 .... **TCLC 105**
See also CA 85-88; 162

Bermant, Chaim (Icyk) 1929-1998 ... **CLC 40**
See also CA 57-60; CANR 6, 31, 57, 105;
CN 7

Bern, Victoria
See Fisher, M(ary) F(rances) K(ennedy)

Bernanos, (Paul Louis) Georges
1888-1948 .... **TCLC 3**
See also CA 104; 130; CANR 94; DLB 72;
EWL 3; GFL 1789 to the Present; RGWL
2, 3

Bernard, April 1956- .... **CLC 59**
See also CA 131

Bernard of Clairvaux 1090-1153 .. **CMLC 71**
See also DLB 208

Berne, Victoria
See Fisher, M(ary) F(rances) K(ennedy)

Bernhard, Thomas 1931-1989 ..... **CLC 3, 32,
61; DC 14**
See also CA 85-88; 127; CANR 32, 57; CD-
WLB 2; DLB 85, 124; EWL 3; MTCW 1;
RGWL 2, 3

Bernhardt, Sarah (Henriette Rosine)
1844-1923 .... **TCLC 75**
See also CA 157

Bernstein, Charles 1950- .... **CLC 142**
See also CA 129; CAAS 24; CANR 90; CP
7; DLB 169

Bernstein, Ingrid
See Kirsch, Sarah

Berriault, Gina 1926-1999 .... **CLC 54, 109;
SSC 30**
See also CA 116; 129; 185; CANR 66; DLB
130; SSFS 7,11

Berrigan, Daniel 1921- .... **CLC 4**
See also CA 33-36R, 187; CAAE 187;
CAAS 1; CANR 11, 43, 78; CP 7; DLB 5

Berrigan, Edmund Joseph Michael, Jr.
1934-1983
See Berrigan, Ted
See also CA 61-64; 110; CANR 14, 102

Berrigan, Ted .... **CLC 37**
See Berrigan, Edmund Joseph Michael, Jr.
See also DLB 5, 169; WP

Berry, Charles Edward Anderson 1931-
See Berry, Chuck
See also CA 115

Berry, Chuck .... **CLC 17**
See Berry, Charles Edward Anderson

Berry, Jonas
See Ashbery, John (Lawrence)
See also GLL 1

Berry, Wendell (Erdman) 1934- ... **CLC 4, 6,
8, 27, 46; PC 28**
See also AITN 1; AMWS 10; ANW; CA
73-76; CANR 50, 73, 101, 132; CP 7;
CSW; DAM POET; DLB 5, 6, 234, 275;
MTCW 1

Berryman, John 1914-1972 ... **CLC 1, 2, 3, 4,
6, 8, 10, 13, 25, 62**
See also AMW; CA 13-16; 33-36R; CABS
2; CANR 35; CAP 1; CDALB 1941-1968;
DAM POET; DLB 48; EWL 3; MTCW 1,
2; PAB; RGAL 4; WP

Bertolucci, Bernardo 1940- ...... **CLC 16, 157**
See also CA 106; CANR 125

Berton, Pierre (Francis Demarigny)
1920-2004 .... **CLC 104**
See also CA 1-4R; CANR 2, 56; CPW;
DLB 68; SATA 99

Bertrand, Aloysius 1807-1841 .... **NCLC 31**
See Bertrand, Louis oAloysiusc

Bertrand, Louis oAloysiusc
See Bertrand, Aloysius
See also DLB 217

Bertran de Born c. 1140-1215 .... **CMLC 5**

Besant, Annie (Wood) 1847-1933 ..... **TCLC 9**
See also CA 105; 185

Bessie, Alvah 1904-1985 .... **CLC 23**
See also CA 5-8R; 116; CANR 2, 80; DLB 26

Bestuzhev, Aleksandr Aleksandrovich
1797-1837 .... **NCLC 131**
See also DLB 198

Bethlen, T. D.
See Silverberg, Robert

Beti, Mongo .... **BLC 1; CLC 27**
See Biyidi, Alexandre
See also AFW; CANR 79; DAM MULT; EWL 3; WLIT 2

Betjeman, John 1906-1984 ...... **CLC 2, 6, 10, 34, 43**
See also BRW 7; CA 9-12R; 112; CANR 33, 56; CDBLB 1945-1960; DA3; DAB; DAM MST, POET; DLB 20; DLBY 1984; EWL 3; MTCW 1, 2

Bettelheim, Bruno 1903-1990 .... **CLC 79; TCLC 143**
See also CA 81-84; 131; CANR 23, 61; DA3; MTCW 1, 2

Betti, Ugo 1892-1953 .... **TCLC 5**
See also CA 104; 155; EWL 3; RGWL 2, 3

Betts, Doris (Waugh) 1932- ..... **CLC 3, 6, 28; SSC 45**
See also CA 13-16R; CANR 9, 66, 77; CN 7; CSW; DLB 218; DLBY 1982; INT CANR-9; RGAL 4

Bevan, Alistair
See Roberts, Keith (John Kingston)

Bey, Pilaff
See Douglas, (George) Norman

Bialik, Chaim Nachman
1873-1934 .... **TCLC 25**
See also CA 170; EWL 3

Bickerstaff, Isaac
See Swift, Jonathan

Bidart, Frank 1939- .... **CLC 33**
See also CA 140; CANR 106; CP 7

Bienek, Horst 1930- .... **CLC 7, 11**
See also CA 73-76; DLB 75

Bierce, Ambrose (Gwinett)
1842-1914(?) ..... **SSC 9, 72; TCLC 1, 7, 44; WLC**
See also AAYA 55; AMW; BYA 11; CA 104; 139; CANR 78; CDALB 1865-1917; DA; DA3; DAC; DAM MST; DLB 11, 12, 23, 71, 74, 186; EWL 3; EXPS; HGG; LAIT 2; RGAL 4; RGSF 2; SSFS 9; SUFW 1

Biggers, Earl Derr 1884-1933 .... **TCLC 65**
See also CA 108; 153; DLB 306

Billiken, Bud
See Motley, Willard (Francis)

Billings, Josh
See Shaw, Henry Wheeler

Billington, (Lady) Rachel (Mary)
1942- .... **CLC 43**
See also AITN 2; CA 33-36R; CANR 44; CN 7

Binchy, Maeve 1940- .... **CLC 153**
See also BEST 90:1; BPFB 1; CA 127; 134; CANR 50, 96, 134; CN 7; CPW; DA3; DAM POP; INT CA-134; MTCW 1; RHW

Binyon, T(imothy) J(ohn) 1936- .... **CLC 34**
See also CA 111; CANR 28

Bion 335B.C.-245B.C. .... **CMLC 39**

Bioy Casares, Adolfo 1914-1999 ... **CLC 4, 8, 13, 88; HLC 1; SSC 17**
See Casares, Adolfo Bioy; Miranda, Javier; Sacastru, Martin
See also CA 29-32R; 177; CANR 19, 43, 66; CWW 2; DAM MULT; DLB 113; EWL 3; HW 1, 2; LAW; MTCW 1, 2

Birch, Allison .... **CLC 65**

Bird, Cordwainer
See Ellison, Harlan (Jay)

Bird, Robert Montgomery
1806-1854 .... **NCLC 1**
See also DLB 202; RGAL 4

Birkerts, Sven 1951- .... **CLC 116**
See also CA 128; 133, 176; CAAE 176; CAAS 29; INT CA-133

Birney, (Alfred) Earle 1904-1995 .. **CLC 1, 4, 6, 11; PC 52**
See also CA 1-4R; CANR 5, 20; CP 7; DAC; DAM MST, POET; DLB 88; MTCW 1; PFS 8; RGEL 2

Biruni, al 973-1048(?) .... **CMLC 28**

Bishop, Elizabeth 1911-1979 ..... **CLC 1, 4, 9, 13, 15, 32; PC 3, 34; TCLC 121**
See also AMWR 2; AMWS 1; CA 5-8R; 89-92; CABS 2; CANR 26, 61, 108; CDALB 1968-1988; DA; DA3; DAC; DAM MST, POET; DLB 5, 169; EWL 3; GLL 2; MAWW; MTCW 1, 2; PAB; PFS 6, 12; RGAL 4; SATA-Obit 24; TUS; WP

Bishop, John 1935- .... **CLC 10**
See also CA 105

Bishop, John Peale 1892-1944 ..... **TCLC 103**
See also CA 107; 155; DLB 4, 9, 45; RGAL 4

Bissett, Bill 1939- .... **CLC 18; PC 14**
See also CA 69-72; CAAS 19; CANR 15; CCA 1; CP 7; DLB 53; MTCW 1

Bissoondath, Neil (Devindra)
1955- .... **CLC 120**
See also CA 136; CANR 123; CN 7; DAC

Bitov, Andrei (Georgievich) 1937- ... **CLC 57**
See also CA 142; DLB 302

Biyidi, Alexandre 1932-
See Beti, Mongo
See also BW 1, 3; CA 114; 124; CANR 81; DA3; MTCW 1, 2

Bjarme, Brynjolf
See Ibsen, Henrik (Johan)

Bjoernson, Bjoernstjerne (Martinius)
1832-1910 .... **TCLC 7, 37**
See also CA 104

Black, Robert
See Holdstock, Robert P.

Blackburn, Paul 1926-1971 .... **CLC 9, 43**
See also BG 2; CA 81-84; 33-36R; CANR 34; DLB 16; DLBY 1981

Black Elk 1863-1950 .... **NNAL; TCLC 33**
See also CA 144; DAM MULT; MTCW 1; WP

Black Hawk 1767-1838 .... **NNAL**

Black Hobart
See Sanders, (James) Ed(ward)

Blacklin, Malcolm
See Chambers, Aidan

Blackmore, R(ichard) D(oddridge)
1825-1900 .... **TCLC 27**
See also CA 120; DLB 18; RGEL 2

Blackmur, R(ichard) P(almer)
1904-1965 .... **CLC 2, 24**
See also AMWS 2; CA 11-12; 25-28R; CANR 71; CAP 1; DLB 63; EWL 3

Black Tarantula
See Acker, Kathy

Blackwood, Algernon (Henry)
1869-1951 .... **TCLC 5**
See also CA 105; 150; DLB 153, 156, 178; HGG; SUFW 1

Blackwood, Caroline 1931-1996 .... **CLC 6, 9, 100**
See also BRWS 9; CA 85-88; 151; CANR 32, 61, 65; CN 7; DLB 14, 207; HGG; MTCW 1

Blade, Alexander
See Hamilton, Edmond; Silverberg, Robert

Blaga, Lucian 1895-1961 .... **CLC 75**
See also CA 157; DLB 220; EWL 3

Blair, Eric (Arthur) 1903-1950 .... **TCLC 123**
See Orwell, George
See also CA 104; 132; DA; DA3; DAB; DAC; DAM MST, NOV; MTCW 1, 2; SATA 29

Blair, Hugh 1718-1800 .... **NCLC 75**

Blais, Marie-Claire 1939- .... **CLC 2, 4, 6, 13, 22**
See also CA 21-24R; CAAS 4; CANR 38, 75, 93; CWW 2; DAC; DAM MST; DLB 53; EWL 3; FW; MTCW 1, 2; TWA

Blaise, Clark 1940- .... **CLC 29**
See also AITN 2; CA 53-56; CAAS 3; CANR 5, 66, 106; CN 7; DLB 53; RGSF 2

Blake, Fairley
See De Voto, Bernard (Augustine)

Blake, Nicholas
See Day Lewis, C(ecil)
See also DLB 77; MSW

Blake, Sterling
See Benford, Gregory (Albert)

Blake, William 1757-1827 . **NCLC 13, 37, 57, 127; PC 12; WLC**
See also AAYA 47; BRW 3; BRWR 1; CDBLB 1789-1832; CLR 52; DA; DA3; DAB; DAC; DAM MST, POET; DLB 93, 163; EXPP; LATS 1:1; LMFS 1; MAICYA 1, 2; PAB; PFS 2, 12; SATA 30; TEA; WCH; WLIT 3; WP

Blanchot, Maurice 1907-2003 .... **CLC 135**
See also CA 117; 144; 213; DLB 72, 296; EWL 3

Blasco Ibanez, Vicente 1867-1928 . **TCLC 12**
See also BPFB 1; CA 110; 131; CANR 81; DA3; DAM NOV; EW 8; EWL 3; HW 1, 2; MTCW 1

Blatty, William Peter 1928- .... **CLC 2**
See also CA 5-8R; CANR 9, 124; DAM POP; HGG

Bleeck, Oliver
See Thomas, Ross (Elmore)

Blessing, Lee 1949- .... **CLC 54**
See also CAD; CD 5

Blight, Rose
See Greer, Germaine

Blish, James (Benjamin) 1921-1975 . **CLC 14**
See also BPFB 1; CA 1-4R; 57-60; CANR 3; DLB 8; MTCW 1; SATA 66; SCFW 2; SFW 4

Bliss, Frederick
See Card, Orson Scott

Bliss, Reginald
See Wells, H(erbert) G(eorge)

Blixen, Karen (Christentze Dinesen)
1885-1962
See Dinesen, Isak
See also CA 25-28; CANR 22, 50; CAP 2; DA3; DLB 214; LMFS 1; MTCW 1, 2; SATA 44; SSFS 20

Bloch, Robert (Albert) 1917-1994 .... **CLC 33**
See also AAYA 29; CA 5-8R; 179; 146; CAAE 179; CAAS 20; CANR 5, 78; DA3; DLB 44; HGG; INT CANR-5; MTCW 1; SATA 12; SATA-Obit 82; SFW 4; SUFW 1, 2

Blok, Alexander (Alexandrovich)
1880-1921 .... **PC 21; TCLC 5**
See also CA 104; 183; DLB 295; EW 9; EWL 3; LMFS 2; RGWL 2, 3

Blom, Jan
See Breytenbach, Breyten

Bloom, Harold 1930- .... **CLC 24, 103**
See also CA 13-16R; CANR 39, 75, 92, 133; DLB 67; EWL 3; MTCW 1; RGAL 4

Bloomfield, Aurelius
See Bourne, Randolph S(illiman)

Bloomfield, Robert 1766-1823 ..... **NCLC 145**
See also DLB 93

Blount, Roy (Alton), Jr. 1941- .... **CLC 38**
See also CA 53-56; CANR 10, 28, 61, 125;
CSW; INT CANR-28; MTCW 1, 2

Blowsnake, Sam 1875-(?) .... **NNAL**

Bloy, Leon 1846-1917 .... **TCLC 22**
See also CA 121; 183; DLB 123; GFL 1789
to the Present

Blue Cloud, Peter (Aroniawenrate)
1933- .... **NNAL**
See also CA 117; CANR 40; DAM MULT

Bluggage, Oranthy
See Alcott, Louisa May

Blume, Judy (Sussman) 1938- .... **CLC 12, 30**
See also AAYA 3, 26; BYA 1, 8, 12; CA 29-
32R; CANR 13, 37, 66, 124; CLR 2, 15,
69; CPW; DA3; DAM NOV, POP; DLB
52; JRDA; MAICYA 1, 2; MAICYAS 1;
MTCW 1, 2; SATA 2, 31, 79, 142; WYA;
YAW

Blunden, Edmund (Charles)
1896-1974 .... **CLC 2, 56**
See also BRW 6; CA 17-18; 45-48; CANR
54; CAP 2; DLB 20, 100, 155; MTCW 1;
PAB

Bly, Robert (Elwood) 1926- .... **CLC 1, 2, 5,**
10, 15, 38, 128; PC 39
See also AMWS 4; CA 5-8R; CANR 41,
73, 125; CP 7; DA3; DAM POET; DLB
5; EWL 3; MTCW 1, 2; PFS 6, 17; RGAL
4

Boas, Franz 1858-1942 .... **TCLC 56**
See also CA 115; 181

Bobette
See Simenon, Georges (Jacques Christian)

Boccaccio, Giovanni 1313-1375 ... **CMLC 13,**
57; SSC 10
See also EW 2; RGSF 2; RGWL 2, 3; TWA

Bochco, Steven 1943- .... **CLC 35**
See also AAYA 11; CA 124; 138

Bode, Sigmund
See O'Doherty, Brian

Bodel, Jean 1167(?)-1210 .... **CMLC 28**

Bodenheim, Maxwell 1892-1954 .... **TCLC 44**
See also CA 110; 187; DLB 9, 45; RGAL 4

Bodenheimer, Maxwell
See Bodenheim, Maxwell

Bodker, Cecil 1927-
See Bodker, Cecil

Bodker, Cecil 1927- .... **CLC 21**
See also CA 73-76; CANR 13, 44, 111;
CLR 23; MAICYA 1, 2; SATA 14, 133

Boell, Heinrich (Theodor)
1917-1985 ..... **CLC 2, 3, 6, 9, 11, 15, 27,**
32, 72; SSC 23; WLC
See Boll, Heinrich
See also CA 21-24R; 116; CANR 24; DA;
DA3; DAB; DAC; DAM MST, NOV;
DLB 69; DLBY 1985; MTCW 1, 2; SSFS
20; TWA

Boerne, Alfred
See Doeblin, Alfred

Boethius c. 480-c. 524 .... **CMLC 15**
See also DLB 115; RGWL 2, 3

Boff, Leonardo (Genezio Darci)
1938- .... **CLC 70; HLC 1**
See also CA 150; DAM MULT; HW 2

Bogan, Louise 1897-1970 .... **CLC 4, 39, 46,**
93; PC 12
See also AMWS 3; CA 73-76; 25-28R;
CANR 33, 82; DAM POET; DLB 45, 169;
EWL 3; MAWW; MTCW 1, 2; PFS 21;
RGAL 4

Bogarde, Dirk
See Van Den Bogarde, Derek Jules Gaspard
Ulric Niven
See also DLB 14

Bogosian, Eric 1953- .... **CLC 45, 141**
See also CA 138; CAD; CANR 102; CD 5

Bograd, Larry 1953- .... **CLC 35**
See also CA 93-96; CANR 57; SAAS 21;
SATA 33, 89; WYA

Boiardo, Matteo Maria 1441-1494 .... **LC 6**

Boileau-Despreaux, Nicolas 1636-1711 . **LC 3**
See also DLB 268; EW 3; GFL Beginnings
to 1789; RGWL 2, 3

Boissard, Maurice
See Leautaud, Paul

Bojer, Johan 1872-1959 .... **TCLC 64**
See also CA 189; EWL 3

Bok, Edward W(illiam)
1863-1930 .... **TCLC 101**
See also CA 217; DLB 91; DLBD 16

Boker, George Henry 1823-1890 . **NCLC 125**
See also RGAL 4

Boland, Eavan (Aisling) 1944- .. **CLC 40, 67,**
113; PC 58
See also BRWS 5; CA 143, 207; CAAE
207; CANR 61; CP 7; CWP; DAM POET;
DLB 40; FW; MTCW 2; PFS 12

Boll, Heinrich
See Boell, Heinrich (Theodor)
See also BPFB 1; CDWLB 2; EW 13; EWL
3; RGSF 2; RGWL 2, 3

Bolt, Lee
See Faust, Frederick (Schiller)

Bolt, Robert (Oxton) 1924-1995 .... **CLC 14**
See also CA 17-20R; 147; CANR 35, 67;
CBD; DAM DRAM; DFS 2; DLB 13,
233; EWL 3; LAIT 1; MTCW 1

Bombal, Maria Luisa 1910-1980 .... **HLCS 1;**
SSC 37
See also CA 127; CANR 72; EWL 3; HW
1; LAW; RGSF 2

Bombet, Louis-Alexandre-Cesar
See Stendhal

Bomkauf
See Kaufman, Bob (Garnell)

Bonaventura .... **NCLC 35**
See also DLB 90

Bond, Edward 1934- .... **CLC 4, 6, 13, 23**
See also AAYA 50; BRWS 1; CA 25-28R;
CANR 38, 67, 106; CBD; CD 5; DAM
DRAM; DFS 3, 8; DLB 13; EWL 3;
MTCW 1

Bonham, Frank 1914-1989 .... **CLC 12**
See also AAYA 1; BYA 1, 3; CA 9-12R;
CANR 4, 36; JRDA; MAICYA 1, 2;
SAAS 3; SATA 1, 49; SATA-Obit 62;
TCWW 2; YAW

Bonnefoy, Yves 1923- . **CLC 9, 15, 58; PC 58**
See also CA 85-88; CANR 33, 75, 97;
CWW 2; DAM MST, POET; DLB 258;
EWL 3; GFL 1789 to the Present; MTCW
1, 2

Bonner, Marita .... **HR 2**
See Occomy, Marita (Odette) Bonner

Bonnin, Gertrude 1876-1938 .... **NNAL**
See Zitkala-Sa
See also CA 150; DAM MULT

Bontemps, Arna(ud Wendell)
1902-1973 ..... **BLC 1; CLC 1, 18; HR 2**
See also BW 1; CA 1-4R; 41-44R; CANR
4, 35; CLR 6; CWRI 5; DA3; DAM
MULT, NOV, POET; DLB 48, 51; JRDA;
MAICYA 1, 2; MTCW 1, 2; SATA 2, 44;
SATA-Obit 24; WCH; WP

Boot, William
See Stoppard, Tom

Booth, Martin 1944-2004 .... **CLC 13**
See also CA 93-96, 188; 223; CAAE 188;
CAAS 2; CANR 92

Booth, Philip 1925- .... **CLC 23**
See also CA 5-8R; CANR 5, 88; CP 7;
DLBY 1982

Booth, Wayne C(layson) 1921- .... **CLC 24**
See also CA 1-4R; CAAS 5; CANR 3, 43,
117; DLB 67

Borchert, Wolfgang 1921-1947 .... **TCLC 5**
See also CA 104; 188; DLB 69, 124; EWL
3

Borel, Petrus 1809-1859 .... **NCLC 41**
See also DLB 119; GFL 1789 to the Present

Borges, Jorge Luis 1899-1986 ... **CLC 1, 2, 3,**
4, 6, 8, 9, 10, 13, 19, 44, 48, 83; HLC 1;
PC 22, 32; SSC 4, 41; TCLC 109;
WLC
See also AAYA 26; BPFB 1; CA 21-24R;
CANR 19, 33, 75, 105, 133; CDWLB 3;
DA; DA3; DAB; DAC; DAM MST,
MULT; DLB 113, 283; DLBY 1986;
DNFS 1, 2; EWL 3; HW 1, 2; LAW;
LMFS 2; MSW; MTCW 1, 2; RGSF 2;
RGWL 2, 3; SFW 4; SSFS 17; TWA;
WLIT 1

Borowski, Tadeusz 1922-1951 .... **SSC 48;**
TCLC 9
See also CA 106; 154; CDWLB 4; DLB
215; EWL 3; RGSF 2; RGWL 3; SSFS
13

Borrow, George (Henry)
1803-1881 .... **NCLC 9**
See also DLB 21, 55, 166

Bosch (Gavino), Juan 1909-2001 ..... **HLCS 1**
See also CA 151; 204; DAM MST, MULT;
DLB 145; HW 1, 2

Bosman, Herman Charles
1905-1951 .... **TCLC 49**
See Malan, Herman
See also CA 160; DLB 225; RGSF 2

Bosschere, Jean de 1878(?)-1953 ... **TCLC 19**
See also CA 115; 186

Boswell, James 1740-1795 ... **LC 4, 50; WLC**
See also BRW 3; CDBLB 1660-1789; DA;
DAB; DAC; DAM MST; DLB 104, 142;
TEA; WLIT 3

Bottomley, Gordon 1874-1948 ..... **TCLC 107**
See also CA 120; 192; DLB 10

Bottoms, David 1949- .... **CLC 53**
See also CA 105; CANR 22; CSW; DLB
120; DLBY 1983

Boucicault, Dion 1820-1890 .... **NCLC 41**

Boucolon, Maryse
See Conde, Maryse

Bourdieu, Pierre 1930-2002 .... **CLC 198**
See also CA 130; 204

Bourget, Paul (Charles Joseph)
1852-1935 .... **TCLC 12**
See also CA 107; 196; DLB 123; GFL 1789
to the Present

Bourjaily, Vance (Nye) 1922- .... **CLC 8, 62**
See also CA 1-4R; CAAS 1; CANR 2, 72;
CN 7; DLB 2, 143

Bourne, Randolph S(illiman)
1886-1918 .... **TCLC 16**
See also AMW; CA 117; 155; DLB 63

Bova, Ben(jamin William) 1932- ...... **CLC 45**
See also AAYA 16; CA 5-8R; CAAS 18;
CANR 11, 56, 94, 111; CLR 3, 96; DLBY
1981; INT CANR-11; MAICYA 1, 2;
MTCW 1; SATA 6, 68, 133; SFW 4

Bowen, Elizabeth (Dorothea Cole)
1899-1973 . **CLC 1, 3, 6, 11, 15, 22, 118;**
SSC 3, 28, 66; TCLC 148
See also BRWS 2; CA 17-18; 41-44R;
CANR 35, 105; CAP 2; CDBLB 1945-
1960; DA3; DAM NOV; DLB 15, 162;
EWL 3; EXPS; FW; HGG; MTCW 1, 2;
NFS 13; RGSF 2; SSFS 5; SUFW 1;
TEA; WLIT 4

Bowering, George 1935- .... **CLC 15, 47**
See also CA 21-24R; CAAS 16; CANR 10;
CP 7; DLB 53

Breytenbach, Breyten 1939(?)- .. **CLC 23, 37, 126**
See also CA 113; 129; CANR 61, 122; CWW 2; DAM POET; DLB 225; EWL 3

Bridgers, Sue Ellen 1942- .... **CLC 26**
See also AAYA 8, 49; BYA 7, 8; CA 65-68; CANR 11, 36; CLR 18; DLB 52; JRDA; MAICYA 1, 2; SAAS 1; SATA 22, 90; SATA-Essay 109; WYA; YAW

Bridges, Robert (Seymour)
1844-1930 .... **PC 28; TCLC 1**
See also BRW 6; CA 104; 152; CDBLB 1890-1914; DAM POET; DLB 19, 98

Bridie, James .... **TCLC 3**
See Mavor, Osborne Henry
See also DLB 10; EWL 3

Brin, David 1950- .... **CLC 34**
See also AAYA 21; CA 102; CANR 24, 70, 125, 127; INT CANR-24; SATA 65; SCFW 2; SFW 4

Brink, Andre (Philippus) 1935- . **CLC 18, 36, 106**
See also AFW; BRWS 6; CA 104; CANR 39, 62, 109, 133; CN 7; DLB 225; EWL 3; INT CA-103; LATS 1:2; MTCW 1, 2; WLIT 2

Brinsmead, H. F(ay)
See Brinsmead, H(esba) F(ay)

Brinsmead, H. F.
See Brinsmead, H(esba) F(ay)

Brinsmead, H(esba) F(ay) 1922- ...... **CLC 21**
See also CA 21-24R; CANR 10; CLR 47; CWRI 5; MAICYA 1, 2; SAAS 5; SATA 18, 78

Brittain, Vera (Mary) 1893(?)-1970 . **CLC 23**
See also BRWS 10; CA 13-16; 25-28R; CANR 58; CAP 1; DLB 191; FW; MTCW 1, 2

Broch, Hermann 1886-1951 .... **TCLC 20**
See also CA 117; 211; CDWLB 2; DLB 85, 124; EW 10; EWL 3; RGWL 2, 3

Brock, Rose
See Hansen, Joseph
See also GLL 1

Brod, Max 1884-1968 .... **TCLC 115**
See also CA 5-8R; 25-28R; CANR 7; DLB 81; EWL 3

Brodkey, Harold (Roy) 1930-1996 .. **CLC 56; TCLC 123**
See also CA 111; 151; CANR 71; CN 7; DLB 130

Brodsky, Iosif Alexandrovich 1940-1996
See Brodsky, Joseph
See also AITN 1; CA 41-44R; 151; CANR 37, 106; DA3; DAM POET; MTCW 1, 2; RGWL 2, 3

Brodsky, Joseph . **CLC 4, 6, 13, 36, 100; PC 9**
See Brodsky, Iosif Alexandrovich
See also AMWS 8; CWW 2; DLB 285; EWL 3; MTCW 1

Brodsky, Michael (Mark) 1948- .... **CLC 19**
See also CA 102; CANR 18, 41, 58; DLB 244

Brodzki, Bella ed. .... **CLC 65**

Brome, Richard 1590(?)-1652 .... **LC 61**
See also BRWS 10; DLB 58

Bromell, Henry 1947- .... **CLC 5**
See also CA 53-56; CANR 9, 115, 116

Bromfield, Louis (Brucker)
1896-1956 .... **TCLC 11**
See also CA 107; 155; DLB 4, 9, 86; RGAL 4; RHW

Broner, E(sther) M(asserman)
1930- .... **CLC 19**
See also CA 17-20R; CANR 8, 25, 72; CN 7; DLB 28

Bronk, William (M.) 1918-1999 .... **CLC 10**
See also CA 89-92; 177; CANR 23; CP 7; DLB 165

Bronstein, Lev Davidovich
See Trotsky, Leon

Bronte, Anne 1820-1849 ..... **NCLC 4, 71, 102**
See also BRW 5; BRWR 1; DA3; DLB 21, 199; TEA

Bronte, (Patrick) Branwell
1817-1848 .... **NCLC 109**

Bronte, Charlotte 1816-1855 ...... **NCLC 3, 8, 33, 58, 105; WLC**
See also AAYA 17; BRW 5; BRWC 2; BRWR 1; BYA 2; CDBLB 1832-1890; DA; DA3; DAB; DAC; DAM MST, NOV; DLB 21, 159, 199; EXPN; LAIT 2; NFS 4; TEA; WLIT 4

Bronte, Emily (Jane) 1818-1848 ... **NCLC 16, 35; PC 8; WLC**
See also AAYA 17; BPFB 1; BRW 5; BRWC 1; BRWR 1; BYA 3; CDBLB 1832-1890; DA; DA3; DAB; DAC; DAM MST, NOV, POET; DLB 21, 32, 199; EXPN; LAIT 1; TEA; WLIT 3

Brontes
See Bronte, Anne; Bronte, Charlotte; Bronte, Emily (Jane)

Brooke, Frances 1724-1789 .... **LC 6, 48**
See also DLB 39, 99

Brooke, Henry 1703(?)-1783 .... **LC 1**
See also DLB 39

Brooke, Rupert (Chawner)
1887-1915 ..... **PC 24; TCLC 2, 7; WLC**
See also BRWS 3; CA 104; 132; CANR 61; CDBLB 1914-1945; DA; DAB; DAC; DAM MST, POET; DLB 19, 216; EXPP; GLL 2; MTCW 1, 2; PFS 7; TEA

Brooke-Haven, P.
See Wodehouse, P(elham) G(renville)

Brooke-Rose, Christine 1926(?)- ..... **CLC 40, 184**
See also BRWS 4; CA 13-16R; CANR 58, 118; CN 7; DLB 14, 231; EWL 3; SFW 4

Brookner, Anita 1928- .. **CLC 32, 34, 51, 136**
See also BRWS 4; CA 114; 120; CANR 37, 56, 87, 130; CN 7; CPW; DA3; DAB; DAM POP; DLB 194; DLBY 1987; EWL 3; MTCW 1, 2; TEA

Brooks, Cleanth 1906-1994 . **CLC 24, 86, 110**
See also AMWS 14; CA 17-20R; 145; CANR 33, 35; CSW; DLB 63; DLBY 1994; EWL 3; INT CANR-35; MTCW 1, 2

Brooks, George
See Baum, L(yman) Frank

Brooks, Gwendolyn (Elizabeth)
1917-2000 ... **BLC 1; CLC 1, 2, 4, 5, 15, 49, 125; PC 7; WLC**
See also AAYA 20; AFAW 1, 2; AITN 1; AMWS 3; BW 2, 3; CA 1-4R; 190; CANR 1, 27, 52, 75, 132; CDALB 1941-1968; CLR 27; CP 7; CWP; DA; DA3; DAC; DAM MST, MULT, POET; DLB 5, 76, 165; EWL 3; EXPP; MAWW; MTCW 1, 2; PFS 1, 2, 4, 6; RGAL 4; SATA 6; SATA-Obit 123; TUS; WP

Brooks, Mel .... **CLC 12**
See Kaminsky, Melvin
See also AAYA 13, 48; DLB 26

Brooks, Peter (Preston) 1938- .... **CLC 34**
See also CA 45-48; CANR 1, 107

Brooks, Van Wyck 1886-1963 .... **CLC 29**
See also AMW; CA 1-4R; CANR 6; DLB 45, 63, 103; TUS

Brophy, Brigid (Antonia)
1929-1995 .... **CLC 6, 11, 29, 105**
See also CA 5-8R; 149; CAAS 4; CANR 25, 53; CBD; CN 7; CWD; DA3; DLB 14, 271; EWL 3; MTCW 1, 2

Brosman, Catharine Savage 1934- ..... **CLC 9**
See also CA 61-64; CANR 21, 46

Brossard, Nicole 1943- .... **CLC 115, 169**
See also CA 122; CAAS 16; CCA 1; CWP; CWW 2; DLB 53; EWL 3; FW; GLL 2; RGWL 3

Brother Antoninus
See Everson, William (Oliver)

The Brothers Quay
See Quay, Stephen; Quay, Timothy

Broughton, T(homas) Alan 1936- ..... **CLC 19**
See also CA 45-48; CANR 2, 23, 48, 111

Broumas, Olga 1949- .... **CLC 10, 73**
See also CA 85-88; CANR 20, 69, 110; CP 7; CWP; GLL 2

Broun, Heywood 1888-1939 .... **TCLC 104**
See also DLB 29, 171

Brown, Alan 1950- .... **CLC 99**
See also CA 156

Brown, Charles Brockden
1771-1810 .... **NCLC 22, 74, 122**
See also AMWS 1; CDALB 1640-1865; DLB 37, 59, 73; FW; HGG; LMFS 1; RGAL 4; TUS

Brown, Christy 1932-1981 .... **CLC 63**
See also BYA 13; CA 105; 104; CANR 72; DLB 14

Brown, Claude 1937-2002 ... **BLC 1; CLC 30**
See also AAYA 7; BW 1, 3; CA 73-76; 205; CANR 81; DAM MULT

Brown, Dee (Alexander)
1908-2002 .... **CLC 18, 47**
See also AAYA 30; CA 13-16R; 212; CAAS 6; CANR 11, 45, 60; CPW; CSW; DA3; DAM POP; DLBY 1980; LAIT 2; MTCW 1, 2; NCFS 5; SATA 5, 110; SATA-Obit 141; TCWW 2

Brown, George
See Wertmueller, Lina

Brown, George Douglas
1869-1902 .... **TCLC 28**
See Douglas, George
See also CA 162

Brown, George Mackay 1921-1996 ... **CLC 5, 48, 100**
See also BRWS 6; CA 21-24R; 151; CAAS 6; CANR 12, 37, 67; CN 7; CP 7; DLB 14, 27, 139, 271; MTCW 1; RGSF 2; SATA 35

Brown, (William) Larry 1951-2004 . **CLC 73**
See also CA 130; 134; CANR 117; CSW; DLB 234; INT CA-134

Brown, Moses
See Barrett, William (Christopher)

Brown, Rita Mae 1944- .... **CLC 18, 43, 79**
See also BPFB 1; CA 45-48; CANR 2, 11, 35, 62, 95; CN 7; CPW; CSW; DA3; DAM NOV, POP; FW; INT CANR-11; MTCW 1, 2; NFS 9; RGAL 4; TUS

Brown, Roderick (Langmere) Haig-
See Haig-Brown, Roderick (Langmere)

Brown, Rosellen 1939- .... **CLC 32, 170**
See also CA 77-80; CAAS 10; CANR 14, 44, 98; CN 7

Brown, Sterling Allen 1901-1989 ...... **BLC 1; CLC 1, 23, 59; HR 2; PC 55**
See also AFAW 1, 2; BW 1, 3; CA 85-88; 127; CANR 26; DA3; DAM MULT, POET; DLB 48, 51, 63; MTCW 1, 2; RGAL 4; WP

Brown, Will
See Ainsworth, William Harrison

Brown, William Hill 1765-1793 .... **LC 93**
See also DLB 37

Brown, William Wells 1815-1884 ...... **BLC 1; DC 1; NCLC 2, 89**
See also DAM MULT; DLB 3, 50, 183, 248; RGAL 4

Burroughs, William S(eward)
1914-1997 .. **CLC 1, 2, 5, 15, 22, 42, 75, 109; TCLC 121; WLC**
See Lee, William; Lee, Willy
See also AAYA 60; AITN 2; AMWS 3; BG 2; BPFB 1; CA 9-12R; 160; CANR 20, 52, 104; CN 7; CPW; DA; DA3; DAB; DAC; DAM MST, NOV, POP; DLB 2, 8, 16, 152, 237; DLBY 1981, 1997; EWL 3; HGG; LMFS 2; MTCW 1, 2; RGAL 4; SFW 4

Burton, Sir Richard F(rancis)
1821-1890 .... **NCLC 42**
See also DLB 55, 166, 184

Burton, Robert 1577-1640 .... **LC 74**
See also DLB 151; RGEL 2

Buruma, Ian 1951- .... **CLC 163**
See also CA 128; CANR 65

Busch, Frederick 1941- ... **CLC 7, 10, 18, 47, 166**
See also CA 33-36R; CAAS 1; CANR 45, 73, 92; CN 7; DLB 6, 218

Bush, Barney (Furman) 1946- .... **NNAL**
See also CA 145

Bush, Ronald 1946- .... **CLC 34**
See also CA 136

Bustos, F(rancisco)
See Borges, Jorge Luis

Bustos Domecq, H(onorio)
See Bioy Casares, Adolfo; Borges, Jorge Luis

Butler, Octavia E(stelle) 1947- .. **BLCS; CLC 38, 121**
See also AAYA 18, 48; AFAW 2; AMWS 13; BPFB 1; BW 2, 3; CA 73-76; CANR 12, 24, 38, 73; CLR 65; CPW; DA3; DAM MULT, POP; DLB 33; LATS 1:2; MTCW 1, 2; NFS 8; SATA 84; SCFW 2; SFW 4; SSFS 6; YAW

Butler, Robert Olen, (Jr.) 1945- ...... **CLC 81, 162**
See also AMWS 12; BPFB 1; CA 112; CANR 66; CSW; DAM POP; DLB 173; INT CA-112; MTCW 1; SSFS 11

Butler, Samuel 1612-1680 .... **LC 16, 43**
See also DLB 101, 126; RGEL 2

Butler, Samuel 1835-1902 .... **TCLC 1, 33; WLC**
See also BRWS 2; CA 143; CDBLB 1890-1914; DA; DA3; DAB; DAC; DAM MST, NOV; DLB 18, 57, 174; RGEL 2; SFW 4; TEA

Butler, Walter C.
See Faust, Frederick (Schiller)

Butor, Michel (Marie Francois)
1926- .... **CLC 1, 3, 8, 11, 15, 161**
See also CA 9-12R; CANR 33, 66; CWW 2; DLB 83; EW 13; EWL 3; GFL 1789 to the Present; MTCW 1, 2

Butts, Mary 1890(?)-1937 .... **TCLC 77**
See also CA 148; DLB 240

Buxton, Ralph
See Silverstein, Alvin; Silverstein, Virginia B(arbara Opshelor)

Buzo, Alex
See Buzo, Alexander (John)
See also DLB 289

Buzo, Alexander (John) 1944- .... **CLC 61**
See also CA 97-100; CANR 17, 39, 69; CD 5

Buzzati, Dino 1906-1972 .... **CLC 36**
See also CA 160; 33-36R; DLB 177; RGWL 2, 3; SFW 4

Byars, Betsy (Cromer) 1928- .... **CLC 35**
See also AAYA 19; BYA 3; CA 33-36R, 183; CAAE 183; CANR 18, 36, 57, 102; CLR 1, 16, 72; DLB 52; INT CANR-18; JRDA; MAICYA 1, 2; MAICYAS 1; MTCW 1; SAAS 1; SATA 4, 46, 80; SATA-Essay 108; WYA; YAW

Byatt, A(ntonia) S(usan Drabble)
1936- .... **CLC 19, 65, 136**
See also BPFB 1; BRWC 2; BRWS 4; CA 13-16R; CANR 13, 33, 50, 75, 96, 133; DA3; DAM NOV, POP; DLB 14, 194; EWL 3; MTCW 1, 2; RGSF 2; RHW; TEA

Byrne, David 1952- .... **CLC 26**
See also CA 127

Byrne, John Keyes 1926-
See Leonard, Hugh
See also CA 102; CANR 78; INT CA-102

Byron, George Gordon (Noel)
1788-1824 ..... **DC 24; NCLC 2, 12, 109, 149; PC 16; WLC**
See also BRW 4; BRWC 2; CDBLB 1789-1832; DA; DA3; DAB; DAC; DAM MST, POET; DLB 96, 110; EXPP; LMFS 1; PAB; PFS 1, 14; RGEL 2; TEA; WLIT 3; WP

Byron, Robert 1905-1941 .... **TCLC 67**
See also CA 160; DLB 195

C. 3. 3.
See Wilde, Oscar (Fingal O'Flahertie Wills)

Caballero, Fernan 1796-1877 .... **NCLC 10**

Cabell, Branch
See Cabell, James Branch

Cabell, James Branch 1879-1958 .... **TCLC 6**
See also CA 105; 152; DLB 9, 78; FANT; MTCW 1; RGAL 4; SUFW 1

Cabeza de Vaca, Alvar Nunez
1490-1557(?) .... **LC 61**

Cable, George Washington
1844-1925 .... **SSC 4; TCLC 4**
See also CA 104; 155; DLB 12, 74; DLBD 13; RGAL 4; TUS

Cabral de Melo Neto, Joao
1920-1999 .... **CLC 76**
See Melo Neto, Joao Cabral de
See also CA 151; DAM MULT; DLB 307; LAW; LAWS 1

Cabrera Infante, G(uillermo) 1929- . **CLC 5, 25, 45, 120; HLC 1; SSC 39**
See also CA 85-88; CANR 29, 65, 110; CD-WLB 3; CWW 2; DA3; DAM MULT; DLB 113; EWL 3; HW 1, 2; LAW; LAWS 1; MTCW 1, 2; RGSF 2; WLIT 1

Cade, Toni
See Bambara, Toni Cade

Cadmus and Harmonia
See Buchan, John

Caedmon fl. 658-680 .... **CMLC 7**
See also DLB 146

Caeiro, Alberto
See Pessoa, Fernando (Antonio Nogueira)

Caesar, Julius .... **CMLC 47**
See Julius Caesar
See also AW 1; RGWL 2, 3

Cage, John (Milton, Jr.)
1912-1992 .... **CLC 41; PC 58**
See also CA 13-16R; 169; CANR 9, 78; DLB 193; INT CANR-9

Cahan, Abraham 1860-1951 .... **TCLC 71**
See also CA 108; 154; DLB 9, 25, 28; RGAL 4

Cain, G.
See Cabrera Infante, G(uillermo)

Cain, Guillermo
See Cabrera Infante, G(uillermo)

Cain, James M(allahan) 1892-1977 .. **CLC 3, 11, 28**
See also AITN 1; BPFB 1; CA 17-20R; 73-76; CANR 8, 34, 61; CMW 4; DLB 226; EWL 3; MSW; MTCW 1; RGAL 4

Caine, Hall 1853-1931 .... **TCLC 97**
See also RHW

Caine, Mark
See Raphael, Frederic (Michael)

Calasso, Roberto 1941- .... **CLC 81**
See also CA 143; CANR 89

Calderon de la Barca, Pedro
1600-1681 .... **DC 3; HLCS 1; LC 23**
See also EW 2; RGWL 2, 3; TWA

Caldwell, Erskine (Preston)
1903-1987 .... **CLC 1, 8, 14, 50, 60; SSC 19; TCLC 117**
See also AITN 1; AMW; BPFB 1; CA 1-4R; 121; CAAS 1; CANR 2, 33; DA3; DAM NOV; DLB 9, 86; EWL 3; MTCW 1, 2; RGAL 4; RGSF 2; TUS

Caldwell, (Janet Miriam) Taylor (Holland)
1900-1985 .... **CLC 2, 28, 39**
See also BPFB 1; CA 5-8R; 116; CANR 5; DA3; DAM NOV, POP; DLBD 17; RHW

Calhoun, John Caldwell
1782-1850 .... **NCLC 15**
See also DLB 3, 248

Calisher, Hortense 1911- ..... **CLC 2, 4, 8, 38, 134; SSC 15**
See also CA 1-4R; CANR 1, 22, 117; CN 7; DA3; DAM NOV; DLB 2, 218; INT CANR-22; MTCW 1, 2; RGAL 4; RGSF 2

Callaghan, Morley Edward
1903-1990 ..... **CLC 3, 14, 41, 65; TCLC 145**
See also CA 9-12R; 132; CANR 33, 73; DAC; DAM MST; DLB 68; EWL 3; MTCW 1, 2; RGEL 2; RGSF 2; SSFS 19

Callimachus c. 305B.C.-c.
240B.C. .... **CMLC 18**
See also AW 1; DLB 176; RGWL 2, 3

Calvin, Jean
See Calvin, John
See also GFL Beginnings to 1789

Calvin, John 1509-1564 .... **LC 37**
See Calvin, Jean

Calvino, Italo 1923-1985 .... **CLC 5, 8, 11, 22, 33, 39, 73; SSC 3, 48**
See also AAYA 58; CA 85-88; 116; CANR 23, 61, 132; DAM NOV; DLB 196; EW 13; EWL 3; MTCW 1, 2; RGSF 2; RGWL 2, 3; SFW 4; SSFS 12

Camara Laye
See Laye, Camara
See also EWL 3

Camden, William 1551-1623 .... **LC 77**
See also DLB 172

Cameron, Carey 1952- .... **CLC 59**
See also CA 135

Cameron, Peter 1959- .... **CLC 44**
See also AMWS 12; CA 125; CANR 50, 117; DLB 234; GLL 2

Camoens, Luis Vaz de 1524(?)-1580
See Camoes, Luis de
See also EW 2

Camoes, Luis de 1524(?)-1580 . **HLCS 1; LC 62; PC 31**
See Camoens, Luis Vaz de
See also DLB 287; RGWL 2, 3

Campana, Dino 1885-1932 .... **TCLC 20**
See also CA 117; DLB 114; EWL 3

Campanella, Tommaso 1568-1639 .... **LC 32**
See also RGWL 2, 3

Campbell, John W(ood, Jr.)
1910-1971 .... **CLC 32**
See also CA 21-22; 29-32R; CANR 34; CAP 2; DLB 8; MTCW 1; SCFW; SFW 4

Campbell, Joseph 1904-1987 .... **CLC 69; TCLC 140**
See also AAYA 3; BEST 89:2; CA 1-4R; 124; CANR 3, 28, 61, 107; DA3; MTCW 1, 2

Campbell, Maria 1940- .... **CLC 85; NNAL**
See also CA 102; CANR 54; CCA 1; DAC

Chopin, Katherine 1851-1904
See Chopin, Kate
See also CA 104; 122; DA3; DAC; DAM
MST, NOV

Chretien de Troyes c. 12th cent. - . **CMLC 10**
See also DLB 208; EW 1; RGWL 2, 3;
TWA

Christie
See Ichikawa, Kon

Christie, Agatha (Mary Clarissa)
1890-1976 .. **CLC 1, 6, 8, 12, 39, 48, 110**
See also AAYA 9; AITN 1, 2; BPFB 1;
BRWS 2; CA 17-20R; 61-64; CANR 10,
37, 108; CBD; CDBLB 1914-1945; CMW
4; CPW; CWD; DA3; DAB; DAC; DAM
NOV; DFS 2; DLB 13, 77, 245; MSW;
MTCW 1, 2; NFS 8; RGEL 2; RHW;
SATA 36; TEA; YAW

Christie, Philippa .... **CLC 21**
See Pearce, Philippa
See also BYA 5; CANR 109; CLR 9; DLB
161; MAICYA 1; SATA 1, 67, 129

Christine de Pizan 1365(?)-1431(?) .... **LC 9**
See also DLB 208; RGWL 2, 3

Chuang Tzu c. 369B.C.-c.
286B.C. .... **CMLC 57**

Chubb, Elmer
See Masters, Edgar Lee

Chulkov, Mikhail Dmitrievich
1743-1792 .... **LC 2**
See also DLB 150

Churchill, Caryl 1938- .... **CLC 31, 55, 157;**
DC 5
See Churchill, Chick
See also BRWS 4; CA 102; CANR 22, 46,
108; CBD; CWD; DFS 12, 16; DLB 13;
EWL 3; FW; MTCW 1; RGEL 2

Churchill, Charles 1731-1764 .... **LC 3**
See also DLB 109; RGEL 2

Churchill, Chick
See Churchill, Caryl
See also CD 5

Churchill, Sir Winston (Leonard Spencer)
1874-1965 .... **TCLC 113**
See also BRW 6; CA 97-100; CDBLB
1890-1914; DA3; DLB 100; DLBD 16;
LAIT 4; MTCW 1, 2

Chute, Carolyn 1947- .... **CLC 39**
See also CA 123; CANR 135

Ciardi, John (Anthony) 1916-1986 . **CLC 10,**
40, 44, 129
See also CA 5-8R; 118; CAAS 2; CANR 5,
33; CLR 19; CWRI 5; DAM POET; DLB
5; DLBY 1986; INT CANR-5; MAICYA
1, 2; MTCW 1, 2; RGAL 4; SAAS 26;
SATA 1, 65; SATA-Obit 46

Cibber, Colley 1671-1757 .... **LC 66**
See also DLB 84; RGEL 2

Cicero, Marcus Tullius
106B.C.-43B.C. .... **CMLC 3**
See also AW 1; CDWLB 1; DLB 211;
RGWL 2, 3

Cimino, Michael 1943- .... **CLC 16**
See also CA 105

Cioran, E(mil) M. 1911-1995 .... **CLC 64**
See also CA 25-28R; 149; CANR 91; DLB
220; EWL 3

Cisneros, Sandra 1954- .... **CLC 69, 118, 193;**
HLC 1; PC 52; SSC 32, 72
See also AAYA 9, 53; AMWS 7; CA 131;
CANR 64, 118; CWP; DA3; DAM MULT;
DLB 122, 152; EWL 3; EXPN; FW; HW
1, 2; LAIT 5; LATS 1:2; LLW 1; MAI-
CYA 2; MTCW 2; NFS 2; PFS 19; RGAL
4; RGSF 2; SSFS 3, 13; WLIT 1; YAW

Cixous, Helene 1937- .... **CLC 92**
See also CA 126; CANR 55, 123; CWW 2;
DLB 83, 242; EWL 3; FW; GLL 2;
MTCW 1, 2; TWA

Clair, Rene .... **CLC 20**
See Chomette, Rene Lucien

Clampitt, Amy 1920-1994 .... **CLC 32; PC 19**
See also AMWS 9; CA 110; 146; CANR
29, 79; DLB 105

Clancy, Thomas L., Jr. 1947-
See Clancy, Tom
See also CA 125; 131; CANR 62, 105;
DA3; INT CA-131; MTCW 1, 2

Clancy, Tom .... **CLC 45, 112**
See Clancy, Thomas L., Jr.
See also AAYA 9, 51; BEST 89:1, 90:1;
BPFB 1; BYA 10, 11; CANR 132; CMW
4; CPW; DAM NOV, POP; DLB 227

Clare, John 1793-1864 .. **NCLC 9, 86; PC 23**
See also DAB; DAM POET; DLB 55, 96;
RGEL 2

Clarin
See Alas (y Urena), Leopoldo (Enrique
Garcia)

Clark, Al C.
See Goines, Donald

Clark, (Robert) Brian 1932- .... **CLC 29**
See also CA 41-44R; CANR 67; CBD; CD
5

Clark, Curt
See Westlake, Donald E(dwin)

Clark, Eleanor 1913-1996 .... **CLC 5, 19**
See also CA 9-12R; 151; CANR 41; CN 7;
DLB 6

Clark, J. P.
See Clark Bekederemo, J(ohnson) P(epper)
See also CDWLB 3; DLB 117

Clark, John Pepper
See Clark Bekederemo, J(ohnson) P(epper)
See also AFW; CD 5; CP 7; RGEL 2

Clark, Kenneth (Mackenzie)
1903-1983 .... **TCLC 147**
See also CA 93-96; 109; CANR 36; MTCW
1, 2

Clark, M. R.
See Clark, Mavis Thorpe

Clark, Mavis Thorpe 1909-1999 ...... **CLC 12**
See also CA 57-60; CANR 8, 37, 107; CLR
30; CWRI 5; MAICYA 1, 2; SAAS 5;
SATA 8, 74

Clark, Walter Van Tilburg
1909-1971 .... **CLC 28**
See also CA 9-12R; 33-36R; CANR 63,
113; DLB 9, 206; LAIT 2; RGAL 4;
SATA 8

Clark Bekederemo, J(ohnson) P(epper)
1935- .... **BLC 1; CLC 38; DC 5**
See Clark, J. P.; Clark, John Pepper
See also BW 1; CA 65-68; CANR 16, 72;
DAM DRAM, MULT; DFS 13; EWL 3;
MTCW 1

Clarke, Arthur C(harles) 1917- .... **CLC 1, 4,**
13, 18, 35, 136; SSC 3
See also AAYA 4, 33; BPFB 1; BYA 13;
CA 1-4R; CANR 2, 28, 55, 74, 130; CN
7; CPW; DA3; DAM POP; DLB 261;
JRDA; LAIT 5; MAICYA 1, 2; MTCW 1,
2; SATA 13, 70, 115; SCFW; SFW 4;
SSFS 4, 18; YAW

Clarke, Austin 1896-1974 .... **CLC 6, 9**
See also CA 29-32; 49-52; CAP 2; DAM
POET; DLB 10, 20; EWL 3; RGEL 2

Clarke, Austin C(hesterfield) 1934- .. **BLC 1;**
CLC 8, 53; SSC 45
See also BW 1; CA 25-28R; CAAS 16;
CANR 14, 32, 68; CN 7; DAC; DAM
MULT; DLB 53, 125; DNFS 2; RGSF 2

Clarke, Gillian 1937- .... **CLC 61**
See also CA 106; CP 7; CWP; DLB 40

Clarke, Marcus (Andrew Hislop)
1846-1881 .... **NCLC 19**
See also DLB 230; RGEL 2; RGSF 2

Clarke, Shirley 1925-1997 .... **CLC 16**
See also CA 189

Clash, The
See Headon, (Nicky) Topper; Jones, Mick;
Simonon, Paul; Strummer, Joe

Claudel, Paul (Louis Charles Marie)
1868-1955 .... **TCLC 2, 10**
See also CA 104; 165; DLB 192, 258; EW
8; EWL 3; GFL 1789 to the Present;
RGWL 2, 3; TWA

Claudian 370(?)-404(?) .... **CMLC 46**
See also RGWL 2, 3

Claudius, Matthias 1740-1815 .... **NCLC 75**
See also DLB 97

Clavell, James (duMaresq)
1925-1994 .... **CLC 6, 25, 87**
See also BPFB 1; CA 25-28R; 146; CANR
26, 48; CPW; DA3; DAM NOV, POP;
MTCW 1, 2; NFS 10; RHW

Clayman, Gregory .... **CLC 65**

Cleaver, (Leroy) Eldridge
1935-1998 .... **BLC 1; CLC 30, 119**
See also BW 1, 3; CA 21-24R; 167; CANR
16, 75; DA3; DAM MULT; MTCW 2;
YAW

Cleese, John (Marwood) 1939- .... **CLC 21**
See Monty Python
See also CA 112; 116; CANR 35; MTCW 1

Cleishbotham, Jebediah
See Scott, Sir Walter

Cleland, John 1710-1789 .... **LC 2, 48**
See also DLB 39; RGEL 2

Clemens, Samuel Langhorne 1835-1910
See Twain, Mark
See also CA 104; 135; CDALB 1865-1917;
DA; DA3; DAB; DAC; DAM MST, NOV;
DLB 12, 23, 64, 74, 186, 189; JRDA;
LMFS 1; MAICYA 1, 2; NCFS 4; NFS
20; SATA 100; SSFS 16; YABC 2

Clement of Alexandria
150(?)-215(?) .... **CMLC 41**

Cleophil
See Congreve, William

Clerihew, E.
See Bentley, E(dmund) C(lerihew)

Clerk, N. W.
See Lewis, C(live) S(taples)

Cleveland, John 1613-1658 .... **LC 106**
See also DLB 126; RGEL 2

Cliff, Jimmy .... **CLC 21**
See Chambers, James
See also CA 193

Cliff, Michelle 1946- .... **BLCS; CLC 120**
See also BW 2; CA 116; CANR 39, 72; CD-
WLB 3; DLB 157; FW; GLL 2

Clifford, Lady Anne 1590-1676 .... **LC 76**
See also DLB 151

Clifton, (Thelma) Lucille 1936- .... **BLC 1;**
CLC 19, 66, 162; PC 17
See also AFAW 2; BW 2, 3; CA 49-52;
CANR 2, 24, 42, 76, 97; CLR 5; CP 7;
CSW; CWP; CWRI 5; DA3; DAM MULT,
POET; DLB 5, 41; EXPP; MAICYA 1, 2;
MTCW 1, 2; PFS 1, 14; SATA 20, 69,
128; WP

Clinton, Dirk
See Silverberg, Robert

Clough, Arthur Hugh 1819-1861 ... **NCLC 27**
See also BRW 5; DLB 32; RGEL 2

Clutha, Janet Paterson Frame 1924-2004
See Frame, Janet
See also CA 1-4R; 224; CANR 2, 36, 76,
135; MTCW 1, 2; SATA 119

Clyne, Terence
See Blatty, William Peter

Cobalt, Martin
See Mayne, William (James Carter)

Cook, Michael 1933-1994 .... **CLC 58**
See also CA 93-96; CANR 68; DLB 53
Cook, Robin 1940- .... **CLC 14**
See also AAYA 32; BEST 90:2; BPFB 1;
CA 108; 111; CANR 41, 90, 109; CPW;
DA3; DAM POP; HGG; INT CA-111
Cook, Roy
See Silverberg, Robert
Cooke, Elizabeth 1948- .... **CLC 55**
See also CA 129
Cooke, John Esten 1830-1886 .... **NCLC 5**
See also DLB 3, 248; RGAL 4
Cooke, John Estes
See Baum, L(yman) Frank
Cooke, M. E.
See Creasey, John
Cooke, Margaret
See Creasey, John
Cooke, Rose Terry 1827-1892 ...... **NCLC 110**
See also DLB 12, 74
Cook-Lynn, Elizabeth 1930- .... **CLC 93;
NNAL**
See also CA 133; DAM MULT; DLB 175
Cooney, Ray .... **CLC 62**
See also CBD
Cooper, Anthony Ashley 1671-1713 .. **LC 107**
See also DLB 101
Cooper, Douglas 1960- .... **CLC 86**
Cooper, Henry St. John
See Creasey, John
Cooper, J(oan) California (?)- .... **CLC 56**
See also AAYA 12; BW 1; CA 125; CANR
55; DAM MULT; DLB 212
Cooper, James Fenimore
1789-1851 .... **NCLC 1, 27, 54**
See also AAYA 22; AMW; BPFB 1;
CDALB 1640-1865; DA3; DLB 3, 183,
250, 254; LAIT 1; NFS 9; RGAL 4; SATA
19; TUS; WCH
Cooper, Susan Fenimore
1813-1894 .... **NCLC 129**
See also ANW; DLB 239, 254
Coover, Robert (Lowell) 1932- ...... **CLC 3, 7,
15, 32, 46, 87, 161; SSC 15**
See also AMWS 5; BPFB 1; CA 45-48;
CANR 3, 37, 58, 115; CN 7; DAM NOV;
DLB 2, 227; DLBY 1981; EWL 3;
MTCW 1, 2; RGAL 4; RGSF 2
Copeland, Stewart (Armstrong)
1952- .... **CLC 26**
Copernicus, Nicolaus 1473-1543 .... **LC 45**
Coppard, A(lfred) E(dgar)
1878-1957 .... **SSC 21; TCLC 5**
See also BRWS 8; CA 114; 167; DLB 162;
EWL 3; HGG; RGEL 2; RGSF 2; SUFW
1; YABC 1
Coppee, Francois 1842-1908 .... **TCLC 25**
See also CA 170; DLB 217
Coppola, Francis Ford 1939- ... **CLC 16, 126**
See also AAYA 39; CA 77-80; CANR 40,
78; DLB 44
Copway, George 1818-1869 .... **NNAL**
See also DAM MULT; DLB 175, 183
Corbiere, Tristan 1845-1875 .... **NCLC 43**
See also DLB 217; GFL 1789 to the Present
Corcoran, Barbara (Asenath)
1911- .... **CLC 17**
See also AAYA 14; CA 21-24R, 191; CAAE
191; CAAS 2; CANR 11, 28, 48; CLR
50; DLB 52; JRDA; MAICYA 2; MAIC-
YAS 1; RHW; SAAS 20; SATA 3, 77;
SATA-Essay 125
Cordelier, Maurice
See Giraudoux, Jean(-Hippolyte)
Corelli, Marie .... **TCLC 51**
See Mackay, Mary
See also DLB 34, 156; RGEL 2; SUFW 1
Corinna c. 225B.C.-c. 305B.C. ...... **CMLC 72**

Corman, Cid .... **CLC 9**
See Corman, Sidney
See also CAAS 2; DLB 5, 193
Corman, Sidney 1924-2004
See Corman, Cid
See also CA 85-88; 225; CANR 44; CP 7;
DAM POET
Cormier, Robert (Edmund)
1925-2000 .... **CLC 12, 30**
See also AAYA 3, 19; BYA 1, 2, 6, 8, 9;
CA 1-4R; CANR 5, 23, 76, 93; CDALB
1968-1988; CLR 12, 55; DA; DAB; DAC;
DAM MST, NOV; DLB 52; EXPN; INT
CANR-23; JRDA; LAIT 5; MAICYA 1,
2; MTCW 1, 2; NFS 2, 18; SATA 10, 45,
83; SATA-Obit 122; WYA; YAW
Corn, Alfred (DeWitt III) 1943- .... **CLC 33**
See also CA 179; CAAE 179; CAAS 25;
CANR 44; CP 7; CSW; DLB 120, 282;
DLBY 1980
Corneille, Pierre 1606-1684 ... **DC 21; LC 28**
See also DAB; DAM MST; DLB 268; EW
3; GFL Beginnings to 1789; RGWL 2, 3;
TWA
Cornwell, David (John Moore)
1931- .... **CLC 9, 15**
See le Carre, John
See also CA 5-8R; CANR 13, 33, 59, 107,
132; DA3; DAM POP; MTCW 1, 2
Cornwell, Patricia (Daniels) 1956- . **CLC 155**
See also AAYA 16, 56; BPFB 1; CA 134;
CANR 53, 131; CMW 4; CPW; CSW;
DAM POP; DLB 306; MSW; MTCW 1
Corso, (Nunzio) Gregory 1930-2001 . **CLC 1,
11; PC 33**
See also AMWS 12; BG 2; CA 5-8R; 193;
CANR 41, 76, 132; CP 7; DA3; DLB 5,
16, 237; LMFS 2; MTCW 1, 2; WP
Cortazar, Julio 1914-1984 ... **CLC 2, 3, 5, 10,
13, 15, 33, 34, 92; HLC 1; SSC 7, 76**
See also BPFB 1; CA 21-24R; CANR 12,
32, 81; CDWLB 3; DA3; DAM MULT,
NOV; DLB 113; EWL 3; EXPS; HW 1,
2; LAW; MTCW 1, 2; RGSF 2; RGWL 2,
3; SSFS 3, 20; TWA; WLIT 1
Cortes, Hernan 1485-1547 .... **LC 31**
Corvinus, Jakob
See Raabe, Wilhelm (Karl)
Corwin, Cecil
See Kornbluth, C(yril) M.
Cosic, Dobrica 1921- .... **CLC 14**
See also CA 122; 138; CDWLB 4; CWW
2; DLB 181; EWL 3
Costain, Thomas B(ertram)
1885-1965 .... **CLC 30**
See also BYA 3; CA 5-8R; 25-28R; DLB 9;
RHW
Costantini, Humberto 1924(?)-1987 . **CLC 49**
See also CA 131; 122; EWL 3; HW 1
Costello, Elvis 1954- .... **CLC 21**
See also CA 204
Costenoble, Philostene
See Ghelderode, Michel de
Cotes, Cecil V.
See Duncan, Sara Jeannette
Cotter, Joseph Seamon Sr.
1861-1949 .... **BLC 1; TCLC 28**
See also BW 1; CA 124; DAM MULT; DLB
50
Couch, Arthur Thomas Quiller
See Quiller-Couch, Sir Arthur (Thomas)
Coulton, James
See Hansen, Joseph
Couperus, Louis (Marie Anne)
1863-1923 .... **TCLC 15**
See also CA 115; EWL 3; RGWL 2, 3
Coupland, Douglas 1961- .... **CLC 85, 133**
See also AAYA 34; CA 142; CANR 57, 90,
130; CCA 1; CPW; DAC; DAM POP

Court, Wesli
See Turco, Lewis (Putnam)
Courtenay, Bryce 1933- .... **CLC 59**
See also CA 138; CPW
Courtney, Robert
See Ellison, Harlan (Jay)
Cousteau, Jacques-Yves 1910-1997 .. **CLC 30**
See also CA 65-68; 159; CANR 15, 67;
MTCW 1; SATA 38, 98
Coventry, Francis 1725-1754 .... **LC 46**
Coverdale, Miles c. 1487-1569 .... **LC 77**
See also DLB 167
Cowan, Peter (Walkinshaw)
1914-2002 .... **SSC 28**
See also CA 21-24R; CANR 9, 25, 50, 83;
CN 7; DLB 260; RGSF 2
Coward, Noel (Peirce) 1899-1973 . **CLC 1, 9,
29, 51**
See also AITN 1; BRWS 2; CA 17-18; 41-
44R; CANR 35, 132; CAP 2; CDBLB
1914-1945; DA3; DAM DRAM; DFS 3,
6; DLB 10, 245; EWL 3; IDFW 3, 4;
MTCW 1, 2; RGEL 2; TEA
Cowley, Abraham 1618-1667 .... **LC 43**
See also BRW 2; DLB 131, 151; PAB;
RGEL 2
Cowley, Malcolm 1898-1989 .... **CLC 39**
See also AMWS 2; CA 5-8R; 128; CANR
3, 55; DLB 4, 48; DLBY 1981, 1989;
EWL 3; MTCW 1, 2
Cowper, William 1731-1800 ..... **NCLC 8, 94;
PC 40**
See also BRW 3; DA3; DAM POET; DLB
104, 109; RGEL 2
Cox, William Trevor 1928-
See Trevor, William
See also CA 9-12R; CANR 4, 37, 55, 76,
102; DAM NOV; INT CANR-37; MTCW
1, 2; TEA
Coyne, P. J.
See Masters, Hilary
Cozzens, James Gould 1903-1978 . **CLC 1, 4,
11, 92**
See also AMW; BPFB 1; CA 9-12R; 81-84;
CANR 19; CDALB 1941-1968; DLB 9,
294; DLBD 2; DLBY 1984, 1997; EWL
3; MTCW 1, 2; RGAL 4
Crabbe, George 1754-1832 .... **NCLC 26, 121**
See also BRW 3; DLB 93; RGEL 2
Crace, Jim 1946- .... **CLC 157; SSC 61**
See also CA 128; 135; CANR 55, 70, 123;
CN 7; DLB 231; INT CA-135
Craddock, Charles Egbert
See Murfree, Mary Noailles
Craig, A. A.
See Anderson, Poul (William)
Craik, Mrs.
See Craik, Dinah Maria (Mulock)
See also RGEL 2
Craik, Dinah Maria (Mulock)
1826-1887 .... **NCLC 38**
See Craik, Mrs.; Mulock, Dinah Maria
See also DLB 35, 163; MAICYA 1, 2;
SATA 34
Cram, Ralph Adams 1863-1942 ..... **TCLC 45**
See also CA 160
Cranch, Christopher Pearse
1813-1892 .... **NCLC 115**
See also DLB 1, 42, 243
Crane, (Harold) Hart 1899-1932 .... **PC 3;
TCLC 2, 5, 80; WLC**
See also AMW; AMWR 2; CA 104; 127;
CDALB 1917-1929; DA; DA3; DAB;
DAC; DAM MST, POET; DLB 4, 48;
EWL 3; MTCW 1, 2; RGAL 4; TUS
Crane, R(onald) S(almon)
1886-1967 .... **CLC 27**
See also CA 85-88; DLB 63

Dabrowska, Maria (Szumska)
1889-1965 .... **CLC 15**
See also CA 106; CDWLB 4; DLB 215;
EWL 3

Dabydeen, David 1955- .... **CLC 34**
See also BW 1; CA 125; CANR 56, 92; CN
7; CP 7

Dacey, Philip 1939- .... **CLC 51**
See also CA 37-40R; CAAS 17; CANR 14,
32, 64; CP 7; DLB 105

Dafydd ap Gwilym c. 1320-c. 1380 ..... **PC 56**

Dagerman, Stig (Halvard)
1923-1954 .... **TCLC 17**
See also CA 117; 155; DLB 259; EWL 3

D'Aguiar, Fred 1960- .... **CLC 145**
See also CA 148; CANR 83, 101; CP 7;
DLB 157; EWL 3

Dahl, Roald 1916-1990 .... **CLC 1, 6, 18, 79**
See also AAYA 15; BPFB 1; BRWS 4; BYA
5; CA 1-4R; 133; CANR 6, 32, 37, 62;
CLR 1, 7, 41; CPW; DA3; DAB; DAC;
DAM MST, NOV, POP; DLB 139, 255;
HGG; JRDA; MAICYA 1, 2; MTCW 1,
2; RGSF 2; SATA 1, 26, 73; SATA-Obit
65; SSFS 4; TEA; YAW

Dahlberg, Edward 1900-1977 .. **CLC 1, 7, 14**
See also CA 9-12R; 69-72; CANR 31, 62;
DLB 48; MTCW 1; RGAL 4

Daitch, Susan 1954- .... **CLC 103**
See also CA 161

Dale, Colin .... **TCLC 18**
See Lawrence, T(homas) E(dward)

Dale, George E.
See Asimov, Isaac

Dalton, Roque 1935-1975(?) ..... **HLCS 1; PC
36**
See also CA 176; DLB 283; HW 2

Daly, Elizabeth 1878-1967 .... **CLC 52**
See also CA 23-24; 25-28R; CANR 60;
CAP 2; CMW 4

Daly, Mary 1928- .... **CLC 173**
See also CA 25-28R; CANR 30, 62; FW;
GLL 1; MTCW 1

Daly, Maureen 1921- .... **CLC 17**
See also AAYA 5, 58; BYA 6; CANR 37,
83, 108; CLR 96; JRDA; MAICYA 1, 2;
SAAS 1; SATA 2, 129; WYA; YAW

Damas, Leon-Gontran 1912-1978 .... **CLC 84**
See also BW 1; CA 125; 73-76; EWL 3

Dana, Richard Henry Sr.
1787-1879 .... **NCLC 53**

Daniel, Samuel 1562(?)-1619 .... **LC 24**
See also DLB 62; RGEL 2

Daniels, Brett
See Adler, Renata

Dannay, Frederic 1905-1982 .... **CLC 11**
See Queen, Ellery
See also CA 1-4R; 107; CANR 1, 39; CMW
4; DAM POP; DLB 137; MTCW 1

D'Annunzio, Gabriele 1863-1938 ... **TCLC 6,
40**
See also CA 104; 155; EW 8; EWL 3;
RGWL 2, 3; TWA

Danois, N. le
See Gourmont, Remy(-Marie-Charles) de

Dante 1265-1321 .... **CMLC 3, 18, 39, 70; PC
21; WLCS**
See also DA; DA3; DAB; DAC; DAM
MST, POET; EFS 1; EW 1; LAIT 1;
RGWL 2, 3; TWA; WP

d'Antibes, Germain
See Simenon, Georges (Jacques Christian)

Danticat, Edwidge 1969- .... **CLC 94, 139**
See also AAYA 29; CA 152, 192; CAAE
192; CANR 73, 129; DNFS 1; EXPS;
LATS 1:2; MTCW 1; SSFS 1; YAW

Danvers, Dennis 1947- .... **CLC 70**

Danziger, Paula 1944-2004 .... **CLC 21**
See also AAYA 4, 36; BYA 6, 7, 14; CA
112; 115; 229; CANR 37, 132; CLR 20;
JRDA; MAICYA 1, 2; SATA 36, 63, 102,
149; SATA-Brief 30; WYA; YAW

Da Ponte, Lorenzo 1749-1838 .... **NCLC 50**

Dario, Ruben 1867-1916 .... **HLC 1; PC 15;
TCLC 4**
See also CA 131; CANR 81; DAM MULT;
DLB 290; EWL 3; HW 1, 2; LAW;
MTCW 1, 2; RGWL 2, 3

Darley, George 1795-1846 .... **NCLC 2**
See also DLB 96; RGEL 2

Darrow, Clarence (Seward)
1857-1938 .... **TCLC 81**
See also CA 164; DLB 303

Darwin, Charles 1809-1882 .... **NCLC 57**
See also BRWS 7; DLB 57, 166; LATS 1:1;
RGEL 2; TEA; WLIT 4

Darwin, Erasmus 1731-1802 .... **NCLC 106**
See also DLB 93; RGEL 2

Daryush, Elizabeth 1887-1977 ...... **CLC 6, 19**
See also CA 49-52; CANR 3, 81; DLB 20

Das, Kamala 1934- .... **CLC 191; PC 43**
See also CA 101; CANR 27, 59; CP 7;
CWP; FW

Dasgupta, Surendranath
1887-1952 .... **TCLC 81**
See also CA 157

**Dashwood, Edmee Elizabeth Monica de la
Pasture** 1890-1943
See Delafield, E. M.
See also CA 119; 154

da Silva, Antonio Jose
1705-1739 .... **NCLC 114**

Daudet, (Louis Marie) Alphonse
1840-1897 .... **NCLC 1**
See also DLB 123; GFL 1789 to the Present;
RGSF 2

d'Aulnoy, Marie-Catherine c.
1650-1705 .... **LC 100**

Daumal, Rene 1908-1944 .... **TCLC 14**
See also CA 114; EWL 3

Davenant, William 1606-1668 .... **LC 13**
See also DLB 58, 126; RGEL 2

Davenport, Guy (Mattison, Jr.)
1927-2005 .... **CLC 6, 14, 38; SSC 16**
See also CA 33-36R; CANR 23, 73; CN 7;
CSW; DLB 130

David, Robert
See Nezval, Vitezslav

Davidson, Avram (James) 1923-1993
See Queen, Ellery
See also CA 101; 171; CANR 26; DLB 8;
FANT; SFW 4; SUFW 1, 2

Davidson, Donald (Grady)
1893-1968 .... **CLC 2, 13, 19**
See also CA 5-8R; 25-28R; CANR 4, 84;
DLB 45

Davidson, Hugh
See Hamilton, Edmond

Davidson, John 1857-1909 .... **TCLC 24**
See also CA 118; 217; DLB 19; RGEL 2

Davidson, Sara 1943- .... **CLC 9**
See also CA 81-84; CANR 44, 68; DLB
185

Davie, Donald (Alfred) 1922-1995 .... **CLC 5,
8, 10, 31; PC 29**
See also BRWS 6; CA 1-4R; 149; CAAS 3;
CANR 1, 44; CP 7; DLB 27; MTCW 1;
RGEL 2

Davie, Elspeth 1919-1995 .... **SSC 52**
See also CA 120; 126; 150; DLB 139

Davies, Ray(mond Douglas) 1944- .. **CLC 21**
See also CA 116; 146; CANR 92

Davies, Rhys 1901-1978 .... **CLC 23**
See also CA 9-12R; 81-84; CANR 4; DLB
139, 191

Davies, (William) Robertson
1913-1995 .... **CLC 2, 7, 13, 25, 42, 75,
91; WLC**
See Marchbanks, Samuel
See also BEST 89:2; BPFB 1; CA 33-36R;
150; CANR 17, 42, 103; CN 7; CPW;
DA; DA3; DAB; DAC; DAM MST, NOV,
POP; DLB 68; EWL 3; HGG; INT CANR-
17; MTCW 1, 2; RGEL 2; TWA

Davies, Sir John 1569-1626 .... **LC 85**
See also DLB 172

Davies, Walter C.
See Kornbluth, C(yril) M.

Davies, William Henry 1871-1940 ... **TCLC 5**
See also CA 104; 179; DLB 19, 174; EWL
3; RGEL 2

Da Vinci, Leonardo 1452-1519 ..... **LC 12, 57,
60**
See also AAYA 40

Davis, Angela (Yvonne) 1944- .... **CLC 77**
See also BW 2, 3; CA 57-60; CANR 10,
81; CSW; DA3; DAM MULT; FW

Davis, B. Lynch
See Bioy Casares, Adolfo; Borges, Jorge
Luis

Davis, Frank Marshall 1905-1987 ...... **BLC 1**
See also BW 2, 3; CA 125; 123; CANR 42,
80; DAM MULT; DLB 51

Davis, Gordon
See Hunt, E(verette) Howard, (Jr.)

Davis, H(arold) L(enoir) 1896-1960 . **CLC 49**
See also ANW; CA 178; 89-92; DLB 9,
206; SATA 114

Davis, Rebecca (Blaine) Harding
1831-1910 .... **SSC 38; TCLC 6**
See also CA 104; 179; DLB 74, 239; FW;
NFS 14; RGAL 4; TUS

Davis, Richard Harding
1864-1916 .... **TCLC 24**
See also CA 114; 179; DLB 12, 23, 78, 79,
189; DLBD 13; RGAL 4

Davison, Frank Dalby 1893-1970 ..... **CLC 15**
See also CA 217; 116; DLB 260

Davison, Lawrence H.
See Lawrence, D(avid) H(erbert Richards)

Davison, Peter (Hubert) 1928- .... **CLC 28**
See also CA 9-12R; CAAS 4; CANR 3, 43,
84; CP 7; DLB 5

Davys, Mary 1674-1732 .... **LC 1, 46**
See also DLB 39

Dawson, (Guy) Fielding (Lewis)
1930-2002 .... **CLC 6**
See also CA 85-88; 202; CANR 108; DLB
130; DLBY 2002

Dawson, Peter
See Faust, Frederick (Schiller)
See also TCWW 2, 2

Day, Clarence (Shepard, Jr.)
1874-1935 .... **TCLC 25**
See also CA 108; 199; DLB 11

Day, John 1574(?)-1640(?) .... **LC 70**
See also DLB 62, 170; RGEL 2

Day, Thomas 1748-1789 .... **LC 1**
See also DLB 39; YABC 1

Day Lewis, C(ecil) 1904-1972 . **CLC 1, 6, 10;
PC 11**
See Blake, Nicholas
See also BRWS 3; CA 13-16; 33-36R;
CANR 34; CAP 1; CWRI 5; DAM POET;
DLB 15, 20; EWL 3; MTCW 1, 2; RGEL
2

Dazai Osamu .... **SSC 41; TCLC 11**
See Tsushima, Shuji
See also CA 164; DLB 182; EWL 3; MJW;
RGSF 2; RGWL 2, 3; TWA

de Andrade, Carlos Drummond
See Drummond de Andrade, Carlos

Derleth, August (William)
1909-1971 .... **CLC 31**
See also BPFB 1; BYA 9, 10; CA 1-4R; 29-32R; CANR 4; CMW 4; DLB 9; DLBD 17; HGG; SATA 5; SUFW 1

Der Nister 1884-1950 .... **TCLC 56**
See Nister, Der

de Routisie, Albert
See Aragon, Louis

Derrida, Jacques 1930-2004 .... **CLC 24, 87**
See also CA 124; 127; CANR 76, 98, 133; DLB 242; EWL 3; LMFS 2; MTCW 1; TWA

Derry Down Derry
See Lear, Edward

Dersonnes, Jacques
See Simenon, Georges (Jacques Christian)

Desai, Anita 1937- .... **CLC 19, 37, 97, 175**
See also BRWS 5; CA 81-84; CANR 33, 53, 95, 133; CN 7; CWRI 5; DA3; DAB; DAM NOV; DLB 271; DNFS 2; EWL 3; FW; MTCW 1, 2; SATA 63, 126

Desai, Kiran 1971- .... **CLC 119**
See also BYA 16; CA 171; CANR 127

de Saint-Luc, Jean
See Glassco, John

de Saint Roman, Arnaud
See Aragon, Louis

Desbordes-Valmore, Marceline
1786-1859 .... **NCLC 97**
See also DLB 217

Descartes, Rene 1596-1650 .... **LC 20, 35**
See also DLB 268; EW 3; GFL Beginnings to 1789

Deschamps, Eustache 1340(?)-1404 .. **LC 103**
See also DLB 208

De Sica, Vittorio 1901(?)-1974 .... **CLC 20**
See also CA 117

Desnos, Robert 1900-1945 .... **TCLC 22**
See also CA 121; 151; CANR 107; DLB 258; EWL 3; LMFS 2

Destouches, Louis-Ferdinand
1894-1961 .... **CLC 9, 15**
See Celine, Louis-Ferdinand
See also CA 85-88; CANR 28; MTCW 1

de Tolignac, Gaston
See Griffith, D(avid Lewelyn) W(ark)

Deutsch, Babette 1895-1982 .... **CLC 18**
See also BYA 3; CA 1-4R; 108; CANR 4, 79; DLB 45; SATA 1; SATA-Obit 33

Devenant, William 1606-1649 .... **LC 13**

Devkota, Laxmiprasad 1909-1959 . **TCLC 23**
See also CA 123

De Voto, Bernard (Augustine)
1897-1955 .... **TCLC 29**
See also CA 113; 160; DLB 9, 256

De Vries, Peter 1910-1993 ..... **CLC 1, 2, 3, 7, 10, 28, 46**
See also CA 17-20R; 142; CANR 41; DAM NOV; DLB 6; DLBY 1982; MTCW 1, 2

Dewey, John 1859-1952 .... **TCLC 95**
See also CA 114; 170; DLB 246, 270; RGAL 4

Dexter, John
See Bradley, Marion Zimmer
See also GLL 1

Dexter, Martin
See Faust, Frederick (Schiller)
See also TCWW 2

Dexter, Pete 1943- .... **CLC 34, 55**
See also BEST 89:2; CA 127; 131; CANR 129; CPW; DAM POP; INT CA-131; MTCW 1

Diamano, Silmang
See Senghor, Leopold Sedar

Diamond, Neil 1941- .... **CLC 30**
See also CA 108

Diaz del Castillo, Bernal
1496-1584 .... **HLCS 1; LC 31**
See also LAW

di Bassetto, Corno
See Shaw, George Bernard

Dick, Philip K(indred) 1928-1982 ... **CLC 10, 30, 72; SSC 57**
See also AAYA 24; BPFB 1; BYA 11; CA 49-52; 106; CANR 2, 16, 132; CPW; DA3; DAM NOV, POP; DLB 8; MTCW 1, 2; NFS 5; SCFW; SFW 4

Dickens, Charles (John Huffam)
1812-1870 .... **NCLC 3, 8, 18, 26, 37, 50, 86, 105, 113; SSC 17, 49; WLC**
See also AAYA 23; BRW 5; BRWC 1, 2; BYA 1, 2, 3, 13, 14; CDBLB 1832-1890; CLR 95; CMW 4; DA; DA3; DAB; DAC; DAM MST, NOV; DLB 21, 55, 70, 159, 166; EXPN; HGG; JRDA; LAIT 1, 2; LATS 1:1; LMFS 1; MAICYA 1, 2; NFS 4, 5, 10, 14, 20; RGEL 2; RGSF 2; SATA 15; SUFW 1; TEA; WCH; WLIT 4; WYA

Dickey, James (Lafayette)
1923-1997 .... **CLC 1, 2, 4, 7, 10, 15, 47, 109; PC 40; TCLC 151**
See also AAYA 50; AITN 1, 2; AMWS 4; BPFB 1; CA 9-12R; 156; CABS 2; CANR 10, 48, 61, 105; CDALB 1968-1988; CP 7; CPW; CSW; DA3; DAM NOV, POET, POP; DLB 5, 193; DLBD 7; DLBY 1982, 1993, 1996, 1997, 1998; EWL 3; INT CANR-10; MTCW 1, 2; NFS 9; PFS 6, 11; RGAL 4; TUS

Dickey, William 1928-1994 .... **CLC 3, 28**
See also CA 9-12R; 145; CANR 24, 79; DLB 5

Dickinson, Charles 1951- .... **CLC 49**
See also CA 128

Dickinson, Emily (Elizabeth)
1830-1886 ... **NCLC 21, 77; PC 1; WLC**
See also AAYA 22; AMW; AMWR 1; CDALB 1865-1917; DA; DA3; DAB; DAC; DAM MST, POET; DLB 1, 243; EXPP; MAWW; PAB; PFS 1, 2, 3, 4, 5, 6, 8, 10, 11, 13, 16; RGAL 4; SATA 29; TUS; WP; WYA

Dickinson, Mrs. Herbert Ward
See Phelps, Elizabeth Stuart

Dickinson, Peter (Malcolm de Brissac)
1927- .... **CLC 12, 35**
See also AAYA 9, 49; BYA 5; CA 41-44R; CANR 31, 58, 88, 134; CLR 29; CMW 4; DLB 87, 161, 276; JRDA; MAICYA 1, 2; SATA 5, 62, 95, 150; SFW 4; WYA; YAW

Dickson, Carr
See Carr, John Dickson

Dickson, Carter
See Carr, John Dickson

Diderot, Denis 1713-1784 .... **LC 26**
See also EW 4; GFL Beginnings to 1789; LMFS 1; RGWL 2, 3

Didion, Joan 1934- . **CLC 1, 3, 8, 14, 32, 129**
See also AITN 1; AMWS 4; CA 5-8R; CANR 14, 52, 76, 125; CDALB 1968-1988; CN 7; DA3; DAM NOV; DLB 2, 173, 185; DLBY 1981, 1986; EWL 3; MAWW; MTCW 1, 2; NFS 3; RGAL 4; TCWW 2; TUS

di Donato, Pietro 1911-1992 .... **TCLC 159**
See also CA 101; 136; DLB 9

Dietrich, Robert
See Hunt, E(verette) Howard, (Jr.)

Difusa, Pati
See Almodovar, Pedro

Dillard, Annie 1945- .... **CLC 9, 60, 115**
See also AAYA 6, 43; AMWS 6; ANW; CA 49-52; CANR 3, 43, 62, 90, 125; DA3; DAM NOV; DLB 275, 278; DLBY 1980; LAIT 4, 5; MTCW 1, 2; NCFS 1; RGAL 4; SATA 10, 140; TUS

Dillard, R(ichard) H(enry) W(ilde)
1937- .... **CLC 5**
See also CA 21-24R; CAAS 7; CANR 10; CP 7; CSW; DLB 5, 244

Dillon, Eilis 1920-1994 .... **CLC 17**
See also CA 9-12R; 182; 147; CAAE 182; CAAS 3; CANR 4, 38, 78; CLR 26; MAI-CYA 1, 2; MAICYAS 1; SATA 2, 74; SATA-Essay 105; SATA-Obit 83; YAW

Dimont, Penelope
See Mortimer, Penelope (Ruth)

Dinesen, Isak ..... **CLC 10, 29, 95; SSC 7, 75**
See Blixen, Karen (Christentze Dinesen)
See also EW 10; EWL 3; EXPS; FW; HGG; LAIT 3; MTCW 1; NCFS 2; NFS 9; RGSF 2; RGWL 2, 3; SSFS 3, 6, 13; WLIT 2

Ding Ling .... **CLC 68**
See Chiang, Pin-chin
See also RGWL 3

Diphusa, Patty
See Almodovar, Pedro

Disch, Thomas M(ichael) 1940- ... **CLC 7, 36**
See Disch, Tom
See also AAYA 17; BPFB 1; CA 21-24R; CAAS 4; CANR 17, 36, 54, 89; CLR 18; CP 7; DA3; DLB 8; HGG; MAICYA 1, 2; MTCW 1, 2; SAAS 15; SATA 92; SCFW; SFW 4; SUFW 2

Disch, Tom
See Disch, Thomas M(ichael)
See also DLB 282

d'Isly, Georges
See Simenon, Georges (Jacques Christian)

Disraeli, Benjamin 1804-1881 ... **NCLC 2, 39, 79**
See also BRW 4; DLB 21, 55; RGEL 2

Ditcum, Steve
See Crumb, R(obert)

Dixon, Paige
See Corcoran, Barbara (Asenath)

Dixon, Stephen 1936- .... **CLC 52; SSC 16**
See also AMWS 12; CA 89-92; CANR 17, 40, 54, 91; CN 7; DLB 130

Djebar, Assia 1936- .... **CLC 182**
See also CA 188; EWL 3; RGWL 3; WLIT 2

Doak, Annie
See Dillard, Annie

Dobell, Sydney Thompson
1824-1874 .... **NCLC 43**
See also DLB 32; RGEL 2

Doblin, Alfred .... **TCLC 13**
See Doeblin, Alfred
See also CDWLB 2; EWL 3; RGWL 2, 3

Dobroliubov, Nikolai Aleksandrovich
See Dobrolyubov, Nikolai Alexandrovich
See also DLB 277

Dobrolyubov, Nikolai Alexandrovich
1836-1861 .... **NCLC 5**
See Dobroliubov, Nikolai Aleksandrovich

Dobson, Austin 1840-1921 .... **TCLC 79**
See also DLB 35, 144

Dobyns, Stephen 1941- .... **CLC 37**
See also AMWS 13; CA 45-48; CANR 2, 18, 99; CMW 4; CP 7

Doctorow, E(dgar) L(aurence)
1931- .... **CLC 6, 11, 15, 18, 37, 44, 65, 113**
See also AAYA 22; AITN 2; AMWS 4; BEST 89:3; BPFB 1; CA 45-48; CANR 2, 33, 51, 76, 97, 133; CDALB 1968-1988; CN 7; CPW; DA3; DAM NOV, POP; DLB 2, 28, 173; DLBY 1980; EWL 3; LAIT 3; MTCW 1, 2; NFS 6; RGAL 4; RHW; TUS

Dodgson, Charles L(utwidge) 1832-1898
See Carroll, Lewis
See also CLR 2; DA; DA3; DAB; DAC;
DAM MST, NOV, POET; MAICYA 1, 2;
SATA 100; YABC 2

Dodsley, Robert 1703-1764 .... **LC 97**
See also DLB 95; RGEL 2

Dodson, Owen (Vincent) 1914-1983 .. **BLC 1;
CLC 79**
See also BW 1; CA 65-68; 110; CANR 24;
DAM MULT; DLB 76

Doeblin, Alfred 1878-1957 .... **TCLC 13**
See Doblin, Alfred
See also CA 110; 141; DLB 66

Doerr, Harriet 1910-2002 .... **CLC 34**
See also CA 117; 122; 213; CANR 47; INT
CA-122; LATS 1:2

Domecq, H(onorio Bustos)
See Bioy Casares, Adolfo

Domecq, H(onorio) Bustos
See Bioy Casares, Adolfo; Borges, Jorge
Luis

Domini, Rey
See Lorde, Audre (Geraldine)
See also GLL 1

Dominique
See Proust, (Valentin-Louis-George-Eugene)
Marcel

Don, A
See Stephen, Sir Leslie

Donaldson, Stephen R(eeder)
1947- .... **CLC 46, 138**
See also AAYA 36; BPFB 1; CA 89-92;
CANR 13, 55, 99; CPW; DAM POP;
FANT; INT CANR-13; SATA 121; SFW
4; SUFW 1, 2

Donleavy, J(ames) P(atrick) 1926- .... **CLC 1,
4, 6, 10, 45**
See also AITN 2; BPFB 1; CA 9-12R;
CANR 24, 49, 62, 80, 124; CBD; CD 5;
CN 7; DLB 6, 173; INT CANR-24;
MTCW 1, 2; RGAL 4

Donnadieu, Marguerite
See Duras, Marguerite

Donne, John 1572-1631 ... **LC 10, 24, 91; PC
1, 43; WLC**
See also BRW 1; BRWC 1; BRWR 2; CD-
BLB Before 1660; DA; DAB; DAC;
DAM MST, POET; DLB 121, 151; EXPP;
PAB; PFS 2, 11; RGEL 3; TEA; WLIT 3;
WP

Donnell, David 1939(?)- .... **CLC 34**
See also CA 197

Donoghue, P. S.
See Hunt, E(verette) Howard, (Jr.)

Donoso (Yanez), Jose 1924-1996 ... **CLC 4, 8,
11, 32, 99; HLC 1; SSC 34; TCLC 133**
See also CA 81-84; 155; CANR 32, 73; CD-
WLB 3; CWW 2; DAM MULT; DLB 113;
EWL 3; HW 1, 2; LAW; LAWS 1; MTCW
1, 2; RGSF 2; WLIT 1

Donovan, John 1928-1992 .... **CLC 35**
See also AAYA 20; CA 97-100; 137; CLR
3; MAICYA 1, 2; SATA 72; SATA-Brief
29; YAW

Don Roberto
See Cunninghame Graham, Robert
(Gallnigad) Bontine

Doolittle, Hilda 1886-1961 . **CLC 3, 8, 14, 31,
34, 73; PC 5; WLC**
See H. D.
See also AMWS 1; CA 97-100; CANR 35,
131; DA; DAC; DAM MST, POET; DLB
4, 45; EWL 3; FW; GLL 1; LMFS 2;
MAWW; MTCW 1, 2; PFS 6; RGAL 4

Doppo, Kunikida .... **TCLC 99**
See Kunikida Doppo

Dorfman, Ariel 1942- .... **CLC 48, 77, 189;
HLC 1**
See also CA 124; 130; CANR 67, 70, 135;
CWW 2; DAM MULT; DFS 4; EWL 3;
HW 1, 2; INT CA-130; WLIT 1

Dorn, Edward (Merton)
1929-1999 .... **CLC 10, 18**
See also CA 93-96; 187; CANR 42, 79; CP
7; DLB 5; INT CA-93-96; WP

Dor-Ner, Zvi .... **CLC 70**

Dorris, Michael (Anthony)
1945-1997 .... **CLC 109; NNAL**
See also AAYA 20; BEST 90:1; BYA 12;
CA 102; 157; CANR 19, 46, 75; CLR 58;
DA3; DAM MULT, NOV; DLB 175;
LAIT 5; MTCW 2; NFS 3; RGAL 4;
SATA 75; SATA-Obit 94; TCWW 2; YAW

Dorris, Michael A.
See Dorris, Michael (Anthony)

Dorsan, Luc
See Simenon, Georges (Jacques Christian)

Dorsange, Jean
See Simenon, Georges (Jacques Christian)

Dorset
See Sackville, Thomas

Dos Passos, John (Roderigo)
1896-1970 ... **CLC 1, 4, 8, 11, 15, 25, 34,
82; WLC**
See also AMW; BPFB 1; CA 1-4R; 29-32R;
CANR 3; CDALB 1929-1941; DA; DA3;
DAB; DAC; DAM MST, NOV; DLB 4,
9, 274; DLBD 1, 15; DLBY 1996; EWL
3; MTCW 1, 2; NFS 14; RGAL 4; TUS

Dossage, Jean
See Simenon, Georges (Jacques Christian)

Dostoevsky, Fedor Mikhailovich
1821-1881 .. **NCLC 2, 7, 21, 33, 43, 119;
SSC 2, 33, 44; WLC**
See Dostoevsky, Fyodor
See also AAYA 40; DA; DA3; DAB; DAC;
DAM MST, NOV; EW 7; EXPN; NFS 3,
8; RGSF 2; RGWL 2, 3; SSFS 8; TWA

Dostoevsky, Fyodor
See Dostoevsky, Fedor Mikhailovich
See also DLB 238; LATS 1:1; LMFS 1, 2

Doty, M. R.
See Doty, Mark (Alan)

Doty, Mark
See Doty, Mark (Alan)

Doty, Mark (Alan) 1953(?)- .... **CLC 176; PC
53**
See also AMWS 11; CA 161, 183; CAAE
183; CANR 110

Doty, Mark A.
See Doty, Mark (Alan)

Doughty, Charles M(ontagu)
1843-1926 .... **TCLC 27**
See also CA 115; 178; DLB 19, 57, 174

Douglas, Ellen .... **CLC 73**
See Haxton, Josephine Ayres; Williamson,
Ellen Douglas
See also CN 7; CSW; DLB 292

Douglas, Gavin 1475(?)-1522 .... **LC 20**
See also DLB 132; RGEL 2

Douglas, George
See Brown, George Douglas
See also RGEL 2

Douglas, Keith (Castellain)
1920-1944 .... **TCLC 40**
See also BRW 7; CA 160; DLB 27; EWL
3; PAB; RGEL 2

Douglas, Leonard
See Bradbury, Ray (Douglas)

Douglas, Michael
See Crichton, (John) Michael

Douglas, (George) Norman
1868-1952 .... **TCLC 68**
See also BRW 6; CA 119; 157; DLB 34,
195; RGEL 2

Douglas, William
See Brown, George Douglas

Douglass, Frederick 1817(?)-1895 ..... **BLC 1;
NCLC 7, 55, 141; WLC**
See also AAYA 48; AFAW 1, 2; AMWC 1;
AMWS 3; CDALB 1640-1865; DA; DA3;
DAC; DAM MST, MULT; DLB 1, 43, 50,
79, 243; FW; LAIT 2; NCFS 2; RGAL 4;
SATA 29

Dourado, (Waldomiro Freitas) Autran
1926- .... **CLC 23, 60**
See also CA 25-28R; 179; CANR 34, 81;
DLB 145, 307; HW 2

Dourado, Waldomiro Freitas Autran
See Dourado, (Waldomiro Freitas) Autran

Dove, Rita (Frances) 1952- . **BLCS; CLC 50,
81; PC 6**
See also AAYA 46; AMWS 4; BW 2; CA
109; CAAS 19; CANR 27, 42, 68, 76, 97,
132; CDALBS; CP 7; CSW; CWP; DA3;
DAM MULT, POET; DLB 120; EWL 3;
EXPP; MTCW 1; PFS 1, 15; RGAL 4

Doveglion
See Villa, Jose Garcia

Dowell, Coleman 1925-1985 .... **CLC 60**
See also CA 25-28R; 117; CANR 10; DLB
130; GLL 2

Dowson, Ernest (Christopher)
1867-1900 .... **TCLC 4**
See also CA 105; 150; DLB 19, 135; RGEL
2

Doyle, A. Conan
See Doyle, Sir Arthur Conan

Doyle, Sir Arthur Conan
1859-1930 .... **SSC 12; TCLC 7; WLC**
See Conan Doyle, Arthur
See also AAYA 14; BRWS 2; CA 104; 122;
CANR 131; CDBLB 1890-1914; CMW
4; DA; DA3; DAB; DAC; DAM MST,
NOV; DLB 18, 70, 156, 178; EXPS;
HGG; LAIT 2; MSW; MTCW 1, 2; RGEL
2; RGSF 2; RHW; SATA 24; SCFW 2;
SFW 4; SSFS 2; TEA; WCH; WLIT 4;
WYA; YAW

Doyle, Conan
See Doyle, Sir Arthur Conan

Doyle, John
See Graves, Robert (von Ranke)

Doyle, Roddy 1958(?)- .... **CLC 81, 178**
See also AAYA 14; BRWS 5; CA 143;
CANR 73, 128; CN 7; DA3; DLB 194

Doyle, Sir A. Conan
See Doyle, Sir Arthur Conan

Dr. A
See Asimov, Isaac; Silverstein, Alvin; Silverstein, Virginia B(arbara Opshelor)

Drabble, Margaret 1939- ...... **CLC 2, 3, 5, 8,
10, 22, 53, 129**
See also BRWS 4; CA 13-16R; CANR 18,
35, 63, 112, 131; CDBLB 1960 to Present;
CN 7; CPW; DA3; DAB; DAC; DAM
MST, NOV, POP; DLB 14, 155, 231;
EWL 3; FW; MTCW 1, 2; RGEL 2; SATA
48; TEA

Drakulic, Slavenka 1949- .... **CLC 173**
See also CA 144; CANR 92

Drakulic-Ilic, Slavenka
See Drakulic, Slavenka

Drapier, M. B.
See Swift, Jonathan

Drayham, James
See Mencken, H(enry) L(ouis)

Drayton, Michael 1563-1631 .... **LC 8**
See also DAM POET; DLB 121; RGEL 2

Dreadstone, Carl
See Campbell, (John) Ramsey

Dreiser, Theodore (Herman Albert)
1871-1945 .... **SSC 30; TCLC 10, 18, 35, 83; WLC**
See also AMW; AMWC 2; AMWR 2; BYA 15, 16; CA 106; 132; CDALB 1865-1917; DA; DA3; DAC; DAM MST, NOV; DLB 9, 12, 102, 137; DLBD 1; EWL 3; LAIT 2; LMFS 2; MTCW 1, 2; NFS 8, 17; RGAL 4; TUS

Drexler, Rosalyn 1926- .... **CLC 2, 6**
See also CA 81-84; CAD; CANR 68, 124; CD 5; CWD

Dreyer, Carl Theodor 1889-1968 ...... **CLC 16**
See also CA 116

Drieu la Rochelle, Pierre(-Eugene)
1893-1945 .... **TCLC 21**
See also CA 117; DLB 72; EWL 3; GFL 1789 to the Present

Drinkwater, John 1882-1937 .... **TCLC 57**
See also CA 109; 149; DLB 10, 19, 149; RGEL 2

Drop Shot
See Cable, George Washington

Droste-Hulshoff, Annette Freiin von
1797-1848 .... **NCLC 3, 133**
See also CDWLB 2; DLB 133; RGSF 2; RGWL 2, 3

Drummond, Walter
See Silverberg, Robert

Drummond, William Henry
1854-1907 .... **TCLC 25**
See also CA 160; DLB 92

Drummond de Andrade, Carlos
1902-1987 .... **CLC 18; TCLC 139**
See Andrade, Carlos Drummond de
See also CA 132; 123; DLB 307; LAW

Drummond of Hawthornden, William
1585-1649 .... **LC 83**
See also DLB 121, 213; RGEL 2

Drury, Allen (Stuart) 1918-1998 .... **CLC 37**
See also CA 57-60; 170; CANR 18, 52; CN 7; INT CANR-18

Druse, Eleanor
See King, Stephen (Edwin)

Dryden, John 1631-1700 ..... **DC 3; LC 3, 21; PC 25; WLC**
See also BRW 2; CDBLB 1660-1789; DA; DAB; DAC; DAM DRAM, MST, POET; DLB 80, 101, 131; EXPP; IDTP; LMFS 1; RGEL 2; TEA; WLIT 3

du Bellay, Joachim 1524-1560 .... **LC 92**
See also GFL Beginnings to 1789; RGWL 2, 3

Duberman, Martin (Bauml) 1930- ..... **CLC 8**
See also CA 1-4R; CAD; CANR 2, 63; CD 5

Dubie, Norman (Evans) 1945- .... **CLC 36**
See also CA 69-72; CANR 12, 115; CP 7; DLB 120; PFS 12

Du Bois, W(illiam) E(dward) B(urghardt)
1868-1963 ..... **BLC 1; CLC 1, 2, 13, 64, 96; HR 2; WLC**
See also AAYA 40; AFAW 1, 2; AMWC 1; AMWS 2; BW 1, 3; CA 85-88; CANR 34, 82, 132; CDALB 1865-1917; DA; DA3; DAC; DAM MST, MULT, NOV; DLB 47, 50, 91, 246, 284; EWL 3; EXPP; LAIT 2; LMFS 2; MTCW 1, 2; NCFS 1; PFS 13; RGAL 4; SATA 42

Dubus, Andre 1936-1999 ..... **CLC 13, 36, 97; SSC 15**
See also AMWS 7; CA 21-24R; 177; CANR 17; CN 7; CSW; DLB 130; INT CANR-17; RGAL 4; SSFS 10

Duca Minimo
See D'Annunzio, Gabriele

Ducharme, Rejean 1941- .... **CLC 74**
See also CA 165; DLB 60

du Chatelet, Emilie 1706-1749 .... **LC 96**

Duchen, Claire .... **CLC 65**

Duclos, Charles Pinot- 1704-1772 .... **LC 1**
See also GFL Beginnings to 1789

Dudek, Louis 1918-2001 .... **CLC 11, 19**
See also CA 45-48; 215; CAAS 14; CANR 1; CP 7; DLB 88

Duerrenmatt, Friedrich 1921-1990 ... **CLC 1, 4, 8, 11, 15, 43, 102**
See Durrenmatt, Friedrich
See also CA 17-20R; CANR 33; CMW 4; DAM DRAM; DLB 69, 124; MTCW 1, 2

Duffy, Bruce 1953(?)- .... **CLC 50**
See also CA 172

Duffy, Maureen 1933- .... **CLC 37**
See also CA 25-28R; CANR 33, 68; CBD; CN 7; CP 7; CWD; CWP; DFS 15; DLB 14; FW; MTCW 1

Du Fu
See Tu Fu
See also RGWL 2, 3

Dugan, Alan 1923-2003 .... **CLC 2, 6**
See also CA 81-84; 220; CANR 119; CP 7; DLB 5; PFS 10

du Gard, Roger Martin
See Martin du Gard, Roger

Duhamel, Georges 1884-1966 .... **CLC 8**
See also CA 81-84; 25-28R; CANR 35; DLB 65; EWL 3; GFL 1789 to the Present; MTCW 1

Dujardin, Edouard (Emile Louis)
1861-1949 .... **TCLC 13**
See also CA 109; DLB 123

Duke, Raoul
See Thompson, Hunter S(tockton)

Dulles, John Foster 1888-1959 .... **TCLC 72**
See also CA 115; 149

Dumas, Alexandre (pere)
1802-1870 .... **NCLC 11, 71; WLC**
See also AAYA 22; BYA 3; DA; DA3; DAB; DAC; DAM MST, NOV; DLB 119, 192; EW 6; GFL 1789 to the Present; LAIT 1, 2; NFS 14, 19; RGWL 2, 3; SATA 18; TWA; WCH

Dumas, Alexandre (fils) 1824-1895 ...... **DC 1; NCLC 9**
See also DLB 192; GFL 1789 to the Present; RGWL 2, 3

Dumas, Claudine
See Malzberg, Barry N(athaniel)

Dumas, Henry L. 1934-1968 .... **CLC 6, 62**
See also BW 1; CA 85-88; DLB 41; RGAL 4

du Maurier, Daphne 1907-1989 .. **CLC 6, 11, 59; SSC 18**
See also AAYA 37; BPFB 1; BRWS 3; CA 5-8R; 128; CANR 6, 55; CMW 4; CPW; DA3; DAB; DAC; DAM MST, POP; DLB 191; HGG; LAIT 3; MSW; MTCW 1, 2; NFS 12; RGEL 2; RGSF 2; RHW; SATA 27; SATA-Obit 60; SSFS 14, 16; TEA

Du Maurier, George 1834-1896 ..... **NCLC 86**
See also DLB 153, 178; RGEL 2

Dunbar, Paul Laurence 1872-1906 .. **BLC 1; PC 5; SSC 8; TCLC 2, 12; WLC**
See also AFAW 1, 2; AMWS 2; BW 1, 3; CA 104; 124; CANR 79; CDALB 1865-1917; DA; DA3; DAC; DAM MST, MULT, POET; DLB 50, 54, 78; EXPP; RGAL 4; SATA 34

Dunbar, William 1460(?)-1520(?) .... **LC 20**
See also BRWS 8; DLB 132, 146; RGEL 2

Dunbar-Nelson, Alice .... **HR 2**
See Nelson, Alice Ruth Moore Dunbar

Duncan, Dora Angela
See Duncan, Isadora

Duncan, Isadora 1877(?)-1927 .... **TCLC 68**
See also CA 118; 149

Duncan, Lois 1934- .... **CLC 26**
See also AAYA 4, 34; BYA 6, 8; CA 1-4R; CANR 2, 23, 36, 111; CLR 29; JRDA; MAICYA 1, 2; MAICYAS 1; SAAS 2; SATA 1, 36, 75, 133, 141; SATA-Essay 141; WYA; YAW

Duncan, Robert (Edward)
1919-1988 .... **CLC 1, 2, 4, 7, 15, 41, 55; PC 2**
See also BG 2; CA 9-12R; 124; CANR 28, 62; DAM POET; DLB 5, 16, 193; EWL 3; MTCW 1, 2; PFS 13; RGAL 4; WP

Duncan, Sara Jeannette
1861-1922 .... **TCLC 60**
See also CA 157; DLB 92

Dunlap, William 1766-1839 .... **NCLC 2**
See also DLB 30, 37, 59; RGAL 4

Dunn, Douglas (Eaglesham) 1942- .... **CLC 6, 40**
See also BRWS 10; CA 45-48; CANR 2, 33, 126; CP 7; DLB 40; MTCW 1

Dunn, Katherine (Karen) 1945- .... **CLC 71**
See also CA 33-36R; CANR 72; HGG; MTCW 1

Dunn, Stephen (Elliott) 1939- .... **CLC 36**
See also AMWS 11; CA 33-36R; CANR 12, 48, 53, 105; CP 7; DLB 105; PFS 21

Dunne, Finley Peter 1867-1936 ...... **TCLC 28**
See also CA 108; 178; DLB 11, 23; RGAL 4

Dunne, John Gregory 1932-2003 ..... **CLC 28**
See also CA 25-28R; 222; CANR 14, 50; CN 7; DLBY 1980

Dunsany, Lord .... **TCLC 2, 59**
See Dunsany, Edward John Moreton Drax Plunkett
See also DLB 77, 153, 156, 255; FANT; IDTP; RGEL 2; SFW 4; SUFW 1

Dunsany, Edward John Moreton Drax
Plunkett 1878-1957
See Dunsany, Lord
See also CA 104; 148; DLB 10; MTCW 1

Duns Scotus, John 1266(?)-1308 .... **CMLC 59**
See also DLB 115

du Perry, Jean
See Simenon, Georges (Jacques Christian)

Durang, Christopher (Ferdinand)
1949- .... **CLC 27, 38**
See also CA 105; CAD; CANR 50, 76, 130; CD 5; MTCW 1

Duras, Marguerite 1914-1996 . **CLC 3, 6, 11, 20, 34, 40, 68, 100; SSC 40**
See also BPFB 1; CA 25-28R; 151; CANR 50; CWW 2; DLB 83; EWL 3; GFL 1789 to the Present; IDFW 4; MTCW 1, 2; RGWL 2, 3; TWA

Durban, (Rosa) Pam 1947- .... **CLC 39**
See also CA 123; CANR 98; CSW

Durcan, Paul 1944- .... **CLC 43, 70**
See also CA 134; CANR 123; CP 7; DAM POET; EWL 3

Durfey, Thomas 1653-1723 .... **LC 94**
See also DLB 80; RGEL 2

Durkheim, Emile 1858-1917 .... **TCLC 55**

Durrell, Lawrence (George)
1912-1990 ..... **CLC 1, 4, 6, 8, 13, 27, 41**
See also BPFB 1; BRWS 1; CA 9-12R; 132; CANR 40, 77; CDBLB 1945-1960; DAM NOV; DLB 15, 27, 204; DLBY 1990; EWL 3; MTCW 1, 2; RGEL 2; SFW 4; TEA

Durrenmatt, Friedrich
See Duerrenmatt, Friedrich
See also CDWLB 2; EW 13; EWL 3; RGWL 2, 3

Dutt, Michael Madhusudan
1824-1873 .... **NCLC 118**

Dutt, Toru 1856-1877 .... **NCLC 29**
See also DLB 240

Feiffer, Jules (Ralph) 1929- ...... **CLC 2, 8, 64**
See also AAYA 3; CA 17-20R; CAD; CANR 30, 59, 129; CD 5; DAM DRAM; DLB 7, 44; INT CANR-30; MTCW 1; SATA 8, 61, 111

Feige, Hermann Albert Otto Maximilian
See Traven, B.

Feinberg, David B. 1956-1994 .... **CLC 59**
See also CA 135; 147

Feinstein, Elaine 1930- .... **CLC 36**
See also CA 69-72; CAAS 1; CANR 31, 68, 121; CN 7; CP 7; CWP; DLB 14, 40; MTCW 1

Feke, Gilbert David .... **CLC 65**

Feldman, Irving (Mordecai) 1928- ..... **CLC 7**
See also CA 1-4R; CANR 1; CP 7; DLB 169

Felix-Tchicaya, Gerald
See Tchicaya, Gerald Felix

Fellini, Federico 1920-1993 .... **CLC 16, 85**
See also CA 65-68; 143; CANR 33

Felltham, Owen 1602(?)-1668 .... **LC 92**
See also DLB 126, 151

Felsen, Henry Gregor 1916-1995 ..... **CLC 17**
See also CA 1-4R; 180; CANR 1; SAAS 2; SATA 1

Felski, Rita .... **CLC 65**

Fenno, Jack
See Calisher, Hortense

Fenollosa, Ernest (Francisco) 1853-1908 .... **TCLC 91**

Fenton, James Martin 1949- .... **CLC 32**
See also CA 102; CANR 108; CP 7; DLB 40; PFS 11

Ferber, Edna 1887-1968 .... **CLC 18, 93**
See also AITN 1; CA 5-8R; 25-28R; CANR 68, 105; DLB 9, 28, 86, 266; MTCW 1, 2; RGAL 4; RHW; SATA 7; TCWW 2

Ferdowsi, Abu'l Qasem 940-1020 . **CMLC 43**
See also RGWL 2, 3

Ferguson, Helen
See Kavan, Anna

Ferguson, Niall 1964- .... **CLC 134**
See also CA 190

Ferguson, Samuel 1810-1886 .... **NCLC 33**
See also DLB 32; RGEL 2

Fergusson, Robert 1750-1774 .... **LC 29**
See also DLB 109; RGEL 2

Ferling, Lawrence
See Ferlinghetti, Lawrence (Monsanto)

Ferlinghetti, Lawrence (Monsanto)
1919(?)- ..... **CLC 2, 6, 10, 27, 111; PC 1**
See also CA 5-8R; CANR 3, 41, 73, 125; CDALB 1941-1968; CP 7; DA3; DAM POET; DLB 5, 16; MTCW 1, 2; RGAL 4; WP

Fern, Fanny
See Parton, Sara Payson Willis

Fernandez, Vicente Garcia Huidobro
See Huidobro Fernandez, Vicente Garcia

Fernandez-Armesto, Felipe .... **CLC 70**

Fernandez de Lizardi, Jose Joaquin
See Lizardi, Jose Joaquin Fernandez de

Ferre, Rosario 1938- ...... **CLC 139; HLCS 1; SSC 36**
See also CA 131; CANR 55, 81, 134; CWW 2; DLB 145; EWL 3; HW 1, 2; LAWS 1; MTCW 1; WLIT 1

Ferrer, Gabriel (Francisco Victor) Miro
See Miro (Ferrer), Gabriel (Francisco Victor)

Ferrier, Susan (Edmonstone)
1782-1854 .... **NCLC 8**
See also DLB 116; RGEL 2

Ferrigno, Robert 1948(?)- .... **CLC 65**
See also CA 140; CANR 125

Ferron, Jacques 1921-1985 .... **CLC 94**
See also CA 117; 129; CCA 1; DAC; DLB 60; EWL 3

Feuchtwanger, Lion 1884-1958 .... **TCLC 3**
See also CA 104; 187; DLB 66; EWL 3

Feuerbach, Ludwig 1804-1872 ..... **NCLC 139**
See also DLB 133

Feuillet, Octave 1821-1890 .... **NCLC 45**
See also DLB 192

Feydeau, Georges (Leon Jules Marie)
1862-1921 .... **TCLC 22**
See also CA 113; 152; CANR 84; DAM DRAM; DLB 192; EWL 3; GFL 1789 to the Present; RGWL 2, 3

Fichte, Johann Gottlieb
1762-1814 .... **NCLC 62**
See also DLB 90

Ficino, Marsilio 1433-1499 .... **LC 12**
See also LMFS 1

Fiedeler, Hans
See Doeblin, Alfred

Fiedler, Leslie A(aron) 1917-2003 ..... **CLC 4, 13, 24**
See also AMWS 13; CA 9-12R; 212; CANR 7, 63; CN 7; DLB 28, 67; EWL 3; MTCW 1, 2; RGAL 4; TUS

Field, Andrew 1938- .... **CLC 44**
See also CA 97-100; CANR 25

Field, Eugene 1850-1895 .... **NCLC 3**
See also DLB 23, 42, 140; DLBD 13; MAICYA 1, 2; RGAL 4; SATA 16

Field, Gans T.
See Wellman, Manly Wade

Field, Michael 1915-1971 .... **TCLC 43**
See also CA 29-32R

Field, Peter
See Hobson, Laura Z(ametkin)
See also TCWW 2

Fielding, Helen 1958- .... **CLC 146**
See also CA 172; CANR 127; DLB 231

Fielding, Henry 1707-1754 .... **LC 1, 46, 85; WLC**
See also BRW 3; BRWR 1; CDBLB 1660-1789; DA; DA3; DAB; DAC; DAM DRAM, MST, NOV; DLB 39, 84, 101; NFS 18; RGEL 2; TEA; WLIT 3

Fielding, Sarah 1710-1768 .... **LC 1, 44**
See also DLB 39; RGEL 2; TEA

Fields, W. C. 1880-1946 .... **TCLC 80**
See also DLB 44

Fierstein, Harvey (Forbes) 1954- ..... **CLC 33**
See also CA 123; 129; CAD; CD 5; CPW; DA3; DAM DRAM, POP; DFS 6; DLB 266; GLL

Figes, Eva 1932- .... **CLC 31**
See also CA 53-56; CANR 4, 44, 83; CN 7; DLB 14, 271; FW

Filippo, Eduardo de
See de Filippo, Eduardo

Finch, Anne 1661-1720 .... **LC 3; PC 21**
See also BRWS 9; DLB 95

Finch, Robert (Duer Claydon)
1900-1995 .... **CLC 18**
See also CA 57-60; CANR 9, 24, 49; CP 7; DLB 88

Findley, Timothy (Irving Frederick)
1930-2002 .... **CLC 27, 102**
See also CA 25-28R; 206; CANR 12, 42, 69, 109; CCA 1; CN 7; DAC; DAM MST; DLB 53; FANT; RHW

Fink, William
See Mencken, H(enry) L(ouis)

Firbank, Louis 1942-
See Reed, Lou
See also CA 117

Firbank, (Arthur Annesley) Ronald
1886-1926 .... **TCLC 1**
See also BRWS 2; CA 104; 177; DLB 36; EWL 3; RGEL 2

Fish, Stanley
See Fish, Stanley Eugene

Fish, Stanley E.
See Fish, Stanley Eugene

Fish, Stanley Eugene 1938- .... **CLC 142**
See also CA 112; 132; CANR 90; DLB 67

Fisher, Dorothy (Frances) Canfield
1879-1958 .... **TCLC 87**
See also CA 114; 136; CANR 80; CLR 71,; CWRI 5; DLB 9, 102, 284; MAICYA 1, 2; YABC 1

Fisher, M(ary) F(rances) K(ennedy)
1908-1992 .... **CLC 76, 87**
See also CA 77-80; 138; CANR 44; MTCW 1

Fisher, Roy 1930- .... **CLC 25**
See also CA 81-84; CAAS 10; CANR 16; CP 7; DLB 40

Fisher, Rudolph 1897-1934 .... **BLC 2; HR 2; SSC 25; TCLC 11**
See also BW 1, 3; CA 107; 124; CANR 80; DAM MULT; DLB 51, 102

Fisher, Vardis (Alvero) 1895-1968 .... **CLC 7; TCLC 140**
See also CA 5-8R; 25-28R; CANR 68; DLB 9, 206; RGAL 4; TCWW 2

Fiske, Tarleton
See Bloch, Robert (Albert)

Fitch, Clarke
See Sinclair, Upton (Beall)

Fitch, John IV
See Cormier, Robert (Edmund)

Fitzgerald, Captain Hugh
See Baum, L(yman) Frank

FitzGerald, Edward 1809-1883 .... **NCLC 9**
See also BRW 4; DLB 32; RGEL 2

Fitzgerald, F(rancis) Scott (Key)
1896-1940 ... **SSC 6, 31, 75; TCLC 1, 6, 14, 28, 55, 157; WLC**
See also AAYA 24; AITN 1; AMW; AMWC 2; AMWR 1; BPFB 1; CA 110; 123; CDALB 1917-1929; DA; DA3; DAB; DAC; DAM MST, NOV; DLB 4, 9, 86, 219, 273; DLBD 1, 15, 16; DLBY 1981, 1996; EWL 3; EXPN; EXPS; LAIT 3; MTCW 1, 2; NFS 2, 19, 20; RGAL 4; RGSF 2; SSFS 4, 15; TUS

Fitzgerald, Penelope 1916-2000 . **CLC 19, 51, 61, 143**
See also BRWS 5; CA 85-88; 190; CAAS 10; CANR 56, 86, 131; CN 7; DLB 14, 194; EWL 3; MTCW 2

Fitzgerald, Robert (Stuart)
1910-1985 .... **CLC 39**
See also CA 1-4R; 114; CANR 1; DLBY 1980

FitzGerald, Robert D(avid)
1902-1987 .... **CLC 19**
See also CA 17-20R; DLB 260; RGEL 2

Fitzgerald, Zelda (Sayre)
1900-1948 .... **TCLC 52**
See also AMWS 9; CA 117; 126; DLBY 1984

Flanagan, Thomas (James Bonner)
1923-2002 .... **CLC 25, 52**
See also CA 108; 206; CANR 55; CN 7; DLBY 1980; INT CA-108; MTCW 1; RHW

Flaubert, Gustave 1821-1880 .... **NCLC 2, 10, 19, 62, 66, 135; SSC 11, 60; WLC**
See also DA; DA3; DAB; DAC; DAM MST, NOV; DLB 119, 301; EW 7; EXPS; GFL 1789 to the Present; LAIT 2; LMFS 1; NFS 14; RGSF 2; RGWL 2, 3; SSFS 6; TWA

Flavius Josephus
See Josephus, Flavius

Flecker, Herman Elroy
See Flecker, (Herman) James Elroy

Flecker, (Herman) James Elroy
 1884-1915 .... **TCLC 43**
 See also CA 109; 150; DLB 10, 19; RGEL
 2

Fleming, Ian (Lancaster) 1908-1964 . **CLC 3, 30**
 See also AAYA 26; BPFB 1; CA 5-8R;
 CANR 59; CDBLB 1945-1960; CMW 4;
 CPW; DA3; DAM POP; DLB 87, 201;
 MSW; MTCW 1, 2; RGEL 2; SATA 9;
 TEA; YAW

Fleming, Thomas (James) 1927- ...... **CLC 37**
 See also CA 5-8R; CANR 10, 102; INT
 CANR-10; SATA 8

Fletcher, John 1579-1625 .... **DC 6; LC 33**
 See also BRW 2; CDBLB Before 1660;
 DLB 58; RGEL 2; TEA

Fletcher, John Gould 1886-1950 .... **TCLC 35**
 See also CA 107; 167; DLB 4, 45; LMFS
 2; RGAL 4

Fleur, Paul
 See Pohl, Frederik

Flieg, Helmut
 See Heym, Stefan

Flooglebuckle, Al
 See Spiegelman, Art

Flora, Fletcher 1914-1969
 See Queen, Ellery
 See also CA 1-4R; CANR 3, 85

Flying Officer X
 See Bates, H(erbert) E(rnest)

Fo, Dario 1926- .... **CLC 32, 109; DC 10**
 See also CA 116; 128; CANR 68, 114, 134;
 CWW 2; DA3; DAM DRAM; DLBY
 1997; EWL 3; MTCW 1, 2

Fogarty, Jonathan Titulescu Esq.
 See Farrell, James T(homas)

Follett, Ken(neth Martin) 1949- .... **CLC 18**
 See also AAYA 6, 50; BEST 89:4; BPFB 1;
 CA 81-84; CANR 13, 33, 54, 102; CMW
 4; CPW; DA3; DAM NOV, POP; DLB
 87; DLBY 1981; INT CANR-33; MTCW
 1

Fondane, Benjamin 1898-1944 ..... **TCLC 159**

Fontane, Theodor 1819-1898 .... **NCLC 26**
 See also CDWLB 2; DLB 129; EW 6;
 RGWL 2, 3; TWA

Fontenot, Chester .... **CLC 65**

Fonvizin, Denis Ivanovich
 1744(?)-1792 .... **LC 81**
 See also DLB 150; RGWL 2, 3

Foote, Horton 1916- .... **CLC 51, 91**
 See also CA 73-76; CAD; CANR 34, 51,
 110; CD 5; CSW; DA3; DAM DRAM;
 DFS 20; DLB 26, 266; EWL 3; INT
 CANR-34

Foote, Mary Hallock 1847-1938 .. **TCLC 108**
 See also DLB 186, 188, 202, 221

Foote, Samuel 1721-1777 .... **LC 106**
 See also DLB 89; RGEL 2

Foote, Shelby 1916- .... **CLC 75**
 See also AAYA 40; CA 5-8R; CANR 3, 45,
 74, 131; CN 7; CPW; CSW; DA3; DAM
 NOV, POP; DLB 2, 17; MTCW 2; RHW

Forbes, Cosmo
 See Lewton, Val

Forbes, Esther 1891-1967 .... **CLC 12**
 See also AAYA 17; BYA 2; CA 13-14; 25-
 28R; CAP 1; CLR 27; DLB 22; JRDA;
 MAICYA 1, 2; RHW; SATA 2, 100; YAW

Forche, Carolyn (Louise) 1950- .... **CLC 25, 83, 86; PC 10**
 See also CA 109; 117; CANR 50, 74; CP 7;
 CWP; DA3; DAM POET; DLB 5, 193;
 INT CA-117; MTCW 1; PFS 18; RGAL 4

Ford, Elbur
 See Hibbert, Eleanor Alice Burford

Ford, Ford Madox 1873-1939 ... **TCLC 1, 15, 39, 57**
 See Chaucer, Daniel
 See also BRW 6; CA 104; 132; CANR 74;
 CDBLB 1914-1945; DA3; DAM NOV;
 DLB 34, 98, 162; EWL 3; MTCW 1, 2;
 RGEL 2; TEA

Ford, Henry 1863-1947 .... **TCLC 73**
 See also CA 115; 148

Ford, Jack
 See Ford, John

Ford, John 1586-1639 .... **DC 8; LC 68**
 See also BRW 2; CDBLB Before 1660;
 DA3; DAM DRAM; DFS 7; DLB 58;
 IDTP; RGEL 2

Ford, John 1895-1973 .... **CLC 16**
 See also CA 187; 45-48

Ford, Richard 1944- .... **CLC 46, 99**
 See also AMWS 5; CA 69-72; CANR 11,
 47, 86, 128; CN 7; CSW; DLB 227; EWL
 3; MTCW 1; RGAL 4; RGSF 2

Ford, Webster
 See Masters, Edgar Lee

Foreman, Richard 1937- .... **CLC 50**
 See also CA 65-68; CAD; CANR 32, 63;
 CD 5

Forester, C(ecil) S(cott) 1899-1966 . **CLC 35; TCLC 152**
 See also CA 73-76; 25-28R; CANR 83;
 DLB 191; RGEL 2; RHW; SATA 13

Forez
 See Mauriac, Francois (Charles)

Forman, James
 See Forman, James D(ouglas)

Forman, James D(ouglas) 1932- .... **CLC 21**
 See also AAYA 17; CA 9-12R; CANR 4,
 19, 42; JRDA; MAICYA 1, 2; SATA 8,
 70; YAW

Forman, Milos 1932- .... **CLC 164**
 See also CA 109

Fornes, Maria Irene 1930- .... **CLC 39, 61, 187; DC 10; HLCS 1**
 See also CA 25-28R; CAD; CANR 28, 81;
 CD 5; CWD; DLB 7; HW 1, 2; INT
 CANR-28; LLW 1; MTCW 1; RGAL 4

Forrest, Leon (Richard)
 1937-1997 .... **BLCS; CLC 4**
 See also AFAW 2; BW 2; CA 89-92; 162;
 CAAS 7; CANR 25, 52, 87; CN 7; DLB
 33

Forster, E(dward) M(organ)
 1879-1970 ...... **CLC 1, 2, 3, 4, 9, 10, 13, 15, 22, 45, 77; SSC 27; TCLC 125; WLC**
 See also AAYA 2, 37; BRW 6; BRWR 2;
 BYA 12; CA 13-14; 25-28R; CANR 45;
 CAP 1; CDBLB 1914-1945; DA; DA3;
 DAB; DAC; DAM MST, NOV; DLB 34,
 98, 162, 178, 195; DLBD 10; EWL 3;
 EXPN; LAIT 3; LMFS 1; MTCW 1, 2;
 NCFS 1; NFS 3, 10, 11; RGEL 2; RGSF
 2; SATA 57; SUFW 1; TEA; WLIT 4

Forster, John 1812-1876 .... **NCLC 11**
 See also DLB 144, 184

Forster, Margaret 1938- .... **CLC 149**
 See also CA 133; CANR 62, 115; CN 7;
 DLB 155, 271

Forsyth, Frederick 1938- .... **CLC 2, 5, 36**
 See also BEST 89:4; CA 85-88; CANR 38,
 62, 115; CMW 4; CN 7; CPW; DAM
 NOV, POP; DLB 87; MTCW 1, 2

Forten, Charlotte L. 1837-1914 .... **BLC 2; TCLC 16**
 See Grimke, Charlotte L(ottie) Forten
 See also DLB 50, 239

Fortinbras
 See Grieg, (Johan) Nordahl (Brun)

Foscolo, Ugo 1778-1827 .... **NCLC 8, 97**
 See also EW 5

Fosse, Bob .... **CLC 20**
 See Fosse, Robert Louis

Fosse, Robert Louis 1927-1987
 See Fosse, Bob
 See also CA 110; 123

Foster, Hannah Webster
 1758-1840 .... **NCLC 99**
 See also DLB 37, 200; RGAL 4

Foster, Stephen Collins
 1826-1864 .... **NCLC 26**
 See also RGAL 4

Foucault, Michel 1926-1984 . **CLC 31, 34, 69**
 See also CA 105; 113; CANR 34; DLB 242;
 EW 13; EWL 3; GFL 1789 to the Present;
 GLL 1; LMFS 2; MTCW 1, 2; TWA

Fouque, Friedrich (Heinrich Karl) de la
 Motte 1777-1843 .... **NCLC 2**
 See also DLB 90; RGWL 2, 3; SUFW 1

Fourier, Charles 1772-1837 .... **NCLC 51**

Fournier, Henri-Alban 1886-1914
 See Alain-Fournier
 See also CA 104; 179

Fournier, Pierre 1916- .... **CLC 11**
 See Gascar, Pierre
 See also CA 89-92; CANR 16, 40

Fowles, John (Robert) 1926- . **CLC 1, 2, 3, 4, 6, 9, 10, 15, 33, 87; SSC 33**
 See also BPFB 1; BRWS 1; CA 5-8R;
 CANR 25, 71, 103; CDBLB 1960 to
 Present; CN 7; DA3; DAB; DAC; DAM
 MST; DLB 14, 139, 207; EWL 3; HGG;
 MTCW 1, 2; RGEL 2; RHW; SATA 22;
 TEA; WLIT 4

Fox, Paula 1923- .... **CLC 2, 8, 121**
 See also AAYA 3, 37; BYA 3, 8; CA 73-76;
 CANR 20, 36, 62, 105; CLR 1, 44, 96;
 DLB 52; JRDA; MAICYA 1, 2; MTCW
 1; NFS 12; SATA 17, 60, 120; WYA;
 YAW

Fox, William Price (Jr.) 1926- .... **CLC 22**
 See also CA 17-20R; CAAS 19; CANR 11;
 CSW; DLB 2; DLBY 1981

Foxe, John 1517(?)-1587 .... **LC 14**
 See also DLB 132

Frame, Janet .. **CLC 2, 3, 6, 22, 66, 96; SSC 29**
 See Clutha, Janet Paterson Frame
 See also CN 7; CWP; EWL 3; RGEL 2;
 RGSF 2; TWA

France, Anatole .... **TCLC 9**
 See Thibault, Jacques Anatole Francois
 See also DLB 123; EWL 3; GFL 1789 to
 the Present; MTCW 1; RGWL 2, 3;
 SUFW 1

Francis, Claude .... **CLC 50**
 See also CA 192

Francis, Richard Stanley 1920- ... **CLC 2, 22, 42, 102**
 See also AAYA 5, 21; BEST 89:3; BPFB 1;
 CA 5-8R; CANR 9, 42, 68, 100; CDBLB
 1960 to Present; CMW 4; CN 7; DA3;
 DAM POP; DLB 87; INT CANR-9;
 MSW; MTCW 1, 2

Francis, Robert (Churchill)
 1901-1987 .... **CLC 15; PC 34**
 See also AMWS 9; CA 1-4R; 123; CANR
 1; EXPP; PFS 12

Francis, Lord Jeffrey
 See Jeffrey, Francis
 See also DLB 107

Frank, Anne(lies Marie)
 1929-1945 .... **TCLC 17; WLC**
 See also AAYA 12; BYA 1; CA 113; 133;
 CANR 68; CLR 101; DA; DA3; DAB;
 DAC; DAM MST; LAIT 4; MAICYA 2;
 MAICYAS 1; MTCW 1, 2; NCFS 2;
 SATA 87; SATA-Brief 42; WYA; YAW

Frank, Bruno 1887-1945 .... **TCLC 81**
 See also CA 189; DLB 118; EWL 3

Frank, Elizabeth 1945- .... **CLC 39**
See also CA 121; 126; CANR 78; INT CA-126

Frankl, Viktor E(mil) 1905-1997 ...... **CLC 93**
See also CA 65-68; 161

Franklin, Benjamin
See Hasek, Jaroslav (Matej Frantisek)

Franklin, Benjamin 1706-1790 .... **LC 25;
WLCS**
See also AMW; CDALB 1640-1865; DA;
DA3; DAB; DAC; DAM MST; DLB 24,
43, 73, 183; LAIT 1; RGAL 4; TUS

**Franklin, (Stella Maria Sarah) Miles
(Lampe)** 1879-1954 .... **TCLC 7**
See also CA 104; 164; DLB 230; FW;
MTCW 2; RGEL 2; TWA

Fraser, Antonia (Pakenham) 1932- . **CLC 32,
107**
See also AAYA 57; CA 85-88; CANR 44,
65, 119; CMW; DLB 276; MTCW 1, 2;
SATA-Brief 32

Fraser, George MacDonald 1925- ...... **CLC 7**
See also AAYA 48; CA 45-48; 180; CAAE
180; CANR 2, 48, 74; MTCW 1; RHW

Fraser, Sylvia 1935- .... **CLC 64**
See also CA 45-48; CANR 1, 16, 60; CCA
1

Frayn, Michael 1933- . **CLC 3, 7, 31, 47, 176**
See also BRWC 2; BRWS 7; CA 5-8R;
CANR 30, 69, 114, 133; CBD; CD 5; CN
7; DAM DRAM, NOV; DLB 13, 14, 194,
245; FANT; MTCW 1, 2; SFW 4

Fraze, Candida (Merrill) 1945- .... **CLC 50**
See also CA 126

Frazer, Andrew
See Marlowe, Stephen

Frazer, J(ames) G(eorge)
1854-1941 .... **TCLC 32**
See also BRWS 3; CA 118; NCFS 5

Frazer, Robert Caine
See Creasey, John

Frazer, Sir James George
See Frazer, J(ames) G(eorge)

Frazier, Charles 1950- .... **CLC 109**
See also AAYA 34; CA 161; CANR 126;
CSW; DLB 292

Frazier, Ian 1951- .... **CLC 46**
See also CA 130; CANR 54, 93

Frederic, Harold 1856-1898 .... **NCLC 10**
See also AMW; DLB 12, 23; DLBD 13;
RGAL 4

Frederick, John
See Faust, Frederick (Schiller)
See also TCWW 2

Frederick the Great 1712-1786 .... **LC 14**

Fredro, Aleksander 1793-1876 .... **NCLC 8**

Freeling, Nicolas 1927-2003 .... **CLC 38**
See also CA 49-52; 218; CAAS 12; CANR
1, 17, 50, 84; CMW 4; CN 7; DLB 87

Freeman, Douglas Southall
1886-1953 .... **TCLC 11**
See also CA 109; 195; DLB 17; DLBD 17

Freeman, Judith 1946- .... **CLC 55**
See also CA 148; CANR 120; DLB 256

Freeman, Mary E(leanor) Wilkins
1852-1930 .... **SSC 1, 47; TCLC 9**
See also CA 106; 177; DLB 12, 78, 221;
EXPS; FW; HGG; MAWW; RGAL 4;
RGSF 2; SSFS 4, 8; SUFW 1; TUS

Freeman, R(ichard) Austin
1862-1943 .... **TCLC 21**
See also CA 113; CANR 84; CMW 4; DLB
70

French, Albert 1943- .... **CLC 86**
See also BW 3; CA 167

French, Antonia
See Kureishi, Hanif

French, Marilyn 1929- .. **CLC 10, 18, 60, 177**
See also BPFB 1; CA 69-72; CANR 3, 31,
134; CN 7; CPW; DAM DRAM, NOV,
POP; FW; INT CANR-31; MTCW 1, 2

French, Paul
See Asimov, Isaac

Freneau, Philip Morin 1752-1832 .. **NCLC 1,
111**
See also AMWS 2; DLB 37, 43; RGAL 4

Freud, Sigmund 1856-1939 .... **TCLC 52**
See also CA 115; 133; CANR 69; DLB 296;
EW 8; EWL 3; LATS 1:1; MTCW 1, 2;
NCFS 3; TWA

Freytag, Gustav 1816-1895 .... **NCLC 109**
See also DLB 129

Friedan, Betty (Naomi) 1921- .... **CLC 74**
See also CA 65-68; CANR 18, 45, 74; DLB
246; FW; MTCW 1, 2; NCFS 5

Friedlander, Saul 1932- .... **CLC 90**
See also CA 117; 130; CANR 72

Friedman, B(ernard) H(arper)
1926- .... **CLC 7**
See also CA 1-4R; CANR 3, 48

Friedman, Bruce Jay 1930- ...... **CLC 3, 5, 56**
See also CA 9-12R; CAD; CANR 25, 52,
101; CD 5; CN 7; DLB 2, 28, 244; INT
CANR-25; SSFS 18

Friel, Brian 1929- .... **CLC 5, 42, 59, 115; DC
8; SSC 76**
See also BRWS 5; CA 21-24R; CANR 33,
69, 131; CBD; CD 5; DFS 11; DLB 13;
EWL 3; MTCW 1; RGEL 2; TEA

Friis-Baastad, Babbis Ellinor
1921-1970 .... **CLC 12**
See also CA 17-20R; 134; SATA 7

Frisch, Max (Rudolf) 1911-1991 ... **CLC 3, 9,
14, 18, 32, 44; TCLC 121**
See also CA 85-88; 134; CANR 32, 74; CD-
WLB 2; DAM DRAM, NOV; DLB 69,
124; EW 13; EWL 3; MTCW 1, 2; RGWL
2, 3

Fromentin, Eugene (Samuel Auguste)
1820-1876 .... **NCLC 10, 125**
See also DLB 123; GFL 1789 to the Present

Frost, Frederick
See Faust, Frederick (Schiller)
See also TCWW 2

Frost, Robert (Lee) 1874-1963 .. **CLC 1, 3, 4,
9, 10, 13, 15, 26, 34, 44; PC 1, 39;
WLC**
See also AAYA 21; AMW; AMWR 1; CA
89-92; CANR 33; CDALB 1917-1929;
CLR 67; DA; DA3; DAB; DAC; DAM
MST, POET; DLB 54, 284; DLBD 7;
EWL 3; EXPP; MTCW 1, 2; PAB; PFS 1,
2, 3, 4, 5, 6, 7, 10, 13; RGAL 4; SATA
14; TUS; WP; WYA

Froude, James Anthony
1818-1894 .... **NCLC 43**
See also DLB 18, 57, 144

Froy, Herald
See Waterhouse, Keith (Spencer)

Fry, Christopher 1907- .... **CLC 2, 10, 14**
See also BRWS 3; CA 17-20R; CAAS 23;
CANR 9, 30, 74, 132; CBD; CD 5; CP 7;
DAM DRAM; DLB 13; EWL 3; MTCW
1, 2; RGEL 2; SATA 66; TEA

Frye, (Herman) Northrop
1912-1991 .... **CLC 24, 70**
See also CA 5-8R; 133; CANR 8, 37; DLB
67, 68, 246; EWL 3; MTCW 1, 2; RGAL
4; TWA

Fuchs, Daniel 1909-1993 .... **CLC 8, 22**
See also CA 81-84; 142; CAAS 5; CANR
40; DLB 9, 26, 28; DLBY 1993

Fuchs, Daniel 1934- .... **CLC 34**
See also CA 37-40R; CANR 14, 48

Fuentes, Carlos 1928- .. **CLC 3, 8, 10, 13, 22,
41, 60, 113; HLC 1; SSC 24; WLC**
See also AAYA 4, 45; AITN 2; BPFB 1;
CA 69-72; CANR 10, 32, 68, 104; CD-
WLB 3; CWW 2; DA; DA3; DAB; DAC;
DAM MST, MULT, NOV; DLB 113;
DNFS 2; EWL 3; HW 1, 2; LAIT 3; LATS
1:2; LAW; LAWS 1; LMFS 2; MTCW 1,
2; NFS 8; RGSF 2; RGWL 2, 3; TWA;
WLIT 1

Fuentes, Gregorio Lopez y
See Lopez y Fuentes, Gregorio

Fuertes, Gloria 1918-1998 .... **PC 27**
See also CA 178; 180; DLB 108; HW 2;
SATA 115

Fugard, (Harold) Athol 1932- . **CLC 5, 9, 14,
25, 40, 80; DC 3**
See also AAYA 17; AFW; CA 85-88; CANR
32, 54, 118; CD 5; DAM DRAM; DFS 3,
6, 10; DLB 225; DNFS 1, 2; EWL 3;
LATS 1:2; MTCW 1; RGEL 2; WLIT 2

Fugard, Sheila 1932- .... **CLC 48**
See also CA 125

Fukuyama, Francis 1952- .... **CLC 131**
See also CA 140; CANR 72, 125

Fuller, Charles (H.), (Jr.) 1939- .... **BLC 2;
CLC 25; DC 1**
See also BW 2; CA 108; 112; CAD; CANR
87; CD 5; DAM DRAM, MULT; DFS 8;
DLB 38, 266; EWL 3; INT CA-112;
MTCW 1

Fuller, Henry Blake 1857-1929 .... **TCLC 103**
See also CA 108; 177; DLB 12; RGAL 4

Fuller, John (Leopold) 1937- .... **CLC 62**
See also CA 21-24R; CANR 9, 44; CP 7;
DLB 40

Fuller, Margaret
See Ossoli, Sarah Margaret (Fuller)
See also AMWS 2; DLB 183, 223, 239

Fuller, Roy (Broadbent) 1912-1991 ... **CLC 4,
28**
See also BRWS 7; CA 5-8R; 135; CAAS
10; CANR 53, 83; CWRI 5; DLB 15, 20;
EWL 3; RGEL 2; SATA 87

Fuller, Sarah Margaret
See Ossoli, Sarah Margaret (Fuller)

Fuller, Sarah Margaret
See Ossoli, Sarah Margaret (Fuller)
See also DLB 1, 59, 73

Fuller, Thomas 1608-1661 .... **LC 111**
See also DLB 151

Fulton, Alice 1952- .... **CLC 52**
See also CA 116; CANR 57, 88; CP 7;
CWP; DLB 193

Furphy, Joseph 1843-1912 .... **TCLC 25**
See Collins, Tom
See also CA 163; DLB 230; EWL 3; RGEL
2

Fuson, Robert H(enderson) 1927- .... **CLC 70**
See also CA 89-92; CANR 103

Fussell, Paul 1924- .... **CLC 74**
See also BEST 90:1; CA 17-20R; CANR 8,
21, 35, 69, 135; INT CANR-21; MTCW
1, 2

Futabatei, Shimei 1864-1909 .... **TCLC 44**
See Futabatei Shimei
See also CA 162; MJW

Futabatei Shimei
See Futabatei, Shimei
See also DLB 180; EWL 3

Futrelle, Jacques 1875-1912 .... **TCLC 19**
See also CA 113; 155; CMW 4

Gaboriau, Emile 1835-1873 .... **NCLC 14**
See also CMW 4; MSW

Gadda, Carlo Emilio 1893-1973 ...... **CLC 11;
TCLC 144**
See also CA 89-92; DLB 177; EWL 3

Gaddis, William 1922-1998 ... **CLC 1, 3, 6, 8, 10, 19, 43, 86**
See also AMWS 4; BPFB 1; CA 17-20R; 172; CANR 21, 48; CN 7; DLB 2, 278; EWL 3; MTCW 1, 2; RGAL 4

Gaelique, Moruen le
See Jacob, (Cyprien-)Max

Gage, Walter
See Inge, William (Motter)

Gaiman, Neil (Richard) 1960- .... **CLC 195**
See also AAYA 19, 42; CA 133; CANR 81, 129; DLB 261; HGG; SATA 85, 146; SFW 4; SUFW 2

Gaines, Ernest J(ames) 1933- .. **BLC 2; CLC 3, 11, 18, 86, 181; SSC 68**
See also AAYA 18; AFAW 1, 2; AITN 1; BPFB 2; BW 2, 3; BYA 6; CA 9-12R; CANR 6, 24, 42, 75, 126; CDALB 1968-1988; CLR 62; CN 7; CSW; DA3; DAM MULT; DLB 2, 33, 152; DLBY 1980; EWL 3; EXPN; LAIT 5; LATS 1:2; MTCW 1, 2; NFS 5, 7, 16; RGAL 4; RGSF; RHW; SATA 86; SSFS 5; YAW

Gaitskill, Mary (Lawrence) 1954- .... **CLC 69**
See also CA 128; CANR 61; DLB 244

Gaius Suetonius Tranquillus
See Suetonius

Galdos, Benito Perez
See Perez Galdos, Benito
See also EW 7

Gale, Zona 1874-1938 .... **TCLC 7**
See also CA 105; 153; CANR 84; DAM DRAM; DFS 17; DLB 9, 78, 228; RGAL 4

Galeano, Eduardo (Hughes) 1940- . **CLC 72; HLCS 1**
See also CA 29-32R; CANR 13, 32, 100; HW 1

Galiano, Juan Valera y Alcala
See Valera y Alcala-Galiano, Juan

Galilei, Galileo 1564-1642 .... **LC 45**

Gallagher, Tess 1943- .... **CLC 18, 63; PC 9**
See also CA 106; CP 7; CWP; DAM POET; DLB 120, 212, 244; PFS 16

Gallant, Mavis 1922- ..... **CLC 7, 18, 38, 172; SSC 5, 78**
See also CA 69-72; CANR 29, 69, 117; CCA 1; CN 7; DAC; DAM MST; DLB 53; EWL 3; MTCW 1, 2; RGEL 2; RGSF 2

Gallant, Roy A(rthur) 1924- .... **CLC 17**
See also CA 5-8R; CANR 4, 29, 54, 117; CLR 30; MAICYA 1, 2; SATA 4, 68, 110

Gallico, Paul (William) 1897-1976 ..... **CLC 2**
See also AITN 1; CA 5-8R; 69-72; CANR 23; DLB 9, 171; FANT; MAICYA 1, 2; SATA 13

Gallo, Max Louis 1932- .... **CLC 95**
See also CA 85-88

Gallois, Lucien
See Desnos, Robert

Gallup, Ralph
See Whitemore, Hugh (John)

Galsworthy, John 1867-1933 .... **SSC 22; TCLC 1, 45; WLC**
See also BRW 6; CA 104; 141; CANR 75; CDBLB 1890-1914; DA; DA3; DAB; DAC; DAM DRAM, MST, NOV; DLB 10, 34, 98, 162; DLBD 16; EWL 3; MTCW 1; RGEL 2; SSFS 3; TEA

Galt, John 1779-1839 .... **NCLC 1, 110**
See also DLB 99, 116, 159; RGEL 2; RGSF 2

Galvin, James 1951- .... **CLC 38**
See also CA 108; CANR 26

Gamboa, Federico 1864-1939 .... **TCLC 36**
See also CA 167; HW 2; LAW

Gandhi, M. K.
See Gandhi, Mohandas Karamchand

Gandhi, Mahatma
See Gandhi, Mohandas Karamchand

Gandhi, Mohandas Karamchand
1869-1948 .... **TCLC 59**
See also CA 121; 132; DA3; DAM MULT; MTCW 1, 2

Gann, Ernest Kellogg 1910-1991 ..... **CLC 23**
See also AITN 1; BPFB 2; CA 1-4R; 136; CANR 1, 83; RHW

Gao Xingjian 1940- .... **CLC 167**
See Xingjian, Gao

Garber, Eric 1943(?)-
See Holleran, Andrew
See also CANR 89

Garcia, Cristina 1958- .... **CLC 76**
See also AMWS 11; CA 141; CANR 73, 130; DLB 292; DNFS 1; EWL 3; HW 2; LLW 1

Garcia Lorca, Federico 1898-1936 ...... **DC 2; HLC 2; PC 3; TCLC 1, 7, 49; WLC**
See Lorca, Federico Garcia
See also AAYA 46; CA 104; 131; CANR 81; DA; DA3; DAB; DAC; DAM DRAM, MST, MULT, POET; DFS 4, 10; DLB 108; EWL 3; HW 1, 2; LATS 1:2; MTCW 1, 2; TWA

Garcia Marquez, Gabriel (Jose)
1928- .... **CLC 2, 3, 8, 10, 15, 27, 47, 55, 68, 170; HLC 1; SSC 8; WLC**
See also AAYA 3, 33; BEST 89:1, 90:4; BPFB 2; BYA 12, 16; CA 33-36R; CANR 10, 28, 50, 75, 82, 128; CDWLB 3; CPW; CWW 2; DA; DA3; DAB; DAC; DAM MST, MULT, NOV, POP; DLB 113; DNFS 1, 2; EWL 3; EXPN; EXPS; HW 1, 2; LAIT 2; LATS 1:2; LAW; LAWS 1; LMFS 2; MTCW 1, 2; NCFS 3; NFS 1, 5, 10; RGSF 2; RGWL 2, 3; SSFS 1, 6, 16; TWA; WLIT 1

Garcilaso de la Vega, El Inca
1503-1536 .... **HLCS 1**
See also LAW

Gard, Janice
See Latham, Jean Lee

Gard, Roger Martin du
See Martin du Gard, Roger

Gardam, Jane (Mary) 1928- .... **CLC 43**
See also CA 49-52; CANR 2, 18, 33, 54, 106; CLR 12; DLB 14, 161, 231; MAICYA 1, 2; MTCW 1; SAAS 9; SATA 39, 76, 130; SATA-Brief 28; YAW

Gardner, Herb(ert George)
1934-2003 .... **CLC 44**
See also CA 149; 220; CAD; CANR 119; CD 5; DFS 18, 20

Gardner, John (Champlin), Jr.
1933-1982 ...... **CLC 2, 3, 5, 7, 8, 10, 18, 28, 34; SSC 7**
See also AAYA 45; AITN 1; AMWS 6; BPFB 2; CA 65-68; 107; CANR 33, 73; CDALBS; CPW; DA3; DAM NOV, POP; DLB 2; DLBY 1982; EWL 3; FANT; LATS 1:2; MTCW 1; NFS 3; RGAL 4; RGSF 2; SATA 40; SATA-Obit 31; SSFS 8

Gardner, John (Edmund) 1926- .... **CLC 30**
See also CA 103; CANR 15, 69, 127; CMW 4; CPW; DAM POP; MTCW 1

Gardner, Miriam
See Bradley, Marion Zimmer
See also GLL 1

Gardner, Noel
See Kuttner, Henry

Gardons, S. S.
See Snodgrass, W(illiam) D(e Witt)

Garfield, Leon 1921-1996 .... **CLC 12**
See also AAYA 8; BYA 1, 3; CA 17-20R; 152; CANR 38, 41, 78; CLR 21; DLB 161; JRDA; MAICYA 1, 2; MAICYAS 1; SATA 1, 32, 76; SATA-Obit 90; TEA; WYA; YAW

Garland, (Hannibal) Hamlin
1860-1940 .... **SSC 18; TCLC 3**
See also CA 104; DLB 12, 71, 78, 186; RGAL 4; RGSF 2; TCWW 2

Garneau, (Hector de) Saint-Denys
1912-1943 .... **TCLC 13**
See also CA 111; DLB 88

Garner, Alan 1934- .... **CLC 17**
See also AAYA 18; BYA 3, 5; CA 73-76, 178; CAAE 178; CANR 15, 64, 134; CLR 20; CPW; DAB; DAM POP; DLB 161, 261; FANT; MAICYA 1, 2; MTCW 1, 2; SATA 18, 69; SATA-Essay 108; SUFW 1, 2; YAW

Garner, Hugh 1913-1979 .... **CLC 13**
See Warwick, Jarvis
See also CA 69-72; CANR 31; CCA 1; DLB 68

Garnett, David 1892-1981 .... **CLC 3**
See also CA 5-8R; 103; CANR 17, 79; DLB 34; FANT; MTCW 2; RGEL 2; SFW 4; SUFW 1

Garos, Stephanie
See Katz, Steve

Garrett, George (Palmer) 1929- .. **CLC 3, 11, 51; SSC 30**
See also AMWS 7; BPFB 2; CA 1-4R, 202; CAAE 202; CAAS 5; CANR 1, 42, 67, 109; CN 7; CP 7; CSW; DLB 2, 5, 130, 152; DLBY 1983

Garrick, David 1717-1779 .... **LC 15**
See also DAM DRAM; DLB 84, 213; RGEL 2

Garrigue, Jean 1914-1972 .... **CLC 2, 8**
See also CA 5-8R; 37-40R; CANR 20

Garrison, Frederick
See Sinclair, Upton (Beall)

Garrison, William Lloyd
1805-1879 .... **NCLC 149**
See also CDALB 1640-1865; DLB 1, 43, 235

Garro, Elena 1920(?)-1998 .. **HLCS 1; TCLC 153**
See also CA 131; 169; CWW 2; DLB 145; EWL 3; HW 1; LAWS 1; WLIT 1

Garth, Will
See Hamilton, Edmond; Kuttner, Henry

Garvey, Marcus (Moziah, Jr.)
1887-1940 .... **BLC 2; HR 2; TCLC 41**
See also BW 1; CA 120; 124; CANR 79; DAM MULT

Gary, Romain .... **CLC 25**
See Kacew, Romain
See also DLB 83, 299

Gascar, Pierre .... **CLC 11**
See Fournier, Pierre
See also EWL 3

Gascoigne, George 1539-1577 .... **LC 108**
See also DLB 136; RGEL 2

Gascoyne, David (Emery)
1916-2001 .... **CLC 45**
See also CA 65-68; 200; CANR 10, 28, 54; CP 7; DLB 20; MTCW 1; RGEL 2

Gaskell, Elizabeth Cleghorn
1810-1865 .... **NCLC 5, 70, 97, 137; SSC 25**
See also BRW 5; CDBLB 1832-1890; DAB; DAM MST; DLB 21, 144, 159; RGEL 2; RGSF 2; TEA

Gass, William H(oward) 1924- . **CLC 1, 2, 8, 11, 15, 39, 132; SSC 12**
See also AMWS 6; CA 17-20R; CANR 30, 71, 100; CN 7; DLB 2, 227; EWL 3; MTCW 1, 2; RGAL 4

Gassendi, Pierre 1592-1655 .... **LC 54**
See also GFL Beginnings to 1789

Gasset, Jose Ortega y
See Ortega y Gasset, Jose

Gates, Henry Louis, Jr. 1950- ... **BLCS; CLC 65**
See also BW 2, 3; CA 109; CANR 25, 53, 75, 125; CSW; DA3; DAM MULT; DLB 67; EWL 3; MTCW 1; RGAL 4

Gautier, Theophile 1811-1872 .. **NCLC 1, 59; PC 18; SSC 20**
See also DAM POET; DLB 119; EW 6; GFL 1789 to the Present; RGWL 2, 3; SUFW; TWA

Gawsworth, John
See Bates, H(erbert) E(rnest)

Gay, John 1685-1732 .... **LC 49**
See also BRW 3; DAM DRAM; DLB 84, 95; RGEL 2; WLIT 3

Gay, Oliver
See Gogarty, Oliver St. John

Gay, Peter (Jack) 1923- .... **CLC 158**
See also CA 13-16R; CANR 18, 41, 77; INT CANR-18

Gaye, Marvin (Pentz, Jr.)
1939-1984 .... **CLC 26**
See also CA 195; 112

Gebler, Carlo (Ernest) 1954- .... **CLC 39**
See also CA 119; 133; CANR 96; DLB 271

Gee, Maggie (Mary) 1948- .... **CLC 57**
See also CA 130; CANR 125; CN 7; DLB 207

Gee, Maurice (Gough) 1931- .... **CLC 29**
See also AAYA 42; CA 97-100; CANR 67, 123; CLR 56; CN 7; CWRI 5; EWL 3; MAICYA 2; RGSF 2; SATA 46, 101

Geiogamah, Hanay 1945- .... **NNAL**
See also CA 153; DAM MULT; DLB 175

Gelbart, Larry (Simon) 1928- .... **CLC 21, 61**
See Gelbart, Larry
See also CA 73-76; CANR 45, 94

Gelbart, Larry 1928-
See Gelbart, Larry (Simon)
See also CAD; CD 5

Gelber, Jack 1932-2003 ...... **CLC 1, 6, 14, 79**
See also CA 1-4R; 216; CAD; CANR 2; DLB 7, 228

Gellhorn, Martha (Ellis)
1908-1998 .... **CLC 14, 60**
See also CA 77-80; 164; CANR 44; CN 7; DLBY 1982, 1998

Genet, Jean 1910-1986 . **DC 25; CLC 1, 2, 5, 10, 14, 44, 46; TCLC 128**
See also CA 13-16R; CANR 18; DA3; DAM DRAM; DFS 10; DLB 72; DLBY 1986; EW 13; EWL 3; GFL 1789 to the Present; GLL 1; LMFS 2; MTCW 1, 2; RGWL 2, 3; TWA

Gent, Peter 1942- .... **CLC 29**
See also AITN 1; CA 89-92; DLBY 1982

Gentile, Giovanni 1875-1944 .... **TCLC 96**
See also CA 119

Gentlewoman in New England, A
See Bradstreet, Anne

Gentlewoman in Those Parts, A
See Bradstreet, Anne

Geoffrey of Monmouth c.
1100-1155 .... **CMLC 44**
See also DLB 146; TEA

George, Jean
See George, Jean Craighead

George, Jean Craighead 1919- .... **CLC 35**
See also AAYA 8; BYA 2, 4; CA 5-8R; CANR 25; CLR 1; 80; DLB 52; JRDA; MAICYA 1, 2; SATA 2, 68, 124; WYA; YAW

George, Stefan (Anton) 1868-1933 . **TCLC 2, 14**
See also CA 104; 193; EW 8; EWL 3

Georges, Georges Martin
See Simenon, Georges (Jacques Christian)

Gerald of Wales c. 1146-c. 1223 ... **CMLC 60**

Gerhardi, William Alexander
See Gerhardie, William Alexander

Gerhardie, William Alexander
1895-1977 .... **CLC 5**
See also CA 25-28R; 73-76; CANR 18; DLB 36; RGEL 2

Gerson, Jean 1363-1429 .... **LC 77**
See also DLB 208

Gersonides 1288-1344 .... **CMLC 49**
See also DLB 115

Gerstler, Amy 1956- .... **CLC 70**
See also CA 146; CANR 99

Gertler, T. .... **CLC 34**
See also CA 116; 121

Gertsen, Aleksandr Ivanovich
See Herzen, Aleksandr Ivanovich

Ghalib .... **NCLC 39, 78**
See Ghalib, Asadullah Khan

Ghalib, Asadullah Khan 1797-1869
See Ghalib
See also DAM POET; RGWL 2, 3

Ghelderode, Michel de 1898-1962 ..... **CLC 6, 11; DC 15**
See also CA 85-88; CANR 40, 77; DAM DRAM; EW 11; EWL 3; TWA

Ghiselin, Brewster 1903-2001 .... **CLC 23**
See also CA 13-16R; CAAS 10; CANR 13; CP 7

Ghose, Aurabinda 1872-1950 .... **TCLC 63**
See Ghose, Aurobindo
See also CA 163

Ghose, Aurobindo
See Ghose, Aurabinda
See also EWL 3

Ghose, Zulfikar 1935- .... **CLC 42, 200**
See also CA 65-68; CANR 67; CN 7; CP 7; EWL 3

Ghosh, Amitav 1956- .... **CLC 44, 153**
See also CA 147; CANR 80; CN 7; WWE 1

Giacosa, Giuseppe 1847-1906 .... **TCLC 7**
See also CA 104

Gibb, Lee
See Waterhouse, Keith (Spencer)

Gibbon, Edward 1737-1794 .... **LC 97**
See also BRW 3; DLB 104; RGEL 2

Gibbon, Lewis Grassic .... **TCLC 4**
See Mitchell, James Leslie
See also RGEL 2

Gibbons, Kaye 1960- .... **CLC 50, 88, 145**
See also AAYA 34; AMWS 10; CA 151; CANR 75, 127; CSW; DA3; DAM POP; DLB 292; MTCW 1; NFS 3; RGAL 4; SATA 117

Gibran, Kahlil 1883-1931 . **PC 9; TCLC 1, 9**
See also CA 104; 150; DA3; DAM POET, POP; EWL 3; MTCW 2

Gibran, Khalil
See Gibran, Kahlil

Gibson, William 1914- .... **CLC 23**
See also CA 9-12R; CAD 2; CANR 9, 42, 75, 125; CD 5; DA; DAB; DAC; DAM DRAM, MST; DFS 2; DLB 7; LAIT 2; MTCW 2; SATA 66; YAW

Gibson, William (Ford) 1948- ... **CLC 39, 63, 186, 192; SSC 52**
See also AAYA 12, 59; BPFB 2; CA 126; 133; CANR 52, 90, 106; CN 7; CPW; DA3; DAM POP; DLB 251; MTCW 2; SCFW 2; SFW 4

Gide, Andre (Paul Guillaume)
1869-1951 ..... **SSC 13; TCLC 5, 12, 36; WLC**
See also CA 104; 124; DA; DA3; DAB; DAC; DAM MST, NOV; DLB 65; EW 8; EWL 3; GFL 1789 to the Present; MTCW 1, 2; RGSF 2; RGWL 2, 3; TWA

Gifford, Barry (Colby) 1946- .... **CLC 34**
See also CA 65-68; CANR 9, 30, 40, 90

Gilbert, Frank
See De Voto, Bernard (Augustine)

Gilbert, W(illiam) S(chwenck)
1836-1911 .... **TCLC 3**
See also CA 104; 173; DAM DRAM, POET; RGEL 2; SATA 36

Gilbreth, Frank B(unker), Jr.
1911-2001 .... **CLC 17**
See also CA 9-12R; SATA 2

Gilchrist, Ellen (Louise) 1935- .. **CLC 34, 48, 143; SSC 14, 63**
See also BPFB 2; CA 113; 116; CANR 41, 61, 104; CN 7; CPW; CSW; DAM POP; DLB 130; EWL 3; EXPS; MTCW 1, 2; RGAL 4; RGSF 2; SSFS 9

Giles, Molly 1942- .... **CLC 39**
See also CA 126; CANR 98

Gill, Eric 1882-1940 .... **TCLC 85**
See Gill, (Arthur) Eric (Rowton Peter Joseph)

Gill, (Arthur) Eric (Rowton Peter Joseph)
1882-1940
See Gill, Eric
See also CA 120; DLB 98

Gill, Patrick
See Creasey, John

Gillette, Douglas .... **CLC 70**

Gilliam, Terry (Vance) 1940- .... **CLC 21, 141**
See Monty Python
See also AAYA 19, 59; CA 108; 113; CANR 35; INT CA-113

Gillian, Jerry
See Gilliam, Terry (Vance)

Gilliatt, Penelope (Ann Douglass)
1932-1993 .... **CLC 2, 10, 13, 53**
See also AITN 2; CA 13-16R; 141; CANR 49; DLB 14

Gilman, Charlotte (Anna) Perkins (Stetson)
1860-1935 ...... **SSC 13, 62; TCLC 9, 37, 117**
See also AMWS 11; BYA 11; CA 106; 150; DLB 221; EXPS; FW; HGG; LAIT 2; MAWW; MTCW 1; RGAL 4; RGSF 2; SFW 4; SSFS 1, 18

Gilmour, David 1946- .... **CLC 35**

Gilpin, William 1724-1804 .... **NCLC 30**

Gilray, J. D.
See Mencken, H(enry) L(ouis)

Gilroy, Frank D(aniel) 1925- .... **CLC 2**
See also CA 81-84; CAD; CANR 32, 64, 86; CD 5; DFS 17; DLB 7

Gilstrap, John 1957(?)- .... **CLC 99**
See also CA 160; CANR 101

Ginsberg, Allen 1926-1997 .... **CLC 1, 2, 3, 4, 6, 13, 36, 69, 109; PC 4, 47; TCLC 120; WLC**
See also AAYA 33; AITN 1; AMWC 1; AMWS 2; BG 2; CA 1-4R; 157; CANR 2, 41, 63, 95; CDALB 1941-1968; CP 7; DA; DA3; DAB; DAC; DAM MST, POET; DLB 5, 16, 169, 237; EWL 3; GLL 1; LMFS 2; MTCW 1, 2; PAB; PFS 5; RGAL 4; TUS; WP

Ginzburg, Eugenia .... **CLC 59**
See Ginzburg, Evgeniia

Ginzburg, Evgeniia 1904-1977
See Ginzburg, Eugenia
See also DLB 302

Ginzburg, Natalia 1916-1991 .... **CLC 5, 11, 54, 70; SSC 65; TCLC 156**
See also CA 85-88; 135; CANR 33; DFS 14; DLB 177; EW 13; EWL 3; MTCW 1, 2; RGWL 2, 3

Giono, Jean 1895-1970 .... **CLC 4, 11; TCLC 124**
See also CA 45-48; 29-32R; CANR 2, 35; DLB 72; EWL 3; GFL 1789 to the Present; MTCW 1; RGWL 2, 3

Gordimer, Nadine 1923- ...... **CLC 3, 5, 7, 10, 18, 33, 51, 70, 123, 160, 161; SSC 17; WLCS**
See also AAYA 39; AFW; BRWS 2; CA 5-8R; CANR 3, 28, 56, 88, 131; CN 7; DA; DA3; DAB; DAC; DAM MST, NOV; DLB 225; EWL 3; EXPS; INT CANR-28; LATS 1:2; MTCW 1, 2; NFS 4; RGEL 2; RGSF 2; SSFS 2, 14, 19; TWA; WLIT 2; YAW

Gordon, Adam Lindsay
1833-1870 .... **NCLC 21**
See also DLB 230

Gordon, Caroline 1895-1981 . **CLC 6, 13, 29, 83; SSC 15**
See also AMW; CA 11-12; 103; CANR 36; CAP 1; DLB 4, 9, 102; DLBD 17; DLBY 1981; EWL 3; MTCW 1, 2; RGAL 4; RGSF 2

Gordon, Charles William 1860-1937
See Connor, Ralph
See also CA 109

Gordon, Mary (Catherine) 1949- .... **CLC 13, 22, 128; SSC 59**
See also AMWS 4; BPFB 2; CA 102; CANR 44, 92; CN 7; DLB 6; DLBY 1981; FW; INT CA-102; MTCW 1

Gordon, N. J.
See Bosman, Herman Charles

Gordon, Sol 1923- .... **CLC 26**
See also CA 53-56; CANR 4; SATA 11

Gordone, Charles 1925-1995 .. **CLC 1, 4; DC 8**
See also BW 1, 3; CA 93-96; 180; 150; CAAE 180; CAD; CANR 55; DAM DRAM; DLB 7; INT CA-93-96; MTCW 1

Gore, Catherine 1800-1861 .... **NCLC 65**
See also DLB 116; RGEL 2

Gorenko, Anna Andreevna
See Akhmatova, Anna

Gorky, Maxim .... **SSC 28; TCLC 8; WLC**
See Peshkov, Alexei Maximovich
See also DAB; DFS 9; DLB 295; EW 8; EWL 3; MTCW 2; TWA

Goryan, Sirak
See Saroyan, William

Gosse, Edmund (William)
1849-1928 .... **TCLC 28**
See also CA 117; DLB 57, 144, 184; RGEL 2

Gotlieb, Phyllis (Fay Bloom) 1926- .. **CLC 18**
See also CA 13-16R; CANR 7, 135; DLB 88, 251; SFW 4

Gottesman, S. D.
See Kornbluth, C(yril) M.; Pohl, Frederik

Gottfried von Strassburg fl. c.
1170-1215 .... **CMLC 10**
See also CDWLB 2; DLB 138; EW 1; RGWL 2, 3

Gotthelf, Jeremias 1797-1854 .... **NCLC 117**
See also DLB 133; RGWL 2, 3

Gottschalk, Laura Riding
See Jackson, Laura (Riding)

Gould, Lois 1932(?)-2002 .... **CLC 4, 10**
See also CA 77-80; 208; CANR 29; MTCW 1

Gould, Stephen Jay 1941-2002 .... **CLC 163**
See also AAYA 26; BEST 90:2; CA 77-80; 205; CANR 10, 27, 56, 75, 125; CPW; INT CANR-27; MTCW 1, 2

Gourmont, Remy(-Marie-Charles) de
1858-1915 .... **TCLC 17**
See also CA 109; 150; GFL 1789 to the Present; MTCW 2

Gournay, Marie le Jars de
See de Gournay, Marie le Jars

Govier, Katherine 1948- .... **CLC 51**
See also CA 101; CANR 18, 40, 128; CCA 1

Gower, John c. 1330-1408 .... **LC 76; PC 59**
See also BRW 1; DLB 146; RGEL 2

Goyen, (Charles) William
1915-1983 .... **CLC 5, 8, 14, 40**
See also AITN 2; CA 5-8R; 110; CANR 6, 71; DLB 2, 218; DLBY 1983; EWL 3; INT CANR-6

Goytisolo, Juan 1931- .... **CLC 5, 10, 23, 133; HLC 1**
See also CA 85-88; CANR 32, 61, 131; CWW 2; DAM MULT; EWL 3; GLL 2; HW 1, 2; MTCW 1, 2

Gozzano, Guido 1883-1916 .... **PC 10**
See also CA 154; DLB 114; EWL 3

Gozzi, (Conte) Carlo 1720-1806 .... **NCLC 23**

Grabbe, Christian Dietrich
1801-1836 .... **NCLC 2**
See also DLB 133; RGWL 2, 3

Grace, Patricia Frances 1937- .... **CLC 56**
See also CA 176; CANR 118; CN 7; EWL 3; RGSF 2

Gracian y Morales, Baltasar
1601-1658 .... **LC 15**

Gracq, Julien .... **CLC 11, 48**
See Poirier, Louis
See also CWW 2; DLB 83; GFL 1789 to the Present

Grade, Chaim 1910-1982 .... **CLC 10**
See also CA 93-96; 107; EWL 3

Graduate of Oxford, A
See Ruskin, John

Grafton, Garth
See Duncan, Sara Jeannette

Grafton, Sue 1940- .... **CLC 163**
See also AAYA 11, 49; BEST 90:3; CA 108; CANR 31, 55, 111, 134; CMW 4; CPW; CSW; DA3; DAM POP; DLB 226; FW; MSW

Graham, John
See Phillips, David Graham

Graham, Jorie 1951- .... **CLC 48, 118; PC 59**
See also CA 111; CANR 63, 118; CP 7; CWP; DLB 120; EWL 3; PFS 10, 17

Graham, R(obert) B(ontine) Cunninghame
See Cunninghame Graham, Robert (Gallnigad) Bontine
See also DLB 98, 135, 174; RGEL 2; RGSF 2

Graham, Robert
See Haldeman, Joe (William)

Graham, Tom
See Lewis, (Harry) Sinclair

Graham, W(illiam) S(idney)
1918-1986 .... **CLC 29**
See also BRWS 7; CA 73-76; 118; DLB 20; RGEL 2

Graham, Winston (Mawdsley)
1910-2003 .... **CLC 23**
See also CA 49-52; 218; CANR 2, 22, 45, 66; CMW 4; CN 7; DLB 77; RHW

Grahame, Kenneth 1859-1932 ...... **TCLC 64, 136**
See also BYA 5; CA 108; 136; CANR 80; CLR 5; CWRI 5; DA3; DAB; DLB 34, 141, 178; FANT; MAICYA 1, 2; MTCW 2; RGEL 2; SATA 100; TEA; WCH; YABC 1

Granger, Darius John
See Marlowe, Stephen

Granin, Daniil 1918- .... **CLC 59**
See also DLB 302

Granovsky, Timofei Nikolaevich
1813-1855 .... **NCLC 75**
See also DLB 198

Grant, Skeeter
See Spiegelman, Art

Granville-Barker, Harley
1877-1946 .... **TCLC 2**
See Barker, Harley Granville
See also CA 104; 204; DAM DRAM; RGEL 2

Granzotto, Gianni
See Granzotto, Giovanni Battista

Granzotto, Giovanni Battista
1914-1985 .... **CLC 70**
See also CA 166

Grass, Guenter (Wilhelm) 1927- ... **CLC 1, 2, 4, 6, 11, 15, 22, 32, 49, 88; WLC**
See Grass, Gunter (Wilhelm)
See also BPFB 2; CA 13-16R; CANR 20, 75, 93, 133; CDWLB 2; DA; DA3; DAB; DAC; DAM MST, NOV; DLB 75, 124; EW 13; EWL 3; MTCW 1, 2; RGWL 2, 3; TWA

Grass, Gunter (Wilhelm)
See Grass, Guenter (Wilhelm)
See also CWW 2

Gratton, Thomas
See Hulme, T(homas) E(rnest)

Grau, Shirley Ann 1929- .... **CLC 4, 9, 146; SSC 15**
See also CA 89-92; CANR 22, 69; CN 7; CSW; DLB 2, 218; INT CA-89-92; CANR-22; MTCW 1

Gravel, Fern
See Hall, James Norman

Graver, Elizabeth 1964- .... **CLC 70**
See also CA 135; CANR 71, 129

Graves, Richard Perceval
1895-1985 .... **CLC 44**
See also CA 65-68; CANR 9, 26, 51

Graves, Robert (von Ranke)
1895-1985 .. **CLC 1, 2, 6, 11, 39, 44, 45; PC 6**
See also BPFB 2; BRW 7; BYA 4; CA 5-8R; 117; CANR 5, 36; CDBLB 1914-1945; DA3; DAB; DAC; DAM MST, POET; DLB 20, 100, 191; DLBD 18; DLBY 1985; EWL 3; LATS 1:1; MTCW 1, 2; NCFS 2; RGEL 2; RHW; SATA 45; TEA

Graves, Valerie
See Bradley, Marion Zimmer

Gray, Alasdair (James) 1934- .... **CLC 41**
See also BRWS 9; CA 126; CANR 47, 69, 106; CN 7; DLB 194, 261; HGG; INT CA-126; MTCW 1, 2; RGSF 2; SUFW 2

Gray, Amlin 1946- .... **CLC 29**
See also CA 138

Gray, Francine du Plessix 1930- ..... **CLC 22, 153**
See also BEST 90:3; CA 61-64; CAAS 2; CANR 11, 33, 75, 81; DAM NOV; INT CANR-11; MTCW 1, 2

Gray, John (Henry) 1866-1934 ...... **TCLC 19**
See also CA 119; 162; RGEL 2

Gray, Simon (James Holliday)
1936- .... **CLC 9, 14, 36**
See also AITN 1; CA 21-24R; CAAS 3; CANR 32, 69; CD 5; DLB 13; EWL 3; MTCW 1; RGEL 2

Gray, Spalding 1941-2004 .... **CLC 49, 112; DC 7**
See also CA 128; 225; CAD; CANR 74; CD 5; CPW; DAM POP; MTCW 2

Gray, Thomas 1716-1771 .... **LC 4, 40; PC 2; WLC**
See also BRW 3; CDBLB 1660-1789; DA; DA3; DAB; DAC; DAM MST; DLB 109; EXPP; PAB; PFS 9; RGEL 2; TEA; WP

Grayson, David
See Baker, Ray Stannard

Grayson, Richard (A.) 1951- .... **CLC 38**
See also CA 85-88; 210; CAAE 210; CANR 14, 31, 57; DLB 234

Greeley, Andrew M(oran) 1928- ...... **CLC 28**
See also BPFB 2; CA 5-8R; CAAS 7;
CANR 7, 43, 69, 104; CMW 4; CPW;
DA3; DAM POP; MTCW 1, 2

Green, Anna Katharine
1846-1935 .... **TCLC 63**
See also CA 112; 159; CMW 4; DLB 202,
221; MSW

Green, Brian
See Card, Orson Scott

Green, Hannah
See Greenberg, Joanne (Goldenberg)

Green, Hannah 1927(?)-1996 .... **CLC 3**
See also CA 73-76; CANR 59, 93; NFS 10

Green, Henry .... **CLC 2, 13, 97**
See Yorke, Henry Vincent
See also BRWS 2; CA 175; DLB 15; EWL
3; RGEL 2

Green, Julian (Hartridge) 1900-1998
See Green, Julian
See also CA 21-24R; 169; CANR 33, 87;
CWW 2; DLB 4, 72; MTCW 1

Green, Julian .... **CLC 3, 11, 77**
See Green, Julien (Hartridge)
See also EWL 3; GFL 1789 to the Present;
MTCW 2

Green, Paul (Eliot) 1894-1981 .... **CLC 25**
See also AITN 1; CA 5-8R; 103; CANR 3;
DAM DRAM; DLB 7, 9, 249; DLBY
1981; RGAL 4

Greenaway, Peter 1942- .... **CLC 159**
See also CA 127

Greenberg, Ivan 1908-1973
See Rahv, Philip
See also CA 85-88

Greenberg, Joanne (Goldenberg)
1932- .... **CLC 7, 30**
See also AAYA 12; CA 5-8R; CANR 14,
32, 69; CN 7; SATA 25; YAW

Greenberg, Richard 1959(?)- .... **CLC 57**
See also CA 138; CAD; CD 5

Greenblatt, Stephen J(ay) 1943- ...... **CLC 70**
See also CA 49-52; CANR 115

Greene, Bette 1934- .... **CLC 30**
See also AAYA 7; BYA 3; CA 53-56; CANR
4; CLR 2; CWRI 5; JRDA; LAIT 4; MAI-
CYA 1, 2; NFS 10; SAAS 16; SATA 8,
102; WYA; YAW

Greene, Gael .... **CLC 8**
See also CA 13-16R; CANR 10

Greene, Graham (Henry)
1904-1991 .... **CLC 1, 3, 6, 9, 14, 18, 27,
37, 70, 72, 125; SSC 29; WLC**
See also AITN 2; BPFB 2; BRWR 2; BRWS
1; BYA 3; CA 13-16R; 133; CANR 35,
61, 131; CBD; CDBLB 1945-1960; CMW
4; DA; DA3; DAB; DAC; DAM MST,
NOV; DLB 13, 15, 77, 100, 162, 201,
204; DLBY 1991; EWL 3; MSW; MTCW
1, 2; NFS 16; RGEL 2; SATA 20; SSFS
14; TEA; WLIT 4

Greene, Robert 1558-1592 .... **LC 41**
See also BRWS 8; DLB 62, 167; IDTP;
RGEL 2; TEA

Greer, Germaine 1939- .... **CLC 131**
See also AITN 1; CA 81-84; CANR 33, 70,
115, 133; FW; MTCW 1, 2

Greer, Richard
See Silverberg, Robert

Gregor, Arthur 1923- .... **CLC 9**
See also CA 25-28R; CAAS 10; CANR 11;
CP 7; SATA 36

Gregor, Lee
See Pohl, Frederik

Gregory, Lady Isabella Augusta (Persse)
1852-1932 .... **TCLC 1**
See also BRW 6; CA 104; 184; DLB 10;
IDTP; RGEL 2

Gregory, J. Dennis
See Williams, John A(lfred)

Grekova, I. .... **CLC 59**
See Ventsel, Elena Sergeevna
See also CWW 2

Grendon, Stephen
See Derleth, August (William)

Grenville, Kate 1950- .... **CLC 61**
See also CA 118; CANR 53, 93

Grenville, Pelham
See Wodehouse, P(elham) G(renville)

Greve, Felix Paul (Berthold Friedrich)
1879-1948
See Grove, Frederick Philip
See also CA 104; 141, 175; CANR 79;
DAC; DAM MST

Greville, Fulke 1554-1628 .... **LC 79**
See also DLB 62, 172; RGEL 2

Grey, Lady Jane 1537-1554 .... **LC 93**
See also DLB 132

Grey, Zane 1872-1939 .... **TCLC 6**
See also BPFB 2; CA 104; 132; DA3; DAM
POP; DLB 9, 212; MTCW 1, 2; RGAL 4;
TCWW 2; TUS

Griboedov, Aleksandr Sergeevich
1795(?)-1829 .... **NCLC 129**
See also DLB 205; RGWL 2, 3

Grieg, (Johan) Nordahl (Brun)
1902-1943 .... **TCLC 10**
See also CA 107; 189; EWL 3

Grieve, C(hristopher) M(urray)
1892-1978 .... **CLC 11, 19**
See MacDiarmid, Hugh; Grieve, C. M.
See also CA 5-8R; 85-88; CANR 33, 107;
DAM POET; MTCW 1; RGEL 2

Griffin, Gerald 1803-1840 .... **NCLC 7**
See also DLB 159; RGEL 2

Griffin, John Howard 1920-1980 ..... **CLC 68**
See also AITN 1; CA 1-4R; 101; CANR 2

Griffin, Peter 1942- .... **CLC 39**
See also CA 136

Griffith, D(avid Lewelyn) W(ark)
1875(?)-1948 .... **TCLC 68**
See also CA 119; 150; CANR 80

Griffith, Lawrence
See Griffith, D(avid Lewelyn) W(ark)

Griffiths, Trevor 1935- .... **CLC 13, 52**
See also CA 97-100; CANR 45; CBD; CD
5; DLB 13, 245

Griggs, Sutton (Elbert)
1872-1930 .... **TCLC 77**
See also CA 123; 186; DLB 50

Grigson, Geoffrey (Edward Harvey)
1905-1985 .... **CLC 7, 39**
See also CA 25-28R; 118; CANR 20, 33;
DLB 27; MTCW 1, 2

Grile, Dod
See Bierce, Ambrose (Gwinett)

Grillparzer, Franz 1791-1872 .... **DC 14;
NCLC 1, 102; SSC 37**
See also CDWLB 2; DLB 133; EW 5;
RGWL 2, 3; TWA

Grimble, Reverend Charles James
See Eliot, T(homas) S(tearns)

Grimke, Angelina (Emily) Weld
1880-1958 .... **HR 2**
See Weld, Angelina (Emily) Grimke
See also BW 1; CA 124; DAM POET; DLB
50, 54

Grimke, Charlotte L(ottie) Forten
1837(?)-1914
See Forten, Charlotte L.
See also BW 1; CA 117; 124; DAM MULT,
POET

Grimm, Jacob Ludwig Karl
1785-1863 .... **NCLC 3, 77; SSC 36**
See also DLB 90; MAICYA 1, 2; RGSF 2;
RGWL 2, 3; SATA 22; WCH

Grimm, Wilhelm Karl 1786-1859 .. **NCLC 3,
77; SSC 36**
See also CDWLB 2; DLB 90; MAICYA 1,
2; RGSF 2; RGWL 2, 3; SATA 22; WCH

**Grimmelshausen, Hans Jakob Christoffel
von**
See Grimmelshausen, Johann Jakob Christoffel von
See also RGWL 2, 3

**Grimmelshausen, Johann Jakob Christoffel
von** 1621-1676 .... **LC 6**
See Grimmelshausen, Hans Jakob Christof-
fel von
See also CDWLB 2; DLB 168

Grindel, Eugene 1895-1952
See Eluard, Paul
See also CA 104; 193; LMFS 2

Grisham, John 1955- .... **CLC 84**
See also AAYA 14, 47; BPFB 2; CA 138;
CANR 47, 69, 114, 133; CMW 4; CN 7;
CPW; CSW; DA3; DAM POP; MSW;
MTCW 2

Grosseteste, Robert 1175(?)-1253 . **CMLC 62**
See also DLB 115

Grossman, David 1954- .... **CLC 67**
See also CA 138; CANR 114; CWW 2;
DLB 299; EWL 3

Grossman, Vasilii Semenovich
See Grossman, Vasily (Semenovich)
See also DLB 272

Grossman, Vasily (Semenovich)
1905-1964 .... **CLC 41**
See Grossman, Vasilii Semenovich
See also CA 124; 130; MTCW 1

Grove, Frederick Philip .... **TCLC 4**
See Greve, Felix Paul (Berthold Friedrich)
See also DLB 92; RGEL 2

Grubb
See Crumb, R(obert)

Grumbach, Doris (Isaac) 1918- . **CLC 13, 22,
64**
See also CA 5-8R; CAAS 2; CANR 9, 42,
70, 127; CN 7; INT CANR-9; MTCW 2

Grundtvig, Nicolai Frederik Severin
1783-1872 .... **NCLC 1**
See also DLB 300

Grunge
See Crumb, R(obert)

Grunwald, Lisa 1959- .... **CLC 44**
See also CA 120

Gryphius, Andreas 1616-1664 .... **LC 89**
See also CDWLB 2; DLB 164; RGWL 2, 3

Guare, John 1938- .... **CLC 8, 14, 29, 67; DC
20**
See also CA 73-76; CAD; CANR 21, 69,
118; CD 5; DAM DRAM; DFS 8, 13;
DLB 7, 249; EWL 3; MTCW 1, 2; RGAL
4

Guarini, Battista 1537-1612 .... **LC 102**

Gubar, Susan (David) 1944- .... **CLC 145**
See also CA 108; CANR 45, 70; FW;
MTCW 1; RGAL 4

Gudjonsson, Halldor Kiljan 1902-1998
See Halldor Laxness
See also CA 103; 164

Guenter, Erich
See Eich, Gunter

Guest, Barbara 1920- .... **CLC 34; PC 55**
See also BG 2; CA 25-28R; CANR 11, 44,
84; CP 7; CWP; DLB 5, 193

Guest, Edgar A(lbert) 1881-1959 ... **TCLC 95**
See also CA 112; 168

Guest, Judith (Ann) 1936- .... **CLC 8, 30**
See also AAYA 7; CA 77-80; CANR 15,
75; DA3; DAM NOV, POP; EXPN; INT
CANR-15; LAIT 5; MTCW 1, 2; NFS 1

Guevara, Che .... **CLC 87; HLC 1**
See Guevara (Serna), Ernesto

Guevara (Serna), Ernesto
1928-1967 .... **CLC 87; HLC 1**
See Guevara, Che
See also CA 127; 111; CANR 56; DAM
MULT; HW 1

Guicciardini, Francesco 1483-1540 ..... **LC 49**

Guild, Nicholas M. 1944- .... **CLC 33**
See also CA 93-96

Guillemin, Jacques
See Sartre, Jean-Paul

Guillen, Jorge 1893-1984 . **CLC 11; HLCS 1;
PC 35**
See also CA 89-92; 112; DAM MULT;
POET; DLB 108; EWL 3; HW 1; RGWL
2, 3

Guillen, Nicolas (Cristobal)
1902-1989 .... **BLC 2; CLC 48, 79; HLC
1; PC 23**
See also BW 2; CA 116; 125; 129; CANR
84; DAM MST, MULT, POET; DLB 283;
EWL 3; HW 1; LAW; RGWL 2, 3; WP

Guillen y Alvarez, Jorge
See Guillen, Jorge

Guillevic, (Eugene) 1907-1997 .... **CLC 33**
See also CA 93-96; CWW 2

Guillois
See Desnos, Robert

Guillois, Valentin
See Desnos, Robert

Guimaraes Rosa, Joao 1908-1967 .... **HLCS 2**
See Rosa, Joao Guimaraes
See also CA 175; LAW; RGSF 2; RGWL 2,
3

Guiney, Louise Imogen
1861-1920 .... **TCLC 41**
See also CA 160; DLB 54; RGAL 4

Guinizelli, Guido c. 1230-1276 ...... **CMLC 49**

Guiraldes, Ricardo (Guillermo)
1886-1927 .... **TCLC 39**
See also CA 131; EWL 3; HW 1; LAW;
MTCW 1

Gumilev, Nikolai (Stepanovich)
1886-1921 .... **TCLC 60**
See Gumilyov, Nikolay Stepanovich
See also CA 165; DLB 295

Gumilyov, Nikolay Stepanovich
See Gumilev, Nikolai (Stepanovich)
See also EWL 3

Gump, P. Q.
See Card, Orson Scott

Gunesekera, Romesh 1954- .... **CLC 91**
See also BRWS 10; CA 159; CN 7; DLB
267

Gunn, Bill .... **CLC 5**
See Gunn, William Harrison
See also DLB 38

Gunn, Thom(son William)
1929-2004 . **CLC 3, 6, 18, 32, 81; PC 26**
See also BRWS 4; CA 17-20R; 227; CANR
9, 33, 116; CDBLB 1960 to Present; CP
7; DAM POET; DLB 27; INT CANR-33;
MTCW 1; PFS 9; RGEL 2

Gunn, William Harrison 1934(?)-1989
See Gunn, Bill
See also AITN 1; BW 1, 3; CA 13-16R;
128; CANR 12, 25, 76

Gunn Allen, Paula
See Allen, Paula Gunn

Gunnars, Kristjana 1948- .... **CLC 69**
See also CA 113; CCA 1; CP 7; CWP; DLB
60

Gunter, Erich
See Eich, Gunter

Gurdjieff, G(eorgei) I(vanovich)
1877(?)-1949 .... **TCLC 71**
See also CA 157

Gurganus, Allan 1947- .... **CLC 70**
See also BEST 90:1; CA 135; CANR 114;
CN 7; CPW; CSW; DAM POP; GLL 1

Gurney, A. R.
See Gurney, A(lbert) R(amsdell), Jr.
See also DLB 266

Gurney, A(lbert) R(amsdell), Jr.
1930- .... **CLC 32, 50, 54**
See Gurney, A. R.
See also AMWS 5; CA 77-80; CAD; CANR
32, 64, 121; CD 5; DAM DRAM; EWL 3

Gurney, Ivor (Bertie) 1890-1937 ... **TCLC 33**
See also BRW 6; CA 167; DLBY 2002;
PAB; RGEL 2

Gurney, Peter
See Gurney, A(lbert) R(amsdell), Jr.

Guro, Elena (Genrikhovna)
1877-1913 .... **TCLC 56**
See also DLB 295

Gustafson, James M(oody) 1925- ... **CLC 100**
See also CA 25-28R; CANR 37

Gustafson, Ralph (Barker)
1909-1995 .... **CLC 36**
See also CA 21-24R; CANR 8, 45, 84; CP
7; DLB 88; RGEL 2

Gut, Gom
See Simenon, Georges (Jacques Christian)

Guterson, David 1956- .... **CLC 91**
See also CA 132; CANR 73, 126; DLB 292;
MTCW 2; NFS 13

Guthrie, A(lfred) B(ertram), Jr.
1901-1991 .... **CLC 23**
See also CA 57-60; 134; CANR 24; DLB 6,
212; SATA 62; SATA-Obit 67

Guthrie, Isobel
See Grieve, C(hristopher) M(urray)

Guthrie, Woodrow Wilson 1912-1967
See Guthrie, Woody
See also CA 113; 93-96

Guthrie, Woody .... **CLC 35**
See Guthrie, Woodrow Wilson
See also DLB 303; LAIT 3

Gutierrez Najera, Manuel
1859-1895 .... **HLCS 2; NCLC 133**
See also DLB 290; LAW

Guy, Rosa (Cuthbert) 1925- .... **CLC 26**
See also AAYA 4, 37; BW 2; CA 17-20R;
CANR 14, 34, 83; CLR 13; DLB 33;
DNFS 1; JRDA; MAICYA 1, 2; SATA 14,
62, 122; YAW

Gwendolyn
See Bennett, (Enoch) Arnold

H. D. .... **CLC 3, 8, 14, 31, 34, 73; PC 5**
See Doolittle, Hilda

H. de V.
See Buchan, John

Haavikko, Paavo Juhani 1931- .. **CLC 18, 34**
See also CA 106; CWW 2; EWL 3

Habbema, Koos
See Heijermans, Herman

Habermas, Juergen 1929- .... **CLC 104**
See also CA 109; CANR 85; DLB 242

Habermas, Jurgen
See Habermas, Juergen

Hacker, Marilyn 1942- ...... **CLC 5, 9, 23, 72,
91; PC 47**
See also CA 77-80; CANR 68, 129; CP 7;
CWP; DAM POET; DLB 120, 282; FW;
GLL 2; PFS 19

Hadewijch of Antwerp fl. 1250- ... **CMLC 61**
See also RGWL 3

Hadrian 76-138 .... **CMLC 52**

Haeckel, Ernst Heinrich (Philipp August)
1834-1919 .... **TCLC 83**
See also CA 157

Hafiz c. 1326-1389(?) .... **CMLC 34**
See also RGWL 2, 3

Hagedorn, Jessica T(arahata)
1949- .... **CLC 185**
See also CA 139; CANR 69; CWP; RGAL
4

Haggard, H(enry) Rider
1856-1925 .... **TCLC 11**
See also BRWS 3; BYA 4, 5; CA 108; 148;
CANR 112; DLB 70, 156, 174, 178;
FANT; LMFS 1; MTCW 2; RGEL 2;
RHW; SATA 16; SCFW; SFW 4; SUFW
1; WLIT 4

Hagiosy, L.
See Larbaud, Valery (Nicolas)

Hagiwara, Sakutaro 1886-1942 .... **PC 18;
TCLC 60**
See Hagiwara Sakutaro
See also CA 154; RGWL 3

Hagiwara Sakutaro
See Hagiwara, Sakutaro
See also EWL 3

Haig, Fenil
See Ford, Ford Madox

Haig-Brown, Roderick (Langmere)
1908-1976 .... **CLC 21**
See also CA 5-8R; 69-72; CANR 4, 38, 83;
CLR 31; CWRI 5; DLB 88; MAICYA 1,
2; SATA 12

Haight, Rip
See Carpenter, John (Howard)

Hailey, Arthur 1920- .... **CLC 5**
See also AITN 2; BEST 90:3; BPFB 2; CA
1-4R; CANR 2, 36, 75; CCA 1; CN 7;
CPW; DAM NOV, POP; DLB 88; DLBY
1982; MTCW 1, 2

Hailey, Elizabeth Forsythe 1938- ..... **CLC 40**
See also CA 93-96, 188; CAAE 188; CAAS
1; CANR 15, 48; INT CANR-15

Haines, John (Meade) 1924- .... **CLC 58**
See also AMWS 12; CA 17-20R; CANR
13, 34; CSW; DLB 5, 212

Hakluyt, Richard 1552-1616 .... **LC 31**
See also DLB 136; RGEL 2

Haldeman, Joe (William) 1943- .... **CLC 61**
See Graham, Robert
See also AAYA 38; CA 53-56, 179; CAAE
179; CAAS 25; CANR 6, 70, 72, 130;
DLB 8; INT CANR-6; SCFW 2; SFW 4

Hale, Janet Campbell 1947- .... **NNAL**
See also CA 49-52; CANR 45, 75; DAM
MULT; DLB 175; MTCW 2

Hale, Sarah Josepha (Buell)
1788-1879 .... **NCLC 75**
See also DLB 1, 42, 73, 243

Halevy, Elie 1870-1937 .... **TCLC 104**

Haley, Alex(ander Murray Palmer)
1921-1992 .... **BLC 2; CLC 8, 12, 76;
TCLC 147**
See also AAYA 26; BPFB 2; BW 2, 3; CA
77-80; 136; CANR 61; CDALBS; CPW;
CSW; DA; DA3; DAB; DAC; DAM MST,
MULT, POP; DLB 38; LAIT 5; MTCW
1, 2; NFS 9

Haliburton, Thomas Chandler
1796-1865 .... **NCLC 15, 149**
See also DLB 11, 99; RGEL 2; RGSF 2

Hall, Donald (Andrew, Jr.) 1928- ...... **CLC 1,
13, 37, 59, 151**
See also CA 5-8R; CAAS 7; CANR 2, 44,
64, 106, 133; CP 7; DAM POET; DLB 5;
MTCW 1; RGAL 4; SATA 23, 97

Hall, Frederic Sauser
See Sauser-Hall, Frederic

Hall, James
See Kuttner, Henry

Hall, James Norman 1887-1951 ..... **TCLC 23**
See also CA 123; 173; LAIT 1; RHW 1;
SATA 21

Hall, Joseph 1574-1656 .... **LC 91**
See also DLB 121, 151; RGEL 2

Hall, (Marguerite) Radclyffe
1880-1943 .... **TCLC 12**
See also BRWS 6; CA 110; 150; CANR 83;
DLB 191; MTCW 2; RGEL 2; RHW

Harrison, Tony 1937- .... **CLC 43, 129**
See also BRWS 5; CA 65-68; CANR 44, 98; CBD; CD 5; CP 7; DLB 40, 245; MTCW 1; RGEL 2

Harriss, Will(ard Irvin) 1922- .... **CLC 34**
See also CA 111

Hart, Ellis
See Ellison, Harlan (Jay)

Hart, Josephine 1942(?)- .... **CLC 70**
See also CA 138; CANR 70; CPW; DAM POP

Hart, Moss 1904-1961 .... **CLC 66**
See also CA 109; 89-92; CANR 84; DAM DRAM; DFS 1; DLB 7, 266; RGAL 4

Harte, (Francis) Bret(t)
1836(?)-1902 ... **SSC 8, 59; TCLC 1, 25; WLC**
See also AMWS 2; CA 104; 140; CANR 80; CDALB 1865-1917; DA; DA3; DAC; DAM MST; DLB 12, 64, 74, 79, 186; EXPS; LAIT 2; RGAL 4; RGSF 2; SATA 26; SSFS 3; TUS

Hartley, L(eslie) P(oles) 1895-1972 ... **CLC 2, 22**
See also BRWS 7; CA 45-48; 37-40R; CANR 33; DLB 15, 139; EWL 3; HGG; MTCW 1, 2; RGEL 2; RGSF 2; SUFW 1

Hartman, Geoffrey H. 1929- .... **CLC 27**
See also CA 117; 125; CANR 79; DLB 67

Hartmann, Sadakichi 1869-1944 ... **TCLC 73**
See also CA 157; DLB 54

Hartmann von Aue c. 1170-c.
1210 .... **CMLC 15**
See also CDWLB 2; DLB 138; RGWL 2, 3

Hartog, Jan de
See de Hartog, Jan

Haruf, Kent 1943- .... **CLC 34**
See also AAYA 44; CA 149; CANR 91, 131

Harvey, Caroline
See Trollope, Joanna

Harvey, Gabriel 1550(?)-1631 .... **LC 88**
See also DLB 167, 213, 281

Harwood, Ronald 1934- .... **CLC 32**
See also CA 1-4R; CANR 4, 55; CBD; CD 5; DAM DRAM, MST; DLB 13

Hasegawa Tatsunosuke
See Futabatei, Shimei

Hasek, Jaroslav (Matej Frantisek)
1883-1923 .... **SSC 69; TCLC 4**
See also CA 104; 129; CDWLB 4; DLB 215; EW 9; EWL 3; MTCW 1, 2; RGSF 2; RGWL 2, 3

Hass, Robert 1941- ... **CLC 18, 39, 99; PC 16**
See also AMWS 6; CA 111; CANR 30, 50, 71; CP 7; DLB 105, 206; EWL 3; RGAL 4; SATA 94

Hastings, Hudson
See Kuttner, Henry

Hastings, Selina .... **CLC 44**

Hathorne, John 1641-1717 .... **LC 38**

Hatteras, Amelia
See Mencken, H(enry) L(ouis)

Hatteras, Owen .... **TCLC 18**
See Mencken, H(enry) L(ouis); Nathan, George Jean

Hauptmann, Gerhart (Johann Robert)
1862-1946 .... **SSC 37; TCLC 4**
See also CA 104; 153; CDWLB 2; DAM DRAM; DLB 66, 118; EW 8; EWL 3; RGSF 2; RGWL 2, 3; TWA

Havel, Vaclav 1936- ..... **CLC 25, 58, 65, 123; DC 6**
See also CA 104; CANR 36, 63, 124; CD-WLB 4; CWW 2; DA3; DAM DRAM; DFS 10; DLB 232; EWL 3; LMFS 2; MTCW 1, 2; RGWL 3

Haviaras, Stratis .... **CLC 33**
See Chaviaras, Strates

Hawes, Stephen 1475(?)-1529(?) .... **LC 17**
See also DLB 132; RGEL 2

Hawkes, John (Clendennin Burne, Jr.)
1925-1998 .. **CLC 1, 2, 3, 4, 7, 9, 14, 15, 27, 49**
See also BPFB 2; CA 1-4R; 167; CANR 2, 47, 64; CN 7; DLB 2, 7, 227; DLBY 1980, 1998; EWL 3; MTCW 1, 2; RGAL 4

Hawking, S. W.
See Hawking, Stephen W(illiam)

Hawking, Stephen W(illiam) 1942- . **CLC 63, 105**
See also AAYA 13; BEST 89:1; CA 126; 129; CANR 48, 115; CPW; DA3; MTCW 2

Hawkins, Anthony Hope
See Hope, Anthony

Hawthorne, Julian 1846-1934 .... **TCLC 25**
See also CA 165; HGG

Hawthorne, Nathaniel 1804-1864 ... **NCLC 2, 10, 17, 23, 39, 79, 95; SSC 3, 29, 39; WLC**
See also AAYA 18; AMW; AMWC 1; AMWR 1; BPFB 2; BYA 3; CDALB 1640-1865; DA; DA3; DAB; DAC; DAM MST, NOV; DLB 1, 74, 183, 223, 269; EXPN; EXPS; HGG; LAIT 1; NFS 1, 20; RGAL 4; RGSF 2; SSFS 1, 7, 11, 15; SUFW 1; TUS; WCH; YABC 2

Hawthorne, Sophia Peabody
1809-1871 .... **NCLC 150**
See also DLB 183, 239

Haxton, Josephine Ayres 1921-
See Douglas, Ellen
See also CA 115; CANR 41, 83

Hayaseca y Eizaguirre, Jorge
See Echegaray (y Eizaguirre), Jose (Maria Waldo)

Hayashi, Fumiko 1904-1951 .... **TCLC 27**
See Hayashi Fumiko
See also CA 161

Hayashi Fumiko
See Hayashi, Fumiko
See also DLB 180; EWL 3

Haycraft, Anna (Margaret) 1932-
See Ellis, Alice Thomas
See also CA 122; CANR 85, 90; MTCW 2

Hayden, Robert E(arl) 1913-1980 ..... **BLC 2; CLC 5, 9, 14, 37; PC 6**
See also AFAW 1, 2; AMWS 2; BW 1, 3; CA 69-72; 97-100; CABS 2; CANR 24, 75, 82; CDALB 1941-1968; DA; DAC; DAM MST, MULT, POET; DLB 5, 76; EWL 3; EXPP; MTCW 1, 2; PFS 1; RGAL 4; SATA 19; SATA-Obit 26; WP

Haydon, Benjamin Robert
1786-1846 .... **NCLC 146**
See also DLB 110

Hayek, F(riedrich) A(ugust von)
1899-1992 .... **TCLC 109**
See also CA 93-96; 137; CANR 20; MTCW 1, 2

Hayford, J(oseph) E(phraim) Casely
See Casely-Hayford, J(oseph) E(phraim)

Hayman, Ronald 1932- .... **CLC 44**
See also CA 25-28R; CANR 18, 50, 88; CD 5; DLB 155

Hayne, Paul Hamilton 1830-1886 . **NCLC 94**
See also DLB 3, 64, 79, 248; RGAL 4

Hays, Mary 1760-1843 .... **NCLC 114**
See also DLB 142, 158; RGEL 2

Haywood, Eliza (Fowler)
1693(?)-1756 .... **LC 1, 44**
See also DLB 39; RGEL 2

Hazlitt, William 1778-1830 ...... **NCLC 29, 82**
See also BRW 4; DLB 110, 158; RGEL 2; TEA

Hazzard, Shirley 1931- .... **CLC 18**
See also CA 9-12R; CANR 4, 70, 127; CN 7; DLB 289; DLBY 1982; MTCW 1

Head, Bessie 1937-1986 ...... **BLC 2; CLC 25, 67; SSC 52**
See also AFW; BW 2, 3; CA 29-32R; 119; CANR 25, 82; CDWLB 3; DA3; DAM MULT; DLB 117, 225; EWL 3; EXPS; FW; MTCW 1, 2; RGSF 2; SSFS 5, 13; WLIT 2; WWE 1

Headon, (Nicky) Topper 1956(?)- .... **CLC 30**

Heaney, Seamus (Justin) 1939- ..... **CLC 5, 7, 14, 25, 37, 74, 91, 171; PC 18; WLCS**
See also BRWR 1; BRWS 2; CA 85-88; CANR 25, 48, 75, 91, 128; CDBLB 1960 to Present; CP 7; DA3; DAB; DAM POET; DLB 40; DLBY 1995; EWL 3; EXPP; MTCW 1, 2; PAB; PFS 2, 5, 8, 17; RGEL 2; TEA; WLIT 4

Hearn, (Patricio) Lafcadio (Tessima Carlos)
1850-1904 .... **TCLC 9**
See also CA 105; 166; DLB 12, 78, 189; HGG; RGAL 4

Hearne, Samuel 1745-1792 .... **LC 95**
See also DLB 99

Hearne, Vicki 1946-2001 .... **CLC 56**
See also CA 139; 201

Hearon, Shelby 1931- .... **CLC 63**
See also AITN 2; AMWS 8; CA 25-28R; CANR 18, 48, 103; CSW

Heat-Moon, William Least .... **CLC 29**
See Trogdon, William (Lewis)
See also AAYA 9

Hebbel, Friedrich 1813-1863 . **DC 21; NCLC 43**
See also CDWLB 2; DAM DRAM; DLB 129; EW 6; RGWL 2, 3

Hebert, Anne 1916-2000 .... **CLC 4, 13, 29**
See also CA 85-88; 187; CANR 69, 126; CCA 1; CWP; CWW 2; DA3; DAC; DAM MST, POET; DLB 68; EWL 3; GFL 1789 to the Present; MTCW 1, 2; PFS 20

Hecht, Anthony (Evan) 1923-2004 .... **CLC 8, 13, 19**
See also AMWS 10; CA 9-12R; CANR 6, 108; CP 7; DAM POET; DLB 5, 169; EWL 3; PFS 6; WP

Hecht, Ben 1894-1964 ..... **CLC 8; TCLC 101**
See also CA 85-88; DFS 9; DLB 7, 9, 25, 26, 28, 86; FANT; IDFW 3, 4; RGAL 4

Hedayat, Sadeq 1903-1951 .... **TCLC 21**
See also CA 120; EWL 3; RGSF 2

Hegel, Georg Wilhelm Friedrich
1770-1831 .... **NCLC 46**
See also DLB 90; TWA

Heidegger, Martin 1889-1976 .... **CLC 24**
See also CA 81-84; 65-68; CANR 34; DLB 296; MTCW 1, 2

Heidenstam, (Carl Gustaf) Verner von
1859-1940 .... **TCLC 5**
See also CA 104

Heidi Louise
See Erdrich, Louise

Heifner, Jack 1946- .... **CLC 11**
See also CA 105; CANR 47

Heijermans, Herman 1864-1924 .... **TCLC 24**
See also CA 123; EWL 3

Heilbrun, Carolyn G(old)
1926-2003 .... **CLC 25, 173**
See Cross, Amanda
See also CA 45-48; 220; CANR 1, 28, 58, 94; FW

Hein, Christoph 1944- .... **CLC 154**
See also CA 158; CANR 108; CDWLB 2; CWW 2; DLB 124

Heine, Heinrich 1797-1856 .... **NCLC 4, 54, 147; PC 25**
See also CDWLB 2; DLB 90; EW 5; RGWL 2, 3; TWA

Lampedusa, Giuseppe (Tomasi) di
　... **TCLC 13**
　See Tomasi di Lampedusa, Giuseppe
　See also CA 164; EW 11; MTCW 2; RGWL
　2, 3

Lampman, Archibald 1861-1899 ... **NCLC 25**
　See also DLB 92; RGEL 2; TWA

Lancaster, Bruce 1896-1963 .... **CLC 36**
　See also CA 9-10; CANR 70; CAP 1; SATA
　9

Lanchester, John 1962- .... **CLC 99**
　See also CA 194; DLB 267

Landau, Mark Alexandrovich
　See Aldanov, Mark (Alexandrovich)

Landau-Aldanov, Mark Alexandrovich
　See Aldanov, Mark (Alexandrovich)

Landis, Jerry
　See Simon, Paul (Frederick)

Landis, John 1950- .... **CLC 26**
　See also CA 112; 122; CANR 128

Landolfi, Tommaso 1908-1979 .... **CLC 11, 49**
　See also CA 127; 117; DLB 177; EWL 3

Landon, Letitia Elizabeth
　1802-1838 .... **NCLC 15**
　See also DLB 96

Landor, Walter Savage
　1775-1864 .... **NCLC 14**
　See also BRW 4; DLB 93, 107; RGEL 2

Landwirth, Heinz 1927-
　See Lind, Jakov
　See also CA 9-12R; CANR 7

Lane, Patrick 1939- .... **CLC 25**
　See also CA 97-100; CANR 54; CP 7; DAM
　POET; DLB 53; INT CA-97-100

Lang, Andrew 1844-1912 .... **TCLC 16**
　See also CA 114; 137; CANR 85; CLR 101;
　DLB 98, 141, 184; FANT; MAICYA 1, 2;
　RGEL 2; SATA 16; WCH

Lang, Fritz 1890-1976 .... **CLC 20, 103**
　See also CA 77-80; 69-72; CANR 30

Lange, John
　See Crichton, (John) Michael

Langer, Elinor 1939- .... **CLC 34**
　See also CA 121

Langland, William 1332(?)-1400(?) ..... **LC 19**
　See also BRW 1; DA; DAB; DAC; DAM
　MST, POET; DLB 146; RGEL 2; TEA;
　WLIT 3

Langstaff, Launcelot
　See Irving, Washington

Lanier, Sidney 1842-1881 . **NCLC 6, 118; PC
　50**
　See also AMWS 1; DAM POET; DLB 64;
　DLBD 13; EXPP; MAICYA 1; PFS 14;
　RGAL 4; SATA 18

Lanyer, Aemilia 1569-1645 .... **LC 10, 30, 83;
　PC 60**
　See also DLB 121

Lao-Tzu
　See Lao Tzu

Lao Tzu c. 6th cent. B.C.-3rd cent.
　B.C. .... **CMLC 7**

Lapine, James (Elliot) 1949- .... **CLC 39**
　See also CA 123; 130; CANR 54, 128; INT
　CA-130

Larbaud, Valery (Nicolas)
　1881-1957 .... **TCLC 9**
　See also CA 106; 152; EWL 3; GFL 1789
　to the Present

Lardner, Ring
　See Lardner, Ring(gold) W(ilmer)
　See also BPFB 2; CDALB 1917-1929; DLB
　11, 25, 86, 171; DLBD 16; RGAL 4;
　RGSF 2

Lardner, Ring W., Jr.
　See Lardner, Ring(gold) W(ilmer)

Lardner, Ring(gold) W(ilmer)
　1885-1933 .... **SSC 32; TCLC 2, 14**
　See Lardner, Ring
　See also AMW; CA 104; 131; MTCW 1, 2;
　TUS

Laredo, Betty
　See Codrescu, Andrei

Larkin, Maia
　See Wojciechowska, Maia (Teresa)

Larkin, Philip (Arthur) 1922-1985 ... **CLC 3,
　5, 8, 9, 13, 18, 33, 39, 64; PC 21**
　See also BRWS 1; CA 5-8R; 117; CANR
　24, 62; CDBLB 1960 to Present; DA3;
　DAB; DAM MST, POET; DLB 27; EWL
　3; MTCW 1, 2; PFS 3, 4, 12; RGEL 2

La Roche, Sophie von
　1730-1807 .... **NCLC 121**
　See also DLB 94

La Rochefoucauld, Francois
　1613-1680 .... **LC 108**

**Larra (y Sanchez de Castro), Mariano Jose
　de** 1809-1837 .... **NCLC 17, 130**

Larsen, Eric 1941- .... **CLC 55**
　See also CA 132

Larsen, Nella 1893(?)-1963 .... **BLC 2; CLC
　37; HR 3**
　See also AFAW 1, 2; BW 1; CA 125; CANR
　83; DAM MULT; DLB 51; FW; LATS
　1:1; LMFS 2

Larson, Charles R(aymond) 1938- ... **CLC 31**
　See also CA 53-56; CANR 4, 121

Larson, Jonathan 1961-1996 .... **CLC 99**
　See also AAYA 28; CA 156

La Sale, Antoine de c. 1386-1460(?) . **LC 104**
　See also DLB 208

Las Casas, Bartolome de
　1474-1566 .... **HLCS; LC 31**
　See Casas, Bartolome de las
　See also LAW

Lasch, Christopher 1932-1994 .... **CLC 102**
　See also CA 73-76; 144; CANR 25, 118;
　DLB 246; MTCW 1, 2

Lasker-Schueler, Else 1869-1945 ... **TCLC 57**
　See Lasker-Schuler, Else
　See also CA 183; DLB 66, 124

Lasker-Schuler, Else
　See Lasker-Schueler, Else
　See also EWL 3

Laski, Harold J(oseph) 1893-1950 . **TCLC 79**
　See also CA 188

Latham, Jean Lee 1902-1995 .... **CLC 12**
　See also AITN 1; BYA 1; CA 5-8R; CANR
　7, 84; CLR 50; MAICYA 1, 2; SATA 2,
　68; YAW

Latham, Mavis
　See Clark, Mavis Thorpe

Lathen, Emma .... **CLC 2**
　See Hennissart, Martha; Latsis, Mary J(ane)
　See also BPFB 2; CMW 4; DLB 306

Lathrop, Francis
　See Leiber, Fritz (Reuter, Jr.)

Latsis, Mary J(ane) 1927-1997
　See Lathen, Emma
　See also CA 85-88; 162; CMW 4

Lattany, Kristin
　See Lattany, Kristin (Elaine Eggleston)
　Hunter

Lattany, Kristin (Elaine Eggleston) Hunter
　1931- .... **CLC 35**
　See also AITN 1; BW 1; BYA 3; CA 13-
　16R; CANR 13, 108; CLR 3; CN 7; DLB
　33; INT CANR-13; MAICYA 1, 2; SAAS
　10; SATA 12, 132; YAW

Lattimore, Richmond (Alexander)
　1906-1984 .... **CLC 3**
　See also CA 1-4R; 112; CANR 1

Laughlin, James 1914-1997 .... **CLC 49**
　See also CA 21-24R; 162; CAAS 22; CANR
　9, 47; CP 7; DLB 48; DLBY 1996, 1997

Laurence, (Jean) Margaret (Wemyss)
　1926-1987 . **CLC 3, 6, 13, 50, 62; SSC 7**
　See also BYA 13; CA 5-8R; 121; CANR
　33; DAC; DAM MST; DLB 53; EWL 3;
　FW; MTCW 1, 2; NFS 11; RGEL 2;
　RGSF 2; SATA-Obit 50; TCWW 2

Laurent, Antoine 1952- .... **CLC 50**

Lauscher, Hermann
　See Hesse, Hermann

Lautreamont 1846-1870 .. **NCLC 12; SSC 14**
　See Lautreamont, Isidore Lucien Ducasse
　See also GFL 1789 to the Present; RGWL
　2, 3

Lautreamont, Isidore Lucien Ducasse
　See Lautreamont
　See also DLB 217

Lavater, Johann Kaspar
　1741-1801 .... **NCLC 142**
　See also DLB 97

Laverty, Donald
　See Blish, James (Benjamin)

Lavin, Mary 1912-1996 . **CLC 4, 18, 99; SSC
　4, 67**
　See also CA 9-12R; 151; CANR 33; CN 7;
　DLB 15; FW; MTCW 1; RGEL 2; RGSF
　2

Lavond, Paul Dennis
　See Kornbluth, C(yril) M.; Pohl, Frederik

Lawler, Ray
　See Lawler, Raymond Evenor
　See also DLB 289

Lawler, Raymond Evenor 1922- .... **CLC 58**
　See Lawler, Ray
　See also CA 103; CD 5; RGEL 2

Lawrence, D(avid) H(erbert Richards)
　1885-1930 .... **PC 54; SSC 4, 19, 73;
　TCLC 2, 9, 16, 33, 48, 61, 93; WLC**
　See Chambers, Jessie
　See also BPFB 2; BRW 7; BRWR 2; CA
　104; 121; CANR 131; CDBLB 1914-
　1945; DA; DA3; DAB; DAC; DAM MST,
　NOV, POET; DLB 10, 19, 36, 98, 162,
　195; EWL 3; EXPP; EXPS; LAIT 2, 3;
　MTCW 1, 2; NFS 18; PFS 6; RGEL 2;
　RGSF 2; SSFS 2, 6; TEA; WLIT 4; WP

Lawrence, T(homas) E(dward)
　1888-1935 .... **TCLC 18**
　See Dale, Colin
　See also BRWS 2; CA 115; 167; DLB 195

Lawrence of Arabia
　See Lawrence, T(homas) E(dward)

Lawson, Henry (Archibald Hertzberg)
　1867-1922 .... **SSC 18; TCLC 27**
　See also CA 120; 181; DLB 230; RGEL 2;
　RGSF 2

Lawton, Dennis
　See Faust, Frederick (Schiller)

Layamon fl. c. 1200- .... **CMLC 10**
　See Laȝamon
　See also DLB 146; RGEL 2

Laye, Camara 1928-1980 ..... **BLC 2; CLC 4,
　38**
　See Camara Laye
　See also AFW; BW 1; CA 85-88; 97-100;
　CANR 25; DAM MULT; MTCW 1, 2;
　WLIT 2

Layton, Irving (Peter) 1912- .... **CLC 2, 15,
　164**
　See also CA 1-4R; CANR 2, 33, 43, 66,
　129; CP 7; DAC; DAM MST, POET;
　DLB 88; EWL 3; MTCW 1, 2; PFS 12;
　RGEL 2

Lazarus, Emma 1849-1887 ...... **NCLC 8, 109**

Lazarus, Felix
　See Cable, George Washington

Lazarus, Henry
　See Slavitt, David R(ytman)

Lea, Joan
　See Neufeld, John (Arthur)

Lenz, Jakob Michael Reinhold
1751-1792 .... **LC 100**
See also DLB 94; RGWL 2, 3
Lenz, Siegfried 1926- .... **CLC 27; SSC 33**
See also CA 89-92; CANR 80; CWW 2;
DLB 75; EWL 3; RGSF 2; RGWL 2, 3
Leon, David
See Jacob, (Cyprien-)Max
Leonard, Elmore (John, Jr.) 1925- . **CLC 28,
34, 71, 120**
See also AAYA 22, 59; AITN 1; BEST 89:1,
90:4; BPFB 2; CA 81-84; CANR 12, 28,
53, 76, 96, 133; CMW 4; CN 7; CPW;
DA3; DAM POP; DLB 173, 226; INT
CANR-28; MSW; MTCW 1, 2; RGAL 4;
TCWW 2
Leonard, Hugh .... **CLC 19**
See Byrne, John Keyes
See also CBD; CD 5; DFS 13; DLB 13
Leonov, Leonid (Maximovich)
1899-1994 .... **CLC 92**
See Leonov, Leonid Maksimovich
See also CA 129; CANR 74, 76; DAM
NOV; EWL 3; MTCW 1, 2
Leonov, Leonid Maksimovich
See Leonov, Leonid (Maximovich)
See also DLB 272
Leopardi, (Conte) Giacomo
1798-1837 .... **NCLC 22, 129; PC 37**
See also EW 5; RGWL 2, 3; WP
Le Reveler
See Artaud, Antonin (Marie Joseph)
Lerman, Eleanor 1952- .... **CLC 9**
See also CA 85-88; CANR 69, 124
Lerman, Rhoda 1936- .... **CLC 56**
See also CA 49-52; CANR 70
Lermontov, Mikhail Iur'evich
See Lermontov, Mikhail Yuryevich
See also DLB 205
Lermontov, Mikhail Yuryevich
1814-1841 .... **NCLC 5, 47, 126; PC 18**
See Lermontov, Mikhail Iur'evich
See also EW 6; RGWL 2, 3; TWA
Leroux, Gaston 1868-1927 .... **TCLC 25**
See also CA 108; 136; CANR 69; CMW 4;
NFS 20; SATA 65
Lesage, Alain-Rene 1668-1747 .... **LC 2, 28**
See also EW 3; GFL Beginnings to 1789;
RGWL 2, 3
Leskov, N(ikolai) S(emenovich) 1831-1895
See Leskov, Nikolai (Semyonovich)
Leskov, Nikolai (Semyonovich)
1831-1895 .... **NCLC 25; SSC 34**
See Leskov, Nikolai Semenovich
Leskov, Nikolai Semenovich
See Leskov, Nikolai (Semyonovich)
See also DLB 238
Lesser, Milton
See Marlowe, Stephen
Lessing, Doris (May) 1919- ... **CLC 1, 2, 3, 6,
10, 15, 22, 40, 94, 170; SSC 6, 61;
WLCS**
See also AAYA 57; AFW; BRWS 1; CA
9-12R; CAAS 14; CANR 33, 54, 76, 122;
CD 5; CDBLB 1960 to Present; CN 7;
DA; DA3; DAB; DAC; DAM MST, NOV;
DFS 20; DLB 15, 139; DLBY 1985; EWL
3; EXPS; FW; LAIT 4; MTCW 1, 2;
RGEL 2; RGSF 2; SFW 4; SSFS 1, 12,
20; TEA; WLIT 2, 4
Lessing, Gotthold Ephraim 1729-1781 . **LC 8**
See also CDWLB 2; DLB 97; EW 4; RGWL
2, 3
Lester, Richard 1932- .... **CLC 20**
Levenson, Jay .... **CLC 70**
Lever, Charles (James)
1806-1872 .... **NCLC 23**
See also DLB 21; RGEL 2

Leverson, Ada Esther
1862(?)-1933(?) .... **TCLC 18**
See Elaine
See also CA 117; 202; DLB 153; RGEL 2
Levertov, Denise 1923-1997 .. **CLC 1, 2, 3, 5,
8, 15, 28, 66; PC 11**
See also AMWS 3; CA 1-4R; 178; 163;
CAAE 178; CAAS 19; CANR 3, 29, 50,
108; CDALBS; CP 7; CWP; DAM POET;
DLB 5, 165; EWL 3; EXPP; FW; INT
CANR-29; MTCW 1, 2; PAB; PFS 7, 17;
RGAL 4; TUS; WP
Levi, Carlo 1902-1975 .... **TCLC 125**
See also CA 65-68; 53-56; CANR 10; EWL
3; RGWL 2, 3
Levi, Jonathan .... **CLC 76**
See also CA 197
Levi, Peter (Chad Tigar)
1931-2000 .... **CLC 41**
See also CA 5-8R; 187; CANR 34, 80; CP
7; DLB 40
Levi, Primo 1919-1987 ...... **CLC 37, 50; SSC
12; TCLC 109**
See also CA 13-16R; 122; CANR 12, 33,
61, 70, 132; DLB 177, 299; EWL 3;
MTCW 1, 2; RGWL 2, 3
Levin, Ira 1929- .... **CLC 3, 6**
See also CA 21-24R; CANR 17, 44, 74;
CMW 4; CN 7; CPW; DA3; DAM POP;
HGG; MTCW 1, 2; SATA 66; SFW 4
Levin, Meyer 1905-1981 .... **CLC 7**
See also AITN 1; CA 9-12R; 104; CANR
15; DAM POP; DLB 9, 28; DLBY 1981;
SATA 21; SATA-Obit 27
Levine, Norman 1924- .... **CLC 54**
See also CA 73-76; CAAS 23; CANR 14,
70; DLB 88
Levine, Philip 1928- .. **CLC 2, 4, 5, 9, 14, 33,
118; PC 22**
See also AMWS 5; CA 9-12R; CANR 9,
37, 52, 116; CP 7; DAM POET; DLB 5;
EWL 3; PFS 8
Levinson, Deirdre 1931- .... **CLC 49**
See also CA 73-76; CANR 70
Levi-Strauss, Claude 1908- .... **CLC 38**
See also CA 1-4R; CANR 6, 32, 57; DLB
242; EWL 3; GFL 1789 to the Present;
MTCW 1, 2; TWA
Levitin, Sonia (Wolff) 1934- .... **CLC 17**
See also AAYA 13, 48; CA 29-32R; CANR
14, 32, 79; CLR 53; JRDA; MAICYA 1,
2; SAAS 2; SATA 4, 68, 119, 131; SATA-
Essay 131; YAW
Levon, O. U.
See Kesey, Ken (Elton)
Levy, Amy 1861-1889 .... **NCLC 59**
See also DLB 156, 240
Lewes, George Henry 1817-1878 ... **NCLC 25**
See also DLB 55, 144
Lewis, Alun 1915-1944 .... **SSC 40; TCLC 3**
See also BRW 7; CA 104; 188; DLB 20,
162; PAB; RGEL 2
Lewis, C. Day
See Day Lewis, C(ecil)
Lewis, C(live) S(taples) 1898-1963 .... **CLC 1,
3, 6, 14, 27, 124; WLC**
See also AAYA 3, 39; BPFB 2; BRWS 3;
BYA 15, 16; CA 81-84; CANR 33, 71,
132; CDBLB 1945-1960; CLR 3, 27;
CWRI 5; DA; DA3; DAB; DAC; DAM
MST, NOV, POP; DLB 15, 100, 160, 255;
EWL 3; FANT; JRDA; LMFS 2; MAI-
CYA 1, 2; MTCW 1, 2; RGEL 2; SATA
13, 100; SCFW; SFW 4; SUFW 1; TEA;
WCH; WYA; YAW
Lewis, Cecil Day
See Day Lewis, C(ecil)

Lewis, Janet 1899-1998 .... **CLC 41**
See Winters, Janet Lewis
See also CA 9-12R; 172; CANR 29, 63;
CAP 1; CN 7; DLBY 1987; RHW;
TCWW 2
Lewis, Matthew Gregory
1775-1818 .... **NCLC 11, 62**
See also DLB 39, 158, 178; HGG; LMFS
1; RGEL 2; SUFW
Lewis, (Harry) Sinclair 1885-1951 . **TCLC 4,
13, 23, 39; WLC**
See also AMW; AMWC 1; BPFB 2; CA
104; 133; CANR 132; CDALB 1917-
1929; DA; DA3; DAB; DAC; DAM MST,
NOV; DLB 9, 102, 284; DLBD 1; EWL
3; LAIT 3; MTCW 1, 2; NFS 15, 19;
RGAL 4; TUS
Lewis, (Percy) Wyndham
1884(?)-1957 .. **SSC 34; TCLC 2, 9, 104**
See also BRW 7; CA 104; 157; DLB 15;
EWL 3; FANT; MTCW 2; RGEL 2
Lewisohn, Ludwig 1883-1955 .... **TCLC 19**
See also CA 107; 203; DLB 4, 9, 28, 102
Lewton, Val 1904-1951 .... **TCLC 76**
See also CA 199; IDFW 3, 4
Leyner, Mark 1956- .... **CLC 92**
See also CA 110; CANR 28, 53; DA3; DLB
292; MTCW 2
Lezama Lima, Jose 1910-1976 .... **CLC 4, 10,
101; HLCS 2**
See also CA 77-80; CANR 71; DAM
MULT; DLB 113, 283; EWL 3; HW 1, 2;
LAW; RGWL 2, 3
L'Heureux, John (Clarke) 1934- ...... **CLC 52**
See also CA 13-16R; CANR 23, 45, 88;
DLB 244
Li Ch'ing-chao 1081(?)-1141(?) .... **CMLC 71**
Liddell, C. H.
See Kuttner, Henry
Lie, Jonas (Lauritz Idemil)
1833-1908(?) .... **TCLC 5**
See also CA 115
Lieber, Joel 1937-1971 .... **CLC 6**
See also CA 73-76; 29-32R
Lieber, Stanley Martin
See Lee, Stan
Lieberman, Laurence (James)
1935- .... **CLC 4, 36**
See also CA 17-20R; CANR 8, 36, 89; CP
7
Lieh Tzu fl. 7th cent. B.C.-5th cent.
B.C. .... **CMLC 27**
Lieksman, Anders
See Haavikko, Paavo Juhani
Li Fei-kan 1904-
See Pa Chin
See also CA 105; TWA
Lifton, Robert Jay 1926- .... **CLC 67**
See also CA 17-20R; CANR 27, 78; INT
CANR-27; SATA 66
Lightfoot, Gordon 1938- .... **CLC 26**
See also CA 109
Lightman, Alan P(aige) 1948- .... **CLC 81**
See also CA 141; CANR 63, 105
Ligotti, Thomas (Robert) 1953- ...... **CLC 44;
SSC 16**
See also CA 123; CANR 49, 135; HGG;
SUFW 2
Li Ho 791-817 .... **PC 13**
Li Ju-chen c. 1763-c. 1830 .... **NCLC 137**
Lilar, Francoise
See Mallet-Joris, Francoise
**Liliencron, (Friedrich Adolf Axel) Detlev
von** 1844-1909 .... **TCLC 18**
See also CA 117
Lille, Alain de
See Alain de Lille
Lilly, William 1602-1681 .... **LC 27**

Loreaux, Nichol .... **CLC 65**

Lorenzini, Carlo 1826-1890
See Collodi, Carlo
See also MAICYA 1, 2; SATA 29, 100

Lorenzo, Heberto Padilla
See Padilla (Lorenzo), Heberto

Loris
See Hofmannsthal, Hugo von

Loti, Pierre .... **TCLC 11**
See Viaud, (Louis Marie) Julien
See also DLB 123; GFL 1789 to the Present

Lou, Henri
See Andreas-Salome, Lou

Louie, David Wong 1954- .... **CLC 70**
See also CA 139; CANR 120

Louis, Adrian C. .... **NNAL**
See also CA 223

Louis, Father M.
See Merton, Thomas (James)

Louise, Heidi
See Erdrich, Louise

Lovecraft, H(oward) P(hillips)
1890-1937 .... **SSC 3, 52; TCLC 4, 22**
See also AAYA 14; BPFB 2; CA 104; 133;
CANR 106; DA3; DAM POP; HGG;
MTCW 1, 2; RGAL 4; SCFW; SFW 4;
SUFW

Lovelace, Earl 1935- .... **CLC 51**
See also BW 2; CA 77-80; CANR 41, 72,
114; CD 5; CDWLB 3; CN 7; DLB 125;
EWL 3; MTCW 1

Lovelace, Richard 1618-1657 .... **LC 24**
See also BRW 2; DLB 131; EXPP; PAB;
RGEL 2

Lowe, Pardee 1904- .... **AAL**

Lowell, Amy 1874-1925 ... **PC 13; TCLC 1, 8**
See also AAYA 57; AMW; CA 104; 151;
DAM POET; DLB 54, 140; EWL 3;
EXPP; LMFS 2; MAWW; MTCW 2;
RGAL 4; TUS

Lowell, James Russell 1819-1891 ... **NCLC 2, 90**
See also AMWS 1; CDALB 1640-1865;
DLB 1, 11, 64, 79, 189, 235; RGAL 4

Lowell, Robert (Traill Spence, Jr.)
1917-1977 ... **CLC 1, 2, 3, 4, 5, 8, 9, 11, 15, 37, 124; PC 3; WLC**
See also AMW; AMWC 2; AMWR 2; CA
9-12R; 73-76; CABS 2; CANR 26, 60;
CDALBS; DA; DA3; DAB; DAC; DAM
MST, NOV; DLB 5, 169; EWL 3; MTCW
1, 2; PAB; PFS 6, 7; RGAL 4; WP

Lowenthal, Michael (Francis)
1969- .... **CLC 119**
See also CA 150; CANR 115

Lowndes, Marie Adelaide (Belloc)
1868-1947 .... **TCLC 12**
See also CA 107; CMW 4; DLB 70; RHW

Lowry, (Clarence) Malcolm
1909-1957 .... **SSC 31; TCLC 6, 40**
See also BPFB 2; BRWS 3; CA 105; 131;
CANR 62, 105; CDBLB 1945-1960; DLB
15; EWL 3; MTCW 1, 2; RGEL 2

Lowry, Mina Gertrude 1882-1966
See Loy, Mina
See also CA 113

Loxsmith, John
See Brunner, John (Kilian Houston)

Loy, Mina .... **CLC 28; PC 16**
See Lowry, Mina Gertrude
See also DAM POET; DLB 4, 54; PFS 20

Loyson-Bridet
See Schwob, Marcel (Mayer Andre)

Lucan 39-65 .... **CMLC 33**
See also AW 2; DLB 211; EFS 2; RGWL 2, 3

Lucas, Craig 1951- .... **CLC 64**
See also CA 137; CAD; CANR 71, 109;
CD 5; GLL 2

Lucas, E(dward) V(errall)
1868-1938 .... **TCLC 73**
See also CA 176; DLB 98, 149, 153; SATA
20

Lucas, George 1944- .... **CLC 16**
See also AAYA 1, 23; CA 77-80; CANR
30; SATA 56

Lucas, Hans
See Godard, Jean-Luc

Lucas, Victoria
See Plath, Sylvia

Lucian c. 125-c. 180 .... **CMLC 32**
See also AW 2; DLB 176; RGWL 2, 3

Lucretius c. 94B.C.-c. 49B.C. .... **CMLC 48**
See also AW 2; CDWLB 1; DLB 211; EFS
2; RGWL 2, 3

Ludlam, Charles 1943-1987 .... **CLC 46, 50**
See also CA 85-88; 122; CAD; CANR 72,
86; DLB 266

Ludlum, Robert 1927-2001 .... **CLC 22, 43**
See also AAYA 10, 59; BEST 89:1, 90:3;
BPFB 2; CA 33-36R; 195; CANR 25, 41,
68, 105, 131; CMW 4; CPW; DA3; DAM
NOV, POP; DLBY 1982; MSW; MTCW
1, 2

Ludwig, Ken .... **CLC 60**
See also CA 195; CAD

Ludwig, Otto 1813-1865 .... **NCLC 4**
See also DLB 129

Lugones, Leopoldo 1874-1938 .... **HLCS 2; TCLC 15**
See also CA 116; 131; CANR 104; DLB
283; EWL 3; HW 1; LAW

Lu Hsun .... **SSC 20; TCLC 3**
See Shu-Jen, Chou
See also EWL 3

Lukacs, George .... **CLC 24**
See Lukacs, Gyorgy (Szegeny von)

Lukacs, Gyorgy (Szegeny von) 1885-1971
See Lukacs, George
See also CA 101; 29-32R; CANR 62; CD-
WLB 4; DLB 215, 242; EW 10; EWL 3;
MTCW 2

Luke, Peter (Ambrose Cyprian)
1919-1995 .... **CLC 38**
See also CA 81-84; 147; CANR 72; CBD;
CD 5; DLB 13

Lunar, Dennis
See Mungo, Raymond

Lurie, Alison 1926- ..... **CLC 4, 5, 18, 39, 175**
See also BPFB 2; CA 1-4R; CANR 2, 17,
50, 88; CN 7; DLB 2; MTCW 1; SATA
46, 112

Lustig, Arnost 1926- .... **CLC 56**
See also AAYA 3; CA 69-72; CANR 47,
102; CWW 2; DLB 232, 299; EWL 3;
SATA 56

Luther, Martin 1483-1546 .... **LC 9, 37**
See also CDWLB 2; DLB 179; EW 2;
RGWL 2, 3

Luxemburg, Rosa 1870(?)-1919 ..... **TCLC 63**
See also CA 118

Luzi, Mario 1914- .... **CLC 13**
See also CA 61-64; CANR 9, 70; CWW 2;
DLB 128; EWL 3

L'vov, Arkady .... **CLC 59**

Lydgate, John c. 1370-1450(?) .... **LC 81**
See also BRW 1; DLB 146; RGEL 2

Lyly, John 1554(?)-1606 .... **DC 7; LC 41**
See also BRW 1; DAM DRAM; DLB 62,
167; RGEL 2

L'Ymagier
See Gourmont, Remy(-Marie-Charles) de

Lynch, B. Suarez
See Borges, Jorge Luis

Lynch, David (Keith) 1946- ...... **CLC 66, 162**
See also AAYA 55; CA 124; 129; CANR
111

Lynch, James
See Andreyev, Leonid (Nikolaevich)

Lyndsay, Sir David 1485-1555 .... **LC 20**
See also RGEL 2

Lynn, Kenneth S(chuyler)
1923-2001 .... **CLC 50**
See also CA 1-4R; 196; CANR 3, 27, 65

Lynx
See West, Rebecca

Lyons, Marcus
See Blish, James (Benjamin)

Lyotard, Jean-Francois
1924-1998 .... **TCLC 103**
See also DLB 242; EWL 3

Lyre, Pinchbeck
See Sassoon, Siegfried (Lorraine)

Lytle, Andrew (Nelson) 1902-1995 ... **CLC 22**
See also CA 9-12R; 150; CANR 70; CN 7;
CSW; DLB 6; DLBY 1995; RGAL 4;
RHW

Lyttelton, George 1709-1773 .... **LC 10**
See also RGEL 2

Lytton of Knebworth, Baron
See Bulwer-Lytton, Edward (George Earle
Lytton)

Maas, Peter 1929-2001 .... **CLC 29**
See also CA 93-96; 201; INT CA-93-96;
MTCW 2

Macaulay, Catherine 1731-1791 .... **LC 64**
See also DLB 104

Macaulay, (Emilie) Rose
1881(?)-1958 .... **TCLC 7, 44**
See also CA 104; DLB 36; EWL 3; RGEL
2; RHW

Macaulay, Thomas Babington
1800-1859 .... **NCLC 42**
See also BRW 4; CDBLB 1832-1890; DLB
32, 55; RGEL 2

MacBeth, George (Mann)
1932-1992 .... **CLC 2, 5, 9**
See also CA 25-28R; 136; CANR 61, 66;
DLB 40; MTCW 1; PFS 8; SATA 4;
SATA-Obit 70

MacCaig, Norman (Alexander)
1910-1996 .... **CLC 36**
See also BRWS 6; CA 9-12R; CANR 3, 34;
CP 7; DAB; DAM POET; DLB 27; EWL
3; RGEL 2

MacCarthy, Sir (Charles Otto) Desmond
1877-1952 .... **TCLC 36**
See also CA 167

MacDiarmid, Hugh .... **CLC 2, 4, 11, 19, 63; PC 9**
See Grieve, C(hristopher) M(urray)
See also CDBLB 1945-1960; DLB 20;
EWL 3; RGEL 2

MacDonald, Anson
See Heinlein, Robert A(nson)

Macdonald, Cynthia 1928- .... **CLC 13, 19**
See also CA 49-52; CANR 4, 44; DLB 105

MacDonald, George 1824-1905 .... **TCLC 9, 113**
See also AAYA 57; BYA 5; CA 106; 137;
CANR 80; CLR 67; DLB 18, 163, 178;
FANT; MAICYA 1, 2; RGEL 2; SATA 33,
100; SFW 4; SUFW; WCH

Macdonald, John
See Millar, Kenneth

MacDonald, John D(ann)
1916-1986 .... **CLC 3, 27, 44**
See also BPFB 2; CA 1-4R; 121; CANR 1,
19, 60; CMW 4; CPW; DAM NOV, POP;
DLB 8, 306; DLBY 1986; MSW; MTCW
1, 2; SFW 4

Macdonald, John Ross
See Millar, Kenneth

Marquis, Don(ald Robert Perry)
1878-1937 .... **TCLC 7**
See also CA 104; 166; DLB 11, 25; RGAL
4

Marquis de Sade
See Sade, Donatien Alphonse Francois

Marric, J. J.
See Creasey, John
See also MSW

Marryat, Frederick 1792-1848 .... **NCLC 3**
See also DLB 21, 163; RGEL 2; WCH

Marsden, James
See Creasey, John

Marsh, Edward 1872-1953 .... **TCLC 99**

Marsh, (Edith) Ngaio 1895-1982 .. **CLC 7, 53**
See also CA 9-12R; CANR 6, 58; CMW 4;
CPW; DAM POP; DLB 77; MSW;
MTCW 1, 2; RGEL 2; TEA

Marshall, Garry 1934- .... **CLC 17**
See also AAYA 3; CA 111; SATA 60

Marshall, Paule 1929- .. **BLC 3; CLC 27, 72;**
SSC 3
See also AFAW 1, 2; AMWS 11; BPFB 2;
BW 2, 3; CA 77-80; CANR 25, 73, 129;
CN 7; DA3; DAM MULT; DLB 33, 157,
227; EWL 3; LATS 1:2; MTCW 1, 2;
RGAL 4; SSFS 15

Marshallik
See Zangwill, Israel

Marsten, Richard
See Hunter, Evan

Marston, John 1576-1634 .... **LC 33**
See also BRW 2; DAM DRAM; DLB 58,
172; RGEL 2

Martel, Yann 1963- .... **CLC 192**
See also CA 146; CANR 114

Martha, Henry
See Harris, Mark

Marti, Jose
See Marti (y Perez), Jose (Julian)
See also DLB 290

Marti (y Perez), Jose (Julian)
1853-1895 .... **HLC 2; NCLC 63**
See Marti, Jose
See also DAM MULT; HW 2; LAW; RGWL
2, 3; WLIT 1

Martial c. 40-c. 104 .... **CMLC 35; PC 10**
See also AW 2; CDWLB 1; DLB 211;
RGWL 2, 3

Martin, Ken
See Hubbard, L(afayette) Ron(ald)

Martin, Richard
See Creasey, John

Martin, Steve 1945- .... **CLC 30**
See also AAYA 53; CA 97-100; CANR 30,
100; DFS 19; MTCW 1

Martin, Valerie 1948- .... **CLC 89**
See also BEST 90:2; CA 85-88; CANR 49,
89

Martin, Violet Florence 1862-1915 .. **SSC 56;**
TCLC 51

Martin, Webber
See Silverberg, Robert

Martindale, Patrick Victor
See White, Patrick (Victor Martindale)

Martin du Gard, Roger
1881-1958 .... **TCLC 24**
See also CA 118; CANR 94; DLB 65; EWL
3; GFL 1789 to the Present; RGWL 2, 3

Martineau, Harriet 1802-1876 ...... **NCLC 26,**
137
See also DLB 21, 55, 159, 163, 166, 190;
FW; RGEL 2; YABC 2

Martines, Julia
See O'Faolain, Julia

Martinez, Enrique Gonzalez
See Gonzalez Martinez, Enrique

Martinez, Jacinto Benavente y
See Benavente (y Martinez), Jacinto

Martinez de la Rosa, Francisco de Paula
1787-1862 .... **NCLC 102**
See also TWA

Martinez Ruiz, Jose 1873-1967
See Azorin; Ruiz, Jose Martinez
See also CA 93-96; HW 1

Martinez Sierra, Gregorio
1881-1947 .... **TCLC 6**
See also CA 115; EWL 3

Martinez Sierra, Maria (de la O'LeJarraga)
1874-1974 .... **TCLC 6**
See also CA 115; EWL 3

Martinsen, Martin
See Follett, Ken(neth Martin)

Martinson, Harry (Edmund)
1904-1978 .... **CLC 14**
See also CA 77-80; CANR 34, 130; DLB
259; EWL 3

Martyn, Edward 1859-1923 .... **TCLC 131**
See also CA 179; DLB 10; RGEL 2

Marut, Ret
See Traven, B.

Marut, Robert
See Traven, B.

Marvell, Andrew 1621-1678 .... **LC 4, 43; PC**
10; WLC
See also BRW 2; BRWR 2; CDBLB 1660-
1789; DA; DAB; DAC; DAM MST,
POET; DLB 131; EXPP; PFS 5; RGEL 2;
TEA; WP

Marx, Karl (Heinrich)
1818-1883 .... **NCLC 17, 114**
See also DLB 129; LATS 1:1; TWA

Masaoka, Shiki -1902 .... **TCLC 18**
See Masaoka, Tsunenori
See also RGWL 3

Masaoka, Tsunenori 1867-1902
See Masaoka, Shiki
See also CA 117; 191; TWA

Masefield, John (Edward)
1878-1967 .... **CLC 11, 47**
See also CA 19-20; 25-28R; CANR 33;
CAP 2; CDBLB 1890-1914; DAM POET;
DLB 10, 19, 153, 160; EWL 3; EXPP;
FANT; MTCW 1, 2; PFS 5; RGEL 2;
SATA 19

Maso, Carole 19(?)- .... **CLC 44**
See also CA 170; GLL 2; RGAL 4

Mason, Bobbie Ann 1940- ... **CLC 28, 43, 82,**
154; SSC 4
See also AAYA 5, 42; AMWS 8; BPFB 2;
CA 53-56; CANR 11, 31, 58, 83, 125;
CDALBS; CN 7; CSW; DA3; DLB 173;
DLBY 1987; EWL 3; EXPS; INT CANR-
31; MTCW 1, 2; NFS 4; RGAL 4; RGSF
2; SSFS 3, 8, 20; YAW

Mason, Ernst
See Pohl, Frederik

Mason, Hunni B.
See Sternheim, (William Adolf) Carl

Mason, Lee W.
See Malzberg, Barry N(athaniel)

Mason, Nick 1945- .... **CLC 35**

Mason, Tally
See Derleth, August (William)

Mass, Anna .... **CLC 59**

Mass, William
See Gibson, William

Massinger, Philip 1583-1640 .... **LC 70**
See also DLB 58; RGEL 2

Master Lao
See Lao Tzu

Masters, Edgar Lee 1868-1950 ...... **PC 1, 36;**
TCLC 2, 25; WLCS
See also AMWS 1; CA 104; 133; CDALB
1865-1917; DA; DAC; DAM MST,
POET; DLB 54; EWL 3; EXPP; MTCW
1, 2; RGAL 4; TUS; WP

Masters, Hilary 1928- .... **CLC 48**
See also CA 25-28R, 217; CAAE 217;
CANR 13, 47, 97; CN 7; DLB 244

Mastrosimone, William 19(?)- .... **CLC 36**
See also CA 186; CAD; CD 5

Mathe, Albert
See Camus, Albert

Mather, Cotton 1663-1728 .... **LC 38**
See also AMWS 2; CDALB 1640-1865;
DLB 24, 30, 140; RGAL 4; TUS

Mather, Increase 1639-1723 .... **LC 38**
See also DLB 24

Matheson, Richard (Burton) 1926- .. **CLC 37**
See also AAYA 31; CA 97-100; CANR 88,
99; DLB 8, 44; HGG; INT CA-97-100;
SCFW 2; SFW 4; SUFW 2

Mathews, Harry 1930- .... **CLC 6, 52**
See also CA 21-24R; CAAS 6; CANR 18,
40, 98; CN 7

Mathews, John Joseph 1894-1979 .. **CLC 84;**
NNAL
See also CA 19-20; 142; CANR 45; CAP 2;
DAM MULT; DLB 175

Mathias, Roland (Glyn) 1915- .... **CLC 45**
See also CA 97-100; CANR 19, 41; CP 7;
DLB 27

Matsuo Basho 1644-1694 .... **LC 62; PC 3**
See Basho, Matsuo
See also DAM POET; PFS 2, 7

Mattheson, Rodney
See Creasey, John

Matthews, (James) Brander
1852-1929 .... **TCLC 95**
See also DLB 71, 78; DLBD 13

Matthews, (James) Brander
1852-1929 .... **TCLC 95**
See also CA 181; DLB 71, 78; DLBD 13

Matthews, Greg 1949- .... **CLC 45**
See also CA 135

Matthews, William (Procter III)
1942-1997 .... **CLC 40**
See also AMWS 9; CA 29-32R; 162; CAAS
18; CANR 12, 57; CP 7; DLB 5

Matthias, John (Edward) 1941- .... **CLC 9**
See also CA 33-36R; CANR 56; CP 7

Matthiessen, F(rancis) O(tto)
1902-1950 .... **TCLC 100**
See also CA 185; DLB 63

Matthiessen, Peter 1927- ... **CLC 5, 7, 11, 32,**
64
See also AAYA 6, 40; AMWS 5; ANW;
BEST 90:4; BPFB 2; CA 9-12R; CANR
21, 50, 73, 100; CN 7; DA3; DAM NOV;
DLB 6, 173, 275; MTCW 1, 2; SATA 27

Maturin, Charles Robert
1780(?)-1824 .... **NCLC 6**
See also BRWS 8; DLB 178; HGG; LMFS
1; RGEL 2; SUFW

Matute (Ausejo), Ana Maria 1925- .. **CLC 11**
See also CA 89-92; CANR 129; CWW 2;
EWL 3; MTCW 1; RGSF 2

Maugham, W. S.
See Maugham, W(illiam) Somerset

Maugham, W(illiam) Somerset
1874-1965 .. **CLC 1, 11, 15, 67, 93; SSC**
8; WLC
See also AAYA 55; BPFB 2; BRW 6; CA
5-8R; 25-28R; CANR 40, 127; CDBLB
1914-1945; CMW 4; DA; DA3; DAB;
DAC; DAM DRAM, MST, NOV; DLB
10, 36, 77, 100, 162, 195; EWL 3; LAIT
3; MTCW 1, 2; RGEL 2; RGSF 2; SATA
54; SSFS 17

Maugham, William Somerset
See Maugham, W(illiam) Somerset

Maupassant, (Henri Rene Albert) Guy de
1850-1893 . **NCLC 1, 42, 83; SSC 1, 64;**
WLC
See also BYA 14; DA; DA3; DAB; DAC;
DAM MST; DLB 123; EW 7; EXPS; GFL
1789 to the Present; LAIT 2; LMFS 1;
RGSF 2; RGWL 2, 3; SSFS 4; SUFW;
TWA

Maupin, Armistead (Jones, Jr.)
1944- .... **CLC 95**
See also CA 125; 130; CANR 58, 101;
CPW; DA3; DAM POP; DLB 278; GLL
1; INT CA-130; MTCW 2

Maurhut, Richard
See Traven, B.

Mauriac, Claude 1914-1996 .... **CLC 9**
See also CA 89-92; 152; CWW 2; DLB 83;
EWL 3; GFL 1789 to the Present

Mauriac, Francois (Charles)
1885-1970 .... **CLC 4, 9, 56; SSC 24**
See also CA 25-28; CAP 2; DLB 65; EW
10; EWL 3; GFL 1789 to the Present;
MTCW 1, 2; RGWL 2, 3; TWA

Mavor, Osborne Henry 1888-1951
See Bridie, James
See also CA 104

Maxwell, William (Keepers, Jr.)
1908-2000 .... **CLC 19**
See also AMWS 8; CA 93-96; 189; CANR
54, 95; CN 7; DLB 218, 278; DLBY
1980; INT CA-93-96; SATA-Obit 128

May, Elaine 1932- .... **CLC 16**
See also CA 124; 142; CAD; CWD; DLB
44

Mayakovski, Vladimir (Vladimirovich)
1893-1930 .... **TCLC 4, 18**
See Maiakovskii, Vladimir; Mayakovsky,
Vladimir
See also CA 104; 158; EWL 3; MTCW 2;
SFW 4; TWA

Mayakovsky, Vladimir
See Mayakovski, Vladimir (Vladimirovich)
See also EW 11; WP

Mayhew, Henry 1812-1887 .... **NCLC 31**
See also DLB 18, 55, 190

Mayle, Peter 1939(?)- .... **CLC 89**
See also CA 139; CANR 64, 109

Maynard, Joyce 1953- .... **CLC 23**
See also CA 111; 129; CANR 64

Mayne, William (James Carter)
1928- .... **CLC 12**
See also AAYA 20; CA 9-12R; CANR 37,
80, 100; CLR 25; FANT; JRDA; MAI-
CYA 1, 2; MAICYAS 1; SAAS 11; SATA
6, 68, 122; SUFW 2; YAW

Mayo, Jim
See L'Amour, Louis (Dearborn)
See also TCWW 2

Maysles, Albert 1926- .... **CLC 16**
See also CA 29-32R

Maysles, David 1932-1987 .... **CLC 16**
See also CA 191

Mazer, Norma Fox 1931- .... **CLC 26**
See also AAYA 5, 36; BYA 1, 8; CA 69-72;
CANR 12, 32, 66, 129; CLR 23; JRDA;
MAICYA 1, 2; SAAS 1; SATA 24, 67,
105; WYA; YAW

Mazzini, Guiseppe 1805-1872 .... **NCLC 34**

McAlmon, Robert (Menzies)
1895-1956 .... **TCLC 97**
See also CA 107; 168; DLB 4, 45; DLBD
15; GLL 1

McAuley, James Phillip 1917-1976 .. **CLC 45**
See also CA 97-100; DLB 260; RGEL 2

McBain, Ed
See Hunter, Evan
See also MSW

McBrien, William (Augustine)
1930- .... **CLC 44**
See also CA 107; CANR 90

McCabe, Patrick 1955- .... **CLC 133**
See also BRWS 9; CA 130; CANR 50, 90;
CN 7; DLB 194

McCaffrey, Anne (Inez) 1926- .... **CLC 17**
See also AAYA 6, 34; AITN 2; BEST 89:2;
BPFB 2; BYA 5; CA 25-28R, 227; CAAE
227; CANR 15, 35, 55, 96; CLR 49;
CPW; DA3; DAM NOV, POP; DLB 8;
JRDA; MAICYA 1, 2; MTCW 1, 2; SAAS
11; SATA 8, 70, 116, 152; SATA-Essay
152; SFW 4; SUFW 2; WYA; YAW

McCall, Nathan 1955(?)- .... **CLC 86**
See also AAYA 59; BW 3; CA 146; CANR
88

McCann, Arthur
See Campbell, John W(ood, Jr.)

McCann, Edson
See Pohl, Frederik

McCarthy, Charles, Jr. 1933-
See McCarthy, Cormac
See also CANR 42, 69, 101; CN 7; CPW;
CSW; DA3; DAM POP; MTCW 2

McCarthy, Cormac .... **CLC 4, 57, 101**
See McCarthy, Charles, Jr.
See also AAYA 41; AMWS 8; BPFB 2; CA
13-16R; CANR 10; DLB 6, 143, 256;
EWL 3; LATS 1:2; TCWW 2

McCarthy, Mary (Therese)
1912-1989 .. **CLC 1, 3, 5, 14, 24, 39, 59;**
SSC 24
See also AMW; BPFB 2; CA 5-8R; 129;
CANR 16, 50, 64; DA3; DLB 2; DLBY
1981; EWL 3; FW; INT CANR-16;
MAWW; MTCW 1, 2; RGAL 4; TUS

McCartney, (James) Paul 1942- . **CLC 12, 35**
See also CA 146; CANR 111

McCauley, Stephen (D.) 1955- .... **CLC 50**
See also CA 141

McClaren, Peter .... **CLC 70**

McClure, Michael (Thomas) 1932- ... **CLC 6,**
10
See also BG 3; CA 21-24R; CAD; CANR
17, 46, 77, 131; CD 5; CP 7; DLB 16;
WP

McCorkle, Jill (Collins) 1958- .... **CLC 51**
See also CA 121; CANR 113; CSW; DLB
234; DLBY 1987

McCourt, Frank 1930- .... **CLC 109**
See also AMWS 12; CA 157; CANR 97;
NCFS 1

McCourt, James 1941- .... **CLC 5**
See also CA 57-60; CANR 98

McCourt, Malachy 1931- .... **CLC 119**
See also SATA 126

McCoy, Horace (Stanley)
1897-1955 .... **TCLC 28**
See also AMWS 13; CA 108; 155; CMW 4;
DLB 9

McCrae, John 1872-1918 .... **TCLC 12**
See also CA 109; DLB 92; PFS 5

McCreigh, James
See Pohl, Frederik

McCullers, (Lula) Carson (Smith)
1917-1967 .... **CLC 1, 4, 10, 12, 48, 100;**
SSC 9, 24; TCLC 155; WLC
See also AAYA 21; AMW; AMWC 2; BPFB
2; CA 5-8R; 25-28R; CABS 1, 3; CANR
18, 132; CDALB 1941-1968; DA; DA3;
DAB; DAC; DAM MST, NOV; DFS 5,
18; DLB 2, 7, 173, 228; EWL 3; EXPS;
FW; GLL 1; LAIT 3, 4; MAWW; MTCW
1, 2; NFS 6, 13; RGAL 4; RGSF 2; SATA
27; SSFS 5; TUS; YAW

McCulloch, John Tyler
See Burroughs, Edgar Rice

McCullough, Colleen 1938(?)- .. **CLC 27, 107**
See also AAYA 36; BPFB 2; CA 81-84;
CANR 17, 46, 67, 98; CPW; DA3; DAM
NOV, POP; MTCW 1, 2; RHW

McCunn, Ruthanne Lum 1946- .... **AAL**
See also CA 119; CANR 43, 96; LAIT 2;
SATA 63

McDermott, Alice 1953- .... **CLC 90**
See also CA 109; CANR 40, 90, 126; DLB
292

McElroy, Joseph 1930- .... **CLC 5, 47**
See also CA 17-20R; CN 7

McEwan, Ian (Russell) 1948- .... **CLC 13, 66,**
169
See also BEST 90:4; BRWS 4; CA 61-64;
CANR 14, 41, 69, 87, 132; CN 7; DAM
NOV; DLB 14, 194; HGG; MTCW 1, 2;
RGSF 2; SUFW 2; TEA

McFadden, David 1940- .... **CLC 48**
See also CA 104; CP 7; DLB 60; INT CA-
104

McFarland, Dennis 1950- .... **CLC 65**
See also CA 165; CANR 110

McGahern, John 1934- ... **CLC 5, 9, 48, 156;**
SSC 17
See also CA 17-20R; CANR 29, 68, 113;
CN 7; DLB 14, 231; MTCW 1

McGinley, Patrick (Anthony) 1937- . **CLC 41**
See also CA 120; 127; CANR 56; INT CA-
127

McGinley, Phyllis 1905-1978 .... **CLC 14**
See also CA 9-12R; 77-80; CANR 19;
CWRI 5; DLB 11, 48; PFS 9, 13; SATA
2, 44; SATA-Obit 24

McGinniss, Joe 1942- .... **CLC 32**
See also AITN 2; BEST 89:2; CA 25-28R;
CANR 26, 70; CPW; DLB 185; INT
CANR-26

McGivern, Maureen Daly
See Daly, Maureen

McGrath, Patrick 1950- .... **CLC 55**
See also CA 136; CANR 65; CN 7; DLB
231; HGG; SUFW 2

McGrath, Thomas (Matthew)
1916-1990 .... **CLC 28, 59**
See also AMWS 10; CA 9-12R; 132; CANR
6, 33, 95; DAM POET; MTCW 1; SATA
41; SATA-Obit 66

McGuane, Thomas (Francis III)
1939- .... **CLC 3, 7, 18, 45, 127**
See also AITN 2; BPFB 2; CA 49-52;
CANR 5, 24, 49, 94; CN 7; DLB 2, 212;
DLBY 1980; EWL 3; INT CANR-24;
MTCW 1; TCWW 2

McGuckian, Medbh 1950- .... **CLC 48, 174;**
PC 27
See also BRWS 5; CA 143; CP 7; CWP;
DAM POET; DLB 40

McHale, Tom 1942(?)-1982 .... **CLC 3, 5**
See also AITN 1; CA 77-80; 106

McHugh, Heather 1948- .... **PC 61**
See also CA 69-72; CANR 11, 28, 55, 92;
CP 7; CWP

McIlvanney, William 1936- .... **CLC 42**
See also CA 25-28R; CANR 61; CMW 4;
DLB 14, 207

McIlwraith, Maureen Mollie Hunter
See Hunter, Mollie
See also SATA 2

McInerney, Jay 1955- .... **CLC 34, 112**
See also AAYA 18; BPFB 2; CA 116; 123;
CANR 45, 68, 116; CN 7; CPW; DA3;
DAM POP; DLB 292; INT CA-123;
MTCW 2

McIntyre, Vonda N(eel) 1948- .... **CLC 18**
See also CA 81-84; CANR 17, 34, 69;
MTCW 1; SFW 4; YAW

McKay, Claude .... BLC 3; HR 3; PC 2;
TCLC 7, 41; WLC
See McKay, Festus Claudius
See also AFAW 1, 2; AMWS 10; DAB;
DLB 4, 45, 51, 117; EWL 3; EXPP; GLL
2; LAIT 3; LMFS 2; PAB; PFS 4; RGAL
4; WP

McKay, Festus Claudius 1889-1948
See McKay, Claude
See also BW 1, 3; CA 104; 124; CANR 73;
DA; DAC; DAM MST, MULT, NOV,
POET; MTCW 1, 2; TUS

McKuen, Rod 1933- .... CLC 1, 3
See also AITN 1; CA 41-44R; CANR 40

McLoughlin, R. B.
See Mencken, H(enry) L(ouis)

McLuhan, (Herbert) Marshall
1911-1980 .... CLC 37, 83
See also CA 9-12R; 102; CANR 12, 34, 61;
DLB 88; INT CANR-12; MTCW 1, 2

McManus, Declan Patrick Aloysius
See Costello, Elvis

McMillan, Terry (L.) 1951- . BLCS; CLC 50,
61, 112
See also AAYA 21; AMWS 13; BPFB 2;
BW 2, 3; CA 140; CANR 60, 104, 131;
CPW; DA3; DAM MULT, NOV, POP;
MTCW 2; RGAL 4; YAW

McMurtry, Larry (Jeff) 1936- .. CLC 2, 3, 7,
11, 27, 44, 127
See also AAYA 15; AITN 2; AMWS 5;
BEST 89:2; BPFB 2; CA 5-8R; CANR
19, 43, 64, 103; CDALB 1968-1988; CN
7; CPW; CSW; DA3; DAM NOV, POP;
DLB 2, 143, 256; DLBY 1980, 1987;
EWL 3; MTCW 1, 2; RGAL 4; TCWW 2

McNally, T. M. 1961- .... CLC 82

McNally, Terrence 1939- .... CLC 4, 7, 41, 91
See also AMWS 13; CA 45-48; CAD;
CANR 2, 56, 116; CD 5; DA3; DAM
DRAM; DFS 16, 19; DLB 7, 249; EWL
3; GLL 1; MTCW 2

McNamer, Deirdre 1950- .... CLC 70

McNeal, Tom .... CLC 119

McNeile, Herman Cyril 1888-1937
See Sapper
See also CA 184; CMW 4; DLB 77

McNickle, (William) D'Arcy
1904-1977 .... CLC 89; NNAL
See also CA 9-12R; 85-88; CANR 5, 45;
DAM MULT; DLB 175, 212; RGAL 4;
SATA-Obit 22

McPhee, John (Angus) 1931- .... CLC 36
See also AMWS 3; ANW; BEST 90:1; CA
65-68; CANR 20, 46, 64, 69, 121; CPW;
DLB 185, 275; MTCW 1, 2; TUS

McPherson, James Alan 1943- . BLCS; CLC
19, 77
See also BW 1, 3; CA 25-28R; CAAS 17;
CANR 24, 74; CN 7; CSW; DLB 38, 244;
EWL 3; MTCW 1, 2; RGAL 4; RGSF 2

McPherson, William (Alexander)
1933- .... CLC 34
See also CA 69-72; CANR 28; INT
CANR-28

McTaggart, J. McT. Ellis
See McTaggart, John McTaggart Ellis

McTaggart, John McTaggart Ellis
1866-1925 .... TCLC 105
See also CA 120; DLB 262

Mead, George Herbert 1863-1931 . TCLC 89
See also CA 212; DLB 270

Mead, Margaret 1901-1978 .... CLC 37
See also AITN 1; CA 1-4R; 81-84; CANR
4; DA3; FW; MTCW 1, 2; SATA-Obit 20

Meaker, Marijane (Agnes) 1927-
See Kerr, M. E.
See also CA 107; CANR 37, 63; INT CA-
107; JRDA; MAICYA 1, 2; MAICYAS 1;
MTCW 1; SATA 20, 61, 99; SATA-Essay
111; YAW

Medoff, Mark (Howard) 1940- .... CLC 6, 23
See also AITN 1; CA 53-56; CAD; CANR
5; CD 5; DAM DRAM; DFS 4; DLB 7;
INT CANR-5

Medvedev, P. N.
See Bakhtin, Mikhail Mikhailovich

Meged, Aharon
See Megged, Aharon

Meged, Aron
See Megged, Aharon

Megged, Aharon 1920- .... CLC 9
See also CA 49-52; CAAS 13; CANR 1;
EWL 3

Mehta, Gita 1943- .... CLC 179
See also CA 225; DNFS 2

Mehta, Ved (Parkash) 1934- .... CLC 37
See also CA 1-4R, 212; CAAE 212; CANR
2, 23, 69; MTCW 1

Melanchthon, Philipp 1497-1560 .... LC 90
See also DLB 179

Melanter
See Blackmore, R(ichard) D(oddridge)

Meleager c. 140B.C.-c. 70B.C. ...... CMLC 53

Melies, Georges 1861-1938 .... TCLC 81

Melikow, Loris
See Hofmannsthal, Hugo von

Melmoth, Sebastian
See Wilde, Oscar (Fingal O'Flahertie Wills)

Melo Neto, Joao Cabral de
See Cabral de Melo Neto, Joao
See also CWW 2; EWL 3

Meltzer, Milton 1915- .... CLC 26
See also AAYA 8, 45; BYA 2, 6; CA 13-
16R; CANR 38, 92, 107; CLR 13; DLB
61; JRDA; MAICYA 1, 2; SAAS 1; SATA
1, 50, 80, 128; SATA-Essay 124; WYA;
YAW

Melville, Herman 1819-1891 ..... NCLC 3, 12,
29, 45, 49, 91, 93, 123; SSC 1, 17, 46;
WLC
See also AAYA 25; AMW; AMWR 1;
CDALB 1640-1865; DA; DA3; DAB;
DAC; DAM MST, NOV; DLB 3, 74, 250,
254; EXPN; EXPS; LAIT 1, 2; NFS 7, 9;
RGAL 4; RGSF 2; SATA 59; SSFS 3;
TUS

Members, Mark
See Powell, Anthony (Dymoke)

Membreno, Alejandro .... CLC 59

Menander c. 342B.C.-c. 293B.C. .... CMLC 9,
51; DC 3
See also AW 1; CDWLB 1; DAM DRAM;
DLB 176; LMFS 1; RGWL 2, 3

Menchu, Rigoberta 1959- .. CLC 160; HLCS
2
See also CA 175; DNFS 1; WLIT 1

Mencken, H(enry) L(ouis)
1880-1956 .... TCLC 13
See also AMW; CA 105; 125; CDALB
1917-1929; DLB 11, 29, 63, 137, 222;
EWL 3; MTCW 1, 2; NCFS 4; RGAL 4;
TUS

Mendelsohn, Jane 1965- .... CLC 99
See also CA 154; CANR 94

Menton, Francisco de
See Chin, Frank (Chew, Jr.)

Mercer, David 1928-1980 .... CLC 5
See also CA 9-12R; 102; CANR 23; CBD;
DAM DRAM; DLB 13; MTCW 1; RGEL
2

Merchant, Paul
See Ellison, Harlan (Jay)

Meredith, George 1828-1909 .. PC 60; TCLC
17, 43
See also CA 117; 153; CANR 80; CDBLB
1832-1890; DAM POET; DLB 18, 35, 57,
159; RGEL 2; TEA

Meredith, William (Morris) 1919- .... CLC 4,
13, 22, 55; PC 28
See also CA 9-12R; CAAS 14; CANR 6,
40, 129; CP 7; DAM POET; DLB 5

Merezhkovsky, Dmitrii Sergeevich
See Merezhkovsky, Dmitry Sergeyevich
See also DLB 295

Merezhkovsky, Dmitry Sergeevich
See Merezhkovsky, Dmitry Sergeyevich
See also EWL 3

Merezhkovsky, Dmitry Sergeyevich
1865-1941 .... TCLC 29
See Merezhkovsky, Dmitrii Sergeevich;
Merezhkovsky, Dmitry Sergeevich
See also CA 169

Merimee, Prosper 1803-1870 ... NCLC 6, 65;
SSC 7, 77
See also DLB 119, 192; EW 6; EXPS; GFL
1789 to the Present; RGSF 2; RGWL 2,
3; SSFS 8; SUFW

Merkin, Daphne 1954- .... CLC 44
See also CA 123

Merleau-Ponty, Maurice
1908-1961 .... TCLC 156
See also CA 114; 89-92; DLB 296; GFL
1789 to the Present

Merlin, Arthur
See Blish, James (Benjamin)

Mernissi, Fatima 1940- .... CLC 171
See also CA 152; FW

Merrill, James (Ingram) 1926-1995 .. CLC 2,
3, 6, 8, 13, 18, 34, 91; PC 28
See also AMWS 3; CA 13-16R; 147; CANR
10, 49, 63, 108; DA3; DAM POET; DLB
5, 165; DLBY 1985; EWL 3; INT CANR-
10; MTCW 1, 2; PAB; RGAL 4

Merriman, Alex
See Silverberg, Robert

Merriman, Brian 1747-1805 .... NCLC 70

Merritt, E. B.
See Waddington, Miriam

Merton, Thomas (James)
1915-1968 . CLC 1, 3, 11, 34, 83; PC 10
See also AMWS 8; CA 5-8R; 25-28R;
CANR 22, 53, 111, 131; DA3; DLB 48;
DLBY 1981; MTCW 1, 2

Merwin, W(illiam) S(tanley) 1927- ... CLC 1,
2, 3, 5, 8, 13, 18, 45, 88; PC 45
See also AMWS 3; CA 13-16R; CANR 15,
51, 112; CP 7; DA3; DAM POET; DLB
5, 169; EWL 3; INT CANR-15; MTCW
1, 2; PAB; PFS 5, 15; RGAL 4

Metcalf, John 1938- .... CLC 37; SSC 43
See also CA 113; CN 7; DLB 60; RGSF 2;
TWA

Metcalf, Suzanne
See Baum, L(yman) Frank

Mew, Charlotte (Mary) 1870-1928 .. TCLC 8
See also CA 105; 189; DLB 19, 135; RGEL
2

Mewshaw, Michael 1943- .... CLC 9
See also CA 53-56; CANR 7, 47; DLBY
1980

Meyer, Conrad Ferdinand
1825-1898 .... NCLC 81; SSC 30
See also DLB 129; EW; RGWL 2, 3

Meyer, Gustav 1868-1932
See Meyrink, Gustav
See also CA 117; 190

Meyer, June
See Jordan, June (Meyer)

Meyer, Lynn
See Slavitt, David R(ytman)

Meyers, Jeffrey 1939- .... **CLC 39**
See also CA 73-76, 186; CAAE 186; CANR 54, 102; DLB 111

Meynell, Alice (Christina Gertrude Thompson) 1847-1922 .... **TCLC 6**
See also CA 104; 177; DLB 19, 98; RGEL 2

Meyrink, Gustav .... **TCLC 21**
See Meyer, Gustav
See also DLB 81; EWL 3

Michaels, Leonard 1933-2003 ..... **CLC 6, 25; SSC 16**
See also CA 61-64; 216; CANR 21, 62, 119; CN 7; DLB 130; MTCW 1

Michaux, Henri 1899-1984 .... **CLC 8, 19**
See also CA 85-88; 114; DLB 258; EWL 3; GFL 1789 to the Present; RGWL 2, 3

Micheaux, Oscar (Devereaux) 1884-1951 .... **TCLC 76**
See also BW 3; CA 174; DLB 50; TCWW 2

Michelangelo 1475-1564 .... **LC 12**
See also AAYA 43

Michelet, Jules 1798-1874 .... **NCLC 31**
See also EW 5; GFL 1789 to the Present

Michels, Robert 1876-1936 .... **TCLC 88**
See also CA 212

Michener, James A(lbert) 1907(?)-1997 .. **CLC 1, 5, 11, 29, 60, 109**
See also AAYA 27; AITN 1; BEST 90:1; BPFB 2; CA 5-8R; 161; CANR 21, 45, 68; CN 7; CPW; DA3; DAM NOV, POP; DLB 6; MTCW 1, 2; RHW

Mickiewicz, Adam 1798-1855 . **NCLC 3, 101; PC 38**
See also EW 5; RGWL 2, 3

Middleton, (John) Christopher 1926- .... **CLC 13**
See also CA 13-16R; CANR 29, 54, 117; CP 7; DLB 40

Middleton, Richard (Barham) 1882-1911 .... **TCLC 56**
See also CA 187; DLB 156; HGG

Middleton, Stanley 1919- .... **CLC 7, 38**
See also CA 25-28R; CAAS 23; CANR 21, 46, 81; CN 7; DLB 14

Middleton, Thomas 1580-1627 ...... **DC 5; LC 33**
See also BRW 2; DAM DRAM, MST; DFS 18; DLB 58; RGEL 2

Migueis, Jose Rodrigues 1901-1980 . **CLC 10**
See also DLB 287

Mikszath, Kalman 1847-1910 .... **TCLC 31**
See also CA 170

Miles, Jack .... **CLC 100**
See also CA 200

Miles, John Russiano
See Miles, Jack

Miles, Josephine (Louise) 1911-1985 .... **CLC 1, 2, 14, 34, 39**
See also CA 1-4R; 116; CANR 2, 55; DAM POET; DLB 48

Militant
See Sandburg, Carl (August)

Mill, Harriet (Hardy) Taylor 1807-1858 .... **NCLC 102**
See also FW

Mill, John Stuart 1806-1873 .... **NCLC 11, 58**
See also CDBLB 1832-1890; DLB 55, 190, 262; FW 1; RGEL 2; TEA

Millar, Kenneth 1915-1983 .... **CLC 14**
See Macdonald, Ross
See also CA 9-12R; 110; CANR 16, 63, 107; CMW 4; CPW; DA3; DAM POP; DLB 2, 226; DLBD 6; DLBY 1983; MTCW 1, 2

Millay, E. Vincent
See Millay, Edna St. Vincent

Millay, Edna St. Vincent 1892-1950 ..... **PC 6, 61; TCLC 4, 49; WLCS**
See Boyd, Nancy
See also AMW; CA 104; 130; CDALB 1917-1929; DA; DA3; DAB; DAC; DAM MST, POET; DLB 45, 249; EWL 3; EXPP; MAWW; MTCW 1, 2; PAB; PFS 3, 17; RGAL 4; TUS; WP

Miller, Arthur 1915- ...... **CLC 1, 2, 6, 10, 15, 26, 47, 78, 179; DC 1; WLC**
See also AAYA 15; AITN 1; AMW; AMWC 1; CA 1-4R; CABS 3; CAD; CANR 2, 30, 54, 76, 132; CD 5; CDALB 1941-1968; DA; DA3; DAB; DAC; DAM DRAM, MST; DFS 1, 3, 8; DLB 7, 266; EWL 3; LAIT 1, 4; MTCW 1, 2; RGAL 4; TUS; WYAS 1

Miller, Henry (Valentine) 1891-1980 .... **CLC 1, 2, 4, 9, 14, 43, 84; WLC**
See also AMW; BPFB 2; CA 9-12R; 97-100; CANR 33, 64; CDALB 1929-1941; DA; DA3; DAB; DAC; DAM MST, NOV; DLB 4, 9; DLBY 1980; EWL 3; MTCW 1, 2; RGAL 4; TUS

Miller, Hugh 1802-1856 .... **NCLC 143**
See also DLB 190

Miller, Jason 1939(?)-2001 .... **CLC 2**
See also AITN 1; CA 73-76; 197; CAD; CANR 130; DFS 12; DLB 7

Miller, Sue 1943- .... **CLC 44**
See also AMWS 12; BEST 90:3; CA 139; CANR 59, 91, 128; DA3; DAM POP; DLB 143

Miller, Walter M(ichael), Jr. 1923-1996 .... **CLC 4, 30**
See also BPFB 2; CA 85-88; CANR 108; DLB 8; SCFW; SFW 4

Millett, Kate 1934- .... **CLC 67**
See also AITN 1; CA 73-76; CANR 32, 53, 76, 110; DA3; DLB 246; FW; GLL 1; MTCW 1, 2

Millhauser, Steven (Lewis) 1943- .... **CLC 21, 54, 109; SSC 57**
See also CA 110; 111; CANR 63, 114, 133; CN 7; DA3; DLB 2; FANT; INT CA-111; MTCW 2

Millin, Sarah Gertrude 1889-1968 ... **CLC 49**
See also CA 102; 93-96; DLB 225; EWL 3

Milne, A(lan) A(lexander) 1882-1956 .... **TCLC 6, 88**
See also BRWS 5; CA 104; 133; CLR 1, 26; CMW 4; CWRI 5; DA3; DAB; DAC; DAM MST; DLB 10, 77, 100, 160; FANT; MAICYA 1, 2; MTCW 1, 2; RGEL 2; SATA 100; WCH; YABC 1

Milner, Ron(ald) 1938-2004 ..... **BLC 3; CLC 56**
See also AITN 1; BW 1; CA 73-76; CAD; CANR 24, 81; CD 5; DAM MULT; DLB 38; MTCW 1

Milnes, Richard Monckton 1809-1885 .... **NCLC 61**
See also DLB 32, 184

Milosz, Czeslaw 1911- ...... **CLC 5, 11, 22, 31, 56, 82; PC 8; WLCS**
See also CA 81-84; CANR 23, 51, 91, 126; CDWLB 4; CWW 2; DA3; DAM MST, POET; DLB 215; EW 13; EWL 3; MTCW 1, 2; PFS 16; RGWL 2, 3

Milton, John 1608-1674 ..... **LC 9, 43, 92; PC 19, 29; WLC**
See also BRW 2; BRWR 2; CDBLB 1660-1789; DA; DA3; DAB; DAC; DAM MST, POET; DLB 131, 151, 281; EFS 1; EXPP; LAIT 1; PAB; PFS 3, 17; RGEL 2; TEA; WLIT 3; WP

Min, Anchee 1957- .... **CLC 86**
See also CA 146; CANR 94

Minehaha, Cornelius
See Wedekind, (Benjamin) Frank(lin)

Miner, Valerie 1947- .... **CLC 40**
See also CA 97-100; CANR 59; FW; GLL 2

Minimo, Duca
See D'Annunzio, Gabriele

Minot, Susan 1956- .... **CLC 44, 159**
See also AMWS 6; CA 134; CANR 118; CN 7

Minus, Ed 1938- .... **CLC 39**
See also CA 185

Mirabai 1498(?)-1550(?) .... **PC 48**

Miranda, Javier
See Bioy Casares, Adolfo
See also CWW 2

Mirbeau, Octave 1848-1917 .... **TCLC 55**
See also CA 216; DLB 123, 192; GFL 1789 to the Present

Mirikitani, Janice 1942- .... **AAL**
See also CA 211; RGAL 4

Mirk, John (?)-c. 1414 .... **LC 105**
See also DLB 146

Miro (Ferrer), Gabriel (Francisco Victor) 1879-1930 .... **TCLC 5**
See also CA 104; 185; EWL 3

Misharin, Alexandr .... **CLC 59**

Mishima, Yukio ... **CLC 2, 4, 6, 9, 27; DC 1; SSC 4**
See Hiraoka, Kimitake
See also AAYA 50; BPFB 2; GLL 1; MJW; MTCW 2; RGSF 2; RGWL 2, 3; SSFS 5, 12

Mistral, Frederic 1830-1914 .... **TCLC 51**
See also CA 122; 213; GFL 1789 to the Present

Mistral, Gabriela
See Godoy Alcayaga, Lucila
See also DLB 283; DNFS 1; EWL 3; LAW; RGWL 2, 3; WP

Mistry, Rohinton 1952- ... **CLC 71, 196; SSC 73**
See also BRWS 10; CA 141; CANR 86, 114; CCA 1; CN 7; DAC; SSFS 6

Mitchell, Clyde
See Ellison, Harlan (Jay)

Mitchell, Emerson Blackhorse Barney 1945- .... **NNAL**
See also CA 45-48

Mitchell, James Leslie 1901-1935
See Gibbon, Lewis Grassic
See also CA 104; 188; DLB 15

Mitchell, Joni 1943- .... **CLC 12**
See also CA 112; CCA 1

Mitchell, Joseph (Quincy) 1908-1996 .... **CLC 98**
See also CA 77-80; 152; CANR 69; CN 7; CSW; DLB 185; DLBY 1996

Mitchell, Margaret (Munnerlyn) 1900-1949 .... **TCLC 11**
See also AAYA 23; BPFB 2; BYA 1; CA 109; 125; CANR 55, 94; CDALBS; DA3; DAM NOV, POP; DLB 9; LAIT 2; MTCW 1, 2; NFS 9; RGAL 4; RHW; TUS; WYAS 1; YAW

Mitchell, Peggy
See Mitchell, Margaret (Munnerlyn)

Mitchell, S(ilas) Weir 1829-1914 .... **TCLC 36**
See also CA 165; DLB 202; RGAL 4

Mitchell, W(illiam) O(rmond) 1914-1998 .... **CLC 25**
See also CA 77-80; 165; CANR 15, 43; CN 7; DAC; DAM MST; DLB 88

Mitchell, William (Lendrum) 1879-1936 .... **TCLC 81**
See also CA 213

Mitford, Mary Russell 1787-1855 ... **NCLC 4**
See also DLB 110, 116; RGEL 2

Newlove, Donald 1928- .... **CLC 6**
See also CA 29-32R; CANR 25

Newlove, John (Herbert) 1938- .... **CLC 14**
See also CA 21-24R; CANR 9, 25; CP 7

Newman, Charles 1938- .... **CLC 2, 8**
See also CA 21-24R; CANR 84; CN 7

Newman, Edwin (Harold) 1919- ...... **CLC 14**
See also AITN 1; CA 69-72; CANR 5

Newman, John Henry 1801-1890 . **NCLC 38, 99**
See also BRWS 7; DLB 18, 32, 55; RGEL 2

Newton, (Sir) Isaac 1642-1727 ...... **LC 35, 53**
See also DLB 252

Newton, Suzanne 1936- .... **CLC 35**
See also BYA 7; CA 41-44R; CANR 14; JRDA; SATA 5, 77

New York Dept. of Ed. .... **CLC 70**

Nexo, Martin Andersen 1869-1954 .... **TCLC 43**
See also CA 202; DLB 214; EWL 3

Nezval, Vitezslav 1900-1958 .... **TCLC 44**
See also CA 123; CDWLB 4; DLB 215; EWL 3

Ng, Fae Myenne 1957(?)- .... **CLC 81**
See also BYA 11; CA 146

Ngema, Mbongeni 1955- .... **CLC 57**
See also BW 2; CA 143; CANR 84; CD 5

Ngugi, James T(hiong'o) . **CLC 3, 7, 13, 182**
See Ngugi wa Thiong'o

Ngugi wa Thiong'o
See Ngugi wa Thiong'o
See also DLB 125; EWL 3

Ngugi wa Thiong'o 1938- .. **BLC 3; CLC 36, 182**
See Ngugi, James T(hiong'o); Ngugi wa Thiong'o
See also AFW; BRWS 8; BW 2; CA 81-84; CANR 27, 58; CDWLB 3; DAM MULT, NOV; DNFS 2; MTCW 1, 2; RGEL 2; WWE 1

Niatum, Duane 1938- .... **NNAL**
See also CA 41-44R; CANR 21, 45, 83; DLB 175

Nichol, B(arrie) P(hillip) 1944-1988 . **CLC 18**
See also CA 53-56; DLB 53; SATA 66

Nicholas of Cusa 1401-1464 .... **LC 80**
See also DLB 115

Nichols, John (Treadwell) 1940- .... **CLC 38**
See also AMWS 13; CA 9-12R, 190; CAAE 190; CAAS 2; CANR 6, 70, 121; DLBY 1982; LATS 1:2; TCWW 2

Nichols, Leigh
See Koontz, Dean R(ay)

Nichols, Peter (Richard) 1927- .... **CLC 5, 36, 65**
See also CA 104; CANR 33, 86; CBD; CD 5; DLB 13, 245; MTCW 1

Nicholson, Linda ed. .... **CLC 65**

Ni Chuilleanain, Eilean 1942- .... **PC 34**
See also CA 126; CANR 53, 83; CP 7; CWP; DLB 40

Nicolas, F. R. E.
See Freeling, Nicolas

Niedecker, Lorine 1903-1970 ..... **CLC 10, 42; PC 42**
See also CA 25-28; CAP 2; DAM POET; DLB 48

Nietzsche, Friedrich (Wilhelm) 1844-1900 .... **TCLC 10, 18, 55**
See also CA 107; 121; CDWLB 2; DLB 129; EW 7; RGWL 2, 3; TWA

Nievo, Ippolito 1831-1861 .... **NCLC 22**

Nightingale, Anne Redmon 1943-
See Redmon, Anne
See also CA 103

Nightingale, Florence 1820-1910 ... **TCLC 85**
See also CA 188; DLB 166

Nijo Yoshimoto 1320-1388 .... **CMLC 49**
See also DLB 203

Nik. T. O.
See Annensky, Innokenty (Fyodorovich)

Nin, Anais 1903-1977 ..... **CLC 1, 4, 8, 11, 14, 60, 127; SSC 10**
See also AITN 2; AMWS 10; BPFB 2; CA 13-16R; 69-72; CANR 22, 53; DAM NOV, POP; DLB 2, 4, 152; EWL 3; GLL 2; MAWW; MTCW 1, 2; RGAL 4; RGSF 2

Nisbet, Robert A(lexander) 1913-1996 .... **TCLC 117**
See also CA 25-28R; 153; CANR 17; INT CANR-17

Nishida, Kitaro 1870-1945 .... **TCLC 83**

Nishiwaki, Junzaburo
See Nishiwaki, Junzaburo
See also CA 194

Nishiwaki, Junzaburo 1894-1982 .... **PC 15**
See Nishiwaki, Junzaburo; Nishiwaki Junzaburo
See also CA 194; 107; MJW; RGWL 3

Nishiwaki Junzaburo
See Nishiwaki, Junzaburo
See also EWL 3

Nissenson, Hugh 1933- .... **CLC 4, 9**
See also CA 17-20R; CANR 27, 108; CN 7; DLB 28

Nister, Der
See Der Nister
See also EWL 3

Niven, Larry .... **CLC 8**
See Niven, Laurence Van Cott
See also AAYA 27; BPFB 2; BYA 10; DLB 8; SCFW 2

Niven, Laurence Van Cott 1938-
See Niven, Larry
See also CA 21-24R, 207; CAAE 207; CAAS 12; CANR 14, 44, 66, 113; CPW; DAM POP; MTCW 1, 2; SATA 95; SFW 4

Nixon, Agnes Eckhardt 1927- .... **CLC 21**
See also CA 110

Nizan, Paul 1905-1940 .... **TCLC 40**
See also CA 161; DLB 72; EWL 3; GFL 1789 to the Present

Nkosi, Lewis 1936- .... **BLC 3; CLC 45**
See also BW 1, 3; CA 65-68; CANR 27, 81; CBD; CD 5; DAM MULT; DLB 157, 225; WWE 1

Nodier, (Jean) Charles (Emmanuel) 1780-1844 .... **NCLC 19**
See also DLB 119; GFL 1789 to the Present

Noguchi, Yone 1875-1947 .... **TCLC 80**

Nolan, Christopher 1965- .... **CLC 58**
See also CA 111; CANR 88

Noon, Jeff 1957- .... **CLC 91**
See also CA 148; CANR 83; DLB 267; SFW 4

Norden, Charles
See Durrell, Lawrence (George)

Nordhoff, Charles Bernard 1887-1947 .... **TCLC 23**
See also CA 108; 211; DLB 9; LAIT 1; RHW 1; SATA 23

Norfolk, Lawrence 1963- .... **CLC 76**
See also CA 144; CANR 85; CN 7; DLB 267

Norman, Marsha 1947- . **CLC 28, 186; DC 8**
See also CA 105; CABS 3; CAD; CANR 41, 131; CD 5; CSW; CWD; DAM DRAM; DFS 2; DLB 266; DLBY 1984; FW

Normyx
See Douglas, (George) Norman

Norris, (Benjamin) Frank(lin, Jr.) 1870-1902 .... **SSC 28; TCLC 24, 155**
See also AAYA 57; AMW; AMWC 2; BPFB 2; CA 110; 160; CDALB 1865-1917; DLB 12, 71, 186; LMFS 2; NFS 12; RGAL 4; TCWW 2; TUS

Norris, Leslie 1921- .... **CLC 14**
See also CA 11-12; CANR 14, 117; CAP 1; CP 7; DLB 27, 256

North, Andrew
See Norton, Andre

North, Anthony
See Koontz, Dean R(ay)

North, Captain George
See Stevenson, Robert Louis (Balfour)

North, Captain George
See Stevenson, Robert Louis (Balfour)

North, Milou
See Erdrich, Louise

Northrup, B. A.
See Hubbard, L(afayette) Ron(ald)

North Staffs
See Hulme, T(homas) E(rnest)

Northup, Solomon 1808-1863 ...... **NCLC 105**

Norton, Alice Mary
See Norton, Andre
See also MAICYA 1; SATA 1, 43

Norton, Andre 1912- .... **CLC 12**
See Norton, Alice Mary
See also AAYA 14; BPFB 2; BYA 4, 10, 12; CA 1-4R; CANR 68; CLR 50; DLB 8, 52; JRDA; MAICYA 2; MTCW 1; SATA 91; SUFW 1, 2; YAW

Norton, Caroline 1808-1877 .... **NCLC 47**
See also DLB 21, 159, 199

Norway, Nevil Shute 1899-1960
See Shute, Nevil
See also CA 102; 93-96; CANR 85; MTCW 2

Norwid, Cyprian Kamil 1821-1883 .... **NCLC 17**
See also RGWL 3

Nosille, Nabrah
See Ellison, Harlan (Jay)

Nossack, Hans Erich 1901-1978 .... **CLC 6**
See also CA 93-96; 85-88; DLB 69; EWL 3

Nostradamus 1503-1566 .... **LC 27**

Nosu, Chuji
See Ozu, Yasujiro

Notenburg, Eleanora (Genrikhovna) von
See Guro, Elena (Genrikhovna)

Nova, Craig 1945- .... **CLC 7, 31**
See also CA 45-48; CANR 2, 53, 127

Novak, Joseph
See Kosinski, Jerzy (Nikodem)

Novalis 1772-1801 .... **NCLC 13**
See also CDWLB 2; DLB 90; EW 5; RGWL 2, 3

Novick, Peter 1934- .... **CLC 164**
See also CA 188

Novis, Emile
See Weil, Simone (Adolphine)

Nowlan, Alden (Albert) 1933-1983 ... **CLC 15**
See also CA 9-12R; CANR 5; DAC; DAM MST; DLB 53; PFS 12

Noyes, Alfred 1880-1958 ...... **PC 27; TCLC 7**
See also CA 104; 188; DLB 20; EXPP; FANT; PFS 4; RGEL 2

Nugent, Richard Bruce 1906(?)-1987 ... **HR 3**
See also BW 1; CA 125; DLB 51; GLL 2

Nunn, Kem .... **CLC 34**
See also CA 159

Nwapa, Flora (Nwanzuruaha) 1931-1993 .... **BLCS; CLC 133**
See also BW 2; CA 143; CANR 83; CDWLB 3; CWRI 5; DLB 125; EWL 3; WLIT 2

Oneal, Zibby .... **CLC 30**
 See Oneal, Elizabeth
 See also AAYA 5, 41; BYA 13; CLR 13;
  JRDA; WYA

O'Neill, Eugene (Gladstone)
  1888-1953 ... **DC 20; TCLC 1, 6, 27, 49;**
  WLC
 See also AAYA 54; AITN 1; AMW; AMWC
  1; CA 110; 132; CAD; CANR 131;
  CDALB 1929-1941; DA; DA3; DAB;
  DAC; DAM DRAM, MST; DFS 2, 4, 5,
  6, 9, 11, 12, 16, 20; DLB 7; LAIT
  3; LMFS 2; MTCW 1, 2; RGAL 4; TUS

Onetti, Juan Carlos 1909-1994 ... **CLC 7, 10;**
  HLCS 2; SSC 23; TCLC 131
 See also CA 85-88; 145; CANR 32, 63; CD-
  WLB 3; CWW 2; DAM MULT, NOV;
  DLB 113; EWL 3; HW 1, 2; LAW;
  MTCW 1, 2; RGSF 2

O Nuallain, Brian 1911-1966
 See O'Brien, Flann
 See also CA 21-22; 25-28R; CAP 2; DLB
  231; FANT; TEA

Ophuls, Max 1902-1957 .... **TCLC 79**
 See also CA 113

Opie, Amelia 1769-1853 .... **NCLC 65**
 See also DLB 116, 159; RGEL 2

Oppen, George 1908-1984 ..... **CLC 7, 13, 34;**
  PC 35; TCLC 107
 See also CA 13-16R; 113; CANR 8, 82;
  DLB 5, 165

Oppenheim, E(dward) Phillips
  1866-1946 .... **TCLC 45**
 See also CA 111; 202; CMW 4; DLB 70

Opuls, Max
 See Ophuls, Max

Orage, A(lfred) R(ichard)
  1873-1934 .... **TCLC 157**
 See also CA 122

Origen c. 185-c. 254 .... **CMLC 19**

Orlovitz, Gil 1918-1973 .... **CLC 22**
 See also CA 77-80; 45-48; DLB 2, 5

Orris
 See Ingelow, Jean

Ortega y Gasset, Jose 1883-1955 ...... **HLC 2;**
  TCLC 9
 See also CA 106; 130; DAM MULT; EW 9;
  EWL 3; HW 1, 2; MTCW 1, 2

Ortese, Anna Maria 1914-1998 .... **CLC 89**
 See also DLB 177; EWL 3

Ortiz, Simon J(oseph) 1941- .... **CLC 45;**
  NNAL; PC 17
 See also AMWS 4; CA 134; CANR 69, 118;
  CP 7; DAM MULT, POET; DLB 120,
  175, 256; EXPP; PFS 4, 16; RGAL 4

Orton, Joe ...... **CLC 4, 13, 43; DC 3; TCLC**
  157
 See Orton, John Kingsley
 See also BRWS 5; CBD; CDBLB 1960 to
  Present; DFS 3, 6; DLB 13; GLL 1;
  MTCW 2; RGEL 2; TEA; WLIT 4

Orton, John Kingsley 1933-1967
 See Orton, Joe
 See also CA 85-88; CANR 35, 66; DAM
  DRAM; MTCW 1, 2

Orwell, George ...... **SSC 68; TCLC 2, 6, 15,**
  31, 51, 128, 129; WLC
 See Blair, Eric (Arthur)
 See also BPFB 3; BRW 7; BYA 5; CDBLB
  1945-1960; CLR 68; DAB; DLB 15, 98,
  195, 255; EWL 3; EXPN; LAIT 4, 5;
  LATS 1:1; NFS 3, 7; RGEL 2; SCFW 2;
  SFW 4; SSFS 4; TEA; WLIT 4; YAW

Osborne, David
 See Silverberg, Robert

Osborne, George
 See Silverberg, Robert

Osborne, John (James) 1929-1994 .... **CLC 1,**
  2, 5, 11, 45; TCLC 153; WLC
 See also BRWS 1; CA 13-16R; 147; CANR
  21, 56; CDBLB 1945-1960; DA; DAB;
  DAC; DAM DRAM, MST; DFS 4, 19;
  DLB 13; EWL 3; MTCW 1, 2; RGEL 2

Osborne, Lawrence 1958- .... **CLC 50**
 See also CA 189

Osbourne, Lloyd 1868-1947 .... **TCLC 93**

Osgood, Frances Sargent
  1811-1850 .... **NCLC 141**
 See also DLB 250

Oshima, Nagisa 1932- .... **CLC 20**
 See also CA 116; 121; CANR 78

Oskison, John Milton
  1874-1947 .... **NNAL; TCLC 35**
 See also CA 144; CANR 84; DAM MULT;
  DLB 175

Ossian c. 3rd cent. - .... **CMLC 28**
 See Macpherson, James

Ossoli, Sarah Margaret (Fuller)
  1810-1850 .... **NCLC 5, 50**
 See Fuller, Margaret; Fuller, Sarah Margaret
 See also CDALB 1640-1865; FW; LMFS 1;
  SATA 25

Ostriker, Alicia (Suskin) 1937- .... **CLC 132**
 See also CA 25-28R; CAAS 24; CANR 10,
  30, 62, 99; CWP; DLB 120; EXPP; PFS
  19

Ostrovsky, Aleksandr Nikolaevich
 See Ostrovsky, Alexander
 See also DLB 277

Ostrovsky, Alexander 1823-1886 .. **NCLC 30,**
  57
 See Ostrovsky, Aleksandr Nikolaevich

Otero, Blas de 1916-1979 .... **CLC 11**
 See also CA 89-92; DLB 134; EWL 3

O'Trigger, Sir Lucius
 See Horne, Richard Henry Hengist

Otto, Rudolf 1869-1937 .... **TCLC 85**

Otto, Whitney 1955- .... **CLC 70**
 See also CA 140; CANR 120

Otway, Thomas 1652-1685 ... **DC 24; LC 106**
 See also DAM DRAM; DLB 80; RGEL 2

Ouida .... **TCLC 43**
 See De la Ramee, Marie Louise (Ouida)
 See also DLB 18, 156; RGEL 2

Ouologuem, Yambo 1940- .... **CLC 146**
 See also CA 111; 176

Ousmane, Sembene 1923- ..... **BLC 3; CLC 66**
 See Sembene, Ousmane
 See also BW 1, 3; CA 117; 125; CANR 81;
  CWW 2; MTCW 1

Ovid 43B.C.-17 .... **CMLC 7; PC 2**
 See also AW 2; CDWLB 1; DA3; DAM
  POET; DLB 211; RGWL 2, 3; WP

Owen, Hugh
 See Faust, Frederick (Schiller)

Owen, Wilfred (Edward Salter)
  1893-1918 ... **PC 19; TCLC 5, 27; WLC**
 See also BRW 6; CA 104; 141; CDBLB
  1914-1945; DA; DAB; DAC; DAM MST,
  POET; DLB 20; EWL 3; EXPP; MTCW
  2; PFS 10; RGEL 2; WLIT 4

Owens, Louis (Dean) 1948-2002 .... **NNAL**
 See also CA 137, 179; 207; CAAE 179;
  CAAS 24; CANR 71

Owens, Rochelle 1936- .... **CLC 8**
 See also CA 17-20R; CAAS 2; CAD;
  CANR 39; CD 5; CP 7; CWD; CWP

Oz, Amos 1939- ...... **CLC 5, 8, 11, 27, 33, 54;**
  SSC 66
 See also CA 53-56; CANR 27, 47, 65, 113;
  CWW 2; DAM NOV; EWL 3; MTCW 1,
  2; RGSF 2; RGWL 3

Ozick, Cynthia 1928- .... **CLC 3, 7, 28, 62,**
  155; SSC 15, 60
 See also AMWS 5; BEST 90:1; CA 17-20R;
  CANR 23, 58, 116; CN 7; CPW; DA3;
  DAM NOV, POP; DLB 28, 152, 299;
  DLBY 1982; EWL 3; EXPS; INT CANR-
  23; MTCW 1, 2; RGAL 4; RGSF 2; SSFS
  3, 12

Ozu, Yasujiro 1903-1963 .... **CLC 16**
 See also CA 112

Pabst, G. W. 1885-1967 .... **TCLC 127**

Pacheco, C.
 See Pessoa, Fernando (Antonio Nogueira)

Pacheco, Jose Emilio 1939- .... **HLC 2**
 See also CA 111; 131; CANR 65; CWW 2;
  DAM MULT; DLB 290; EWL 3; HW 1,
  2; RGSF 2

Pa Chin .... **CLC 18**
 See Li Fei-kan
 See also EWL 3

Pack, Robert 1929- .... **CLC 13**
 See also CA 1-4R; CANR 3, 44, 82; CP 7;
  DLB 5; SATA 118

Padgett, Lewis
 See Kuttner, Henry

Padilla (Lorenzo), Heberto
  1932-2000 .... **CLC 38**
 See also AITN 1; CA 123; 131; 189; CWW
  2; EWL 3; HW 1

Page, James Patrick 1944-
 See Page, Jimmy
 See also CA 204

Page, Jimmy 1944- .... **CLC 12**
 See Page, James Patrick

Page, Louise 1955- .... **CLC 40**
 See also CA 140; CANR 76; CBD; CD 5;
  CWD; DLB 233

Page, P(atricia) K(athleen) 1916- ...... **CLC 7,**
  18; PC 12
 See Cape, Judith
 See also CA 53-56; CANR 4, 22, 65; CP 7;
  DAC; DAM MST; DLB 68; MTCW 1;
  RGEL 2

Page, Stanton
 See Fuller, Henry Blake

Page, Stanton
 See Fuller, Henry Blake

Page, Thomas Nelson 1853-1922 .... **SSC 23**
 See also CA 118; 177; DLB 12, 78; DLBD
  13; RGAL 4

Pagels, Elaine Hiesey 1943- .... **CLC 104**
 See also CA 45-48; CANR 2, 24, 51; FW;
  NCFS 4

Paget, Violet 1856-1935
 See Lee, Vernon
 See also CA 104; 166; GLL 1; HGG

Paget-Lowe, Henry
 See Lovecraft, H(oward) P(hillips)

Paglia, Camille (Anna) 1947- .... **CLC 68**
 See also CA 140; CANR 72; CPW; FW;
  GLL 2; MTCW 2

Paige, Richard
 See Koontz, Dean R(ay)

Paine, Thomas 1737-1809 .... **NCLC 62**
 See also AMWS 1; CDALB 1640-1865;
  DLB 31, 43, 73, 158; LAIT 1; RGAL 4;
  RGEL 2; TUS

Pakenham, Antonia
 See Fraser, Antonia (Pakenham)

Palamas, Costis
 See Palamas, Kostes

Palamas, Kostes 1859-1943 .... **TCLC 5**
 See Palamas, Kostis
 See also CA 105; 190; RGWL 2, 3

Palamas, Kostis
 See Palamas, Kostes
 See also EWL 3

p'Bitek, Okot 1931-1982 .... **BLC 3; CLC 96; TCLC 149**
See also AFW; BW 2, 3; CA 124; 107; CANR 82; DAM MULT; DLB 125; EWL 3; MTCW 1, 2; RGEL 2; WLIT 2

Peacock, Molly 1947- .... **CLC 60**
See also CA 103; CAAS 21; CANR 52, 84; CP 7; CWP; DLB 120, 282

Peacock, Thomas Love
1785-1866 .... **NCLC 22**
See also BRW 4; DLB 96, 116; RGEL 2; RGSF 2

Peake, Mervyn 1911-1968 .... **CLC 7, 54**
See also CA 5-8R; 25-28R; CANR 3; DLB 15, 160, 255; FANT; MTCW 1; RGEL 2; SATA 23; SFW 4

Pearce, Philippa
See Christie, Philippa
See also CA 5-8R; CANR 4, 109; CWRI 5; FANT; MAICYA 2

Pearl, Eric
See Elman, Richard (Martin)

Pearson, T(homas) R(eid) 1956- .... **CLC 39**
See also CA 120; 130; CANR 97; CSW; INT CA-130

Peck, Dale 1967- .... **CLC 81**
See also CA 146; CANR 72, 127; GLL 2

Peck, John (Frederick) 1941- .... **CLC 3**
See also CA 49-52; CANR 3, 100; CP 7

Peck, Richard (Wayne) 1934- .... **CLC 21**
See also AAYA 1, 24; BYA 1, 6, 8, 11; CA 85-88; CANR 19, 38, 129; CLR 15; INT CANR-19; JRDA; MAICYA 1, 2; SAAS 2; SATA 18, 55, 97; SATA-Essay 110; WYA; YAW

Peck, Robert Newton 1928- .... **CLC 17**
See also AAYA 3, 43; BYA 1, 6; CA 81-84, 182; CAAE 182; CANR 31, 63, 127; CLR 45; DA; DAC; DAM MST; JRDA; LAIT 3; MAICYA 1, 2; SAAS 1; SATA 21, 62, 111; SATA-Essay 108; WYA; YAW

Peckinpah, (David) Sam(uel)
1925-1984 .... **CLC 20**
See also CA 109; 114; CANR 82

Pedersen, Knut 1859-1952
See Hamsun, Knut
See also CA 104; 119; CANR 63; MTCW 1, 2

Peeslake, Gaffer
See Durrell, Lawrence (George)

Peguy, Charles (Pierre)
1873-1914 .... **TCLC 10**
See also CA 107; 193; DLB 258; EWL 3; GFL 1789 to the Present

Peirce, Charles Sanders
1839-1914 .... **TCLC 81**
See also CA 194; DLB 270

Pellicer, Carlos 1897(?)-1977 .... **HLCS 2**
See also CA 153; 69-72; DLB 290; EWL 3; HW 1

Pena, Ramon del Valle y
See Valle-Inclan, Ramon (Maria) del

Pendennis, Arthur Esquir
See Thackeray, William Makepeace

Penn, Arthur
See Matthews, (James) Brander

Penn, William 1644-1718 .... **LC 25**
See also DLB 24

PEPECE
See Prado (Calvo), Pedro

Pepys, Samuel 1633-1703 ... **LC 11, 58; WLC**
See also BRW 2; CDBLB 1660-1789; DA; DA3; DAB; DAC; DAM MST; DLB 101, 213; NCFS 4; RGEL 2; TEA; WLIT 3

Percy, Thomas 1729-1811 .... **NCLC 95**
See also DLB 104

Percy, Walker 1916-1990 .... **CLC 2, 3, 6, 8, 14, 18, 47, 65**
See also AMWS 3; BPFB 3; CA 1-4R; 131; CANR 1, 23, 64; CPW; CSW; DA3; DAM NOV, POP; DLB 2; DLBY 1980, 1990; EWL 3; MTCW 1, 2; RGAL 4; TUS

Percy, William Alexander
1885-1942 .... **TCLC 84**
See also CA 163; MTCW 2

Perec, Georges 1936-1982 .... **CLC 56, 116**
See also CA 141; DLB 83, 299; EWL 3; GFL 1789 to the Present; RGWL 3

Pereda (y Sanchez de Porrua), Jose Maria de 1833-1906 .... **TCLC 16**
See also CA 117

Pereda y Porrua, Jose Maria de
See Pereda (y Sanchez de Porrua), Jose Maria de

Peregoy, George Weems
See Mencken, H(enry) L(ouis)

Perelman, S(idney) J(oseph)
1904-1979 .. **CLC 3, 5, 9, 15, 23, 44, 49; SSC 32**
See also AITN 1, 2; BPFB 3; CA 73-76; 89-92; CANR 18; DAM DRAM; DLB 11, 44; MTCW 1, 2; RGAL 4

Peret, Benjamin 1899-1959 .... **PC 33; TCLC 20**
See also CA 117; 186; GFL 1789 to the Present

Peretz, Isaac Leib
See Peretz, Isaac Loeb
See also CA 201

Peretz, Isaac Loeb 1851(?)-1915 ...... **SSC 26; TCLC 16**
See Peretz, Isaac Leib
See also CA 109

Peretz, Yitzhok Leibush
See Peretz, Isaac Loeb

Perez Galdos, Benito 1843-1920 ..... **HLCS 2; TCLC 27**
See Galdos, Benito Perez
See also CA 125; 153; EWL 3; HW 1; RGWL 2, 3

Peri Rossi, Cristina 1941- .. **CLC 156; HLCS 2**
See also CA 131; CANR 59, 81; CWW 2; DLB 145, 290; EWL 3; HW 1, 2

Perlata
See Peret, Benjamin

Perloff, Marjorie G(abrielle)
1931- .... **CLC 137**
See also CA 57-60; CANR 7, 22, 49, 104

Perrault, Charles 1628-1703 .... **LC 2, 56**
See also BYA 4; CLR 79; DLB 268; GFL Beginnings to 1789; MAICYA 1, 2; RGWL 2, 3; SATA 25; WCH

Perry, Anne 1938- .... **CLC 126**
See also CA 101; CANR 22, 50, 84; CMW 4; CN 7; CPW; DLB 276

Perry, Brighton
See Sherwood, Robert E(mmet)

Perse, St.-John
See Leger, (Marie-Rene Auguste) Alexis Saint-Leger

Perse, Saint-John
See Leger, (Marie-Rene Auguste) Alexis Saint-Leger
See also DLB 258; RGWL 3

Perutz, Leo(pold) 1882-1957 .... **TCLC 60**
See also CA 147; DLB 81

Peseenz, Tulio F.
See Lopez y Fuentes, Gregorio

Pesetsky, Bette 1932- .... **CLC 28**
See also CA 133; DLB 130

Peshkov, Alexei Maximovich 1868-1936
See Gorky, Maxim
See also CA 105; 141; CANR 83; DA; DAC; DAM DRAM, MST, NOV; MTCW 2

Pessoa, Fernando (Antonio Nogueira)
1888-1935 ..... **HLC 2; PC 20; TCLC 27**
See also CA 125; 183; DAM MULT; DLB 287; EW 10; EWL 3; RGWL 2, 3; WP

Peterkin, Julia Mood 1880-1961 ...... **CLC 31**
See also CA 102; DLB 9

Peters, Joan K(aren) 1945- .... **CLC 39**
See also CA 158; CANR 109

Peters, Robert L(ouis) 1924- .... **CLC 7**
See also CA 13-16R; CAAS 8; CP 7; DLB 105

Petofi, Sandor 1823-1849 .... **NCLC 21**
See also RGWL 2, 3

Petrakis, Harry Mark 1923- .... **CLC 3**
See also CA 9-12R; CANR 4, 30, 85; CN 7

Petrarch 1304-1374 .... **CMLC 20; PC 8**
See also DA3; DAM POET; EW 2; LMFS 1; RGWL 2. 3

Petronius c. 20-66 .... **CMLC 34**
See also AW 2; CDWLB 1; DLB 211; RGWL 2, 3

Petrov, Evgeny .... **TCLC 21**
See Kataev, Evgeny Petrovich

Petry, Ann (Lane) 1908-1997 .. **CLC 1, 7, 18; TCLC 112**
See also AFAW 1, 2; BPFB 3; BW 1, 3; BYA 2; CA 5-8R; 157; CAAS 6; CANR 4, 46; CLR 12; CN 7; DLB 76; EWL 3; JRDA; LAIT 1; MAICYA 1, 2; MAIC-YAS 1; MTCW 1; RGAL 4; SATA 5; SATA-Obit 94; TUS

Petursson, Halligrimur 1614-1674 .... **LC 8**

Peychinovich
See Vazov, Ivan (Minchov)

Phaedrus c. 15B.C.-c. 50 .... **CMLC 25**
See also DLB 211

Phelps (Ward), Elizabeth Stuart
See Phelps, Elizabeth Stuart
See also FW

Phelps, Elizabeth Stuart
1844-1911 .... **TCLC 113**
See Phelps (Ward), Elizabeth Stuart
See also DLB 74

Philips, Katherine 1632-1664 . **LC 30; PC 40**
See also DLB 131; RGEL 2

Philipson, Morris H. 1926- .... **CLC 53**
See also CA 1-4R; CANR 4

Phillips, Caryl 1958- .... **BLCS; CLC 96**
See also BRWS 5; BW 2; CA 141; CANR 63, 104; CBD; CD 5; CN 7; DA3; DAM MULT; DLB 157; EWL 3; MTCW 2; WLIT 4; WWE 1

Phillips, David Graham
1867-1911 .... **TCLC 44**
See also CA 108; 176; DLB 9, 12, 303; RGAL 4

Phillips, Jack
See Sandburg, Carl (August)

Phillips, Jayne Anne 1952- .... **CLC 15, 33, 139; SSC 16**
See also AAYA 57; BPFB 3; CA 101; CANR 24, 50, 96; CN 7; CSW; DLBY 1980; INT CANR-24; MTCW 1, 2; RGAL 4; RGSF 2; SSFS 4

Phillips, Richard
See Dick, Philip K(indred)

Phillips, Robert (Schaeffer) 1938- .... **CLC 28**
See also CA 17-20R; CAAS 13; CANR 8; DLB 105

Phillips, Ward
See Lovecraft, H(oward) P(hillips)

Philostratus, Flavius c. 179-c.
244 .... **CMLC 62**

Pomerance, Bernard 1940- .... **CLC 13**
See also CA 101; CAD; CANR 49, 134;
CD 5; DAM DRAM; DFS 9; LAIT 2

Ponge, Francis 1899-1988 .... **CLC 6, 18**
See also CA 85-88; 126; CANR 40, 86;
DAM POET; DLBY 2002; EWL 3; GFL
1789 to the Present; RGWL 2, 3

Poniatowska, Elena 1933- . **CLC 140; HLC 2**
See also CA 101; CANR 32, 66, 107; CD-
WLB 3; CWW 2; DAM MULT; DLB 113;
EWL 3; HW 1, 2; LAWS 1; WLIT 1

Pontoppidan, Henrik 1857-1943 .... **TCLC 29**
See also CA 170; DLB 300

Ponty, Maurice Merleau
See Merleau-Ponty, Maurice

Poole, Josephine .... **CLC 17**
See Helyar, Jane Penelope Josephine
See also SAAS 2; SATA 5

Popa, Vasko 1922-1991 .... **CLC 19**
See also CA 112; 148; CDWLB 4; DLB
181; EWL 3; RGWL 2, 3

Pope, Alexander 1688-1744 ...... **LC 3, 58, 60,
64; PC 26; WLC**
See also BRW 3; BRWC 1; BRWR 1; CD-
BLB 1660-1789; DA; DA3; DAB; DAC;
DAM MST, POET; DLB 95, 101, 213;
EXPP; PAB; PFS 12; RGEL 2; WLIT 3;
WP

Popov, Evgenii Anatol'evich
See Popov, Yevgeny
See also DLB 285

Popov, Yevgeny .... **CLC 59**
See Popov, Evgenii Anatol'evich

Poquelin, Jean-Baptiste
See Moliere

Porete, Marguerite c. 1250-1310 .. **CMLC 73**
See also DLB 208

Porphyry c. 233-c. 305 .... **CMLC 71**

Porter, Connie (Rose) 1959(?)- .... **CLC 70**
See also BW 2, 3; CA 142; CANR 90, 109;
SATA 81, 129

Porter, Gene(va Grace) Stratton .. **TCLC 21**
See Stratton-Porter, Gene(va Grace)
See also BPFB 3; CA 112; CWRI 5; RHW

Porter, Katherine Anne 1890-1980 ... **CLC 1,
3, 7, 10, 13, 15, 27, 101; SSC 4, 31, 43**
See also AAYA 42; AITN 2; AMW; BPFB
3; CA 1-4R; 101; CANR 1, 65; CDALBS;
DA; DA3; DAB; DAC; DAM MST, NOV;
DLB 4, 9, 102; DLBD 12; DLBY 1980;
EWL 3; EXPS; LAIT 3; MAWW; MTCW
1, 2; NFS 14; RGAL 4; RGSF 2; SATA
39; SATA-Obit 23; SSFS 1, 8, 11, 16;
TUS

Porter, Peter (Neville Frederick)
1929- .... **CLC 5, 13, 33**
See also CA 85-88; CP 7; DLB 40, 289;
WWE 1

Porter, William Sydney 1862-1910
See Henry, O.
See also CA 104; 131; CDALB 1865-1917;
DA; DA3; DAB; DAC; DAM MST; DLB
12, 78, 79; MTCW 1, 2; TUS; YABC 2

Portillo (y Pacheco), Jose Lopez
See Lopez Portillo (y Pacheco), Jose

Portillo Trambley, Estela 1927-1998 .. **HLC 2**
See Trambley, Estela Portillo
See also CANR 32; DAM MULT; DLB
209; HW 1

Posey, Alexander (Lawrence)
1873-1908 .... **NNAL**
See also CA 144; CANR 80; DAM MULT;
DLB 175

Posse, Abel .... **CLC 70**

Post, Melville Davisson
1869-1930 .... **TCLC 39**
See also CA 110; 202; CMW 4

Potok, Chaim 1929-2002 ... **CLC 2, 7, 14, 26,
112**
See also AAYA 15, 50; AITN 1, 2; BPFB 3;
BYA 1; CA 17-20R; 208; CANR 19, 35,
64, 98; CLR 92; CN 7; DA3; DAM NOV;
DLB 28, 152; EXPN; INT CANR-19;
LAIT 4; MTCW 1, 2; NFS 4; SATA 33,
106; SATA-Obit 134; TUS; YAW

Potok, Herbert Harold -2002
See Potok, Chaim

Potok, Herman Harold
See Potok, Chaim

Potter, Dennis (Christopher George)
1935-1994 .... **CLC 58, 86, 123**
See also BRWS 10; CA 107; 145; CANR
33, 61; CBD; DLB 233; MTCW 1

Pound, Ezra (Weston Loomis)
1885-1972 .. **CLC 1, 2, 3, 4, 5, 7, 10, 13,
18, 34, 48, 50, 112; PC 4; WLC**
See also AAYA 47; AMW; AMWR 1; CA
5-8R; 37-40R; CANR 40; CDALB 1917-
1929; DA; DA3; DAC; DAM MST,
POET; DLB 4, 45, 63; DLBD 15; EFS 2;
EWL 3; EXPP; LMFS 2; MTCW 1, 2;
PAB; PFS 2, 8, 16; RGAL 4; TUS; WP

Povod, Reinaldo 1959-1994 .... **CLC 44**
See also CA 136; 146; CANR 83

Powell, Adam Clayton, Jr.
1908-1972 .... **BLC 3; CLC 89**
See also BW 1, 3; CA 102; 33-36R; CANR
86; DAM MULT

Powell, Anthony (Dymoke)
1905-2000 .... **CLC 1, 3, 7, 9, 10, 31**
See also BRW 7; CA 1-4R; 189; CANR 1,
32, 62, 107; CDBLB 1945-1960; CN 7;
DLB 15; EWL 3; MTCW 1, 2; RGEL 2;
TEA

Powell, Dawn 1896(?)-1965 .... **CLC 66**
See also CA 5-8R; CANR 121; DLBY 1997

Powell, Padgett 1952- .... **CLC 34**
See also CA 126; CANR 63, 101; CSW;
DLB 234; DLBY 01

Powell, (Oval) Talmage 1920-2000
See Queen, Ellery
See also CA 5-8R; CANR 2, 80

Power, Susan 1961- .... **CLC 91**
See also BYA 14; CA 160; CANR 135; NFS
11

Powers, J(ames) F(arl) 1917-1999 ..... **CLC 1,
4, 8, 57; SSC 4**
See also CA 1-4R; 181; CANR 2, 61; CN
7; DLB 130; MTCW 1; RGAL 4; RGSF
2

Powers, John J(ames) 1945-
See Powers, John R.
See also CA 69-72

Powers, John R. .... **CLC 66**
See Powers, John J(ames)

Powers, Richard (S.) 1957- .... **CLC 93**
See also AMWS 9; BPFB 3; CA 148;
CANR 80; CN 7

Pownall, David 1938- .... **CLC 10**
See also CA 89-92, 180; CAAS 18; CANR
49, 101; CBD; CD 5; CN 7; DLB 14

Powys, John Cowper 1872-1963 ... **CLC 7, 9,
15, 46, 125**
See also CA 85-88; CANR 106; DLB 15,
255; EWL 3; FANT; MTCW 1, 2; RGEL
2; SUFW

Powys, T(heodore) F(rancis)
1875-1953 .... **TCLC 9**
See also BRWS 8; CA 106; 189; DLB 36,
162; EWL 3; FANT; RGEL 2; SUFW

Prado (Calvo), Pedro 1886-1952 ... **TCLC 75**
See also CA 131; DLB 283; HW 1; LAW

Prager, Emily 1952- .... **CLC 56**
See also CA 204

Pratchett, Terry 1948- .... **CLC 197**
See also AAYA 19, 54; BPFB 3; CA 143;
CANR 87, 126; CLR 64; CN 7; CPW;
CWRI 5; FANT; SATA 82, 139; SFW 4;
SUFW 2

Pratolini, Vasco 1913-1991 .... **TCLC 124**
See also CA 211; DLB 177; EWL 3; RGWL
2, 3

Pratt, E(dwin) J(ohn) 1883(?)-1964 . **CLC 19**
See also CA 141; 93-96; CANR 77; DAC;
DAM POET; DLB 92; EWL 3; RGEL 2;
TWA

Premchand .... **TCLC 21**
See Srivastava, Dhanpat Rai
See also EWL 3

Preseren, France 1800-1849 .... **NCLC 127**
See also CDWLB 4; DLB 147

Preussler, Otfried 1923- .... **CLC 17**
See also CA 77-80; SATA 24

Prevert, Jacques (Henri Marie)
1900-1977 .... **CLC 15**
See also CA 77-80; 69-72; CANR 29, 61;
DLB 258; EWL 3; GFL 1789 to the
Present; IDFW 3, 4; MTCW 1; RGWL 2,
3; SATA-Obit 30

Prevost, (Antoine Francois)
1697-1763 .... **LC 1**
See also EW 4; GFL Beginnings to 1789;
RGWL 2, 3

Price, (Edward) Reynolds 1933- ... **CLC 3, 6,
13, 43, 50, 63; SSC 22**
See also AMWS 6; CA 1-4R; CANR 1, 37,
57, 87, 128; CN 7; CSW; DAM NOV;
DLB 2, 218, 278; EWL 3; INT CANR-
37; NFS 18

Price, Richard 1949- .... **CLC 6, 12**
See also CA 49-52; CANR 3; DLBY 1981

Prichard, Katharine Susannah
1883-1969 .... **CLC 46**
See also CA 11-12; CANR 33; CAP 1; DLB
260; MTCW 1; RGEL 2; RGSF 2; SATA
66

Priestley, J(ohn) B(oynton)
1894-1984 .... **CLC 2, 5, 9, 34**
See also BRW 7; CA 9-12R; 113; CANR
33; CDBLB 1914-1945; DA3; DAM
DRAM, NOV; DLB 10, 34, 77, 100, 139;
DLBY 1984; EWL 3; MTCW 1, 2; RGEL
2; SFW 4

Prince 1958- .... **CLC 35**
See also CA 213

Prince, F(rank) T(empleton)
1912-2003 .... **CLC 22**
See also CA 101; 219; CANR 43, 79; CP 7;
DLB 20

Prince Kropotkin
See Kropotkin, Peter (Aleksieevich)

Prior, Matthew 1664-1721 .... **LC 4**
See also DLB 95; RGEL 2

Prishvin, Mikhail 1873-1954 .... **TCLC 75**
See Prishvin, Mikhail Mikhailovich

Prishvin, Mikhail Mikhailovich
See Prishvin, Mikhail
See also DLB 272; EWL 3

Pritchard, William H(arrison)
1932- .... **CLC 34**
See also CA 65-68; CANR 23, 95; DLB
111

Pritchett, V(ictor) S(awdon)
1900-1997 ... **CLC 5, 13, 15, 41; SSC 14**
See also BPFB 3; BRWS 3; CA 61-64; 157;
CANR 31, 63; CN 7; DA3; DAM NOV;
DLB 15, 139; EWL 3; MTCW 1, 2;
RGEL 2; RGSF 2; TEA

Private 19022
See Manning, Frederic

Probst, Mark 1925- .... **CLC 59**
See also CA 130

Ross, Martin 1862-1915
See Martin, Violet Florence
See also DLB 135; GLL 2; RGEL 2; RGSF 2

Ross, (James) Sinclair 1908-1996 ... **CLC 13; SSC 24**
See also CA 73-76; CANR 81; CN 7; DAC; DAM MST; DLB 88; RGEL 2; RGSF 2; TCWW 2

Rossetti, Christina (Georgina) 1830-1894 .... **NCLC 2, 50, 66; PC 7; WLC**
See also AAYA 51; BRW 5; BYA 4; DA; DA3; DAB; DAC; DAM MST, POET; DLB 35, 163, 240; EXPP; LATS 1:1; MAICYA 1, 2; PFS 10, 14; RGEL 2; SATA 20; TEA; WCH

Rossetti, Dante Gabriel 1828-1882 . **NCLC 4, 77; PC 44; WLC**
See also AAYA 51; BRW 5; CDBLB 1832-1890; DA; DAB; DAC; DAM MST, POET; DLB 35; EXPP; RGEL 2; TEA

Rossi, Cristina Peri
See Peri Rossi, Cristina

Rossi, Jean-Baptiste 1931-2003
See Japrisot, Sebastien
See also CA 201; 215

Rossner, Judith (Perelman) 1935- . **CLC 6, 9, 29**
See also AITN 2; BEST 90:3; BPFB 3; CA 17-20R; CANR 18, 51, 73; CN 7; DLB 6; INT CANR-18; MTCW 1, 2

Rostand, Edmond (Eugene Alexis) 1868-1918 .... **DC 10; TCLC 6, 37**
See also CA 104; 126; DA; DA3; DAB; DAC; DAM DRAM, MST; DFS 1; DLB 192; LAIT 1; MTCW 1; RGWL 2, 3; TWA

Roth, Henry 1906-1995 ..... **CLC 2, 6, 11, 104**
See also AMWS 9; CA 11-12; 149; CANR 38, 63; CAP 1; CN 7; DA3; DLB 28; EWL 3; MTCW 1, 2; RGAL 4

Roth, (Moses) Joseph 1894-1939 ... **TCLC 33**
See also CA 160; DLB 85; EWL 3; RGWL 2, 3

Roth, Philip (Milton) 1933- ... **CLC 1, 2, 3, 4, 6, 9, 15, 22, 31, 47, 66, 86, 119; SSC 26; WLC**
See also AMWR 2; AMWS 3; BEST 90:3; BPFB 3; CA 1-4R; CANR 1, 22, 36, 55, 89, 132; CDALB 1968-1988; CN 7; CPW 1; DA; DA3; DAB; DAC; DAM MST, NOV, POP; DLB 2, 28, 173; DLBY 1982; EWL 3; MTCW 1, 2; RGAL 4; RGSF 2; SSFS 12, 18; TUS

Rothenberg, Jerome 1931- .... **CLC 6, 57**
See also CA 45-48; CANR 1, 106; CP 7; DLB 5, 193

Rotter, Pat ed. .... **CLC 65**

Roumain, Jacques (Jean Baptiste) 1907-1944 .... **BLC 3; TCLC 19**
See also BW 1; CA 117; 125; DAM MULT; EWL 3

Rourke, Constance Mayfield 1885-1941 .... **TCLC 12**
See also CA 107; 200; YABC 1

Rousseau, Jean-Baptiste 1671-1741 ...... **LC 9**

Rousseau, Jean-Jacques 1712-1778 .... **LC 14, 36; WLC**
See also DA; DA3; DAB; DAC; DAM MST; EW 4; GFL Beginnings to 1789; LMFS 1; RGWL 2, 3; TWA

Roussel, Raymond 1877-1933 .... **TCLC 20**
See also CA 117; 201; EWL 3; GFL 1789 to the Present

Rovit, Earl (Herbert) 1927- .... **CLC 7**
See also CA 5-8R; CANR 12

Rowe, Elizabeth Singer 1674-1737 ..... **LC 44**
See also DLB 39, 95

Rowe, Nicholas 1674-1718 .... **LC 8**
See also DLB 84; RGEL 2

Rowlandson, Mary 1637(?)-1678 .... **LC 66**
See also DLB 24, 200; RGAL 4

Rowley, Ames Dorrance
See Lovecraft, H(oward) P(hillips)

Rowley, William 1585(?)-1626 .... **LC 100**
See also DLB 58; RGEL 2

Rowling, J(oanne) K(athleen) 1966- .... **CLC 137**
See also AAYA 34; BYA 11, 13, 14; CA 173; CANR 128; CLR 66, 80; MAICYA 2; SATA 109; SUFW 2

Rowson, Susanna Haswell 1762(?)-1824 .... **NCLC 5, 69**
See also DLB 37, 200; RGAL 4

Roy, Arundhati 1960(?)- .... **CLC 109**
See also CA 163; CANR 90, 126; DLBY 1997; EWL 3; LATS 1:2; WWE 1

Roy, Gabrielle 1909-1983 .... **CLC 10, 14**
See also CA 53-56; 110; CANR 5, 61; CCA 1; DAB; DAC; DAM MST; DLB 68; EWL 3; MTCW 1; RGWL 2, 3; SATA 104

Royko, Mike 1932-1997 .... **CLC 109**
See also CA 89-92; 157; CANR 26, 111; CPW

Rozanov, Vasilii Vasil'evich
See Rozanov, Vassili
See also DLB 295

Rozanov, Vasily Vasilyevich
See Rozanov, Vassili
See also EWL 3

Rozanov, Vassili 1856-1919 .... **TCLC 104**
See Rozanov, Vasilii Vasil'evich; Rozanov, Vasily Vasilyevich

Rozewicz, Tadeusz 1921- ...... **CLC 9, 23, 139**
See also CA 108; CANR 36, 66; CWW 2; DA3; DAM POET; DLB 232; EWL 3; MTCW 1, 2; RGWL 3

Ruark, Gibbons 1941- .... **CLC 3**
See also CA 33-36R; CAAS 23; CANR 14, 31, 57; DLB 120

Rubens, Bernice (Ruth) 1923-2004 . **CLC 19, 31**
See also CA 25-28R; CANR 33, 65, 128; CN 7; DLB 14, 207; MTCW 1

Rubin, Harold
See Robbins, Harold

Rudkin, (James) David 1936- .... **CLC 14**
See also CA 89-92; CBD; CD 5; DLB 13

Rudnik, Raphael 1933- .... **CLC 7**
See also CA 29-32R

Ruffian, M.
See Hasek, Jaroslav (Matej Frantisek)

Ruiz, Jose Martinez .... **CLC 11**
See Martinez Ruiz, Jose

Ruiz, Juan c. 1283-c. 1350 .... **CMLC 66**

Rukeyser, Muriel 1913-1980 . **CLC 6, 10, 15, 27; PC 12**
See also AMWS 6; CA 5-8R; 93-96; CANR 26, 60; DA3; DAM POET; DLB 48; EWL 3; FW; GLL 2; MTCW 1, 2; PFS 10; RGAL 4; SATA-Obit 22

Rule, Jane (Vance) 1931- .... **CLC 27**
See also CA 25-28R; CAAS 18; CANR 12, 87; CN 7; DLB 60; FW

Rulfo, Juan 1918-1986 .. **CLC 8, 80; HLC 2; SSC 25**
See also CA 85-88; 118; CANR 26; CD-WLB 3; DAM MULT; DLB 113; EWL 3; HW 1, 2; LAW; MTCW 1, 2; RGSF 2; RGWL 2, 3; WLIT 1

Rumi, Jalal al-Din 1207-1273 ...... **CMLC 20; PC 45**
See also RGWL 2, 3; WP

Runeberg, Johan 1804-1877 .... **NCLC 41**

Runyon, (Alfred) Damon 1884(?)-1946 .... **TCLC 10**
See also CA 107; 165; DLB 11, 86, 171; MTCW 2; RGAL 4

Rush, Norman 1933- .... **CLC 44**
See also CA 121; 126; CANR 130; INT CA-126

Rushdie, (Ahmed) Salman 1947- .... **CLC 23, 31, 55, 100, 191; WLCS**
See also BEST 89:3; BPFB 3; BRWS 4; CA 108; 111; CANR 33, 56, 108, 133; CN 7; CPW 1; DA3; DAB; DAC; DAM MST, NOV, POP; DLB 194; EWL 3; FANT; INT CA-111; LATS 1:2; LMFS 2; MTCW 1, 2; RGEL 2; RGSF 2; TEA; WLIT 4; WWE 1

Rushforth, Peter (Scott) 1945- .... **CLC 19**
See also CA 101

Ruskin, John 1819-1900 .... **TCLC 63**
See also BRW 5; BYA 5; CA 114; 129; CDBLB 1832-1890; DLB 55, 163, 190; RGEL 2; SATA 24; TEA; WCH

Russ, Joanna 1937- .... **CLC 15**
See also BPFB 3; CA 5-28R; CANR 11, 31, 65; CN 7; DLB 8; FW; GLL 1; MTCW 1; SCFW 2; SFW 4

Russ, Richard Patrick
See O'Brian, Patrick

Russell, George William 1867-1935
See A.E.; Baker, Jean H.
See also BRWS 8; CA 104; 153; CDBLB 1890-1914; DAM POET; EWL 3; RGEL 2

Russell, Jeffrey Burton 1934- .... **CLC 70**
See also CA 25-28R; CANR 11, 28, 52

Russell, (Henry) Ken(neth Alfred) 1927- .... **CLC 16**
See also CA 105

Russell, William Martin 1947-
See Russell, Willy
See also CA 164; CANR 107

Russell, Willy .... **CLC 60**
See Russell, William Martin
See also CBD; CD 5; DLB 233

Russo, Richard 1949- .... **CLC 181**
See also AMWS 12; CA 127; 133; CANR 87, 114

Rutherford, Mark .... **TCLC 25**
See White, William Hale
See also DLB 18; RGEL 2

Ruyslinck, Ward .... **CLC 14**
See Belser, Reimond Karel Maria de

Ryan, Cornelius (John) 1920-1974 ..... **CLC 7**
See also CA 69-72; 53-56; CANR 38

Ryan, Michael 1946- .... **CLC 65**
See also CA 49-52; CANR 109; DLBY 1982

Ryan, Tim
See Dent, Lester

Rybakov, Anatoli (Naumovich) 1911-1998 .... **CLC 23, 53**
See Rybakov, Anatolii (Naumovich)
See also CA 126; 135; 172; SATA 79; SATA-Obit 108

Rybakov, Anatolii (Naumovich)
See Rybakov, Anatoli (Naumovich)
See also DLB 302

Ryder, Jonathan
See Ludlum, Robert

Ryga, George 1932-1987 .... **CLC 14**
See also CA 101; 124; CANR 43, 90; CCA 1; DAC; DAM MST; DLB 60

S. H.
See Hartmann, Sadakichi

S. S.
See Sassoon, Siegfried (Lorraine)

Sa'adawi, al- Nawal
See El Saadawi, Nawal
See also AFW; EWL 3

Schumacher, E(rnst) F(riedrich)
1911-1977 .... **CLC 80**
See also CA 81-84; 73-76; CANR 34, 85

Schumann, Robert 1810-1856 ...... **NCLC 143**

Schuyler, George Samuel 1895-1977 .... **HR 3**
See also BW 2; CA 81-84; 73-76; CANR
42; DLB 29, 51

Schuyler, James Marcus 1923-1991 .. **CLC 5,
23**
See also CA 101; 134; DAM POET; DLB
5, 169; EWL 3; INT CA-101; WP

Schwartz, Delmore (David)
1913-1966 ... **CLC 2, 4, 10, 45, 87; PC 8**
See also AMWS 2; CA 17-18; 25-28R;
CANR 35; CAP 2; DLB 28, 48; EWL 3;
MTCW 1, 2; PAB; RGAL 4; TUS

Schwartz, Ernst
See Ozu, Yasujiro

Schwartz, John Burnham 1965- .... **CLC 59**
See also CA 132; CANR 116

Schwartz, Lynne Sharon 1939- .... **CLC 31**
See also CA 103; CANR 44, 89; DLB 218;
MTCW 2

Schwartz, Muriel A.
See Eliot, T(homas) S(tearns)

Schwarz-Bart, Andre 1928- .... **CLC 2, 4**
See also CA 89-92; CANR 109; DLB 299

Schwarz-Bart, Simone 1938- . **BLCS; CLC 7**
See also BW 2; CA 97-100; CANR 117;
EWL 3

Schwerner, Armand 1927-1999 .... **PC 42**
See also CA 9-12R; 179; CANR 50, 85; CP
7; DLB 165

**Schwitters, Kurt (Hermann Edward Karl
Julius)** 1887-1948 .... **TCLC 95**
See also CA 158

Schwob, Marcel (Mayer Andre)
1867-1905 .... **TCLC 20**
See also CA 117; 168; DLB 123; GFL 1789
to the Present

Sciascia, Leonardo 1921-1989 .. **CLC 8, 9, 41**
See also CA 85-88; 130; CANR 35; DLB
177; EWL 3; MTCW 1; RGWL 2, 3

Scoppettone, Sandra 1936- .... **CLC 26**
See Early, Jack
See also AAYA 11; BYA 8; CA 5-8R;
CANR 41, 73; GLL 1; MAICYA 2; MAI-
CYAS 1; SATA 9, 92; WYA; YAW

Scorsese, Martin 1942- .... **CLC 20, 89**
See also AAYA 38; CA 110; 114; CANR
46, 85

Scotland, Jay
See Jakes, John (William)

Scott, Duncan Campbell
1862-1947 .... **TCLC 6**
See also CA 104; 153; DAC; DLB 92;
RGEL 2

Scott, Evelyn 1893-1963 .... **CLC 43**
See also CA 104; 112; CANR 64; DLB 9,
48; RHW

Scott, F(rancis) R(eginald)
1899-1985 .... **CLC 22**
See also CA 101; 114; CANR 87; DLB 88;
INT CA-101; RGEL 2

Scott, Frank
See Scott, F(rancis) R(eginald)

Scott, Joan .... **CLC 65**

Scott, Joanna 1960- .... **CLC 50**
See also CA 126; CANR 53, 92

Scott, Paul (Mark) 1920-1978 ...... **CLC 9, 60**
See also BRWS 1; CA 81-84; 77-80; CANR
33; DLB 14, 207; EWL 3; MTCW 1;
RGEL 2; RHW; WWE 1

Scott, Ridley 1937- .... **CLC 183**
See also AAYA 13, 43

Scott, Sarah 1723-1795 .... **LC 44**
See also DLB 39

Scott, Sir Walter 1771-1832 .... **NCLC 15, 69,
110; PC 13; SSC 32; WLC**
See also AAYA 22; BRW 4; BYA 2; CD-
BLB 1789-1832; DA; DAB; DAC; DAM
MST, NOV, POET; DLB 93, 107, 116,
144, 159; HGG; LAIT 1; RGEL 2; RGSF
2; SSFS 10; SUFW 1; TEA; WLIT 3;
YABC 2

Scribe, (Augustin) Eugene 1791-1861 . **DC 5;
NCLC 16**
See also DAM DRAM; DLB 192; GFL
1789 to the Present; RGWL 2, 3

Scrum, R.
See Crumb, R(obert)

Scudery, Georges de 1601-1667 .... **LC 75**
See also GFL Beginnings to 1789

Scudery, Madeleine de 1607-1701 .. **LC 2, 58**
See also DLB 268; GFL Beginnings to 1789

Scum
See Crumb, R(obert)

Scumbag, Little Bobby
See Crumb, R(obert)

Seabrook, John
See Hubbard, L(afayette) Ron(ald)

Seacole, Mary Jane Grant
1805-1881 .... **NCLC 147**
See also DLB 166

Sealy, I(rwin) Allan 1951- .... **CLC 55**
See also CA 136; CN 7

Search, Alexander
See Pessoa, Fernando (Antonio Nogueira)

Sebald, W(infried) G(eorg)
1944-2001 .... **CLC 194**
See also BRWS 8; CA 159; 202; CANR 98

Sebastian, Lee
See Silverberg, Robert

Sebastian Owl
See Thompson, Hunter S(tockton)

Sebestyen, Igen
See Sebestyen, Ouida

Sebestyen, Ouida 1924- .... **CLC 30**
See also AAYA 8; BYA 7; CA 107; CANR
40, 114; CLR 17; JRDA; MAICYA 1, 2;
SAAS 10; SATA 39, 140; WYA; YAW

Sebold, Alice 1963(?)- .... **CLC 193**
See also AAYA 56; CA 203

Second Duke of Buckingham
See Villiers, George

Secundus, H. Scriblerus
See Fielding, Henry

Sedges, John
See Buck, Pearl S(ydenstricker)

Sedgwick, Catharine Maria
1789-1867 .... **NCLC 19, 98**
See also DLB 1, 74, 183, 239, 243, 254;
RGAL 4

Seelye, John (Douglas) 1931- .... **CLC 7**
See also CA 97-100; CANR 70; INT CA-
97-100; TCWW 2

Seferiades, Giorgos Stylianou 1900-1971
See Seferis, George
See also CA 5-8R; 33-36R; CANR 5, 36;
MTCW 1

Seferis, George .... **CLC 5, 11**
See Seferiades, Giorgos Stylianou
See also EW 12; EWL 3; RGWL 2, 3

Segal, Erich (Wolf) 1937- .... **CLC 3, 10**
See also BEST 89:1; BPFB 3; CA 25-28R;
CANR 20, 36, 65, 113; CPW; DAM POP;
DLBY 1986; INT CANR-20; MTCW 1

Seger, Bob 1945- .... **CLC 35**

Seghers, Anna .... **CLC 7**
See Radvanyi, Netty
See also CDWLB 2; DLB 69; EWL 3

Seidel, Frederick (Lewis) 1936- .... **CLC 18**
See also CA 13-16R; CANR 8, 99; CP 7;
DLBY 1984

Seifert, Jaroslav 1901-1986 . **CLC 34, 44, 93;
PC 47**
See also CA 127; CDWLB 4; DLB 215;
EWL 3; MTCW 1, 2

Sei Shonagon c. 966-1017(?) .... **CMLC 6**

Sejour, Victor 1817-1874 .... **DC 10**
See also DLB 50

Sejour Marcou et Ferrand, Juan Victor
See Sejour, Victor

Selby, Hubert, Jr. 1928-2004 ..... **CLC 1, 2, 4,
8; SSC 20**
See also CA 13-16R; 226; CANR 33, 85;
CN 7; DLB 2, 227

Selzer, Richard 1928- .... **CLC 74**
See also CA 65-68; CANR 14, 106

Sembene, Ousmane
See Ousmane, Sembene
See also AFW; EWL 3; WLIT 2

Senancour, Etienne Pivert de
1770-1846 .... **NCLC 16**
See also DLB 119; GFL 1789 to the Present

Sender, Ramon (Jose) 1902-1982 ...... **CLC 8;
HLC 2; TCLC 136**
See also CA 5-8R; 105; CANR 8; DAM
MULT; EWL 3; HW 1; MTCW 1; RGWL
2, 3

Seneca, Lucius Annaeus c. 4B.C.-c.
65 .... **CMLC 6; DC 5**
See also AW 2; CDWLB 1; DAM DRAM;
DLB 211; RGWL 2, 3; TWA

Senghor, Leopold Sedar 1906-2001 ... **BLC 3;
CLC 54, 130; PC 25**
See also AFW; BW 1; CA 116; 125; 203;
CANR 47, 74, 134; CWW 2; DAM
MULT, POET; DNFS 2; EWL 3; GFL
1789 to the Present; MTCW 1, 2; TWA

Senior, Olive (Marjorie) 1941- .... **SSC 78**
See also BW 3; CA 154; CANR 86, 126;
CN 7; CP 7; CWP; DLB 157; EWL 3;
RGSF 2

Senna, Danzy 1970- .... **CLC 119**
See also CA 169; CANR 130

Serling, (Edward) Rod(man)
1924-1975 .... **CLC 30**
See also AAYA 14; AITN 1; CA 162; 57-
60; DLB 26; SFW 4

Serna, Ramon Gomez de la
See Gomez de la Serna, Ramon

Serpieres
See Guillevic, (Eugene)

Service, Robert
See Service, Robert W(illiam)
See also BYA 4; DAB; DLB 92

Service, Robert W(illiam)
1874(?)-1958 .... **TCLC 15; WLC**
See Service, Robert
See also CA 115; 140; CANR 84; DA;
DAC; DAM MST, POET; PFS 10; RGEL
2; SATA 20

Seth, Vikram 1952- .... **CLC 43, 90**
See also BRWS 10; CA 121; 127; CANR
50, 74, 131; CN 7; CP 7; DA3; DAM
MULT; DLB 120, 271, 282; EWL 3; INT
CA-127; MTCW 2; WWE 1

Seton, Cynthia Propper 1926-1982 .. **CLC 27**
See also CA 5-8R; 108; CANR 7

Seton, Ernest (Evan) Thompson
1860-1946 .... **TCLC 31**
See also ANW; BYA 3; CA 109; 204; CLR
59; DLB 92; DLBD 13; JRDA; SATA 18

Seton-Thompson, Ernest
See Seton, Ernest (Evan) Thompson

Settle, Mary Lee 1918- .... **CLC 19, 61**
See also BPFB 3; CA 89-92; CAAS 1;
CANR 44, 87, 126; CN 7; CSW; DLB 6;
INT CA-89-92

Seuphor, Michel
See Arp, Jean

Sholokhov, Mikhail (Aleksandrovich)
1905-1984 .... **CLC 7, 15**
See also CA 101; 112; DLB 272; EWL 3;
MTCW 1, 2; RGWL 2, 3; SATA-Obit 36

Shone, Patric
See Hanley, James

Showalter, Elaine 1941- .... **CLC 169**
See also CA 57-60; CANR 58, 106; DLB
67; FW; GLL 2

Shreve, Susan
See Shreve, Susan Richards

Shreve, Susan Richards 1939- .... **CLC 23**
See also CA 49-52; CAAS 5; CANR 5, 38,
69, 100; MAICYA 1, 2; SATA 46, 95, 152;
SATA-Brief 41

Shue, Larry 1946-1985 .... **CLC 52**
See also CA 145; 117; DAM DRAM; DFS
7

Shu-Jen, Chou 1881-1936
See Lu Hsun
See also CA 104

Shulman, Alix Kates 1932- .... **CLC 2, 10**
See also CA 29-32R; CANR 43; FW; SATA
7

Shuster, Joe 1914-1992 .... **CLC 21**
See also AAYA 50

Shute, Nevil .... **CLC 30**
See Norway, Nevil Shute
See also BPFB 3; DLB 255; NFS 9; RHW;
SFW 4

Shuttle, Penelope (Diane) 1947- .... **CLC 7**
See also CA 93-96; CANR 39, 84, 92, 108;
CP 7; CWP; DLB 14, 40

Shvarts, Elena 1948- .... **PC 50**
See also CA 147

Sidhwa, Bapsy (N.) 1938- .... **CLC 168**
See also CA 108; CANR 25, 57; CN 7; FW

Sidney, Mary 1561-1621 .... **LC 19, 39**
See Sidney Herbert, Mary

Sidney, Sir Philip 1554-1586 . **LC 19, 39; PC
32**
See also BRW 1; BRWR 2; CDBLB Before
1660; DA; DA3; DAB; DAC; DAM MST,
POET; DLB 167; EXPP; PAB; RGEL 2;
TEA; WP

Sidney Herbert, Mary
See Sidney, Mary
See also DLB 167

Siegel, Jerome 1914-1996 .... **CLC 21**
See Siegel, Jerry
See also CA 116; 169; 151

Siegel, Jerry
See Siegel, Jerome
See also AAYA 50

Sienkiewicz, Henryk (Adam Alexander Pius)
1846-1916 .... **TCLC 3**
See also CA 104; 134; CANR 84; EWL 3;
RGSF 2; RGWL 2, 3

Sierra, Gregorio Martinez
See Martinez Sierra, Gregorio

Sierra, Maria (de la O'LeJarraga) Martinez
See Martinez Sierra, Maria (de la
O'LeJarraga)

Sigal, Clancy 1926- .... **CLC 7**
See also CA 1-4R; CANR 85; CN 7

Siger of Brabant 1240(?)-1284(?) . **CMLC 69**
See also DLB 115

Sigourney, Lydia H.
See Sigourney, Lydia Howard (Huntley)
See also DLB 73, 183

Sigourney, Lydia Howard (Huntley)
1791-1865 .... **NCLC 21, 87**
See Sigourney, Lydia H.; Sigourney, Lydia
Huntley
See also DLB 1

Sigourney, Lydia Huntley
See Sigourney, Lydia Howard (Huntley)
See also DLB 42, 239, 243

Siguenza y Gongora, Carlos de
1645-1700 .... **HLCS 2; LC 8**
See also LAW

Sigurjonsson, Johann
See Sigurjonsson, Johann

Sigurjonsson, Johann 1880-1919 ... **TCLC 27**
See also CA 170; DLB 293; EWL 3

Sikelianos, Angelos 1884-1951 .... **PC 29;
TCLC 39**
See also EWL 3; RGWL 2, 3

Silkin, Jon 1930-1997 .... **CLC 2, 6, 43**
See also CA 5-8R; CAAS 5; CANR 89; CP
7; DLB 27

Silko, Leslie (Marmon) 1948- .... **CLC 23, 74,
114; NNAL; SSC 37, 66; WLCS**
See also AAYA 14; AMWS 4; ANW; BYA
12; CA 115; 122; CANR 45, 65, 118; CN
7; CP 7; CPW 1; CWP; DA; DA3; DAC;
DAM MST, MULT, POP; DLB 143, 175,
256, 275; EWL 3; EXPP; EXPS; LAIT 4;
MTCW 2; NFS 4; PFS 9, 16; RGAL 4;
RGSF 2; SSFS 4, 8, 10, 11

Sillanpaa, Frans Eemil 1888-1964 ... **CLC 19**
See also CA 129; 93-96; EWL 3; MTCW 1

Sillitoe, Alan 1928- .. **CLC 1, 3, 6, 10, 19, 57,
148**
See also AITN 1; BRWS 5; CA 9-12R, 191;
CAAE 191; CAAS 2; CANR 8, 26, 55;
CDBLB 1960 to Present; CN 7; DLB 14,
139; EWL 3; MTCW 1, 2; RGEL 2;
RGSF 2; SATA 61

Silone, Ignazio 1900-1978 .... **CLC 4**
See also CA 25-28; 81-84; CANR 34; CAP
2; DLB 264; EW 12; EWL 3; MTCW 1;
RGSF 2; RGWL 2, 3

Silone, Ignazione
See Silone, Ignazio

Silver, Joan Micklin 1935- .... **CLC 20**
See also CA 114; 121; INT CA-121

Silver, Nicholas
See Faust, Frederick (Schiller)
See also TCWW 2

Silverberg, Robert 1935- .... **CLC 7, 140**
See also AAYA 24; BPFB 3; BYA 7, 9; CA
1-4R, 186; CAAE 186; CAAS 3; CANR
1, 20, 36, 85; CLR 59; CN 7; CPW; DAM
POP; DLB 8; INT CANR-20; MAICYA
1, 2; MTCW 1, 2; SATA 13, 91; SATA-
Essay 104; SCFW 2; SFW 4; SUFW 2

Silverstein, Alvin 1933- .... **CLC 17**
See also CA 49-52; CANR 2; CLR 25;
JRDA; MAICYA 1, 2; SATA 8, 69, 124

Silverstein, Shel(don Allan)
1932-1999 .... **PC 49**
See also AAYA 40; BW 3; CA 107; 179;
CANR 47, 74, 81; CLR 5, 96; CWRI 5;
JRDA; MAICYA 1, 2; MTCW 2; SATA
33, 92; SATA-Brief 27; SATA-Obit 116

Silverstein, Virginia B(arbara Opshelor)
1937- .... **CLC 17**
See also CA 49-52; CANR 2; CLR 25;
JRDA; MAICYA 1, 2; SATA 8, 69, 124

Sim, Georges
See Simenon, Georges (Jacques Christian)

Simak, Clifford D(onald) 1904-1988 . **CLC 1,
55**
See also CA 1-4R; 125; CANR 1, 35; DLB
8; MTCW 1; SATA-Obit 56; SFW 4

Simenon, Georges (Jacques Christian)
1903-1989 .... **CLC 1, 2, 3, 8, 18, 47**
See also BPFB 3; CA 85-88; 129; CANR
35; CMW 4; DA3; DAM POP; DLB 72;
DLBY 1989; EW 12; EWL 3; GFL 1789
to the Present; MSW; MTCW 1, 2; RGWL
2, 3

Simic, Charles 1938- .... **CLC 6, 9, 22, 49, 68,
130**
See also AMWS 8; CA 29-32R; CAAS 4;
CANR 12, 33, 52, 61, 96; CP 7; DA3;
DAM POET; DLB 105; MTCW 2; PFS 7;
RGAL 4; WP

Simmel, Georg 1858-1918 .... **TCLC 64**
See also CA 157; DLB 296

Simmons, Charles (Paul) 1924- .... **CLC 57**
See also CA 89-92; INT CA-89-92

Simmons, Dan 1948- .... **CLC 44**
See also AAYA 16, 54; CA 138; CANR 53,
81, 126; CPW; DAM POP; HGG; SUFW
2

Simmons, James (Stewart Alexander)
1933- .... **CLC 43**
See also CA 105; CAAS 21; CP 7; DLB 40

Simms, William Gilmore
1806-1870 .... **NCLC 3**
See also DLB 3, 30, 59, 73, 248, 254;
RGAL 4

Simon, Carly 1945- .... **CLC 26**
See also CA 105

Simon, Claude (Eugene Henri)
1913-1984 .... **CLC 4, 9, 15, 39**
See also CA 89-92; CANR 33, 117; CWW
2; DAM NOV; DLB 83; EW 13; EWL 3;
GFL 1789 to the Present; MTCW 1

Simon, Myles
See Follett, Ken(neth Martin)

Simon, (Marvin) Neil 1927- ... **CLC 6, 11, 31,
39, 70; DC 14**
See also AAYA 32; AITN 1; AMWS 4; CA
21-24R; CANR 26, 54, 87, 126; CD 5;
DA3; DAM DRAM; DFS 2, 6, 12, 18;
DLB 7, 266; LAIT 4; MTCW 1, 2; RGAL
4; TUS

Simon, Paul (Frederick) 1941(?)- ..... **CLC 17**
See also CA 116; 153

Simonon, Paul 1956(?)- .... **CLC 30**

Simonson, Rick ed. .... **CLC 70**

Simpson, Harriette
See Arnow, Harriette (Louisa) Simpson

Simpson, Louis (Aston Marantz)
1923- .... **CLC 4, 7, 9, 32, 149**
See also AMWS 9; CA 1-4R; CAAS 4;
CANR 1, 61; CP 7; DAM POET; DLB 5;
MTCW 1, 2; PFS 7, 11, 14; RGAL 4

Simpson, Mona (Elizabeth) 1957- ... **CLC 44,
146**
See also CA 122; 135; CANR 68, 103; CN
7; EWL 3

Simpson, N(orman) F(rederick)
1919- .... **CLC 29**
See also CA 13-16R; CBD; DLB 13; RGEL
2

Sinclair, Andrew (Annandale) 1935- . **CLC 2,
14**
See also CA 9-12R; CAAS 5; CANR 14,
38, 91; CN 7; DLB 14; FANT; MTCW 1

Sinclair, Emil
See Hesse, Hermann

Sinclair, Iain 1943- .... **CLC 76**
See also CA 132; CANR 81; CP 7; HGG

Sinclair, Iain MacGregor
See Sinclair, Iain

Sinclair, Irene
See Griffith, D(avid Lewelyn) W(ark)

Sinclair, Mary Amelia St. Clair 1865(?)-1946
See Sinclair, May
See also CA 104; HGG; RHW

Sinclair, May .... **TCLC 3, 11**
See Sinclair, Mary Amelia St. Clair
See also CA 166; DLB 36, 135; EWL 3;
RGEL 2; SUFW

Sinclair, Roy
See Griffith, D(avid Lewelyn) W(ark)

Sinclair, Upton (Beall) 1878-1968 ..... **CLC 1,
11, 15, 63; WLC**
See also AMWS 5; BPFB 3; BYA 2; CA
5-8R; 25-28R; CANR 7; CDALB 1929-
1941; DA; DA3; DAB; DAC; DAM MST,
NOV; DLB 9; EWL 3; INT CANR-7;
LAIT 3; MTCW 1, 2; NFS 6; RGAL 4;
SATA 9; TUS; YAW

Singe, (Edmund) J(ohn) M(illington)
1871-1909 .... **WLC**

Singer, Isaac
See Singer, Isaac Bashevis

Singer, Isaac Bashevis 1904-1991 .. **CLC 1, 3, 6, 9, 11, 15, 23, 38, 69, 111; SSC 3, 53; WLC**
See also AAYA 32; AITN 1, 2; AMW; AMWR 2; BPFB 3; BYA 1, 4; CA 1-4R; 134; CANR 1, 39, 106; CDALB 1941-1968; CLR 1; CWRI 5; DA; DA3; DAB; DAC; DAM MST, NOV; DLB 6, 28, 52, 278; DLBY 1991; EWL 3; EXPS; HGG; JRDA; LAIT 3; MAICYA 1, 2; MTCW 1, 2; RGAL 4; RGSF 2; SATA 3, 27; SATA-Obit 68; SSFS 2, 12, 16; TUS; TWA

Singer, Israel Joshua 1893-1944 .... **TCLC 33**
See also CA 169; EWL 3

Singh, Khushwant 1915- .... **CLC 11**
See also CA 9-12R; CAAS 9; CANR 6, 84; CN 7; EWL 3; RGEL 2

Singleton, Ann
See Benedict, Ruth (Fulton)

Singleton, John 1968(?)- .... **CLC 156**
See also AAYA 50; BW 2, 3; CA 138; CANR 67, 82; DAM MULT

Siniavskii, Andrei
See Sinyavsky, Andrei (Donatevich)
See also CWW 2

Sinjohn, John
See Galsworthy, John

Sinyavsky, Andrei (Donatevich)
1925-1997 .... **CLC 8**
See Siniavskii, Andrei; Sinyavsky, Andrey Donatovich; Tertz, Abram
See also CA 85-88; 159

Sinyavsky, Andrey Donatovich
See Sinyavsky, Andrei (Donatevich)
See also EWL 3

Sirin, V.
See Nabokov, Vladimir (Vladimirovich)

Sissman, L(ouis) E(dward)
1928-1976 .... **CLC 9, 18**
See also CA 21-24R; 65-68; CANR 13; DLB 5

Sisson, C(harles) H(ubert)
1914-2003 .... **CLC 8**
See also CA 1-4R; 220; CAAS 3; CANR 3, 48, 84; CP 7; DLB 27

Sitting Bull 1831(?)-1890 .... **NNAL**
See also DA3; DAM MULT

Sitwell, Dame Edith 1887-1964 ..... **CLC 2, 9, 67; PC 3**
See also BRW 7; CA 9-12R; CANR 35; CDBLB 1945-1960; DAM POET; DLB 20; EWL 3; MTCW 1, 2; RGEL 2; TEA

Siwaarmill, H. P.
See Sharp, William

Sjoewall, Maj 1935- .... **CLC 7**
See Sjowall, Maj
See also CA 65-68; CANR 73

Sjowall, Maj
See Sjoewall, Maj
See also BPFB 3; CMW 4; MSW

Skelton, John 1460(?)-1529 ..... **LC 71; PC 25**
See also BRW 1; DLB 136; RGEL 2

Skelton, Robin 1925-1997 .... **CLC 13**
See Zuk, Georges
See also AITN 2; CA 5-8R; 160; CAAS 5; CANR 28, 89; CCA 1; CP 7; DLB 27, 53

Skolimowski, Jerzy 1938- .... **CLC 20**
See also CA 128

Skram, Amalie (Bertha)
1847-1905 .... **TCLC 25**
See also CA 165

Skvorecky, Josef (Vaclav) 1924- ...... **CLC 15, 39, 69, 152**
See also CA 61-64; CAAS 1; CANR 10, 34, 63, 108; CDWLB 4; CWW 2; DA3; DAC; DAM NOV; DLB 232; EWL 3; MTCW 1, 2

Slade, Bernard .... **CLC 11, 46**
See Newbound, Bernard Slade
See also CAAS 9; CCA 1; DLB 53

Slaughter, Carolyn 1946- .... **CLC 56**
See also CA 85-88; CANR 85; CN 7

Slaughter, Frank G(ill) 1908-2001 ... **CLC 29**
See also AITN 2; CA 5-8R; 197; CANR 5, 85; INT CANR-5; RHW

Slavitt, David R(ytman) 1935- ...... **CLC 5, 14**
See also CA 21-24R; CAAS 3; CANR 41, 83; CP 7; DLB 5, 6

Slesinger, Tess 1905-1945 .... **TCLC 10**
See also CA 107; 199; DLB 102

Slessor, Kenneth 1901-1971 .... **CLC 14**
See also CA 102; 89-92; DLB 260; RGEL 2

Slowacki, Juliusz 1809-1849 .... **NCLC 15**
See also RGWL 3

Smart, Christopher 1722-1771 . **LC 3; PC 13**
See also DAM POET; DLB 109; RGEL 2

Smart, Elizabeth 1913-1986 .... **CLC 54**
See also CA 81-84; 118; DLB 88

Smiley, Jane (Graves) 1949- ...... **CLC 53, 76, 144**
See also AMWS 6; BPFB 3; CA 104; CANR 30, 50, 74, 96; CN 7; CPW 1; DA3; DAM POP; DLB 227, 234; EWL 3; INT CANR-30; SSFS 19

Smith, A(rthur) J(ames) M(arshall)
1902-1980 .... **CLC 15**
See also CA 1-4R; 102; CANR 4; DAC; DLB 88; RGEL 2

Smith, Adam 1723(?)-1790 .... **LC 36**
See also DLB 104, 252; RGEL 2

Smith, Alexander 1829-1867 .... **NCLC 59**
See also DLB 32, 55

Smith, Anna Deavere 1950- .... **CLC 86**
See also CA 133; CANR 103; CD 5; DFS 2

Smith, Betty (Wehner) 1904-1972 .... **CLC 19**
See also BPFB 3; BYA 3; CA 5-8R; 33-36R; DLBY 1982; LAIT 3; RGAL 4; SATA 6

Smith, Charlotte (Turner)
1749-1806 .... **NCLC 23, 115**
See also DLB 39, 109; RGEL 2; TEA

Smith, Clark Ashton 1893-1961 .... **CLC 43**
See also CA 143; CANR 81; FANT; HGG; MTCW 2; SCFW 2; SFW 4; SUFW

Smith, Dave .... **CLC 22, 42**
See Smith, David (Jeddie)
See also CAAS 7; DLB 5

Smith, David (Jeddie) 1942-
See Smith, Dave
See also CA 49-52; CANR 1, 59, 120; CP 7; CSW; DAM POET

Smith, Florence Margaret 1902-1971
See Smith, Stevie
See also CA 17-18; 29-32R; CANR 35; CAP 2; DAM POET; MTCW 1, 2; TEA

Smith, Iain Crichton 1928-1998 .... **CLC 64**
See also BRWS 9; CA 21-24R; 171; CN 7; CP 7; DLB 40, 139; RGSF 2

Smith, John 1580(?)-1631 .... **LC 9**
See also DLB 24, 30; TUS

Smith, Johnston
See Crane, Stephen (Townley)

Smith, Joseph, Jr. 1805-1844 .... **NCLC 53**

Smith, Lee 1944- .... **CLC 25, 73**
See also CA 114; 119; CANR 46, 118; CSW; DLB 143; DLBY 1983; EWL 3; INT CA-119; RGAL 4

Smith, Martin
See Smith, Martin Cruz

Smith, Martin Cruz 1942- .. **CLC 25; NNAL**
See also BEST 89:4; BPFB 3; CA 85-88; CANR 6, 23, 43, 65, 119; CMW 4; CPW; DAM MULT, POP; HGG; INT CANR-23; MTCW 2; RGAL 4

Smith, Patti 1946- .... **CLC 12**
See also CA 93-96; CANR 63

Smith, Pauline (Urmson)
1882-1959 .... **TCLC 25**
See also DLB 225; EWL 3

Smith, Rosamond
See Oates, Joyce Carol

Smith, Sheila Kaye
See Kaye-Smith, Sheila

Smith, Stevie .... **CLC 3, 8, 25, 44; PC 12**
See Smith, Florence Margaret
See also BRWS 2; DLB 20; EWL 3; MTCW 2; PAB; PFS 3; RGEL 2

Smith, Wilbur (Addison) 1933- .... **CLC 33**
See also CA 13-16R; CANR 7, 46, 66, 134; CPW; MTCW 1, 2

Smith, William Jay 1918- .... **CLC 6**
See also AMWS 13; CA 5-8R; CANR 44, 106; CP 7; CSW; CWRI 5; DLB 5; MAICYA 1, 2; SAAS 22; SATA 2, 68, 154; SATA-Essay 154

Smith, Woodrow Wilson
See Kuttner, Henry

Smith, Zadie 1976- .... **CLC 158**
See also AAYA 50; CA 193

Smolenskin, Peretz 1842-1885 .... **NCLC 30**

Smollett, Tobias (George) 1721-1771 ... **LC 2, 46**
See also BRW 3; CDBLB 1660-1789; DLB 39, 104; RGEL 2; TEA

Snodgrass, W(illiam) D(e Witt)
1926- .... **CLC 2, 6, 10, 18, 68**
See also AMWS 6; CA 1-4R; CANR 6, 36, 65, 85; CP 7; DAM POET; DLB 5; MTCW 1, 2; RGAL 4

Snorri Sturluson 1179-1241 .... **CMLC 56**
See also RGWL 2, 3

Snow, C(harles) P(ercy) 1905-1980 ... **CLC 1, 4, 6, 9, 13, 19**
See also BRW 7; CA 5-8R; 101; CANR 28; CDBLB 1945-1960; DAM NOV; DLB 15, 77; DLBD 17; EWL 3; MTCW 1, 2; RGEL 2; TEA

Snow, Frances Compton
See Adams, Henry (Brooks)

Snyder, Gary (Sherman) 1930- . **CLC 1, 2, 5, 9, 32, 120; PC 21**
See also AMWS 8; ANW; BG 3; CA 17-20R; CANR 30, 60, 125; CP 7; DA3; DAM POET; DLB 5, 16, 165, 212, 237, 275; EWL 3; MTCW 2; PFS 9, 19; RGAL 4; WP

Snyder, Zilpha Keatley 1927- .... **CLC 17**
See also AAYA 15; BYA 1; CA 9-12R; CANR 38; CLR 31; JRDA; MAICYA 1, 2; SAAS 2; SATA 1, 28, 75, 110; SATA-Essay 112; YAW

Soares, Bernardo
See Pessoa, Fernando (Antonio Nogueira)

Sobh, A.
See Shamlu, Ahmad

Sobh, Alef
See Shamlu, Ahmad

Sobol, Joshua 1939- .... **CLC 60**
See Sobol, Yehoshua
See also CA 200

Sobol, Yehoshua 1939-
See Sobol, Joshua
See also CWW 2

Socrates 470B.C.-399B.C. .... **CMLC 27**

Soderberg, Hjalmar 1869-1941 ...... **TCLC 39**
See also DLB 259; EWL 3; RGSF 2

Soderbergh, Steven 1963- .... **CLC 154**
See also AAYA 43

Sodergran, Edith (Irene) 1892-1923
See Soedergran, Edith (Irene)
See also CA 202; DLB 259; EW 11; EWL 3; RGWL 2, 3
Soedergran, Edith (Irene)
1892-1923 .... **TCLC 31**
See Sodergran, Edith (Irene)
Softly, Edgar
See Lovecraft, H(oward) P(hillips)
Softly, Edward
See Lovecraft, H(oward) P(hillips)
Sokolov, Alexander V(sevolodovich) 1943-
See Sokolov, Sasha
See also CA 73-76
Sokolov, Raymond 1941- .... **CLC 7**
See also CA 85-88
Sokolov, Sasha .... **CLC 59**
See Sokolov, Alexander V(sevolodovich)
See also CWW 2; DLB 285; EWL 3; RGWL 2, 3
Solo, Jay
See Ellison, Harlan (Jay)
Sologub, Fyodor .... **TCLC 9**
See Teternikov, Fyodor Kuzmich
See also EWL 3
Solomons, Ikey Esquir
See Thackeray, William Makepeace
Solomos, Dionysios 1798-1857 .... **NCLC 15**
Solwoska, Mara
See French, Marilyn
Solzhenitsyn, Aleksandr I(sayevich)
1918- .. **CLC 1, 2, 4, 7, 9, 10, 18, 26, 34, 78, 134; SSC 32; WLC**
See Solzhenitsyn, Aleksandr Isaevich
See also AAYA 49; AITN 1; BPFB 3; CA 69-72; CANR 40, 65, 116; DA; DA3; DAB; DAC; DAM MST, NOV; DLB 302; EW 13; EXPS; LAIT 4; MTCW 1, 2; NFS 6; RGSF 2; RGWL 2, 3; SSFS 9; TWA
Solzhenitsyn, Aleksandr Isaevich
See Solzhenitsyn, Aleksandr I(sayevich)
See also CWW 2; EWL 3
Somers, Jane
See Lessing, Doris (May)
Somerville, Edith Oenone
1858-1949 .... **SSC 56; TCLC 51**
See also CA 196; DLB 135; RGEL 2; RGSF 2
Somerville & Ross
See Martin, Violet Florence; Somerville, Edith Oenone
Sommer, Scott 1951- .... **CLC 25**
See also CA 106
Sommers, Christina Hoff 1950- ...... **CLC 197**
See also CA 153; CANR 95
Sondheim, Stephen (Joshua) 1930- . **CLC 30, 39, 147; DC 22**
See also AAYA 11; CA 103; CANR 47, 67, 125; DAM DRAM; LAIT 4
Sone, Monica 1919- .... **AAL**
Song, Cathy 1955- .... **AAL; PC 21**
See also CA 154; CANR 118; CWP; DLB 169; EXPP; FW; PFS 5
Sontag, Susan 1933- .... **CLC 1, 2, 10, 13, 31, 105, 195**
See also AMWS 3; CA 17-20R; CANR 25, 51, 74, 97; CN 7; CPW; DA3; DAM POP; DLB 2, 67; EWL 3; MAWW; MTCW 1, 2; RGAL 4; RHW; SSFS 10
Sophocles 496(?)B.C.-406(?)B.C. .... **CMLC 2, 47, 51; DC 1; WLCS**
See also AW 1; CDWLB 1; DA; DA3; DAB; DAC; DAM DRAM, MST; DFS 1, 4, 8; DLB 176; LAIT 1; LATS 1:1; LMFS 1; RGWL 2, 3; TWA
Sordello 1189-1269 .... **CMLC 15**
Sorel, Georges 1847-1922 .... **TCLC 91**
See also CA 118; 188

Sorel, Julia
See Drexler, Rosalyn
Sorokin, Vladimir .... **CLC 59**
See Sorokin, Vladimir Georgievich
Sorokin, Vladimir Georgievich
See Sorokin, Vladimir
See also DLB 285
Sorrentino, Gilbert 1929- .. **CLC 3, 7, 14, 22, 40**
See also CA 77-80; CANR 14, 33, 115; CN 7; CP 7; DLB 5, 173; DLBY 1980; INT CANR-14
Soseki
See Natsume, Soseki
See also MJW
Soto, Gary 1952- ... **CLC 32, 80; HLC 2; PC 28**
See also AAYA 10, 37; BYA 11; CA 119; 125; CANR 50, 74, 107; CLR 38; CP 7; DAM MULT; DLB 82; EWL 3; EXPP; HW 1, 2; INT CA-125; JRDA; LLW 1; MAICYA 2; MAICYAS 1; MTCW 2; PFS 7; RGAL 4; SATA 80, 120; WYA; YAW
Soupault, Philippe 1897-1990 .... **CLC 68**
See also CA 116; 147; 131; EWL 3; GFL 1789 to the Present; LMFS 2
Souster, (Holmes) Raymond 1921- .... **CLC 5, 14**
See also CA 13-16R; CAAS 14; CANR 13, 29, 53; CP 7; DA3; DAC; DAM POET; DLB 88; RGEL 2; SATA 63
Southern, Terry 1924(?)-1995 .... **CLC 7**
See also AMWS 11; BPFB 3; CA 1-4R; 150; CANR 1, 55, 107; CN 7; DLB 2; IDFW 3, 4
Southerne, Thomas 1660-1746 .... **LC 99**
See also DLB 80; RGEL 2
Southey, Robert 1774-1843 .... **NCLC 8, 97**
See also BRW 4; DLB 93, 107, 142; RGEL 2; SATA 54
Southwell, Robert 1561(?)-1595 .... **LC 108**
See also DLB 167; RGEL 2
Southworth, Emma Dorothy Eliza Nevitte
1819-1899 .... **NCLC 26**
See also DLB 239
Souza, Ernest
See Scott, Evelyn
Soyinka, Wole 1934- .. **BLC 3; CLC 3, 5, 14, 36, 44, 179; DC 2; WLC**
See also AFW; BW 2, 3; CA 13-16R; CANR 27, 39, 82; CD 5; CDWLB 3; CN 7; CP 7; DA; DA3; DAB; DAC; DAM DRAM, MST, MULT; DFS 10; DLB 125; EWL 3; MTCW 1, 2; RGEL 2; TWA; WLIT 2; WWE 1
Spackman, W(illiam) M(ode)
1905-1990 .... **CLC 46**
See also CA 81-84; 132
Spacks, Barry (Bernard) 1931- .... **CLC 14**
See also CA 154; CANR 33, 109; CP 7; DLB 105
Spanidou, Irini 1946- .... **CLC 44**
See also CA 185
Spark, Muriel (Sarah) 1918- ..... **CLC 2, 3, 5, 8, 13, 18, 40, 94; SSC 10**
See also BRWS 1; CA 5-8R; CANR 12, 36, 76, 89, 131; CDBLB 1945-1960; CN 7; CP 7; DA3; DAB; DAC; DAM MST, NOV; DLB 15, 139; EWL 3; FW; INT CANR-12; LAIT 4; MTCW 1, 2; RGEL 2; TEA; WLIT 4; YAW
Spaulding, Douglas
See Bradbury, Ray (Douglas)
Spaulding, Leonard
See Bradbury, Ray (Douglas)
Speght, Rachel 1597-c. 1630 .... **LC 97**
See also DLB 126
Spelman, Elizabeth .... **CLC 65**

Spence, J. A. D.
See Eliot, T(homas) S(tearns)
Spencer, Anne 1882-1975 .... **HR 3**
See also BW 2; CA 161; DLB 51, 54
Spencer, Elizabeth 1921- .... **CLC 22; SSC 57**
See also CA 13-16R; CANR 32, 65, 87; CN 7; CSW; DLB 6, 218; EWL 3; MTCW 1; RGAL 4; SATA 14
Spencer, Leonard G.
See Silverberg, Robert
Spencer, Scott 1945- .... **CLC 30**
See also CA 113; CANR 51; DLBY 1986
Spender, Stephen (Harold)
1909-1995 .... **CLC 1, 2, 5, 10, 41, 91**
See also BRWS 2; CA 9-12R; 149; CANR 31, 54; CDBLB 1945-1960; CP 7; DA3; DAM POET; DLB 20; EWL 3; MTCW 1, 2; PAB; RGEL 2; TEA
Spengler, Oswald (Arnold Gottfried)
1880-1936 .... **TCLC 25**
See also CA 118; 189
Spenser, Edmund 1552(?)-1599 ..... **LC 5, 39; PC 8, 42; WLC**
See also AAYA 60; BRW 1; CDBLB Before 1660; DA; DA3; DAB; DAC; DAM MST, POET; DLB 167; EFS 2; EXPP; PAB; RGEL 2; TEA; WLIT 3; WP
Spicer, Jack 1925-1965 .... **CLC 8, 18, 72**
See also BG 3; CA 85-88; DAM POET; DLB 5, 16, 193; GLL 1; WP
Spiegelman, Art 1948- .... **CLC 76, 178**
See also AAYA 10, 46; CA 125; CANR 41, 55, 74, 124; DLB 299; MTCW 2; SATA 109; YAW
Spielberg, Peter 1929- .... **CLC 6**
See also CA 5-8R; CANR 4, 48; DLBY 1981
Spielberg, Steven 1947- .... **CLC 20, 188**
See also AAYA 8, 24; CA 77-80; CANR 32; SATA 32
Spillane, Frank Morrison 1918-
See Spillane, Mickey
See also CA 25-28R; CANR 28, 63, 125; DA3; MTCW 1, 2; SATA 66
Spillane, Mickey .... **CLC 3, 13**
See Spillane, Frank Morrison
See also BPFB 3; CMW 4; DLB 226; MSW; MTCW 2
Spinoza, Benedictus de 1632-1677 .. **LC 9, 58**
Spinrad, Norman (Richard) 1940- ... **CLC 46**
See also BPFB 3; CA 37-40R; CAAS 19; CANR 20, 91; DLB 8; INT CANR-20; SFW 4
Spitteler, Carl (Friedrich Georg)
1845-1924 .... **TCLC 12**
See also CA 109; DLB 129; EWL 3
Spivack, Kathleen (Romola Drucker)
1938- .... **CLC 6**
See also CA 49-52
Spoto, Donald 1941- .... **CLC 39**
See also CA 65-68; CANR 11, 57, 93
Springsteen, Bruce (F.) 1949- .... **CLC 17**
See also CA 111
Spurling, (Susan) Hilary 1940- .... **CLC 34**
See also CA 104; CANR 25, 52, 94
Spyker, John Howland
See Elman, Richard (Martin)
Squared, A.
See Abbott, Edwin A.
Squires, (James) Radcliffe
1917-1993 .... **CLC 51**
See also CA 1-4R; 140; CANR 6, 21
Srivastava, Dhanpat Rai 1880(?)-1936
See Premchand
See also CA 118; 197
Stacy, Donald
See Pohl, Frederik

Stoddard, Charles
See Kuttner, Henry

Stoker, Abraham 1847-1912
See Stoker, Bram
See also CA 105; 150; DA; DA3; DAC;
DAM MST, NOV; HGG; SATA 29

Stoker, Bram . **SSC 62; TCLC 8, 144; WLC**
See Stoker, Abraham
See also AAYA 23; BPFB 3; BRWS 3; BYA
5; CDBLB 1890-1914; DAB; DLB 304;
LATS 1:1; NFS 18; RGEL 2; SUFW;
TEA; WLIT 4

Stolz, Mary (Slattery) 1920- .... **CLC 12**
See also AAYA 8; AITN 1; CA 5-8R;
CANR 13, 41, 112; JRDA; MAICYA 1,
2; SAAS 3; SATA 10, 71, 133; YAW

Stone, Irving 1903-1989 .... **CLC 7**
See also AITN 1; BPFB 3; CA 1-4R; 129;
CAAS 3; CANR 1, 23; CPW; DA3; DAM
POP; INT CANR-23; MTCW 1, 2; RHW;
SATA 3; SATA-Obit 64

Stone, Oliver (William) 1946- .... **CLC 73**
See also AAYA 15; CA 110; CANR 55, 125

Stone, Robert (Anthony) 1937- ... **CLC 5, 23,
42, 175**
See also AMWS 5; BPFB 3; CA 85-88;
CANR 23, 66, 95; CN 7; DLB 152; EWL
3; INT CANR-23; MTCW 1

Stone, Ruth 1915- .... **PC 53**
See also CA 45-48; CANR 2, 91; CP 7;
CSW; DLB 105; PFS 19

Stone, Zachary
See Follett, Ken(neth Martin)

Stoppard, Tom 1937- ... **CLC 1, 3, 4, 5, 8, 15,
29, 34, 63, 91; DC 6; WLC**
See also BRWC 1; BRWR 2; BRWS 1; CA
81-84; CANR 39, 67, 125; CBD; CD 5;
CDBLB 1960 to Present; DA; DA3;
DAB; DAC; DAM DRAM, MST; DFS 2,
5, 8, 11, 13, 16; DLB 13, 233; DLBY
1985; EWL 3; LATS 1:2; MTCW 1, 2;
RGEL 2; TEA; WLIT 4

Storey, David (Malcolm) 1933- . **CLC 2, 4, 5,
8**
See also BRWS 1; CA 81-84; CANR 36;
CBD; CD 5; CN 7; DAM DRAM; DLB
13, 14, 207, 245; EWL 3; MTCW 1;
RGEL 2

Storm, Hyemeyohsts 1935- ... **CLC 3; NNAL**
See also CA 81-84; CANR 45; DAM MULT

Storm, (Hans) Theodor (Woldsen)
1817-1888 .... **NCLC 1; SSC 27**
See also CDWLB 2; DLB 129; EW; RGSF
2; RGWL 2, 3

Storni, Alfonsina 1892-1938 . **HLC 2; PC 33;
TCLC 5**
See also CA 104; 131; DAM MULT; DLB
283; HW 1; LAW

Stoughton, William 1631-1701 .... **LC 38**
See also DLB 24

Stout, Rex (Todhunter) 1886-1975 ..... **CLC 3**
See also AITN 2; BPFB 3; CA 61-64;
CANR 71; CMW 4; DLB 306; MSW;
RGAL 4

Stow, (Julian) Randolph 1935- ... **CLC 23, 48**
See also CA 13-16R; CANR 33; CN 7;
DLB 260; MTCW 1; RGEL 2

Stowe, Harriet (Elizabeth) Beecher
1811-1896 .... **NCLC 3, 50, 133; WLC**
See also AAYA 53; AMWS 1; CDALB
1865-1917; DA; DA3; DAB; DAC; DAM
MST, NOV; DLB 1, 12, 42, 74, 189, 239,
243; EXPN; JRDA; LAIT 2; MAICYA 1,
2; NFS 6; RGAL 4; TUS; YABC 1

Strabo c. 64B.C.-c. 25 .... **CMLC 37**
See also DLB 176

Strachey, (Giles) Lytton
1880-1932 .... **TCLC 12**
See also BRWS 2; CA 110; 178; DLB 149;
DLBD 10; EWL 3; MTCW 2; NCFS 4

Stramm, August 1874-1915 .... **PC 50**
See also CA 195; EWL 3

Strand, Mark 1934- .... **CLC 6, 18, 41, 71**
See also AMWS 4; CA 21-24R; CANR 40,
65, 100; CP 7; DAM POET; DLB 5; EWL
3; PAB; PFS 9, 18; RGAL 4; SATA 41

Stratton-Porter, Gene(va Grace) 1863-1924
See Porter, Gene(va Grace) Stratton
See also ANW; CA 137; CLR 87; DLB 221;
DLBD 14; MAICYA 1, 2; SATA 15

Straub, Peter (Francis) 1943- ... **CLC 28, 107**
See also BEST 89:1; BPFB 3; CA 85-88;
CANR 28, 65, 109; CPW; DAM POP;
DLBY 1984; HGG; MTCW 1, 2; SUFW
2

Strauss, Botho 1944- .... **CLC 22**
See also CA 157; CWW 2; DLB 124

Strauss, Leo 1899-1973 .... **TCLC 141**
See also CA 101; 45-48; CANR 122

Streatfeild, (Mary) Noel
1897(?)-1986 .... **CLC 21**
See also CA 81-84; 120; CANR 31; CLR
17, 83; CWRI 5; DLB 160; MAICYA 1,
2; SATA 20; SATA-Obit 48

Stribling, T(homas) S(igismund)
1881-1965 .... **CLC 23**
See also CA 189; 107; CMW 4; DLB 9;
RGAL 4

Strindberg, (Johan) August
1849-1912 ... **DC 18; TCLC 1, 8, 21, 47;
WLC**
See also CA 104; 135; DA; DA3; DAB;
DAC; DAM DRAM, MST; DFS 4, 9;
DLB 259; EW 7; EWL 3; IDTP; LMFS
2; MTCW 2; RGWL 2, 3; TWA

Stringer, Arthur 1874-1950 .... **TCLC 37**
See also CA 161; DLB 92

Stringer, David
See Roberts, Keith (John Kingston)

Stroheim, Erich von 1885-1957 ..... **TCLC 71**

Strugatskii, Arkadii (Natanovich)
1925-1991 .... **CLC 27**
See Strugatsky, Arkadii Natanovich
See also CA 106; 135; SFW 4

Strugatskii, Boris (Natanovich)
1933- .... **CLC 27**
See Strugatsky, Boris (Natanovich)
See also CA 106; SFW 4

Strugatsky, Arkadii Natanovich
See Strugatskii, Arkadii (Natanovich)
See also DLB 302

Strugatsky, Boris (Natanovich)
See Strugatskii, Boris (Natanovich)
See also DLB 302

Strummer, Joe 1953(?)- .... **CLC 30**

Strunk, William, Jr. 1869-1946 ...... **TCLC 92**
See also CA 118; 164; NCFS 5

Stryk, Lucien 1924- .... **PC 27**
See also CA 13-16R; CANR 10, 28, 55,
110; CP 7

Stuart, Don A.
See Campbell, John W(ood, Jr.)

Stuart, Ian
See MacLean, Alistair (Stuart)

Stuart, Jesse (Hilton) 1906-1984 ... **CLC 1, 8,
11, 14, 34; SSC 31**
See also CA 5-8R; 112; CANR 31; DLB 9,
48, 102; DLBY 1984; SATA 2; SATA-
Obit 36

Stubblefield, Sally
See Trumbo, Dalton

Sturgeon, Theodore (Hamilton)
1918-1985 .... **CLC 22, 39**
See Queen, Ellery
See also AAYA 51; BPFB 3; BYA 9, 10;
CA 81-84; 116; CANR 32, 103; DLB 8;
DLBY 1985; HGG; MTCW 1, 2; SCFW
4; SFW 4; SUFW

Sturges, Preston 1898-1959 .... **TCLC 48**
See also CA 114; 149; DLB 26

Styron, William 1925- .... **CLC 1, 3, 5, 11, 15,
60; SSC 25**
See also AMW; AMWC 2; BEST 90:4;
BPFB 3; CA 5-8R; CANR 6, 33, 74, 126;
CDALB 1968-1988; CN 7; CPW; CSW;
DA3; DAM NOV, POP; DLB 2, 143, 299;
DLBY 1980; EWL 3; INT CANR-6;
LAIT 2; MTCW 1, 2; NCFS 1; RGAL 4;
RHW; TUS

Su, Chien 1884-1918
See Su Man-shu
See also CA 123

Suarez Lynch, B.
See Bioy Casares, Adolfo; Borges, Jorge
Luis

Suassuna, Ariano Vilar 1927- .... **HLCS 1**
See also CA 178; DLB 307; HW 2; LAW

Suckert, Kurt Erich
See Malaparte, Curzio

Suckling, Sir John 1609-1642 . **LC 75; PC 30**
See also BRW 2; DAM POET; DLB 58,
126; EXPP; PAB; RGEL 2

Suckow, Ruth 1892-1960 .... **SSC 18**
See also CA 193; 113; DLB 9, 102; RGAL
4; TCWW 2

Sudermann, Hermann 1857-1928 .. **TCLC 15**
See also CA 107; 201; DLB 118

Sue, Eugene 1804-1857 .... **NCLC 1**
See also DLB 119

Sueskind, Patrick 1949- .... **CLC 44, 182**
See Suskind, Patrick

Suetonius c. 70-c. 130 .... **CMLC 60**
See also AW 2; DLB 211; RGWL 2, 3

Sukenick, Ronald 1932-2004 ..... **CLC 3, 4, 6,
48**
See also CA 25-28R; 209; 229; CAAE 209;
CAAS 8; CANR 32, 89; CN 7; DLB 173;
DLBY 1981

Suknaski, Andrew 1942- .... **CLC 19**
See also CA 101; CP 7; DLB 53

Sullivan, Vernon
See Vian, Boris

Sully Prudhomme, Rene-Francois-Armand
1839-1907 .... **TCLC 31**
See also GFL 1789 to the Present

Su Man-shu .... **TCLC 24**
See Su, Chien
See also EWL 3

Sumarokov, Aleksandr Petrovich
1717-1777 .... **LC 104**
See also DLB 150

Summerforest, Ivy B.
See Kirkup, James

Summers, Andrew James 1942- .... **CLC 26**

Summers, Andy
See Summers, Andrew James

Summers, Hollis (Spurgeon, Jr.)
1916- .... **CLC 10**
See also CA 5-8R; CANR 3; DLB 6

**Summers, (Alphonsus Joseph-Mary
Augustus) Montague**
1880-1948 .... **TCLC 16**
See also CA 118; 163

Sumner, Gordon Matthew .... **CLC 26**
See Police, The; Sting

Sun Tzu c. 400B.C.-c. 320B.C. .... **CMLC 56**

Surrey, Henry Howard 1517-1574 ...... **PC 59**
See also BRW 1; RGEL 2

Surtees, Robert Smith 1805-1864 .. **NCLC 14**
See also DLB 21; RGEL 2

Susann, Jacqueline 1921-1974 .... **CLC 3**
See also AITN 1; BPFB 3; CA 65-68; 53-
56; MTCW 1, 2

Su Shi
See Su Shih
See also RGWL 2, 3

Tranquilli, Secondino
See Silone, Ignazio
Transtroemer, Tomas Gosta
See Transtromer, Tomas (Goesta)
Transtromer, Tomas (Goesta)
See Transtromer, Tomas (Goesta)
See also CWW 2
Transtromer, Tomas (Goesta)
1931- .... **CLC 52, 65**
See Transtromer, Tomas (Goesta)
See also CA 117; 129; CAAS 17; CANR
115; DAM POET; DLB 257; EWL 3; PFS
21
Transtromer, Tomas Gosta
See Transtromer, Tomas (Goesta)
Traven, B. 1882(?)-1969 .... **CLC 8, 11**
See also CA 19-20; 25-28R; CAP 2; DLB
9, 56; EWL 3; MTCW 1; RGAL 4
Trediakovsky, Vasilii Kirillovich
1703-1769 .... **LC 68**
See also DLB 150
Treitel, Jonathan 1959- .... **CLC 70**
See also CA 210; DLB 267
Trelawny, Edward John
1792-1881 .... **NCLC 85**
See also DLB 110, 116, 144
Tremain, Rose 1943- .... **CLC 42**
See also CA 97-100; CANR 44, 95; CN 7;
DLB 14, 271; RGSF 2; RHW
Tremblay, Michel 1942- .... **CLC 29, 102**
See also CA 116; 128; CCA 1; CWW 2;
DAC; DAM MST; DLB 60; EWL 3; GLL
1; MTCW 1, 2
Trevanian .... **CLC 29**
See Whitaker, Rod(ney)
Trevor, Glen
See Hilton, James
Trevor, William .. **CLC 7, 9, 14, 25, 71, 116;
SSC 21, 58**
See Cox, William Trevor
See also BRWS 4; CBD; CD 5; CN 7; DLB
14, 139; EWL 3; LATS 1:2; MTCW 2;
RGEL 2; RGSF 2; SSFS 10
Trifonov, Iurii (Valentinovich)
See Trifonov, Yuri (Valentinovich)
See also DLB 302; RGWL 2, 3
Trifonov, Yuri (Valentinovich)
1925-1981 .... **CLC 45**
See Trifonov, Iurii (Valentinovich); Tri-
fonov, Yury Valentinovich
See also CA 126; 103; MTCW 1
Trifonov, Yury Valentinovich
See Trifonov, Yuri (Valentinovich)
See also EWL 3
Trilling, Diana (Rubin) 1905-1996 . **CLC 129**
See also CA 5-8R; 154; CANR 10, 46; INT
CANR-10; MTCW 1, 2
Trilling, Lionel 1905-1975 ..... **CLC 9, 11, 24;
SSC 75**
See also AMWS 3; CA 9-12R; 61-64;
CANR 10, 105; DLB 28, 63; EWL 3; INT
CANR-10; MTCW 1, 2; RGAL 4; TUS
Trimball, W. H.
See Mencken, H(enry) L(ouis)
Tristan
See Gomez de la Serna, Ramon
Tristram
See Housman, A(lfred) E(dward)
Trogdon, William (Lewis) 1939-
See Heat-Moon, William Least
See also CA 115; 119; CANR 47, 89; CPW;
INT CA-119
Trollope, Anthony 1815-1882 .... **NCLC 6, 33,
101; SSC 28; WLC**
See also BRW 5; CDBLB 1832-1890; DA;
DA3; DAB; DAC; DAM MST, NOV;
DLB 21, 57, 159; RGEL 2; RGSF 2;
SATA 22

Trollope, Frances 1779-1863 .... **NCLC 30**
See also DLB 21, 166
Trollope, Joanna 1943- .... **CLC 186**
See also CA 101; CANR 58, 95; CPW;
DLB 207; RHW
Trotsky, Leon 1879-1940 .... **TCLC 22**
See also CA 118; 167
Trotter (Cockburn), Catharine
1679-1749 .... **LC 8**
See also DLB 84, 252
Trotter, Wilfred 1872-1939 .... **TCLC 97**
Trout, Kilgore
See Farmer, Philip Jose
Trow, George W. S. 1943- .... **CLC 52**
See also CA 126; CANR 91
Troyat, Henri 1911- .... **CLC 23**
See also CA 45-48; CANR 2, 33, 67, 117;
GFL 1789 to the Present; MTCW 1
Trudeau, G(arretson) B(eekman) 1948-
See Trudeau, Garry B.
See also AAYA 60; CA 81-84; CANR 31;
SATA 35
Trudeau, Garry B. .... **CLC 12**
See Trudeau, G(arretson) B(eekman)
See also AAYA 10; AITN 2
Truffaut, Francois 1932-1984 ... **CLC 20, 101**
See also CA 81-84; 113; CANR 34
Trumbo, Dalton 1905-1976 .... **CLC 19**
See also CA 21-24R; 69-72; CANR 10;
DLB 26; IDFW 3, 4; YAW
Trumbull, John 1750-1831 .... **NCLC 30**
See also DLB 31; RGAL 4
Trundlett, Helen B.
See Eliot, T(homas) S(tearns)
Truth, Sojourner 1797(?)-1883 ...... **NCLC 94**
See also DLB 239; FW; LAIT 2
Tryon, Thomas 1926-1991 .... **CLC 3, 11**
See also AITN 1; BPFB 3; CA 29-32R; 135;
CANR 32, 77; CPW; DA3; DAM POP;
HGG; MTCW 1
Tryon, Tom
See Tryon, Thomas
Ts'ao Hsueh-ch'in 1715(?)-1763 .... **LC 1**
Tsushima, Shuji 1909-1948
See Dazai Osamu
See also CA 107
Tsvetaeva (Efron), Marina (Ivanovna)
1892-1941 .... **PC 14; TCLC 7, 35**
See also CA 104; 128; CANR 73; DLB 295;
EW 11; MTCW 1, 2; RGWL 2, 3
Tuck, Lily 1938- .... **CLC 70**
See also CA 139; CANR 90
Tu Fu 712-770 .... **PC 9**
See Du Fu
See also DAM MULT; TWA; WP
Tunis, John R(oberts) 1889-1975 ..... **CLC 12**
See also BYA 1; CA 61-64; CANR 62; DLB
22, 171; JRDA; MAICYA 1, 2; SATA 37;
SATA-Brief 30; YAW
Tuohy, Frank .... **CLC 37**
See Tuohy, John Francis
See also DLB 14, 139
Tuohy, John Francis 1925-
See Tuohy, Frank
See also CA 5-8R; 178; CANR 3, 47; CN 7
Turco, Lewis (Putnam) 1934- ..... **CLC 11, 63**
See also CA 13-16R; CAAS 22; CANR 24,
51; CP 7; DLBY 1984
Turgenev, Ivan (Sergeevich)
1818-1883 ..... **DC 7; NCLC 21, 37, 122;
SSC 7, 57; WLC**
See also AAYA 58; DA; DAB; DAC; DAM
MST, NOV; DFS 6; DLB 238, 284; EW
6; LATS 1:1; NFS 16; RGSF 2; RGWL 2,
3; TWA
Turgot, Anne-Robert-Jacques
1727-1781 .... **LC 26**

Turner, Frederick 1943- .... **CLC 48**
See also CA 73-76, 227; CAAE 227; CAAS
10; CANR 12, 30, 56; DLB 40, 282
Turton, James
See Crace, Jim
Tutu, Desmond M(pilo) 1931- .. **BLC 3; CLC
80**
See also BW 1, 3; CA 125; CANR 67, 81;
DAM MULT
Tutuola, Amos 1920-1997 ..... **BLC 3; CLC 5,
14, 29**
See also AFW; BW 2, 3; CA 9-12R; 159;
CANR 27, 66; CDWLB 3; CN 7; DA3;
DAM MULT; DLB 125; DNFS 2; EWL
3; MTCW 1, 2; RGEL 2; WLIT 2
Twain, Mark .... **SSC 6, 26, 34; TCLC 6, 12,
19, 36, 48, 59; WLC**
See Clemens, Samuel Langhorne
See also AAYA 20; AMW; AMWC 1; BPFB
3; BYA 2, 3, 11, 14; CLR 58, 60, 66; DLB
11; EXPN; EXPS; FANT; LAIT 2; NCFS
4; NFS 1, 6; RGAL 4; RGSF 2; SFW 4;
SSFS 1, 7; SUFW; TUS; WCH; WYA;
YAW
Tyler, Anne 1941- . **CLC 7, 11, 18, 28, 44, 59,
103**
See also AAYA 18, 60; AMWS 4; BEST
89:1; BPFB 3; BYA 12; CA 9-12R; CANR
11, 33, 53, 109, 132; CDALBS; CN 7;
CPW; CSW; DAM NOV, POP; DLB 6,
143; DLBY 1982; EWL 3; EXPN; LATS
1:2; MAWW; MTCW 1, 2; NFS 2, 7, 10;
RGAL 4; SATA 7, 90; SSFS 17; TUS;
YAW
Tyler, Royall 1757-1826 .... **NCLC 3**
See also DLB 37; RGAL 4
Tynan, Katharine 1861-1931 .... **TCLC 3**
See also CA 104; 167; DLB 153, 240; FW
Tyndale, William c. 1484-1536 .... **LC 103**
See also DLB 132
Tyutchev, Fyodor 1803-1873 .... **NCLC 34**
Tzara, Tristan 1896-1963 ..... **CLC 47; PC 27**
See also CA 153; 89-92; DAM POET; EWL
3; MTCW 2
Uchida, Yoshiko 1921-1992 .... **AAL**
See also AAYA 16; BYA 2, 3; CA 13-16R;
139; CANR 6, 22, 47, 61; CDALBS; CLR
6, 56; CWRI 5; JRDA; MAICYA 1, 2;
MTCW 1, 2; SAAS 1; SATA 1, 53; SATA-
Obit 72
Udall, Nicholas 1504-1556 .... **LC 84**
See also DLB 62; RGEL 2
Ueda Akinari 1734-1809 .... **NCLC 131**
Uhry, Alfred 1936- .... **CLC 55**
See also CA 127; 133; CAD; CANR 112;
CD 5; CSW; DA3; DAM DRAM, POP;
DFS 11, 15; INT CA-133
Ulf, Haerved
See Strindberg, (Johan) August
Ulf, Harved
See Strindberg, (Johan) August
Ulibarri, Sabine R(eyes)
1919-2003 .... **CLC 83; HLCS 2**
See also CA 131; 214; CANR 81; DAM
MULT; DLB 82; HW 1, 2; RGSF 2
Unamuno (y Jugo), Miguel de
1864-1936 .. **HLC 2; SSC 11, 69; TCLC
2, 9, 148**
See also CA 104; 131; CANR 81; DAM
MULT, NOV; DLB 108; EW 8; EWL 3;
HW 1, 2; MTCW 1, 2; RGSF 2; RGWL
2, 3; SSFS 20; TWA
Uncle Shelby
See Silverstein, Shel(don Allan)
Undercliffe, Errol
See Campbell, (John) Ramsey
Underwood, Miles
See Glassco, John

Venison, Alfred
 See Pound, Ezra (Weston Loomis)
Ventsel, Elena Sergeevna 1907-2002
 See Grekova, I.
 See also CA 154
Verdi, Marie de
 See Mencken, H(enry) L(ouis)
Verdu, Matilde
 See Cela, Camilo Jose
Verga, Giovanni (Carmelo)
 1840-1922 .... **SSC 21; TCLC 3**
 See also CA 104; 123; CANR 101; EW 7;
 EWL 3; RGSF 2; RGWL 2, 3
Vergil 70B.C.-19B.C. ... **CMLC 9, 40; PC 12;**
 WLCS
 See Virgil
 See also AW 2; DA; DA3; DAB; DAC;
 DAM MST, POET; EFS 1; LMFS 1
Vergil, Polydore c. 1470-1555 .... **LC 108**
 See also DLB 132
Verhaeren, Emile (Adolphe Gustave)
 1855-1916 .... **TCLC 12**
 See also CA 109; EWL 3; GFL 1789 to the
 Present
Verlaine, Paul (Marie) 1844-1896 .. **NCLC 2,**
 51; PC 2, 32
 See also DAM POET; DLB 217; EW 7;
 GFL 1789 to the Present; LMFS 2; RGWL
 2, 3; TWA
Verne, Jules (Gabriel) 1828-1905 ... **TCLC 6,**
 52
 See also AAYA 16; BYA 4; CA 110; 131;
 CLR 88; DA3; DLB 123; GFL 1789 to
 the Present; JRDA; LAIT 2; LMFS 2;
 MAICYA 1, 2; RGWL 2, 3; SATA 21;
 SCFW; SFW 4; TWA; WCH
Verus, Marcus Annius
 See Aurelius, Marcus
Very, Jones 1813-1880 .... **NCLC 9**
 See also DLB 1, 243; RGAL 4
Vesaas, Tarjei 1897-1970 .... **CLC 48**
 See also CA 190; 29-32R; DLB 297; EW
 11; EWL 3; RGWL 3
Vialis, Gaston
 See Simenon, Georges (Jacques Christian)
Vian, Boris 1920-1959(?) .... **TCLC 9**
 See also CA 106; 164; CANR 111; DLB
 72; EWL 3; GFL 1789 to the Present;
 MTCW 2; RGWL 2, 3
Viaud, (Louis Marie) Julien 1850-1923
 See Loti, Pierre
 See also CA 107
Vicar, Henry
 See Felsen, Henry Gregor
Vicente, Gil 1465-c. 1536 .... **LC 99**
 See also DLB 287; RGWL 2, 3
Vicker, Angus
 See Felsen, Henry Gregor
Vidal, (Eugene Luther) Gore 1925- .. **CLC 2,**
 4, 6, 8, 10, 22, 33, 72, 142
 See Box, Edgar
 See also AITN 1; AMWS 4; BEST 90:2;
 BPFB 3; CA 5-8R; CAD; CANR 13, 45,
 65, 100, 132; CD 5; CDALBS; CN 7;
 CPW; DA3; DAM NOV, POP; DFS 2;
 DLB 6, 152; EWL 3; INT CANR-13;
 MTCW 1, 2; RGAL 4; RHW; TUS
Viereck, Peter (Robert Edwin)
 1916- .... **CLC 4; PC 27**
 See also CA 1-4R; CANR 1, 47; CP 7; DLB
 5; PFS 9, 14
Vigny, Alfred (Victor) de
 1797-1863 .... **NCLC 7, 102; PC 26**
 See also DAM POET; DLB 119, 192, 217;
 EW 5; GFL 1789 to the Present; RGWL
 2, 3
Vilakazi, Benedict Wallet
 1906-1947 .... **TCLC 37**
 See also CA 168

Villa, Jose Garcia 1914-1997 .... **AAL; PC 22**
 See also CA 25-28R; CANR 12, 118; EWL
 3; EXPP
Villa, Jose Garcia 1914-1997
 See Villa, Jose Garcia
Villarreal, Jose Antonio 1924- .... **HLC 2**
 See also CA 133; CANR 93; DAM MULT;
 DLB 82; HW 1; LAIT 4; RGAL 4
Villaurrutia, Xavier 1903-1950 ...... **TCLC 80**
 See also CA 192; EWL 3; HW 1; LAW
Villaverde, Cirilo 1812-1894 .... **NCLC 121**
 See also LAW
Villehardouin, Geoffroi de
 1150(?)-1218(?) .... **CMLC 38**
Villiers, George 1628-1687 .... **LC 107**
 See also DLB 80; RGEL 2
Villiers de l'Isle Adam, Jean Marie Mathias
 Philippe Auguste 1838-1889 ... **NCLC 3;**
 SSC 14
 See also DLB 123, 192; GFL 1789 to the
 Present; RGSF 2
Villon, Francois 1431-1463(?) . **LC 62; PC 13**
 See also DLB 208; EW 2; RGWL 2, 3;
 TWA
Vine, Barbara .... **CLC 50**
 See Rendell, Ruth (Barbara)
 See also BEST 90:4
Vinge, Joan (Carol) D(ennison)
 1948- .... **CLC 30; SSC 24**
 See also AAYA 32; BPFB 3; CA 93-96;
 CANR 72; SATA 36, 113; SFW 4; YAW
Viola, Herman J(oseph) 1938- .... **CLC 70**
 See also CA 61-64; CANR 8, 23, 48, 91;
 SATA 126
Violis, G.
 See Simenon, Georges (Jacques Christian)
Viramontes, Helena Maria 1954- .... **HLCS 2**
 See also CA 159; DLB 122; HW 2; LLW 1
Virgil
 See Vergil
 See also CDWLB 1; DLB 211; LAIT 1;
 RGWL 2, 3; WP
Visconti, Luchino 1906-1976 .... **CLC 16**
 See also CA 81-84; 65-68; CANR 39
Vitry, Jacques de
 See Jacques de Vitry
Vittorini, Elio 1908-1966 .... **CLC 6, 9, 14**
 See also CA 133; 25-28R; DLB 264; EW
 12; EWL 3; RGWL 2, 3
Vivekananda, Swami 1863-1902 .... **TCLC 88**
Vizenor, Gerald Robert 1934- .... **CLC 103;**
 NNAL
 See also CA 13-16R, 205; CAAE 205;
 CAAS 22; CANR 5, 21, 44, 67; DAM
 MULT; DLB 175, 227; MTCW 2; TCWW
 2
Vizinczey, Stephen 1933- .... **CLC 40**
 See also CA 128; CCA 1; INT CA-128
Vliet, R(ussell) G(ordon)
 1929-1984 .... **CLC 22**
 See also CA 37-40R; 112; CANR 18
Vogau, Boris Andreyevich 1894-1938
 See Pilnyak, Boris
 See also CA 123; 218
Vogel, Paula A(nne) 1951- ... **CLC 76; DC 19**
 See also CA 108; CAD; CANR 119; CD 5;
 CWD; DFS 14; RGAL 4
Voigt, Cynthia 1942- .... **CLC 30**
 See also AAYA 3, 30; BYA 1, 3, 6, 7, 8;
 CA 106; CANR 18, 37, 40, 94; CLR 13,
 48; INT CANR-18; JRDA; LAIT 5; MAI-
 CYA 1, 2; MAICYAS 1; SATA 48, 79,
 116; SATA-Brief 33; WYA; YAW
Voigt, Ellen Bryant 1943- .... **CLC 54**
 See also CA 69-72; CANR 11, 29, 55, 115;
 CP 7; CSW; CWP; DLB 120

Voinovich, Vladimir (Nikolaevich)
 1932- .... **CLC 10, 49, 147**
 See also CA 81-84; CAAS 12; CANR 33,
 67; CWW 2; DLB 302; MTCW 1
Vollmann, William T. 1959- .... **CLC 89**
 See also CA 134; CANR 67, 116; CPW;
 DA3; DAM NOV, POP; MTCW 2
Voloshinov, V. N.
 See Bakhtin, Mikhail Mikhailovich
Voltaire 1694-1778 . **LC 14, 79, 110; SSC 12;**
 WLC
 See also BYA 13; DA; DA3; DAB; DAC;
 DAM DRAM, MST; EW 4; GFL Begin-
 nings to 1789; LATS 1:1; LMFS 1; NFS
 7; RGWL 2, 3; TWA
von Aschendrof, Baron Ignatz
 See Ford, Ford Madox
von Chamisso, Adelbert
 See Chamisso, Adelbert von
von Daeniken, Erich 1935- .... **CLC 30**
 See also AITN 1; CA 37-40R; CANR 17,
 44
von Daniken, Erich
 See von Daeniken, Erich
von Hartmann, Eduard
 1842-1906 .... **TCLC 96**
von Hayek, Friedrich August
 See Hayek, F(riedrich) A(ugust von)
von Heidenstam, (Carl Gustaf) Verner
 See Heidenstam, (Carl Gustaf) Verner von
von Heyse, Paul (Johann Ludwig)
 See Heyse, Paul (Johann Ludwig von)
von Hofmannsthal, Hugo
 See Hofmannsthal, Hugo von
von Horvath, Odon
 See von Horvath, Odon
von Horvath, Odon
 See von Horvath, Odon
von Horvath, Odon 1901-1938 .... **TCLC 45**
 See von Horvath, Oedoen
 See also CA 118; 194; DLB 85, 124; RGWL
 2, 3
von Horvath, Oedoen
 See von Horvath, Odon
 See also CA 184
von Kleist, Heinrich
 See Kleist, Heinrich von
von Liliencron, (Friedrich Adolf Axel)
 Detlev
 See Liliencron, (Friedrich Adolf Axel) De-
 tlev von
Vonnegut, Kurt, Jr. 1922- . **CLC 1, 2, 3, 4, 5,**
 8, 12, 22, 40, 60, 111; SSC 8; WLC
 See also AAYA 6, 44; AITN 1; AMWS 2;
 BEST 90:4; BPFB 3; BYA 3, 14; CA
 1-4R; CANR 1, 25, 49, 75, 92; CDALB
 1968-1988; CN 7; CPW 1; DA; DA3;
 DAB; DAC; DAM MST, NOV, POP;
 DLB 2, 8, 152; DLBD 3; DLBY 1980;
 EWL 3; EXPN; EXPS; LAIT 4; LMFS 2;
 MTCW 1, 2; NFS 3; RGAL 4; SCFW;
 SFW 4; SSFS 5; TUS; YAW
Von Rachen, Kurt
 See Hubbard, L(afayette) Ron(ald)
von Rezzori (d'Arezzo), Gregor
 See Rezzori (d'Arezzo), Gregor von
von Sternberg, Josef
 See Sternberg, Josef von
Vorster, Gordon 1924- .... **CLC 34**
 See also CA 133
Vosce, Trudie
 See Ozick, Cynthia
Voznesensky, Andrei (Andreievich)
 1933- .... **CLC 1, 15, 57**
 See Voznesensky, Andrey
 See also CA 89-92; CANR 37; CWW 2;
 DAM POET; MTCW 1

Warung, Price .... **TCLC 45**
  See Astley, William
  See also DLB 230; RGEL 2
Warwick, Jarvis
  See Garner, Hugh
  See also CCA 1
Washington, Alex
  See Harris, Mark
Washington, Booker T(aliaferro)
  1856-1915 .... **BLC 3; TCLC 10**
  See also BW 1; CA 114; 125; DA3; DAM
  MULT; LAIT 2; RGAL 4; SATA 28
Washington, George 1732-1799 .... **LC 25**
  See also DLB 31
Wassermann, (Karl) Jakob
  1873-1934 .... **TCLC 6**
  See also CA 104; 163; DLB 66; EWL 3
Wasserstein, Wendy 1950- ... **CLC 32, 59, 90,**
    183; DC 4
  See also CA 121; 129; CABS 3; CAD;
  CANR 53, 75, 128; CD 5; CWD; DA3;
  DAM DRAM; DFS 5, 17; DLB 228;
  EWL 3; FW; INT CA-129; MTCW 2;
  SATA 94
Waterhouse, Keith (Spencer) 1929- . **CLC 47**
  See also CA 5-8R; CANR 38, 67, 109;
  CBD; CN 7; DLB 13, 15; MTCW 1, 2
Waters, Frank (Joseph) 1902-1995 .. **CLC 88**
  See also CA 5-8R; 149; CAAS 13; CANR
  3, 18, 63, 121; DLB 212; DLBY 1986;
  RGAL 4; TCWW 2
Waters, Mary C. .... **CLC 70**
Waters, Roger 1944- .... **CLC 35**
Watkins, Frances Ellen
  See Harper, Frances Ellen Watkins
Watkins, Gerrold
  See Malzberg, Barry N(athaniel)
Watkins, Gloria Jean 1952(?)- .... **CLC 94**
  See also BW 2; CA 143; CANR 87, 126;
  DLB 246; MTCW 2; SATA 115
Watkins, Paul 1964- .... **CLC 55**
  See also CA 132; CANR 62, 98
Watkins, Vernon Phillips
  1906-1967 .... **CLC 43**
  See also CA 9-10; 25-28R; CAP 1; DLB
  20; EWL 3; RGEL 2
Watson, Irving S.
  See Mencken, H(enry) L(ouis)
Watson, John H.
  See Farmer, Philip Jose
Watson, Richard F.
  See Silverberg, Robert
Watts, Ephraim
  See Horne, Richard Henry Hengist
Watts, Isaac 1674-1748 .... **LC 98**
  See also DLB 95; RGEL 2; SATA 52
Waugh, Auberon (Alexander)
  1939-2001 .... **CLC 7**
  See also CA 45-48; 192; CANR 6, 22, 92;
  DLB 14, 194
Waugh, Evelyn (Arthur St. John)
  1903-1966 .. **CLC 1, 3, 8, 13, 19, 27, 44,**
    107; SSC 41; WLC
  See also BPFB 3; BRW 7; CA 85-88; 25-
  28R; CANR 22; CDBLB 1914-1945; DA;
  DA3; DAB; DAC; DAM MST, NOV,
  POP; DLB 15, 162, 195; EWL 3; MTCW
  1, 2; NFS 13, 17; RGEL 2; RGSF 2; TEA;
  WLIT 4
Waugh, Harriet 1944- .... **CLC 6**
  See also CA 85-88; CANR 22
Ways, C. R.
  See Blount, Roy (Alton), Jr.
Waystaff, Simon
  See Swift, Jonathan
Webb, Beatrice (Martha Potter)
  1858-1943 .... **TCLC 22**
  See also CA 117; 162; DLB 190; FW

Webb, Charles (Richard) 1939- .... **CLC 7**
  See also CA 25-28R; CANR 114
Webb, Frank J. .... **NCLC 143**
  See also DLB 50
Webb, James H(enry), Jr. 1946- ...... **CLC 22**
  See also CA 81-84
Webb, Mary Gladys (Meredith)
  1881-1927 .... **TCLC 24**
  See also CA 182; 123; DLB 34; FW
Webb, Mrs. Sidney
  See Webb, Beatrice (Martha Potter)
Webb, Phyllis 1927- .... **CLC 18**
  See also CA 104; CANR 23; CCA 1; CP 7;
  CWP; DLB 53
Webb, Sidney (James) 1859-1947 .. **TCLC 22**
  See also CA 117; 163; DLB 190
Webber, Andrew Lloyd .... **CLC 21**
  See Lloyd Webber, Andrew
  See also DFS 7
Weber, Lenora Mattingly
  1895-1971 .... **CLC 12**
  See also CA 19-20; 29-32R; CAP 1; SATA
  2; SATA-Obit 26
Weber, Max 1864-1920 .... **TCLC 69**
  See also CA 109; 189; DLB 296
Webster, John 1580(?)-1634(?) ...... **DC 2; LC**
    33, 84; WLC
  See also BRW 2; CDBLB Before 1660; DA;
  DAB; DAC; DAM DRAM, MST; DFS
  17, 19; DLB 58; IDTP; RGEL 2; WLIT 3
Webster, Noah 1758-1843 .... **NCLC 30**
  See also DLB 1, 37, 42, 43, 73, 243
Wedekind, (Benjamin) Frank(lin)
  1864-1918 .... **TCLC 7**
  See also CA 104; 153; CANR 121, 122;
  CDWLB 2; DAM DRAM; DLB 118; EW
  8; EWL 3; LMFS 2; RGWL 2, 3
Wehr, Demaris .... **CLC 65**
Weidman, Jerome 1913-1998 .... **CLC 7**
  See also AITN 2; CA 1-4R; 171; CAD;
  CANR 1; DLB 28
Weil, Simone (Adolphine)
  1909-1943 .... **TCLC 23**
  See also CA 117; 159; EW 12; EWL 3; FW;
  GFL 1789 to the Present; MTCW 2
Weininger, Otto 1880-1903 .... **TCLC 84**
Weinstein, Nathan
  See West, Nathanael
Weinstein, Nathan von Wallenstein
  See West, Nathanael
Weir, Peter (Lindsay) 1944- .... **CLC 20**
  See also CA 113; 123
Weiss, Peter (Ulrich) 1916-1982 .. **CLC 3, 15,**
    51; TCLC 152
  See also CA 45-48; 106; CANR 3; DAM
  DRAM; DFS 3; DLB 69, 124; EWL 3;
  RGWL 2, 3
Weiss, Theodore (Russell)
  1916-2003 .... **CLC 3, 8, 14**
  See also CA 9-12R; 189; 216; CAAE 189;
  CAAS 2; CANR 46, 94; CP 7; DLB 5
Welch, (Maurice) Denton
  1915-1948 .... **TCLC 22**
  See also BRWS 8, 9; CA 121; 148; RGEL
  2
Welch, James (Phillip) 1940-2003 ..... **CLC 6,**
    14, 52; NNAL
  See also CA 85-88; 219; CANR 42, 66, 107;
  CN 7; CP 7; CPW; DAM MULT, POP;
  DLB 175, 256; LATS 1:1; RGAL 4;
  TCWW 2
Weldon, Fay 1931- . **CLC 6, 9, 11, 19, 36, 59,**
    122
  See also BRWS 4; CA 21-24R; CANR 16,
  46, 63, 97; CDBLB 1960 to Present; CN
  7; CPW; DAM POP; DLB 14, 194; EWL
  3; FW; HGG; INT CANR-16; MTCW 1,
  2; RGEL 2; RGSF 2

Wellek, Rene 1903-1995 .... **CLC 28**
  See also CA 5-8R; 150; CAAS 7; CANR 8;
  DLB 63; EWL 3; INT CANR-8
Weller, Michael 1942- .... **CLC 10, 53**
  See also CA 85-88; CAD; CD 5
Weller, Paul 1958- .... **CLC 26**
Wellershoff, Dieter 1925- .... **CLC 46**
  See also CA 89-92; CANR 16, 37
Welles, (George) Orson 1915-1985 .. **CLC 20,**
    80
  See also AAYA 40; CA 93-96; 117
Wellman, John McDowell 1945-
  See Wellman, Mac
  See also CA 166; CD 5
Wellman, Mac .... **CLC 65**
  See Wellman, John McDowell; Wellman,
  John McDowell
  See also CAD; RGAL 4
Wellman, Manly Wade 1903-1986 ... **CLC 49**
  See also CA 1-4R; 118; CANR 6, 16, 44;
  FANT; SATA 6; SATA-Obit 47; SFW 4;
  SUFW
Wells, Carolyn 1869(?)-1942 .... **TCLC 35**
  See also CA 113; 185; CMW 4; DLB 11
Wells, H(erbert) G(eorge) 1866-1946 . **SSC 6,**
    70; TCLC 6, 12, 19, 133; WLC
  See also AAYA 18; BPFB 3; BRW 6; CA
  110; 121; CDBLB 1914-1945; CLR 64;
  DA; DA3; DAB; DAM MST, NOV;
  DLB 34, 70, 156, 178; EWL 3; EXPS;
  HGG; LAIT 3; LMFS 2; MTCW 1, 2;
  NFS 17, 20; RGEL 2; RGSF 2; SATA 20;
  SCFW; SFW 4; SSFS 3; SUFW; TEA;
  WCH; WLIT 4; YAW
Wells, Rosemary 1943- .... **CLC 12**
  See also AAYA 13; BYA 7, 8; CA 85-88;
  CANR 48, 120; CLR 16, 69; CWRI 5;
  MAICYA 1, 2; SAAS 1; SATA 18, 69,
  114; YAW
Wells-Barnett, Ida B(ell)
  1862-1931 .... **TCLC 125**
  See also CA 182; DLB 23, 221
Welsh, Irvine 1958- .... **CLC 144**
  See also CA 173; DLB 271
Welty, Eudora (Alice) 1909-2001 .. **CLC 1, 2,**
    5, 14, 22, 33, 105; SSC 1, 27, 51; WLC
  See also AAYA 48; AMW; AMWR 1; BPFB
  3; CA 9-12R; 199; CABS 1; CANR 32,
  65, 128; CDALB 1941-1968; CN 7; CSW;
  DA; DA3; DAB; DAC; DAM MST, NOV;
  DLB 2, 102, 143; DLBD 12; DLBY 1987,
  2001; EWL 3; EXPS; HGG; LAIT 3;
  MAWW; MTCW 1, 2; NFS 13, 15; RGAL
  4; RGSF 2; RHW; SSFS 2, 10; TUS
Wen I-to 1899-1946 .... **TCLC 28**
  See also EWL 3
Wentworth, Robert
  See Hamilton, Edmond
Werfel, Franz (Viktor) 1890-1945 ... **TCLC 8**
  See also CA 104; 161; DLB 81, 124; EWL
  3; RGWL 2, 3
Wergeland, Henrik Arnold
  1808-1845 .... **NCLC 5**
Wersba, Barbara 1932- .... **CLC 30**
  See also AAYA 2, 30; BYA 6, 12, 13; CA
  29-32R, 182; CAAE 182; CANR 16, 38;
  CLR 3, 78; DLB 52; JRDA; MAICYA 1,
  2; SAAS 2; SATA 1, 58; SATA-Essay 103;
  WYA; YAW
Wertmueller, Lina 1928- .... **CLC 16**
  See also CA 97-100; CANR 39, 78
Wescott, Glenway 1901-1987 .. **CLC 13; SSC**
    35
  See also CA 13-16R; 121; CANR 23, 70;
  DLB 4, 9, 102; RGAL 4

Wilson, Robert M. 1941- .... **CLC 7, 9**
See also CA 49-52; CAD; CANR 2, 41; CD
5; MTCW 1

Wilson, Robert McLiam 1964- .... **CLC 59**
See also CA 132; DLB 267

Wilson, Sloan 1920-2003 .... **CLC 32**
See also CA 1-4R; 216; CANR 1, 44; CN 7

Wilson, Snoo 1948- .... **CLC 33**
See also CA 69-72; CBD; CD 5

Wilson, William S(mith) 1932- .... **CLC 49**
See also CA 81-84

Wilson, (Thomas) Woodrow
1856-1924 .... **TCLC 79**
See also CA 166; DLB 47

Wilson and Warnke eds. .... **CLC 65**

Winchilsea, Anne (Kingsmill) Finch
1661-1720
See Finch, Anne
See also RGEL 2

Windham, Basil
See Wodehouse, P(elham) G(renville)

Wingrove, David (John) 1954- .... **CLC 68**
See also CA 133; SFW 4

Winnemucca, Sarah 1844-1891 .... **NCLC 79;**
NNAL
See also DAM MULT; DLB 175; RGAL 4

Winstanley, Gerrard 1609-1676 .... **LC 52**

Wintergreen, Jane
See Duncan, Sara Jeannette

Winters, Janet Lewis .... **CLC 41**
See Lewis, Janet
See also DLBY 1987

Winters, (Arthur) Yvor 1900-1968 .... **CLC 4,**
8, 32
See also AMWS 2; CA 11-12; 25-28R; CAP
1; DLB 48; EWL 3; MTCW 1; RGAL 4

Winterson, Jeanette 1959- .... **CLC 64, 158**
See also BRWS 4; CA 136; CANR 58, 116;
CN 7; CPW; DA3; DAM POP; DLB 207,
261; FANT; FW; GLL 1; MTCW 2; RHW

Winthrop, John 1588-1649 .... **LC 31, 107**
See also DLB 24, 30

Wirth, Louis 1897-1952 .... **TCLC 92**
See also CA 210

Wiseman, Frederick 1930- .... **CLC 20**
See also CA 159

Wister, Owen 1860-1938 .... **TCLC 21**
See also BPFB 3; CA 108; DLB 9, 78,
186; RGAL 4; SATA 62; TCWW 2

Wither, George 1588-1667 .... **LC 96**
See also DLB 121; RGEL 2

Witkacy
See Witkiewicz, Stanislaw Ignacy

Witkiewicz, Stanislaw Ignacy
1885-1939 .... **TCLC 8**
See also CA 105; 162; CDWLB 4; DLB
215; EW 10; EWL 3; RGWL 2, 3; SFW 4

Wittgenstein, Ludwig (Josef Johann)
1889-1951 .... **TCLC 59**
See also CA 113; 164; DLB 262; MTCW 2

Wittig, Monique 1935(?)-2003 .... **CLC 22**
See also CA 116; 135; 212; CWW 2; DLB
83; EWL 3; FW; GLL 1

Wittlin, Jozef 1896-1976 .... **CLC 25**
See also CA 49-52; 65-68; CANR 3; EWL
3

Wodehouse, P(elham) G(renville)
1881-1975 . **CLC 1, 2, 5, 10, 22; SSC 2;**
TCLC 108
See also AITN 2; BRWS 3; CA 45-48; 57-
60; CANR 3, 33; CDBLB 1914-1945;
CPW 1; DA3; DAB; DAC; DAM NOV;
DLB 34, 162; EWL 3; MTCW 1, 2;
RGEL 2; RGSF 2; SATA 22; SSFS 10

Woiwode, L.
See Woiwode, Larry (Alfred)

Woiwode, Larry (Alfred) 1941- ... **CLC 6, 10**
See also CA 73-76; CANR 16, 94; CN 7;
DLB 6; INT CANR-16

Wojciechowska, Maia (Teresa)
1927-2002 .... **CLC 26**
See also AAYA 8, 46; BYA 3; CA 9-12R,
183; 209; CAAE 183; CANR 4, 41; CLR
1; JRDA; MAICYA 1, 2; SAAS 1; SATA
1, 28, 83; SATA-Essay 104; SATA-Obit
134; YAW

Wojtyla, Karol
See John Paul II, Pope

Wolf, Christa 1929- .... **CLC 14, 29, 58, 150**
See also CA 85-88; CANR 45, 123; CD-
WLB 2; CWW 2; DLB 75; EWL 3; FW;
MTCW 1; RGWL 2, 3; SSFS 14

Wolf, Naomi 1962- .... **CLC 157**
See also CA 141; CANR 110; FW

Wolfe, Gene (Rodman) 1931- .... **CLC 25**
See also AAYA 35; CA 57-60; CAAS 9;
CANR 6, 32, 60; CPW; DAM POP; DLB
8; FANT; MTCW 2; SATA 118; SCFW 2;
SFW 4; SUFW 2

Wolfe, George C. 1954- .... **BLCS; CLC 49**
See also CA 149; CAD; CD 5

Wolfe, Thomas (Clayton)
1900-1938 ...... **SSC 33; TCLC 4, 13, 29,**
61; WLC
See also AMW; BPFB 3; CA 104; 132;
CANR 102; CDALB 1929-1941; DA;
DA3; DAB; DAC; DAM MST, NOV;
DLB 9, 102, 229; DLBD 2, 16; DLBY
1985, 1997; EWL 3; MTCW 1, 2; NFS
18; RGAL 4; TUS

Wolfe, Thomas Kennerly, Jr.
1931- .... **CLC 147**
See Wolfe, Tom
See also CA 13-16R; CANR 9, 33, 70, 104;
DA3; DAM POP; DLB 185; EWL 3; INT
CANR-9; MTCW 1, 2; SSFS 18; TUS

Wolfe, Tom .... **CLC 1, 2, 9, 15, 35, 51**
See Wolfe, Thomas Kennerly, Jr.
See also AAYA 8; AITN 2; AMWS 3; BEST
89:1; BPFB 3; CN 7; CPW; CSW; DLB
152; LAIT 5; RGAL 4

Wolff, Geoffrey (Ansell) 1937- .... **CLC 41**
See also CA 29-32R; CANR 29, 43, 78

Wolff, Sonia
See Levitin, Sonia (Wolff)

Wolff, Tobias (Jonathan Ansell)
1945- .... **CLC 39, 64, 172; SSC 63**
See also AAYA 16; AMWS 7; BEST 90:2;
BYA 12; CA 114; 117; CAAS 22; CANR
54, 76, 96; CN 7; CSW; DA3; DLB 130;
EWL 3; INT CA-117; MTCW 2; RGAL
4; RGSF 2; SSFS 4, 11

Wolfram von Eschenbach c. 1170-c.
1220 .... **CMLC 5**
See Eschenbach, Wolfram von
See also CDWLB 2; DLB 138; EW 1;
RGWL 2

Wolitzer, Hilma 1930- .... **CLC 17**
See also CA 65-68; CANR 18, 40; INT
CANR-18; SATA 31; YAW

Wollstonecraft, Mary 1759-1797 .... **LC 5, 50,**
90
See also BRWS 3; CDBLB 1789-1832;
DLB 39, 104, 158, 252; FW; LAIT 1;
RGEL 2; TEA; WLIT 3

Wonder, Stevie .... **CLC 12**
See Morris, Steveland Judkins

Wong, Jade Snow 1922- .... **CLC 17**
See also CA 109; CANR 91; SATA 112

Woodberry, George Edward
1855-1930 .... **TCLC 73**
See also CA 165; DLB 71, 103

Woodcott, Keith
See Brunner, John (Kilian Houston)

Woodruff, Robert W.
See Mencken, H(enry) L(ouis)

Woolf, (Adeline) Virginia 1882-1941 . **SSC 7;**
TCLC 1, 5, 20, 43, 56, 101, 123, 128;
WLC
See also AAYA 44; BPFB 3; BRW 7;
BRWC 2; BRWR 1; CA 104; 130; CANR
64, 132; CDBLB 1914-1945; DA; DA3;
DAB; DAC; DAM MST, NOV; DLB 36,
100, 162; DLBD 10; EWL 3; EXPS; FW;
LAIT 3; LATS 1:1; LMFS 2; MTCW 1,
2; NCFS 2; NFS 8, 12; RGEL 2; RGSF 2;
SSFS 4, 12; TEA; WLIT 4

Woollcott, Alexander (Humphreys)
1887-1943 .... **TCLC 5**
See also CA 105; 161; DLB 29

Woolrich, Cornell .... **CLC 77**
See Hopley-Woolrich, Cornell George
See also MSW

Woolson, Constance Fenimore
1840-1894 .... **NCLC 82**
See also DLB 12, 74, 189, 221; RGAL 4

Wordsworth, Dorothy 1771-1855 . **NCLC 25,**
138
See also DLB 107

Wordsworth, William 1770-1850 .. **NCLC 12,**
38, 111; PC 4; WLC
See also BRW 4; BRWC 1; CDBLB 1789-
1832; DA; DA3; DAB; DAC; DAM MST,
POET; DLB 93, 107; EXPP; LATS 1:1;
LMFS 1; PAB; PFS 2; RGEL 2; TEA;
WLIT 3; WP

Wotton, Sir Henry 1568-1639 .... **LC 68**
See also DLB 121; RGEL 2

Wouk, Herman 1915- .... **CLC 1, 9, 38**
See also BPFB 2, 3; CA 5-8R; CANR 6,
33, 67; CDALBS; CN 7; CPW; DA3;
DAM NOV, POP; DLBY 1982; INT
CANR-6; LAIT 4; MTCW 1, 2; NFS 7;
TUS

Wright, Charles (Penzel, Jr.) 1935- .. **CLC 6,**
13, 28, 119, 146
See also AMWS 5; CA 29-32R; CAAS 7;
CANR 23, 36, 62, 88, 135; CP 7; DLB
165; DLBY 1982; EWL 3; MTCW 1, 2;
PFS 10

Wright, Charles Stevenson 1932- ..... **BLC 3;**
CLC 49
See also BW 1; CA 9-12R; CANR 26; CN
7; DAM MULT, POET; DLB 33

Wright, Frances 1795-1852 .... **NCLC 74**
See also DLB 73

Wright, Frank Lloyd 1867-1959 .... **TCLC 95**
See also AAYA 33; CA 174

Wright, Jack R.
See Harris, Mark

Wright, James (Arlington)
1927-1980 .... **CLC 3, 5, 10, 28; PC 36**
See also AITN 2; AMWS 3; CA 49-52; 97-
100; CANR 4, 34, 64; CDALBS; DAM
POET; DLB 5, 169; EWL 3; EXPP;
MTCW 1, 2; PFS 7, 8; RGAL 4; TUS;
WP

Wright, Judith (Arundell)
1915-2000 .... **CLC 11, 53; PC 14**
See also CA 13-16R; 188; CANR 31, 76,
93; CP 7; CWP; DLB 260; EWL 3;
MTCW 1, 2; PFS 8; RGEL 2; SATA 14;
SATA-Obit 121

Wright, L(aurali) R. 1939- .... **CLC 44**
See also CA 138; CMW 4

Wright, Richard (Nathaniel)
1908-1960 ... **BLC 3; CLC 1, 3, 4, 9, 14,**
21, 48, 74; SSC 2; TCLC 136; WLC
See also AAYA 5, 42; AFAW 1, 2; AMW;
BPFB 3; BW 1; BYA 2; CA 108; CANR
64; CDALB 1929-1941; DA; DA3; DAB;
DAC; DAM MST, MULT, NOV; DLB 76,
102; DLBD 2; EWL 3; EXPN; LAIT 3,
4; MTCW 1, 2; NCFS 1; NFS 1, 7; RGAL
4; RGSF 2; SSFS 3, 9, 15, 20; TUS; YAW

Literary Criticism Series
Cumulative Topic Index

This index lists all topic entries in Gale's *Children's Literature Review* (CLR), *Classical and Medieval Literature Criticism* (CMLC), *Contemporary Literary Criticism* (CLC), *Drama Criticism* (DC), *Literature Criticism from 1400 to 1800* (LC), *Nineteenth-Century Literature Criticism* (NCLC), *Short Story Criticism* (SSC), and *Twentieth-Century Literary Criticism* (TCLC). The index also lists topic entries in the Gale Critical Companion Collection, which includes the following publications: *The Beat Generation* (BG), and *Harlem Renaissance* (HR).

Topic Index

Topic Index

NCLC Cumulative Nationality Index

NCLC-150 Title Index

ISBN 0-7876-8634-4

90000

9 780787 686345